Blacksto

Com**p**any

Blackstone's Statutes

Company Law

....

2003/2004

Seventh Edition

Edited by

Derek French

OXFORD
UNIVERSITY PRESS

OXFORD
UNIVERSITY PRESS

Great Clarendon Street, Oxford OX2 6DP

Oxford University Press is a department of the University of Oxford.
It furthers the University's objective of excellence in research, scholarship,
and education by publishing worldwide in

Oxford New York

Auckland Bangkok Buenos Aires Cape Town Chennai
Dar es Salaam Delhi Hong Kong Istanbul Karachi Kolkata
Kuala Lumpur Madrid Melbourne Mexico City Mumbai Nairobi
São Paulo Shanghai Taipei Tokyo Toronto

Oxford is a registered trade mark of Oxford University Press
in the UK and in certain other countries

Published in the United States
by Oxford University Press Inc., New York

First published by Blackstone Press

This selection © Derek French 2003

The moral rights of the author have been asserted
Database right Oxford University Press (maker)

First published 1997
Second edition 1998
Third edition 1999
Fourth edition 2000
Fifth edition 2001
Sixth edition 2002
Seventh edition 2003

British Library Cataloguing in Publication Data
Data available

Crown Copyright material is reproduced with the permission of
the Controller of HMSO and the Queen's Printer for Scotland

ISBN 0–19–925947–X

1 3 5 7 9 10 8 6 4 2

Typeset in ITC Stone Serif and ITC Stone Sans
by RefineCatch Limited, Bungay, Suffolk
Printed in Great Britain by
Ashford Colour Press Ltd, Gosport, Hampshire

CONTENTS

EDITOR'S PREFACE

This book provides the text of the main statutes and statutory instruments concerning company law in England and Wales. The selection should provide all the legislation that is required for degree-level courses in company law, including courses that cover company insolvency. To keep the book to a handy size, provisions relating only to banking, insurance and oversea companies have been omitted, and there is only a representative sample from the detailed schedules on accounting requirements.

The text of all legislation incorporates all amendments and repeals in force on 10 June 2003. At the end of the book there is a list of sources of amendments so that the legislative history of any provision can be investigated if necessary.

Enactments which had not been brought into force by 10 June 2003 are printed in italics. Where a provision is subject to an amendment or repeal that has not been brought into force (or is only in force for certain purposes), the text of the provision currently in force is printed, accompanied by a note of relevant amendments and repeals. The Department of Trade and Industry has indicated that several amendments made by the Companies Act 1989 will not be brought into force. The text of those amendments is set out under the heading 'Companies Act 1989'.

This is the first edition for which updates will be available on a companion web site, www.oup.com/uk/booksites/law, click on French: Statutes on Company Law, 7e. There will be an update at the beginning of each month with: amendments to the legislation in this edition, new legislation which will be included in the next edition, information about dates on which legislation which will come into force. The first update will be on 1 October 2003.

Editing the texts of legislation for this book has revealed minor drafting anomalies and typographical errors, which are indicated in notes at appropriate points in the book and have been communicated to the Department of Trade and Industry.

Derek French
10 June 2003

PART I

Statutes

Partnership Act 1890
(53 & 54 Vict., c. 39)

An Act to declare and amend the Law of Partnership. [14 August 1890]

Nature of partnership

1 Definition of partnership

(1) Partnership is the relation which subsists between persons carrying on a business in common with a view of profit.

(2) But the relation between members of any company or association which is—

(a) Registered as a company under the Companies Act 1862, or any other Act of Parliament for the time being in force and relating to the registration of joint stock companies; or

(b) Formed or incorporated by or in pursuance of any other Act of Parliament or letters patent, or Royal Charter:

is not a partnership within the meaning of this Act.

2 Rules for determining existence of partnership

In determining whether a partnership does or does not exist, regard shall be had to the following rules:

(1) Joint tenancy, tenancy in common, joint property, common property, or part ownership does not of itself create a partnership as to anything so held or owned, whether the tenants or owners do or do not share any profits made by the use thereof.

(2) The sharing of gross returns does not of itself create a partnership, whether the persons sharing such returns have or have not a joint or common right or interest in any property from which or from the use of which the returns are derived.

(3) The receipt by a person of a share of the profits of a business is prima facie evidence that he is a partner in the business, but the receipt of such a share, or of a payment contingent on or varying with the profits of a business, does not of itself make him a partner in the business; and in particular—

(a) The receipt by a person of a debt or other liquidated amount by instalments or otherwise out of the accruing profits of a business does not of itself make him a partner in the business or liable as such:

(b) A contract for the remuneration of a servant or agent of a person engaged in a business by a share of the profits of the business does not of itself make the servant or agent a partner in the business or liable as such:

(c) A person being the widow or child of a deceased partner, and receiving by way of annuity a portion of the profits made in the business in which the deceased person was a partner, is not by reason only of such receipt a partner in the business or liable as such:

(d) The advance of money by way of loan to a person engaged or about to engage in any business on a contract with that person that the lender shall receive a rate of interest varying with the profits, or shall receive a share of the profits arising from carrying on the business, does not of itself make the lender a partner with the person or persons carrying on the business or liable as such. Provided that the contract is in writing, and signed by or on behalf of all the parties thereto:

(e) A person receiving by way of annuity or otherwise a portion of the profits of a business in consideration of the sale by him of the goodwill of the business is not by reason only of such receipt a partner in the business or liable as such.

3 Postponement of rights of person lending or selling in consideration of share of profits in case of insolvency

In the event of any person to whom money has been advanced by way of loan upon such a contract as is mentioned in the last foregoing section, or of any buyer of a goodwill in consideration of a share of the profits of the business, being adjudged a bankrupt, entering into an arrangement to pay his creditors less than [100p] in the pound, or dying in insolvent circumstances, the lender of the loan shall not be entitled to recover anything in respect of his loan, and the seller of the goodwill shall not be entitled to recover anything in respect of the share of profits contracted for, until the claims of the other creditors of the borrower or buyer for valuable consideration in money or money's worth have been satisfied.

4 Meaning of firm

(1) Persons who have entered into partnership with one another are for the purposes of this Act called collectively a firm, and the name under which their business is carried on is called the firm-name.

(2) In Scotland a firm is a legal person distinct from the partners of whom it is composed, but an individual partner may be charged on a decree or diligence directed against the firm, and on payment of the debts is entitled to relief pro rata from the firm and its other members.

Relations of partners to persons dealing with them

5 Power of partner to bind the firm

Every partner is an agent of the firm and his other partners for the purpose of the business of the partnership; and the acts of every partner who does any act for carrying on in the usual way business of the kind carried on by the firm of which he is a member bind the firm and his partners, unless the partner so acting has in fact no authority to act for the firm in the particular matter, and the person with whom he is dealing either knows that he has no authority, or does not know or believe him to be a partner.

6 Partners bound by acts on behalf of firm

An act or instrument relating to the business of the firm and done or executed in the firm-name, or in any other manner showing an intention to bind the firm, by any person thereto authorised, whether a partner or not, is binding on the firm and all the partners.

Provided that this section shall not affect any general rule of law relating to the execution of deeds or negotiable instruments.

7 Partner using credit of firm for private purposes

Where one partner pledges the credit of the firm for a purpose apparently not connected with the firm's ordinary course of business, the firm is not bound, unless he is in fact specially authorised by the other partners; but this section does not affect any personal liability incurred by an individual partner.

8 Effect of notice that firm will not be bound by acts of partner

If it has been agreed between the partners that any restriction shall be placed on the power of any one or more of them to bind the firm, no act done in contravention of the agreement is binding on the firm with respect to persons having notice of the agreement.

9 Liability of partners

Every partner in a firm is liable jointly with the other partners, and in Scotland severally also, for all debts and obligations of the firm incurred while he is a partner; and after his death his estate is also severally liable in a due course of administration for such debts and obligations, so far as they remain unsatisfied, but subject in England or [Northern Ireland] to the prior payment of his separate debts.

10 Liability of the firm for wrongs

Where, by any wrongful act or omission of any partner acting in the ordinary course of the business of the firm, or with the authority of his co-partners, loss or injury is caused to any person not being a partner in the firm, or any penalty is incurred, the firm is liable therefor to the same extent as the partner so acting or omitting to act.

11 Misapplication of money or property received for or in custody of the firm

In the following cases; namely—
  (a) Where one partner acting within the scope of his apparent authority receives the money or property of a third person and misapplies it; and
  (b) Where a firm in the course of its business receives money or property of a third person, and the money or property so received is misapplied by one or more of the partners while it is in the custody of the firm;
the firm is liable to make good the loss.

12 Liability for wrongs joint and several

Every partner is liable jointly with his co-partners and also severally for everything for which the firm while he is a partner therein becomes liable under either of the two last preceding sections.

13 Improper employment of trust-property for partnership purposes

If a partner, being a trustee, improperly employs trust-property in the business or on the account of the partnership, no other partner is liable for the trust-property to the persons beneficially interested therein.

  Provided as follows:—

  (1) This section shall not affect any liability incurred by any partner by reason of his having notice of a breach of trust; and

  (2) Nothing in this section shall prevent trust money from being followed and recovered from the firm if still in its possession or under its control.

14 Persons liable by 'holding out'

  (1) Every one who by words spoken or written or by conduct represents himself, or who knowingly suffers himself to be represented, as a partner in a particular firm, is liable as a partner to any one who has on the faith of any such representation given credit to the firm, whether the representation has or has not been made or communicated to the person so giving credit by or with the knowledge of the apparent partner making the representation or suffering it to be made.

  (2) Provided that where after a partner's death the partnership business is continued in the old firm-name, the continued use of that name or of the deceased partner's name as part thereof shall not of itself make his executors or administrators estate or effects liable for any partnership debts contracted after his death.

15 Admissions and representations of partners

An admission or representation made by any partner concerning the partnership affairs, and in the ordinary course of its business, is evidence against the firm.

16 Notice to acting partner to be notice to the firm

Notice to any partner who habitually acts in the partnership business of any matter relating to partnership affairs operates as notice to the firm, except in the case of a fraud on the firm committed by or with the consent of that partner.

17 Liabilities of incoming and outgoing partners

(1) A person who is admitted as a partner into an existing firm does not thereby become liable to the creditors of the firm for anything done before he became a partner.

(2) A partner who retires from a firm does not thereby cease to be liable for partnership debts or obligations incurred before his retirement.

(3) A retiring partner may be discharged from any existing liabilities, by an agreement to that effect between himself and the members of the firm as newly constituted and the creditors, and this agreement may be either express or inferred as a fact from the course of dealing between the creditors and the firm as newly constituted.

18 Revocation of continuing guaranty by change in firm

A continuing guaranty or cautionary obligation given either to a firm or to a third person in respect of the transactions of a firm is, in the absence of agreement to the contrary, revoked as to future transactions by any change in the constitution of the firm to which, or of the firm in respect of the transactions of which, the guaranty or obligation was given.

Relations of partners to one another

19 Variation by consent of terms of partnership

The mutual rights and duties of partners, whether ascertained by agreement or defined by this Act, may be varied by the consent of all the partners, and such consent may be either express or inferred from a course of dealing.

20 Partnership property

(1) All property and rights and interests in property originally brought into the partnership stock or acquired, whether by purchase or otherwise, on account of the firm, or for the purposes and in the course of the partnership business, are called in this Act partnership property, and must be held and applied by the partners exclusively for the purposes of the partnership and in accordance with the partnership agreement.

(2) Provided that the legal estate or interest in any land, or in Scotland the title to and interest in any heritable estate, which belongs to the partnership shall devolve according to the nature and tenure thereof, and the general rules of law thereto applicable, but in trust, so far as necessary, for the persons beneficially interested in the land under this section.

(3) Where co-owners of an estate or interest in any land, or in Scotland of any heritable estate, not being itself partnership property, are partners as to profits made by the use of that land or estate, and purchase other land or estate out of the profits to be used in like manner, the land or estate so purchased belongs to them, in the absence of an agreement to the contrary, not as partners, but as co-owners for the same respective estates and interests as are held by them in the land or estate first mentioned at the date of the purchase.

21 Property bought with partnership money

Unless the contrary intention appears, property bought with money belonging to the firm is deemed to have been bought on account of the firm.

23 Procedure against partnership property for a partner's separate judgment debt

(1) A writ of execution shall not issue against any partnership property except on a judgment against the firm.

(2) The High Court, or a judge thereof, or a county court, may, on the application by summons of any judgment creditor of a partner, make an order charging that partner's inter-

est in the partnership property and profits with payment of the amount of the judgment debt and interest thereon, and may by the same or a subsequent order appoint a receiver of that partner's share of profits (whether already declared or accruing), and of any other money which may be coming to him in respect of the partnership, and direct all accounts and inquiries, and give all other orders and directions which might have been directed or given if the charge had been made in favour of the judgment creditor by the partner, or which the circumstances of the case may require.

(3) The other partner or partners shall be at liberty at any time to redeem the interest charged, or in case of a sale being directed, to purchase the same.

(5) This section shall not apply to Scotland.

24   Rules as to interests and duties of partners subject to special agreement

The interests of partners in the partnership property and their rights and duties in relation to the partnership shall be determined, subject to any agreement express or implied between the partners, by the following rules:

(1) All the partners are entitled to share equally in the capital and profits of the business, and must contribute equally towards the losses whether of capital or otherwise sustained by the firm.

(2) The firm must indemnify every partner in respect of payments made and personal liabilities incurred by him—

  (a) In the ordinary and proper conduct of the business of the firm; or,
  (b) In or about anything necessarily done for the preservation of the business or property of the firm.

(3) A partner making, for the purpose of the partnership, any actual payment or advance beyond the amount of capital which he has agreed to subscribe, is entitled to interest at the rate of five per cent per annum from the date of the payment or advance.

(4) A partner is not entitled, before the ascertainment of profits, to interest on the capital subscribed by him.

(5) Every partner may take part in the management of the partnership business.

(6) No partner shall be entitled to remuneration for acting in the partnership business.

(7) No person may be introduced as a partner without the consent of all existing partners.

(8) Any difference arising as to ordinary matters connected with the partnership business may be decided by a majority of the partners, but no change may be made in the nature of the partnership business without the consent of all existing partners.

(9) The partnership books are to be kept at the place of business of the partnership (or the principal place, if there is more than one), and every partner may, when he thinks fit, have access to and inspect and copy any of them.

25   Expulsion of partner

No majority of the partners can expel any partner unless a power to do so has been conferred by express agreement between the partners.

26   Retirement from partnership at will

(1) Where no fixed term has been agreed upon for the duration of the partnership, any partner may determine the partnership at any time on giving notice of his intention so to do to all the other partners.

(2) Where the partnership has originally been constituted by deed, a notice in writing, signed by the partner giving it, shall be sufficient for this purpose.

27   Where partnership for term is continued over, continuance on old terms presumed

(1) Where a partnership entered into for a fixed term is continued after the term has expired, and without any express new agreement, the rights and duties of the partners remain

the same as they were at the expiration of the term, so far as is consistent with the incidents of a partnership at will.

(2) A continuance of the business by the partners or such of them as habitually acted therein during the term, without any settlement or liquidation of the partnership affairs, is presumed to be a continuance of the partnership.

28   Duty of partners to render accounts, &c.
Partners are bound to render true accounts and full information of all things affecting the partnership to any partner or his legal representatives.

29   Accountability of partners for private profits
(1) Every partner must account to the firm for any benefit derived by him without the consent of the other partners from any transaction concerning the partnership, or from any use by him of the partnership property name or business connection.

(2) This section applies also to transactions undertaken after a partnership has been dissolved by the death of a partner, and before the affairs thereof have been completely wound up, either by any surviving partner or by the representatives of the deceased partner.

30   Duty of partner not to compete with firm
If a partner, without the consent of the other partners, carries on any business of the same nature as and competing with that of the firm, he must account for and pay over to the firm all profits made by him in that business.

31   Rights of assignee of share in partnership
(1) An assignment by any partner of his share in the partnership, either absolute or by way of mortgage or redeemable charge, does not, as against the other partners, entitle the assignee, during the continuance of the partnership, to interfere in the management or administration of the partnership business or affairs, or to require any accounts of the partnership transactions, or to inspect the partnership books, but entitles the assignee only to receive the share of profits to which the assigning partner would otherwise be entitled, and the assignee must accept the account of profits agreed to by the partners.

(2) In case of a dissolution of the partnership, whether as respects all the partners or as respects the assigning partner, the assignee is entitled to receive the share of the partnership assets to which the assigning partner is entitled as between himself and the other partners, and, for the purpose of ascertaining that share, to an account as from the date of the dissolution.

Dissolution of partnership, and its consequences

32   Dissolution by expiration or notice
Subject to any agreement between the partners, a partnership is dissolved—
   (a) If entered into for a fixed term, by the expiration of that term:
   (b) If entered into for a single adventure or undertaking, by the termination of that adventure or undertaking:
   (c) If entered into for an undefined time, by any partner giving notice to the other or others of his intention to dissolve the partnership.
In the last-mentioned case the partnership is dissolved as from the date mentioned in the notice as the date of dissolution, or, if no date is so mentioned, as from the date of the communication of the notice.

33   Dissolution by bankruptcy, death, or charge
(1) Subject to any agreement between the partners, every partnership is dissolved as regards all the partners by the death or bankruptcy of any partner.

(2) A partnership may, at the option of the other partners, be dissolved if any partner suffers his share of the partnership property to be charged under this Act for his separate debt.

34   Dissolution by illegality of partnership
A partnership is in every case dissolved by the happening of any event which makes it unlawful for the business of the firm to be carried on or for the members of the firm to carry it on in partnership.

35   Dissolution by the Court
On application by a partner the Court may decree a dissolution of the partnership in any of the following cases:
>   (b)   When a partner, other than the partner suing, becomes in any other way permanently incapable of performing his part of the partnership contract:
>   (c)   When a partner, other than the partner suing, has been guilty of such conduct as, in the opinion of the Court, regard being had to the nature of the business, is calculated to prejudicially affect the carrying on of the business:
>   (d)   When a partner, other than the partner suing, wilfully or persistently commits a breach of the partnership agreement, or otherwise so conducts himself in matters relating to the partnership business that it is not reasonably practicable for the other partner or partners to carry on the business in partnership with him:
>   (e)   When the business of the partnership can only be carried on at a loss:
>   (f)   Whenever in any case circumstances have arisen which, in the opinion of the Court, render it just and equitable that the partnership be dissolved.

36   Rights of persons dealing with firm against apparent members of firm
    (1)   Where a person deals with a firm after a change in its constitution he is entitled to treat all apparent members of the old firm as still being members of the firm until he has notice of the change.
    (2)   An advertisement in the London Gazette as to a firm whose principal place of business is in England or Wales, in the Edinburgh Gazette as to a firm whose principal place of business is in Scotland, and in the [Belfast Gazette] as to a firm whose principal place of business is in [Northern Ireland], shall be notice as to persons who had not dealings with the firm before the date of the dissolution or change so advertised.
    (3)   The estate of a partner who dies, or who becomes bankrupt, or of a partner who, not having been known to the person dealing with the firm to be a partner, retires from the firm, is not liable for partnership debts contracted after the date of the death, bankruptcy, or retirement respectively.

37   Right of partners to notify dissolution
On the dissolution of a partnership or retirement of a partner any partner may publicly notify the same, and may require the other partner or partners to concur for that purpose in all necessary or proper acts, if any, which cannot be done without his or their concurrence.

38   Continuing authority of partners for purposes of winding up
After the dissolution of a partnership the authority of each partner to bind the firm, and the other rights and obligations of the partners, continue notwithstanding the dissolution so far as may be necessary to wind up the affairs of the partnership, and to complete transactions begun but unfinished at the time of the dissolution, but not otherwise.
    Provided that the firm is in no case bound by the acts of a partner who has become bankrupt; but this proviso does not affect the liability of any person who has after the bankruptcy represented himself or knowingly suffered himself to be represented as a partner of the bankrupt.

39   Rights of partners as to application of partnership property
On the dissolution of a partnership every partner is entitled, as against the other partners in the firm, and all persons claiming through them in respect of their interests as partners, to have the property of the partnership applied in payment of the debts and liabilities of the

firm, and to have the surplus assets after such payment applied in payment of what may be due to the partners respectively after deducting what may be due from them as partners to the firm; and for that purpose any partner or his representatives may on the termination of the partnership apply to the Court to wind up the business and affairs of the firm.

40   Apportionment of premium where partnership prematurely dissolved

Where one partner has paid a premium to another on entering into a partnership for a fixed term, and the partnership is dissolved before the expiration of that term otherwise than by the death of a partner, the Court may order the repayment of the premium, or of such part thereof as it thinks just, having regard to the terms of the partnership contract and to the length of time during which the partnership has continued; unless

(a) the dissolution is, in the judgment of the Court, wholly or chiefly due to the misconduct of the partner who paid the premium, or

(b) the partnership has been dissolved by an agreement containing no provision for a return of any part of the premium.

41   Rights where partnership dissolved for fraud or misrepresentation

Where a partnership contract is rescinded on the ground of the fraud or misrepresentation of one of the parties thereto, the party entitled to rescind is, without prejudice to any other right, entitled—

(a) to a lien on, or right of retention of, the surplus of the partnership assets, after satisfying the partnership liabilities, for any sum of money paid by him for the purchase of a share in the partnership and for any capital contributed by him, and is

(b) to stand in the place of the creditors of the firm for any payments made by him in respect of the partnership liabilities, and

(c) to be indemnified by the person guilty of the fraud or making the representation against all the debts and liabilities of the firm.

42   Right of outgoing partner in certain cases to share profits made after dissolution

(1) Where any member of a firm has died or otherwise ceased to be a partner, and the surviving or continuing partners carry on the business of the firm with its capital or assets without any final settlement of accounts as between the firm and the outgoing partner or his estate, then, in the absence of any agreement to the contrary, the outgoing partner or his estate is entitled at the option of himself or his representatives to such share of the profits made since the dissolution as the Court may find to be attributable to the use of his share of the partnership assets, or to interest at the rate of five per cent per annum on the amount of his share of the partnership assets.

(2) Provided that where by the partnership contract an option is given to surviving or continuing partners to purchase the interest of a deceased or outgoing partner, and that option is duly exercised, the estate of the deceased partner, or the outgoing partner or his estate, as the case may be, is not entitled to any further or other share of profits; but if any partner assuming to act in exercise of the option does not in all material respects comply with the terms thereof, he is liable to account under the foregoing provisions of this section.

43   Retiring or deceased partner's share to be a debt

Subject to any agreement between the partners, the amount due from surviving or continuing partners to an outgoing partner or the representatives of a deceased partner in respect of the outgoing or deceased partner's share is a debt accruing at the date of the dissolution or death.

44   Rule for distribution of assets on final settlement of accounts

In settling accounts between the partners after a dissolution of partnership, the following rules shall, subject to any agreement, be observed:

(a) Losses, including losses and deficiencies of capital, shall be paid first out of profits, next out of capital, and lastly, if necessary, by the partners individually in the proportion in which they were entitled to share profits:

(b) The assets of the firm including the sums, if any, contributed by the partners to make up losses or deficiencies of capital, shall be applied in the following manner and order:

    1. In paying the debts and liabilities of the firm to persons who are not partners therein:

    2. In paying to each partner rateably what is due from the firm to him for advances as distinguished from capital:

    3. In paying to each partner rateably what is due from the firm to him in respect of capital:

    4. The ultimate residue, if any, shall be divided among the partners in the proportion in which profits are divisible.

Supplemental

45 Definitions of 'court' and 'business'
In this Act, unless the contrary intention appears,—
The expression 'court' includes every court and judge having jurisdiction in the case;
The expression 'business' includes every trade, occupation, or profession.

46 Saving for rules of equity and common law
The rules of equity and of common law applicable to partnership shall continue in force except so far as they are inconsistent with the express provisions of this Act.

50 Short title
This Act may be cited as the Partnership Act 1890.

Stock Transfer Act 1963
(1963, c. 18)

An Act to amend the law with respect to the transfer of securities. [10 July 1963]

1 Simplified transfer of securities
(1) Registered securities to which this section applies may be transferred by means of an instrument under hand in the form set out in Schedule 1 to this Act (in this Act referred to as a stock transfer), executed by the transferor only and specifying (in addition to the particulars of the consideration, of the description and number or amount of the securities, and of the person by whom the transfer is made) the full name and address of the transferee.

(2) The execution of a stock transfer need not be attested; and where such a transfer has been executed for the purpose of a stock exchange transaction, the particulars of the consideration and of the transferee may either be inserted in that transfer or, as the case may require, supplied by means of separate instruments in the form set out in Schedule 2 to this Act (in this Act referred to as brokers transfers), identifying the stock transfer and specifying the securities to which each such instrument relates and the consideration paid for those securities.

(3) Nothing in this section shall be construed as affecting the validity of any instrument which would be effective to transfer securities apart from this section; and any instrument purporting to be made in any form which was common or usual before the commencement of this Act, or in any other form authorised or required for that purpose apart from this section, shall be sufficient, whether or not it is completed in accordance with the form, if

it complies with the requirements as to execution and contents which apply to a stock transfer.

(4) This section applies to fully paid up registered securities of any description, being—

> (a) securities issued by any company within the meaning of the Companies Act 1985 except a company limited by guarantee or an unlimited company;

. . .

2 Supplementary provisions as to simplified transfer

(1) Section 1 of this Act shall have effect in relation to the transfer of any securities to which that section applies notwithstanding anything to the contrary in any enactment or instrument relating to the transfer of those securities; but nothing in that section affects—

> (a) any right to refuse to register a person as the holder of any securities on any ground other than the form in which those securities purport to be transferred to him: or
>
> (b) any enactment or rule of law regulating the execution of documents by companies or other bodies corporate, or any articles of association or other instrument regulating the execution of documents by any particular company or body corporate.

(2) Subject to the provisions of this section, any enactment or instrument relating to the transfer of securities to which section 1 of this Act applies shall, with any necessary modifications, apply in relation to an instrument of transfer authorised by that section as it applies in relation to an instrument of transfer to which it applies apart from this subsection; and without prejudice to the generality of the foregoing provision, the reference in section 184 of the Companies Act 1985 (certification of transfers) to any instrument of transfer shall be construed as including a reference to a brokers transfer.

(3) In relation to the transfer of securities by means of a stock transfer and a brokers transfer—

> (a) any reference in any enactment or instrument (including in particular section 183(1) and (2) of the Companies Act 1985 *and section 56(4) of the Finance Act 1946*) to the delivery or lodging of an instrument (or proper instrument) of transfer shall be construed as a reference to the delivery or lodging of the stock transfer and the brokers transfer;
>
> (b) any such reference to the date on which an instrument of transfer is delivered or lodged shall be construed as a reference to the date by which the later of those transfers to be delivered or lodged has been delivered or lodged; *and*
>
> (c) *subject to the foregoing provisions of this subsection, the brokers transfer (and not the stock transfer) shall be deemed to be the conveyance or transfer for the purposes of the enactments relating to stamp duty.*

. . .

[*The words in italics will be repealed when the relevant provisions of the Finance Act 1990, sch. 19, part VI, are brought into force.*]

3 Additional provisions as to transfer forms

(1) References in this Act to the forms set out in Schedule 1 and Schedule 2 include references to forms substantially corresponding to those forms respectively.

(2) The Treasury may by order amend the said Schedules either by altering the forms set out therein or by substituting different forms for those forms or by the addition of forms for use as alternatives to those forms; and references in this Act to the forms set out in those Schedules (including references in this section) shall be construed accordingly.

(3) Any order under subsection (2) of this section which substitutes a different form for a form set out in Schedule 1 to this Act may direct that subsection (3) of section 1 of this Act shall apply, with any necessary modifications, in relation to the form for which that form is

substituted as it applies to any form which was common or usual before the commencement of this Act.

(4) Any order of the Treasury under this section shall be made by statutory instrument, and may be varied or revoked by a subsequent order; and any statutory instrument made by virtue of this section shall be subject to annulment in pursuance of a resolution of either House of Parliament.

(5) An order under subsection (2) of this section may—

    (a) provide for forms on which some of the particulars mentioned in subsection (1) of section 1 of this Act are not required to be specified;

    (b) provide for that section to have effect, in relation to such forms as are mentioned in the preceding paragraph or other forms specified in the order, subject to such amendments as are so specified (which may include an amendment of the reference in subsection (1) of that section to an instrument under hand);

    (c) provide for all or any of the provisions of the order to have effect in such cases only as are specified in the order.

4 Interpretation

(1) In this Act the following expressions have the meanings hereby respectively assigned to them, that is to say—

. . .

'registered securities' means transferable securities the holders of which are entered in a register (whether maintained in Great Britain or not);

'securities' means shares, stock, debentures, debenture stock, loan stock, bonds, units of a collective investment scheme within the meaning of the Financial Services and Markets Act 2000, and other securities of any description;

'stock exchange transaction' means a sale and purchase of securities in which each of the parties is a member of a stock exchange acting in the ordinary course of his business as such or is acting through the agency of such a member;

'stock exchange' means the Stock Exchange, London, and any other stock exchange (whether in Great Britain or not) which is declared by order of the Treasury to be a recognised stock exchange for the purposes of this Act.

(2) Any order of the Treasury under this section shall be made by statutory instrument, and may be varied or revoked by a subsequent order.

6 Short title and commencement

(1) This Act may be cited as the Stock Transfer Act 1963.

. . .

Companies Act 1985

(1985, c. 6)

An Act to consolidate the greater part of the Companies Acts   [11 March 1985]

PART I FORMATION AND REGISTRATION OF COMPANIES; JURIDICAL STATUS AND MEMBERSHIP

CHAPTER I COMPANY FORMATION

Memorandum of association

1 Mode of forming incorporated company

(1) Any two or more persons associated for a lawful purpose may, by subscribing their names to a memorandum of association and otherwise complying with the requirements of

this Act in respect of registration, form an incorporated company, with or without limited liability.

(2) A company so formed may be either—

(a) a company having the liability of its members limited by the memorandum to the amount, if any, unpaid on the shares respectively held by them ('a company limited by shares');

(b) a company having the liability of its members limited by the memorandum to such amount as the members may respectively thereby undertake to contribute to the assets of the company in the event of its being wound up ('a company limited by guarantee'); or

(c) a company not having any limit on the liability of its members ('an unlimited company').

(3) A 'public company' is a company limited by shares or limited by guarantee and having a share capital, being a company—

(a) the memorandum of which states that it is to be a public company, and

(b) in relation to which the provisions of this Act or the former Companies Acts as to the registration or re-registration of a company as a public company have been complied with on or after 22 December 1980;

and a 'private company' is a company that is not a public company.

(3A) Notwithstanding subsection (1), one person may, for a lawful purpose, by subscribing his name to a memorandum of association and otherwise complying with the requirements of this Act in respect of registration, form an incorporated company being a private company limited by shares or by guarantee.

(4) With effect from 22 December 1980, a company cannot be formed as, or become, a company limited by guarantee with a share capital.

2 Requirements with respect to memorandum

(1) The memorandum of every company must state—

(a) the name of the company;

(b) whether the registered office of the company is to be situated in England and Wales, or in Scotland;

(c) the objects of the company.

(2) Alternatively to subsection (1)(b), the memorandum may contain a statement that the company's registered office is to be situated in Wales; and a company whose registered office is situated in Wales may by special resolution alter its memorandum so as to provide that its registered office is to be so situated.

(3) The memorandum of a company limited by shares or by guarantee must also state that the liability of its members is limited.

(4) The memorandum of a company limited by guarantee must also state that each member undertakes to contribute to the assets of the company if it should be wound up while he is a member, or within one year after he ceases to be a member, for payment of the debts and liabilities of the company contracted before he ceases to be a member, and of the costs, charges and expenses of winding up, and for adjustment of the rights of the contributories among themselves, such amount as may be required, not exceeding a specified amount.

(5) In the case of a company having a share capital—

(a) the memorandum must also (unless it is an unlimited company) state the amount of the share capital with which the company proposes to be registered and the division of the share capital into shares of a fixed amount;

(b) no subscriber of the memorandum may take less than one share; and

(c) there must be shown in the memorandum against the name of each subscriber the number of shares he takes.

(6) Subject to subsection (6A), the memorandum must be signed by each subscriber in the presence of at least one witness, who must attest the signature. . . .

(6A) Where the memorandum is delivered to the registrar otherwise than in legible form and is authenticated by each subscriber in such manner as is directed by the registrar, the requirements in subsection (6) for signature in the presence of at least one witness and for attestation of the signature do not apply.

(7) A company may not alter the conditions contained in its memorandum except in the cases, in the mode and to the extent, for which express provision is made by this Act.

3 Forms of memorandum

(1) Subject to the provisions of sections 1 and 2, the form of the memorandum of association of—

(a) a public company, being a company limited by shares,
(b) a public company, being a company limited by guarantee and having a share capital,
(c) a private company limited by shares,
(d) a private company limited by guarantee and not having a share capital,
(e) a private company limited by guarantee and having a share capital, and
(f) an unlimited company having a share capital,

shall be as specified respectively for such companies by regulations made by the Secretary of State, or as near to that form as circumstances admit.

(2) Regulations under this section shall be made by statutory instrument subject to annulment in pursuance of a resolution of either House of Parliament.

3A Statement of company's objects: general commercial company

Where the company's memorandum states that the object of the company is to carry on business as a general commercial company—

(a) the object of the company is to carry on any trade or business whatsoever, and
(b) the company has power to do all such things as are incidental or conducive to the carrying on of any trade or business by it.

4 Resolution to alter objects

(1) A company may by special resolution alter its memorandum with respect to the statement of the company's objects.

(2) If an application is made under the following section, an alteration does not have effect except in so far as it is confirmed by the court.

5 Procedure for objecting to alteration

(1) Where a company's memorandum has been altered by special resolution under section 4, application may be made to the court for the alteration to be cancelled.

(2) Such an application may be made—

(a) by the holders of not less in the aggregate than 15 per cent in nominal value of the company's issued share capital or any class of it or, if the company is not limited by shares, not less than 15 per cent of the company's members; or
(b) by the holders of not less than 15 per cent of the company's debentures entitling the holders to object to an alteration of its objects;

but an application shall not be made by any person who has consented to or voted in favour of the alteration.

(3) The application must be made within 21 days after the date on which the resolution altering the company's objects was passed, and may be made on behalf of the persons entitled to make the application by such one or more of their number as they may appoint in writing for the purpose.

(4) The court may on such an application make an order confirming the alteration either wholly or in part and on such terms and conditions as it thinks fit, and may—

(a) if it thinks fit, adjourn the proceedings in order that an arrangement may be made to its satisfaction for the purchase of the interests of dissentient members, and

(b) give such directions and make such orders as it thinks expedient for facilitating or carrying into effect any such arrangement.

(5) The court's order may (if the court thinks fit) provide for the purchase by the company of the shares of any members of the company, and for the reduction accordingly of its capital, and may make such alterations in the company's memorandum and articles as may be required in consequence of that provision.

(6) If the court's order requires the company not to make any, or any specified, alteration in its memorandum or articles, the company does not then have power without the leave of the court to make any such alteration in breach of that requirement.

(7) An alteration in the memorandum or articles of a company made by virtue of an order under this section, other than one made by resolution of the company, is of the same effect as if duly made by resolution; and this Act applies accordingly to the memorandum or articles as so altered.

(7A) For the purposes of subsection (2)(a), any of the company's issued share capital held as treasury shares must be disregarded.

(8) The debentures entitling the holders to object to an alteration of a company's objects are any debentures secured by a floating charge which were issued or first issued before 1 December 1947 or form part of the same series as any debentures so issued; and a special resolution altering a company's objects requires the same notice to the holders of any such debentures as to members of the company.

In the absence of provisions regulating the giving of notice to any such debenture holders, the provisions of the company's articles regulating the giving of notice to members apply.

[*Section 5(7A) is in force from 1 December 2003.*]

6 Provisions supplementing ss. 4, 5

(1) Where a company passes a resolution altering its objects, then—

(a) if with respect to the resolution no application is made under section 5, the company shall within 15 days from the end of the period for making such an application deliver to the registrar of companies a printed copy of its memorandum as altered; and

(b) if such an application is made, the company shall—

(i) forthwith give notice (in the prescribed form) of that fact to the registrar, and

(ii) within 15 days from the date of any order cancelling or confirming the alteration, deliver to the registrar an office copy of the order and, in the case of an order confirming the alteration, a printed copy of the memorandum as altered.

(2) The court may by order at any time extend the time for the delivery of documents to the registrar under subsection (1)(b) for such period as the court may think proper.

(3) If a company makes default in giving notice or delivering any document to the registrar of companies as required by subsection (1), the company and every officer of it who is in default is liable to a fine and, for continued contravention, to a daily default fine.

(4) The validity of an alteration of a company's memorandum with respect to the objects of the company shall not be questioned on the ground that it was not authorised by section 4, except in proceedings taken for the purpose (whether under section 5 or otherwise) before the expiration of 21 days after the date of the resolution in that behalf.

(5) Where such proceedings are taken otherwise than under section 5, subsections (1) to (3) above apply in relation to the proceedings as if they had been taken under that section, and as if an order declaring the alteration invalid were an order cancelling it, and as if an order dismissing the proceedings were an order confirming the alteration.

Articles of association

7   Articles prescribing regulations for companies

(1) There may in the case of a company limited by shares, and there shall in the case of a company limited by guarantee or unlimited, be registered with the memorandum articles of association signed by the subscribers to the memorandum and prescribing regulations for the company.

(2) In the case of an unlimited company having a share capital, the articles must state the amount of share capital with which the company proposes to be registered.

(3) Articles must—

(a) be printed,

(b) be divided into paragraphs numbered consecutively, and

(c) subject to subsection (3A), be signed by each subscriber of the memorandum in the presence of at least one witness who must attest the signature. . . .

(3A) Where the articles are delivered to the registrar otherwise than in legible form and are authenticated by each subscriber to the memorandum in such manner as is directed by the registrar, the requirements in subsection (3)(c) for signature in the presence of at least one witness and for attestation of the signature do not apply.

8   Tables A, C, D and E

(1) Table A is as prescribed by regulations made by the Secretary of State; and a company may for its articles adopt the whole or any part of that Table.

(2) In the case of a company limited by shares, if articles are not registered or, if articles are registered, in so far as they do not exclude or modify Table A, that Table (so far as applicable, and as in force at the date of the company's registration) constitutes the company's articles, in the same manner and to the same extent as if articles in the form of that Table had been duly registered.

(3) If in consequence of regulations under this section Table A is altered, the alteration does not affect a company registered before the alteration takes effect, or repeal as respects that company any portion of the Table.

(4) The form of the articles of association of—

(a) a company limited by guarantee and not having a share capital,

(b) a company limited by guarantee and having a share capital, and

(c) an unlimited company having a share capital,

shall be respectively in accordance with Table C, D or E prescribed by regulations made by the Secretary of State, or as near to that form as circumstances admit.

(5) Regulations under this section shall be made by statutory instrument subject to annulment in pursuance of a resolution of either House of Parliament.

8A   Table G

(1) The Secretary of State may by regulations prescribe a Table G containing articles of association appropriate for a partnership company, that is, a company limited by shares whose shares are intended to be held to a substantial extent by or on behalf of its employees.

(2) A company limited by shares may for its articles adopt the whole or any part of that Table.

(3) If in consequence of regulations under this section Table G is altered, the alteration does not affect a company registered before the alteration takes effect, or repeal as respects that company any portion of the Table.

(4) Regulations under this section shall be made by statutory instrument which shall be subject to annulment in pursuance of a resolution of either House of Parliament.

[*Section 8A will be inserted when the Companies Act 1989, s. 128, is brought into force.*]

9   Alteration of articles by special resolution

(1) Subject to the provisions of this Act and to the conditions contained in its memorandum, a company may by special resolution alter its articles.

(2) Alterations so made in the articles are (subject to this Act) as valid as if originally contained in them, and are subject in like manner to alteration by special resolution.

Registration and its consequences

10   Documents to be sent to registrar

(1) The company's memorandum and articles (if any) shall be delivered—

(a) to the registrar of companies for England and Wales, if the memorandum states that the registered office of the company is to be situated in England and Wales, or that it is to be situated in Wales; and

(b) to the registrar of companies for Scotland, if the memorandum states that the registered office of the company is to be situated in Scotland.

(2) With the memorandum there shall be delivered a statement in the prescribed form containing the names and requisite particulars of—

(a) the person who is, or the persons who are, to be the first director or directors of the company; and

(b) the person who is, or the persons who are, to be the first secretary or joint secretaries of the company;

and the requisite particulars in each case are those set out in Schedule 1.

(2A) Where any statement delivered under subsection (2) includes an address specified in reliance on paragraph 5 of Schedule 1 there shall be delivered with the statement, a statement in the prescribed form containing particulars of the usual residential address of the director or secretary whose address is so specified.

(3) The statement under subsection (2) shall be signed by or on behalf of the subscribers of the memorandum and shall contain a consent signed by each of the persons named in it as a director, as secretary or as one of joint secretaries, to act in the relevant capacity.

(4) Where a memorandum is delivered by a person as agent for the subscribers, the statement shall specify that fact and the person's name and address.

(5) An appointment by any articles delivered with the memorandum of a person as director or secretary of the company is void unless he is named as a director or secretary in the statement.

(6) There shall in the statement be specified the intended situation of the company's registered office on incorporation.

11   Minimum authorised capital (public companies)

When a memorandum delivered to the registrar of companies under section 10 states that the association to be registered is to be a public company, the amount of the share capital stated in the memorandum to be that with which the company proposes to be registered must not be less than the authorised minimum (defined in section 118).

12   Duty of registrar

(1) The registrar of companies shall not register a company's memorandum delivered under section 10 unless he is satisfied that all the requirements of this Act in respect of registration and of matters precedent and incidental to it have been complied with.

(2) Subject to this, the registrar shall retain and register the memorandum and articles (if any) delivered to him under that section.

(3) Subject to subsection (3A), a statutory declaration in the prescribed form by—

(a) a solicitor engaged in the formation of a company, or

(b) a person named as a director or secretary of the company in the statement delivered under section 10(2),

that those requirements have been complied with shall be delivered to the registrar of companies, and the registrar may accept such a declaration as sufficient evidence of compliance.

(3A) In place of the statutory declaration referred to in subsection (3), there may be delivered to the registrar of companies using electronic communications a statement made by a person mentioned in paragraph (a) or (b) of subsection (3) that the requirements mentioned in subsection (1) have been complied with; and the registrar may accept such a statement as sufficient evidence of compliance.

(3B) Any person who makes a false statement under subsection (3A) which he knows to be false or does not believe to be true is liable to imprisonment or a fine, or both.

13   Effect of registration

(1) On the registration of a company's memorandum, the registrar of companies shall give a certificate that the company is incorporated and, in the case of a limited company, that it is limited.

(2) The certificate may be signed by the registrar, or authenticated by his official seal.

(3) From the date of incorporation mentioned in the certificate, the subscribers of the memorandum, together with such other persons as may from time to time become members of the company, shall be a body corporate by the name contained in the memorandum.

(4) That body corporate is then capable forthwith of exercising all the functions of an incorporated company, but with such liability on the part of its members to contribute to its assets in the event of its being wound up as is provided by this Act and the Insolvency Act.

This is subject, in the case of a public company, to section 117 (additional certificate as to amount of allotted share capital).

(5) The persons named in the statement under section 10 as directors, secretary or joint secretaries are, on the company's incorporation, deemed to have been respectively appointed as its first directors, secretary or joint secretaries.

(6) Where the registrar registers an association's memorandum which states that the association is to be a public company, the certificate of incorporation shall contain a statement that the company is a public company.

(7) A certificate of incorporation given in respect of an association is conclusive evidence—

    (a) that the requirements of this Act in respect of registration and of matters precedent and incidental to it have been complied with, and that the association is a company authorised to be registered, and is duly registered, under this Act, and

    (b) if the certificate contains a statement that the company is a public company, that the company is such a company.

14   Effect of memorandum and articles

(1) Subject to the provisions of this Act, the memorandum and articles, when registered, bind the company and its members to the same extent as if they respectively had been signed and sealed by each member, and contained covenants on the part of each member to observe all the provisions of the memorandum and of the articles.

(2) Money payable by a member to the company under the memorandum or articles is a debt due from him to the company, and in England and Wales is of the nature of a specialty debt.

15   Memorandum and articles of company limited by guarantee

(1) In the case of a company limited by guarantee and not having a share capital, every provision in the memorandum or articles, or in any resolution of the company purporting to give any person a right to participate in the divisible profits of the company otherwise than as a member, is void.

(2) For purposes of provisions of this Act relating to the memorandum of a company limited by guarantee, and for those of section 1(4) and this section, every provision in the memorandum or articles, or in any resolution, of a company so limited purporting to divide the company's undertaking into shares or interests is to be treated as a provision for a share

capital, notwithstanding that the nominal amount or number of the shares or interests is not specified by the provision.

16   Effect of alteration on company's members

(1) A member of a company is not bound by an alteration made in the memorandum or articles after the date on which he became a member, if and so far as the alteration—

(a) requires him to take or subscribe for more shares than the number held by him at the date on which the alteration is made; or

(b) in any way increases his liability as at that date to contribute to the company's share capital or otherwise to pay money to the company.

(2) Subsection (1) operates notwithstanding anything in the memorandum or articles; but it does not apply in a case where the member agrees in writing, either before or after the alteration is made, to be bound by the alteration.

17   Conditions in memorandum which could have been in articles

(1) A condition contained in a company's memorandum which could lawfully have been contained in articles of association instead of in the memorandum may be altered by the company by special resolution; but if an application is made to the court for the alteration to be cancelled, the alteration does not have effect except in so far as it is confirmed by the court.

(2) This section—

(a) is subject to section 16, and also to Part XVII (court order protecting minority), and

(b) does not apply where the memorandum itself provides for or prohibits the alteration of all or any of the conditions above referred to, and does not authorise any variation or abrogation of the special rights of any class of members.

(3) Section 5 (except subsections (2)(b) and (8)) and section 6(1) to (3) apply in relation to any alteration and to any application made under this section as they apply in relation to alterations and applications under sections 4 to 6.

18   Amendments of memorandum or articles to be registered

(1) Where an alteration is made in a company's memorandum or articles by any statutory provision, whether contained in an Act of Parliament or in an instrument made under an Act, a printed copy of the Act or instrument shall, not later than 15 days after that provision comes into force, be forwarded to the registrar of companies and recorded by him.

(2) Where a company is required (by this section or otherwise) to send to the registrar any document making or evidencing an alteration in the company's memorandum or articles (other than a special resolution under section 4), the company shall send with it a printed copy of the memorandum or articles as altered.

(3) If a company fails to comply with this section, the company and any officer of it who is in default is liable to a fine and, for continued contravention, to a daily default fine.

19   Copies of memorandum and articles to be given to members

(1) A company shall, on being so required by any member, send to him a copy of the memorandum and of the articles (if any), and a copy of any Act of Parliament which alters the memorandum, subject to payment—

(a) in the case of a copy of the memorandum and of the articles, of 5 pence or such less sum as the company may prescribe, and

(b) in the case of a copy of an Act, of such sum not exceeding its published price as the company may require.

(2) If a company makes default in complying with this section, the company and every officer of it who is in default is liable for each offence to a fine.

20   Issued copy of memorandum to embody alterations

(1) Where an alteration is made in a company's memorandum, every copy of the memorandum issued after the date of the alteration shall be in accordance with the alteration.

(2) If, where any such alteration has been made, the company at any time after the date of the alteration issues any copies of the memorandum which are not in accordance with the alteration, it is liable to a fine, and so too is every officer of the company who is in default.

A company's membership

22 Definition of 'member'

(1) The subscribers of a company's memorandum are deemed to have agreed to become members of the company, and on its registration shall be entered as such in its register of members.

(2) Every other person who agrees to become a member of a company, and whose name is entered in its register of members, is a member of the company.

23 Membership of holding company

(1) Except as mentioned in this section, a body corporate cannot be a member of a company which is its holding company and any allotment or transfer of shares in a company to its subsidiary is void.

(2) The prohibition does not apply where the subsidiary is concerned only as personal representative or trustee unless, in the latter case, the holding company or a subsidiary of it is beneficially interested under the trust.

For the purpose of ascertaining whether the holding company or a subsidiary is so interested, there shall be disregarded—

    (a) any interest held only by way of security for the purposes of a transaction entered into by the holding company or subsidiary in the ordinary course of a business which includes the lending of money;

    (b) any such interest as is mentioned in Part I of Schedule 2.

(3) The prohibition does not apply where shares in the holding company are held by the subsidiary in the ordinary course of its business as an intermediary.

For this purpose a person is an intermediary if that person—

    (a) carries on a bona fide business of dealing in securities;

    (b) is a member of an EEA exchange (and satisfies any requirements for recognition as a dealer in securities laid down by that exchange) or is otherwise approved or supervised as a dealer in securities under the laws of an EEA State; and

    (c) does not carry on an excluded business.

(3A) The excluded businesses are the following—

    (a) any business which consists wholly or mainly in the making or managing of investments;

    (b) any business which consists wholly or mainly in, or is carried on wholly or mainly for the purpose of, providing services to persons who are connected with the person carrying on the business;

    (c) any business which consists in insurance business;

    (d) any business which consists in managing or acting as trustee in relation to a pension scheme or which is carried on by the manager or trustee of such a scheme in connection with or for the purposes of the scheme;

    (e) any business which consists in operating or acting as trustee in relation to a collective investment scheme or is carried on by the operator or trustee of such a scheme in connection with or for the purposes of the scheme.

(3B) For the purposes of subsections (3) and (3A)—

    (a) the question whether a person is connected with another shall be determined in accordance with the provisions of section 839 of the Income and Corporation Taxes Act 1988;

    (b) 'collective investment scheme' has the meaning given in section 236 of the Financial Services and Markets Act 2000;

(c) 'EEA exchange' means a market which appears on the list drawn up by an EEA State pursuant to Article 16 of Council Directive 93/22/EEC on investment services in the securities field;

(d) 'insurance business' means business which consists of the effecting or carrying out of contracts of insurance;

(e) 'securities' includes—
    (i) options,
    (ii) futures, and
    (iii) contracts for differences,
    and rights or interests in those investments;

(f) 'trustee' and 'the operator' shall, in relation to a collective investment scheme, be construed in accordance with section 237(2) of the Financial Services and Markets Act 2000.

(3BA) Subsection (3B) must be read with—
    (a) section 22 of the Financial Services and Markets Act 2000;
    (b) any relevant order under that section; and
    (c) Schedule 2 to that Act.

(3C) Where—
    (a) a subsidiary which is a dealer in securities has purportedly acquired shares in its holding company in contravention of the prohibition in subsection (1); and
    (b) a person acting in good faith has agreed, for value and without notice of that contravention, to acquire shares in the holding company from the subsidiary or from someone who has purportedly acquired the shares after their disposal by the subsidiary, any transfer to that person of the shares mentioned in paragraph (a) shall have the same effect as it would have had if their original acquisition by the subsidiary had not been in contravention of the prohibition.

(4) Where a body corporate became a holder of shares in a company—
    (a) before 1 July 1948, or
    (b) on or after that date and before 20 October 1997, in circumstances in which this section as it then had effect did not apply,
but at any time on or after 20 October 1997 falls within the prohibition in subsection (1) above in respect of those shares, it may continue to be a member of that company; but for so long as that prohibition would apply, apart from this subsection, it has no right to vote in respect of those shares at meetings of the company or of any class of its members.

(5) Where a body corporate becomes a holder of shares in a company on or after 20 October 1997 in circumstances in which the prohibition in subsection (1) does not apply, but subsequently falls within that prohibition in respect of those shares, it may continue to be a member of that company; but for so long as that prohibition would apply, apart from this subsection, it has no right to vote in respect of those shares at meetings of the company or of any class of its members.

(6) Where a body corporate is permitted to continue as a member of a company by virtue of subsection (4) or (5), an allotment to it of fully paid shares in the company may be validly made by way of capitalisation of reserves of the company; but for so long as the prohibition in subsection (1) would apply, apart from subsection (4) or (5), it has no right to vote in respect of those shares at meetings of the company or of any class of its members.

(7) The provisions of this section apply to a nominee acting on behalf of a subsidiary as to the subsidiary itself.

(8) In relation to a company other than a company limited by shares, the references in this section to shares shall be construed as references to the interest of its members as such, whatever the form of that interest.

24 Minimum membership for carrying on business

(1) If a company, other than a private company limited by shares or by guarantee, carries on business without having at least two members and does so for more than 6 months, a person who, for the whole or any part of the period that it so carries on business after those 6 months—

    (a) is a member of the company, and

    (b) knows that it is carrying on business with only one member,

is liable (jointly and severally with the company) for the payment of the company's debts contracted during the period or, as the case may be, that part of it.

(2) For the purposes of this section references to a member of a company do not include the company itself where it is such a member only by virtue of its holding shares as treasury shares.
[*Section 24(2) is in force from 1 December 2003.*]

CHAPTER II   COMPANY NAMES

25 Name as stated in memorandum

(1) The name of a public company must end with the words 'public limited company' or, if the memorandum states that the company's registered office is to be situated in Wales, those words or their equivalent in Welsh ('cwmni cyfyngedig cyhoeddus'); and those words or that equivalent may not be preceded by the word 'limited' or its equivalent in Welsh ('cyfyngedig').

(2) In the case of a company limited by shares or by guarantee (not being a public company), the name must have 'limited' as its last word, except that—

    (a) this is subject to section 30 (exempting, in certain circumstances, a company from the requirement to have 'limited' as part of the name), and

    (b) if the company is to be registered with a memorandum stating that its registered office is to be situated in Wales, the name may have 'cyfyngedig' as its last word.

26 Prohibition on registration of certain names

(1) A company shall not be registered under this Act by a name—

    (a) which includes, otherwise than at the end of the name, any of the following words or expressions, that is to say, 'limited', 'unlimited' or 'public limited company' or their Welsh equivalents ('cyfyngedig', 'anghyfyngedig' and 'cwmni cyfyngedig cyhoeddus' respectively);

    (b) which includes, otherwise than at the end of the name, an abbreviation of any of those words or expressions;

    (bb) which includes, at any place in the name, the expressions 'investment company with variable capital' or 'open-ended investment company' or their Welsh equivalents ('cwmni buddsoddi â chyfalaf newidiol' and 'cwmni buddsoddiant penagored' respectively);

    (bbb) which includes, at any place in the name, the expression 'limited liability partnership' or its Welsh equivalent ('partneriaeth atebolrwydd cyfyngedig');

    (c) which is the same as a name appearing in the registrar's index of company names;

    (d) the use of which by the company would in the opinion of the Secretary of State constitute a criminal offence; or

    (e) which in the opinion of the Secretary of State is offensive.

(2) Except with the approval of the Secretary of State, a company shall not be registered under this Act by a name which—

    (a) in the opinion of the Secretary of State would be likely to give the impression that the company is connected in any way with Her Majesty's Government or with any local authority; or

    (b) includes any word or expression for the time being specified in regulations under section 29.

'Local authority' means any local authority within the meaning of the Local Government Act 1972 or the Local Government (Scotland) Act 1973, the Common Council of the City of London or the Council of the Isles of Scilly.

(3) In determining for purposes of subsection (1)(c) whether one name is the same as another, there are to be disregarded—

    (a) the definite article, where it is the first word of the name;

    (b) the following words and expressions where they appear at the end of the name, that is to say—

        'company' or its Welsh equivalent ('cwmni'),

        'and company' or its Welsh equivalent ('a'r cwmni'),

        'company limited' or its Welsh equivalent ('cwmni cyfyngedig'),

        'and company limited' or its Welsh equivalent ('a'r cwmni cyfyngedig'),

        'limited' or its Welsh equivalent ('cyfyngedig'),

        'unlimited' or its Welsh equivalent ('anghyfyngedig'),

        'public limited company' or its Welsh equivalent ('cwmni cyfyngedig cyhoeddus'), and

        'open-ended investment company' or its Welsh equivalent ('cwmni buddsoddiant penagored');

    (c) abbreviations of any of those words or expressions where they appear at the end of the name; and

    (d) type and case of letters, accents, spaces between letters and punctuation marks;

and 'and' and '&' are to be taken as the same.

27 Alternatives of statutory designations

(1) A company which by any provision of this Act is either required or entitled to include in its name, as its last part, any of the words specified in subsection (4) below may, instead of those words, include as the last part of the name the abbreviations there specified as alternatives in relation to those words.

(2) A reference in this Act to the name of a company or to the inclusion of any of those words in a company's name includes a reference to the name including (in place of any of the words so specified) the appropriate alternative, or to the inclusion of the appropriate alternative, as the case may be.

(3) A provision of this Act requiring a company not to include any of those words in its name also requires it not to include the abbreviated alternative specified in subsection (4).

(4) For the purposes of this section—

    (a) the alternative of 'limited' is 'ltd.';

    (b) the alternative of 'public limited company' is 'p.l.c.';

    (c) the alternative of 'cyfyngedig' is 'cyf.'; and

    (d) the alternative of 'cwmni cyfyngedig cyhoeddus' is 'c.c.c.'.

28 Change of name

(1) A company may by special resolution change its name (but subject to section 31 in the case of a company which has received a direction under subsection (2) of that section from the Secretary of State).

(2) Where a company has been registered by a name which—

    (a) is the same as or, in the opinion of the Secretary of State, too like a name appearing at the time of the registration in the registrar's index of company names, or

    (b) is the same as or, in the opinion of the Secretary of State, too like a name which should have appeared in that index at that time,

the Secretary of State may within 12 months of that time, in writing, direct the company to change its name within such period as he may specify.

Section 26(3) applies in determining under this subsection whether a name is the same as or too like another.

(3) If it appears to the Secretary of State that misleading information has been given for the purpose of a company's registration with a particular name, or that undertakings or assurances have been given for that purpose and have not been fulfilled, he may within 5 years of the date of its registration with that name in writing direct the company to change its name within such period as he may specify.

(4) Where a direction has been given under subsection (2) or (3), the Secretary of State may by a further direction in writing extend the period within which the company is to change its name, at any time before the end of that period.

(5) A company which fails to comply with a direction under this section, and any officer of it who is in default, is liable to a fine and, for continued contravention, to a daily default fine.

(6) Where a company changes its name under this section, the registrar of companies shall (subject to section 26) enter the new name on the register in place of the former name, and shall issue a certificate of incorporation altered to meet the circumstances of the case; and the change of name has effect from the date on which the altered certificate is issued.

(7) A change of name by a company under this section does not affect any rights or obligations of the company or render defective any legal proceedings by or against it; and any legal proceedings that might have been continued or commenced against it by its former name may be continued or commenced against it by its new name.

29 Regulations about names

(1) The Secretary of State may by regulations—

    (a) specify words or expressions for the registration of which as or as part of a company's corporate name his approval is required under section 26(2)(b), and

    (b) in relation to any such word or expression, specify a Government department or other body as the relevant body for purposes of the following subsection.

(2) Where a company proposes to have as, or as part of, its corporate name any such word or expression and a Government department or other body is specified under subsection (1)(b) in relation to that word or expression, a request shall be made (in writing) to the relevant body to indicate whether (and if so why) it has any objections to the proposal; and the person to make the request is—

    (a) in the case of a company seeking to be registered under this Part, the person making the statutory declaration under section 12(3) or statement under section 12(3A) (as the case may be),

    (b) in the case of a company seeking to be registered under section 680, the persons making the statutory declaration under section 686(2) or statement under section 686(2A) (as the case may be), and

    (c) in any other case, a director or secretary of the company concerned.

(3) The person who has made that request to the relevant body shall submit to the registrar of companies a statement that it has been made and a copy of any response received from that body, together with—

    (a) the requisite statutory declaration or statement, or

    (b) a copy of the special resolution changing the company's name, according as the case is one or other of those mentioned in subsection (2).

(4) Sections 709 and 710 (public rights of inspection of documents kept by registrar of companies) do not apply to documents sent under subsection (3) of this section.

(5) Regulations under this section may contain such transitional provisions and savings as the Secretary of State thinks appropriate and may make different provision for different cases or classes of case.

(6) The regulations shall be made by statutory instrument, to be laid before Parliament after it is made; and the regulations shall cease to have effect at the end of 28 days beginning

with the day on which the regulations were made (but without prejudice to anything previously done by virtue of them or to the making of new regulations), unless during that period they are approved by resolution of each House. In reckoning that period, no account is to be taken of any time during which Parliament is dissolved or prorogued or during which both Houses are adjourned for more than 4 days.

30   Exemption from requirement of 'limited' as part of the name

(1) Certain companies are exempt from requirements of this Act relating to the use of 'limited' as part of the company name.

(2) A private company limited by guarantee is exempt from those requirements, and so too is a company which on 25 February 1982 was a private company limited by shares with a name which, by virtue of a licence under section 19 of the Companies Act 1948, did not include 'limited'; but in either case the company must, to have the exemption, comply with the requirements of the following subsection.

(3) Those requirements are that—

(a) the objects of the company are (or, in the case of a company about to be registered, are to be) the promotion of commerce, art, science, education, religion, charity or any profession, and anything incidental or conducive to any of those objects; and

(b) the company's memorandum or articles—

(i) require its profits (if any) or other income to be applied in promoting its objects

(ii) prohibit the payment of dividends to its members, and

(iii) require all the assets which would otherwise be available to its members generally to be transferred on its winding up either to another body with objects similar to its own or to another body the objects of which are the promotion of charity and anything incidental or conducive thereto (whether or not the body is a member of the company).

(4) Subject to subsection (5A), a statutory declaration that a company complies with the requirements of subsection (3) may be delivered to the registrar of companies, who may accept the declaration as sufficient evidence of the matters stated in it.

(5) The statutory declaration must be in the prescribed form and be made—

(a) in the case of a company to be formed, by a solicitor engaged in its formation or by a person named as director or secretary in the statement delivered under section 10(2);

(b) in the case of a company to be registered in pursuance of section 680, by two or more directors or other principal officers of the company; and

(c) in the case of a company proposing to change its name so that it ceases to have the word 'limited' as part of its name, by a director or secretary of the company.

(5A) In place of the statutory declaration referred to in subsection (4), there may be delivered to the registrar of companies using electronic communications a statement made by a person falling within the applicable paragraph of subsection (5) stating that the company complies with the requirements of subsection (3); and the registrar may accept such a statement as sufficient evidence of the matters stated in it.

(5B) The registrar may refuse to register a company by a name which does not include the word 'limited' unless a statutory declaration under subsection (4) or statement under subsection (5A) has been delivered to him.

(5C) Any person who makes a false statement under subsection (5A) which he knows to be false or does not believe to be true is liable to imprisonment or a fine, or both.

(6) References in this section to the word 'limited' include (in an appropriate case) its Welsh equivalent ('cyfyngedig'), and the appropriate alternative ('ltd.' or 'cyf.', as the case may be).

(7) A company which is exempt from requirements relating to the use of 'limited' and does not include that word as part of its name, is also exempt from the requirements of this Act relating to the publication of its name and the sending of lists of members to the registrar of companies.

31   Provisions applying to company exempt under s. 30

(1) A company which is exempt under section 30 and whose name does not include 'limited' shall not alter its memorandum or articles of association so that it ceases to comply with the requirements of subsection (3) of that section.

(2) If it appears to the Secretary of State that such a company—
- (a) has carried on any business other than the promotion of any of the objects mentioned in that subsection, or
- (b) has applied any of its profits or other income otherwise than in promoting such objects, or
- (c) has paid a dividend to any of its members,

he may, in writing, direct the company to change its name by resolution of the directors within such period as may be specified in the direction, so that its name ends with 'limited'.

A resolution passed by the directors in compliance with a direction under this subsection is subject to section 380 of this Act (copy to be forwarded to the registrar of companies within 15 days).

(3) A company which has received a direction under subsection (2) shall not thereafter be registered by a name which does not include 'limited', without the approval of the Secretary of State.

(4) References in this section to the word 'limited' include (in an appropriate case) its Welsh equivalent ('cyfyngedig'), and the appropriate alternative ('ltd.' or 'cyf.', as the case may be).

(5) A company which contravenes subsection (1), and any officer of it who is in default, is liable to a fine and, for continued contravention, to a daily default fine.

(6) A company which fails to comply with a direction by the Secretary of State under subsection (2), and any officer of the company who is in default, is liable to a fine and, for continued contravention, to a daily default fine.

32   Power to require company to abandon misleading name

(1) If in the Secretary of State's opinion the name by which a company is registered gives so misleading an indication of the nature of its activities as to be likely to cause harm to the public, he may direct it to change its name.

(2) The direction must, if not duly made the subject of an application to the court under the following subsection, be complied with within a period of 6 weeks from the date of the direction or such longer period as the Secretary of State may think fit to allow.

(3) The company may, within a period of 3 weeks from the date of the direction, apply to the court to set it aside; and the court may set the direction aside or confirm it and, if it confirms the direction, shall specify a period within which it must be complied with.

(4) If a company makes default in complying with a direction under this section, it is liable to a fine and, for continued contravention, to a daily default fine.

(5) Where a company changes its name under this section, the registrar shall (subject to section 26) enter the new name on the register in place of the former name, and shall issue a certificate of incorporation altered to meet the circumstances of the case; and the change of name has effect from the date on which the altered certificate is issued.

(6) A change of name by a company under this section does not affect any of the rights or obligations of the company, or render defective any legal proceedings by or against it; and any legal proceedings that might have been continued or commenced against it by its former name may be continued or commenced against it by its new name.

33   Prohibition on trading under misleading name

(1) A person who is not a public company is guilty of an offence if he carries on any trade, profession or business under a name which includes, as its last part, the words 'public limited company' or their equivalent in Welsh ('cwmni cyfyngedig cyhoeddus').

(2) A public company is guilty of an offence if, in circumstances in which the fact that it is a public company is likely to be material to any person, it uses a name which may reasonably be expected to give the impression that it is a private company.

(3) A person guilty of an offence under subsection (1) or (2) and, if that person is a company, any officer of the company who is in default, is liable to a fine and, for continued contravention, to a daily default fine.

34   Penalty for improper use of 'limited' or 'cyfyngedig'

If any person trades or carries on business under a name or title of which 'limited' or 'cyfynge-dig', or any contraction or imitation of either of those words, is the last word, that person, unless duly incorporated with limited liability, is liable to a fine and, for continued contravention, to a daily default fine.

35   A company's capacity not limited by its memorandum

(1) The validity of an act done by a company shall not be called into question on the ground of lack of capacity by reason of anything in the company's memorandum.

(2) A member of a company may bring proceedings to restrain the doing of an act which but for subsection (1) would be beyond the company's capacity; but no such proceedings shall lie in respect of an act to be done in fulfilment of a legal obligation arising from a previous act of the company.

(3) It remains the duty of the directors to observe any limitations on their powers flowing from the company's memorandum; and action by the directors which but for subsection (1) would be beyond the company's capacity may only be ratified by the company by special resolution.

A resolution ratifying such action shall not affect any liability incurred by the directors or any other person; relief from any such liability must be agreed to separately by special resolution.

(4) The operation of this section is restricted by section 65(1) of the Charities Act 1993 and section 112(3) of the Companies Act 1989 in relation to companies which are charities; and section 322A below (invalidity of certain transactions to which directors or their associates are parties) has effect notwithstanding this section.

35A   Power of directors to bind the company

(1) In favour of a person dealing with a company in good faith, the power of the board of directors to bind the company, or authorise others to do so, shall be deemed to be free of any limitation under the company's constitution.

(2) For this purpose—

(a) a person 'deals with' a company if he is a party to any transaction or other act to which the company is a party;

(b) a person shall not be regarded as acting in bad faith by reason only of his knowing that an act is beyond the powers of the directors under the company's constitution; and

(c) a person shall be presumed to have acted in good faith unless the contrary is proved.

(3) The references above to limitations on the directors' powers under the company's constitution include limitations deriving—

(a) from a resolution of the company in general meeting or a meeting of any class of shareholders, or

(b) from any agreement between the members of the company or of any class of shareholders.

(4) Subsection (1) does not affect any right of a member of the company to bring proceedings to restrain the doing of an act which is beyond the powers of the directors; but no such proceedings shall lie in respect of an act to be done in fulfilment of a legal obligation arising from a previous act of the company.

(5) Nor does that subsection affect any liability incurred by the directors, or any other person, by reason of the directors' exceeding their powers.

(6) The operation of this section is restricted by section 65(1) of the Charities Act 1993 and section 112(3) of the Companies Act 1989 in relation to companies which are charities; and section 322A below (invalidity of certain transactions to which directors or their associates are parties) has effect notwithstanding this section.

35B   No duty to enquire as to capacity of company or authority of directors
A party to a transaction with a company is not bound to enquire as to whether it is permitted by the company's memorandum or as to any limitation on the powers of the board of directors to bind the company or authorise others to do so.

36   Company contracts: England and Wales
Under the law of England and Wales a contract may be made—
   (a) by a company, by writing under its common seal, or
   (b) on behalf of a company, by any person acting under its authority, express or implied;
and any formalities required by law in the case of a contract made by an individual also apply, unless a contrary intention appears, to a contract made by or on behalf of a company.

36A   Execution of documents: England and Wales
(1) Under the law of England and Wales the following provisions have effect with respect to the execution of documents by a company.

(2) A document is executed by a company by the affixing of its common seal.

(3) A company need not have a common seal, however, and the following subsections apply whether it does or not.

(4) A document signed by a director and the secretary of a company, or by two directors of a company, and expressed (in whatever form of words) to be executed by the company has the same effect as if executed under the common seal of the company.

(5) A document executed by a company which makes it clear on its face that it is intended by the person or persons making it to be a deed has effect, upon delivery, as a deed; and it shall be presumed, unless a contrary intention is proved, to be delivered upon its being so executed.

(6) In favour of a purchaser a document shall be deemed to have been duly executed by a company if it purports to be signed by a director and the secretary of the company, or by two directors of the company, and where it makes it clear on its face that it is intended by the person or persons making it to be a deed, to have been delivered upon its being executed.

A 'purchaser' means a purchaser in good faith for valuable consideration and includes a lessee, mortgagee or other person who for valuable consideration acquires an interest in property.

36C   Pre-incorporation contracts, deeds and obligations
(1) A contract which purports to be made by or on behalf of a company at a time when the company has not been formed has effect, subject to any agreement to the contrary, as one made with the person purporting to act for the company or as agent for it, and he is personally liable on the contract accordingly.

(2) Subsection (1) applies—
   (a) to the making of a deed under the law of England and Wales, and
   (b) to the undertaking of an obligation under the law of Scotland,
as it applies to the making of a contract.

37   Bills of exchange and promissory notes

A bill of exchange or promissory note is deemed to have been made, accepted or endorsed on behalf of a company if made, accepted or endorsed in the name of, or by or on behalf or on account of, the company by a person acting under its authority.

38   Execution of deeds abroad

(1) A company may, by writing under its common seal, empower any person, either generally or in respect of any specified matters, as its attorney, to execute deeds on its behalf in any place elsewhere than in the United Kingdom.

(2) A deed executed by such an attorney on behalf of the company has the same effect as if it were executed under the company's common seal.

39   Power of company to have official seal for use abroad

(1) A company which has a common seal whose objects require or comprise the transaction of business in foreign countries may, if authorised by its articles, have for use in any territory, district or place elsewhere than in the United Kingdom, an official seal, which shall be a facsimile of its common seal, with the addition on its face of the name of every territory, district or place where it is to be used.

(2) The official seal when duly affixed to a document has the same effect as the company's common seal.

(3) A company having an official seal for use in any such territory, district or place may, by writing under its common seal, authorise any person appointed for the purpose in that territory, district or place to affix the official seal to any deed or other document to which the company is party in that territory, district or place.

(4) As between the company and a person dealing with such an agent, the agent's authority continues during the period (if any) mentioned in the instrument conferring the authority, or if no period is there mentioned, then until notice of the revocation or determination of the agent's authority has been given to the person dealing with him.

(5) The person affixing the official seal shall certify in writing on the deed or other instrument to which the seal is affixed the date on which and the place at which it is affixed.

40   Official seal for share certificates, etc.

A company which has a common seal may have, for use for sealing securities issued by the company and for sealing documents creating or evidencing securities so issued, an official seal which is a facsimile of its common seal with the addition on its face of the word 'Securities'.

The official seal when duly affixed to a document has the same effect as the company's common seal.

41   Authentication of documents

A document or proceeding requiring authentication by a company is sufficiently authenticated for the purposes of the law of England and Wales by the signature of a director, secretary or other authorised officer of the company.

42   Events affecting a company's status

(1) A company is not entitled to rely against other persons on the happening of any of the following events—

    (a) the making of a winding-up order in respect of the company, or the appointment of a liquidator in a voluntary winding up of the company, or

    (b) any alteration of the company's memorandum or articles, or

    (c) any change among the company's directors, or

    (d) (as regards service of any document on the company) any change in the situation of the company's registered office,

if the event had not been officially notified at the material time and is not shown by the company to have been known at that time to the person concerned, or if the material time fell on or before the 15th day after the date of official notification (or, where the 15th day was a non-business day, on or before the next day that was not) and it is shown that the person concerned was unavoidably prevented from knowing of the event at that time.

(2) In subsection (1)—

(a) 'official notification' and 'officially notified' have the meanings given by section 711(2) (registrar of companies to give public notice of the issue or receipt by him of certain documents), and

(b) 'non-business day' means a Saturday or Sunday, Christmas Day, Good Friday and any other day which is a bank holiday in the part of Great Britain where the company is registered.

PART II   RE-REGISTRATION AS A MEANS OF ALTERING A COMPANY'S STATUS

Private company becoming public

43   Re-registration of private company as public

(1) Subject to this and the following five sections, a private company (other than a company not having a share capital) may be re-registered as a public company if—

(a) a special resolution that it should be so re-registered is passed; and

(b) an application for re-registration is delivered to the registrar of companies, together with the necessary documents.

A company cannot be re-registered under this section if it has previously been re-registered as unlimited.

(2) The special resolution must—

(a) alter the company's memorandum so that it states that the company is to be a public company; and

(b) make such other alterations in the memorandum as are necessary to bring it (in substance and in form) into conformity with the requirements of this Act with respect to the memorandum of a public company (the alterations to include compliance with section 25(1) as regards the company's name); and

(c) make such alterations in the company's articles as are requisite in the circumstances.

(3) The application must be in the prescribed form and be signed by a director or secretary of the company; and the documents to be delivered with it are the following—

(a) a printed copy of the memorandum and articles as altered in pursuance of the resolution;

(b) a copy of a written statement by the company's auditors that in their opinion the relevant balance sheet shows that at the balance sheet date the amount of the company's net assets (within the meaning given to that expression by section 264(2)) was not less than the aggregate of its called-up share capital and undistributable reserves;

(c) a copy of the relevant balance sheet, together with a copy of an unqualified report (defined in section 46) by the company's auditors in relation to that balance sheet;

(d) if section 44 applies, a copy of the valuation report under subsection (2)(b) of that section; and

(e) subject to subsection (3A), a statutory declaration in the prescribed form by a director or secretary of the company—

(i) that the special resolution required by this section has been passed and that the conditions of the following two sections (so far as applicable) have been satisfied, and

(ii) that, between the balance sheet date and the application for re-registration, there has been no change in the company's financial position that has resulted in the amount of its net assets becoming less than the aggregate of its called-up share capital and undistributable reserves.

(3A) In place of the statutory declaration referred to in paragraph (e) of subsection (3), there may be delivered to the registrar of companies using electronic communications a statement made by a director or secretary of the company as to the matters set out in sub-paragraphs (i) and (ii) of that paragraph.

(3B) Any person who makes a false statement under subsection (3A) which he knows to be false or does not believe to be true is liable to imprisonment or a fine, or both.

(4) 'Relevant balance sheet' means a balance sheet prepared as at a date not more than 7 months before the company's application under this section.

(5) A resolution that a company be re-registered as a public company may change the company name by deleting the word 'company' or the words 'and company', or its or their equivalent in Welsh ('cwmni', 'a'r cwmni'), including any abbreviation of them.

44 Consideration for shares recently allotted to be valued

(1) The following applies if shares have been allotted by the company between the date as at which the relevant balance sheet was prepared and the passing of the special resolution under section 43, and those shares were allotted as fully or partly paid up as to their nominal value or any premium on them otherwise than in cash.

(2) Subject to the following provisions, the registrar of companies shall not entertain an application by the company under section 43 unless beforehand—

(a) the consideration for the allotment has been valued in accordance with section 108, and

(b) a report with respect to the value of the consideration has been made to the company (in accordance with that section) during the 6 months immediately preceding the allotment of the shares.

(3) Where an amount standing to the credit of any of the company's reserve accounts, or of its profit and loss account, has been applied in paying up (to any extent) any of the shares allotted or any premium on those shares, the amount applied does not count as consideration for the allotment, and accordingly subsection (2) does not apply to it.

(4) Subsection (2) does not apply if the allotment is in connection with an arrangement providing for it to be on terms that the whole or part of the consideration for the shares allotted is to be provided by the transfer to the company or the cancellation of all or some of the shares, or of all or some of the shares of a particular class, in another company (with or without the issue to the company applying under section 43 of shares, or of shares of any particular class, in that other company).

(5) But subsection (4) does not exclude the application of subsection (2), unless under the arrangement it is open to all the holders of the shares of the other company in question (or, where the arrangement applies only to shares of a particular class, all the holders of the other company's shares of that class) to take part in the arrangement.

In determining whether that is the case, shares held by or by a nominee of the company allotting shares in connection with the arrangement, or by or by a nominee of a company which is that company's holding company or subsidiary or a company which is a subsidiary of its holding company, are to be disregarded.

(6) Subsection (2) does not apply to preclude an application under section 43, if the allotment of the company's shares is in connection with its proposed merger with another company; that is, where one of the companies concerned proposes to acquire all the assets and liabilities of the other in exchange for the issue of shares or other securities of that one to shareholders of the other, with or without any cash payment to shareholders.

(7) In this section—

(a) 'arrangement' means any agreement, scheme or arrangement, including an arrangement sanctioned in accordance with section 425 (company compromise with creditors and members) or section 110 of the Insolvency Act (liquidator in winding up accepting shares as consideration for sale of company's property), and

(b) 'another company' includes any body corporate and any body to which letters patent have been issued under the Chartered Companies Act 1837.

45 Additional requirements relating to share capital

(1) For a private company to be re-registered under section 43 as a public company, the following conditions with respect to its share capital must be satisfied at the time the special resolution under that section is passed.

(2) Subject to subsections (5) to (7) below—

(a) the nominal value of the company's allotted share capital must be not less than the authorised minimum, and

(b) each of the company's allotted shares must be paid up at least as to one-quarter of the nominal value of that share and the whole of any premium on it.

(3) Subject to subsection (5), if any shares in the company or any premium on them have been fully or partly paid up by an undertaking given by any person that he or another should do work or perform services (whether for the company or any other person), the undertaking must have been performed or otherwise discharged.

(4) Subject to subsection (5), if shares have been allotted as fully or partly paid up as to their nominal value or any premium on them otherwise than in cash, and the consideration for the allotment consists of or includes an undertaking to the company (other than one to which subsection (3) applies), then either—

(a) the undertaking must have been performed or otherwise discharged, or

(b) there must be a contract between the company and some person pursuant to which the undertaking is to be performed within 5 years from the time the resolution under section 43 is passed.

(5) For the purpose of determining whether subsections (2)(b), (3) and (4) are complied with, certain shares in the company may be disregarded; and these are—

(a) subject to the next subsection, any share which was allotted before 22 June 1982, and

(b) any share which was allotted in pursuance of an employees' share scheme and by reason of which the company would, but for this subsection, be precluded under subsection (2)(b) (but not otherwise) from being re-registered as a public company.

(6) A share is not to be disregarded under subsection (5)(a) if the aggregate in nominal value of that share and other shares proposed to be so disregarded is more than one-tenth of the nominal value of the company's allotted share capital; but for this purpose the allotted share capital is treated as not including any shares disregarded under subsection (5)(b).

(7) Any shares disregarded under subsection (5) are treated as not forming part of the allotted share capital for the purposes of subsection (2)(a).

46 Meaning of 'unqualified report' in s. 43(3)

(1) The following subsections explain the reference in section 43(3)(c) to an unqualified report of the company's auditors on the relevant balance sheet.

(2) If the balance sheet was prepared for a financial year of the company, the reference is to an auditors' report stating without material qualification the auditors' opinion that the balance sheet has been properly prepared in accordance with this Act.

(3) If the balance sheet was not prepared for a financial year of the company, the reference is to an auditors' report stating without material qualification the auditors' opinion that

the balance sheet has been properly prepared in accordance with the provisions of this Act which would have applied if it had been so prepared.

For the purposes of an auditors' report under this subsection the provisions of this Act shall be deemed to apply with such modifications as are necessary by reason of the fact that the balance sheet is not prepared for a financial year of the company.

(4) A qualification shall be regarded as material unless the auditors state in their report that the matter giving rise to the qualification is not material for the purpose of determining (by reference to the company's balance sheet) whether at the balance sheet date the amount of the company's net assets was not less than the aggregate of its called up share capital and undistributable reserves.

In this subsection 'net assets' and 'undistributable reserves' have the meaning given by section 264(2) and (3).

47 Certificate of re-registration under s. 43

(1) If the registrar of companies is satisfied, on an application under section 43, that a company may be re-registered under that section as a public company, he shall—

(a) retain the application and other documents delivered to him under the section; and

(b) issue the company with a certificate of incorporation stating that the company is a public company.

(2) The registrar may accept a declaration under section 43(3)(e) or a statement under section 43(3A) as sufficient evidence that the special resolution required by that section has been passed and the other conditions of re-registration satisfied.

(3) The registrar shall not issue the certificate if it appears to him that the court has made an order confirming a reduction of the company's capital which has the effect of Companies Act 1985 33 bringing the nominal value of the company's allotted share capital below the authorised minimum.

(4) Upon the issue to a company of a certificate of incorporation under this section—

(a) the company by virtue of the issue of that certificate becomes a public company; and

(b) any alteration in the memorandum and articles set out in the resolution take effect accordingly.

(5) The certificate is conclusive evidence—

(a) that the requirements of this Act in respect of re-registration and of matters precedent and incidental thereto have been complied with; and

(b) that the company is a public company.

48 Modification for unlimited company re-registering

(1) In their application to unlimited companies, sections 43 to 47 are modified as follows.

(2) The special resolution required by section 43(1) must, in addition to the matters mentioned in subsection (2) of that section—

(a) state that the liability of the members is to be limited by shares, and what the company's share capital is to be; and

(b) make such alterations in the company's memorandum as are necessary to bring it in substance and in form into conformity with the requirements of this Act with respect to the memorandum of a company limited by shares.

(3) The certificate of incorporation issued under section 47(1) shall, in addition to containing the statement required by paragraph (b) of that subsection, state that the company has been incorporated as a company limited by shares; and—

(a) the company by virtue of the issue of the certificate becomes a public company so limited; and

(b) the certificate is conclusive evidence of the fact that it is such a company.

Limited company becoming unlimited

49   Re-registration of limited company as unlimited

(1) Subject as follows, a company which is registered as limited may be re-registered as unlimited in pursuance of an application in that behalf complying with the requirements of this section.

(2) A company is excluded from re-registering under this section if it is limited by virtue of re-registration under section 44 of the Companies Act 1967 or section 51 of this Act.

(3) A public company cannot be re-registered under this section; nor can a company which has previously been re-registered as unlimited.

(4) An application under this section must be in the prescribed form and be signed by a director or the secretary of the company, and be lodged with the registrar of companies, together with the documents specified in subsection (8) below.

(5) The application must set out such alterations in the company's memorandum as—

   (a) if it is to have a share capital, are requisite to bring it (in substance and in form) into conformity with the requirements of this Act with respect to the memorandum of a company to be formed as an unlimited company having a share capital; or

   (b) if it is not to have a share capital, are requisite in the circumstances.

(6) If articles have been registered, the application must set out such alterations in them as—

   (a) if the company is to have a share capital, are requisite to bring the articles (in substance and in form) into conformity with the requirements of this Act with respect to the articles of a company to be formed as an unlimited company having a share capital; or

   (b) if the company is not to have a share capital, are requisite in the circumstances.

(7) If articles have not been registered, the application must have annexed to it, and request the registration of, printed articles; and these must, if the company is to have a share capital, comply with the requirements mentioned in subsection (6)(a) and, if not, be articles appropriate to the circumstances.

(8) The documents to be lodged with the registrar are—

   (a) the prescribed form of assent to the company's being registered as unlimited, subscribed by or on behalf of all the members of the company;

   (b) subject to subsection (8A), a statutory declaration made by the directors of the company—

      (i) that the persons by whom or on whose behalf the form of assent is subscribed constitute the whole membership of the company, and

      (ii) if any of the members have not subscribed that form themselves, that the directors have taken all reasonable steps to satisfy themselves that each person who subscribed it on behalf of a member was lawfully empowered to do so;

   (c) a printed copy of the memorandum incorporating the alterations in it set out in the application; and

   (d) if articles have been registered, a printed copy of them incorporating the alterations set out in the application.

(8A) In place of the lodging of a statutory declaration under paragraph (b) of subsection (8), there may be delivered to the registrar of companies using electronic communications a statement made by the directors of the company as to the matters set out in sub-paragraphs (i) and (ii) of that paragraph.

(8B) Any person who makes a false statement under subsection (8A) which he knows to be false or does not believe to be true is liable to imprisonment or a fine, or both.

(9) For purposes of this section—

(a) subscription to a form of assent by the legal personal representative of a deceased member of a company is deemed subscription by him; and

(b) a trustee in bankruptcy of a member of a company is, to the exclusion of the latter, deemed a member of the company.

50   Certificate of re-registration under s. 49

(1) The registrar of companies shall retain the application and other documents lodged with him under section 49 and shall—

(a) if articles are annexed to the application, register them; and

(b) issue to the company a certificate of incorporation appropriate to the status to be assumed by it by virtue of that section.

(2) On the issue of the certificate—

(a) the status of the company, by virtue of the issue, is changed from limited to unlimited; and

(b) the alterations in the memorandum set out in the application and (if articles have been previously registered) any alterations to the articles so set out take effect as if duly made by resolution of the company; and

(c) the provisions of this Act apply accordingly to the memorandum and articles as altered.

(3) The certificate is conclusive evidence that the requirements of section 49 in respect of re-registration and of matters precedent and incidental to it have been complied with, and that the company was authorised to be re-registered under this Act in pursuance of that section and was duly so re-registered.

Unlimited company becoming limited

51   Re-registration of unlimited company as limited

(1) Subject as follows, a company which is registered as unlimited may be re-registered as limited if a special resolution that it should be so re-registered is passed, and the requirements of this section are complied with in respect of the resolution and otherwise.

(2) A company cannot under this section be re-registered as a public company; and a company is excluded from re-registering under it if it is unlimited by virtue of re-registration under section 43 of the Companies Act 1967 or section 49 of this Act.

(3) The special resolution must state whether the company is to be limited by shares or by guarantee and—

(a) if it is to be limited by shares, must state what the share capital is to be and provide for the making of such alterations in the memorandum as are necessary to bring it (in substance and in form) into conformity with the requirements of this Act with respect to the memorandum of a company so limited, and such alterations in the articles as are requisite in the circumstances;

(b) if it is to be limited by guarantee, must provide for the making of such alterations in its memorandum and articles as are necessary to bring them (in substance and in form) into conformity with the requirements of this Act with respect to the memorandum and articles of a company so limited.

(4) The special resolution is subject to section 380 of this Act (copy to be forwarded to registrar within 15 days); and an application for the company to be re-registered as limited, framed in the prescribed form and signed by a director or by the secretary of the company, must be lodged with the registrar of companies, together with the necessary documents, not earlier than the day on which the copy of the resolution forwarded under section 380 is received by him.

(5) The documents to be lodged with the registrar are—

(a) a printed copy of the memorandum as altered in pursuance of the resolution; and

(b) a printed copy of the articles as so altered.

(6) This section does not apply in relation to the re-registration of an unlimited company as a public company under section 43.

52 Certification of re-registration under s. 51

(1) The registrar shall retain the application and other documents lodged with him under section 51, and shall issue to the company a certificate of incorporation appropriate to the status to be assumed by the company by virtue of that section.

(2) On the issue of the certificate—

(a) the status of the company is, by virtue of the issue, changed from unlimited to limited; and

(b) the alterations in the memorandum specified in the resolution and the alterations in, and additions to, the articles so specified take effect.

(3) The certificate is conclusive evidence that the requirements of section 51 in respect of re-registration and of matters precedent and incidental to it have been complied with, and that the company was authorised to be re-registered in pursuance of that section and was duly so re-registered.

Public company becoming private

53 Re-registration of public company as private

(1) A public company may be re-registered as a private company if—

(a) a special resolution complying with subsection (2) below that it should be so re-registered is passed and has not been cancelled by the court under the following section;

(b) an application for the purpose in the prescribed form and signed by a director or the secretary of the company is delivered to the registrar of companies, together with a printed copy of the memorandum and articles of the company as altered by the resolution; and

(c) the period during which an application for the cancellation of the resolution under the following section may be made has expired without any such application having been made; or

(d) where such an application has been made, the application has been withdrawn or an order has been made under section 54(5) confirming the resolution and a copy of that order has been delivered to the registrar.

(2) The special resolution must alter the company's memorandum so that it no longer states that the company is to be a public company and must make such other alterations in the company's memorandum and articles as are requisite in the circumstances.

(3) A company cannot under this section be re-registered otherwise than as a company limited by shares or by guarantee.

54 Litigated objection to resolution under s. 53

(1) Where a special resolution by a public company to be re-registered under section 53 as a private company has been passed, an application may be made to the court for the cancellation of that resolution.

(2) The application may be made—

(a) by the holders of not less in the aggregate than 5 per cent in nominal value of the company's issued share capital or any class thereof;

(b) if the company is not limited by shares, by not less than 5 per cent of its members; or

(c) by not less than 50 of the company's members; but not by a person who has consented to or voted in favour of the resolution.

(2A) For the purposes of subsection (2)(a), any of the company's issued share capital held as treasury shares must be disregarded.

(3) The application must be made within 28 days after the passing of the resolution and may be made on behalf of the persons entitled to make the application by such one or more of their number as they may appoint in writing for the purpose.

(4) If such an application is made, the company shall forthwith give notice in the prescribed form of that fact to the registrar of companies.

(5) On the hearing of the application, the court shall make an order either cancelling or confirming the resolution and—

(a) may make that order on such terms and conditions as it thinks fit, and may (if it thinks fit) adjourn the proceedings in order that an arrangement may be made to the satisfaction of the court for the purchase of the interests of dissentient members; and

(b) may give such directions and make such orders as it thinks expedient for facilitating or carrying into effect any such arrangement.

(6) The court's order may, if the court thinks fit, provide for the purchase by the company of the shares of any of its members and for the reduction accordingly of the company's capital, and may make such alterations in the company's memorandum and articles as may be required in consequence of that provision.

(7) The company shall, within 15 days from the making of the court's order, or within such longer period as the court may at any time by order direct, deliver to the registrar of companies an office copy of the order.

(8) If the court's order requires the company not to make any, or any specified, alteration in its memorandum or articles, the company has not then power without the leave of the court to make any such alteration in breach of the requirement.

(9) An alteration in the memorandum or articles made by virtue of an order under this section, if not made by resolution of the company, is of the same effect as if duly made by resolution; and this Act applies accordingly to the memorandum or articles as so altered.

(10) A company which fails to comply with subsection (4) or subsection (7), and any officer of it who is in default, is liable to a fine and, for continued contravention, to a daily default fine.

[*Section 54(2A) is in force from 1 December 2003.*]

55   Certificate of re-registration under s. 53

(1) If the registrar of companies is satisfied that a company may be re-registered under section 53, he shall—

(a) retain the application and other documents delivered to him under that section; and

(b) issue the company with a certificate of incorporation appropriate to a private company.

(2) On the issue of the certificate—

(a) the company by virtue of the issue becomes a private company; and

(b) the alterations in the memorandum and articles set out in the resolution under section 53 take effect accordingly.

(3) The certificate is conclusive evidence—

(a) that the requirements of section 53 in respect of re-registration and of matters precedent and incidental to it have been complied with; and

(b) that the company is a private company.

PART III   CAPITAL ISSUES

CHAPTER I   ISSUES BY COMPANIES REGISTERED, OR TO BE REGISTERED,
IN GREAT BRITAIN

The prospectus

58   Document offering shares etc. for sale deemed a prospectus

(1) If a company allots or agrees to allot its shares or debentures with a view to all or any of them being offered for sale to the public, any document by which the offer for sale to the public is made is deemed for all purposes a prospectus issued by the company.

(2) All enactments and rules of law as to the contents of prospectuses, and to liability in respect of statements in and omissions from prospectuses, or otherwise relating to prospectuses, apply and have effect accordingly, as if the shares or debentures had been offered to the public for subscription and as if persons accepting the offer in respect of any shares or debentures were subscribers for those shares or debentures.

This is without prejudice to the liability (if any) of the persons by whom the offer is made, in respect of misstatements in the document or otherwise in respect of it.

(3) For purposes of this Act it is evidence (unless the contrary is proved) that an allotment of, or an agreement to allot, shares or debentures was made with a view to their being offered for sale to the public if it is shown—

    (a) *that an offer of the shares or debentures (or of any of them) for sale to the public was made within 6 months after the allotment or agreement to allot, or*

    (b) *that at the date when the offer was made the whole consideration to be received by the company in respect of the shares or debentures had not been so received.*

(4) Section 56 as applied by this section has effect as if it required a prospectus to state, in addition to the matters required by that section—

    (a) *the net amount of the consideration received or to be received by the company in respect of the shares or debentures to which the offer relates, and*

    (b) *the place and time at which the contract under which those shares or debentures have been or are to be allotted may be inspected.*

[*The Financial Services Act 1986, sch. 17, part I, repealed the Companies Act 1985, s. 58, except so far as it is necessary for the purposes of ss. 81, 83, 246, 248 and 744 (Financial Services Act 1986 (Commencement) (No. 13) Order 1995 (SI 1995/1538), art. 2(a)(i)).*]

62   Meaning of 'expert'

The expression 'expert', in both Chapters of this Part, includes engineer, valuer, accountant and any other person whose profession gives authority to a statement made by him.

[*The Financial Services Act 1986, sch. 17, part I, repealed the Companies Act 1985, s. 62, except so far as it is necessary for the purposes of s. 744 (Financial Services Act 1986 (Commencement) (No. 13) Order 1995 (SI 1995/1538), art. 2(a)(iii)).*]

PART IV   ALLOTMENT OF SHARES AND DEBENTURES

General provisions as to allotment

80   Authority of company required for certain allotments

(1) The directors of a company shall not exercise any power of the company to allot relevant securities, unless they are, in accordance with this section or section 80A, authorised to do so by—

    (a) the company in general meeting; or

    (b) the company's articles.

(2) In this section 'relevant securities' means—

(a) shares in the company other than shares shown in the memorandum to have been taken by the subscribers to it or shares allotted in pursuance of an employees' share scheme, and

(b) any right to subscribe for, or to convert any security into, shares in the company (other than shares so allotted);

and a reference to the allotment of relevant securities includes the grant of such a right but (subject to subsection (6) below), not the allotment of shares pursuant to such a right.

(3) Authority under this section may be given for a particular exercise of the power or for its exercise generally, and may be unconditional or subject to conditions.

(4) The authority must state the maximum amount of relevant securities that may be allotted under it and the date on which it will expire, which must be not more than 5 years from whichever is relevant of the following dates—

(a) in the case of an authority contained in the company's articles at the time of its original incorporation, the date of that incorporation; and

(b) in any other case, the date on which the resolution is passed by virtue of which the authority is given;

but such an authority (including an authority contained in the articles) may be previously revoked or varied by the company in general meeting.

(5) The authority may be renewed or further renewed by the company in general meeting for a further period not exceeding 5 years; but the resolution must state (or restate) the amount of relevant securities which may be allotted under the authority or, as the case may be, the amount remaining to be allotted under it, and must specify the date on which the renewed authority will expire.

(6) In relation to authority under this section for the grant of such rights as are mentioned in subsection (2)(b), the reference in subsection (4) (as also the corresponding reference in subsection (5)) to the maximum amount of relevant securities that may be allotted under the authority is to the maximum amount of shares which may be allotted pursuant to the rights.

(7) The directors may allot relevant securities, notwithstanding that authority under this section has expired, if they are allotted in pursuance of an offer or agreement made by the company before the authority expired and the authority allowed it to make an offer or agreement which would or might require relevant securities to be allotted after the authority expired.

(8) A resolution of a company to give, vary, revoke or renew such an authority may, notwithstanding that it alters the company's articles, be an ordinary resolution; but it is in any case subject to section 380 of this Act (copy to be forwarded to registrar within 15 days).

(9) A director who knowingly and wilfully contravenes, or permits or authorises a contravention of, this section is liable to a fine.

(10) Nothing in this section affects the validity of any allotment.

(11) This section does not apply to any allotment of relevant securities by a company, other than a public company registered as such on its original incorporation, if it is made in pursuance of an offer or agreement made before the earlier of the following two dates—

(a) the date of the holding of the first general meeting of the company after its registration or re-registration as a public company, and

(b) 22 June 1982;

but any resolution to give, vary or revoke an authority for the purposes of section 14 of the Companies Act 1980 or this section has effect for those purposes if passed at any time after the end of April 1980.

80A   Election by private company as to duration of authority

(1) A private company may elect (by elective resolution in accordance with section 379A) that the provisions of this section shall apply, instead of the provisions of section

80(4) and (5), in relation to the giving or renewal, after the election, of an authority under that section.

(2) The authority must state the maximum amount of relevant securities that may be allotted under it and may be given—

(a) for an indefinite period, or

(b) for a fixed period, in which case it must state the date on which it will expire.

(3) In either case an authority (including an authority contained in the articles) may be revoked or varied by the company in general meeting.

(4) An authority given for a fixed period may be renewed or further renewed by the company in general meeting.

(5) A resolution renewing an authority—

(a) must state, or restate, the amount of relevant securities which may be allotted under the authority or, as the case may be, as the amount remaining to be allotted under it, and

(b) must state whether the authority is renewed for an indefinite period or for a fixed period, in which case it must state the date on which the renewed authority will expire.

(6) The references in this section to the maximum amount of relevant securities that may be allotted shall be construed in accordance with section 80(6).

(7) If an election under this section ceases to have effect, an authority then in force which was given for an indefinite period or for a fixed period of more than five years—

(a) if given five years or more before the election ceases to have effect, shall expire forthwith, and

(b) otherwise, shall have effect as if it had been given for a fixed period of five years.

81   Restriction on public offers by private company

(1) A private limited company (other than a company limited by guarantee and not having a share capital) commits an offence if it—

(a) *offers to the public (whether for cash or otherwise) any shares in or debentures of the company; or*

(b) *allots or agrees to allot (whether for cash or otherwise) any shares in or debentures of the company with a view to all or any of those shares or debentures being offered for sale to the public (within the meaning given to that expression by sections 58 to 60).*

(2) A company guilty of an offence under this section, and any officer of it who is in default, is liable to a fine.

(3) Nothing in this section affects the validity of any allotment or sale of shares or debentures, or of any agreement to allot or sell shares or debentures.

[*The Financial Services Act 1986, sch. 17, part I, repealed the Companies Act 1985, s. 81, and the words in italics in ss. 84, 85 and 97, to the extent to which they would apply in relation to: (a) any investment which is listed or the subject of an application for listing in accordance with part IV of the Financial Services Act 1986 (Financial Services Act 1986 (Commencement No. 3) Order 1986 (SI 1986/2246), art. 5 and sch. 4); (b) a prospectus offering for subscription, or any form of application for, units in a body corporate which is a recognised scheme (Financial Services Act 1986 (Commencement) (No. 8) Order 1988 (SI 1988/740), art. 2 and sch.).*]

82   Application for, and allotment of, shares and debentures

(1) No allotment shall be made of a company's shares or debentures in pursuance of a prospectus issued generally, and no proceedings shall be taken on applications made in pursuance of a prospectus so issued, until the beginning of the third day after that on which the prospectus is first so issued or such later time (if any) as may be specified in the prospectus.

(2) The beginning of that third day, or that later time, is 'the time of the opening of the subscription lists'.

(3) In subsection (1), the reference to the day on which the prospectus is first issued generally is to the day when it is first so issued as a newspaper advertisement; and if it is not so issued as a newspaper advertisement before the third day after that on which it is first so issued in any other manner, the reference is to the day on which it is first so issued in any manner.

(4) In reckoning for this purpose the third day after another day—

(a) any intervening day which is a Saturday or Sunday, or is a bank holiday in any part of Great Britain, is to be disregarded; and

(b) if the third day (as so reckoned) is itself a Saturday or Sunday, or a bank holiday, there is to be substituted the first day after that which is none of them.

(5) The validity of an allotment is not affected by any contravention of subsections (1) to (4); but in the event of contravention, the company and every officer of it who is in default is liable to a fine.

(6) As applying to a prospectus offering shares or debentures for sale, the above provisions are modified as follows—

(a) for references to allotment, substitute references to sale; and

(b) for the reference to the company and every officer of it who is in default, substitute a reference to any person by or through whom the offer is made and who knowingly and wilfully authorises or permits the contravention.

(7) An application for shares in or debentures of a company which is made in pursuance of a prospectus issued generally is not revocable until after the expiration of the third day after the time of the opening of the subscription lists, or the giving before the expiration of that day of the appropriate public notice; and that notice is one given by some person responsible under sections 67 to 69 for the prospectus and having the effect under those sections of excluding or limiting the responsibility of the giver.

[The Financial Services Act 1986, sch. 17, part I, repealed the Companies Act 1985, ss. 82 and 83, except for the purposes of prospectuses to which reg. 8 of the Public Offers of Securities Regulations 1995 (SI 1995/1537) applies (Financial Services Act 1986 (Commencement) (No. 14) Order 1999 (SI 1999/727)).]

83   No allotment unless minimum subscription received

(1) No allotment shall be made of any share capital of a company offered to the public for subscription unless—

(a) there has been subscribed the amount stated in the prospectus as the minimum amount which, in the opinion of the directors, must be raised by the issue of share capital in order to provide for the matters specified in paragraph 2 of Schedule 3 (preliminary expenses, purchase of property, working capital, etc.); and

(b) the sum payable on application for the amount so stated has been paid to and received by the company.

(2) For purposes of subsection (1)(b), a sum is deemed paid to the company, and received by it, if a cheque for that sum has been received in good faith by the company and the directors have no reason for suspecting that the cheque will not be paid.

(3) The amount so stated in the prospectus is to be reckoned exclusively of any amount payable otherwise than in cash and is known as 'the minimum subscription'.

(4) If the above conditions have not been complied with on the expiration of 40 days after the first issue of the prospectus, all money received from applicants for shares shall be forthwith repaid to them without interest.

(5) If any of the money is not repaid within 48 days after the issue of the prospectus, the directors of the company are jointly and severally liable to repay it with interest at the rate of 5 per cent per annum from the expiration of the 48th day; except that a director is not so liable if he proves that the default in the repayment of the money was not due to any misconduct or negligence on his part.

(6) Any condition requiring or binding an applicant for shares to waive compliance with any requirement of this section is void.

(7) This section does not apply to an allotment of shares subsequent to the first allotment of shares offered to the public for subscription.
[*See note after s. 82.*]

84   Allotment where issue not fully subscribed

(1) No allotment shall be made of any share capital of a public company offered for subscription unless—

  (a) that capital is subscribed for in full; or
  (b) the offer states that, even if the capital is not subscribed for in full, the amount of that capital subscribed for may be allotted in any event or in the event of the conditions specified in the offer being satisfied;

and, where conditions are so specified, no allotment of the capital shall be made by virtue of paragraph (b) unless those conditions are satisfied.

This is without prejudice to section 83.

(2) If shares are prohibited from being allotted by subsection (1) and 40 days have elapsed after the first issue of the prospectus, all money received from applicants for shares shall be forthwith repaid to them without interest.

(3) If any of the money is not repaid within 48 days after the issue of the prospectus, the directors of the company are jointly and severally liable to repay it with interest at the rate of 5 per cent per annum from the expiration of the 48th day; except that a director is not so liable if he proves that the default in repayment was not due to any misconduct or negligence on his part.

(4) This section applies in the case of shares offered as wholly or partly payable otherwise than in cash as it applies in the case of shares offered for subscription (the word 'subscribed' in subsection (1) being construed accordingly).

(5) In subsections (2) and (3) as they apply to the case of shares offered as wholly or partly payable otherwise than in cash, references to the repayment of money received from applicants for shares include—

  (a) the return of any other consideration so received (including, if the case so requires, the release of the applicant from any undertaking), or
  (b) if it is not reasonably practicable to return the consideration, the payment of money equal to its value at the time it was so received,

and references to interest apply accordingly.

(6) Any condition requiring or binding an applicant for shares to waive compliance with any requirement of this section is void.
[*See note after s. 81.*]

85   Effect of irregular allotment

(1) An allotment made by a company to an applicant in contravention of section *83 or* 84 is voidable at the instance of the applicant within one month after the date of the allotment, and not later, and is so voidable notwithstanding that the company is in the course of being wound up.

(2) If a director of a company knowingly contravenes, or permits or authorises the contravention of, any provision of either of those sections with respect to allotment, he is liable to compensate the company and the allottee respectively for any loss, damages or costs which the company or the allottee may have sustained or incurred by the contravention.

(3) But proceedings to recover any such loss, damages or costs shall not be commenced after the expiration of 2 years from the date of the allotment.
[*See note after s. 81.*]

88   Return as to allotments, etc.

(1) This section applies to a company limited by shares and to a company limited by guarantee and having a share capital.

(2) When such a company makes an allotment of its shares, the company shall within one month thereafter deliver to the registrar of companies for registration—

    (a) a return of the allotments (in the prescribed form) stating the number and nominal amount of the shares comprised in the allotment, the names and addresses of the allottees, and the amount (if any) paid or due and payable on each share, whether on account of the nominal value of the share or by way of premium; and

    (b) in the case of shares allotted as fully or partly paid up otherwise than in cash—

        (i) a contract in writing constituting the title of the allottee to the allotment together with any contract of sale, or for services or other consideration in respect of which that allotment was made (such contracts being duly stamped), and

        (ii) a return stating the number and nominal amount of shares so allotted, the extent to which they are to be treated as paid up, and the consideration for which they have been allotted.

(3) Where such a contract as above mentioned is not reduced to writing, the company shall within one month after the allotment deliver to the registrar of companies for registration the prescribed particulars of the contract stamped with the same stamp duty as would have been payable if the contract had been reduced to writing.

(4) Those particulars are deemed an instrument within the meaning of the Stamp Act 1891; and the registrar may, as a condition of filing the particulars, require that the duty payable on them be adjudicated under section 12 of that Act.

(5) If default is made in complying with this section, every officer of the company who is in default is liable to a fine and, for continued contravention, to a daily default fine, but subject as follows.

(6) In the case of default in delivering to the registrar within one month after the allotment any document required by this section to be delivered, the company, or any officer liable for the default, may apply to the court for relief; and the court, if satisfied that the omission to deliver the document was accidental or due to inadvertence, or that it is just and equitable to grant relief, may make an order extending the time for the delivery of the document for such period as the court thinks proper.

Pre-emption rights

89 Offers to shareholders to be on pre-emptive basis

(1) Subject to the provisions of this section and the seven sections next following, a company proposing to allot equity securities (defined in section 94)—

    (a) shall not allot any of them on any terms to a person unless it has made an offer to each person who holds relevant shares or relevant employee shares to allot to him on the same or more favourable terms a proportion of those securities which is as nearly as practicable equal to the proportion in nominal value held by him of the aggregate of relevant shares and relevant employee shares, and

    (b) shall not allot any of those securities to a person unless the period during which any such offer may be accepted has expired or the company has received notice of the acceptance or refusal of every offer so made.

(2) Subsection (3) below applies to any provision of a company's memorandum or articles which requires the company, when proposing to allot equity securities consisting of relevant shares of any particular class, not to allot those securities on any terms unless it has complied with the condition that it makes such an offer as is described in subsection (1) to each person who holds relevant shares or relevant employee shares of that class.

(3) If in accordance with a provision to which this subsection applies—

    (a) a company makes an offer to allot securities to such a holder, and

(b) he or anyone in whose favour he has renounced his right to their allotment accepts the offer,

subsection (1) does not appy to the allotment of those securities, and the company may allot them accordingly; but this is without prejudice to the application of subsection (1) in any other case.

(4) Subsection (1) does not apply to a particular allotment of equity securities if these are, or are to be, wholly or partly paid up otherwise than in cash; and securities which a company has offered to allot to a holder of relevant shares or relevant employee shares may be allotted to him, or anyone in whose favour he has renounced his right to their allotment, without contravening subsection (1)(b).

(5) Subsection (1) does not apply to the allotment of securities which would, apart from a renunciation or assignment of the right to their allotment, be held under an employees' share scheme.

(6) For the purposes of subsections (1) and (2), where a company is holding relevant shares as treasury shares the company is not a 'person who holds relevant shares'.

[*Section 89(6) is in force from 1 December 2003.*]

90   Communication of pre-emption offers to shareholders

(1) This section has effect as to the manner in which offers required by section 89(1), or by a provision to which section 89(3) applies, are to be made to holders of a company's shares.

(2) Subject to the following subsections, an offer shall be in writing and shall be made to a holder of shares either personally or by sending it by post (that is to say prepaying and posting a letter containing the offer) to him or to his registered address or, if he has no registered address in the United Kingdom, to the address in the United Kingdom supplied by him to the company for the giving of notice to him.

If sent by post, the offer is deemed to be made at the time at which the letter would be delivered in the ordinary course of post.

(3) Where shares are held by two or more persons jointly, the offer may be made to the joint holder first named in the register of members in respect of the shares.

(4) In the case of a holder's death or bankruptcy, the offer may be made—

(a) by sending it by post in a prepaid letter addressed to the persons claiming to be entitled to the shares in consequence of the death or bankruptcy by name, or by the title of representatives of the deceased, or trustee of the bankrupt, or by any like description, at the address in the United Kingdom supplied for the purpose by those so claiming, or

(b) (until such an address has been so supplied) by giving the notice in any manner in which it might have been given if the death or bankruptcy had not occurred.

(5) If the holder—

(a) has no registered address in the United Kingdom and has not given to the company an address in the United Kingdom for the service of notices on him, or

(b) is the holder of a share warrant,

the offer may be made by causing it, or a notice specifying where a copy of it can be obtained or inspected, to be published in the Gazette.

(6) The offer must state a period of not less than 21 days during which it may be accepted; and the offer shall not be withdrawn before the end of that period.

(7) This section does not invalidate a provision to which section 89(3) applies by reason that that provision requires or authorises an offer under it to be made in contravention of any of subsections (1) to (6) above; but, to the extent that the provision requires or authorises such an offer to be so made, it is of no effect.

91   Exclusion of ss. 89, 90 by private company

(1) Section 89(1), section 90(1) to (5) or section 90(6) may, as applying to allotments by a

private company of equity securities or to such allotments of a particular description, be excluded by a provision contained in the memorandum or articles of that company.

(2) A requirement or authority contained in the memorandum or articles of a private company, if it is inconsistent with any of those subsections, has effect as a provision excluding that subsection; but a provision to which section 89(3) applies is not to be treated as inconsistent with section 89(1).

92   Consequences of contravening ss. 89, 90

(1) If there is a contravention of section 89(1), or of section 90(1) to (5) or section 90(6), or of a provision to which section 89(3) applies, the company, and every officer of it who knowingly authorised or permitted the contravention, are jointly and severally liable to compensate any person to whom an offer should have been made under the subsection or provision contravened for any loss, damage, costs or expenses which the person has sustained or incurred by reason of the contravention.

(2) However, no proceedings to recover any such loss, damage, costs or expenses shall be commenced after the expiration of 2 years from the delivery to the registrar of companies of the return of allotments in question or, where equity securities other than shares are granted, from the date of the grant.

93   Savings for other restrictions as to offers

(1) Sections 89 to 92 are without prejudice to any enactment by virtue of which a company is prohibited (whether generally or in specified circumstances) from offering or allotting equity securities to any person.

(2) Where a company cannot by virtue of such an enactment offer or allot equity securities to a holder of relevant shares or relevant employee shares, those sections have effect as if the shares held by that holder were not relevant shares or relevant employee shares.

94   Definitions for ss. 89–96

(1) The following subsections apply for the interpretation of sections 89 to 96.

(2) 'Equity security', in relation to a company, means a relevant share in the company (other than a share shown in the memorandum to have been taken by a subscriber to the memorandum or a bonus share), or a right to subscribe for, or to convert securities into, relevant shares in the company.

(3) A reference to the allotment of equity securities or of equity securities consisting of relevant shares of a particular class includes the grant of a right to subscribe for, or to convert any securities into, relevant shares in the company or (as the case may be) relevant shares of a particular class; but such a reference does not include the allotment of any relevant shares pursuant to such a right.

(3A) A reference to the allotment of equity securities or of equity securities consisting of relevant shares of a particular class also includes the sale of any relevant shares in the company or (as the case may be) relevant shares of a particular class if, immediately before the sale, the shares were held by the company as treasury shares.

(4) 'Relevant employee shares', in relation to a company, means shares of the company which would be relevant shares in it but for the fact that they are held by a person who acquired them in pursuance of an employees' share scheme.

(5) 'Relevant shares', in relation to a company, means shares in the company other than—

(a) shares which as respects dividends and capital carry a right to participate only up to a specified amount in a distribution, and

(b) shares which are held by a person who acquired them in pursuance of an employees' share scheme or, in the case of shares which have not been allotted, are to be allotted in pursuance of such a scheme *or, in the case of shares held by the company as treasury shares, are to be transferred in pursuance of such a scheme.*

(6) A reference to a class of shares is to shares to which the same rights are attached as to voting and as to participation, both as respects dividends and as respects capital, in a distribution.

(7) In relation to an offer to allot securities required by section 89(1) or by any provision to which section 89(3) applies, a reference in sections 89 to 94 (however expressed) to the holder of shares of any description is to whoever was at the close of business on a date, to be specified in the offer and to fall in the period of 28 days immediately before the date of the offer, the holder of shares of that description.

[*Section 94(3A) and the words in italics in s. 94(5)(b) are in force from 1 December 2003.*]

95   Disapplication of pre-emption rights

(1) Where the directors of a company are generally authorised for purposes of section 80, they may be given power by the articles, or by a special resolution of the company, to allot equity securities pursuant to that authority as if—

(a) section 89(1) did not apply to the allotment, or

(b) that subsection applied to the allotment with such modifications as the directors may determine;

and where the directors make an allotment under this subsection, sections 89 to 94 have effect accordingly.

(2) Where the directors of a company are authorised for purposes of section 80 (whether generally or otherwise), the company may by special resolution resolve either—

(a) that section 89(1) shall not apply to a specified allotment of equity securities to be made pursuant to that authority, or

(b) that that subsection shall apply to the allotment with such modifications as may be specified in the resolution;

and where such a resolution is passed, sections 89 to 94 have effect accordingly.

(2A) Subsections (1) and (2) apply in relation to a sale of shares which is an allotment of equity securities by virtue of section 94(3A) as if—

(a) in subsection (1) for 'Where the directors of a company are generally authorised for purposes of section 80, they' there were substituted 'The directors of a company' and the words 'pursuant to that authority' were omitted, and

(b) in subsection (2), the words from 'Where' to 'otherwise),' and, in paragraph (a), the words 'to be made pursuant to that authority' were omitted.

(3) The power conferred by subsection (1) or a special resolution under subsection (2) ceases to have effect when the authority to which it relates is revoked or would (if not renewed) expire; but if the authority is renewed, the power or (as the case may be) the resolution may also be renewed, for a period not longer than that for which the authority is renewed, by a special resolution of the company.

(4) Notwithstanding that any such power or resolution has expired, the directors may allot equity securities in pursuance of an offer or agreement previously made by the company, if the power or resolution enabled the company to make an offer or agreement which would or might require equity securities to be allotted after it expired.

(5) A special resolution under subsection (2), or a special resolution to renew such a resolution, shall not be proposed unless it is recommended by the directors and there has been circulated, with the notice of the meeting at which the resolution is proposed, to the members entitled to have that notice a written statement by the directors setting out—

(a) their reasons for making the recommendation,

(b) the amount to be paid to the company in respect of the equity securities to be allotted, and

(c) the directors' justification of that amount.

(6) A person who knowingly or recklessly authorises or permits the inclusion in a statement circulated under subsection (5) of any matter which is misleading, false or deceptive in a material particular is liable to imprisonment or a fine, or both.
[*Section 95(2A) is in force from 1 December 2003.*]

96   Saving for company's pre-emption procedure operative before 1982

(1) Where a company which is re-registered or registered as a public company is or, but for the provisions of the Companies Act 1980 and the enactments replacing it, would be subject at the time of re-registration or (as the case may be) registration to a pre-1982 pre-emption requirement, sections 89 to 95 do not apply to an allotment of the equity securities which are subject to that requirement.

(2) A 'pre-1982 pre-emption requirement' is a requirement imposed (whether by the company's memorandum or articles, or otherwise) before the relevant date in 1982 by virtue of which the company must, when making an allotment of equity securities, make an offer to allot those securities or some of them in a manner which (otherwise than because involving a contravention of section 90(1) to (5) or 90(6)) is inconsistent with sections 89 to 94; and 'the relevant date in 1982' is—

    (a) except in a case falling within the following paragraph, 22 June in that year, and

    (b) in the case of a company which was re-registered or registered as a public company on an application made before that date, the date on which the application was made.

(3) A requirement which—

    (a) is imposed on a private company (having been so imposed before the relevant date in 1982) otherwise than by the company's memorandum or articles, and

    (b) if contained in the company's memorandum or articles, would have effect under section 91 to the exclusion of any provisions of sections 89 to 94,

has effect, so long as the company remains a private company, as if it were contained in the memorandum or articles.

(4) If on the relevant date in 1982 a company, other than a public company registered as such on its original incorporation, was subject to such a requirement as is mentioned in section 89(2) imposed otherwise than by the memorandum or articles, the requirement is to be treated for purposes of sections 89 to 94 as if it were contained in the memorandum or articles.

Commissions and discounts

97   Power of company to pay commissions

(1) It is lawful for a company to pay a commission to any person in consideration of his subscribing or agreeing to subscribe (whether absolutely or conditionally) for any shares in the company, or procuring or agreeing to procure subscriptions (whether absolute or conditional) for any shares in the company, if the following conditions are satisfied.

(2) The payment of the commission must be authorised by the company's articles; and—

    (a) the commission paid or agreed to be paid must not exceed 10 per cent of the price at which the shares are issued or the amount or rate authorised by the articles, whichever is the less; *and*

    (b) *the amount or rate per cent of commission paid or agreed to be paid, and the number of shares which persons have agreed for a commission to subscribe absolutely, must be disclosed in the manner required by the following subsection.*

(3) *Those matters must, in the case of shares offered to the public for subscription, be disclosed in the prospectus; and in the case of shares not so offered—*

    (a) *they must be disclosed in a statement in the prescribed form signed by every director of the company or by his agent authorised in writing, and delivered (before payment of the commission) to the registrar of companies for registration; and*

(b) where a circular or notice (not being a prospectus) inviting subscription for the shares is issued, they must also be disclosed in that circular or notice.

(4) If default is made in complying with subsection (3)(a) as regards delivery to the registrar of the statement in prescribed form, the company and every officer of it who is in default is liable to a fine. [See note after s. 81.]

98   Apart from s. 97, commissions and discounts barred

(1) Except as permitted by section 97, no company shall apply any of its shares or capital money, either directly or indirectly in payment of any commission, discount or allowance to any person in consideration of his subscribing or agreeing to subscribe (whether absolutely or conditionally) for any shares in the company, or procuring or agreeing to procure subscriptions (whether absolute or conditional) for any shares in the company.

(2) This applies whether the shares or money be so applied by being added to the purchase money of any property acquired by the company or to the contract price of any work to be executed for the company, or the money be paid out of the nominal purchase money or contract price, or otherwise.

(3) Nothing in section 97 or this section affects the power of a company to pay such brokerage as has previously been lawful.

(4) A vendor to, or promoter of, or other person who receives payment in money or shares from, a company has, and is deemed always to have had, power to apply any part of the money or shares so received in payment of any commission, the payment of which, if made directly by the company, would have been lawful under section 97 and this section.

Amount to be paid for shares; the means of payment

99   General rules as to payment for shares on allotment

(1) Subject to the following provisions of this Part, shares allotted by a company, and any premium on them, may be paid up in money or money's worth (including goodwill and know-how).

(2) A public company shall not accept at any time, in payment up of its shares or any premium on them, an undertaking given by any person that he or another should do work or perform services for the company or any other person.

(3) If a public company accepts such an undertaking in payment up of its shares or any premium on them, the holder of the shares when they or the premium are treated as paid up (in whole or in part) by the undertaking is liable—

(a) to pay the company in respect of those shares an amount equal to their nominal value, together with the whole of any premium or, if the case so requires, such proportion of that amount as is treated as paid up by the undertaking; and

(b) to pay interest at the appropriate rate on the amount payable under paragraph (a) above.

(4) This section does not prevent a company from allotting bonus shares to its members or from paying up, with sums available for the purpose, any amounts for the time being unpaid on any of its shares (whether on account of the nominal value of the shares or by way of premium).

(5) The reference in subsection (3) to the holder of shares includes any person who has an unconditional right to be included in the company's register of members in respect of those shares or to have an instrument of transfer of them executed in his favour.

100   Prohibition on allotment of shares at a discount

(1) A company's shares shall not be allotted at a discount.

(2) If shares are allotted in contravention of this section, the allottee is liable to pay the company an amount equal to the amount of the discount, with interest at the appropriate rate.

101 Shares to be allotted as at least one-quarter paid-up

(1) A public company shall not allot a share except as paid up at least as to one-quarter of its nominal value and the whole of any premium on it.

(2) Subsection (1) does not apply to shares allotted in pursuance of an employees' share scheme.

(3) If a company allots a share in contravention of subsection (1), the share is to be treated as if one-quarter of its nominal value, together with the whole of any premium on it, had been received.

(4) But the allottee is liable to pay the company the minimum amount which should have been received in respect of the share under subsection (1) (less the value of any consideration actually applied in payment up, to any extent, of the share and any premium on it), with interest at the appropriate rate.

(5) Subsections (3) and (4) do not apply to the allotment of bonus shares, unless the allottee knew or ought to have known the shares were allotted in contravention of subsection (1).

102 Restriction on payment by long-term undertaking

(1) A public company shall not allot shares as fully or partly paid up (as to their nominal value or any premium on them) otherwise than in cash if the consideration for the allotment is or includes an undertaking which is to be, or may be, performed more than 5 years after the date of the allotment.

(2) If a company allots shares in contravention of subsection (1), the allottee is liable to pay the company an amount equal to the aggregate of their nominal value and the whole of any premium (or, if the case so requires, so much of that aggregate as is treated as paid up by the undertaking), with interest at the appropriate rate.

(3) Where a contract for the allotment of shares does not contravene subsection (1), any variation of the contract which has the effect that the contract would have contravened the subsection, if the terms of the contract as varied had been its original terms, is void.

(4) Subsection (3) applies also to the variation by a public company of the terms of a contract entered into before the company was re-registered as a public company.

(5) The following subsection applies where a public company allots shares for a consideration which consists of or includes (in accordance with subsection (1)) an undertaking which is to be performed within 5 years of the allotment, but the undertaking is not performed within the period allowed by the contract for the allotment of the shares.

(6) The allottee is then liable to pay the company, at the end of the period so allowed, an amount equal to the aggregate of the nominal value of the shares and the whole of any premium (or, if the case so requires, so much of that aggregate as is treated as paid up by the undertaking), with interest at the appropriate rate.

(7) A reference in this section to a contract for the allotment of shares includes an ancillary contract relating to payment in respect of them.

103 Non-cash consideration to be valued before allotment

(1) A public company shall not allot shares as fully or partly paid up (as to their nominal value or any premium on them) otherwise than in cash unless—

(a) the consideration for the allotment has been independently valued under section 108; and

(b) a report with respect to its value has been made to the company by a person appointed by the company (in accordance with that section) during the 6 months immediately preceding the allotment of the shares; and

(c) a copy of the report has been sent to the proposed allottee.

(2) Where an amount standing to the credit of any of a company's reserve accounts, or of its profit and loss account, is applied in paying up (to any extent) any shares allotted to

members of the company or any premiums on shares so allotted, the amount applied does not count as consideration for the allotment, and accordingly subsection (1) does not apply in that case.

(3) Subsection (1) does not apply to the allotment of shares by a company in connection with an arrangement providing for the allotment of shares in that company on terms that the whole or part of the consideration for the shares allotted is to be provided by the transfer to that company (or the cancellation) of all or some of the shares, or of all or some of the shares of a particular class, in another company (with or without the issue to that company of shares, or of shares of any particular class, in that other company).

(4) But subsection (3) does not exclude the application of subsection (1) unless under the arrangement it is open to all the holders of the shares in the other company in question (or, where the arrangement applies only to shares of a particular class, to all the holders of shares in that other company, being holders of shares of that class) to take part in the arrangement.

In determining whether that is the case, shares held by or by a nominee of the company proposing to allot the shares in connection with the arrangement, or by a nominee of a company which is that company's holding company or subsidiary or a company which is a subsidiary of its holding company, shall be disregarded.

(5) Subsection (1) also does not apply to the allotment of shares by a company in connection with its proposed merger with another company; that is, where one of the companies proposes to acquire all the assets and liabilities of the other in exchange for the issue of shares or other securities of that one to shareholders of the other, with or without any cash payment to shareholders.

(6) If a company allots shares in contravention of subsection (1) and either—

    (a) the allottee has not received the valuer's report required by that subsection to be sent to him; or

    (b) there has been some other contravention of this section or section 108 which the allottee knew or ought to have known amounted to a contravention,

the allottee is liable to pay the company an amount equal to the aggregate of the nominal value of the shares and the whole of any premium (or, if the case so requires, so much of that aggregate as is treated as paid up by the consideration), with interest at the appropriate rate.

(7) In this section—

    (a) 'arrangement' means any agreement, scheme or arrangement (including an arrangement sanctioned in accordance with section 425 (company compromise with creditors and members) or section 110 of the Insolvency Act (liquidator in winding up accepting shares as consideration for sale of company property)), and

    (b) any reference to a company, except where it is or is to be construed as a reference to a public company, includes any body corporate and any body to which letters patent have been issued under the Chartered Companies Act 1837.

[As from 1 December 2003, s. 103(4) is:

(4) But subsection (3) does not exclude the application of subsection (1) unless under the arrangement it is open to all the holders of the shares in the other company in question ('the relevant company') (or, where the arrangement applies only to shares of a particular class, to all the holders of shares in the relevant company, being holders of shares of that class) to take part in the arrangement.

In determining whether that is the case, the following shall be disregarded—

    (a) shares held by or by a nominee of the company proposing to allot the shares in connection with the arrangement ('the allotting company');

    (b) shares held by or by a nominee of a company which is—

        (i) the holding company, or a subsidiary, of the allotting company, or

        (ii) a subsidiary of that holding company; and

    (c) shares held as treasury shares by the relevant company.]

104   Transfer to public company of non-cash asset in initial period

(1) A public company formed as such shall not, unless the conditions of this section have been complied with, enter into an agreement with a person for the transfer by him during the initial period of one or more non-cash assets to the company or another, if—

    (a) that person is a subscriber to the company's memorandum, and

    (b) the consideration for the transfer to be given by the company is equal in value at the time of the agreement to one-tenth or more of the company's nominal share capital issued at that time.

(2) The 'initial period' for this purpose is 2 years beginning with the date of the company being issued with a certificate under section 117 (or the previous corresponding provision) that it was entitled to do business.

(3) This section applies also to a company re-registered as a public company (except one re-registered under section 8 of the Companies Act 1980 or section 2 of the Consequential Provisions Act), or registered under section 685 (joint stock company) or the previous corresponding provision; but in that case—

    (a) there is substituted a reference in subsection (1)(a) to a person who is a member of the company on the date of registration or re-registration, and

    (b) the initial period is then 2 years beginning with that date.

In this subsection the reference to a company re-registered as a public company includes a private company so re-registered which was a public company before it was a private company.

(4) The conditions of this section are as follows—

    (a) the consideration to be received by the company, and any consideration other than cash to be given by the company, must have been independently valued under section 109;

    (b) a report with respect to the consideration to be so received and given must have been made to the company in accordance with that section during the 6 months immediately preceding the date of the agreement;

    (c) the terms of the agreement must have been approved by an ordinary resolution of the company; and

    (d) not later than the giving of the notice of the meeting at which the resolution is proposed, copies of the resolution and report must have been circulated to the members of the company entitled to receive the notice and, if the person with whom the agreement in question is proposed to be made is not then a member of the company so entitled, to that person.

(5) In subsection (4)(a)—

    (a) the reference to the consideration to be received by the company is to the asset to be transferred to it or the advantage to the company of the asset's transfer to another person; and

    (b) the specified condition is without prejudice to any requirement to value any consideration for purposes of section 103.

(6) In the case of the following agreements, this section does not apply—

    (a) where it is part of the company's ordinary business to acquire, or arrange for other persons to acquire, assets of a particular description, an agreement entered into by the company in the ordinary course of its business for the transfer of an asset of that description to it or to such a person, as the case may be;

    (b) an agreement entered into by the company under the supervision of the court, or of an officer authorised by the court for the purpose, for the transfer of an asset to the company or to another.

105   Agreements contravening s. 104

(1) The following subsection applies if a public company enters into an agreement contravening section 104, the agreement being made with the person referred to in subsection

(1)(a) or (as the case may be) subsection (3) of that section, and either—

    (a) that person has not received the valuer's report required for compliance with the conditions of the section, or

    (b) there has been some other contravention of the section or of section 108(1), (2) or (5) or section 109, which he knew or ought to have known amounted to a contravention.

(2) The company is then entitled to recover from that person any consideration given by it under the agreement, or an amount equal to the value of the consideration at the time of the agreement; and the agreement, so far as not carried out, is void.

(3) However, if the agreement is or includes an agreement for the allotment of shares in the company, then—

    (a) whether or not the agreement also contravenes section 103, subsection (2) above does not apply to it in so far as it is for the allotment of shares; and

    (b) the allottee is liable to pay the company an amount equal to the aggregate of the nominal value of the shares and the whole of any premium (or, if the case so requires, so much of that aggregate as is treated as paid up by the consideration), with interest at the appropriate rate.

106   Shares issued to subscribers of memorandum

Shares taken by a subscriber to the memorandum of a public company in pursuance of an undertaking of his in the memorandum, and any premium on the shares, shall be paid up in cash.

107   Meaning of 'the appropriate rate'

In sections 99 to 105 'the appropriate rate', in relation to interest, means 5 per cent per annum or such other rate as may be specified by order made by the Secretary of State by statutory instrument subject to annulment in pursuance of a resolution of either House of Parliament.

Valuation provisions

108   Valuation and report (s. 103)

(1) The valuation and report required by section 103 (or, where applicable, section 44) shall be made by an independent person, that is to say a person qualified at the time of the report to be appointed, or continue to be, an auditor of the company.

(2) However, where it appears to the independent person (from here on referred to as 'the valuer') to be reasonable for the valuation of the consideration, or part of it, to be made (or for him to accept such a valuation) by another person who—

    (a) appears to him to have the requisite knowledge and experience to value the consideration or that part of it; and

    (b) is not an officer or servant of the company or any other body corporate which is that company's subsidiary or holding company or a subsidiary of that company's holding company or a partner or employee of such an officer or servant,

he may arrange for or accept such a valuation, together with a report which will enable him to make his own report under this section and provide the note required by subsection (6) below.

(3) The reference in subsection (2)(b) to an officer or servant does not include an auditor.

(4) The valuer's report shall state—

    (a) the nominal value of the shares to be wholly or partly paid for by the consideration in question;

    (b) the amount of any premium payable on the shares;

    (c) the description of the consideration and, as respects so much of the consideration as he himself has valued, a description of that part of the consideration, the method used to value it and the date of the valuation;

    (d) the extent to which the nominal value of the shares and any premium are to be treated as paid up—

        (i) by the consideration;

        (ii) in cash.

  (5) Where the consideration or part of it is valued by a person other than the valuer himself, the latter's report shall state that fact and shall also—

    (a) state the former's name and what knowledge and experience he has to carry out the valuation, and

    (b) describe so much of the consideration as was valued by the other person, and the method used to value it, and specify the date of the valuation.

  (6) The valuer's report shall contain or be accompanied by a note by him—

    (a) in the case of a valuation made by a person other than himself, that it appeared to himself reasonable to arrange for it to be so made or to accept a valuation so made;

    (b) whoever made the valuation, that the method of valuation was reasonable in all the circumstances;

    (c) that it appears to the valuer that there has been no material change in the value of the consideration in question since the valuation; and

    (d) that on the basis of the valuation the value of the consideration, together with any cash by which the nominal value of the shares or any premium payable on them is to be paid up, is not less than so much of the aggregate of the nominal value and the whole of any such premium as is treated as paid up by the consideration and any such cash.

  (7) Where the consideration to be valued is accepted partly in payment up of the nominal value of the shares and any premium and partly for some other consideration given by the company, section 103 (and, where applicable, section 44) and the foregoing provisions of this section apply as if references to the consideration accepted by the company included the proportion of that consideration which is properly attributable to the payment up of that value and any premium; and—

    (a) the valuer shall carry out, or arrange for, such other valuations as will enable him to determine that proportion; and

    (b) his report shall state what valuations have been made under this subsection and also the reason for, and method and date of, any such valuation and any other matters which may be relevant to the determination.

109 Valuation and report (s. 104)

  (1) Subsections (1) to (3) and (5) of section 108 apply also as respects the valuation and report for the purposes of section 104.

  (2) The valuer's report for those purposes shall—

    (a) state the consideration to be received by the company, describing the asset in question (specifying the amount to be received in cash) and the consideration to be given by the company (specifying the amount to be given in cash);

    (b) state the method and date of valuation;

    (c) contain or be accompanied by a note as to the matters mentioned in section 108(6)(a) to (c); and

    (d) contain or be accompanied by a note that on the basis of the valuation the value of the consideration to be received by the company is not less than the value of the consideration to be given by it.

  (3) A reference in section 104 or this section to consideration given for the transfer of an asset includes consideration given partly for its transfer; but—

    (a) the value of any consideration partly so given is to be taken as the proportion of the consideration properly attributable to its transfer;

   (b) the valuer shall carry out or arrange for such valuations of anything else as will enable him to determine that proportion; and

   (c) his report for purposes of section 104 shall state what valuation has been made under this subsection and also the reason for and method and date of any such valuation and any other matters which may be relevant to that determination.

110   Entitlement of valuer to full disclosure

(1) A person carrying out a valuation or making a report under section 103 or 104, with respect to any consideration proposed to be accepted or given by a company, is entitled to require from the officers of the company such information and explanation as he thinks necessary to enable him to carry out the valuation or make the report and provide a note under section 108(6) or (as the case may be) section 109(2)(c).

(2) A person who knowingly or recklessly makes a statement which—

   (a) is misleading, false or deceptive in a material particular, and

   (b) is a statement to which this subsection applies,

is guilty of an offence and liable to imprisonment or a fine, or both.

(3) Subsection (2) applies to any statement made (whether orally or in writing) to a person carrying out a valuation or making a report under section 108 or 109, being a statement which conveys or purports to convey any information or explanation which that person requires, or is entitled to require, under subsection (1) of this section.

111   Matters to be communicated to registrar

(1) A company to which a report is made under section 108 as to the value of any consideration for which, or partly for which, it proposes to allot shares shall deliver a copy of the report to the registrar of companies for registration at the same time that it files the return of the allotments of those shares under section 88.

(2) A company which has passed a resolution under section 104 with respect to the transfer of an asset shall, within 15 days of so doing, deliver to the registrar of companies a copy of the resolution together with the valuer's report required by that section.

(3) If default is made in complying with subsection (1), every officer of the company who is in default is liable to a fine and, for continued contravention, to a daily default fine; but this is subject to the same exception as is made by section 88(6) (relief on application to the court) in the case of default in complying with that section.

(4) If a company fails to comply with subsection (2), it and every officer of it who is in default is liable to a fine and, for continued contravention, to a daily default fine.

Other matters arising out of allotment &c.

111A   Right to damages, &c. not affected

A person is not debarred from obtaining damages or other compensation from a company by reason only of his holding or having held shares in the company or any right to apply or subscribe for shares or to be included in the company's register in respect of shares.

112   Liability of subsequent holders of shares allotted

(1) If a person becomes a holder of shares in respect of which—

   (a) there has been a contravention of section 99, 100, 101 or 103; and

   (b) by virtue of that contravention, another is liable to pay any amount under the section contravened,

that person is also liable to pay that amount (jointly and severally with any other person so liable), unless he is exempted from liability by subsection (3) below.

(2) If a company enters into an agreement in contravention of section 104 and—

   (a) the agreement is or includes an agreement for the allotment of shares in the company; and

   (b) a person becomes a holder of shares allotted under the agreement; and

(c) by virtue of the agreement and allotment under it, another person is liable to pay any amount under section 105,

the person who becomes the holder of the shares is also liable to pay that amount (jointly and severally with any other person so liable), unless he is exempted from liability by the following subsection; and this applies whether or not the agreement also contravenes section 103.

(3) A person otherwise liable under subsection (1) or (2) is exempted from that liability if either—

(a) he is a purchaser for value and, at the time of the purchase, he did not have actual notice of the contravention concerned; or

(b) he derived title to the shares (directly or indirectly) from a person who became a holder of them after the contravention and was not liable under subsection (1) or (as the case may be) subsection (2).

(4) References in this section to a holder, in relation to shares in a company, include any person who has an unconditional right to be included in the company's register of members in respect of those shares or to have an instrument of transfer of the shares executed in his favour.

(5) As subsection (1) and (3) apply in relation to the contraventions there mentioned, they also apply—

(a) to a contravention of section 102; and

(b) to a failure to carry out a term of a contract as mentioned in subsections (5) and (6) of that section.

113   Relief in respect of certain liabilities under ss. 99 ff.

(1) Where a person is liable to a company under—

(a) section 99, 102, 103 or 105;

(b) section 112(1) by reference to a contravention of section 99 or 103; or

(c) section 112(2) or (5),

in relation to payment in respect of any shares in the company, or is liable by virtue of an undertaking given to it in, or in connection with, payment for any such shares, the person so liable may make an application to the court to be exempted in whole or in part from the liability.

(2) If the liability mentioned in subsection (1) arises in relation to payment in respect of any shares, the court may, on an application under that subsection, exempt the applicant from the liability only—

(a) if and to the extent that it appears to the court just and equitable to do so having regard to the matters mentioned in the following subsection,

(b) if and to the extent that it appears to the court just and equitable to do so in respect of any interest which he is liable to pay the company under any of the relevant sections.

(3) The matters to be taken into account by the court under subsection (2)(a) are—

(a) whether the applicant has paid, or is liable to pay, any amount in respect of any other liability arising in relation to those shares under any of the relevant sections, or of any liability arising by virtue of any undertaking given in or in connection with payment for those shares;

(b) whether any person other than the applicant has paid or is likely to pay (whether in pursuance of an order of the court or otherwise) any such amount; and

(c) whether the applicant or any other person has performed in whole or in part, or is likely so to perform, any such undertaking, or has done or is likely to do any other thing in payment or part payment for the shares.

(4) Where the liability arises by virtue of an undertaking given to the company in, or in connection with, payment for shares in it, the court may, on an application under subsection

(1), exempt the applicant from the liability only if and to the extent that it appears to the court just and equitable to do so having regard to—

(a) whether the applicant has paid or is liable to pay any amount in respect of liability arising in relation to the shares under any of the provisions mentioned in that subsection; and

(b) whether any person other than the applicant has paid or is likely to pay (whether in pursuance of an order of the court or otherwise) any such amount.

(5) In determining whether it should exempt the applicant in whole or in part from any liability, the court shall have regard to the following overriding principles, namely—

(a) that a company which has allotted shares should receive money or money's worth at least equal in value to the aggregate of the nominal value of those shares and the whole of any premium or, if the case so requires, so much of that aggregate as is treated as paid up; and

(b) subject to this, that where such a company would, if the court did not grant the exemption, have more than one remedy against a particular person, it should be for the company to decide which remedy it should remain entitled to pursue.

(6) If a person brings proceedings against another ('the contributor') for a contribution in respect of liability to a company arising under any of sections 99 to 105 or 112, and it appears to the court that the contributor is liable to make such a contribution, the court may exercise the powers of the following subsection.

(7) The court may, if and to the extent that it appears to it, having regard to the respective culpability (in respect of the liability to the company) of the contributor and the person bringing the proceedings, that it is just and equitable to do so—

(a) exempt the contributor in whole or in part from his liability to make such a contribution; or

(b) order the contributor to make a larger contribution than, but for this subsection, he would be liable to make.

(8) Where a person is liable to a company under section 105(2), the court may, on application, exempt him in whole or in part from that liability if and to the extent that it appears to the court just and equitable to do so having regard to any benefit accruing to the company by virtue of anything done by him towards the carrying out of the agreement mentioned in that subsection.

114   Penalty for contravention
If a company contravenes any of the provisions of sections 99 to 104 and 106 the company and any officer of it who is in default is liable to a fine.

115   Undertakings to do work, etc.
(1) Subject to section 113, an undertaking given by any person, in or in connection with payment for shares in a company, to do work or perform services or to do any other thing, if it is enforceable by the company apart from this Act, is so enforceable notwithstanding that there has been a contravention in relation to it of, 102 or 103.

(2) Where such an undertaking is given in contravention of section 104 in respect of the allotment of shares, it is so enforceable notwithstanding the contravention.

116   Application of ss. 99 ff. to special cases
Except as provided by section 9 of the Consequential Provisions Act (transitional cases dealt with by section 31 of the Companies Act 1980), sections 99, 101 to 103, 106, 108, 110, 111 and 112 to 115 apply—

(a) to a company which has passed and not revoked a resolution to be re-registered under section 43 as a public company, and

(b) to a joint stock company which has passed, and not revoked, a resolution that the company be a public company,

as those sections apply to a public company.

PART V   SHARE CAPITAL, ITS INCREASE, MAINTENANCE AND REDUCTION

CHAPTER I   GENERAL PROVISIONS ABOUT SHARE CAPITAL

117   Public company share capital requirements

(1) A company registered as a public company on its original incorporation shall not do business or exercise any borrowing powers unless the registrar of companies has issued it with a certificate under this section or the company is re-registered as a private company.

(2) The registrar shall issue a company with such a certificate if, on an application made to him by the company in the prescribed form, he is satisfied that the nominal value of the company's allotted share capital is not less than the authorised minimum, and there is delivered to him a statutory declaration complying with the following subsection. This subsection is subject to subsection (3A).

(3) The statutory declaration must be in the prescribed form and be signed by a director or secretary of the company; and it must—

  (a) state that the nominal value of the company's allotted share capital is not less than the authorised minimum;

  (b) specify the amount paid up, at the time of the application, on the allotted share capital of the company;

  (c) specify the amount, or estimated amount, of the company's preliminary expenses and the persons by whom any of those expenses have been paid or are payable; and

  (d) specify any amount or benefit paid or given, or intended to be paid or given, to any promoter of the company, and the consideration for the payment or benefit.

(3A) In place of the statutory declaration referred to in subsection (2), there may be delivered to the registrar of companies using electronic communications a statement made by a director or secretary of the company complying with the requirements of subsection (3)(a) to (d).

(4) For the purposes of subsection (2), a share allotted in pursuance of an employees' share scheme may not be taken into account in determining the nominal value of the company's allotted share capital unless it is paid up at least as to one-quarter of the nominal value of the share and the whole of any premium on the share.

(5) The registrar may accept a statutory declaration or statement delivered to him under this section as sufficient evidence of the matters stated in it.

(6) A certificate under this section in respect of a company is conclusive evidence that the company is entitled to do business and exercise any borrowing powers.

(7) If a company does business or exercises borrowing powers in contravention of this section, the company and any officer of it who is in default is liable to a fine.

(7A) Any person who makes a false statement under subsection (3A) which he knows to be false or does not believe to be true is liable to imprisonment or a fine, or both.

(8) Nothing in this section affects the validity of any transaction entered into by a company; but, if a company enters into a transaction in contravention of this section and fails to comply with its obligations in that connection within 21 days from being called upon to do so, the directors of the company are jointly and severally liable to indemnify the other party to the transaction in respect of any loss or damage suffered by him by reason of the company's failure to comply with those obligations.

118   The authorised minimum

(1) In this Act, 'the authorised minimum' means £50,000, or such other sum as the Secretary of State may by order made by statutory instrument specify instead.

(2) An order under this section which increases the authorised minimum may—

(a) require any public company having an allotted share capital of which the nominal value is less than the amount specified in the order as the authorised minimum to increase that value to not less than that amount or make application to be re-registered as a private company;

(b) make, in connection with any such requirement, provision for any of the matters for which provision is made by this Act relating to a company's registration, re-registration or change of name, to payment for any share comprised in a company's capital and to offers of shares in or debentures of a company to the public, including provision as to the consequences (whether in criminal law or otherwise) of a failure to comply with any requirement of the order; and

(c) contain such supplemental and transitional provisions as the Secretary of State thinks appropriate, make different provision for different cases and, in particular, provide for any provision of the order to come into operation on different days for different purposes.

(3) An order shall not be made under this section unless a draft of it has been laid before Parliament and approved by resolution of each House.

119 Provision for different amounts to be paid on shares
A company, if so authorised by its articles, may do any one or more of the following things—

(a) make arrangements on the issue of shares for a difference between the shareholders in the amounts and times of payment of calls on their shares;

(b) accept from any member the whole or a part of the amount remaining unpaid on any shares held by him, although no part of that amount has been called up;

(c) pay dividend in proportion to the amount paid up on each share where a larger amount is paid up on some shares than on others.

120 Reserve liability of limited company
A limited company may by special resolution determine that any portion of its share capital which has not been already called up shall not be capable of being called up except in the event and for the purposes of the company being wound up; and that portion of its share capital is then not capable of being called up except in that event and for those purposes.

121 Alteration of share capital (limited companies)
(1) A company limited by shares or a company limited by guarantee and having a share capital, if so authorised by its articles, may alter the conditions of its memorandum in any of the following ways.

(2) The company may—

(a) increase its share capital by new shares of such amount as it thinks expedient;

(b) consolidate and divide all or any of its share capital into shares of larger amount than its existing shares;

(c) convert all or any of its paid-up shares into stock, and reconvert that stock into paid-up shares of any denomination;

(d) subdivide its shares, or any of them, into shares of smaller amount than is fixed by the memorandum (but subject to the following subsection);

(e) cancel shares which, at the date of the passing of the resolution to cancel them, have not been taken or agreed to be taken by any person, and diminish the amount of the company's share capital by the amount of the shares so cancelled.

(3) In any subdivision under subsection (2)(d) the proportion between the amount paid and the amount, if any, unpaid on each reduced share must be the same as it was in the case of the share from which the reduced share is derived.

(4) The powers conferred by this section must be exercised by the company in general meeting.

(5) A cancellation of shares under this section does not for purposes of this Act constitute a reduction of share capital.

122   Notice to registrar of alteration

(1) If a company having a share capital has—
- (a) consolidated and divided its share capital into shares of larger amount than its existing shares; or
- (b) converted any shares into stock; or
- (c) reconverted stock into shares; or
- (d) subdivided its shares or any of them; or
- (e) redeemed any redeemable shares; or
- (f) cancelled any shares (otherwise than in connection with a reduction of share capital under section 135),

it shall within one month after so doing give notice in the prescribed form to the registrar of companies, specifying (as the case may be) the shares consolidated, divided, converted, subdivided, redeemed or cancelled, or the stock reconverted.

(2) If default is made in complying with this section, the company and every officer of it who is in default is liable to a fine and, for continued contravention, to a daily default fine.

123   Notice to registrar of increased share capital

(1) If a company having a share capital (whether or not its shares have been converted into stock) increases its share capital beyond the registered capital, it shall within 15 days after the passing of the resolution authorising the increase, give to the registrar of companies notice of the increase, and the registrar shall record the increase.

(2) The notice must include such particulars as may be prescribed with respect to the classes of shares affected and the conditions subject to which the new shares have been or are to be issued.

(3) There shall be fowarded to the registrar together with the notice a printed copy of the resolution authorising the increase, or a copy of the resolution in some other form approved by the registrar.

(4) If default is made in complying with this section, the company and every officer of it who is in default is liable to a fine and, for continued contravention, to a daily default fine.

124   Reserve capital of unlimited company

An unlimited company having a share capital may by its resolution for re-registration as a public company under section 43, or as a limited company under section 51—
- (a) increase the nominal amount of its share capital by increasing the nominal amount of each of its shares (but subject to the condition that no part of the increased capital is to be capable of being called up except in the event and for the purpose of the company being wound up), and
- (b) alternatively or in addition, provide that a specified portion of its uncalled share capital is not to be capable of being called up except in that event and for that purpose.

CHAPTER II   CLASS RIGHTS

125   Variation of class rights

(1) This section is concerned with the variation of the rights attached to any class of shares in a company whose share capital is divided into shares of different classes.

(2) Where the rights are attached to a class of shares otherwise than by the company's memorandum, and the company's articles do not contain provision with respect to the variation of the rights, those rights may be varied if, but only if—

    (a) the holders of three-quarters in nominal value of the issued shares of that class *(excluding any shares of that class held as treasury shares)* consent in writing to the variation; or

    (b) an extraordinary resolution passed at a separate general meeting of the holders of that class sanctions the variation;

and any requirement (howsoever imposed) in relation to the variation of those rights is complied with to the extent that it is not comprised in paragraphs (a) and (b) above.

(3) Where—

    (a) the rights are attached to a class of shares by the memorandum or otherwise;

    (b) the memorandum or articles contain provision for the variation of those rights; and

    (c) the variation of those rights is connected with the giving, variation, revocation or renewal of an authority for allotment under section 80 or with a reduction of the company's share capital under section 135;

those rights shall not be varied unless—

    (i) the condition mentioned in subsection 2(a) or (b) above is satisfied; and

    (ii) any requirement of the memorandum or articles in relation to the variation of rights of that class is complied with to the extent that it is not comprised in that condition.

(4) If the rights are attached to a class of shares in the company by the memorandum or otherwise and—

    (a) where they are so attached by the memorandum, the articles contain provision with respect to their variation which had been included in the articles at the time of the company's original incorporation; or

    (b) where they are so attached otherwise, the articles contain such provision (whenever first so included),

and in either case the variation is not connected as mentioned in subsection (3)(c), those rights may only be varied in accordance with that provision of the articles.

(5) If the rights are attached to a class of shares by the memorandum, and the memorandum and articles do not contain provision with respect to the variation of those rights, those rights may be varied if all the members of the company *(excluding any member holding shares as treasury shares)* agree to the variation.

(6) The provisions of section 369 (length of notice for calling company meetings), section 370 (general provisions as to meetings and votes), and sections 376 and 377 (circulation of members' resolutions) and the provisions of the articles relating to general meetings shall, so far as applicable, apply in relation to any meeting of shareholders required by this section or otherwise to take place in connection with the variation of the rights attached to a class of shares, and shall so apply with the necessary modifications and subject to the following provisions, namely—

    (a) the necessary quorum at any such meeting other than an adjourned meeting shall be two persons holding or representing by proxy at least one-third in nominal value of the issued shares of the class in question *(excluding any shares of that class held as treasury shares)* and at an adjourned meeting one person holding shares of the class in question or his proxy;

    (b) any holder of shares of the class in question present in person or by proxy may demand a poll.

(7) Any alteration of a provision contained in a company's articles for the variation of the rights attached to a class of shares, or the insertion of any such provision into the articles, is itself to be treated as a variation of those rights.

(8) In this section and (except where the context otherwise requires) in any provision for the variation of the rights attached to a class of shares contained in a company's

memorandum or articles, references to the variation of those rights are to be read as including references to their abrogation.

[*The words in italics in s. 125(2)(a), (5) and (6)(a) are in force from 1 December 2003.*]

126   Saving for court's powers under other provisions

Nothing in subsections (2) to (5) of section 125 derogates from the powers of the court under the following sections of this Act, namely—

sections 4 to 6 (company resolution to alter objects),

section 54 (litigated objection to public company becoming private by re-registration),

section 425 (court control of company compromising with members and creditors),

section 427 (company reconstruction or amalgamation),

sections 459 to 461 (protection of minorities).

127   Shareholders' right to object to variation

(1) This section applies if, in the case of a company whose share capital is divided into different classes of shares—

    (a) provision is made by the memorandum or articles for authorising the variation of the rights attached to any class of shares in the company, subject to—

        (i) the consent of any specified proportion of the holders of the issued shares of that class, or

        (ii) the sanction of a resolution passed at a separate meeting of the holders of those shares,

and in pursuance of that provision the rights attached to any such class of shares are at any time varied; or

    (b) the rights attached to any class of shares in the company are varied under section 125(2).

(2) The holders of not less in the aggregate than 15 per cent of the issued shares of the class in question (being persons who did not consent to or vote in favour of the resolution for the variation), may apply to the court to have the variation cancelled; and if such an application is made, the variation has no effect unless and until it is confirmed by the court.

(2A) For the purposes of subsection (2), any of the company's issued share capital held as treasury shares must be disregarded.

(3) Application to the court must be made within 21 days after the date on which the consent was given or the resolution was passed (as the case may be), and may be made on behalf of the shareholders entitled to make the application by such one or more of their number as they may appoint in writing for the purpose.

(4) The court, after hearing the applicant and any other persons who apply to the court to be heard and appear to the court to be interested in the application, may, if satisfied having regard to all the circumstances of the case, that the variation would unfairly prejudice the shareholders of the class represented by the applicant, disallow the variation and shall, if not so satisfied, confirm it.

The decision of the court on any such application is final.

(5) The company shall within 15 days after the making of an order by the court on such an application forward a copy of the order to the registrar of companies; and, if default is made in complying with this provision, the company and every officer of it who is in default is liable to a fine and, for continued contravention, to a daily default fine.

(6) 'Variation', in this section, includes abrogation; and 'varied' is to be construed accordingly.

[*Section 127(2A) is in force from 1 December 2003.*]

128   Registration of particulars of special rights

(1) If a company allots shares with rights which are not stated in its memorandum or articles, or in any resolution or agreement which is required by section 380 to be sent to the

registrar of companies, the company shall deliver to the registrar of companies, within one month from allotting the shares, a statement in the prescribed form containing particulars of those rights.

(2) This does not apply if the shares are in all respects uniform with shares previously allotted; and shares are not for this purpose to be treated as different from shares previously allotted by reason only that the former do not carry the same rights to dividends as the latter during the 12 months immediately following the former's allotment.

(3) Where the rights attached to any shares of a company are varied otherwise than by an amendment of the company's memorandum or articles or by a resolution or agreement subject to section 380, the company shall within one month from the date on which the variation is made deliver to the registrar of companies a statement in the prescribed form containing particulars of the variation.

(4) Where a company (otherwise than by any such amendment, resolution or agreement as is mentioned above) assigns a name or other designation, or a new name or other designation, to any class of its shares, it shall within one month from doing so deliver to the registrar of companies a notice in the prescribed form giving particulars of the name or designation so assigned.

(5) If a company fails to comply with this section, the company and every officer of it who is in default is liable to a fine and, for continued contravention, to a daily default fine.

129   Registration of newly created class rights

(1) If a company not having a share capital creates a class of members with rights which are not stated in its memorandum or articles or in a resolution or agreement to which section 380 applies, the company shall deliver to the registrar of companies within one month from the date on which the new class is created a statement in the prescribed form containing particulars of the rights attached to that class.

(2) If the rights of any class of members of the company are varied otherwise than by an amendment of the memorandum or articles or by a resolution or agreement subject to section 380, the company shall within one month from the date on which the variation is made deliver to the registrar a statement in the prescribed form containing particulars of the variation.

(3) If a company (otherwise than by such an amendment, resolution or agreement as is mentioned above) assigns a name or other designation, or a new name or other designation, to any class of its members, it shall within one month from doing so deliver to the registrar a notice in the prescribed form giving particulars of the name or designation so assigned.

(4) If a company fails to comply with this section, the company and every officer of it who is in default is liable to a fine and, for continued contravention, to a daily default fine.

CHAPTER III   SHARE PREMIUMS

130   Application of share premiums

(1) If a company issues shares at a premium, whether for cash or otherwise, a sum equal to the aggregate amount or value of the premiums on those shares shall be transferred to an account called 'the share premium account'.

(2) The share premium account may be applied by the company in paying up unissued shares to be allotted to members as fully paid bonus shares, or in writing off—

(a)   the company's preliminary expenses; or
(b)   the expenses of, or the commission paid or discount allowed on, any issue of shares or debentures of the company,

or in providing for the premium payable on redemption of debentures of the company.

(3) Subject to this, the provisions of this Act relating to the reduction of a company's share capital apply as if the share premium account were part of its paid-up share capital.

(4) Sections 131 and 132 below give relief from the requirements of this section, and in those sections references to the issuing company are to the company issuing shares as above mentioned.

131   Merger relief

(1) With the exception made by section 132(8) (group reconstruction) this section applies where the issuing company has secured at least a 90 per cent equity holding in another company in pursuance of an arrangement providing for the allotment of equity shares in the issuing company on terms that the consideration for the shares allotted is to be provided—

(a) by the issue or transfer to the issuing company of equity shares in the other company, or

(b) by the cancellation of any such shares not held by the issuing company.

(2) If the equity shares in the issuing company allotted in pursuance of the arrangement in consideration for the acquisition or cancellation of equity shares in the other company are issued at a premium, section 130 does not apply to the premiums on those shares.

(3) Where the arrangement also provides for the allotment of any shares in the issuing company on terms that the consideration for those shares is to be provided by the issue or transfer to the issuing company of non-equity shares in the other company or by the cancellation of any such shares in that company not held by the issuing company, relief under subsection (2) extends to any shares in the issuing company allotted on those terms in pursuance of the arrangement.

(4) Subject to the next subsection, the issuing company is to be regarded for purposes of this section as having secured at least a 90 per cent equity holding in another company in pursuance of such an arrangement as is mentioned in subsection (1) if in consequence of an acquisition or cancellation of equity shares in that company (in pursuance of that arrangement) it holds equity shares in that company (whether all or any of those shares were acquired in pursuance of that arrangement, or not) of an aggregate nominal value equal to 90 per cent or more of the nominal value of that company's equity share capital *(excluding any shares in that company held as treasury shares)*.

(5) Where the equity share capital of the other company is divided into different classes of shares, this section does not apply unless the requirements of subsection (1) are satisfied in relation to each of those classes of shares taken separately.

(6) Shares held by a company which is the issuing company's holding company or subsidiary, or a subsidiary of the issuing company's holding company, or by its or their nominees, are to be regarded for purposes of this section as held by the issuing company.

(7) In relation to a company and its shares and capital, the following definitions apply for purposes of this section—

(a) 'equity shares' means shares comprised in the company's equity share capital; and

(b) 'non-equity shares' means shares (of any class) not so comprised;

and 'arrangement' means any agreement, scheme or arrangement (including an arrangement sanctioned under section 425 (company compromise with members and creditors) or section 110 of the Insolvency Act (liquidator accepting shares etc. as consideration for sale of company property)).

(8) The relief allowed by this section does not apply if the issue of shares took place before 4 February 1981.

[*The words in italics in s. 131(4) are in force from 1 December 2003.*]

132   Relief in respect of group reconstructions

(1) This section applies where the issuing company—

(a) is a wholly-owned subsidiary of another company ('the holding company'), and

(b) allots shares to the holding company or to another wholly-owned subsidiary of the holding company in consideration for the transfer to the issuing company of assets other than cash, being assets of any company ('the transferor company') which is a member of the group of companies which comprises the holding company and all its wholly-owned subsidiaries.

(2) Where the shares in the issuing company allotted in consideration for the transfer are issued at a premium, the issuing company is not required by section 130 to transfer any amount in excess of the minimum premium value to the share premium account.

(3) In subsection (2), 'the minimum premium value' means the amount (if any) by which the base value of the consideration for the shares allotted exceeds the aggregate nominal value of those shares.

(4) For the purposes of subsection (3), the base value of the consideration for the shares allotted is the amount by which the base value of the assets transferred exceeds the base value of any liabilities of the transferor company assumed by the issuing company as part of the consideration for the assets transferred.

(5) For the purposes of subsection (4)—

    (a) the base value of the assets transferred is to be taken as—

        (i) the cost of those assets to the transferor company, or

        (ii) the amount at which those assets are stated in the transferor company's accounting records immediately before the transfer,

       whichever is the less; and

    (b) the base value of the liabilities assumed is to be taken as the amount at which they are stated in the transferor company's accounting records immediately before the transfer.

(6) The relief allowed by this section does not apply (subject to the next subsection) if the issue of shares took place before the date of the coming into force of the Companies (Share Premium Account) Regulations 1984 (which were made on 21 December 1984).

(7) To the extent that the relief allowed by this section would have been allowed by section 38 of the Companies Act 1981 as originally enacted (the text of which section is set out in Schedule 25 to this Act), the relief applies where the issue of shares took place before the date of the coming into force of those Regulations, but not if the issue took place before 4 February 1981.

(8) Section 131 does not apply in a case falling within this section.

133   Provisions supplementing ss. 131, 132

(1) An amount corresponding to one representing the premiums or part of the premiums on shares issued by a company which by virtue of sections 131 or 132 of this Act, or section 12 of the Consequential Provisions Act, is not included in the company's share premium account may also be disregarded in determining the amount at which any shares or other consideration provided for the shares issued is to be included in the company's balance sheet.

(2) References in this Chapter (however expressed) to—

    (a) the acquisition by a company of shares in another company; and

    (b) the issue or allotment of shares to, or the transfer of shares to or by, a company,

include (respectively) the acquisition of any of those shares by, and the issue or allotment or (as the case may be) the transfer of any of those shares to or by, nominees of that company; and the reference in section 132 to the company transferring the shares is to be construed accordingly.

(3) References in this Chapter to the transfer of shares in a company include the transfer of a right to be included in the company's register of members in respect of those shares.

(4) In sections 131 to 133 'company', except in references to the issuing company, includes any body corporate.

134   Provision for extending or restricting relief from s. 130

(1) The Secretary of State may by regulations in a statutory instrument make such provision as appears to him to be appropriate—

(a) for relieving companies from the requirements of section 130 in relation to premiums other than cash premiums, or

(b) for restricting or otherwise modifying any relief from those requirements provided by this Chapter.

(2) Regulations under this section may make different provision for different cases or classes of case and may contain such incidental and supplementary provisions as the Secretary of State thinks fit.

(3) No such regulations shall be made unless a draft of the instrument containing them has been laid before Parliament and approved by a resolution of each House.

CHAPTER IV   REDUCTION OF SHARE CAPITAL

135   Special resolution for reduction of share capital

(1) Subject to confirmation by the court, a company limited by shares or a company limited by guarantee and having a share capital may, if so authorised by its articles, by special resolution reduce its share capital in any way.

(2) In particular, and without prejudice to subsection (1), the company may—

(a) extinguish or reduce the liability on any of its shares in respect of share capital not paid up; or

(b) either with or without extinguishing or reducing liability on any of its shares, cancel any paid-up share capital which is lost or unrepresented by available assets; or

(c) either with or without extinguishing or reducing liability on any of its shares, pay off any paid-up share capital which is in excess of the company's wants;

and the company may, if and so far as is necessary, alter its memorandum by reducing the amount of its share capital and of its shares accordingly.

(3) A special resolution under this section is in this Act referred to as 'a resolution for reducing share capital'.

136   Application to court for order of confirmation

(1) Where a company has passed a resolution for reducing share capital, it may apply to the court for an order confirming the reduction.

(2) If the proposed reduction of share capital involves either—

(a) diminution of liability in respect of unpaid share capital; or

(b) the payment to a shareholder of any paid-up share capital, and in any other case if the court so directs, the next three subsections have effect, but subject throughout to subsection (6).

(3) Every creditor of the company who at the date fixed by the court is entitled to any debt or claim which, if that date were the commencement of the winding up of the company, would be admissible in proof against the company is entitled to object to the reduction of capital.

(4) The court shall settle a list of creditors entitled to object, and for that purpose—

(a) shall ascertain, as far as possible without requiring an application from any creditor, the names of those creditors and the nature and amount of their debts or claims; and

(b) may publish notices fixing a day or days within which creditors not entered on the list are to claim to be so entered or are to be excluded from the right of objecting to the reduction of capital.

(5) If a creditor entered on the list whose debt or claim is not discharged or has not determined does not consent to the reduction, the court may, if it thinks fit, dispense with the consent of that creditor, on the company securing payment of his debt or claim by appropriating (as the court may direct) the following amount—

    (a) if the company admits the full amount of the debt or claim or, though not admitting it, is willing to provide for it, then the full amount of the debt or claim;

    (b) if the company does not admit, and is not willing to provide for, the full amount of the debt or claim, or if the amount is contingent or not ascertained, then an amount fixed by the court after the like enquiry and adjudication as if the company were being wound up by the court.

(6) If a proposed reduction of share capital involves either the diminution of any liability in respect of unpaid share capital or the payment to any shareholder of any paid-up share capital, the court may, if having regard to any special circumstances of the case it thinks proper to do so, direct that subsections (3) to (5) of this section shall not apply as regards any class or any classes of creditors.

137   Court order confirming reduction

(1) The court, if satisfied with respect to every creditor of the company who under section 136 is entitled to object to the reduction of capital that either—

    (a) his consent to the reduction has been obtained; or

    (b) his debt or claim has been discharged or has determined, or has been secured, may make an order confirming the reduction on such terms and conditions as it thinks fit.

(2) Where the court so orders, it may also—

    (a) if for any special reason it thinks proper to do so, make an order directing that the company shall, during such period (commencing on or at any time after the date of the order) as is specified in the order, add to its name as its last words the words 'and reduced'; and

    (b) make an order requiring the company to publish (as the court directs) the reasons for reduction of capital or such other information in regard to it as the court thinks expedient with a view to giving proper information to the public and (if the court thinks fit) the causes which led to the reduction.

(3) Where a company is ordered to add to its name the words 'and reduced', those words are, until the expiration of the period specified in the order, deemed to be part of the company's name.

138   Registration of order and minute of reduction

(1) The registrar of companies, on production to him of an order of the court confirming the reduction of a company's share capital, and the delivery to him of a copy of the order and of a minute (approved by the court) showing, with respect to the company's share capital as altered by the order—

    (a) the amount of the share capital;

    (b) the number of shares into which it is to be divided, and the amount of each share; and

    (c) the amount (if any) at the date of the registration deemed to be paid up on each share,

shall register the order and minute (but subject to section 139).

(2) On the registration of the order and minute, and not before, the resolution for reducing share capital as confirmed by the order so registered takes effect.

(3) Notice of the registration shall be published in such manner as the court may direct.

(4) The registrar shall certify the registration of the order and minute; and the certificate—

    (a) may be either signed by the registrar, or authenticated by his official seal;

    (b) is conclusive evidence that all the requirements of this Act with respect to the reduction of share capital have been complied with, and that the company's share capital is as stated in the minute.

(5) The minute when registered is deemed to be substituted for the corresponding part of the company's memorandum, and is valid and alterable as if it had been originally contained therein.

(6) The substitution of such a minute for part of the company's memorandum is deemed an alteration of the memorandum for purposes of section 20.

139   Public company reducing capital below authorised minimum

(1) This section applies where the court makes an order confirming a reduction of a public company's capital which has the effect of bringing the nominal value of its allotted share capital below the authorised minimum.

(2) The registrar of companies shall not register the order under section 138 unless the court otherwise directs, or the company is first re-registered as a private company.

(3) The court may authorise the company to be so re-registered without its having passed the special resolution required by section 53; and where that authority is given, the court shall specify in the order the alterations in the company's memorandum and articles to be made in connection with that re-registration.

(4) The company may then be re-registered as a private company, if an application in the prescribed form and signed by a director or secretary of the company is delivered to the registrar, together with a printed copy of the memorandum and articles as altered by the court's order.

(5) On receipt of such an application, the registrar shall retain it and the other documents delivered with it and issue the company with a certificate of incorporation appropriate to a company that is not a public company; and—

    (a) the company by virtue of the issue of the certificate becomes a private company, and the alterations in the memorandum and articles set out in the court's order take effect; and

    (b) the certificate is conclusive evidence that the requirements of this section in respect of re-registration and of matters precedent and incidental thereto have been complied with, and that the company is a private company.

140   Liability of members on reduced shares

(1) Where a company's share capital is reduced, a member of the company (past or present) is not liable in respect of any share to any call or contribution exceeding in amount the difference (if any) between the amount of the share as fixed by the minute and the amount paid on the share or the reduced amount (if any), which is deemed to have been paid on it, as the case may be.

(2) But the following two subsections apply if—

    (a) a creditor, entitled in respect of a debt or claim to object to the reduction of share capital, by reason of his ignorance of the proceedings for reduction of share capital, or of their nature and effect with respect to his claim, is not entered on the list of creditors; and

    (b) after the reduction of capital, the company is unable (within the meaning of section 123 of the Insolvency Act) to pay the amount of his debt or claim.

(3) Every person who was a member of the company at the date of the registration of the order for reduction and minute is then liable to contribute for the payment of the debt or claim in question an amount not exceeding that which he would have been liable to contribute if the company had commenced to be wound up on the day before that date.

(4) If the company is wound up, the court, on the application of the creditor in question and proof of ignorance referred to in subsection (2)(a), may (if it thinks fit) settle accordingly a list of persons so liable to contribute, and make and enforce calls and orders on the contributories settled on the list, as if they were ordinary contributories in a winding up.

(5) Nothing in this section affects the rights of the contributories among themselves.

141   Penalty for concealing name of creditor, etc.
If an officer of the company—
(a) wilfully conceals the name of a creditor entitled to object to the reduction of capital; or
(b) wilfully misrepresents the nature or amount of the debt or claim of any creditor; or
(c) aids, abets or is privy to any such concealment or misrepresentation as is mentioned above,
he is guilty of an offence and liable to a fine.

CHAPTER V   MAINTENANCE OF CAPITAL

142   Duty of directors on serious loss of capital
(1) Where the net assets of a public company are half or less of its called-up share capital, the directors shall, not later than 28 days from the earliest day on which that fact is known to a director of the company, duly convene an extraordinary general meeting of the company for a date not later than 56 days from that day for the purpose of considering whether any, and if so what, steps should be taken to deal with the situation.
(2) If there is a failure to convene an extraordinary general meeting as required by subsection (1), each of the directors of the company who—
(a) knowingly and wilfully authorises or permits the failure, or
(b) after the expiry of the period during which that meeting should have been convened, knowingly and wilfully authorises or permits the failure to continue,
is liable to a fine.
(3) Nothing in this section authorises the consideration, at a meeting convened in pursuance of subsection (1), of any matter which could not have been considered at that meeting apart from this section.

143   General rule against company acquiring own shares
(1) Subject to the following provisions, a company limited by shares or limited by guarantee and having a share capital shall not acquire its own shares, whether by purchase, subscription or otherwise.
(2) If a company purports to act in contravention of this section, the company is liable to a fine, and every officer of the company who is in default is liable to imprisonment or a fine, or both; and, *subject to subsection (2A),* the purported acquisition is void.
(2A) Where a company purchases qualifying shares out of distributable profits under section 162, any contravention by the company of any provision of section 162B(1) or (2) shall not render the acquisition void under subsection (2) above.
(3) A company limited by shares may acquire any of its own fully paid shares otherwise than for valuable consideration; and subsection (1) does not apply in relation to—
(a) the redemption or purchase of shares in accordance with Chapter VII of this Part,
(b) the acquisition of shares in a reduction of capital duly made,
(c) the purchase of shares in pursuance of an order of the court under section 5 (alteration of objects), section 54 (litigated objection to resolution for company to be re-registered as private) or Part XVII (relief to members unfairly prejudiced), or
(d) the forfeiture of shares, or the acceptance of shares surrendered in lieu, in pursuance of the articles, for failure to pay any sum payable in respect of the shares.
[*The words in italics in s. 143(2) and s. 143(2A) are in force from 1 December 2003.*]

144   Acquisition of shares by company's nominee
(1) Subject to section 145, where shares are issued to a nominee of a company mentioned in section 143(1), or are acquired by a nominee of such a company from a third person as partly paid up, then, for all purposes—

(a) the shares are to be treated as held by the nominee on his own account; and

(b) the company is to be regarded as having no beneficial interest in them.

(2) Subject to that section, if a person is called on to pay any amount for the purpose of paying up, or paying any premium on, any shares in such a company which were issued to him, or which he otherwise acquired, as the company's nominee and he fails to pay that amount within 21 days from being called on to do so, then—

(a) if the shares were issued to him as subscriber to the memorandum by virtue of an undertaking of his in the memorandum, the other subscribers to the memorandum, or

(b) if the shares were otherwise issued to or acquired by him, the directors of the company at the time of the issue or acquisition,

are jointly and severally liable with him to pay that amount.

(3) If in proceedings for the recovery of any such amount from any such subscriber or director under this section it appears to the court—

(a) that he is or may be liable to pay that amount, but

(b) that he has acted honestly and reasonably and, having regard to all the circumstances of the case, he ought fairly to be excused from liability,

the court may relieve him, either wholly or partly, from his liability on such terms as the court thinks fit.

(4) Where any such subscriber or director has reason to apprehend that a claim will or might be made for the recovery of any such amount from him, he may apply to the court for relief; and the court has the same power to relieve him as it would have had in proceedings for the recovery of that amount.

145   Exceptions from s. 144

(1) Section 144(1) does not apply to shares acquired otherwise than by subscription by a nominee of a public company, where a person acquires shares in the company with financial assistance given to him directly or indirectly by the company for the purpose of or in connection with the acquisition, and the company has a beneficial interest in the shares.

(2) Section 144(1) and (2) do not apply—

(a) to shares acquired by a nominee of a company when the company has no beneficial interest in those shares, or

(b) to shares issued in consequence of an application made before 22 December 1980, or transferred in pursuance of an agreement to acquire them made before that date.

(3) Schedule 2 to this Act has effect for the interpretation of references in this section to a company having, or not having, a beneficial interest in shares.

146   Treatment of shares held by or for public company

(1) Except as provided by section 148, the following applies to a public company—

(a) where shares in the company are forfeited, or surrendered to the company in lieu, in pursuance of the articles, for failure to pay any sum payable in respect of the shares;

(b) where shares in the company are acquired by it (otherwise than by any of the methods mentioned in section 143(3)(a) to (d)) and the company has a beneficial interest in the shares;

(c) where the nominee of the company acquires shares in the company from a third person without financial assistance being given directly or indirectly by the company and the company has a beneficial interest in the shares; or

(d) where a person acquires shares in the company with financial assistance given to him directly or indirectly by the company for the purpose of or in connection with the acquisition, and the company has a beneficial interest in the shares.

Schedule 2 to this Act has effect for the interpretation of references in this subsection to the company having a beneficial interest in shares.

(2) Unless the shares or any interest of the company in them are previously disposed of, the company must, not later than the end of the relevant period from their forfeiture or surrender or, in a case within subsection (1)(b), (c) or (d), their acquisition—

(a) cancel them and diminish the amount of the share capital by the nominal value of the shares cancelled, and

(b) where the effect of cancelling the shares will be that the nominal value of the company's allotted share capital is brought below the authorised minimum, apply for re-registration as a private company, stating the effect of the cancellation.

(3) For this purpose 'the relevant period' is—

(a) 3 years in the case of shares forfeited or surrendered to the company in lieu of forfeiture, or acquired as mentioned in subsection (1)(b) or (c);

(b) one year in the case of shares acquired as mentioned in subsection (1)(d).

(4) The company and, in a case within subsection (1)(c) or (d), the company's nominee or (as the case may be) the other shareholder must not exercise any voting rights in respect of the shares; and any purported exercise of those rights is void.

147 Matters arising out of compliance with s. 146(2)

(1) The directors may take such steps as are requisite to enable the company to carry out its obligations under section 146(2) without complying with sections 135 and 136 (resolution to reduce share capital; application to court for approval).

(2) The steps taken may include the passing of a resolution to alter the company's memorandum so that it no longer states that the company is to be a public company; and the resolution may make such other alterations in the memorandum as are requisite in the circumstances.

Such a resolution is subject to section 380 (copy to be forwarded to registrar within 15 days).

(3) The application for re-registration required by section 146(2)(b) must be in the prescribed form and be signed by a director or secretary of the company, and must be delivered to the registrar of companies together with a printed copy of the memorandum and articles of the company as altered by the resolution.

(4) If the registrar is satisfied that the company may be re-registered under section 146, he shall retain the application and other documents delivered with it and issue the company with a certificate of incorporation appropriate to a company that is not a public company; and—

(a) the company by virtue of the issue of the certificate becomes a private company, and the alterations in the memorandum and articles set out in the resolution take effect accordingly, and

(b) the certificate is conclusive evidence that the requirements of sections 146 to 148 in respect of re-registration and of matters precedent and incidental to it have been complied with, and that the company is a private company.

148 Further provisions supplementing ss. 146, 147

(1) Where, after shares in a private company—

(a) are forfeited in pursuance of the company's articles or are surrendered to the company in lieu of forfeiture, or

(b) are acquired by the company (otherwise than by such surrender or forfeiture, and otherwise than by any of the methods mentioned in section 143(3)), the company having a beneficial interest in the shares, or

(c) are acquired by the nominee of a company in the circumstances mentioned in section 146(1)(c), or

(d) are acquired by any person in the circumstances mentioned in section 146(1)(d),

the company is re-registered as a public company, sections 146 and 147, and also section 149, apply to the company as if it had been a public company at the time of the forfeiture, surrender or acquisition, but with the modification required by the following subsection.

(2) That modification is to treat any reference to the relevant period from the forfeiture, surrender or acquisition as referring to the relevant period from the re-registration of the company as a public company.

(3) Schedule 2 to this Act has effect for the interpretation of the reference in subsection (1)(b) to the company having a beneficial interest in shares.

(4) Where a public company or a nominee of a public company acquires shares in the company or an interest in such shares, and those shares are (or that interest is) shown in a balance sheet of the company as an asset, an amount equal to the value of the shares or (as the case may be) the value to the company of its interest in them shall be transferred out of profits available for dividend to a reserve fund and are not then available for distribution.

149   Sanctions for non-compliance

(1) If a public company required by section 146(2) to apply to be re-registered as a private company fails to do so before the end of the relevant period referred to in that subsection, section 81 (restriction on public offers) applies to it as if it were a private company such as is mentioned in that section; but, subject to this, the company continues to be treated for the purpose of this Act as a public company until it is so re-registered.

(2) If a company when required to do so by section 146(2) (including that subsection as applied by section 148(1)) fails to cancel any shares in accordance with paragraph (a) of that subsection or to make an application for re-registration in accordance with paragraph (b) of it, the company and every officer of it who is in default is liable to a fine and, for continued contravention, to a daily default fine.

150   Charges of public companies on own shares

(1) A lien or other charge of a public company on its own shares (whether taken expressly or otherwise), except a charge permitted by any of the following subsections, is void.

This is subject to section 6 of the Consequential Provisions Act (saving for charges of old public companies on their own shares).

(2) In the case of any description of company, a charge on its own shares is permitted if the shares are not fully paid and the charge is for any amount payable in respect of the shares.

(3) In the case of a company whose ordinary business—

(a) includes the lending of money, or

(b) consists of the provision of credit or the bailment (in Scotland, hiring) of goods under a hire-purchase agreement, or both,

a charge of the company on its own shares is permitted (whether the shares are fully paid or not) if it arises in connection with a transaction entered into by the company in the ordinary course of its business.

(4) In the case of a company which is re-registered or is registered under section 680 as a public company, a charge on its own shares is permitted if the charge was in existence immediately before the company's application for re-registration or (as the case may be) registration.

This subsection does not apply in the case of such a company as is referred to in section 6(3) of the Consequential Provisions Act (old public company remaining such after 22 March 1982, not having applied to be re-registered as public company).

CHAPTER VI   FINANCIAL ASSISTANCE BY A COMPANY FOR ACQUISITION
OF ITS OWN SHARES

Provisions applying to both public and private companies

151   Financial assistance generally prohibited

(1) Subject to the following provisions of this Chapter, where a person is acquiring or is proposing to acquire shares in a company, it is not lawful for the company or any of its subsidiaries to give financial assistance directly or indirectly for the purpose of that acquisition before or at the same time as the acquisition takes place.

(2) Subject to those provisions, where a person has acquired shares in a company and any liability has been incurred (by that or any other person), for the purpose of that acquisition, it is not lawful for the company or any of its subsidiaries to give financial assistance directly or indirectly for the purpose of reducing or discharging the liability so incurred.

(3) If a company acts in contravention of this section, it is liable to a fine, and every officer of it who is in default is liable to imprisonment or a fine, or both.

152   Definitions for this Chapter

(1) In this Chapter—

    (a) 'financial assistance' means—

        (i) financial assistance given by way of gift,

        (ii) financial assistance given by way of guarantee, security or indemnity, other than an indemnity in respect of the indemnifier's own neglect or default, or by way of release or waiver,

        (iii) financial assistance given by way of a loan or any other agreement under which any of the obligations of the person giving the assistance are to be fulfilled at a time when in accordance with the agreement any obligation of another party to the agreement remains unfulfilled, or by way of the novation of, or the assignment of rights arising under, a loan or such other agreement, or

        (iv) any other financial assistance given by a company the net assets of which are thereby reduced to a material extent or which has no net assets;

    (b) 'distributable profits', in relation to the giving of any financial assistance—

        (i) means those profits out of which the company could lawfully make a distribution equal in value to that assistance, and

        (ii) includes, in a case where the financial assistance is or includes a non-cash asset, any profit which, if the company were to make a distribution of that asset, would under section 276 (distributions in kind) be available for that purpose,

    and

    (c) 'distribution' has the meaning given by section 263(2).

(2) In subsection (1)(a)(iv), 'net assets' means the aggregate of the company's assets, less the aggregate of its liabilities ('liabilities' to include any provision for liabilities or charges within paragraph 89 of Schedule 4).

(3) In this Chapter—

    (a) a reference to a person incurring a liability includes his changing his financial position by making an agreement or arrangement (whether enforceable or unenforceable, and whether made on his own account or with any other person) or by any other means, and

    (b) a reference to a company giving financial assistance for the purpose of reducing or discharging a liability incurred by a person for the purpose of the acquisition of shares includes its giving such assistance for the purpose of wholly or partly restoring his financial position to what it was before the acquisition took place.

153 Transactions not prohibited by s. 151

(1) Section 151(1) does not prohibit a company from giving financial assistance for the purpose of an acquisition of shares in it or its holding company if—

(a) the company's principal purpose in giving that assistance is not to give it for the purpose of any such acquisition, or the giving of the assistance for that purpose is but an incidental part of some larger purpose of the company, and

(b) the assistance is given in good faith in the interests of the company.

(2) Section 151(2) does not prohibit a company from giving financial assistance if—

(a) the company's principal purpose in giving the assistance is not to reduce or discharge any liability incurred by a person for the purpose of the acquisition of shares in the company or its holding company, or the reduction or discharge of any such liability is but an incidental part of some larger purpose of the company, and

(b) the assistance is given in good faith in the interests of the company.

(3) Section 151 does not prohibit—

(a) a distribution of a company's assets by way of dividend lawfully made or a distribution made in the course of the company's winding up,

(b) the allotment of bonus shares,

(c) a reduction of capital confirmed by order of the court under section 137,

(d) a redemption or purchase of shares made in accordance with Chapter VII of this part,

(e) anything done in pursuance of an order of the court under section 425 (compromises and arrangements with creditors and members),

(f) anything done under an arrangement made in pursuance of section 110 of the Insolvency Act (acceptance of shares by liquidator in winding up as consideration for sale of property), or

(g) anything done under an arrangement made between a company and its creditors which is binding on the creditors by virtue of Part I of the Insolvency Act.

(4) Section 151 does not prohibit—

(a) where the lending of money is part of the ordinary business of the company, the lending of money by the company in the ordinary course of its business,

(b) the provision by a company, in good faith in the interests of the company, of financial assistance for the purposes of an employees' share scheme,

(bb) without prejudice to paragraph (b), the provision of financial assistance by a company or any of its subsidiaries for the purposes of or in connection with anything done by the company (or a company in the same group) for the purpose of enabling or facilitating transactions in shares in the first-mentioned company between, and involving the acquisition of beneficial ownership of those shares by, any of the following persons—

(i) the bona fide employees or former employees of that company or of another company in the same group; or

(ii) the wives, husbands, widows, widowers, children or stepchildren under the age of eighteen of any such employees or former employees,

(c) the making by a company of loans to persons (other than directors) employed in goodfaith by the company with a viewto enabling those persons to acquire fully paid shares in the company or its holding company to be held by themby way of beneficial ownership.

(5) For the purposes of subsection (4)(bb) a company is in the same group as another company if it is a holding company or subsidiary of that company, or a subsidiary of a holding company of that company.

154   Special restriction for public companies

(1) In the case of a public company, section 153(4) authorises the giving of financial assistance only if the company has net assets which are not thereby reduced or, to the extent that those assets are thereby reduced, if the assistance is provided out of distributable profits.

(2) For this purpose the following definitions apply—

(a) 'net assets' means the amount by which the aggregate of the company's assets exceeds the aggregate of its liabilities (taking the amount of both assets and liabilities to be as stated in the company's accounting records immediately before the financial assistance is given);

(b) 'liabilities' includes any amount retained as reasonable necessary for the purpose of providing for any liability or loss which is either likely to be incurred, or certain to be incurred but uncertain as to amount or as to the date on which it will arise.

Private companies

155   Relaxation of s. 151 for private companies

(1) Section 151 does not prohibit a private company from giving financial assistance in a case where the acquisition of shares in question is or was an acquisition of shares in the company or, if it is a subsidiary of another private company, in that other company if the following provisions of this section, and sections 156 to 158, are complied with as respects the giving of that assistance.

(2) The financial assistance may only be given if the company has net assets which are not thereby reduced or, to the extent that they are reduced, if the assistance is provided out of distributable profits.

Section 154(2) applies for the interpretation of this subsection.

(3) This section does not permit financial assistance to be given by a subsidiary, in a case where the acquisition of shares in question is or was an acquisition of shares in its holding company, if it is also a subsidiary of a public company which is itself a subsidiary of that holding company.

(4) Unless the company proposing to give the financial assistance is a wholly-owned subsidiary, the giving of assistance under this section must be approved by special resolution of the company in general meeting.

(5) Where the financial assistance is to be given by the company in a case where the acquisition of shares in question is or was an acquisition of shares in its holding company, that holding company and any other company which is both the company's holding company and a subsidiary of that other holding company (except, in any case, a company which is a wholly-owned subsidiary) shall also approve by special resolution in general meeting the giving of the financial assistance.

(6) Subject to subsection (6A), the directors of the company proposing to give the financial assistance and, where the shares acquired or to be acquired are shares in its holding company, the directors of that company and of any other company which is both the company's holding company and a subsidiary of that other holding company shall before the financial assistance is given make a statutory declaration in the prescribed form complying with the section next following.

(6A) In place of the statutory declaration referred to in subsection (6), there may be delivered to the registrar of companies under section 156(5) a statement made by the persons mentioned in subsection (6) above complying with the section next following.

156   Statutory declaration under s. 155

(1) A statutory declaration made by a company's directors under section 155(6) shall contain such particulars of the financial assistance to be given, and of the business of the company of which they are directors, as may be prescribed, and shall identify the person to whom the assistance is to be given.

(1A) A statement made by a company's directors under section 155(6A) shall state—

- (a) the names and addresses of all the directors of the company,
- (b) whether the business of the company is that of a banking company or insurance company or some other business,
- (c) that the company or (as the case may be) a company (naming such company) of which it is the holding company is proposing to give financial assistance in connection with the acquisition of shares in the company or (as the case may be) its holding company (naming that holding company),
- (d) whether the assistance is for the purpose of that acquisition or for reducing or discharging a liability incurred for the purpose of that acquisition,
- (e) the name and address of the person to whom the assistance is to be given (and in the case of a company its registered office),
- (f) the name of the person who has acquired or will acquire the shares and the number and class of the shares acquired or to be acquired,
- (g) the principal terms on which the assistance will be given,
- (h) the form the financial assistance will take (stating the amount of cash or value of any asset to be transferred to the person assisted), and
- (i) the date on which the assistance is to be given.

(2) The declaration under section 155(6) or (as the case may be) statement under section 155(6A) shall state that the directors have formed the opinion, as regards the company's initial situation immediately following the date on which the assistance is proposed to be given, that there will be no ground on which it could then be found to be unable to pay its debts; and either—

- (a) if it is intended to commence the winding up of the company within 12 months of that date, that the company will be able to pay it debts in full within 12 months of the commencement of the winding up, or
- (b) in any other case, that the company will be able to pay its debts as they fall due during the year immediately following that date.

(3) In forming their opinion for purposes of subsection (2), the directors shall take into account the same liabilities (including contingent and prospective liabilities) as would be relevant under section 122 of the Insolvency Act (winding up by the court) to the question whether the company is unable to pay its debts.

(4) The directors' statutory declaration or statement shall have annexed to it a report addressed to them by their company's auditors stating that—

- (a) they have enquired into the state of affairs of the company, and
- (b) they are not aware of anything to indicate that the opinion expressed by the directors in the declaration or statement as to any of the matters mentioned in subsection (2) of this section is unreasonable in all the circumstances.

(5) The statutory declaration or statement and auditors' report shall be delivered to the registrar of companies—

- (a) together with a copy of any special resolution passed by the company under section 155 and delivered to the registrar in compliance with section 380, or
- (b) where no such resolution is required to be passed, within 15 days after the making of the declaration or statement.

(6) If a company fails to comply with subsection (5), the company and every officer of it who is in default is liable to a fine and, for continued contravention, to a daily default fine.

(7) A director of a company who makes a statutory declaration or statement under section 155 without having reasonable grounds for the opinion expressed in it is liable to imprisonment or a fine, or both.

157   Special resolution under s. 155

(1) A special resolution required by section 155 to be passed by a company approving the giving of financial assistance must be passed on the date on which the directors of that company make the statutory declaration required by that section in connection with the giving of that assistance, or within the week immediately following that date.

(2) Where such a resolution has been passed, an application may be made to the court for the cancellation of the resolution—

    (a) by the holders of not less in the aggregate than 10 per cent in nominal value of the company's issued share capital or any class of it, or

    (b) if the company is not limited by shares, by not less than 10 per cent of the company's members;

but the application shall not be made by a person who has consented to or voted in favour of the resolution.

(3) Subsections (3) to (10) of section 54 (litigation to cancel resolution under section 53) apply to applications under this section as to applications under section 54.

(4) A special resolution passed by a company is not effective for purposes of section 155—

    (a) unless the declaration made in compliance with subsection (6) of that section by the directors of the company, together with the auditors' report annexed to it, is available for inspection by members of the company at the meeting at which the resolution is passed,

    (b) if it is cancelled by the court on an application under this section.

[*Amendments to s. 157 are made by the Companies Act 1985 (Electronic Communications) Order 2000 (SI 2000/3373), art. 31(2), but, as printed, they do not make sense. For example, art. 31(2) asks for words to be inserted after the word 'declaration' in s. 157(2), though that word is not in that subsection, and also asks for amendments to be made to subsections (5) and (7), which do not exist. In this edition no amendments have been made to s. 157 pending clarification of what amendments should be made.*]

158   Time for giving financial assistance under s. 155

(1) This section applies as to the time before and after which financial assistance may not be given by a company in pursuance of section 155.

(2) Where a special resolution is required by that section to be passed approving the giving of the assistance, the assistance shall not be given before the expiry of the period of 4 weeks beginning with—

    (a) the date on which the special resolution is passed, or

    (b) where more than one such resolution is passed, the date on which the last of them is passed,

unless, as respects that resolution (or, if more than one, each of them), every member of the company which passed the resolution who is entitled to vote at general meetings of the company voted in favour of the resolution.

(3) If application for the cancellation of any such resolution is made under section 157, the financial assistance shall not be given before the final determination of the application unless the court otherwise orders.

(4) The assistance shall not be given after the expiry of the period of 8 weeks beginning with—

    (a) the date on which the directors of the company proposing to give the assistance made their statutory declaration or statement under section 155, or

    (b) where that company is a subsidiary and both its directors and the directors of any of its holding companies made such a declaration or statement, the date on which the earliest of the declarations or statements is made,

unless the court, on an application under section 157, otherwise orders.

CHAPTER VII   REDEEMABLE SHARES: PURCHASE BY A COMPANY OF
ITS OWN SHARES

Redemption and purchase generally

159   Power to issue redeemable shares

(1) Subject to the provisions of this Chapter, a company limited by shares or limited by guarantee and having a share capital may, if authorised to do so by its articles, issue shares which are to be redeemed or are liable to be redeemed at the option of the company or the shareholder.

(2) No redeemable shares may be issued at a time when there are no issued shares of the company which are not redeemable.

(3) Redeemable shares may not be redeemed unless they are fully paid; and the terms of redemption must provide for payment on redemption.

[*A new s. 159A would be inserted if s. 133 of the Companies Act 1989 were brought into force.*]

160   Financing etc. of redemption

(1) Subject to the next subsection and to sections 171 (private companies redeeming or purchasing own shares out of capital) and 178(4) (terms of redemption or purchase enforceable in a winding up)—

   (a) redeemable shares may only be redeemed out of distributable profits of the company or out of the proceeds of a fresh issue of shares made for the purposes of the redemption; and

   (b) any premium payable on redemption must be paid out of distributable profits of the company.

(2) If the redeemable shares were issued at a premium, any premium payable on their redemption may be paid out of the proceeds of a fresh issue of shares made for the purposes of the redemption, up to an amount equal to—

   (a) the aggregate of the premiums received by the company on the issue of the shares redeemed, or

   (b) the current amount of the company's share premium account (including any sum transferred to that account in respect of premiums on the new shares),

whichever is the less; and in that case the amount of the company's share premium account shall be reduced by a sum corresponding (or by sums in the aggregate corresponding) to the amount of any payment made by virtue of this subsection out of the proceeds of the issue of the new shares.

(3) Subject to the following provisions of this Chapter, redemption of shares may be effected on such terms and in such manner as may be provided by the company's articles.

(4) Shares redeemed under this section shall be treated as cancelled on redemption, and the amount of the company's issued share capital shall be diminished by the nominal value of those shares accordingly; but the redemption of shares by a company is not to be taken as reducing the amount of the company's authorised share capital.

(5) Without prejudice to subsection (4), where a company is about to redeem shares, it has power to issue shares up to the nominal value of the shares to be redeemed as if those shares had never been issued.

[*Section 160(3) would be repealed and s. 160(4) amended if s. 133 of the Companies Act 1989 were brought into force.*]

162   Power of company to purchase own shares

[*This version of s. 162 is in force until 30 November 2003.*]

(1) Subject to the following provisions of this Chapter, a company limited by shares or limited by guarantee and having a share capital may, if authorised to do so by its articles, purchase its own shares (including any redeemable shares).

(2) Sections 159 to 161 apply to the purchase by a company under this section of its own shares as they apply to the redemption of redeemable shares, save that the terms and manner of purchase need not be determined by the articles as required by section 160(3).

(3) A company may not under this section purchase its shares if as a result of the purchase there would no longer be any member of the company holding shares other than redeemable shares.

[*The following version of s. 162 is in force from 1 December 2003.*]

(1) Subject to the following provisions of this Chapter, a company limited by shares or limited by guarantee and having a share capital may, if authorised to do so by its articles, purchase its own shares (including any redeemable shares).

(2) Sections 159 and 160 apply to the purchase by a company under this section of its own shares as they apply to the redemption of redeemable shares.

This is subject to subsections (2A) and (2B).

(2A) The terms and manner of a purchase under this section need not be determined by the articles as required by section 160(3).

(2B) Where a company makes a purchase of qualifying shares out of distributable profits under this section, section 162A applies to the shares purchased; and accordingly section 160(4) does not apply to those shares.

(3) A company may not under this section purchase its shares if as a result of the purchase there would no longer be any member of the company holding shares other than redeemable shares or shares held as treasury shares.

(4) For the purposes of this Chapter 'qualifying shares' are shares which—

(a) are included in the official list in accordance with the provisions of Part VI of the Financial Services and Markets Act 2000,

(b) are traded on the market known as the Alternative Investment Market established under the rules of London Stock Exchange plc,

(c) are officially listed in an EEA State, or

(d) are traded on a market established in an EEA State which is a regulated market for the purposes of Article 16 of Council Directive 93/22/EEC on investment services in the securities field

and in paragraph (a) 'the official list' has the meaning given in section 103(1) of the Financial Services and Markets Act 2000.

162A   Treasury shares

[*Section 162A is in force from 1 December 2003.*]

(1) Where qualifying shares are purchased by a company out of distributable profits in accordance with section 162, the company may—

(a) hold the shares (or any of them), or

(b) deal with any of them, at any time, in accordance with section 162D.

(2) Where shares are held under subsection (1)(a) then, for the purposes of section 352, the company must be entered in the register as the member holding those shares.

(3) In this Act, references to a company holding shares as treasury shares are references to the company holding shares which—

(a) were (or are treated as having been) purchased by it in circumstances in which this section applies, and

(b) have been held by the company continuously since they were so purchased.

162B   Treasury shares: maximum holdings

[*Section 162B is in force from 1 December 2003.*]

(1) Where a company has shares of only one class, the aggregate nominal value of shares held as treasury shares must not at any time exceed 10 per cent of the nominal value of the issued share capital of the company at that time.

(2) *Where the share capital of a company is divided into shares of different classes, the aggregate nominal value of the shares of any class held as treasury shares must not at any time exceed 10 per cent of the nominal value of the issued share capital of the shares in that class at that time.*

(3) *Where subsection (1) or (2) is contravened by a company, the company must dispose of or cancel the excess shares, in accordance with section 162D, before the end of the period of 12 months beginning with the day on which that contravention occurs.*

For this purpose 'the excess shares' means such number of the shares, held by the company as treasury shares at the time in question, as resulted in the limit being exceeded.

162C   Treasury shares: voting and other rights
[*Section 162C is in force from 1 December 2003.*]

(1) *This section applies to shares which are held by a company as treasury shares ('the treasury shares').*

(2) *The company must not exercise any right in respect of the treasury shares, and any purported exercise of such a right is void.*

(3) *The rights to which subsection (2) applies include any right to attend or vote at meetings (including meetings under section 425).*

(4) *No dividend may be paid, and no other distribution (whether in cash or otherwise) of the company's assets (including any distribution of assets to members on a winding up) may be made, to the company in respect of the treasury shares.*

(5) *Nothing in this section is to be taken as preventing—*

   (a) *an allotment of shares as fully paid bonus shares in respect of the treasury shares, or*
   (b) *the payment of any amount payable on the redemption of the treasury shares (if they are redeemable shares).*

(6) *Any shares allotted as fully paid bonus shares in respect of the treasury shares shall be treated for the purposes of this Act as if they were purchased by the company at the time they were allotted, in circumstances in which section 162A(1) applied.*

162D   Treasury shares: disposal and cancellation
[*Section 162D is in force from 1 December 2003.*]

(1) *Where shares are held as treasury shares, a company may at any time—*

   (a) *sell the shares (or any of them) for cash,*
   (b) *transfer the shares (or any of them) for the purposes of or pursuant to an employees' share scheme, or*
   (c) *cancel the shares (or any of them).*

(2) *For the purposes of subsection (1)(a), 'cash', in relation to a sale of shares by a company, means—*

   (a) *cash (including foreign currency) received by the company, or*
   (b) *a cheque received by the company in good faith which the directors have no reason for suspecting will not be paid, or*
   (c) *a release of a liability of the company for a liquidated sum, or*
   (d) *an undertaking to pay cash to the company on or before a date not more than 90 days after the date on which the company agrees to sell the shares.*

(3) *But if the company receives a notice under section 429 (right of offeror to buy out minority shareholders) that a person desires to acquire any of the shares, the company must not, under subsection (1), sell or transfer the shares to which the notice relates except to that person.*

(4) *If under subsection (1) the company cancels shares held as treasury shares, the company must diminish the amount of the issued share capital by the nominal value of the shares cancelled; but the cancellation is not to be taken as reducing the amount of the company's authorised share capital.*

(5) *The directors may take such steps as are requisite to enable the company to cancel its shares under subsection (1) without complying with sections 135 and 136 (resolution to reduce issued share capital; application to court for approval).*

162E   Treasury shares: mandatory cancellation

[*Section 162E is in force from 1 December 2003.*]

(1) If shares held as treasury shares cease to be qualifying shares, the company must forthwith cancel the shares in accordance with section 162D.

(2) For the purposes of subsection (1), shares are not to be regarded as ceasing to be qualifying shares by virtue only of—

  (a) *the suspension of their listing in accordance with the applicable rules in the EEA State in which the shares are officially listed, or*

  (b) *the suspension of their trading in accordance with—*

    (i) *in the case of shares traded on the market known as the Alternative Investment Market, the rules of London Stock Exchange plc, and*

    (ii) *in any other case, the rules of the regulated market on which they are traded.*

(3) For the purposes of this section 'regulated market' means a market which is a regulated market for the purposes of Article 16 of Council Directive 93/22/EEC on investment services in the securities field.

162F   Treasury shares: proceeds of sale

[*Section 162F is in force from 1 December 2003.*]

(1) Where shares held as treasury shares are sold, the proceeds of sale shall be dealt with in accordance with this section.

(2) Where the proceeds of sale are equal to or less than the purchase price paid by the company for the shares, the proceeds shall be treated for the purposes of Part VIII as a realised profit of the company.

(3) Where the proceeds of sale exceed the purchase price paid by the company for the shares—

  (a) *that part of the proceeds of sale that is equal to the purchase price paid shall be treated for the purposes of Part VIII as a realised profit of the company, and*

  (b) *a sum equal to the excess shall be transferred to the company's share premium account.*

(4) The purchase price paid by the company for the shares shall be determined by the application of a weighted average price method.

(5) Where the shares were allotted to the company as fully paid bonus shares, the purchase price paid for them shall, for the purposes of subsection (4), be treated as being nil.

162G   Treasury shares: penalty for contravention

[*Section 162G is in force from 1 December 2003.*]

If a company contravenes any provision of sections 162A to 162F every officer of it who is in default is liable to a fine.

163   Definitions of 'off-market' and 'market' purchase

(1) A purchase by a company of its own shares is 'off-market' if the shares either—

  (a) are purchased otherwise than on a recognised investment exchange, or

  (b) are purchased on a recognised investment exchange but are not subject to a marketing arrangement on that investment exchange.

(2) For this purpose, a company's shares are subject to a marketing arrangement on a recognised investment exchange if either—

  (a) they are listed under Part VI of the Financial Services and Markets Act 2000; or

  (b) the company has been afforded facilities for dealings in those shares to take place on that investment exchange without prior permission for individual transactions from the authority governing that investment exchange and without limit as to the time during which those facilities are to be available.

(3) A purchase by a company of its own shares is a 'market purchase' if it is a purchase made on a recognised investment exchange, other than a purchase which is an off-market purchase by virtue of subsection (1)(b).

(4) 'Recognised investment exchange' means a recognised investment exchange other than an overseas investment exchange.

(5) Expressions used in the definition contained in subsection (4) have the same meaning as in Part XVIII of the Financial Services and Markets Act 2000.

164   Authority for off-market purchase

(1) A company may only make an off-market purchase of its own shares in pursuance of a contract approved in advance in accordance with this section or under section 165 below.

(2) The terms of the proposed contract must be authorised by a special resolution of the company before the contract is entered into; and the following subsections apply with respect to that authority and to resolutions conferring it.

(3) Subject to the next subsection, the authority may be varied, revoked or from time to time renewed by special resolution of the company.

(4) In the case of a public company, the authority conferred by the resolution must specify a date on which the authority is to expire; and in a resolution conferring or renewing authority that date must not be later than 18 months after that on which the resolution is passed.

(5) A special resolution to confer, vary, revoke or renew authority is not effective if any member of the company holding shares to which the resolution relates exercises the voting rights carried by any of those shares in voting on the resolution and the resolution would not have been passed if he had not done so.

For this purpose—

(a) a member who holds shares to which the resolution relates is regarded as exercising the voting rights carried by those shares not only if he votes in respect of them on a poll on the question whether the resolution shall be passed, but also if he votes on the resolution otherwise than on a poll;

(b) notwithstanding anything in the company's articles, any member of the company may demand a poll on that question; and

(c) a vote and a demand for a poll by a person as proxy for a member are the same respectively as a vote and a demand by the member.

(6) Such a resolution is not effective for the purposes of this section unless (if the proposed contract is in writing) a copy of the contract or (if not) a written memorandum of its terms is available for inspection by members of the company both—

(a) at the company's registered office for not less than 15 days ending with the date of the meeting at which the resolution is passed, and

(b) at the meeting itself.

A memorandum of contract terms so made available must include the names of any members holding shares to which the contract relates; and a copy of the contract so made available must have annexed to it a written memorandum specifying any such names which do not appear in the contract itself.

(7) A company may agree to a variation of an existing contract so approved, but only if the variation is authorised by a special resolution of the company before it is agreed to; and subsections (3) to (6) above apply to the authority for a proposed variation as they apply to the authority for a proposed contract, save that a copy of the original contract or (as the case may require) a memorandum of its terms, together with any variations previously made, must also be available for inspection in accordance with subsection (6).

165   Authority for contingent purchase contract

(1) A contingent purchase contract is a contract entered into by a company and relating to any of its shares—

(a) which does not amount to a contract to purchase those shares, but

(b) under which the company may (subject to any conditions) become entitled or obliged to purchase those shares.

(2) A company may only make a purchase of its own shares in pursuance of a contingent purchase contract if the contract is approved in advance by a special resolution of the company before the contract is entered into; and subsections (3) to (7) of section 164 apply to the contract and its terms.

166   Authority for market purchase

(1) A company shall not make a market purchase of its own shares unless the purchase has first been authorised by the company in general meeting.

(2) That authority—

(a) may be general for that purpose, or limited to the purchase of shares of any particular class or description, and

(b) may be unconditional or subject to conditions.

(3) The authority must—

(a) specify the maximum number of shares authorised to be acquired,

(b) determine both the maximum and the minimum prices which may be paid for the shares, and

(c) specify a date on which it is to expire.

(4) The authority may be varied, revoked or from time to time renewed by the company in general meeting, but this is subject to subsection (3) above; and in a resolution to confer or renew authority, the date on which the authority is to expire must not be later than 18 months after that on which the resolution is passed.

(5) A company may under this section make a purchase of its own shares after the expiry of the time limit imposed to comply with subsection (3)(c), if the contract of purchase was concluded before the authority expired and the terms of the authority permitted the company to make a contract of purchase which would or might be executed wholly or partly after its expiration.

(6) A resolution to confer or vary authority under this section may determine either or both the maximum and minimum prices for purchase by—

(a) specifying a particular sum, or

(b) providing a basis or formula for calculating the amount of the price in question without reference to any person's discretion or opinion.

(7) A resolution of a company conferring, varying, revoking or renewing authority under this section is subject to section 380 (resolution to be sent to registrar of companies within 15 days).

167   Assignment or release of company's right to purchase own shares

(1) The rights of a company under a contract approved under section 164 or 165, or under a contract for a purchase authorised under section 166, are not capable of being assigned.

(2) An agreement by a company to release its rights under a contract approved under section 164 or 165 is void unless the terms of the release agreement are approved in advance by a special resolution of the company before the agreement is entered into; and subsections (3) to (7) of section 164 apply to approval for a proposed release agreement as to authority for a proposed variation of an existing contract.

168   Payments apart from purchase price to be made out of distributable profits

(1) A payment made by a company in consideration of—

(a) acquiring any right with respect to the purchase of its own shares in pursuance of a contract approved under section 165, or

(b) the variation of a contract approved under section 164 or 165, or

(c) the release of any of the company's obligations with respect to the purchase of any of its own shares under a contract approved under section 164 or 165 or under a contract for a purchase authorised under section 166,

must be made out of the company's distributable profits.

(2) If the requirements of subsection (1) are not satisfied in relation to a contract—

    (a) in a case within paragraph (a) of the subsection, no purchase by the company of its own shares in pursuance of that contract is lawful under this Chapter,

    (b) in a case within paragraph (b), no such purchase following the variation is lawful under this Chapter, and

    (c) in a case within paragraph (c), the purported release is void.

169   Disclosure by company of purchase of own shares

(1) Within the period of 28 days beginning with the date on which any shares purchased by a company under this Chapter are delivered to it, the company shall deliver to the registrar of companies for registration a return in the prescribed form stating with respect to shares of each class purchased the number and nominal value of those shares and the date on which they were delivered to the company.

(1A) But in the case of a company which has purchased its own shares in circumstances in which section 162A applies, the requirement to deliver a return under subsection (1) shall apply only where some or all of the shares have been cancelled forthwith after the date of their delivery in accordance with section 162D(1) and in those circumstances the particulars required by that subsection to be stated with respect to the shares purchased shall apply only to such of the shares as have been so cancelled.

(1B) Where a company has purchased its own shares in circumstances in which section 162A applies, the company shall within the period of 28 days beginning with the date on which such shares are delivered to it (except where all of the shares have been cancelled forthwith after the date of their delivery in the circumstances referred to in subsection (1A)) deliver to the registrar of companies for registration a return in the prescribed form stating with respect to shares of each class purchased (other than any shares which have been cancelled in the circumstances referred to in subsection (1A)) the number and nominal value of each of those shares which are held as treasury shares and the date on which they were delivered to the company.

(2) In the case of a public company, the return shall also state—

    (a) the aggregate amount paid by the company for the shares; and

    (b) the maximum and minimum prices paid in respect of shares of each class purchased.

(3) Particulars of shares delivered to the company on different dates and under different contracts may be included in a single return *under either subsection (1) or (1B)* to the registrar; and in such a case the amount required to be stated under subsection (2)(a) is the aggregate amount paid by the company for all the shares to which the return relates.

(4) Where a company enters into a contract approved under section 164 or 165, or a contract for a purchase authorised under section 166, the company shall keep at its registered office—

    (a) if the contract is in writing, a copy of it; and

    (b) if not, a memorandum of its terms,

from the conclusion of the contract until the end of the period of 10 years beginning with the date on which the purchase of all the shares in pursuance of the contract is completed or (as the case may be) the date on which the contract otherwise determines.

(5) Every copy and memorandum so required to be kept shall be open to inspection without charge—

    (a) by any member of the company, and

    (b) if it is a public company, by any other person.

(6) If default is made in delivering to the registrar any return required by this section, every officer of the company who is in default is liable to a fine and, for continued contravention, to a daily default fine.

(7) If default is made in complying with subsection (4), or if an inspection required under subsection (5) is refused, the company and every officer of it who is in default is liable to a fine and, for continued contravention, to a daily default fine.

(8) In the case of a refusal of an inspection required under subsection (5) of a copy or memorandum, the court may by order compel an immediate inspection of it.

(9) The obligation of a company under subsection (4) to keep a copy of any contract or (as the case may be) a memorandum of its terms applies to any variation of the contract so long as it applies to the contract.

[*Section 169(1A) and (1B) and the words in italics in s. 169(3) are in force from 1 December 2003. Also from that date the words 'the return' in s. 169(2) are replaced by 'any return under subsection (1) or (1B)'.*]

169A   Disclosure by company of cancellation or disposal of treasury shares
[*Section 169A is in force from 1 December 2003.*]

(1) *Subsection (2) applies in relation to any shares held by a company as treasury shares if—*
  (a) *the company is or was required to make a return under section 169(1B) in relation to the shares, and*
  (b) *the shares have—*
    (i) *been cancelled in accordance with section 162D(1), or*
    (ii) *been sold or transferred for the purposes of or pursuant to an employees' share scheme under section 162D(1).*

(2) *Within the period of 28 days beginning with the date on which such shares are cancelled or disposed of, the company shall deliver to the registrar of companies for registration a return in the prescribed form stating with respect to shares of each class cancelled or disposed of—*
  (a) *the number and nominal value of those shares, and*
  (b) *the date on which they were cancelled or disposed of.*

(3) *Particulars of shares cancelled or disposed of on different dates may be included in a single return to the registrar.*

(4) *If default is made in delivering to the registrar any return required by this section, every officer of the company who is in default is liable to a fine and, for continued contravention, to a daily default fine.*

170   The capital redemption reserve

(1) Where under this Chapter shares of a company are redeemed or purchased wholly out of the company's profits, the amount by which the company's issued share capital is diminished in accordance with section 160(4) on cancellation of the shares redeemed or purchased, *or in accordance with section 162D(4) on cancellation of shares held as treasury shares,* shall be transferred to a reserve, called 'the capital redemption reserve'.

(2) If the shares are redeemed or purchased wholly or partly out of the proceeds of a fresh issue and the aggregate amount of those proceeds is less than the aggregate nominal value of the shares redeemed or purchased, the amount of the difference shall be transferred to the capital redemption reserve.

(3) But subsection (2) does not apply if the proceeds of the fresh issue are applied by the company in making a redemption or purchase of its own shares in addition to a payment out of capital under section 171;

(4) The provisions of this Act relating to the reduction of a company's share capital apply as if the capital redemption reserve were paid-up share capital of the company, except that the reserve may be applied by the company in paying up its unissued shares to be allotted to members of the company as fully paid bonus shares.

[*The words in italics in s. 170(1) are in force from 1 December 2003.*]

Redemption or purchase of own shares out of capital (private companies only)

171   Power of private companies to redeem or purchase own shares out of capital

(1) Subject to the following provisions of this Chapter, a private company limited by shares or limited by guarantee and having a share capital may, if so authorised by its articles,

make a payment in respect of the redemption or purchase under section 160 or (as the case may be) section 162, of its own shares otherwise than out of its distributable profits or the proceeds of a fresh issue of shares.

(2) References below in this Chapter to payment out of capital are (subject to subsection (6)) to any payment so made, whether or not it would be regarded apart from this section as a payment out of capital.

(3) The payment which may (if authorised in accordance with the following provisions of this Chapter) be made by a company out of capital in respect of the redemption or purchase of its own shares is such an amount as, taken together with—

(a) any available profits of the company, and
(b) the proceeds of any fresh issue of shares made for the purposes of the redemption or purchase,

is equal to the price of redemption or purchase; and the payment permissible under this subsection is referred to below in this Chapter as the permissible capital payment for the shares.

(4) Subject to subsection (6), if the permissible capital payment for shares redeemed or purchased is less than their nominal amount, the amount of the difference shall be transferred to the company's capital redemption reserve.

(5) Subject to subsection (6), if the permissible capital payment is greater than the nominal amount of the shares redeemed or purchased—

(a) the amount of any capital redemption reserve, share premium account or fully paid share capital of the company, and
(b) any amount representing unrealised profits of thg company for the time being standing to the credit of any reserve maintained by the company in accordance with paragraph 34 of Schedule 4 or paragraph 34 of Schedule 8 (revaluation reserve),

may be reduced by a sum not exceeding (or by sums not in the aggregate exceeding) the amount by which the permissible capital payment exceeds the nominal amount of the shares.

(6) Where the proceeds of a fresh issue are applied by a company in making any redemption or purchase of its own shares in addition to a payment out of capital under this section, the references in subsections (4) and (5) to the permissible capital payment are to be read as referring to the aggregate of that payment and those proceeds.

172   Availability of profits for purposes of s. 171

(1) The reference in section 171(3)(a) to available profits of the company is to the company's profits which are available for distribution (within the meaning of Part VIII); but the question whether a company has any profits so available and the amount of any such profits are to be determined for purposes of that section in accordance with the following subsections, instead of sections 270 to 275 in that Part.

(2) Subject to the next subsection, that question is to be determined by reference to—

(a) profits, losses, assets and liabilities,
(b) provisions of any of the kinds mentioned in paragraphs 88 and 89 of Schedule 4 (depreciation, diminution in value of assets, retentions to meet liabilities, etc.), and
(c) share capital and reserves (including undistributable reserves),

as stated in the relevant accounts for determining the permissible capital payment of shares.

(3) The relevant accounts for this purpose are such accounts, prepared as at any date within the period for determining the amount of the permissible capital payment, as are necessary to enable a reasonable judgment to be made as to the amounts of any of the items mentioned in subsection (2)(a) to (c) above.

(4) For purposes of determining the amount of the permissible capital payment for shares, the amount of the company's available profits (if any) determined in accordance with

subsections (2) and (3) is treated as reduced by the amount of any distributions lawfully made by the company after the date of the relevant accounts and before the end of the period for determining the amount of that payment.

(5) The reference in subsection (4) to distributions lawfully made by the company includes—

(a) financial assistance lawfully given out of distributable profits in a case falling within section 154 or 155,

(b) any payment lawfully made by the company in respect of the purchase by it of any shares in the company (except a payment lawfully made otherwise than out of distributable profits), and

(c) a payment of any description specified in section 168(1) lawfully made by the company.

(6) References in this section to the period for determining the amount of the permissible capital payment for shares are to the period of 3 months ending with the date on which the statutory declaration of the directors purporting to specify the amount of that payment is made in accordance with subsection (3) of the section next following.

173   Conditions for payment out of capital

(1) Subject to any order of the court under section 177, a payment out of capital by a private company for the redemption or purchase of its own shares is not lawful unless the requirements of this and the next two sections are satisfied.

(2) The payment out of capital must be approved by a special resolution of the company.

(3) The company's directors must make a statutory declaration specifying the amount of the permissible capital payment for the shares in question and stating that, having made full inquiry into the affairs and prospects of the company, they have formed the opinion—

(a) as regards its initial situation immediately following the date on which the payment out of capital is proposed to be made, that there will be no grounds on which the company could then be found unable to pay its debts, and

(b) as regards its prospects for the year immediately following that date, that, having regard to their intentions with respect to the management of the company's business during that year and to the amount and character of the financial resources which will in their view be available to the company during that year, the company will be able to continue to carry on business as a going concern (and will accordingly be able to pay its debts as they fall due) throughout that year.

(4) In forming their opinion for purposes of subsection (3)(a), the directors shall take into account the same liabilities (including prospective and contingent liabilities) as would be relevant under section 122 of the Insolvency Act (winding up by the court) to the question whether a company is unable to pay its debts.

(5) The directors' statutory declaration must be in the prescribed form and contain such information with respect to the nature of the company's business as may be prescribed, and must in addition have annexed to it a report addressed to the directors by the company's auditors stating that—

(a) they have inquired into the company's state of affairs; and

(b) the amount specified in the declaration as the permissible capital payment for the shares in question is in their view properly determined in accordance with sections 171 and 172; and

(c) they are not aware of anything to indicate that the opinion expressed by the directors in the declaration as to any of the matters mentioned in subsection (3) is unreasonable in all the circumstances.

(6) A director who makes a declaration under this section without having reasonable grounds for the opinion expressed in the declaration is liable to imprisonment or a fine, or both.

174 Procedure for special resolution under s. 173

(1) The resolution required by section 173 must be passed on, or within the week immediately following, the date on which the directors make the statutory declaration required by that section; and the payment out of capital must be made no earlier than 5 nor more than 7 weeks after the date of the resolution.

(2) The resolution is ineffective if any member of the company holding shares to which the resolution relates exercises the voting rights carried by any of those shares in voting on the resolution and the resolution would not have been passed if he had not done so.

(3) For purposes of subsection (2), a member who holds such shares is to be regarded as exercising the voting rights carried by them in voting on the resolution not only if he votes in respect of them on a poll on the question whether the resolution shall be passed, but also if he votes on the resolution otherwise than on a poll; and, notwithstanding anything in a company's articles, any member of the company may demand a poll on that question.

(4) The resolution is ineffective unless the statutory declaration and auditors' report required by the section are available for inspection by members of the company at the meeting at which the resolution is passed.

(5) For purposes of this section a vote and a demand for a poll by a person as proxy for a member are the same (respectively) as a vote and demand by the member.

175 Publicity for proposed payment out of capital

(1) Within the week immediately following the date of the resolution for payment out of capital the company must cause to be published in the Gazette a notice—

    (a) stating that the company has approved a payment out of capital for the purpose of acquiring its own shares by redemption or purchase or both (as the case may be);

    (b) specifying the amount of the permissible capital payment for the shares in question and the date of the resolution under section 173;

    (c) stating that the statutory declaration of the directors and the auditors' report required by that section are available for inspection at the company's registered office; and

    (d) stating that any creditor of the company may at any time within the 5 weeks immediately following the date of the resolution for payment out of capital apply to the court under section 176 for an order prohibiting the payment.

(2) Within the week immediately following the date of the resolution the company must also either cause a notice to the same effect as that required by subsection (1) to be published in an appropriate national newspaper or give notice in writing to that effect to each of its creditors.

(3) 'An appropriate national newspaper' means a newspaper circulating throughout England and Wales (in the case of a company registered in England and Wales), and a newspaper circulating throughout Scotland (in the case of a company registered in Scotland).

(4) References below in this section to the first notice date are to the day on which the company first publishes the notice required by subsection (1) or first publishes or gives the notice required by subsection (2) (whichever is the earlier).

(5) Not later than the first notice date the company must deliver to the registrar of companies a copy of the statutory declaration of the directors and of the auditors' report required by section 173.

(6) The statutory declaration and auditors' report—

    (a) shall be kept at the company's registered office throughout the period beginning with the first notice date and ending 5 weeks after the date of the resolution for payment out of capital, and

    (b) shall be open to the inspection of any member or creditor of the company without charge.

(7) If an inspection required under subsection (6) is refused, the company and every officer of it who is in default is liable to a fine and, for continued contravention, to a daily default fine.

(8) In the case of refusal of an inspection required under subsection (6) of a declaration or report, the court may by order compel an immediate inspection of that declaration or report.

176 Objections by company's members or creditors

(1) Where a private company passes a special resolution approving for purposes of this Chapter any payment out of capital for the redemption or purchase of any of its shares—

- (a) any member of the company other than one who consented to or voted in favour of the resolution; and
- (b) any creditor of the company,

may within 5 weeks of the date on which the resolution was passed apply to the court for cancellation of the resolution.

(2) The application may be made on behalf of the persons entitled to make it by such one or more of their number as they may appoint in writing for the purpose.

(3) If an application is made, the company shall—

- (a) forthwith give notice in the prescribed form of that fact to the registrar of companies; and
- (b) within 15 days from the making of any order of the court on the hearing of the application, or such longer period as the court may by order direct, deliver an office copy of the order to the registrar.

(4) A company which fails to comply with subsection (3), and any officer of it who is in default, is liable to a fine and for continued contravention, to a daily default fine.

177 Powers of court on application under s. 176

(1) On the hearing of an application under section 176 the court may, if it thinks fit, adjourn the proceedings in order that an arrangement may be made to the court's satisfaction for the purchase of the interests of dissentient members or for the protection of dissentient creditors (as the case may be); and the court may give such directions and make such orders as it thinks expedient for facilitating or carrying into effect any such arrangement.

(2) Without prejudice to its powers under subsection (1), the court shall make an order on such terms and conditions as it thinks fit either confirming or cancelling the resolution; and, if the court confirms the resolution, it may in particular by order alter or extend any date or period of time specified in the resolution or in any provision in this Chapter which applies to the redemption or purchase of shares to which the resolution refers.

(3) The court's order may, if the court thinks fit, provide for the purchase by the company of the shares of any of its members and for the reduction accordingly of the company's capital, and may make such alterations in the company's memorandum and articles as may be required in consequence of that provision.

(4) If the court's order requires the company not to make any, or any specified, alteration in its memorandum or articles, the company has not then power without leave of the court to make any such alteration in breach of the requirement.

(5) An alteration in the memorandum or articles made by virtue of an order under this section, if not made by resolution of the company, is of the same effect as if duly made by resolution; and this Act applies accordingly to the memorandum or articles as so altered.

Supplementary

178 Effect of company's failure to redeem or purchase

(1) This section has effect where a company has, on or after 15 June 1982,—

- (a) issued shares on terms that they are or are liable to be redeemed, or
- (b) agreed to purchase any of its own shares.

(2) The company is not liable in damages in respect of any failure on its part to redeem or purchase any of the shares.

(3) Subsection (2) is without prejudice to any right of the holder of the shares other than his right to sue the company for damages in respect of its failure; but the court shall not grant an order for specific performance of the terms of redemption or purchase if the company shows that it is unable to meet the costs of redeeming or purchasing the shares in question out of distributable profits.

(4) If the company is wound up and at the commencement of the winding up any of the shares have not been redeemed or purchased, the terms of redemption or purchase may be enforced against the company; and when shares are redeemed or purchased under this subsection, they are treated as cancelled.

(5) However, subsection (4) does not apply if—

    (a) the terms provided for the redemption or purchase to take place at a date later than that of the commencement of the winding up, or

    (b) during the period beginning with the date on which the redemption or purchase was to have taken place and ending with the commencement of the winding up the company could not at any time have lawfully made a distribution equal in value to the price at which the shares were to have been redeemed or purchased.

(6) There shall be paid in priority to any amount which the company is liable under subsection (4) to pay in respect of any shares—

    (a) all other debts and liabilities of the company (other than any due to members in their character as such),

    (b) if other shares carry rights (whether as to capital or as to income) which are preferred to the rights as to capital attaching to the first-mentioned shares, any amount due in satisfaction of those preferred rights;

but, subject to that, any such amount shall be paid in priority to any amounts due to members in satisfaction of their rights (whether as to capital or income) as members.

179   Power for Secretary of State to modify this Chapter

(1) The Secretary of State may by regulations made by statutory instrument modify the provisions of this Chapter with respect to any of the following matters—

    (a) the authority required for a purchase by a company of its own shares,

    (b) the authority required for the release by a company of its rights under a contract for the purchase of its own shares or a contract under which the company may (subject to any conditions) become entitled or obliged to purchase its own shares,

    (c) the information to be included in a return delivered by a company to the registrar of companies in accordance with section 169(1),

    (d) the matters to be dealt with in the statutory declaration of the directors under section 173 with a view to indicating their opinion of their company's ability to make a proposed payment out of capital with due regard to its financial situationand prospects, and

    (e) the contents of the auditors' report required by that section to be annexed to that declaration.

(2) The Secretary of State may also by regulations so made make such provision (including modification of the provisions of this Chapter) as appears to him to be appropriate—

    (a) for wholly or partly relieving companies from the requirement of section 171(3)(a) that any available profits must be taken into account in determining the amount of the permissible capital payment for shares under that section, or

    (b) for permitting a company's share premium account to be applied, to an extent appearing to the Secretary of State to be appropriate, in providing for the premiums payable on the redemption or purchase by the company of any of its own shares.

(3) Regulations under this section—

(a) may make such further modification of any provisions of this Chapter as appears to the Secretary of State to be reasonably necessary in consequence of any provision made under such regulations by virtue of subsection (1) or (2),

(b) may make different provision for different cases or classes of case, and

(c) may contain such further consequential provisions, and such incidental and supplementary provisions, as the Secretary of State thinks fit.

(4) No regulations shall be made under this section unless a draft of the instrument containing them has been laid before Parliament and approved by resolution of each House.

180 Transitional cases arising under this Chapter; and savings

(1) Any preference shares issued by a company before 15 June 1982 which could but for the repeal by the Companies Act 1981 of section 58 of the Companies Act 1948 (power to issue redeemable preference shares) have been redeemed under that section are subject to redemption in accordance with the provisions of this Chapter.

(2) In a case to which sections 159 and 160 apply by virtue of this section, any premium payable on redemption may, notwithstanding the repeal by the 1981 Act of any provision of the 1948 Act, be paid out of the share premium account instead of out of profits, or partly out of that account and partly out of profits (but subject to the provisions of this Chapter so far as payment is out of profits).

(3) Any capital redemption reserve fund established before 15 June 1982 by a company for the purposes of section 58 of the Act of 1948 is to be known as the company's capital redemption reserve and be treated as if it had been established for the purposes of section 170 of this Act; and accordingly, a reference in any enactment or in the articles of any company, or in any other instrument, to a company's capital redemption reserve fund is to be construed as a reference to the company's capital redemption reserve.

181 Definitions for Chapter VII

In this Chapter—

(a) 'distributable profits', in relation to the making of any payment by a company, means those profits out of which it could lawfully make a distribution (within the meaning given by section 263(2)) equal in value to the payment, and

(b) 'permissible capital payment' means the payment permitted by section 171; and references to payment out of capital are to be construed in accordance with section 171.

CHAPTER VIII   MISCELLANEOUS PROVISIONS ABOUT SHARES AND DEBENTURES

Share and debenture certificates, transfers and warrants

182 Nature, transfer and numbering of shares

(1) The shares or other interest of any member in a company—

(a) are personal estate or, in Scotland, movable property and are not in the nature of real estate or heritage,

(b) are transferable in manner provided by the company's articles, but subject to the Stock Transfer Act 1963 (which enables securities of certain descriptions to be transferred by a simplified process) and to regulations made under section 207 of the Companies Act 1989 (which enable title to securities to be evidenced and transferred without a written instrument).

(2) Each share in a company having a share capital shall be distinguished by its appropriate number; except that, if at any time all the issued shares in a company, or all the issued shares in it of a particular class, are fully paid up and rank *pari passu* for all purposes, none of those shares need thereafter have a distinguishing number so long as it remains fully paid up and ranks *pari passu* for all purposes with all shares of the same class for the time being issued and fully paid up.

183   Transfer and registration

(1) It is not lawful for a company to register a transfer of shares in or debentures of the company unless a proper instrument of transfer has been delivered to it, or the transfer is an exempt transfer within the Stock Transfer Act 1982 or is in accordance with regulations made under section 207 of the Companies Act 1989.

This applies notwithstanding anything in the company's articles.

(2) Subsection (1) does not prejudice any power of the company to register as shareholder or debenture holder a person to whom the right to any shares in or debentures of the company has been transmitted by operation of law.

(3) A transfer of the share or other interest of a deceased member of a company made by his personal representative, although the personal representative is not himself a member of the company, is as valid as if he had been such a member at the time of the execution of the instrument of transfer.

(4) On the application of the transferor of any share or interest in a company, the company shall enter in its register of members the name of the transferee in the same manner and subject to the same conditions as if the application for the entry were made by the transferee.

(5) If a company refuses to register a transfer of shares or debentures, the company shall, within 2 months after the date on which the transfer was lodged with it, send to the transferee notice of the refusal.

(6) If default is made in complying with subsection (5), the company and every officer of it who is in default is liable to a fine and, for continued contravention, to a daily default fine.

184   Certification of transfers

(1) The certification by a company of any instrument of transfer of any shares in, or debentures of, the company is to be taken as a representation by the company to any person acting on the faith of the certification that there have been produced to the company such documents as on their face show a prima facie title to the shares or debentures in the transferor named in the instrument.

However, the certification is not to be taken as a representation that the transferor has any title to the shares or debentures.

(2) Where a person acts on the faith of a false certification by a company made negligently, the company is under the same liability to him as if the certification had been made fraudulently.

(3) For purposes of this section—

(a) an instrument of transfer is deemed certificated if it bears the words 'certificate lodged' (or words to the like effect);

(b) the certification of an instrument of transfer is deemed made by a company if—

(i) the person issuing the instrument is a person authorised to issue certificated instruments of transfer on the company's behalf, and

(ii) the certification is signed by a person authorised to certificate transfers on the company's behalf or by an officer or servant either of the company or of a body corporate so authorised;

(c) a certification is deemed signed by a person if—

(i) it purports to be authenticated by his signature or initials (whether handwritten or not), and

(ii) it is not shown that the signature or initials was or were placed there neither by himself nor by a person authorised to use the signature or initials for the purpose of certificating transfers on the company's behalf.

185   Duty of company as to issue of certificates

(1) Subject to the following provisions, every company shall—

(a) within 2 months after the allotment of any of its shares, debentures or debenture stock, and

(b) within 2 months after the date on which a transfer of any such shares, debentures or debenture stock is lodged with the company,

complete and have ready for delivery the certificates of all shares, the debentures and the certificates of all debenture stock allotted or transferred (unless the conditions of issue of the shares, debentures or debenture stock otherwise provide).

(2) For this purpose, 'transfer' means a transfer duly stamped and otherwise valid, or an exempt transfer within the Stock Transfer Act 1982, and does not include such a transfer as the company is for any reason entitled to refuse to register and does not register.

(3) Subsection (1) does not apply in the case of a transfer to any person where, by virtue of regulations under section 3 of the Stock Transfer Act 1982, he is not entitled to a certificate or other document of or evidencing title in respect of the securities transferred; but if in such a case the transferee—

(a) subsequently becomes entitled to such a certificate or other document by virtue of any provision of those regulations, and

(b) gives notice in writing of that fact to the company,

this section has effect as if the reference in subsection (1)(b) to the date of the lodging of the transfer were a reference to the date of the notice.

(4) Subsection (4A) applies in relation to a company—

(a) of which shares or debentures are allotted to a financial institution,

(b) of which debenture stock is allotted to a financial institution, or

(c) with which a transfer for transferring shares, debentures or debenture stock to a financial institution is lodged.

(4A) The company is not required, in consequence of that allotment or transfer, to comply with subsection (1).

(4B) 'Financial institution' means—

(a) a recognised clearing house acting in relation to a recognised investment exchange; or

(b) a nominee of—

(i)   a recognised clearing house acting in that way; or

(ii) a recognised investment exchange.

(4C) No person may be a nominee for the purposes of this section unless he is a person designated for those purposes in the rules of the recognised investment exchange in question.

(4D) Expressions used in subsections (4B) and (4C) have the same meaning as in Part XVIII of the Financial Services and Markets Act 2000.

(5) If default is made in complying with subsection (1), the company and every officer of it who is in default is liable to a fine and, for continued contravention, to a daily default fine.

(6) If a company on which a notice has been served requiring it to make good any default in complying with subsection (1) fails to make good the default within 10 days after service of the notice, the court may, on the application of the person entitled to have the certificates or the debentures delivered to him, exercise the power of the following subsection.

(7) The court may make an order directing the company and any officer of it to make good the default within such time as may be specified in the order; and the order may provide that all costs of and incidental to the application shall be borne by the company or by an officer of it responsible for the default.

186 Certificate to be evidence of title

A certificate under the common seal of the company specifying any shares held by a member is—

(a) in England and Wales, prima facie evidence, and

(b) in Scotland, sufficient evidence unless the contrary is shown,

of his title to the shares.

187   Evidence of grant of probate or confirmation as executor

The production to a company of any document which is by law sufficient evidence of probate of the will, or letters of administration of the estate, or confirmation as executor, of a deceased person having been granted to some person shall be accepted by the company as sufficient evidence of the grant.

This has effect notwithstanding anything in the company's articles.

188   Issue and effect of share warrant to bearer

(1) A company limited by shares may, if so authorised by its articles, issue with respect to any fully paid shares a warrant (a 'share warrant') stating that the bearer of the warrant is entitled to the shares specified in it.

(2) A share warrant issued under the company's common seal entitles the bearer to the shares specified in it; and the shares may be transferred by delivery of the warrant.

(3) A company which issues a share warrant may, if so authorised by its articles, provide (by coupons or otherwise) for the payment of the future dividends on the shares included in the warrant.

Debentures

190   Register of debenture holders

(1) A company registered in England and Wales shall not keep in Scotland any register of holders of debentures of the company or any duplicate of any such register or part of any such register which is kept outside Great Britain.

(2) A company registered in Scotland shall not keep in England and Wales any such register or duplicate as above-mentioned.

(3) Neither a register of holders of debentures of a company nor a duplicate of any such register or part of any such register which is kept outside Great Britain shall be kept in England and Wales (in the case of a company registered in England and Wales) or in Scotland (in the case of a company registered in Scotland) elsewhere than—

    (a) at the company's registered office; or

    (b) at any office of the company at which the work of making it up is done; or

    (c) if the company arranges with some other person for the making up of the register or duplicate to be undertaken on its behalf by that other person, at the office of that other person at which the work is done.

(4) Where a company keeps (in England and Wales or in Scotland, as the case may be) both such a register and such a duplicate, it shall keep them at the same place.

(5) Every company which keeps any such register or duplicate in England and Wales or Scotland shall send to the registrar of companies notice (in the prescribed form) of the place where the register or duplicate is kept and of any change in that place.

(6) But a company is not bound to send notice under subsection (5) where the register or duplicate has, at all times since it came into existence, been kept at the company's registered office.

191   Right to inspect register

(1) Every register of holders of debentures of a company shall, except when duly closed, be open to the inspection—

    (a) of the registered holder of any such debentures or any holder of shares in the company without fee; and

    (b) of any other person on payment of such fee as may be prescribed.

(2) Any such registered holder of debentures or holder of shares, or any other person, may require a copy of the register of the holders of debentures of the company or any part of it, on payment of such fee as may be prescribed.

(3) A copy of any trust deed for securing an issue of debentures shall be forwarded to every holder of any such debentures at his request on payment of such fee as may be prescribed.

(4) If inspection is refused, or a copy is refused or not forwarded, the company and every officer of it who is in default is liable to a fine and, for continued contravention, to a daily default fine.

(5) Where a company is in default as above-mentioned, the court may by order compel an immediate inspection of the register or direct that the copies required be sent to the person requiring them.

(6) For purposes of this section, a register is deemed to be duly closed if closed in accordance with provisions contained in the articles or in the debentures or, in the case of debenture stock, in the stock certificates, or in the trust deed or other document securing the debentures or debenture stock, during such period or periods, not exceeding in the whole 30 days in any year, as may be therein specified.

(7) Liability incurred by a company from the making or deletion of an entry in its register of debenture holders, or from a failure to make or delete any such entry, is not enforceable more than 20 years after the date on which the entry was made or deleted or, in the case of any such failure, the failure first occurred.

This is without prejudice to any lesser period of limitation.

192   Liability of trustees of debentures

(1) Subject to this section, any provision contained—
   (a) in a trust deed for securing an issue of debentures, or
   (b) in any contract with the holders of debentures secured by a trust deed,
is void in so far as it would have the effect of exempting a trustee of the deed from, or indemnifying him against, liability for breach of trust where he fails to show the degree of care and diligence required of him as trustee, having regard to the provisions of the trust deed conferring on him any powers, authorities or discretions.

(2) Subsection (1) does not invalidate—
   (a) a release otherwise validly given in respect of anything done or omitted to be done by a trustee before the giving of the release; or
   (b) any provision enabling such a release to be given—
      (i) on the agreement thereto of a majority of not less than three-fourths in value of the debenture holders present and voting in person or, where proxies are permitted, by proxy at a meeting summoned for the purpose, and
      (ii) either with respect to specific acts or omissions or on the trustee dying or ceasing to act.

(3) Subsection (1) does not operate—
   (a) to invalidate any provision in force on 1 July 1948 so long as any person then entitled to the benefit of that provision or afterwards given the benefit of that provision under the following subsection remains a trustee of the deed in question; or
   (b) to deprive any person of any exemption or right to be indemnified in respect of anything done or omitted to be done by him while any such provision was in force.

(4) While any trustee of a trust deed remains entitled to the benefit of a provision saved by subsection (3), the benefit of that provision may be given either—
   (a) to all trustees of the deed, present and future; or
   (b) to any named trustees or proposed trustees of it,
by a resolution passed by a majority of not less than three-fourths in value of the debenture holders present in person or, where proxies are permitted, by proxy at a meeting summoned for the purpose in accordance with the provisions of the deed or, if the deed makes no

provision for summoning meetings, a meeting summoned for the purpose in any manner approved by the court.

193   Perpetual debentures

A condition contained in debentures, or in a deed for securing debentures, is not invalid by reason only that the debentures are thereby made irredeemable or redeemable only on the happening of a contingency (however remote), or on the expiration of a period (however long), any rule of equity to the contrary notwithstanding.

This applies to debentures whenever issued, and to deeds whenever executed.

194   Power to reissue redeemed debentures

(1) Where (at any time) a company has redeemed debentures previously issued, then—

  (a) unless provision to the contrary, whether express or implied, is contained in the articles or in any contract entered into by the company; or

  (b) unless the company has, by passing a resolution to that effect or by some other act, manifested its intention that the debentures shall be cancelled,

the company has, and is deemed always to have had, power to reissue the debentures, either by reissuing the same debentures or by issuing other debentures in their place.

(2) On a reissue of redeemed debentures, the person entitled to the debentures has, and is deemed always to have had, the same priorities as if the debentures had never been redeemed.

(3) Where a company has (at any time) deposited any of its debentures to secure advances from time to time on current account or otherwise, the debentures are not deemed to have been redeemed by reason only of the company's account having ceased to be in debit while the debentures remained so deposited.

(4) The reissue of a debenture or the issue of another debenture in its place under the power which by this section is given to or deemed to be possessed by a company is to be treated as the issue of a new debenture for purposes of stamp duty; but it is not to be so treated for the purposes of any provision limiting the amount or number of debentures to be issued.

This applies whenever the issue or reissue was made.

(5) A person lending money on the security of a debenture reissued under this section which appears to be duly stamped may give the debenture in evidence in any proceedings for enforcing his security without payment of the stamp duty or any penalty in respect of it, unless he had notice (or, but for his negligence, might have discovered) that the debenture was not duly stamped; but in that case the company is liable to pay the proper stamp duty and penalty.

195   Contract to subscribe for debentures

A contract with a company to take up and pay for debentures of the company may be enforced by an order for specific performance.

196

(1) The following applies in the case of a company registered in England and Wales, where debentures of the company are secured by a charge which, as created, was a floating charge.

(2) If possession is taken, by or on behalf of the holders of any of the debentures, of any property comprised in or subject to the charge, and the company is not at that time in course of being wound up, the company's preferential debts shall be paid out of assets coming to the hands of the person taking possession in priority to any claims for principal or interest in respect of the debentures.

(3) 'Preferential debts' means the categories of debts listed in Schedule 6 to the Insolvency Act; and for the purposes of that Schedule 'the relevant date' is the date of possession being taken as above-mentioned.

(4) Payments made under this section shall be recouped, as far as may be, out of the assets of the company available for payment of general creditors.

[*The s. 196 substituted by the Insolvency Act 1986, sch. 13, part I, has no section title.*]

PART VI   DISCLOSURE OF INTERESTS IN SHARES

Individual and group acquisitions

198   Obligation of disclosure: the cases in which it may arise and 'the relevant time'

(1) Where a person either—

    (a) to his knowledge acquires an interest in shares comprised in a public company's relevant share capital, or ceases to be interested in shares so comprised (whether or not retaining an interest in other shares so comprised), or

    (b) becomes aware that he has acquired an interest in shares so comprised or that he has ceased to be interested in shares so comprised in which he was previously interested, then in certain circumstances he comes under an obligation ('the obligation of disclosure') to make notification to the company with respect to his interests (if any) in its shares.

(2) In relation to a public company, 'relevant share capital' means the company's issued share capital of a class carrying rights to vote in all circumstances at general meetings of the company *(excluding any shares in the company held as treasury shares)*; and it is hereby declared for the avoidance of doubt that—

    (a) where a company's share capital is divided into different classes of shares, references in this Part to a percentage of the nominal value of its relevant share capital are to a percentage of the nominal value of the issued shares comprised in each of the classes taken separately *(excluding any shares of each class held as treasury shares)*, and

    (b) the temporary suspension of voting rights in respect of shares comprised in issued share capital of a company of any such class does not affect the application of this Part in relation to interests in those or any other shares comprised in that class.

(3) Where, otherwise than in circumstances within subsection (1), a person—

    (a) is aware at the time when it occurs of any change of circumstances affecting facts relevant to the application of the next following section to an existing interest of his in shares comprised in a company's share capital of any description, or

    (b) otherwise becomes aware of any such facts (whether or not arising from any such change of circumstances),

then in certain circumstances he comes under the obligation of disclosure.

(4) The existence of the obligation in a particular case depends (in part) on circumstances obtaining before and after whatever is in that case the relevant time; and that is—

    (a) in a case within subsection (1)(a) or (3)(a), the time of the event or change of circumstances there mentioned, and

    (b) in a case within subsection (1)(b) or (3)(b), the time at which the person became aware of the facts in question.

[*The words in italics in s. 198(2) are in force from 1 December 2003.*]

199   Interests to be disclosed

(1) For purposes of the obligation of disclosure, the interests to be taken into account are those in relevant share capital of the company concerned.

(2) Where a person is interested in shares comprised in relevant share capital, then—

    (a) if in some or all of those shares he has interests which are material interests, he has a notifiable interest at any time when the aggregate nominal value of the shares in which those material interests subsist is equal to or more than 3 per cent of the nominal value of that share capital; and

    (b) he has a notifiable interest at any time when, not having such an interest by virtue of paragraph (a), the aggregate nominal value of the shares in which he has interests (whether or not including material interests) is equal to or more than 10 per cent of the nominal value of the relevant share capital.

(2A) For the purposes of this Part, a material interest is any interest other than—

(a) an interest which a person who may lawfully manage investments belonging to another has by virtue of having the management of such investments under an agreement in or evidenced in writing;

(b) an interest which a person has by virtue of being the operator of—

(i)   an authorised unit trust scheme;

(ii) a recognised scheme; or

(iii) a UCITS (as defined in subsection (8));

(bb) an interest belonging to an open-ended investment company;

(c) an interest in shares in a listed company which, if that company were not listed, would fall to be disregarded by virtue of section 209(10); or

(d) an interest of another which a person is taken to have by virtue of the application of section 203 or 205, where the interest of that other person falls within paragraph (a), (b), (bb) or (c).

(3) All facts relevant to determining whether a person has a notifiable interest at any time (or the percentage level of his interest) are taken to be what he knows the facts to be at that time.

(4) The obligation of disclosure arises under section 198(1) or (3) where the person has a notifiable interest immediately after the relevant time, but did not have such an interest immediately before that time.

(5) The obligation also arises under section 198(1) or (3) where—

(a) the person had a notifiable interest immediately before the relevant time, but does not have such an interest immediately after it, or

(b) he had a notifiable interest immediately before that time, and has such an interest immediately after it, but the percentage levels of his interest immediately before and immediately after that time are not the same.

(6) For the purposes of subsection (2A), a person ('A') may lawfully manage investments belonging to another if—

(a) A can manage those investments in accordance with a permission which A has under Part IV of the Financial Services and Markets Act 2000;

(b) A is an EEA firm of the kind mentioned in sub-paragraph (a) or (b) of paragraph 5 of Schedule 3 to that Act, and can manage those investments in accordance with its EEA authorisation;

(c) A can, in accordance with section 327 of that Act, manage those investments without contravening the prohibition contained in section 19 of that Act; or

(d) A can lawfully manage those investments in another Member State and would, if he were to manage those investments in the United Kingdom, require permission under Part IV of that Act.

(7) References in this section to the management of investments must be read with—

(a) section 22 of the Financial Services and Markets Act 2000;

(b) any relevant order under that section; and

(c) Schedule 2 to that Act.

(8) In this Part 'UCITS' means a collective investment scheme which—

(a) is constituted in a member State other than the United Kingdom, and

(b) is certified by the competent authority in that member State as complying with the conditions imposed by Council Directive 85/611/EEC coordinating the laws, regulations and administrative provisions relating to undertakings for collective investment in transferable securities;

and subsection (5) of section 264 of the Financial Services and Markets Act 2000 (meaning of 'constituted in a member State') applies for the purposes of paragraph (a) of this subsection as it applies for the purposes of that section.

200 'Percentage level' in relation to notifiable interests

(1) Subject to the qualifications mentioned below, 'percentage level', in section 199(5)(b), means the percentage figure found by expressing the aggregate nominal value of all the shares comprised in the share capital concerned in which the person has material interests immediately before or (as the case may be) immediately after the relevant time as a percentage of the nominal value of that share capital and rounding that figure down, if it is not a whole number, to the next whole number.

(2) In relation to a notifiable interest which a person has when the aggregate nominal value of the shares in which he is interested is equal to or more than 10 per cent of the nominal value of that relevant share capital, subsection (1) shall have effect as if for the words 'has material interests' there were substituted 'is interested'.

(3) Where the nominal value of the share capital is greater immediately after the relevant time than it was immediately before, the percentage level of the person's interest immediately before (as well as immediately after) that time is determined by reference to the larger amount.

202 Particulars to be contained in notification

(1) Where notification is required by section 198 with respect to a person's interest (if any) in shares comprised in relevant share capital of a public company, the obligation to make the notification must be performed within the period of 2 days next following the day on which that obligation arises; and the notification must be in writing to the company.

(2) The notification must specify the share capital to which it relates, and must also—

(a) subject to subsections (2A) and (2B), state the number of shares comprised in that share capital in which the person making the notification knows he had material interests immediately after the time when the obligation arose, or

(b) in a case where the person no longer has a notifiable interest in shares comprised in that share capital, state that he no longer has that interest.

(2A) Where, immediately after the relevant time, the aggregate nominal value of the shares in which the person making the notification is interested is equal to or more than 10 per cent of the nominal value of that relevant share capital, subsection (2)(a) shall have effect as if for the words 'had material interests' there were substituted 'was interested'.

(2B) Nothing in subsection (2) or (2A) requires a notification to state, in relation to any shares, whether the interest of the person making the notification is (or is not) a material interest.

(3) A notification (other than one stating that a person no longer has a notifiable interest) shall include the following particulars, so far as known to the person making the notification at the date when it is made—

(a) the identity of each registered holder of shares to which the notification relates and the number of such shares held by each of them, and

(b) the number of such shares in which the interest of the person giving the notification is such an interest as is mentioned in section 208(5).

(4) A person who has an interest in shares comprised in a company's relevant share capital, that interest being notifiable, is under obligation to notify the company in writing—

(a) of any particulars in relation to those shares which are specified in subsection (3), and

(b) of any change in those particulars,

of which in either case he becomes aware at any time after any interest notification date and before the first occasion following that date on which he comes under any further obligation of disclosure with respect to his interest in shares comprised in that share capital.

An obligation arising under this subsection must be performed within the period of 2 days next following the day on which it arises.

(5) The reference in subsection (4) to an interest notification date, in relation to a person's interest in shares comprised in a public company's relevant share capital, is to either of the following—

(a) the date of any notification made by him with respect to his interest under this Part, and

(b) where he has failed to make a notification, the date on which the period allowed for making it came to an end.

(6) A person who at any time has an interest in shares which is notifiable is to be regarded under subsection (4) as continuing to have a notifiable interest in them unless and until he comes under obligation to make a notification stating that he no longer has such an interest in those shares.

203 Notification of family and corporate interests

(1) For purposes of sections 198 to 202, a person is taken to be interested in any shares in which his spouse or any infant child or stepchild of his is interested; and 'infant' means, in relation to Scotland, pupil or minor.

(2) For those purposes, a person is taken to be interested in shares if a body corporate is interested in them and—

(a) that body or its directors are accustomed to act in accordance with his directions or instructions, or

(b) he is entitled to exercise or control the exercise of one-third or more of the voting power at general meetings of that body corporate.

(3) Where a person is entitled to exercise or control the exercise of one-third or more of the voting power at general meetings of a body corporate and that body corporate is entitled to exercise or control the exercise of any of the voting power at general meetings of another body corporate ('the effective voting power') then, for purposes of subsection (2)(b), the effective voting power is taken as exercisable by that person.

(4) For purposes of subsections (2) and (3), a person is entitled to exercise or control the exercise of voting power if—

(a) he has a right (whether subject to conditions or not) the exercise of which would make him so entitled, or

(b) he is under an obligation (whether or not so subject) the fulfilment of which would make him so entitled.

204 Agreement to acquire interests in a particular company

(1) In certain circumstances the obligation of disclosure may arise from an agreement between two or more persons which includes provision for the acquisition by any one or more of them of interests in shares of a particular public company ('the target company'), being shares comprised in the relevant share capital of that company.

(2) This section applies to such an agreement if—

(a) the agreement also includes provisions imposing obligations or restrictions on any one or more of the parties to it with respect to their use, retention or disposal of their interests in that company's shares acquired in pursuance of the agreement (whether or not together with any other interests of theirs in the company's shares to which the agreement relates), and

(b) any interest in the company's shares is in fact acquired by any of the parties in pursuance of the agreement;

and in relation to such an agreement references below in this section, and in sections 205 and 206, to the target company are to the company which is the target company for that agreement in accordance with this and the previous subsection.

(3) The reference in subsection (2)(a) to the use of interests in shares in the target

company is to the exercise of any rights or of any control or influence arising from those interests (including the right to enter into any agreement for the exercise, or for control of the exercise, of any of those rights by another person).

(4) Once any interest in shares in the target company has been acquired in pursuance of such an agreement as is mentioned above, this section continues to apply to that agreement irrespective of—

(a) whether or not any further acquisitions of interests in the company's shares take place in pursuance of the agreement, and

(b) any change in the persons who are for the time being parties to it, and

(c) any variation of the agreement, so long as the agreement continues to include provisions of any description mentioned in subsection (2)(a).

References in this subsection to the agreement include any agreement having effect (whether directly or indirectly) in substitution for the original agreement.

(5) In this section, and also in references elsewhere in this Part to an agreement to which this section applies, 'agreement' includes any agreement or arrangement; and references in this section to provisions of an agreement—

(a) accordingly include undertakings, expectations or understandings operative under any arrangement, and

(b) (without prejudice to the above) also include any provisions, whether express or implied and whether absolute or not.

(6) However, this section does not apply to an agreement which is not legally binding unless it involves mutuality in the undertakings, expectations or understandings of the parties to it; nor does the section apply to an agreement to underwrite or sub-underwrite any offer of shares in a company, provided the agreement is confined to that purpose and any matters incidental to it.

205   Obligation of disclosure arising under s. 204

(1) In the case of an agreement to which section 204 applies, each party to the agreement is taken (for purposes of the obligation of disclosure) to be interested in all shares in the target company in which any other party to it is interested apart from the agreement (whether or not the interest of the other party in question was acquired, or includes any interest which was acquired, in pursuance of the agreement).

(2) For those purposes, and also for those of the next section, an interest of a party to such an agreement in shares in the target company is an interest apart from the agreement if he is interested in those shares otherwise than by virtue of the application of section 204 and this section in relation to the agreement.

(3) Accordingly, any such interest of the person (apart from the agreement) includes for those purposes any interest treated as his under section 203 or by the application of section 204 and this section in relation to any other agreement with respect to shares in the target company to which he is a party.

(4) A notification with respect to his interest in shares in the target company made to that company under this Part by a person who is for the time being a party to an agreement to which section 204 applies shall—

(a) state that the person making the notification is a party to such an agreement,

(b) include the names and (so far as known to him) the addresses of the other parties to the agreement, identifying them as such, and

(c) state whether or not any of the shares to which the notification relates are shares in which he is interested by virtue of section 204 and this section and, if so, the number of those shares.

(5) Where a person makes a notification to a company under this part in consequence of ceasing to be interested in any shares of that company by virtue of the fact that he or any other person has ceased to be a party to an agreement to which section 204 applies, the notification

shall include a statement that he or that other person has ceased to be a party to the agreement (as the case may require) and also (in the latter case) the name and (if known to him) the address of that other.

206   Obligation of persons acting together to keep each other informed

(1) A person who is a party to an agreement to which section 204 applies is subject to the requirements of this section at any time when—

(a) the target company is a public company, and he knows it to be so, and

(b) the shares in that company to which the agreement relates consist of or include shares comprised in relevant share capital of the company, and he knows that to be the case; and

(c) he knows the facts which make the agreement one to which section 204 applies.

(2) Such a person is under obligation to notify every other party to the agreement, in writing, of the relevant particulars of his interest (if any) apart from the agreement in shares comprised in relevant share capital of the target company—

(a) on his first becoming subject to the requirements of this section, and

(b) on each occurrence after that time while he is still subject to those requirements of any event or circumstances within section 198(1) (as it applies to his case otherwise than by reference to interests treated as his under section 205 as applying to that agreement).

(3) The relevant particulars to be notified under subsection (2) are—

(a) the number of shares (if any) comprised in the target company's relevant share capital in which the person giving the notice would be required to state his interest if he were under the wide obligation of disclosure with respect to that interest (apart from the agreement) immediately after the time when the obligation to give notice under subsection (2) arose, and

(b) the relevant particulars with respect to the registered ownership of those shares, so far as known to him at the date of the notice, and

(c) except in the circumstance mentioned in subsection (3A), the number of shares (if any) out of the number given under paragraph (a) in which he knows that, immediately after the time when the obligation to give the notice arose, he had interests (apart from the agreement) which were not material interests.

(3A) The circumstance referred to in subsection (3)(c) is that the aggregate nominal value of the shares comprised in relevant share capital in which the person is interested (apart from the agreement) is equal to or more than 10 per cent of the nominal value of the relevant share capital.

(3B) For the purposes of subsection (3)(a) 'the wide obligation of disclosure' means the obligation to disclose the number of shares in which the person concerned has any interest (material or otherwise).

(4) A person who is for the time being subject to the requirements of this section is also under obligation to notify every other party to the agreement, in writing—

(a) of any relevant particulars with respect to the registered ownership of any shares comprised in relevant share capital of the target company in which he is interested apart from the agreement, and

(b) of any change in those particulars,

of which in either case he becomes aware at any time after any interest notification date and before the first occasion following that date on which he becomes subject to any further obligation to give notice under subsection (2) with respect to his interest in shares comprised in that share capital.

(5) The reference in subsection (4) to an interest notification date, in relation to a person's interest in shares comprised in the target company's relevant share capital, is to either of the following—

(a) the date of any notice given by him with respect to his interest under subsection (2), and

(b) where he has failed to give that notice, the date on which the period allowed by this section for giving the notice came to an end.

(6) A person who is a party to an agreement to which section 204 applies is under an obligation to notify each other party to the agreement, in writing, of his current address—

(a) on his first becoming subject to the requirements of this section, and

(b) on any change in his address occurring after that time and while he is still subject to those requirements.

(7) A reference to the relevant particulars with respect to the registered ownership of shares is to such particulars in relation to those shares as are mentioned in section 202(3)(a) or (b).

(8) A person's obligation to give any notice required by this section to any other person must be performed within the period of 2 days next following the day on which that obligation arose.

207 Interests in shares by attribution

(1) Where section 198 or 199 refers to a person acquiring an interest in shares or ceasing to be interested in shares, that reference in certain cases includes his becoming or ceasing to be interested in those shares by virtue of another person's interest.

(2) Such is the case where he becomes or ceases to be interested by virtue of section 203 or (as the case may be) section 205 whether—

(a) by virtue of the fact that the person who is interested in the shares becomes or ceases to be a person whose interests (if any) fall by virtue of either section to be treated as his, or

(b) in consequence of the fact that such a person has become or ceased to be interested in the shares, or

(c) in consequence of the fact that he himself becomes or ceases to be a party to an agreement to which section 204 applies to which the person interested in the shares is for the time being a party, or

(d) in consequence of the fact that an agreement to which both he and that person are parties becomes or ceases to be one to which that section applies.

(3) The person is then to be treated as knowing he has acquired an interest in the shares or (as the case may be) that he has ceased to be interested in them, if and when he knows both—

(a) the relevant facts with respect to the other person's interest in the shares, and

(b) the relevant facts by virtue of which he himself has become or ceased to be interested in them in accordance with section 203 or 205.

(4) He has the knowledge referred to in subsection (3)(a) if he knows (whether contemporaneously or not) either of the subsistence of the other person's interest at any material time or of the fact that the other has become or ceased to be interested in the shares at any such time; and 'material time' is any time at which the other's interests (if any) fall or fell to be treated as his under section 203 or 205.

(5) A person is to be regarded as knowing of the subsistence of another's interest in shares or (as the case may be) that another has become or ceased to be interested in shares if he has been notified under section 206 of facts with respect to the other's interest which indicate that he is or has become or ceased to be interested in the shares (whether on his own account or by virtue of a third party's interest in them).

208 Interests in shares which are to be notified

(1) This section applies, subject to the section next following, in determining for purposes of sections 198 to 202 whether a person has a notifiable interest in shares.

(2) A reference to an interest in shares is to be read as including an interest of any kind whatsoever in the shares; and accordingly there are to be disregarded any restraints or restrictions to which the exercise of any right attached to the interest is or may be subject.

(3) Where property is held on trust and an interest in shares is comprised in the property, a beneficiary of the trust who apart from this subsection does not have an interest in the shares is to be taken as having such an interest.

(4) A person is taken to have an interest in shares if—

    (a) he enters into a contract for their purchase by him (whether for cash or other consideration), or

    (b) not being the registered holder, he is entitled to exercise any right conferred by the holding of the shares or is entitled to control the exercise of any such right.

(5) A person is taken to have an interest in shares if, otherwise than by virtue of having an interest under a trust—

    (a) he has a right to call for delivery of the shares to himself or to his order, or

    (b) he has a right to acquire an interest in shares or is under an obligation to take an interest in shares,

whether in any case the right or obligation is conditional or absolute.

(6) For purposes of subsection (4)(b), a person is entitled to exercise or control the exercise of any right conferred by the holding of shares if he—

    (a) has a right (whether subject to conditions or not) the exercise of which would make him so entitled, or

    (b) is under an obligation (whether so subject or not) the fulfilment of which would make him so entitled.

(7) Persons having a joint interest are taken each of them to have that interest.

(8) It is immaterial that shares in which a person has an interest are unidentifiable.

209   Interests to be disregarded

(1) Subject to subsections (5) and (6), the following interests in shares are disregarded for the purposes of sections 198 to 202—

    (a) where property is held on trust and an interest in shares is comprised in that property, an interest of a person, being a discretionary interest or an interest in reversion or remainder or an interest of a bare trustee;

    (b) an interest which a person has by virtue of holding units in—

        (i)   an authorised unit trust scheme;

        (ii) a recognised scheme; or

        (iii) a UCITS;

    (c) an interest of a person which is an exempt security interest within the meaning of subsection (2);

    (d) an interest which a person has by virtue of his being a beneficiary under a retirement benefits scheme as defined in section 611 of the Income and Corporation Taxes Act 1988;

    (e) an interest which a person has in shares as a result of the acceptance of a takeover offer made by him (either alone or jointly with one or more other persons) for shares where—

        (i) the offer is subject to a threshold acceptance condition; and

        (ii) the threshold acceptance condition is not fulfilled;

    (f) an interest of a person which is an exempt custodian interest within the meaning of subsection (4);

    (g) an interest which a person has by virtue of his being a personal representative of any estate;

    (h) an interest which a person has—

        (i) by virtue of his being a trustee of an authorised unit trust scheme,

        (ii) in relation to a recognised scheme or a UCITS, by virtue of his being entrusted with the custody of the property in question (whether or not under a trust), or

(iii) by virtue of his being a depositary, within the meaning of the Open-Ended Investment Companies Regulations 2001, of an open-ended investment company.

(2) An interest in shares is an exempt security interest for the purposes of subsection (1)(c) if the condition mentioned in subsection (2A) is satisfied and it is held by—

(a) a person who has permission under Part IV of the Financial Services and Markets Act 2000 to accept deposits;

(b) an EEA firm of the kind mentioned in paragraph 5(b) of Schedule 3 to that Act which falls within article 1(1)(a) of the banking consolidation directive (within the meaning of that Schedule);

(c) a person authorised under the law of a member State other than the United Kingdom to accept deposits who—

(i) would not qualify for authorisation under paragraph 12 of Schedule 3 to that Act; and

(ii) would require permission under another provision of that Act to accept such deposits in the United Kingdom;

(d) an authorised insurance undertaking;

(e) a person authorised under the law of a member State to deal in securities or derivatives, who deals in securities or derivatives on a relevant stock exchange or a relevant investment exchange, whether as a member or otherwise;

(f) a relevant stock exchange;

(g) a relevant investment exchange;

(h) a recognised clearing house;

(i) the Bank of England; or

(j) the central bank of a member State other than the United Kingdom.

(2A) The condition is that the interest in the shares must be held by way of security only for the purposes of a transaction entered into in the ordinary course of his or its business as a person or other body falling within any of paragraphs (a) to (j) of subsection (2).

(2B) Paragraphs (a) to (c) of subsection (2) must be read with—

(a) section 22 of the Financial Services and Markets Act 2000;

(b) any relevant order under that section; and

(c) Schedule 2 to that Act.

(2C) But paragraph (a) of subsection (2) does not include—

(a) a building society incorporated, or deemed to be incorporated, under the Building Societies Act 1986; or

(b) a credit union, within the meaning of the Credit Unions Act 1979 [or] the Credit Unions (Northern Ireland) Order 1985.

(3) For the purposes of subsection (1)(e)—

(a) 'takeover offer' has the same meaning as in Part XIIIA; and

(b) 'a threshold acceptance condition' means a condition that acceptances are received in respect of such proportion of the shares for which the takeover offer is made as is specified in or determined in accordance with the terms of the takeover offer.

(4) For the purposes of subsection (1)(f) an interest of a person is an exempt custodian interest if it is held by him—

(a) as a custodian (whether under a trust or by a contract); or

(b) under an arrangement pursuant to which he has issued, or is to issue, depositary receipts in respect of the shares concerned.

(5) An interest referred to in any paragraph of subsection (1) (except for paragraph (c)) is disregarded only if the person referred to in the relevant paragraph or in subsection (4) is not entitled to exercise or control the exercise of voting rights in respect of the shares concerned; and for this purpose he is not so entitled if he is bound (whether by contract or otherwise) not

to exercise the voting rights, or not to exercise them otherwise than in accordance with the instructions of another.

(6) In the case of an interest referred to in paragraph (c) of subsection (1), an interest of a person referred to in subsection (2) is disregarded only if that person—

(a) is not entitled (within the meaning of subsection (5)) to exercise or control the exercise of voting rights in respect of the shares concerned; or

(b) is so entitled, but has not evidenced any intention to exercise them or control their exercise nor taken any step to do so.

(7) For the purposes of subsection (5) and (6), voting rights which a person is entitled to exercise or of which he is entitled to control the exercise only in certain circumstances shall be taken into account only when the circumstances have arisen and for so long as they continue to obtain.

(8) An interest in shares of a company is also disregarded for the purposes of sections 198 to 202—

(a) if it is held by a market maker in securities or derivatives for the purposes of his business, but

(b) only in so far as it is not used by him for the purpose of intervening in the management of the company.

(9) For the purposes of subsection (8) a person is a market maker in securities or derivatives if—

(a) he is authorised under the law of a member State to deal in securities or derivatives and so deals on a relevant stock exchange or on a relevant investment exchange (whether as a member or otherwise); and

(b) he holds himself out at all normal times as willing to acquire and dispose of securities or derivatives at prices specified by him and in so doing is subject to the rules of that exchange;

and he holds an interest for the purposes of his business if he holds it for the purposes of a business carried on by him as a market maker in a member State.

(9A) Where—

(a) in pursuance of arrangements made with the operator of a relevant system—

(i) securities of a particular aggregate value are on any day transferred by means of that system from a person ('A') to another person ('B');

(ii) the securities are of kinds and amounts determined by the operator-system; and

(iii) the securities, or securities of the same kinds and amounts, are on the following day transferred by means of the relevant system from B to A; and

(b) the securities comprise any shares of a company,

any interest of B in those shares is also disregarded for the purposes of sections 198 to 202.

(9B) For the purposes of subsection (9A)—

(a) any day which, in England and Wales, is a non-business day for the purposes of the Bills of Exchange Act 1882 is disregarded; and

(b) expressions which are used in the Uncertificated Securities Regulations 2001 have the same meanings as in those Regulations.

(10) The following interests in shares in a public company which is not listed are also disregarded for the purposes of sections 198 to 202—

(a) an interest which subsists by virtue of—

(i) a scheme made under section 24 or 25 of the Charities Act 1993, section 25 of the Charities Act (Northern Ireland) 1964, section 11 of the Trustee Investments Act 1961 or section 42 of the Administration of Justice Act 1982, or

(ii) the scheme set out in the Schedule to the Church Funds Investment Measure 1958;

(b) an interest of the Church of Scotland General Trustees, the Church of Scotland Trust or the Church of Scotland Investors Trust in shares held by them or of any other person in shares held by those Trustees or Trusts otherwise than as simple trustees;

(c) an interest for the life of himself or another of a person under a settlement in the case of which the property comprised in the settlement consists of or includes shares, and the conditions mentioned in subsection (11) are satisfied;

(e) an interest of the Accountant General of the Supreme Court in shares held by him

(f) an interest of the Public Trustee;

(g) an interest of the Probate Judge subsisting by virtue of section 3 of the Administration of Estates Act (Northern Ireland) 1955.

(11) The conditions referred to in subsection (10)(c) are, in relation to a settlement—

(a) that it is irrevocable, and

(b) that the settlor (within the meaning of section 670 of the Income and Corporation Taxes Act 1988) has no interest in any income arising under, or property comprised in, the settlement.

(12) A person is not by virtue of section 208(4)(b) taken to be interested in shares by reason only that he has been appointed a proxy to vote at a specified meeting of a company or of any class of its members and at any adjournment of that meeting, or has been appointed by a corporation to act as its representative at any meeting of a company or of any class of its members.

(13) In the application of subsection (1)(a) to property held on trust according to the law of Scotland, for the words 'or remainder or an interest of a bare trustee' there shall be substituted 'or in fee or an interest of a simple trustee'.

[In s. 209(2C)(b), which was inserted by SI 2001/3649, the word 'or' which is in square brackets in this edition is mistakenly printed as 'of' in SI 2001/3649.]

210   Other provisions about notification under this Part

(1) Where a person authorises another ('the agent') to acquire or dispose of, on his behalf, interests in shares comprised in relevant share capital of a public company, he shall secure that the agent notifies him immediately of acquisitions or disposals effected by the agent which will or may give rise to any obligation of disclosure imposed on him by this Part with respect to his interest in that share capital.

(2) An obligation of disclosure imposed on a person by any provision of sections 198 to 202 is treated as not being fulfilled unless the notice by means of which it purports to be fulfilled identifies him and gives his address and, in a case where he is a director of the company, is expressed to be given in fulfilment of that obligation.

(3) A person who—

(a) fails to fulfil, within the proper period, an obligation of disclosure imposed on him by this Part, or

(b) in purported fulfilment of any such obligation makes to a company a statement which he knows to be false, or recklessly makes to a company a statement which is false, or

(c) fails to fulfil, within the proper period, an obligation to give another person a notice required by section 206, or

(d) fails without reasonable excuse to comply with subsection (1) of this section, is guilty of an offence and liable to imprisonment or a fine, or both.

(4) It is a defence for a person charged with an offence under subsection (3)(c) to prove that it was not possible for him to give the notice to the other person required by section 206 within the proper period, and either—

(a) that it has not since become possible for him to give the notice so required, or

(b) that he gave the notice as soon after the end of that period as it became possible for him to do so.

(5) Where a person is convicted of an offence under this section (other than an offence relating to his ceasing to be interested in a company's shares), the Secretary of State may by order direct that the shares in relation to which the offence was committed shall, until further order, be subject to the restrictions of Part XV of this Act; and such an order may be made notwithstanding any power in the company's memorandum or articles enabling the company to impose similar restrictions on those shares.

(5A) If the Secretary of State is satisfied that an order under subsection (5) may unfairly affect the rights of third parties in respect of shares then the Secretary of State, for the purpose of protecting such rights and subject to such terms as he thinks fit, may direct that such acts by such persons or descriptions of persons and for such purposes as may be set out in the order, shall not constitute a breach of the restrictions of Part XV of this Act.

(6) Sections 732 (restriction on prosecutions) and 733(2) and (3) (liability of directors, etc.) apply to offences under this section.

210A   Power to make further provision by regulations

(1) The Secretary of State may by regulations amend—
   (a) the definition of 'relevant share capital' (section 198(2)),
   (b) the percentage giving rise to a 'notifiable interest' (section 199(2)),
   (c) the periods within which an obligation of disclosure must be fulfilled or a notice must be given (sections 202(1) and (4) and 206(8)),
   (d) the provisions as to what is taken to be an interest in shares (section 208) and what interests are to be disregarded (section 209), and
   (e) the provisions as to company investigations (section 212); and the regulations may amend, replace or repeal the provisions referred to above and make such other consequential amendments or repeals of provisions of this part as appear to the Secretary of State to be appropriate.

(2) The regulations may in any case make different provision for different descriptions of company; and regulations under subsection (1)(b), (c) or (d) may make different provision for different descriptions of person, interest or share capital.

(3) The regulations may contain such transitional and other supplementary and incidental provisions as appear to the Secretary of State to be appropriate, and may in particular make provision as to the obligations of a person whose interest in a company's shares becomes or ceases to be notifiable by virtue of the regulations.

(4) Regulations under this section shall be made by statutory instrument.

(5) No regulations shall be made under this section unless a draft of the regulations has been laid before and approved by a resolution of each House of Parliament.

Registration and investigation of share acquisitions and disposals

211   Register of interests in shares

(1) Every public company shall keep a register for purposes of sections 198 to 202, and whenever the company receives information from a person in consequence of the fulfilment of an obligation imposed on him by any of those sections, it is under obligation to inscribe in the register, against that person's name, that information and the date of the inscription.

(2) Without prejudice to subsection (1), where a company receives a notification under this Part which includes a statement that the person making the notification, or any other person, has ceased to be a party to an agreement to which section 204 applies, the company is under obligation to record that information against the name of that person in every place where his name appears in the register as a party to that agreement (including any entry relating to him made against another person's name).

(3) An obligation imposed by subsection (1) or (2) must be fulfilled within the period of 3 days next following the day on which it arises.

(4) The company is not, by virtue of anything done for the purposes of this section, affected with notice of, or put upon enquiry as to, the rights of any person in relation to any shares.

(5) The register must be so made up that the entries against the several names entered in it appear in chronological order.

(6) Unless the register is in such form as to constitute in itself an index, the company shall keep an index of the names entered in the register which shall in respect of each name contain a sufficient indication to enable the information entered against it to be readily found; and the company shall, within 10 days after the date on which a name is entered in the register, make any necessary alteration in the index.

(7) If the company ceases to be a public company it shall continue to keep the register and any associated index until the end of the period of 6 years beginning with the day next following that on which it ceases to be such a company.

(8) The register and any associated index—

(a) shall be kept at the place at which the register required to be kept by the company by section 325 (register of directors' interests) is kept, and

(b) subject to the next subsection, shall be available for inspection in accordance with section 219 below.

(9) Neither the register nor any associated index shall be available for inspection in accordance with that section in so far as it contains information with respect to a company for the time being entitled to avail itself of the benefit conferred by section 231(3) (disclosure of shareholdings not required if it would be harmful to company's business).

(10) If default is made in complying with subsection (1) or (2), or with any of subsections (5) to (7), the company and every officer of it who is in default is liable to a fine and, for continued contravention, to a daily default fine.

(11) Any register kept by a company immediately before 15 June 1982 under section 34 of the Companies Act 1967 shall continue to be kept by the company under and for the purposes of this section.

212   Company investigations

(1) A public company may by notice in writing require a person whom the company knows or has reasonable cause to believe to be or, at any time during the 3 years immediately preceding the date on which the notice is issued, to have been interested in shares comprised in the company's relevant share capital—

(a) to confirm that fact or (as the case may be) to indicate whether or not it is the case, and

(b) where he holds or has during that time held an interest in shares so comprised, to give such further information as may be required in accordance with the following subsection.

(2) A notice under this section may require the person to whom it is addressed—

(a) to give particulars of his own past or present interest in shares comprised in relevant share capital of the company (held by him at any time during the 3-year period mentioned in subsection (1)),

(b) where the interest is a present interest and any other interest in the shares subsists or, in any case, where another interest in the shares subsisted during that 3-year period at any time when his own interest subsisted, to give (so far as lies within his knowledge) such particulars with respect to that other interest as may be required by the notice,

(c) where his interest is a past interest, to give (so far as lies within his knowledge) particulars of the identity of the person who held that interest immediately upon his ceasing to hold it.

(3) The particulars referred to in subsection (2)(a) and (b) include particulars of the identity of persons interested in the shares in question and of whether persons interested in the same shares are or were parties to any agreement to which section 204 applies or to any agreement or arrangement relating to the exercise of any rights conferred by the holding of the shares.

(4) A notice under this section shall require any information given in response to the notice to be given in writing within such reasonable time as may be specified in the notice.

(5) Sections 203 to 205 and 208 apply for the purpose of construing references in this section to persons interested in shares and to interests in shares respectively, as they apply in relation to sections 198 to 201 (but with the omission of any reference to section 209).

(6) This section applies in relation to a person who has or previously had, or is or was entitled to acquire, a right to subscribe for shares in a public company which would on issue be comprised in relevant share capital of that company as it applies in relation to a person who is or was interested in shares so comprised; and references above in this section to an interest in shares so comprised and to shares so comprised are to be read accordingly in any such case as including respectively any such right and shares which would on issue be so comprised.

213   Registration of interests disclosed under s. 212

(1) Whenever in pursuance of a requirement imposed on a person under section 212 a company receives information to which this section applies relating to shares comprised in its relevant share capital, it is under obligation to enter against the name of the registered holder of those shares, in a separate part of its register of interests in shares—

  (a) the fact that the requirement was imposed and the date on which it was imposed, and
  (b) any information to which this section applies received in pursuance of the requirement.

(2) This section applies to any information received in pursuance of a requirement imposed by section 212 which relates to the present interests held by any persons in shares comprised in relevant share capital of the company in question.

(3) Subsections (3) to (10) of section 211 apply in relation to any part of the register maintained in accordance with subsection (1) of this section as they apply in relation to the remainder of the register, reading references to subsection (1) of that section to include subsection (1) of this.

(4) In the case of a register kept by a company immediately before 15 June 1982 under section 34 of the Companies Act 1967, and part of the register so kept for the purposes of scetion 27 of the Companies Act 1976 shall continue to be kept by the company under and for the purposes of this section.

214   Company investigation on requisition by members

(1) A company may be required to exercise its powers under section 212 on the requisition of members of the company holding at the date of the deposit of the requisition not less than one-tenth of such of the paid-up capital of the company as carries at that date the right of voting at general meetings of the company *(excluding any shares in the company held as treasury shares)*.

(2) The requisition must—

  (a) state that the requisitions are requiring the company to exercise its powers under section 212,
  (b) specify the manner in which they require those powers to be exercised, and
  (c) give reasonable grounds for requiring the company to exercise those powers in the manner specified,

and must be signed by the requisitions and deposited at the company's registered office.

(3) The requisition may consist of several documents in like form each signed by one or more requisitionists.

(4) On the deposit of a requisition complying with this section it is the company's duty to exercise its powers under section 212 in the manner specified in the requisition.

(5) If default is made in complying with subsection (4), the company and every officer of it who is in default is liable to a fine.

[*The words in italics in s. 214(1) are in force from 1 December 2003.*]

215 Company report to members

(1) On the conclusion of an investigation carried out by a company in pursuance of a requisition under section 214, it is the company's duty to cause a report of the information received in pursuance of that investigation to be prepared, and the report shall be made available at the company's registered office within a reasonable period after the conclusion of that investigation.

(2) Where—

(a) a company undertakes an investigation in pursuance of a requisition under section 214, and

(b) the investigation is not concluded before the end of 3 months beginning with the date immediately following the date of the deposit of the requisition,

it is the duty of the company to cause to be prepared, in respect of that period and each successive period of 3 months ending before the conclusion of the investigation, an interim report of the information received during that period in pursuance of the investigation. Each such report shall be made available at the company's registered office within a reasonable period after the end of the period to which it relates.

(3) The period for making any report prepared under this section available as required by subsection (1) or (2) shall not exceed 15 days.

(4) Such a report shall not include any information with respect to a company entitled to avail itself of the benefit conferred by section 231(3) (disclosure of shareholdings not required if it would be harmful to company's business); but where any such information is omitted, that fact shall be stated in the report.

(5) The company shall, within 3 days of making any report prepared under this section available at its registered office, notify the requisitionists that the report is so available.

(6) An investigation carried out by a company in pursuance of a requisition under section 214 is regarded for purposes of this section as concluded when the company has made all such inquiries as are necessary or expedient for the purposes of the requisition and in the case of each such inquiry, either a response has been received by the company or the time allowed for a response has elapsed.

(7) A report prepared under this section—

(a) shall be kept at the company's registered office from the day on which it is first available there in accordance with subsection (1) or (2) until the expiration of 6 years beginning with the day next following that day, and

(b) shall be available for inspection in accordance with section 219 below so long as it is so kept.

(8) If default is made in complying with subsection (1), (2), (5) or (7)(a), the company and every officer of it who is in default is liable to a fine.

216 Penalty for failure to provide information

(1) Where notice is served by a company under section 212 on a person who is or was interested in shares of the company and that person fails to give the company any information required by the notice within the time specified in it, the company may apply to the court for an order directing that the shares in question be subject to the restrictions of Part XV of this Act.

(1A) On an application made under subsection (1) the court may make an interim order and any such order may be made unconditionally or on such terms as the court thinks fit.

(1B) If the court is satisfied that an order under subsection (1) may unfairly affect the rights of third parties in respect of shares then the court, for the purpose of protecting such rights and subject to such terms as it thinks fit, may direct that such acts by such persons or descriptions of persons and for such purposes as may be set out in the order, shall not constitute a breach of the restrictions of Part XV of this Act.

(2) An order under this section may be made by the court notwithstanding any power contained in the applicant company's memorandum or articles enabling the company itself to impose similar restrictions on the shares in question.

(3) Subject to the following subsections, a person who fails to comply with a notice under section 212 or who, in purported compliance with such a notice, makes any statement which he knows to be false in a material particular or recklessly makes any statement which is false in a material particular is guilty of an offence and liable to imprisonment or a fine, or both.

Section 733(2) and (3) of this Act (liability of individuals for corporate default) apply to offences under this subsection.

(4) A person is not guilty of an offence by virtue of failing to comply with a notice under section 212 if he proves that the requirement to give the information was frivolous or vexatious.

(5) A person is not obliged to comply with a notice under section 212 if he is for the time being exempted by the Secretary of State from the operation of that section; but the Secretary of State shall not grant any such exemption unless—

(a) he has consulted with the Governor of the Bank of England, and
(b) he (the Secretary of State) is satisfied that, having regard to any undertaking given by the person in question with respect to any interest held or to be held by him in any shares, there are special reasons why that person should not be subject to the obligations imposed by that section.

217   Removal of entries from register

(1) A company may remove an entry against a person's name from its register of interests in shares if more than 6 years have elapsed since the date of the entry being made, and either—

(a) that entry recorded the fact that the person in question had ceased to have an interest notifiable under this Part in relevant share capital of the company, or
(b) it has been superseded by a later entry made under section 211 against the same person's name;

and in a case within paragraph (a) the company may also remove that person's name from the register.

(2) If a person in pursuance of an obligation imposed on him by any provision of this Part gives to a company the name and address of another person as being interested in shares in the company, the company shall, within 15 days of the date on which it was given that information, notify the other person that he has been so named and shall include in that notification—

(a) particulars of any entry relating to him made, in consequence of its being given that information, by the company in its register of interests in shares, and
(b) a statement informing him of his right to apply to have the entry removed in accordance with the following provisions of this section.

(3) A person who has been notified by a company in pursuance of subsection (2) that an entry relating to him has been made in the company's register of interests in shares may apply in writing to the company for the removal of that entry from the register; and the company shall remove the entry if satisfied that the information in pursuance of which the entry was made was incorrect.

(4) If a person who is identified in a company's register of interests in shares as being a party to an agreement to which section 204 applies (whether by an entry against his own

name or by an entry relating to him made against another person's name as mentioned in subsection (2)(a)) ceases to be a party to that agreement, he may apply in writing to the company for the inclusion of that information in the register; and if the company is satisfied that he has ceased to be a party to the agreement, it shall record that information (if not already recorded) in every place where his name appears as a party to that agreement in the register.

(5) If an application under subsection (3) or (4) is refused (in a case within subsection (4)), otherwise than on the ground that the information has already been recorded) the applicant may apply to the court for an order directing the company to remove the entry in question from the register or (as the case may be) to include the information in question in the register; and the court may, if it thinks fit, make such an order.

(6) Where a name is removed from a company's register of interests in shares in pursuance of subsection (1) or (3) or an order under subsection (5), the company shall within 14 days of the date of that removal make any necessary alteration in any associated index.

(7) If default is made in complying with subsection (2) or (6), the company and every officer of it who is in default is liable to a fine and, for continued contravention, to a daily default fine.

218   Otherwise, entries not to be removed

(1) Entries in a company's register of interests in shares shall not be deleted except in accordance with section 217.

(2) If an entry is deleted from a company's register of interests in shares in contravention of subsection (1), the company shall restore that entry to the register as soon as is reasonably practicable.

(3) If default is made in complying with subsection (1) or (2), the company and every officer of it who is in default is liable to a fine and, for continued contravention of subsection (2), to a daily default fine.

219   Inspection of register and reports

(1) Any register of interests in shares and any report which is required by section 215(7) to be available for inspection in accordance with this section shall be open to the inspection of any member of the company or of any other person without charge.

(2) Any such member or other person may require a copy of any such register or report, or any part of it, on payment of such fee as may be prescribed; and the company shall cause any copy so required by a person to be sent to him before the expiration of the period of 10 days beginning with the day next following that on which the requirement is received by the company.

(3) If an inspection required under this section is refused or a copy so required is not sent within the proper period, the company and every officer of it who is in default is liable to a fine and, for continued contravention, to a daily default fine.

(4) In the case of a refusal of an inspection required under this section of any register or report, the court may by order compel an immediate inspection of it; and in the case of failure to send a copy required under this section, the court may by order direct that the copy required shall be sent to the person requiring it.

(5) The Secretary of State may by regulations made by statutory instrument substitute a sum specified in the regulations for the sum for the time being mentioned in subsection (2).
[*No sum is now mentioned in s. 219(2), following amendment by the Companies Act 1989, s. 143(5)(b).*]

Supplementary

220   Definitions for Part VI

(1) In this Part of this Act—

'associated index', in relation to a register, means the index kept in relation to that register in pursuance of section 211(6);

'authorised insurance undertaking' means an insurance undertaking which has been authorised in accordance with Article 6 or 23 of Council Directive 73/239/EEC or Article 6 or 27 of Council Directive 79/267/EEC, or is authorised under the law of a member State to carry on insurance business restricted to reinsurance;

'authorised unit trust scheme' has the same meaning as in Part XVII of the Financial Services and Markets Act 2000;

'depositary receipt' means a certificate or other record (whether or not in the form of a document)—

(a) which is issued by or on behalf of a person who holds shares or who holds evidence of the right to receive shares, or has an interest in shares, in a particular company; and

(b) which evidences or acknowledges that another person is entitled to rights in relation to those shares or shares of the same kind, which shall include the right to receive such shares (or evidence of the right to receive such shares) from the person mentioned in paragraph (a);

'derivatives' means options and futures in relation to shares;

'EEA authorisation' has the same meaning as in paragraph 6 of Schedule 3 to the Financial Services and Markets Act 2000;

'listed company' means a company any of the shares in which are officially listed on a relevant stock exchange and 'listed' shall be construed accordingly;

'material interest' shall be construed in accordance with section 199(2A);

'open-ended investment company' has the same meaning as in the Open-Ended Investment Companies Regulations 2001;

'operator', in relation to a collective investment scheme, shall be construed in accordance with section 237(2) of the Financial Services and Markets Act 2000;

'recognised clearing house' has the same meaning as in the Financial Services and Markets Act 2000;

'recognised scheme' has the same meaning as in Part XVII of the Financial Services and Markets Act 2000;

'register of interest in shares' means the register kept in pursuance of section 211 including, except where the context otherwise requires, that part of the register kept in pursuance of section 213;

'relevant investment exchange' means an exchange situated or operating in a member State on which derivatives are traded;

'relevant share capital' has the meaning given by section 198(2);

'relevant stock exchange' means a stock exchange situated or operating in a member State;

'UCITS' has the meaning given by section 199(8);

'units' has the same meaning as in section 237(2) of the Financial Services and Markets Act 2000.

(1A) References in subsection (1) to contracts of insurance (of any description), options and futures must be read with—

(a) section 22 of the Financial Services and Markets Act 2000;

(b) any relevant order under that section; and

(c) Schedule 2 to that Act.

(2) Where the period allowed by any provision of this Part for fulfilling an obligation is expressed as a number of days, any day that is a Saturday or Sunday or a bank holiday in any part of Great Britain is to be disregarded in reckoning that period.

PART VII   ACCOUNTS AND AUDIT

CHAPTER I   PROVISIONS APPLYING TO COMPANIES GENERALLY

Accounting records

221   Duty to keep accounting records

(1) Every company shall keep accounting records which are sufficient to show and explain the company's transactions and are such as to—

    (a) disclose with reasonable accuracy, at any time, the financial position of the company at that time, and

    (b) enable the directors to ensure that any balance sheet and profit and loss account prepared under this Part complies with the requirements of this Act.

(2) The accounting records shall in particular contain—

    (a) entries from day to day of all sums of money received and expended by the company, and the matters in respect of which the receipt and expenditure takes place, and

    (b) a record of the assets and liabilities of the company.

(3) If the company's business involves dealing in goods, the accounting records shall contain—

    (a) statements of stock held by the company at the end of each financial year of the company,

    (b) all statements of stocktakings from which any such statement of stock as is mentioned in paragraph (a) has been or is to be prepared, and

    (c) except in the case of goods sold by way of ordinary retail trade, statements of all goods sold and purchased, showing the goods and the buyers and sellers in sufficient detail to enable all these to be identified.

(4) A parent company which has a subsidiary undertaking in relation to which the above requirements do not apply shall take reasonable steps to secure that the undertaking keeps such accounting records as to enable the directors of the parent company to ensure that any balance sheet and profit and loss account prepared under this Part complies with the requirements of this Act.

(5) If a company fails to comply with any provision of this section, every officer of the company who is in default is guilty of an offence unless he shows that he acted honestly and that in the circumstances in which the company's business was carried on the default was excusable.

(6) A person guilty of an offence under this section is liable to imprisonment or a fine, or both.

[*In s. 221(2)(a), it may be that 'the receipt and expenditure takes place' is a mistake for 'the receipt or expenditure takes place'.*]

222   Where and for how long records to be kept

(1) A company's accounting records shall be kept at its registered office or such other place as the directors think fit, and shall at all times be open to inspection by the company's officers.

(2) If accounting records are kept at a place outside Great Britain, accounts and returns with respect to the business dealt with in the accounting records so kept shall be sent to, and kept at, a place in Great Britain, and shall at all times be open to such inspection.

(3) The accounts and returns to be sent to Great Britain shall be such as to—

    (a) disclose with reasonable accuracy the financial position of the business in question at intervals of not more than six months, and

    (b) enable the directors to ensure that the company's balance sheet and profit and loss account comply with the requirements of this Act.

(4) If a company fails to comply with any provision of subsections (1) to (3), every officer of the company who is in default is guilty of an offence, and liable to imprisonment or a fine or both, unless he shows that he acted honestly and that in the circumstances in which the company's business was carried on the default was excusable.

(5) Accounting records which a company is required by section 221 to keep shall be preserved by it—

(a) in the case of a private company, for three years from the date on which they are made, and

(b) in the case of a public company, for six years from the date on which they are made.

This is subject to any provision contained in rules made under section 411 of the Insolvency Act 1986 (company insolvency rules).

(6) An officer of a company is guilty of an offence, and liable to imprisonment or a fine or both, if he fails to take all reasonable steps for securing compliance by the company with subsection (5) or intentionally causes any default by the company under that subsection.

A company's financial year and accounting reference periods

223   A company's financial year

(1) A company's 'financial year' is determined as follows.

(2) Its first financial year begins with the first day of its first accounting reference period and ends with the last day of that period or such other date, not more than seven days before or after the end of that period, as the directors may determine.

(3) Subsequent financial years begin with the day immediately following the end of the company's previous financial year and end with the last day of its next accounting reference period or such other date, not more than seven days before or after the end of that period, as the directors may determine.

(4) In relation to an undertaking which is not a company, references in this Act to its financial year are to any period in respect of which a profit and loss account of the undertaking is required to be made up (by its constitution or by the law under which it is established), whether that period is a year or not.

(5) The directors of a parent company shall secure that, except where in their opinion there are good reasons against it, the financial year of each of its subsidiary undertakings coincides with the company's own financial year.

224   Accounting reference periods and accounting reference date

(1) A company's accounting reference periods are determined according to its accounting reference date.

(2) A company incorporated before 1 April 1996 may, at any time before the end of the period of nine months beginning with the date of its incorporation, by notice in the prescribed form given to the registrar specify its accounting reference date, that is, the date on which its accounting reference period ends in each calendar year.

(3) Failing such notice, the accounting reference date of such a company is—

(a) in the case of a company incorporated before 1 April 1990, 31 March;

(b) in the case of a company incorporated after 1 April 1990, the last day of the month in which the anniversary of its incorporation falls.

(3A) The accounting reference date of a company incorporated on or after 1 April 1996 is the last day of the month in which the anniversary of its incorporation falls.

(4) A company's first accounting reference period is the period of more than six months, but not more than 18 months, beginning with the date of its incorporation and ending with its accounting reference date.

(5) Its subsequent accounting reference periods are successive periods of twelve months beginning immediately after the end of the previous accounting reference period and ending with its accounting reference date.

(6) This section has effect subject to the provisions of section 225 relating to the alteration of accounting reference dates and the consequences of such alteration.

225   Alteration of accounting reference date

(1) A company may by notice in the prescribed form given to the registrar specify a new accounting reference date having effect in relation to—

(a) the company's current accounting reference period and subsequent periods; or

(b) the company's previous accounting reference period and subsequent periods.

A company's 'previous accounting reference period' means that immediately preceding its current accounting reference period.

(3) The notice shall state whether the current or previous accounting reference period—

(a) is to be shortened, so as to come to an end on the first occasion on which the new accounting reference date falls or fell after the beginning of the period, or

(b) is to be extended, so as to come to an end on the second occasion on which that date falls or fell after the beginning of the period.

(4) A notice under subsection (1) stating that the current or previous accounting reference period is to be extended is ineffective, except as mentioned below, if given less than five years after the end of an earlier accounting reference period of the company which was extended by virtue of this section.

This subsection does not apply—

(a) to a notice given by a company which is a subsidiary undertaking or parent undertaking of another EEA undertaking if the new accounting reference date coincides with that of the other EEA undertaking or, where that undertaking is not a company, with the last day of its financial year, or

(b) where *an administration order is in force* under Part II of the Insolvency Act 1986, or where the Secretary of State directs that it should not apply, which he may do with respect to a notice which has been given or which may be given.

(5) A notice under subsection (1) may not be given in respect of a previous accounting reference period if the period allowed for laying and delivering accounts and reports in relation to that period has already expired.

(6) *An accounting reference period may not in any case, unless an administration order is in force* under Part II of the Insolvency Act 1986, be extended so as to exceed 18 months and a notice under this section is ineffective if the current or previous accounting reference period as extended in accordance with the notice would exceed that limit.

(7) In this section 'EEA undertaking' means an undertaking established under the law of any part of the United Kingdom or the law of any other EEA State.

[*When the Enterprise Act 2002, sch. 17, is brought into force, the words in italics in the Companies Act 1985, s. 225(4), will be replaced by:*
    the company is in administration
and the words in italics in s. 225(6) will be replaced by:
    A company's accounting reference period may not in any case, unless the company is in administration]

Annual accounts

226   Duty to prepare individual company accounts

(1) The directors of every company shall prepare for each financial year of the company—

(a) a balance sheet as at the last day of the year, and

(b) a profit and loss account.

Those accounts are referred to in this Part as the company's 'individual accounts'.

(2) The balance sheet shall give a true and fair view of the state of affairs of the company as at the end of the financial year; and the profit and loss account shall give a true and fair view of the profit or loss of the company for the financial year.

(3) A company's individual accounts shall comply with the provisions of Schedule 4 as to the form and content of the balance sheet and profit and loss account and additional information to be provided by way of notes to the accounts.

(4) Where compliance with the provisions of that Schedule, and the other provisions of this Act as to the matters to be included in a company's individual accounts or in notes to those accounts, would not be sufficient to give a true and fair view, the necessary additional information shall be given in the accounts or in a note to them.

(5) If in special circumstances compliance with any of those provisions is inconsistent with the requirement to give a true and fair view, the directors shall depart from that provision to the extent necessary to give a true and fair view.

Particulars of any such departure, the reasons for it and its effect shall be given in a note to the accounts.

227   Duty to prepare group accounts

(1) If at the end of a financial year a company is a parent company the directors shall, as well as preparing individual accounts for the year, prepare group accounts.

(2) Group accounts shall be consolidated accounts comprising—

(a) a consolidated balance sheet dealing with the state of affairs of the parent company and its subsidiary undertakings, and

(b) a consolidated profit and loss account dealing with the profit or loss of the parent company and its subsidiary undertakings.

(3) The accounts shall give a true and fair view of the state of affairs as at the end of the financial year, and the profit or loss for the financial year, of the undertakings included in the consolidation as a whole, so far as concerns members of the company.

(4) A company's group accounts shall comply with the provisions of Schedule 4A as to the form and content of the consolidated balance sheet and consolidated profit and loss account and additional information to be provided by way of notes to the accounts.

(5) Where compliance with the provisions of that Schedule, and the other provisions of this Act, as to the matters to be included in a company's group accounts or in notes to those accounts, would not be sufficient to give a true and fair view, the necessary additional information shall be given in the accounts or in a note to them.

(6) If in special circumstances compliance with any of those provisions is inconsistent with the requirement to give a true and fair view, the directors shall depart from that provision to the extent necessary to give a true and fair view.

Particulars of any such departure, the reasons for it and its effect shall be given in a note to the accounts.

228   Exemption for parent companies included in accounts of larger group

(1) A company is exempt from the requirement to prepare group accounts if it is itself a subsidiary undertaking and its immediate parent undertaking is established under the law of a member State of the European Economic Community, in the following cases—

(a) where the company is a wholly-owned subsidiary of that parent undertaking;

(b) where that parent undertaking holds more than 50 per cent of the shares in the company and notice requesting the preparation of group accounts has not been served on the company by shareholders holding in aggregate—

(i)   more than half of the remaining shares in the company, or

(ii) 5 per cent of the total shares in the company.

Such notice must be served not later than six months after the end of the financial year before that to which it relates.

(2) Exemption is conditional upon compliance with all of the following conditions—

    (a) that the company is included in consolidated accounts for a larger group drawn up to the same date, or to an earlier date in the same financial year, by a parent undertaking established under the law of a member State of the European Economic Community;

    (b) that those accounts are drawn up and audited, and that parent undertaking's annual report is drawn up, according to that law, in accordance with the provisions of the Seventh Directive (83/349/EEC) (where applicable as modified by the provisions of the Bank Accounts Directive (86/635/EEC) or the Insurance Accounts Directive (91/ 674/EEC));

    (c) that the company discloses in its individual accounts that it is exempt from the obligation to prepare and deliver group accounts;

    (d) that the company states in its individual accounts the name of the parent undertaking which draws up the group accounts referred to above and—

        (i) if it is incorporated outside Great Britain, the country in which it is incorporated,

        (iii) if it is unincorporated, the address of its principal place of business;

    (e) that the company delivers to the registrar, within the period allowed for delivering its individual accounts, copies of those group accounts and of the parent undertaking's annual report, together with the auditors' report on them; and

    (f) (subject to section 710B(6) (delivery of certain Welsh documents without a translation)) that if any document comprised in accounts and reports delivered in accordance with paragraph (e) is in a language other than English, there is annexed to the copy of that document delivered a translation of it into English, certified in the prescribed manner to be a correct translation.

(3) The exemption does not apply to a company any of whose securities are listed on a stock exchange in any member State of the European Economic Community.

(4) Shares held by directors of a company for the purpose of complying with any share qualification requirement shall be disregarded in determining for the purposes of subsection (1)(a) whether the company is a wholly-owned subsidiary.

(5) For the purposes of subsection (1)(b) shares held by a wholly-owned subsidiary of the parent undertaking, or held on behalf of the parent undertaking or a wholly-owned subsidiary, shall be attributed to the parent undertaking.

(6) In subsection (3) 'securities' includes—

    (a) shares and stock,

    (b) debentures, including debenture stock, loan stock, bonds, certificates of deposit and other instruments creating or acknowledging indebtedness,

    (c) warrants or other instruments entitling the holder to subscribe for securities falling within paragraph (a) or (b), and

    (d) certificates or other instruments which confer—

        (i) property rights in respect of a security falling within paragraph (a), (b) or (c),

        (ii) any right to acquire, dispose of, underwrite or convert a security, being a right to which the holder would be entitled if he held any such security to which the certificate or other instrument relates, or

        (iii) a contractual right (other than an option) to acquire any such security otherwise than by subscription.

229   Subsidiary undertakings included in the consolidation

(1) Subject to the exceptions authorised or required by this section, all the subsidiary undertakings of the parent company shall be included in the consolidation.

(2) A subsidiary undertaking may be excluded from consolidation if its inclusion is not material for the purpose of giving a true and fair view; but two or more undertakings may be excluded only if they are not material taken together.

(3) In addition, a subsidiary undertaking may be excluded from consolidation where—

(a) severe long-term restrictions substantially hinder the exercise of the rights of the parent company over the assets or management of that undertaking, or

(b) the information necessary for the preparation of group accounts cannot be obtained without disproportionate expense or undue delay, or

(c) the interest of the parent company is held exclusively with a view to subsequent resale and the undertaking has not previously been included in consolidated group accounts prepared by the parent company.

The reference in paragraph (a) to the rights of the parent company and the reference in paragraph (c) to the interest of the parent company are, respectively, to rights and interests held by or attributed to the company for the purposes of section 258 (definition of 'parent undertaking') in the absence of which it would not be the parent company.

(4) Where the activities of one or more subsidiary undertakings are so different from those of other undertakings to be included in the consolidation that their inclusion would be incompatible with the obligation to give a true and fair view, those undertakings shall be excluded from consolidation.

This subsection does not apply merely because some of the undertakings are industrial, some commercial and some provide services, or because they carry on industrial or commercial activities involving different products or provide different services.

(5) Where all the subsidiary undertakings of a parent company fall within the above exclusions, no group accounts are required.

230 Treatment of individual profit and loss account where group accounts prepared

(1) The following provisions apply with respect to the individual profit and loss account of a parent company where—

(a) the company is required to prepare and does prepare group accounts in accordance with this Act, and

(b) the notes to the company's individual balance sheet show the company's profit or loss for the financial year determined in accordance with this Act.

(2) The profit and loss account need not contain the information specified in paragraphs 52 to 57 of Schedule 4 (information supplementing the profit and loss account).

(3) The profit and loss account must be approved in accordance with section 233(1) (approval by board of directors) but may be omitted from the company's annual accounts for the purposes of the other provisions below in this Chapter.

(4) The exemption conferred by this section is conditional upon its being disclosed in the company's annual accounts that the exemption applies.

231 Disclosure required in notes to accounts: related undertakings

(1) The information specified in Schedule 5 shall be given in notes to a company's annual accounts.

(2) Where the company is not required to prepare group accounts, the information specified in Part I of that Schedule shall be given; and where the company is required to prepare group accounts, the information specified in Part II of that Schedule shall be given.

(3) The information required by Schedule 5 need not be disclosed with respect to an undertaking which—

(a) is established under the law of a country outside the United Kingdom, or

(b) carries on business outside the United Kingdom,

if in the opinion of the directors of the company the disclosure would be seriously prejudicial to the business of that undertaking, or to the business of the company or any of its subsidiary undertakings, and the Secretary of State agrees that the information need not be disclosed.

This subsection does not apply in relation to the information required under paragraph 6, 9A, 20 or 28A of that Schedule.

(4) Where advantage is taken of subsection (3), that fact shall be stated in a note to the company's annual accounts.

(5) If the directors of the company are of the opinion that the number of undertakings in respect of which the company is required to disclose information under any provision of Schedule 5 to this Act is such that compliance with that provision would result in information of excessive length being given, the information need only be given in respect of—

(a) the undertakings whose results or financial position, in the opinion of the directors, principally affected the figures shown in the company's annual accounts, and

(b) undertakings excluded from consolidation under section 229(3) or (4).

(6) If advantage is taken of subsection (5)—

(a) there shall be included in the notes to the company's annual accounts a statement that the information is given only with respect to such undertakings as are mentioned in that subsection, and

(b) the full information (both that which is disclosed in the notes to the accounts and that which is not) shall be annexed to the company's next annual return.

For this purpose the 'next annual return' means that next delivered to the registrar after the accounts in question have been approved under section 233.

(7) If a company fails to comply with subsection (6)(b), the company and every officer of it who is in default is liable to a fine and, for continued contravention, to a daily default fine.

232   Disclosure required in notes to accounts: emoluments and other benefits of directors and others

(1) The information specified in Schedule 6 shall be given in notes to a company's annual accounts, save that the information specified in paragraphs 2–14 in Part I of Schedule 6 shall be given only in the case of a company which is not a quoted company.

(2) In that Schedule—

Part I relates to the emoluments of directors (including emoluments waived), pensions of directors and past directors, compensation for loss of office to directors and past directors and sums paid to third parties in respect of directors' services,

Part II relates to loans, quasi-loans and other dealings in favour of directors and connected persons, and

Part III relates to transactions, arrangements and agreements made by the company or a subsidiary undertaking for officers of the company other than directors.

(3) It is the duty of any director of a company, and any person who is or has at any time in the preceding five years been an officer of the company, to give notice to the company of such matters relating to himself as may be necessary for the purposes of Part I of Schedule 6.

(4) A person who makes default in complying with subsection (3) commits an offence and is liable to a fine.

Approval and signing of accounts

233   Approval and signing of accounts

(1) A company's annual accounts shall be approved by the board of directors and signed on behalf of the board by a director of the company.

(2) The signature shall be on the company's balance sheet.

(3) Every copy of the balance sheet which is laid before the company in general meeting, or which is otherwise circulated, published or issued, shall state the name of the person who signed the balance sheet on behalf of the board.

(4) The copy of the company's balance sheet which is delivered to the registrar shall be signed on behalf of the board by a director of the company.

(5) If annual accounts are approved which do not comply with the requirements of this Act, every director of the company who is party to their approval and who knows that they do not comply or is reckless as to whether they comply is guilty of an offence and liable to a fine.

For this purpose every director of the company at the time the accounts are approved shall be taken to be a party to their approval unless he shows that he took all reasonable steps to prevent their being approved.

(6) If a copy of the balance sheet—

(a) is laid before the company, or otherwise circulated, published or issued, without the balance sheet having been signed as required by this section or without the required statement of the signatory's name being included, or

(b) is delivered to the registrar without being signed as required by this section, the company and every officer of it who is in default is guilty of an offence and liable to a fine.

Directors' report

234   Duty to prepare directors' report

(1) The directors of a company shall for each financial year prepare a report—

(a) containing a fair review of the development of the business of the company and its subsidiary undertakings during the financial year and of their position at the end of it, and

(b) stating the amount (if any) which they recommend should be paid as dividend.

(2) The report shall state the names of the persons who, at any time during the financial year, were directors of the company, and the principal activities of the company and its subsidiary undertakings in the course of the year and any significant change in those activities in the year.

(3) The report shall also comply with Schedule 7 as regards the disclosure of the matters mentioned there.

(4) In Schedule 7—

Part I relates to matters of a general nature, including changes in asset values, directors' shareholdings and other interests and contributions for political and charitable purposes,

Part II relates to the acquisition by a company of its own shares or a charge on them,

Part III relates to the employment, training and advancement of disabled persons,

Part V relates to the involvement of employees in the affairs, policy and performance of the company,

Part VI relates to the company's policy and practice on the payment of creditors.

(5) In the case of any failure to comply with the provisions of this Part as to the preparation of a directors' report and the contents of the report, every person who was a director of the company immediately before the end of the period of laying and delivering accounts and reports for the financial year in question is guilty of an offence and liable to a fine.

(6) In proceedings against a person for an offence under this section it is a defence for him to prove that he took all reasonable steps for securing compliance with the requirements in question.

234A   Approval and signing of directors' report

(1) The directors' report shall be approved by the board of directors and signed on behalf of the board by a director or the secretary of the company.

(2) Every copy of the directors' report which is laid before the company in general meeting, or which is otherwise circulated, published or issued, shall state the name of the person who signed it on behalf of the board.

(3) The copy of the directors' report which is delivered to the registrar shall be signed on behalf of the board by a director or the secretary of the company.

(4) If a copy of the directors' report—

    (a) is laid before the company, or otherwise circulated, published or issued, without the report having been signed as required by this section or without the required statement of the signatory's name being included, or

    (b) is delivered to the registrar without being signed as required by this section, the company and every officer of it who is in default is guilty of an offence and liable to a fine.

Quoted companies: directors' remuneration report

234B   Duty to prepare directors' remuneration report

(1) The directors of a quoted company shall for each financial year prepare a directors' remuneration report which shall contain the information specified in Schedule 7A and comply with any requirement of that Schedule as to how information is to be set out in the report.

(2) In Schedule 7A—

Part 1 is introductory,

Part 2 relates to information about remuneration committees, performance related remuneration and liabilities in respect of directors' contracts,

Part 3 relates to detailed information about directors' remuneration (information included under Part 3 is required to be reported on by the auditors, see section 235), and

Part 4 contains interpretative and supplementary provisions.

(3) In the case of any failure to comply with the provisions of this Part as to the preparation of a directors' remuneration report and the contents of the report, every person who was a director of the quoted company immediately before the end of the period for laying and delivering accounts and reports for the financial year in question is guilty of an offence and liable to a fine.

(4) In proceedings against a person for an offence under subsection (3) it is a defence for him to prove that he took all reasonable steps for securing compliance with the requirements in question.

(5) It is the duty of any director of a company, and any person who has at any time in the preceding five years been a director of the company, to give notice to the company of such matters relating to himself as may be necessary for the purposes of Parts 2 and 3 of Schedule 7A.

(6) A person who makes default in complying with subsection (5) commits an offence and is liable to a fine.

234C   Approval and signing of directors' remuneration report

(1) The directors' remuneration report shall be approved by the board of directors and signed on behalf of the board by a director or the secretary of the company.

(2) Every copy of the directors' remuneration report which is laid before the company in general meeting, or which is otherwise circulated, published or issued, shall state the name of the person who signed it on behalf of the board.

(3) The copy of the directors' remuneration report which is delivered to the registrar shall be signed on behalf of the board by a director or the secretary of the company.

(4) If a copy of the directors' remuneration report—

    (a) is laid before the company, or otherwise circulated, published or issued, without the report having been signed as required by this section or without the required statement of the signatory's name being included, or

    (b) is delivered to the registrar without being signed as required by this section,

the company and every officer of it who is in default is guilty of an offence and liable to a fine.

Auditors' report

235 Auditors' report

(1) A company's auditors shall make a report to the company's members on all annual accounts of the company of which copies are to be laid before the company in general meeting during their tenure of office.

(2) The auditors' report shall state whether in the auditors' opinion the annual accounts have been properly prepared in accordance with this Act, and in particular whether a true and fair view is given—

(a) in the case of an individual balance sheet, of the state of affairs of the company as at the end of the financial year,

(b) in the case of an individual profit and loss account, of the profit or loss of the company for the financial year,

(c) in the case of group accounts, of the state of affairs as at the end of the financial year, and the profit or loss for the financial year, of the undertakings included in the consolidation as a whole, so far as concerns members of the company.

(3) The auditors shall consider whether the information given in the directors' report for the financial year for which the annual accounts are prepared is consistent with those accounts; and if they are of opinion that it is not they shall state that fact in their report.

(4) If a directors' remuneration report is prepared for the financial year for which the annual accounts are prepared the auditors shall in their report—

(a) report to the company's members on the auditable part of the directors' remuneration report, and

(b) state whether in their opinion that part of the directors' remuneration report has been properly prepared in accordance with this Act.

(5) For the purposes of this Part, 'the auditable part' of a directors' remuneration report is the part containing the information required by Part 3 of Schedule 7A.

236 Signature of auditors' report

(1) The auditors' report shall state the names of the auditors and be signed by them.

(2) Every copy of the auditors' report which is laid before the company in general meeting, or which is otherwise circulated, published or issued, shall state the names of the auditors.

(3) The copy of the auditors' report which is delivered to the registrar shall state the names of the auditors and be signed by them.

(4) If a copy of the auditors' report—

(a) is laid before the company, or otherwise circulated, published or issued, without the required statement of the auditors' names, or

(b) is delivered to the registrar without the required statement of the auditors' names or without being signed as required by this section,

the company and every officer of it who is in default is guilty of an offence and liable to a fine.

(5) References in this section to signature by the auditors are, where the office of auditor is held by a body corporate or partnership, to signature in the name of the body corporate or partnership by a person authorised to sign on its behalf.

237 Duties of auditors

(1) A company's auditors shall, in preparing their report, carry out such investigations as will enable them to form an opinion as to—

(a) whether proper accounting records have been kept by the company and proper returns adequate for their audit have been received from branches not visited by them, and

(b) whether the company's individual accounts are in agreement with the accounting records and returns, and

(c) (in the case of a quoted company) whether the auditable part of the company's directors' remuneration report is in agreement with the accounting records and returns.

(2) If the auditors are of opinion that proper accounting records have not been kept, or that proper returns adequate for their audit have not been received from branches not visited by them, or if the company's individual accounts are not in agreement with the accounting records and returns, or if in the case of a quoted company the auditable part of its directors' remuneration report is not in agreement with the accounting records and returns, the auditors shall state the fact in their report.

(3) If the auditors fail to obtain all the information and explanations which, to the best of their knowledge and belief, are necessary for the purposes of their audit, they shall state that fact in their report.

(4) If—

(a) the requirements of Schedule 6 (disclosure of information: emoluments and other benefits of directors and others) are not complied with in the annual accounts, or

(b) where a directors' remuneration report is required to be prepared, the requirements of Part 3 of Schedule 7A (directors' remuneration report) are not complied with in that report,

the auditors shall include in their report, so far as they are reasonably able to do so, a statement giving the required particulars.

(4A) If the directors of the company have taken advantage of the exemption conferred by section 248 (exemption for small and medium-sized groups from the need to prepare group accounts) and in the auditors' opinion they were not entitled so to do, the auditors shall state that fact in their report.

Publication of accounts and reports

238 Persons entitled to receive copies of accounts and reports

(1) A copy of each of the documents mentioned in subsection (1A) shall be sent to—

(a) every member of the company,

(b) every holder of the company's debentures, and

(c) every person who is entitled to receive notice of general meetings,

not less than 21 days before the date of the meeting at which copies of those documents are to be laid in accordance with section 241.

(1A) Those documents are—

(a) the company's annual accounts for the financial year,

(b) the directors' report for that financial year,

(c) (in the case of a quoted company) the directors' remuneration report for that financial year, and

(d) the auditors' report on those accounts or (in the case of a quoted company) on those accounts and the auditable part of the directors' remuneration report.

(2) Copies need not be sent—

(a) to a person who is not entitled to receive notices of general meetings and of whose address the company is unaware, or

(b) to more than one of the joint holders of shares or debentures none of whom is entitled to receive such notices, or

(c) in the case of joint holders of shares or debentures some of whom are, and some not, entitled to receive such notices, to those who are not so entitled.

(3) In the case of a company not having a share capital, copies need not be sent to anyone who is not entitled to receive notices of general meetings of the company.

(4) If copies are sent less than 21 days before the date of the meeting, they shall, notwithstanding that fact, be deemed to have been duly sent if it is so agreed by all the members entitled to attend and vote at the meeting.

(4A) References in this section to sending to any person copies of the documents mentioned in subsection (1A) include references to using electronic communications for sending copies of those documents to such address as may for the time being be notified to the company by that person for that purpose.

(4B) For the purposes of this section copies of those documents are also to be treated as sent to a person where—

(a) the company and that person have agreed to his having access to the documents on a web site (instead of their being sent to him);

(b) the documents are documents to which that agreement applies; and

(c) that person is notified, in a manner for the time being agreed for the purpose between him and the company, of—

(i) the publication of the documents on a web site;

(ii) the address of that web site; and

(iii) the place on that web site where the documents may be accessed, and how they may be accessed.

(4C) For the purposes of this section documents treated in accordance with subsection (4B) as sent to any person are to be treated as sent to him not less than 21 days before the date of a meeting if, and only if—

(a) the documents are published on the web site throughout a period beginning at least 21 days before the date of the meeting and ending with the conclusion of the meeting; and

(b) the notification given for the purposes of paragraph (c) of that subsection is given not less than 21 days before the date of the meeting.

(4D) Nothing in subsection (4C) shall invalidate the proceedings of a meeting where—

(a) any documents that are required to be published as mentioned in paragraph (a) of that subsection are published for a part, but not all, of the period mentioned in that paragraph; and

(b) the failure to publish those documents throughout that period is wholly attributable to circumstances which it would not be reasonable to have expected the company to prevent or avoid.

(4E) A company may, notwithstanding any provision to the contrary in its articles, take advantage of any of subsections (4A) to (4D).

(5) If default is made in complying with this section, the company and every officer of it who is in default is guilty of an offence and liable to a fine.

(6) Where copies are sent out under this section over a period of days, references elsewhere in this Act to the day on which copies are sent out shall be construed as references to the last day of that period.

239   Right to demand copies of accounts and reports

(1) Any member of a company and any holder of a company's debentures is entitled to be furnished, on demand and without charge, with a copy of—

(a) the company's last annual accounts,

(b) the last directors' report,

(c) (in the case of a quoted company) the last directors' remuneration report, and

(d) the auditors' report on those accounts or (in the case of a quoted company) on those accounts and the auditable part of the directors' remuneration report for the financial year for which those accounts are prepared.

(2) The entitlement under this section is to a single copy of those documents, but that is in addition to any copy to which a person may be entitled under section 238.

(2A) Any obligation by virtue of subsection (1) to furnish a person with a document may be complied with by using electronic communications for sending that document to such address as may for the time being be notified to the company by that person for that purpose.

(2B) A company may, notwithstanding any provision to the contrary in its articles, take advantage of subsection (2A).

(3) If a demand under this section is not complied with within seven days, the company and every officer of it who is in default is guilty of an offence and liable to a fine and, for continued contravention, to a daily default fine.

(4) If in proceedings for such an offence the issue arises whether a person had already been furnished with a copy of the relevant document under this section, it is for the defendant to prove that he had.

240 Requirements in connection with publication of accounts

(1) If a company publishes any of its statutory accounts, they must be accompanied by the relevant auditors' report under section 235 or, as the case may be, the relevant report made for the purposes of section 249A(2).

(2) A company which is required to prepare group accounts for a financial year shall not publish its statutory individual accounts for that year without also publishing with them its statutory group accounts.

(3) If a company publishes non-statutory accounts, it shall publish with them a statement indicating—

(a) that they are not the company's statutory accounts,

(b) whether statutory accounts dealing with any financial year with which the non-statutory accounts purport to deal have been delivered to the registrar,

(c) whether the company's auditors have made a report under section 235 on the statutory accounts for any such financial year and, if no such report has been made, whether the company's reporting accountant has made a report for the purposes of section 249A(2) on the statutory accounts for any such financial year, and

(d) whether any auditors' report so made was qualified or contained a statement under section 237(2) or (3) (accounting records or returns inadequate, accounts not agreeing with records and returns or failure to obtain necessary information and explanations) or whether any report made for the purposes of section 249A(2) was qualified;

and it shall not publish with the non-statutory accounts any auditors' report under section 235 or any report made for the purposes of section 249A(2).

(4) For the purposes of this section a company shall be regarded as publishing a document if it publishes, issues or circulates it or otherwise makes it available for public inspection in a manner calculated to invite members of the public generally, or any class of members of the public, to read it.

(5) References in this section to a company's statutory accounts are to its individual or group accounts for a financial year as required to be delivered to the registrar under section 242; and references to the publication by a company of 'non-statutory accounts' are to the publication of—

(a) any balance sheet or profit and loss account relating to, or purporting to deal with, a financial year of the company, or

(b) an account in any form purporting to be a balance sheet or profit and loss account for the group consisting of the company and its subsidiary undertakings relating to, or purporting to deal with, a financial year of the company,

otherwise than as part of the company's statutory accounts.

(6) A company which contravenes any provision of this section, and any officer of it who is in default, is guilty of an offence and liable to a fine.

Laying and delivering of accounts and reports

241   Accounts and reports to be laid before company in general meeting

(1) The directors of a company shall in respect of each financial year lay before the company in general meeting copies of—

- (a) the company's annual accounts,
- (b) the directors' report,
- (c) (in the case of a quoted company) the directors' remuneration report, and
- (d) the auditors' report on those accounts or (in the case of a quoted company) on those accounts and the auditable part of the directors' remuneration report.

(2) If the requirements of subsection (1) are not complied with before the end of the period allowed for laying and delivering accounts and reports, every person who immediately before the end of that period was a director of the company is guilty of an offence and liable to a fine and, for continued contravention, to a daily default fine.

(3) It is a defence for a person charged with such an offence to prove that he took all reasonable steps for securing that those requirements would be complied with before the end of that period.

(4) It is not a defence to prove that the documents in question were not in fact prepared as required by this Part.

241A   Members' approval of directors' remuneration report

(1) This section applies to every company that is a quoted company immediately before the end of a financial year.

(2) In this section 'the meeting' means the general meeting of the company before which the company's annual accounts for the financial year are to be laid.

(3) The company must, prior to the meeting, give to the members of the company entitled to be sent notice of the meeting notice of the intention to move at the meeting, as an ordinary resolution, a resolution approving the directors' remuneration report for the financial year.

(4) Notice under subsection (3) shall be given to each such member in any manner permitted for the service on him of notice of the meeting.

(5) The business that may be dealt with at the meeting includes the resolution.

(6) The existing directors must ensure that the resolution is put to the vote of the meeting.

(7) Subsection (5) has effect notwithstanding—

- (a) any default in complying with subsections (3) and (4);
- (b) anything in the company's articles.

(8) No entitlement of a person to remuneration is made conditional on the resolution being passed by reason only of the provision made by this section.

(9) In the event of default in complying with the requirements of subsections (3) and (4), every officer of the company who is in default is liable to a fine.

(10) If the resolution is not put to the vote of the meeting, each existing director is guilty of an offence and liable to a fine.

(11) If an existing director is charged with an offence under subsection (10), it is a defence for him to prove that he took all reasonable steps for securing that the resolution was put to the vote of the meeting.

(12) In this section 'existing director' means a person who, immediately before the meeting, is a director of the company.

242   Accounts and reports to be delivered to the registrar

(1) The directors of a company shall in respect of each financial year deliver to the registrar a copy of—

- (a) the company's annual accounts,
- (b) the directors' report,
- (c) (in the case of a quoted company) the directors' remuneration report, and

(d) the auditors' report on those accounts or (in the case of a quoted company) on those accounts and the auditable part of the directors' remuneration report.

If any document comprised in those accounts or reports is in a language other than English then, subject to section 710B(6) (delivery of certain Welsh documents without a translation), the directors shall annex to the copy of that document delivered a translation of it into English, certified in the prescribed manner to be a correct translation.

(2) If the requirements of subsection (1) are not complied with before the end of the period allowed for laying and delivering accounts and reports, every person who immediately before the end of that period was a director of the company is guilty of an offence and liable to a fine and, for continued contravention, to a daily default fine.

(3) Further, if the directors of the company fail to make good the default within 14 days after the service of a notice on them requiring compliance, the court may on the application of any member or creditor of the company or of the registrar, make an order directing the directors (or any of them) to make good the default within such time as may be specified in the order.

The court's order may provide that all costs of and incidental to the application shall be borne by the directors.

(4) It is a defence of a person charged with an offence under this section to prove that he took all reasonable steps for securing that the requirements of subsection (1) would be complied with before the end of the period allowed for laying and delivering accounts and reports.

(5) It is not a defence in any proceedings under this section to prove that the documents in question were not in fact prepared as required by this Part.

[*The amendment to s. 242(1) made by SI 2002/1986, reg. 10(8), is expressed in such a way that it repeals the second paragraph of the subsection, but that repeal is clearly not intended.*]

242A   Civil penalty for failure to deliver accounts

(1) Where the requirements of section 242(1) are not complied with before the end of the period allowed for laying and delivering accounts and reports, the company is liable to a civil penalty.

This is in addition to any liability of the directors under section 242.

(2) The amount of the penalty is determined by reference to the length of the period between the end of the period allowed for laying and delivering accounts and reports and the day on which the requirements are complied with, and whether the company is a public or private company, as follows:—

Length of period	Public company	Private company
Not more than 3 months.	£500	£100
More than 3 months but not more than 6 months.	£1,000	£250
More than 6 months but not more than 12 months.	£2,000	£500
More than 12 months.	£5,000	£1,000

(3) The penalty may be recovered by the registrar and shall be paid by him into the Consolidated Fund.

(4) It is not a defence in proceedings under this section to prove that the documents in question were not in fact prepared as required by this Part.

242B   Delivery and publication of accounts in ECUs

(1) The amount set out in the annual accounts of a company may also be shown in the same accounts translated into ECUs.

(2) When complying with section 242, the directors of a company may deliver to the registrar an additional copy of the company's annual accounts in which the amounts have been translated into ECUs.

(3) In both cases—

(a) the amounts must have been translated at the relevant exchange rate prevailing on the balance sheet date, and

(b) that rate must be disclosed in the notes to the accounts.

(4) For the purposes of section 240 any additional copy of the company's annual accounts delivered to the registrar under subsection (2) shall be treated as statutory accounts of the company and, in the case of such a copy, references in section 240 to the auditors' report under section 235 shall be read as references to the auditors' report on the annual accounts of which it is a copy.

(5) In this section—

'ECU' means a unit with a value equal to the value of the unit of account known as the ecu used in the European Monetary System, and

'relevant exchange rate' means the rate of exchange used for translating the value of the ecu for the purposes of that System.

243   Accounts of subsidiary undertakings to be appended in certain cases

(1) The following provisions apply where at the end of the financial year a parent company has as a subsidiary undertaking—

    (a) a body corporate incorporated outside Great Britain which does not have an established place of business in Great Britain, or

    (b) an unincorporated undertaking, which is excluded from consolidation in accordance with section 229(4) (undertaking with activities different from the undertakings included in the consolidation).

(2) There shall be appended to the copy of the company's annual accounts delivered to the registrar in accordance with section 242 a copy of the undertaking's latest individual accounts and, if it is a parent undertaking, its latest group accounts.

If the accounts appended are required by law to be audited, a copy of the auditors' report shall also be appended.

(3) The accounts must be for a period ending not more than twelve months before the end of the financial year for which the parent company's accounts are made up.

(4) If any document required to be appended is in a language other than English then, subject to section 710B(6) (delivery of certain Welsh documents without a translation), the directors shall annex to the copy of that document delivered a translation of it into English certified in the prescribed manner to be a correct translation.

(5) The above requirements are subject to the following qualifications—

    (a) an undertaking is not required to prepare for the purposes of this section accounts which would not otherwise be prepared, and if no accounts satisfying the above requirements are prepared none need be appended;

    (b) a document need not be appended if it would not otherwise be required to be published, or made available for public inspection, anywhere in the world, but in that case the reason for not appending it shall be stated in a note to the company's accounts;

    (c) where an undertaking and all its subsidiary undertakings are excluded from consolidation in accordance with section 229(4), the accounts of such of the subsidiary undertakings of that undertaking as are included in its consolidated group accounts need not be appended.

(6) Subsections (2) to (4) of section 242 (penalties, &c. in case of default) apply in relation to the requirements of this section as they apply in relation to the requirements of subsection (1) of that section.

244   Period allowed for laying and delivering accounts and reports

(1) The period allowed for laying and delivering accounts and reports is—

    (a) for a private company, 10 months after the end of the relevant accounting reference period, and

    (b) for a public company, 7 months after the end of that period.

This is subject to the following provisions of this section.

(2) If the relevant accounting reference period is the company's first and is a period of more than 12 months, the period allowed is—

    (a) 10 months or 7 months, as the case may be, from the first anniversary of the incorporation of the company, or

    (b) 3 months from the end of the accounting reference period, whichever last expires.

(3) Where a company carries on business, or has interests, outside the United Kingdom, the Channel Islands and the Isle of Man, the directors may, in respect of any financial year, give to the registrar before the end of the period allowed by subsection (1) or (2) a notice in the prescribed form—

    (a) stating that the company so carries on business or has such interests, and

    (b) claiming a 3 month extension of the period allowed for laying and delivering accounts and reports;

and upon such a notice being given the period is extended accordingly.

(4) If the relevant accounting period is treated as shortened by virtue of a notice given by the company under section 225 (alteration of accounting reference date), the period allowed for laying and delivering accounts is that applicable in accordance with the above provisions or 3 months from the date of the notice under that section, whichever last expires.

(5) If for any special reason the Secretary of State thinks fit he may, on an application made before the expiry of the period otherwise allowed, by notice in writing to a company extend that period by such further period as may be specified in the notice.

(6) In this section 'the relevant accounting reference period' means the accounting reference period by reference to which the financial year for the accounts in question was determined.

Revision of defective accounts and reports

245   Voluntary revision of annual accounts or directors' report

(1) If it appears to the directors of a company that any annual accounts of the company, or any directors' report or directors' remuneration report, did not comply with the requirements of this Act, they may prepare revised accounts or a revised report.

(2) Where copies of the previous accounts or report have been laid before the company in general meeting or delivered to the registrar, the revisions shall be confined to—

    (a) the correction of those respects in which the previous accounts or report did not comply with the requirements of this Act, and

    (b) the making of any necessary consequential alterations.

(3) The Secretary of State may make provision by regulations as to the application of the provisions of this Act in relation to revised annual accounts or a revised directors' report or a revised directors' remuneration report.

(4) The regulations may, in particular—

    (a) make different provision according to whether the previous accounts or report are replaced or are supplemented by a document indicating the corrections to be made;

    (b) make provision with respect to the functions of the company's auditors or reporting accountant in relation to the revised accounts or report;

    (c) require the directors to take such steps as may be specified in the regulations where the previous accounts or report have been—

        (i) sent out to members and others under section 238(1),

        (ii) laid before the company in general meeting, or

        (iii) delivered to the registrar,

or where a summary financial statement based on the previous accounts or report has been sent to members under section 251;

    (d) apply the provisions of this Act (including those creating criminal offences) subject to such additions, exceptions and modifications as are specified in the regulations.

(5) Regulations under this section shall be made by statutory instrument which shall be subject to annulment in pursuance of a resolution of either House of Parliament.

245A   Secretary of State's notice in respect of annual accounts

(1) Where copies of a company's annual accounts have been sent out under section 238, or a copy of a company's annual accounts has been laid before the company in general meeting or delivered to the registrar, and it appears to the Secretary of State that there is, or may be, a question whether the accounts comply with the requirements of this Act, he may give notice to the directors of the company indicating the respects in which it appears to him that such a question arises, or may arise.

(2) The notice shall specify a period of not less than one month for the directors to give him an explanation of the accounts or prepare revised accounts.

(3) If at the end of the specified period, or such longer period as he may allow, it appears to the Secretary of State that no satisfactory explanation of the accounts has been given and that the accounts have not been revised so as to comply with the requirements of this Act, he may if he thinks fit apply to the court.

(4) The provisions of this section apply equally to revised annual accounts, in which case the references to revised accounts shall be read as references to further revised accounts.

245B   Application to court in respect of defective accounts

(1) An application may be made to the court—
    (a) by the Secretary of State, after having complied with section 245A, or
    (b) by a person authorised by the Secretary of State for the purposes of this section,
for a declaration or declarator that the annual accounts of a company do not comply with the requirements of this Act and for an order requiring the directors of the company to prepare revised accounts.

(2) Notice of the application, together with a general statement of the matters at issue in the proceedings, shall be given by the applicant to the registrar for registration.

(3) If the court orders the preparation of revised accounts, it may give directions with respect to—
    (a) the auditing of the accounts,
    (b) the revision of any directors' report, directors' remuneration report or summary financial statement, and
    (c) the taking of steps by the directors to bring the making of the order to the notice of persons likely to rely on the previous accounts,
and such other matters as the court thinks fit.

(4) If the court finds that the accounts did not comply with the requirements of this Act it may order that all or part of—
    (a) the costs (or in Scotland expenses) of and incidental to the application, and
    (b) any reasonable expenses incurred by the company in connection with or in consequence of the preparation of revised accounts,
shall be borne by such of the directors as were party to the approval of the defective accounts.

For this purpose every director of the company at the time the accounts were approved shall be taken to have been a party to their approval unless he shows that he took all reasonable steps to prevent their being approved.

(5) Where the court makes an order under subsection (4) it shall have regard to whether the directors party to the approval of the defective accounts knew or ought to have known that the accounts did not comply with the requirements of this Act, and it may exclude one or more directors from the order or order the payment of different amounts by different directors.

(6) On the conclusion of proceedings on an application under this section, the applicant shall give to the registrar for registration an office copy of the court order or, as the case may be, notice that the application has failed or been withdrawn.

(7) The provisions of this section apply equally to revised annual accounts, in which case the references to revised accounts shall be read as references to further revised accounts.

245C   Other persons authorised to apply to court

(1) The Secretary of State may authorise for the purposes of section 245B any person appearing to him—

   (a) to have an interest in, and to have satisfactory procedures directed to securing, compliance by companies with the accounting requirements of this Act.

   (b) to have satisfactory procedures for receiving and investigating complaints about the annual accounts of companies, and

   (c) otherwise to be a fit and proper person to be authorised.

(2) A person may be authorised generally or in respect of particular classes of case, and different persons may be authorised in respect of different classes of case.

(3) The Secretary of State may refuse to authorise a person if he considers that his authorisation is unnecessary having regard to the fact that there are one or more other persons who have been or are likely to be authorised.

(4) Authorisation shall be by order made by statutory instrument which shall be subject to annulment in pursuance of a resolution of either House of Parliament.

(5) Where authorisation is revoked, the revoking order may make such provision as the Secretary of State thinks fit with respect to pending proceedings.

(6) Neither a person authorised under this section, nor any officer, servant or member of the governing body of such a person, shall be liable in damages for anything done or purporting to be done for the purposes of or in connection with—

   (a) the taking of steps to discover whether there are grounds for an application to the court,

   (b) the determination whether or not to make such an application, or

   (c) the publication of its reasons for any such decision, unless the act or omission is shown to have been in bad faith.

CHAPTER II   EXEMPTIONS, EXCEPTIONS AND SPECIAL PROVISIONS

Small and medium-sized companies and groups

246   Special provisions for small companies

(1) Subject to section 247A, this section applies where a company qualifies as a small company in relation to a financial year.

(2) If the company's individual accounts for the year—

   (a) comply with the provisions of Schedule 8, or

   (b) fail to comply with those provisions only in so far as they comply instead with one or more corresponding provisions of Schedule 4,

they need not comply with the provisions or, as the case may be, the remaining provisions of Schedule 4; and where advantage is taken of this subsection, references in section 226 to compliance with the provisions of Schedule 4 shall be construed accordingly.

(3) The company's individual accounts for the year—

   (a) may give the total of the aggregates required by paragraphs (a), (c) and (d) of paragraph 1(1) of Schedule 6 (emoluments and other benefits etc. of directors) instead of giving those aggregates individually; and

   (b) need not give the information required by—

      (i) paragraph 4 of Schedule 5 (financial years of subsidiary undertakings);

      (ii) paragraph 1(2)(b) of Schedule 6 (numbers of directors exercising share options and receiving shares under long term incentive schemes);

      (iii) paragraph 2 of Schedule 6 (details of highest paid director's emoluments etc.); or

(iv) paragraph 7 of Schedule 6 (excess retirement benefits of directors and past directors).

(4) The directors' report for the year need not give the information required by—

(a) section 234(1)(a) and (b) (fair review of business and amount to be paid as dividend);

(b) paragraph 1(2) of Schedule 7 (statement of market value of fixed assets where substantially different from balance sheet amount);

(c) paragraph 6 of Schedule 7 (miscellaneous disclosures); or

(d) paragraph 11 of Schedule 7 (employee involvement).

(5) Notwithstanding anything in section 242(1), the directors of the company need not deliver to the registrar any of the following, namely—

(a) a copy of the company's profit and loss account for the year;

(b) a copy of the directors' report for the year; and

(c) if they deliver a copy of a balance sheet drawn up as at the last day of the year which complies with the requirements of Schedule 8A, a copy of the company's balance sheet drawn up as at that day.

(6) Neither a copy of the company's accounts for the year delivered to the registrar under section 242(1), nor a copy of a balance sheet delivered to the registrar under subsection (5)(c), need give the information required by—

(a) paragraph 4 of Schedule 5 (financial years of subsidiary undertakings);

(b) paragraph 6 of Schedule 5 (shares of company held by subsidiary undertakings);

(c) Part I of Schedule 6 (directors' and chairman's emoluments, pensions and compensation for loss of office); or

(d) section 390A(3) (amount of auditors' remuneration).

(7) The provisions of section 233 as to the signing of the copy of the balance sheet delivered to the registrar apply to a copy of a balance sheet delivered under subsection (5)(c).

(8) Subject to subsection (9), each of the following, namely—

(a) accounts prepared in accordance with subsection (2) or (3),

(b) a report prepared in accordance with subsection (4), and

(c) a copy of accounts delivered to the registrar in accordance with subsection (5) or (6),

shall contain a statement in a prominent position on the balance sheet, in the report or, as the case may be, on the copy of the balance sheet, above the signature required by section 233, 234A or subsection (7), that they are prepared in accordance with the special provisions of this Part relating to small companies.

(9) Subsection (8) does not apply where the directors of the company have taken advantage of the exemption from audit conferred by section 249AA (dormant companies).

246A   Special provisions for medium-sized companies

(1) Subject to section 247A, this section applies where a company qualifies as a medium-sized company in relation to a financial year.

(2) The company's individual accounts for the year need not comply with the requirements of paragraph 36A of Schedule 4 (disclosure with respect to compliance with accounting standards).

(3) The company may deliver to the registrar a copy of the company's accounts for the year—

(a) which includes a profit and loss account in which the following items listed in the profit and loss account formats set out in Part I of Schedule 4 are combined as one item under the heading 'gross profit or loss'—

Items 1, 2, 3 and 6 in Format 1;

Items 1 to 5 in Format 2;

Items A.1, B.1 and B.2 in Format 3;

Items A.1, A.2 and B.1 to B.4 in Format 4;

    (b) which does not contain the information required by paragraph 55 of Schedule 4 (particulars of turnover).

    (4) A copy of accounts delivered to the registrar in accordance with subsection (3) shall contain a statement in a prominent position on the copy of the balance sheet, above the signature required by section 233, that the accounts are prepared in accordance with the special provisions of this Part relating to medium-sized companies.

247   Qualification of company as small or medium-sized

    (1) A company qualifies as small or medium-sized in relation to a financial year if the qualifying conditions are met—

    (a) in the case of the company's first financial year, in that year, and

    (b) in the case of any subsequent financial year, in that year and the preceding year.

    (2) A company shall be treated as qualifying as small or medium-sized in relation to a financial year—

    (a) if it so qualified in relation to the previous financial year under subsection (1) above or was treated as so qualifying under paragraph (b) below; or

    (b) if it was treated as so qualifying in relation to the previous year by virtue of paragraph (a) and the qualifying conditions are met in the year in question.

    (3) The qualifying conditions are met by a company in a year in which it satisfies two or more of the following requirements—

Small company

1. Turnover	Not more than £2.8 million
2. Balance sheet total	Not more than £1.4 million
3. Number of employees	Not more than 50

Medium-sized company

1. Turnover	Not more than £11.2 million
2. Balance sheet total	Not more than £5.6 million
3. Number of employees	Not more than 250

    (4) For a period which is a company's financial year but not in fact a year the maximum figures for turnover shall be proportionately adjusted.

    (5) The balance sheet total means—

    (a) where in the company's accounts Format 1 of the balance sheet formats set out in Part I of Schedule 4 or Part I of Schedule 8 is adopted, the aggregate of the amounts shown in the balance sheet under the headings corresponding to items A to D in that Format, and

    (b) where Format 2 is adopted, the aggregate of the amounts shown under the general heading 'Assets'.

    (6) The number of employees means the average number of persons employed by the company in the year (determined on a monthly basis).

    That number shall be determined by applying the method of calculation prescribed by paragraph 56(2) and (3) of Schedule 4 for determining the corresponding number required to be stated in a note to the company's accounts.

247A   Cases in which special provisions do not apply

    (1) Nothing in section 246 or 246A shall apply where—

    (a) the company is, or was at any time within the financial year to which the accounts relate—

       (i) a public company,

      (ii) a person who has permission under Part IV of the Financial Services and Markets Act 2000 to carry on one or more regulated activities, or

(iii) a person who carries on insurance market activity; or

(b) the company is, or was at any time during that year, a member of an ineligible group.

(2) A group is ineligible if any of its members is—

(a) a public company or a body corporate which (not being a company) has power under its constitution to offer its shares or debentures to the public and may lawfully exercise that power,

(b) a person who has permission under Part IV of the Financial Services and Markets Act 2000 to carry on a regulated activity, or

(c) a person who carries on an insurance market activity.

(3) A parent company shall not be treated as qualifying as a small company in relation to a financial year unless the group headed by it qualifies as a small group, and shall not be treated as qualifying as a medium-sized company in relation to a financial year unless that group qualifies as a medium-sized group (see section 249).

247B   Special auditors' report

(1) This section applies where—

(a) the directors of a company propose to deliver to the registrar copies of accounts ('abbreviated accounts') prepared in accordance with section 246(5) or (6) or 246A(3) ('the relevant provision'),

(b) the directors have not taken advantage of the exemption from audit conferred by section 249A(1) or (2) or section 249AA.

(2) If abbreviated accounts prepared in accordance with the relevant provision are delivered to the registrar, they shall be accompanied by a copy of a special report of the auditors stating that in their opinion—

(a) the company is entitled to deliver abbreviated accounts prepared in accordance with that provision, and

(b) the abbreviated accounts to be delivered are properly prepared in accordance with that provision.

(3) In such a case a copy of the auditors' report under section 235 need not be delivered, but—

(a) if that report was qualified, the special report shall set out that report in full together with any further material necessary to understand the qualification; and

(b) if that report contained a statement under—

(i) section 237(2) (accounts, records or returns inadequate or accounts not agreeing with records and returns), or

(ii) section 237(3) (failure to obtain necessary information and explanations), the special report shall set out that statement in full.

(4) Section 236 (signature of auditors' report) applies to a special report under this section as it applies to a report under section 235.

(5) If abbreviated accounts prepared in accordance with the relevant provision are delivered to the registrar, references in section 240 (requirements in connection with publication of accounts) to the auditors' report under section 235 shall be read as references to the special auditors' report under this section.

248   Exemption for small and medium-sized groups

(1) A parent company need not prepare group accounts for a financial year in relation to which the group headed by that company qualifies as a small or medium-sized group and is not an ineligible group.

(2) A group is ineligible if any of its members is—

(a) a public company or a body corporate which (not being a company) has power under its constitution to offer its shares or debentures to the public and may lawfully exercise that power,

(b) a person who has permission under Part IV of the Financial Services and Markets Act 2000 to carry on a regulated activity, or

(c) a person who carries on an insurance market activity.

248A Group accounts prepared by small company

(1) This section applies where a small company—

(a) has prepared individual accounts for a financial year in accordance with section 246(2) or (3), and

(b) is preparing group accounts in respect of the same year.

(2) If the group accounts—

(a) comply with the provisions of Schedule 8, or

(b) fail to comply with those provisions only in so far as they comply instead with one or more corresponding provisions of Schedule 4,

they need not comply with the provisions or, as the case may be, the remaining provisions of Schedule 4; and where advantage is taken of this subsection, references in Schedule 4A to compliance with the provisions of Schedule 4 shall be construed accordingly.

(3) For the purposes of this section, Schedule 8 shall have effect as if, in each balance sheet format set out in that Schedule, for item B.III there were substituted the following item—

'B.III Investments

1. Shares in group undertakings

2. Interests in associated undertakings

3. Other participating interests

4. Loans to group undertakings and undertakings in which a participating interest is held

5. Other investments other than loans

6. Others.'

(4) The group accounts need not give the information required by the provisions specified in section 246(3).

(5) Group accounts prepared in accordance with this section shall contain a statement in a prominent position on the balance sheet, above the signature required by section 233, that they are prepared in accordance with the special provisions of this Part relating to small companies.

249 Qualification of group as small or medium-sized

(1) A group qualifies as small or medium-sized in relation to a financial year if the qualifying conditions are met—

(a) in the case of the parent company's first financial year, in that year, and

(b) in the case of any subsequent financial year, in that year and the preceding year.

(2) A group shall be treated as qualifying as small or medium-sized in relation to a financial year—

(a) if it so qualified in relation to the previous financial year under subsection (1) above or was treated as so qualifying under paragraph (b) below; or

(b) if it was treated as so qualifying in relation to the previous year by virtue of paragraph (a) and the qualifying conditions are met in the year in question.

(3) The qualifying conditions are met by a group in a year in which it satisfies two or more of the following requirements—

Small group

1.	Aggregate turnover	Not more than £2.8 million net (or £3.36 million gross)
2.	Aggregate balance sheet total	Not more than £1.4 million net (or £1.68 million gross)
3.	Aggregatenumberofemployees	Not more than 50

Medium-sized group

1. Aggregate turnover
2. Aggregate balance sheet total
3. Aggregate number of employees

Not more than £11.2 million net (or £13.44 million gross)
Not more than £5.6 million net (or £6.72 million gross)
Not more than 50

(4) The aggregate figures shall be ascertained by aggregating the relevant figures determined in accordance with section 247 for each member of the group.

In relation to the aggregate figures for turnover and balance sheet total, 'net' means with the set-offs and other adjustments required by Schedule 4A in the case of group accounts and 'gross' means without those set-offs and other adjustments; and a company may satisfy the relevant requirement on the basis of either the net or the gross figure.

(5) The figures for each subsidiary undertaking shall be those included in its accounts for the relevant financial year, that is—

(a) if its financial year ends with that of the parent company, that financial year, and
(b) if not, its financial year ending last before the end of the financial year of the parent company.

(6) If those figures cannot be obtained without disproportionate expense or undue delay, the latest available figures shall be taken.

Exemptions from audit for certain categories of small company

249A   Exemptions from audit

(1) Subject to section 249B, a company which meets the total exemption conditions set out below in respect of a financial year is exempt from the provisions of this Part relating to the audit of accounts in respect of that year.

(2) Subject to section 249B, a company which is a charity and which meets the report conditions set out below in respect of a financial year is exempt from the provisions of this Part relating to the audit of accounts in respect of that year if the directors cause a report in respect of the company's individual accounts for that year to be prepared in accordance with section 249C and made to the company's members.

(3) The total exemption conditions are met by a company in respect of a financial year if—

(a) it qualifies as a small company in relation to that year for the purposes of section 246,
(b) its turnover in that year is not more than £1 million, and
(c) its balance sheet total for that year is not more than £1.4 million.

(3A) In relation to any company which is a charity, subsection (3)(b) shall have effect with the substitution—

(a) for the reference to turnover of a reference to gross income, and
(b) for the reference to £1 million of a reference to £90,000.

(4) The report conditions are met by a company which is a charity in respect of a financial year if—

(a) it qualifies as a small company in relation to that year for the purposes of section 246,
(b) its gross income in that year is more than £90,000 but not more than £250,000, and
(c) its balance sheet total for that year is not more than £1.4 million.

(6) For a period which is a company's financial year but not in fact a year the maximum figures for turnover or gross income shall be proportionately adjusted.

(6A) A company is entitled to the exemption conferred by subsection (1) or (2) notwithstanding that it falls within paragraph (a) or (b) of section 249AA(1).

(7) In this section—

'balance sheet total' has the meaning given by section 247(5), and

'gross income' means the company's income from all sources, as shown in the company's income and expenditure account.

249AA   Dormant companies

(1) Subject to section 249B(2) to (5), a company is exempt from the provisions of this Part relating to the audit of accounts in respect of a financial year if—

    (a) it has been dormant since its formation, or

    (b) it has been dormant since the end of the previous financial year and subsection (2) applies.

(2) This subsection applies if the company—

    (a) is entitled in respect of its individual accounts for the financial year in question to prepare accounts in accordance with section 246, or would be so entitled but for the application of section 247A(1)(a)(i) or (b), and

    (b) is not required to prepare group accounts for that year.

(3) Subsection (1) does not apply if at any time in the financial year in question the company was—

    (a) a person who has permission under Part IV of the Financial Services and Markets Act 2000 to carry on one or more regulated activities; or

    (b) a person who carries on insurance market activity.

(4) A company is 'dormant' during any period in which it has no significant accounting transaction.

(5) 'Significant accounting transaction' means a transaction which—

    (a) is required by section 221 to be entered in the company's accounting records; but

    (b) is not a transaction to which subsection (6) or (7) applies.

(6) This subsection applies to a transaction arising from the taking of shares in the company by a subscriber to the memorandum as a result of an undertaking of his in the memorandum.

(7) This subsection applies to a transaction consisting of the payment of—

    (a) a fee to the registrar on a change of name under section 28 (change of name),

    (b) a fee to the registrar on the re-registration of a company under Part II (re-registration as a means of altering a company's status),

    (c) a penalty under section 242A (penalty for failure to deliver accounts), or

    (d) a fee to the registrar for the registration of an annual return under Chapter III of Part XI.

249B   Cases where exemptions not available

(1) Subject to subsections (1A) to (1C), a company is not entitled to the exemption conferred by subsection (1) or (2) of section 249A in respect of a financial year if at any time within that year—

    (a) it was a public company,

    (b) it was a person who had permission under Part IV of the Financial Services and Markets Act 2000 to carry on a regulated activity,

    (bb) it carried on an insurance market activity,

    (d) it was an appointed representative, within the meaning of section 39 of the Financial Services and Markets Act 2000,

    (e) it was a special register body as defined in section 117(1) of the Trade Union and Labour Relations (Consolidation) Act 1992 or an employers' association as defined in section 122 of that Act, or

    (f) it was a parent company or a subsidiary undertaking.

(1A) A company which, apart from this subsection, would fall within subsection (1)(f) by virtue of its being a subsidiary undertaking for any period within a financial year shall not be treated as so falling if it is dormant (within the meaning of section 249AA) throughout that period.

(1AB) A company which, apart from this subsection, would fall within subsection (1)(f) by virtue of its being a parent company or a subsidiary undertaking for any period within a financial year, shall not be treated as so falling if throughout that period it was a member of a group meeting the conditions set out in subsection (1C).

(1C) The conditions referred to in subsection (1B) are—

(a) that the group qualifies as a small group, in relation to the financial year within which the period falls, for the purposes of section 249 (or if all bodies corporate in such group were companies, would so qualify) and is not, and was not at any time within that year, an ineligible group within the meaning of section 248(2),

(b) that the group's aggregate turnover in that year (calculated in accordance with section 249) is, where the company referred to in subsection (1B) is a charity, not more than £350,000 net (or £420,000 gross) or, where the company so referred to is not a charity, not more than £1 million net (or £1.2 million gross), and

(c) that the group's aggregate balance sheet total for that year (calculated in accordance with section 249) is not more than £1.4 million net (or £1.68 million gross).

(2) Any member or members holding not less in the aggregate than 10 per cent in nominal value of the company's issued share capital or any class of it or, if the company does not have a share capital, not less than 10 per cent in number of the members of the company, may, by notice in writing deposited at the registered office of the company during a financial year but not later than one month before the end of that year, require the company to obtain an audit of its accounts for that year.

(3) Where a notice has been deposited under subsection (2), the company is not entitled to the exemption conferred by subsection (1) or (2) of section 249A or by subsection (1) of section 249AA in respect of the financial year to which the notice relates.

(4) A company is not entitled to the exemption conferred by subsection (1) or (2) of section 249A or by subsection (1) of section 249AA unless its balance sheet contains a statement by the directors—

(a) to the effect that for the year in question the company was entitled to exemption under subsection (1) or (2) of section 249A or subsection (1) of section 249AA,

(b) to the effect that members have not required the company to obtain an audit of its accounts for the year in question in accordance with subsection (2) of this section, and

(c) to the effect that the directors acknowledge their responsibilities for—

(i) ensuring that the company keeps accounting records which comply with section 221, and

(ii) preparing accounts which give a true and fair view of the state of affairs of the company as at the end of the financial year and of its profit or loss for the financial year in accordance with the requirements of section 226, and which otherwise comply with the requirements of this Act relating to accounts, so far as applicable to the company.

(5) The statement required by subsection (4) shall appear in the balance sheet above the signature required by section 233.

249E   Effect of exemptions

(1) Where the directors of a company have taken advantage of the exemption conferred by section 249A(1) or 249AA(1)—

(a) sections 238 and 239 (right to receive or demand copies of accounts and reports) shall have effect with the omission of references to the auditors' report;

(b) no copy of an auditors' report need be delivered to the registrar or laid before the company in general meeting;

(c) subsections (3) to (5) of section 271 (accounts by reference to which distribution to be justified) shall not apply.

(1A) Where the directors of a company have taken advantage of the exemption conferred by section 249AA, then for the purposes of that section the company shall be treated as a company entitled to prepare accounts in accordance with section 246 even though it is a member of an ineligible group.

. . .

Listed public companies

251   Provision of summary financial statement to shareholders

(1) A public company whose shares or debentures, or any class of whose shares or debentures, are listed need not, in such cases as may be specified by regulations made by the Secretary of State, and provided any conditions so specified are complied with, send copies of the documents referred to in section 238(1) to entitled persons, but may instead send them a summary financial statement.

In this section—

'entitled persons', in relation to a company, means such of the persons specified in paragraphs (a) to (c) of subsection (1) of section 238 as are or would apart from this section be entitled to be sent copies of those documents relating to the company which are referred to in that subsection;

'listed' means included in the official list by the competent authority for the purposes of Part VI of the Financial Services and Markets Act 2000 (official listing); and

'the official list' has the meaning given in section 103(1) of that Act.

(2) Copies of the documents referred to in section 238(1) shall, however, be sent to any entitled person who wishes to receive them; and the Secretary of State may by regulations make provision as to the manner in which it is to be ascertained (whether before or after he becomes an entitled person) whether an entitled person wishes to receive them.

(2A) References in this section to sending a summary financial statement to an entitled person include references to using electronic communications for sending the statement to such address as may for the time being be notified to the company by that person for that purpose.

(2B) For the purposes of this section a summary financial statement is also to be treated as sent to an entitled person where—

(a) the company and that person have agreed to his having access to summary financial statements on a web site (instead of their being sent to him);

(b) the statement is a statement to which that agreement applies; and

(c) that person is notified, in a manner for the time being agreed for the purpose between him and the company, of—

(i)   the publication of the statement on a web site;

(ii) the address of that web site; and

(iii) the place on that web site where the statement may be accessed, and how it may be accessed.

(2C) For the purposes of this section a statement treated in accordance with subsection (2B) as sent to an entitled person is to be treated as sent to him if, and only if—

(a) the statement is published on the web site throughout a period beginning at least 21 days before the date of the meeting at which the accounts and directors' report from which the statement is derived are to be laid and ending with the conclusion of that meeting; and

(b) the notification given for the purposes of paragraph (c) of that subsection is given not less than 21 days before the date of the meeting.

(2D) Nothing in subsection (2C) shall invalidate the proceedings of a meeting where—
  (a) any statement that is required to be published as mentioned in paragraph (a) of that subsection is published for a part, but not all, of the period mentioned in that paragraph; and
  (b) the failure to publish that statement throughout that period is wholly attributable to circumstances which it would not be reasonable to have expected the company to prevent or avoid.

(2E) A company may, notwithstanding any provision to the contrary in its articles, take advantage of any of subsections (2A) to (2D).

(3) The summary financial statement—
  (a) shall be derived from the company's annual accounts, the directors' report and (in the case of a quoted company) the directors' remuneration report, and
  (b) shall be in such form and contain such information as may be specified by regulations made by the Secretary of State.

(4) Every summary financial statement shall—
  (a) state that it is only a summary of information in the company's annual accounts, the directors' report and (in the case of a quoted company) the directors' remuneration report;
  (b) contain a statement by the company's auditors of their opinion as to whether the summary financial statement is consistent with those accounts and those reports and complies with the requirements of this section and regulations made under it;
  (c) state whether the auditors' report on the annual accounts, or on the annual accounts and the auditable part of the directors' remuneration report, was unqualified or qualified, and if it was qualified set out the report in full together with any further material needed to understand the qualification;
  (d) state whether that auditors' report contained a statement under—
    (i) section 237(2) (accounting records or returns inadequate or accounts or directors' remuneration report not agreeing with records and returns); or
    (ii) section 237(3) (failure to obtain necessary information and explanations),
and if so, set out the statement in full.

(5) Regulations under this section shall be made by statutory instrument which shall be subject to annulment in pursuance of a resolution of either House of Parliament.

(6) If default is made in complying with this section or regulations made under it, the company and every officer of it who is in default is guilty of an offence and liable to a fine.

(7) Section 240 (requirements in connection with publication of accounts) does not apply in relation to the provision to entitled persons of a summary financial statement in accordance with this section.

Private companies

252 Election to dispense with laying of accounts and reports before general meeting

(1) A private company may elect (by elective resolution in accordance with section 379A) to dispense with the laying of accounts and reports before the company in general meeting.

(2) An election has effect in relation to the accounts and reports in respect of the financial year in which the election is made and subsequent financial years.

(3) Whilst an election is in force, the references in the following provisions of this Act to the laying of accounts before the company in general meeting shall be read as references to the sending of copies of the accounts to members and others under section 238(1)—
  (a) section 235(1) (accounts on which auditors are to report),
  (b) section 270(3) and (4) (accounts by reference to which distributions are justified), and

(c) section 320(2) (accounts relevant for determining company's net assets for purposes of ascertaining whether approval required for certain transactions);
and the requirement in section 271(4) that the auditors' statement under that provision be
laid before the company in general meeting shall be read as a requirement that it be sent to
members and others along with the copies of the accounts sent to them under section 238(1).

(4) If an election under this section ceases to have effect, section 241 applies in relation to
the accounts and reports in respect of the financial year in which the election ceases to have
effect and subsequent financial years.

253   Right of shareholder to require laying of accounts

(1) Where an election under section 252 is in force, the copies of the accounts and reports
sent out in accordance with section 238(1)—

(a) shall be sent not less than 28 days before the end of the period allowed for laying
and delivering accounts and reports, and

(b) shall be accompanied, in the case of a member of the company, by a notice
informing him of his right to require the laying of the accounts and reports before
a general meeting;

and section 238(5) (penalty for default) applies in relation to the above requirements as to the
requirements contained in that section.

(2) Before the end of the period of 28 days beginning with the day on which the accounts
and reports are sent out in accordance with section 238(1), any member or auditor of the
company may by notice in writing deposited at the registered office of the company require
that a general meeting be held for the purpose of laying the accounts and reports before the
company.

(2A) The power of a member or auditor under subsection (2) to require the holding of
a general meeting is exercisable not only by the deposit of a notice in writing but also by
the transmission to the company at such address as may for the time being be specified for the
purpose by or on behalf of the company of an electronic communication containing the
requirement.

(3) If the directors do not within 21 days from the date of—

(a) the deposit of a notice containing a requirement under subsection (2), or

(b) the receipt of such a requirement contained in an electronic communication,
proceed duly to convene a meeting, the person who required the holding of the
meeting may do so himself.

(4) A meeting so convened shall not be held more than three months from that date and
shall be convened in the same manner, as nearly as possible, as that in which meetings are to
be convened by directors.

(5) Where the directors do not duly convene a meeting, any reasonable expenses incurred
by reason of that failure by the person who required the holding of the meeting shall be made
good to him by the company, and shall be recouped by the company out of any fees, or other
remuneration in respect of their services, due or to become due to such of the directors as were
in default.

(6) The directors shall be deemed not to have duly convened a meeting if they convene a
meeting for a date more than28 days after the date of the notice convening it.

Unlimited companies

254   Exemption from requirement to deliver accounts and reports

(1) The directors of an unlimited company are not required to deliver accounts and
reports to the registrar in respect of a financial year if the following conditions are met.

(2) The conditions are that at no time during the relevant accounting reference period—

(a) has the company been, to its knowledge, a subsidiary undertaking of an undertaking which was then limited, or

(b) have there been, to its knowledge, exercisable by or on behalf of two or more undertakings which were then limited, rights which if exercisable by one of them would have made the company a subsidiary undertaking of it, or

(c) has the company been a parent company of an undertaking which was then limited.

The references above to an undertaking being limited at a particular time are to an undertaking (under whatever law established) the liability of whose members is at that time limited.

(3) The exemption conferred by this section does not apply if—

(a) the company is a banking or insurance company or the parent company of a banking or insurance group, or

(b) the company is a qualifying company within the meaning of the Partnerships and Unlimited Companies (Accounts) Regulations 1993, or

(c) at any time during the relevant accounting period the company carried on business as the promoter of a trading stamp scheme within the Trading Stamps Act 1964.

(4) Where a company is exempt by virtue of this section from the obligation to deliver accounts, section 240 (requirements in connection with publication of accounts) has effect with the following modifications—

(a) in subsection (3)(b) for the words from 'whether statutory accounts' to 'have been delivered to the registrar' substitute 'that the company is exempt from the requirement to deliver statutory accounts', and

(b) in subsection (5) for 'as required to be delivered to the registrar under section 242' substitute 'as prepared in accordance with this Part and approved by the board of directors'.

CHAPTER III   SUPPLEMENTARY PROVISIONS

Accounting standards

256   Accounting standards

(1) In this Part 'accounting standards' means statements of standard accounting practice issued by such body or bodies as may be prescribed by regulations.

(2) References in this Part to accounting standards applicable to a company's annual accounts are to such standards as are, in accordance with their terms, relevant to the company's circumstances and to the accounts.

(3) The Secretary of State may make grants to or for the purposes of bodies concerned with—

(a) issuing accounting standards,

(b) overseeing and directing the issuing of such standards, or

(c) investigating departures from such standards or from the accounting requirements of this Act and taking steps to secure compliance with them.

(4) Regulations under this section may contain such transitional and other supplementary and incidental provisions as appear to the Secretary of State to be appropriate.

Power to alter accounting requirements

257   Power of Secretary of State to alter accounting requirements

(1) The Secretary of State may by regulations made by statutory instrument modify the provisions of this Part.

(2) Regulations which—

(a) add to the classes of documents required to be prepared, laid before the company in general meeting or delivered to the registrar,

(b) restrict the classes of company which have the benefit of any exemption, exception or special provision,

(c) require additional matter to be included in a document of any class, or

(d) otherwise render the requirements of this Part more onerous,
shall not be made unless a draft of the instrument containing the regulations has been laid before Parliament and approved by a resolution of each House.

(3) Otherwise, a statutory instrument containing regulations under this section shall be subject to annulment in pursuance of a resolution of either House of Parliament.

(4) Regulations under this section may—

(a) make different provision for different cases or classes of case,

(b) repeal and re-enact provisions with modifications of form or arrangement, whether or not they are modified in substance,

(c) make consequential amendments or repeals in other provisions of this Act, or in other enactments, and

(d) contain such transitional and other incidental and supplementary provisions as the Secretary of State thinks fit.

(5) Any modification by regulations under this section of section 258 or Schedule 10A (parent and subsidiary undertakings) does not apply for the purposes of enactments outside the Companies Acts unless the regulations so provide.

Parent and subsidiary undertakings

258   Parent and subsidiary undertakings

(1) The expressions 'parent undertaking' and 'subsidiary undertaking' in this Part shall be construed as follows; and a 'parent company' means a parent undertaking which is a company.

(2) An undertaking is a parent undertaking in relation to another undertaking, a subsidiary undertaking, if—

(a) it holds a majority of the voting rights in the undertaking, or

(b) it is a member of the undertaking and has the right to appoint or remove a majority of its board of directors, or

(c) it has the right to exercise a dominant influence over the undertaking—

(i) by virtue of provisions contained in the undertaking's memorandum or articles, or

(ii) by virtue of a control contract, or

(d) it is a member of the undertaking and controls alone, pursuant to an agreement with other shareholders or members, a majority of the voting rights in the undertaking.

(3) For the purposes of subsection (2) an undertaking shall be treated as a member of another undertaking—

(a) if any of its subsidiary undertakings is a member of that undertaking, or

(b) if any shares in that other undertaking are held by a person acting on behalf of the undertaking or any of its subsidiary undertakings.

(4) An undertaking is also a parent undertaking in relation to another undertaking, a subsidiary undertaking, if it has a participating interest in the undertaking and—

(a) it actually exercises a dominant influence over it, or

(b) it and the subsidiary undertaking are managed on a unified basis.

(5) A parent undertaking shall be treated as the parent undertaking of undertakings in relation to which any of its subsidiary undertakings are, or are to be treated as, parent undertakings; and references to its subsidiary undertakings shall be construed accordingly.

(6) Schedule 10A contains provisions explaining expressions used in this section and otherwise supplementing this section.

Other interpretation provisions

259   Meaning of 'undertaking' and related expressions

(1) In this Part 'undertaking' means—

(a) a body corporate or partnership, or

(b) an unincorporated association carrying on a trade or business, with or without a view to profit.

(2) In this part references to shares—

(a) in relation to an undertaking with a share capital, are to allotted shares;

(b) in relation to an undertaking with capital but no share capital, are to rights to share in the capital of the undertaking; and

(c) in relation to an undertaking without capital, are to interests—

(i) conferring any right to share in the profits or liability or contribute to the losses of the undertaking, or

(ii) giving rise to an obligation to contribute to the debts or expenses of the undertaking in the event of a winding up.

(3) Other expressions appropriate to companies shall be construed, in relation to an undertaking which is not a company, as references to the corresponding persons, officers, documents or organs, as the case may be, appropriate to undertakings of that description.

This is subject to provision in any specific context providing for the translation of such expressions.

(4) References in this part to 'fellow subsidiary undertakings' are to undertakings which are subsidiary undertakings of the same parent undertaking but are not parent undertakings or subsidiary undertakings of each other.

(5) In this Part 'group undertaking', in relation to an undertaking, means an undertaking which is—

(a) a parent undertaking or subsidiary undertaking of that undertaking, or

(b) a subsidiary undertaking of any parent undertaking of that undertaking.

260   Participating interests

(1) In this Part a 'participating interest' means an interest held by an undertaking in the shares of another undertaking which it holds on a long-term basis for the purpose of securing a contribution to its activities by the exercise of control or influence arising from or related to that interest.

(2) A holding of 20 per cent or more of the shares of an undertaking shall be presumed to be a participating interest unless the contrary is shown.

(3) The reference in subsection (1) to an interest in shares includes—

(a) an interest which is convertible into an interest in shares, and

(b) an option to acquire shares or any such interest;

and an interest or option falls within paragraph (a) or (b) notwithstanding that the shares to which it relates are, until the conversion or the exercise of the option, unissued.

(4) For the purposes of this section an interest held on behalf of an undertaking shall be treated as held by it.

(5) For the purposes of this section as it applies in relation to the expression 'participating interest' in section 258(4) (definition of 'subsidiary undertaking')—

(a) there shall be attributed to an undertaking any interests held by any of its subsidiary undertakings, and

(b) the references in subsection (1) to the purpose and activities of an undertaking include the purposes and activities of any of its subsidiary undertakings and of the group as a whole.

(6) In the balance sheet and profit and loss formats set out in Part I of Schedule 4, Part I of Schedule 8, Schedule 8A, Chapter I of Part I of Schedule 9 and Chapter I of Part I of Schedule 9A, 'participating interest' does not include an interest in a group undertaking.

(7) For the purposes of this section as it applies in relation to the expression 'participating interest'—

(a) in those formats as they apply in relation to group accounts, and

    (b) in paragraph 20 of Schedule 4A (group accounts: undertakings to be accounted for as associated undertakings),

the references in subsections (1) to (4) to the interest held by, and the purposes and activities of, the undertaking concerned shall be construed as references to the interest held by, and the purposes and activities of, the group (within the meaning of paragraph 1 of that Schedule).

261 Notes to the accounts

    (1) Information required by this Part to be given in notes to a company's annual accounts may be contained in the accounts or in a separate document annexed to the accounts.

    (2) References in this Part to a company's annual accounts, or to a balance sheet or profit and loss account, include notes to the accounts giving information which is required by any provision of this Act, and required or allowed by any such provision to be given in a note to company accounts.

262 Minor definitions

    (1) In this Part—

'address', except in section 228, in relation to electronic communications, includes any number or address used for the purposes of such communications;

'annual accounts' means—

    (a) the individual accounts required by section 226, and

    (b) any group accounts required by section 227,

(but see also section 230 (treatment of individual profit and loss account where group accounts prepared));

'annual report', in relation to a company, means the directors' report required by section 234;

'balance sheet date' means the date as at which the balance sheet was made up;

'capitalisation', in relation to work or costs, means treating that work or those costs as a fixed asset;

'credit institution' means a credit institution as defined in article 1(1)(a) of Directive 2000/12/EC of the European Parliament and of the Council of 20 March 2000 relating to the taking up and pursuit of the business of credit institutions, that is to say an undertaking whose business is to receive deposits or other repayable funds from the public and to grant credits for its own account;

'fixed assets' means assets of a company which are intended for use on a continuing basis in the company's activities, and 'current assets' means assets not intended for such use;

'group' means a parent undertaking and its subsidiary undertakings;

'included in the consolidation', in relation to group accounts, or 'included in consolidated group accounts', means that the undertaking is included in the accounts by the method of full (and not proportional) consolidation, and references to an undertaking excluded from consolidation shall be construed accordingly;

'purchase price', in relation to an asset of a company or any raw materials or consumables used in the production of such an asset, includes any consideration (whether in cash or otherwise) given by the company in respect of that asset or those materials or consumables, as the case may be;

'qualified', in relation to an auditors' report, means that the report does not state the auditors' unqualified opinion that the accounts have been properly prepared in accordance with this Act or, in the case of an undertaking not required to prepare accounts in accordance with this Act, under any corresponding legislation under which it is required to prepare accounts;

'quoted company' means a company whose equity share capital—

    (a) has been included in the official list in accordance with the provisions of Part VI of the Financial Services and Markets Act 2000; or

(b) is officially listed in an EEA State; or

(c) is admitted to dealing on either the New York Stock Exchange or the exchange known as Nasdaq;

and in paragraph (a) 'the official list' shall have the meaning given it by section 103(1) of the Financial Services and Markets Act 2000;

'true and fair view' refers—

(a) in the case of individual accounts, to the requirement of section 226(2), and

(b) in the case of group accounts, to the requirement of section 227(3);

'turnover', in relation to a company, means the amounts derived from the provision of goods and services falling within the company's ordinary activities, after deduction of—

(i) trade discounts,

(ii) value added tax, and

(iii) any other taxes based on the amounts so derived.

(2) In the case of an undertaking not trading for profit, any reference in this Part to a profit and loss account is to an income and expenditure account; and references to profit and loss and, in relation to group accounts, to a consolidated profit and loss account shall be construed accordingly.

(3) References in this Part to 'realised profits' and 'realised losses', in relation to a company's accounts, are to such profits or losses of the company as fall to be treated as realised in accordance with principles generally accepted, at the time when the accounts are prepared, with respect to the determination for accounting purposes of realised profits or losses.

This is without prejudice to—

(a) the construction of any other expression (where appropriate) by reference to accepted accounting principles or practice, or

(b) any specific provision for the treatment of profits or losses of any description as realised.

262A   Index of defined expressions

The following Table shows the provisions of this Part defining or otherwise explaining expressions used in this part (other than expressions used only in the same section or paragraph)—

the 1982 Act (in Schedule 9A)	paragraph 81 of Part I of that Schedule
accounting reference date and accounting reference period	section 224
accounting standards and applicable accounting standards	section 256
address	section 262(1)
annual accounts	
(generally)	section 262(1)
(includes notes to the accounts)	section 261(2)
annual report	section 262(1)
associated undertaking (in Schedule 4A)	paragraph 20 of that Schedule
auditable part (of a directors' remuneration report)	section 235(5)
balance sheet (includes notes)	section 261(2)
balance sheet date	section 262(1)
banking group	section 255A(4)
capitalisation (in relation to work or costs)	section 262(1)
credit institution	section 262(1)
current assets	section 262(1)
fellow subsidiary undertaking	section 259(4)
financial fixed assets (in Schedule 9)	paragraph 82 of Part I of that Schedule
financial year	section 223
fixed assets	section 262(1)
general business (in Schedule 9A)	paragraph 81 of Part I of that Schedule
group	section 262(1)

group undertaking	section 259(5)
historical cost accounting rules	
—in Schedule 4	paragraph 29 of that Schedule
—in Schedule 8	paragraph 29 of that Schedule
—in Schedule 9	paragraph 39 of Part I of that Schedule
—in Schedule 9A	paragraph 20(1) of Part I of that Schedule
included in the consolidation and related expressions	section 262(1)
individual accounts	section 262(1)
insurance group	section 255A(5)
land of freehold tenure and land of leasehold tenure (in relation to Scotland)	
—in Schedule 4	paragraph 93 of that Schedule
—in Schedule 9	paragraph 86 of Part I of that Schedule
—in Schedule 9A	paragraph 85 of Part I of that Schedule
lease, long lease and short lease	
—in Schedule 4	paragraph 83 of that Schedule
—in Schedule 9	paragraph 82 of Part I of that Schedule
—in Schedule 9A	paragraph 81 of Part I of that Schedule
listed investment	
—in Schedule 4	paragraph 84 of that Schedule
—in Schedule 8	paragraph 54 of that Schedule
—in Schedule 9A	paragraph 81 of Part I of that Schedule
listed security (in Schedule 9)	paragraph 82 of Part I of that Schedule
long term business (in Schedule 9A)	paragraph 81 of Part I of that Schedule
long term fund (in Schedule 9A)	paragraph 81 of Part I of that Schedule
notes to the accounts	section 261(1)
parent undertaking (and parent company)	section 258 and Schedule 10A
participating interest	section 260
pension costs	
—in Schedule 4	paragraph 94(2) of that Schedule
—in Schedule 8	paragraph 59(2) of that Schedule
—in Schedule 9	paragraph 87(b) of Part I of that Schedule
—in Schedule 9A	paragraph 86(b) of Part I of that Schedule
period allowed for laying and delivering accounts and reports	section 244
policy holder (in Schedule 9A)	paragraph 81 of Part I of that Schedule
profit and loss account	
(includes notes)	section 261(2)
(in relation to a company not trading for profit)	section 262(2)
provision	
—in Schedule 4	paragraphs 88 and 89 of that Schedule
—in Schedule 8	paragraphs 57 and 58 of that Schedule
—in Schedule 9	paragraph 85 of Part I of that Schedule
—in Schedule 9A	paragraph 84 of Part I of that Schedule
provision for unexpired risks (in Schedule 9A)	paragraph 81 of Part I of that Schedule
purchase price	section 262(1)
qualified	section 262(1)
quoted company	section 262(1)
realised losses and realised profits	section 262(3)
repayable on demand (in Schedule 9)	paragraph 82 of Part I of that Schedule
reporting account	section 249C(1)
reserve (in Schedule 9A)	paragraph 32 of that Schedule *
sale and repurchase transaction (in Schedule 9)	paragraph 82 of Part I of that Schedule
sale and option to resell transaction (in Schedule 9)	paragraph 82 of Part I of that Schedule
shares	section 259(2)

social security costs

— in Schedule 4	paragraph 94(1) and (3) of that Schedule
— in Schedule 8	paragraph 59(1) and (3) of that Schedule
— in Schedule 9	paragraph 87(a) and (c) of Part I of that Schedule
— in Schedule 9A	paragraph 86(a) and (c) of Part I of that Schedule
special provisions for banking and insurance companies and groups	sections 255 and 255A
subsidiary undertaking	section 258 and Schedule 10A
true and fair view	section 262(1)
turnover	section 262(1)
undertaking and related expressions	section 259(1) to (3)

[* *This entry was not changed when a new sch. 9A was substituted by the Companies Act 1985 (Insurance Companies Accounts) Regulations 1993 (SI 1993/3246) and is no longer accurate.*]

PART VIII   DISTRIBUTION OF PROFITS AND ASSETS

Limits of company's power of distribution

263   Certain distributions prohibited

(1) A company shall not make a distribution except out of profits available for the purpose.

(2) In this Part, 'distribution' means every description of distribution of a company's assets to its members, whether in cash or otherwise, except distribution by way of—

(a) an issue of shares as fully or partly paid bonus shares,

(b) the redemption or purchase of any of the company's own shares out of capital (including the proceeds of any fresh issue of shares) or out of unrealised profits in accordance with Chapter VII of Part V,

(c) the reduction of share capital by extinguishing or reducing the liability of any of the members on any of the company's shares in respect of share capital not paid up, or by paying off paid-up share capital, and

(d) a distribution of assets to members of the company on its winding up.

(3) For purposes of this Part, a company's profits available for distribution are its accumulated, realised profits, so far as not previously utilised by distribution or capitalisation, less its accumulated, realised losses, so far as not previously written off in a reduction or reorganisation of capital duly made.

This is subject to the provision made by sections 265 and 266 for investment and other companies.

(4) A company shall not apply an unrealised profit in paying up debentures, or any amounts unpaid on its issued shares.

(5) Where the directors of a company are, after making all reasonable enquiries, unable to determine whether a particular profit made before 22 December 1980 is realised or unrealised, they may treat the profit as realised; and where after making such enquiries they are unable to determine whether a particular loss so made is realised or unrealised, they may treat the loss as unrealised.

264   Restriction on distribution of assets

(1) A public company may only make a distribution at any time—

(a) if at that time the amount of its net assets is not less than the aggregate of its called-up share capital and undistributable reserves, and

(b) if, and to the extent that, the distribution does not reduce the amount of those assets to less than that aggregate.

This is subject to the provision made by sections 265 and 266 for investment and other companies.

(2) In subsection (1), 'net assets' means the aggregate of the company's assets less the aggregate of its liabilities ('liabilities' to include any provision for liabilities or charges within paragraph 89 of Schedule 4).

(3) A company's undistributable reserves are—

(a) the share premium account,

(b) the capital redemption reserve,

(c) the amount by which the company's accumulated, unrealised profits, so far as not previously utilised by capitalisation of a description to which this paragraph applies, exceed its accumulated, unrealised losses (so far as not previously written off in a reduction or reorganisation of capital duly made), and

(d) any other reserve which the company is prohibited from distributing by any enactment (other than one contained in this Part) or by its memorandum or articles; and paragraph (c) applies to every description of capitalisation except a transfer of profits of the company to its capital redemption reserve on or after 22 December 1980.

(4) A public company shall not include any uncalled share capital as an asset in any accounts relevant for purposes of this section.

265   Other distributions by investment companies

(1) Subject to the following provisions of this section, an investment company (defined in section 266) may also make a distribution at any time out of its accumulated, realised revenue profits, so far as not previously utilised by distribution or capitalisation, less its accumulated revenue losses (whether realised or unrealised), so far as not previously written off in a reduction or reorganisation of capital duly made—

(a) if at that time the amount of its assets is at least equal to one and a half times the aggregate of its liabilities, and

(b) if, and to the extent that, the distribution does not reduce that amount to less than one and a half times that aggregate.

(2) In subsection (1)(a), 'liabilities' includes any provision for liabilities or charges (within the meaning of paragraph 89 of Schedule 4).

(3) The company shall not include any uncalled share capital as an asset in any accounts relevant for purposes of this section.

(4) An investment company may not make a distribution by virtue of subsection (1) unless—

(a) its shares are listed on a recognised investment exchange other than an overseas investment exchange, and

(b) during the relevant period it has not—

(i) distributed any of its capital profits otherwise than by way of the redemption or purchase of any of the company's own shares in accordance with section 160 or 162 in Chapter VII of Part V, or

(ii) applied any unrealised profits or any capital profits (realised or unrealised) in paying up debentures or amounts unpaid on its issued shares.

(4A) In subsection (4)(a) 'recognised investment exchange' and 'overseas investment exchange' have the same meaning as in Part XVIII of the Financial Services and Markets Act 2000.

(5) The 'relevant period' under subsection (4) is the period beginning with—

(a) the first day of the accounting reference period immediately preceding that in which the proposed distribution is to be made, or

(b) where the distribution is to be made in the company's first accounting reference period, the first day of that period,

and ending with the date of the distribution.

(6) An investment company may not make a distribution by virtue of subsection (1) unless the company gave to the registrar of companies the requisite notice (that is, notice under section 266(1)) of the company's intention to carry on business as an investment company—

(a) before the beginning of the relevant period under subsection (4), or

(b) in the case of a company incorporated on or after 22 December 1980, as soon as may have been reasonably practicable after the date of its incorporation.

266   Meaning of 'investment company'

(1) In section 265 'investment company' means a public company which has given notice in the prescribed form (which has not been revoked) to the registrar of companies of its intention to carry on business as an investment company, and has since the date of that notice complied with the requirements specified below.

(2) Those requirements are—

(a) that the business of the company consists of investing its funds mainly in securities, with the aim of spreading investment risk and giving members of the company the benefit of the results of the management of its funds,

(b) that none of the company's holdings in companies (other than those which are for the time being in investment companies) represents more than 15 per cent by value of the investing company's investments,

(c) that subject to subsection (2A), distribution of the company's capital profits is prohibited by its memorandum or articles of association,

(d) that the company has not retained, otherwise than in compliance with this Part, in respect of any accounting reference period more than 15 per cent of the income it derives from securities.

(2A) An investment company need not be prohibited by its memorandum or articles from redeeming or purchasing its own shares in accordance with section 160 or 162 in Chapter VII of Part V out of its capital profits.

(3) Notice to the registrar of companies under subsection (1) may be revoked at any time by the company on giving notice in the prescribed form to the registrar that it no longer wishes to be an investment company within the meaning of this section; and, on giving such notice, the company ceases to be such a company.

(4) Subsections (1A) to (3) of section 842 of the Income and Corporation Taxes Act 1988 apply for the purposes of subsection (2)(b) above as for those of subsection (1)(b) of that section.

267   Extension of ss. 265, 266 to other companies

(1) The Secretary of State may by regulations in a statutory instrument extend the provisions of sections 265 and 266 (with or without modifications) to companies whose principal business consists of investing their funds in securities, land or other assets with the aim of spreading investment risk and giving their members the benefit of the results of the management of the assets.

(2) Regulations under this section—

(a) may make different provision for different classes of companies and may contain such transitional and supplemental provisions as the Secretary of State considers necessary, and

(b) shall not be made unless a draft of the statutory instrument containing them has been laid before Parliament and approved by a resolution of each House.

269   Treatment of development costs

(1) Subject as follows, where development costs are shown as an asset in a company's accounts, any amount shown in respect of those costs is to be treated—

(a) under section 263, as a realised loss, and

(b) under section 265, as a realised revenue loss.

(2) This does not apply to any part of that amount representing an unrealised profit made on revaluation of those costs; nor does it apply if—

(a) there are special circumstances in the company's case justifying the directors in deciding that the amount there mentioned is not to be treated as required by subsection (1), and

(b) the note to the accounts required by paragraph 20 of Schedule 4 [or] paragraph 20 of Schedule 8 (reasons for showing development costs as an asset) states that the amount is not to be so treated and explains the circumstances relied upon to justify the decision of the directors to that effect.

[*It is clear that the word 'or' has been accidentally omitted from s. 269(2)(b).*]

Relevant accounts

270   Distribution to be justified by reference to company's accounts

(1) This section and sections 271 to 276 below are for determining the question whether a distribution may be made by a company without contravening sections 263, 264 or 265.

(2) The amount of a distribution which may be made is determined by reference to the following items as stated in the company's accounts—

(a) profits, losses, assets and liabilities,

(b) provisions of any of the kinds mentioned in paragraphs 88 and 89 of Schedule 4 (depreciation, diminution in value of assets, retentions to meet liabilities, etc.), and

(c) share capital and reserves (including undistributable reserves).

(3) Except in a case falling within the next subsection, the company's accounts which are relevant for this purpose are its last annual accounts, that is to say those prepared under Part VII which were laid in respect of the last preceding accounting reference period in respect of which accounts so prepared were laid; and for this purpose accounts are laid if section 241(1) has been complied with in relation to them.

(4) In the following two cases—

(a) where the distribution would be found to contravene the relevant section if reference were made only to the company's last annual accounts, or

(b) where the distribution is proposed to be declared during the company's first accounting reference period, or before any accounts are laid in respect of that period, the accounts relevant under this section (called 'interim accounts' in the first case, and 'initial accounts' in the second) are those necessary to enable a reasonable judgment to be made as to the amounts of the items mentioned in subsection (2) above.

(5) The relevant section is treated as contravened in the case of a distribution unless the statutory requirements about the relevant accounts (that is, the requirements of this and the following three sections, as and where applicable) are complied with in relation to that distribution.

271   Requirements for last annual accounts

(1) If the company's last annual accounts constitute the only accounts relevant under section 270, the statutory requirements in respect of them are as follows.

(2) The accounts must have been properly prepared in accordance with this Act, or have been so prepared subject only to matters which are not material for determining, by reference to items mentioned in section 270(2), whether the distribution would contravene the relevant section; and, without prejudice to the foregoing—

(a) so much of the accounts as consists of a balance sheet must give a true and fair view of the state of the company's affairs as at the balance sheet date, and

(b) so much of the accounts as consists of a profit and loss account must give a true and fair view of the company's profit or loss for the period in respect of which the accounts were prepared.

(3) The auditors must have made their report on the accounts under section 235; and the following subsection applies if the report is a qualified report, that is to say, it is not a report without qualification to the effect that in the auditors' opinion the accounts have been properly prepared in accordance with this Act.

(4) The auditors must in that case also have stated in writing (either at the time of their report or subsequently) whether, in their opinion, the matter in respect of which their report is qualified is material for determining, by reference to items mentioned in section 270(2), whether the distribution would contravene the relevant section; and a copy of the statement must have been laid before the company in general meeting.

(5) A statement under subsection (4) suffices for purposes of a particular distribution not only if it relates to a distribution which has been proposed but also if it relates to distributions of any description which includes that particular distribution, notwithstanding that at the time of the statement it has not been proposed.

272 Requirements for interim accounts

(1) The following are the statutory requirements in respect of interim accounts prepared for a proposed distribution by a public company.

(2) The accounts must have been properly prepared, or have been so prepared subject only to matters which are not material for determining, by reference to items mentioned in section 270(2), whether the proposed distribution would contravene the relevant section.

(3) 'Properly prepared' means that the accounts must comply with section 226 (applying that section and Schedule 4 with such modifications as are necessary because the accounts are prepared otherwise than in respect of an accounting reference period) and any balance sheet comprised in the accounts must have been signed in accordance with section 233; and, without prejudice to the foregoing—

(a) so much of the accounts as consists of a balance sheet must give a true and fair view of the state of the company's affairs as at the balance sheet date, and

(b) so much of the accounts as consists of a profit and loss account must give a true and fair view of the company's profit or loss for the period in respect of which the accounts were prepared.

(4) A copy of the accounts must have been delivered to the registrar of companies.

(5) If the accounts are in a language other than English and the second sentence of section 242(1) (translation) does not apply then, subject to section 710B(6) (delivery of certain Welsh documents without a translation), a translation into English of the accounts, certified in the prescribed manner to be a correct translation, must also have been delivered to the registrar.

273 Requirements for initial accounts

(1) The following are the statutory requirements in respect of initial accounts prepared for a proposed distribution by a public company.

(2) The accounts must have been properly prepared, or they must have been so prepared subject only to matters which are not material for determining, by reference to items mentioned in section 270(2), whether the proposed distribution would contravene the relevant section.

(3) Section 272(3) applies as respects the meaning of 'properly prepared'.

(4) The company's auditors must have made a report stating whether, in their opinion, the accounts have been properly prepared; and the following subsection applies if their report is a qualified report, that is to say it is not a report without qualification to the effect that in the auditors' opinion the accounts have been so prepared.

(5) The auditors must in that case also have stated in writing whether, in their opinion, the matter in respect of which their report is qualified is material for determining, by reference

to items mentioned in section 270(2), whether the distribution would contravene the relevant section.

(6) A copy of the accounts, of the auditors' report under subsection (4) and of the auditors' statement (if any) under subsection (5) must have been delivered to the registrar of companies.

(7) If the accounts are, or the auditors' report under subsection (4) or their statement (if any) under subsection (5) is, in a language other than English and the second sentence of section 242(1) (translation) does not apply then, subject to section 710B(6) (delivery of certain Welsh documents without a translation), a translation into English of the accounts, the report or the statement (as the case may be), certified in the prescribed manner to be a correct translation, must also have been delivered to the registrar.

274   Method of applying s. 270 to successive distributions

(1) For the purpose of determining by reference to particular accounts whether a proposed distribution may be made by a company, section 270 has effect, in a case where one or more distributions have already been made in pursuance of determinations made by reference to those same accounts, as if the amount of the proposed distribution was increased by the amount of the distributions so made.

(2) Subsection (1) of this section applies (if it would not otherwise do so) to—

(a) financial assistance lawfully given by a public company out of its distributable profits in a case where the assistance is required to be so given by section 154,

(b) financial assistance lawfully given by a private company out of its distributable profits in a case where the assistance is required to be so given by section 155(2),

(c) financial assistance given by a company in contravention of section 151, in a case where the giving of that assistance reduces the company's net assets or increases its net liabilities,

(d) a payment made by a company in respect of the purchase by it of shares in the company (except a payment lawfully made otherwise than out of distributable profits), and

(e) a payment of any description specified in section 168 (company's purchase of right to acquire its own shares, etc.),

being financial assistance given or payment made since the relevant accounts were prepared, as if any such financial assistance or payment were a distribution already made in pursuance of a determination made by reference to those accounts.

(3) In this section the following definitions apply—

'financial assistance' means the same as in Chapter VI of Part V;

'net assets' has the meaning given by section 154(2)(a); and

'net liabilities', in relation to the giving of financial assistance by a company, means the amount by which the aggregate amount of the company's liabilities (within the meaning of section 154(2)(b)) exceeds the aggregate amount of its assets, taking the amount of the assets and liabilities to be as stated in the company's accounting records immediately before the financial assistance is given.

(4) Subsections (2) and (3) of this section are deemed to be included in Chapter VII of Part V for purposes of the Secretary of State's power to make regulations under section 179.

275   Treatment of assets in the relevant accounts

(1) For purposes of sections 263 and 264, a provision of any kind mentioned in paragraphs 88 and 89 of Schedule 4, other than one in respect of a diminution in value of a fixed asset appearing on a revaluation of all the fixed assets of the company, or of all of its fixed assets other than goodwill, is treated as a realised loss.

(2) If, on the revaluation of a fixed asset, an unrealised profit is shown to have been made and, on or after the revaluation, a sum is written off or retained for depreciation of that asset over a period, then an amount equal to the amount by which that sum exceeds the sum which

would have been so written off or retained for the depreciation of that asset over that period, if that profit had not been made, is treated for purposes of sections 263 and 264 as a realised profit made over that period.

(3) Where there is no record of the original cost of an asset, or a record cannot be obtained without unreasonable expense or delay, then for the purpose of determining whether the company has made a profit or loss in respect of that asset, its cost is taken to be the value ascribed to it in the earliest available record of its value made on or after its acquisition by the company.

(4) Subject to subsection (6), any consideration by the directors of the value at a particular time of a fixed asset is treated as a revaluation of the asset for the purposes of determining whether any such revaluation of the company's fixed assets as is required for purposes of the exception from subsection (1) has taken place at that time.

(5) But where any such assets which have not actually been revalued are treated as revalued for those purposes under subsection (4), that exception applies only if the directors are satisfied that their aggregate value at the time in question is not less than the aggregate amount at which they are for the time being stated in the company's accounts.

(6) Where section 271(2), 272(2) or 273(2) applies to the relevant accounts, subsections (4) and (5) above do not apply for the purpose of determining whether a revaluation of the company's fixed assets affecting the amount of the relevant items (that is, the items mentioned in section 270(2)) as stated in those accounts has taken place, unless it is stated in a note to the accounts—

(a) that the directors have considered the value at any time of any fixed assets of the company, without actually revaluing those assets,

(b) that they are satisfied that the aggregate value of those assets at the time in question is or was not less than the aggregate amount at which they are or were for the time being stated in the company's accounts, and

(c) that the relevant items in question are accordingly stated in the relevant accounts on the basis that a revaluation of the company's fixed assets which by virtue of subsections (4) and (5) included the assets in question took place at that time.

276   Distributions in kind

Where a company makes a distribution of or including a non-cash asset, and any part of the amount at which that asset is stated in the accounts relevant for the purposes of the distribution in accordance with sections 270 to 275 represents an unrealised profit, that profit is to be treated as a realised profit—

(a) for the purpose of determining the lawfulness of the distribution in accordance with this Part (whether before or after the distribution takes place), and

(b) for the purpose of the application of paragraphs 12(a) and 34(3)(a) of Schedule 4 or paragraphs 12(a) and 34(3)(a) of Schedule 8 (only realised profits to be included in or transferred to the profit and loss account) in relation to anything done with a view to or in connection with the making of that distribution.

Supplementary

277   Consequences of unlawful distribution

(1) Where a distribution, or part of one, made by a company to one of its members is made in contravention of this Part and, at the time of the distribution, he knows or has reasonable grounds for believing that it is so made, he is liable to repay it (or that part of it, as the case may be) to the company or (in the case of a distribution made otherwise than in cash) to pay the company a sum equal to the value of the distribution (or part) at that time.

(2) The above is without prejudice to any obligation imposed apart from this section on a member of a company to repay a distribution unlawfully made to him; but this section does not apply in relation to—

(a) financial assistance given by a company in contravention of section 151, or

(b) any payment made by a company in respect of the redemption or purchase by the company of shares in itself.

(3) Subsection (2) of this section is deemed included in Chapter VII of Part V for purposes of the Secretary of State's power to make regulations under section 179.

278 Saving for provision in articles operative before Act of 1980
Where immediately before 22 December 1980 a company was authorised by a provision of its articles to apply its unrealised profits in paying up in full or in part unissued shares to be allotted to members of the company as fully or partly paid bonus shares, that provision continues (subject to any alteration of the articles) as authority for those profits to be so applied after that date.

280 Definitions for Part VIII
(1) The following has effect for the interpretation of this Part.

(2) 'Capitalisation', in relation to a company's profits, means any of the following operations (whenever carried out)—
    (a) applying the profits in wholly or partly paying up unissued shares in the company to be allotted to members of the company as fully or partly paid bonus shares, or
    (b) transferring the profits to capital redemption reserve.

(3) References to profits and losses of any description are (respectively) to profits and losses of that description made at any time and, except where the context otherwise requires, are (respectively) to revenue and capital profits and revenue and capital losses.

281 Saving for other restraints on distribution
The provisions of this Part are without prejudice to any enactment or rule of law, or any provision of a company's memorandum or articles, restricting the sums out of which, or the cases in which, a distribution may be made.

PART IX   A COMPANY'S MANAGEMENT; DIRECTORS AND SECRETARIES; THEIR QUALIFICATIONS, DUTIES AND RESPONSIBILITIES

Officers and registered office

282 Directors
(1) Every company registered on or after 1 November 1929 (other than a private company) shall have at least two directors.

(2) Every company registered before that date (other than a private company) shall have at least one director.

(3) Every private company shall have at least one director.

283 Secretary
(1) Every company shall have a secretary.

(2) A sole director shall not also be secretary.

(3) Anything required or authorised to be done by or to the secretary may, if the office is vacant or there is for any other reason no secretary capable of acting, be done by or to any assistant or deputy secretary or, if there is no assistant or deputy secretary capable of acting, by or to any officer of the company authorised generally or specially in that behalf by the directors.

(4) No company shall—
    (a) have as secretary to the company a corporation the sole director of which is a sole director of the company;
    (b) have as sole director of the company a corporation the sole director of which is secretary to the company.

284   Acts done by person in dual capacity

A provision requiring or authorising a thing to be done by or to a director and the secretary is not satisfied by its being done by or to the same person acting both as director and as, or in place of, the secretary.

285   Validity of acts of directors

The acts of a director or manager are valid notwithstanding any defect that may afterwards be discovered in his appointment or qualification; and this provision is not excluded by section 292(2) (void resolution to appoint).

286   Qualifications of company secretaries

(1) It is the duty of the directors of a public company to take all reasonable steps to secure that the secretary (or each joint secretary) of the company is a person who appears to them to have the requisite knowledge and experience to discharge the functions of secretary of the company and who—

    (a) on 22 December 1980 held the office of secretary or assistant or deputy secretary of the company; or

    (b) for at least 3 of the 5 years immediately preceding his appointment as secretary held the office of secretary of a company other than a private company; or

    (c) is a member of any of the bodies specified in the following subsection; or

    (d) is a barrister, advocate or solicitor called or admitted in any part of the United Kingdom; or

    (e) is a person who, by virtue of his holding or having held any other position or his being a member of any other body, appears to the directors to be capable of discharging those functions.

(2) The bodies referred to in subsection (1)(c) are—

    (a) the Institute of Chartered Accountants in England and Wales;

    (b) the Institute of Chartered Accountants of Scotland;

    (c) the Chartered Association of Certified Accountants;

    (d) the Institute of Chartered Accountants in Ireland;

    (e) the Institute of Chartered Secretaries and Administrators;

    (f) the Institute of Cost and Management Accountants;

    (g) the Chartered Institute of Public Finance and Accountancy.

287   Registered office

(1) A company shall at all times have a registered office to which all communications and notices may be addressed.

(2) On incorporation the situation of the company's registered office is that specified in the statement sent to the registrar under section 10.

(3) The company may change the situation of its registered office from time to time by giving notice in the prescribed form to the registrar.

(4) The change takes effect upon the notice being registered by the registrar, but until the end of the period of 14 days beginning with the date on which it is registered a person may validly serve any document on the company at its previous registered office.

(5) For the purposes of any duty of a company—

    (a) to keep at its registered office, or make available for public inspection there, any register, index or other document, or

    (b) to mention the address of its registered office in any document, a company which has given notice to the registrar of a change in the situation of its registered office may act on the change as from such date, not more than 14 days after the notice is given, as it may determine.

(6) Where a company unavoidably ceases to perform at its registered office any such duty as is mentioned in subsection (5)(a) in circumstances in which it was not practicable to give prior notice to the registrar of a change in the situation of its registered office, but—

    (a) resumes performance of that duty at other premises as soon as practicable,

    (b) gives notice accordingly to the registrar of a change in the situation of its registered office within 14 days of doing so,

it shall not be treated as having failed to comply with that duty.

    (7) In proceedings for an offence of failing to comply with any such duty as is mentioned in subsection (5), it is for the person charged to show that by reason of the matters referred to in that subsection or subsection (6) no offence was committed.

288   Register of directors and secretaries

    (1) Every company shall keep at its registered office a register of its directors and secretaries; and the register shall, with respect to the particulars to be contained in it of those persons, comply with sections 289 and 290 below.

    (2) The company shall, within the period of 14 days from the occurrence of—

    (a) any change among its directors or in its secretary, or

    (b) any change in the particulars contained in the register,

send to the registrar of companies a notification in the prescribed form of the change and of the date on which it occurred; and a notification of a person having become a director or secretary, or one of joint secretaries, of the company shall contain a consent, signed by that person, to act in the relevant capacity.

    (3) The register shall be open to the inspection of any member of the company without charge and of any other person on payment of such fee as may be prescribed.

    (4) If an inspection required under this section is refused, or if default is made in complying with subsection (1) or (2), the company and every officer of it who is in default is liable to a fine and, for continued contravention, to a daily default fine.

    (5) In the case of a refusal of inspection of the register, the court may by order compel an immediate inspection of it.

    (5A) Where a confidentiality order made under section 723B is in force in respect of a director or secretary of a company, subsections (3) and (5) shall not apply in relation to that part of the register of the company as contains particulars of the usual residential address of that individual.

    (6) For purposes of this and the next section, a shadow director of a company is deemed a director and officer of it.

288A

If an individual in respect of whom a confidentiality order under section 723B as applied to limited liability partnerships becomes a member of a limited liability partnership—

    (a) the notice to be delivered to the registrar under section 9(1) of the Limited Liability Partnerships Act 2000 shall contain the address for the time being notified by the member to the limited liability partnership under the Limited Liability Partnerships (Particulars of Usual Residential Address) (Confidentiality Orders) Regulations 2002 but shall not contain his usual residential address; and

    (b) with that notice the limited liability partnership shall deliver to the registrar a notice in the prescribed form containing the usual residential address of that member.

[*No section title has been given to s. 288A.*]

289   Particulars of directors to be registered under s. 288

    (1) Subject to the provisions of this section, the register kept by a company under section 288 shall contain the following particulars with respect to each director—

    (a) in the case of an individual—

        (i)   his present name,

        (ii) any former name,

        (iii) his usual residential address,

(iv) his nationality,

(v)   his business occupation (if any),

(vi) particulars of any other directorships held by him or which have been held by him, and

(vii) the date of his birth;

(b) in the case of a corporation or Scottish firm, its corporate or firm name and registered or principal office.

(1A) Where a confidentiality order made under section 723B is in force in respect of a director, the register shall contain, in addition to the particulars specified in subsection (1)(a), such address as is for the time being notified by the director to the company under regulations made under sections 723B to 723F.

(2) In subsection (1)(a)—

(a) 'name' means a person's Christian name (or other forename) and surname, except that in the case of a peer, or an individual usually known by a title, the title may be stated instead of his Christian name (or other forename) and surname, or in addition to either or both of them; and

(b) the reference to a former name does not include—

(i) in the case of a peer, or an individual normally known by a British title, the name by which he was known previous to the adoption of or succession to the title, or

(ii) in the case of any person, a former name which was changed or disused before he attained the age of 18 years or which has been changed or disused for 20 years or more, or

(iii) in the case of a married woman, the name by which she was known previous to the marriage.

(3) It is not necessary for the register to contain on any day particulars of a directorship—

(a) which has not been held by a director at any time during the 5 years preceding that day,

(b) which is held by a director in a company which—

(i) is dormant or grouped with the company keeping the register, and

(ii) if he also held that directorship for any period during those 5 years, was for the whole of that period either dormant or so grouped,

(c) which was held by a director for any period during those 5 years in a company which for the whole of that period was either dormant or grouped with the company keeping the register.

(4) For purposes of subsection (3), 'company' includes any body corporate incorporated in Great Britain; and—

(a) section 249AA(3) applies as regards whether and when a company is or has been dormant, and

(b) a company is to be regarded as being, or having been, grouped with another at any time if at that time it is or was a company of which the other is or was a wholly-owned subsidiary, or if it is or was a wholly-owned subsidiary of the other or of another company of which that other is or was a wholly-owned subsidiary.

290 Particulars of secretaries to be registered under s. 288

(1) The register to be kept by a company under section 288 shall contain the following particulars with respect to the secretary or, where there are joint secretaries, with respect to each of them—

(a) in the case of an individual, his present name, any former name and his usual residential address, and

(b) in the case of a corporation or a Scottish firm, its corporate or firm name and registered or principal office.

(1A) Where a confidentiality order made under section 723B is in force in respect of a secretary the register shall contain, in addition to the particulars specified in subsection (1)(a), such address as is for the time being notified by the secretary to the company under regulations made under sections 723B to 723F.

(2) Where all the partners in a firm are joint secretaries, the name and principal office of the firm may be stated instead of the particulars specified above.

(3) Section 289(2)(a) and (b) apply for the purposes of the obligation under subsection (1)(a) of this section to state the name or former name of an individual.

Provisions governing appointment of directors

291   Share qualification of directors

(1) It is the duty of every director who is by the company's articles required to hold a specified share qualification, and who is not already qualified, to obtain his qualification within 2 months after his appointment, or such shorter time as may be fixed by the articles.

(2) For the purpose of any provision of the articles requiring a director or manager to hold any specified share qualification, the bearer of a share warrant is not deemed the holder of the shares specified in the warrant.

(3) The office of director of a company is vacated if the director does not within 2 months from the date of his appointment (or within such shorter time as may be fixed by the articles) obtain his qualification, or if after the expiration of that period or shorter time he ceases at any time to hold his qualification.

(4) A person vacating office under this section is incapable of being reappointed to be a director of the company until he has obtained his qualification.

(5) If after the expiration of that period or shorter time any unqualified person acts as a director of the company, he is liable to a fine and, for continued contravention, to a daily default fine.

292   Appointment of directors to be voted on individually

(1) At a general meeting of a public company, a motion for the appointment of two or more persons as directors of the company by a single resolution shall not be made, unless a resolution that it shall be so made has first been agreed to by the meeting without any vote being given against it.

(2) A resolution moved in contravention of this section is void, whether or not its being so moved was objected to at the time; but where a resolution so moved is passed, no provision for the automatic reappointment of retiring directors in default of another appointment applies.

(3) For purposes of this section, a motion for approving a person's appointment, or for nominating a person for appointment, is to be treated as a motion for his appointment.

(4) Nothing in this section applies to a resolution altering the company's articles.

293   Age limit for directors

(1) A company is subject to this section if—
   (a) it is a public company, or
   (b) being a private company, it is a subsidiary of a public company or of a body corporate registered under the law relating to companies for the time being in force in Northern Ireland as a public company.

(2) No person is capable of being appointed a director of a company which is subject to this section if at the time of his appointment he has attained the age of 70.

(3) A director of such a company shall vacate his office at the conclusion of the annual general meeting commencing next after he attains the age of 70; but acts done by a person as director are valid notwithstanding that it is afterwards discovered that his appointment had terminated under this subsection.

(4) Where a person retires under subsection (3), no provision for the automatic reappointment of retiring directors in default of another appointment applies; and if at the meeting at which he retires the vacancy is not filled, it may be filled as a casual vacancy.

(5) Nothing in subsections (2) to (4) prevents the appointment of a director at any age, or requires a director to retire at any time, if his apointment is or was made or approved by the company in general meeting; but special notice is required of a resolution appointing or approving the appointment of a director for it to have effect under this subsection, and the notice of the resolution given to the company, and by the company to its members, must state, or have stated, the age of the person to whom it relates.

(6) A person reappointed director on retiring under subsection (3), or appointed in place of a director so retiring, is to be treated, for the purpose of determining the time at which he or any other director is to retire, as if he had become director on the day on which the retiring director was last appointed before his retirement.

Subject to this, the retirement of a director out of turn under subsection (3) is to be disregarded in determining when any other directors are to retire.

(7) In the case of a company first registered after the beginning of 1947, this section has effect subject to the provisions of the company's articles; and in the case of a company first registered before the beginning of that year—

(a) this section has effect subject to any alterations of the company's articles made after the beginning of that year; and

(b) if at the beginning of that year the company's articles contained provision for retirement of directors under an age limit, or for preventing or restricting appointments of directors over a given age, this section does not apply to directors to whom that provision applies.

294   Duty of director to disclose his age

(1) A person who is appointed or to his knowledge proposed to be appointed director of a company subject to section 293 at a time when he has attained any retiring age applicable to him under that section or under the company's articles shall give notice of his age to the company.

(2) For purposes of this section, a company is deemed subject to section 293 notwithstanding that all or any of the section's provisions are excluded or modified by the company's articles.

(3) Subsection (1) does not apply in relation to a person's reappointment on the termination of a previous appointment as director of the company.

(4) A person who—

(a) fails to give notice of his age as required by this section; or

(b) acts as director under any appointment which is invalid or has terminated by reason of his age,

is liable to a fine and, for continued contravention, to a daily default fine.

(5) For purposes of subsection (4), a person who has acted as director under an appointment which is invalid or has terminated is deemed to have continued so to act throughout the period from the invalid appointment or the date on which the appointment terminated (as the case may be), until the last day on which he is shown to have acted thereunder.

Removal of directors

303   Resolution to remove director

(1) A company may by ordinary resolution remove a director before the expiration of his period of office, notwithstanding anything in its articles or in any agreement between it and him.

(2) Special notice is required of a resolution to remove a director under this section or to appoint somebody instead of a director so removed at the meeting at which he is removed.

(3) A vacancy created by the removal of a director under this section, if not filled at the meeting at which he is removed, may be filled as a casual vacancy.

(4) A person appointed director in place of a person removed under this section is treated, for the purpose of determining the time at which he or any other director is to retire, as if he had become director on the day on which the person in whose place he is appointed was last appointed a director.

(5) This section is not to be taken as depriving a person removed under it of compensation or damages payable to him in respect of the termination of his appointment as director or of any appointment terminating with that as director, or as derogating from any power to remove a director which may exist apart from this section.

304 Director's right to protest removal

(1) On receipt of notice of an intended resolution to remove a director under section 303, the company shall forthwith send a copy of the notice to the director concerned; and he (whether or not a member of the company) is entitled to be heard on the resolution at the meeting.

(2) Where notice is given of an intended resolution to remove a director under that section, and the director concerned makes with respect to it representations in writing to the company (not exceeding a reasonable length) and requests their notification to members of the company, the company shall, unless the representations are received by it too late for it to do so—

(a) in any notice of the resolution given to members of the company state the fact of the representations having been made; and

(b) send a copy of the representations to every member of the company to whom notice of the meeting is sent (whether before or after receipt of the representations by the company).

(3) If a copy of the representations is not sent as required by subsection (2) because received too late or because of the company's default, the director may (without prejudice to his right to be heard orally) require that the representations shall be read out at the meeting.

(4) But copies of the representations need not be sent out and the representations need not be read out at the meeting if, on the application either of the company or of any other person who claims to be aggrieved, the court is satisfied that the rights conferred by this section are being abused to secure needless publicity for defamatory matter.

(5) The court may order the company's costs on an application under this section to be paid in whole or in part by the director, notwithstanding that he is not a party to the application.

Other provisions about directors and officers

305 Directors' names on company correspondence, etc.

(1) A company to which this section applies shall not state, in any form, the name of any of its directors (otherwise than in the text or as a signatory) on any business letter on which the company's name appears unless it states on the letter in legible characters the name of every director of the company.

(2) This section applies to—

(a) every company registered under this Act or under the former Companies Acts (except a company registered before 23 November 1916); and

(b) every company incorporated outside Great Britain which has an established place of business within Great Britain, unless it had established such a place of business before that date.

(3) If a company makes default in complying with this section, every officer of the company who is in default is liable for each offence to a fine; and for this purpose, where a corporation is an officer of the company, any officer of the corporation is deemed an officer of the company.

(4) For the purposes of the obligation under subsection (1) to state the name of every director of the company, a person's 'name' means—

    (a) in the case of an individual, his Christian name (or other forename) and surname; and

    (b) in the case of a corporation or Scottish firm, its corporate or firm name.

(5) The initial or a recognised abbreviation of a person's Christian name or other forename may be stated instead of the full Christian name or other forename.

(6) In the case of a peer, or an individual usually known by a title, the title may be stated instead of his Christian name (or other forename) and surname or in addition to either or both of them.

(7) In this section 'director' includes a shadow director and the reference in subsection (3) to an 'officer' shall be construed accordingly.

306   Limited company may have directors with unlimited liability

(1) In the case of a limited company the liability of the directors or managers, or of the managing director, may, if so provided by the memorandum, be unlimited.

(2) In the case of a limited company in which the liability of a director or manager is unlimited, the directors and any managers of the company and the member who proposes any person for election or appointment to the office of director or manager, shall add to that proposal a statement that the liability of the person holding that office will be unlimited.

(3) Before the person accepts the office or acts in it, notice in writing that his liability will be unlimited shall be given to him by the following or one of the following persons, namely—

    (a) the promoters of the company,

    (b) the directors of the company,

    (c) any managers of the company,

    (d) the company secretary.

(4) If a director, manager or proposer makes default in adding such a statement, or if a promoter, director, manager or secretary makes default in giving the notice required by subsection (3), then—

    (a) he is liable to a fine, and

    (b) he is also liable for any damage which the person so elected or appointed may sustain from the default;

but the liability of the person elected or appointed is not affected by the default.

307   Special resolution making liability of directors unlimited

(1) A limited company, if so authorised by its articles, may by special resolution after its memorandum so as to render unlimited the liability of its directors or managers, or of any managing director.

(2) When such a special resolution is passed, its provisions are as valid as if they had been originally contained in the memorandum.

308   Assignment of office by directors

If provision is made by a company's articles, or by any agreement entered into between any person and the company, for empowering a director or manager of the company to assign his office as such to another person, any assignment of office made in pursuance of that provision is (notwithstanding anything to the contrary contained in the provision) of no effect unless and until it is approved by a special resolution of the company.

309   Directors to have regard to interests of employees

(1) The matters to which the directors of a company are to have regard in the performance of their functions include the interests of the company's employees in general, as well as the interests of its members.

(2) Accordingly, the duty imposed by this section on the directors is owed by them to the company (and the company alone) and is enforceable in the same way as any other fiduciary duty owed to a company by its directors.

(3) This section applies to shadow directors as it does to directors.

310 Provisions exempting officers and auditors from liability

(1) This section applies to any provision, whether contained in a company's articles or in any contract with the company or otherwise, for exempting any officer of the company or any person (whether an officer or not) employed by the company as auditor from, or indemnifying him against, any liability which by virtue of any rule of law would otherwise attach to him in respect of any negligence, default, breach of duty or breach of trust of which he may be guilty in relation to the company.

(2) Except as provided by the following subsection, any such provision is void.

(3) This section does not prevent a company—

    (a) from purchasing and maintaining for any such officer or auditor insurance against any such liability, or

    (b) from indemnifying any such officer or auditor against any liability incurred by him—

        (i) in defending any proceedings (whether civil or criminal) in which judgment is given in his favour or he is acquitted, or

        (ii) in connection with any application under section 144(3) or (4) (acquisition of shares by innocent nominee) or section 727 (general power to grant relief in case of honest and reasonable conduct) in which relief is granted to him by the court.

PART X   ENFORCEMENT OF FAIR DEALING BY DIRECTORS

Restrictions on directors taking financial advantage

311 Prohibition on tax-free payments to directors

(1) It is not lawful for a company to pay a director remuneration (whether as director or otherwise) free of income tax, or otherwise calculated by reference to or varying with the amount of his income tax, or to or with any rate of income tax.

(2) Any provision contained in a company's articles, or in any contract, or in any resolution of a company or a company's directors, for payment to a director of remuneration as above-mentioned has effect as if it provided for payment, as a gross sum subject to income tax, of the net sum for which it actually provides.

312 Payment to director for loss of office etc.

It is not lawful for a company to make to a director of the company any payment by way of compensation for loss of office, or as consideration for or in connection with his retirement from office, without particulars of the proposed payment (including its amount) being disclosed to members of the company and the proposal being approved by the company.

313 Company approval for property transfer

(1) It is not lawful, in connection with the transfer of the whole or any part of the undertaking or property of a company, for any payment to be made to a director of the company by way of compensation for loss of office, or as consideration for or in connection with his retirement from office, unless particulars of the proposed payment (including its amount) have been disclosed to members of the company and the proposal approved by the company.

(2) Where a payment unlawful under this section is made to a director, the amount received is deemed to be received by him in trust for the company.

314   Director's duty of disclosure on takeover, etc.

(1) This section applies where, in connection with the transfer to any persons of all or any of the shares in a company, being a transfer resulting from—

(a) an offer made to the general body of shareholders; or

(b) an offer made by or on behalf of some other body corporate with a view to the company becoming its subsidiary or a subsidiary of its holding company; or

(c) an offer made by or on behalf of an individual with a view to his obtaining the right to exercise or control the exercise of not less than one-third of the voting power at any general meeting of the company; or

(d) any other offer which is conditional on acceptance to a given extent, a payment is to be made to a director of the company by way of compensation for loss of office, or as consideration for or in connection with his retirement from office.

(2) It is in those circumstances the director's duty to take all reasonable steps to secure that particulars of the proposed payment (including its amount) are included in or sent with any notice of the offer made for their shares which is given to any shareholders.

(3) If—

(a) the director fails to take those steps, or

(b) any person who has been properly required by the director to include those particulars in or send them with the notice required by subsection (2) fails to do so, he is liable to a fine.

315   Consequences of non-compliance with s. 314

(1) If in the case of any such payment to a director as is mentioned in section 314(1)—

(a) his duty under that section is not complied with, or

(b) the making of the proposed payment is not, before the transfer of any shares in pursuance of the offer, approved by a meeting (summoned for the purpose) of the holders of the shares to which the offer relates and of other holders of shares of the same class as any of those shares,

any sum received by the director on account of the payment is deemed to have been received by him in trust for persons who have sold their shares as a result of the offer made; and the expenses incurred by him in distributing that sum amongst those persons shall be borne by him and not retained out of that sum.

(2) Where—

(a) the shareholders referred to in subsection (1)(b) are not all the members of the company, and

(b) no provision is made by the articles for summoning or regulating the meeting referred to in that paragraph,

the provisions of this Act and of the company's articles relating to general meetings of the company apply (for that purpose) to the meeting either without modification or with such modifications as the Secretary of State on the application of any person concerned may direct for the purpose of adapting them to the circumstances of the meeting.

(3) If at a meeting summoned for the purpose of approving any payment as required by subsection (1)(b) a quorum is not present and, after the meeting has been adjourned to a later date, a quorum is again not present, the payment is deemed for the purposes of that subsection to have been approved.

316   Provisions supplementing ss. 312 to 315

(1) Where in proceedings for the recovery of any payment as having, by virtue of section 313(2) or 315(1), been received by any person in trust, it is shown that—

(a) the payment was made in pursuance of any arrangement entered into as part of the agreement for the transfer in question, or within one year before or two years after that agreement or the offer leading to it; and

(b) the company or any person to whom the transfer was made was privy to that arrangement,

the payment is deemed, except in so far as the contrary is shown, to be one to which the provisions mentioned above in this subsection apply.

(2) If in connection with any such transfer as is mentioned in any of sections 313 to 315—

(a) the price to be paid to a director of the company whose office is to be abolished or who is to retire from office for any shares in the company held by him is in excess of the price which could at the time have been obtained by other holders of the like shares; or

(b) any valuable consideration is given to any such director,

the excess or the money value of the consideration (as the case may be) is deemed for the purposes of that section to have been a payment made to him by way of compensation for loss of office or as consideration for or in conection with his retirement from office.

(3) References in sections 312 to 315 to payments made to a director by way of compensation for loss of office or as consideration for or in connection with his retirement from office, do not include any bona fide payment by way of damages for breach of contract or by way of pension in respect of past services.

'Pension' here includes any superannuation allowance, superannuation gratuity or similar payment.

(4) Nothing in sections 313 to 315 prejudices the operation of any rule of law requiring disclosure to be made with respect to such payments as are there mentioned, or with respect to any other like payments made or to be made to a company's directors.

317 Directors to disclose interest in contracts

(1) It is the duty of a director of a company who is in any way, whether directly or indirectly, interested in a contract or proposed contract with the company to declare the nature of his interest at a meeting of the directors of the company.

(2) In the case of a proposed contract, the declaration shall be made—

(a) at the meeting of the directors at which the question of entering into the contract is first taken into consideration; or

(b) if the director was not at the date of that meeting interested in the proposed contract, at the next meeting of the directors held after he became so interested;

and, in a case where the director becomes interested in a contract after it is made, the declaration shall be made at the first meeting of the directors held after he becomes so interested.

(3) For purposes of this section, a general notice given to the directors of a company by a director to the effect that—

(a) he is a member of a specified company or firm and is to be regarded as interested in any contract which may, after the date of the notice, be made with that company or firm; or

(b) he is to be regarded as interested in any contract which may after the date of the notice be made with a specified person who is connected with him (within the meaning of section 346 below),

is deemed a sufficient declaration of interest in relation to any such contract.

(4) However, no such notice is of effect unless either it is given at a meeting of the directors or the director takes reasonable steps to secure that it is brought up and read at the next meeting of the directors after it is given.

(5) A reference in this section to a contract includes any transaction or arrangement (whether or not constituting a contract) made or entered into on or after 22 December 1980.

(6) For purposes of this section, a transaction or arrangement of a kind described in section 330 (prohibition of loans, quasi-loans etc. to directors) made by a company for a

director of the company or a person connected with such a director is treated (if it would not otherwise be so treated, and whether or not it is prohibited by that section) as a transaction or arrangement in which that director is interested.

(7) A director who fails to comply with this section is liable to a fine.

(8) This section applies to a shadow director as it applies to a director, except that a shadow director shall declare his interest, not at a meeting of the directors, but by a notice in writing to the directors which is either—

(a) a specific notice given before the date of the meeting at which, if he had been a director, the declaration would be required by subsection (2) to be made; or

(b) a notice which under subsection (3) falls to be treated as a sufficient declaration of that interest (or would fall to be so treated apart from subsection (4)).

(9) Nothing in this section prejudices the operation of any rule of law restricting directors of a company from having an interest in contracts with the company.

318   Directors' service contracts to be open to inspection

(1) Subject to the following provisions, every company shall keep at an appropriate place—

(a) in the case of each director whose contract of service with the company is in writing, a copy of that contract;

(b) in the case of each director whose contract of service with the company is not in writing, a written memorandum setting out its terms; and

(c) in the case of each director who is employed under a contract of service with a subsidiary of the company, a copy of that contract or, if it is not in writing, a written memorandum setting out its terms.

(2) All copies and memoranda kept by a company in pursuance of subsection (1) shall be kept at the same place.

(3) The following are appropriate places for the purposes of subsection (1)—

(a) the company's registered office;

(b) the place where its register of members is kept (if other than its registered office);

(c) its principal place of business, provided that is situated in that part of Great Britain in which the company is registered.

(4) Every company shall send notice in the prescribed form to the registrar of companies of the place where copies and memoranda are kept in compliance with subsection (1), and of any change in that place, save in a case in which they have at all times been kept at the company's registered office.

(5) Subsection (1) does not apply to a director's contract of service with the company or with a subsidiary of it if that contract required him to work wholly or mainly outside the United Kingdom; but the company shall keep a memorandum—

(a) in the case of a contract of service with the company, giving the director's name and setting out the provisions of the contract relating to its duration;

(b) in the case of a contract of service with a subsidiary, giving the director's name and the name and place of incorporation of the subsidiary, and setting out the provisions of the contract relating to its duration,

at the same place as copies and memoranda are kept by the company in pursuance of subsection (1).

(6) A shadow director is treated for purposes of this section as a director.

(7) Every copy and memorandum required by subsection (1) or (5) to be kept shall be open to inspection of any member of the company without charge.

(8) If—

(a) default is made in complying with subsection (1) or (5), or

(b) an inspection required under subsection (7) is refused, or

(c) default is made for 14 days in complying with subsection (4), the company and every officer of it who is in default is liable to a fine and, for continued contravention, to a daily default fine.

(9) In the case of a refusal of an inspection required under subsection (7) of a copy or memorandum, the court may by order compel an immediate inspection of it.

(10) Subsections (1) and (5) apply to a variation of a director's contract of service as they apply to the contract.

(11) This section does not require that there be kept a copy of, or memorandum setting out the terms of, a contract (or its variation) at a time when the unexpired portion of the term for which the contract is to be in force is less than 12 months, or at a time at which the contract can, within the next ensuing 12 months, be terminated by the company without payment of compensation.

319   Director's contract of employment for more than 5 years

(1) This section applies in respect of any term of an agreement whereby a director's employment with the company of which he is a director or, where he is the director of a holding company, his employment within the group is to continue, or may be continued, otherwise than at the instance of the company (whether under the original agreement or under a new agreement entered into in pursuance of it), for a period of more than 5 years during which the employment—

(a) cannot be terminated by the company by notice; or

(b) can be so terminated only in specified circumstances.

(2) In any case where—

(a) a person is or is to be employed with a company under an agreement which cannot be terminated by the company by notice or can be so terminated only in specified circumstances; and

(b) more than 6 months before the expiration of the period for which he is or is to be so employed, the company enters into a further agreement (otherwise than in pursuance of a right conferred by or under the original agreement on the other party to it) under which he is to be employed with the company or, where he is a director of a holding company, within the group,

this section applies as if to the period for which he is to be employed under that further agreement there were added a further period equal to the unexpired period of the original agreement.

(3) A company shall not incorporate in an agreement such a term as is mentioned in subsection (1), unless the term is first approved by a resolution of the company in general meeting and, in the case of a director of a holding company, by a resolution of that company in general meeting.

(4) No approval is required to be given under this section by any body corporate unless it is a company within the meaning of this Act, or is registered under section 680, or if it is a wholly-owned subsidiary of any body corporate, wherever incorporated.

(5) A resolution of a company approving such a term as is mentioned in subsection (1) shall not be passed at a general meeting of the company unless a written memorandum setting out the proposed agreement incorporating the term is available for inspection by members of the company both—

(a) at the company's registered office for not less than 15 days ending with the date of the meeting; and

(b) at the meeting itself.

(6) A term incorporated in an agreement in contravention of this section is, to the extent that it contravenes the section, void; and that agreement and, in a case where subsection (2) applies, the original agreement are deemed to contain a term entitling the company to terminate it at any time by the giving of reasonable notice.

(7) In this section—

(a) 'employment' includes employment under a contract for services; and

(b) 'group', in relation to a director of a holding company, means the group which consists of that company and its subsidiaries;

and for purposes of this section a shadow director is treated as a director.

320   Substantial property transactions involving directors, etc.

(1) With the exceptions provided by the section next following, a company shall not enter into an arrangement—

(a) whereby a director of the company or its holding company, or a person connected with such a director, acquires or is to acquire one or more non-cash assets of the requisite value from the company; or

(b) whereby the company acquires or is to acquire one or more non-cash assets of the requisite value from such a director or a person so connected,

unless the arrangement is first approved by a resolution of the company in general meeting and, if the director or connected person is a director of its holding company or a person connected with such a director, by a resolution in general meeting of the holding company.

(2) For this purpose a non-cash asset is of the requisite value if at the time the arrangement in question is entered into its value is not less than £2,000 but (subject to that) exceeds £100,000 or 10 per cent of the company's asset value, that is—

(a) except in a case falling within paragraph (b) below, the value of the company's net assets determined by reference to the accounts prepared and laid under Part VII in respect of the last preceding financial year in respect of which such accounts were so laid; and

(b) where no accounts have been so prepared and laid before that time, the amount of the company's called-up share capital.

(3) For purposes of this section and sections 321 and 322, a shadow director is treated as a director.

321   Exceptions from s. 320

(1) No approval is required to be given under section 320 by any body corporate unless it is a company within the meaning of this Act or registered under section 680 or, if it is a wholly-owned subsidiary of any body corporate, wherever incorporated.

(2) Section 320(1) does not apply to an arrangement for the acquisition of a non-cash asset—

(a) if the asset is to be acquired by a holding company from any of its wholly-owned subsidiaries or from a holding company by any of its wholly-owned subsidiaries, or by one wholly-owned subsidiary of a holding company from another wholly-owned subsidiary of that same holding company, or

(b) if the arrangement is entered into by a company which is being wound up, unless the winding up is a member's voluntary winding up.

(3) Section 320(1)(a) does not apply to an arrangement whereby a person is to acquire an asset from a company of which he is a member, if the arrangement is made with that person in his character as a member.

(4) Section 320(1) does not apply to a transaction on a recognised investment exchange which is effected by a director, or a person connected with him, through the agency of a person who in relation to the transaction acts as an independent broker.

For this purpose an 'independent broker' means—

(a) in relation to a transaction on behalf of a director, a person who independently of the director selects the person with whom the transaction is to be effected, and

(b) in relation to a transaction on behalf of a person connected with a director, a person who independently of that person or the director selects the person with whom the transaction is to be effected;

and 'recognised', in relation to an investment exchange, means recognised under the Financial Services and Markets Act 2000.

322   Liabilities arising from contravention of s. 320

(1) An arrangement entered into by a company in contravention of section 320, and any transaction entered into in pursuance of the arrangement (whether by the company or any other person) is voidable at the instance of the company unless one or more of the conditions specified in the next subsection is satisfied.

(2) Those conditions are that—

- (a) restitution of any money or other asset which is the subject matter of the arrangement or transaction is no longer possible or the company has been indemnified in pursuance of this section by any other person for the loss or damage suffered by it; or
- (b) any rights acquired bona fide for value and without actual notice of the contravention by any person who is not a party to the arrangement or transaction would be affected by its avoidance; or
- (c) the arrangement is, within a reasonable period, affirmed by the company in general meeting and, if it is an arrangement for the transfer of an asset to or by a director of its holding company or a person who is connected with such a director, is so affirmed with the approval of the holding company given by a resolution in general meeting.

(3) If an arrangement is entered into with a company by a director of the company or its holding company or a person connected with him in contravention of section 320, that director and the person so connected, and any other director of the company who authorised the arrangement or any transaction entered into in pursuance of such an arrangement, is liable—

- (a) to account to the company for any gain which he has made directly or indirectly by the arrangement or transaction, and
- (b) (jointly and severally with any other person liable under this subsection) to indemnify the company for any loss or damage resulting from the arrangement or transaction.

(4) Subsection (3) is without prejudice to any liability imposed otherwise than by that subsection, and is subject to the following two subsections; and the liability under subsection (3) arises whether or not the arrangement or transaction entered into has been avoided in pursuance of subsection (1).

(5) If an arrangement is entered into by a company and a person connected with a director of the company or its holding company in contravention of section 320, that director is not liable under subsection (3) if he shows that he took all reasonable steps to secure the company's compliance with that section.

(6) In any case, a person so connected and any such other director as is mentioned in subsection (3) is not so liable if he shows that, at the time the arrangement was entered into, he did not know the relevant circumstances constituting the contravention.

322A   Invalidity of certain transactions involving directors, etc.

(1) This section applies where a company enters into a transaction to which the parties include—

- (a) a director of the company or of its holding company, or
- (b) a person connected with such a director or a company with whom such a director is associated,

and the board of directors, in connection with the transaction, exceed any limitation on their powers under the company's constitution.

(2) The transaction is voidable at the instance of the company.

(3) Whether or not it is avoided, any such party to the transaction as is mentioned in subsection (1)(a) or (b), and any director of the company who authorised the transaction, is liable—

- (a) to account to the company for any gain which he has made directly or indirectly by the transaction, and
- (b) to indemnify the company for any loss or damage resulting from the transaction.

(4) Nothing in the above provisions shall be construed as excluding the operation of any other enactment or rule of law by virtue of which the transaction may be called in question or any liability to the company may arise.

(5) The transaction ceases to be voidable if—

    (a) restitution of any money or other asset which was the subject matter of the transaction is no longer possible, or

    (b) the company is indemnified for any loss or damage resulting from the transaction, or

    (c) rights acquired bona fide for value and without actual notice of the directors' exceeding their powers by a person who is not party to the transaction would be affected by the avoidance, or

    (d) the transaction is ratified by the company in general meeting, by ordinary or special resolution or otherwise as the case may require.

(6) A person other than a director of the company is not liable under subsection (3) if he shows that at the time the transaction was entered into he did not know that the directors were exceeding their powers.

(7) This section does not affect the operation of section 35A in relation to any party to the transaction not within subsection (1)(a) or (b).

But where a transaction is voidable by virtue of this section and valid by virtue of that section in favour of such a person, the court may, on the application of that person or of the company, make such order affirming, severing or setting aside the transaction, on such terms, as appear to the court to be just.

(8) In this section 'transaction' includes any act; and the reference in subsection (1) to limitations under the company's constitution includes limitations deriving—

    (a) from a resolution of the company in general meeting or a meeting of any class of shareholders, or

    (b) from any agreement between the members of the company or of any class of shareholders.

322B   Contracts with sole members who are directors

(1) Subject to subsection (2), where a private company limited by shares or by guarantee having only one member enters into a contract with the sole member of the company and the sole member is also a director of the company, the company shall, unless the contract is in writing, ensure that the terms of the contract are either set out in a written memorandum or are recorded in the minutes of the first meeting of the directors of the company following the making of the contract.

(2) Subsection (1) shall not apply to contracts entered into in the ordinary course of the company's business.

(3) For the purposes of this section a sole member who is a shadow director is treated as a director.

(4) If a company fails to comply with subsection (1), the company and every officer of it who is in default is liable to a fine.

(5) Subject to subsection (6), nothing in this section shall be construed as excluding the operation of any other enactment or rule of law applying to contracts between a company and a director of that company.

(6) Failure to comply with subsection (1) with respect to a contract shall not affect the validity of that contract.

Share dealings by directors and their families

323   Prohibition on directors dealing in share options

(1) It is an offence for a director of a company to buy—

(a) a right to call for delivery at a specified price and within a specified time of a specified number of relevant shares or a specified amount of relevant debentures; or

(b) a right to make delivery at a specified price and within a specified time of a specified number of relevant shares or a specified amount of relevant debentures; or

(c) a right (as he may elect) to call for delivery at a specified price and within a specified time or to make delivery at a specified price and within a specified time of a specified number of relevant shares or a specified amount of relevant debentures.

(2) A person guilty of an offence under subsection (1) is liable to imprisonment or a fine, or both.

(3) In subsection (1)—

(a) 'relevant shares', in relation to a director of a company, means shares in the company or in any other body corporate, being the company's subsidiary or holding company, or a subsidiary of the company's holding company, being shares as respects which there has been granted a listing on a stock exchange (whether in Great Britain or elsewhere);

(b) 'relevant debentures', in relation to a director of a company, means debentures of the company or of any other body corporate, being the company's subsidiary or holding company or a subsidiary of the company's holding company, being debentures as respects which there has been granted such a listing; and

(c) 'price' includes any consideration other than money.

(4) This section applies to a shadow director as to a director.

(5) This section is not to be taken as penalising a person who buys a right to subscribe for shares in, or debentures of, a body corporate or buys debentures of a body corporate that confer upon the holder of them a right to subscribe for, or to convert the debentures (in whole or in part) into, shares of that body.

324   Duty of director to disclose shareholdings in own company

(1) A person who becomes a director of a company and at the time when he does so is interested in shares in, or debentures of, the company or any other body corporate, being the company's subsidiary or holding company or a subsidiary of the company's holding company, is under obligation to notify the company in writing—

(a) of the subsistence of his interests at that time; and

(b) of the number of shares of each class in, and the amount of debentures of each class of, the company or other such body corporate in which each interest of his subsists at that time.

(2) A director of a company is under obligation to notify the company in writing of the occurrence, while he is a director, of any of the following events—

(a) any event in consequence of whose occurrence he becomes, or ceases to be, interested in shares in, or debentures of, the company or any other body corporate, being the company's subsidiary or holding company or a subsidiary of the company's holding company;

(b) the entering into by him of a contract to sell any such shares or debentures;

(c) the assignment by him of a right granted to him by the company to subscribe for shares in, or debentures of, the company; and

(d) the grant to him by another body corporate, being the company's subsidiary or holding company or a subsidiary of the company's holding company, of a right to subscribe for shares in, or debentures of, that other body corporate, the exercise of such a right granted to him and the assignment by him of such a right so granted;

and notification to the company must state the number or amount, and class, of shares or debentures involved.

(3) Schedule 13 has effect in connection with subsections (1) and (2) above; and of that Schedule—

(a) Part I contains rules for the interpretation of, and otherwise in relation to, those subsections and applies in determining, for purposes of those subsections, whether a person has an interest in shares or debentures;

(b) Part II applies with respect to the periods within which obligations imposed by the subsections must be fulfilled; and

(c) Part III specifies certain circumstances in which obligations arising from subsection (2) are to be treated as not discharged; and

subsections (1) and (2) are subject to any exceptions for which provision may be made by regulations made by the Secretary of State by statutory instrument.

(4) Subsection (2) does not require the notification by a person of the occurrence of an event whose occurrence comes to his knowledge after he has ceased to be a director.

(5) An obligation imposed by this section is treated as not discharged unless the notice by means of which it purports to be discharged is expressed to be given in fulfilment of that obligation.

(6) This section applies to shadow directors as to directors; but nothing in it operates so as to impose an obligation with respect to shares in a body corporate which is the wholly-owned subsidiary of another body corporate.

(7) A person who—

(a) fails to discharge, within the proper period, an obligation to which he is subject under subsection (1) or (2), or

(b) in purported discharge of an obligation to which he is so subject, makes to the company a statement which he knows to be false, or recklessly makes to it a statement which is false,

is guilty of an offence and liable to imprisonment or a fine, or both.

(8) Section 732 (restriction on prosecutions) applies to an offence under this section.

325   Register of directors' interests notified under s. 324

(1) Every company shall keep a register for the purposes of section 324.

(2) Whenever a company receives information from a director given in fulfilment of an obligation imposed on him by that section, it is under obligation to enter in the register, against the director's name, the information received and the date of the entry.

(3) The company is also under obligation, whenever it grants to a director a right to subscribe for shares in, or debentures of, the company to enter in the register against his name—

(a) the date on which the right is granted,

(b) the period during which, or time at which, it is exercisable,

(c) the consideration for the grant (or, if there is no consideration, that fact), and

(d) the description of shares or debentures involved and the number or amount of them, and the price to be paid for them (or the consideration, if otherwise than in money).

(4) Whenever such a right as is mentioned above is exercised by a director, the company is under obligation to enter in the register against his name that fact (identifying the right), the number or amount of shares or debentures in respect of which it is exercised and, if they were registered in his name, that fact and, if not, the name or names of the person or persons in whose name or names they were registered, together (if they were registered in the names of two persons or more) with the number or amount of the shares or debentures registered in the name of each of them.

(5) Part IV of Schedule 13 has effect with respect to the register to be kept under this section, to the way in which entries in it are to be made, to the right of inspection, and generally.

(6) For purposes of this section, a shadow director is deemed a director.

326   Sanctions for non-compliance

(1) The following applies with respect to defaults in complying with, and to contraventions of, section 325 and Part IV of Schedule 13.

(2) If default is made in complying with any of the following provisions—

    (a)   section 325(1), (2), (3) or (4), or

    (b)   Schedule 13, paragraph 21, 22 or 28,

the company and every officer of it who is in default is liable to a fine and, for continued contravention, to a daily default fine.

(3) If an inspection of the register required under paragraph 25 of the Schedule is refused, or a copy required under paragraph 26 is not sent within the proper period, the company and every officer of it who is in default is liable to a fine and, for continued contravention, to a daily default fine.

(4) If default is made for 14 days in complying with paragraph 27 of the Schedule (notice to registrar of where register is kept), the company and every officer of it who is in default is liable to a fine and, for continued contravention, to a daily default fine.

(5) If default is made in complying with paragraph 29 of the Schedule (register to be produced at annual general meeting), the company and every officer of it who is in default is liable to a fine.

(6) In the case of a refusal of an inspection of the register required under paragraph 25 of the Schedule, the court may by order compel an immediate inspection of it; and in the case of failure to send within the proper period a copy required under paragraph 26, the court may by order direct that the copy be sent to the person requiring it.

327   Extension of s. 323 to spouses and children

(1) Section 323 applies to—

    (a)   the wife or husband of a director of a company (not being herself or himself a director of it), and

    (b)   an infant son or infant daughter of a director (not being himself or herself a director of the company),

as it applies to the director; but it is a defence for a person charged by virtue of this section with an offence under section 323 to prove that he (she) had no reason to believe that his (her) spouse or, as the case may be, parent was a director of the company in question.

(2) For purposes of this section—

    (a)   'son' includes stepson and 'daughter' includes stepdaughter ('parent' being construed accordingly),

    (b)   'infant' means, in relation to Scotland, pupil or minor, and

    (c)   a shadow director of a company is deemed a director of it.

328   Extension of s. 324 to spouses and children

(1) For the purposes of section 324—

    (a)   an interest of the wife or husband of a director of a company (not being herself or himself a director of it) in shares or debentures is to be treated as the director's interest; and

    (b)   the same applies to an interest of an infant son or infant daughter of a director of a company (not being himself or herself a director of it) in shares or debentures.

(2) For those purposes—

    (a)   a contract, assignment or right of subscription entered into, exercised or made by, or a grant made to, the wife or husband of a director of a company (not being herself or himself a director of it) is to be treated as having been entered into, exercised or made by, or (as the case may be) as having been made to, the director; and

    (b)   the same applies to a contract, assignment or right of subscription entered into, exercised or made by, or grant made to, an infant son or infant daughter of a director of a company (not being himself or herself a director of it).

(3) A director of a company is under obligation to notify the company in writing of the occurrence while he or she is a director, of either of the following events, namely—

(a) the grant by the company to his (her) spouse, or to his or her infant son or infant daughter, of a right to subscribe for shares in, or debentures of, the company; and

(b) the exercise by his (her) spouse or by his or her infant son or infant daughter of such a right granted by the company to the wife, husband, son or daughter.

(4) In a notice given to the company under subsection (3) there shall be stated—

(a) in the case of the grant of a right, the like information as is required by section 324 to be stated by the director on the grant to him by another body corporate of a right to subscribe for shares in, or debentures of, that other body corporate; and

(b) in the case of the exercise of a right, the like information as is required by that section to be stated by the director on the exercise of a right granted to him by another body corporate to subscribe for shares in, or debentures of, that other body corporate.

(5) An obligation imposed by subsection (3) on a director must be fulfilled by him before the end of 5 days beginning with the day following that on which the occurrence of the event giving rise to it comes to his knowledge; but in reckoning that period of days there is disregarded any Saturday or Sunday, and any day which is a bank holiday in any part of Great Britain.

(6) A person who—

(a) fails to fulfil, within the proper period, an obligation to which he is subject under subsection (3), or

(b) in purported fulfilment of such an obligation, makes to a company a statement which he knows to be false, or recklessly makes to a company a statement which is false, is guilty of an offence and liable to imprisonment or a fine, or both.

(7) The rules set out in Part I of Schedule 13 have effect for the interpretation of, and otherwise in relation to, subsections (1) and (2); and subsections (5), (6) and (8) of section 324 apply with any requisite modification.

(8) In this section, 'son' includes stepson 'daughter' includes stepdaughter, and 'infant' means, in relation to Scotland, pupil or minor.

(9) For purposes of section 325, an obligation imposed on a director by this section is to be treated as if imposed by section 324.

329   Duty to notify stock exchange of matters notified under preceding sections

(1) Whenever a company whose shares or debentures are listed on a recognised investment exchange other than an overseas investment exchange is notified of any matter by a director in consequence of the fulfilment of an obligation imposed by section 324 or 328, and that matter relates to shares or debentures so listed, the company is under obligation to notify that investment exchange of that matter; and the investment exchange may publish, in such manner as it may determine, any information received by it under this subsection.

(2) An obligation imposed by subsection (1) must be fulfilled before the end of the day next following that on which it arises; but there is disregarded for this purpose a day which is a Saturday or a Sunday or a bank holiday in any part of Great Britain.

(3) If default is made in complying with this section, the company and every officer of it who is in default is guilty of an offence and liable to a fine and, for continued contravention, to a daily default fine.

Section 732 (restriction on prosecutions) applies to an offence under this section.

(4) In subsection (1) 'recognised investment exchange' and 'overseas investment exchange' have the same meaning as in Part XVIII of the Financial Services and Markets Act 2000.

Restrictions on a company's power to make loans, etc., to directors and persons connected with them

330   General restriction on loans etc. to directors and persons connected with them

(1) The prohibitions listed below in this section are subject to the exceptions in sections 332 to 338.

(2) A company shall not—

(a)   make a loan to a director of the company or of its holding company;

(b)   enter into any guarantee or provide any security in connection with a loan made by any person to such a director.

(3) A relevant company shall not—

(a)   make a quasi-loan to a director of the company or of its holding company;

(b)   make a loan or a quasi-loan to a person connected with such a director;

(c)   enter into a guarantee or provide any security in connection with a loan or quasi-loan made by any other person for such a director or a person so connected.

(4) A relevant company shall not—

(a)   enter into a credit transaction as creditor for such a director or a person so connected;

(b)   enter into any guarantee or provide any security in connection with a credit transaction made by any other person for such a director or a person so connected.

(5) For purposes of sections 330 to 346, a shadow director is treated as a director.

(6) A company shall not arrange for the assignment to it, or the assumption by it, of any rights, obligations or liabilities under a transaction which, if it had been entered into by the company, would have contravened subsection (2), (3) or (4); but for the purposes of sections 330 to 347 the transaction is to be treated as having been entered into on the date of the arrangement.

(7) A company shall not take part in any arrangement whereby—

(a)   another person enters into a transaction which, if it had been entered into by the company, would have contravened any of subsections (2), (3), (4) or (6); and

(b)   that other person, in pursuance of the arrangement, has obtained or is to obtain any benefit from the company or its holding company or a subsidiary of the company or its holding company.

331   Definitions for ss. 330 ff.

(1) The following subsections apply for the interpretation of sections 330 to 346.

(2) 'Guarantee' includes indemnity, and cognate expressions are to be construed accordingly.

(3) A quasi-loan is a transaction under which one party ('the creditor') agrees to pay, or pays otherwise than in pursuance of an agreement, a sum for another ('the borrower') or agrees to reimburse, or reimburses otherwise than in pursuance of an agreement, expenditure incurred by another party for another ('the borrower')—

(a)   on terms that the borrower (or a person on his behalf) will reimburse the creditor; or

(b)   in circumstances giving rise to a liability on the borrower to reimburse the creditor.

(4) Any reference to the person to whom a quasi-loan is made is a reference to the borrower; and the liabilities of a borrower under a quasi-loan include the liabilities of any person who has agreed to reimburse the creditor on behalf of the borrower.

(6) 'Relevant company' means a company which—

(a)   is a public company, or

(b)   is a subsidiary of a public company, or

(c)   is a subsidiary of a company which has as another subsidiary a public company, or

(d)   has a subsidiary which is a public company.

(7) A credit transaction is a transaction under which one party ('the creditor')—

    (a) supplies any goods or sells any land under a hire-purchase agreement or a conditional sale agreement;

    (b) leases or hires any land or goods in return for periodical payments;

    (c) otherwise disposes of land or supplies goods or services on the understanding that payment (whether in a lump sum or instalments or by way of periodical payments or otherwise) is to be deferred.

(8) 'Services' means anything other than goods or land.

(9) A transaction or arrangement is made 'for' a person if—

    (a) in the case of a loan or quasi-loan, it is made to him;

    (b) in the case of a credit transaction, he is the person to whom goods or services are supplied, or land is sold or otherwise disposed of, under the transaction;

    (c) in the case of a guarantee or security, it is entered into or provided in connection with a loan or quasi-loan made to him or a credit transaction made for him;

    (d) in the case of an arrangement within subsection (6) or (7) of section 330, the transaction to which the arrangement relates was made for him; and

    (e) in the case of any other transaction or arrangement for the supply or transfer of, or of any interest in, goods, land or services, he is the person to whom the goods, land or services (or the interest) are supplied or transferred.

(10) 'Conditional sale agreement' means the same as in the Consumer Credit Act 1974.

332   Short-term quasi-loans

(1) Subsection (3) of section 330 does not prohibit a company ('the creditor') from making a quasi-loan to one of its directors or to a director of its holding company if—

    (a) the quasi-loan contains a term requiring the director or a person on his behalf to reimburse the creditor his expenditure within 2 months of its being incurred; and

    (b) the aggregate of the amount of that quasi-loan and of the amount outstanding under each relevant quasi-loan does not exceed £5,000.

(2) A quasi-loan is relevant for this purpose if it was made to the director by virtue of this section by the creditor or its subsidiary or, where the director is a director of the creditor's holding company, any other subsidiary of that company; and 'the amount outstanding' is the amount of the outstanding liabilities of the person to whom the quasi-loan was made.

333   Inter-company loans in same group

In the case of a relevant company which is a member of a group of companies (meaning a holding company and its subsidiaries), paragraphs (b) and (c) of section 330(3) do not prohibit the company from—

    (a) making a loan or quasi-loan to another member of that group; or

    (b) entering into a guarantee or providing any security in connection with a loan or quasi-loan made by any person to another member of the group,

by reason only that a director of one member of the group is associated with another.

334   Loans of small amounts

Without prejudice to any other provision of sections 332 to 338, paragraph (a) of section 330(2) does not prohibit a company from making a loan to a director of the company or of its holding company if the aggregate of the relevant amounts does not exceed £5,000.

335   Minor and business transactions

(1) Section 330(4) does not prohibit a company from entering into a transaction for a person if the aggregate of the relevant amounts does not exceed £10,000.

(2) Section 330(4) does not prohibit a company from entering into a transaction for a person if—

    (a) the transaction is entered into by the company in the ordinary course of its business; and

(b) the value of the transaction is not greater, and the terms on which it is entered into are no more favourable, in respect of the person for whom the transaction is made, than that or those which it is reasonable to expect the company to have offered to or in respect of a person of the same financial standing but unconnected with the company.

336   Transactions at behest of holding company

The following transactions are excepted from the prohibitions of section 330—

(a) a loan or quasi-loan by a company to its holding company, or a company entering into a guarantee or providing any security in connection with a loan or quasi-loan made by any person to its holding company;

(b) a company entering into a credit transaction as creditor for its holding company, or entering into a guarantee or providing any security in connection with a credit transaction made by any other person for its holding company.

337   Funding of director's expenditure on duty to company

(1) A company is not prohibited by section 330 from doing anything to provide a director with funds to meet expenditure incurred or to be incurred by him for the purposes of the company or for the purpose of enabling him properly to perform his duties as an officer of the company.

(2) Nor does the section prohibit a company from doing anything to enable a director to avoid incurring such expenditure.

(3) Subsections (1) and (2) apply only if one of the following conditions is satisfied—

(a) the thing in question is done with prior approval of the company given at a general meeting at which there are disclosed all the matters mentioned in the next subsection;

(b) that thing is done on condition that, if the approval of the company is not so given at or before the next annual general meeting, the loan is to be repaid, or any other liability arising under any such transaction discharged, within 6 months from the conclusion of that meeting;

but those subsections do not authorise a relevant company to enter into any transaction if the aggregate of the relevant amounts exceeds £20,000.

(4) The matters to be disclosed under subsection (3)(a) are—

(a) the purpose of the expenditure incurred or to be incurred, or which would other-wise be incurred, by the director,

(b) the amount of the funds to be provided by the company, and

(c) the extent of the company's liability under any transaction which is or is con-nected with the thing in question.

338   Loan or quasi-loan by money-lending company

(1) There is excepted from the prohibitions in section 330—

(a) a loan or quasi-loan made by a money-lending company to any person; or

(b) a money-lending company entering into a guarantee in connection with any other loan or quasi-loan.

(2) 'Money-lending company' means a company whose ordinary business includes the making of loans or quasi-loans, or the giving of guarantees in connection with loans or quasi-loans.

(3) Subsection (1) applies only if both the following conditions are satisfied—

(a) the loan or quasi-loan in question is made by the company, or it enters into the guarantee, in the ordinary course of the company's business; and

(b) the amount of the loan or quasi-loan, or the amount guaranteed, is not greater, and the terms of the loan, quasi-loan or guarantee are not more favourable, in the case of the person to whom the loan or quasi-loan is made or in respect of whom the guarantee is entered into, than that or those which it is reasonable to expect that company to have offered to or in respect of a person of the same financial standing but unconnected with the company.

(4) But subsection (1) does not authorise a relevant company (unless it is a banking company) to enter into any transaction if the aggregate of the relevant amounts exceeds £100,000.

(5) In determining that aggregate, a company which a director does not control is deemed not to be connected with him.

(6) The condition specified in subsection (3)(b) does not of itself prevent a company from making a loan to one of its directors or a director of its holding company—

(a) for the purpose of facilitating the purchase, for use as that director's only or main residence, of the whole or part of any dwelling house together with any land to be occupied and enjoyed with it;

(b) for the purpose of improving a dwelling house or part of a dwelling house so used or any land occupied and enjoyed with it;

(c) in substitution for any loan made by any person and falling within paragraph (a) or (b) of this subsection,

if loans of that description are ordinarily made by the company to its employees and on terms no less favourable than those on which the transaction in question is made, and the aggregate of the relevant amounts does not exceed £100,000.

339 'Relevant amounts' for purposes of ss. 334 ff.

(1) This section has effect for defining the 'relevant amounts' to be aggregated under sections 334, 335(1), 337(3) and 338(4); and in relation to any proposed transaction or arrangement and the question whether it falls within one or other of the exceptions provided by those sections, 'the relevant exception' is that exception; but where the relevant exception is the one provided by section 334 (loan of small amount), references in this section to a person connected with a director are to be disregarded.

(2) Subject as follows, the relevant amounts in relation to a proposed transaction or arrangement are—

(a) the value of the proposed transaction or arrangement,

(b) the value of any existing arrangement which—

(i) falls within subsection (6) or (7) of section 330, and

(ii) also falls within subsection (3) of this section, and

(iii) was entered into by virtue of the relevant exception by the company or by a subsidiary of the company or, where the proposed transaction or arrangement is to be made for a director of its holding company or a person connected with such a director, by that holding company or any of its subsidiaries;

(c) the amount outstanding under any other transaction—

(i) falling within subsection (3) below, and

(ii) made by virtue of the relevant exception, and

(iii) made by the company or by a subsidiary of the company or, where the proposed transaction or arrangement is to be made for a director of its holding company or a person connected with such a director, by that holding company or any of its subsidiaries.

(3) A transaction falls within this subsection if it was made—

(a) for the director for whom the proposed transaction or arrangement is to be made, or for any person connected with that director; or

(b) where the proposed transaction or arrangement is to be made for a person connected with a director of a company, for that director or any person connected with him;

and an arrangement also falls within this subsection if it relates to a transaction which does so.

(4) But where the proposed transaction falls within section 338 and is one which a banking company proposes to enter into under subsection (6) of that section (housing loans, etc.), any other transaction or arrangement which apart from this subsection would fall within subsection (3) of this section does not do so unless it was entered into in pursuance of section 338(6).

(5) A transaction entered into by a company which is (at the time of that transaction being entered into) a subsidiary of the company which is to make the proposed transaction, or is a subsidiary of that company's holding company, does not fall within subsection (3) if at the time when the question arises (that is to say, the question whether the proposed transaction or arrangement falls within any relevant exception), it no longer is such a subsidiary.

(6) Values for purposes of subsection (2) of this section are to be determined in accordance with the section next following; and 'the amount outstanding' for purposes of subsection (2)(c) above is the value of the transaction less any amount by which that value has been reduced.

340 **'Value' of transactions and arrangements**

(1) This section has effect for determining the value of a transaction or arrangement for purposes of sections 330 to 339.

(2) The value of a loan is the amount of its principal.

(3) The value of a quasi-loan is the amount, or maximum amount, which the person to whom the quasi-loan is made is liable to reimburse the creditor.

(4) The value of a guarantee or security is the amount guaranteed or secured.

(5) The value of an arrangement to which section 330(6) or (7) applies is the value of the transaction to which the arrangement relates less any amount by which the liabilities under the arrangement or transaction of the person for whom the transaction was made have been reduced.

(6) The value of a transaction or arrangement not falling within subsections (2) to (5) above is the price which it is reasonable to expect could be obtained for the goods, land or services to which the transaction or arrangement relates if they had been supplied (at the time the transaction or arrangement is entered into) in the ordinary course of business and on the same terms (apart from price) as they have been supplied, or are to be supplied, under the transaction or arrangement in question.

(7) For purposes of this section, the value of a transaction or arrangement which is not capable of being expressed as a specific sum of money (because the amount of any liability arising under the transaction or arrangement is unascertainable, or for any other reason), whether or not any liability under the transaction or arrangement has been reduced, is deemed to exceed £100,000.

341 **Civil remedies for breach of s. 330**

(1) If a company enters into a transaction or arrangement in contravention of section 330, the transaction or arrangement is voidable at the instance of the company unless—

(a) restitution of any money or any other asset which is the subject matter of the arrangement or transaction is no longer possible, or the company has been indemnified in pursuance of subsection (2)(b) below for the loss or damage suffered by it, or

(b) any rights acquired bona fide for value and without actual notice of the contravention by a person other than the person for whom the transaction or arrangement was made would be affected by its avoidance.

(2) Where an arrangement or transaction is made by a company for a director of the company or its holding company or a person connected with such a director in contravention of section 330, that director and the person so connected and any other director of the company who authorised the transaction or arrangement (whether or not it has been avoided in pursuance of subsection (1)) is liable—

(a) to account to the company for any gain which he has made directly or indirectly by the arrangement or transaction; and

(b) (jointly and severally with any other person liable under this subsection) to indemnify the company for any loss or damage resulting from the arrangement or transaction.

(3) Subsection (2) is without prejudice to any liability imposed otherwise than by that subsection, but is subject to the next two subsections.

(4) Where an arrangement or transaction is entered into by a company and a person connected with a director of the company or its holding company in contravention of section 330, that director is not liable under subsection (2) of this section if he shows that he took all reasonable steps to secure the company's compliance with that section.

(5) In any case, a person so connected and any such other director as is mentioned in subsection (2) is not so liable if he shows that, at the time the arrangement or transaction was entered into, he did not know the relevant circumstances constituting the contravention.

342   Criminal penalties for breach of s. 330

(1) A director of a relevant company who authorises or permits the company to enter into a transaction or arrangement knowing or having reasonable cause to believe that the company was thereby contravening section 330 is guilty of an offence.

(2) A relevant company which enters into a transaction or arrangement for one of its directors or for a director of its holding company in contravention of section 330 is guilty of an offence.

(3) A person who procures a relevant company to enter into a transaction or arrangement knowing or having reasonable cause to believe that the company was thereby contravening section 330 is guilty of an offence.

(4) A person guilty of an offence under this section is liable to imprisonment or a fine, or both.

(5) A relevant company is not guilty of an offence under subsection (2) if it shows that, at the time the transaction or arrangement was entered into, it did not know the relevant circumstances.

Supplementary

345   Power to increase financial limits

(1) The Secretary of State may by order in a statutory instrument substitute for any sum of money specified in this Part a larger sum specified in the order.

(2) An order under this section is subject to annulment in pursuance of a resolution of either House of Parliament.

(3) Such an order does not have effect in relation to anything done or not done before its coming into force; and accordingly, proceedings in respect of any liability (whether civil or criminal) incurred before that time may be continued or instituted as if the order had not been made.

346   'Connected persons', etc.

(1) This section has effect with respect to references in this Part to a person being 'connected' with a director of a company, and to a director being 'associated with' or 'controlling' a body corporate.

(2) A person is connected with a director of a company if, but only if, he (not being himself a director of it) is—

(a) that director's spouse, child or stepchild; or

(b) except where the context otherwise requires, a body corporate with which the director is associated; or

(c) a person acting in his capacity as trustee of any trust the beneficiaries of which include—

    (i) the director, his spouse or any children or stepchildren of his, or

    (ii) a body corporate with which he is associated,

    or of a trust whose terms confer a power on the trustees that may be exercised for the benefit of the director, his spouse, or any children or stepchildren of his, or any such body corporate; or

  (d) a person acting in his capacity as partner of that director or of any person who, by virtue of paragraph (a), (b) or (c) of this subsection, is connected with that director; or

  (e) a Scottish firm in which—

    (i) that director is a partner,

    (ii) a partner is a person who, by virtue of paragraph (a), (b) or (c) above, is connected with that director, or

    (iii) a partner is a Scottish firm in which that director is a partner or in which there is a partner who, by virtue of paragraph (a), (b) or (c) above, is connected with that director.

(3) In subsection (2)—

  (a) a reference to the child or stepchild of any person includes an illegitimate child of his, but does not include any person who has attained the age of 18; and

  (b) paragraph (c) does not apply to a person acting in his capacity as trustee under an employees' share scheme or a pension scheme.

(4) A director of a company is associated with a body corporate if, but only if, he and the persons connected with him, together—

  (a) are interested in shares comprised in the equity share capital of that body corporate of a nominal value equal to at least one-fifth of that share capital *(excluding any shares in the company held as treasury shares)*; or

  (b) are entitled to exercise or control the exercise of more than one-fifth of the voting power at any general meeting of that body *(excluding any voting rights attached to any shares in the company held as treasury shares).*

(5) A director of a company is deemed to control a body corporate if, but only if—

  (a) he or any person connected with him is interested in any part of the equity share capital of that body or is entitled to exercise or control the exercise of any part of the voting power at any general meeting of that body; and

  (b) that director, the persons connected with him and the other directors of that company, together, are interested in more than one-half of that share capital *(excluding any shares in the company held as treasury shares)* or are entitled to exercise or control the exercise of more than one-half of that voting power *(excluding any voting rights attached to any shares in the company held as treasury shares).*

(6) For purposes of subsections (4) and (5)—

  (a) a body corporate with which a director is associated is not to be treated as connected with that director unless it is also connected with him by virtue of subsection (2)(c) or (d); and

  (b) a trustee of a trust the beneficiaries of which include (or may include) a body corporate with which a director is associated is not to be treated as connected with a director by reason only of that fact.

(7) The rules set out in Part I of Schedule 13 apply for the purposes of subsections (4) and (5).

(8) References in those subsections to voting power the exercise of which is controlled by a director include voting power whose exercise is controlled by a body corporate controlled by him; but this is without prejudice to other provisions of subsections (4) and (5).

[*The words in italics in s. 346(4)(a) and (b) and (5)(b) are in force from 1 December 2003.*]

347   Transactions under foreign law

For purposes of sections 319 to 322 and 330 to 343, it is immaterial whether the law which (apart from this Act) governs any arrangement or transaction is the law of the United Kingdom, or of a part of it, or not.

PART XA   CONTROL OF POLITICAL DONATIONS

347A   Introductory provisions

(1) This Part has effect for controlling—

  (a) contributions and other donations made by companies to registered parties and other EU political organisations; and

  (b) EU political expenditure incurred by companies.

(2) The following provisions have effect for the purposes of this Part, but subsections (4) and (7) have effect subject to section 347B.

(3) 'Director' includes shadow director.

(4) 'Donation', in relation to an organisation, means anything that would constitute a donation for the purposes of Part IV of the Political Parties, Elections and Referendums Act 2000 in accordance with sections 50 to 52 of that Act (references in those sections to a registered party being read as applying equally to an organisation which is not such a party); and—

  (a) subsections (3) to (8) of section 50 of that Act shall apply, with any necessary modifications, for the purpose of determining whether something is a donation to an organisation for the purposes of this Part as they apply for the purpose of determining whether something is a donation to a registered party for the purposes of Part IV of that Act; and

  (b) section 53 of that Act shall similarly apply for the purpose of determining, for the purposes of this Part, the value of any donation.

(5) 'EU political expenditure', in relation to a company, means any expenditure incurred by the company—

  (a) in respect of the preparation, publication or dissemination of any advertising or any other promotional or publicity material—

    (i) of whatever nature, and

    (ii) however published or otherwise disseminated,

    which, at the time of publication or dissemination, is capable of being reasonably regarded as intended to affect public support for any EU political organisation, or

  (b) in respect of any activities on the part of the company such as are mentioned in subsection (7)(b) or (c).

(6) 'EU political organisation' means—

  (a) a registered party; or

  (b) any other organisation to which subsection (7) applies.

(7) This subsection applies to an organisation if—

  (a) it is a political party which carries on, or proposes to carry on, activities for the purpose of or in connection with the participation of the party in any election or elections to public office held in a member State other than the United Kingdom;

  (b) it carries on, or proposes to carry on, activities which are capable of being reasonably regarded as intended to affect public support for—

    (i) any registered party,

    (ii) any other political party within paragraph (a), or

    (iii) independent candidates at any election or elections of the kind mentioned in that paragraph; or

  (c) it carries on, or proposes to carry on, activities which are capable of being reasonably regarded as intended to influence voters in relation to any national or regional referendum held under the law of any member State.

(8) 'Organisation' includes any body corporate and any combination of persons or other unincorporated association.

(9) 'Registered party' means a party registered under Part II of the Political Parties, Elections and Referendums Act 2000.

(10) 'The relevant time', in relation to any donation or expenditure made or incurred by a company or subsidiary undertaking, means—

(a) the time when the donation or expenditure is made or incurred; or

(b) if earlier, the time when any contract is entered into by the company or undertaking in pursuance of which the donation or expenditure is made or incurred.

(11) 'Subsidiary undertaking' has the same meaning as in Part VII.

347B   Exemptions

(1) Section 347A(4) does not extend to a subscription paid to an EU trade association for membership of the association, and accordingly such a payment is not a donation to the association for the purposes of this Part.

(2) In subsection (1)—

'EU trade association' means any organisation formed for the purpose of furthering the trade interests—

(a) of its members, or

(b) of persons represented by its members,

which carries on its activities wholly or mainly in one or more of the member States;

'subscription', in relation to a trade association, does not include any payment to the association to the extent that it is made for the purpose of financing any particular activity of the association.

(3) Section 347A(7) does not apply to any all-party parliamentary group composed of members of one or both of the Houses of Parliament (or of such members and other persons), and accordingly any such group is not an EU political organisation for the purposes of this Part.

(4) For the purposes of this Part—

(a) a company does not need to be authorised as mentioned in section 347C(1) or section 347D(2) or (3), and

(b) a subsidiary undertaking does not need to be authorised as mentioned in section 347E(2),

in connection with any donation or donations to any EU political organisation or organisations made in a particular qualifying period, except to the extent (if any) that the amount or aggregate amount of any such donation or donations made in that period exceeds £5,000.

(5) The restrictions imposed by sections 347C(1), 347D(2) and (3) and 347E(2) accordingly have effect subject to subsection (4); and, where a resolution is passed for the purposes of any of those provisions, any amount of donations in relation to which, by virtue of subsection (4), no authorisation is needed shall accordingly not count towards the sum specified in the resolution.

(6) In subsection (4) 'qualifying period' means—

(a) the period of 12 months beginning with the relevant date for the company or (in the case of a subsidiary undertaking) the parent company; and

(b) each succeeding period of twelve months.

(7) For the purposes of subsection (6) the relevant date for a company is—

(a) if an annual general meeting of the company is held within the period of 12 months beginning with the date of the coming into force of this section, the date of that meeting; and

(b) otherwise, the date immediately following the end of that period.

(8) For the purposes of this Part—

(a) a company does not need to be authorised as mentioned in section 347C(1) or section 347D(2) or (3), and

(b) a subsidiary undertaking does not need to be authorised as mentioned in section 347E(2),

in connection with any EU political expenditure in relation to which an exemption is conferred on the company or (as the case may be) subsidiary undertaking by virtue of an order made by the Secretary of State by statutory instrument.

(9) The restrictions imposed by sections 347C(1), 347D(2) and (3) and 347E(2) accordingly have effect subject to subsection (8); and, where a resolution is passed for the purposes of any of those provisions, any amount of EU political expenditure in relation to which, by virtue of subsection (8), no authorisation is needed shall accordingly not count towards the sum specified in the resolution.

(10) An order under subsection (8) may confer an exemption for the purposes of that subsection in relation to—

(a) companies or subsidiary undertakings of any description or category specified in the order, or

(b) expenditure of any description or category so specified (whether framed by reference to goods, services or other matters in respect of which such expenditure is incurred or otherwise),

or both.

(11) An order shall not be made under subsection (8) unless a draft of the statutory instrument containing the order has been laid before and approved by each House of Parliament.

347C   Prohibition on donations and political expenditure by companies

(1) A company must not—

(a) make any donation to any registered party or to any other EU political organisation, or

(b) incur any EU political expenditure,

unless the donation or expenditure is authorised by virtue of an approval resolution passed by the company in general meeting before the relevant time.

This subsection has effect subject to section 347D(3).

(2) For the purposes of this section an approval resolution is a qualifying resolution which authorises the company to do either (or both) of the following, namely—

(a) make donations to EU political organisations not exceeding in total a sum specified in the resolution, or

(b) incur EU political expenditure not exceeding in total a sum so specified, during the requisite period beginning with the date of the resolution.

(3) In subsection (2)—

(a) 'qualifying resolution' means an ordinary resolution or, if the directors so determine or the articles so require—

(i) a special resolution, or

(ii) a resolution passed by any percentage of the members greater than that required for an ordinary resolution;

(b) 'the requisite period' means four years or such shorter period as the directors may determine or the articles may require;

and the directors may make a determination for the purposes of paragraph (a) or (b) above except where any provision of the articles operates to prevent them from doing so.

(4) The resolution must be expressed in general terms conforming with subsection (2), and accordingly may not purport to authorise particular donations or expenditure.

(5) Where a company makes any donation or incurs any expenditure in contravention of subsection (1), no ratification or other approval made or given by the company or its members after the relevant time is capable of operating to nullify that contravention.

(6) Nothing in this section enables a company to be authorised to do anything that it could not lawfully do apart from this section.

347D   Special rules for subsidiaries

(1) This section applies where a company is a subsidiary of another company ('the holding company').

(2) Where the subsidiary is not a wholly-owned subsidiary of the holding company—

    (a) it must not make any donation or incur any expenditure to which subsection (1) of section 347C applies unless the donation or expenditure is authorised by virtue of a subsidiary approval resolution passed by the holding company in general meeting before the relevant time; and

    (b) this requirement applies in addition to that imposed by that subsection.

(3) Where the subsidiary is a wholly-owned subsidiary of the holding company—

    (a) it must not make any donation or incur any expenditure to which subsection (1) of section 347C applies unless the donation or expenditure is authorised by virtue of a subsidiary approval resolution passed by the holding company in general meeting before the relevant time; and

    (b) this requirement applies in place of that imposed by that subsection.

(4) For the purposes of this section a subsidiary approval resolution is a qualifying resolution of the holding company which authorises the subsidiary to do either (or both) of the following, namely—

    (a) make donations to EU political organisations not exceeding in total a sum specified in the resolution, or

    (b) incur EU political expenditure not exceeding in total a sum so specified, during the requisite period beginning with the date of the resolution.

(5) Subsection (3) of section 347C shall apply for the purposes of subsection (4) above as it applies for the purposes of subsection (2) of that section.

(6) The resolution must be expressed in general terms conforming with subsection (4), and accordingly may not purport to authorise particular donations or expenditure.

(7) The resolution may not relate to donations or expenditure by more than one subsidiary.

(8) Where a subsidiary makes any donation or incurs any expenditure in contravention of subsection (2) or (3), no ratification or other approval made or given by the holding company or its members after the relevant time is capable of operating to nullify that contravention.

(9) Nothing in this section enables a company to be authorised to do anything that it could not lawfully do apart from this section.

347E   Special rule for parent company of non-GB subsidiary undertaking

(1) This section applies where a company ('the parent company') has a subsidiary undertaking which is incorporated or otherwise established outside Great Britain.

(2) The parent company shall take all such steps as are reasonably open to it to secure that the subsidiary undertaking does not make any donation or incur any expenditure to which subsection (1) of section 347C applies except to the extent that the donation or expenditure is authorised by virtue of a subsidiary approval resolution passed by the parent company in general meeting before the relevant time.

(3) For the purposes of this section a subsidiary approval resolution is a qualifying resolution of the parent company which authorises the subsidiary undertaking to do either (or both) of the following, namely—

    (a) make donations to EU political organisations not exceeding in total a sum specified in the resolution, or

    (b) incur EU political expenditure not exceeding in total a sum so specified, during the requisite period beginning with the date of the resolution.

(4) Subsection (3) of section 347C shall apply for the purposes of subsection (3) above as it applies for the purposes of subsection (2) of that section.

(5) The resolution must be expressed in general terms conforming with subsection (3), and accordingly may not purport to authorise particular donations or expenditure.

(6) The resolution may not relate to donations or expenditure by more than one subsidiary undertaking.

(7) Where a subsidiary undertaking makes any donation or incurs any expenditure which (to any extent) is not authorised as mentioned in subsection (2), no ratification or other approval made or given by the parent company or its members after the relevant time is capable of operating to authorise that donation or expenditure.

347F   Remedies for breach of prohibitions on company donations etc.

(1) This section applies where a company has made any donation or incurred any expenditure in contravention of any of the provisions of sections 347C and 347D.

(2) Every person who was a director of the company at the relevant time is liable to pay the company—
    (a) the amount of the donation or expenditure made or incurred in contravention of the provisions in question; and
    (b) damages in respect of any loss or damage sustained by the company as a result of the donation or expenditure having been made or incurred in contravention of those provisions.

(3) Every such person is also liable to pay the company interest on the amount mentioned in subsection (2)(a) in respect of the period—
    (a) beginning with the date when the donation or expenditure was made or incurred, and
    (b) ending with the date when that amount is paid to the company by any such person;

and such interest shall be payable at such rate as the Secretary of State may prescribe by regulations.

(4) Where two or more persons are subject to a particular liability arising by virtue of any provision of this section, each of those persons is jointly and severally liable.

(5) Where only part of any donation or expenditure was made or incurred in contravention of any of the provisions of sections 347C and 347D, this section applies only to so much of it as was so made or incurred.

(6) Where—
    (a) this section applies as mentioned in subsection (1), and
    (b) the company in question is a subsidiary of another company ('the holding company'),

then (subject to subsection (7)) subsections (2) to (5) shall, in connection with the donation or expenditure made or incurred by the subsidiary, apply in relation to the holding company as they apply in relation to the subsidiary.

(7) Those subsections do not apply in relation to the holding company if—
    (a) the subsidiary is not a wholly-owned subsidiary of the holding company; and
    (b) the donation or expenditure was authorised by such a resolution of the holding company as is mentioned in section 347D(2)(a).

(8) Nothing in section 727 shall apply in relation to any liability of any person arising under this section.

347G   Remedy for unauthorised donation or expenditure by non-GB subsidiary

(1) This section applies where—
    (a) a company ('the parent company') has a subsidiary undertaking falling within subsection (1) of section 347E;
    (b) the subsidiary undertaking has made any donation or incurred any expenditure to which subsection (1) of section 347C applies; and

(c) the parent company has, in relation to that donation or expenditure, failed to discharge its duty under subsection (2) of section 347E to take all such steps as are mentioned in that subsection.

(2) Subsections (2) to (4) of section 347F shall, in connection with the donation or expenditure made or incurred by the subsidiary undertaking, apply in relation to the holding company as if—

(a) it were a company falling within subsection (1) of that section, and

(b) the donation or expenditure had been made or incurred by it in contravention of section 347C or 347D.

(3) Where only part of the donation or expenditure was not authorised as mentioned in section 347E(2), those subsections shall so apply only to that part of it.

(4) Section 347F(8) applies to any liability of any person arising under section 347F by virtue of this section.

347H   Exemption of directors from liability in respect of unauthorised donation or expenditure

(1) Where proceedings are brought against a director or former director of a company in respect of any liability arising under section 347F(2)(a) in connection with a donation or expenditure made or incurred by the company, it shall be a defence for that person to show that—

(a) the unauthorised amount has been repaid to the company, together with any interest on that amount due under section 347F(3);

(b) that repayment has been approved by the company in general meeting; and

(c) in the notice of the relevant resolution submitted to that meeting full disclosure was made—

(i) of the circumstances in which the donation or expenditure was made or incurred in contravention of section 347C or 347D, and

(ii) of the circumstances in which, and the person or persons by whom, the repayment was made.

(2) Where proceedings are brought against a director or former director of a holding company in respect of any liability arising under section 347F(2)(a) in connection with a donation or expenditure made or incurred by a subsidiary of the company, it shall be a defence for that person to show that—

(a) the unauthorised amount has been repaid either to the subsidiary or to the holding company, together with any interest on that amount due under section 347F(3);

(b) that repayment has been approved—

(i) (if made to the subsidiary) by both the subsidiary and the holding company in general meeting, or

(ii) (if made to the holding company) by the holding company in general meeting; and

(c) in the notice of the relevant resolution submitted to each of those meetings or (as the case may be) to that meeting, full disclosure was made—

(i) of the circumstances in which the donation or expenditure was made in contravention of section 347D, and

(ii) of the circumstances in which, and the person or persons by whom, the repayment was made.

(3) If the subsidiary is a wholly-owned subsidiary of the holding company, it is not necessary for the purposes of subsection (2) to show (where the repayment was made to the subsidiary) that the repayment has been approved by the subsidiary, and paragraphs (b) and (c) of that subsection shall apply accordingly.

(4) Where proceedings are brought against a director or former director of a holding company in respect of any liability arising under section 347F(2)(a) in connection with a

donation or expenditure made or incurred by a subsidiary of the company which is not a wholly-owned subsidiary, then (subject to subsection (5)) it shall be a defence for that person to show that—

  (a) proceedings have been instituted by the subsidiary against all or any of its directors in respect of the unauthorised amount; and

  (b) those proceedings are being pursued with due diligence by the subsidiary.

(5) A person may not avail himself of the defence provided by subsection (4) except with the leave of the court; and on an application for leave under this subsection the court may make such order as it thinks fit, including an order adjourning, or sanctioning the continuation of, the proceedings against the applicant on such terms and conditions as it thinks fit.

(6) Where proceedings are brought against a director or former director of a company in respect of any liability arising under section 347F(2)(a) (as applied by virtue of section 347G) in connection with a donation or expenditure made or incurred by a subsidiary undertaking of the company, it shall be a defence for that person to show that—

  (a) the unauthorised amount has been repaid to the subsidiary undertaking, together with any interest on that amount due under section 347F(3) (as so applied);

  (b) that repayment has been approved by the company in general meeting; and

  (c) in the notice of the relevant resolution submitted to that meeting full disclosure was made—

    (i) of the circumstances in which the donation or expenditure was made without having been authorised as mentioned in section 347E(2), and

    (ii) of the circumstances in which, and the person or persons by whom, the repayment was made.

(7) In this section 'the unauthorised amount', in relation to any donation or expenditure, means the amount of the donation or expenditure—

  (a) which was made or incurred in contravention of section 347C or 347D, or

  (b) which was not authorised as mentioned in section 347E(2), as the case may be.

347I   Enforcement of directors' liabilities by shareholder action

(1) Any liability of any person under section 347F or 347G as a director or former director of a company is (in addition to being enforceable by proceedings brought by the company) enforceable by proceedings brought under this section in the name of the company by an authorised group of members of the company.

(2) For the purposes of this section 'authorised group', in relation to the members of a company, means any such combination of members as is specified in section 54(2)(a), (b) or (c).

(3) An authorised group of members of a company may not bring proceedings under this section unless—

  (a) the group has given written notice to the company stating—

    (i) the cause of action and a summary of the facts on which the proceedings are to be based,

    (ii) the names and addresses of the members of the company comprising the group, and

    (iii) the grounds on which it is alleged that those members constitute an authorised group; and

  (b) not less than 28 days have elapsed between the date of the giving of the notice to the company and the institution of the proceedings.

(4) Where such a notice is given to a company, any director may apply to the court within the period of 28 days beginning with the date of the giving of the notice for an order directing that the proposed proceedings are not to be instituted.

(5) An application under subsection (4) may be made on one or more of the following grounds—

(a) that the unauthorised amount within the meaning of section 347H has been repaid to the company or subsidiary undertaking as mentioned in subsection (1), (2), (4) or (6) of that section (as the case may be) and the other conditions mentioned in that subsection were satisfied with respect to that repayment;

(b) that proceedings to enforce the liability have been instituted by the company and are being pursued with due diligence by the company;

(c) that the members proposing to institute proceedings under this section do not constitute an authorised group.

(6) Where such an application is made on the ground mentioned in subsection (5)(b), the court may make such order as it thinks fit; and such an order may, as an alternative to directing that the proposed proceedings under this section are not to be instituted, direct—

(a) that those proceedings may be instituted on such terms and conditions as the court thinks fit;

(b) that the proceedings instituted by the company are to be discontinued;

(c) that the proceedings instituted by the company may be continued on such terms and conditions as the court thinks fit.

(7) If proceedings are brought under this section by an authorised group of members of a company, the group shall owe the same duties to the company in relation to the bringing of those proceedings on behalf of the company as would be owed by the directors of the company if the proceedings were being brought by the company itself; but no proceedings to enforce any duty owed by virtue of this subsection shall be brought by the company except with the leave of the court.

(8) Proceedings brought under this section may not be discontinued or settled by the group except with the leave of the court; and the court may grant leave under this subsection on such terms as it thinks fit.

347J   Costs of shareholder action

(1) This section applies in relation to proceedings brought under section 347I by an authorised group of members of a company ('the group').

(2) The group may apply to the court for an order directing the company to indemnify the group in respect of costs incurred or to be incurred by the group in connection with the proceedings; and on such an application the court may make such an order on such terms as it thinks fit.

(3) The group shall not be entitled to be paid any such costs out of the assets of the company except by virtue of such an order.

(4) If—

(a) the company is awarded costs in connection with the proceedings or it is agreed that costs incurred by the company in connection with the proceedings should be paid by any defendant, and

(b) no order has been made with respect to the proceedings under subsection (2), the costs shall be paid to the group.

(5) If—

(a) any defendant is awarded costs in connection with the proceedings or it is agreed that any defendant should be paid costs incurred by him in connection with the proceedings, and

(b) no order has been made with respect to the proceedings under subsection (2), the costs shall be paid by the group.

(6) In the application of this section to Scotland references to costs are to expenses and references to any defendant are to any defender.

347K   Information for purposes of shareholder action

(1) Where any proceedings have been instituted under section 347I by an authorised group within the meaning of that section, the group is entitled to require the company to

provide the group with all information relating to the subject matter of the proceedings which is in the company's possession or under its control or which is reasonably obtainable by it.

(2) If the company, having been required by the group to provide the information referred to in subsection (1), refuses to provide the group with all or any of the information, the court may, on an application made by the group, make an order directing—

(a) the company, and

(b) any of its officers or employees specified in the application, to provide the group with the information in question in such form and by such means as the court may direct.

PART XI   COMPANY ADMINISTRATION AND PROCEDURE

CHAPTER I   COMPANY IDENTIFICATION

348   Company name to appear outside place of business

(1) Every company shall paint or affix, and keep painted or affixed, its name on the outside of every office or place in which its business is carried on, in a conspicuous position and in letters easily legible.

(2) If a company does not paint or affix its name as required above, the company and every officer of it who is in default is liable to a fine; and if a company does not keep its name painted or affixed as so required, the company and every officer of it who is in default is liable to a fine and, for continued contravention, to a daily default fine.

349   Company's name to appear in its correspondence, etc.

(1) Every company shall have its name mentioned in legible characters—

(a) in all business letters of the company,

(b) in all its notices and other official publications,

(c) in all bills of exchange, promissory notes, endorsements, cheques and orders for money or goods purporting to be signed by or on behalf of the company, and

(d) in all its bills of parcels, invoices, receipts and letters of credit.

(2) If a company fails to comply with subsection (1) it is liable to a fine.

(3) If an officer of a company or a person on its behalf—

(a) issues or authorises the issue of any business letter of the company, or any notice or other official publication of the company, in which the company's name is not mentioned as required by subsection (1), or

(b) issues or authorises the issue of any bill of parcels, invoice, receipt or letter of credit of the company in which its name is not so mentioned,

he is liable to a fine.

(4) If an officer of a company or a person on its behalf signs or authorises to be signed on behalf of the company any bill of exchange, promissory note, endorsement, cheque or order for money or goods in which the company's name is not mentioned as required by subsection (1), he is liable to a fine; and he is further personally liable to the holder of the bill of exchange, promissory note, cheque or order for money or goods for the amount of it (unless it is duly paid by the company).

350   Company seal

(1) A company which has a common seal shall have its name engraved in legible characters on the seal; and if it fails to comply with this subsection it is liable to a fine.

(2) If an officer of a company or a person on its behalf uses or authorises the use of any seal purporting to be a seal of the company on which its name is not engraved as required by subsection (1), he is liable to a fine.

351   Particulars in correspondence, etc.

(1) Every company shall have the following particulars mentioned in legible characters in all business letters and order forms of the company, that is to say—

    (a) the company's place of registration and the number with which it is registered,

    (b) the address of its registered office,

    (c) in the case of an investment company (as defined in section 266), the fact that it is such a company, and

    (d) in the case of a limited company exempt from the obligation to use the word 'limited' as part of its name, the fact that it is a limited company.

(2) If in the case of a company having a share capital there is on the stationery used for any such letters, or on the company's order forms, a reference to the amount of share capital, the reference must be to paid-up share capital.

(5) As to contraventions of this section, the following applies—

    (a) if a company fails to comply with subsection (1) or (2), it is liable to a fine,

    (b) if an officer of a company or a person on its behalf issues or authorises the issue of any business letter or order form not complying with those subsections, he is liable to a fine.

CHAPTER II   REGISTER OF MEMBERS

352   Obligation to keep and enter up register

(1) Every company shall keep a register of its members and enter in it the particulars required by this section.

(2) There shall be entered in the register—

    (a) the names and addresses of the members;

    (b) the date on which each person was registered as a member; and

    (c) the date at which any person ceased to be a member.

(3) The following applies in the case of a company having a share capital—

    (a) with the names and addresses of the members there shall be entered a statement—

        (i) of the shares held by each member, distinguishing each share by its number (so long as the share has a number) and, where the company has more than one class of issued shares, by its class, and

        (ii) of the amount paid or agreed to be considered as paid on the shares of each member;

    (b) where the company has converted any of its shares into stock and given notice of the conversion to the registrar of companies, the register shall show the amount and class of stock held by each member, instead of the amount of shares and the particulars relating to shares specified in paragraph (a).

(3A) Where a company purchases one or more of its own shares in circumstances in which section 162A applies—

    (a) the requirements of subsection (2) and (3) must be complied with unless the company cancels all of the shares forthwith after the purchase in accordance with section 162D(1), but

    (b) any share which is so cancelled must be disregarded for the purposes of subsection (3).

(4) In the case of a company which does not have a share capital but has more than one class of members, there shall be entered in the register, with the names and addresses of the members, the class to which each member belongs.

(5) If a company makes default in complying with this section, the company and every officer of it who is in default is liable to a fine and, for continued contravention, to a daily default fine.

(6) An entry relating to a former member of the company may be removed from the register after the expiration of 20 years from the date on which he ceased to be a member.

(7) Liability incurred by a company from the making or deletion of an entry in its register of members, or from a failure to make or delete any such entry, is not enforceable more than 20 years after the date on which the entry was made or deleted or, in the case of any such failure, the failure first occurred.

This is without prejudice to any lesser period of limitation.

[*Section 352(3A) is in force from 1 December 2003.*]

352A   Statement that company has only one member

(1) If the number of members of a private company limited by shares or by guarantee falls to one there shall upon the occurrence of that event be entered in the company's register of members with the name and address of the sole member—

(i)   a statement that the company has only one member, and

(ii) the date on which the company became a company having only one member.

(2) If the membership of a private company limited by shares or by guarantee increases from one to two or more members there shall upon the occurrence of that event be entered in the company's register of members, with the name and address of the person who was formerly the sole member, a statement that the company has ceased to have only one member together with the date on which that event occurred.

(3) If a company makes default in complying with this section, the company and every officer of it who is in default is liable to a fine and, for continued contravention, to a daily default fine.

353   Location of register

(1) A company's register of members shall be kept at its registered office, except that—

(a) if the work of making it up is done at another office of the company, it may be kept there; and

(b) if the company arranges with some other person for the making up of the register to be undertaken on its behalf by that other, it may be kept at the office of the other at which the work is done;

but it must not be kept, in the case of a company registered in England and Wales, at any place elsewhere than in England and Wales or, in the case of a company registered in Scotland, at any place elsewhere than in Scotland.

(2) Subject as follows, every company shall send notice in the prescribed form to the registrar of companies of the place where its register of members is kept, and of any change in that place.

(3) The notice need not be sent if the register has, at all times since it came into existence (or, in the case of a register in existence on 1 July 1948, at all times since then) been kept at the company's registered office.

(4) If a company makes default for 14 days in complying with subsection (2), the company and every officer of it who is in default is liable to a fine and, for continued contravention, to a daily default fine.

354   Index of members

(1) Every company having more than 50 members shall, unless the register of members is in such a form as to constitute in itself an index, keep an index of the names of the members of the company and shall, within 14 days after the date on which any alteration is made in the register of members, make any necessary alteration in the index.

(2) The index shall in respect of each member contain a sufficient indication to enable the account of that member in the register to be readily found.

(3) The index shall be at all times kept at the same place as the register of members.

(4) If default is made in complying with this section, the company and every officer of it who is in default is liable to a fine and, for continued contravention, to a daily default fine.

355   Entries in register in relation to share warrants

(1) On the issue of a share warrant the company shall strike out of its register of members the name of the member then entered in it as holding the shares specified in the warrant as if he had ceased to be a member, and shall enter in the register the following particulars, namely—

  (a) the fact of the issue of the warrant;

  (b) a statement of the shares included in the warrant, distinguishing each share by its number so long as the share has a number; and

  (c) the date of the issue of the warrant.

(2) Subject to the company's articles, the bearer of a share warrant is entitled, on surrendering it for cancellation, to have his name entered as a member in the register of members.

(3) The company is responsible for any loss incurred by any person by reason of the company entering in the register the name of a bearer of a share warrant in respect of the shares specified in it without the warrant being surrendered and cancelled.

(4) Until the warrant is surrendered, the particulars specified in subsection (1) are deemed to be those required by this Act to be entered in the register of members; and, on the surrender, the date of the surrender must be entered.

(5) Except as provided by section 291(2) (director's share qualification), the bearer of a share warrant may, if the articles of the company so provide, be deemed a member of the company within the meaning of this Act, either to the full extent or for any purposes defined in the articles.

356   Inspection of register and index

(1) Except when the register of members is closed under the provisions of this Act, the register and the index of members' names shall be open to the inspection of any member of the company without charge, and of any other person on payment of such fee as may be prescribed.

(3) Any member of the company or other person may require a copy of the register, or of any part of it, on payment of such fee as may be prescribed; and the company shall cause any copy so required by a person to be sent to him within 10 days beginning with the day next following that on which the requirement is received by the company.

(5) If an inspection required under this section is refused, or if a copy so required is not sent within the proper period, the company and every officer of it who is in default is liable in respect of each offence to a fine.

(6) In the case of such refusal or default, the court may by order compel an immediate inspection of the register and index, or direct that the copies required be sent to the persons requiring them.

357   Non-compliance with ss. 353, 354, 356; agent's default

Where under section 353(1)(b), the register of members is kept at the office of some person other than the company, and by reason of any default of his the company fails to comply with—

  section 353(2) (notice to registrar),

  section 354(3) (index to be kept with register), or

  section 356 (inspection),

or with any requirement of this Act as to the production of the register, that other person is liable to the same penalties as if he were an officer of the company who was in default, and the power of the court under section 356(6) extends to the making of orders against that other and his officers and servants.

358   Power to close register

A company may, on giving notice by advertisement in a newspaper circulating in the district in which the company's registered office is situated, close the register of members for any time or times not exceeding in the whole 30 days in each year.

359   Power of court to rectify register

    (1) If—

        (a) the name of any person is, without sufficient cause, entered in or omitted from a company's register of members, or

        (b) default is made or unnecessary delay takes place in entering on the register the fact of any person having ceased to be a member,

the person aggrieved, or any member of the company, or the company, may apply to the court for rectification of the register.

    (2) The court may either refuse the application or may order rectification of the register and payment by the company of any damages sustained by any party aggrieved.

    (3) On such an application the court may decide any question relating to the title of a person who is a party to the application to have his name entered in or omitted from the register, whether the question arises between members or alleged members, or between members or alleged members on the one hand and the company on the other hand, and generally may decide any question necessary or expedient to be decided for rectification of the register.

    (4) In the case of a company required by this Act to send a list of its members to the registrar of companies, the court, when making an order for rectification of the register, shall by its order direct notice of the rectification to be given to the registrar.

360   Trusts not to be entered on register in England and Wales

No notice of any trust, expressed, implied or constructive, shall be entered on the register, or be receivable by the registrar, in the case of companies registered in England and Wales.

361   Register to be evidence

The register of members is prima facie evidence of any matters which are by this Act directed or authorised to be inserted in it.

362   Overseas branch registers

    (1) A company having a share capital whose objects comprise the transaction of business in any of the countries or territories specified in Part I of Schedule 14 to this Act may cause to be kept in any such country or territory in which it transacts business a branch register of members resident in that country or territory.

    (2) Such a branch register is to be known as an 'overseas branch register'; and—

        (a) any dominion register kept by a company under section 119 of the Companies Act 1948 is to become known as an overseas branch register of the company;

        (b) where any Act or instrument (including in particular a company's articles) refers to a company's dominion register, that reference is to be read (unless the context otherwise requires) as being to an overseas branch register kept under this section; and

        (c) references to a colonial register occurring in articles registered before 1 November 1929 are to be read as referring to an overseas branch register.

    (3) Part II of Schedule 14 has effect with respect to overseas branch registers kept under this section; and Part III of the Schedule enables corresponding facilities in Great Britain to be accorded to companies incorporated in other parts of the world.

. . .

CHAPTER III   ANNUAL RETURN

363   Duty to deliver annual returns

    (1) Every company shall deliver to the registrar successive annual returns each of which is made up to a date not later than the date which is from time to time the company's 'return date', that is—

        (a) the anniversary of the company's incorporation, or

        (b) if the company's last return delivered in accordance with this Chapter was made up to a different date, the anniversary of that date.

(2) Each return shall—
- (a) be in the prescribed form,
- (b) contain the information required by or under the following provisions of this Chapter, and
- (c) be signed by a director or the secretary of the company; and it shall be delivered to the registrar within 28 days after the date to which it is made up.

(3) If a company fails to deliver an annual return in accordance with this Chapter before the end of the period of 28 days after a return date, the company is guilty of an offence and liable to a fine and, in the case of continued contravention, to a daily default fine.

The contravention continues until such time as an annual return made up to that return date and complying with the requirements of subsection (2) (except as to date of delivery) is delivered by the company to the registrar.

(4) Where a company is guilty of an offence under subsection (3), every director or secretary of the company is similarly liable unless he shows that he took all reasonable steps to avoid the commission or continuation of the offence.

(5) The references in this section to a return being delivered 'in accordance with this Chapter' are—
- (a) in relation to a return made on or after 1 October 1990, to a return with respect to which all the requirements of subsection (2) are complied with;
- (b) in relation to a return made before 1 October 1990, to a return with respect to which the formal and substantive requirements of this Chapter as it then had effect were complied with, whether or not the return was delivered in time.

364 Contents of annual return: general

(1) Every annual return shall state the date to which it is made up and shall contain the following information—
- (a) the address of the company's registered office;
- (b) the type of company it is and its principal business activities;
- (c) the name and address of the company secretary;
- (d) the name and address of every director of the company;
- (e) in the case of each individual director—
  - (i) his nationality, date of birth and business occupation;
- (g) if the register of members is not kept at the company's registered office, the address of the place where it is kept;
- (h) if any register of debenture holders (or a duplicate of any such register or a part of it) is not kept at the company's registered office, the address of the place where it is kept.

(2) The information as to the company's type shall be given by reference to the classification scheme prescribed for the purposes of this section.

(3) The information as to the company's principal business activities may be given by reference to one or more categories of any prescribed system of classifying business activities.

(4) A person's 'name' and 'address' mean, respectively—
- (a) in the case of an individual, his Christian name (or other forename) and surname and his usual residential address;
- (b) in the case of a corporation or Scottish firm, its corporate or firm name and its registered or principal office.

(5) In the case of a peer, or an individual usually known by a title, the title may be stated instead of his Christian name (or other forename) and surname or in addition to either or both of them.

(6) Where all the partners in a firm are joint secretaries, the name and principal office of the firm may be stated instead of the names and addresses of the partners.

364A   Contents of annual return: particulars of share capital and shareholders
(1) The annual return of a company having a share capital shall contain the following information with respect to its share capital and members.

(2) The return shall state the total number of issued shares of the company at the date to which the return is made up and the aggregate nominal value of those shares.

(3) The return shall state with respect to each class of shares in the company—
(a) the nature of the class, and
(b) the total number and aggregate nominal value of issued shares of that class at the date to which the return is made up.

(4) The return shall contain a list of the names and addresses of every person who—
(a) is a member of the company on the date to which the return is made up, or
(b) has ceased to be a member of the company since the date to which the last return was made up (or, in the case of the first return, since the incorporation of the company);
and if the names are not arranged in alphabetical order the return shall have annexed to it an index sufficient to enable the name of any person in the list to be easily found.

(5) The return shall also state—
(a) the number of shares of each class held by each member of the company at the date to which the return is made up, and
(b) the number of shares of each class transferred since the date to which the last return was made up (or, in the case of the first return, since the incorporation of the company) by each member or person who has ceased to be a member, and the dates of registration of the transfers.

(6) The return may, if either of the two immediately preceding returns has given the full particulars required by subsection (4) and (5), give only such particulars as relate to persons ceasing to be or becoming members since the date of the last return and to shares transferred since that date.

(7) Subsections (4) and (5) do not require the inclusion of particulars entered in an overseas branch register if copies of those entries have not been received at the company's registered office by the date to which the return is made up.
Those particulars shall be included in the company's next annual return after they are received.

(8) Where the company has converted any of its shares into stock, the return shall give the corresponding information in relation to that stock, stating the amount of stock instead of the number or nominal value of shares.

365   Supplementary provisions: regulations and interpretation
(1) The Secretary of State may by regulations make further provision as to the information to be given in a company's annual return, which may amend or repeal the provisions of sections 364 and 364A.

(2) Regulations under this section shall be made by statutory instrument which shall be subject to annulment in pursuance of a resolution of either House of Parliament.

(3) For the purposes of this Chapter, except section 363(2)(c) (signature of annual return), a shadow director shall be deemed to be a director.

CHAPTER IV   MEETINGS AND RESOLUTIONS
Meetings

366   Annual general meeting
(1) Every company shall in each year hold a general meeting as its annual general meeting in addition to any other meetings in that year, and shall specify the meeting as such in the notices calling it.

(2) However, so long as a company holds its first annual general meeting within 18 months of its incorporation, it need not hold it in the year of its incorporation or in the following year.

(3) Not more than 15 months shall elapse between the date of one annual general meeting of a company and that of the next.

(4) If default is made in holding a meeting in accordance with this section, the company and every officer of it who is in default is liable to a fine.

366A   Election by private company to dispense with annual general meetings

(1) A private company may elect (by elective resolution in accordance with section 379A) to dispense with the holding of annual general meetings.

(2) An election has effect for the year in which it is made and subsequent years, but does not affect any liability already incurred by reason of default in holding an annual general meeting.

(3) In any year in which an annual general meeting would be required to be held but for the election, and in which no such meeting has been held, any member of the company may, by notice to the company not later than three months before the end of the year, require the holding of an annual general meeting in that year.

(3A) The power of a member under subsection (3) to require the holding of an annual general meeting is exercisable not only by the giving of a notice but also by the transmission to the company at such address as may for the time being be specified for the purpose by or on behalf of the company of an electronic communication containing the requirement.

(4) If such a notice is given or electronic communication is transmitted, the provisions of section 366(1) and (4) apply with respect to the calling of the meeting and the consequences of default.

(5) If the election ceases to have effect, the company is not obliged under section 366 to hold an annual general meeting in that year if, when the election ceases to have effect, less than three months of the year remains.

This does not affect any obligation of the company to hold an annual general meeting in that year in pursuance of a notice given or electronic communication transmitted under subsection (3).

(5A) In this section, 'address' includes any number or address used for the purposes of electronic communications.

367   Secretary of State's power to call meeting in default

(1) If default is made in holding a meeting in accordance with section 366, the Secretary of State may, on the application of any member of the company, call, or direct the calling of, a general meeting of the company and give such ancillary or consequential directions as he thinks expedient, including directions modifying or supplementing, in relation to the calling, holding and conduct of the meeting, the operation of the company's articles.

(2) The directions that may be given under subsection (1) include a direction that one member of the company present in person or by proxy shall be deemed to constitute a meeting.

(3) If default is made in complying with directions of the Secretary of State under subsection (1), the company and every officer of it who is in default is liable to a fine.

(4) A general meeting held under this section shall, subject to any directions of the Secretary of State, be deemed to be an annual general meeting of the company; but, where a meeting so held is not held in the year in which the default in holding the company's annual general meeting occurred, the meeting so held shall not be treated as the annual general meeting for the year in which it is held unless at that meeting the company resolves that it be so treated.

(5) Where a company so resolves, a copy of the resolution shall, within 15 days after its passing, be forwarded to the registrar of companies and recorded by him; and if default is

made in complying with this subsection, the company and every officer of it who is in default is liable to a fine and, for continued contravention, to a daily default fine.

368   Extraordinary general meeting on members' requisition

(1) The directors of a company shall, on a members' requisition, forthwith proceed duly to convene an extraordinary general meeting of the company.

This applies notwithstanding anything in the company's articles.

(2) A members' requisition is a requisition of—

    (a) members of the company holding at the date of the deposit of the requisition not less than one-tenth of such of the paid-up capital of the company as at that date carries the right of voting at general meetings of the company; or

    (b) in the case of a company not having a share capital, members of it representing not less than one-tenth of the total voting rights of all the members having at the date of deposit of the requisition a right to vote at general meetings.

(2A) For the purposes of subsection (2)(a) any of the company's paid up capital held as treasury shares must be disregarded.

(3) The requisition must state the objects of the meeting, and must be signed by the requisitionists and deposited at the registered office of the company, and may consist of several documents in like form each signed by one or more requisitionists.

(4) If the directors do not within 21 days from the date of the deposit of the requisition proceed duly to convene a meeting, the requisitionists, or any of them representing more than one-half of the total voting rights of all of them, may themselves convene a meeting, but any meeting so convened shall not be held after the expiration of 3 months from that date.

(5) A meeting convened under this section by requisitionists shall be convened in the same manner, as nearly as possible, as that in which meetings are to be convened by directors.

(6) Any reasonable expenses incurred by the requisitionists by reason of the failure of the directors duly to convene a meeting shall be repaid to the requisitionists by the company, and any sum so repaid shall be retained by the company out of any sums due or to become due from the company by way of fees or other remuneration in respect of their services to such of the directors as were in default.

(7) In the case of a meeting at which a resolution is to be proposed as a special resolution, the directors are deemed not to have duly convened the meeting if they do not give the notice required for special resolutions by section 378(2).

(8) The directors are deemed not to have duly convened a meeting if they convene a meeting for a date more than 28 days after the date of the notice convening the meeting.

[*Section 368(2A) is in force from 1 December 2003.*]

369   Length of notice for calling meetings

(1) A provision of a company's articles is void in so far as it provides for the calling of a meeting of the company (other than an adjourned meeting) by a shorter notice than—

    (a) in the case of the annual general meeting, 21 days' notice in writing; and

    (b) in the case of a meeting other than an annual general meeting or a meeting for the passing of a special resolution—

        (i) 7 days' notice in writing in the case of an unlimited company, and

        (ii) otherwise, 14 days' notice in writing.

(2) Save in so far as the articles of a company make other provision in that behalf (not being a provision avoided by subsection (1)), a meeting of the company (other than an adjourned meeting) may be called—

    (a) in the case of the annual general meeting, by 21 days' notice in writing; and

    (b) in the case of a meeting other than an annual general meeting or a meeting for the passing of a special resolution—

        (i) by 7 days' notice in writing in the case of an unlimited company, and

        (ii) otherwise, 14 days' notice in writing.

(3) Notwithstanding that a meeting is called by shorter notice than that specified in subsection (2) or in the company's articles (as the case may be), it is deemed to have been duly called if it is so agreed—

(a) in the case of a meeting called as the annual general meeting, by all the members entitled to attend and vote at it; and

(b) otherwise by the requisite majority.

(4) The requisite majority for this purpose is a majority in number of the members having a right to attend and vote at the meeting, being a majority—

(a) together holding not less than 95 per cent in nominal value of the shares giving a right to attend and vote at the meeting *(excluding any shares in the company held as treasury shares)*; or

(b) in the case of a company not having a share capital, together representing not less than 95 per cent of the total voting rights at that meeting of all the members.

A private company may elect (by elective resolution in accordance with section 379A) that the above provisions shall have effect in relation to the company as if for the references to 95 per cent there were substituted references to such lesser percentage, but not less than 90 per cent, as may be specified in the resolution or subsequently determined by the company in general meeting.

(4A) For the purposes of this section the cases in which notice in writing of a meeting is to be taken as given to a person include any case in which notice of the meeting is sent using electronic communications to such address as may for the time being be notified by that person to the company for that purpose.

(4B) For the purposes of this section a notice in writing of a meeting is also to be treated as given to a person where—

(a) the company and that person have agreed that notices of meetings required to be given to that person may instead be accessed by him on a web site;

(b) the meeting is a meeting to which that agreement applies;

(c) that person is notified, in a manner for the time being agreed between him and the company for the purpose, of—

(i) the publication of the notice on a web site;

(ii) the address of that web site; and

(iii) the place on that web site where the notice may be accessed, and how it may be accessed;

and

(d) the notice continues to be published on that web site throughout the period beginning with the giving of that notification and ending with the conclusion of the meeting;

and for the purposes of this section a notice treated in accordance with this subsection as given to any person is to be treated as so given at the time of the notification mentioned in paragraph (c).

(4C) A notification given for the purposes of subsection (4B)(c) must—

(a) state that it concerns a notice of a company meeting served in accordance with this Act,

(b) specify the place, date and time of the meeting, and

(c) state whether the meeting is to be an annual or extraordinary general meeting.

(4D) Nothing in subsection (4B) shall invalidate the proceedings of a meeting where—

(a) any notice that is required to be published as mentioned in paragraph (d) of that subsection is published for a part, but not all, of the period mentioned in that paragraph; and

(b) the failure to publish that notice throughout that period is wholly attributable to circumstances which it would not be reasonable to have expected the company to prevent or avoid.

(4E) A company may, notwithstanding any provision to the contrary in a company's articles, take advantage of any of subsections (4A) to (4D).

(4F) In so far as the articles of the company do not provide for notices and notifications to be served using electronic communications, the provisions of Table A (as for the time being in force) as to such service shall apply.

(4G) In this section, 'address' includes any number or address used for the purposes of electronic communications.

[*The words in italics in s. 369(4)(a) are in force from 1 December 2003.*]

370   General provisions as to meetings and votes

(1) The following provisions have effect in so far as the articles of the company do not make other provision in that behalf.

(2) Notice of the meeting of a company shall be served on every member of it in the manner in which notices are required to be served by Table A (as for the time being in force).

(3) Two or more members holding not less than one-tenth of the issued share capital *(excluding any shares in the company held as treasury shares)* or, if the company does not have a share capital, not less than 5 per cent in number of the members of the company may call a meeting.

(4) Two members personally present are a quorum.

(5) Any member elected by the members present at a meeting may be chairman of

(6) In the case of a company originally having a share capital, every member has one vote in respect of each share or each £10 of stock held by him; and in any other case every member has one vote.

[*The words in italics in s. 370(3) are in force from 1 December 2003.*]

370A   Quorum at meetings of the sole member

Notwithstanding any provision to the contrary in the articles of a private company limited by shares or by guarantee having only one member, one member present in person or by proxy shall be a quorum.

371   Power of court to order meeting

(1) If for any reason it is impracticable to call a meeting of a company in any manner in which meetings of that company may be called, or to conduct the meeting in manner prescribed by the articles or this Act, the court may, either of its own motion or on the application—

> (a) of any director of the company, or
> (b) of any member of the company who would be entitled to vote at the meeting, order a meeting to be called, held and conducted in any manner the court thinks fit.

(2) Where such an order is made, the court may give such ancillary or consequential directions as it thinks expedient; and these may include a direction that one member of the company present in person or by proxy be deemed to constitute a meeting.

(3) A meeting called, held and conducted in accordance with an order under subsection (1) is deemed for all purposes a meeting of the company duly called, held and conducted.

372   Proxies

(1) Any member of a company entitled to attend and vote at a meeting of it is entitled to appoint another person (whether a member or not) as his proxy to attend and vote instead of him; and in the case of a private company a proxy appointed to attend and vote instead of a member has also the same right as the member to speak at the meeting.

(2) But, unless the articles otherwise provide—

> (a) subsection (1) does not apply in the case of a company not having a share capital; and

(b) a member of a private company is not entitled to appoint more than one proxy to attend on the same occasion; and

(c) a proxy is not entitled to vote except on a poll.

(2A) The appointment of a proxy may, notwithstanding any provision to the contrary in a company's articles, be contained in an electronic communication sent to such address as may be notified by or on behalf of the company for that purpose.

(2B) In so far as the articles of the company do not make other provision in that behalf, the appointment of a proxy may be contained in an electronic communication in accordance with the provisions of Table A (as for the time being in force).

(3) In the case of a company having a share capital, in every notice calling a meeting of the company there shall appear with reasonable prominence a statement that a member entitled to attend and vote is entitled to appoint a proxy or, where that is allowed, one or more proxies to attend and vote instead of him, and that a proxy need not also be a member.

(4) If default is made in complying with subsection (3) as respects any meeting, every officer of the company who is in default is liable to a fine.

(5) A provision contained in a company's articles is void in so far as it would have the effect of requiring the appointment of a proxy or any document necessary to show the validity of, or otherwise relating to, the appointment of a proxy, to be received by the company or any other person more than 48 hours before a meeting or adjourned meeting in order that the appointment may be effective.

(6) If for the purpose of any meeting of a company invitations to appoint as proxy a person or one of a number of persons specified in the invitations are issued at the company's expense to some only of the members entitled to be sent a notice of the meeting and to vote at it by proxy, then every officer of the company who knowingly and wilfully authorises or permits their issue in that manner is liable to a fine.

However, an officer is not so liable by reason only of the issue to a member at his request of a form of appointment naming the proxy, or of a list of persons willing to act as proxy, if the form or list is available on request to every member entitled to vote at the meeting by proxy.

(6A) In this section, 'address' includes any number or address used for the purposes of electronic communications.

(7) This section applies to meetings of any class of members of a company as it applies to general meetings of the company.

373   Right to demand a poll

(1) A provision contained in a company's articles is void in so far as it would have the effect either—

(a) of excluding the right to demand a poll at a general meeting on any question other than the election of the chairman of the meeting or the adjournment of the meeting; or

(b) of making ineffective a demand for a poll on any such question which is made either—

  (i) by not less than 5 members having the right to vote at the meeting *(excluding any voting rights attached to any shares in the company held as treasury shares)*; or

  (ii) by a member or members representing not less than one-tenth of the total voting rights of all the members having the right to vote at the meeting; or

  (iii) by a member or members holding shares in the company conferring a right to vote at the meeting, being shares on which an aggregate sum has been paid up equal to not less than one-tenth of the total sum paid up on all the shares conferring that right *(excluding any shares in the company conferring a right to vote at the meeting which are held as treasury shares)*.

(2) The appointment of a proxy to vote at a meeting of a company is deemed also to confer authority to demand or join in demanding a poll; and for the purposes of subsection (1) a demand by a person as proxy for a member is the same as a demand by the member.
[*The words in italics in s. 373(1)(b) are in force from 1 December 2003.*]

374   Voting on a poll
On a poll taken at a meeting of a company or a meeting of any class of members of a company, a member entitled to more than one vote need not, if he votes, use all his votes or cast all the votes he uses in the same way.

375   Representation of corporations at meetings
(1) A corporation, whether or not a company within the meaning of this Act, may—
    (a) if it is a member of another corporation, being such a company, by resolution of its directors or other governing body authorise such person as it thinks fit to act as its representative at any meeting of the company or at any meeting of any class of members of the company;
    (b) if it is a creditor (including a holder of debentures) of another corporation, being such a company, by resolution of its directors or other governing body authorise such person as it thinks fit to act as its representative at any meeting of creditors of the company held in pursuance of this Act or of rules made under it, or in pursuance of the provisions contained in any debenture or trust deed, as the case may be.

(2) A person so authorised is entitled to exercise the same powers on behalf of the corporation which he represents as that corporation could exercise if it were an individual shareholder, creditor or debenture-holder of the other company.

Resolutions

376   Circulation of members' resolutions
(1) Subject to the section next following, it is the duty of a company, on the requisition in writing of such number of members as is specified below and (unless the company otherwise resolves) at the expense of the requisitionists—
    (a) to give to members of the company entitled to receive notice of the next annual general meeting notice of any resolution which may properly be moved and is intended to be moved at that meeting;
    (b) to circulate to members entitled to have notice of any general meeting sent to them any statement of not more than 1,000 words with respect to the matter referred to in any proposed resolution or the business to be dealt with at that meeting.

(2) The number of members necessary for a requisition under subsection (1) is—
    (a) any number representing not less than one-twentieth of the total voting rights of all the members having at the date of the requisition a right to vote at the meeting to which the requisition relates *(excluding any voting rights attached to any shares in the company held as treasury shares)*; or
    (b) not less than 100 members holding shares in the company on which there has been paid up an average sum, per member, of not less than £100.

(3) Notice of any such resolution shall be given, and any such statement shall be circulated, to members of the company entitled to have notice of the meeting sent to them, by serving a copy of the resolution or statement on each such member in any manner permitted for service of notice of the meeting.

(4) Notice of any such resolution shall be given to any other member of the company by giving notice of the general effect of the resolution in any manner permitted for giving him notice of meetings of the company.

(5) For compliance with subsections (3) and (4), the copy must be served, or notice of the effect of the resolution be given (as the case may be), in the same manner and (so far as practicable) at the same time as notice of the meeting; and, where it is not practicable for it to be served or given at the same time, it must be served or given as soon as practicable thereafter.

(6) The business which may be dealt with at an annual general meeting includes any resolution of which notice is given in accordance with this section; and for purposes of this subsection notice is deemed to have been so given notwithstanding the accidental omission, in giving it, of one or more members. This has effect notwithstanding anything in the company's articles.

(7) In the event of default in complying with this section, every officer of the company who is in default is liable to a fine.

[*The words in italics in s. 376(2)(a) are in force from 1 December 2003.*]

377 In certain cases, compliance with s. 376 not required

(1) A company is not bound under section 376 to give notice of a resolution or to circulate a statement unless—

   (a) a copy of the requisition signed by the requisitionists (or two or more copies which between them contain the signatures of all the requisitionists) is deposited at the registered office of the company—

      (i) in the case of a requisition requiring notice of a resolution, not less than 6 weeks before the meeting, and

      (ii) otherwise, not less than one week before the meeting; and

   (b) there is deposited or tendered with the requisition a sum reasonably sufficient to meet the company's expenses in giving effect to it.

(2) But if, after a copy of a requisition requiring notice of a resolution has been deposited at the company's registered office, an annual general meeting is called for a date 6 weeks or less after the copy has been deposited, the copy (though not deposited within the time required by subsection (1)) is deemed properly deposited for the purposes of that subsection.

(3) The company is also not bound under section 376 to circulate a statement if, on the application either of the company or of any other person who claims to be aggrieved, the court is satisfied that the rights conferred by that section are being abused to secure needless publicity for defamatory matter; and the court may order the company's costs on such an application to be paid in whole or in part by the requisitionists, notwithstanding that they are not parties to the application.

378 Extraordinary and special resolutions

(1) A resolution is an extraordinary resolution when it has been passed by a majority of not less than three-fourths of such members as (being entitled to do so) vote in person or, where proxies are allowed, by proxy, at a general meeting of which notice specifying the intention to propose the resolution as an extraordinary resolution has been duly given.

(2) A resolution is a special resolution when it has been passed by such a majority as is required for the passing of an extraordinary resolution and at a general meeting of which not less than 21 days' notice, specifying the intention to propose the resolution as a special resolution, has been duly given.

(3) If it is so agreed by a majority in number of the members having the right to attend and vote at such a meeting, being a majority—

   (a) together holding not less than 95 per cent in nominal value of the shares giving that right *(excluding any shares in the company held as treasury shares)*; or

   (b) in the case of a company not having a share capital, together representing not less than 95 per cent of the total voting rights at that meeting of all the members,

a resolution may be proposed and passed as a special resolution at a meeting of which less than 21 days' notice has been given.

A private company may elect (by elective resolution in accordance with section 379A) that the above provisions shall have effect in relation to the company as if for the references to 95 per cent there were substituted references to such lesser percentage, but not less than 90 per cent, as may be specified in the resolution or subsequently determined by the company in general meeting.

(4) At any meeting at which an extraordinary resolution or a special resolution is submitted to be passed, a declaration by the chairman that the resolution is carried is, unless a poll is demanded, conclusive evidence of the fact without proof of the number or proportion of the votes recorded in favour of or against the resolution.

(5) In computing the majority on a poll demanded on the question that an extraordinary resolution or a special resolution be passed, reference is to be had to the number of votes cast for and against the resolution.

(6) For purposes of this section, notice of a meeting is deemed duly given, and the meeting duly held, when the notice is given and the meeting held in the manner provided by this Act or the company's articles.

[*The words in italics in s. 378(3)(a) are in force from 1 December 2003.*]

379   Resolution requiring special notice

(1) Where by any provision of this Act special notice is required of a resolution, the resolution is not effective unless notice of the intention to move it has been given to the company at least 28 days before the meeting at which it is moved.

(2) The company shall give its members notice of any such resolution at the same time and in the same manner as it gives notice of the meeting or, if that is not practicable, shall give them notice either by advertisement in a newspaper having an appropriate circulation or in any other mode allowed by the company's articles, at least 21 days before the meeting.

(3) If, after notice of the intention to move such a resolution has been given to the company, a meeting is called for a date 28 days or less after the notice has been given, the notice is deemed properly given, though not given within the time required.

379A   Elective resolution of private company

(1) An election by a private company for the purposes of—

(a) section 80A (election as to duration of authority to allot shares),

(b) section 252 (election to dispense with laying of accounts and reports before general meeting),

(c) section 366A (election to dispense with holding of annual general meeting),

(d) section 369(4) or 378(3) (election as to majority required to authorise short notice of meeting), or

(e) section 386 (election to dispense with appointment of auditors annually), shall be made by resolution of the company in general meeting in accordance with this section.

Such a resolution is referred to in this Act as an 'elective resolution'.

(2) An elective resolution is not effective unless—

(a) at least 21 days' notice in writing is given of the meeting, stating that an elective resolution is to be proposed and stating the terms of the resolution, and

(b) the resolution is agreed to at the meeting, in person or by proxy, by all the members entitled to attend and vote at the meeting.

(2A) An elective resolution is effective notwithstanding the fact that less than 21 days' notice in writing of the meeting is given if all the members entitled to attend and vote at the meeting so agree.

(2B) For the purposes of this section, notice in writing of the meeting is to be taken as given to a person where notice of the meeting is sent using electronic communications to such address as may for the time being be notified by that person to the company for that purpose.

(2C) For the purposes of this section a notice in writing of the meeting is also to be treated as given to a person where—

    (a) the company and that person have agreed that notices of meetings required to be given to that person may instead be accessed by him on a web site;

    (b) the meeting is a meeting to which that agreement applies;

    (c) that person is notified, in a manner for the time being agreed between him and the company for the purpose, of—

        (i)   the publication of the notice on a web site;

        (ii) the address of that web site; and

        (iii) the place on that web site where the notice may be accessed, and how it may be accessed; and

    (d) the notice continues to be published on that web site throughout the period beginning with the giving of that notification and ending with the conclusion of the meeting;

and for the purposes of this section a notice treated in accordance with this subsection as given to any person is to be treated as so given at the time of the notification mentioned in paragraph (c).

(2D) A notification given for the purposes of subsection (2C)(c) must—

    (a) state that it concerns a notice of a company meeting at which an elective resolution is to be proposed, and

    (b) specify the place, date and time of the meeting.

(2E) Nothing in subsection (2C) shall invalidate the proceedings of a meeting where—

    (a) any notice that is required to be published as mentioned in paragraph (d) of that subsection is published for a part, but not all, of the period mentioned in that paragraph; and

    (b) the failure to publish that notice throughout that period is wholly attributable to circumstances which it would not be reasonable to have expected the company to prevent or avoid.

(2F) In so far as the articles of the company do not provide for notices and notifications to be served using electronic communications, the provisions of Table A (as for the time being in force) as to such service shall apply.

(3) The company may revoke an elective resolution by passing an ordinary resolution to that effect.

(4) An elective resolution shall cease to have effect if the company is re-registered as a public company.

(5) An elective resolution may be passed or revoked in accordance with this section, and the provisions referred to in subsections (1) and (2B) to (2E) have effect, notwithstanding any contrary provision in the company's articles of association.

(5A) In this section, 'address' includes any number or address used for the purposes of electronic communications.

380 Registration, etc. of resolutions and agreements

(1) A copy of every resolution or agreement to which this section applies shall, within 15 days after it is passed or made, be forwarded to the registrar of companies and recorded by him; and it must be either a printed copy or else a copy in some other form approved by the registrar.

(2) Where articles have been registered, a copy of every such resolution or agreement for the time being in force shall be embodied in or annexed to every copy of the articles issued after the passing of the resolution or the making of the agreement.

(3) Where articles have not been registered, a printed copy of every such resolution or agreement shall be forwarded to any member at his request on payment of 5 pence or such less sum as the company may direct.

(4) This section applies to—

(a) special resolutions;

(b) extraordinary resolutions;

(bb) an elective resolution or a resolution revoking such a resolution;

(c) resolutions or agreements which have been agreed to by all the members of a company but which, if not so agreed to, would not have been effective for their purpose unless (as the case may be) they had been passed as special resolutions or as extraordinary resolutions;

(d) resolutions or agreements which have been agreed to by all the members of some class of shareholders but which, if not so agreed to, would not have been effective for their purpose unless they had been passed by some particular majority or otherwise in some particular manner, and all resolutions or agreements which effectively bind all the members of any class of shareholders though not agreed to by all those members;

(e) a resolution passed by the directors of a company in compliance with a direction under section 31(2) (change of name on Secretary of State's direction);

(f) a resolution of a company to give, vary, revoke or renew an authority to the directors for the purposes of section 80 (allotment of relevant securities);

(g) a resolution of the directors passed under section 147(2) (alteration of memorandum on company ceasing to be a public company, following acquisition of its own shares);

(h) a resolution conferring, varying, revoking or renewing authority under section 166 (market purchase of company's own shares);

(j) a resolution for voluntary winding up, passed under section 84(1)(a) of the Insolvency Act;

(k) a resolution passed by the directors of an old public company, under section 2(1) of the Consequential Provisions Act, that the company should be re-registered as a public company;

(l) a resolution of the directors passed by virtue of regulation 16(2) of the Uncertificated Securities Regulations 2001 (which allow title to a company's shares to be evidenced and transferred without written instrument); and

(m) a resolution of a company passed by virtue of regulation 16(6) of the Uncertificated Securities Regulations 2001 (which prevents or reverses a resolution of the directors under regulation 16(2) of those Regulations).

(4A) For the purposes of this section, references to a member of a company do not include the company itself where it is such a member by virtue only of its holding shares as treasury shares, and accordingly, in such circumstances, the company is not, for those purposes, to be treated as a member of any class of the company's shareholders.

(5) If a company fails to comply with subsection (1), the company and every officer of it who is in default is liable to a fine and, for continued contravention, to a daily default fine.

(6) If a company fails to comply with subsection (2) or (3), the company and every officer of it who is in default is liable to a fine.

(7) For purposes of subsections (5) and (6), a liquidator of a company is deemed an officer of it.

[*Section 380(4A) is in force from 1 December 2003.*]

381 Resolution passed at adjourned meeting

Where a resolution is passed at an adjourned meeting of—

(a) a company;

(b) the holders of any class of shares in a company;

(c) the directors of a company;

the resolution is for all purposes to be treated as having been passed on the date on which it was in fact passed, and is not to be deemed passed on any earlier date.

Written resolutions of private companies

381A   Written resolutions of private companies

(1) Anything which in the case of a private company may be done—

    (a) by resolution of the company in general meeting, or

    (b) by resolution of a meeting of any class of members of the company,

may be done, without a meeting and without any previous notice being required, by resolution in writing signed by or on behalf of all the members of the company who at the date of the resolution would be entitled to attend and vote at such meeting.

(2) The signatures need not be on a single document provided each is on a document which accurately states the terms of the resolution.

(3) The date of the resolution means when the resolution is signed by or on behalf of the last member to sign.

(4) A resolution agreed to in accordance with this section has effect as if passed—

    (a) by the company in general meeting, or

    (b) by a meeting of the relevant class of members of the company,

as the case may be; and any reference in any enactment to a meeting at which a resolution is passed or to members voting in favour of a resolution shall be construed accordingly.

(5) Any reference in any enactment to the date of passing of a resolution is, in relation to a resolution agreed to in accordance with this section, a reference to the date of the resolution.

(6) A resolution may be agreed to in accordance with this section which would otherwise be required to be passed as a special, extraordinary or elective resolution; and any reference in any enactment to a special, extraordinary or elective resolution includes such a resolution.

(7) This section has effect subject to the exceptions specified in Part I of Schedule 15A; and in relation to certain descriptions of resolution under this section the procedural requirements of this Act have effect with the adaptations specified in Part II of that Schedule.

381B   Duty to notify auditors of proposed written resolution

(1) If a director or secretary of a company—

    (a) knows that it is proposed to seek agreement to a resolution in accordance with section 381A, and

    (b) knows the terms of the resolution,

he shall, if the company has auditors, secure that a copy of the resolution is sent to them, or that they are otherwise notified of its contents, at or before the time the resolution is supplied to a member for signature.

(2) A person who fails to comply with subsection (1) is liable to a fine.

(3) In any proceedings for an offence under this section it is a defence for the accused to prove—

    (a) that the circumstances were such that it was not practicable for him to comply with subsection (1), or

    (b) that he believed on reasonable grounds that a copy of the resolution had been sent to the company's auditors or that they had otherwise been informed of its contents.

(4) Nothing in this section affects the validity of any resolution.

381C   Written resolutions: supplementary provisions

(1) Sections 381A and 381B have effect notwithstanding any provision of the company's memorandum or articles, but do not prejudice any power conferred by any such provision.

(2) Nothing in those sections affects any enactment or rule of law as to—

    (a) things done otherwise than by passing a resolution, or

    (b) cases in which a resolution is treated as having been passed, or a person is precluded from alleging that a resolution has not been duly passed.

Records of proceedings

382 Minutes of meetings

(1) Every company shall cause minutes of all proceedings of general meetings, all proceedings at meetings of its directors and, where there are managers, all proceedings at meetings of its managers to be entered in books kept for that purpose.

(2) Any such minute, if purporting to be signed by the chairman of the meeting at which the proceedings were had, or by the chairman of the next succeeding meeting, is evidence of the proceedings.

(3) Where a shadow director by means of a notice required by section 317(8) declares an interest in a contract or proposed contract, this section applies—

    (a) if it is a specific notice under paragraph (a) of that subsection, as if the declaration had been made at the meeting there referred to, and

    (b) otherwise, as if it had been made at the meeting of the directors next following the giving of the notice;

and the making of the declaration is in either case deemed to form part of the proceedings at the meeting.

(4) Where minutes have been made in accordance with this section of the proceedings at any general meeting of the company or meeting of directors or managers, then, until the contrary is proved, the meeting is deemed duly held and convened, and all proceedings had at the meeting to have been duly had; and all appointments of directors, managers or liquidators are deemed valid.

(5) If a company fails to comply with subsection (1), the company and every officer of it who is in default is liable to a fine and, for continued contravention, to a daily default fine.

382A Recording of written resolutions

(1) Where a written resolution is agreed to in accordance with section 381A which has effect as if agreed by the company in general meeting, the company shall cause a record of the resolution (and of the signatures) to be entered in a book in the same way as minutes of proceedings of a general meeting of the company.

(2) Any such record, if purporting to be signed by a director of the company or by the company secretary, is evidence of the proceedings in agreeing to the resolution; and where a record is made in accordance with this section, then, until the contrary is proved, the requirements of this Act with respect to those proceedings shall be deemed to be complied with.

(3) Section 382(5) (penalties) applies in relation to a failure to comply with subsection (1) above as it applies in relation to a failure to comply with subsection (1) of that section; and section 383 (inspection of minute books) applies in relation to a record made in accordance with this section as it applies in relation to the minutes of a general meeting.

382B Recording of decisions by the sole member

(1) Where a private company limited by shares or by guarantee has only one member and he takes any decision which may be taken by the company in general meeting and which has effect as if agreed by the company in general meeting, he shall (unless that decision is taken by way of a written resolution) provide the company with a written record of that decision.

(2) If the sole member fails to comply with subsection (1) he shall be liable to a fine.

(3) Failure by the sole member to comply with subsection (1) shall not affect the validity of any decision referred to in that subsection.

383 Inspection of minute books

(1) The books containing the minutes of proceedings of any general meeting of a company held on or after 1 November 1929 shall be kept at the company's registered office, and shall be open to the inspection of any member without charge.

(3) Any member shall be entitled on payment of such fee as may be prescribed to be furnished, within 7 days after he has made a request in that behalf to the company, with a copy of any such minutes as are referred to above.

(4) If an inspection required under this section is refused or if a copy required under this section is not sent within the proper time, the company and every officer of it who is in default is liable in respect of each offence to a fine.

(5) In the case of any such refusal or default, the court may by order compel an immediate inspection of the books in respect of all proceedings of general meetings, or direct that the copies required be sent to the persons requiring them.

CHAPTER V   AUDITORS

Appointment of auditors

384   Duty to appoint auditors

(1) Every company shall appoint an auditor or auditors in accordance with this Chapter.
This is subject to section 388A (certain companies exempt from obligation to appoint auditors).

(2) Auditors shall be appointed in accordance with section 385 (appointment at general meeting at which accounts are laid), except in the case of a private company which has elected to dispense with the laying of accounts in which case the appointment shall be made in accordance with section 385A.

(3) References in this Chapter to the end of the time for appointing auditors are to the end of the time within which an appointment must be made under section 385(2) or 385A(2), according to whichever of those sections applies.

(4) Sections 385 and 385A have effect subject to section 386 under which a private company may elect to dispense with the obligation to appoint auditors annually.

385   Appointment at general meeting at which accounts laid

(1) This section applies to every public company and to a private company which has not elected to dispense with the laying of accounts.

(2) The company shall, at each general meeting at which accounts are laid, appoint an auditor or auditors to hold office from the conclusion of that meeting until the conclusion of the next general meeting at which accounts are laid.

(3) The first auditors of the company may be appointed by the directors at any time before the first general meeting of the company at which accounts are laid; and auditors so appointed shall hold office until the conclusion of that meeting.

(4) If the directors fail to exercise their powers under subsection (3), the powers may be exercised by the company in general meeting.

385A   Appointment by private company which is not obliged to lay accounts

(1) This section applies to a private company which has elected in accordance with section 252 to dispense with the laying of accounts before the company in general meeting.

(2) Auditors shall be appointed by the company in general meeting before the end of the period of 28 days beginning with the day on which copies of the company's annual accounts for the previous financial year are sent to members under section 238 or, if notice is given under section 253(2) requiring the laying of the accounts before the company in general meeting, the conclusion of that meeting.

Auditors so appointed shall hold office from the end of that period or, as the case may be, the conclusion of that meeting until the end of the time for appointing auditors for the next financial year.

(3) The first auditors of the company may be appointed by the directors at any time before—

    (a) the end of the period of 28 days beginning with the day on which copies of the company's first annual accounts are sent to members under section 238, or

    (b) if notice is given under section 253(2) requiring the laying of the accounts before the company in general meeting, the beginning of that meeting;

and auditors so appointed shall hold office until the end of that period or, as the case may be, the conclusion of that meeting.

    (4) If the directors fail to exercise their powers under subsection (3), the powers may be exercised by the company in general meeting.

    (5) Auditors holding office when the election is made shall, unless the company in general meeting determines otherwise, continue to hold office until the end of the time for appointing auditors for the next financial year; and auditors holding office when an election ceases to have effect shall continue to hold office until the conclusion of the next general meeting of the company at which accounts are laid.

386   Election by private company to dispense with annual appointment

    (1) A private company may elect (by elective resolution in accordance with section 379A) to dispense with the obligation to appoint auditors annually.

    (2) When such an election is in force the company's auditors shall be deemed to be reappointed for each succeeding financial year on the expiry of the time for appointing auditors for that year, unless—

    (a) the directors of the company have taken advantage of the exemption conferred by section 249A or 249AA, or

    (b) a resolution has been passed under section 393 to the effect that their appointment should be brought to an end.

    (3) If the election ceases to be in force, the auditors then holding office shall continue to hold office—

    (a) where section 385 then applies, until the conclusion of the next general meeting of the company at which accounts are laid;

    (b) where section 385A then applies, until the end of the time for appointing auditors for the next financial year under that section.

    (4) No account shall be taken of any loss of the opportunity of further deemed reappointment under this section in ascertaining the amount of any compensation or damages payable to an auditor on his ceasing to hold office for any reason.

387   Appointment by Secretary of State in default of appointment by company

    (1) If in any case no auditors are appointed, reappointed or deemed to be reappointed before the end of the time for appointing auditors, the Secretary of State may appoint a person to fill the vacancy.

    (2) In such a case the company shall within one week of the end of the time for appointing auditors give notice to the Secretary of State of his power having become exercisable.

    If a company fails to give the notice required by this subsection, the company and every officer of it who is in default is guilty of an offence and liable to a fine and, for continued contravention, to a daily default fine.

388   Filling of casual vacancies

    (1) The directors, or the company in general meeting, may fill a casual vacancy in the office of auditor.

    (2) While such a vacancy continues, any surviving or continuing auditor or auditors may continue to act.

    (3) Special notice is required for a resolution at a general meeting of a company—

    (a) filling a casual vacancy in the office of auditor, or

    (b) reappointing as auditor a retiring auditor who was appointed by the directors to fill a casual vacancy.

(4) On receipt of notice of such an intended resolution the company shall forthwith send a copy of it—

    (a) to the person proposed to be appointed, and

    (b) if the casual vacancy was caused by the resignation of an auditor, to the auditor who resigned.

388A   Certain companies exempt from obligation to appoint auditors

(1) A company which by virtue of section 249A (certain categories of small company) or section 249AA (dormant companies) is exempt from the provisions of Part VII relating to the audit of accounts is also exempt from the obligation to appoint auditors.

(2) The following provisions apply if a company which has been exempt from those provisions ceases to be so exempt.

(3) Where section 385 applies (appointment at general meeting at which accounts are laid), the directors may appoint auditors at any time before the next meeting of the company at which accounts are to be laid; and auditors so appointed shall hold office until the conclusion of that meeting.

(4) Where section 385A applies (appointment by private company not obliged to lay accounts), the directors may appoint auditors at any time before—

    (a) the end of the period of 28 days beginning with the day on which copies of the company's annual accounts are next sent to members under section 238, or

    (b) if notice is given under section 253(2) requiring the laying of the accounts before the company in general meeting, the beginning of that meeting;

and auditors so appointed shall hold office until the end of that period or, as the case may be, the conclusion of that meeting.

(5) If the directors fail to exercise their powers under subsection (3) or (4), the powers may be exercised by the company in general meeting.

Rights of auditors

389A   Rights to information

(1) The auditors of a company have a right of access at all times to the company's books, accounts and vouchers, and are entitled to require from the company's officers such information and explanations as they think necessary for the performance of their duties as auditors.

(2) An officer of a company commits an offence if he knowingly or recklessly makes to the company's auditors a statement (whether written or oral) which—

    (a) conveys or purports to convey any information or explanations which the auditors require, or are entitled to require, as auditors of the company, and

    (b) is misleading, false or deceptive in a material particular.

A person guilty of an offence under this subsection is liable to imprisonment or a fine, or both.

(3) A subsidiary undertaking which is a body corporate incorporated in Great Britain, and the auditors of such an undertaking, shall give to the auditors of any parent company of the undertaking such information and explanations as they may reasonably require for the purposes of their duties as auditors of that company.

If a subsidiary undertaking fails to comply with this subsection, the undertaking and every officer of it who is in default is guilty of an offence and liable to a fine; and if an auditor fails without reasonable excuse to comply with this subsection he is guilty of an offence and liable to a fine.

(4) A parent company having a subsidiary undertaking which is not a body corporate incorporated in Great Britain shall, if required by its auditors to do so, take all such steps as are reasonably open to it to obtain from the subsidiary undertaking such information and explanations as they may reasonably require for the purposes of their duties as auditors of that company.

If a parent company fails to comply with this subsection, the company and every officer of it who is in default is guilty of an offence and liable to a fine.

(5) Section 734 (criminal proceedings against unincorporated bodies) applies to an offence under subsection (3).

390   Right to attend company meetings, &c.

(1) A company's auditors are entitled—
- (a) to receive all notices of, and other communications relating to, any general meeting which a member of the company is entitled to receive;
- (b) to attend any general meeting of the company; and
- (c) to be heard at any general meeting which they attend on any part of the business of the meeting which concerns them as auditors.

(1A) Subsections (4A) to (4G) of section 369 (electronic communication of notices of meetings) apply for the purpose of determining whether notice of a meeting is received by the company's auditors as they apply in determining whether such a notice is given to any person.

(2) In relation to a written resolution proposed to be agreed to by a private company in accordance with section 381A, the company's auditors are entitled—
- (a) to receive all such communications relating to the resolution as, by virtue of any provision of Schedule 15A, are required to be supplied to a member of the company.

(3) The right to attend or be heard at a meeting is exercisable in the case of a body corporate or partnership by an individual authorised by it in writing to act as its representative at the meeting.

Remuneration of auditors

390A   Remuneration of auditors

(1) The remuneration of auditors appointed by the company in general meeting shall be fixed by the company in general meeting or in such manner as the company in general meeting may determine.

(2) The remuneration of auditors appointed by the directors or the Secretary of State shall be fixed by the directors or the Secretary of State, as the case may be.

(3) There shall be stated in a note to the company's annual accounts the amount of the remuneration of the company's auditors in their capacity as such.

(4) For the purposes of this section 'remuneration' includes sums paid in respect of expenses.

(5) This section applies in relation to benefits in kind as to payments in cash, and in relation to any such benefit references to its amount are to its estimated money value.
 The nature of any such benefit shall also be disclosed.

390B   Remuneration of auditors or their associates for non-audit work

(1) The Secretary of State may make provision by regulations for securing the disclosure of the amount of any remuneration received or receivable by a company's auditors or their associates in respect of services other than those of auditors in their capacity as such.

(2) The regulations may—
- (a) provide that 'remuneration' includes sums paid in respect of expenses,
- (b) apply in relation to benefits in kind as to payments in cash, and in relation to any such benefit require disclosure of its nature and its estimated money value,
- (c) define 'associate' in relation to an auditor,
- (d) require the disclosure of remuneration in respect of services rendered to associated undertakings of the company, and
- (e) define 'associated undertaking' for that purpose.

(3) The regulations may require the auditors to disclose the relevant information in their report or require the relevant information to be disclosed in a note to the company's accounts and require the auditors to supply the directors of the company with such information as is necessary to enable that disclosure to be made.

(4) The regulations may make different provision for different cases.

(5) Regulations under this section shall be made by statutory instrument which shall be subject to annulment in pursuance of a resolution of either House of parliament.

Removal, resignation, &c. of auditors

391   Removal of auditors

(1) A company may by ordinary resolution at any time remove an auditor from office, notwithstanding anything in any agreement between it and him.

(2) Where a resolution removing an auditor is passed at a general meeting of a company, the company shall within 14 days give notice of that fact in the prescribed form to the registrar.

If a company fails to give the notice required by this subsection, the company and every officer of it who is in default is guilty of an offence and liable to a fine and, for continued contravention, to a daily default fine.

(3) Nothing in this section shall be taken as depriving a person removed under it of compensation or damages payable to him in respect of the termination of his appointment as auditor or of any appointment terminating with that as auditor.

(4) An auditor of a company who has been removed has, notwithstanding his removal, the rights conferred by section 390 in relation to any general meeting of the company—

(a) at which his term of office would otherwise have expired, or

(b) at which it is proposed to fill the vacancy caused by his removal.

In such a case the references in that section to matters concerning the auditors as auditors shall be construed as references to matters concerning him as a former auditor.

391A   Rights of auditors who are removed or not reappointed

(1) Special notice is required for a resolution at a general meeting of a company—

(a) removing an auditor before the expiration of his term of office, or

(b) appointing as auditor a person other than a retiring auditor.

(2) On receipt of notice of such an intended resolution the company shall forthwith send a copy of it to the person proposed to be removed or, as the case may be, to the person proposed to be appointed and to the retiring auditor.

(3) The auditor proposed to be removed or (as the case may be) the retiring auditor may make with respect to the intended resolution representations in writing to the company (not exceeding a reasonable length) and request their notification to members of the company.

(4) The company shall (unless the representations are received by it too late for it to do so)—

(a) in any notice of the resolution given to members of the company, state the fact of the representations having been made, and

(b) send a copy of the representations to every member of the company to whom notice of the meeting is or has been sent.

(5) If a copy of any such representations is not sent out as required because received too late or because of the company's default, the auditor may (without prejudice to his right to be heard orally) require that the representations be read out at the meeting.

(6) Copies of the representations need not be sent out and the representations need not be read at the meeting if, on the application either of the company or of any other person claiming to be aggrieved, the court is satisfied that the rights conferred by this section are being abused to secure needless publicity for defamatory matter; and the court may order the company's costs on the application to be paid in whole or in part by the auditor, notwithstanding that he is not a party to the application.

392   Resignation of auditors

(1) An auditor of a company may resign his office by depositing a notice in writing to that effect at the company's registered office.

The notice is not effective unless it is accompanied by the statement required by section 394.

(2) An effective notice of resignation operates to bring the auditor's term of office to an end as of the date on which the notice is deposited or on such later date as may be specified in it.

(3) The company shall within 14 days of the deposit of a notice of resignation send a copy of the notice to the registrar of companies.

If default is made in complying with this subsection, the company and every officer of it who is in default is guilty of an offence and liable to a fine and, for continued contravention, a daily default fine.

392A   Rights of resigning auditors

(1) This section applies where an auditor's notice of resignation is accompanied by a statement of circumstances which he considers should be brought to the attention of members or creditors of the company.

(2) He may deposit with the notice a signed requisition calling on the directors of the company forthwith duly to convene an extraordinary general meeting of the company for the purpose of receiving and considering such explanation of the circumstances connected with his resignation as he may wish to place before the meeting.

(3) He may request the company to circulate to its members—

(a) before the meeting convened on his requisition, or

(b) before any general meeting at which his term of office would otherwise have expired or at which it is proposed to fill the vacancy caused by his resignation,

a statement in writing (not exceeding a reasonable length) of the circumstances connected with his resignation.

(4) The company shall (unless the statement is received too late for it to comply)—

(a) in any notice of the meeting given to members of the company, state the fact of the statement having been made, and

(b) send a copy of the statement to every member of the company to whom notice of the meeting is or has been sent.

(5) If the directors do not within 21 days from the date of the deposit of a requisition under this section proceed duly to convene a meeting for a day not more than 28 days after the date on which the notice convening the meeting is given, every director who failed to take all reasonable steps to secure that a meeting was convened as mentioned above is guilty of an offence and liable to a fine.

(6) If a copy of the statement mentioned above is not sent out as required because received too late or because of the company's default, the auditor may (without prejudice to his right to be heard orally) require that the statement be read out at the meeting.

(7) Copies of a statement need not be sent out and the statement need not be read out at the meeting if, on the application either of the company or of any other person who claims to be aggrieved, the court is satisfied that the rights conferred by this section are being abused to secure needless publicity for defamatory matters; and the court may order the company's costs on such an application to be paid in whole or in part by the auditor, notwithstanding that he is not a party to the application.

(8) An auditor who has resigned has, notwithstanding his resignation, the rights conferred by section 390 in relation to any such general meeting of the company as is mentioned in subsection (3)(a) or (b).

In such a case the references in that section to matters concerning the auditors as auditors shall be construed as references to matters concerning him as a former auditor.

393   Termination of appointment of auditors not appointed annually

(1) When an election is in force under section 386 (election by private company to dispense with annual appointment), any member of the company may deposit notice in writing at the company's registered office proposing that the appointment of the company's auditors be brought to an end.

No member may deposit more than one such notice in any financial year of the company.

(2) If such a notice is deposited it is the duty of the directors—

    (a) to convene a general meeting of the company for a date not more than 28 days after the date on which the notice was given, and

    (b) to propose at the meeting a resolution in a form enabling the company to decide whether the appointment of the company's auditors should be brought to an end.

(3) If the decision of the company at the meeting is that the appointment of the auditors should be brought to an end, the auditors shall not be deemed to be reappointed when next they would be and, if the notice was deposited within the period immediately following the distribution of accounts, any deemed reappointment for the financial year following that to which those accounts relate which has already occurred shall cease to have effect.

The period immediately following the distribution of accounts means the period beginning with the day on which copies of the company's annual accounts are sent to members of the company under section 238 and ending 14 days after that day.

(4) If the directors do not within 14 days from the date of the deposit of the notice proceed duly to convene a meeting, the member who deposited the notice (or, if there was more than one, any of them) may himself convene the meeting; but any meeting so convened shall not be held after the expiration of three months from that date.

(5) A meeting convened under this section by member shall be convened in the same manner, as nearly as possible, as that in which meetings are to be convened by directors.

(6) Any reasonable expenses incurred by a member by reason of the failure of the directors duly to convene a meeting shall be made good to him by the company; and any such sums shall be recouped by the company from such of the directors as were in default out of any sums payable, or to become payable, by the company by way of fees or other remuneration in respect of their services.

(7) This section has effect notwithstanding anything in any agreement between the company and its auditors; and no compensation or damages shall be payable by reason of the auditors' appointment being terminated under this section.

394   Statement by person ceasing to hold office as auditor

(1) Where an auditor ceases for any reason to hold office, he shall deposit at the company's registered office a statement of any circumstances connected with his ceasing to hold office which he considers should be brought to the attention of the members or creditors of the company or, if he considers that there are no such circumstances, a statement that there are none.

(2) In the case of resignation, the statement shall be deposited along with the notice of resignation; in the case of failure to seek reappointment, the statement shall be deposited not less than 14 days before the end of the time allowed for next appointing auditors; in any other case, the statement shall be deposited not later than the end of the period of 14 days beginning with the date on which he ceases to hold office.

(3) If the statement is of circumstances which the auditor considers should be brought to the attention of the members or creditors of the company, the company shall within 14 days of the deposit of the statement either—

    (a) send a copy of it to every person who under section 238 is entitled to be sent copies of the accounts, or

    (b) apply to the court.

(4) The company shall if it applies to the court notify the auditor of the application.

(5) Unless the auditor receives notice of such an application before the end of the period of 21 days beginning with the day on which he deposited the statement, he shall within a further seven days send a copy of the statement to the registrar.

(6) If the court is satisfied that the auditor is using the statement to secure needless publicity for defamatory matter—

(a) it shall direct that copies of the statement need not be sent out, and

(b) it may further order the company's costs on the application to be paid in whole or in part by the auditor, notwithstanding that he is not a party to the application;

and the company shall within 14 days of the court's decision send to the persons mentioned in subsection (3)(a) a statement setting out the effect of the order.

(7) If the court is not so satisfied, the company shall within 14 days of the court's decision—

(a) send copies of the statement to the persons mentioned in subsection (3)(a),

(b) notify the auditor of the court's decision;

and the auditor shall within seven days of receiving such notice send a copy of the statement to the registrar.

394A   Offences of failing to comply with s. 394

(1) If a person ceasing to hold office as auditor fails to comply with section 394 he is guilty of an offence and liable to a fine.

(2) In proceedings for an offence under subsection (1) it is a defence for the person charged to show that he took all reasonable steps and exercised all due diligence to avoid the commission of the offence.

(3) Sections 733 (liability of individuals for corporate default) and 734 (criminal proceedings against unincorporated bodies) apply to an offence under subsection (1).

(4) If a company makes default in complying with section 394, the company and every officer of it who is in default is guilty of an offence and liable to a fine and, for continued contravention, to a daily default fine.

PART XII   REGISTRATION OF CHARGES

[Part XII would be replaced by new provisions if Part IV of the Companies Act 1989 were brought into force. The Department of Trade and Industry has indicated that Part IV of the 1989 Act will not be brought into force.]

CHAPTER I   REGISTRATION OF CHARGES (ENGLAND AND WALES)

395   Certain charges void if not registered

(1) Subject to the provisions of this Chapter, a charge created by a company registered in England and Wales and being a charge to which this section applies is, so far as any security on the company's property or undertaking is conferred by the charge, void against the liquidator or administrator and any creditor of the company, unless the prescribed particulars of the charge together with the instrument (if any) by which the charge is created or evidenced, are delivered to or received by the registrar of companies for registration in the manner required by this Chapter within 21 days after the date of the charge's creation.

(2) Subsection (1) is without prejudice to any contract or obligation for repayment of the money secured by the charge; and when a charge becomes void under this section, the money secured by it immediately becomes payable.

396   Charges which have to be registered

(1) Section 395 applies to the following charges—

(a) a charge for the purpose of securing any issue of debentures,

    (b) a charge on uncalled share capital of the company,

    (c) a charge created or evidenced by an instrument which, if executed by an individual, would require registration as a bill of sale,

    (d) a charge on land (wherever situated) or any interest in it, but not including a charge for any rent or other periodical sum issuing out of the land,

    (e) a charge on book debts of the company,

    (f) a floating charge on the company's undertaking or property,

    (g) a charge on calls made but not paid,

    (h) a charge on a ship or aircraft, or any share in a ship,

    (j) a charge on goodwill, or on any intellectual property.

(2) Where a negotiable instrument has been given to secure the payment of any book debts of a company, the deposit of the instrument for the purpose of securing an advance to the company is not, for purposes of section 395, to be treated as a charge on those book debts.

(3) The holding of debentures entitling the holder to a charge on land is not for purposes of this section deemed to be an interest in land.

(3A) The following are 'intellectual property' for the purposes of this section—

    (a) any patent, trade mark, registered design, copyright or design right;

    (b) any licence under or in respect of any such right.

(4) In this Chapter, 'charge' includes mortgage.

397 Formalities of registration (debentures)

(1) Where a series of debentures containing, or giving by reference to another instrument, any charge to the benefit of which the debenture holders of that series are entitled *pari passu* is created by a company, it is for purposes of section 395 sufficient if there are delivered to or received by the registrar, within 21 days after the execution of the deed containing the charge (or, if there is no such deed, after the execution of any debentures of the series), the following particulars in the prescribed form—

    (a) the total amount secured by the whole series, and

    (b) the dates of the resolutions authorising the issue of the series and the date of the covering deed (if any) by which the security is created or defined, and

    (c) a general description of the property charged, and

    (d) the names of the trustees (if any) for the debenture holders,

together with the deed containing the charge or, if there is no such deed, one of the debentures of the series:

  Provided that there shall be sent to the registrar of companies, for entry in the register, particulars in the prescribed form of the date and amount of each issue of debentures of the series, but any omission to do this does not affect the validity of any of those debentures.

(2) Where any commission, allowance or discount has been paid or made either directly or indirectly by a company to a person in consideration of his—

    (a) subscribing or agreeing to subscribe, whether absolutely or conditionally, for debentures of the company, or

    (b) procuring or agreeing to procure subscriptions, whether absolute or conditional, for such debentures,

the particulars required to be sent for registration under section 395 shall include particulars as to the amount or rate per cent of the commission, discount or allowance so paid or made, but omission to do this does not affect the validity of the debentures issued.

(3) The deposit of debentures as security for a debt of the company is not, for the purposes of subsection (2), treated as the issue of the debentures at a discount.

398 Verification of charge on property outside United Kingdom

(1) In the case of a charge created out of the United Kingdom comprising property situated outside the United Kingdom, the delivery to and the receipt by the registrar of companies of the copy (verified in the prescribed manner) of the instrument by which the charge is

created or evidenced has the same effect for purposes of sections 395 to 398 as the delivery and receipt of the instrument itself.

(2) In that case, 21 days after the date on which the instrument or copy could, in due course of post (and if dispatched with due diligence), have been received in the United Kingdom are substituted for the 21 days mentioned in section 395(1) (or as the case may be, section 397(1)) as the time within which the particulars and instrument or copy are to be delivered to the registrar.

(3) Where a charge is created in the United Kingdom but comprises property outside the United Kingdom, the instrument creating or purporting to create the charge may be sent for registration under section 395 notwithstanding that further proceedings may be necessary to make the charge valid or effectual according to the law of the country in which the property is situated.

(4) Where a charge comprises property situated in Scotland or Northern Ireland and registration in the country where the property is situated is necessary to make the charge valid or effectual according to the law of that country, the delivery to and the receipt by the registrar of a copy (verified in the prescribed manner) of the instrument by which the charge is created or evidenced, together with a certificate in the prescribed form stating that the charge was presented for registration in Scotland or Northern Ireland (as the case may be) on the date on which it was so presented has, for purposes of sections 395 to 398, the same effect as the delivery and receipt of the instrument itself.

399 Company's duty to register charges it creates

(1) It is a company's duty to send to the registrar of companies for registration the particulars of every charge created by the company and of the issues of debentures of a series requiring registration under sections 395 to 398; but registration of any such charge may be effected on the application of any person interested in it.

(2) Where registration is effected on the application of some person other than the company, that person is entitled to recover from the company the amount of any fees properly paid by him to the registrar on the registration.

(3) If a company fails to comply with subsection (1), then, unless the registration has been effected on the application of some other person, the company and every officer of it who is in default is liable to a fine and, for continued contravention, to a daily default fine.

400 Charges existing on property acquired

(1) This section applies where a company registered in England and Wales acquires property which is subject to a charge of any such kind as would, if it had been created by the company after the acquisition of the property, have been required to be registered under this Chapter.

(2) The company shall cause the prescribed particulars of the charge, together with a copy (certified in the prescribed manner to be a correct copy) of the instrument (if any) by which the charge was created or is evidenced, to be delivered to the registrar of companies for registration in manner required by this Chapter within 21 days after the date on which the acquisition is completed.

(3) However, if the property is situated and the charge was created outside Great Britain, 21 days after the date on which the copy of the instrument could in due course of post, and if dispatched with due diligence, have been received in the United Kingdom is substituted for the 21 days above-mentioned as the time within which the particulars and copy of the instrument are to be delivered to the registrar.

(4) If default is made in complying with this section, the company and every officer of it who is in default is liable to a fine and, for continued contravention, to a daily default fine.

401 Register of charges to be kept by registrar of companies

(1) The registrar of companies shall keep, with respect to each company, a register in the prescribed form of all the charges requiring registration under this Chapter; and he shall enter in the register with respect to such charges the following particulars—

(a) in the case of a charge to the benefit of which the holders of a series of debentures are entitled, the particulars specified in section 397(1),

(b) in the case of any other charge—

  (i) if it is a charge created by the company, the date of its creation, and if it is a charge which was existing on property acquired by the company, the date of the acquisition of the property, and

  (ii) the amount secured by the charge, and

  (iii) short particulars of the property charged, and

  (iv) the persons entitled to the charge.

(2) The registrar shall give a certificate of the registration of any charge registered in pursuance of this Chapter, stating the amount secured by the charge.

The certificate—

(a) shall be either signed by the registrar, or authenticated by his official seal, and

(b) is conclusive evidence that the requirements of this Chapter as to registration have been satisfied.

(3) The register kept in pursuance of this section shall be open to inspection by any person.

402   Endorsement of certificate on debentures

(1) The company shall cause a copy of every certificate of registration given under section 401 to be endorsed on every debenture or certificate of debenture stock which is issued by the company, and the payment of which is secured by the charge so registered.

(2) But this does not require a company to cause a certificate of registration of any charge so given to be endorsed on any debenture or certificate of debenture stock issued by the company before the charge was created.

(3) If a person knowingly and wilfully authorises or permits the delivery of a debenture or certificate of debenture stock which under this section is required to have endorsed on it a copy of a certificate of registration, without the copy being so endorsed upon it, he is liable (without prejudice to any other liability) to a fine.

403   Entries of satisfaction and release

(1) Subject to subsection (1A), the registrar of companies, on receipt of a statutory declaration in the prescribed form verifying, with respect to a registered charge,—

(a) that the debt for which the charge was given has been paid or satisfied in whole or in part, or

(b) that part of the property or undertaking charged has been released from the charge or has ceased to form part of the company's property or undertaking,

may enter on the register a memorandum of satisfaction in whole or in part, or of the fact that part of the property or undertaking has been released from the charge or has ceased to form part of the company's property or undertaking (as the case may be).

(1A) The registrar of companies may make any such entry as is mentioned in subsection (1) where, instead of receiving such a statutory declaration as is mentioned in that subsection, he receives a statement by a director, secretary, administrator or administrative receiver of the company which is contained in an electronic communication and that statement—

(a) verifies the matters set out in paragraph (a) or (b) of that subsection,

(b) contains a description of the charge,

(c) states the date of creation of the charge and the date of its registration under this Chapter,

(d) states the name and address of the chargee or, in the case of a debenture, trustee, and

(e) where paragraph (b) of subsection (1) applies, contains short particulars of the property or undertaking which has been released from the charge, or which has ceased to form part of the company's property or undertaking (as the case may be).

(2) Where the registrar enters a memorandum of satisfaction in whole, he shall if required furnish the company with a copy of it.

(2A) Any person who makes a false statement under subsection (1A) which he knows to be false or does not believe to be true is liable to imprisonment or a fine, or both.

404   Rectification of register of charges

(1) The following applies if the court is satisfied that the omission to register a charge within the time required by this Chapter or that the omission or misstatement of any particular with respect to any such charge or in a memorandum of satisfaction was accidental, or due to inadvertence or to some other sufficient cause, or is not of a nature to prejudice the position of creditors or shareholders of the company, or that on other grounds it is just and equitable to grant relief.

(2) The court may, on the application of the company or a person interested, and on such terms and conditions as seem to the court just and expedient, order that the time for registration shall be extended or, as the case may be, that the omission or misstatement shall be rectified.

405   Registration of enforcement of security

(1) If a person obtains an order for the appointment of a receiver or manager of a company's property, or appoints such a receiver or manager under powers contained in an instrument, he shall within 7 days of the order or of the appointment under those powers, give notice of the fact to the registrar of companies; and the registrar shall enter the fact in the register of charges.

(2) Where a person appointed receiver or manager of a company's property under powers contained in an instrument ceases to act as such receiver or manager, he shall, on so ceasing, give the registrar notice to that effect, and the registrar shall enter the fact in the register of charges.

(3) A notice under this section shall be in the prescribed form.

(4) If a person makes default in complying with the requirements of this section, he is liable to a fine and, for continued contravention, to a daily default fine.

406   Companies to keep copies of instruments creating charges

(1) Every company shall cause a copy of every instrument creating a charge requiring registration under this Chapter to be kept at its registered office.

(2) In the case of a series of uniform debentures, a copy of one debenture of the series is sufficient.

407   Company's register of charges

(1) Every limited company shall keep at its registered office a register of charges and enter in it all charges specifically affecting property of the company and all floating charges on the company's undertaking or any of its property.

(2) The entry shall in each case give a short description of the property charged, the amount of the charge and, except in the case of securities to bearer, the names of the persons entitled to it.

(3) If an officer of the company knowingly and wilfully authorises or permits the omission of an entry required to be made in pursuance of this section, he is liable to a fine.

408   Right to inspect instruments which create charges, etc.

(1) The copies of instruments creating any charge requiring registration under this Chapter with the registrar of companies, and the register of charges kept in pursuance of section 407, shall be open during business hours (but subject to such reasonable restrictions as the company in general meeting may impose, so that not less than 2 hours in each day be allowed for inspection) to the inspection of any creditor or member of the company without fee.

(2) The register of charges shall also be open to the inspection of any other person on payment of such fee, not exceeding 5 pence, for each inspection, as the company may prescribe.

(3) If inspection of the copies referred to, or of the register, is refused, every officer of the company who is in default is liable to a fine and, for continued contravention, to a daily default fine.

(4) If such a refusal occurs in relation to a company registered in England and Wales, the court may by order compel an immediate inspection of the copies or register.

PART XIII   ARRANGEMENTS AND RECONSTRUCTIONS

425   Power of company to compromise with creditors and members

(1) Where a compromise or arrangement is proposed between a company and its creditors, or any class of them, or between the company and its members, or any class of them, the court may on the application of the company or any creditor or member of it or, in the case of a company being wound up or *an administration order being in force in relation to a company*, of the liquidator or administrator, order a meeting of the creditors or class of creditors, or of the members of the company or class of members (as the case may be), to be summoned in such manner as the court directs.

(2) If a majority in number representing three-fourths in value of the creditors or class of creditors or members or class of members (as the case may be), present and voting either in person or by proxy at the meeting, agree to any compromise or arrangement, the compromise or arrangement, if sanctioned by the court, is binding on all creditors or the class of creditors or on the members or class of members (as the case may be), and also on the company or, in the case of a company in the course of being wound up, on the liquidator and contributories of the company.

(3) The court's order under subsection (2) has no effect until an office copy of it has been delivered to the registrar of companies for registration; and a copy of every such order shall be annexed to every copy of the company's memorandum issued after the order has been made or, in the case of a company not having a memorandum, of every copy so issued of the instrument constituting the company or defining its constitution.

(4) If a company makes default in complying with subsection (3), the company and every officer of it who is in default is liable to a fine.

(6) In this section and the next—
  (a) 'company' means any company liable to be wound up under this Act, and
  (b) 'arrangement' includes a reorganisation of the company's share capital by the consolidation of shares of different classes or by the division of shares into shares of different classes, or by both of those methods.

[*When the Enterprise Act 2002, sch. 17, is brought into force, the words in italics in the Companies Act 1985, s. 425(1), will be replaced by:*
  in administration]

426   Information as to compromise to be circulated

(1) The following applies where a meeting of creditors or any class of creditors, or of members or any class of members, is summoned under section 425.

(2) With every notice summoning the meeting which is sent to a creditor or member there shall be sent also a statement explaining the effect of the compromise or arrangement and in particular stating any material interests of the directors of the company (whether as directors or as members or as creditors of the company or otherwise) and the effect on those interests of the compromise or arrangement, in so far as it is different from the effect on the like interests of other persons.

(3) In every notice summoning the meeting which is given by advertisement there shall be included either such a statement as above-mentioned or a notification of the place at

which, and the manner in which, creditors or members entitled to attend the meeting may obtain copies of the statement.

(4) Where the compromise or arrangement affects the rights of debenture holders of the company, the statement shall give the like explanation as respects the trustees of any deed for securing the issue of the debentures as it is required to give as respects the company's directors.

(5) Where a notice given by advertisement includes a notification that copies of a statement explaining the effect of the compromise or arrangement proposed can be obtained by creditors or members entitled to attend the meeting, every such creditor or member shall, on making application in the manner indicated by the notice, be furnished by the company free of charge with a copy of the statement.

(6) If a company makes default in complying with any requirement of this section, the company and every officer of it who is in default is liable to a fine; and for this purpose a liquidator or administrator of the company and a trustee of a deed for securing the issue of debentures of the company is deemed an officer of it.

However, a person is not liable under this subsection if he shows that the default was due to the refusal of another person, being a director or trustee for debenture holders, to supply the necessary particulars of his interests.

(7) It is the duty of any director of the company, and of any trustee for its debenture holders, to give notice to the company of such matters relating to himself as may be necessary for purposes of this section; and any person who makes default in complying with this subsection is liable to a fine.

427   Provisions for facilitating company reconstruction or amalgamation

(1) The following applies where application is made to the court under section 425 for the sanctioning of a compromise or arrangement proposed between a company and any such persons as are mentioned in that section.

(2) If it is shown—

    (a) that the compromise or arrangement has been proposed for the purposes of, or in connection with, a scheme for the reconstruction of any company or companies, or the amalgamation of any two or more companies, and

    (b) that under the scheme the whole or any part of the undertaking or the property of any company concerned in the scheme ('a transferor company') is to be transferred to another company ('the transferee company'),

the court may, either by the order sanctioning the compromise or arrangement or by any subsequent order, make provision for all or any of the following matters.

(3) The matters for which the court's order may make provision are—

    (a) the transfer to the transferee company of the whole or any part of the undertaking and of the property or liabilities of any transferor company,

    (b) the allotting or appropriation by the transferee company of any shares, debentures, policies or other like interests in that company which under the compromise or arrangement are to be allotted or appropriated by that company to or for any person,

    (c) the continuation by or against the transferee company of any legal proceedings pending by or against any transferor company,

    (d) the dissolution, without winding up, of any transferor company,

    (e) the provision to be made for any persons who, within such time and in such manner as the court directs, dissent from the compromise or arrangement,

    (f) such incidental, consequential and supplemental matters as are necessary to secure that the reconstruction or amalgamation is fully and effectively carried out.

(4) If an order under this section provides for the transfer of property or liabilities, then—

    (a) that property is by virtue of the order transferred to, and vests in, the transferee company, and

(b) those liabilities are, by virtue of the order, transferred to and become liabilities of that company;

and property (if the order so directs) vests freed from any charge which is by virtue of the compromise or arrangement to cease to have effect.

(5) Where an order is made under this section, every company in relation to which the order is made shall cause an office copy of the order to be delivered to the registrar of companies for registration within 7 days after its making; and if default is made in complying with this subsection, the company and every officer of it who is in default is liable to a fine and, for continued contravention, to a daily default fine.

(6) In this section the expression 'property' includes property, rights and powers of every description; the expression 'liabilities' includes duties and 'company' includes only a company as defined in section 735(1).

427A   Application of ss. 425–427 to mergers and divisions of public companies
(1) Where—
    (a) a compromise or arrangement is proposed between a public company and any such persons as are mentioned in section 425(1) for the purposes of, or in connection with, a scheme for the reconstruction of any company or companies or the amalgamation of any two or more companies,
    (b) the circumstances are as specified in any of the Cases described in subsection (2), and
    (c) the consideration for the transfer or each of the transfers envisaged in the Case in question is to be shares in the transferee company or any of the transferee companies receivable by members of the transferor company or transferor companies, with or without any cash payment to members,

sections 425 to 427 shall, as regards that compromise or arrangement, have effect subject to the provisions of this section and Schedule 15B.

(2) The Cases referred to in subsection (1) are as follows—

Case 1

Where under the scheme the undertaking, property and liabilities of the company in respect of which the compromise or arrangement in question is proposed are to be transferred to another public company, other than one formed for the purpose of, or in connection with, the scheme.

Case 2

Where under the scheme the undertaking, property and liabilities of each of two or more public companies concerned in the scheme, including the company in respect of which the compromise or arrangement in question is proposed, are to be transferred to a company (whether or not a public company) formed for the purpose of, or in connection with, the scheme.

Case 3

Where under the scheme the undertaking, property and liabilities of the company in respect of which the compromise or arrangement in question is proposed are to be divided among and transferred to two or more companies each of which is either—
    (a) a public company, or
    (b) a company (whether or not a public company) formed for the purposes of, or in connection with, the scheme.

(3) Before sanctioning any compromise or arrangement under section 425(2) the court may, on the application of any pre-existing transferee company or any member or creditor of

it or, *an administration order being in force in relation to the company,* the administrator, order a meeting of the members of the company or any class of them or of the creditors of the company or any class of them to be summoned in such manner as the court directs.

(4) This section does not apply where the company in respect of which the compromise or arrangement is proposed is being wound up.

(5) This section does not apply to compromises or arrangements in respect of which an application has been made to the court for an order under section 425(1) before 1 January 1988.

(6) Where section 427 would apply in the case of a scheme but for the fact that the transferee company or any of the transferee companies is a company within the meaning of Article 3 of the Companies (Northern Ireland) Order 1986 (and thus not within the definition of 'company' in subsection (6) of section 427), section 427 shall apply notwithstanding that fact.

(7) In the case of a scheme mentioned in subsection (1), for a company within the meaning of Article 3 of the Companies (Northern Ireland) Order 1986, the reference in section 427(5) to the registrar of companies shall have effect as a reference to the registrar as defined in Article 2 of that Order.

(8) In this section and Schedule 15B—

'transferor company' means a company whose undertaking, property and liabilities are to be transferred by means of a transfer envisaged in any of the Cases specified in subsection (2);

'transferee company' means a company to which a transfer envisaged in any of those Cases is to be made;

'pre-existing transferee company' means a transferee company other than one formed for the purpose of, or in connection with, the scheme;

'compromise or arrangement' means a compromise or arrangement to which subsection (1) applies;

'the scheme' means the scheme mentioned in subsection (1)(a);

'company' includes only a company as defined in section 735(1) except that, in the case of a transferee company, it also includes a company as defined in Article 3 of the companies (Northern Ireland) Order 1986 (referred to in these definitions as a 'Northern Ireland company');

'public company' means, in relation to a transferee company which is a Northern Ireland company, a public company within the meaning of Article 12 of the Companies (Northern Ireland) Order 1986;

'the registrar of companies' means, in relation to a transferee company which is a Northern Ireland company, the registrar as defined in Article 2 of the Companies (Northern Ireland) Order 1986;

'the Gazette' means, in relation to a transferee company which is a Northern Ireland company, the Belfast Gazette;

'Case 1 Scheme', 'Case 2 Scheme' and 'Case 3 Scheme' mean a scheme of the kind described in Cases 1, 2 and 3 of subsection (2) respectively;

'property' and 'liabilities' have the same meaning as in section 427.

[*When the Enterprise Act 2002, sch. 17, is brought into force, the words in italics in the Companies Act 1985, s. 427A(3), will be replaced by:*

where the company is in administration]

PART XIIIA   TAKEOVER OFFERS

428 'Takeover offers'

(1) In this Part of this Act 'a takeover offer' means an offer to acquire all the shares, or all the shares of any class or classes, in a company (other than shares which at the date of the offer are already held by the offeror), being an offer on terms which are the same in relation to all

the shares to which the offer relates or, where those shares include shares of different classes, in relation to all the shares of each class.

(2) In subsection (1) 'shares' means shares which have been allotted on the date of the offer but a takeover offer may include among the shares to which it relates all or any shares that are subsequently allotted before a date specified in or determined in accordance with the terms of the offer.

(3) The terms offered in relation to any shares shall for the purposes of this section be treated as being the same in relation to all the shares or, as the case may be, all the shares of a class to which the offer relates notwithstanding any variation permitted by subsection (4).

(4) A variation is permitted by this subsection where—

(a) the law of a country or territory outside the United Kingdom precludes an offer of consideration in the form or any of the forms specified in the terms in question or precludes it except after compliance by the offeror with conditions with which he is unable to comply or which he regards as unduly onerous; and

(b) the variation is such that the persons to whom an offer of consideration in that form is precluded are able to receive consideration otherwise than in that form but of substantially equivalent value.

(5) The reference in subsection (1) to shares already held by the offeror includes a reference to shares which he has contracted to acquire but that shall not be construed as including shares which are the subject of a contract binding the holder to accept the offer when it is made, being a contract entered into by the holder either for no consideration and under seal or for no consideration other than a promise by the offeror to make the offer.

(6) In the application of subsection (5) to Scotland, the words 'and under seal' shall be omitted.

(7) Where the terms of an offer make provision for their revision and for acceptances on the previous terms to be treated as acceptances on the revised terms, the revision shall not be regarded for the purposes of this Part of this Act as the making of a fresh offer and references in this part of this Act to the date of the offer shall accordingly be construed as references to the date on which the original offer was made.

(8) In this Part of this Act 'the offeror' means, subject to section 430D, the person making a takeover offer and 'the company' means the company whose shares are the subject of the offer.

429   Right of offeror to buy out minority shareholders

(1) If, in a case in which a takeover offer does not relate to shares of different classes, the offeror has by virtue of acceptances of the offer acquired or contracted to acquire not less than nine-tenths in value of the shares to which the offer relates *(excluding any shares in the company held as treasury shares)* he may give notice to the holder of any shares to which the offer relates which the offeror has not acquired or contracted to acquire that he desires to acquire those shares.

(2) If, in a case in which a takeover offer relates to shares of different classes, the offeror has by virtue of acceptances of the offer acquired or contracted to acquire not less than nine-tenths in value of the shares of any class to which the offer relates *(excluding any shares in the company held as treasury shares)*, he may give notice to the holder of any shares of that class which the offeror has not acquired or contracted to acquire that he desires to acquire those shares.

(3) No notice shall be given under subsection (1) or (2) unless the offeror has acquired or contracted to acquire the shares necessary to satisfy the minimum specified in that subsection before the end of the period of four months beginning with the date of the offer; and no such notice shall be given after the end of the period of two months beginning with the date on which he has acquired or contracted to acquire shares which satisfy that minimum.

(4) Any notice under this section shall be given in the prescribed manner; and when the offeror gives the first notice in relation to an offer he shall send a copy of it to the company

together with a statutory declaration by him in the prescribed form stating that the conditions for the giving of the notice are satisfied.

(5) Where the offeror is a company (whether or not a company within the meaning of this Act) the statutory declaration shall be signed by a director.

(6) Any person who fails to send a copy of a notice or a statutory declaration as required by subsection (4) or makes such a declaration for the purposes of that subsection knowing it to be false or without having reasonable grounds for believing it to be true shall be liable to imprisonment or a fine, or both, and for continued failure to send the copy or declaration, to a daily default fine.

(7) If any person is charged with an offence for failing to send a copy of a notice as required by subsection (4) it is a defence for him to prove that he took reasonable steps for securing compliance with that subsection.

(8) Where during the period within which a takeover offer can be accepted the offeror acquires or contracts to acquire any of the shares to which the offer relates but otherwise than by virtue of acceptances of the offer, then, if—

(a) the value of the consideration for which they are acquired or contracted to be acquired ('the acquisition consideration') does not at that time exceed the value of the consideration specified in the terms of the offer; or

(b) those terms are subsequently revised so that when the revision is announced the value of the acquisition consideration, at the time mentioned in paragraph (a) above, no longer exceeds the value of the consideration specified in those terms,

the offeror shall be treated for the purposes of this section as having acquired or contracted to acquire those shares by virtue of acceptances of the offer; but in any other case those shares shall be treated as excluded from those to which the offer relates.

[*The words in italics in s. 429(1) and (2) are in force from 1 December 2003.*]

430   Effect of notice under s. 429

(1) The following provisions shall, subject to section 430C, have effect where a notice is given in respect of any shares under section 429.

(2) The offeror shall be entitled and bound to acquire those shares on the terms of the offer.

(3) Where the terms of an offer are such as to give the holder of any shares a choice of consideration the notice shall give particulars of the choice and state—

(a) that the holder of the shares may within six weeks from the date of the notice indicate his choice by a written communication sent to the offeror at an address specified in the notice; and

(b) which consideration specified in the offer is to be taken as applying in default of his indicating a choice as aforesaid;

and the terms of the offer mentioned in subsection (2) shall be determined accordingly.

(4) Subsection (3) applies whether or not any time limit or other conditions applicable to the choice under the terms of the offer can still be complied with; and if the consideration chosen by the holder of the shares—

(a) is not cash and the offeror is no longer able to provide it; or

(b) was to have been provided by a third party who is no longer bound or able to provide it,

the consideration shall be taken to consist of an amount of cash payable by the offeror which at the date of the notice is equivalent to the chosen consideration.

(5) At the end of six weeks from the date of the notice the offeror shall forthwith—

(a) send a copy of the notice to the company; and

(b) pay or transfer to the company the consideration for the shares to which the notice relates.

(6) If the shares to which the notice relates are registered the copy of the notice sent to company under subsection (5)(a) shall be accompanied by an instrument of transfer executed

on behalf of the shareholder by a person appointed by the offeror; and on receipt of that instrument the company shall register the offeror as the holder of those shares.

(7) If the shares to which the notice relates are transferable by the delivery of warrants or other instruments the copy of the notice sent to the company under subsection (5)(a) shall be accompanied by a statement to that effect; and the company shall on receipt of the statement issue the offeror with warrants or other instruments in respect of the shares and those already in issue in respect of the shares shall become void.

(8) Where the consideration referred to in paragraph (b) of subsection (5) consists of shares or securities to be allotted by the offeror the reference in that paragraph to the transfer of the consideration shall be construed as a reference to the allotment of the shares or securities to the company.

(9) Any sum received by a company under paragraph (b) of subsection (5) and any other consideration received under that paragraph shall be held by the company on trust for the person entitled to the shares in respect of which the sum or other consideration was received.

(10) Any sum received by a company under paragraph (b) of subsection (5), and any dividend or other sum accruing from any other consideration received by a company under that paragraph, shall be paid into a separate bank account, being an account the balance on which bears interest at an appropriate rate and can be withdrawn by such notice (if any) as is appropriate.

(11) Where after reasonable enquiry made at such intervals as are reasonable the person entitled to any consideration held on trust by virtue of subsection (9) cannot be found and twelve years have elapsed since the consideration was received or the company is wound up the consideration (together with any interest, dividend or other benefit that has accrued from it) shall be paid into court.

(12) In relation to a company registered in Scotland, subsections (13) and (14) shall apply in place of subsection (11).

(13) Where after reasonable enquiry made at such intervals as are reasonable the person entitled to any consideration held on trust by virtue of subsection (9) cannot be found and twelve years have elapsed since the consideration was received or the company is wound up—

    (a) the trust shall terminate;

    (b) the company or, as the case may be, the liquidator shall sell any consideration other than cash and any benefit other than cash that has accrued from the consideration; and

    (c) a sum representing—

        (i) the consideration so far as it is cash;

        (ii) the proceeds of any sale under paragraph (b) above; and

        (iii) any interest, dividend or other benefit that has accrued from the consideration,

shall be deposited in the name of the Accountant of Court in a bank account such as is referred to in subsection (10) and the receipt for the deposit shall be transmitted to the Accountant of Court.

(14) Section 58 of the Bankruptcy (Scotland) Act 1985 (so far as consistent with this Act) shall apply with any necessary modifications to sums deposited under subsection (13) as that section applies to sums deposited under section 57(1)(a) of that Act.

(15) The expenses of any such enquiry as is mentioned in subsection (11) or (13) may be defrayed out of the money or other property held on trust for the person or persons to whom the enquiry relates.

430A   Right of minority shareholder to be bought out by offeror

(1) If a takeover offer relates to all the shares in a company and at any time before the end of the period within which the offer can be accepted—

(a) the offeror has by virtue of acceptances of the offer acquired or contracted to acquire some (but not all) of the shares to which the offer relates; and

(b) those shares, with or without any other shares in the company which he has acquired or contracted to acquire, amount to not less than nine-tenths in value of all the shares in the company *(excluding any shares in the company held as treasury shares)*,

the holder of any shares to which the offer relates who has not accepted the offer may by a written communication addressed to the offeror require him to acquire those shares.

(2) If a takeover offer relates to shares of any class or classes and at any time before the end of the period within which the offer can be accepted—

(a) the offeror has by virtue of acceptances of the offer acquired or contracted to acquire some (but not all) of the shares of any class to which the offer relates; and

(b) those shares, with or without any other shares of that class which he has acquired or contracted to acquire, amount to not less than nine-tenths in value of all the shares of that class *(excluding any shares in the company held as treasury shares)*,

the holder of any shares of that class who has not accepted the offer may by a written communication addressed to the offeror require him to acquire those shares.

(3) Within one month of the time specified in subsection (1) or, as the case may be, subsection (2) the offeror shall give any shareholder who has not accepted the offer notice in the prescribed manner of the rights that are exercisable by him under that subsection; and if the notice is given before the end of the period mentioned in that subsection it shall state that the offer is still open for acceptance.

(4) A notice under subsection (3) may specify a period for the exercise of the rights conferred by this section and in that event the rights shall not be exercisable after the end of that period; but no such period shall end less than three months after the end of the period within which the offer can be accepted.

(5) Subsection (3) does not apply if the offeror has given the shareholder a notice in respect of the shares in question under section 429.

(6) If the offeror fails to comply with subsection (3) he and, if the offeror is a company, every officer of the company who is in default or to whose neglect the failure is attributable, shall be liable to a fine and, for continued contravention, to a daily default fine.

(7) If an offeror other than a company is charged with an offence for failing to comply with subsection (3) it is a defence for him to prove that he took all reasonable steps for securing compliance with that subsection.

[*The words in italics in s. 430A(1)(b) and (2)(b) are in force from 1 December 2003.*]

430B   Effect of requirement under s. 430A

(1) The following provisions shall, subject to section 430C, have effect where a shareholder exercises his rights in respect of any shares under section 430A.

(2) The offeror shall be entitled and bound to acquire those shares on the terms of the offer or on such other terms as may be agreed.

(3) Where the terms of an offer are such as to give the holder of shares a choice of consideration the holder of the shares may indicate his choice when requiring the offeror to acquire them and the notice given to the holder under section 430A(3)—

(a) shall give particulars of the choice and of the rights conferred by this subsection; and

(b) may state which consideration specified in the offer is to be taken as applying in default of his indicating a choice;

and the terms of the offer mentioned in subsection (2) shall be determined accordingly.

(4) Subsection (3) applies whether or not any time limit or other conditions applicable to the choice under the terms of the offer can still be complied with; and if the consideration chosen by the holder of the shares—

    (a) is not cash and the offeror is no longer able to provide it; or

    (b) was to have been provided by a third party who is no longer bound or able to provide it,

the consideration shall be taken to consist of an amount of cash payable by the offeror which at the date when the holder of the shares requires the offeror to acquire them is equivalent to the chosen consideration.

430C Applications to the court

    (1) Where a notice is given under section 429 to the holder of any shares the court may, on an application made by him within six weeks from the date on which the notice was given—

    (a) order that the offeror shall not be entitled and bound to acquire the shares; or

    (b) specify terms of acquisition different from those of the offer.

    (2) If an application to the court under subsection (1) is pending at the end of the period mentioned in subsection (5) of section 430 that subsection shall not have effect until the application has been disposed of.

    (3) Where the holder of any shares exercises his rights under section 430A the court may, on an application made by him or the offeror, order that the terms on which the offeror is entitled and bound to acquire the shares shall be such as the court thinks fit.

    (4) No order for costs or expenses shall be made against a shareholder making an application under subsection (1) or (3) unless the court considers—

    (a) that the application was unnecessary, improper or vexatious; or

    (b) that there has been unreasonable delay in making the application or unreasonable conduct on his part in conducting the proceedings on the application.

    (5) Where a takeover offer has not been accepted to the extent necessary for entitling the offeror to give notices under subsection (1) or (2) of section 429 the court may, on the application of the offeror, make an order authorising him to give notices under that subsection if satisfied—

    (a) that the offeror has after reasonable enquiry been unable to trace one or more of the persons holding shares to which the offer relates;

    (b) that the shares which the offeror has acquired or contracted to acquire by virtue of acceptances of the offer, together with the shares held by the person or persons mentioned in paragraph (a), amount to not less than the minimum specified in that subsection; and

    (c) that the consideration offered is fair and reasonable; but the court shall not make an order under this subsection unless it considers that it is just and equitable to do so having regard, in particular, to the number of shareholders who have been traced but who have not accepted the offer.

430D Joint offers

    (1) A takeover offer may be made by two or more persons jointly and in that event this Part of this Act has effect with the following modifications.

    (2) The conditions for the exercise of the rights conferred by sections 429 and 430A shall be satisfied by the joint offerors acquiring or contracting to acquire the necessary shares jointly (as respects acquisitions by virtue of acceptances of the offer) and either jointly or separately (in other cases); and, subject to the following provisions, the rights and obligations of the offeror under those sections and sections 430 and 430B shall be respectively joint rights and joint and several obligations of the joint offerors.

    (3) It shall be a sufficient compliance with any provision of those sections requiring or authorising a notice or other document to be given or sent by or to the joint offerors that it is given or sent by or to any of them; but the statutory declaration required by section 429(4) shall be made by all of them and, in the case of a joint offeror being a company, signed by a director of that company.

(4) In sections 428, 430(8) and 430E references to the offeror shall be construed as references to the joint offerors or any of them.

(5) In section 430(6) and (7) references to the offeror shall be construed as references to the joint offerors or such of them as they may determine.

(6) In sections 430(4)(a) and 430B(4)(a) references to the offeror being no longer able to provide the relevant consideration shall be construed as references to none of the joint offerors being able to do so.

(7) In section 430C references to the offeror shall be construed as references to the joint offerors except that any application under subsection (3) or (5) may be made by any of them and the reference in subsection (5)(a) to the offeror having been unable to trace one or more of the persons holding shares shall be construed as a reference to none of the offerors having been able to do so.

430E   Associates

(1) The requirement in section 428(1) that a takeover offer must extend to all the shares, or all the shares of any class or classes, in a company shall be regarded as satisfied notwithstanding that the offer does not extend to shares which associates of the offeror hold or have contracted to acquire; but, subject to subsection (2), shares which any such associate holds or has contracted to acquire, whether at the time when the offer is made or subsequently, shall be disregarded for the purposes of any reference in this Part of this Act to the shares to which a takeover offer relates.

(2) Where during the period within which a takeover offer can be accepted any associate of the offeror acquires or contracts to acquire any of the shares to which the offer relates, then, if the condition specified in subsection (8)(a) or (b) of section 429 is satisfied as respects those shares they shall be treated for the purposes of that section as shares to which the offer relates.

(3) In section 430A(1)(b) and (2)(b) the reference to shares which the offeror has acquired or contracted to acquire shall include a reference to shares which any associate of his has acquired or contracted to acquire.

(4) In this section 'associate', in relation to an offeror means—
   (a) a nominee of the offeror;
   (b) a holding company, subsidiary or fellow subsidiary of the offeror or a nominee of such a holding company, subsidiary or fellow subsidiary;
   (c) a body corporate in which the offeror is substantially interested; or
   (d) any person who is, or is a nominee of, a party to an agreement with the offeror for the acquisition of, or of an interest in, the shares which are the subject of the takeover offer, being an agreement which includes provisions imposing obligations or restrictions such as are mentioned in section 204(2)(a).

(5) For the purposes of subsection (4)(b) a company is a fellow subsidiary of another body corporate if both are subsidiaries of the same body corporate but neither is a subsidiary of the other.

(6) For the purposes of subsection (4)(c) an offeror has a substantial interest in a body corporate if—
   (a) that body or its directors are accustomed to act in accordance with his directions or instructions; or
   (b) he is entitled to exercise or control the exercise of one-third or more of the voting power at general meetings of that body.

(7) Subsections (5) and (6) of section 204 shall apply to subsection (4)(d) above as they apply to that section and subsections (3) and (4) of section 203 shall apply for the purposes of subsection (6) above as they apply for the purposes of subsection (2)(b) of that section.

(8) Where the offeror is an individual his associates shall also include his spouse and any minor child or stepchild of his.

430F   Convertible securities
(1) For the purposes of this Part of this Act securities of a company shall be treated as shares in the company if they are convertible into or entitle the holder to subscribe for such shares; and references to the holder of shares or a shareholder shall be construed accordingly.
(2) Subsection (1) shall not be construed as requiring any securities to be treated—
   (a) as shares of the same class as those into which they are convertible or for which the holder is entitled to subscribe; or
   (b) as shares of the same class as other securities by reason only that the shares into which they are convertible or for which the holder is entitled to subscribe are of the same class.

PART XIV   INVESTIGATION OF COMPANIES AND THEIR AFFAIRS; REQUISITION OF DOCUMENTS

Appointment and functions of inspectors

431   Investigation of a company on its own application or that of its members
(1) The Secretary of State may appoint one or more competent inspectors to investigate the affairs of a company and to report on them in such manner as he may direct.
(2) The appointment may be made—
   (a) in the case of a company having a share capital, on the application either of not less than 200 members or of members holding not less than one-tenth of the shares issued *(excluding any shares held as treasury shares)*,
   (b) in the case of a company not having a share capital, on the application of not less than one-fifth in number of the persons on the company's register of members, and
   (c) in any case, on application of the company.
(3) The application shall be supported by such evidence as the Secretary of State may require for the purpose of showing that the applicant or applicants have good reason for requiring the investigation.
(4) The Secretary of State may, before appointing inspectors, require the applicant or applicants to give security, to an amount not exceeding £5,000, or such other sum as he may by order specify, for payment of the costs of the investigation.
   An order under this subsection shall be made by statutory instrument subject to annulment in pursuance of a resolution of either House of Parliament.
[*The words in italics in s. 431(2)(a) are in force from 1 December 2003.*]

432   Other company investigations
(1) The Secretary of State shall appoint one or more competent inspectors to investigate the affairs of a company and report on them in such manner as he directs, if the court by order declares that its affairs ought to be so investigated.
(2) The Secretary of State may make such an appointment if it appears to him that there are circumstances suggesting—
   (a) that the company's affairs are being or have been conducted with intent to defraud its creditors or the creditors of any other person, or otherwise for a fraudulent or unlawful purpose, or in a manner which is unfairly prejudicial to some part of its members, or
   (b) that any actual or proposed act or omission of the company (including an act or omission on its behalf) is or would be so prejudicial, or that the company was formed for any fraudulent or unlawful purpose, or
   (c) that persons concerned with the company's formation or the management of its affairs have in connection therewith been guilty of fraud, misfeasance or other misconduct towards it or towards its members, or

(d) that the company's members have not been given all the information with respect to its affairs which they might reasonably expect.

(2A) Inspectors may be appointed under subsection (2) on terms that any report they may make is not for publication; and in such a case, the provisions of section 437(3) (availability and publication of inspectors' reports) do not apply.

(3) Subsections (1) and (2) are without prejudice to the powers of the Secretary of State under section 431; and the power conferred by subsection (2) is exercisable with respect to a body corporate notwithstanding that it is in course of being voluntarily wound up.

(4) The reference in subsection (2)(a) to a company's members includes any person who is not a member but to whom shares in the company have been transferred or transmitted by operation of law.

433 Inspectors' powers during investigation

(1) If inspectors appointed under section 431 or 432 to investigate the affairs of a company think it necessary for the purposes of their investigation to investigate also the affairs of another body corporate which is or at any relevant time has been the company's subsidiary or holding company, or a subsidiary of its holding company or a holding company of its subsidiary, they have power to do so; and they shall report on the affairs of the other body corporate so far as they think that the results of their investigation of its affairs are relevant to the investigation of the affairs of the company first mentioned above.

434 Production of documents and evidence to inspectors

(1) When inspectors are appointed under section 431 or 432, it is the duty of all officers and agents of the company, and of all officers and agents of any other body corporate whose affairs are investigated under section 433(1)—

(a) to produce to the inspectors all documents of or relating to the company or, as the case may be, the other body corporate which are in their custody or power,

(b) to attend before the inspectors when required to do so, and

(c) otherwise to give the inspectors all assistance in connection with the investigation which they are reasonably able to give.

(2) If the inspectors consider that an officer or agent of the company or other body corporate, or any other person, is or may be in possession of information relating to a matter which they believe to be relevant to the investigation, they may require him—

(a) to produce to them any documents in his custody or power relating to that matter,

(b) to attend before them, and

(c) otherwise to give them all assistance in connection with the investigation which he is reasonably able to give;

and it is that person's duty to comply with the requirement.

(3) An inspector may for the purposes of the investigation examine any person on oath, and may administer an oath accordingly.

(4) In this section a reference to officers or to agents includes past, as well as present, officers or agents (as the case maybe); and 'agents', in relation to a company or other body corporate, includes its bankers and solicitors and persons employed by it as auditors, whether these persons are or are not officers of the company or other body corporate.

(5) An answer given by a person to a question put to him in exercise of powers conferred by this section (whether as it has effect in relation to an investigation under any of sections 431 to 433, or as applied by any other section in this Part) may be used in evidence against him.

(5A) However, in criminal proceedings in which that person is charged with an offence to which this subsection applies—

(a) no evidence relating to the answer may be adduced, and

(b) no question relating to it may be asked,

by or on behalf of the prosecution, unless evidence relating to it is adduced, or a question relating to it is asked, in the proceedings by or on behalf of that person.

(5B) Subsection (5A) applies to any offence other than—

    (a) an offence under section 2 or 5 of the Perjury Act 1911 (false statements made on oath otherwise than in judicial proceedings or made otherwise than on oath); or

    (b) an offence under section 44(1) or (2) of the Criminal Law (Consolidation) (Scotland) Act 1995 (false statements made on oath or otherwise than on oath).

(6) In this section 'documents' includes information recorded in any form; and, in relation to information recorded otherwise than in legible form, the power to require its production includes power to require the production of a copy of the information in legible form, or in a form from which it can readily be produced in visible and legible form.

436 Obstruction of inspectors treated as contempt of court

(1) If any person—

    (a) fails to comply with section 434(1)(a) or (c),

    (b) refuses to comply with a requirement under section 434(1)(b) or (2), or

    (c) refuses to answer any question put to him by the inspectors for the purposes of the investigation,

the inspectors may certify that fact in writing to the court.

(2) If that person—

    (a) refuses to produce any book or document which it is his duty under section 434 or 435 to produce, or

    (b) refuses to attend before the inspectors when required to do so, or

    (c) refuses to answer any question put to him by the inspectors with respect to the affairs of the company or other body corporate (as the case may be),

the inspectors may certify the refusal in writing to the court.

(3) The court may thereupon enquire into the case; and, after hearing any witnesses who may be produced against or on behalf of the alleged offender and after hearing any statement which may be offered in defence, the court may punish the offender in like manner as if he had been guilty of contempt of the court.

437 Inspectors' reports

(1) The inspectors may, and if so directed by the Secretary of State shall, make interim reports to the Secretary of State, and on the conclusion of their investigation shall make a final report to him.

Any such report shall be written or printed, as the Secretary of State directs.

(1A) Any persons who have been appointed under section 431 or 432 may at any time and, if the Secretary of State directs them to do so, shall inform him of any matters coming to their knowledge as a result of their investigations.

(1B) If it appears to the Secretary of State that matters have come to light in the course of the inspectors' investigation which suggest that a criminal offence has been committed, and those matters have been referred to the appropriate prosecuting authority, he may direct the inspectors to take no further steps in the investigation or to take only such further steps as are specified in the direction.

(1C) Where an investigation is the subject of a direction under subsection (1B), the inspectors shall make a final report to the Secretary of State only where—

    (a) they were appointed under section 432(1) (appointment in pursuance of an order of the court), or

    (b) the Secretary of State directs them to do so.

(2) If the inspectors were appointed under section 432 in pursuance of an order of the court, the Secretary of State shall furnish a copy of any report of theirs to the court.

(3) In any case the Secretary of State may, if he thinks fit—

    (a) forward a copy of any report made by the inspectors to the company's registered office,

    (b) furnish a copy on request and on payment of the prescribed fee to—

    (i) any member of the company or other body corporate which is the subject of the report,

    (ii) any person whose conduct is referred to in the report,

    (iii) the auditors of that company or body corporate,

    (iv) the applicants for the investigation,

    (v) any other person whose financial interests appear to the Secretary of State to be affected by the matters dealt with in the report, whether as a creditor of the company or body corporate, or otherwise, and

  (c) cause any such report to be printed and published.

438 Power to bring civil proceedings on company's behalf

(1) If from any report made or information obtained under this Part it appears to the Secretary of State that any civil proceedings ought in the public interest to be brought by any body corporate, he may himself bring such proceedings in the name and on behalf of the body corporate.

(2) The Secretary of State shall indemnify the body corporate against any costs or expenses incurred by it in or in connection with proceedings brought under this section.

439 Expenses of investigating a company's affairs

(1) The expenses of an investigation under any of the powers conferred by this Part shall be defrayed in the first instance by the Secretary of State, but he may recover those expenses from the persons liable in accordance with this section.

There shall be treated as expenses of the investigation, in particular, such reasonable sums as the Secretary of State may determine in respect of general staff costs and overheads.

(2) A person who is convicted on a prosecution instituted as a result of the investigation, or is ordered to pay the whole or any part of the costs of proceedings brought under section 438, may in the same proceedings be ordered to pay those expenses to such extent as may be specified in the order.

(3) A body corporate in whose name proceedings are brought under that section is liable to the amount or value of any sums or property recovered by it as a result of those proceedings; and any amount for which a body corporate is liable under this subsection is a first charge on the sums or property recovered.

(4) A body corporate dealt with by an inspectors' report, where the inspectors were appointed otherwise than of the Secretary of State's own motion, is liable except where it was the applicant for the investigation, and except so far as the Secretary of State otherwise directs.

(5) Where inspectors were appointed—

  (a) under section 431, or

  (b) on an application under section 442(3),

the applicant or applicants for the investigation is or are liable to such extent (if any) as the Secretary of State may direct.

(6) The report of inspectors appointed otherwise than of the Secretary of State's own motion may, if they think fit, and shall if the Secretary of State so directs, include a recommendation as to the directions (if any) which they think appropriate, in the light of their investigation, to be given under subsection (4) or (5) of this section.

(7) For purposes of this section, any costs or expenses incurred by the Secretary of State in or in connection with proceedings brought under section 438 (including expenses incurred under subsection (2) of it) are to be treated as expenses of the investigation giving rise to the proceedings.

(8) Any liability to repay the Secretary of State imposed by subsection (2) and (3) above is (subject to satisfaction of his right to repayment) a liability also to indemnify all persons against liability under subsections (4) and (5); and any such liability imposed by subsection (2) is (subject as mentioned above) a liability also to indemnify all persons against liability under subsection (3).

(9) A person liable under any one of those subsections is entitled to contribution from any other person liable under the same subsection, according to the amount of their respective liabilities under it.

(10) Expenses to be defrayed by the Secretary of State under this section shall, so far as not recovered under it, be paid out of money provided by Parliament.

441   Inspectors' report to be evidence

(1) A copy of any report of inspectors appointed under this Part, certified by the Secretary of State to be a true copy, is admissible in any legal proceedings as evidence of the opinion of the inspectors in relation to any matter contained in the report and, in proceedings on an application under section 8 of the Company Directors Disqualification Act 1986, as evidence of any fact stated therein.

(2) A document purporting to be such a certificate as is mentioned above shall be received in evidence and be deemed to be such a certificate, unless the contrary is proved.

Other powers of investigation available to the Secretary of State

442   Power to investigate company ownership

(1) Where it appears to the Secretary of State that there is good reason to do so, he may appoint one or more competent inspectors to investigate and report on the membership of any company, and otherwise with respect to the company, for the purpose of determining the true persons who are or have been financially interested in the success or failure (real or apparent) of the company or able to control or materially to influence its policy.

(2) The appointment of inspectors under this section may define the scope of their investigation (whether as respects the matter or the period to which it is to extend or otherwise) and in particular may limit the investigation to matters connected with particular shares or debentures.

(3) If an application for investigation under this section with respect to particular shares or debentures of a company is made to the Secretary of State by members of the company, and the number of applicants or the amount of shares held by them is not less than that required for an application for the appointment of inspectors under section 431(2)(a) or (b), then, subject to the following provisions, the Secretary of State shall appoint inspectors to conduct the investigation applied for.

(3A) The Secretary of State shall not appoint inspectors if he is satisfied that the application is vexatious; and where inspectors are appointed their terms of appointment shall exclude any matter in so far as the Secretary of State is satisfied that it is unreasonable for it to be investigated.

(3B) The Secretary of State may, before appointing inspectors, require the applicant or applicants to give security, to an amount not exceeding £5,000, or such other sum as he may by order specify, for payment of the costs of the investigation.

An order under this subsection shall be made by statutory instrument which shall be subject to annulment in pursuance of a resolution of either House of Parliament.

(3C) If on an application under subsection (3) it appears to the Secretary of State that the powers conferred by section 444 are sufficient for the purposes of investigating the matters which inspectors would be appointed to investigate, he may instead conduct the investigation under that section.

(4) Subject to the terms of their appointment, the inspectors' powers extend to the investigation of any circumstances suggesting the existence of an arrangement or understanding which, though not legally binding, is or was observed or likely to be observed in practice and which is relevant to the purposes of the investigation.

443   Provisions applicable on investigation under s. 442

(1) For purposes of an investigation under section 442, sections 433(1), 434, 436 and 437 apply with the necessary modifications of references to the affairs of the company or to those of any other body corporate, subject however to the following subsections.

(2) Those sections apply to—

(a) all persons who are or have been, or whom the inspector has reasonable cause to believe to be or have been, financially interested in the success or failure or the apparent success or failure of the company or any other body corporate whose membership is investigated with that of the company, or able to control or materially influence its policy (including persons concerned only on behalf of others), and

(b) any other person whom the inspector has reasonable cause to believe possesses information relevant to the investigation,

as they apply in relation to officers and agents of the company or the other body corporate (as the case may be).

(3) If the Secretary of State is of opinion that there is good reason for not divulging any part of a report made by virtue of section 442 and this section, he may under section 437 disclose the report with the omission of that part; and he may cause to be kept by the registrar of companies a copy of the report with that part omitted or, in the case of any other such report, a copy of the whole report.

444   Power to obtain information as to those interested in shares, etc.

(1) If it appears to the Secretary of State that there is good reason to investigate the ownership of any shares in or debentures of a company and that it is unnecessary to appoint inspectors for the purpose, he may require any person whom he has reasonable cause to believe to have or to be able to obtain any information as to the present and past interests in those shares or debentures and the names and addresses of the persons interested and of any persons who act or have acted on their behalf in relation to the shares or debentures to give any such information to the Secretary of State.

(2) For this purpose a person is deemed to have an interest in shares or debentures if he has any right to acquire or dispose of them or of any interest in them, or to vote in respect of them, or if his consent is necessary for the exercise of any of the rights of other persons interested in them, or if other persons interested in them can be required, or are accustomed, to exercise their rights in accordance with his instructions.

(3) A person who fails to give information required of him under this section, or who in giving such information makes any statement which he knows to be false in a material particular, or recklessly makes any statement which is false in a material particular, is liable to imprisonment or a fine, or both.

445   Power to impose restrictions on shares and debentures

(1) If in connection with an investigation under either section 442 or 444 it appears to the Secretary of State that there is difficulty in finding out the relevant facts about any shares (whether issued or to be issued), he may by order direct that the shares shall until further order be subject to the restrictions of Part XV of this Act.

(1A) If the Secretary of State is satisfied that an order under subsection (1) may unfairly affect the rights of third parties in respect of shares then the Secretary of State, for the purpose of protecting such rights and subject to such terms as he thinks fit, may direct that such acts by such persons or descriptions of persons and for such purposes as may be set out in the order, shall not constitute a breach of the restrictions of Part XV of this Act.

(2) This section, and Part XV in its application to orders under it, apply in relation to debentures as in relation to shares save that subsection (1A) shall not so apply.

446   Investigation of share dealings

(1) If it appears to the Secretary of State that there are circumstances suggesting that contraventions may have occurred, in relation to a company's shares or debentures, of section 323 or 324 (taken with Schedule 13), or of subsections (3) to (5) of section 328 (restrictions on share dealings by directors and their families; obligation of director to disclose shareholding in his own company), he may appoint one or more competent inspectors to carry out such

investigations as are requisite to establish whether or not such contraventions have occurred and to report the result of their investigations to him.

(2) The appointment of inspectors under this section may limit the period to which their investigation is to extend or confine it to shares or debentures of a particular class, or both.

(3) For purposes of an investigation under this section, sections 434 to 437 apply—

    (a) with the substitution, for references to any other body corporate whose affairs are investigated under section 433(1), of a reference to any other body corporate which is, or has at any relevant time been, the company's subsidiary or holding company, or a subsidiary of its holding company.

(4) Sections 434 to 436 apply for the purposes of an investigation under this section to the following persons as they apply to officers of the company or of the other body corporate—

    (a) an authorised person;

    (b) a relevant professional;

    (c) a person not falling within paragraph (a) or (b) who may carry on a regulated activity without contravening the prohibition imposed by section 19 of the Financial Services and Markets Act 2000; and

    (d) in relation to an authorised person, to a relevant professional or to a person falling within paragraph (c)—

        (i) if it is a body corporate, any person who is or has been an officer of it;

        (ii) if it is a partnership, any person who is or has been a partner in it;

        (iii) if it is an unincorporated association, any person who is or has been a member of its governing body or an officer of it.

(4A) In subsection (4)—

'authorised person' has the meaning given in section 31(2) of the Financial Services and Markets Act 2000;

'relevant professional' means a member of a profession in relation to which a body has been designated under section 326(1) of that Act, and, in relation to such a profession, 'member' has the meaning given in section 325(2) of that Act.

Requisition and seizure of books and papers

447   Secretary of State's power to require production of documents

    (2) The Secretary of State may at any time, if he thinks there is good reason to do so, give directions to a company requiring it, at such time and place as may be specified in the directions, to produce such documents as may be so specified.

    (3) The Secretary of State may at any time, if he thinks there is good reason to do so, authorise an officer of his or any other competent person, on producing (if so required) evidence of his authority, to require a company to produce to him (the officer or other person) forthwith any documents which he (the officer or other person) may specify.

    (4) Where by virtue of subsection (2) or (3) the Secretary of State or an officer of his or other person has power to require the production of documents from a company, he or the officer or other person has the like power to require production of those documents from any person who appears to him or the officer or other person to be in possession of them; but where any such person claims a lien on books or papers produced by him, the production is without prejudice to the lien.

    (5) The power under this section to require a company or other person to produce documents includes power—

    (a) if the documents are produced—

        (i) to take copies of them or extracts from them, and

        (ii) to require that person, or any other person who is a present or past officer of, or is or was at any time employed by, the company in question, to provide an explanation of any of them;

(b) if the documents are not produced, to require the person who was required to produce them to state, to the best of his knowledge and belief, where they are.

(6) If the requirement to produce documents or provide an explanation or make a statement is not complied with, the company or other person on whom the requirement was so imposed is guilty of an offence and liable to a fine.

Sections 732 (restriction on prosecutions), 733 (liability of individuals for corporate default) and 734 (criminal proceedings against unincorporated bodies) apply to this offence.

(7) However, where a person is charged with an offence under subsection (6) in respect of a requirement to produce any documents, it is a defence to prove that they were not in his possession or under his control and that it was not reasonably practicable for him to comply with the requirement.

(8) A statement made by a person in compliance with such a requirement may be used in evidence against him.

(8A) However, in criminal proceedings in which that person is charged with an offence to which this subsection applies—

(a) no evidence relating to the statement may be adduced, and

(b) no question relating to it may be asked,

by or on behalf of the prosecution, unless evidence relating to it is adduced, or a question relating to it is asked, in the proceedings by or on behalf of that person.

(8B) Subsection (8A) applies to any offence other than—

(a) an offence under subsection (6) or section 451;

(b) an offence under section 5 of the Perjury Act 1911 (false statements made otherwise than on oath); or

(c) an offence under section 44(2) of the Criminal Law (Consolidation) (Scotland) Act 1995 (false statements made on oath or otherwise than on oath).

(9) In this section 'documents' includes information recorded in any form; and, in relation to information recorded otherwise than in legible form, the power to require its production includes power to require the production of a copy of it in legible form, or in a form from which it can readily be produced in visible and legible form.

448 Entry and search of premises

(1) A justice of the peace may issue a warrant under this section if satisfied on information on oath given by or on behalf of the Secretary of State, or by a person appointed or authorised to exercise powers under this Part, that there are reasonable grounds for believing that there are on any premises documents whose production has been required under this Part and which have not been produced in compliance with the requirement.

(2) A justice of the peace may also issue a warrant under this section if satisfied on information on oath given by or on behalf of the Secretary of State, or by a person appointed or authorised to exercise powers under this Part—

(a) that there are reasonable grounds for believing that an offence has been committed for which the penalty on conviction on indictment is imprisonment for a term of not less than two years and that there are on any premises documents relating to whether the offence has been committed,

(b) that the Secretary of State, or the person so appointed or authorised, has power to require the production of the documents under this Part, and

(c) that there are reasonable grounds for believing that if production was so required the documents would not be produced but would be removed from the premises, hidden, tampered with or destroyed.

(3) A warrant under this section shall authorise a constable, together with any other person named in it and any other constables—

(a) to enter the premises specified in the information, using such force as is reasonably necessary for the purpose;

(b) to search the premises and take possession of any documents appearing to be such documents as are mentioned in subsection (1) or (2), as the case may be, or to take, in relation to any such documents, any other steps which may appear to be necessary for preserving them or preventing interference with them;

(c) to take copies of any such documents; and

(d) to require any person named in the warrant to provide an explanation of them or to state where they may be found.

(4) If in the case of a warrant under subsection (2) the justice of the peace is satisfied on information on oath that there are reasonable grounds for believing that there are also on the premises other documents relevant to the investigation, the warrant shall also authorise the actions mentioned in subsection (3) to be taken in relation to such documents.

(5) A warrant under this section shall continue in force until the end of the period of one month beginning with the day on which it is issued.

(6) Any documents of which possession is taken under this section may be retained—

(a) for a period of three months; or

(b) if within that period proceedings to which the documents are relevant are commenced against any person for any criminal offence, until the conclusion of those proceedings.

(7) Any person who intentionally obstructs the exercise of any rights conferred by a warrant issued under this section or fails without reasonable excuse to comply with any requirement imposed in accordance with subsection (3)(d) is guilty of an offence and liable to a fine.

Sections 732 (restriction on prosecutions), 733 (liability of individuals for corporate default) and 734 (criminal proceedings against unincorporated bodies) apply to this offence.

(8) For the purposes of sections 449 and 451A (provision for security of information) documents obtained under this section shall be treated as if they had been obtained under the provision of this Part under which their production was or, as the case may be, could have been required.

(9) In the application of this section to Scotland for the references to a justice of the peace substitute references to a justice of the peace or a sheriff, and for the references to information on oath substitute references to evidence on oath.

(10) In this section 'document' includes information recorded in any form.

449   Provision for security of information obtained

(1) No information or document relating to a company which has been obtained under section 447 shall, without the previous consent in writing of that company, be published or disclosed, except to a competent authority, unless the publication or disclosure is required—

(a) with a view to the institution of or otherwise for the purposes of criminal proceedings;

(ba) with a view to the institution of, or otherwise for the purposes of, any proceedings on an application under section 6, 7 or 8 of the Company Directors Disqualification Act 1986;

(c) for the purposes of enabling or assisting any inspector appointed under this Part to discharge his functions;

(cc) for the purpose of enabling or assisting any person authorised to exercise powers [under] section 447 of this Act or section 84 of the Companies Act 1989 to discharge his functions;

(cd) for the purposes of enabling or assisting a person appointed under—

(i) section 167 of the Financial Services and Markets Act 2000 (general investigations),

(ii) section 168 of that Act (investigations in particular cases),

(iii) section 169(1)(b) of that Act (investigation in support of overseas regulator),

(iv) section 284 of that Act (investigations into affairs of certain collective investment schemes), or

(v) regulations made as a result of section 262(2)(k) of that Act (investigations into open-ended investment companies),

to conduct an investigation to discharge his functions;

(d) for the purpose of enabling or assisting the Secretary of State or the Treasury to exercise any of their functions under this Act, the insider dealing legislation, *the Prevention of Fraud (Investments) Act 1958,* the Insolvency Act 1986, the Company Directors Disqualification Act 1986, Part II, III or VII of the Companies Act 1989 or the Financial Services and Markets Act 2000;

(dd) for the purpose of enabling or assisting the Department of Economic Development for Northern Ireland to exercise any powers conferred on it by the enactments relating to companies or insolvency or for the purpose of enabling or assisting any inspector appointed by it under the enactments relating to companies to discharge his functions;

(dg) for the purpose of enabling or assisting the Occupational Pensions Regulatory Authority to discharge their functions under the Pension Schemes Act 1993 or the Pensions Act 1995 or any enactment in force in Northern Ireland corresponding to either of them;

(f) for the purpose of enabling or assisting the Bank of England to discharge its functions;

(fa) for the purposes of enabling or assisting the Financial Services Authority to discharge its functions under the legislation relating to friendly societies or to industrial and provident societies, under the Building Societies Act 1986, under Part VII of the Companies Act 1989 or under the Financial Services and Markets Act 2000;

(fb) for the purposes of enabling or assisting the competent authority for the purposes of Part VI of the Financial Services and Markets Act 2000 to discharge its functions under that Part;

(g) for the purposes of enabling or assisting a body corporate established in accordance with section 212(1) of the Financial Services and Markets Act 2000 (compensation scheme manager) to discharge its functions;

(h) for the purposes of any proceedings before the Financial Services Tribunal by virtue of the Financial Services and Markets Act 2000 (Transitional Provisions) (Partly Completed Procedures) Order 2001;

(ha) with a view to the institution of, or otherwise for the purposes of, proceedings before the Financial Services and Markets Tribunal;

(hb) for the purpose of enabling or assisting a recognised investment exchange or a recognised clearing house to discharge its functions as such;

(hc) for the purpose of enabling or assisting a body designated under section 326(1) of the Financial Services and Markets Act 2000 (designated professional bodies) to discharge its functions in its capacity as a body designated under that section;

(hh) for the purpose of enabling or assisting a body established by order under section 46 of the Companies Act 1989 to discharge its functions under Part II of that Act, or of enabling or assisting a recognised supervisory or qualifying body within the meaning of that Part to discharge its functions as such;

(k) for the purpose of enabling or assisting an official receiver to discharge his functions under the enactments relating to insolvency or for the purpose of enabling or assisting a body which is for the time being a recognised professional body for the purposes of section 391 of the Insolvency Act 1986 to discharge its functions as such;

(l) with a view to the institution of, or otherwise for the purposes of, any disciplinary proceedings relating to the exercise by a solicitor, auditor, accountant, valuer or actuary of his professional duties;

(ll) with a view to the institution of, or otherwise for the purposes of, any disciplinary proceedings relating to the discharge by a public servant of his duties;

(m) for the purpose of enabling or assisting an overseas regulatory authority to exercise its regulatory functions.

(1A) In subsection (1)—

(aa) in paragraph (hb) 'recognised investment exchange' and 'recognised clearing house' [have] the same meaning as in section 285 of the Financial Services and Markets Act 2000;

(a) in paragraph (ll) 'public servant' means an officer or servant of the Crown or of any public or other authority for the time being designated for the purposes of that paragraph by the Secretary of State by order made by statutory instrument; and

(b) in paragraph (m) 'overseas regulatory authority' and 'regulatory functions' have the same meaning as in section 82 of the Companies Act 1989.

(1B) Subject to subsection (1C), subsection (1) shall not preclude publication or disclosure for the purpose of enabling or assisting any public or other authority for the time being designated for the purposes of this subsection by the Secretary of State by an order in a statutory instrument to discharge any functions which are specified in the order.

(1C) An order under subsection (1B) designating an authority for the purpose of that subsection may—

(a) impose conditions subject to which the publication or disclosure of any information or document is permitted by that subsection; and

(b) otherwise restrict the circumstances in which that subsection permits publication or disclosure.

(2) A person who publishes or discloses any information or document in contravention of this section is guilty of an offence and liable to imprisonment or a fine, or both.

Sections 732 (restriction on prosecutions), 733 (liability of individuals for corporate default) and 734 (criminal proceedings against unincorporated bodies) apply to this offence.

(3) For the purposes of this section each of the following is a competent authority—

(a) the Secretary of State,

(b) an inspector appointed under this Part,

(ba) a person appointed under—

(i) section 167 of the Financial Services and Markets Act 2000 (general investigations),

(ii) section 168 of that Act (investigations in particular cases),

(iii) section 169(1)(b) of that Act (investigation in support of overseas regulator),

(iv) section 284 of that Act (investigations into affairs of certain collective investment schemes), or

(v) regulations made as a result of section 262(2)(k) of that Act (investigations into open-ended investment companies),

to conduct an investigation;

(c) any person authorised to exercise powers under section 447 of this Act or section 84 of the Companies Act 1989,

(d) the Department of Economic Development in Northern Ireland,

(e) the Treasury,

(f) the Bank of England,

(g) the Lord Advocate,

(h) the Director of Public Prosecutions and the Director of Public Prosecutions for Northern Ireland,

(ha)the Financial Services Authority,

(l) any constable,

(m) any procurator fiscal,

(n) the Scottish Ministers.

(3A) Any information which may by virtue of this section be disclosed to a competent authority may be disclosed to any officer or servant of the authority.

(4) A statutory instrument containing an order under subsection (1A)(a) or (1B) is subject to annulment in pursuance of a resolution of either House of Parliament.

[*The words in italics in s. 449(1)(d) ('the Prevention of Fraud (Investments) Act 1958,') were repealed by the Financial Services Act 1986, sch. 17, part I, but this repeal was brought into force only in so far as the words applied to a prospectus offering for subscription, or to any form of application for, units in a body corporate which was a recognised scheme (Financial Services Act 1986 (Commencement) (No. 8) Order 1988 (SI 1988/740), art. 2 and sch.). However, the words are now redundant as the 1958 Act was repealed for all purposes as from 1 October 1989 by the Financial Services Act 1986, sch. 17, part I, and the Financial Services Act (Commencement) (No. 12) Order 1989 (SI 1989/1583), art. 2(2)(a).*

The amendment to s. 449(1)(c) made by SI 2001/3649, art. 22(3), omitted the word 'under', which seems to be required and has been added editorially.

Section 449(1)(hh) has not been brought into force to the extent that it refers to a body established by order under the Companies Act 1989, s. 46 (Companies Act 1989 (Commencement No. 2) Order 1990 (SI 1990/142), art. 4(a)).

The word 'have' in s. 449(1A)(aa) has been substituted editorially for the ungrammatical 'has' in the paragraph as enacted in SI 2001/3649, art. 22(7).]

450   Punishment for destroying, mutilating etc. company documents

(1) An officer of a company who—

    (a) destroys, mutilates or falsifies, or is privy to the destruction, mutilation or falsification of a document affecting or relating to the company's property or affairs, or

    (b) makes, or is privy to the making of, a false entry in such a document,

is guilty of an offence, unless he proves that he had no intention to conceal the state of affairs of the company or to defeat the law.

(1A) Subsection (1) applies to an officer of an authorised insurance company which is not a body corporate as it applies to an officer of a company.

(2) Such a person as above mentioned who fraudulently either parts with, alters or makes an omission in any such document or is privy to fraudulent parting with, fraudulent altering or fraudulent making of an omission in, any such document, is guilty of an offence.

(3) A person guilty of an offence under this section is liable to imprisonment or a fine, or both.

(4) Sections 732 (restriction on prosecutions), 733 (liability of individuals for corporate default) and 734 (criminal proceedings against unincorporated bodies) apply to an offence under this section.

(5) In this section 'document' includes information recorded in any form.

451   Punishment for furnishing false information

A person who, in purported compliance with a requirement imposed under section 447 to provide an explanation or make a statement, provides or makes an explanation or statement which he knows to be false in a material particular or recklessly provides or makes an explanation or statement which is so false, is guilty of an offence and liable to imprisonment or a fine, or both.

Sections 732 (restriction on prosecutions), 733 (liability of individuals for corporate default) and 734 (criminal proceedings against unincorporated bodies) apply to this offence.

451A   Disclosure of information by Secretary of State or inspector

(1) This section applies to information obtained under sections 434 to 446.

(2) The Secretary of State may, if he thinks fit—

    (a) disclose any information to which this section applies to any person to whom, or for any purpose for which, disclosure is permitted under section 449, or

    (b) authorise or require an inspector appointed under this Part to disclose such information to any such person or for any such purpose.

(3) Information to which this section applies may also be disclosed by an inspector appointed under this Part to—
- (a) another inspector appointed under this Part;
- (b) a person appointed under—
    - (i) section 167 of the Financial Services and Markets Act 2000 (general investigations),
    - (ii) section 168 of that Act (investigations in particular cases),
    - (iii) section 169(1)(b) of that Act (investigation in support of overseas regulator),
    - (iv) section 284 of that Act (investigations into affairs of certain collective investment schemes), or
    - (v) regulations made as a result of section 262(2)(k) of that Act (investigations into open-ended investment companies),

    to conduct an investigation; or
- (c) a person authorised to exercise powers under—
    - (i) section 447 of this Act; or
    - (ii) section 84 of the Companies Act 1989 (exercise of powers to assist overseas regulatory authority).

(4) Any information which may by virtue of subsection (3) be disclosed to any person may be disclosed to any officer or servant of that person.

(5) The Secretary of State may, if he thinks fit, disclose any information obtained under section 444 to—
- (a) the company whose ownership was the subject of the investigation,
- (b) any member of the company,
- (c) any person whose conduct was investigated in the course of the investigation,
- (d) the auditors of the company, or
- (e) any person whose financial interests appear to the Secretary of State to be affected by matters covered by the investigation.

Supplementary

452   Privileged information

(1) Nothing in sections 431 to 446 requires the disclosure to the Secretary of State or to an inspector appointed by him—
- (a) by any person of information which he would in an action in the High Court or the Court of Session be entitled to refuse to disclose on grounds of legal professional privilege except, if he is a lawyer, the name and address of his client.

(1A) Nothing in section 434, 443 or 446 requires a person (except as mentioned in subsection (1B) below) to disclose information or produce documents in respect of which he owes an obligation of confidence by virtue of carrying on the business of banking unless—
- (a) the person to whom the obligation of confidence is owed is the company or other body corporate under investigation,
- (b) the person to whom the obligation of confidence is owed consents to the disclosure or production, or
- (c) the making of the requirement is authorised by the Secretary of State.

(1B) Subsection (1A) does not apply where the person owing the obligation of confidence is the company or other body corporate under investigation under section 431, 432 or 433.

(2) Nothing in section 447 to 451 compels the production by any person of a document which he would in an action in the High Court or the Court of Session be entitled to refuse to produce on grounds of legal professional privilege, or authorises the taking of possession of any such document which is in the person's possession.

(3) The Secretary of State shall not under section 447 require, or authorise an officer of his or other person to require, the production by a person carrying on the business of banking of a

document relating to the affairs of a customer of his unless either it appears to the Secretary of State that it is necessary to do so for the purpose of investigating the affairs of the first-mentioned person, or the customer is—

    (a) a person on whom a requirement has been imposed under that section, or

    (b) a person on whom a requirement to produce information or documents has been imposed by the Secretary of State, or by a person appointed by the Secretary of State to conduct an investigation, under section 171 or 173 of the Financial Services and Markets Act 2000.

453   Investigation of oversea companies

(1) The provisions of this Part apply to bodies corporate incorporated outside Great Britain which are carrying on business in Great Britain, or have at any time carried on business there, as they apply to companies under this Act; but subject to the following exceptions, adaptations and modifications.

(1A) The following provisions do not apply to such bodies—

    (a) section 431 (investigation on application of company or its members),

    (b) section 438 (power to bring civil proceedings on the company's behalf),

    (c) sections 442 to 445 (investigation of company ownership and power to obtain information as to those interested in shares, &c.), and

    (d) section 446 (investigation of share dealings).

(1B) The other provisions of this Part apply to such bodies subject to such adaptations and modifications as may be specified by regulations made by the Secretary of State.

(2) Regulations under this section shall be made by statutory instrument subject to annulment in pursuance of a resolution of either House of Parliament.

PART XV   ORDERS IMPOSING RESTRICTIONS ON SHARES (SECTIONS 210, 216, 445)

454   Consequence of order imposing restrictions

(1) So long as any shares are directed to be subject to the restrictions of this Part then, subject to any directions made in relation to an order pursuant to sections 210(5A), 216(1B), 445(1A) or 456(1A) or subject in the case of an interim order pursuant to section 216(1A) to the terms of that order—

    (a) any transfer of those shares or, in the case of unissued shares, any transfer of the right to be issued with them, and any issue of them, is void;

    (b) no voting rights are exercisable in respect of the shares;

    (c) no further shares shall be issued in right of them or in pursuance of any offer made to their holder; and

    (d) except in a liquidation, no payment shall be made of any sums due from the company on the shares, whether in respect of capital or otherwise.

(2) Where shares are subject to the restrictions of subsection (1)(a), any agreement to transfer the shares or, in the case of unissued shares, the right to be issued with them is void (except such agreement or right as may be made or exercised under the terms of directions made by the Secretary of State or the court under sections 210(5A), 216(1B), 445(1A), 456(1A) or of an interim order made under section 216(1A) or an agreement to transfer the shares on the making of an order under section 456(3)(b) below).

(3) Where shares are subject to the restrictions of subsection (1)(c) or (d), an agreement to transfer any right to be issued with other shares in right of those shares, or to receive any payment on them (otherwise than in a liquidation) is void (except such agreement or right as may be made or exercised under the terms of directions made by the Secretary of State or the court under sections 210(5A), 216(1B), 445(1A), 456(1A) or of an interim order made under section 216(1A) or an agreement to transfer any such right on the transfer of the shares on the making of an order under section 456(3)(b) below).

455   Punishment for attempted evasion of restrictions

(1) Subject to the terms of any directions made under sections 210(5A), 216(1B) or 445(1A) or 456 or of an interim order made under section 216(1A) a person is liable to a fine if he—

    (a) exercises or purports to exercise any right to dispose of any shares which, to his knowledge, are for the time being subject to the restrictions of this Part or of any right to be issued with any such shares, or

    (b) votes in respect of any such shares (whether as holder or proxy), or appoints a proxy to vote in respect of them, or

    (c) being the holder of any such shares, fails to notify of their being subject to those restrictions any person whom he does not know to be aware of that fact but does know to be entitled (apart from the restrictions) to vote in respect of those shares whether as holder or as proxy, or

    (d) being the holder of any such shares, or being entitled to any right to be issued with other shares in right of them, or to receive any payment on them (otherwise than in a liquidation), enters into any agreement which is void under section 454(2) or (3).

(2) Subject to the terms of any directions made under sections 210(5A), 216(1B), 445(1A) or 456 or of an interim order made under section 216(1A) if shares in a company are issued in contravention of the restrictions, the company and every officer of it who is in default is liable to a fine.

(3) Section 732 (restriction on prosecutions) applies to an offence under this section.

456   Relaxation and removal of restrictions

(1) Where shares in a company are by order made subject to the restrictions of this Part, application may be made to the court for an order directing that the shares be no longer so subject.

(1A) Where the court is satisfied that an order subjecting the shares to the restrictions of this Part unfairly affects the rights of third parties in respect of shares then the court, for the purpose of protecting such rights and subject to such terms as it thinks fit and in addition to any order it may make under subsection (1), may direct on an application made under that subsection that such acts by such persons or descriptions of persons and for such purposes, as may be set out in the order, shall not constitute a breach of the restrictions of Part XV of this Act.

Subsection (3) does not apply to an order made under this subsection.

(2) If the order applying the restrictions was made by the Secretary of State, or he has refused to make an order disapplying them, the application may be made by any person aggrieved; and if the order was made by the court under section 216 (non-disclosure of share holding), it may be made by any such person or by the company.

(3) Subject as follows, an order of the court or the Secretary of State directing that shares shall cease to be subject to the restrictions may be made only if—

    (a) the court or (as the case may be) the Secretary of State is satisfied that the relevant facts about the shares have been disclosed to the company and no unfair advantage has accrued to any person as a result of the earlier failure to make that disclosure, or

    (b) the shares are to be transferred for valuable consideration and the court (in any case) or the Secretary of State (if the order was made under section 210 or 445) approves the transfer.

(4) Without prejudice to the power of the court to give directions under subsection (1A), where shares in a company are subject to the restrictions, the court may on application order the shares to be sold, subject to the court's approval as to the sale, and may also direct that the shares shall cease to be subject to the restrictions.

An application to the court under this subsection may be made by the Secretary of State (unless the restrictions were imposed by court order under section 216), or by the company.

(5) Where an order has been made under subsection (4), the court may on application make such further order relating to the sale or transfer of the shares as it thinks fit.

An application to the court under this subsection may be made—

(a) by the Secretary of State (unless the restrictions on the shares were imposed by court order under section 216), or

(b) by the company, or

(c) by the person appointed by or in pursuance of the order to effect the sale, or

(d) by any person interested in the shares.

(6) An order (whether of the Secretary of State or the court) directing that shares shall cease to be subject to the restrictions of this Part, if it is—

(a) expressed to be made with a view to permitting a transfer of the shares, or

(b) made under subsection (4) of this section, may continue the restrictions mentioned in paragraphs (c) and (d) or section 454(1), either in whole or in part, so far as they relate to any right acquired or offer made before the transfer.

(7) Subsection (3) does not apply to an order directing that shares shall cease to be subject to any restrictions which have been continued in force in relation to those shares under subsection (6).

457   Further provisions on sale by court order of restricted shares

(1) Where shares are sold in pursuance of an order of the court under section 456(4) the proceeds of sale, less the costs of the sale, shall be paid into court for the benefit of the persons who are beneficially interested in the shares; and any such person may apply to the court for the whole or part of those proceeds to be paid to him.

(2) On application under subsection (1) the court shall (subject as provided below) order the payment to the applicant of the whole of the proceeds of sale together with any interest thereon or, if any other person had a beneficial interest in the shares at the time of their sale, such proportion of those proceeds and interest as is equal to the proportion which the value of the applicant's interest in the shares bears to the total value of the shares.

(3) On granting an application for an order under section 456(4) or (5) the court may order that the applicant's costs be paid out of the proceeds of sale; and if that order is made, the applicant is entitled to payment of his costs out of those proceeds before any person interested in the shares in question receives any part of those proceeds.

PART XVI   FRAUDULENT TRADING BY A COMPANY

458   Punishment for fraudulent trading

If any business of a company is carried on with intent to defraud creditors of the company or creditors of any other person, or for any fraudulent purpose, every person who was knowingly a party to the carrying on of the business in that manner is liable to imprisonment or a fine, or both.

This applies whether or not the company has been, or is in the course of being, wound up.

PART XVII   PROTECTION OF COMPANY'S MEMBERS AGAINST UNFAIR PREJUDICE

459   Order on application of company member

(1) A member of a company may apply to the court by petition for an order under this Part on the ground that the company's affairs are being or have been conducted in a manner which is unfairly prejudicial to the interests of its members generally or of some part of its

members (including at least himself) or that any actual or proposed act or omission of the company (including an act or omission on its behalf) is or would be so prejudicial.

(2) The provisions of this Part apply to a person who is not a member of a company but to whom shares in the company have been transferred or transmitted by operation of law, as those provisions apply to a member of the company; and references to a member or members are to be construed accordingly.

(3) In this section (and so far as applicable for the purposes of this section, in section 461(2)) 'company' means any company within the meaning of this Act or any company which is not such a company but is a statutory water company within the meaning of the Statutory Water Companies Act 1991.

460   Order on application of Secretary of State

(1) If it appears to the Secretary of State that—
  (a) the affairs of a company to which this subsection applies are being or have been conducted in a manner which is unfairly prejudicial to the interests of its members generally or of some part of its members, or
  (b) any actual or proposed act or omission of a company to which this subsection applies, including an act or omission on its behalf, is or would be so prejudicial,
he may himself (in addition to or instead of presenting a petition for the winding up of the company) apply to the court by petition for an order under this Part.

(1A) Subsection (1) applies to a company in respect of which—
  (a) the Secretary of State has received a report under section 437 of this Act;
  (b) the Secretary of State has exercised his powers under section 447 or 448 of this Act;
  (c) the Secretary of State or the Financial Services Authority has exercised his or its powers under Part XI of the Financial Services and Markets Act 2000; or
  (d) the Secretary of State has received a report from an investigator appointed by him or the Financial Services Authority under that Part.

(2) In this section (and, so far as applicable for its purposes, in the section next following) 'company' means any body corporate which is liable to be wound up under this Act.

461   Provisions as to petitions and orders under this Part

(1) If the court is satisfied that a petition under this Part is well founded, it may make such order as it thinks fit for giving relief in respect of the matters complained of.

(2) Without prejudice to the generality of subsection (1), the court's order may—
  (a) regulate the conduct of the company's affairs in the future,
  (b) require the company to refrain from doing or continuing an act complained of by the petitioner or to do an act which the petitioner has complained it has omitted to do,
  (c) authorise civil proceedings to be brought in the name and on behalf of the company by such person or persons and on such terms as the court may direct,
  (d) provide for the purchase of the shares of any members of the company by other members or by the company itself and, in the case of a purchase by the company itself, the reduction of the company's capital accordingly.

(3) If an order under this Part requires the company not to make any, or any specified, alteration in the memorandum or articles, the company does not then have power without leave of the court to make any such alteration in breach of that requirement.

(4) Any alteration in the company's memorandum or articles made by virtue of an order under this Part is of the same effect as if duly made by resolution of the company, and the provisions of this Act apply to the memorandum or articles as so altered accordingly.

(5) An office copy of an order under this part altering, or giving leave to alter, a company's memorandum or articles shall, within 14 days from the making of the order or such longer period as the court may allow, be delivered by the company to the registrar of companies for registration; and if a company makes default in complying with this subsection, the company

and every officer of it who is in default is liable to a fine and, for continued contravention, to a daily default fine.

(6) The power under section 411 of the Insolvency Act to make rules shall, so far as it relates to a winding-up petition, apply for the purposes of a petition under this Part.

PART XX   WINDING UP OF COMPANIES REGISTERED UNDER THIS ACT OR THE FORMER COMPANIES ACTS

CHAPTER VI   MATTERS ARISING SUBSEQUENT TO WINDING UP

651   Power of court to declare dissolution of company void

(1) Where a company has been dissolved, the court may, on an application made for the purpose by the liquidator of the company or by any other person appearing to the court to be interested, make an order, on such terms as the court thinks fit, declaring the dissolution to have been void.

(2) Thereupon such proceedings may be taken as might have been taken if the company had not been dissolved.

(3) It is the duty of the person on whose application the order was made, within 7 days after its making (or such further time as the court may allow), to deliver to the registrar of companies for registration an office copy of the order.

If the person fails to do so, he is liable to a fine and, for continued contravention, to a daily default fine.

(4) Subject to the following provisions, an application under this section may not be made after the end of the period of two years from the date of the dissolution of the company.

(5) An application for the purpose of bringing proceedings against the company—

    (a) for damages in respect of personal injuries (including any sum claimed by virtue of section 1(2)(c) of the Law Reform (Miscellaneous Provisions) Act 1934 (funeral expenses)), or

    (b) for damages under the Fatal Accidents Act 1976 or the Damages (Scotland) Act 1976,

may be made at any time; but no order shall be made on such an application if it appears to the court that the proceedings would fail by virtue of any enactment as to the time within which proceedings must be brought.

(6) Nothing in subsection (5) affects the power of the court on making an order under this section to direct that the period between the dissolution of the company and the making of the order shall not count for the purposes of any such enactment.

(7) In subsection (5)(a) 'personal injuries' includes any disease and any impairment of a person's physical or mental condition.

652   Registrar may strike defunct company off register

(1) If the registrar of companies has reasonable cause to believe that a company is not carrying on business or in operation, he may send to the company by post a letter inquiring whether the company is carrying on business or in operation.

(2) If the registrar does not within one month of sending the letter receive any answer to it, he shall within 14 days after the expiration of that month send to the company by post a registered letter referring to the first letter, and stating that no answer to it has been received, and that if an answer is not received to the second letter within one month from its date, a notice will be published in the Gazette with a view to striking the company's name off the register.

(3) If the registrar either receives an answer to the effect that the company is not carrying on business or in operation, or does not within one month after sending the second letter receive any answer, he may publish in the Gazette, and send to the company by post, a notice that at the expiration of 3 months from the date of that notice the name of the company

mentioned in it will, unless cause is shown to the contrary, be struck off the register and the company will be dissolved.

(4) If, in a case where a company is being wound up, the registrar has reasonable cause to believe either that no liquidator is acting, or that the affairs of the company are fully wound up, and the returns required to be made by the liquidator have not been made for a period of 6 consecutive months, the registrar shall publish in the Gazette and send to the company or the liquidator (if any) a like notice as is provided in subsection (3).

(5) At the expiration of the time mentioned in the notice the registrar may, unless cause to the contrary is previously shown by the company, strike its name off the register, and shall publish notice of this in the Gazette; and on the publication of that notice in the Gazette the company is dissolved.

(6) However—

    (a) the liability (if any) of every director, managing officer and member of the company continues and may be enforced as if the company had not been dissolved, and

    (b) nothing in subsection (5) affects the power of the court to wind up a company the name of which has been struck off the register.

(7) A notice to be sent to a liquidator under this section may be addressed to him at his last known place of business; and a letter or notice to be sent under this section to a company may be addressed to the company at its registered office or, if no office has been registered, to the care of some officer of the company.

If there is no officer of the company whose name and address are known to the registrar of companies, the letter or notice may be sent to each of the persons who subscribed the memorandum, addressed to him at the address mentioned in the memorandum.

652A   Registrar may strike private company off register on application

(1) On application by a private company, the registrar of companies may strike the company's name off the register.

(2) An application by a company under this section shall—

    (a) be made on its behalf by its directors or by a majority of them,

    (b) be in the prescribed form, and

    (c) contain the prescribed information.

(3) The registrar shall not strike a company off under this section until after the expiration of 3 months from the publication by him in the Gazette of a notice—

    (a) stating that he may exercise his power under this section in relation to the company, and

    (b) inviting any person to show cause why he should not do so.

(4) Where the registrar strikes a company off under this section, he shall publish notice of that fact in the Gazette.

(5) On the publication in the Gazette of a notice under subsection (4), the company to which the notice relates is dissolved.

(6) However, the liability (if any) of every director, managing officer and member of the company continues and may be enforced as if the company had not been dissolved.

(7) Nothing in this section affects the power of the court to wind up a company the name of which has been struck off the register.

652B   Duties in connection with making application under section 652A

(1) A person shall not make an application under section 652A on behalf of a company if, at any time in the previous 3 months, the company has—

    (a) changed its name,

    (b) traded or otherwise carried on business,

    (c) made a disposal for value of property or rights which, immediately before ceasing to trade or otherwise carry on business, it held for the purpose of disposal for gain in the normal course of trading or otherwise carrying on business, or

    (d) engaged in any other activity, except one which is—
        (i) necessary or expedient for the purpose of making an application under section 652A, or deciding whether to do so,
        (ii) necessary or expedient for the purpose of concluding the affairs of the company,
        (iii) necessary or expedient for the purpose of complying with any statutory requirement, or
        (iv) specified by the Secretary of State by order for the purposes of this sub-paragraph.

    (2) For the purposes of subsection (1), a company shall not be treated as trading or otherwise carrying on business by virtue only of the fact that it makes a payment in respect of a liability incurred in the course of trading or otherwise carrying on business.

    (3) A person shall not make an application under section 652A on behalf of a company at a time when any of the following is the case—
    (a) an application has been made to the court under section 425 on behalf of the company for the sanctioning of a compromise or arrangement and the matter has not been finally concluded;
    (b) a voluntary arrangement in relation to the company has been proposed under Part I of the Insolvency Act 1986 and the matter has not been finally concluded;
    (c) an administration order in relation to the company is in force under Part II of that Act or a petition for such an order has been presented and not finally dealt with or withdrawn;
    (d) the company is being wound up under Part IV of that Act, whether voluntarily or by the court, or a petition under that Part for the winding up of the company by the court has been presented and not finally dealt with or withdrawn;
    (e) there is a receiver or manager of the company's property;
    (f) the company's estate is being administered by a judicial factor.

    (4) For the purposes of subsection (3)(a), the matter is finally concluded if—
    (a) the application has been withdrawn,
    (b) the application has been finally dealt with without a compromise or arrangement being sanctioned by the court, or
    (c) a compromise or arrangement has been sanctioned by the court and has, together with anything required to be done under any provision made in relation to the matter by order of the court, been fully carried out.

    (5) For the purposes of subsection (3)(b), the matter is finally concluded if—
    (a) no meetings are to be summoned under section 3 of the Insolvency Act 1986,
    (b) meetings summoned under that section fail to approve the arrangement with no, or the same modifications,
    (c) an arrangement approved by meetings summoned under that section, or in consequence of a direction under section 6(4)(b) of that Act, has been fully implemented, or
    (d) the court makes an order under subsection (5) of section 6 of that Act revoking approval given at previous meetings and, if the court gives any directions under subsection (6) of that section, the company has done whatever it is required to do under those directions.

    (6) A person who makes an application under section 652A on behalf of a company shall secure that a copy of the application is given, within 7 days from the day on which the application is made, to every person who, at any time on that day, is—
    (a) a member of the company,
    (b) an employee of the company,
    (c) a creditor of the company,
    (d) a director of the company,

(e) a manager or trustee of any pension fund established for the benefit of employees of the company, or

(f) a person of a description specified for the purposes of this paragraph by regulations made by the Secretary of State.

(7) Subsection (6) shall not require a copy of the application to be given to a director who is a party to the application.

(8) The duty imposed by subection (6) shall cease to apply if the application is withdrawn before the end of the period for giving the copy application.

(9) The Secretary of State may by order amend subsection (1) for the purpose of altering the period in relation to which the doing of the things mentioned in paragraphs (a) to (d) of that subsection is relevant.

[*When the Enterprise Act 2002, sch. 17, is brought into force, the words in italics in the Companies Act 1985, s. 225(4), will be replaced by:*

(c) *the company is in administration under Part II of that Act;*

(ca) *an application to the court for an administration order in respect of the company has been made and not finally dealt with or withdrawn;*

(cb) *a copy of notice of intention to appoint an administrator of the company under paragraph 14 of Schedule B1 to that Act has been filed with the court and neither of the events mentioned in paragraph 44(2)(a) and (b) of that Schedule has occurred;*

(cc) *a copy of notice of intention to appoint an administrator of the company under paragraph 22 of that Schedule has been filed with the court and neither of the events mentioned in paragraph 44(4)(a) and (b) of that Schedule has occurred;*]

652C   Directors' duties following application under section 652A

(1) Subsection (2) applies in relation to any time after the day on which a company makes an application under section 652A and before the day on which the application is finally dealt with or withdrawn.

(2) A person who is a director of the company at the end of a day on which a person other than himself becomes—

(a) a member of the company,

(b) an employee of the company,

(c) a creditor of the company,

(d) a director of the company,

(e) a manager or trustee of any pension fund established for the benefit of employees of the company, or

(f) a person of a description specified for the purposes of this paragraph by regulations made by the Secretary of State,

shall secure that a copy of the application is given to that person within 7 days from that day.

(3) The duty imposed by subsection (2) shall cease to apply if the application is finally dealt with or withdrawn before the end of the period for giving the copy application.

(4) Subsection (5) applies where, at any time on or after the day on which a company makes an application under section 652A and before the day on which the application is finally dealt with or withdrawn—

(a) the company—

(i) changes its name,

(ii) trades or otherwise carries on business,

(iii) makes a disposal for value of any property or rights other than those which it was necessary or expedient for it to hold for the purpose of making, or proceeding with, an application under section 652A, or

(iv) engages in any other activity, except one to which subsection (6)applies;

(b) an application is made to the court under section 425 on behalf of the company for the sanctioning of a compromise or arrangement;

(c) a voluntary arrangement in relation to the company is proposed under Part I of the Insolvency Act 1986;

(d) *a petition is presented for the making of an administration order under Part II of that Act in relation to the company;*

(e) there arise any of the circumstances in which, under section 84(1) of that Act, the company may be voluntarily wound up;

(f) a petition is presented for the winding up of the company by the court under Part IV of that Act;

(g) a receiver or manager of the company's property is appointed; or

(h) a judicial factor is appointed to administer the company's estate.

(5) A person who, at the end of a day on which an event mentioned in any of paragraphs (a) to (h) of subsection (4) occurs, is a director of the company shall secure that the company's application is withdrawn forthwith.

(6) This subsection applies to any activity which is—

(a) necessary or expedient for the purpose of making, or proceeding with, an application under section 652A.

(b) necessary or expedient for the purpose of concluding affairs of the company which are outstanding because of what has been necessary or expedient for the purpose of making, or proceeding with, such an application,

(c) necessary or expedient for the purpose of complying with any statutory requirement, or

(d) specified by the Secretary of State by order for the purposes of this subsection.

(7) For the purposes of subsection (4)(a), a company shall not be treated as trading or otherwise carrying on business by virtue only of the fact that it makes a payment in respect of a liability incurred in the course of trading or otherwise carrying on business.

[*When the Enterprise Act 2002, sch. 17, is brought into force, the words in italics in the Companies Act 1985, s. 225(4), will be replaced by:*

(d) *an application to the court for an administration order in respect of the company is made under paragraph 12 of Schedule B1 to that Act;*

(da) *an administrator is appointed in respect of the company under paragraph 14 or 22 of that Schedule;*

(db) *a copy of notice of intention to appoint an administrator of the company under paragraph 14 or 22 of that Schedule is filed with the court;*]

652D   Sections 652B and 652C: supplementary provisions

(1) For the purposes of sections 652B(6) and 652C(2), a document shall be treated as given to a person if it is delivered to him or left at his proper address or sent by post to him at that address.

(2) For the purposes of subsection (1) and section 7 of the Interpretation Act 1978 (which relates to the service of documents by post) in its application to that subsection, the proper address of any person shall be his last known address, except that—

(a) in the case of a body corporate, other than one to which subsection (3) applies, it shall be the address of its registered or principal office,

(b) in the case of a partnership, other than one to which subsection (3) applies, it shall be the address of its principal office, and

(c) in the case of a body corporate or partnership to which subsection (3) applies, it shall be the address of its principal office in the United Kingdom.

(3) This subsection applies to a body corporate or partnership which—

(a) is incorporated or formed under the law of a country or territory outside the United Kingdom, and

(b) has a place of business in the United Kingdom.

(4) Where a creditor of the company has more than one place of business, subsection (1)

shall have effect, so far as concerns the giving of a document to him, as if for the words from 'delivered' to the end there were substituted 'left, or sent by post to him, at each place of business of his with which the company has had dealings in relation to a matter by virtue of which he is a creditor of the company'.

(5) Any power to make an order or regulations under section 652B or 652C shall—

(a) include power to make different provision for different cases or classes of case,

(b) include power to make such transitional provisions as the Secretary of State considers appropriate, and

(c) be exercisable by statutory instrument subject to annulment in pursuance of a resolution of either House of Parliament.

(6) For the purposes of sections 652B and 652C, an application under section 652A is withdrawn if notice of withdrawal in the prescribed form is given to the registrar of companies.

(7) In sections 652B and 652C, 'disposal' includes part disposal.

(8) In sections 652B and 652C and this section, 'creditor' includes a contingent or prospective creditor.

652E   Sections 652B and 652C: enforcement

(1) A person who breaches or fails to perform a duty imposed on him by section 652B or 652C is guilty of an offence and liable to a fine.

(2) A person who fails to perform a duty imposed on him by section 652B(6) or 652C(2) with the intention of concealing the making of the application in question from the person concerned is guilty of an offence and liable to imprisonment or a fine, or both.

(3) In any proceedings for an offence under subsection (1) consisting of breach of a duty imposed by section 652B(1) or (3), it shall be a defence for the accused to prove that he did not know, and could not reasonably have known, of the existence of the facts which led to the breach.

(4) In any proceedings for an offence under subsection (1) consisting of failure to perform the duty imposed by section 652B(6), it shall be a defence for the accused to prove that he took all reasonable steps to perform the duty.

(5) In any proceedings for an offence under subsection (1) consisting of failure to perform a duty imposed by section 652C(2) or (5), it shall be a defence for the accused to prove—

(a) that at the time of the failure he was not aware of the fact that the company had made an application under section 652A, or

(b) that he took all reasonable steps to perform the duty.

652F   Other offences connected with section 652A

(1) Where a company makes an application under section 652A, any person who, in connection with the application, knowingly or recklessly furnishes any information to the registrar of companies which is false or misleading in a material particular is guilty of an offence and liable to a fine.

(2) Any person who knowingly or recklessly makes an application to the registrar of companies which purports to be an application under section 652A, but which is not, is guilty of an offence and liable to a fine.

653   Objection to striking off by person aggrieved

(1) Subsection (2) applies if a company or any member or creditor of it feels aggrieved by the company having been struck off the register under section 652.

(2) The court, on an application by the company or the member or creditor made before the expiration of 20 years from publication in the Gazette of notice under section 652, may, if satisfied that the company was at the time of the striking off carrying on business or in operation, or otherwise that it is just that the company be restored to the register, order the company's name to be restored.

(2A) Subsections (2B) and (2D) apply if a company has been struck off the register under section 652A.

(2B) The court, on an application by a notifiable person made before the expiration of 20 years from publication in the Gazette of notice under section 652A(4), may, if satisfied—

(a) that any duty under section 652B or 652C with respect to the giving to that person of a copy of the company's application under section 652A was not performed,

(b) that the making of the company's application under section 652A involved a breach of duty under section 652B(1) or (3), or

(c) that it is for some other reason just to do so, order the company's name to be restored to the register.

(2C) In subsection (2B), 'notifiable person' means a person to whom a copy of the company's application under section 652A was required to be given under section 652B or 652C.

(2D) The court, on an application by the Secretary of State made before the expiration of 20 years from publication in the Gazette of notice under section 652A(4), may, if satisfied that it is in the public interest to do so, order the company's name to be restored.

(3) On an office copy of an order under subsection (2), (2B) or (2D) being delivered to the registrar of companies for registration the company to which the order relates is deemed to have continued in existence as if its name had not been struck off; and the court may by the order give such directions and make such provisions as seem just for placing the company and all other persons in the same position (as nearly as may be) as if the company's name had not been struck off.

654   Property of dissolved company to be bona vacantia

(1) When a company is dissolved, all property and rights whatsoever vested in or held on trust for the company immediately before its dissolution (including leasehold property, but not including property held by the company on trust for any other person) are deemed to be bona vacantia and—

(a) accordingly belong to the Crown, or to the Duchy of Lancaster or to the Duke of Cornwall for the time being (as the case may be), and

(b) vest and may be dealt with in the same manner as other bona vacantia accruing to the Crown, to the Duchy of Lancaster or to the Duke of Cornwall.

(2) Except as provided by the section next following, the above has effect subject and without prejudice to any order made by the court under section 651 or 653.

655   Effect on s. 654 of company's revival after dissolution

(1) The person in whom any property or right is vested by section 654 may dispose of, or of an interest in, that property or right notwithstanding that an order may be made under section 651 or 653.

(2) Where such an order is made—

(a) it does not affect the disposition (but without prejudice to the order so far as it relates to any other property or right previously vested in or held on trust for the company), and

(b) the Crown or, as the case may be, the Duke of Cornwall shall pay to the company an amount equal to—

(i) the amount of any consideration received for the property or right, or interest therein, or

(ii) the value of any such consideration at the time of the disposition, or, if no consideration was received, an amount equal to the value of the property, right or interest disposed of, as at the date of the disposition.

(3) Where a liability accrues under subsection (2) in respect of any property or right which, before the order under section 651 or 653 was made, had accrued as bona vacantia to the Duchy of Lancaster, the Attorney General of the Duchy shall represent Her Majesty in any proceedings arising in connection with that liability.

(4) Where a liability accrues under subsection (2) in respect of any property or right which, before the order under section 651 or 653 was made, had accrued as bona vacantia to the Duchy of Cornwall, such persons as the Duke of Cornwall (or other possessor for the time being of the Duchy) may appoint shall represent the Duke (or other possessor) in any proceedings arising out of that liability.

(5) This section applies in relation to the disposition of any property, right or interest on or after 22 December 1981, whether the company concerned was dissolved before, on or after that day.

656   Crown disclaimer of property vesting as bona vacantia

(1) Where property vests in the Crown under section 654, the Crown's title to it under that section may be disclaimed by a notice signed by the Crown representative, that is to say the Treasury Solicitor, or, in relation to property in Scotland, the Queen's and Lord Treasurer's Remembrancer.

(2) The right to execute a notice of disclaimer under this section may be waived by or on behalf of the Crown either expressly or by taking possession or other act evincing that intention.

(3) A notice of disclaimer under this section is of no effect unless it is executed—

    (a) within 12 months of the date on which the vesting of the property under section 654 came to the notice of the Crown representative, or

    (b) if an application in writing is made to the Crown representative by any person interested in the property requiring him to decide whether he will or will not disclaim, within a period of 3 months after the receipt of the application or such further period as may be allowed by the court which would have had jurisdiction to wind up the company if it had not been dissolved.

(4) A statement in a notice of disclaimer of any property under this section that the vesting of it came to the notice of the Crown representative on a specified date, or that no such application as above mentioned was received by him with respect to the property before a specified date, is sufficient evidence of the fact stated, until the contrary is proved.

(5) A notice of disclaimer under this section shall be delivered to the registrar of companies and retained and registered by him; and copies of it shall be published in the Gazette and sent to any persons who have given the Crown representative notice that they claim to be interested in the property.

(6) This section applies to property vested in the Duchy of Lancaster or the Duke of Cornwall under section 654 as if for references to the Crown and the Crown representative there were respectively substituted references to the Duchy of Lancaster and to the Solicitor to that Duchy, or to the Duke of Cornwall and to the Solicitor to the Duchy of Cornwall, as the case may be.

657   Effect of Crown disclaimer under s. 656

(1) Where notice of disclaimer is executed under section 656 as respects any property, that property is deemed not to have vested in the Crown under section 654.

(2) As regards property in England and Wales, section 178(4) and sections 179 to 182 of the Insolvency Act shall apply as if the property had been disclaimed by the liquidator under the said section 91 immediately before the dissolution of the company.

[*Before an amendment was made by the Insolvency Act 1986, sch. 13, this subsection read:*

    As regards property in England and Wales, subsections (3) and (5) to (7) of section 91 of the Insolvency Act 1985 and section 92 of that Act shall apply as if the property had been disclaimed by the liquidator under the said section 91 immediately before the dissolution of the company.

The Insolvency Act 1986 updated the first mention of the Insolvency Act 1985, s. 91, but not the second: the words 'under the said section 91' should have been changed to 'under section 178' (or omitted altogether).]

(3) As regards property in Scotland, the following 4 subsections apply.

(4) The Crown's disclaimer operates to determine, as from the date of the disclaimer, the rights, interests and liabilities of the company, and the property of the company, in or in respect of the property disclaimed; but it does not (except so far as is necessary for the purpose of releasing the company and its property from liability) affect the rights or liabilities of any other person.

(5) The court may, on application by a person who either claims an interest in disclaimed property or is under a liability not discharged by this Act in respect of disclaimed property, and on hearing such persons as it thinks fit, make an order for the vesting of the property in or its delivery to any persons entitled to it, or to whom it may seem just that the property should be delivered by way of compensation for such liability, or a trustee for him, and on such terms as the court thinks just.

(6) On such a vesting order being made, the property comprised in it vests accordingly in the person named in that behalf in the order, without conveyance or assignation for that purpose.

(7) Part II of Schedule 20 has effect for the protection of third parties where the property disclaimed is held under a lease.

658   Liability for rentcharge on company's land after dissolution

(1) Section 180 of the Insolvency Act shall apply to land in England and Wales which by operation of law vests subject to a rentcharge in the Crown or any other person on the dissolution of a company as it applies to land so vesting on a disclaimer under that section.

(2) In this section 'company' includes any body corporate.

PART XXII   BODIES CORPORATE SUBJECT, OR BECOMING SUBJECT, TO THIS ACT (OTHERWISE THAN BY ORIGINAL FORMATION UNDER PART I)

CHAPTER I   COMPANIES FORMED OR REGISTERED UNDER FORMER COMPANIES ACTS

675   Companies formed and registered under former Companies Acts

(1) In its application to existing companies, this Act applies in the same manner—
 (a) in the case of a limited company (other than a company limited by guarantee), as if the company had been formed and registered under Part I of this Act as a company limited by shares,
 (b) in the case of a company limited by guarantee, as if the company had been formed and registered under that Part as a company limited by guarantee, and
 (c) in the case of a company other than a limited company, as if the company had been formed and registered under that Part as an unlimited company.

(2) But reference, express or implied, to the date of registration is to be read as the date at which the company was registered under the Joint Stock Companies Acts, the Companies Act 1862, the Companies (Consolidation) Act 1908, the Companies Act 1929, or the Companies Act 1948.

679   Northern Ireland and Irish companies

Nothing in sections 675 to 678 applies to companies registered in Northern Ireland or the Republic of Ireland.

CHAPTER II   COMPANIES NOT FORMED UNDER COMPANIES LEGISLATION, BUT AUTHORISED TO REGISTER

680   Companies capable of being registered under this Chapter

(1) With the exceptions and subject to the provisions contained in this section and the next—

(a) any company consisting of two or more members, which was in existence on 2 November 1862, including any company registered under the Joint Stock Companies Acts, and

(b) any company formed after that date (whether before or after the commencement of this Act), in pursuance of any Act of Parliament (other than this Act), or of letters patent, or being otherwise duly constituted according to law, and consisting of two or more members,

may at any time, on making application in the prescribed form, register under this Act as an unlimited company, or as a company limited by shares, or as a company limited by guarantee; and the registration is not invalid by reason that it has taken place with a view to the company's being wound up.

(1A) A company shall not be prevented from registering under this Act as a private company limited by shares or by guarantee solely because it has only one member.

(2) A company registered in any part of the United Kingdom under the Companies Act 1862, the Companies (Consolidation) Act 1908, the Companies Act 1929 or the Companies Act 1948 shall not register under this section.

(3) A company having the liability of its members limited by Act of Parliament or letters patent, and not being a joint stock company, shall not register under this section.

(4) A company having the liability of its members limited by Act of Parliament or letters patent shall not register in pursuance of this section as an unlimited company or as a company limited by guarantee.

(5) A company that is not a joint stock company shall not register under this section as a company limited by shares.

681   Procedural requirements for registration

(1) A company shall not register under section 680 without the assent of a majority of such of its members as are present in person or by proxy (in cases where proxies are allowed) at a general meeting summoned for the purpose.

(2) Where a company not having the liability of its members limited by Act of Parliament or letters patent is about to register as a limited company, the majority required to assent as required by subsection (1) shall consist of not less than three-fourths of the members present in person or by proxy at the meeting.

(3) In computing any majority under this section when a poll is demanded, regard is to be had to the number of votes to which each member is entitled according to the company's regulations.

(4) Where a company is about to register (under section 680) as a company limited by guarantee, the assent to its being so registered shall be accompanied by a resolution declaring that each member undertakes to contribute to the company's assets, in the event of its being wound up while he is a member, or within one year after he ceases to be a member, for payment of the company's debts and liabilities contracted before he ceased to be a member, and of the costs and expenses of winding up and for the adjustment of the rights of the contributories among themselves, such amount as may be required, not exceeding a specified amount.

(5) Before a company is registered under section 680, it shall deliver to the registrar of companies—

(a) a statement that the registered office of the company is to be situated in England and Wales, or in Wales, or in Scotland (as the case may be),

(b) a statement specifying the intended situation of the company's registered office after registration, and

(c) in an appropriate case, if the company wishes to be registered with the Welsh equivalent of 'public limited company' or, as the case may be, 'limited' as the last words or word of its name, a statement to that effect.

(6) Any statement delivered to the registrar under subsection (5) shall be made in the prescribed form.

682 Change of name on registration
(1) Where the name of a company seeking registration under section 680 is a name by which it is precluded from registration by section 26 of this Act, either because it falls within subsection (1) of that section or, if it falls within subsection (2), because the Secretary of State would not approve the company's being registered with the name, the company may change its name with effect from the date on which it is registered under this chapter.

(2) A change of name under this section requires the like assent of the company's members as is required by section 681 for registration.

683 Definition of 'joint stock company'
(1) For purposes of this Chapter, as far as relates to registration of companies as companies limited by shares, 'joint stock company' means a company—

(a) having a permanent paid-up or nominal share capital of fixed amount divided into shares, also of fixed amount, or held and transferable as stock, or divided and held partly in one way and partly in the other, and

(b) formed on the principle of having for its members the holders of those shares or that stock, and no other persons.

(2) Such a company when registered with limited liability under this Act is deemed a company limited by shares.

684 Requirements for registration by joint stock companies
(1) Before the registration under section 680 of a joint stock company, there shall be delivered to the registrar of companies the following documents—

(a) a statement in the prescribed form specifying the name with which the company is proposed to be registered,

(b) a list in the prescribed form showing the names and addresses of all persons who on a day named in the list (not more than 28 clear days before the day of registration) were members of the company, with the addition of the shares or stock held by them respectively (distinguishing, in cases where the shares are numbered, each share by its number), and

(c) a copy of any Act of Parliament, royal charter, letters patent, deed of settlement, contract of copartnery or other instrument constituting or regulating the company.

(2) If the company is intended to be registered as a limited company, there shall also be delivered to the registrar of companies a statement in the prescribed form specifying the following particulars—

(a) the nominal share capital of the company and the number of shares into which it is divided, or the amount of stock of which it consists, and

(b) the number of shares taken and the amount paid on each share.

685 Registration of joint stock company as public company
(1) A joint stock company applying to be registered under section 680 as a company limited by shares may, subject to—

(a) satisfying the conditions set out in section 44(2)(a) and (b) (where applicable) and section 45(2) to (4) as applied by this section, and

(b) complying with subsection (4) below, apply to be so registered as a public company.

(2) Sections 44 and 45 apply for this purpose as in the case of a private company applying to be re-registered under section 43, but as if a reference to the special resolution required by section 43 were to the joint stock company's resolution that it be a public company.

(3) The resolution may change the company's name by deleting the word 'company' or the words 'and company', or its or their equivalent in Welsh ('cwmni', 'a'r cwmni'), including any abbreviation of them.

(4) The joint stock company's application shall be made in the form prescribed for the purpose, and shall be delivered to the registrar of companies together with the following documents as well as those required by section 684, namely—

(a) a copy of the resolution that the company be a public company,

(b) a copy of a written statement by an accountant with the appropriate qualifications that in his opinion a relevant balance sheet shows that at the balance sheet date the amount of the company's net assets was not less than the aggregate of its called up share capital and undistributable reserves,

(c) a copy of the relevant balance sheet, together with a copy of an unqualified report (by an accountant with such qualifications) in relation to the balance sheet,

(d) a copy of any valuation report prepared under section 44(2)(b) as applied by this section, and

(e) subject to subsection (4A), a statutory declaration in the prescribed form by a director or secretary of the company—

    (i) that the conditions set out in section 44(2)(a) and (b) (where applicable) and section 45(2) to (4) have been satisfied, and

    (ii) that, between the balance sheet date referred to in paragraph (b) of this subsection and the joint stock company's application, there has been no change in the company's financial position that has resulted in the amount of its net assets becoming less than the aggregate of its called up share capital and undistributable reserves.

(4A) In place of the statutory declaration referred to in paragraph (e) of subsection (4), there may be delivered to the registrar of companies using electronic communications a statement made by a director or secretary of the company as to the matters set out in subparagraphs (i) and (ii) of that paragraph.

(5) The registrar may accept a declaration under subsection (4)(e) or statement under subsection (4A) as sufficient evidence that the conditions referred to in that paragraph have been satisfied.

(6) In this section—

'accountant with the appropriate qualifications' means a person who would be eligible for appointment as the company's auditor, if it were a company registered under this Act,

'relevant balance sheet' means a balance sheet prepared as at a date not more than 7 months before the joint stock company's application to be registered as a public company limited by shares, and

'undistributable reserves' has the meaning given by section 264(3);

and section 46 applies (with necessary modifications) for the interpretation of the reference in subsection (4)(c) above to an unqualified report by the accountant.

(6A) Any person who makes a false statement under subsection (4A) which he knows to be false or does not believe to be true is liable to imprisonment or a fine, or both.

686   Other requirements for registration

(1) Before the registration in pursuance of this Chapter of any company (not being a joint stock company), there shall be delivered to the registrar of companies—

(a) a statement in the prescribed form specifying the name with which the company is proposed to be registered,

(b) a list showing with respect to each director or manager of the company—

    (i) in the case of an individual, his name, address, occupation and date of birth,

    (ii) in the case of a corporation or Scottish firm, its corporate or firm name and registered or principal office,

(c) a copy of any Act of Parliament, letters patent, deed of settlement, contract of copartnery or other instrument constituting or regulating the company, and

(d) in the case of a company intended to be registered as a company limited by guarantee, a copy of the resolution declaring the amount of the guarantee.

(1A) For the purposes of subsection (1)(b)(i) a person's 'name' means his Christian name (or other forename) and surname, except that in the case of a peer, or an individual usually known by a title, the title may be stated instead of his Christian name (or other forename) and surname or in addition to either or both of them.

(2) Subject to subsection (2A), the lists of members and directors and any other particulars relating to the company which are required by this Chapter to be delivered to the registrar shall be verified by a statutory declaration in the prescribed form made by any two or more directors or other principal officers of the company.

(2A) In place of the statutory declaration referred to in subsection (2), there may be delivered to the registrar of companies using electronic communications a statement made by any two or more directors or other principal officers of the company verifying the matters set out in that subsection.

(3) The registrar may require such evidence as he thinks necessary for the purpose of satisfying himself whether a company proposing to be registered is or is not a joint stock company as defined by section 683.

(3A) Any person who makes a false statement under subsection (2A) which he knows to be false or does not believe to be true is liable to imprisonment or a fine, or both.

687   Name of company registering

(1) The following applies with respect to the name of a company registering under this Chapter (whether a joint stock company or not).

(2) If the company is to be registered as a public company, its name must end with the words 'public limited company' or, if it is stated that the company's registered office is to be situated in Wales, with those words or their equivalent in Welsh ('cwmni cyfyngedig cyhoeddus'); and those words or that equivalent may not be preceded by the word 'limited' or its equivalent in Welsh ('cyfyngedig').

(3) In the case of a company limited by shares or by guarantee (not being a public company), the name must have 'limited' as its last word (or, if the company's registered office is to be situated in Wales, 'cyfyngedig'); but this is subject to section 30 (exempting a company, in certain circumstances, from having 'limited' as part of the name).

(4) If the company is registered with limited liability, then any additions to the company's name set out in the statements delivered under section 684(1)(a) or 686(1)(a) shall form and be registered as the last part of the company's name.

688   Certificate of registration under this Chapter

(1) On compliance with the requirements of this Chapter with respect to registration, the registrar of companies shall give a certificate (which may be signed by him, or authenticated by his official seal) that the company applying for registration is incorporated as a company under this Act and, in the case of a limited company, that it is limited.

(2) On the issue of the certificate, the company shall be so incorporated; and a banking company in Scotland so incorporated is deemed a bank incorporated, constituted or established by or under Act of Parliament.

(3) The certificate is conclusive evidence that the requirements of this Chapter in respect of registration, and of matters precedent and incidental to it, have been complied with.

(4) Where on an application by a joint stock company to register as a public company limited by shares the registrar of companies is satisfied that the company may be registered as a public company so limited, the certificate of incorporation given under this section shall state that the company is a public company; and that statement is conclusive evidence that

the requirements of section 685 have been complied with and that the company is a public company so limited.

689   Effect of registration

Schedule 21 to this Act has effect with respect to the consequences of registration under this Chapter, the vesting of property, savings for existing liabilities, continuation of existing actions, status of the company following registration, and other connected matters.

690   Power to substitute memorandum and articles for deed of settlement

(1) Subject as follows, a company registered in pursuance of this Chapter may by special resolution alter the form of its constitution by substituting a memorandum and articles for a deed of settlement.

(2) The provisions of sections 4 to 6 of this Act with respect to applications to the court for cancellation of alterations of the objects of a company and matters consequential on the passing of resolutions for such alterations (so far as applicable) apply, but with the following modifications—

    (a) there is substituted for the printed copy of the altered memorandum required to be delivered to the registrar of companies a printed copy of the substituted memorandum and articles, and

    (b) on the delivery to the registrar of the substituted memorandum and articles or the date when the alteration is no longer liable to be cancelled by order of the court (whichever is the later)—

        (i) the substituted memorandum and articles apply to the company in the same manner as if it were a company registered under Part I with that memorandum and those articles, and

        (ii) the company's deed of settlement ceases to apply to the company.

(3) An alteration under this section may be made either with or without alteration of the company's objects.

(4) In this section 'deed of settlement' includes any contract of copartnery or other instrument constituting or regulating the company, not being an Act of Parliament, a royal charter or letters patent.

PART XXIII   OVERSEA COMPANIES

CHAPTER I   REGISTRATION, ETC.

698   Definitions

. . .

(2) For the purposes of this Part (except section 699A and Schedule 21C):

. . .

    (b) 'branch' means a branch within the meaning of the Council Directive concerning disclosure requirements in respect of branches opened in a Member State by certain types of company governed by the law of another State (the Eleventh Company Law Directive, 89/666/EEC).

PART XXIV   THE REGISTRAR OF COMPANIES, HIS FUNCTIONS AND OFFICES

704   Registration offices

(1) For the purposes of the registration of companies under the Companies Acts, there shall continue to be offices in England and Wales and in Scotland, at such places as the Secretary of State thinks fit.

(2) The Secretary of State may appoint such registrars, assistant registrars, clerks and servants as he thinks necessary for that purpose, and may make regulations with respect to their duties, and may remove any persons so appointed.

(3) The salaries of the persons so appointed continue to be fixed by the Secretary of State, with the concurrence of the Treasury, and shall be paid out of money provided by Parliament.

(4) The Secretary of State may direct a seal or seals to be prepared for the authentication of documents required for or in connection with the registration of companies; and any seal so prepared is referred to in this Act as the Registrar's official seal.

(5) Wherever any act is by the Companies Acts directed to be done to or by the registrar of companies, it shall (until the Secretary of State otherwise directs) be done to or by the existing registrar of companies in England and Wales or in Scotland (as the case may be), or to or by such person as the Secretary of State may for the time being authorise.

(6) In the event of the Secretary of State altering the constitution of the existing registration offices or any of them, any such act shall be done to or by such officer and at such place with reference to the local situation of the registered offices of the companies to be registered as the Secretary of State may appoint.

(7) Subsection (8) below applies where by virtue of an order made under section 69 of the Deregulation and Contracting Out Act 1994 a person is authorised by the registrar of companies to accept delivery of any class of documents which are under any provision of the Companies Acts to be delivered to the registrar.

(8) If—
    (a) the registrar directs that documents of that class shall be delivered to a specified address of the authorised person; and
    (b) the direction is printed and made available to the public (with or without payment),
any document of that class which is delivered to an address other than the specified address shall be treated for the purposes of those Acts as not having been delivered.

705 Companies' registered numbers

(1) The registrar shall allocate to every company a number, which shall be known as the company's registered number.

(2) Companies' registered numbers shall be in such form, consisting of one or more sequences of figures or letters, as the registrar may from time to time determine.

(3) The registrar may upon adopting a new form of registered number make such changes of existing registered numbers as appear to him necessary.

(4) A change of a company's registered number has effect from the date on which the company is notified by the registrar of the change; but for a period of three years beginning with the date on which that notification is sent by the registrar the requirement of section 351(1)(a) as to the use of the company's registered number on business letters and order forms is satisfied by the use of either the old number or the new.

(5) In this section 'company' includes—
    (za) any oversea company which has complied with paragraph 1 of Schedule 21A other than a company which appears to the registrar not to have a branch in Great Britain;
    (a) any oversea company which has complied with section 691 (delivery of statutes to registrar, &c.), other than a company which appears to the registrar not to have a place of business in Great Britain; and
    (b) any body to which any provision of this Act applies by virtue of section 718 (unregistered companies).

706 Delivery to the registrar of documents in legible form

(1) This section applies to the delivery to the registrar under any provision of the Companies Acts of documents in legible form.

(2) The document must—

    (a) state in a prominent position the registered number of the company to which it relates, and, if the document is delivered under sections 659A(3), 703P or 703Q or Schedules 21A or 21D the registered number of the branch to which it relates,

    (b) satisfy any requirements prescribed by regulations for the purposes of this section, and

    (c) conform to such requirements as the registrar may specify for the purpose of enabling him to copy the document.

(3) If a document is delivered to the registrar which does not comply with the requirements of this section, he may serve on the person by whom the document was delivered (or, if there are two or more such persons, on any of them) a notice indicating the respect in which the document does not comply.

(4) Where the registrar serves such a notice, then, unless a replacement document—

    (a) is delivered to him within 14 days after the service of the notice, and

    (b) complies with the requirements of this section (or section 707B) or is not rejected by him for failure to comply with those requirements,

the original document shall be deemed not to have been delivered to him.

But for the purposes of any enactment imposing a penalty for failure to deliver, so far as it imposes a penalty for continued contravention, no account shall be taken of the period between the delivery of the original document and the end of the period of 14 days after service of the registrar's notice.

(5) Regulations made for the purposes of this section may make different provision with respect to different descriptions of document.

707A   The keeping of company records by the registrar

(1) The information contained in a document delivered to the registrar under the Companies Acts may be recorded and kept by him in any form he thinks fit, provided it is possible to inspect the information and to produce a copy of it in legible form.

This is sufficient compliance with any duty of his to keep, file or register the document.

(2) The originals of documents delivered to the registrar in legible form shall be kept by him for ten years, after which they may be destroyed.

(3) Where a company has been dissolved, the registrar may, at any time after the expiration of two years from the date of the dissolution, direct that any records in his custody relating to the company may be removed to the Public Record Office; and records in respect of which such a direction is given shall be disposed of in accordance with the enactments relating to that Office and the rules made under them.

This subsection does not extend to Scotland.

(4) In subsection (3) 'company' includes a company provisionally or completely registered under the Joint Stock Companies Act 1844.

707B   Delivery to the registrar using electronic communications

(1) Electronic communications may be used for the delivery of any document to the registrar under any provision of the Companies Acts (including delivery of a document in the prescribed form), provided that such delivery is in such form and manner as is directed by the registrar.

(2) Where the document is required under any provision of the Companies Acts to be signed or sealed, it shall instead be authenticated in such manner as is directed by the registrar.

(3) The document must contain in a prominent position—

    (a) the name and registered number of the company to which it relates, or

    (b) if the document is delivered under Part XXIII, the registered number of the branch or place of business of the company to which it relates.

(4) If a document is delivered to the registrar which does not comply with the requirements imposed by or under this section, he may serve on the person by whom the document

was delivered (or, if there are two or more such persons, on any of them) a notice indicating the respect in which the document does not comply.

(5) Where the registrar serves such a notice, then unless a replacement document—

(a) is delivered to him within 14 days after the service of the notice, and

(b) complies with the requirements of this section (or section 706) or is not rejected by him for failure to comply with those requirements,

the original document shall be deemed not to have been delivered to him.

But for the purposes of any enactment imposing a penalty for failure to deliver, so far as it imposes a penalty for continued contravention, no account shall be taken of the period between the delivery of the original document and the end of the period of 14 days after service of the registrar's notice.

(6) In this section references to the delivery of a document include references to the forwarding, lodging, registering, sending or submission of a document and to the giving of a notice, and cognate expressions are to be construed accordingly.

708   Fees payable to registrar

(1) The Secretary of State may by regulations made by statutory instrument require the payment to the registrar of companies of such fees as may be specified in the regulations in respect of—

(a) the performance by the registrar of such functions under the Companies Acts as may be so specified, including the receipt by him of any document which under those Acts is required to be delivered to him,

(b) the inspection of documents kept by him under those Acts.

(2) A statutory instrument containing regulations under this section requiring the payment of a fee in respect of a matter for which no fee was previously payable, or increasing a fee, shall be laid before Parliament after being made and shall cease to have effect at the end of the period of 28 days beginning with the day on which the regulations were made (but without prejudice to anything previously done under the regulations or to the making of further regulations) unless in that period the regulations are approved by resolution of each House of Parliament.

In reckoning that period of 28 days no account is to be taken of any time during which Parliament is dissolved or prorogued or during which both Houses are adjourned for more than 4 days.

(3) A statutory instrument containing regulations under this section, where subsection (2) does not apply, is subject to annulment in pursuance of a resolution of either House of Parliament.

(4) Fees paid to the registrar under the Companies Acts shall be paid into the Consolidated Fund.

(5) It is hereby declared that the registrar may charge a fee for any services provided by him otherwise than in pursuance of an obligation on him by law.

709   Inspection, &c. of records kept by the registrar

(1) Subject to section 723B, any person may inspect any records kept by the registrar for the purposes of the Companies Acts and may require—

(a) a copy, in such form as the registrar considers appropriate, of any information contained in those records, or

(b) a certified copy of, or extract from, any such record.

(2) The right of inspection extends to the originals of documents delivered to the registrar in legible form only where the record kept by the registrar of the contents of the documents is illegible or unavailable.

(3) A copy of or extract from a record kept at any of the offices for the registration of companies in England and Wales or Scotland, certified in writing by the registrar (whose official position it is unnecessary to prove) to be an accurate record of the contents of any

document delivered to him under the Companies Acts, is in all legal proceedings admissible in evidence as of equal validity with the original document and as evidence of any fact stated therein of which direct oral evidence would be admissible.

(4) Copies of or extracts from records furnished by the registrar may, instead of being certified by him in writing to be an accurate record, be sealed with his official seal.

(5) No process for compelling the production of a record kept by the registrar shall issue from any court except with the leave of the court; and any such process shall bear on it a statement that it is issued with the leave of the court.

710   Certificate of incorporation
Any person may require a certificate of the incorporation of a company, signed by the registrar or authenticated by his official seal.

710A   Provision and authentication by registrar of documents in non-legible form
(1) Any requirement of the Companies Acts as to the supply by the registrar of a document may, if the registrar thinks fit, be satisfied by the communication by the registrar of the requisite information in any non-legible form prescribed for the purposes of this section by regulations or approved by him.

(2) Where the document is required to be signed by him or sealed with his official seal, it shall instead be authenticated in such manner as may be prescribed by regulations or approved by the registrar.

710B   Documents relating to Welsh companies
(1) This section applies to any document which—
   (a) is delivered to the registrar under this Act or the Insolvency Act 1986, and
   (b) relates to a company (whether already registered or to be registered) whose memorandum states that its registered office is to be situated in Wales.

(2) A document to which this section applies may be in Welsh but, subject to subsection (3), shall on delivery to the registrar be accompanied by a certified translation into English.

(3) The requirement for a translation imposed by subsection (2) shall not apply—
   (a) to documents of such descriptions as may be prescribed for the purposes of this paragraph, or
   (b) to documents in a form prescribed in Welsh (or partly in Welsh and partly in English) by virtue of section 26 of the Welsh Language Act 1993.

(4) Where by virtue of subsection (3) the registrar receives a document in Welsh without a certified translation into English, he shall, if that document is to be available for inspection, himself obtain such a translation; and that translation shall be treated as delivered to him in accordance with the same provision as the original.

(5) A company whose memorandum states that its registered office is to be situated in Wales may deliver to the registrar a certified translation into Welsh of any document in English which relates to the company and which is or has been delivered to the registrar.

(6) The provisions within subsection (7) (which require certified translations into English of certain documents delivered to the registrar) shall not apply where a translation is required by subsection (2) or would be required but for subsection (3).

(7) The provisions within this subsection are section 228(2)(f), the second sentence of section 242(1), sections 243(4), 272(5) and 273(7) and paragraph 7(3) of Part II of Schedule 9.

(8) In this section 'certified translation' means a translation certified in the prescribed manner to be a correct translation.

711   Public notice by registrar of receipt and issue of certain documents
(1) The registrar of companies shall cause to be published in the Gazette notice of the issue or receipt by him of documents of any of the following descriptions (stating in the notice the name of the company, the description of document and the date of issue or receipt)—

(a) any certificate of incorporation of a company,
(b) any document making or evidencing an alteration in a company's memorandum or articles,
(c) any notification of a change among the directors of a company,
(d) any copy of a resolution of a public company which gives, varies, revokes or renews an authority for the purposes of section 80 (allotment of relevant securities),
(e) any copy of a special resolution of a public company passed under section 95(1), (2) or (3) (disapplication of pre-emption rights),
(f) any report under section 103 or 104 as to the value of a non-cash asset,
(g) any statutory declaration or statement delivered under section 117 (public company share capital requirements),
(h) any notification (given under section 122) of the redemption of shares,
(j) any statement or notice delivered by a public company under section 128 (registration of particulars of special rights),
(k) any documents delivered by a company under section 242(1) (accounts and reports),
(l) a copy of any resolution or agreement to which section 380 applies and which—
   (i) states the rights attached to any shares in a public company, other than shares which are in all respects uniform (for purposes of section 128) with shares previously allotted, or
   (ii) varies rights attached to any shares in a public company, or
   (iii) assigns a name or other designation, or a new name or designation, to any class of shares in a public company,
(m) any return of allotments of a public company,
(n) any notice of a change in the situation of a company's registered office,
(p) any copy of a winding-up order in respect of a company,
(q) any order for the dissolution of a company on a winding up,
(r) any return by a liquidator of the final meeting of a company on a winding up,
(s) any copy of a draft of the terms of a scheme delivered to the registrar of companies under paragraph 2(1) of Schedule 15A,
(t) any copy of an order under section 425(2) or section 427 in respect of a compromise or arrangement to which section 427A(1) applies,
(u) any return delivered under paragraph 1, 7 or 8 of Schedule 21A (branch registration),
(v) any document delivered under paragraph 1 or 8 of that Schedule,
(w) any notice under section 695A(3) of the closure of a branch,
(x) any document delivered under Schedule 21C (accounts and reports of foreign credit and financial institutions),
(y) any document delivered under Schedule 21D (accounts and reports of oversea companies subject to branch registration, other than credit and financial institutions),
(z) any return delivered under section 703P (particulars of winding up of oversea companies subject to branch registration).
(2) In section 42 'official notification' means—
   (a) in relation to anything stated in a document of any of the above descriptions, the notification of that document in the Gazette under this section, and
   (b) in relation to the appointment of a liquidator in a voluntary winding up, the notification of it in the Gazette under section 109 of the Insolvency Act; and 'officially notified' is to be construed accordingly.
[*A new s. 711A would be inserted if s. 142(1) of the Companies Act 1989 were brought into force.*]

713   Enforcement of company's duty to make returns

(1) If a company, having made default in complying with any provision of the Companies Acts which requires it to deliver a document to the registrar of companies, or to give notice to him of any matter, fails to make good the default within 14 days after the service of a notice on the company requiring it to do so, the court may, on an application made to it by any member or creditor of the company or by the registrar of companies, make an order directing the company and any officer of it to make good the default within such time as may be specified in the order.

(2) The court's order may provide that all costs of and incidental to the application shall be borne by the company or by any officers of it responsible for the default.

(3) Nothing in this section prejudices the operation of any enactment imposing penalties on a company or its officers in respect of any such default as is mentioned above.

714   Registrar's index of company and corporate names

(1) The registrar of companies shall keep an index of the names of the following bodies—

(a) companies as defined by this Act,

(aa) companies incorporated outside the United Kingdom and Gibraltar which have complied with paragraph 1 of Schedule 21A and which do not appear to the registrar of companies not to have a branch in Great Britain,

(b) companies incorporated outside Great Britain which have complied with section 691 and which do not appear to the registrar of companies not to have a place of business in Great Britain,

(c) incorporated and unincorporated bodies to which any provision of this Act applies by virtue of section 718 (unregistered companies),

(d) limited partnerships registered under the Limited Partnerships Act 1907,

(da) limited liability partnerships incorporated under the Limited Liability Partnerships Act 2000,

(e) companies within the meaning of the Companies Act (Northern Ireland) 1960,

(f) companies incorporated outside Northern Ireland which have complied with section 356 of that Act (which corresponds with section 691 of this Act), and which do not appear to the registrar not to have a place of business in Northern Ireland, and

(g) societies registered under the Industrial and Provident Societies Act 1965 or the Industrial and Provident Societies Act (Northern Ireland) 1969.

(2) The Secretary of State may by order in a statutory instrument vary subsection (1) by the addition or deletion of any class of body, except any within paragraph (a) or (b) of the subsection, whether incorporated or unincorporated; and any such statutory instrument is subject to annulment in pursuance of a resolution of either House of Parliament.

715A   Interpretation

(1) In this Part—

'document' includes information recorded in any form; and 'legible', in the context of documents in legible or non-legible form, means capable of being read with the naked eye.

(2) References in this Part to delivering a document include sending, forwarding, producing or (in the case of a notice) giving it.

PART XXV   MISCELLANEOUS AND SUPPLEMENTARY PROVISIONS

719   Power of company to provide for employees on cessation or transfer of business

(1) The powers of a company include (if they would not otherwise do so apart from this section) power to make the following provision for the benefit of persons employed or

formerly employed by the company or any of its subsidiaries, that is to say, provision in connection with the cessation or the transfer to any person of the whole or part of the undertaking of the company or that subsidiary.

(2) The power conferred by subsection (1) is exercisable notwithstanding that its exercise is not in the best interests of the company.

(3) The power which a company may exercise by virtue only of subsection (1) shall only be exercised by the company if sanctioned—

 (a) in a case not falling within paragraph (b) or (c) below, by an ordinary resolution of the company, or

 (b) if so authorised by the memorandum or articles, a resolution of the directors, or

 (c) if the memorandum or articles require the exercise of the power to be sanctioned by a resolution of the company of some other description for which more than a simple majority of the members voting is necessary, with the sanction of a resolution of that description;

and in any case after compliance with any other requirements of the memorandum or articles applicable to its exercise.

(4) Any payment which may be made by a company under this section may, if made before the commencement of any winding up of the company, be made out of profits of the company which are available for dividend.

721   Production and inspection of books where offence suspected

(1) The following applies if on an application made—

 (a) in England and Wales, to a judge of the High Court by the Director of Public Prosecutions, the Secretary of State or a chief officer of police, or

 (b) in Scotland, to one of the Lords Commissioners of Justiciary by the Lord Advocate,

there is shown to be reasonable cause to believe that any person has, while an officer of a company, committed an offence in connection with the management of the company's affairs and that evidence of the commission of the offence is to be found in any books or papers of or under the control of the company.

(2) An order may be made—

 (a) authorising any person named in it to inspect the books or papers in question, or any of them, for the purpose of investigating and obtaining evidence of the offence, or

 (b) requiring the secretary of the company or such other officer of it as may be named in the order to produce the books or papers (or any of them) to a person named in the order at a place so named.

(3) The above applies also in relation to any books or papers of a person carrying on the business of banking so far as they relate to the company's affairs, as it applies to any books or papers of or under the control of the company, except that no such order as is referred to in subsection (2)(b) shall be made by virtue of this subsection.

(4) The decision of a judge of the High Court or of any of the Lords Commissioners of Justiciary on an application under this section is not appealable.

722   Form of company registers, etc.

(1) Any register, index, minute book or accounting records required by the Companies Acts to be kept by a company may be kept either by making entries in bound books or by recording the matters in question in any other manner.

(2) Where any such register, index, minute book or accounting record is not kept by making entries in a bound book, but by some other means, adequate precautions shall be taken for guarding against falsification and facilitating its discovery.

(3) If default is made in complying with subsection (2), the company and every officer of it who is in default is liable to a fine and, for continued contravention, to a daily default fine.

723   Use of computers for company records

(1) The power conferred on a company by section 722(1) to keep a register or other record by recording the matters in question otherwise than by making entries in bound books includes power to keep the register or other record by recording those matters otherwise than in a legible form, so long as the recording is capable of being reproduced in a legible form.

(2) Any provision of an instrument made by a company before 12 February 1979 which requires a register of holders of the company's debentures to be kept in a legible form is to be read as requiring the register to be kept in a legible or non-legible form.

(3) If any such register or other record of a company as is mentioned in section 722(1), or a register of holders of a company's debentures, is kept by the company by recording the matters in question otherwise than in a legible form, any duty imposed on the company by this Act to allow inspection of, or to furnish a copy of, the register or other record or any part of it is to be treated as a duty to allow inspection of, or to furnish, a reproduction of the recording or of the relevant part of it in a legible form.

(4) The Secretary of State may by regulations in a statutory instrument make such provision in addition to subsection (3) as he considers appropriate in connection with such registers or other records as are mentioned in that subsection, and are kept as so mentioned; and the regulations may make modifications of provisions of this Act relating to such registers or other records.

(5) A statutory instrument under subsection (4) is subject to annulment in pursuance of a resolution of either House of Parliament.

723A   Obligations of company as to inspection of registers, &c.

(1) The Secretary of State may make provision by regulations as to the obligations of a company which is required by any provision of this Act—

    (a)   to make available for inspection any register, index or document, or

    (b)   to provide copies of any such register, index or document, or part of it;

and a company which fails to comply with the regulations shall be deemed to have refused inspection or, as the case may be, to have failed to provide a copy.

(2) The regulations may make provision as to the time, duration and manner of inspection, including the circumstances in which and extent to which the copying of information is permitted in the course of inspection.

(3) The regulations may define what may be required of the company as regards the nature, extent and manner of extracting or presenting any information for the purposes of inspection or the provision of copies.

(4) Where there is power to charge a fee, the regulations may make provision as to the amount of the fee and the basis of its calculation.

(5) Regulations under this section may make different provision for different classes of case.

(6) Nothing in any provision of this Act or in the regulations shall be construed as preventing a company from affording more extensive facilities than are required by the regulations or, where a fee may be charged, from charging a lesser fee than that prescribed or no fee at all.

(7) Regulations under this section shall be made by statutory instrument which shall be subject to annulment in pursuance of a resolution of either House of Parliament.

723B   Confidentiality orders

(1) Subject to the provisions of this section, an individual may make an application under this section to the Secretary of State where the condition in subsection (2) is satisfied.

(2) That condition is that the individual—

    (a)   is or proposes to become a director, secretary or permanent representative of a relevant company; and

    (b)   considers that the availability for inspection by members of the public of particulars of his usual residential address creates, or (if an order is not made under this section) is likely to create, a serious risk that he or a person who lives with him will be subjected to violence or intimidation.

(3) Where, on an application made by an individual under this section, the Secretary of State is satisfied that the availability for inspection by members of the public of particulars of the individual's usual residential address creates, or (if an order is not made under this section) is likely to create, a serious risk that the individual, or a person who lives with him, will be subjected to violence or intimidation, he shall make an order under this section ('a confidentiality order') in relation to him.

(4) Otherwise, he shall dismiss the application.

(5) An application under this section shall specify, in relation to each company of which the individual is a director, secretary or permanent representative, an address satisfying such conditions as may be prescribed.

(6) The Secretary of State shall give the applicant notice of his decision under subsection (3) or (4); and a notice under this subsection shall be given within the prescribed period after the making of the decision and contain such information as may be prescribed.

(7) Regulations may make provision about applications for confidentiality orders; and the regulations may in particular—

    (a) require the payment, on the making of an application, of such fees as may be specified in the regulations;

    (b) make provision about the form and manner in which applications are to be made;

    (c) provide that applications shall contain such information, and be accompanied by such evidence, as the Secretary of State may from time to time direct.

(8) Regulations may make provision—

    (a) about the manner in which determinations are to be made under subsection (3) or (4);

    (b) for questions to be referred to such persons as the Secretary of State thinks fit for the purposes of such determinations;

    (c) about the review of such determinations;

    (d) about the period for which confidentiality orders shall remain in force and the renewal of confidentiality orders.

(9) The Secretary of State may at any time revoke a confidentiality order if he is satisfied that such conditions as may be prescribed are satisfied.

(10) Regulations may make provision about the manner in which a determination under subsection (9) is to be made and notified to the individual concerned.

723C   Effect of confidentiality orders

(1) At any time when a confidentiality order is in force in relation to an individual—

    (a) section 709(1) shall not apply to so much of any record kept by the registrar as contains information which is recorded as particulars of the individual's usual residential address that were contained in a document delivered to the registrar after the order came into force;

    (b) section 364 shall have effect in relation to each affected company of which the individual is a director or secretary as if the reference in subsection (4)(a) of that section to the individual's usual residential address were a reference to the address for the time being specified by the individual in relation to that company under section 723B(5) or subsection (7) below.

(2) Regulations may make provision about the inspection and copying of confidential records, and such provision may include—

    (a) provision as to the persons by whom, and the circumstances in which, confidential records may be inspected or copies taken of such records;

    (b) provision under which the registrar may be required to provide certified copies of, or of extracts from, such records.

(3) Provision under subsection (2) may include provision—
  (a) for persons of a prescribed description to be entitled to apply to the court for authority to inspect or take copies of confidential records;
  (b) as to the criteria to be used by the court in determining whether an authorisation should be given.

(4) Regulations may make provision for restricting the persons to whom, and the purposes for which, relevant information may be disclosed.

(5) In subsection (4) 'relevant information' means information, relating to the usual residential address of an individual in relation to whom a confidentiality order is in force, which has been obtained in prescribed circumstances.

(6) Regulations may—
  (a) provide that, where a confidentiality order is in force in relation to an individual who is a director or secretary of a company, subsections (3) and (5) of section 288 shall not apply in relation to so much of the register kept by the company under that section as contains particulars of the usual residential address of that individual ('the protected part of the register'); and
  (b) make provision as to the persons by whom the protected part of the register may be inspected and the conditions (which may include conditions as to the payment of a fee) on which they may inspect it.

(7) Regulations may make provision—
  (a) requiring any individual in relation to whom a confidentiality order is in force to specify in the prescribed manner, in relation to each company of which he becomes a director, secretary or permanent representative at a time when the order is in force, an address satisfying such conditions as may be prescribed;
  (b) as to the manner in which the address specified in relation to a company under section 723B(5) or this subsection may be changed.

(8) A company is an affected company for the purposes of subsection (1) if—
  (a) it is required to deliver annual returns in accordance with section 363; and
  (b) the individual has specified an address in relation to it under section 723B(5) or subsection (7) above.

723D   Construction of sections 723B and 723C
(1) In section 723B 'relevant company' means—
  (a) a company formed and registered under this Act or an existing company; or
  (b) an oversea company.

(2) For the purposes of sections 723B and 723C, an individual is a permanent representative of a company if—
  (a) the company is a company to which section 690A applies; and
  (b) he is authorised to represent the company as a permanent representative of the company for the business of one or more of its branches in Great Britain.

(3) In section 723C 'confidential records' means so much of any records kept by the registrar for the purposes of the Companies Acts as contains information—
  (a) which relates to an individual in relation to whom a confidentiality order is in force; and
  (b) is recorded as particulars of the individual's usual residential address that were contained in a document delivered to the registrar after the order came into force.

(4) In sections 723B and 723C—
'confidentiality order' means an order under section 723B;
'the court' means such court as may be specified in regulations;
'director' and 'secretary', in relation to an oversea company, have the same meanings as in Chapter 1 of Part 23 of this Act;
'document' has the same meaning as in Part 24 of this Act;

'prescribed' means prescribed by regulations.

(5) Section 715A(2) applies in relation to sections 723B and 723C as it applies in relation to Part 24 of this Act.

(6) Regulations mayprovide that indetermining for the purposes of sections 723B and 723C whether a document has been delivered after the coming into force of a confidentiality order, any document delivered to the registrar after the latest time permitted for the delivery of that document shall be deemed to have been delivered at that time.

(7) For the purposes of section 723B(2)(a) and subsection (2) above it is immaterial whether or not the company in question has already been incorporated or become a relevant company or a company to which section 690A applies at the time of the application under section 723B.

(8) For the purposes of section 723C(1) and subsection (3) above, it is immaterial whether the record in question consists in the original document concerned.

723E   Sections 723B and 723C: offences

(1) Regulations may provide—
   (a) that any person who in an application under section 723B makes a statement which he knows to be false in a material particular, or recklessly makes a statement which is false in a material particular, shall be guilty of an offence;
   (b) that any person who discloses information in contravention of regulations under section 723C(4) shall be guilty of an offence.

(2) Regulations may provide that a person guilty of an offence under subsection (1) shall be liable—
   (a) on conviction on indictment, to imprisonment for a term not exceeding two years, or to a fine, or to both; and
   (b) on summary conviction, to imprisonment for a term not exceeding six months, or to a fine not exceeding the statutory maximum, or to both.

723F   Regulations under sections 723B to 723E

(1) In sections 723B to 723E 'regulations' means regulations made by the Secretary of State.

(2) Any power of the Secretary of State to make regulations under any of those sections shall be exercisable by statutory instrument.

(3) Regulations under sections 723B to 723E—
   (a) may make different provision for different cases;
   (b) may contain such incidental, supplemental, consequential and transitional provision, as the Secretary of State thinks fit.

(4) The provision that may be made by virtue of subsection (3)(b) includes provision repealing or modifying any enactment.

(5) No regulations shall be made under any of sections 723B to 723E unless a draft of the instrument containing them has been laid before Parliament and approved by a resolution of each House.

725   Service of documents

(1) A document may be served on a company by leaving it at, or sending it by post to, the company's registered office.

(2) Where a company registered in Scotland carries on business in England and Wales, the process of any court in England and Wales may be served on the company by leaving it at, or sending it by post to, the company's principal place of business in England and Wales, addressed to the manager or other head officer in England and Wales of the company.

(3) Where process is served on a company under subsection (2), the person issuing out the process shall send a copy of it by post to the company's registered office.

726 Costs and expenses in actions by certain limited companies

(1) Where in England and Wales a limited company is plaintiff in an action or other legal proceeding, the court having jurisdiction in the matter may, if it appears by credible testimony that there is reason to believe that the company will be unable to pay the defendant's costs if successful in his defence, require sufficient security to be given for those costs, and may stay all proceedings until the security is given.

(2) Where in Scotland a limited company is pursuer in an action or other legal proceeding, the court having jurisdiction in the matter may, if it appears by credible testimony that there is reason to believe that the company will be unable to pay the defender's expenses if successful in his defence, order the company to find caution and sist the proceedings until caution is found.

727 Power of court to grant relief in certain cases

(1) If in any proceedings for negligence, default, breach of duty or breach of trust against an officer of a company or a person employed by a company as auditor (whether he is or is not an officer of the company) it appears to the court hearing the case that that officer or person is or may be liable in respect of the negligence, default, breach of duty or breach of trust, but that he has acted honestly and reasonably, and that having regard to all the circumstances of the case (including those connected with his appointment) he ought fairly to be excused for the negligence, default, breach of duty or breach of trust, that court may relieve him, either wholly or partly, from his liability on such terms as it thinks fit.

(2) If any such officer or person as above-mentioned has reason to apprehend that any claim will or might be made against him in respect of any negligence, default, breach of duty or breach of trust, he may apply to the court for relief; and the court on the application has the same power to relieve him as under this section it would have had if it had been a court before which proceedings against that person for negligence, default, breach of duty or breach of trust had been brought.

(3) Where a case to which subsection (1) applies is being tried by a judge with a jury, the judge, after hearing the evidence, may, if he is satisfied that the defendant or defender ought in pursuance of that subsection to be relieved either in whole or in part from the liability sought to be enforced against him, withdraw the case in whole or in part from the jury and forthwith direct judgment to be entered for the defendant or defender on such terms as to costs or otherwise as the judge may think proper.

728 Enforcement of High Court orders

Orders made by the High Court under this Act may be enforced in the same manner as orders made in an action pending in that court.

729 Annual report by Secretary of State

The Secretary of State shall cause a general annual report of matters within the Companies Acts to be prepared and laid before both Houses of Parliament.

730 Punishment of offences

(1) Schedule 24 to this Act has effect with respect to the way in which offences under this Act are punishable on conviction.

(2) In relation to an offence under a provision of this Act specified in the first column of the Schedule (the general nature of the offence being described in the second column), the third column shows whether the offence is punishable on conviction on indictment, or on summary conviction, or either in the one way or the other.

(3) The fourth column of the Schedule shows, in relation to an offence, the maximum punishment by way of fine or imprisonment under this Act which may be imposed on a person convicted of the offence in the way specified in relation to it in the third column (that is to say, on indictment or summarily), a reference to a period of years or months being to a term of imprisonment of that duration.

(4) The fifth column shows (in relation to an offence for which there is an entry in that column) that a person convicted of the offence after continued contravention is liable to a daily default fine; that is to say, he is liable on a second or subsequent summary conviction of the offence to the fine specified in that column for each day on which the contravention is continued (instead of the penalty specified for the offence in the fourth column of the Schedule).

(5) For the purpose of any enactment in the Companies Acts which provides that an officer of a company or other body who is in default is liable to a fine or penalty, the expression 'officer who is in default' means any officer of the company or other body who knowingly and wilfully authorises or permits the default, refusal or contravention mentioned in the enactment.

731   Summary proceedings

(1) Summary proceedings for any offence under the Companies Acts may (without prejudice to any jurisdiction exercisable apart from this subsection) be taken against a body corporate at any place at which the body has a place of business, and against any other person at any place at which he is for the time being.

(2) Notwithstanding anything in section 127(1) of the Magistrates' Courts Act 1980, an information relating to an offence under the Companies Acts which is triable by a magistrates' court in England and Wales may be so tried if it is laid at any time within 3 years after the commission of the offence and within 12 months after the date on which evidence sufficient in the opinion of the Director of Public Prosecutions or the Secretary of State (as the case may be) to justify the proceedings comes to his knowledge.

(3) Summary proceedings in Scotland for an offence under the Companies Acts shall not be commenced after the expiration of 3 years from the commission of the offence.

Subject to this (and notwithstanding anything in section 136 of the Criminal Procedure (Scotland) Act 1995), such proceedings may (in Scotland) be commenced at any time within 12 months after the date on which evidence sufficient in the Lord Advocate's opinion to justify the proceedings came to his knowledge or, where such evidence was reported to him by the Secretary of State, within 12 months after the date on which it came to the knowledge of the latter; and subsection (3) of that section applies for the purpose of this subsection as it applies for the purpose of that section.

(4) For purposes of this section, a certificate of the Director of Public Prosecutions, the Lord Advocate or the Secretary of State (as the case may be) as to the date on which such evidence as is referred to above came to his knowledge is conclusive evidence.

732   Prosecution by public authorities

(1) In respect of an offence under any of sections 210, 324, 329, 447 to 451 and 455, proceedings shall not, in England and Wales, be instituted except by or with the consent of the appropriate authority.

(2) That authority is—
  (a) for an offence under any of sections 210, 324 and 329, the Secretary of State or the Director of Public Prosecutions,
  (b) for an offence under any of sections 447 to 451, either one of those two persons or the Industrial Assurance Commissioner, and
  (c) for an offence under section 455, the Secretary of State.

(3) Where proceedings are instituted under the Companies Acts against any person by the Director of Public Prosecutions or by or on behalf of the Secretary of State or the Lord Advocate, nothing in those acts is to be taken to require any person to disclose any information which he is entitled to refuse to disclose on grounds of legal professional privilege.

733   Offences by bodies corporate

(1) The following applies to offences under any of sections 210, 216(3), 394A(1) and 447 to 451.

(2) Where a body corporate is guilty of such an offence and it is proved that the offence occurred with the consent or connivance of, or was attributable to any neglect on the part of any director, manager, secretary or other similar officer of the body, or any person who was purporting to act in any such capacity, he as well as the body corporate is guilty of that offence and is liable to be proceeded against and punished accordingly.

(3) Where the affairs of a body corporate are managed by its members, subsection (2) above applies in relation to the acts and defaults of a member in connection with his functions of management as if he were a director of the body corporate.

(4) In this section 'director', in relation to an offence under any of sections 447 to 451, includes a shadow director.

734 Criminal proceedings against unincorporated bodies

(1) Proceedings for an offence alleged to have been committed under section 389A(3) or section 394A(1) or any of sections 447 to 451 by an unincorporated body shall be brought in the name of that body (and not in that of any of its members), and for the purposes of any such proceedings, any rules of court relating to the service of documents apply as if that body were a corporation.

(2) A fine imposed on an unincorporated body on its conviction of such an offence shall be paid out of the funds of that body.

(3) In a case in which an unincorporated body is charged in England and Wales with such an offence, section 33 of the Criminal Justice Act 1925 and Schedule 3 to the Magistrates' Courts Act 1980 (procedure on charge of an offence against a corporation) have effect in like manner as in the case of a corporation so charged.

(4) In relation to proceedings on indictment in Scotland for such an offence alleged to have been committed by an unincorporated body, section 70 of the Criminal Procedure (Scotland) Act 1995 (proceedings on indictment against bodies corporate) has effect as if that body were a body corporate.

(5) Where such an offence committed by a partnership is proved to have been committed with the consent or connivance of, or to be attributable to any neglect on the part of, a partner, he as well as the partnership is guilty of the offence and liable to be proceeded against and punished accordingly.

(6) Where such an offence committed by an unincorporated body (other than a partnership) is proved to have been committed with the consent or connivance of, or to be attributable to any neglect on the part of, any officer of the body or any member of its governing body, he as well as the body is guilty of the offence and liable to be proceeded against and punished accordingly.

PART XXVI   INTERPRETATION

735 'Company'

(1) In this Act—

    (a) 'company' means a company formed and registered under this Act, or an existing company;

    (b) 'existing company' means a company formed and registered under the former Companies Acts, but does not include a company registered under the Joint Stock Companies Acts, the Companies Act 1862 or the Companies (Consolidation) Act 1908 in what was then Ireland;

    (c) 'the former Companies Acts' means the Joint Stock Companies Acts, the Companies Act 1862, the Companies (Consolidation) Act 1908, the Companies Act 1929 and the Companies Acts 1948 to 1983.

(2) 'Public company' and 'private company' have the meanings given by section 1(3).

(3) 'The Joint Stock Companies Acts' means the Joint Stock Companies Act 1856, the Joint Stock Companies Acts 1856, 1857, the Joint Stock Banking Companies Act 1857 and the

Act to enable Joint Stock Banking Companies to be formed on the principle of limited liability, or any one or more of those Acts (as the case may require), but does not include the Joint Stock Companies Act 1844.

(4) The definitions in this section apply unless the contrary intention appears.

735A   Relationship of this Act to Insolvency Act

(1) In this Act 'the Insolvency Act' means the Insolvency Act 1986; and in the following provisions of this Act, namely, sections 375(1)(b), 425(6)(a), 460(2), 675, 676, 677, 699(1), 728 and Schedule 21, paragraph 6(1), the words 'this Act' are to be read as including Parts I to VII of that Act, sections 411, 413, 414, 416 and 417 in Part XV of that Act, and also the Company Directors Disqualification Act 1986.

(2) In sections 704(5), (7) and (8), 706(1), 707B(1), 707A(1), 708(1)(a) and (4), 709(1) and (3), 710A, 713(1), 729 and 732(3) references to the Companies Acts include Parts I to VII of the Insolvency Act, sections 411, 413, 414, 416 and 417 in Part XV of that Act, and also the Company Directors Disqualification Act 1986.

(3) Subsections (1) and (2) apply unless the contrary intention appears.

735B   Relationship of this Act to Parts IV and V of the Financial Services Act 1986

In sections 704(5), (7) and (8), 706(1), 707(1), 707A(1), 708(1)(a) and (4), 709(1) and (3), 710A and 713(1) references to the Companies Acts include Part VI of the Financial Services and Markets Act 2000.

736   'Subsidiary', 'holding company' and 'wholly-owned subsidiary'

(1) A company is a 'subsidiary' of another company, its 'holding company', if that other company—

(a) holds a majority of the voting rights in it, or

(b) is a member of it and has the right to appoint or remove a majority of its board of directors, or

(c) is a member of it and controls alone, pursuant to an agreement with other shareholders or members, a majority of the voting rights in it,

or if it is a subsidiary of a company which is itself a subsidiary of that other company.

(2) A company is a 'wholly-owned subsidiary' of another company if it has no members except that other and that other's wholly-owned subsidiaries or persons acting on behalf of that other or its wholly-owned subsidiaries.

(3) In this section 'company' includes any body corporate.

736A   Provisions supplementing s. 736

(1) The provisions of this section explain expressions used in section 736 and otherwise supplement that section.

(2) In section 736(1)(a) and (c) the references to the voting rights in a company are to the rights conferred on shareholders in respect of their shares or, in the case of a company not having a share capital, on members, to vote at general meetings of the company on all, or substantially all, matters.

(3) In section 736(1)(b) the reference to the right to appoint or remove a majority of the board of directors is to the right to appoint or remove directors holding a majority of the voting rights at meetings of the board on all, or substantially all, matters; and for the purposes of that provision—

(a) a company shall be treated as having the right to appoint to a directorship if—

(i) a person's appointment to it follows necessarily from his appointment as director of the company, or

(ii) the directorship is held by the company itself; and

(b) a right to appoint or remove which is exercisable only with the consent or concurrence of another person shall be left out of account unless no other person has a right to appoint or, as the case may be, remove in relation to that directorship.

(4) Rights which are exercisable only in certain circumstances shall be taken into account only—

  (a) when the circumstances have arisen, and for so long as they continue to obtain, or
  (b) when the circumstances are within the control of the person having the rights; and rights which are normally exercisable but are temporarily incapable of exercise shall continue to be taken into account.

(5) Rights held by a person in a fiduciary capacity shall be treated as not held by him.

(6) Rights held by a person as nominee for another shall be treated as held by the other; and rights shall be regarded as held as nominee for another if they are exercisable only on his instructions or with his consent or concurrence.

(7) Rights attached to shares held by way of security shall be treated as held by the person providing the security—

  (a) where apart from the right to exercise them for the purpose of preserving the value of the security, or of realising it, the rights are exercisable only in accordance with his instructions;
  (b) where the shares are held in connection with the granting of loans as part of normal business activities and apart from the right to exercise them for the purpose of preserving the value of the security, or of realising it, the rights are exercisable only in his interests.

(8) Rights shall be treated as held by a company if they are held by any of its subsidiaries; and nothing in subsection (6) or (7) shall be construed as requiring rights held by a company to be treated as held by any of its subsidiaries.

(9) For the purposes of subsection (7) rights shall be treated as being exercisable in accordance with the instructions or in the interests of a company if they are exercisable in accordance with the instructions of or, as the case may be, in the interests of—

  (a) any subsidiary or holding company of that company, or
  (b) any subsidiary of a holding company of that company.

(10) The voting rights in a company shall be reduced by any rights held by the company itself.

(11) References in any provision of subsections (5) to (10) to rights held by a person include rights falling to be treated as held by him by virtue of any other provision of those subsections but not rights which by virtue of any such provision are to be treated as not held by him.

(12) In this section 'company' includes any body corporate.

736B Power to amend ss. 736 and 736A

(1) The Secretary of State may by regulations amend sections 736 and 736A so as to alter the meaning of the expressions 'holding company', 'subsidiary' or 'wholly-owned subsidiary'.

(2) The regulations may make different provision for different cases or classes of case and may contain such incidental and supplementary provisions as the Secretary of State thinks fit.

(3) Regulations under this section shall be made by statutory instrument which shall be subject to annulment in pursuance of a resolution of either House of Parliament.

(4) Any amendment made by regulations under this section does not apply for the purposes of enactments outside the Companies Acts unless the regulations so provide.

(5) So much of section 23(3) of the Interpretation Act 1978 as applies section 17(2)(a) of that Act (effect of repeal and re-enactment) to deeds, instruments and documents other than enactments shall not apply in relation to any repeal and re-enactment effected by regulations made under this section.

737 'Called-up share capital'

(1) In this Act, 'called-up share capital', in relation to a company, means so much of its share capital as equals the aggregate amount of the calls made on its shares (whether or not

those calls have been paid), together with any share capital paid up without being called and any share capital to be paid on a specified future date under the articles, the terms of allotment of the relevant shares or any other arrangements for payment of those shares.

(2) 'Uncalled share capital' is to be construed accordingly.

(3) The definitions in this section apply unless the contrary intention appears.

738 'Allotment' and 'paid up'

(1) In relation to an allotment of shares in a company, the shares are to be taken for the purposes of this Act to be allotted when a person acquires the unconditional right to be included in the company's register of members in respect of those shares.

(2) For purposes of this Act, a share in a company is deemed paid up (as to its nominal value or any premium on it) in cash, or allotted for cash, if the consideration for the allotment or payment up is cash received by the company, or is a cheque received by it in good faith which the directors have no reason for suspecting will not be paid, or is a release of a liability of the company for a liquidated sum, or is an undertaking to pay cash to the company at a future date.

(3) In relation to the allotment or payment up of any shares in a company, references in this Act (except sections 89 to 94) to consideration other than cash and to the payment up of shares and premiums on shares otherwise than in cash include the payment of, or any undertaking to pay, cash to any person other than the company.

(4) For the purpose of determining whether a share is or is to be allotted for cash, or paid up in cash, 'cash' includes foreign currency.

739 'Non-cash asset'

(1) In this Act 'non-cash asset' means any property or interest in property other than cash; and for this purpose 'cash' includes foreign currency.

(2) A reference to the transfer or acquisition of a non-cash asset includes the creation or extinction of an estate or interest in, or a right over, any property and also the discharge of any person's liability, other than a liability for a liquidated sum.

740 'Body corporate' and 'corporation'

References in this Act to a body corporate or to a corporation do not include a corporation sole, but include a company incorporated elsewhere than in Great Britain.

Such references to a body corporate do not include a Scottish firm.

741 'Director' and 'shadow director'

(1) In this Act, 'director' includes any person occupying the position of director, by whatever name called.

(2) In relation to a company, 'shadow director' means a person in accordance with whose directions or instructions the directors of the company are accustomed to act.

However, a person is not deemed a shadow director by reason only that the directors act on advice given by him in a professional capacity.

(3) For the purposes of the following provisions of this Act, namely—

section 309 (directors' duty to have regard to interests of employees),

section 319 (directors' long-term contracts of employment),

sections 320 to 322 (substantial property transactions involving directors),

section 322B (contracts with sole members who are directors), and

sections 330 to 346 (general restrictions on power of companies to make loans, etc., to directors and others connected with them),

(being provisions under which shadow directors are treated as directors), a body corporate is not to be treated as a shadow director of any of its subsidiary companies by reason only that the directors of the subsidiary are accustomed to act in accordance with its directions or instructions.

742   Expressions used in connection with accounts

(1) In this Act, unless a contrary intention appears, the following expressions have the same meaning as in Part VII (accounts)—

'annual accounts',

'accounting reference date' and 'accounting reference period',

'balance sheet' and 'balance sheet date',

'current assets',

'financial year', in relation to a company,

'fixed assets',

'parent company' and 'parent undertaking',

'profit and loss account', and

'subsidiary undertaking'.

(2) References in this Act to 'realised profits' and 'realised losses', in relation to a company's accounts, shall be construed in accordance with section 262(3).

(2A) References in this Act to sending or sending out copies of any of the documents referred to in section 238(1) include sending or sending out such copies in accordance with section 238(4A) or (4B).

742A   Meaning of 'offer to the public'

(1) Any reference in Part IV (allotment of shares and debentures) or Part VII (accounts) to offering shares or debentures to the public is to be read as including a reference to offering them to any section of the public, however selected.

(2) This section does not require an offer to be treated as made to the public if it can properly be regarded, in all the circumstances—

(a) as not being calculated to result, directly or indirectly, in the shares or debentures becoming available for subscription or purchase by persons other than those receiving the offer; or

(b) as being a domestic concern of the persons receiving and making it.

(3) An offer of shares in or debentures of a private company (other than an offer to which subsection (5) applies) is to be regarded (unless the contrary is proved) as being a domestic concern of the persons making and receiving it if—

(a) it is made to—

(i) an existing member of the company making the offer,

(ii) an existing employee of that company,

(iii) the widow or widower of a person who was a member or employee of that company,

(iv) a member of the family of a person who is or was a member or employee of that company, or

(v) an existing debenture holder; or

(b) it is an offer to subscribe for shares or debentures to be held under an employee's share scheme.

(4) Subsection (5) applies to an offer—

(a) which falls within paragraph (a) or (b) of subsection (3); but

(b) which is made on terms which permit the person to whom it is made to renounce his right to the allotment of shares or issue of debentures.

(5) The offer is to be regarded (unless the contrary is proved) as being a domestic concern of the persons making and receiving it if the terms are such that the right may be renounced only in favour—

(a) of any person mentioned in subsection (3)(a); or

(b) in the case of an employee's share scheme, of a person entitled to hold shares or debentures under the scheme.

(6) For the purposes of subsection (3)(a)(iv), the members of a person's family are—

(a) the person's spouse and children (including stepchildren) and their descendants, and

(b) any trustee (acting in his capacity as such) of a trust the principal beneficiary of which is the person him or herself or of any of those relatives.

(7) Where an application has been made to the competent authority in any EEA State for the admission of any securities to official listing, then an offer of those securities for subscription or sale to a person whose ordinary business it is to buy or sell shares or debentures (whether as principal or agent) is not to be regarded as an offer to the public for the purposes of this Part.

(8) For the purposes of subsection (7)—

(a) 'competent authority' means a competent authority appointed for the purposes of the Council Directive of 28 May 2001 on the admission of securities to official stock exchange listing and on information to be published on those securities; and

(b) 'official listing' means official listing pursuant to that directive.

742B   Meaning of 'banking company'

(1) Subject to subsection (2), 'banking company' means a person who has permission under Part IV of the Financial Services and Markets Act 2000 to accept deposits.

(2) A banking company does not include—

(a) a person who is not a company, and

(b) a person who has permission to accept deposits only for the purpose of carrying on another regulated activity in accordance with that permission.

(3) This section must be read with—

(a) section 22 of the Financial Services and Markets Act 2000;

(b) any relevant order under that section; and

(c) Schedule 2 to that Act.

742C   Meaning of 'insurance company' and 'authorised insurance company'

(1) For the purposes of this Act, 'insurance company' has the meaning given in subsection (2) and 'authorised insurance company' has the meaning given in subsection (4).

(2) Subject to subsection (3), 'insurance company' means a person (whether incorporated or not)—

(a) who has permission under Part IV of the Financial Services and Markets Act 2000 to effect or carry out contracts of insurance; or

(b) who carries on insurance market activity; or

(c) who may effect or carry out contracts of insurance under which the benefits provided by that person are exclusively or primarily benefits in kind in the event of accident to or breakdown of a vehicle, and does not fall within paragraph (a).

(3) An insurance company does not include a friendly society, within the meaning of section 116 of the Friendly Societies Act 1992.

(4) An 'authorised insurance company' means a person falling within paragraph (a) of subsection (2).

(5) References in this section to contracts of insurance and the effecting or carrying out of such contracts must be read with—

(a) section 22 of the Financial Services and Markets Act 2000;

(b) any relevant order under that section; and

(c) Schedule 2 to that Act.

743   'Employees' share scheme'

For purposes of this Act, an employees' share scheme is a scheme for encouraging or facilitating the holding of shares or debentures in a company by or for the benefit of—

(a) the bona fide employees or former employees of the company, the company's subsidiary or holding company or a subsidiary of the company's holding company, or

(b) the wives, husbands, widows, widowers or children or stepchildren under the age of 18 of such employees or former employees.

744 Expressions used generally in this Act
In this Act, unless the contrary intention appears, the following definitions apply—
'agent' does not include a person's counsel acting as such;
'articles' means, in relation to a company, its articles of association, as originally framed or as altered by resolution, including (so far as applicable to the company) regulations contained in or annexed to any enactment relating to companies passed before this Act, as altered by or under any such enactment;
'authorised minimum' has the meaning given by section 118;
'bank holiday' means a holiday under the Banking and Financial Dealings Act 1971;
'books and papers' and 'books or papers' include accounts, deeds, writings and documents;
'communication' means the same as in the Electronic Communications Act 2000;
'the Companies Acts' means this Act, the insider dealing legislation and the Consequential Provisions Act;
'the Consequential Provisions Act' means the Companies Consolidation (Consequential Provisions) Act 1985;
'the court', in relation to a company, means the court having jurisdiction to wind up the company;
'debenture' includes debenture stock, bonds and any other securities of a company, whether constituting a charge on the assets of the company or not;
'document' includes summons, notice, order, and other legal process, and registers;
'EEA State' means a State which is a Contracting Party to the Agreement on the European Economic Area signed at Oporto on 2 May 1992 as adjusted by the protocol signed at Brussels on 17 March 1993;
'electronic communication' means the same as in the Electronic Communications Act 2000;
'equity share capital' means, in relation to a company, its issued share capital excluding any part of that capital which, neither as respects dividends nor as respects capital, carries any right to participate beyond a specified amount in a distribution;
'expert' has the meaning given by section 62;
'floating charge' includes a floating charge within the meaning given by section 462;
'the Gazette' means, as respects companies registered in England and Wales, the London Gazette and, as respects companies registered in Scotland, the Edinburgh Gazette;
'hire-purchase agreement' has the same meaning as in the Consumer Credit Act 1974;
'the insider dealing legislation' means Part V of the Criminal Justice Act 1993 (insider dealing);
'insurance market activity' has the meaning given in section 316(3) of the Financial Services and Markets Act 2000;
'joint stock company' has the meaning given by section 683;
'memorandum', in relation to a company, means its memorandum of association, as originally framed or as altered in pursuance of any enactment;
'number', in relation to shares, includes amount, where the context admits of the reference to shares being construed to include stock;
'officer', in relation to a body corporate, includes a director, manager or secretary;
'official seal', in relation to the registrar of companies, means a seal prepared under section 704(4) for the authentication of documents required for or in connection with the registration of companies;

'oversea company' means—

(a) a company incorporated elsewhere than in Great Britain which, after the commencement of this Act, establishes a place of business in Great Britain, and

(b) a company so incorporated which has, before that commencement, established a place of business and continues to have an established place of business in Great Britain at that commencement;

'place of business' includes a share transfer or share registration office;

'prescribed' means—

(a) as respects provisions of this Act relating to winding up, prescribed by general rules, and

(b) otherwise, prescribed by statutory instrument made by the Secretary of State; 'prospectus' means any prospectus, notice, circular, advertisement, or other invitation, offering to the public for subscription or purchase any shares in or debentures of a company;

'prospectus issued generally' means a prospectus issued to persons who are not existing members of the company or holders of its debentures;

'the registrar of companies' and 'the registrar' mean the registrar or other officer performing under this Act the duty of registration of companies in England and Wales or in Scotland, as the case may require;

'regulated activity' has the meaning given in section 22 of the Financial Services and Markets Act 2000;

'share' means share in the share capital of a company, and includes stock (except where a distinction between shares and stock is express or implied); and

'undistributable reserves' has the meaning given by section 264(3).

[*The definitions of 'authorised minimum', 'expert', 'floating charge', 'joint stock company' and 'undistributable reserves' would be repealed if the relevant provisions of sch. 24 to the Companies Act 1989 were brought into force.*

The definition of 'prospectus issued generally' was repealed by the Financial Services Act 1986, sch. 17, part I, but this repeal was brought into force only in so far as was necessary to have the effect that the definition ceased to apply to a prospectus offering for subscription, or to any form of application for, units in a body corporate which was a recognised scheme (Financial Services Act 1986 (Commencement) (No. 8) Order 1988 (SI 1988/740), art. 2 and sch.).]

744A   Index of defined expressions

The following Table shows provisions defining or otherwise explaining expressions for the purposes of this Act generally—

accounting reference date, accounting reference period	sections 224 and 742(1)
acquisition (in relation to a non-cash asset)	section 739(2)
agent	section 744
allotment (and related expressions)	section 738
annual accounts	sections 261(2), 262(1) and 742(1)
annual general meeting	section 366
annual return	section 363
articles	section 744
authorised insurance company	section 742C
authorised minimum	section 118
balance sheet and balance sheet date	sections 261(2), 262(1) and 742(1)
bank holiday	section 744
banking company	section 742B
body corporate	section 740

resolution for reducing share capital	section 135(3)
shadow director	section 741(2) and (3)
share	section 744
share premium account	section 130(1)
share warrant	section 188
special notice (in relation to a resolution)	section 379
special resolution	section 378(2)
subsidiary	section 736
subsidiary undertaking	sections 258 and 742(1)
transfer (in relation to a non-cash asset)	section 739(2)
treasury shares	*section 162A(3)*
uncalled share capital	section 737(2)
undistributable reserves	section 264(3)
unlimited company	section 1(2)
unregistered company	section 718
wholly-owned subsidiary	section 736(2)

[*The entry relating to treasury shares is in force from 1 December 2003.*]

PART XXVII   FINAL PROVISIONS

745   Northern Ireland
(1) Except where otherwise expressly provided, nothing in this Act (except provisions relating expressly to companies registered or incorporated in Northern Ireland or outside Great Britain) applies to or in relation to companies so registered or incorporated.

(2) Subject to any such provision, and to any express provision as to extent, this Act does not extend to Northern Ireland.

746   Commencement
This Act comes into force on 1 July 1985.

747   Citation
This Act may be cited as the Companies Act 1985.

SCHEDULES
Section 10
SCHEDULE 1
PARTICULARS OF DIRECTORS ETC. TO BE CONTAINED IN STATEMENT UNDER SECTION 10

Directors

1.   Subject as provided below, the statement under section 10(2) shall contain the following particulars with respect to each person named as director—
   (a) in the case of an individual, his present name, any former name, his usual residential address, his nationality, his business occupation (if any), particulars of any other directorships held by him, or which have been held by him and his date of birth;
   (b) in the case of a corporation or Scottish firm, its corporate or firm name and registered or principal office.

2.—(1) It is not necessary for the statement to contain particulars of a directorship—
   (a) which has not been held by a director at any time during the 5 years preceding the date on which the statement is delivered to the registrar,

(b) which is held by a director in a company which—
   (i) is dormant or grouped with the company delivering the statement, and
   (ii) if he also held that directorship for any period during those 5 years, was for the whole of that period either dormant or so grouped,

(c) which was held by a director for any period during those 5 years in a company which for the whole of that period was either dormant or grouped with the company delivering the statement.

(2) For these purposes, 'company' includes any body corporate incorporated in Great Britain; and—

(a) section 249AA(3) applies as regards whether and when a company is or has been 'dormant', and

(b) a company is treated as being or having been at any time grouped with another company if at that time it is or was a company of which that other is or was a wholly-owned subsidiary, or if it is or was a wholly-owned subsidiary of the other or of another company of which that other is or was a wholly-owned subsidiary.

Secretaries

3.—(1) The statement shall contain the following particulars with respect to the person named as secretary or, where there are to be joint secretaries, with respect to each person named as one of them—

(a) in the case of an individual, his present name, any former name and his usual residential address,

(b) in the case of a corporation or a Scottish firm, its corporate or firm name and registered or principal office.

(2) However, if all the partners in a firm are joint secretaries, the name and principal office of the firm may be stated instead of the particulars otherwise required by this paragraph.

Interpretation

4. In paragraphs 1(a) and 3(1)(a) above—

(a) 'name' means a person's Christian name (or other forename) and surname, except that in the case of a peer, or an individual usually known by a title, the title may be stated instead of his Christain name (or other forename) and surname or in addition to either or both of them; and

(b) the reference to a former name does not include—
   (i) in the case of a peer, or an individual normally known by a British title, the name by which he was known previous to the adoption of or succession to the title, or
   (ii) in the case of any person, a former name which was changed or disused before he attained the age of 18 years or which has been changed or disused for 20 years or more, or
   (iii) in the case of a married woman, the name by which she was known previous to the marriage.

5. Where a confidentiality order made under section 723B is in force in respect of any individual named as a director or secretary, paragraphs 1(a) and 3(1)(a) have effect as if the references to the usual residential address of the individual were references to the address for the time being notified by him under regulations made under sections 723B to 723F to any companies or oversea companies of which he is a director, secretary or permanent representative, or, if he is not such a director, secretary or permanent representative either the address specified in his application for a confidentiality order under regulations made under section

723B or the address last notified by him under regulations made under sections 723B to 723F as the case may be.

Section 56

SCHEDULE 3
MANDATORY CONTENTS OF PROSPECTUS
PART I   MATTERS TO BE STATED

The company's proprietorship, management and its capital requirement

2.   Where shares are offered to the public for subscription, the prospectus must give particulars as to—
    (a)   the minimum amount which, in the opinion of the directors, must be raised by the issue of those shares in order to provide the sums (or, if any part of them is to be defrayed in any other manner, the balance of the sums) required to be provided in respect of each of the following—
        (i)   the purchase price of any property purchased or to be purchased which is to be defrayed in whole or in part out of the proceeds of the issue,
        (ii)   any preliminary expenses payable by the company, and any commission so payable to any person in consideration of his agreeing to subscribe for, or of his procuring or agreeing to procure subscriptions for, any shares in the company,
        (iii) the repayment of any money borrowed by the company in respect of any of the foregoing matters,
        (iv) working capital, and
    (b)   the amounts to be provided in respect of the matters above mentioned otherwise than out of the proceeds of the issue and the sources out of which those amounts are to be provided.

[*The Financial Services Act 1986, sch. 17, part I, repealed the Companies Act 1985, sch. 3, except for para. 2 in so far as it is necessary for the purposes of s. 83(1)(a) (Financial Services Act 1986 (Commencement) (No. 13) Order 1995 (SI 1995/1538)).*]

Section 226

SCHEDULE 4
FORM AND CONTENT OF COMPANY ACCOUNTS
PART I   GENERAL RULES AND FORMATS
SECTION A   GENERAL RULES

1.—(1) Subject to the following provisions of this Schedule—
    (a)   every balance sheet of a company shall show the items listed in either of the balance sheet formats set out below in section B of this Part; and
    (b)   every profit and loss account of a company shall show the items listed in any one of the profit and loss account formats so set out;
in either case in the order and under the headings and sub-headings given in the format adopted.

(2) Sub-paragraph (1) above is not to be read as requiring the heading or sub-heading for any item to be distinguished by any letter or number assigned to that item in the format adopted.

2.—(1) Where in accordance with paragraph 1 a company's balance sheet or profit and loss account for any financial year has been prepared by reference to one of the formats set out in section B below, the directors of the company shall adopt the same format in preparing the accounts for subsequent financial years of the company unless in their opinion there are special reasons for a change.

(2) Particulars of any change in the format adopted in preparing a company's balance sheet or profit and loss account in accordance with paragraph 1 shall be disclosed, and the reasons for the change shall be explained, in a note to the accounts in which the new format is first adopted.

3.—(1) Any item required in accordance with paragraph 1 to be shown in a company's balance sheet or profit and loss account may be shown in greater detail than required by the format adopted.

(2) A company's balance sheet or profit and loss account may include an item representing or covering the amount of any asset or liability, income or expenditure not otherwise covered by any of the items listed in the format adopted, but the following shall not be treated as assets in any company's balance sheet—

    (a) preliminary expenses;

    (b) expenses of and commission on any issue of shares or debentures; and

    (c) costs of reserach.

(3) In preparing a company's balance sheet or profit and loss account the directors of the company shall adapt the arrangement and headings and sub-headings otherwise required by paragraph 1 in respect of items to which an Arabic number is assigned in the format adopted, in any case where the special nature of the company's business requires such adaptation.

(4) Items to which Arabic numbers are assigned in any of the formats set out in section B below may be combined in a company's accounts for any financial year if either—

    (a) their individual amounts are not material to assessing the state of affairs or profit or loss of the company for that year; or

    (b) the combination facilitates that assessment; but in a case within paragraph (b) the individual amounts of any items so combined shall be disclosed in a note to the accounts.

(5) Subject to paragraph 4(3) below, a heading or sub-heading corresponding to an item listed in the format adopted in preparing a company's balance sheet or profit and loss account shall not be included if there is no amount to be shown for that item in respect of the financial year to which the balance sheet or profit and loss account relates.

(6) Every profit and loss account of a company shall show the amounts of the company's profit or loss on ordinary activities before taxation.

(7) Every profit and loss account of a company shall show separately as additional items—

    (a) any amount set aside or proposed to be set aside to, or withdrawn or proposed to be withdrawn from, reserves;

    (b) the agreement amount of any dividends paid and proposed;

    (c) if it is not shown in the notes to the accounts, the aggregate amount of any dividends proposed.

4.—(1) In respect of every item shown in a company's balance sheet or profit and loss account the corresponding amount for the financial year immediately preceding that to which the balance sheet or profit and loss account relates shall also be shown.

(2) Where that corresponding amount is not comparable with the amount to be shown for the item in question in respect of the financial year to which the balance sheet or profit and loss account relates, the former amount shall be adjusted and particulars of the adjustment and the reasons for it shall be disclosed in a note to the accounts.

(3) Paragraph 3(5) does not apply in any case where an amount can be shown for the item in question in respect of the financial year immediately preceding that to which the balance sheet or profit and loss account relates, and that amount shall be shown under the heading or sub-heading required by paragraph 1 for the item.

5. Amounts in respect of items representing assets or income may not be set off against amounts in respect of items representing liabilities or expenditure (as the case may be), or vice versa.

SECTION B   THE REQUIRED FORMATS FOR ACCOUNTS

Preliminary

6. References in this Part of this Schedule to the items listed in any of the formats set out below are to those items read together with any of the notes following the formats which apply to any of those items, and the requirement imposed by paragraph 1 to show the items listed in any such format in the order adopted in the format is subject to any provision in those notes for alternative positions for any particular items.

7. A number in brackets following any item in any of the formats set out below is a reference to the note of that number in the notes following the formats.

8. In the notes following the formats—
 (a) the heading of each note gives the required heading or sub-heading for the item to which it applies and a reference to any letters and numbers assigned to that item in the formats set out below (taking a reference in the case of Format 2 of the balance sheet formats to the item listed under 'Assets' or under 'Liabilities' as the case may require); and
 (b) references to a numbered format are to the balance sheet format or (as the case may require) to the profit and loss account format of that number set out below.

Balance Sheet Formats

Format 1

A. Called-up share capital not paid *(1)*
B. Fixed assets I
   I   Intangible assets
       1. Development costs
       2. Concessions, patents, licences, trade marks and similar rights and assets *(2)*
       3. Goodwill *(3)*
       4. Payments on account
   II   Tangible assets
       1. Land and buildings
       2. Plant and machinery
       3. Fixtures, fittings, tools and equipment
       4. Payments on account and assets in course of construction
   III Investments
       1. Shares in group undertakings
       2. Loans to group undertakings
       3. Participating interests
       4. Loans to undertakings in which the company has a participating interest
       5. Other investments other than loans
       6. Other loans
       7. Own shares *(4)*
C. Current assets
   I   Stocks
       1. Raw materials and consumables
       2. Work in progress

    3. Finished goods and goods for resale
    4. Payments on account
  II Debtors *(5)*
    1. Trade debtors
    2. Amounts owed by group undertakings
    3. Amounts owed by undertakings in which the company has a participating interest
    4. Other debtors
    5. Called-up share capital not paid *(1)*
    6. Prepayments and accrued income *(6)*
  III Investments
    1. Shares in group undertakings
    2. Own shares *(4)*
    3. Other investments
  IV Cash at bank and in hand
D. Prepayments and accrued income *(6)*
E. Creditors: amounts falling due within one year
    1. Debenture loans *(7)*
    2. Bank loans and overdrafts
    3. Payments received on account *(8)*
    4. Trade creditors
    5. Bills of exchange payable
    6. Amounts owed to group undertakings
    7. Amounts owed to undertakings in which the company has a participating interest
    8. Other creditors including taxation and social security *(9)*
    9. Accruals and deferred income *(10)*
F. Net current assets (liabilities) *(11)*
G. Total assets less current liabilities
H. Creditors: amounts falling due after more than one year
    1. Debenture loans *(7)*
    2. Bank loans and overdrafts
    3. Payments received on account *(8)*
    4. Trade creditors
    5. Bills of exchange payable
    6. Amounts owed to group undertakings
    7. Amounts owed to undertakings in which the company has a participating interest
    8. Other creditors including taxation and social security *(9)*
    9. Accruals and deferred income *(10)*
I. Provisions for liabilities and charges
    1. Pensions and similar obligations
    2. Taxation, including deferred taxation
    3. Other provisions
J. Accruals and deferred income *(10)*
K. Capital and reserves I
  I Called-up share capital *(12)*
  II Share premium account
  III Revaluation reserve
  IV Other reserves
    1. Capital redemption reserve
    2. Reserve for own shares

      3.   Reserves provided for by the articles of association
      4.   Other reserves
  V   Profit and loss account

Balance Sheet Formats

Format 2

ASSETS

  A. Called-up share capital not paid *(1)*
  B. Fixed assets I
     I   Intangible assets
       1. Development costs
       2. Concessions, patents, licences, trade marks and similar rights and assets *(2)*
       3. Goodwill *(3)*
       4. Payments on account
     II Tangible assets
       1. Land and buildings
       2. Plant and machinery
       3. Fixtures, fittings, tools and equipment
       4. Payments on account and assets in course of construction
     III Investments
       1. Shares in group undertakings
       2. Loans to group undertakings
       3. Participating interests
       4. Loans to undertakings in which the company has a participating interest
       5. Other investments other than loans
       6. Other loans
       7. Own shares *(4)*
  C. Current assets
     I   Stocks
       1. Raw materials and consumables
       2. Work in progress
       3. Finished goods and goods for resale
       4. Payments on account
     II Debtors *(5)*
       1. Trade debtors
       2. Amounts owed by group undertakings
       3. Amounts owed by undertakings in which the company has a participating interest
       4. Other debtors
       5. Called-up share capital not paid *(1)*
       6. Prepayments and accrued income *(6)*
     III Investments
       1. Shares in group undertakings
       2. Own shares *(4)*
       3. Other investments
     IV Cash at bank and in hand
  D. Prepayments and accrued income *(6)*

LIABILITIES

    A. Capital and reserves
        I   Called-up share capital *(12)*
        II   Share premium account
        III Revaluation reserve
        IV Other reserves
            1.   Capital redemption reserve
            2.   Reserve for own shares
            3.   Reserves provided for by the articles of association
            4.   Other reserves
        V   Profit and loss account
    B. Provisions for liabilities and charges
            1.   Pensions and similar obligations
            2.   Taxation including deferred taxation
            3.   Other provisions
    C. Creditors *(13)*
            1.   Debenture loans *(7)*
            2.   Bank loans and overdrafts
            3.   Payments received on account *(8)*
            4.   Trade creditors
            5.   Bills of exchange payable
            6.   Amounts owed to group undertakings
            7.   Amounts owed to undertakings in which the company has a participating interest
            8.   Other creditors including taxation and social security *(9)*
            9.   Accruals and deferred income *(10)*
    D. Accruals and deferred income *(10)*

Notes on the balance sheet formats

(1) Called-up share capital not paid
(Formats 1 and 2, items A and C.II.5.)
This item may be shown in either of the two positions given in Formats 1 and 2.
(2) Concessions, patents, licences, trade marks and similar rights and assets
(Formats 1 and 2, item B.I.2.)
Amounts in respect of assets shall only be included in a company's balance sheet under this item if either—
    (a) the assets were acquired for valuable consideration and are not required to be shown under goodwill; or
    (b) the assets in question were created by the company itself.
(3) Goodwill
(Formats 1 and 2, item B.I.3.)
Amounts representing goodwill shall only be included to the extent that the goodwill was acquired for valuable consideration.
(4) Own shares
(Formats 1 and 2, items B.III.7 and C.III.2.)
The nominal value of the shares held shall be shown separately.
(5) Debtors
(Formats 1 and 2, items C.II.1 to 6.)
The amount falling due after more than one year shall be shown separately for each item included under debtors.

(6) Prepayments and accrued income
(Formats 1 and 2, items C.II.6 and D.)
This item may be shown in either of the two positions given in Formats 1 and 2.

(7) Debenture loans
(Format 1, items E.1 and H.1 and Format 2, item C.1.)
The amount of any convertible loans shall be shown separately.

(8) Payments received on account
(Format 1, items E.3 and H.3 and Format 2, item C.3.)
Payments received on account of orders shall be shown for each of these items in so far as they are not shown as deductions from stocks.

(9) Other creditors including taxation and social security
(Format 1, items E. 8 and H. 8 and Format 2, item C.8.)
The amount for creditors in respect of taxation and social security shall be shown separately from the amount for other creditors.

(10) Accruals and deferred income
(Format 1, items E.9, H.9 and J and Format 2, items C.9 and D.)
The two positions given for this item in Format 1 at E.9 and H.9 are an alternative to the position at J, but if the item is not shown in a position corresponding to that at J it may be shown in either or both of the other two positions (as the case may require).

The two positions given for this item in Format 2 are alternatives.

(11) Net current assets (liabilities)
(Format 1, item F.)
In determining the amount to be shown for this item any amounts shown under 'prepayments and accrued income' shall be taken into account wherever shown.

(12) Called-up share capital
(Format 1, item K.I and Format 2, item A.I.)
The amount of allotted share capital and the amount of called-up share capital which has been paid up shall be shown separately.

(13) Creditors
(Format 2, items C.1 to 9.)
Amounts falling due within one year and after one year shall be shown separately for each of these items and for the aggregate of all these items.

Profit and loss account formats

Format 1
(see note *(17)* below)
1. Turnover
2. Cost of sales *(14)*
3. Gross profit or loss
4. Distribution costs *(14)*
5. Administrative expenses *(14)*
6. Other operating income
7. Income from shares in group undertakings
8. Income from participating interests
9. Income from other fixed asset investments *(15)*
10. Other interest receivable and similar income *(15)*
11. Amounts written off investments
12. Interest payable and similar charges *(16)*
13. Tax on profit or loss on ordinary activities
14. Profit or loss on ordinary activities after taxation
15. Extraordinary income

16. Extraordinary charges
17. Extraordinary profit or loss
18. Tax on extraordinary profit or loss
19. Other taxes not shown under the above items
20. Profit or loss for the financial year

Profit and loss account formats

Format 2
1. Turnover
2. Change in stocks of finished goods and in work in progress
3. Own work capitalised
4. Other operating income
5. (a) Raw materials and consumables
   (b) Other external charges
6. Staff costs:
   (a) wages and salaries
   (b) social security costs
   (c) other pension costs
7. (a) Depreciation and other amounts written off tangible and intangible fixed assets
   (b) Exceptional amounts written off current assets
8. Other operating charges
9. Income from shares in group undertakings
10. Income from participating interests
11. Income from other fixed asset investments *(15)*
12. Other interest receivable and similar income *(15)*
13. Amounts written off investments
14. Interest payable and similar charges *(16)*
15. Tax on profit or loss on ordinary activities
16. Profit or loss on ordinary activities after taxation
17. Extraordinary income
18. Extraordinary charges
19. Extraordinary profit or loss
20. Tax on extraordinary profit or loss
21. Other taxes not shown under the above items
22. Profit or loss for the financial year

Profit and loss account formats

Format 3
(see note *(17)* below)
A. Charges
1. Cost of sales *(14)*
2. Distribution costs *(14)*
3. Administrative expenses *(14)*
4. Amounts written off investments
5. Interest payable and similar charges *(16)*
6. Tax on profit or loss on ordinary activities
7. Profit or loss on ordinary activities after taxation
8. Extraordinary charges

        9. Tax on extraordinary profit or loss
     10. Other taxes not shown under the above items
     11. Profit or loss for the financial year
  B. Income
      1. Turnover
      2. Other operating income
      3. Income from shares in group undertakings
      4. Income from participating interests
      5. Income from other fixed asset investments *(15)*
      6. Other interest receivable and similar income *(15)*
      7. Profit or loss on ordinary activities after taxation
      8. Extraordinary income
      9. Profit or loss for the financial year

Profit and loss account formats

Format 4
  A. Charges
      1. Reduction in stocks of finished goods and in work in progress
      2. (a)Raw materials and consumables
         (b) Other external charges
      3. Staff costs:
         (a) wages and salaries
         (b) social security costs
         (c) other pension costs
      4. (a) Depreciation and other amounts written off tangible and intangible fixed assets
         (b) Exceptional amounts written off current assets
      5. Other operating charges
      6. Amounts written off investments
      7. Interest payable and similar charges *(16)*
      8. Tax on profit or loss on ordinary activities
      9. Profit or loss on ordinary activities after taxation
     10. Extraordinary income
     11. Tax on extraordinary profit or loss
     12. Other taxes not shown under the above items
     13. Profit or loss for the financial year
  B. Income
      1. Turnover
      2. Increase in stocks of finished goods and in work in progress
      3. Own work capitalised
      4. Other operating income
      5. Income from shares in group undertakings
      6. Income from participating interests
      7. Income from other fixed asset investments *(15)*
      8. Other interest receivable and similar income *(15)*
      9. Profit or loss on ordinary activities after taxation
     10. Extraordinary income
     11. Profit or loss for the financial year

Notes on the profit and loss account formats

(14) Cost of sales: distribution costs: administrative expenses
(Format 1, items 2, 4 and 5 and Format 3, items A.1, 2 and 3.)
These items shall be stated after taking into account any necessary provisions for depreciation or diminution in value of assets.

(15) Income from other fixed asset investments: other interest receivable and similar income
(Format 1, items 9 and 10: Format 2, items 11 and 12: Format 3, items B.5 and 6: Format 4, items B.7 and 8.)
Income and interest derived from group undertakings shall be shown separately from income and interest derived from other sources.

(16) Interest payable and similar charges
(Format 1, item 12: Format 2, item 14: Format 3, item A.5: Format 4, item A.7.)
The amount payable to group undertakings shall be shown separately.

(17) Formats 1 and 3
The amount of any provisions for depreciation and diminution in value of tangible and intangible fixed assets falling to be shown under items 7(a) and A.4(a) respectively in Formats 2 and 4 shall be disclosed in a note to the accounts in any case where the profit and loss account is prepared by reference to Format 1 or Format 3.

PART II   ACCOUNTING PRINCIPLES AND RULES

SECTION A   ACCOUNTING PRINCIPLES

Preliminary
9. Subject to paragraph 15 below, the amounts to be included in respect of all items shown in a company's accounts shall be determined in accordance with the principles set out in paragraphs 10 to 14.

Accounting principles
10. The company shall be presumed to be carrying on business as a going concern.
11. Accounting policies shall be applied consistently within the same accounts and from one financial year to the next.
12. The amount of any item shall be determined on a prudent basis, and in particular—
  (a) only profits realised at the balance sheet date shall be included in the profit and loss account; and
  (b) all liabilities and losses which have arisen or are likely to arise in respect of the financial year to which the accounts relate or a previous financial year shall be taken into account, including those which only become apparent between the balance sheet date and the date on which it is signed on behalf of the board of directors in pursuance of section 223 of this Act.
13. All income and charges relating to the financial year to which the accounts relate shall be taken into account, without regard to the date of receipt or payment.
14. In determining the aggregate amount of any item the amount of each individual asset or liability that falls to be taken into account shall be determined separately.

Departure from the accounting principles
15. If it appears to the directors of a company that there are special reasons for departing from any of the principles stated above in preparing the company's accounts in respect of any financial year they may do so, but particulars of the departure, the reasons for it and its effect shall be given in a note to the accounts.

SECTION B   HISTORICAL COST ACCOUNTING RULES

Preliminary

16. Subject to section C of this Part of this Schedule, the amounts to be included in respect of all items shown in a company's accounts shall be determined in accordance with the rules set out in paragraphs 17 to 28.

Fixed assets

General rules

17. Subject to any provision for depreciation or diminution in value made in accordance with paragraph 18 or 19 the amount to be included in respect of any fixed asset shall be its purchase price or production cost.

18. In the case of any fixed asset which has a limited useful economic life, the amount of—

(a) its purchase price or production cost; or

(b) where it is estimated that any such asset will have a residual value at the end of the period of its useful economic life, its purchase price or production cost less that estimated residual value;

shall be reduced by provisions for depreciation calculated to write off that amount systematically over the period of the asset's useful economic life.

19.—(1) Where a fixed asset investment of a description falling to be included under item B.III of either of the balance sheet formats set out in part I of this Schedule has diminished in value provisions for diminution in value may be made in respect of it and the amount to be included in respect of it may be reduced accordingly; and any such provisions which are not shown in the profit and loss account shall be disclosed (either separately or in aggregate) in a note to the accounts.

(2) Provisions for diminution in value shall be made in respect of any fixed asset which has diminished in value if the reduction in its value is expected to be permanent (whether its useful economic life is limited or not), and the amount to be included in respect of it shall be reduced accordingly; and any such provisions which are not shown in the profit and loss account shall be disclosed (either separately or in aggregate) in a note to the accounts.

(3) Where the reasons for which any provision was made in accordance with sub-paragraph (1) or (2) have ceased to apply to any extent, that provision shall be written back to the extent that it is no longer necessary; and any amounts written back in accordance with this sub-paragraph which are not shown in the profit and loss account shall be disclosed (either separately or in aggregate) in a note to the accounts.

Rules for determining particular fixed asset items

20.—(1) Notwithstanding that an item in respect of 'development costs' is included under 'fixed assets' in the balance sheet formats set out in Part I of this Schedule, an amount may only be included in a company's balance sheet in respect of development costs in special circumstances.

(2) If any amount is included in a company's balance sheet in respect of development costs the following information shall be given in a note to the accounts—

(a) the period over which the amount of those costs originally capitalised is being or is to be written off; and

(b) the reasons for capitalising the development costs in question.

21.—(1) The application of paragraphs 17 to 19 in relation to goodwill (in any case where goodwill is treated as an asset) is subject to the following provisions of this paragraph.

(2) Subject to sub-paragraph (3) below, the amount of the consideration for any goodwill acquired by a company shall be reduced by provisions for depreciation calculated to write off that amount systematically over a period chosen by the directors of the company.

(3) The period chosen shall not exceed the useful economic life of the goodwill in question.

(4) In any case where any goodwill acquired by a company is shown or included as an asset in the company's balance sheet the period chosen for writing off the consideration for that goodwill and the reasons for choosing that period shall be disclosed in a note to the accounts.

Current assets

22.   Subject to paragraph 23, the amount to be included in respect of any current asset shall be its purchase price or production cost.

23.—(1) If the net realisable value of any current asset is lower than its purchase price or production cost the amount to be included in respect of that asset shall be the net realisable value.

(2) Where the reasons for which any provision for diminution in value was made in accordance with sub-paragraph (1) have ceased to apply to any extent, that provision shall be written back to the extent that it is no longer necessary.

Miscellaneous and supplementary provisions

Excess of money owed over value received as an asset item

24.—(1) Where the amount repayable on any debt owed by a company is greater than the value of the consideration received in the transaction giving rise to the debt, the amount of the difference may be treated as an asset.

(2) Where any such amount is so treated—
   (a) it shall be written off by reasonable amounts each year and must be completely written off before repayment of the debt; and
   (b) if the current amount is not shown as a separate item in the company's balance sheet it must be disclosed in a note to the accounts.

Assets included at a fixed amount

25.—(1) Subject to the following sub-paragraph, assets which fall to be included—
   (a) amongst the fixed assets of a company under the item 'tangible assets'; or
   (b) amongst the current assets of a company under the item 'raw materials and consumables';
may be included at a fixed quantity and value.

(2) Sub-paragraph (1) applies to assets of a kind which are constantly being replaced, where—
   (a) their overall value is not material to assessing the company's state of affairs; and
   (b) their quantity, value and composition are not subject to material variation.

Determination of purchase price or production cost

26.—(1) The purchase price of an asset shall be determined by adding to the actual price paid any expenses incidental to its acquisition.

(2) The production cost of an asset shall be determined by adding to the purchase price of the raw materials and consumables used the amount of the costs incurred by the company which are directly attributable to the production of that asset.

(3) In addition, there may be included in the production cost of an asset—
   (a) a reasonable proportion of the costs incurred by the company which are only indirectly attributable to the production of that asset, but only to the extent that they relate to the period of production; and
   (b) interest on capital borrowed to finance the production of that asset to the extent that it accrues in respect of the period of production;
provided, however, in a case within paragraph (b) above, that the inclusion of the interest in

determining the cost of that asset and the amount of the interest so included is disclosed in a note to the accounts.

(4) In the case of current assets distribution costs may not be included in production costs.

27.—(1) Subject to the qualification mentioned below, the purchase price or production cost of—

(a) any assets which fall to be included under any item shown in a company's balance sheet under the general item 'stocks'; and

(b) any assets which are fungible assets (including investments);

may be determined by the application of any of the methods mentioned in subparagraph (2) below in relation to any such assets of the same class.

The method chosen must be one which appears to the directors to be appropriate in the circumstances of the company.

(2) Those methods are—

(a) the method known as 'first in, first out' (FIFO);

(b) the method known as 'last in, first out' (LIFO);

(c) a weighted average price; and

(d) any other method similar to any of the methods mentioned above.

(3) Where in the case of any company—

(a) the purchase price or production cost of assets falling to be included under any item shown in the company's balance sheet has been determined by the application of any method permitted by this paragraph; and

(b) the amount shown in respect of that item differs materially from the relevant alternative amount given below in this paragraph;

the amount of that difference shall be disclosed in a note to the accounts.

(4) Subject to sub-paragraph (5) below, for the purposes of sub-paragraph (3)(b) above, the relevant alternative amount, in relation to any item shown in a company's balance sheet, is the amount which would have been shown in respect of that item if assets of any class included under that item at an amount determined by any method permitted by this paragraph had instead been included at their replacement cost as at the balance sheet date.

(5) The relevant alternative amount may be determined by reference to the most recent actual purchase price or production cost before the balance sheet date of assets of any class included under the item in question instead of by reference to their replacement cost as at that date, but only if the former appears to the directors of the company to constitute the more appropriate standard of comparison in the case of assets of that class.

(6) For the purposes of this paragraph, assets of any description shall be regarded as fungible if assets of that description are substantially indistinguishable one from another.

Substitution of original stated amount where price or cost unknown

28.   Where there is no record of the purchase price or production cost of any asset of a company or of any price, expenses or costs relevant for determining its purchase price or production cost in accordance with paragraph 26, or any such record cannot be obtained without unreasonable expense or delay, its purchase price or production cost shall be taken for the purposes of paragraphs 17 to 23 to be the value ascribed to it in the earliest available record of its value made on or after its acquisition or production by the company.

SECTION C   ALTERNATIVE ACCOUNTING RULES

Preliminary

29.—(1) The rules set out in section B are referred to below in this Schedule as the historical cost accounting rules.

(2) Those rules, with the omission of paragraphs 16, 21 and 25 to 28, are referred to below in this Part of this Schedule as the depreciation rules; and references below in this Schedule to

the historical cost accounting rules do not include the depreciation rules as they apply by virtue of paragraph 32.

30.   Subject to paragraphs 32 to 34, the amounts to be included in respect of assets of any description mentioned in paragraph 31 may be determined on any basis so mentioned.

Alternative accounting rules

31.—(1) Intangible fixed assets, other than goodwill, may be included at their current cost.

(2) Tangible fixed assets may be included at a market value determined as at the date of their last valuation or at their current cost.

(3) Investments of any description falling to be included under item B.III of either of the balance sheet formats set out in Part I of this Schedule may be included either—

(a) at a market value determined as at the date of their last valuation; or

(b) at a value determined on any basis which appears to the directors to be appropriate in the circumstances of the company;

but in the latter case particulars of the method of valuation adopted and of the reasons for adopting it shall be disclosed in a note to the accounts.

(4) Investments of any description falling to be included under item C.III of either of the balance sheet formats set out in Part I of this Schedule may be included at their current cost.

(5) Stocks may be included at their current cost.

Application of the depreciation rules

32.—(1) Where the value of any asset of a company is determined on any basis mentioned in paragraph 31, that value shall be, or (as the case may require) be the starting point for determining, the amount to be included in respect of that asset in the company's accounts, instead of its purchase price or production cost or any value previously so determined for that asset; and the depreciation rules shall apply accordingly in relation to any such asset with the substitution for any reference to its purchase price or production cost of a reference to the value most recently determined for that asset on any basis mentioned in paragraph 31.

(2) The amount of any provision for depreciation required in the case of any fixed asset by paragraph 18 or 19 as it applies by virtue of sub-paragraph (1) is referred to below in this paragraph as the adjusted amount, and the amount of any provision which would be required by that paragraph in the case of that asset according to the historical cost accounting rules is referred to as the historical cost amount.

(3) Where sub-paragraph (1) applies in the case of any fixed asset the amount of any provision for depreciation in respect of that asset—

(a) included in any item shown in the profit and loss account in respect of amounts written off assets of the description in question; or

(b) taken into account in stating any item so shown which is required by note *(14)* of the notes on the profit and loss account formats set out in Part I of this Schedule to be stated after taking into account any necessary provisions for depreciation or diminution in value of assets included under it;

may be the historical cost amount instead of the adjusted amount, provided that the amount of any difference between the two is shown separately in the profit and loss account or in a note to the accounts.

Additional information to be provided in case of departure from historical cost accounting rules

33.—(1) This paragraph applies where the amounts to be included in respect of assets covered by any items shown in a company's accounts have been determined on any basis mentioned in paragraph 31.

(2) The items affected and the basis of valuation adopted in determining the amounts of the assets in question in the case of each such item shall be disclosed in a note to the accounts.

(3) In the case of each balance sheet item affected (except stocks) either—
- (a) the comparable amounts determined according to the historical cost accounting rules; or
- (b) the differences between those amounts and the corresponding amounts actually shown in the balance sheet in respect of that item;

shall be shown separately in the balance sheet or in a note to the accounts.

(4) In sub-paragraph (3) above, references in relation to any item to the comparable amounts determined as there mentioned are references to—
- (a) the aggregate amount which would be required to be shown in respect of that item if the amounts to be included in respect of all the assets covered by that item were determined according to the historical cost accounting rules; and
- (b) the aggregate amount of the cumulative provisions for depreciation or diminution in value which would be permitted or required in determining those amounts according to those rules.

Revaluation reserve

34.—(1) With respect to any determination of the value of an asset of a company on any basis mentioned in paragraph 31, the amount of any profit or loss arising from that determination (after allowing, where appropriate, for any provisions for depreciation or diminution in value made otherwise than by reference to the value so determined and any adjustments of any such provisions made in the light of that determination) shall be credited or (as the case may be) debited to a separate reserve ('the revaluation reserve').

(2) The amount of the revaluation reserve shall be shown in the company's balance sheet under a separate sub-heading in the position given for the item 'revaluation reserve' in Format 1 or 2 of the balance sheet formats set out in Part I of this Schedule, but need not be shown under that name.

(3) An amount may be transferred—
- (a) from the revaluation reserve—
  - (i) to the profit and loss account, if the amount was previously charged to that account or represents realised profit, or
  - (ii) on capitalisation,
- (b) to or from the revaluation reserve in respect of the taxation relating to any profit or loss credited or debited to the reserve;

and the revaluation reserve shall be reduced to the extent that the amounts transferred to it are no longer necessary for the purposes of the valuation method used.

(3A) In sub-paragraph (3)(a)(ii) 'capitalisation', in relation to an amount standing to the credit of the revaluation reserve, means applying it in wholly or partly paying up unissued shares in the company to be allotted to members of the company as fully or partly paid shares.

(3B) The revaluation reserve shall not be reduced except as mentioned in this paragraph.

(4) The treatment for taxation purposes of amounts credited or debited to the revaluation reserve shall be disclosed in a note to the accounts.

PART VII   INTERPRETATION OF SCHEDULE

76. The following paragraphs apply for the purposes of this Schedule and its interpretation.

Historical cost accounting rules

82. References to the historical cost accounting rules shall be read in accordance with paragraph 29.

Leases

83.—(1) 'Long lease' means a lease in the case of which the portion of the term for which it was granted remaining unexpired at the end of the financial year is not less than 50 years.

(2) 'Short lease' means a lease which is not a long lease.

(3) 'Lease' includes an agreement for a lease.

Listed investments

84.—(1) 'Listed investment' means an investment as respects which there has been granted a listing on—

(a) a recognised investment exchange other than an overseas investment exchange; or

(b) a stock exchange of repute outside Great Britain.

(2) 'Recognised investment exchange' and 'overseas investment exchange' have the meaning given in Part XVIII of the Financial Services and Markets Act 2000.

Loans

85.   A loan is treated as falling due for repayment, and an instalment of a loan is treated as falling due for payment, on the earliest date on which the lender could require repayment or (as the case may be) payment, if he exercised all options and rights available to him.

Materiality

86.   Amounts which in the particular context of any provision of this Schedule are not material may be disregarded for the purposes of that provision.

Provisions

88.—(1) References to provisions for depreciation or diminution in value of assets are to any amount written off by way of providing for depreciation or diminution in value of assets.

(2) Any reference in the profit and loss account formats set out in Part I of this Schedule to the depreciation of, or amounts written off, assets of any description is to any provision for depreciation or diminution in value of assets of that description.

89.   References to provisions for liabilities or charges are to any amount retained as reasonably necessary for the purpose of providing for any liability or loss which is either likely to be incurred, or certain to be incurred but uncertain as to amount or as to the date on which it will arise.

Scots land tenure

93.   In the application of this Schedule to Scotland, 'land of freehold tenure' means land in respect of which the company *is the proprietor of the dominium utile or, in the case of land not held on feudal tenure,* is the owner; 'land of leasehold tenure' means land of which the company is the tenant under a lease; *and the reference to ground-rents, rates and other outgoings includes feu-duty and ground annual.*

[*In Scotland, the words in italics will be repealed when the Abolition of Feudal Tenure etc. (Scotland) Act 2000 (asp 5), sch. 12, para. 46, is brought into force.*]

Staff costs

94.—(1) 'Social security costs' means any contributions by the company to any state social security or pension scheme, fund or arrangement.

(2) 'Pension costs' includes any costs incurred by the company in respect of any pension scheme established for the purpose of providing pensions for persons currently or formerly employed by the company, any sums set aside for the future payment of pensions directly by the company to current or former employees and any pensions paid directly to such persons without having first been set aside.

(3) Any amount stated in respect of the item 'social security costs' or in respect of the item 'wages and salaries' in the company's profit and loss account shall be determined by reference to payments made or costs incurred in respect of all persons employed by the company during the financial year who are taken into account in determining the relevant annual number for the purposes of paragraph 56(1)(a).

Section 232

SCHEDULE 6
DISCLOSURE OF INFORMATION: EMOLUMENTS AND OTHER BENEFITS OF DIRECTORS AND OTHERS

PART I   CHAIRMAN'S AND DIRECTORS' EMOLUMENTS, PENSIONS AND COMPENSATION FOR LOSS OF OFFICE

CHAPTER 1   PROVISIONS APPLYING TO QUOTED AND UNQUOTED COMPANIES

Aggregate amount of directors' emoluments etc.

1.—(1) Subject to sub-paragraph (2), the following shall be shown, namely—
- (a) the aggregate amount of emoluments paid to or receivable by directors in respect of qualifying services;
- (b) the aggregate of the amount of gains made by directors on the exercise of share options;
- (c) the aggregate of the following, namely—
  - (i) the amount of money paid to or receivable by directors under long term incentive schemes in respect of qualifying services; and
  - (ii) the net value of assets (other than money and share options) received or receivable by directors under such schemes in respect of such services;
- (d) the aggregate value of any company contributions paid, or treated as paid, to a pension scheme in respect of directors' qualifying services, being contributions by reference to which the rate or amount of any money purchase benefits that may become payable will be calculated; and
- (e) in the case of each of the following, namely—
  - (i) money purchase schemes; and
  - (ii) defined benefit schemes, the number of directors (if any) to whom retirement benefits are accruing under such schemes in respect of qualifying services.

(2) In the case of a company which is not a quoted company and whose equity share capital is not listed on the market known as AIM—
- (a) sub-paragraph (1) shall have effect as if paragraph (b) were omitted and, in paragraph (c)(ii), 'assets' did not include shares; and
- (b) the number of each of the following (if any) shall be shown, namely—
  - (i) the directors who exercised share options; and
  - (ii) the directors in respect of whose qualifying services shares were received or receivable under long term incentive schemes.

(3) In this paragraph 'emoluments' of a director—
- (a) includes salary, fees and bonuses, sums paid by way of expenses allowance (so far as they are chargeable to United Kingdom income tax) and, subject to paragraph (b), the estimated money value of any other benefits received by him otherwise than in cash; but

 (b) does not include any of the following, namely—
  (i) the value of any share options granted to him or the amount of any gains made on the exercise of any such options;
  (ii) any company contributions paid, or treated as paid, in respect of him under any pension scheme or any benefits to which he is entitled under any such scheme; or
  (iii) any money or other assets paid to or received or receivable by him under any long term incentive scheme.

(4) In this paragraph 'long term incentive scheme' means any agreement or arrangement under which money or other assets may become receivable by a director and which includes one or more qualifying conditions with respect to service or performance which cannot be fulfilled within a single financial year; and for this purpose the following shall be disregarded, namely—

 (a) bonuses the amount of which falls to be determined by reference to service or performance within a single financial year;
 (b) compensation for loss of office, payments for breach of contract and other termination payments; and
 (c) retirement benefits.

(5) In this paragraph—'amount', in relation to a gain made on the exercise of a share option, means the difference between—

 (a) the market price of the shares on the day on which the option was exercised; and
 (b) the price actually paid for the shares;

'company contributions', in relation to a pension scheme and a director, means any payments (including insurance premiums) made, or treated as made, to the scheme in respect of the director by a person other than the director;

'defined benefits' means retirement benefits payable under a pension scheme which are not money purchase benefits;

'defined benefit scheme', in relation to a director, means a pension scheme which is not a money purchase scheme;

'money purchase benefits', in relation to a director, means retirement benefits payable under a pension scheme the rate or amount of which is calculated by reference to payments made, or treated as made, by the director or by any other person in respect of the director and which are not average salary benefits;

'money purchase scheme', in relation to a director, means a pension scheme under which all of the benefits that may become payable to or in respect of the director are money purchase benefits;

'net value', in relation to any assets received or receivable by a director, means value after deducting any money paid or other value given by the director in respect of those assets;

'the official list' has the meaning given in section 103(1) of the Financial Services and Markets Act 2000;

'qualifying services', in relation to any person, means his services as a director of the company, and his services while director of the company—

 (a) as director of any of its subsidiary undertakings; or
 (b) otherwise in connection with the management of the affairs of the company or any of its subsidiary undertakings;

'recognised investment exchange' has the same meaning as in the Financial Services and Markets Act 2000;

'shares' means shares (whether allotted or not) in the company, or any undertaking which is a group undertaking in relation to the company, and includes a share warrant as defined by section 188(1);

'share option' means a right to acquire shares;

'value', in relation to shares received or receivable by a director on any day, means the market price of the shares on that day.

(6) For the purposes of this paragraph—

(a) any information, other than the aggregate amount of gains made by directors on the exercise of share options, shall be treated as shown if it is capable of being readily ascertained from other information which is shown; and

(b) emoluments paid or receivable or share options granted in respect of a person's accepting office as a director shall be treated as emoluments paid or receivable or share options granted in respect of his services as a director.

(7) Where a pension scheme provides for any benefits that may become payable to or in respect of any director to be whichever are the greater of—

(a) money purchase benefits as determined by or under the scheme; and

(b) defined benefits as so determined, the company may assume for the purposes of this paragraph that those benefits will be money purchase benefits, or defined benefits, according to whichever appears more likely at the end of the financial year.

(8) For the purpose of determining whether a pension scheme is a money purchase or defined benefit scheme, any death in service benefits provided for by the scheme shall be disregarded.

CHAPTER 2   PROVISIONS APPLYING ONLY TO UNQUOTED COMPANIES

Details of highest paid director's emoluments etc.

2.—(1) Where the aggregates shown under paragraph 1(1)(a), (b) and (c) total £200,000 or more, the following shall be shown, namely—

(a) so much of the total of those aggregates as is attributable to the highest paid director; and

(b) so much of the aggregate mentioned in paragraph 1(1)(d) as is so attributable.

(2) Where sub-paragraph (1) applies and the highest paid director has performed qualifying services during the financial year by reference to which the rate or amount of any defined benefits that may become payable will be calculated, there shall also be shown—

(a) the amount at the end of the year of his accrued pension; and

(b) where applicable, the amount at the end of the year of his accrued lump sum.

(3) Subject to sub-paragraph (4), where sub-paragraph (1) applies in the case of a company which is not a listed company, there shall also be shown—

(a) whether the highest paid director exercised any share options; and

(b) whether any shares were received or receivable by that director in respect of qualifying services under a long term incentive scheme.

(4) Where the highest paid director has not been involved in any of the transactions specified in sub-paragraph (3), that fact need not be stated.

(5) In this paragraph—

'accrued pension' and 'accrued lump sum', in relation to any pension scheme and any director, mean respectively the amount of the annual pension, and the amount of the lump sum, which would be payable under the scheme on his attaining normal pension age if—

(a) he had left the company's service at the end of the financial year;

(b) there were no increase in the general level of prices in Great Britain during the period beginning with the end of that year and ending with his attaining that age;

(c) no question arose of any commutation of the pension or inverse commutation of the lump sum; and

(d) any amounts attributable to voluntary contributions paid by the director to the scheme, and any money purchase benefits which would be payable under the scheme, were disregarded;

'the highest paid director' means the director to whom is attributable the greatest part of the total of the aggregates shown under paragraph 1(1)(a), (b) and (c);

'normal pension age', in relation to any pension scheme and any director, means the age at which the director will first become entitled to receive a full pension on retirement of an amount determined without reduction to take account of its payment before a later age (but disregarding any entitlement to pension upon retirement in the event of illness, incapacity or redundancy).

(6) Sub-paragraphs (4) to (8) of paragraph 1 apply for the purposes of this paragraph as they apply for the purposes of that paragraph.

Excess retirement benefits of directors and past directors

7.—(1) Subject to sub-paragraph (2), there shall be shown the aggregate amount of—
- (a) so much of retirement benefits paid to or receivable by directors under pension schemes; and
- (b) so much of retirement benefits paid to or receivable by past directors under such schemes,

as (in each case) is in excess of the retirement benefits to which they were respectively entitled on the date on which the benefits first became payable or 31 March 1997, whichever is the later.

(2) Amounts paid or receivable under a pension scheme need not be included in the aggregate amount if—
- (a) the funding of the scheme was such that the amounts were or, as the case may be, could have been paid without recourse to additional contributions; and
- (b) amounts were paid to or receivable by all pensioner members of the scheme on the same basis;

and in this sub-paragraph 'pensioner member', in relation to a pension scheme, means any person who is entitled to the present payment of retirement benefits under the scheme.

(3) In this paragraph—
- (a) references to retirement benefits include benefits otherwise than in cash; and
- (b) in relation to so much of retirement benefits as consists of a benefit otherwise than in cash, references to their amount are to the estimated money value of the benefit; and the nature of any such benefit shall also be disclosed.

Compensation to directors for loss of office

8.—(1) There shall be shown the aggregate amount of any compensation to directors or past directors in respect of loss of office.

(2) This amount includes compensation received or receivable by a director or past director for—
- (a) loss of office as director of the company, or
- (b) loss, while director of the company or on or in connection with his ceasing to be a director of it, of—
  - (i) any other office in connection with the management of the company's affairs, or
  - (ii) any office as director or otherwise in connection with the management of the affairs of any subsidiary undertaking of the company.

(3) References to compensation include benefits otherwise than in cash; and in relation to such compensation references to its amount are to the estimated money value of the benefit.

The nature of any such compensation shall be disclosed.

(4) In this paragraph, references to compensation for loss of office include the following, namely—

(a) compensation in consideration for, or in connection with, a person's retirement from office; and

(b) where such a retirement is occasioned by a breach of the person's contract with the company or with a subsidiary undertaking of the company—

(i) payments made by way of damages for the breach; or

(ii) payments made by way of settlement or compromise of any claim in respect of the breach.

(5) Sub-paragraph (6)(a) of paragraph 1 applies for the purposes of this paragraph as it applies for the purposes of that paragraph.

Sums paid to third parties in respect of directors' services

9.—(1) There shall be shown the aggregate amount of any consideration paid to or receivable by third parties for making available the services of any person—

(a) as a director of the company, or

(b) while director of the company—

(i) as director of any of its subsidiary undertakings, or

(ii) otherwise in connection with the management of the affairs of the company or any of its subsidiary undertakings.

(2) The reference to consideration includes benefits otherwise than in cash; and in relation to such consideration the reference to its amount is to the estimated money value of the benefit.

The nature of any such consideration shall be disclosed.

(3) The reference to third parties is to persons other than—

(a) the director himself or a person connected with him or body corporate controlled by him, and

(b) the company or any of its subsidiary undertakings.

Supplementary

10.—(1) The following applies with respect to the amounts to be shown under this Part of this Schedule.

(2) The amount in each case includes all relevant sums paid by or receivable from—

(a) the company; and

(b) the company's subsidiary undertakings; and

(c) any other person,

except sums to be accounted for to the company or any of its subsidiary undertakings or, by virtue of sections 314 and 315 of this Act (duty of directors to make disclosure on company takeover; consequence of non-compliance), to past or present members of the company or any of its subsidiaries or any class of those members.

(4) References to amounts paid to or receivable by a person include amounts paid to or receivable by a person connected with him or a body corporate controlled by him (but not so as to require an amount to be counted twice).

11.—(1) The amounts to be shown for any financial year under this Part of this Schedule are the sums receivable in respect of that year (whenever paid) or, in the case of sums not receivable in respect of a period, the sums paid during that year.

(2) But where—

(a) any sums are not shown in a note to the accounts for the relevant financial year on the ground that the person receiving them is liable to account for them as mentioned in paragraph 10(2), but the liability is thereafter wholly or partly released or is not enforced within a period of 2 years; or

(b) any sums paid by way of expenses allowance are charged to United Kingdom income tax after the end of the relevant financial year, those sums shall, to the extent to which the liability is released or not enforced or they are charged as mentioned above (as the case may be), be shown in a note to the first accounts in which it is practicable to show them and shall be distinguished from the amounts to be shown apart from this provision.

12.   Where it is necessary to do so for the purpose of making any distinction required by the preceding paragraphs in an amount to be shown in compliance with this Part of this Schedule, the directors may apportion any payments between the matters in respect of which these have been paid or are receivable in such manner as they think appropriate.

Interpretation

13.—(1)   The following applies for the interpretation of this Part of this Schedule.

(2)   A reference to a subsidiary undertaking of the company—

    (a)   in relation to a person who is or was, while a director of the company, a director also, by virtue of the company's nomination (direct or indirect) of any other undertaking, includes (subject to the following sub-paragraph) that undertaking, whether or not it is or was in fact a subsidiary undertaking of the company, and

    (b)   for the purposes of paragraphs 1 to 7 is to an undertaking which is a subsidiary undertaking at the time the services were rendered, and for the purposes of paragraph 8 to a subsidiary undertaking immediately before the loss of office as director.

(3)   The following definitions apply—

    (a)   'pension scheme' has the meaning assigned to 'retirement benefits scheme' by section 611 of the Income and Corporation Taxes Act 1988;

    (b)   'retirement benefits' has the meaning assigned to relevant benefits by section 612(1) of that Act.

(4)   References in this Part of this Schedule to a person being 'connected' with a director, and to a director 'controlling' a body corporate, shall be construed in accordance with section 346.

Supplementary

14.   This Part of this Schedule requires information to be given only so far as it is contained in the company's books and papers or the company has the right to obtain it from the persons concerned.

Section 234   SCHEDULE 7
MATTERS TO BE DEALT WITH IN DIRECTORS' REPORT

PART I   MATTERS OF A GENERAL NATURE

Asset values

1.—(2)   If, in the case of such of the fixed assets of the company or of any of its subsidiary undertakings as consist in interests in land, their market value (as at the end of the financial year) differs substantially from the amount at which they are included in the balance sheet, and the difference is, in the directors' opinion of such significance as to require that the attention of members of the company or of holders of its debentures should be drawn to it, the report shall indicate the difference with such degree of precision as is practicable.

Directors' interests

2.—(1)   The information required by paragraphs 2A and 2B shall be given in the directors' report, or by way of notes to the company's annual accounts, with respect to each person who at the end of the financial year was a director of the company.

(2) In those paragraphs—

  (a) 'the register' means the register of directors' interests kept by the company under section 325; and

  (b) references to a body corporate being in the same group as the company are to its being a subsidiary or holding company, or another subsidiary of a holding company, of the company.

2A.—(1) It shall be stated with respect to each director whether, according to the register, he was at the end of the financial year interested in shares in or debentures of the company or any other body corporate in the same group.

(2) If he was so interested, there shall be stated the number of shares in and amount of debentures of each body (specifying it) in which, according to the register, he was then interested.

(3) If a director was interested at the end of the financial year in shares in or debentures of the company or any other body corporate in the same group—

  (a) it shall also be stated whether, according to the register, he was at the beginning of the financial year (or, if he was not then a director, when he became one) interested in shares in or debentures of the company or any other body corporate in the same group, and

  (b) if he was so interested, there shall be stated the number of shares in and amount of debentures of each body (specifying it) in which, according to the register, he was then interested.

(4) In this paragraph references to an interest in shares or debentures have the same meaning as in section 324; and references to the interest of a director include any interest falling to be treated as his for the purposes of that section.

(5) The reference above to the time when a person became a director is, in the case of a person who became a director on more than one occasion, to the time when he first became a director.

2B.—(1) It shall be stated with respect to each director whether, according to the register, any right to subscribe for shares in or debentures of the company or another body corporate in the same group was during the financial year granted to, or exercised by, the director or a member of his immediate family.

(2) If any such right was granted to, or exercised by, any such person during the financial year, there shall be stated the number of shares in and amount of debentures of each body (specifying it) in respect of which, according to the register, the right was granted or exercised.

(3) A director's 'immediate family' means his or her spouse and infant children; and for this purpose 'children' includes stepchildren, and 'infant', in relation to Scotland, means pupil or minor.

(4) The reference above to a member of the director's immediate family does not include a person who is himself or herself a director of the company.

Political donations and expenditure

3.—(1) If—

  (a) the company (not being the wholly-owned subsidiary of a company incorporated in Great Britain) has in the financial year—

   (i) made any donation to any registered party or to any other EU political organisation, or

   (ii) incurred any EU political expenditure, and

  (b) the amount of the donation or expenditure, or (as the case may be) the aggregate amount of all donations and expenditure falling within paragraph (a), exceeded £200, the directors' report for the year shall contain the particulars specified in sub-paragraph (2).

(2) Those particulars are—
   (a) as respects donations falling within sub-paragraph (1)(a)(i)—
       (i) the name of each registered party or other organisation to whom any such donation has been made, and
       (ii) the total amount given to that party or organisation by way of such donations in the financial year; and
   (b) as respects expenditure falling within sub-paragraph (1)(a)(ii), the total amount incurred by way of such expenditure in the financial year.
(3) If—
   (a) at the end of the financial year the company has subsidiaries which have, in that year, made any donations or incurred any such expenditure as is mentioned in sub-paragraph (1)(a), and
   (b) it is not itself the wholly-owned subsidiary of a company incorporated in Great Britain,
the directors' report for the year is not, by virtue of sub-paragraph (1), required to contain the particulars specified in sub-paragraph (2); but, if the total amount of any such donations or expenditure (or both) made or incurred in that year by the company and the subsidiaries between them exceeds £200, the directors' report for the year shall contain those particulars in relation to each body by whom any such donation or expenditure has been made or incurred.
(4) Any expression used in this paragraph which is also used in Part XA of this Act has the same meaning as in that Part.
   4.—(1) If the company (not being the wholly-owned subsidiary of a company incorporated in Great Britain) has in the financial year made any contribution to a non-EU political party, the directors' report for the year shall contain—
   (a) a statement of the amount of the contribution, or
   (b) (if it has made two or more such contributions in the year) a statement of the total amount of the contributions.
(2) If—
   (a) at the end of the financial year the company has subsidiaries which have, in that year, made any such contributions as are mentioned in sub-paragraph (1), and
   (b) it is not itself the wholly-owned subsidiary of a company incorporated in Great Britain,
the directors' report for the year is not, by virtue of sub-paragraph (1), required to contain any such statement as is there mentioned, but it shall instead contain a statement of the total amount of the contributions made in the year by the company and the subsidiaries between them.
(3) In this paragraph 'contribution', in relation to an organisation, means—
   (a) any gift of money to the organisation (whether made directly or indirectly);
   (b) any subscription or other fee paid for affiliation to, or membership of, the organisation; or
   (c) any money spent (otherwise than by the organisation or a person acting on its behalf) in paying any expenses incurred directly or indirectly by the organisation.
(4) In this paragraph 'non-EU political party' means any political party which carries on, or proposes to carry on, its activities wholly outside the member States.

Charitable donations

   5.—(1) If—
   (a) the company (not being the wholly-owned subsidiary of a company incorporated in Great Britain) has in the financial year given money for charitable purposes, and
   (b) the money given exceeded £200 in amount,

the directors' report for the year shall contain, in the case of each of the purposes for which money has been given, a statement of the amount of money given for that purpose.

(2) If—

(a) at the end of the financial year the company has subsidiaries which have, in that year, given money for charitable purposes, and

(b) it is not itself the wholly-owned subsidiary of a company incorporated in Great Britain,

sub-paragraph (1) does not apply to the company; but, if the amount given in that year for charitable purposes by the company and the subsidiaries between them exceeds £200, the directors' report for the year shall contain, in the case of each of the purposes for which money has been given by the company and the subsidiaries between them, a statement of the amount of money given for that purpose.

(3) Money given for charitable purposes to a person who, when it was given, was ordinarily resident outside the United Kingdom is to be left out of account for the purposes of this paragraph.

(4) For the purposes of this paragraph 'charitable purposes' means purposes which are exclusively charitable, and as respects Scotland 'charitable' is to be construed as if it were contained in the Income Tax Acts.

Miscellaneous

6. The directors' report shall contain—

(a) particulars of any important events affecting the company or any of its subsidiary undertakings which have occurred since the end of the financial year,

(b) an indication of likely future developments in the business of the company and of its subsidiary undertakings,

(c) an indication of the activities (if any) of the company and its subsidiary undertakings in the field of research and development, and

(d) (unless the company is an unlimited company) an indication of the existence of branches (as defined in section 698(2)) of the company outside the United Kingdom.

PART II   DISCLOSURE REQUIRED BY COMPANY ACQUIRING
ITS OWN SHARES, ETC.

7. This Part of this Schedule applies where shares in a company—

(a) are purchased by the company or are acquired by it by forfeiture or surrender in lieu of forfeiture, or in pursuance of section 143(3) of this Act (acquisition of own shares by company limited by shares), or

(b) are acquired by another person in circumstances where paragraph (c) or (d) of section 146(1) applies (acquisition by company's nominee, or by another with company financial assistance, the company having a beneficial interest), or

(c) are made subject to a lien or other charge taken (whether expressly or otherwise) by the company and permitted by section 150(2) or (4), or section 6(3) of the Consequential Provisions Act (exceptions from general rule against a company having a lien or charge on its own shares).

8. The directors' report with respect to a financial year shall state—

(a) the number and nominal value of the shares so purchased, the aggregate amount of the consideration paid by the company for such shares and the reasons for their purchase;

(b) the number and nominal value of the shares so acquired by the company, acquired by another person in such circumstances and so charged respectively during the financial year;

(c) the maximum number and nominal value of shares which, having been so acquired by the company, acquired by another person in such circumstances or so charged (whether or not during that year) are held at any time by the company or that other person during that year;

(d) the number and nominal value of the shares so acquired by the company, acquired by another person in such circumstances or so charged (whether or not during that year) which are disposed of by the company or that other person or cancelled by the company during that year;

(e) where the number and nominal value of the shares of any particular description are stated in pursuance of any of the preceding sub-paragraphs, the percentage of the called-up share capital which shares of that description represent;

(f) where any of the shares have been so charged the amount of the charge in each case; and

(g) where any of the shares have been disposed of by the company or the person who acquired them in such circumstances for money or money's worth the amount or value of the consideration in each case.

PART III   DISCLOSURE CONCERNING EMPLOYMENT, ETC.
OF DISABLED PERSONS

9.—(1) This Part of this Schedule applies to the directors' report where the average number of persons employed by the company in each week during the financial year exceeded 250.

(2) That average number is the quotient derived by dividing, by the number of weeks in the financial year, the number derived by ascertaining, in relation to each of those weeks, the number of persons who, under contracts of service, were employed in the week (whether throughout it or not) by the company, and adding up the numbers ascertained.

(3) The directors' report shall in that case contain a statement describing such policy as the company has applied during the financial year—

(a) for giving full and fair consideration to applications for employment by the company made by disabled persons, having regard to their particular aptitudes and abilities,

(b) for continuing the employment of, and for arranging appropriate training for, employees of the company who have become disabled persons during the period when they were employed by the company, and

(c) otherwise for the training, career development and promotion of disabled persons employed by the company.

(4) In this Part—

(a) 'employment' means employment other than employment to work wholly or mainly outside the United Kingdom, and 'employed' and 'employee' shall be construed accordingly; and

(b) 'disabled person' means the same as in the Disability Discrimination Act 1995.

PART V   EMPLOYEE INVOLVEMENT

11.—(1) This Part of this Schedule applies to the directors' report where the average number of persons employed by the company in each week during the financial year exceeded 250.

(2) That average number is the quotient derived by dividing by the number of weeks in the financial year the number derived by ascertaining, in relation to each of those weeks, the number of persons who, under contracts of service, were employed in the week (whether throughout it or not) by the company, and adding up the numbers ascertained.

(3) The directors' report shall in that case contain a statement describing the action that has been taken during the financial year to introduce, maintain or develop arrangements aimed at—

(a) providing employees systematically with information on matters of concern to them as employees,

(b) consulting employees or their representatives on a regular basis so that the views of employees can be taken into account in making decisions which are likely to affect their interests,

(c) encouraging the involvement of employees in the company's performance through an employees' share scheme or by some other means,

(d) achieving a common awareness on the part of all employees of the financial and economic factors affecting the performance of the company.

(4) In sub-paragraph (3) 'employee' does not include a person employed to work wholly or mainly outside the United Kingdom; and for the purposes of sub-paragraph (2) no regard is to be had to such a person.

PART VI   POLICY AND PRACTICE ON PAYMENT OF CREDITORS

12.—(1) This Part of this Schedule applies to the directors' report for a financial year if—

(a) the company was at any time within the year a public company, or

(b) the company did not qualify as small or medium-sized in relation to the year by virtue of section 247 and was at any time within the year a member of a group of which the parent company was a public company.

(2) The report shall state, with respect to the next following financial year—

(a) whether in respect of some or all of its suppliers it is the company's policy to follow any code or standard on payment practice and, if so, the name of the code or standard and the place where information about, and copies of, the code or standard can be obtained,

(b) whether in respect of some or all of its suppliers it is the company's policy—

(i) to settle the terms of payment with those suppliers when agreeing the terms of each transaction,

(ii) to ensure that those suppliers are made aware of the terms of payment, and

(iii) to abide by the terms of payment,

(c) where the company's policy is not as mentioned in paragraph (a) or (b) in respect of some or all of its suppliers, what its policy is with respect to the payment of those suppliers;

and if the company's policy is different for different suppliers or classes of suppliers, the report shall identify the suppliers to which the different policies apply.

In this sub-paragraph references to the company's suppliers are references to persons who are or may become its suppliers.

(3) The report shall also state the number of days which bears to the number of days in the financial year the same proportion as X bears to Y where—

X = the aggregate of the amounts which were owed to trade creditors at the end of the year; and

Y = the aggregate of the amounts in which the company was invoiced by suppliers during the year.

(4) For the purposes of sub-paragraphs (2) and (3) a person is a supplier of the company at any time if—

(a) at that time, he is owed an amount in respect of goods or services supplied, and

(b) that amount would be included under the heading corresponding to item E.4 (trade creditors) in Format 1 if—

(i)   the company's accounts fell to be prepared as at that time,

(ii) those accounts were prepared in accordance with Schedule 4, and

(iii) that Format were adopted.

(5) For the purpose of sub-paragraph (3), the aggregate of the amounts which at the end of the financial year were owed to trade creditors shall be taken to be—

(a)   where in the company's accounts Format 1 of the balance sheet formats set out in Part I of Schedule 4 is adopted, the amount shown under the heading corresponding to item E.4 (trade creditors) in that Format,

(b)   where Format 2 is adopted, the amount which, under the heading corresponding to item C.4 (trade creditors) in that Format, is shown as falling due within one year, and

(c)   where the company's accounts are prepared in accordance with Schedule 9 or 9A, the amount which would be shown under the heading corresponding to item E.4 (trade creditors) in Format 1 if the company's accounts were prepared in accordance with Schedule 4 and that Format were adopted.

SCHEDULE 7A   DIRECTORS' REMUNERATION REPORT

[schedule introduced by section 234B]

PART 1   INTRODUCTORY

1.—(1) In the directors' remuneration report for a financial year ('the relevant financial year') there shall be shown the information specified in Parts 2 and 3 below.

(2) Information required to be shown in the report for or in respect of a particular person shall be shown in the report in a manner that links the information to that person identified by name.

PART 2   INFORMATION NOT SUBJECT TO AUDIT

Consideration by the directors of matters relating to directors' remuneration

2.—(1) If a committee of the company's directors has considered matters relating to the directors' remuneration for the relevant financial year, the directors' remuneration report shall—

(a)   name each director who was a member of the committee at any time when the committee was considering any such matter;

(b)   name any person who provided to the committee advice, or services, that materially assisted the committee in their consideration of any such matter;

(c)   in the case of any person named under paragraph (b), who is not a director of the company, state—

(i)   the nature of any other services that that person has provided to the company during the relevant financial year; and

(ii) whether that person was appointed by the committee.

(2) In sub-paragraph (1)(b) 'person' includes (in particular) any director of the company who does not fall within sub-paragraph (1)(a).

Statement of company's policy on directors' remuneration

3.—(1) The directors' remuneration report shall contain a statement of the company's policy on directors' remuneration for the following financial year and for financial years subsequent to that.

    (2) The policy statement shall include—

        (a) for each director, a detailed summary of any performance conditions to which any entitlement of the director—

            (i)   to share options, or

            (ii) under a long term incentive scheme,

         is subject;

        (b) an explanation as to why any such performance conditions were chosen;

        (c) a summary of the methods to be used in assessing whether any such performance conditions are met and an explanation as to why those methods were chosen;

        (d) if any such performance condition involves any comparison with factors external to the company—

            (i)   a summary of the factors to be used in making each such comparison, and

            (ii) if any of the factors relates to the performance of another company, of two or more other companies or of an index on which the securities of a company or companies are listed, the identity of that company, of each of those companies or of the index;

        (e) a description of, and an explanation for, any significant amendment proposed to be made to the terms and conditions of any entitlement of a director to share options or under a long term incentive scheme; and

        (f) if any entitlement of a director to share options, or under a long term incentive scheme, is not subject to performance conditions, an explanation as to why that is the case.

    (3) The policy statement shall, in respect of each director's terms and conditions relating to remuneration, explain the relative importance of those elements which are, and those which are not, related to performance.

    (4) The policy statement shall summarise, and explain, the company's policy on—

        (a) the duration of contracts with directors, and

        (b) notice periods, and termination payments, under such contracts.

    (5) In sub-paragraphs (2) and (3), references to a director are to any person who serves as a director of the company at any time in the period beginning with the end of the relevant financial year and ending with date [*sic*] on which the directors' remuneration report is laid before the company in general meeting.

Performance graph

    4.—(1) The directors' remuneration report shall—

        (a) contain a line graph that shows for each of—

            (i)   a holding of shares of that class of the company's equity share capital whose listing, or admission to dealing, has resulted in the company falling within the definition of 'quoted company', and

            (ii) a hypothetical holding of shares made up of shares of the same kinds and number as those by reference to which a broad equity market index is calculated,

         a line drawn by joining up points plotted to represent, for each of the financial years in the relevant period, the total shareholder return on that holding; and

        (b) state the name of the index selected for the purposes of the graph and set out the reasons for selecting that index.

    (2) For the purposes of sub-paragraphs (1) and (4), 'relevant period' means the five financial years of which the last is the relevant financial year.

    (3) Where the relevant financial year—

        (a) is the company's second, third or fourth financial year, sub-paragraph (2) has effect with the substitution of 'two', 'three' or 'four' (as the case may be) for 'five'; and

(b) is the company's first financial year, 'relevant period', for the purposes of sub-paragraphs (1) and (4), means the relevant financial year.

(4) For the purposes of sub-paragraph (1), the 'total shareholder return' for a relevant period on a holding of shares must be calculated using a fair method that—

(a) takes as its starting point the percentage change over the period in the market price of the holding;

(b) involves making—

(i) the assumptions specified in sub-paragraph (5) as to reinvestment of income, and

(ii) the assumption specified in sub-paragraph (7) as to the funding of liabilities; and

(c) makes provision for any replacement of shares in the holding by shares of a different description;

and the same method must be used for each of the holdings mentioned in sub-paragraph (1).

(5) The assumptions as to reinvestment of income are—

(a) that any benefit in the form of shares of the same kind as those in the holding is added to the holding at the time the benefit becomes receivable; and

(b) that any benefit in cash, and an amount equal to the value of any benefit not in cash and not falling within paragraph (a), is applied at the time the benefit becomes receivable in the purchase at their market price of shares of the same kind as those in the holding and that the shares purchased are added to the holding at that time.

(6) In sub-paragraph (5) 'benefit' means any benefit (including, in particular, any dividend) receivable in respect of any shares in the holding by the holder from the company of whose share capital the shares form part.

(7) The assumption as to the funding of liabilities is that, where the holder has a liability to the company of whose capital the shares in the holding form part, shares are sold from the holding—

(a) immediately before the time by which the liability is due to be satisfied, and

(b) in such numbers that, at the time of the sale, the market price of the shares sold equals the amount of the liability in respect of the shares in the holding that are not being sold.

(8) In sub-paragraph (7) 'liability' means a liability arising in respect of any shares in the holding or from the exercise of a right attached to any of those shares.

Service contracts

5.—(1) The directors' remuneration report shall contain, in respect of the contract of service or contract for services of each person who has served as a director of the company at any time during the relevant financial year, the following information—

(a) the date of the contract, the unexpired term and the details of any notice periods;

(b) any provision for compensation payable upon early termination of the contract; and

(c) such details of other provisions in the contract as are necessary to enable members of the company to estimate the liability of the company in the event of early termination of the contract.

(2) The directors' remuneration report shall contain an explanation for any significant award made to a person in the circumstances described in paragraph 14.

PART 3   INFORMATION SUBJECT TO AUDIT

Amount of each director's emoluments and compensation in the relevant financial year

6.—(1) The directors' remuneration report shall for the relevant financial year show, for each person who has served as a director of the company at any time during that year, each of the following—

    (a) the total amount of salary and fees paid to or receivable by the person in respect of qualifying services;

    (b) the total amount of bonuses so paid or receivable;

    (c) the total amount of sums paid by way of expenses allowance that are—

        (i) chargeable to United Kingdom income tax (or would be if the person were an individual); and

        (ii) paid to or receivable by the person in respect of qualifying services;

    (d) the total amount of—

        (i) any compensation for loss of office paid to or receivable by the person, and

        (ii) any other payments paid to or receivable by the person in connection with the termination of qualifying services;

    (e) the total estimated value of any benefits received by the person otherwise than in cash that—

        (i) do not fall within any of sub-paragraphs (a)–(d) or paragraphs 7–11 below,

        (ii) are emoluments of the person, and

        (iii) are received by the person in respect of qualifying services; and

    (f) the amount that is the total of the sums mentioned in paragraphs (a) to (e).

(2) The directors' remuneration report shall show, for each person who has served as a director of the company at any time during the relevant financial year, the amount that for the financial year preceding the relevant financial year is the total of the sums mentioned in paragraphs (a) to (e) of sub-paragraph (1).

(3) The directors' remuneration report shall also state the nature of any element of a remuneration package which is not cash.

(4) The information required by sub-paragraphs (1) and (2) shall be presented in tabular form.

Share options

7.—(1) The directors' remuneration report shall contain, in respect of each person who has served as a director of the company at any time in the relevant financial year, the information specified in paragraph 8.

(2) Sub-paragraph (1) is subject to paragraph 9 (aggregation of information to avoid excessively lengthy reports).

(3) The information specified in paragraphs (a) to (c) of paragraph 8 shall be presented in tabular form in the report.

(4) In paragraph 8 'share option', in relation to a person, means a share option granted in respect of qualifying services of the person.

8.   The information required by sub-paragraph (1) of paragraph 7 in respect of such a person as is mentioned in that sub-paragraph is—

    (a) the number of shares that are subject to a share option—

        (i) at the beginning of the relevant financial year or, if later, on the date of the appointment of the person as a director of the company, and

        (ii) at the end of the relevant financial year or, if earlier, on the cessation of the person's appointment as a director of the company,

        in each case differentiating between share options having different terms and conditions;

(b) information identifying those share options that have been awarded in the relevant financial year, those that have been exercised in that year, those that in that year have expired unexercised and those whose terms and conditions have been varied in that year;

(c) for each share option that is unexpired at any time in the relevant financial year—
    (i)   the price paid, if any, for its award,
    (ii) the exercise price,
    (iii) the date from which the option may be exercised, and
    (iv) the date on which the option expires;

(d) a description of any variation made in the relevant financial year in the terms and conditions of a share option;

(e) a summary of any performance criteria upon which the award or exercise of a share option is conditional, including a description of any variation made in such performance criteria during the relevant financial year;

(f) for each share option that has been exercised during the relevant financial year, the market price of the shares, in relation to which it is exercised, at the time of exercise; and

(g) for each share option that is unexpired at the end of the relevant financial year—
    (i) the market price at the end of that year, and
    (ii) the highest and lowest market prices during that year, of each share that is subject to the option.

9.—(1) If, in the opinion of the directors of the company, disclosure in accordance with paragraphs 7 and 8 would result in a disclosure of excessive length then, (subject to sub-paragraphs (2) and (3))—

(a) information disclosed for a person under paragraph 8(a) need not differentiate between share options having different terms and conditions;

(b) for the purposes of disclosure in respect of a person under paragraph 8(c)(i) and (ii) and (g), share options may be aggregated and (instead of disclosing prices for each share option) disclosure may be made of weighted average prices of aggregations of share options;

(c) for the purposes of disclosure in respect of a person under paragraph 8(c)(iii) and (iv), share options may be aggregated and (instead of disclosing dates for each share option) disclosure may be made of ranges of dates for aggregation of share options.

(2) Sub-paragraph (1)(b) and (c) does not permit the aggregation of—

(a) share options in respect of shares whose market price at the end of the relevant financial year is below the option exercise price, with

(b) share options in respect of shares whose market price at the end of the relevant financial year is equal to, or exceeds, the option exercise price.

(3) Sub-paragraph (1) does not apply (and accordingly, full disclosure must be made in accordance with paragraphs 7 and 8) in respect of share options that during the relevant financial year have been awarded or exercised or had their terms and conditions varied.

Long term incentive schemes

10.—(1) The directors' remuneration report shall contain, in respect of each person who has served as a director of the company at any time in the relevant financial year, the information specified in paragraph 11.

(2) Sub-paragraph (1) does not require the report to contain share option details that are contained in the report in compliance with paragraphs 7 to 9.

(3) The information specified in paragraph 11 shall be presented in tabular form in the report.

(4) For the purposes of paragraph 11—

(a) 'scheme interest', in relation to a person, means an interest under a long term incentive scheme that is an interest in respect of which assets may become receivable under the scheme in respect of qualifying services of the person; and

(b) such an interest 'vests' at the earliest time when—

(i) it has been ascertained that the qualifying conditions have been fulfilled, and

(ii) the nature and quantity of the assets receivable under the scheme in respect of the interest have been ascertained.

(5) In this Schedule 'long term incentive scheme' means any agreement or arrangement under which money or other assets may become receivable by a person and which includes one or more qualifying conditions with respect to service or performance that cannot be fulfilled within a single financial year, and for this purpose the following shall be disregarded, namely—

(a) any bonus the amount of which falls to be determined by reference to service or performance within a single financial year;

(b) compensation in respect of loss of office, payments for breach of contract and other termination payments; and

(c) retirement benefits.

11.—(1) The information required by sub-paragraph (1) of paragraph 10 in respect of such a person as is mentioned in that sub-paragraph is—

(a) details of the scheme interests that the person has at the beginning of the relevant financial year or if later on the date of the appointment of the person as a director of the company;

(b) details of the scheme interests awarded to the person during the relevant financial year;

(c) details of the scheme interests that the person has at the end of the relevant financial year or if earlier on the cessation of the person's appointment as a director of the company;

(d) for each scheme interest within paragraphs (a) to (c)—

(i) the end of the period over which the qualifying conditions for that interest have to be fulfilled (or if there are different periods for different conditions, the end of whichever of those periods ends last); and

(ii) a description of any variation made in the terms and conditions of the scheme interests during the relevant financial year; and

(e) for each scheme interest that has vested in the relevant financial year—

(i) the relevant details (see sub-paragraph (3)) of any shares,

(ii) the amount of any money, and

(iii) the value of any other assets,

that have become receivable in respect of the interest.

(2) The details that sub-paragraph (1)(b) requires of a scheme interest awarded during the relevant financial year include, if shares may become receivable in respect of the interest, the following—

(a) the number of those shares;

(b) the market price of each of those shares when the scheme interest was awarded; and

(c) details of qualifying conditions that are conditions with respect to performance.

(3) In sub-paragraph (1)(e)(i) 'the relevant details', in relation to any shares that have become receivable in respect of a scheme interest, means—

(a) the number of those shares;

(b) the date on which the scheme interest was awarded;

(c) the market price of each of those shares when the scheme interest was awarded;

(d) the market price of each of those shares when the scheme interest vested; and

(e) details of qualifying conditions that were conditions with respect to performance.

Pensions

12.—(1) The directors' remuneration report shall, for each person who has served as a director of the company at any time during the relevant financial year, contain the information in respect of pensions that is specified in sub-paragraphs (2) and (3).

(2) Where the person has rights under a pension scheme that is a defined benefit scheme in relation to the person and any of those rights are rights to which he has become entitled in respect of qualifying services of his—

  (a) details—

    (i) of any changes during the relevant financial year in the person's accrued benefits under the scheme, and

    (ii) of the person's accrued benefits under the scheme as at the end of that year;

  (b) the transfer value, calculated in a manner consistent with 'Retirement Benefit Schemes—Transfer Values (GN 11)' published by the Institute of Actuaries and the Faculty of Actuaries and dated 6th April 2001, of the person's accrued benefits under the scheme at the end of the relevant financial year;

  (c) the transfer value of the person's accrued benefits under the scheme that in compliance with paragraph (b) was contained in the director's remuneration report for the previous financial year or, if there was no such report or no such value was contained in that report, the transfer value, calculated in such a manner as is mentioned in paragraph (b), of the person's accrued benefits under the scheme at the beginning of the relevant financial year;

  (d) the amount obtained by subtracting—

    (i) the transfer value of the person's accrued benefits under the scheme that is required to be contained in the report by paragraph (c), from

    (ii) the transfer value of those benefits that is required to be contained in the report by paragraph (b),

  and then subtracting from the result of that calculation the amount of any contributions made to the scheme by the person in the relevant financial year.

(3) Where—

  (a) the person has rights under a pension scheme that is a money purchase scheme in relation to the person, and

  (b) any of those rights are rights to which he has become entitled in respect of qualifying services of his,

details of any contribution to the scheme in respect of the person that is paid or payable by the company for the relevant financial year or paid by the company in that year for another financial year.

Excess retirement benefits of directors and past directors

13.—(1) Subject to sub-paragraph (3), the directors' remuneration report shall show in respect of each person who has served as a director of the company—

  (a) at any time during the relevant financial year, or

  (b) at any time before the beginning of that year,

the amount of so much of retirement benefits paid to or receivable by the person under pension schemes as is in excess of the retirement benefits to which he was entitled on the date on which the benefits first became payable or 31st March 1997, whichever is the later.

(2) In subsection (1) 'retirement benefits' means retirement benefits to which the person became entitled in respect of qualifying services of his.

(3) Amounts paid or receivable under a pension scheme need not be included in an amount required to be shown under sub-paragraph (1) if—

 (a) the funding of the scheme was such that the amounts were or, as the case may be, could have been paid without recourse to additional contributions; and

 (b) amounts were paid to or receivable by all pensioner members of the scheme on the same basis;

and in this sub-paragraph 'pensioner member', in relation to a pension scheme, means any person who is entitled to the present payment of retirement benefits under the scheme.

(4) In this paragraph—

 (a) references to retirement benefits include benefits otherwise than in cash; and

 (b) in relation to so much of retirement benefits as consists of a benefit otherwise than in cash, references to their amount are to the estimated money value of the benefit;

and the nature of any such benefit shall also be shown in the report.

Compensation for past directors

14. The directors' remuneration report shall contain details of any significant award made in the relevant financial year to any person who was not a director of the company at the time the award was made but had previously been a director of the company, including (in particular) compensation in respect of loss of office and pensions but excluding any sums which have already been shown in the report under paragraph 6(1)(d).

Sums paid to third parties in respect of a director's services

15.—(1) The directors' remuneration report shall show, in respect of each person who served as a director of the company at any time during the relevant financial year, the aggregate amount of any consideration paid to or receivable by third parties for making available the services of the person—

 (a) as a director of the company, or

 (b) while director of the company—

  (i) as director of any of its subsidiary undertakings, or

  (ii) as director of any other undertaking of which he was (while director of the company) a director by virtue of the company's nomination (direct or indirect), or

  (iii) otherwise in connection with the management of the affairs of the company or any such other undertaking.

(2) The reference to consideration includes benefits otherwise than in cash; and in relation to such consideration the reference to its amount is to the estimated money value of the benefit.

The nature of any such consideration shall be shown in the report.

(3) The reference to third parties is to persons other than—

 (a) the person himself or a person connected with him or a body corporate controlled by him, and

 (b) the company or any such other undertaking as is mentioned in sub-paragraph (1)(b)(ii).

PART 4 INTERPRETATION AND SUPPLEMENTARY

16.—(1) In this Schedule—

'amount', in relation to a gain made on the exercise of a share option, means the difference between—

(a) the market price of the shares on the day on which the option was exercised; and

(b) the price actually paid for the shares;

'company contributions', in relation to a pension scheme and a person, means any payments (including insurance premiums) made, or treated as made, to the scheme in respect of the person by anyone other than the person;

'defined benefit scheme', in relation to a person, means a pension scheme which is not a money purchase scheme in relation to the person;

'emoluments' of a person—

(a) includes salary, fees and bonuses, sums paid by way of expenses allowance (so far as they are chargeable to United Kingdom income tax or would be if the person were an individual) but,

(b) does not include any of the following, namely—

(i) the value of any share options granted to him or the amount of any gains made on the exercise of any such options;

(ii) any company contributions paid, or treated as paid, in respect of him under any pension scheme or any benefits to which he is entitled under any such scheme; or

(iii) any money or other assets paid to or received or receivable by him under any long term incentive scheme;

'long term incentive scheme' has the meaning given by paragraph 10(5);

'money purchase benefits', in relation to a person, means retirement benefits the rate or amount of which is calculated by reference to payments made, or treated as made, by the person or by any other person in respect of that person and which are not average salary benefits;

'money purchase scheme', in relation to a person, means a pension scheme under which all of the benefits that may become payable to or in respect of the person are money purchase benefits in relation to the person;

'pension scheme' means a retirement benefits scheme within the meaning given by section 611 of the Income and Corporation Taxes Act 1988;

'qualifying services', in relation to any person, means his services as a director of the company, and his services at any time while he is a director of the company—

(a) as a director of an undertaking that is a subsidiary undertaking of the company at that time;

(b) as a director of any other undertaking of which he is a director by virtue of the company's nomination (direct or indirect); or

(c) otherwise in connection with the management of the affairs of the company or any such subsidiary undertaking or any such other undertaking;

'retirement benefits' means relevant benefits within the meaning given by section 612(1) of the Income and Corporation Taxes Act 1988;

'shares' means shares (whether allotted or not) in the company, or any undertaking which is a group undertaking in relation to the company, and includes a share warrant as defined by section 188(1);

'share option' means a right to acquire shares;

'value', in relation to shares received or receivable on any day by a person who is or has been a director of the company, means the market price of the shares on that day.

(2) In this Schedule 'compensation in respect of loss of office' includes compensation received or receivable by a person for—

(a) loss of office as director of the company, or

(b) loss, while director of the company or on or in connection with his ceasing to be a director of it, of—

(i) any other office in connection with the management of the company's affairs, or

(ii) any office as director or otherwise in connection with the management of the affairs of any undertaking that, immediately before the loss, is a subsidiary undertaking of the company or an undertaking of which he is a director by virtue of the company's nomination (direct or indirect);

(c) compensation in consideration for, or in connection with, a person's retirement from office; and

(d) where such a retirement is occasioned by a breach of the person's contract with the company or with an undertaking that, immediately before the breach, is a subsidiary undertaking of the company or an undertaking of which he is a director by virtue of the company' s nomination (direct or indirect)—

(i) payments made by way of damages for the breach; or

(ii) payments made by way of settlement or compromise of any claim in respect of the breach.

(3) References in this Schedule to compensation include benefits otherwise than in cash; and in relation to such compensation references in this Schedule to its amount are to the estimated money value of the benefit.

(4) References in this Schedule to a person being 'connected' with a director, and to a director 'controlling' a body corporate, shall be construed in accordance with section 346.

17.—(1) For the purposes of this Schedule emoluments paid or receivable or share options granted in respect of a person's accepting office as a director shall be treated as emoluments paid or receivable or share options granted in respect of his services as a director.

(2) Where a pension scheme provides for any benefits that may become payable to or in respect of a person to be whichever are the greater of—

(a) such benefits determined by or under the scheme as are money purchase benefits in relation to the person; and

(b) such retirement benefits determined by or under the scheme to be payable to or in respect of the person as are not money purchase benefits in relation to the person,

the company may assume for the purposes of this Schedule that those benefits will be money purchase benefits in relation to the person, or not, according to whichever appears more likely at the end of the relevant financial year.

(3) In determining for the purposes of this Schedule whether a pension scheme is a money purchase scheme in relation to a person or a defined benefit scheme in relation to a person, any death in service benefits provided for by the scheme shall be disregarded.

18.—(1) The following applies with respect to the amounts to be shown under this Schedule.

(2) The amount in each case includes all relevant sums paid by or receivable from—

(a) the company; and

(b) the company's subsidiary undertakings; and

(c) any other person,

except sums to be accounted for to the company or any of its subsidiary undertakings or any other undertaking of which any person has been a director while director of the company, by virtue of sections 314 and 315 of this Act (duty of directors to make disclosure on company takeover; consequence of non-compliance), to past or present members of the company or any of its subsidiaries or any class of those members.

(3) References to amounts paid to or receivable by a person include amounts paid to or receivable by a person connected with him or a body corporate controlled by him (but not so as to require an amount to be counted twice).

19.—(1) The amounts to be shown for any financial year under Part 3 of this Schedule are the sums receivable in respect of that year (whenever paid) or, in the case of sums not receivable in respect of a period, the sums paid during that year.

(2) But where—

(a) any sums are not shown in the directors' remuneration report for the relevant financial year on the ground that the person receiving them is liable to account for them as mentioned in paragraph 18(2), but the liability is thereafter wholly or partly released or is not enforced within a period of 2 years; or

(b) any sums paid by way of expenses allowance are charged to United Kingdom income tax after the end of the relevant financial year or, in the case of any such sums paid otherwise than to an individual, it does not become clear until the end of the relevant financial year that those sums would be charged to such tax were the person an individual,

those sums shall, to the extent to which the liability is released or not enforced or they are charged as mentioned above (as the case may be), be shown in the first directors' remuneration report in which it is practicable to show them and shall be distinguished from the amounts to be shown apart from this provision.

20.   Where it is necessary to do so for the purpose of making any distinction required by the preceding paragraphs in an amount to be shown in compliance with this Part of this Schedule, the directors may apportion any payments between the matters in respect of which these have been paid or are receivable in such manner as they think appropriate.

21.   This Schedule requires information to be given only so far as it is contained in the company's books and papers, available to members of the public or the company has the right to obtain it.

Section 258   SCHEDULE 10A
PARENT AND SUBSIDIARY UNDERTAKINGS:
SUPPLEMENTARY PROVISIONS

Introduction

1.   The provisions of this Schedule explain expressions used in section 258 (parent and subsidiary undertakings) and otherwise supplement that section.

Voting rights in an undertaking

2.—(1) In section 258(2)(a) and (d) the references to the voting rights in an undertaking are to the rights conferred on shareholders in respect of their shares or, in the case of an undertaking not having a share capital, on members, to vote at general meetings of the undertaking on all, or substantially all, matters.

(2) In relation to an undertaking which does not have general meetings at which matters are decided by the exercise of voting rights, the references to holding a majority of the voting rights in the undertaking shall be construed as references to having the right under the constitution of the undertaking to direct the overall policy of the undertaking or to alter the terms of its constitution.

Right to appoint or remove a majority of the directors

3.—(1) In section 258(2)(b) the reference to the right to appoint or remove a majority of the board of directors is to the right to appoint or remove directors holding a majority of the voting rights at meetings of the board on all, or substantially all, matters.

(2) An undertaking shall be treated as having the right to appoint to a directorship if—

(a) a person's appointment to it follows necessarily from his appointment as director of the undertaking, or

(b) the directorship is held by the undertaking itself.

(3) A right to appoint or remove which is exercisable only with the consent or concurrence of another person shall be left out of account unless no other person has a right to appoint or, as the case may be, remove in relation to that directorship.

Right to exercise dominant influence

4.—(1) For the purposes of section 258(2)(c) an undertaking shall not be regarded as having the right to exercise a dominant influence over another undertaking unless it has a right to give directions with respect to the operating and financial policies of that other undertaking which its directors are obliged to comply with whether or not they are for the benefit of that other undertaking.

(2) A 'control contract' means a contract in writing conferring such a right which—
   (a) is of a kind authorised by the memorandum or articles of the undertaking in relation to which the right is exercisable, and
   (b) is permitted by the law under which that undertaking is established.

(3) This paragraph shall not be read as affecting the construction of the expression 'actually exercises a dominant influence' in section 258(4)(a).

Rights exercisable only in certain circumstances or temporarily incapable of exercise

5.—(1) Rights which are exercisable only in certain circumstances shall be taken into account only—
   (a) when the circumstances have arisen, and for so long as they continue to obtain, or
   (b) when the circumstances are within the control of the person having the rights.

(2) Rights which are normally exercisable but are temporarily incapable of exercise shall continue to be taken into account.

Rights held by one person on behalf of another

6.   Rights held by a person in a fiduciary capacity shall be treated as not held by him.

7.—(1) Rights held by a person as nominee for another shall be treated as held by the other.

(2) Rights shall be regarded as held as nominee for another if they are exercisable only on his instructions or with his consent or concurrence.

Rights attached to shares held by way of security

8.   Rights attached to shares held by way of security shall be treated as held by the person providing the security—
   (a) where apart from the right to exercise them for the purpose of preserving the value of the security, or of realising it, the rights are exercisable only in accordance with his instructions, and
   (b) where the shares are held in connection with the granting of loans as part of normal business activities and apart from the right to exercise them for the purpose of preserving the value of the security, or of realising it, the rights are exercisable only in his interests.

Rights attributed to parent undertaking

9.—(1) Rights shall be treated as held by a parent undertaking if they are held by any of its subsidiary undertakings.

(2) Nothing in paragraph 7 or 8 shall be construed as requiring rights held by a parent undertaking to be treated as held by any of its subsidiary undertakings.

(3) For the purposes of paragraph 8 rights shall be treated as being exercisable in accordance with the instructions or in the interests of an undertaking if they are excercisable in accordance with the instructions of or, as the case may be, in the interests of any group undertaking.

Disregard of certain rights

10.   The voting rights in an undertaking shall be reduced by any rights held by the undertaking itself.

Supplementary

11.   References in any provision of paragraphs 6 to 10 to rights held by a person include rights falling to be treated as held by him by virtue of any other provision of those paragraphs but not rights which by virtue of any such provision are to be treated as not held by him.

Sections 324, 325, 326, 328 and 346

SCHEDULE 13

PROVISIONS SUPPLEMENTING AND INTERPRETING SECTIONS 324 TO 328

PART I   RULES FOR INTERPRETATION OF THE SECTIONS AND ALSO SECTION 346(4) AND (5)

1.—(1) A reference to an interest in shares or debentures is to be read as including any interest of any kind whatsoever in shares or debentures.

(2) Accordingly, there are to be disregarded any restraints or restrictions to which the exercise of any right attached to the interest is or may be subject.

2.   Where property is held on trust and any interest in shares or debentures is comprised in the property, any beneficiary of the trust who (apart from this paragraph) does not have an interest in the shares or debentures is to be taken as having such an interest, but this paragraph is without prejudice to the following provisions of this Part of this Schedule.

3.—(1) A person is taken to have an interest in shares or debentures if—

(a)   he enters into a contract for their purchase by him (whether for cash or other consideration), or

(b)   not being the registered holder, he is entitled to exercise any right conferred by the holding of the shares or debentures, or is entitled to control the exercise of any such right.

(2) For purposes of sub-paragraph (1)(b), a person is taken to be entitled to exercise or control the exercise of a right conferred by the holding of shares or debentures if he—

(a)   has a right (whether subject to conditions or not) the exercise of which would make him so entitled, or

(b)   is under an obligation (whether or not so subject) the fulfilment of which would make him so entitled.

(3) A person is not by virtue of sub-paragraph (1)(b) taken to be interested in shares or debentures by reason only that he—

(a)   has been appointed a proxy to vote at a specified meeting of a company or of any class of its members and at any adjournment of that meeting, or

(b)   has been appointed by a corporation to act as its representative at any meeting of a company or of any class of its members.

4.   A person is taken to be interested in shares or debentures if a body corporate is interested in them and—

(a) that body corporate or its directors are accustomed to act in accordance with his directions or instructions, or

(b) he is entitled to exercise or control the exercise of one-third or more of the voting power at general meetings of that body corporate.

As this paragraph applies for the purposes of section 346(4) and (5), 'more than one-half' is substituted for 'one-third or more'.

5. Where a person is entitled to exercise or control the exercise of one-third or more of the voting power at general meetings of a body corporate, and that body corporate is entitled to exercise or control the exercise of any of the voting power at general meetings of another body corporate ('the effective voting power'), then, for purposes of paragraph 4(b), the effective voting power is taken to be exercisable by that person.

As this paragraph applies for the purposes of section 346(4) and (5), 'more than one-half' is substituted for 'one-third or more'.

6.—(1) A person is taken to have an interest in shares or debentures if, otherwise than by virtue of having an interest under a trust—

(a) he has a right to call for delivery of the shares or debentures to himself or to his order, or

(b) he has a right to acquire an interest in shares or debentures or is under an obligation to take an interest in shares or debentures;

whether in any case the right or obligation is conditional or absolute.

(2) Rights or obligations to subscribe for shares or debentures are not to be taken, for purposes of sub-paragraph (1), to be rights to acquire, or obligations to take, an interest in shares or debentures.

This is without prejudice to paragraph 1.

7. Persons having a joint interest are deemed each of them to have that interest.

8. It is immaterial that shares or debentures in which a person has an interest are unidentifiable.

9. So long as a person is entitled to receive, during the lifetime of himself or another, income from trust property comprising shares or debentures, an interest in the shares or debentures in reversion or remainder or (as regards Scotland) in fee, are to be disregarded.

10. A person is to be treated as uninterested in shares or debentures if, and so long as, he holds them under the law in force in England and Wales as a bare trustee or as a custodian trustee, or under the law in force in Scotland, as a simple trustee.

11.—(1) There is to be disregarded an interest of a person subsisting by virtue of—

(a) any unit trust scheme which is an authorised unit trust scheme;

(b) a scheme made under section 22 or 22A of the Charities Act 1960 or section 24 or 25 of the Charities Act 1993, section 11 of the Trustee Investments Act 1961 or section 1 of the administration of Justice Act 1965; or

(c) the scheme set out in the Schedule to the Church Funds Investment Measure 1958.

(2) 'Unit trust scheme' and 'authorised unit trust scheme' have the meaning given in section 237 of the Financial Services and Markets Act 2000.

12. There is to be disregarded any interest—

(a) of the Church of Scotland General Trustees, the Church of Scotland Trust or the Church of Scotland Investors Trust in shares or debentures held by them;

(b) of any other person in shares or debentures held by those Trustees or those Trusts otherwise than as simple trustees.

'The Church of Scotland General Trustees' are the body incorporated by the order confirmed by the Church of Scotland (General Trustees) Order Confirmation Act 1921; and 'the Church of Scotland Trust' is the body incorporated by the order confirmed by the Church of Scotland Trust Order Confirmation Act 1932 and 'the Church of Scotland Investors Trust' is the body incorporated by Part III of the Order confirmed by the Church of Scotland (Properties and Investments) Order Confirmation Act 1994.

13.   Delivery to a person's order of shares or debentures in fulfilment of a contract for the purchase of them by him or in satisfaction of a right of his to call for their delivery, or failure to deliver shares or debentures in accordance with the terms of such a contract or on which such a right falls to be satisfied, is deemed to constitute an event in consequence of the occurrence of which he ceases to be interested in them, and so is the lapse of a person's right to call for delivery of shares or debentures.

PART II   PERIODS WITHIN WHICH OBLIGATIONS IMPOSED BY SECTION 324 MUST BE FULFILLED

14.—(1) An obligation imposed on a person by section 324(1) to notify an interest must, if he knows of the existence of the interest on the day on which he becomes a director, be fulfilled before the expiration of the period of 5 days beginning with the day following that day.

(2) Otherwise, the obligation must be fulfilled before the expiration of the period of 5 days beginning with the day following that on which the existence of the interest comes to his knowledge.

15.—(1) An obligation imposed on a person by section 324(2) to notify the occurrence of an event must, if at the time at which the event occurs he knows of its occurrence and of the fact that its occurrence gives rise to the obligation, be fulfilled before the expiration of the period of 5 days beginning with the day following that on which the event occurs.

(2) Otherwise, the obligation must be fulfilled before the expiration of a period of 5 days beginning with the day following that on which the fact that the occurrence of the event gives rise to the obligation comes to his knowledge.

16.   In reckoning, for purposes of paragraphs 14 and 15, any period of days, a day that is a Saturday or Sunday, or a bank holiday in any part of Great Britain, is to be disregarded.

PART III   CIRCUMSTANCES IN WHICH OBLIGATION IMPOSED BY SECTION 324 IS NOT DISCHARGED

17.—(1) Where an event of whose occurrence a director is, by virtue of section 324(2)(a), under obligation to notify a company consists of his entering into a contract for the purchase by him of shares or debentures, the obligation is not discharged in the absence of inclusion in the notice of a statement of the price to be paid by him under the contract.

(2) An obligation imposed on a director by section 324(2)(b) is not discharged in the absence of inclusion in the notice of the price to be received by him under the contract.

18.—(1) An obligation imposed on a director by virtue of section 324(2)(c) to notify a company is not discharged in the absence of inclusion in the notice of a statement of the consideration for the assignment (or, if it be the case that there is no consideration, that fact).

(2) Where an event of whose occurrence a director is, by virtue of section 324(2)(d), under obligation to notify a company consists in his assigning a right, the obligation is not discharged in the absence of inclusion in the notice of a similar statement.

19.—(1) Where an event of whose occurrence a director is, by virtue of section 324(2)(d), under obligation to notify a company consists in the grant to him of a right to subscribe for shares or debentures, the obligation is not discharged in the absence of inclusion in the notice of a statement of—

(a) the date on which the right was granted,
(b) the period during which or the time at which the right is exercisable,

   (c) the consideration for the grant (or, if it be the case that there is no consideration, that fact), and

   (d) the price to be paid for the shares or debentures.

(2) Where an event of whose occurrence a director is, by section 324(2)(d), under obligation to notify a company consists in the exercise of a right granted to him to subscribe for shares or debentures, the obligation is not discharged in the absence of inclusion in the notice of a statement of—

   (a) the number of shares or amount of debentures in respect of which the right was exercised, and

   (b) if it be the case that they were registered in his name, that fact, and, if not, the name or names of the person or persons in whose name or names they were registered, together (if they were registered in the names of 2 persons or more) with the number or amount registered in the name of each of them.

20.   In this Part, a reference to price paid or received includes any consideration other than money.

PART IV   PROVISIONS WITH RESPECT TO REGISTER OF
DIRECTORS' INTERESTS TO BE KEPT UNDER SECTION 325

21.   The register must be so made up that the entries in it against the several names appear in chronological order.

22.   An obligation imposed by section 325(2) to (4) must be fulfilled before the expiration of the period of 3 days beginning with the day after that on which the obligation arises; but in reckoning that period, a day which is a Saturday or Sunday or a bank holiday in any part of Great Britain is to be disregarded.

23.   The nature and extent of an interest recorded in the register of a director in any shares or debentures shall, if he so requires, be recorded in the register.

24.   The company is not, by virtue of anything done for the purposes of section 325 or this Part of this Schedule, affected with notice of, or put upon enquiry as to, the rights of any person in relation to any shares or debentures.

25.   The register shall—

   (a) if the company's register of members is kept at its registered office, be kept there;

   (b) if the company's register of members is not so kept, be kept at the company's registered office or at the place where its register of members is kept;

and shall be open to the inspection of any member of the company without charge and of any other person on payment of such fee as may be prescribed.

26.—(1) Any member of the company or other person may require a copy of the register, or of any part of it, on payment of such fee as may be prescribed.

(2) The company shall cause any copy so required by a person to be sent to him within the period of 10 days beginning with the day after that on which the requirement is received by the company.

27.   The company shall send notice in the prescribed form to the registrar of companies of the place where the register is kept and of any change in that place, save in a case in which it has at all times been kept at its registered office.

28.   Unless the register is in such a form as to constitute in itself an index, the company shall keep an index of the names inscribed in it, which shall—

   (a) in respect of each name, contain a sufficient indication to enable the information entered against it to be readily found; and

   (b) be kept at the same place as the register; and the company shall, within 14 days after the date on which a name is entered in the register, make any necessary alteration in the index.

29. The register shall be produced at the commencement of the company's annual general meeting and remain open and accessible during the continuance of the meeting to any person attending the meeting.

Section 362   SCHEDULE 14

OVERSEAS BRANCH REGISTERS

PART I COUNTRIES AND TERRITORIES IN WHICH
OVERSEAS BRANCH REGISTER MAY BE KEPT

Northern Ireland
Any part of Her Majesty's dominions outside the United Kingdom, the Channel Islands or the Isle of Man
  Bangladesh
  Cyprus
  Dominica
  The Gambia
  Ghana
  Guyana
  The Hong Kong Special Administrative Region of the People's Republic of China
  India
  Kenya
  Kiribati
  Lesotho
  Malawi
  Malaysia
  Malta
  Nigeria
  Pakistan
  Republic of Ireland
  Seychelles
  Sierra Leone
  Singapore
  South Africa
  Sri Lanka
  Swaziland
  Trinidad and Tobago
  Uganda
  Zimbabwe

PART II GENERAL PROVISIONS WITH RESPECT TO
OVERSEAS BRANCH REGISTERS

1.—(1) A company keeping an overseas branch register shall give to the registrar of companies notice in the prescribed form of the situation of the office where any overseas branch register is kept and of any change in its situation, and, if it is discontinued, of its discontinuance.

(2) Any such notice shall be given within 14 days of the opening of the office or of the change or discontinuance, as the case may be.

(3) If default is made in complying with this paragraph, the company and every officer of it who is in default is liable to a fine and, for continued contravention, to a daily default fine.

2.—(1) An overseas branch register is deemed to be part of the company's register of members ('the principal register').

(2) It shall be kept in the same manner in which the principal register is by this Act required to be kept, except that the advertisement before closing the register shall be inserted in a newspaper circulating in the district where the overseas branch register is kept.

3.—(1) A competent court in a country or territory where an overseas branch register is kept may exercise the same jurisdiction of rectifying the register as is under this Act exercisable by the court in Great Britain; and the offences of refusing inspection or copies of the register, and of authorising or permitting the refusal, may be prosecuted summarily before any tribunal having summary criminal jurisdiction.

(2) This paragraph extends only to those countries and territories where, immediately before the coming into force of this Act, provision to the same effect made by section 120(2) of the Companies Act 1948 had effect as part of the local law.

4.—(1) The company shall—
(a) transmit to its registered office a copy of every entry in its overseas branch register as soon as may be after the entry is made, and
(b) cause to be kept at the place where the company's principal register is kept a duplicate of its overseas branch register duly entered up from time to time.

Every such duplicate is deemed for all purposes of this Act to be part of the principal register.

(2) If default is made in complying with sub-paragraph (1), the company and every officer of it who is in default is liable to a fine and, for continued contravention, to a daily default fine.

(3) Where, by virtue of section 353(1)(b), the principal register is kept at the office of some person other than the company, and by reason of any default of his the company fails to comply with sub-paragraph (1)(b) above he is liable to the same penalty as if he were an officer of the company who was in default.

5. Subject to the above provisions with respect to the duplicate register, the shares registered in an overseas branch register shall be distinguished from those registered in the principal register; and no transaction with respect to any shares registered in an overseas branch register shall, during the continuance of that registration, be registered in any other register.

6. A company may discontinue to keep an overseas branch register, and thereupon all entries in that register shall be transferred to some other overseas branch register kept by the company in the same country or territory, or to the principal register.

7. Subject to the provisions of this Act, any company may, by its articles, make such provisions as it thinks fit respecting the keeping of overseas branch registers.

8. An instrument of transfer of a share registered in an overseas branch register (other than such a register kept in Northern Ireland) is deemed a transfer of property situated outside the United Kingdom *and, unless executed in a part of the United Kingdom, is exempt from stamp duty chargeable in Great Britain.*

[*The words in italics in para. 8 will be repealed when the relevant provision of the Finance Act 1990, sch. 19, part VI, is brought into force.*]

Section 381A   SCHEDULE 15A
WRITTEN RESOLUTIONS OF PRIVATE COMPANIES

PART I   EXCEPTIONS

1. Section 381A does not apply to—
(a) a resolution under section 303 removing a director before the expiration of his period of office, or
(b) a resolution under section 391 removing an auditor before the expiration of his term of office.

PART II   ADAPTATION OF PROCEDURAL REQUIREMENTS

Introductory

2.—(1) In this Part of this Schedule (which adapts certain requirements of this Act in relation to proceedings under section 381A)—

   (a) a 'written resolution' means a resolution agreed to, or proposed to be agreed to, in accordance with that section, and
   (b) a 'relevant member' means a member by whom, or on whose behalf, the resolution is required to be signed in accordance with that section.

(2) A written resolution is not effective if any of the requirements of this Part of this Schedule is not complied with.

Section 95 (disapplication of pre-emption rights)

3.—(1) The following adaptations have effect in relation to a written resolution under section 95(2) (disapplication of pre-emption rights), or renewing a resolution under that provision.

(2) So much of section 95(5) as requires the circulation of a written statement by the directors with a notice of meeting does not apply, but such a statement must be supplied to each relevant member at or before the time at which the resolution is supplied to him for signature.

(3) Section 95(6) (offences) applies in relation to the inclusion in any such statement of matter which is misleading, false or deceptive in a material particular.

Section 155 (financial assistance for purchase of company's own shares or those of holding company)

4.   In relation to a written resolution giving approval under section 155(4) or (5) (financial assistance for purchase of company's own shares or those of holding company), section 157(4)(a) (documents to be available at meeting) does not apply, but the documents referred to in that provision must be supplied to each relevant member at or before the time at which the resolution is supplied to him for signature.

Sections 164, 165 and 167 (authority for off-market purchase or contingent purchase contract of company's own shares)

5.—(1) The following adaptations have effect in relation to a written resolution—

   (a) conferring authority to make an off-market purchase of the company's own shares under section 164(2),
   (b) conferring authority to vary a contract for an off-market purchase of the company's own shares under section 164(7), or
   (c) varying, revoking or renewing any such authority under section 164(3).

(2) Section 164(5) (resolution ineffective if passed by exercise of voting rights by member holding shares to which the resolution relates) does not apply; but for the purposes of section 381A(1) a member holding shares to which the resolution relates shall not be regarded as a member who would be entitled to attend and vote.

(3) Section 164(6) (documents to be available at company's registered office and at meeting) does not apply, but the documents referred to in that provision and, where that provision applies by virtue of section 164(7), the further documents referred to in that provision must be supplied to each relevant member at or before the time at which the resolution is supplied to him for signature.

(4) The above adaptations also have effect in relation to a written resolution in relation to which the provisions of section 164(3) to (7) apply by virtue of—

(a) section 165(2) (authority for contingent purchase contract), or

(b) section 167(2) (approval of release of rights under contract approved under section 164 or 165).

Section 173 (approval for payment out of capital)

6.—(1) The following adaptations have effect in relation to a written resolution giving approval under section 173(2) (redemption or purchase of company's own shares out of capital).

(2) Section 174(2) (resolution ineffective if passed by exercise of voting rights by member holding shares to which the resolution relates) does not apply; but for the purposes of section 381A(1) a member holding shares to which the resolution relates shall not be regarded as a member who would be entitled to attend and vote.

(3) Section 174(4) (documents to be available at meeting) does not apply, but the documents referred to in that provision must be supplied to each relevant member at or before the time at which the resolution is supplied to him for signature.

Section 319 (approval of director's service contract)

7. In relation to a written resolution approving any such term as is mentioned in section 319(1) (director's contract of employment for more than five years), section 319(5) (documents to be available at company's registered office and at meeting) does not apply, but the documents referred to in that provision must be supplied to each relevant member at or before the time at which the resolution is supplied to him for signature.

Section 337 (funding of director's expenditure in performing his duties)

8. In relation to a written resolution giving approval under section 337(3)(a) (funding a director's expenditure in performing his duties), the requirement of that provision that certain matters be disclosed at the meeting at which the resolution is passed does not apply, but those matters must be disclosed to each relevant member at or before the time at which the resolution is supplied to him for signature.

Section 730

SCHEDULE 24
PUNISHMENT OF OFFENCES UNDER THIS ACT

Section of Act creating offence	General nature of offence	Mode of prosecution	Punishment	Daily default fine (where applicable)
6(3)	Company failing to deliver to registrar notice or other document, following alteration of its objects.	Summary.	One-fifth of the statutory maximum.	One-fiftieth of the statutory maximum.
12(3B)	Person making false statement under section 12(3A) which he knows to be false or does not believe to be true.	1. On indictment. 2. Summary.	2 years or a fine; or both. 6 months or the statutory maximum; or both.	
18(3)	Company failing to register change in memorandum or articles.	Summary	One-fifth of the statutory maximum.	One-fiftieth of the statutory maximum.
19(2)	Company failing to send to one of its members a copy of the memorandum or articles, when so required by the member.	Summary.	One-fifth of the statutory maximum.	
20(2)	Where company's memorandum altered, company issuing copy of the memorandum without the alteration.	Summary.	One-fifth of the statutory maximum for each occasion on which copies are so issued after the date of the alteration.	
28(5)	Company failing to change name on direction of Secretary of State.	Summary.	One-fifth of the statutory maximum.	One-fiftieth of the statutory maximum.
30(5C)	Person making false statement under section 30(5A) which he knows to be false or does not believe to be true.	1. On indictment. 2. Summary.	2 years or a fine; or both. 6 months or the statutory maximum; or both.	

Continued

Schedule 24 continued

Section of Act creating offence	General nature of offence	Mode of prosecution	Punishment	Daily default fine (where applicable)
31(5)	Company altering its memorandum or articles, so ceasing to be exempt from having 'limited' as part of its name.	Summary.	The statutory maximum.	One-tenth of the statutory maximum.
31(6)	Company failing to change name, on Secretary of State's direction, so as to have 'limited' (or Welsh equivalent) at the end.	Summary.	One-fifth of the statutory maximum.	One-fiftieth of the statutory maximum.
32(4)	Company failing to comply with Secretary of State's direction to change its name, on grounds that the name is misleading.	Summary.	One-fifth of the statutory maximum.	One-fiftieth of the statutory maximum.
33	Trading under misleading name (use of 'public limited company' or Welsh equivalent when not so entitled); purporting to be a private company.	Summary.	One-fifth of the statutory maximum.	One-fiftieth of the statutory maximum.
34	Trading or carrying on business with improper use of 'limited' or 'cyfyngedig'.	Summary.	One-fifth of the statutory maximum.	One-fiftieth of the statutory maximum.
43(3B)	Person making false statement under section 43(3A) which he knows to be false or does not believe to be true.	1. On indictment. 2. Summary.	2 years or a fine; or both. 6 months or the statutory maximum; or both.	
49(8B)	Person making false statement under section 49(8A) which he knows to be false or does not believe to be true.	1. On indictment. 2. Summary.	2 years or a fine; or both. 6 months or the statutory maximum; or both.	
54(10)	Public company failing to give notice, or copy of court order, to registrar, concerning application to re-register as private company.	Summary.	One-fifth of the statutory maximum.	One-fiftieth of the statutory maximum.

Section	General nature of offence	Mode of prosecution	Punishment	Daily default fine
80(9)	Directors exercising company's power of allotment without the authority required by section 80(1).	1. On indictment. 2. Summary.	A fine. The statutory maximum.	One-tenth of the statutory maximum.
81(2)	Private limited company offering shares to the public, or allotting shares with a view to their being so offered. [See note 1 at the end of the schedule.]	1. On indictment. 2. Summary.	A fine. The statutory maximum.	
82(5)	Allotting shares or debentures before third day after issue of prospectus. [See note 1 at the end of the schedule.]	1. On indictment. 2. Summary.	A fine. The statutory maximum.	
86(6)	Company failing to keep money in separate bank accounts, where received in pursuance of prospectus stating that stock exchange listing is to be applied for. [See note 1 at the end of the schedule.]	1. On indictment. 2. Summary.	A fine. The statutory maximum.	
87(4)	Offeror of shares for sale failing to keep proceeds in separate bank account. [See note 1 at the end of the schedule.]	1. On indictment. 2. Summary.	A fine. The statutory maximum.	
88(5)	Officer of company failing to deliver return of allotments, etc., to registrar.	1. On indictment. 2. Summary.	A fine. The statutory maximum.	
95(6)	Knowingly or recklessly authorising or permitting misleading, false or deceptive material in statement by directors under section 95(5).	1. On indictment. 2. Summary.	2 years or a fine; or both. 6 months or the statutory maximum; or both	
97(4)	Company failing to deliver to registrar the prescribed form disclosing amount or rate of share commission [See note 1 at the end of the schedule.]	Summary.	One-fifth of the statutory maximum.	
110(2)	Making misleading, false or deceptive statement in connection with valuation under section 103 or 104.	1. On indictment. 2. Summary.	2 years or a fine; or both. 6 months or the statutory maximum; or both	
111(3)	Officer of company failing to deliver copy of asset valuation report to registrar.	1. On indictment. 2. Summary.	A fine. The statutory maximum.	One-tenth of the statutory maximum.

Continued

Schedule 24 continued

Section of Act creating offence	General nature of offence	Mode of prosecution	Punishment	Daily default fine (where applicable)
111(4)	Company failing to deliver to registrar copy of resolution under section 104(4), with respect to transfer of an asset as consideration for allotment.	Summary.	One-fifth of the statutory maximum.	One-fiftieth of the statutory maximum.
114	Contravention of any of the provisions of sections 99 to 104, 106.	1. On indictment. 2. Summary.	A fine. The statutory maximum.	
117(7)	Company doing business or exercising borrowing powers contrary to section 117.	1. On indictment. 2. Summary.	A fine. The statutory maximum.	
117(7A)	Person making false statement under section 117(3A) which he knows to be false or does not believe to be true.	1. On indictment. 2. Summary.	2 years or a fine; or both. 6 months or the statutory maximum; or both.	
122(2)	Company failing to give notice to registrar of reorganisation of share capital.	Summary.	One-fifth of the statutory maximum.	One-fiftieth of the statutory maximum.
123(4)	Company failing to give notice to registrar of increase of share capital.	Summary.	One-fifth of the statutory maximum.	One-fiftieth of the statutory maximum.
127(5)	Company failing to forward to registrar copy of court order, when application made to cancel resolution varying shareholders' rights.	Summary.	One-fifth of the statutory maximum.	One-fiftieth of the statutory maximum.
128(5)	Company failing to send to registrar statement or notice required by section 128 (particulars of shares carrying special rights).	Summary.	One-fifth of the statutory maximum.	One-fiftieth of the statutory maximum.
129(4)	Company failing to deliver to registrar statement or notice required by section 129 (registration of newly created class rights).	Summary.	One-fifth of the statutory maximum.	One-fiftieth of the statutory maximum.

Section	General nature of offence	Mode of prosecution	Punishment	Daily default fine
141	Officer of company concealing name of creditor entitled to object to reduction of capital, or wilfully misrepresenting nature or amount of debt or claim, etc.	1. On indictment. 2. Summary.	A fine. The statutory maximum.	
142(2)	Director authorising or permitting non-compliance with section 142 (requirement to convene company meeting to consider serious loss of capital).	1. On indictment. 2. Summary.	A fine. The statutory maximum.	
143(2)	Company acquiring its own shares in breach of section 143.	1. On indictment.	In the case of the company, a fine. In the case of an officer of the company who is in default, 2 years or a fine; or both.	
		2. Summary.	In the case of the company, the statutory maximum. In the case of an officer of the company who is in default, 6 months or the statutory maximum; or both.	
149(2)	Company failing to cancel its own shares, acquired by itself, as required by section 146(2); or failing to apply for re-registration as private company as so required in the case there mentioned.	Summary.	One-fifth of the statutory maximum.	One-fiftieth of the statutory maximum.
151(3)	Company giving financial assistance towards acquisition of its own shares.	1. On indictment.	Where the company is convicted, a fine. Where an officer of the company is convicted, 2 years or a fine; or both.	

Continued

Schedule 24 continued

Section of Act creating offence	General nature of offence	Mode of prosecution	Punishment	Daily default fine (where applicable)
		2. Summary.	Where the company is convicted, the statutory maximum. Where an officer of the company is convicted, 6 months or the statutory maximum; or both.	
156(6)	Company failing to register statutory declaration or statement under section 155.	Summary.	The statutory maximum.	One-fiftieth of the statutory maximum.
156(7)	Director making statutory declaration or statement under section 155, without having reasonable grounds for opinion expressed in it.	1. On indictment. 2. Summary.	2 years or a fine; or both. 6 months or the statutory maximum; or both.	
162G	Contravention of any provision of sections 162A–162F (dealings by company in treasury shares, etc.).	1. On indictment. 2. Summary.	A fine. The statutory maximum.	
169(6)	Default by company's officer in delivering to registrar the return required by section 169 (disclosure by company of purchase of own shares).	1. On indictment. 2. Summary.	A fine. The statutory maximum.	
169(7)	Company failing to keep copy of contract, etc., at registered office; refusal of inspection to person demanding it.	Summary.	One-fifth of the statutory maximum.	One-tenth of the statutory maximum.
169A(4)	Default by company's officer in delivering to registrar the return required by section 169A (disclosure by company of cancellation or disposal of treasury shares).	1. On indictment. 2. Summary.	A fine. The statutory maximum.	One-fiftieth of the statutory maximum.
173(6)	Director making statutory declaration under section 173 without having reasonable grounds for the opinion expressed in the declaration.	1. On indictment. 2. Summary.	2 years or a fine; or both. 6 months or the statutory maximum; or both.	One-tenth of the statutory maximum.

175(7)	Refusal of inspection of statutory declaration and auditors' report under section 173, etc.	Summary.	One-fifth of the statutory maximum.	One-fiftieth of the statutory maximum.
176(4)	Company failing to give notice to registrar of application to court under section 176, or to register court order.	Summary.	One-fifth of the statutory maximum.	One-fiftieth of the statutory maximum.
183(6)	Company failing to send notice of refusal to register a transfer of shares or debentures.	Summary.	One-fifth of the statutory maximum.	One-fiftieth of the statutory maximum.
185(5)	Company default in compliance with section 185(1) (certificates to be made ready following allotment or transfer of shares, etc.).	Summary.	One-fifth of the statutory maximum.	One-fiftieth of the statutory maximum.
. . .				
191(4)	Refusal of inspection or copy of register of debenture-holders, etc.	Summary.	One-fifth of the statutory maximum.	One-fiftieth of the statutory maximum.
210(3)	Failure to discharge obligation of disclosure under Part VI; other forms of non-compliance with that Part.	1. On indictment. 2. Summary.	2 years or a fine; or both. 6 months or the statutory maximum; or both.	
211(10)	Company failing to keep register of interests disclosed under Part VI; other contraventions of section 211.	Summary.	One-fifth of the statutory maximum.	One-fiftieth of the statutory maximum.
214(5)	Company failing to exercise powers under section 212, when so required by the members.	1. On indictment. 2. Summary.	A fine. The statutory maximum.	
215(8)	Company default in compliance with section 215 (company report of investigation of shareholdings on members' requisition).	1. On indictment. 2. Summary.	A fine. The statutory maximum.	
216(3)	Failure to comply with company notice under section 212; making false statement in response, etc.	1. On indictment. 2. Summary.	2 years or a fine; or both. 6 months or the statutory maximum; or both.	

Continued

Schedule 24 continued

Section of Act creating offence	General nature of offence	Mode of prosecution	Punishment	Daily default fine (where applicable)
217(7)	Company failing to notify a person that he has been named as a shareholder; on removal of name from register, failing to alter associated index.	Summary.	One-fifth of the statutory maximum.	One-fiftieth of the statutory maximum.
218(3)	Improper removal of entry from register of interests disclosed; company failing to restore entry improperly removed.	Summary.	One-fifth of the statutory maximum.	For continued contravention of section 218(2) one-fiftieth of the statutory maximum.
219(3)	Refusal of inspection of register or report under Part VI; failure to send copy when required.	Summary.	One-fifth of the statutory maximum.	One-fiftieth of the statutory maximum.
221(5) or 222(4)	Company failing to keep accounting records (liability of officers).	1. On indictment. 2. Summary.	2 years or a fine; or both. 6 months or the statutory maximum; or both.	
222(6)	Officer of company failing to secure compliance with, or intentionally causing default under, section 222(5) (preservation of accounting records for requisite number of years).	1. On indictment. 2. Summary.	2 years or a fine; or both. 6 months or the statutory maximum; or both.	
231(6)	Company failing to annex to its annual return certain particulars required by Schedule 5 and not included in annual accounts.	Summary.	One-fifth of the statutory maximum.	One-fiftieth of the statutory maximum.
232(4)	Default by director or officer of a company in giving notice of matters relating to himself for purposes of Schedule 6 Part I.	Summary.	One-fifth of the statutory maximum.	
233(5)	Approving defective accounts.	1. On indictment. 2. Summary.	A fine. The statutory maximum.	
233(6)	Laying or delivery of unsigned balance sheet; circulating copies of balance sheet without signatures.	Summary.	One-fifth of the statutory maximum.	
234(5)	Non-compliance with Part VII, as to directors' report and its content; directors individually liable.	1. On indictment. 2. Summary.	A fine. The statutory maximum.	

Section	Offence	Mode of prosecution	Punishment	Daily default fine
234A(4)	Laying, circulating or delivering directors' report without required signature.	Summary.	One-fifth of the statutory maximum.	
234B(3)	Non-compliance with requirements as to preparation and content of directors' remuneration report.	Summary.	One-fifth of the statutory maximum.	
234B(6)	Default in complying with section 234B(5).	Summary.	One-fifth of the statutory maximum.	
236(4)	Laying, circulating or delivering auditors' report without required signature.	Summary.	One-fifth of the statutory maximum.	
238(5)	Failing to send company's annual accounts, directors' report and auditors' report to those entitled to receive them.	1. On indictment. 2. Summary.	A fine. The statutory maximum.	
239(3)	Company failing to supply copy of accounts and reports to shareholder on his demand.	Summary.	One-fifth of the statutory maximum.	One-fiftieth of the statutory maximum.
240(6)	Failure to comply with requirements in connection with publication of accounts.	Summary.	One-fifth of the statutory maximum.	
241(2) or 242(2)	Director in default as regards duty to lay and deliver company's annual accounts, directors' report and auditors' report.	Summary.	The statutory maximum.	One-tenth of the statutory maximum.
241A(9)	Default in complying with the requirements of section 241A(3) and (4).	Summary.	One-fifth of the statutory maximum.	
241A(10)	Failure to put resolution to vote of meeting.	Summary.	One-fifth of the statutory maximum.	
251(6)	Failure to comply with requirements in relation to summary financial statements.	Summary.	One-fifth of the statutory maximum.	
288(4)	Default in complying with section 288 (keeping register of directors and secretaries, refusal of inspection).	Summary.	The statutory maximum.	One-tenth of the statutory maximum.
291(5)	Acting as director of a company without having the requisite share qualification.	Summary.	One-fifth of the statutory maximum.	One-fiftieth of the statutory maximum.

Continued

Schedule 24 continued

Section of Act creating offence	General nature of offence	Mode of prosecution	Punishment	Daily default fine (where applicable)
294(3)	Director failing to give notice of his attaining retirement age; acting as director under appointment invalid due to his attaining it.	Summary.	One-fiftieth of the statutory maximum.	One-fiftieth of the statutory maximum.
305(3)	Company default in complying with section 305 (directors' names to appear on company correspondence, etc.).	Summary.	One-fifth of the statutory maximum.	
306(4)	Failure to state that liability of proposed director or manager is unlimited; failure to give notice of that fact to person accepting office.	1. On indictment. 2. Summary.	A fine. The statutory maximum.	
314(3)	Director failing to comply with section 314 (duty to disclose compensation payable on takeover, etc.); a person's failure to include required particulars in a notice he has to give of such matters.	Summary.	One-fifth of the statutory maximum.	
317(7)	Director failing to disclose interest in contract.	1. On indictment. 2. Summary.	A fine. The statutory maximum.	
318(8)	Company default in complying with section 318(1) or (5) (directors' service contracts to be open to inspection); 14 days' default in complying with section 318(4) (notice to registrar as to where copies of contracts and memoranda are kept); refusal of inspection required under section 318(7).	Summary.	One-fifth of the statutory maximum.	One-fiftieth of the statutory maximum.
322B(4)	Terms of unwritten contract between sole member of a private company limited by shares or by guarantee and the company not set out in a written memorandum or recorded in minutes of a directors' meeting.	Summary.	Level 5 on the standard scale.	

323(2)	Director dealing in options to buy or sell company's listed shares or debentures.	1. On indictment. 2. Summary.	2 years or a fine; or both. 6 months or the statutory maximum; or both.	
324(7)	Director failing to notify interest in company's shares; making false statement in purported notification.	1. On indictment. 2. Summary.	2 years or a fine; or both. 6 months or the statutory maximum; or both.	
326(2), (3), (4), (5)	Various defaults in connection with company register of directors' interests.	Summary.	One-fifth of the statutory maximum.	Except in the case of section 326(5), one-fiftieth of the statutory maximum.
328(6)	Director failing to notify company that members of his family have, or have exercised, options to buy shares or debentures; making false statement in purported notification.	1. On indictment. 2. Summary.	2 years or a fine; or both. 6 months or the statutory maximum; or both.	
329(3)	Company failing to notify investment exchange of acquisition of its securities by a director.	Summary.	One-fifth of the statutory maximum.	One-fiftieth of the statutory maximum.
342(1)	Director of relevant company authorising or permitting company to enter into transaction or arrangement, knowing or suspecting it to contravene section 330.	1. On indictment. 2. Summary.	2 years or a fine; or both. 6 months or the statutory maximum; or both.	
342(2)	Relevant company entering into transaction arrangement for a director in contravention of section 330.	1. On indictment. 2. Summary.	2 years or a fine; or both. 6 months or the statutory maximum; or both.	
342(3)	Procuring a relevant company to enter into transaction or arrangement known to be contrary to section 330.	1. On indictment. 2. Summary.	2 years or a fine; or both. 6 months or the statutory maximum; or both.	

Continued

Schedule 24 continued

Section of Act creating offence	General nature of offence	Mode of prosecution	Punishment	Daily default fine (where applicable)
343(8)	Company failing to maintain register of transactions, etc., made with and for directors and not disclosed in company accounts; failing to make register available at registered office or at company meeting.	1. On indictment. 2. Summary.	A fine. The statutory maximum.	
348(2)	Company failing to paint or affix name; failing to keep it painted or affixed.	Summary.	One-fifth of the statutory maximum.	In the case of failure to keep the name painted or affixed, one-fiftieth of the statutory maximum.
349(2)	Company failing to have name on business correspondence, invoices, etc.	Summary.	One-fifth of the statutory maximum.	
349(3)	Officer of company issuing business letter or document not bearing company's name.	Summary.	One-fifth of the statutory maximum.	
349(4)	Officer of company signing cheque, bill of exchange, etc. on which company's name not mentioned.	Summary.	One-fifth of the statutory maximum.	
350(1)	Company failing to have its name engraved on seal.	Summary.	One-fifth of the statutory maximum.	
350(2)	Officer or company, etc., using company seal without name engraved on it.	Summary.	One-fifth of the statutory maximum.	
351(5)(a)	Company failing to comply with section 351(1) or (2) (matters to be stated on business correspondence, etc.).	Summary.	One-fifth of the statutory maximum.	
351(5)(b)	Officer or agent of company issuing, or authorising issue of, business document not complying with those subsections.	Summary.	One-fifth of the statutory maximum.	
351(5)(c)	Contravention of section 351(3) or (4) (information in English to be stated on Welsh company's business correspondence, etc.).	Summary.	One-fifth of the statutory maximum.	For contravention of section 351(3), one-fiftieth of the statutory maximum.

Section	Offence	Mode of prosecution	Punishment	Daily default fine
352(5)	Company default in complying with section 352 (requirement to keep register of members and their particulars).	Summary.	One-fiftieth of the statutory maximum.	One-fiftieth of the statutory maximum.
352A(3)	Company default in complying with section 352A (statement that company has only one member).	Summary.	Level 2 on the standard scale.	One-tenth of level 2 on the standard scale.
353(4)	Company failing to send notice to registrar as to place where register of members is kept.	Summary.	One-fifth of the statutory maximum.	One-fiftieth of the statutory maximum.
354(4)	Company failing to keep index of members.	Summary.	One-fifth of the statutory maximum.	One-fiftieth of the statutory maximum.
356(5)	Refusal of inspection of members' register; failure to send copy on requisition.	Summary.	One-fifth of the statutory maximum.	One-tenth of the statutory maximum.
363(3)	Company with share capital failing to make annual return.	Summary.	The statutory maximum.	One-tenth of the statutory maximum.
364(4)	Company without share capital failing to complete and register annual return in due time.	Summary.	The statutory maximum.	One-tenth of the statutory maximum.
366(4)	Company default in holding annual general meeting.	1. On indictment. 2. Summary.	A fine. The statutory maximum.	
367(3)	Company default in complying with Secretary of State's direction to hold company meeting.	1. On indictment. 2. Summary.	A fine. The statutory maximum.	
367(5)	Company failing to register resolution that meeting held under section 367 is to be its annual general meeting.	Summary.	One-fifth of the statutory maximum.	One-fiftieth of the statutory maximum.
372(4)	Failure to give notice, to member entitled to vote at company meeting, that he may do so by proxy.	Summary.	One-fifth of the statutory maximum.	
372(6)	Officer of company authorising or permitting issue of irregular invitation to appoint proxies.	Summary.	One-fifth of the statutory maximum.	
376(7)	Officer of company in default as to circulation of members' resolutions for company meeting.	1. On indictment. 2. Summary.	A fine. The statutory maximum.	

Continued

Schedule 24 continued

Section of Act creating offence	General nature of offence	Mode of prosecution	Punishment	Daily default fine (where applicable)
380(5)	Company failing to comply with section 380 (copies of certain resolutions etc. to be sent to registrar of companies).	Summary.	One-fifth of the statutory maximum.	One-fiftieth of the statutory maximum.
380(6)	Company failing to include copy of resolution to which section 380 applies in articles; failing to forward copy to member on request.	Summary.	One-fifth of the statutory maximum for each occasion on which copies are issued or, as the case may be, requested.	
381B(2)	Director or secretary of company failing to notify auditors of proposed written resolution.	Summary.	Level 3 on the standard scale.	
382(5)	Company failing to keep minutes of proceedings at company and board meetings, etc.	Summary.	One-fifth of the statutory maximum.	One-fiftieth of the statutory maximum.
382B(2)	Failure of sole member to provide the company with a written record of decision.	Summary.	Level 2 on the standard scale.	
383(4)	Refusal of inspection of minutes of general meeting; failure to send copy of minutes on member's request.	Summary.	One-fifth of the statutory maximum.	
387(2)	Company failing to give Secretary of State notice of non-appointment of auditors.	Summary.	One-fifth of the statutory maximum.	One-fiftieth of the statutory maximum.
389(10)	Person acting as company auditor knowing himself to be disqualified; failing to give notice vacating office when he becomes disqualified. [*See note 2 at the end of the schedule.*]	1. On indictment. 2. Summary.	A fine. The statutory maximum.	One-tenth of the statutory maximum.
389A(2)	Officer of company making false, misleading or deceptive statement to auditors.	1. On indictment. 2. Summary.	2 years or a fine; or both. 6 months or the statutory maximum; or both.	
389A(3)	Subsidiary undertaking or its auditor failing to give information to auditors of parent company.	Summary.	One-fifth of the statutory maximum.	

389A(4)	Parent company failing to obtain from subsidiary undertaking information for purposes of audit.	Summary.	One-fifth of the statutory maximum.	One-fiftieth of the statutory maximum.
391(2)	Failing to give notice to registrar of removal of auditor.	Summary.	One-fifth of the statutory maximum.	One-tenth of the statutory maximum.
392(3)	Company failing to forward notice of auditor's resignation to registrar.	1. On indictment. 2. Summary.	A fine. The statutory maximum.	
392A(5)	Directors failing to convene meeting requisitioned by resigning auditor.	1. On indictment. 2. Summary.	A fine. The statutory maximum.	
394A(1)	Person ceasing to hold office as auditor failing to deposit statement as to circumstances.	1. On indictment. 2. Summary.	A fine. The statutory maximum.	
394A(4)	Company failing to comply with requirements as to statement of person ceasing to hold office as auditor.	1. On indictment. 2. Summary.	A fine. The statutory maximum.	One-tenth of the statutory maximum.
399(3)	Company failing to send to registrar particulars of charge created by it, or of issue of debentures which requires registration. [*See note 3 at the end of the schedule.*]	1. On indictment. 2. Summary.	A fine. The statutory maximum.	One-tenth of the statutory aximum.
400(4)	Company failing to send to registrar particulars of charge on property acquired. [*See note 3 at the end of the schedule.*]	1. On indictment. 2. Summary.	A fine. The statutory maximum.	One-tenth of the statutory maximum.
402(3)	Authorising or permitting delivery of debenture or certificate of debenture stock, without endorsement on it of certificate of registration of charge. [*See note 3 at the end of the schedule.*]	Summary.	One-fifth of the statutory maximum.	
403(2A)	Person making false statement under section 403(1A) which he knows to be false or does not believe to be true.	1. On indictment. 2. Summary.	2 years or a fine; or both. 6 months or the statutory maximum; or both.	

Continued

Schedule 24 continued

Section of Act creating offence	General nature of offence	Mode of prosecution	Punishment	Daily default fine (where applicable)
405(4)	Failure to give notice to registrar of appointment of receiver or manager, or of his ceasing to act. [*See note 3 at the end of the schedule.*]	Summary.	One-fifth of the statutory maximum.	One-fiftieth of the statutory maximum.
407(3)	Authorising or permitting omission from company register of charges. [*See note 3 at the end of the schedule.*]	1. On indictment. 2. Summary.	A fine. The statutory maximum.	
408(3)	Officer of company refusing inspection of charging instrument, or of register of charges. [*See note 3 at the end of the schedule.*]	Summary.	One-fifth of the statutory maximum.	One-fiftieth of the statutory maximum. . . .
425(4)	Company failing to annex to memorandum court order sanctioning compromise or arrangement with creditors.	Summary.	One-fifth of the statutory maximum.	
426(6)	Company failing to comply with requirements of section 426 (information to members and creditors about compromise or arrangement).	1. On indictment. 2. Summary.	A fine. The statutory maximum.	
426(7)	Director or trustee for debenture holders failing to give notice to company of matters necessary for purposes of section 426.	Summary.	One-fifth of the statutory maximum.	
427(5)	Failure to deliver to registrar office copy of court order under section 427 (company reconstruction or amalgamation).	Summary.	One-fifth of the statutory maximum.	One-fiftieth of the statutory maximum.
429(6)	Offeror failing to send copy of notice or making statutory declaration knowing it to be false, etc.	1. On indictment. 2. Summary.	2 years or a fine; or both. 6 months or the statutory maximum; or both.	One-fiftieth of the statutory maximum.

Section	Offence	Mode of prosecution	Punishment	Daily default fine
430A(6)	Offeror failing to give notice of rights to minority shareholder.	1. On indictment. 2. Summary.	A fine. The statutory maximum.	One-fiftieth of the statutory maximum.
444(3)	Failing to give Secretary of State, when required to do so, information about interests in shares, etc.; giving false information.	1. On indictment. 2. Summary.	2 years or a fine; or both. 6 months or the statutory maximum; or both.	
447(6)	Failure to comply with requirement to produce documents imposed by Secretary of State under section 447.	1. On indictment. 2. Summary.	A fine. The statutory maximum.	
448(7)	Obstructing the exercise of any rights conferred by a warrant or failing to comply with a requirement imposed under subsection (3)(d).	1. On indictment. 2. Summary.	A fine. The statutory maximum.	
449(2)	Wrongful disclosure of information or document obtained under section 447 or 448.	1. On indictment. 2. Summary.	2 years or a fine; or both. 6 months or the statutory maximum; or both.	
450	Destroying or mutilating company documents; falsifying such documents or making false entries; parting with such documents or altering them or making omissions.	1. On indictment. 2. Summary.	7 years or a fine; or both. 6 months or the statutory maximum; or both.	
451	Making false statement or explanation in purported compliance with section 447.	1. On indictment. 2. Summary.	2 years or a fine; or both. 6 months or the statutory maximum; or both.	
455(1)	Exercising a right to dispose of, or vote in respect of, shares which are subject to restrictions under Part XV; failing to give notice in respect of shares so subject; entering into agreement void under section 454(2), (3).	1. On indictment. 2. Summary.	A fine. The statutory maximum.	

Continued

Schedule 24 continued

Section of Act creating offence	General nature of offence	Mode of prosecution	Punishment	Daily default fine (where applicable)
455(2)	Issuing shares in contravention of restrictions of Part XV.	1. On indictment 2. Summary.	A fine. The statutory maximum.	
458	Being a party to carrying on company's business with intent to defraud creditors, or for any fraudulent purpose.	1. On indictment. 2. Summary.	7 years or a fine; or both. 6 months or the statutory maximum; or both.	
461(5)	Failure to register office copy of court order under Part XVII altering, or giving leave to alter, company's memorandum.	Summary.	One-fifth of the statutory maximum.	One-fiftieth of the statutory maximum.
651(3)	Person obtaining court order to declare company's dissolution void, then failing to register the order.	Summary.	One-fifth of the statutory maximum.	One-fiftieth of the statutory maximum.
652E(1)	Person breaching or failing to perform duty imposed by section 652B or 652C.	1. On indictment. 2. Summary.	A fine. The statutory maximum.	
652E(2)	Person failing to perform duty imposed by section 652B(6) or 652C(2) with intent to conceal the making of application under section 652A.	1. On indictment. 2. Summary.	7 years or a fine; or both. 6 months or the statutory maximum; or both.	
652F(1)	Person furnishing false or misleading information in connection with application under section 652A.	1. On indictment. 2. Summary.	A fine. The statutory maximum.	
652F(2)	Person making false application under section 652A.	1. On indictment. 2. Summary.	A fine. The statutory maximum.	
685(6A)	Person making false statement under section 685(4A) which he knows to be false or does not believe to be true.	1. On indictment. 2. Summary.	2 years or a fine; or both. 6 months or the statutory maximum; or both.	

686(3A)	Person making false statement under section 686(2A) which he knows to be false or does not believe to be true.	1. On indictment. 2. Summary.	2 years or a fine; or both. 6 months or the statutory maximum; or both.	
...				
722(3)	Company failing to comply with section 722(2), as regards the manner of keeping registers, minute books and accounting records.	Summary.	One-fifth of the statutory maximum.	One-fiftieth of the statutory maximum.
Sch. 14, Pt II, para. 1(3)	Company failing to give notice of location of overseas branch register, etc.	Summary.	One-fifth of the statutory maximum.	One-fiftieth of the statutory maximum.
Sch. 14, Pt. II, para. 4(2)	Company failing to transmit to its registered office in Great Britain copies of entries in overseas branch register, or to keep a duplicate of overseas branch register.	Summary.	One-fifth of the statutory maximum.	One-fiftieth of the statutory maximum.
...				

[Note 1. The Financial Services Act 1986, sch. 17, part I, has repealed the entries relating to ss. 81(2), 82(5), 86(6), 87(4) and 97(4) to the extent to which they would apply in relation to: (a) any investment which is listed or the subject of an application for listing in accordance with part IV of the Financial Services Act 1986 (Commencement No. 3) Order 1986 (SI 1986/2246), art. 5 and sch. 4); (b) a prospectus offering for subscription, or any form of application for, units in a body corporate which is a recognised scheme (Financial Services Act 1986 (Commencement) (No. 8) Order 1988 (SI 1988/740), art. 2 and sch.). The extent of the repeal of the entries in sch. 24 for ss. 82(5), 86(6) and 87(4) is, through oversight, no longer the same as the extent of the repeal of ss. 82, 86 and 87 themselves.

Note 2. The entry relating to s. 389(10) will be repealed when the relevant provision of the Companies Act 1989, sch. 14, is brought into force. Section 389 itself was repealed as from 1 October 1991 (Companies Act 1989 (Commencement No. 12 and Transitional Provision) Order 1991 (SI 1991/1996), art. 2(1)(c)(i)).

Note 3. The entries relating to ss. 399(3) to 408(3) would be replaced by new provisions if para. 2 of sch. 16 to the Companies Act 1989 were brought into force.]

Business Names Act 1985
(1985, c. 7)

An Act to consolidate certain enactments relating to the names under which persons may carry on business in Great Britain. [11 March 1985]

1   Persons subject to this Act

(1) This Act applies to any person who has a place of business in Great Britain and who carries on business in Great Britain under a name which—

 (a) in the case of a partnership, does not consist of the surnames of all partners who are individuals and the corporate names of all partners who are bodies corporate without any addition other than an addition permitted by this Act;

 (b) in the case of an individual, does not consist of his surname without any addition other than one so permitted;

 (c) in the case of a company, being a company which is capable of being wound up under the Companies Act 1985, does not consist of its corporate name without any addition other than one so permitted;

 (d) in the case of a limited liability partnership, does not consist of its corporate name without any addition other than one so permitted.

(2) The following are permitted additions for the purposes of subsection (1)—

 (a) in the case of a partnership, the forenames of individual partners or the initials of those forenames or, where two or more individual partners have the same surname, the addition of 's' at the end of that surname; or

 (b) in the case of an individual, his forename or its initial;

 (c) in any case, any addition merely indicating that the business is carried on in succession to a former owner of the business.

2   Prohibition of use of certain business names

(1) Subject to the following subsections, a person to whom this Act applies shall not, without the written approval of the Secretary of State, carry on business in Great Britain under a name which—

 (a) would be likely to give the impression that the business is connected with Her Majesty's Government, with any part of the Scottish Administration, or with any local authority; or

 (b) includes any word or expression for the time being specified in regulations made under this Act.

(2) Subsection (1) does not apply to the carrying on of a business by a person—

 (a) to whom the business has been transferred on or after 26 February 1982; and

 (b) who carries on the business under the name which was its lawful business name immediately before that transfer,

during the period of 12 months beginning with the date of that transfer.

(3) Subsection (1) does not apply to the carrying on of a business by a person who—

 (a) carried on that business immediately before 26 February 1982; and

 (b) continues to carry it on under the name which immediately before that date was its lawful business name.

(4) A person who contravenes subsection (1) is guilty of an offence.

3   Words and expressions requiring Secretary of State's approval

(1) The Secretary of State may by regulations—

 (a) specify words or expressions for the use of which as or as part of a business name his approval is required by section 2(1)(b); and

 (b) in relation to any such word or expression, specify a Government department or other body as the relevant body for purposes of the following subsection.

(2) Where a person to whom this Act applies proposes to carry on a business under a name which is or includes any such word or expression, and a Government department or other body is specified under subsection (1)(b) in relation to that word or expression, that person shall—

    (a) request (in writing) the relevant body to indicate whether (and if so why) it has any objections to the proposal; and

    (b) submit to the Secretary of State a statement that such a request has been made and a copy of any response received from the relevant body.

4   Disclosure required of persons using business names

(1) A person to whom this Act applies shall—

    (a) subject to subsections (3) and (3A), state in legible characters on all business letters, written orders for goods or services to be supplied to the business, invoices and receipts issued in the course of the business and written demands for payment of debts arising in the course of the business—

        (i)   in the case of a partnership, the name of each partner,

        (ii) in the case of an individual, his name,

        (iii) in the case of a company, its corporate name,

        (iiia) in the case of a limited liability partnership, its corporate name and the name of each member, and

        (iv) in relation to each person so named, an address in Great Britain at which service of any document relating in any way to the business will be effective; and

    (b) in any premises where the business is carried on and to which the customers of the business or suppliers of any goods or services to the business have access, display in a prominent position so that it may easily be read by such customers or suppliers a notice containing such names and addresses.

(2) A person to whom this Act applies shall secure that the names and addresses required by subsection (1)(a) to be stated on his business letters, or which would have been so required but for subsection (3) or (3A), are immediately given, by written notice to a person with whom anything is done or discussed in the course of the business and who asks for such names and addresses.

(3) Subsection (1)(a) does not apply in relation to any document issued by a partnership of more than 20 persons which maintains at its principal place of business a list of the names of all the partners if—

    (a) none of the names of the partners appears in the document otherwise than in the text or as a signatory; and

    (b) the document states in legible characters the address of the partnership's principal place of business and that the list of the partners' names is open to inspection at that place.

(3A) Subsection (1)(a) does not apply in relation to any document issued by a limited liability partnership with more than 20 members which maintains at its principal place of business a list of the names of all the members if—

    (a) none of the names of the members appears in the document otherwise than in the text or as a signatory; and

    (b) the document states in legible characters the address of the principal place of business of the limited liability partnership and that the list of the members' names is open to inspection at that place.

(4) Where a partnership maintains a list of the partners' names for purposes of subsection (3), any person may inspect the list during office hours.

(4A) Where a limited liability partnership maintains a list of the members' names for the purposes of subsection (3A), any person may inspect the list during office hours.

(5) The Secretary of State may by regulations require notices under subsection (1)(b) or (2) to be displayed or given in a specified form.

(6) A person who without reasonable excuse contravenes subsection (1) or (2), or any regulations made under subsection (5), is guilty of an offence.

(7) Where an inspection required by a person in accordance with subsection (4) or (4A) is refused, any partner of the partnership concerned, or any member of the limited liability partnership concerned, who without reasonable excuse refused that inspection, or permitted it to be refused, is guilty of an offence.

5   Civil remedies for breach of s. 4

(1) Any legal proceedings brought by a person to whom this Act applies to enforce a right arising out of a contract made in the course of a business in respect of which he was, at the time the contract was made, in breach of subsection (1) or (2) of section 4 shall be dismissed if the defendant (or, in Scotland, the defender) to the proceedings shows—

(a) that he has a claim against the plaintiff (pursuer) arising out of that contract which he has been unable to pursue by reason of the latter's breach of section 4(1) or (2), or

(b) that he has suffered some financial loss in connection with the contract by reason of the plaintiff's (pursuer's) breach of section 4(1) or (2),

unless the court before which the proceedings are brought is satisfied that it is just and equitable to permit the proceedings to continue.

(2) This section is without prejudice to the right of any person to enforce such rights as he may have against another person in any proceedings brought by that person.

6   Regulations

(1) Regulations under this Act shall be made by statutory instrument and may contain such transitional provisions and savings as the Secretary of State thinks appropriate, and may make different provision for different cases or classes of case.

(2) In the case of regulations made under section 3, the statutory instrument containing them shall be laid before Parliament after the regulations are made and shall cease to have effect at the end of the period of 28 days beginning with the day on which they were made (but without prejudice to anything previously done by virtue of them or to the making of new regulations) unless during that period they are approved by a resolution of each House of Parliament.

In reckoning this period of 28 days, no account is to be taken of any time during which Parliament is dissolved or prorogued, or during which both Houses are adjourned for more than 4 days.

(3) In the case of regulations made under section 4, the statutory instrument containing them is subject to annulment in pursuance of a resolution of either House of Parliament.

7   Offences

(1) Offences under this Act are punishable on summary conviction.

(2) A person guilty of an offence under this Act is liable to a fine not exceeding one-fifth of the statutory maximum.

(3) If after a person has been convicted summarily of an offence under section 2 or 4(6) the original contravention is continued, he is liable on a second or subsequent summary conviction of the offence to a fine not exceeding one-fiftieth of the statutory maximum for each day on which the contravention is continued (instead of to the penalty which may be imposed on the first conviction of the offence).

(4) Where an offence under section 2 or 4(6) or (7) committed by a body corporate is proved to have been committed with the consent or connivance of, or to be attributable to any neglect on the part of, any director, manager, secretary or other similar officer of the body corporate, or any person who was purporting to act in any such capacity, he as well as the body corporate is guilty of the offence and liable to be proceeded against and punished accordingly.

(5) Where the affairs of a body corporate are managed by its members, subsection (4) applies in relation to the acts and defaults of a member in connection with his functions of management as if he were a director of the body corporate.

(6) For purposes of the following provisions of the Companies Act 1985—
    (a) section 731 (summary proceedings under the Companies Acts), and
    (b) section 732(3) (legal professional privilege),
this Act is to be treated as included in those Acts.

8 Interpretation
(1) The following definitions apply for purposes of this Act—
'business' includes a profession;
'initial' includes any recognised abbreviation of a name;
'lawful business name', in relation to a business, means a name under which the business was carried on without contravening section 2(1) of this Act or section 2 of the Registration of Business Names Act 1916;
'local authority' means any local authority within the meaning of the Local Government Act 1972 or the Local Government (Scotland) Act 1973, the Common Council of the City of London or the Council of the Isles of Scilly;
'partnership' includes a foreign partnership;
and 'surname', in relation to a peer or person usually known by a British title different from his surname, means the title by which he is known.
(2) Any expression used in this Act and also in the Companies Act 1985 has the same meaning in this Act as in that.

9 Northern Ireland
This Act does not extend to Northern Ireland.

10 Commencement
This Act comes into force on 1 July 1985.

11 Citation
This Act may be cited as the Business Names Act 1985.

Insolvency Act 1986
(1986, c. 45)

An Act to consolidate the enactments relating to company insolvency and winding up (including the winding up of companies that are not insolvent, and of unregistered companies); enactments relating to the insolvency and bankruptcy of individuals; and other enactments bearing on those two subject matters, including the functions and qualification of insolvency practitioners, the public administration of insolvency, the penalisation and redress of malpractice and wrongdoing, and the avoidance of certain transactions at an undervalue. [25 July 1986]

THE FIRST GROUP OF PARTS   COMPANY INSOLVENCY;
COMPANIES WINDING UP
PART I   COMPANY VOLUNTARY ARRANGEMENTS

The proposal

1 Those who may propose an arrangement
    (1) The directors of a company (other than one *for which an administration order is in force, or which is* being wound up) may make a proposal under this Part to the company and to its creditors for a composition in satisfaction of its debts or a scheme of arrangement of its affairs (from here on referred to, in either case, as a 'voluntary arrangement').
    (2) A proposal under this Part is one which provides for some person ('the nominee') to act in relation to the voluntary arrangement either as trustee or otherwise for the purpose of

supervising its implementation; and the nominee must be a person who is qualified to act as an insolvency practitioner or authorised to act as nominee, in relation to the voluntary arrangement.

(3) Such a proposal may also be made—

(a) *where an administration order is in force in relation to the company, by the administrator, and*

(b) where the company is being wound up, by the liquidator.

(4) In this Part a reference to a company includes a reference to a company in relation to which a proposal for a voluntary arrangement may be made by virtue of Article 3 of the EC Regulation.

[*When the Enterprise Act 2002, sch. 17, is brought into force, the words in italics in the Insolvency Act 1986, s. 1(1), will be replaced by:*

which is in administration or

and s. 1(3)(a) will be replaced by:

(a) *where the company is in administration, by the administrator, and*]

1A   Moratorium

(1) Where the directors of an eligible company intend to make a proposal for a voluntary arrangement, they may take steps to obtain a moratorium for the company.

(2) The provisions of Schedule A1 to this Act have effect with respect to—

(a) companies eligible for a moratorium under this section,

(b) the procedure for obtaining such a moratorium,

(c) the effects of such a moratorium, and

(d) the procedure applicable (in place of sections 2 to 6 and 7) in relation to the approval and implementation of a voluntary arrangement where such a moratorium is or has been in force.

2   Procedure where nominee is not the liquidator or administrator

(1) This section applies where the nominee under section 1 is not the liquidator or administrator of the company and the directors do not propose to take steps to obtain a moratorium under section 1A for the company.

(2) The nominee shall, within 28 days (or such longer period as the court may allow) after he is given notice of the proposal for a voluntary arrangement, submit a report to the court stating—

(a) whether, in his opinion, the proposed voluntary arrangement has a reasonable prospect of being approved and implemented,

(aa) whether, in his opinion, meetings of the company and of its creditors should be summoned to consider the proposal, and

(b) if in his opinion such meetings should be summoned, the date on which, and time and place at which, he proposes the meetings should be held.

(3) For the purposes of enabling the nominee to prepare his report, the person intending to make the proposal shall submit to the nominee—

(a) a document setting out the terms of the proposed voluntary arrangement, and

(b) a statement of the company's affairs containing—

(i)   such particulars of its creditors and of its debts and other liabilities and of its assets as may be prescribed, and

(ii) such other information as may be prescribed.

(4) The court may—

(a) on an application made by the person intending to make the proposal, in a case where the nominee has failed to submit the report required by this section or has died, or

(b) on an application made by that person or the nominee, in a case where it is impracticable or inappropriate for the nominee to continue to act as such, direct that the nominee be replaced as such by another person qualified to act as an insolvency practitioner, or authorised to act as nominee, in relation to the voluntary arrangement.

3   Summoning of meetings

(1) Where the nominee under section 1 is not the liquidator or administrator, and it has been reported to the court that such meetings as are mentioned in section 2(2) should be summoned, the person making the report shall (unless the court otherwise directs) summon those meetings for the time, date and place proposed in the report.

(2) Where the nominee is the liquidator or administrator, he shall summon meetings of the company and of its creditors to consider the proposal for such a time, date and place as he thinks fit.

(3) The persons to be summoned to a creditors' meeting under this section are every creditor of the company of whose claim and address the person summoning the meeting is aware.

Consideration and implementation of proposal

4   Decisions of meetings

(1) The meetings summoned under section 3 shall decide whether to approve the proposed voluntary arrangement (with or without modifications).

(2) The modifications may include one conferring the functions proposed to be conferred on the nominee on another person qualified to act as an insolvency practitioner or authorised to act as nominee, in relation to the voluntary arrangement.

But they shall not include any modification by virtue of which the proposal ceases to be a proposal such as is mentioned in section 1.

(3) A meeting so summoned shall not approve any proposal or modification which affects the right of a secured creditor of the company to enforce his security, except with the concurrence of the creditor concerned.

(4) Subject as follows, a meeting so summoned shall not approve any proposal or modification under which—

    (a) any preferential debt of the company is to be paid otherwise than in priority to such of its debts as are not preferential debts, or

    (b) a preferential creditor of the company is to be paid an amount in respect of a preferential debt that bears to that debt a smaller proportion than is borne to another preferential debt by the amount that is to be paid in respect of that other debt.

However, the meeting may approve such a proposal or modification with the concurrence of the preferential creditor concerned.

(5) Subject as above, each of the meetings shall be conducted in accordance with the rules.

(6) After the conclusion of either meeting in accordance with the rules, the chairman of the meeting shall report the result of the meeting to the court, and, immediately after reporting to the court, shall give notice of the result of the meeting to such persons as may be prescribed.

(7) References in this section to preferential debts and preferential creditors are to be read in accordance with section 386 in Part XII of this Act.

4A   Approval of arrangement

(1) This section applies to a decision, under section 4, with respect to the approval of a proposed voluntary arrangement.

(2) The decision has effect if, in accordance with the rules—

    (a) it has been taken by both meetings summoned under section 3, or

    (b) (subject to any order made under subsection (4)) it has been taken by the creditors' meeting summoned under that section.

(3) If the decision taken by the creditors' meeting differs from that taken by the company meeting, a member of the company may apply to the court.

(4) An application under subsection (3) shall not be made after the end of the period of 28 days beginning with—

(a) the day on which the decision was taken by the creditors' meeting, or

(b) where the decision of the company meeting was taken on a later day, that day.

(5) Where a member of a regulated company, within the meaning given by paragraph 44 of Schedule A1, applies to the court under subsection (3), the Financial Services Authority is entitled to be heard on the application.

(6) On an application under subsection (3), the court may—

(a) order the decision of the company meeting to have effect instead of the decision of the creditors' meeting, or

(b) make such other order as it thinks fit.

5   Effect of approval

(1) This section applies where a decision approving a voluntary arrangement has effect under section 4A.

(2) The voluntary arrangement—

(a) takes effect as if made by the company at the creditors' meeting, and

(b) binds every person who in accordance with the rules—

(i) was entitled to vote at that meeting (whether or not he was present or represented at it), or

(ii) would have been so entitled if he had had notice of it, as if he were a party to the voluntary arrangement.

(2A) If—

(a) when the arrangement ceases to have effect any amount payable under the arrangement to a person bound by virtue of subsection (2)(b)(ii) has not been paid, and

(b) the arrangement did not come to an end prematurely,

the company shall at that time become liable to pay to that person the amount payable under the arrangement.

(3) Subject as follows, if the company is being wound up or *an administration order is in force*, the court may do one or both of the following, namely—

(a) by order stay or sist all proceedings in the winding up or *discharge the administration order;*

(b) give such directions with respect to the conduct of the winding up or the administration as it thinks appropriate for facilitating the implementation of the voluntary arrangement.

(4) The court shall not make an order under subsection (3)(a)—

(a) at any time before the end of the period of 28 days beginning with the first day on which each of the reports required by section 4(6) has been made to the court, or

(b) at any time when an application under the next section or an appeal in respect of such an application is pending, or at any time in the period within which such an appeal may be brought.

[*When the Enterprise Act 2002, sch. 17, is brought into force, the first set of words in italics in the Insolvency Act 1986, s. 5(3), will be replaced by:*

is in administration,

and the words in italics in s. 5(3)(a) will be replaced by:

provide for the appointment of the administrator to cease to have effect;]

6   Challenge of decisions

(1) Subject to this section, an application to the court may be made, by any of the persons specified below, on one or both of the following grounds, namely—

(a) that a voluntary arrangement which has effect under section 4A unfairly prejudices the interests of a creditor, member or contributory of the company;

(b) that there has been some material irregularity at or in relation to either of the meetings.
(2) The persons who may apply under this section are—
  (a) a person entitled, in accordance with the rules, to vote at either of the meetings;
  (aa) a person who would have been entitled, in accordance with the rules, to vote at the creditors' meeting if he had had notice of it;
  (b) the nominee or any person who has replaced him under section 2(4) or 4(2); and
  (c) if the company is being wound up or *an administration order is in force,* the liquidator or administrator.
(3) An application under this section shall not be made—
  (a) after the end of the period of 28 days beginning with the first day on which each of the reports required by section 4(6) has been made to the court; or
  (b) in the case of a person who was not given notice of the creditors' meeting, after the end of the period of 28 days beginning with the day on which he became aware that the meeting had taken place,
but (subject to that) an application made by a person within subsection (2)(aa) on the ground that the voluntary arrangement prejudices his interests may be made after the arrangement has ceased to have effect, unless it came to an end prematurely.
(4) Where on such an application the court is satisfied as to either of the grounds mentioned in subsection (1), it may do one or both of the following, namely—
  (a) revoke or suspend any decision approving the voluntary arrangement which has effect under section 4A or, in a case falling within subsection (1)(b), any decision taken by the meeting in question which has effect under that section;
  (b) give a direction to any person for the summoning of further meetings to consider any revised proposal the person who made the original proposal may make or, in a case falling within subsection (1)(b), a further company or (as the case may be) creditors' meeting to reconsider the original proposal.
(5) Where at any time after giving a direction under subsection (4)(b) for the summoning of meetings to consider a revised proposal the court is satisfied that the person who made the original proposal does not intend to submit a revised proposal, the court shall revoke the direction and revoke or suspend any decision approving the voluntary arrangement which has effect under section 4A.
(6) In a case where the court, on an application under this section with respect to any meeting—
  (a) gives a direction under subsection (4)(b), or
  (b) revokes or suspends an approval under subsection (4)(a) or (5), the court may give such supplemental directions as it thinks fit and, in particular, directions with respect to things done under the voluntary arrangement since it took effect.
(7) Except in pursuance of the preceding provisions of this section, a decision taken at a meeting summoned under section 3 is not invalidated by any irregularity at or in relation to the meeting.
[*When the Enterprise Act 2002, sch. 17, is brought into force, the words in italics in the Insolvency Act 1986, s. 6(2)(c), will be replaced by:*
  is in administration,]

6A   False representations, etc.
(1) If, for the purpose of obtaining the approval of the members or creditors of a company to a proposal for a voluntary arrangement, a person who is an officer of the company—
  (a) makes any false representation, or
  (b) fraudulently does, or omits to do, anything,
he commits an offence.
(2) Subsection (1) applies even if the proposal is not approved.

(3) For purposes of this section 'officer' includes a shadow director.

(4) A person guilty of an offence under this section is liable to imprisonment or a fine, or both.

7 Implementation of proposal

(1) This section applies where a voluntary arrangement has effect under section 4A.

(2) The person who is for the time being carrying out in relation to the voluntary arrangement the functions conferred—

    (a) on the nominee by virtue of the approval given at one or both of the meetings summoned under section 3

    (b) by virtue of section 2(4) or 4(2) on a person other than the nominee, shall be known as the supervisor of the voluntary arrangement.

(3) If any of the company's creditors or any other person is dissatisfied by any act, omission or decision of the supervisor, he may apply to the court; and on the application the court may—

    (a) confirm, reverse or modify any act or decision of the supervisor,

    (b) give him directions, or

    (c) make such other order as it thinks fit.

(4) The supervisor—

    (a) may apply to the court for directions in relation to any particular matter arising under the voluntary arrangement, and

    (b) is included among the persons who may apply to the court for the winding up of the company or for an administration order to be made in relation to it.

(5) The court may, whenever—

    (a) it is expedient to appoint a person to carry out the functions of the supervisor, and

    (b) it is inexpedient, difficult or impracticable for an appointment to be made without the assistance of the court,

make an order appointing a person who is qualified to act as an insolvency practitioner or authorised to act as supervisor, in relation to the voluntary arrangement, either in substitution for the existing supervisor or to fill a vacancy.

(6) The power conferred by subsection (5) is exercisable so as to increase the number of persons exercising the functions of supervisor or, where there is more than one person exercising those functions, so as to replace one or more of those persons.

7A Prosecution of delinquent officers of company

(1) This section applies where a moratorium under section 1A has been obtained for a company or the approval of a voluntary arrangement in relation to a company has taken effect under section 4A or paragraph 36 of Schedule A1.

(2) If it appears to the nominee or supervisor that any past or present officer of the company has been guilty of any offence in connection with the moratorium or, as the case may be, voluntary arrangement for which he is criminally liable, the nominee or supervisor shall forthwith—

    (a) report the matter to the appropriate authority, and

    (b) provide the appropriate authority with such information and give the authority such access to and facilities for inspecting and taking copies of documents (being information or documents in the possession or under the control of the nominee or supervisor and relating to the matter in question) as the authority requires.

In this subsection, 'the appropriate authority' means—

    (i) in the case of a company registered in England and Wales, the Secretary of State, and

    (ii) in the case of a company registered in Scotland, the Lord Advocate.

(3) Where a report is made to the Secretary of State under subsection (2), he may, for the purpose of investigating the matter reported to him and such other matters relating to the affairs of the company as appear to him to require investigation, exercise any of the powers

which are exercisable by inspectors appointed under section 431 or 432 of the Companies Act to investigate a company's affairs.

(4) For the purpose of such an investigation any obligation imposed on a person by any provision of the Companies Act to produce documents or give information to, or otherwise to assist, inspectors so appointed is to be regarded as an obligation similarly to assist the Secretary of State in his investigation.

(5) An answer given by a person to a question put to him in exercise of the powers conferred by subsection (3) may be used in evidence against him.

(6) However, in criminal proceedings in which that person is charged with an offence to which this subsection applies—

(a) no evidence relating to the answer may be adduced, and

(b) no question relating to it may be asked,

by or on behalf of the prosecution, unless evidence relating to it is adduced, or a question relating to it is asked, in the proceedings by or on behalf of that person.

(7) Subsection (6) applies to any offence other than—

(a) an offence under section 2 or 5 of the Perjury Act 1911 (false statements made on oath otherwise than in judicial proceedings or made otherwise than on oath), or

(b) an offence under section 44(1) or (2) of the Criminal Law (Consolidation) (Scotland) Act 1995 (false statements made on oath or otherwise than on oath).

(8) Where a prosecuting authority institutes criminal proceedings following any report under subsection (2), the nominee or supervisor, and every officer and agent of the company past and present (other than the defendant or defender), shall give the authority all assistance in connection with the prosecution which he is reasonably able to give.

For this purpose—

'agent' includes any banker or solicitor of the company and any person employed by the company as auditor, whether that person is or is not an officer of the company,

'prosecuting authority' means the Director of Public Prosecutions, the Lord Advocate or the Secretary of State.

(9) The court may, on the application of the prosecuting authority, direct any person referred to in subsection (8) to comply with that subsection if he has failed to do so.

7B Arrangements coming to an end prematurely
For the purposes of this Part, a voluntary arrangement the approval of which has taken effect under section 4A or paragraph 36 of Schedule A1 comes to an end prematurely if, when it ceases to have effect, it has not been fully implemented in respect of all persons bound by the arrangement by virtue of section 5(2)(b)(i) or, as the case may be, paragraph 37(2)(b)(i) of Schedule A1.

PART II   ADMINISTRATION ORDERS

[*When s. 248 of the Enterprise Act 2002 is brought into force, Part II of the Insolvency Act 1986 will be replaced by the text set out in italics starting on page 371.*]

Making etc. of administration order

8 Power of court to make order
(1) Subject to this section, if the court—

(a) is satisfied that a company is or is likely to become unable to pay its debts (within the meaning given to that expression by section 123 of this Act), and

(b) considers that the making of an order under this section would be likely to achieve one or more of the purposes mentioned below,

the court may make an administration order in relation to the company.

(1A) For the purposes of a petition presented by the Financial Services Authority alone or together with any other party, an authorised deposit taker who defaults in an obligation to pay any sum due and payable in respect of a relevant deposit is deemed to be unable to pay its debts as mentioned in subsection (1).

(1B) In subsection (1A)—

(a) 'authorised deposit taker' means a person who has permission under Part IV of the Financial Services and Markets Act 2000 to accept deposits, but excludes a person who has such permission only for the purpose of carrying on another regulated activity in accordance with that permission; and

(b) 'relevant deposit' must be read with—

(i) section 22 of the Financial Services and Markets Act 2000,

(ii) any relevant order under that section, and

(iii) Schedule 2 to that Act,

but any restriction on the meaning of deposit which arises from the identity of the person making it is to be disregarded.

(2) An administration order is an order directing that, during the period for which the order is in force, the affairs, business and property of the company shall be managed by a person ('the administrator') appointed for the purpose by the court.

(3) The purposes for whose achievement an administration order may be made are—

(a) the survival of the company, and the whole or any part of its undertaking, as a going concern;

(b) the approval of a voluntary arrangement under Part I;

(c) the sanctioning under section 425 of the Companies Act of a compromise or arrangement between the company and any such persons as are mentioned in that section; and

(d) a more advantageous realisation of the company's assets than would be effected on a winding up;

and the order shall specify the purpose or purposes for which it is made.

(4) An administration order shall not be made in relation to a company after it has gone into liquidation.

(5) An administration order shall not be made against a company if—

(a) it effects or carries out contracts of insurance, but is not—

(i) exempt from the general prohibition, within the meaning of section 19 of the Financial Services and Markets Act 2000, in relation to effecting or carrying out contracts of insurance, or

(ii) an authorised deposit taker within the meaning given by subsection (1B), and effecting or carrying out contracts of insurance in the course of a banking business;

(b) it continues to have a liability in respect of a deposit which was held by it in accordance with the Banking Act 1979 or the Banking Act 1987, but is not an authorised deposit taker, within the meaning given by subsection (1B).

(6) Subsection (5)(a) must be read with—

(a) section 22 of the Financial Services and Markets Act 2000;

(b) any relevant order under that section; and

(c) Schedule 2 to that Act.

(7) In this Part a reference to a company includes a reference to a company in relation to which an administration order may be made by virtue of Article 3 of the EC Regulation.

[*The Insolvency Act 1986, part II, is applied, with modifications, to the companies specified in s. 8(5) by the Banks (Administration Proceedings) Order 1989 (SI 1989/1276) and the Financial Services and Markets Act 2000 (Administration Orders Relating to Insurers) Order 2002 (SI 2002/1242).*]

9   Application for order

(1) An application to the court for an administration order shall be by petition presented either by the company or the directors, or by a creditor or creditors (including any contingent or prospective creditor or creditors), or by a justices' chief executive in the exercise of the

power conferred by section 87A of the Magistrates' Courts Act 1980 (enforcement of fines imposed on companies) or by all or any of those parties, together or separately.

(2) Where a petition is presented to the court—

   (a) notice of the petition shall be given forthwith to any person who has appointed, or is or may be entitled to appoint, an administrative receiver of the company, and to such other persons as may be prescribed, and

   (b) the petition shall not be withdrawn except with the leave of the court.

(3) Where the court is satisfied that there is an administrative receiver of the company, the court shall dismiss the petition unless it is also satisfied either—

   (a) that the person by whom or on whose behalf the receiver was appointed has consented to the making of the order, or

   (b) that, if an administration order were made, any security by virtue of which the receiver was appointed would—

      (i) be liable to be released or discharged under sections 238 to 240 in Part VI (transactions at an undervalue and preferences),

      (ii) be avoided under section 245 in that Part (avoidance of floating charges), or

      (iii) be challengeable under section 242 (gratuitous alienations) or 243 (unfair preferences) in that Part, or under any rule of law in Scotland.

(4) Subject to subsection (3), on hearing a petition the court may dismiss it, or adjourn the hearing conditionally or unconditionally, or make an interim order or any other order that it thinks fit.

(5) Without prejudice to the generality of subsection (4), an interim order under that subsection may restrict the exercise of any powers of the directors or of the company (whether by reference to the consent of the court or of a person qualified to act as an insolvency practitioner in relation to the company, or otherwise).

[*Section 9(3)(b) would be amended if para. 3(2) of sch. 16 to the Companies Act 1989 were brought into force.*]

10   Effect of application

(1) During the period beginning with the presentation of a petition for an administration order and ending with the making of such an order or the dismissal of the petition—

   (a) no resolution may be passed or order made for the winding up of the company;

   (aa) no landlord or other person to whom rent is payable may exercise any right of forfeiture by peaceable re-entry in relation to premises let to the company in respect of a failure by the company to comply with any term or condition of its tenancy of such premises, except with the leave of the court and subject to such terms as the court may impose;

   (b) no steps may be taken to enforce any security over the company's property, or to repossess goods in the company's possession under any hire-purchase agreement, except with the leave of the court and subject to such terms as the court may impose; and

   (c) no other proceedings and no execution or other legal process may be commenced or continued, and no distress may be levied, against the company or its property except with the leave of the court and subject to such terms as aforesaid.

(2) Nothing in subsection (1) requires the leave of the court—

   (a) for the presentation of a petition for the winding up of the company,

   (b) for the appointment of an administrative receiver of the company, or

   (c) for the carrying out by such a receiver (whenever appointed) of any of his functions.

(3) Where—

   (a) a petition for an administration order is presented at a time when there is an administrative receiver of the company, and

   (b) the person by or on whose behalf the receiver was appointed has not consented to the making of the order, the period mentioned in subsection (1) is deemed not to begin unless and until that person so consents.

(4) References in this section and the next to hire-purchase agreements include conditional sale agreements, chattel leasing agreements and retention of title agreements.

(5) In the application of this section and the next to Scotland, references to execution being commenced or continued include references to diligence being carried out or continued, and references to distress being levied shall be omitted.

11   Effect of order

(1) On the making of an administration order—

    (a) any petition for the winding up of the company shall be dismissed, and

    (b) any administrative receiver of the company shall vacate office.

(2) Where an administration order has been made, any receiver of part of the company's property shall vacate office on being required to do so by the administrator.

(3) During the period for which an administration order is in force—

    (a) no resolution may be passed or order made for the winding up of the company;

    (b) no administrative receiver of the company may be appointed;

    (ba) no landlord or other person to whom rent is payable may exercise any right of forfeiture by peaceable re-entry in relation to premises let to the company in respect of a failure by the company to comply with any term or condition of its tenancy of such premises, except with the consent of the administrator or the leave of the court and subject (where the court gives leave) to such terms as the court may impose;

    (c) no other steps may be taken to enforce any security over the company's property, or to repossess goods in the company's possession under any hire-purchase agreement, except with the consent of the administrator or the leave of the court and subject (where the court gives leave) to such terms as the court may impose; and

    (d) no other proceedings and no execution or other legal process may be commenced or continued, and no distress may be levied, against the company or its property except with the consent of the administrator or the leave of the court and subject (where the court gives leave) to such terms as aforesaid.

(4) Where at any time an administrative receiver of the company has vacated office under subsection (1)(b), or a receiver of part of the company's property has vacated office under subsection (2)—

    (a) his remuneration and any expenses properly incurred by him, and

    (b) any indemnity to which he is entitled out of the assets of the company,

shall be charged on and (subject to subsection (3) above) paid out of any property of the company which was in his custody or under his control at that time in priority to any security held by the person by or on whose behalf he was appointed.

(5) Neither an administrative receiver who vacates office under subsection (1)(b) nor a receiver who vacates office under subsection (2) is required on or after so vacating office to take any steps for the purpose of complying with any duty imposed on him by section 40 or 59 of this Act (duty to pay preferential creditors).

12   Notification of order

(1) Every invoice, order for goods or business letter which, at a time when an administration order is in force in relation to a company, is issued by or on behalf of the company or the administrator, being a document on or in which the company's name appears, shall also contain the administrator's name and a statement that the affairs, business and property of the company are being managed by the administrator.

(2) If default is made in complying with this section, the company and any of the following persons who without reasonable excuse authorises or permits the default, namely, the administrator and any officer of the company, is liable to a fine.

Administrators

13 Appointment of administrator

(1) The administrator of a company shall be appointed either by the administration order or by an order under the next subsection.

(2) If a vacancy occurs by death, resignation or otherwise in the office of the administrator, the court may by order fill the vacancy.

(3) An application for an order under subsection (2) may be made—

(a) by any continuing administrator of the company; or

(b) where there is no such administrator, by a creditors' committee established under section 26 below; or

(c) where there is no such administrator and no such committee, by the company or the directors or by any creditor or creditors of the company.

14 General powers

(1) The administrator of a company—

(a) may do all such things as may be necessary for the management of the affairs, business and property of the company, and

(b) without prejudice to the generality of paragraph (a), has the powers specified in Schedule 1 to this Act;

and in the application of that Schedule to the administrator of a company the words 'he' and 'him' refer to the administrator.

(2) The administrator also has power—

(a) to remove any director of the company and to appoint any person to be a director of it, whether to fill a vacancy or otherwise, and

(b) to call any meeting of the members or creditors of the company.

(3) The administrator may apply to the court for directions in relation to any particular matter arising in connection with the carrying out of his functions.

(4) Any power conferred on the company or its officers, whether by this Act or the Companies Act or by the memorandum or articles of association, which could be exercised in such a way as to interfere with the exercise by the administrator of his powers is not exercisable except with the consent of the administrator, which may be given either generally or in relation to particular cases.

(5) In exercising his powers the administrator is deemed to act as the company's agent.

(6) A person dealing with the administrator in good faith and for value is not concerned to inquire whether the administrator is acting within his powers.

15 Power to deal with charged property, etc.

(1) The administrator of a company may dispose of or otherwise exercise his powers in relation to any property of the company which is subject to a security to which this subsection applies as if the property were not subject to the security.

(2) Where, on an application by the administrator, the court is satisfied that the disposal (with or without other assets) of—

(a) any property of the company subject to a security to which this subsection applies, or

(b) any goods in the possession of the company under a hire-purchase agreement, would be likely to promote the purpose or one or more of the purposes specified in the administration order, the court may by order authorise the administrator to dispose of the property as if it were not subject to the security or to dispose of the goods as if all rights of the owner under the hire-purchase agreement were vested in the company.

(3) Subsection (1) applies to any security which, as created, was a floating charge; and subsection (2) applies to any other security.

(4) Where property is disposed of under subsection (1), the holder of the security has the same priority in respect of any property of the company directly or indirectly representing the property disposed of as he would have had in respect of the property subject to the security.

(5) It shall be a condition of an order under subsection (2) that—

(a) the net proceeds of the disposal, and

(b) where those proceeds are less than such amount as may be determined by the court to be the net amount which would be realised on a sale of the property or goods in the open market by a willing vendor, such sums as may be required to make good the deficiency,

shall be applied towards discharging the sums secured by the security or payable under the hire-purchase agreement.

(6) Where a condition imposed in pursuance of subsection (5) relates to two or more securities, that condition requires the net proceeds of the disposal and, where paragraph (b) of that subsection applies, the sums mentioned in that paragraph to be applied towards discharging the sums secured by those securities in the order of their priorities.

(7) An office copy of an order under subsection (2) shall, within 14 days after the making of the order, be sent by the administrator to the registrar of companies.

(8) If the administrator without reasonable excuse fails to comply with subsection (7), he is liable to a fine and, for continued contravention, to a daily default fine.

(9) References in this section to hire-purchase agreements include conditional sale agreements, chattel leasing agreements and retention of title agreements.

17   General duties

(1) The administrator of a company shall, on his appointment, take into his custody or under his control all the property to which the company is or appears to be entitled.

(2) The administrator shall manage the affairs, business and property of the company—

(a) at any time before proposals have been approved (with or without modifications) under section 24 below, in accordance with any directions given by the court, and

(b) at any time after proposals have been so approved, in accordance with those proposals as from time to time revised, whether by him or a predecessor of his.

(3) The administrator shall summon a meeting of the company's creditors if—

(a) he is requested, in accordance with the rules, to do so by one-tenth, in value, of the company's creditors, or

(b) he is directed to do so by the court.

18   Discharge or variation of administration order

(1) The administrator of a company may at any time apply to the court for the administration order to be discharged, or to be varied so as to specify an additional purpose.

(2) The administrator shall make an application under this section if—

(a) it appears to him that the purpose or each of the purposes specified in the order either has been achieved or is incapable of achievement, or

(b) he is required to do so by a meeting of the company's creditors summoned for the purpose in accordance with the rules.

(3) On the hearing of an application under this section, the court may by order discharge or vary the administration order and make such consequential provision as it thinks fit, or adjourn the hearing conditionally or unconditionally, or make an interim order or any other order it thinks fit.

(4) Where the administration order is discharged or varied the administrator shall, within 14 days after the making of the order effecting the discharge or variation, send an office copy of that order to the registrar of companies.

(5) If the administrator without reasonable excuse fails to comply with subsection (4), he is liable to a fine and, for continued contravention, to a daily default fine.

19   Vacation of office

(1) The administrator of a company may at any time be removed from office by order of the court and may, in the prescribed circumstances, resign his office by giving notice of his resignation to the court.

(2) The administrator shall vacate office if—

    (a) he ceases to be qualified to act as an insolvency practitioner in relation to the company, or

    (b) the administration order is discharged.

(3) Where at any time a person ceases to be administrator, the following subsections apply.

(4) His remuneration and any expenses properly incurred by him shall be charged on and paid out of any property of the company which is in his custody or under his control at that time in priority to any security to which section 15(1) then applies.

(5) Any sums payable in respect of debts or liabilities incurred, while he was administrator, under contracts entered into by him or a predecessor of his in the carrying out of his or the predecessor's functions shall be charged on and paid out of any such property as is mentioned in subsection (4) in priority to any charge arising under that subsection.

(6) Any sums payable in respect of liabilities incurred, while he was administrator, under contracts of employment adopted by him or a predecessor of his in the carrying out of his or the predecessor's functions shall, to the extent that the liabilities are qualifying liabilities, be charged on and paid out of any such property as is mentioned in subsection (4) and enjoy the same priority as any sums to which subsection (5) applies.

For this purpose, the administrator is not to be taken to have adopted a contract of employment by reason of anything done or omitted to be done within 14 days after his appointment.

(7) For the purposes of subsection (6), a liability under a contract of employment is a qualifying liability if—

    (a) it is a liability to pay a sum by way of wages or salary or contribution to an occupational pension scheme, and

    (b) it is in respect of services rendered wholly or partly after the adoption of the contract.

(8) There shall be disregarded for the purposes of subsection (6) so much of any qualifying liability as represents payment in respect of services rendered before the adoption of the contract.

(9) For the purposes of subsections (7) and (8)—

    (a) wages or salary payable in respect of a period of holiday or absence from work through sickness or other good cause are deemed to be wages or (as the case may be) salary in respect of services rendered in that period, and

    (b) a sum payable in lieu of holiday is deemed to be wages or (as the case may be) salary in respect of services rendered in the period by reference to which the holiday entitlement arose.

(10) In subsection (9)(a), the reference to wages or salary payable in respect of a period of holiday includes any sums which, if they had been paid, would have been treated for the purposes of the enactments relating to social security as earnings in respect of that period.

20   Release of administrator

(1) A person who has ceased to be the administrator of a company has his release with effect from the following time, that is to say—

    (a) in the case of a person who has died, the time at which notice is given to the court in accordance with the rules that he has ceased to hold office;

    (b) in any other case, such time as the court may determine.

(2) Where a person has his release under this section, he is with effect from the time specified above, discharged from all liability both in respect of acts or omissions of his in the administration and otherwise in relation to his conduct as administrator.

(3) However, nothing in this section prevents the exercise, in relation to a person who has had his release as above, of the court's powers under section 212 in Chapter X of Part IV (summary remedy against delinquent directors, liquidators, etc.).

Ascertainment and investigation of company's affairs

21   Information to be given by administrator

(1) Where an administration order has been made, the administrator shall—

    (a) forthwith send to the company and publish in the prescribed manner a notice of the order, and

    (b) within 28 days after the making of the order, unless the court otherwise directs, send such a notice to all creditors of the company (so far as he is aware of their addresses).

(2) Where an administration order has been made, the administrator shall also, within 14 days after the making of the order, send an office copy of the order to the registrar of companies and to such other persons as may be prescribed.

(3) If the administrator without reasonable excuse fails to comply with this section, he is liable to a fine and, for continued contravention, to a daily default fine.

22   Statement of affairs to be submitted to administrator

(1) Where an administration order has been made, the administrator shall forthwith require some or all of the persons mentioned below to make out and submit to him a statement in the prescribed form as to the affairs of the company.

(2) The statement shall be verified by affidavit by the persons required to submit it and shall show—

    (a) particulars of the company's assets, debts and liabilities;

    (b) the names and addresses of its creditors;

    (c) the securities held by them respectively;

    (d) the dates when the securities were respectively given; and

    (e) such further or other information as may be prescribed.

(3) The persons referred to in subsection (1) are—

    (a) those who are or have been officers of the company;

    (b) those who have taken part in the company's formation at any time within one year before the date of the administration order;

    (c) those who are in the company's employment or have been in its employment within that year, and are in the administrator's opinion capable of giving the information required;

    (d) those who are or have been within that year officers of or in the employment of a company which is, or within that year was, an officer of the company.

In this subsection 'employment' includes employment under a contract for services.

(4) Where any persons are required under this section to submit a statement of affairs to the administrator, they shall do so (subject to the next subsection) before the end of the period of 21 days beginning with the day after that on which the prescribed notice of the requirement is given to them by the administrator.

(5) The administrator, if he thinks fit, may—

    (a) at any time release a person from an obligation imposed on him under subsection (1) or (2), or

    (b) either when giving notice under subsection (4) or subsequently, extend the period so mentioned;

and where the administrator has refused to exercise a power conferred by this subsection, the court, if it thinks fit, may exercise it.

(6) If a person without reasonable excuse fails to comply with any obligation imposed under this section, he is liable to a fine and, for continued contravention, to a daily default fine.

Administrator's proposals

23   Statement of proposals

(1) Where an administration order has been made, the administrator shall, within 3 months (or such longer period as the court may allow) after the making of the order—

  (a) send to the registrar of companies and (so far as he is aware of their addresses) to all creditors a statement of his proposals for achieving the purpose or purposes specified in the order, and

  (b) lay a copy of the statement before a meeting of the company's creditors summoned for the purpose on not less than 14 days' notice.

(2) The administrator shall also, within 3 months (or such longer period as the court may allow) after the making of the order, either—

  (a) send a copy of the statement (so far as he is aware of their addresses) to all members of the company, or

  (b) publish in the prescribed manner a notice stating an address to which members of the company should write for copies of the statement to be sent to them free of charge.

(3) If the administrator without reasonable excuse fails to comply with this section, he is liable to a fine and, for continued contravention, to a daily default fine.

24   Consideration of proposals by creditors' meeting

(1) A meeting of creditors summoned under section 23 shall decide whether to approve the administrator's proposals.

(2) The meeting may approve the proposals with modifications, but shall not do so unless the administrator consents to each modification.

(3) Subject as above, the meeting shall be conducted in accordance with the rules.

(4) After the conclusion of the meeting in accordance with the rules, the administrator shall report the result of the meeting to the court and shall give notice of that result to the registrar of companies and to such persons as may be prescribed.

(5) If a report is given to the court under subsection (4) that the meeting has declined to approve the administrator's proposals (with or without modifications), the court may by order discharge the administration order and make such consequential provision as it thinks fit, or adjourn the hearing conditionally or unconditionally, or make an interim order or any other order that it thinks fit.

(6) Where the administration order is discharged, the administrator shall, within 14 days after the making of the order effecting the discharge, send an office copy of that order to the registrar of companies.

(7) If the administrator without reasonable excuse fails to comply with subsection (6), he is liable to a fine and, for continued contravention, to a daily default fine.

25   Approval of substantial revisions

(1) This section applies where—

  (a) proposals have been approved (with or without modifications) under section 24, and

  (b) the administrator proposes to make revisions of those proposals which appear to him substantial.

(2) The administrator shall—

   (a) send to all creditors of the company (so far as he is aware of their addresses) a
        statement in the prescribed form of his proposed revisions, and
   (b) lay a copy of the statement before a meeting of the company's creditors
        summoned for the purpose on not less than 14 days' notice;
and he shall not make the proposed revisions unless they are approved by the meeting.
   (3) The administrator shall also either—
   (a) send a copy of the statement (so far as he is aware of their addresses) to all mem-
        bers of the company, or
   (b) publish in the prescribed manner a notice stating an address to which members of
        the company should write for copies of the statement to be sent to them free of
        charge.
   (4) The meeting of creditors may approve the proposed revisions with modifications, but
shall not do so unless the administrator consents to each modification.
   (5) Subject as above, the meeting shall be conducted in accordance with the rules.
   (6) After the conclusion of the meeting in accordance with the rules, the administrator
shall give notice of the result of the meeting to the registrar of companies and to such persons
as may be prescribed.

Miscellaneous

26   Creditors' committee
   (1) Where a meeting of creditors summoned under section 23 has approved the administrator's proposals (with or without modifications), the meeting may, if it thinks fit, establish a
committee ('the creditors' committee') to exercise the functions conferred on it by or under
this Act.
   (2) If such a committee is established, the committee may, on giving not less than 7 days'
notice, require the administrator to attend before it at any reasonable time and furnish it with
such information relating to the carrying out of his functions as it may reasonably require.

27   Protection of interests of creditors and members
   (1) At any time when an administration order is in force, a creditor or member of the
company may apply to the court by petition for an order under this section on the ground—
   (a) that the company's affairs, business and property are being or have been managed
        by the administrator in a manner which is unfairly prejudicial to the interests of
        its creditors or members generally, or of some part of its creditors or members
        (including at least himself), or
   (b) that any actual or proposed act or omission of the administrator is or would be so
        prejudicial.
   (2) On an application for an order under this section the court may, subject as follows,
make such order as it thinks fit for giving relief in respect of the matters complained of, or
adjourn the hearing conditionally or unconditionally, or make an interim order or any other
order that it thinks fit.
   (3) An order under this section shall not prejudice or prevent—
   (a) the implementation of a voluntary arrangement approved under Part I, or any
        compromise or arrangement sanctioned under section 425 of the Companies Act;
        or
   (b) where the application for the order was made more than 28 days after the approval
        of any proposals or revised proposals under section 24 or 25, the implementation
        of those proposals or revised proposals.
   (4) Subject as above, an order under this section may in particular—
   (a) regulate the future management by the administrator of the company's affairs,
        business and property;
   (b) require the administrator to refrain from doing or continuing an act complained

of by the petitioner, or to do an act which the petitioner has complained he has omitted to do;

(c) require the summoning of a meeting of creditors or members for the purpose of considering such matters as the court may direct;

(d) discharge the administration order and make such consequential provision as the court thinks fit.

(5) Nothing in section 15 or 16 is to be taken as prejudicing applications to the court under this section.

(6) Where the administration order is discharged, the administrator shall, within 14 days after the making of the order effecting the discharge, send an office copy of that order to the registrar of companies; and if without reasonable excuse he fails to comply with this subsection, he is liable to a fine and, for continued contravention, to a daily default fine.

[*There follows, in italics, the text of part II of the Insolvency Act 1986 as it will be when s. 248 of the Enterprise Act 2002 is brought into force.*]

PART II ADMINISTRATION

8 Administration
Schedule B1 to this Act (which makes provision about the administration of companies) shall have effect.

PART III RECEIVERSHIP

CHAPTER I RECEIVERS AND MANAGERS (ENGLAND AND WALES)

Preliminary and general provisions

28 Extent of this Chapter
This Chapter does not apply to receivers appointed under Chapter II of this Part (Scotland).

29 Definitions
(1) It is hereby declared that, except where the context otherwise requires—

(a) any reference in the Companies Act or this Act to a receiver or manager of the property of a company, or to a receiver of it, includes a receiver or manager, or (as the case may be) a receiver of part only of that property and a receiver only of the income arising from the property or from part of it; and

(b) any reference in the Companies Act or this Act to the appointment of a receiver or manager under powers contained in an instrument includes an appointment made under powers which, by virtue of any enactment, are implied in and have effect as if contained in an instrument.

(2) In this Chapter 'administrative receiver' means—

(a) a receiver or manager of the wholly (or substantially the whole) of a company's property appointed by or on behalf of the holders of any debentures of the company secured by a charge which, as created, was a floating charge, or by such a charge and one or more other securities; or

(b) a person who would be such a receiver or manager but for the appointment of some other person as the receiver of part of the company's property.

30 Disqualification of body corporate from acting as receiver
A body corporate is not qualified for appointment as receiver of the property of a company, and any body corporate which acts as such a receiver is liable to a fine.

31 Disqualification of undischarged bankrupt
If a person being an undischarged bankrupt acts as receiver or manager of the property of a company on behalf of debenture holders, he is liable to imprisonment or a fine, or both.

This does not apply to a receiver or a manager acting under an appointment made by the court.

32 Power for court to appoint official receiver

Where application is made to the court to appoint a receiver on behalf of the debenture holders or other creditors of a company which is being wound up by the court, the official receiver may be appointed.

Receivers and managers appointed out of court

33 Time from which appointment is effective

(1) The appointment of a person as a receiver or manager of a company's property under powers contained in an instrument—

  (a) is of no effect unless it is accepted by that person before the end of the business day next following that on which the instrument of appointment is received by him or on his behalf, and

  (b) subject to this, is deemed to be made at the time at which the instrument of appointment is so received.

(2) This section applies to the appointment of two or more persons as joint receivers or managers of a company's property under powers contained in an instrument, subject to such modifications as may be prescribed by the rules.

34 Liability for invalid appointment

Where the appointment of a person as the receiver or manager of a company's property under powers contained in an instrument is discovered to be invalid (whether by virtue of the invalidity of the instrument or otherwise), the court may order the person by whom or on whose behalf the appointment was made to indemnify the person appointed against any liability which arises solely by reason of the invalidity of the appointment.

35 Application to court for directions

(1) A receiver or manager of the property of a company appointed under powers contained in an instrument, or the persons by whom or on whose behalf a receiver or manager has been so appointed, may apply to the court for directions in relation to any particular matter arising in connection with the performance of the functions of the receiver or manager.

(2) On such an application, the court may give such directions, or may make such order declaring the rights of persons before the court or otherwise, as it thinks just.

36 Court's power to fix remuneration

(1) The court may, on an application made by the liquidator of a company, by order fix the amount to be paid by way of remuneration to a person who, under powers contained in an instrument, has been appointed receiver or manager of the company's property.

(2) The court's power under subsection (1), where no previous order has been made with respect thereto under the subsection—

  (a) extends to fixing the remuneration for any period before the making of the order or the application for it,

  (b) is exercisable notwithstanding that the receiver or manager has died or ceased to act before the making of the order or the application, and

  (c) where the receiver or manager has been paid or has retained for his remuneration for any period before the making of the order any amount in excess of that so fixed for that period, extends to requiring him or his personal representatives to account for the excess or such part of it as may be specified in the order.

But the power conferred by paragraph (c) shall not be exercised as respects any period before the making of the application for the order under this section, unless in the court's opinion there are special circumstances making it proper for the power to be exercised.

(3) The court may from time to time on an application made either by the liquidator or by the receiver or manager, vary or amend an order made under subsection (1).

37 Liability for contracts, etc.

(1) A receiver or manager appointed under powers contained in an instrument (other than an administrative receiver) is, to the same extent as if he had been appointed by order of the court—

    (a) personally liable on any contract entered into by him in the performance of his functions (except in so far as the contract otherwise provides) and on any contract of employment adopted by him in the performance of those functions, and

    (b) entitled in respect of that liability to indemnity out of the assets.

(2) For the purposes of subsection (1)(a), the receiver or manager is not to be taken to have adopted a contract of employment by reason of anything done or omitted to be done within 14 days after his appointment.

(3) Subsection (1) does not limit any right to indemnity which the receiver or manager would have apart from it, nor limit his liability on contracts entered into without authority, nor confer any right to indemnity in respect of that liability.

(4) Where at any time the receiver or manager so appointed vacates office—

    (a) his remuneration and any expenses properly incurred by him, and

    (b) any indemnity to which he is entitled out of the assets of the company,

shall be charged on and paid out of any property of the company which is in his custody or under his control at that time in priority to any charge or other security held by the person by or on whose behalf he was appointed.

38 Receivership accounts to be delivered to registrar

(1) Except in the case of an administrative receiver, every receiver or manager of a company's property who has been appointed under powers contained in an instrument shall deliver to the registrar of companies for registration the requisite accounts of his receipts and payments.

(2) The accounts shall be delivered within one month (or such longer period as the registrar may allow) after the expiration of 12 months from the date of his appointment and of every subsequent period of 6 months, and also within one month after he ceases to act as receiver or manager.

(3) The requisite accounts shall be an abstract in the prescribed form showing—

    (a) receipts and payments during the relevant period of 12 or 6 months, or

    (b) where the receiver or manager ceases to act, receipts and payments during the period from the end of the period of 12 or 6 months to which the last preceding abstract related (or, if no preceding abstract has been delivered under this section, from the date of his appointment) up to the date of his so ceasing, and the aggregate amount of receipts and payments during all preceding periods since his appointment.

(4) In this section 'prescribed' means prescribed by regulations made by statutory instrument by the Secretary of State.

(5) A receiver or manager who makes default in complying with this section is liable to a fine and, for continued contravention, to a daily default fine.

Provisions applicable to every receivership

39 Notification that receiver or manager appointed

(1) When a receiver or manager of the property of a company has been appointed, every invoice, order for goods or business letter issued by or on behalf of the company or the receiver or manager or the liquidator of the company, being a document on or in which the company's name appears, shall contain a statement that a receiver or manager has been appointed.

(2) If default is made in complying with this section, the company and any of the following persons, who knowingly and wilfully authorises or permits the default, namely, any

officer of the company, any liquidator of the company and any receiver or manager, is liable to a fine.

40   Payment of debts out of assets subject to floating charge

(1) The following applies, in the case of a company, where a receiver is appointed on behalf of the holders of any debentures of the company secured by a charge which, as created, was a floating charge.

(2) If the company is not at the time in course of being wound up, its preferential debts (within the meaning given to that expression by section 386 in Part XII) shall be paid out of the assets coming to the hands of the receiver in priority to any claims for principal or interest in respect of the debentures.

(3) Payments made under this section shall be recouped, as far as may be, out of the assets of the company available for payment of general creditors.

41   Enforcement of duty to make returns

(1) If a receiver or manager of a company's property—

    (a) having made default in filing, delivering or making any return, account or other document, or in giving any notice, which a receiver or manager is by law required to file, deliver, make or give, fails to make good the default within 14 days after the service on him of a notice requiring him to do so, or

    (b) having been appointed under powers contained in an instrument, has, after being required at any time by the liquidator of the company to do so, failed to render proper accounts of his receipts and payments and to vouch them and pay over to the liquidator the amount properly payable to him,

the court may, on an application made for the purpose, make an order directing the receiver or manager (as the case may be) to make good the default within such time as may be specified in the order.

(2) In the case of the default mentioned in subsection (1)(a), application to the court may be made by any member or creditor of the company or by the registrar of companies; and in the case of the default mentioned in subsection (1)(b), the application shall be made by the liquidator.

In either case the court's order may provide that all costs of and incidental to the application shall be borne by the receiver or manager, as the case may be.

(3) Nothing in this section prejudices the operation of any enactment imposing penalties on receivers in respect of any such default as is mentioned in subsection (1).

Administrative receivers: general

42   General powers

(1) The powers conferred on the administrative receiver of a company by the debentures by virtue of which he was appointed are deemed to include (except in so far as they are inconsistent with any of the provisions of those debentures) the powers specified in Schedule 1 to this Act.

(2) In the application of Schedule 1 to the administrative receiver of a company—

    (a) the words 'he' and 'him' refer to the administrative receiver, and

    (b) references to the property of the company are to the property of which he is or, but for the appointment of some other person as the receiver of part of the company's property, would be the receiver or manager.

(3) A person dealing with the administrative receiver in good faith and for value is not concerned to inquire whether the receiver is acting within his powers.

43   Power to dispose of charged property, etc.

(1) Where, on an application by the administrative receiver, the court is satisfied that the disposal (with or without other assets) of any relevant property which is subject to a security

would be likely to promote a more advantageous realisation of the company's assets than would otherwise be effected, the court may by order authorise the administrative receiver to dispose of the property as if it were not subject to the security.

(2) Subsection (1) does not apply in the case of any security held by the person by or on whose behalf the administrative receiver was appointed, or of any security to which a security so held has priority.

(3) It shall be a condition of an order under this section that—

(a) the net proceeds of the disposal, and

(b) where those proceeds are less than such amount as may be determined by the court to be the net amount which would be realised on a sale of the property in the open market by a willing vendor, such sums as may be required to make good the deficiency,

shall be applied towards discharging the sums secured by the security.

(4) Where a condition imposed in pursuance of subsection (3) relates to two or more securities, that condition shall require the net proceeds of the disposal and, where paragraph (b) of that subsection applies, the sums mentioned in that paragraph to be applied towards discharging the sums secured by those securities in the order of their priorities.

(5) An office copy of an order under this section shall, within 14 days of the making of the order, be sent by the administrative receiver to the registrar of companies.

(6) If the administrative receiver without reasonable excuse fails to comply with subsection (5), he is liable to a fine and, for continued contravention, to a daily default fine.

(7) In this section 'relevant property', in relation to the administrative receiver, means the property of which he is or, but for the appointment of some other person as the receiver of part of the company's property, would be the receiver or manager.

44   Agency and liability for contracts

(1) The administrative receiver of a company—

(a) is deemed to be the company's agent, unless and until the company goes into liquidation;

(b) is personally liable on any contract entered into by him in the carrying out of his functions (except in so far as the contract otherwise provides) and, to the extent of any qualifying liability, on any contract of employment adopted by him in the carrying out of those functions; and

(c) is entitled in respect of that liability to an indemnity out of the assets of the company.

(2) For the purposes of subsection (1)(b) the administrative receiver is not to be taken to have adopted a contract of employment by reason of anything done or omitted to be done within 14 days after his appointment.

(2A) For the purposes of subsection (1)(b), a liability under a contract of employment is a qualifying liability if—

(a) it is a liability to pay a sum by way of wages or salary or contribution to an occupational pension scheme,

(b) it is incurred while the administrative receiver is in office, and

(c) it is in respect of services rendered wholly or partly after the adoption of the contract.

(2B) Where a sum payable in respect of a liability which is a qualifying liability for the purposes of subsection (1)(b) is payable in respect of services rendered partly before and partly after the adoption of the contract, liability under subsection (1)(b) shall only extend to so much of the sum as is payable in respect of services rendered after the adoption of the contract.

(2C) For the purposes of subsections (2A) and (2B)—

(a) wages or salary payable in respect of a period of holiday or absence from work through sickness or other good cause are deemed to be wages or (as the case may be) salary in respect of services rendered in that period, and

(b) a sum payable in lieu of holiday is deemed to be wages or (as the case may be) salary in respect of services rendered in the period by reference to which the holiday entitlement arose.

(2D) In subsection (2C)(a), the reference to wages or salary payable in respect of a period of holiday includes any sums which, if they had been paid, would have been treated for the purposes of the enactments relating to social security as earnings in respect of that period.

(3) This section does not limit any right to indemnity which the administrative receiver would have apart from it, nor limit his liability on contracts entered into or adopted without authority, nor confer any right to indemnity in respect of that liability.

45 Vacation of office

(1) An administrative receiver of a company may at any time be removed from office by order of the court (but not otherwise) and may resign his office by giving notice of his resignation in the prescribed manner to such persons as may be prescribed.

(2) An administrative receiver shall vacate office if he ceases to be qualified to act as an insolvency practitioner in relation to the company.

(3) Where at any time an administrative receiver vacates office—

(a) his remuneration and any expenses properly incurred by him, and

(b) any indemnity to which he is entitled out of the assets of the company,

shall be charged on and paid out of any property of the company which is in his custody or under his control at that time in priority to any security held by the person by or on whose behalf he was appointed.

(4) Where an administrative receiver vacates office otherwise than by death, he shall, within 14 days after his vacation of office, send a notice to that effect to the registrar of companies.

(5) If an administrative receiver without reasonable excuse fails to comply with subsection (4), he is liable to a fine *and, for continued contravention, to a daily default fine.*

[*The words in italics would be repealed if para. 3(3) of sch. 16 to the Companies Act 1989 were brought into force.*]

Administrative receivers: ascertainment and investigation of company's affairs

46 Information to be given by administrative receiver

(1) Where an administrative receiver is appointed, he shall—

(a) forthwith send to the company and publish in the prescribed manner a notice of his appointment, and

(b) within 28 days after his appointment, unless the court otherwise directs, send such a notice to all the creditors of the company (so far as he is aware of their addresses).

(2) This section and the next do not apply in relation to the appointment of an administrative receiver to act—

(a) with an existing administrative receiver, or

(b) in place of an administrative receiver dying or ceasing to act,

except that, where they apply to an administrative receiver who dies or ceases to act before they have been fully complied with, the references in this section and the next to the administrative receiver include (subject to the next subsection) his successor and any continuing administrative receiver.

(3) If the company is being wound up, this section and the next apply notwithstanding that the administrative receiver and the liquidator are the same person, but with any necessary modifications arising from that fact.

(4) If the administrative receiver without reasonable excuse fails to comply with this section, he is liable to a fine and, for continued contravention, to a daily default fine.

47   Statement of affairs to be submitted

(1) Where an administrative receiver is appointed, he shall forthwith require some or all of the persons mentioned below to make out and submit to him a statement in the prescribed form as to the affairs of the company.

(2) A statement submitted under this section shall be verified by affidavit by the persons required to submit it and shall show—

    (a)   particulars of the company's assets, debts and liabilities;

    (b)   the names and addresses of its creditors;

    (c)   the securities held by them respectively;

    (d)   the dates when the securities were respectively given; and

    (e)   such further or other information as may be prescribed.

(3) The persons referred to in subsection (1) are—

    (a)   those who are or have been officers of the company;

    (b)   those who have taken part in the company's formation at any time within one year before the date of the appointment of the administrative receiver;

    (c)   those who are in the company's employment, or have been in its employment within that year, and are in the administrative receiver's opinion capable of giving the information required;

    (d)   those who are or have been within that year officers of or in the employment of a company which is, or within that year was, an officer of the company.

In this subsection 'employment' includes employment under a contract for services.

(4) Where any persons are required under this section to submit a statement of affairs to the administrative receiver, they shall do so (subject to the next subsection) before the end of the period of 21 days beginning with the day after that on which the prescribed notice of the requirement is given to them by the administrative receiver.

(5) The administrative receiver, if he thinks fit, may—

    (a)   at any time release a person from an obligation imposed on him under subsection (1) or (2), or

    (b)   either when giving notice under subsection (4) or subsequently, extend the period so mentioned;

and where the administrative receiver has refused to exercise a power conferred by this subsection, the court, if it thinks fit, may exercise it.

(6) If a person without reasonable excuse fails to comply with any obligation imposed under this section, he is liable to a fine and, for continued contravention, to a daily default fine.

48   Report by administrative receiver

(1) Where an administrative receiver is appointed, he shall, within 3 months (or such longer period as the court may allow) after his appointment, send to the registrar of companies, to any trustees for secured creditors of the company and (so far as he is aware of their addresses) to all such creditors a report as to the following matters, namely—

    (a)   the events leading up to his appointment, so far as he is aware of them;

    (b)   the disposal or proposed disposal by him of any property of the company and the carrying on or proposed carrying on by him of any business of the company;

    (c)   the amounts of principal and interest payable to the debenture holders by whom or on whose behalf he was appointed and the amounts payable to preferential creditors; and

    (d)   the amount (if any) likely to be available for the payment of other creditors.

(2) The administrative receiver shall also, within 3 months (or such longer period as the court may allow) after his appointment, either—

(a) send a copy of the report (so far as he is aware of their addresses) to all unsecured creditors of the company; or

(b) publish in the prescribed manner a notice stating an address to which unsecured creditors of the company should write for copies of the report to be sent to them free of charge,

and (in either case), unless the court otherwise directs, lay a copy of the report before a meeting of the company's unsecured creditors summoned for the purpose on not less than 14 days' notice.

(3) The court shall not give a direction under subsection (2) unless—

(a) the report states the intention of the administrative receiver to apply for the direction, and

(b) a copy of the report is sent to the person mentioned in paragraph (a) of that subsection, or a notice is published as mentioned in paragraph (b) of that subsection, not less than 14 days before the hearing of the application.

(4) Where the company has gone or goes into liquidation, the administrative receiver—

(a) shall, within 7 days after his compliance with subsection (1) or, if later, the nomination or appointment of the liquidator, send a copy of the report to the liquidator, and

(b) where he does so within the time limited for compliance with subsection (2), is not required to comply with that subsection.

(5) A report under this section shall include a summary of the statement of affairs made out and submitted to the administrative receiver under section 47 and of his comments (if any) upon it.

(6) Nothing in this section is to be taken as requiring any such report to include any information the disclosure of which would seriously prejudice the carrying out by the administrative receiver of his functions.

(7) Section 46(2) applies for the purposes of this section also.

(8) If the administrative receiver without reasonable excuse fails to comply with this section, he is liable to a fine and, for continued contravention, to a daily default fine.

49   Committee of creditors

(1) Where a meeting of creditors is summoned under section 48, the meeting may, if it thinks fit, establish a committee ('the creditors' committee') to exercise the functions conferred on it by or under this Act.

(2) If such a committee is established, the committee may, on giving not less than 7 days' notice, require the administrative receiver to attend before it at any reasonable time and furnish it with such information relating to the carrying out by him of his functions as it may reasonably require.

CHAPTER III   RECEIVERS' POWERS IN GREAT BRITAIN AS A WHOLE

72   Cross-border operation of receivership provisions

(1) A receiver appointed under the law of either part of Great Britain in respect of the whole or any part of any property or undertaking of a company and in consequence of the company having created a charge which, as created, was a floating charge may exercise his powers in the other part of Great Britain so far as their exercise is not inconsistent with the law applicable there.

(2) In subsection (1) 'receiver' includes a manager and a person who is appointed both receiver and manager.

CHAPTER IV   PROHIBITION OF APPOINTMENT OF ADMINISTRATIVE RECEIVER

[On 15 June 2003 the provisions of chapter IV printed in italics below had not been brought into force.]

72A   Floating charge holder not to appoint administrative receiver

(1) The holder of a qualifying floating charge in respect of a company's property may not appoint an administrative receiver of the company.

(2) In Scotland, the holder of a qualifying floating charge in respect of a company's property may not appoint or apply to the court for the appointment of a receiver who on appointment would be an administrative receiver of property of the company.

(3) In subsections (1) and (2)—
'holder of a qualifying floating charge in respect of a company's property' has the same meaning as in paragraph 14 of Schedule B1 to this Act, and
'administrative receiver' has the meaning given by section 251.

(4) This section applies—
(a) to a floating charge created on or after a date appointed by the Secretary of State by order made by statutory instrument, and
(b) in spite of any provision of an agreement or instrument which purports to empower a person to appoint an administrative receiver (by whatever name).

(5) An order under subsection (4)(a) may—
(a) make provision which applies generally or only for a specified purpose;
(b) make different provision for different purposes;
(c) make transitional provision.

(6) This section is subject to the exceptions specified in sections 72B to 72G.

72B   First exception: capital market

(1) Section 72A does not prevent the appointment of an administrative receiver in pursuance of an agreement which is or forms part of a capital market arrangement if—
(a) a party incurs or, when the agreement was entered into was expected to incur, a debt of at least £50 million under the arrangement, and
(b) the arrangement involves the issue of a capital market investment.

(2) In subsection (1)—
'capital market arrangement' means an arrangement of a kind described in paragraph 1 of Schedule 2A, and
'capital market investment' means an investment of a kind described in paragraph 2 or 3 of that Schedule.

72C   Second exception: public—private partnership

(1) Section 72A does not prevent the appointment of an administrative receiver of a project company of a project which—
(a) is a public—private partnership project, and
(b) includes step-in rights.

(2) In this section 'public—private partnership project' means a project—
(a) the resources for which are provided partly by one or more public bodies and partly by one or more private persons, or
(b) which is designed wholly or mainly for the purpose of assisting a public body to discharge a function.

(3) In this section—
'step-in rights' has the meaning given by paragraph 6 of Schedule 2A, and
'project company' has the meaning given by paragraph 7 of that Schedule.

72D   Third exception: utilities

(1) Section 72A does not prevent the appointment of an administrative receiver of a project company of a project which—
(a) is a utility project, and
(b) includes step-in rights.

(2) In this section—

   (a) 'utility project' means a project designed wholly or mainly for the purpose of a regulated business,

   (b) 'regulated business' means a business of a kind listed in paragraph 10 of Schedule 2A,

   (c) 'step-in rights' has the meaning given by paragraph 6 of that Schedule, and

   (d) 'project company' has the meaning given by paragraph 7 of that Schedule.

72E   Fourth exception: project finance

(1) Section 72A does not prevent the appointment of an administrative receiver of a project company of a project which—

   (a) is a financed project, and

   (b) includes step-in rights.

(2) In this section—

   (a) a project is 'financed' if under an agreement relating to the project a project company incurs, or when the agreement is entered into is expected to incur, a debt of at least £50 million for the purposes of carrying out the project,

   (b) 'project company' has the meaning given by paragraph 7 of Schedule 2A, and

   (c) 'step-in rights' has the meaning given by paragraph 6 of that Schedule.

72F   Fifth exception: financial market

Section 72A does not prevent the appointment of an administrative receiver of a company by virtue of—

   (a) a market charge within the meaning of section 173 of the Companies Act 1989 (c. 40),

   (b) a system-charge within the meaning of the Financial Markets and Insolvency Regulations 1996 (SI 1996/1469),

   (c) a collateral security charge within the meaning of the Financial Markets and Insolvency (Settlement Finality) Regulations 1999 (SI 1999/2979).

72G   Sixth exception: registered social landlord

Section 72A does not prevent the appointment of an administrative receiver of a company which is registered as a social landlord under Part I of the Housing Act 1996 (c. 52) or under Part 3 of the Housing (Scotland) Act 2001 (asp 10).

72H   Sections 72A to 72G: supplementary

(1) Schedule 2A (which supplements sections 72B to 72G) shall have effect.

(2) The Secretary of State may by order—

   (a) insert into this Act provision creating an additional exception to section 72A(1) or (2);

   (b) provide for a provision of this Act which creates an exception to section 72A(1) or (2) to cease to have effect;

   (c) amend section 72A in consequence of provision made under paragraph (a) or (b);

   (d) amend any of sections 72B to 72G;

   (e) amend Schedule 2A.

(3) An order under subsection (2) must be made by statutory instrument.

(4) An order under subsection (2) may make—

   (a) provision which applies generally or only for a specified purpose;

   (b) different provision for different purposes;

   (c) consequential or supplementary provision;

   (d) transitional provision.

(5) An order under subsection (2)—

   (a) in the case of an order under subsection (2)(e), shall be subject to annulment in pursuance of a resolution of either House of Parliament,

   (b) in the case of an order under subsection (2)(d) varying the sum specified in section 72B(1)(a) or 72E(2)(a) (whether or not the order also makes consequential or transitional provision), shall be subject to annulment in pursuance of a resolution of either House of Parliament, and

(c) in the case of any other order under subsection (2)(a) to (d), may not be made unless a draft has been laid before and approved by resolution of each House of Parliament.

PART IV WINDING UP OF COMPANIES REGISTERED UNDER THE COMPANIES ACTS

CHAPTER I PRELIMINARY

Modes of winding up

73 Alternative modes of winding up

(1) The winding up of a company, within the meaning given to the expression by section 735 of the Companies Act, may be either voluntary (Chapters II, III, IV and V in this Part) or by the court (Chapter VI).

(2) This Chapter, and Chapters VII to X, relate to winding up generally, except where otherwise stated.

Contributories

74 Liability as contributories of present and past members

(1) When a company is wound up, every present and past member is liable to contribute to its assets to any amount sufficient for payment of its debts and liabilities, and the expenses of the winding up, and for the adjustment of the rights of the contributories among themselves.

(2) This is subject as follows—

(a) a past member is not liable to contribute if he has ceased to be a member for one year or more before the commencement of the winding up;

(b) a past member is not liable to contribute in respect of any debt or liability of the company contracted after he ceased to be a member;

(c) a past member is not liable to contribute, unless it appears to the court that the existing members are unable to satisfy the contributions required to be made by them in pursuance of the Companies Act and this Act;

(d) in the case of a company limited by shares, no contribution is required from any member exceeding the amount (if any) unpaid on the shares in respect of which he is liable as a present or past member;

(e) nothing in the Companies Act or this Act invalidates any provision contained in a policy of insurance or other contract whereby the liability of individual members on the policy or contract is restricted, or whereby the funds of the company are alone made liable in respect of the policy or contract;

(f) a sum due to any member of the company (in his character of a member) by way of dividends, profits or otherwise is not deemed to be a debt of the company, payable to that member in a case of competition between himself and any other creditor not a member of the company, but any such sum may be taken into account for the purpose of the final adjustment of the rights of the contributories among themselves.

(3) In the case of a company limited by guarantee, no contribution is required from any member exceeding the amount undertaken to be contributed by him to the company's assets in the event of its being wound up; but if it is a company with a share capital, every member of it is liable (in addition to the amount so undertaken to be contributed to the assets), to contribute to the extent of any sums unpaid on shares held by him.

75 Directors, etc. with unlimited liability

(1) In the winding up of a limited company, any director or manager (whether past or present) whose liability is under the Companies Act unlimited is liable, in addition to his liability (if any) to contribute as an ordinary member, to make a further contribution as if he were at the commencement of the winding up a member of an unlimited company.

(2) However—

(a) a past director or manager is not liable to make such further contribution if he has ceased to hold office for a year or more before the commencement of the winding up;

(b) a past director or manager is not liable to make such further contribution in respect of any debt or liability of the company contracted after he ceased to hold office;

(c) subject to the company's articles, a director or manager is not liable to make such further contribution unless the court deems it necessary to require that contribution in order to satisfy the company's debts and liabilities, and the expenses of the winding up.

76 Liability of past directors and shareholders

(1) This section applies where a company is being wound up and—

(a) it has under Chapter VII of Part V of the Companies Act (redeemable shares; purchase by a company of its own shares) made a payment out of capital in respect of the redemption or purchase of any of its own shares (the payment being referred to below as 'the relevant payment'), and

(b) the aggregate amount of the company's assets and the amounts paid by way of contribution to its assets (apart from this section) is not sufficient for payment of its debts and liabilities, and the expenses of the winding up.

(2) If the winding up commenced within one year of the date on which the relevant payment was made, then—

(a) the person from whom the shares were redeemed or purchased, and

(b) the directors who signed the statutory declaration made in accordance with section 173(3) of the Companies Act for purposes of the redemption or purchase (except a director who shows that he had reasonable grounds for forming the opinion set out in the declaration),

are, so as to enable that insufficiency to be met, liable to contribute to the following extent to the company's assets.

(3) A person from whom any of the shares were redeemed or purchased is liable to contribute an amount not exceeding so much of the relevant payment as was made by the company in respect of his shares; and the directors are jointly and severally liable with that person to contribute that amount.

(4) A person who has contributed any amount to the assets in pursuance of this section may apply to the court for an order directing any other person jointly and severally liable in respect of that amount to pay him such amount as the court thinks just and equitable.

(5) Sections 74 and 75 do not apply in relation to liability accruing by virtue of this section.

(6) This section is deemed included in Chapter VII of Part V of the Companies Act for the purposes of the Secretary of State's power to make regulations under section 179 of that Act.

77 Limited company formerly unlimited

(1) This section applies in the case of a company being wound up which was at some former time registered as unlimited but has re-registered—

(a) as a public company under section 43 of the Companies Act (or the former corresponding provision, section 5 of the Companies Act 1980), or

(b) as a limited company under section 51 of the Companies Act (or the former corresponding provision, section 44 of the Companies Act 1967).

(2) Notwithstanding section 74(2)(a) above, a past member of the company who was a member of it at the time of re-registration, if the winding up commences within the period of 3 years beginning with the day on which the company was re-registered, is liable to contribute to the assets of the company in respect of debts and liabilities contracted before that time.

(3) If no persons who were members of the company at that time are existing members of it, a person who at that time was a present or past member is liable to contribute as above notwithstanding that the existing members have satisfied the contributions required to be made by them under the Companies Act and this Act.

This applies subject to section 74(2)(a) above and to subsection (2) of this section, but notwithstanding section 74(2)(c).

(4) Notwithstanding section 74(2)(d) and (3), there is no limit on the amount which a person who, at that time, was a past or present member of the company is liable to contribute as above.

78   Unlimited company formerly limited

(1) This section applies in the case of a company being wound up which was at some former time registered as limited but has been re-registered as unlimited under section 49 of the Companies Act (or the former corresponding provision, section 43 of the Companies Act 1967).

(2) A person who, at the time when the application for the company to be re-registered was lodged, was a past member of the company and did not after that again become a member of it is not liable to contribute to the assets of the company more than he would have been liable to contribute had the company not been re-registered.

79   Meaning of 'contributory'

(1) In this Act and the Companies Act the expression 'contributory' means every person liable to contribute to the assets of a company in the event of its being wound up, and for the purposes of all proceedings for determining, and all proceedings prior to the final determination of, the persons who are to be deemed contributories, includes any person alleged to be a contributory.

(2) The reference in subsection (1) to persons liable to contribute to the assets does not include a person so liable by virtue of a declaration by the court under section 213 (imputed responsibility for company's fraudulent trading) or section 214 (wrongful trading) in Chapter X of this Part.

(3) A reference in a company's articles to a contributory does not (unless the context requires) include a person who is a contributory only by virtue of section 76.

This subsection is deemed included in Chapter VII of Part V of the Companies Act for the purposes of the Secretary of State's power to make regulations under section 179 of that Act.

80   Nature of contributory's liability

The liability of a contributory creates a debt (in England and Wales in the nature of a specialty) accruing due from him at the time when his liability commenced, but payable at the times when calls are made for enforcing the liability.

81   Contributories in case of death of a member

(1) If a contributory dies either before or after he has been placed on the list of contributories, his personal representatives, and the heirs and legatees of heritage of his heritable estate in Scotland, are liable in a due course of administration to contribute to the assets of the company in discharge of his liability and are contributories accordingly.

(2) Where the personal representatives are placed on the list of contributories, the heirs or legatees of heritage need not be added, but they may be added as and when the court thinks fit.

(3) If in England and Wales the personal representatives make default in paying any money ordered to be paid by them, proceedings may be taken for administering the estate of the deceased contributory and for compelling payment out of it of the money due.

82 Effect of contributory's bankruptcy

(1) The following applies if a contributory becomes bankrupt, either before or after he has been placed on the list of contributories.

(2) His trustee in bankruptcy represents him for all purposes of the winding up, and is a contributory accordingly.

(3) The trustee may be called on to admit to proof against the bankrupt's estate, or otherwise allow to be paid out of the bankrupt's assets in due course of law, any money due from the bankrupt in respect of his liability to contribute to the company's assets.

(4) There may be proved against the bankrupt's estate the estimated value of his liability to future calls as well as calls already made.

CHAPTER II   VOLUNTARY WINDING UP (INTRODUCTORY AND GENERAL)

Resolutions for, and commencement of, voluntary winding up

84 Circumstances in which company may be wound up voluntarily

(1) A company may be wound up voluntarily—

   (a) when the period (if any) fixed for the duration of the company by the articles expires, or the event (if any) occurs, on the occurrence of which the articles provide that the company is to be dissolved, and the company in general meeting has passed a resolution requiring it to be wound up voluntarily;

   (b) if the company resolves by special resolution that it be wound up voluntarily;

   (c) if the company resolves by extraordinary resolution to the effect that it cannot by reason of its liabilities continue its business, and that it is advisable to wind up.

(2) In this Act the expression 'a resolution for voluntary winding up' means a resolution passed under any of the paragraphs of subsection (1).

(3) A resolution passed under paragraph (a) of subsection (1), as well as a special resolution under paragraph (b) and an extraordinary resolution under paragraph (c), is subject to section 380 of the Companies Act (copy of resolution to be forwarded to registrar of companies within 15 days).

85 Notice of resolution to wind up

(1) When a company has passed a resolution for voluntary winding up, it shall, within 14 days after the passing of the resolution, give notice of the resolution by advertisement in the Gazette.

(2) If default is made in complying with this section, the company and every officer of it who is in default is liable to a fine and, for continued contravention, to a daily default fine.

For purposes of this subsection the liquidator is deemed an officer of the company.

86 Commencement of winding up

A voluntary winding up is deemed to commence at the time of the passing of the resolution for voluntary winding up.

Consequences of resolution to wind up

87 Effect of business and status of company

(1) In case of a voluntary winding up, the company shall from the commencement of the winding up cease to carry on its business, except so far as may be required for its beneficial winding up.

(2) However, the corporate state and corporate powers of the company, notwithstanding anything to the contrary in its articles, continue until the company is dissolved.

88   Avoidance of share transfers, etc. after winding-up resolution

Any transfer of shares, not being a transfer made to or with the sanction of the liquidator, and any alteration in the status of the company's members, made after the commencement of a voluntary winding up, is void.

Declaration of solvency

89   Statutory declaration of solvency

(1) Where it is proposed to wind up a company voluntarily, the directors (or, in the case of a company having more than two directors, the majority of them) may at a directors' meeting make a statutory declaration to the effect that they have made a full inquiry into the company's affairs and that, having done so, they have formed the opinion that the company will be able to pay its debts in full, together with interest at the official rate (as defined in section 251), within such period, not exceeding 12 months from the commencement of the winding up, as may be specified in the declaration.

(2) Such a declaration by the directors has no effect for purposes of this Act unless—

(a) it is made within the 5 weeks immediately preceding the date of the passing of the resolution for winding up, or on that date but before the passing of the resolution, and

(b) it embodies a statement of the company's assets and liabilities as at the latest practicable date before the making of the declaration.

(3) The declaration shall be delivered to the registrar of companies before the expiration of 15 days immediately following the date on which the resolution for winding up is passed.

(4) A director making a declaration under this section without having reasonable grounds for the opinion that the company will be able to pay its debts in full, together with interest at the official rate, within the period specified is liable to imprisonment or a fine, or both.

(5) If the company is wound up in pursuance of a resolution passed within 5 weeks after the making of the declaration, and its debts (together with interest at the official rate) are not paid or provided for in full within the period specified, it is to be presumed (unless the contrary is shown) that the director did not have reasonable grounds for his opinion.

(6) If a declaration required by subsection (3) to be delivered to the registrar is not so delivered within the time prescribed by that subsection, the company and every officer in default is liable to a fine and, for continued contravention, to a daily default fine.

90   Distinction between 'members'' and 'creditors'' voluntary winding up

A winding up in the case of which a directors' statutory declaration under section 89 has been made is a 'members' voluntary winding up'; and a winding up in the case of which such a declaration has not been made is a 'creditors' voluntary winding up'.

CHAPTER III   MEMBERS' VOLUNTARY WINDING UP

91   Appointment of liquidator

(1) In a members' voluntary winding up, the company in general meeting shall appoint one or more liquidators for the purpose of winding up the company's affairs and distributing its assets.

(2) On the appointment of a liquidator all the powers of the directors cease, except so far as the company in general meeting or the liquidator sanctions their continuance.

92   Power to fill vacancy in office of liquidator

(1) If a vacancy occurs by death, resignation or otherwise in the office of liquidator appointed by the company, the company in general meeting may, subject to any arrangement with its creditors, fill the vacancy.

(2) For that purpose a general meeting may be convened by any contributory or, if there were more liquidators than one, by the continuing liquidators.

(3) The meeting shall be held in manner provided by this Act or by the articles, or in such manner as may, on application by any contributory or by the continuing liquidators, be determined by the court.

93   General company meeting at each year's end

(1) Subject to sections 96 and 102, in the event of the winding up continuing for more than one year, the liquidator shall summon a general meeting of the company at the end of the first year from the commencement of the winding up, and of each succeeding year, or at the first convenient date within 3 months from the end of the year or such longer period as the Secretary of State may allow.

(2) The liquidator shall lay before the meeting an account of his acts and dealings, and of the conduct of the winding up, during the preceding year.

(3) If the liquidator fails to comply with this section, he is liable to a fine.

94   Final meeting prior to dissolution

(1) As soon as the company's affairs are fully wound up, the liquidator shall make up an account of the winding up, showing how it has been conducted and the company's property has been disposed of, and thereupon shall call a general meeting of the company for the purpose of laying before it the account, and giving an explanation of it.

(2) The meeting shall be called by advertisement in the Gazette, specifying its time, place and object and published at least one month before the meeting.

(3) Within one week after the meeting, the liquidator shall send to the registrar of companies a copy of the account, and shall make a return to him of the holding of the meeting and of its date.

(4) If the copy is not sent or the return is not made in accordance with subsection (3), the liquidator is liable to a fine and, for continued contravention, to a daily default fine.

(5) If a quorum is not present at the meeting, the liquidator shall, in lieu of the return mentioned above, make a return that the meeting was duly summoned and that no quorum was present; and upon such a return being made, the provisions of subsection (3) as to the making of the return are deemed complied with.

(6) If the liquidator fails to call a general meeting of the company as required by subsection (1), he is liable to a fine.

95   Effect of company's insolvency

(1) This section applies where the liquidator is of the opinion that the company will be unable to pay its debts in full (together with interest at the official rate) within the period stated in the directors' declaration under section 89.

(2) The liquidator shall—
  (a) summon a meeting of creditors for a day not later than the 28th day after the day on which he formed that opinion;
  (b) send notices of the creditors' meeting to the creditors by post not less than 7 days before the day on which that meeting is to be held;
  (c) cause notice of the creditors' meeting to be advertised once in the Gazette and once at least in 2 newspapers circulating in the relevant locality (that is to say the locality in which the company's principal place of business in Great Britain was situated during the relevant period); and
  (d) during the period before the day on which the creditors' meeting is to be held, furnish creditors free of charge with such information concerning the affairs of the company as they may reasonably require;
and the notice of the creditors' meeting shall state the duty imposed by paragraph (d) above.

(3) The liquidator shall also—
  (a) make out a statement in the prescribed form as to the affairs of the company;
  (b) lay that statement before the creditors' meeting; and

(c) attend and preside at that meeting.

(4) The statement as to the affairs of the company shall be verified by affidavit by the liquidator and shall show—

    (a) particulars of the company's assets, debts and liabilities;

    (b) the names and addresses of the company's creditors;

    (c) the securities held by them respectively;

    (d) the dates when the securities were respectively given; and

    (e) such further or other information as may be prescribed.

(5) Where the company's principal place of business in Great Britain was situated in different localities at different times during the relevant period, the duty imposed by subsection (2)(c) applies separately in relation to each of those localities.

(6) Where the company had no place of business in Great Britain during the relevant period, references in subsections (2)(c) and (5) to the company's principal place of business in Great Britain are replaced by references to its registered office.

(7) In this section 'the relevant period' means the period of 6 months immediately preceding the day on which were sent the notices summoning the company meeting at which it was resolved that the company be wound up voluntarily.

(8) If the liquidator without reasonable excuse fails to comply with this section, he is liable to a fine.

96 Conversion to creditors' voluntary winding up

As from the day on which the creditors' meeting is held under section 95, this Act has effect as if—

    (a) the directors' declaration under section 89 had not been made; and

    (b) the creditors' meeting and the company meeting at which it was resolved that the company be wound up voluntarily were the meetings mentioned in section 98 in the next Chapter;

and accordingly the winding up becomes a creditors' voluntary winding up.

CHAPTER IV   CREDITORS' VOLUNTARY WINDING UP

97 Application of this Chapter

(1) Subject as follows, this Chapter applies in relation to a creditors' voluntary winding up.

(2) Sections 98 and 99 do not apply where, under section 96 in Chapter III, a members' voluntary winding up has become a creditors' voluntary winding up.

98 Meeting of creditors

(1) The company shall—

    (a) cause a meeting of its creditors to be summoned for a day not later than the 14th day after the day on which there is to be held the company meeting at which the resolution for voluntary winding up is to be proposed;

    (b) cause the notices of the creditors' meeting to be sent by post to the creditors not less than 7 days before the day on which that meeting is to be held; and

    (c) cause notice of the creditors' meeting to be advertised once in the Gazette and once at least in two newspapers circulating in the relevant locality (that is to say the locality in which the company's principal place of business in Great Britain was situated during the relevant period).

(2) The notice of the creditors' meeting shall state either—

    (a) the name and address of a person qualified to act as an insolvency practitioner in relation to the company who, during the period before the day on which that meeting is to be held, will furnish creditors free of charge with such information concerning the company's affairs as they may reasonably require; or

(b) a place in the relevant locality where, on the two business days falling next before the day on which that meeting is to be held, a list of the names and addresses of the company's creditors will be available for inspection free of charge.

(3) Where the company's principal place of business in Great Britain was situated in different localities at different times during the relevant period, the duties imposed by subsections (1)(c) and (2)(b) above apply separately in relation to each of those localities.

(4) Where the company had no place of business in Great Britain during the relevant period, references in subsections (1)(c) and (3) to the company's principal place of business in Great Britain are replaced by references to its registered office.

(5) In this section 'the relevant period' means the period of 6 months immediately preceding the day on which were sent the notices summoning the company meeting at which it was resolved that the company be wound up voluntarily.

(6) If the company without reasonable excuse fails to comply with subsection (1) or (2), it is guilty of an offence and liable to a fine.

99   Directors to lay statement of affairs before creditors

(1) The directors of the company shall—

(a) make out a statement in the prescribed form as to the affairs of the company;

(b) cause that statement to be laid before the creditors' meeting under section 98; and

(c) appoint one of their number to preside at the meeting; and it is the duty of the director so appointed to attend the meeting and preside over it.

(2) The statement as to the affairs of the company shall be verified by affidavit by some or all of the directors and shall show—

(a) particulars of the company's assets, debts and liabilities;

(b) the names and addresses of the company's creditors;

(c) the securities held by them respectively;

(d) the dates when the securities were respectively given; and

(e) such further or other information as may be prescribed.

(3) If—

(a) the directors without reasonable excuse fail to comply with subsection (1) or (2); or

(b) any director without reasonable excuse fails to comply with subsection (1), so far as requiring him to attend and preside at the creditors' meeting,

the directors are or (as the case may be) the director is guilty of an offence and liable to a fine.

100   Appointment of liquidator

(1) The creditors and the company at their respective meetings mentioned in section 98 may nominate a person to be liquidator for the purpose of winding up the company's affairs and distributing its assets.

(2) The liquidator shall be the person nominated by the creditors or, where no person has been so nominated, the person (if any) nominated by the company.

(3) In the case of different persons being nominated, any director, member or creditor of the company may, within 7 days after the date on which the nomination was made by the creditors, apply to the court for an order either—

(a) directing that the person nominated as liquidator by the company shall be liquidator instead of or jointly with the person nominated by the creditors, or

(b) appointing some other person to be liquidator instead of the person nominated by the creditors.

(4) The court shall grant an application under subsection (3) made by the holder of a qualifying floating charge in respect of the company's property (within the meaning of paragraph 14 of Schedule B1) unless the court thinks it right to refuse the application because of the particular circumstances of the case.

[*On 15 June 2003, s. 100(4) had not been brought into force.*]

101 Appointment of liquidation committee

(1) The creditors at the meeting to be held under section 98 or at any subsequent meeting may, if they think fit, appoint a committee ('the liquidation committee') of not more than 5 persons to exercise the functions conferred on it by or under this Act.

(2) If such a committee is appointed, the company may, either at the meeting at which the resolution for voluntary winding up is passed or at any time subsequently in general meeting, appoint such number of persons as they think fit to act as members of the committee, not exceeding 5.

(3) However, the creditors may, if they think fit, resolve that all or any of the persons so appointed by the company ought not to be members of the liquidation committee; and if the creditors so resolve—

(a) the persons mentioned in the resolution are not then, unless the court otherwise directs, qualified to act as members of the committee; and

(b) on any application to the court under this provision the court may, if it thinks fit, appoint other persons to act as such members in place of the persons mentioned in the resolution.

(4) In Scotland, the liquidation committee has, in addition to the powers and duties conferred and imposed on it by this Act, such of the powers and duties of commissioners on a bankrupt estate as may be conferred and imposed on liquidation committees by the rules.

102 Creditors' meeting where winding up converted under s. 96

Where, in the case of a winding up which was, under section 96 in Chapter III, converted to a creditors' voluntary winding up, a creditors' meeting is held in accordance with section 95, any appointment made or committee established by that meeting is deemed to have been made or established by a meeting held in accordance with section 98 in this Chapter.

103 Cesser of directors' powers

On the appointment of a liquidator, all the powers of the directors cease, except so far as the liquidation committee (or, if there is no such committee, the creditors) sanction their continuance.

104 Vacancy in office of liquidator

If a vacancy occurs, by death, resignation or otherwise, in the office of a liquidator (other than a liquidator appointed by, or by the direction of, the court), the creditors may fill the vacancy.

105 Meetings of company and creditors at each year's end

(1) If the winding up continues for more than one year, the liquidator shall summon a general meeting of the company and a meeting of the creditors at the end of the first year from the commencement of the winding up, and of each succeeding year, or at the first convenient date within 3 months from the end of the year or such longer period as the Secretary of State may allow.

(2) The liquidator shall lay before each of the meetings an account of his acts and dealings and of the conduct of the winding up during the preceding year.

(3) If the liquidator fails to comply with this section, he is liable to a fine.

(4) Where under section 96 a members' voluntary winding up has become a creditors' voluntary winding up, and the creditors' meeting under section 95 is held 3 months or less before the end of the first year from the commencement of the winding up, the liquidator is not required by this section to summon a meeting of creditors at the end of that year.

106 Final meeting prior to dissolution

(1) As soon as the company's affairs are fully wound up, the liquidator shall make an account of the winding up, showing how it has been conducted and the company's property has been disposed of, and thereupon shall call a general meeting of the company and a

meeting of the creditors for the purpose of laying the account before the meetings and giving an explanation of it.

(2) Each such meeting shall be called by advertisement in the Gazette specifying the time, place and object of the meeting, and published at least one month before it.

(3) Within one week after the date of the meetings (or, if they are not held on the same date, after the date of the later one) the liquidator shall send to the registrar of companies a copy of the account, and shall make a return to him of the holding of the meetings and of their dates.

(4) If the copy is not sent or the return is not made in accordance with subsection (3), the liquidator is liable to a fine and, for continued contravention, to a daily default fine.

(5) However, if a quorum is not present at either such meeting, the liquidator shall, in lieu of the return required by subsection (3), make a return that the meeting was duly summoned and that no quorum was present; and upon such return being made the provisions of that subsection as to the making of the return are, in respect of that meeting, deemed complied with.

(6) If the liquidator fails to call a general meeting of the company or a meeting of the creditors as required by this section, he is liable to a fine.

CHAPTER V   PROVISIONS APPLYING TO BOTH KINDS OF VOLUNTARY WINDING UP

107   Distribution of company's property

Subject to the provisions of this Act as to preferential payments, the company's property in a voluntary winding up shall on the winding up be applied in satisfaction of the company's liabilities *pari passu* and, subject to that application, shall (unless the articles otherwise provide) be distributed among the members according to their rights and interests in the company.

108   Appointment or removal of liquidator by the court

(1) If from any cause whatever there is no liquidator acting, the court may appoint a liquidator.

(2) The court may, on cause shown, remove a liquidator and appoint another.

109   Notice by liquidator of his appointment

(1) The liquidator shall, within 14 days after his appointment, publish in the Gazette and deliver to the registrar of companies for registration a notice of his appointment in the form prescribed by statutory instrument made by the Secretary of State.

(2) If the liquidator fails to comply with this section, he is liable to a fine and, for continued contravention, to a daily default fine.

110   Acceptance of shares, etc., as consideration for sale of company property

(1) This section applies, in the case of a company proposed to be, or being, wound up voluntarily, where the whole or part of the company's business or property is proposed to be transferred or sold—

    (a) to another company ('the transferee company'), whether or not the latter is a company within the meaning of the Companies Act, or

    (b) to a limited liability partnership (the 'transferee limited liability partnership').

(2) With the requisite sanction, the liquidator of the company being, or proposed to be, wound up ('the transferor company') may receive, in compensation or part compensation for the transfer or sale—

    (a) in the case of the transferee company, shares, policies or other like interests in the transferee company for distribution among the members of the transferor company, or

(b) in the case of the transferee limited liability partnership, membership in the transferee limited liability partnership for distribution among the members of the transferor company.

(3) The sanction requisite under subsection (2) is—

(a) in the case of a members' voluntary winding up, that of a special resolution of the company, conferring either a general authority on the liquidator or an authority in respect of any particular arrangement, and

(b) in the case of a creditors' voluntary winding up, that of either the court or the liquidation committee.

(4) Alternatively to subsection (2), the liquidator may (with that sanction) enter into any other arrangement whereby the members of the transferor company may—

(a) in the case of the transferee company, in lieu of receiving cash, shares, policies or other like interests (or in addition thereto) participate in the profits of, or receive any other benefit from, the transferee company, or

(b) in the case of the transferee limited liability partnership, in lieu of receiving cash or membership (or in addition thereto), participate in some other way in the profits of, or receive any other benefit from, the transferee limited liability partnership.

(5) A sale or arrangement in pursuance of this section is binding on members of the transferor company.

(6) A special resolution is not invalid for purposes of this section by reason that it is passed before or concurrently with a resolution for voluntary winding up or for appointing liquidators; but, if an order is made within a year for winding up the company by the court, the special resolution is not valid unless sanctioned by the court.

111 Dissent from arrangement under s. 110

(1) This section applies in the case of a voluntary winding up where, for the purposes of section 110(2) or (4), there has been passed a special resolution of the transferor company providing the sanction requisite for the liquidator under that section.

(2) If a member of the transferor company who did not vote in favour of the special resolution expresses his dissent from it in writing, addressed to the liquidator and left at the company's registered office within 7 days after the passing of the resolution, he may require the liquidator either to abstain from carrying the resolution into effect or to purchase his interest at a price to be determined by agreement or by arbitration under this section.

(3) If the liquidator elects to purchase the member's interest, the purchase money must be paid before the company is dissolved and be raised by the liquidator in such manner as may be determined by special resolution.

(4) For purposes of an arbitration under this section, the provisions of the Companies Clauses Consolidation Act 1845 or, in the case of a winding up in Scotland, the Companies Clauses Consolidation (Scotland) Act 1845 with respect to the settlement of disputes by arbitration are incorporated with this Act, and—

(a) in the construction of those provisions this Act is deemed the special Act and 'the company' means the transferor company, and

(b) any appointment by the incorporated provisions directed to be made under the hand of the secretary or any two of the directors may be made in writing by the liquidator (or, if there is more than one liquidator, then any two or more of them).

112 Reference of questions to court

(1) The liquidator or any contributory or creditor may apply to the court to determine any question arising in the winding up of a company, or to exercise, as respects the enforcing of calls or any other matter, all or any of the powers which the court might exercise if the company were being wound up by the court.

(2) The court, if satisfied that the determination of the question or the required exercise of power will be just and beneficial, may accede wholly or partially to the application on such terms and conditions as it thinks fit, or may make such other order on the application as it thinks just.

(3) A copy of an order made by virtue of this section staying the proceedings in the winding up shall forthwith be forwarded by the company, or otherwise as may be prescribed, to the registrar of companies, who shall enter it in his records relating to the company.

114   No liquidator appointed or nominated by company

(1) This section applies where, in the case of a voluntary winding up, no liquidator has been appointed or nominated by the company.

(2) The powers of the directors shall not be exercised, except with the sanction of the court or (in the case of a creditors' voluntary winding up) so far as may be necessary to secure compliance with sections 98 (creditors' meeting) and 99 (statement of affairs), during the period before the appointment or nomination of a liquidator of the company.

(3) Subsection (2) does not apply in relation to the powers of the directors—

    (a) to dispose of perishable goods and other goods the value of which is likely to diminish if they are not immediately disposed of, and

    (b) to do all such other things as may be necessary for the protection of the company's assets.

(4) If the directors of the company without reasonable excuse fail to comply with this section, they are liable to a fine.

115   Expenses of voluntary winding up

All expenses properly incurred in the winding up, including the remuneration of the liquidator, are payable out of the company's assets in priority to all other claims.

116   Saving for certain rights

The voluntary winding up of a company does not bar the right of any creditor or contributory to have it wound up by the court; but in the case of an application by a contributory the court must be satisfied that the rights of the contributories will be prejudiced by a voluntary winding up.

CHAPTER VI   WINDING UP BY THE COURT

Jurisdiction (England and Wales)

117   High Court and county court jurisdiction

(1) The High Court has jurisdiction to wind up any company registered in England and Wales.

(2) Where the amount of a company's share capital paid up or credited as paid up does not exceed £120,000, then (subject to this section) the county court of the district in which the company's registered office is situated has concurrent jurisdiction with the High Court to wind up the company.

(3) The money sum for the time being specified in subsection (2) is subject to increase or reduction by order under section 416 in Part XV.

(4) The Lord Chancellor may by order in a statutory instrument exclude a county court from having winding-up jurisdiction, and for the purposes of that jurisdiction may attach its district, or any part thereof, to any other county court, and may by statutory instrument revoke or vary any such order.

In exercising the powers of this section, the Lord Chancellor shall provide that a county court is not to have winding-up jurisdiction unless it has for the time being jurisdiction for the purposes of Parts VIII to XI of this Act (individual insolvency).

(5) Every court in England and Wales having winding-up jurisdiction has for the purposes of that jurisdiction all the powers of the High Court; and every prescribed officer of the court shall perform any duties which an officer of the High Court may discharge by order of a judge of that court or otherwise in relation to winding up.

(6) For the purposes of this section, a company's 'registered office' is the place which has longest been its registered office during the 6 months immediately preceding the presentation of the petition for winding up.

(7) This section is subject to Article 3 of the EC Regulation (jurisdiction under EC Regulation).

118 Proceedings taken in wrong court

(1) Nothing in section 117 invalidates a proceeding by reason of its being taken in the wrong court.

(2) The winding up of a company by the court in England and Wales, or any proceedings in the winding up, may be retained in the court in which the proceedings were commenced, although it may not be the court in which they ought to have been commenced.

119 Proceedings in county court; case stated for High Court

(1) If any question arises in any winding-up proceedings in a county court which all the parties to the proceedings, or which one of them and the judge of the court, desire to have determined in the first instance in the High Court, the judge shall state the facts in the form of a special case for the opinion of the High Court.

(2) Thereupon the special case and the proceedings (or such of them as may be required) shall be transmitted to the High Court for the purposes of the determination.

Grounds and effect of winding-up petition

122 Circumstances in which company may be wound up by the court

(1) A company may be wound up by the court if—

(a) the company has by special resolution resolved that the company be wound up by the court,

(b) being a public company which was registered as such on its original incorporation, the company has not been issued with a certificate under section 117 of the Companies Act (public company share capital requirements) and more than a year has expired since it was so registered,

(c) it is an old public company, within the meaning of the Consequential Provisions Act,

(d) the company does not commence its business within a year from its incorporation or suspends its business for a whole year,

(e) except in the case of a private company limited by shares or by guarantee, the number of members is reduced below 2,

(f) the company is unable to pay its debts,

(fa) at the time at which a moratorium for the company under section 1A comes to an end, no voluntary arrangement approved under Part I has effect in relation to the company,

(g) the court is of the opinion that it is just and equitable that the company should be wound up.

(2) In Scotland, a company which the Court of Session has jurisdiction to wind up may be wound up by the Court if there is subsisting a floating charge over property comprised in the company's property and undertaking, and the court is satisfied that the security of the creditor entitled to the benefit of the floating charge is in jeopardy.

For this purpose a creditor's security is deemed to be in jeopardy if the Court is satisfied that events have occurred or are about to occur which render it unreasonable in the creditor's interests that the company should retain power to dispose of the property which is subject to the floating charge.

123 Definition of inability to pay debts

(1) A company is deemed unable to pay its debts—

(a) if a creditor (by assignment or otherwise) to whom the company is indebted in a sum exceeding £750 then due has served on the company, by leaving it at the company's registered office, a written demand (in the prescribed form) requiring the company to pay the sum so due and the company has for 3 weeks thereafter neglected to pay the sum or to secure or compound for it to the reasonable satisfaction of the creditor, or

(b) if, in England and Wales, execution or other process issued on a judgment, decree or order of any court in favour of a creditor of the company is returned unsatisfied in whole or in part, or

(c) if, in Scotland, the induciae of a charge for payment on an extract decree, or an extract registered bond, or an extract registered protest, have expired without payment being made, or

(d) if, in Northern Ireland, a certificate of unenforceability has been granted in respect of a judgment against the company, or

(e) if it is proved to the satisfaction of the court that the company is unable to pay its debts as they fall due.

(2) A company is also deemed unable to pay its debts if it is proved to the satisfaction of the court that the value of the company's assets is less than the amount of its liabilities, taking into account its contingent and prospective liabilities.

(3) The money sum for the time being specified in subsection (1)(a) is subject to increase or reduction by order under section 416 in Part XV.

124 Application for winding up

(1) Subject to the provisions of this section, an application to the court for the winding up of a company shall be by petition presented either by the company, or the directors, or by any creditor or creditors (including any contingent or prospective creditor or creditors), contributory or contributories, or by a liquidator (within the meaning of Article 2(b) of the EC Regulation) appointed in proceedings by virtue of Article 3(1) of the EC Regulation or a temporary administrator (within the meaning of Article 38 of the EC Regulation) or by a justices' chief executive in the exercise of the power conferred by section 87A of the Magistrates' Courts Act 1980 (enforcement of fines imposed on companies), or by all or any of those parties, together or separately.

(2) Except as mentioned below, a contributory is not entitled to present a winding-up petition unless either—

(a) the number of members is reduced below 2, or

(b) the shares in respect of which he is a contributory, or some of them, either were originally allotted to him, or have been held by him, and registered in his name, for at least 6 months during the 18 months before the commencement of the winding up, or have devolved on him through the death of a former holder.

(3) A person who is liable under section 76 to contribute to a company's assets in the event of it being wound up may petition on either of the grounds set out in section 122(1)(f) and (g), and subsection (2) above does not then apply; but unless the person is a contributory otherwise than under section 76, he may not in his character as contributory petition on any other ground.

This subsection is deemed included in Chapter VII of Part V of the Companies Act (redeemable shares; purchase by a company of its own shares) for the purposes of the Secretary of State's power to make regulations under section 179 of that Act.

(3A) A winding-up petition on the ground set out in section 122(1)(fa) may only be presented by one or more creditors.

(4) A winding-up petition may be presented by the Secretary of State—
(a) if the ground of the petition is that in section 122(1)(b) or (c), or
(b) in a case falling within section 124A below.

(5) Where a company is being wound up voluntarily in England and Wales, a winding-up petition may be presented by the official receiver attached to the court as well as by any other person authorised in that behalf under the other provisions of this section; but the court shall not make a winding-up order on the petition unless it is satisfied that the voluntary winding up cannot be continued with due regard to the interests of the creditors or contributories.

124A   Petition for winding up on grounds of public interest
(1) Where it appears to the Secretary of State from—
(a) any report made or information obtained under Part XIV of the Companies Act 1985 (company investigations, &c.),
(b) any report made by inspectors under—
(i)   section 167, 168, 169 or 284 of the Financial Services and Markets Act 2000, or
(ii) where the company is an open-ended investment company (within the meaning of that Act), regulations made as a result of section 262(2)(k) of that Act;
(bb) any information or documents obtained under section 165, 171, 172, 173 or 175 of that Act,
(c) any information obtained under section 2 of the Criminal Justice Act 1987 or section 52 of the Criminal Justice (Scotland) Act 1987 (fraud investigations), or
(d) any information obtained under section 83 of the Companies Act 1989 (powers exercisable for purpose of assisting overseas regulatory authorities),
that it is expedient in the public interest that a company should be wound up, he may present a petition for it to be wound up if the court thinks it just and equitable for it to be so.

(2) This section does not apply if the company is already being wound up by the court.

125   Powers of court on hearing of petition
(1) On hearing a winding-up petition the court may dismiss it, or adjourn the hearing conditionally or unconditionally, or make an interim order, or any other order that it thinks fit; but the court shall not refuse to make a winding-up order on the ground only that the company's assets have been mortgaged to an amount equal to or in excess of those assets, or that the company has no assets.

(2) If the petition is presented by members of the company as contributories on the ground that it is just and equitable that the company should be wound up, the court, if it is of opinion—
(a) that the petitioners are entitled to relief either by winding up the company or by some other means, and
(b) that in the absence of any other remedy it would be just and equitable that the company should be wound up,
shall make a winding-up order; but this does not apply if the court is also of the opinion both that some other remedy is available to the petitioners and that they are acting unreasonably in seeking to have the company wound up instead of pursuing that other remedy.

126   Power to stay or restrain proceedings against company
(1) At any time after the presentation of a winding-up petition, and before a winding-up order has been made, the company, or any creditor or contributory, may—
(a) where any action or proceeding against the company is pending in the High Court or Court of Appeal in England and Wales or Northern Ireland, apply to the court in which the action or proceeding is pending for a stay of proceedings therein, and
(b) where any other action or proceeding is pending against the company, apply to

the court having jurisdiction to wind up the company to restrain further proceedings in the action or proceeding;
and the court to which application is so made may (as the case may be) stay, sist or restrain the
proceedings accordingly on such terms as it thinks fit.

(2) In the case of a company registered under section 680 of the Companies Act (pre-1862
companies; companies formed under legislation other than the Companies Acts) or the previous corresponding legislation, where the application to stay, sist or restrain is by a creditor,
this section extends to actions and proceedings against any contributory of the company.

127   Avoidance of property dispositions, etc.

(1) In a winding up by the court, any disposition of the company's property, and any
transfer of shares, or alteration in the status of the company's members, made after the commencement of the winding up is, unless the court otherwise orders, void.

(2) *This section has no effect in respect of anything done by an administrator of a company while a winding-up petition is suspended under paragraph 40 of Schedule B1.*
[*On 15 June 2003, s. 127(2) had not been brought into force.*]

128   Avoidance of attachments, etc.

(1) Where a company registered in England and Wales is being wound up by the court,
any attachment, sequestration, distress or execution put in force against the estate or effects of
the company after the commencement of the winding up is void.

(2) This section, so far as relates to any estate or effects of the company situated in
England and Wales, applies in the case of a company registered in Scotland as it applies in the
case of a company registered in England and Wales.

Commencement of winding up

129   Commencement of winding up by the court

(1) If, before the presentation of a petition for the winding up of a company by the court,
a resolution has been passed by the company for voluntary winding up, the winding up of the
company is deemed to have commenced at the time of the passing of the resolution; and
unless the court, on proof of fraud or mistake, directs otherwise, all proceedings taken in the
voluntary winding up are deemed to have been validly taken.

(1A) *Where the court makes a winding-up order by virtue of paragraph 13(1)(e) of Schedule B1,
the winding up is deemed to commence on the making of the order.*

(2) In any other case, the winding up of a company by the court is deemed to commence
at the time of the presentation of the petition for winding up.
[*On 15 June 2003, s. 129(1A) had not been brought into force.*]

130   Consequences of winding-up order

(1) On the making of a winding-up order, a copy of the order must forthwith be forwarded by the company (or otherwise as may be prescribed) to the registrar of companies, who
shall enter it in his records relating to the company.

(2) When a winding-up order has been made or a provisional liquidator has been
appointed, no action or proceeding shall be proceeded with or commenced against the company or its property, except by leave of the court and subject to such terms as the court may
impose.

(3) When an order has been made for winding up a company registered under section 680
of the Companies Act, no action or proceeding shall be commenced or proceeded with against
the company or its property or any contributory of the company, in respect of any debt of the
company, except by leave of the court, and subject to such terms as the court may impose.

(4) An order for winding up a company operates in favour of all the creditors and of all
contributories of the company as if made on the joint petition of a creditor and of a
contributory.

Investigation procedures

131   Company's statement of affairs

(1) Where the court has made a winding-up order or appointed a provisional liquidator, the official receiver may require some or all of the persons mentioned in subsection (3) below to make out and submit to him a statement in the prescribed form as to the affairs of the company.

(2) The statement shall be verified by affidavit by the persons required to submit it and shall show—

    (a) particulars of the company's assets, debts and liabilities;

    (b) the names and addresses of the company's creditors;

    (c) the securities held by them respectively;

    (d) the dates when the securities were respectively given; and

    (e) such further or other information as may be prescribed or as the official receiver may require.

(3) The persons referred to in subsection (1) are—

    (a) those who are or have been officers of the company;

    (b) those who have taken part in the formation of the company at any time within one year before the relevant date;

    (c) those who are in the company's employment, or have been in its employment within that year, and are in the official receiver's opinion capable of giving the information required;

    (d) those who are or have been within that year officers of, or in the employment of, a company which is, or within that year was, an officer of the company.

(4) Where any persons are required under this section to submit a statement of affairs to the official receiver, they shall do so (subject to the next subsection) before the end of the period of 21 days beginning with the day after that on which the prescribed notice of the requirement is given to them by the official receiver.

(5) The official receiver, if he thinks fit, may—

    (a) at any time release a person from an obligation imposed on him under subsection (1) or (2) above; or

    (b) either when giving the notice mentioned in subsection (4) or subsequently, extend the period so mentioned;

and where the official receiver has refused to exercise a power conferred by this subsection, the court, if it thinks fit, may exercise it.

(6) In this section—

'employment' includes employment under a contract for services; and

'the relevant date' means—

    (a) in a case where a provisional liquidator is appointed, the date of his appointment; and

    (b) in a case where no such appointment is made, the date of the winding-up order.

(7) If a person without reasonable excuse fails to comply with any obligation imposed under this section, he is liable to a fine and, for continued contravention, to a daily default fine.

(8) In the application of this section to Scotland references to the official receiver are to the liquidator or, in a case where a provisional liquidator is appointed, the provisional liquidator.

132   Investigation by official receiver

(1) Where a winding-up order is made by the court in England and Wales, it is the duty of the official receiver to investigate—

    (a) if the company has failed, the causes of the failure; and

    (b) generally, the promotion, formation, business, dealings and affairs of the company, and to make such report (if any) to the court as he thinks fit.

(2) The report is, in any proceedings, prima facie evidence of the facts stated in it.

133   Public examination of officers

(1) Where a company is being wound up by the court, the official receiver or, in Scotland, the liquidator may at any time before the dissolution of the company apply to the court for the public examination of any person who—

(a) is or has been an officer of the company; or

(b) has acted as liquidator or administrator of the company or as receiver or manager or, in Scotland, receiver of its property; or

(c) not being a person falling within paragraph (a) or (b), is or has been concerned, or has taken part, in the promotion, formation or management of the company.

(2) Unless the court otherwise orders, the official receiver or, in Scotland, the liquidator shall make an application under subsection (1) if he is requested in accordance with the rules to do so by—

(a) one-half, in value, of the company's creditors; or

(b) three-quarters, in value, of the company's contributories.

(3) On an application under subsection (1), the court shall direct that a public examination of the person to whom the application relates shall be held on a day appointed by the court; and that person shall attend on that day and be publicly examined as to the promotion, formation or management of the company or as to the conduct of its business and affairs, or his conduct or dealings in relation to the company.

(4) The following may take part in the public examination of a person under this section and may question that person concerning the matters mentioned in subsection (3), namely—

(a) the official receiver;

(b) the liquidator of the company;

(c) any person who has been appointed as special manager of the company's property or business;

(d) any creditor of the company who has tendered a proof or, in Scotland, submitted a claim in the winding up;

(e) any contributory of the company.

134   Enforcement of s. 133

(1) If a person without reasonable excuse fails at any time to attend his public examination under section 133, he is guilty of a contempt of court and liable to be punished accordingly.

(2) In a case where a person without reasonable excuse fails at any time to attend his examination under section 133 or there are reasonable grounds for believing that a person has absconded, or is about to abscond, with a view to avoiding or delaying his examination under that section, the court may cause a warrant to be issued to a constable or prescribed officer of the court—

(a) for the arrest of that person; and

(b) for the seizure of any books, papers, records, money or goods in that person's possession.

(3) In such a case the court may authorise the person arrested under the warrant to be kept in custody, and anything seized under such a warrant to be held, in accordance with the rules, until such time as the court may order.

Appointment of liquidator

135   Appointment and powers of provisional liquidator

(1) Subject to the provisions of this section, the court may, at any time after the presentation of a winding-up petition, appoint a liquidator provisionally.

(2) In England and Wales, the appointment of a provisional liquidator may be made at any time before the making of a winding-up order; and either the official receiver or any other fit person may be appointed.

(3) In Scotland, such an appointment may be made at any time before the first appointment of liquidators.

(4) The provisional liquidator shall carry out such functions as the court may confer on him.

(5) When a liquidator is provisionally appointed by the court, his powers may be limited by the order appointing him.

136   Functions of official receiver in relation to office of liquidator

(1) The following provisions of this section have effect, subject to section 140 below, on a winding-up order being made by the court in England and Wales.

(2) The official receiver, by virtue of his office, becomes the liquidator of the company and continues in office until another person becomes liquidator under the provisions of this Part.

(3) The official receiver is, by virtue of his office, the liquidator during any vacancy.

(4) At any time when he is the liquidator of the company, the official receiver may summon separate meetings of the company's creditors and contributories for the purpose of choosing a person to be liquidator of the company in place of the official receiver.

(5) It is the duty of the official receiver—

(a) as soon as practicable in the period of 12 weeks beginning with the day on which the winding-up order was made, to decide whether to exercise his power under subsection (4) to summon meetings, and

(b) if in pursuance of paragraph (a) he decides not to exercise that power, to give notice of his decision, before the end of that period, to the court and to the company's creditors and contributories, and

(c) (whether or not he has decided to exercise that power) to exercise his power to summon meetings under subsection (4) if he is at any time requested, in accordance with the rules, to do so by one-quarter, in value, of the company's creditors;

and accordingly, where the duty imposed by paragraph (c) arises before the official receiver has performed a duty imposed by paragraph (a) or (b), he is not required to perform the latter duty.

(6) A notice given under subsection (5)(b) to the company's creditors shall contain an explanation of the creditors' power under subsection (5)(c) to require the official receiver to summon meetings of the company's creditors and contributories.

137   Appointment by Secretary of State

(1) In a winding up by the court in England and Wales the official receiver may, at any time when he is the liquidator of the company, apply to the Secretary of State for the appointment of a person as liquidator in his place.

(2) If meetings are held in pursuance of a decision under section 136(5)(a), but no person is chosen to be liquidator as a result of those meetings, it is the duty of the official receiver to decide whether to refer the need for an appointment to the Secretary of State.

(3) On an application under subsection (1), or a reference made in pursuance of a decision under subsection (2), the Secretary of State shall either make an appointment or decline to make one.

(4) Where a liquidator has been appointed by the Secretary of State under subsection (3), the liquidator shall give notice of his appointment to the company's creditors or, if the court so allows, shall advertise his appointment in accordance with the directions of the court.

(5) In that notice or advertisement the liquidator shall—

(a) state whether he proposes to summon a general meeting of the company's creditors under section 141 below for the purpose of determining (together with any meeting of contributories) whether a liquidation committee should be established under that section, and

(b) if he does not propose to summon such a meeting, set out the power of the company's creditors under that section to require him to summon one.

139   Choice of liquidator at meetings of creditors and contributories

(1) This section applies where a company is being wound up by the court and separate meetings of the company's creditors and contributories are summoned for the purpose of choosing a person to be liquidator of the company.

(2) The creditors and the contributories at their respective meetings may nominate a person to be liquidator.

(3) The liquidator shall be the person nominated by the creditors or, where no person has been so nominated, the person (if any) nominated by the contributories.

(4) In the case of different persons being nominated, any contributory or creditor may, within 7 days after the date on which the nomination was made by the creditors, apply to the court for an order either—

(a) appointing the person nominated as liquidator by the contributories to be a liquidator instead of, or jointly with, the person nominated by the creditors; or

(b) appointing some other person to be liquidator instead of the person nominated by the creditors.

140   Appointment by the court following administration or voluntary arrangement

(1) Where a winding-up order is made immediately upon the discharge of an administration order, the court may appoint as liquidator of the company the person who has ceased on the discharge of the administration order to be the administrator of the company.

(2) Where a winding-up order is made at a time when there is a supervisor of a voluntary arrangement approved in relation to the company under Part I, the court may appoint as liquidator of the company the person who is the supervisor at the time when the winding-up order is made.

(3) Where the court makes an appointment under this section, the official receiver does not become the liquidator as otherwise provided by section 136(2), and he has no duty under section 136(5)(a) or (b) in respect of the summoning of creditors' or contributories' meetings. [*When the Enterprise Act 2002, sch. 17, is brought into force, the Insolvency Act 1986, s. 140(1), will be replaced by:*

(1) Where a winding-up order is made immediately upon the appointment of an administrator ceasing to have effect, the court may appoint as liquidator of the company the person whose appointment as administrator has ceased to have effect.]

Liquidation committees

141   Liquidation committee (England and Wales)

(1) Where a winding-up order has been made by the court in England and Wales and separate meetings of creditors and contributories have been summoned for the purpose of choosing a person to be liquidator, those meetings may establish a committee ('the liquidation committee') to exercise the functions conferred on it by or under this Act.

(2) The liquidator (not being the official receiver) may at any time, if he thinks fit, summon separate general meetings of the company's creditors and contributories for the purpose of determining whether such a committee should be established and, if it is so determined, of establishing it.

The liquidator (not being the official receiver) shall summon such a meeting if he is requested, in accordance with the rules, to do so by one-tenth, in value, of the company's creditors.

(3) Where meetings are summoned under this section, or for the purpose of choosing a person to be liquidator, and either the meeting of creditors or the meeting of contributories decides that a liquidation committee should be established, but the other meeting does not so decide or decides that a committee should not be established, the committee shall be established in accordance with the rules, unless the court otherwise orders.

(4) The liquidation committee is not to be able or required to carry out its functions at any time when the official receiver is liquidator; but at any such time its functions are vested in the Secretary of State except to the extent that the rules otherwise provide.

(5) Where there is for the time being no liquidation committee, and the liquidator is a person other than the official receiver, the functions of such a committee are vested in the Secretary of State except to the extent that the rules otherwise provide.

The liquidator's functions

143 General functions in winding up by the court
(1) The functions of the liquidator of a company which is being wound up by the court are to secure that the assets of the company are got in, realised and distributed to the company's creditors and, if there is a surplus, to the persons entitled to it.

(2) It is the duty of the liquidator of a company which is being wound up by the court in England and Wales, if he is not the official receiver—
    (a) to furnish the official receiver with such information,
    (b) to produce to the official receiver, and permit inspection by the official receiver of, such books, papers and other records, and
    (c) to give the official receiver such other assistance, as the official receiver may reasonably require for the purposes of carrying out his functions in relation to the winding up.

144 Custody of company's property
(1) When a winding-up order has been made, or where a provisional liquidator has been appointed, the liquidator or the provisional liquidator (as the case may be) shall take into his custody or under his control all the property and things in action to which the company is or appears to be entitled.

(2) In a winding up by the court in Scotland, if and so long as there is no liquidator, all the property of the company is deemed to be in the custody of the court.

145 Vesting of company property in liquidator
(1) When a company is being wound up by the court, the court may on the application of the liquidator by order direct that all or any part of the property of whatsoever description belonging to the company or held by trustees on its behalf shall vest in the liquidator by his official name; and thereupon the property to which the order relates vests accordingly.

(2) The liquidator may, after giving such indemnity (if any) as the court may direct, bring or defend in his official name any action or other legal proceeding which relates to that property or which it is necessary to bring or defend for the purpose of effectually winding up the company and recovering its property.

146 Duty to summon final meeting
(1) Subject to the next subsection, if it appears to the liquidator of a company which is being wound by the court that the winding up of the company is for practical purposes complete and the liquidator is not the official receiver, the liquidator shall summon a final general meeting of the company's creditors which—
    (a) shall receive the liquidator's report of the winding up, and
    (b) shall determine whether the liquidator should have his release under section 174 in Chapter VII of this Part.

(2) The liquidator may, if he thinks fit, give the notice summoning the final general

meeting at the same time as giving notice of any final distribution of the company's property but, if summoned for an earlier date, that meeting shall be adjourned (and, if necessary, further adjourned) until a date on which the liquidator is able to report to the meeting that the winding up of the company is for practical purposes complete.

(3) In the carrying out of his functions in the winding up it is the duty of the liquidator to retain sufficient sums from the company's property to cover the expenses of summoning and holding the meeting required by this section.

General powers of court

147   Power to stay or sist winding up

(1) The court may at any time after an order for winding up, on the application either of the liquidator or the official receiver or any creditor or contributory, and on proof to the satisfaction of the court that all proceedings in the winding up ought to be stayed or sisted, make an order staying or sisting the proceedings, either altogether or for a limited time, on such terms and conditions as the court thinks fit.

(2) The court may, before making an order, require the official receiver to furnish to it a report with respect to any facts or matters which are in his opinion relevant to the application.

(3) A copy of every order made under this section shall forthwith be forwarded by the company, or otherwise as may be prescribed, to the registrar of companies, who shall enter it in his records relating to the company.

148   Settlement of list of contributories and application of assets

(1) As soon as may be after making a winding-up order, the court shall settle a list of contributories, with power to rectify the register of members in all cases where rectification is required in pursuance of the Companies Act or this Act, and shall cause the company's assets to be collected, and applied in discharge of its liabilities.

(2) If it appears to the court that it will not be necessary to make calls on or adjust the rights of contributories, the court may dispense with the settlement of a list of contributories.

(3) In settling the list, the court shall distinguish between persons who are contributories in their own right and persons who are contributories as being representatives of or liable for the debts of others.

149   Debts due from contributory to company

(1) The court may, at any time after making a winding-up order, make an order on any contributory for the time being on the list of contributories to pay, in manner directed by the order, any money due from him (or from the estate of the person who he represents) to the company, exclusive of any money payable by him or the estate by virtue of any call in pursuance of the Companies Act or this Act.

(2) The court in making such an order may—

    (a) in the case of an unlimited company, allow to the contributory by way of set-off any money due to him or the estate which he represents from the company on any independent dealing or contract with the company, but not any money due to him as a member of the company in respect of any dividend or profit, and

    (b) in the case of a limited company, make to any director or manager whose liability is unlimited or to his estate the like allowance.

(3) In the case of any company, whether limited or unlimited, when all the creditors are paid in full (together with interest at the official rate), any money due on any account whatever to a contributory from the company may be allowed to him by way of set-off against any subsequent call.

150   Power to make calls

(1) The court may, at any time after making a winding-up order, and either before or after it has ascertained the sufficiency of the company's assets, make calls on all or any of the

contributories for the time being settled on the list of the contributories to the extent of their liability, for payment of any money which the court considers necessary to satisfy the company's debts and liabilities, and the expenses of winding up, and for the adjustment of the rights of the contributories among themselves, and make an order for payment of any calls so made.

(2) In making a call the court may take into consideration the probability that some of the contributories may partly or wholly fail to pay it.

151 Payment into bank of money due to company

(1) The court may order any contributory, purchaser or other person from whom money is due to the company to pay the amount due into the Bank of England (or any branch of it) to the account of the liquidator instead of to the liquidator, and such an order may be enforced in the same manner as if it had directed payment to the liquidator.

(2) All money and securities paid or delivered into the Bank of England (or branch) in the event of a winding up by the court are subject in all respects to the orders of the court.

152 Order on contributory to be conclusive evidence

(1) An order made by the court on a contributory is conclusive evidence that the money (if any) thereby appearing to be due or ordered to be paid is due, but subject to any right of appeal.

(2) All other pertinent matters stated in the order are to be taken as truly stated as against all persons and in all proceedings except proceedings in Scotland against the heritable estate of a deceased contributory; and in that case the order is only prima facie evidence for the purpose of charging his heritable estate, unless his heirs or legatees of heritage were on the list of contributories at the time of the order being made.

153 Power to exclude creditors not proving in time

The court may fix a time or times within which creditors are to prove their debts or claims or to be excluded from the benefit of any distribution made before those debts are proved.

154 Adjustment of rights of contributories

The court shall adjust the rights of the contributories among themselves and distribute any surplus among the persons entitled to it.

155 Inspection of books by creditors, etc.

(1) The court may, at any time after making a winding-up order, make such order for inspection of the company's books and papers by creditors and contributories as the court thinks just; and any books and papers in the company's possession may be inspected by creditors and contributories accordingly, but not further or otherwise.

(2) Nothing in this section excludes or restricts any statutory rights of a government department or person acting under the authority of a government department.

(3) For the purposes of subsection (2) above, references to a government department shall be construed as including references to any part of the Scottish Administration.

156 Payment of expenses of winding up

The court may, in the event of the assets being insufficient to satisfy the liabilities, make an order as to the payment out of the assets of the expenses incurred in the winding up in such order of priority as the court thinks just.

158 Power to arrest absconding contributory

The court, at any time either before or after making a winding-up order, on proof of probable cause for believing that a contributory is about to quit the United Kingdom or otherwise to abscond or to remove or conceal any of his property for the purpose of evading payment of calls, may cause the contributory to be arrested and his books and papers and movable personal property to be seized and him and them to be kept safely until such time as the court may order.

159   Powers of court to be cumulative
Powers conferred by this Act and the Companies Act on the court are in addition to, and not in restriction of, any existing powers of instituting proceedings against a contributory or debtor of the company, or the estate of any contributory or debtor, for the recovery of any call or other sums.

160   Delegation of powers to liquidator (England and Wales)
(1) Provision may be made by rules for enabling or requiring all or any of the powers and duties conferred and imposed on the court in England and Wales by the Companies Act and this Act in respect of the following matters—
   (a) the holding and conducting of meetings to ascertain the wishes of creditors and contributories,
   (b) the settling of lists of contributories and the rectifying of the register of members where required, and the collection and application of the assets,
   (c) the payment, delivery, conveyance, surrender or transfer of money, property, books or papers to the liquidator,
   (d) the making of calls,
   (e) the fixing of a time within which debts and claims must be proved,
to be exercised or performed by the liquidator as an officer of the court, and subject to the court's control.

(2) But the liquidator shall not, without the special leave of the court, rectify the register of members, and shall not make any call without either that special leave or the sanction of the liquidation committee.

CHAPTER VII   LIQUIDATORS

Preliminary

163   Style and title of liquidators
The liquidator of a company shall be described—
   (a) where a person other than the official receiver is liquidator, by the style of 'the liquidator' of the particular company, or
   (b) where the official receiver is liquidator, by the style of 'the official receiver and liquidator' of the particular company;
and in neither case shall he be described by an individual name.

164   Corrupt inducement affecting appointment
A person who gives, or agrees or offers to give, to any member or creditor of a company any valuable consideration with a view to securing his own appointment or nomination, or to securing or preventing the appointment or nomination of some person other than himself, as the company's liquidator is liable to a fine.

Liquidator's powers and duties

165   Voluntary winding up
(1) This section has effect where a company is being wound up voluntarily, but subject to section 166 below in the case of a creditors' voluntary winding up.
(2) The liquidator may—
   (a) in the case of a members' voluntary winding up, with the sanction of an extra-ordinary resolution of the company, and
   (b) in the case of a creditors' voluntary winding up, with the sanction of the court or the liquidation committee (or, if there is no such committee, a meeting of the company's creditors),

exercise any of the powers specified in Part I of Schedule 4 to this Act (payment of debts, compromise of claims, etc.).

(3) The liquidator may, without sanction, exercise either of the powers specified in Part II of the Schedule (institution and defence of proceedings; carrying on the business of the company) and any of the general powers specified in Part III of that Schedule.

(4) The liquidator may—

   (a) exercise the court's power of settling a list of contributories (which list is prima facie evidence of the liability of the persons named in it to be contributories),

   (b) exercise the court's power of making calls,

   (c) summon general meetings of the company for the purpose of obtaining its sanction by special or extraordinary resolution or for any other purpose he may think fit.

(5) The liquidator shall pay the company's debts and adjust the rights of the contributories among themselves.

(6) Where the liquidator in exercise of the powers conferred on him by this Act disposes of any property of the company to a person who is connected with the company (within the meaning of section 249 in Part VII), he shall, if there is for the time being a liquidation committee, give notice to the committee of that exercise of his powers.

166 Creditors' voluntary winding up

(1) This section applies where, in the case of a creditors' voluntary winding up, a liquidator has been nominated by the company.

(2) The powers conferred on the liquidator by section 165 shall not be exercised, except with the sanction of the court, during the period before the holding of the creditors' meeting under section 98 in Chapter IV.

(3) Subsection (2) does not apply in relation to the power of the liquidator—

   (a) to take into his custody or under his control all the property to which the company is or appears to be entitled;

   (b) to dispose of perishable goods and other goods the value of which is likely to diminish if they are not immediately disposed of; and

   (c) to do all such other things as may be necessary for the protection of the company's assets.

(4) The liquidator shall attend the creditors' meeting held under section 98 and shall report to the meeting on any exercise by him of his powers (whether or not under this section or under section 112 or 165).

(5) If default is made—

   (a) by the company in complying with subsection (1) or (2) of section 98, or

   (b) by the directors in complying with subsection (1) or (2) of section 99, the liquidator shall, within 7 days of the relevant day, apply to the court for directions as to the manner in which that default is to be remedied.

(6) 'The relevant day' means the day on which the liquidator was nominated by the company or the day on which he first became aware of the default, whichever is the later.

(7) If the liquidator without reasonable excuse fails to comply with this section, he is liable to a fine.

167 Winding up by the court

   (1) Where a company is being wound up by the court, the liquidator may—

   (a) with the sanction of the court or the liquidation committee, exercise any of the powers specified in Parts I and II of Schedule 4 to this Act (payment of debts; compromise of claims, etc.; institution and defence of proceedings; carrying on of the business of the company), and

   (b) with or without that sanction, exercise any of the general powers specified in Part III of that Schedule.

(2) Where the liquidator (not being the official receiver), in exercise of the powers conferred on him by this Act—

  (a) disposes of any property of the company to a person who is connected with the company (within the meaning of section 249 in Part VII), or

  (b) employs a solicitor to assist him in the carrying out of his functions, he shall, if there is for the time being a liquidation committee, give notice to the committee of that exercise of his powers.

(3) The exercise by the liquidator in a winding up by the court of the powers conferred by this section is subject to the control of the court, and any creditor or contributory may apply to the court with respect to any exercise or proposed exercise of any of those powers.

168 Supplementary powers (England and Wales)

(1) This section applies in the case of a company which is being wound up by the court in England and Wales.

(2) The liquidator may summon general meetings of the creditors or contributories for the purpose of ascertaining their wishes; and it is his duty to summon meetings at such times as the creditors or contributories by resolution (either at the meeting appointing the liquidator or otherwise) may direct, or whenever requested in writing to do so by one-tenth in value of the creditors or contributories (as the case may be).

(3) The liquidator may apply to the court (in the prescribed manner) for directions in relation to any particular matter arising in the winding up.

(4) Subject to the provisions of this Act, the liquidator shall use his own discretion in the management of the assets and their distribution among the creditors.

(5) If any person is aggrieved by an act or decision of the liquidator, that person may apply to the court; and the court may confirm, reverse or modify the act or decision complained of, and make such order in the case as it thinks just.

. . .

170 Enforcement of liquidator's duty to make returns, etc.

(1) If a liquidator who has made any default—

  (a) in filing, delivering or making any return, account or other document, or

  (b) in giving any notice which he is by law required to file, deliver, make or give, fails to make good the default within 14 days after the service on him of a notice requiring him to do so, the court has the following powers.

(2) On an application made by any creditor or contributory of the company, or by the registrar of companies, the court may make an order directing the liquidator to make good the default within such time as may be specified in the order.

(3) The court's order may provide that all costs of and incidental to the application shall be borne by the liquidator.

(4) Nothing in this section prejudices the operation of any enactment imposing penalties on a liquidator in respect of any such default as is mentioned above.

Removal; vacation of office

171 Removal, etc. (voluntary winding up)

(1) This section applies with respect to the removal from office and vacation of office of the liquidator of a company which is being wound up voluntarily.

(2) Subject to the next subsection, the liquidator may be removed from office only by an order of the court or—

  (a) in the case of a members' voluntary winding up, by a general meeting of the company summoned specially for that purpose, or

  (b) in the case of a creditors' voluntary winding up, by a general meeting of the company's creditors summoned specially for that purpose in accordance with the rules.

(3) Where the liquidator was appointed by the court under section 108 in Chapter V, a meeting such as is mentioned in subsection (2) above shall be summoned for the purpose of replacing him only if he thinks fit or the court so directs or the meeting is requested, in accordance with the rules—

    (a) in the case of a members' voluntary winding up, by members representing not less than one-half of the total voting rights of all the members having at the date of the request a right to vote at the meeting, or

    (b) in the case of a creditors' voluntary winding up, by not less than one-half, in value, of the company's creditors.

(4) A liquidator shall vacate office if he ceases to be a person who is qualified to act as an insolvency practitioner in relation to the company.

(5) A liquidator may, in the prescribed circumstances, resign his office by giving notice of his resignation to the registrar of companies.

(6) Where—

    (a) in the case of a members' voluntary winding up, a final meeting of the company has been held under section 94 in Chapter III, or

    (b) in the case of a creditors' voluntary winding up, final meetings of the company and of the creditors have been held under section 106 in Chapter IV,

the liquidator whose report was considered at the meeting or meetings shall vacate office as soon as he has complied with subsection (3) of that section and has given notice to the registrar of companies that the meeting or meetings have been held and of the decisions (if any) of the meeting or meetings.

172   Removal, etc. (winding up by the court)

(1) This section applies with respect to the removal from office and vacation of office of the liquidator of a company which is being wound up by the court, or of a provisional liquidator.

(2) Subject as follows, the liquidator may be removed from office only by an order of the court or by a general meeting of the company's creditors summoned specially for that purpose in accordance with the rules; and a provisional liquidator may be removed from office only by an order of the court.

(3) Where—

    (a) the official receiver is liquidator otherwise than in succession under section 136(3) to a person who held office as a result of a nomination by a meeting of the company's creditors or contributories, or

    (b) the liquidator was appointed by the court otherwise than under section 139(4)(a) or 140(1), or was appointed by the Secretary of State,

a general meeting of the company's creditors shall be summoned for the purpose of replacing him only if he thinks fit, or the court so directs, or the meeting is requested, in accordance with the rules, by not less than one-quarter, in value, of the creditors.

(4) If appointed by the Secretary of State, the liquidator may be removed from office by a direction of the Secretary of State.

(5) A liquidator or provisional liquidator, not being the official receiver, shall vacate office if he ceases to be a person who is qualified to act as an insolvency practitioner in relation to the company.

(6) A liquidator may, in the prescribed circumstances, resign his office by giving notice of his resignation to the court.

(7) Where an order is made under section 204 (early dissolution in Scotland) for the dissolution of the company, the liquidator shall vacate office when the dissolution of the company takes effect in accordance with that section.

(8) Where a final meeting has been held under section 146 (liquidator's report on completion of winding up), the liquidator whose report was considered at the meeting shall vacate

office as soon as he has given notice to the court and the registrar of companies that the meeting has been held and of the decisions (if any) of the meeting.

Release of liquidator

173   Release (voluntary winding up)

(1) This section applies with respect to the release of the liquidator of a company which is being wound up voluntarily.

(2) A person who has ceased to be a liquidator shall have his release with effect from the following time, that is to say—

   (a) in the case of a person who has been removed from office by a general meeting of the company or by a general meeting of the company's creditors that has not resolved against his release or who has died, the time at which notice is given to the registrar of companies in accordance with the rules that that person has ceased to hold office;

   (b) in the case of a person who has been removed from office by a general meeting of the company's creditors that has resolved against his release, or by the court, or who has vacated office under section 171(4) above, such time as the Secretary of State may, on the application of that person, determine;

   (c) in the case of a person who has resigned, such time as may be prescribed;

   (d) in the case of a person who has vacated office under subsection (6)(a) of section 171, the time at which he vacated office;

   (e) in the case of a person who has vacated office under subsection (6)(b) of that section—

      (i) if the final meeting of the creditors referred to in that subsection has resolved against that person's release, such time as the Secretary of State may, on an application by that person, determine, and

      (ii) if that meeting has not resolved against that person's release, the time at which he vacated office.

(3) In the application of subsection (2) to the winding up of a company registered in Scotland, the references to a determination by the Secretary of State as to the time from which a person who has ceased to be liquidator shall have his release are to be read as references to such a determination by the Accountant of Court.

(4) Where a liquidator has his release under subsection (2), he is, with effect from the time specified in that subsection, discharged from all liability both in respect of acts or omissions of his in the winding up and otherwise in relation to his conduct as liquidator.

But nothing in this section prevents the exercise, in relation to a person who has had his release under subsection (2), of the court's powers under section 212 of this Act (summary remedy against delinquent directors, liquidators, etc.).

174   Release (winding up by the court)

(1) This section applies with respect to the release of the liquidator of a company which is being wound up by the court, or of a provisional liquidator.

(2) Where the official receiver has ceased to be liquidator and a person becomes liquidator in his stead, the official receiver has his release with effect from the following time, that is to say—

   (a) in a case where that person was nominated by a general meeting of creditors or contributories, or was appointed by the Secretary of State, the time at which the official receiver gives notice to the court that he has been replaced;

   (b) in a case where that person is appointed by the court, such time as the court may determine.

(3) If the official receiver while he is a liquidator gives notice to the Secretary of State that the winding up is for practical purposes complete, he has his release with effect from such time as the Secretary of State may determine.

(4) A person other than the official receiver who has ceased to be a liquidator has his release with effect from the following time, that is to say—

(a) in the case of a person who has been removed from office by a general meeting of creditors that has not resolved against his release or who has died, the time at which notice is given to the court in accordance with the rules that that person has ceased to hold office;

(b) in the case of a person who has been removed from office by a general meeting of creditors that has resolved against his release, or by the court or the Secretary of State, or who has vacated office under section 172(5) or (7), such time as the Secretary of State may, on an application by that person, determine;

(c) in the case of a person who has resigned, such time as may be prescribed;

(d) in the case of a person who has vacated office under section 172(8)—

(i) if the final meeting referred to in that subsection has resolved against that person's release, such time as the Secretary of State may, on an application by that person, determine, and

(ii) if that meeting has not so resolved, the time at which that person vacated office.

(5) A person who has ceased to hold office as a provisional liquidator has his release with effect from such time as the court may, on an application by him, determine.

(6) Where the official receiver or a liquidator or provisional liquidator has his release under this section, he is, with effect from the time specified in the preceding provisions of this section, discharged from all liability both in respect of acts or omissions of his in the winding up and otherwise in relation to his conduct as liquidator or provisional liquidator.

But nothing in this section prevents the exercise, in relation to a person who has had his release under this section, of the court's powers under section 212 (summary remedy against delinquent directors, liquidators, etc.).

(7) In the application of this section to a case where the order for winding up has been made by the court in Scotland, the references to a determination by the Secretary of State as to the time from which a person who has ceased to be liquidator has his release are to such a determination by the Accountant of Court.

CHAPTER VIII   PROVISIONS OF GENERAL APPLICATION IN WINDING UP

Preferential debts

175   Preferential debts (general provision)

(1) In a winding up the company's preferential debts (within the meaning given by section 386 in Part XII) shall be paid in priority to all other debts.

(2) Preferential debts—

(a) rank equally among themselves after the expenses of the winding up and shall be paid in full, unless the assets are insufficient to meet them, in which case they abate in equal proportions; and

(b) so far as the assets of the company available for payment of general creditors are insufficient to meet them, have priority over the claims of holders of debentures secured by, or holders of, any floating charge created by the company, and shall be paid accordingly out of any property comprised in or subject to that charge.

176   Preferential charge on goods distrained

(1) This section applies where a company is being wound up by the court in England and Wales, and is without prejudice to section 128 (avoidance of attachments, etc.).

(2) Where any person (whether or not a landlord or person entitled to rent) has distrained upon the goods or effects of the company in the period of 3 months ending with the date of

the winding-up order, those goods or effects, or the proceeds of their sale, shall be charged for the benefit of the company with the preferential debts of the company to the extent that the company's property is for the time being insufficient for meeting them.

(3) Where by virtue of a charge under subsection (2) any person surrenders any goods or effects to a company or makes a payment to a company, that person ranks, in respect of the amount of the proceeds of sale of those goods or effects by the liquidator or (as the case may be) the amount of the payment, as a preferential creditor of the company, except as against so much of the company's property as is available for the payment of preferential creditors by virtue of the surrender or payment.

Property subject to floating charge

176A   *Share of assets for unsecured creditors*

(1) This section applies where a floating charge relates to property of a company—

    (a) which has gone into liquidation,

    (b) which is in administration,

    (c) of which there is a provisional liquidator, or

    (d) of which there is a receiver.

(2) The liquidator, administrator or receiver—

    (a) shall make a prescribed part of the company's net property available for the satisfaction of unsecured debts, and

    (b) shall not distribute that part to the proprietor of a floating charge except in so far as it exceeds the amount required for the satisfaction of unsecured debts.

(3) Subsection (2) shall not apply to a company if—

    (a) the company's net property is less than the prescribed minimum, and

    (b) the liquidator, administrator or receiver thinks that the cost of making a distribution to unsecured creditors would be disproportionate to the benefits.

(4) Subsection (2) shall also not apply to a company if or in so far as it is disapplied by—

    (a) a voluntary arrangement in respect of the company, or

    (b) a compromise or arrangement agreed under section 425 of the Companies Act (compromise with creditors and members).

(5) Subsection (2) shall also not apply to a company if—

    (a) the liquidator, administrator or receiver applies to the court for an order under this subsection on the ground that the cost of making a distribution to unsecured creditors would be disproportionate to the benefits, and

    (b) the court orders that subsection (2) shall not apply.

(6) In subsections (2) and (3) a company's net property is the amount of its property which would, but for this section, be available for satisfaction of claims of holders of debentures secured by, or holders of, any floating charge created by the company.

(7) An order under subsection (2) prescribing part of a company's net property may, in particular, provide for its calculation—

    (a) as a percentage of the company's net property, or

    (b) as an aggregate of different percentages of different parts of the company's net property.

(8) An order under this section—

    (a) must be made by statutory instrument, and

    (b) shall be subject to annulment pursuant to a resolution of either House of Parliament.

(9) In this section—

'floating charge' means a charge which is a floating charge on its creation and which is created after the first order under subsection (2)(a) comes into force, and

'prescribed' means prescribed by order by the Secretary of State.

(10) An order under this section may include transitional or incidental provision.

[*On 15 June 2003, s. 176A had not been brought into force.*]

Special managers

177 Power to appoint special manager

(1) Where a company has gone into liquidation or a provisional liquidator has been appointed, the court may, on an application under this section, appoint any person to be the special manager of the business or property of the company.

(2) The application may be made by the liquidator or provisional liquidator in any case where it appears to him that the nature of the business or property of the company, or the interests of the company's creditors or contributories or members generally, require the appointment of another person to manage the company's business or property.

(3) The special manager has such powers as may be entrusted to him by the court.

(4) The court's power to entrust powers to the special manager includes power to direct that any provision of this Act that has effect in relation to the provisional liquidator or liquidator of a company shall have the like effect in relation to the special manager for the purposes of the carrying out by him of any of the functions of the provisional liquidator or liquidator.

(5) The special manager shall—
   (a) give such security or, in Scotland, caution as may be prescribed;
   (b) prepare and keep such accounts as may be prescribed; and
   (c) produce those accounts in accordance with the rules to the Secretary of State or to such other persons as may be prescribed.

Disclaimer (England and Wales only)

178 Power to disclaim onerous property

(1) This and the next two sections apply to a company that is being wound up in England and Wales.

(2) Subject as follows, the liquidator may, by the giving of the prescribed notice, disclaim any onerous property and may do so notwithstanding that he has taken possession of it, endeavoured to sell it, or otherwise exercised rights of ownership in relation to it.

(3) The following is onerous property for the purposes of this section—
   (a) any unprofitable contract, and
   (b) any other property of the company which is unsaleable or not readily saleable or is such that it may give rise to a liability to pay money or perform any other onerous act.

(4) A disclaimer under this section—
   (a) operates so as to determine, as from the date of the disclaimer, the rights, interests and liabilities of the company in or in respect of the property disclaimed; but
   (b) does not, except so far as is necessary for the purpose of releasing the company from any liability, affect the rights or liabilities of any other person.

(5) A notice of disclaimer shall not be given under this section in respect of any property if—
   (a) a person interested in the property has applied in writing to the liquidator or one of his predecessors as liquidator requiring the liquidator or that predecessor to decide whether he will disclaim or not, and
   (b) the period of 28 days beginning with the day on which that application was made, or such longer period as the court may allow, has expired without a notice of disclaimer having been given under this section in respect of that property.

(6) Any person sustaining loss or damage in consequence of the operation of a disclaimer under this section is deemed a creditor of the company to the extent of the loss or damage and accordingly may prove for the loss or damage in the winding up.

179   Disclaimer of leaseholds

(1) The disclaimer under section 178 of any property of a leasehold nature does not take effect unless a copy of the disclaimer has been served (so far as the liquidator is aware of their addresses) on every person claiming under the company as underlessee or mortgagee and either—

(a) no application under section 181 below is made with respect to that property before the end of the period of 14 days beginning with the day on which the last notice served under this subsection was served; or

(b) where such an application has been made, the court directs that the disclaimer shall take effect.

(2) Where the court gives a direction under subsection (1)(b) it may also, instead of or in addition to any order it makes under section 181, make such orders with respect to fixtures, tenant's improvements and other matters arising out of the lease as it thinks fit.

180   Land subject to rentcharge

(1) The following applies where, in consequence of the disclaimer under section 178 of any land subject to a rentcharge, that land vests by operation of law in the Crown or any other person (referred to in the next subsection as 'the proprietor').

(2) The proprietor and the successors in title of the proprietor are not subject to any personal liability in respect of any sums becoming due under the rentcharge except sums becoming due after the proprietor, or some person claiming under or through the proprietor, has taken possession or control of the land or has entered into occupation of it.

181   Powers of court (general)

(1) This section and the next apply where the liquidator has disclaimed property under section 178.

(2) An application under this section may be made to the court by—

(a) any person who claims an interest in the disclaimed property, or

(b) any person who is under any liability in respect of the disclaimed property, not being a liability discharged by the disclaimer.

(3) Subject as follows, the court may on the application make an order, on such terms as it thinks fit, for the vesting of the disclaimed property in, or for its delivery to—

(a) a person entitled to it or a trustee for such a person, or

(b) a person subject to such a liability as is mentioned in subsection (2)(b) or a trustee for such a person.

(4) The court shall not make an order under subsection (3)(b) except where it appears to the court that it would be just to do so for the purpose of compensating the person subject to the liability in respect of the disclaimer.

(5) The effect of any order under this section shall be taken into account in assessing for the purpose of section 178(6) the extent of any loss or damage sustained by any person in consequence of the disclaimer.

(6) An order under this section vesting property in any person need not be completed by conveyance, assignment or transfer.

182   Powers of court (leaseholds)

(1) The court shall not make an order under section 181 vesting property of a leasehold nature in any person claiming under the company as underlessee or mortgagee except on terms making that person—

(a) subject to the same liabilities and obligations as the company was subject to under the lease at the commencement of the winding up, or

(b) if the court thinks fit, subject to the same liabilities and obligations as that person would be subject to if the lease had been assigned to him at the commencement of the winding up.

(2) For the purposes of an order under section 181 relating to only part of any property comprised in a lease, the requirements of subsection (1) apply as if the lease comprised only the property to which the order relates.

(3) Where subsection (1) applies and no person claiming under the company as underlessee or mortgagee is willing to accept an order under section 181 on the terms required by virtue of that subsection, the court may, by order under that section, vest the company's estate or interest in the property in any person who is liable (whether personally or in a representative capacity, and whether alone or jointly with the company) to perform the lessee's covenants in the lease.

The court may vest that estate and interest in such a person freed and discharged from all estates, encumbrances and interests created by the company.

(4) Where subsection (1) applies and a person claiming under the company as underlessee or mortgagee declines to accept an order under section 181, that person is excluded from all interest in the property.

Execution, attachment and the Scottish equivalents

183   Effect of execution or attachment (England and Wales)

(1) Where a creditor has issued execution against the goods or land of a company or has attached any debt due to it, and the company is subsequently wound up, he is not entitled to retain the benefit of the execution or attachment against the liquidator unless he has completed the execution or attachment before the commencement of the winding up.

(2) However—

(a) if a creditor has had notice of a meeting having been called at which a resolution for voluntary winding up is to be proposed, the date on which he had notice is substituted, for the purpose of subsection (1), for the date of commencement of the winding up;

(b) a person who purchases in good faith under a sale by the sheriff any goods of a company on which execution has been levied in all cases acquires a good title to them against the liquidator; and

(c) the rights conferred by subsection (1) on the liquidator may be set aside by the court in favour of the creditor to such extent and subject to such terms as the court thinks fit.

(3) For purposes of this Act—

(a) an execution against goods is completed by seizure and sale, or by the making of a charging order under section 1 of the Charging Orders Act 1979;

(b) an attachment of a debt is completed by receipt of the debt; and

(c) an execution against land is completed by seizure, by the appointment of a receiver, or by the making of a charging order under section 1 of the Act abovementioned.

(4) In this section, 'goods' includes all chattels personal; and 'the sheriff' includes any officer charged with the execution of a writ or other process.

(5) This section does not apply in the case of a winding up in Scotland.

184   Duties of sheriff (England and Wales)

(1) The following applies where a company's goods are taken in execution and, before their sale or the completion of the execution (by the receipt or recovery of the full amount of the levy), notice is served on the sheriff that a provisional liquidator has been appointed or that a winding-up order has been made, or that a resolution for voluntary winding up has been passed.

(2) The sheriff shall, on being so required, deliver the goods and any money seized or received in part satisfaction of the execution to the liquidator; but the costs of execution are a first charge on the goods or money so delivered, and the liquidator may sell the goods, or a sufficient part of them, for the purpose of satisfying the charge.

(3) If under an execution in respect of a judgment for a sum exceeding £500 a company's goods are sold or money is paid in order to avoid sale, the sheriff shall deduct the costs of the execution from the proceeds of sale or the money paid and retain the balance for 14 days.

(4) If within that time notice is served on the sheriff of a petition for the winding up of the company having been presented, or of a meeting having been called at which there is to be proposed a resolution for voluntary winding up, and an order is made or a resolution passed (as the case may be), the sheriff shall pay the balance to the liquidator, who is entitled to retain it as against the execution creditor.

(5) The rights conferred by this section on the liquidator may be set aside by the court in favour of the creditor to such extent and subject to such terms as the court thinks fit.

(6) In this section, 'goods' includes all chattels personal; and 'the sheriff' includes any officer charged with the execution of a writ or other process.

(7) The money sum for the time being specified in subsection (3) is subject to increase or reduction by order under section 416 in Part XV.

(8) This section does not apply in the case of a winding up in Scotland.

185   Effect of diligence (Scotland)

(1) In the winding up of a company registered in Scotland, the following provisions of the Bankruptcy (Scotland) Act 1985—

(a) subsections (1) to (6) of section 37 (effect of sequestration on diligence); and

(b) subsections (3), (4), (7) and (8) of section 39 (realisation of estate),

apply, so far as consistent with this Act, in like manner as they apply in the sequestration of a debtor's estate, with the substitutions specified below and with any other necessary modifications.

(2) The substitutions to be made in those sections of the Act of 1985 are as follows—

(a) for references to the debtor, substitute references to the company;

(b) for references to the sequestration, substitute references to the winding up;

(c) for references to the date of sequestration, substitute references to the commencement of the winding up of the company; and

(d) for references to the permanent trustee, substitute references to the liquidator.

(3) In this section, 'the commencement of the winding up of the company' means, where it is being wound up by the court, the day on which the winding-up order is made.

(4) This section, so far as relating to any estate or effects of the company situated in Scotland, applies in the case of a company registered in England and Wales as in the case of one registered in Scotland.

Miscellaneous matters

186   Rescission of contracts by the court

(1) The court may, on the application of a person who is, as against the liquidator, entitled to the benefit or subject to the burden of a contract made with the company, make an order rescinding the contract on such terms as to payment by or to either party of damages for the non-performance of the contract, or otherwise as the court thinks just.

(2) Any damages payable under the order to such a person may be proved by him as a debt in the winding up.

187   Power to make over assets to employees

(1) On the winding up of a company (whether by the court or voluntarily), the liquidator may, subject to the following provisions of this section, make any payment which the company has, before the commencement of the winding up, decided to make under section 719 of the Companies Act (power to provide for employees or former employees on cessation or transfer of business).

(2) The power which a company may exercise by virtue only of that section may be exercised by the liquidator after the winding up has commenced if, after the company's liabilities have been fully satisfied and provision has been made for the expenses of the winding up, the exercise of that power has been sanctioned by such a resolution of the company as would be required of the company itself by section 719(3) before that commencement, if paragraph (b) of that subsection were omitted and any other requirement applicable to its exercise by the company had been met.

(3) Any payment which may be made by a company under this section (that is, a payment after the commencement of its winding up) may be made out of the company's assets which are available to the members on the winding up.

(4) On a winding up by the court, the exercise by the liquidator of his powers under this section is subject to the court's control, and any creditor or contributory may apply to the court with respect to any exercise or proposed exercise of the power.

(5) Subsections (1) and (2) above have effect notwithstanding anything in any rule of law or in section 107 of this Act (property of company after satisfaction of liabilities to be distributed among members).

188 Notification that company is in liquidation

(1) When a company is being wound up, whether by the court or voluntarily, every invoice, order for goods or business letter issued by or on behalf of the company, or a liquidator of the company, or a receiver or manager of the company's property, being a document on or in which the name of the company appears, shall contain a statement that the company is being wound up.

(2) If default is made in complying with this section, the company and any of the following persons who knowingly and wilfully authorises or permits the default, namely, any officer of the company, any liquidator of the company and any receiver or manager, is liable to a fine.

189 Interest on debts

(1) In a winding up interest is payable in accordance with this section on any debt proved in the winding up, including so much of any such debt as represents interest on the remainder.

(2) Any surplus remaining after the payment of the debts proved in a winding up shall, before being applied for any other purpose, be applied in paying interest on those debts in respect of the periods during which they have been outstanding since the company went into liquidation.

(3) All interest under this section ranks equally, whether or not the debts on which it is payable rank equally.

(4) The rate of interest payable under this section in respect of any debt ('the official rate' for the purposes of any provision of this Act in which that expression is used) is whichever is the greater of—

    (a) the rate specified in section 17 of the Judgments Act 1838 on the day on which the company went into liquidation, and

    (b) the rate applicable to that debt apart from the winding up.

(5) In the application of this section to Scotland—

    (a) references to a debt proved in a winding up have effect as references to a claim accepted in a winding up, and

    (b) the reference to section 17 of the Judgments Act 1838 has effect as a reference to the rules.

192 Information as to pending liquidations

(1) If the winding up of a company is not concluded within one year after its commencement, the liquidator shall, at such intervals as may be prescribed, until the winding up is concluded, send to the registrar of companies a statement in the prescribed form and

containing the prescribed particulars with respect to the proceedings in, and position of, the liquidation.

(2) If a liquidator fails to comply with this section, he is liable to a fine and, for continued contravention, to a daily default fine.

194 Resolutions passed at adjourned meetings
Where a resolution is passed at an adjourned meeting of a company's creditors or contributories, the resolution is treated for all purposes as having been passed on the date on which it was in fact passed, and not as having been passed on any earlier date.

195 Meetings to ascertain wishes of creditors or contributories
(1) The court may—
- (a) as to all matters relating to the winding up of a company, have regard to the wishes of the creditors or contributories (as proved to it by any sufficient evidence), and
- (b) if it thinks fit, for the purpose of ascertaining those wishes, direct meetings of the creditors or contributories to be called, held and conducted in such manner as the court directs, and appoint a person to act as chairman of any such meeting and report the result of it to the court.

(2) In the case of creditors, regard shall be had to the value of each creditor's debt.

(3) In the case of contributories, regard shall be had to the number of votes conferred on each contributory by the Companies Act or the articles.

CHAPTER IX   DISSOLUTION OF COMPANIES AFTER WINDING UP

201 Dissolution (voluntary winding up)
(1) This section applies, in the case of a company wound up voluntarily, where the liquidator has sent to the registrar of companies his final account and return under section 94 (members' voluntary) or section 106 (creditors' voluntary).

(2) The registrar on receiving the account and return shall forthwith register them; and on the expiration of 3 months from the registration of the return the company is deemed to be dissolved.

(3) However, the court may, on the application of the liquidator or any other person who appears to the court to be interested, make an order deferring the date at which the dissolution of the company is to take effect for such time as the court thinks fit.

(4) It is the duty of the person on whose application an order of the court under this section is made within 7 days after the making of the order to deliver to the registrar an office copy of the order for registration; and if that person fails to do so he is liable to a fine and, for continued contravention, to a daily default fine.

202 Early dissolution (England and Wales)
(1) This section applies where an order for the winding up of a company has been made by the court in England and Wales.

(2) The official receiver, if—
- (a) he is the liquidator of the company, and
- (b) it appears to him—
  - (i) that the realisable assets of the company are insufficient to cover the expenses of the winding up, and
  - (ii) that the affairs of the company do not require any further investigation, may at any time apply to the registrar of companies for the early dissolution of the company.

(3) Before making that application, the official receiver shall give not less than 28 days' notice of his intention to do so to the company's creditors and contributories and, if there is an administrative receiver of the company, to that receiver.

(4) With the giving of that notice the official receiver ceases (subject to any directions under the next section) to be required to perform any duties imposed on him in relation to the compay, its creditors or contributories by virtue of any provision of this Act, apart from a duty to make an application under subsection (2) of this section.

(5) On the receipt of the official receiver's application under subsection (2) the registrar shall forthwith register it and, at the end of the period of 3 months beginning with the day of the registration of the application, the company shall be dissolved.

However, the Secretary of State may, on the application of the official receiver or any other person who appears to the Secretary of State to be interested, give directions under section 203 at any time before the end of that period.

203   Consequence of notice under s. 202

(1) Where a notice has been given under section 202(3), the official receiver or any creditor or contributory of the company, or the administrative receiver of the company (if there is one) may apply to the Secretary of State for directions under this section.

(2) The grounds on which that application may be made are—

(a)   that the realisable assets of the company are sufficient to cover the expenses of the winding up;

(b)   that the affairs of the company do require further investigation; or

(c)   that for any other reason the early dissolution of the company is inappropriate.

(3) Directions under this section—

(a)   are directions making such provision as the Secretary of State thinks fit for enabling the winding up of the company to proceed as if no notice had been given under section 202(3), and

(b)   may, in the case of an application under section 202(5), include a direction deferring the date at which the dissolution of the company is to take effect for such period as the Secretary of State thinks fit.

(4) An appeal to the court lies from any decision of the Secretary of State on an application for directions under this section.

(5) It is the duty of the person on whose application any directions are given under this section, or in whose favour an appeal with respect to an application for such directions is determined, within 7 days after the giving of the directions or the determination of the appeal, to deliver to the registrar of companies for registration such a copy of the directions or determination as is prescribed.

(6) If a person without reasonable excuse fails to deliver a copy as required by subsection (5), he is liable to a fine and, for continued contravention, to a daily default fine.

205   Dissolution otherwise than under ss. 202–204

(1) This section applies where the registrar of companies receives—

(a)   a notice served for the purposes of section 172(8) (final meeting of creditors and vacation of office by liquidator), or

(b)   a notice from the official receiver that the winding up of a company by the court is complete.

(2) The registrar shall, on receipt of the notice, forthwith register it; and, subject as follows, at the end of the period of 3 months beginning with the day of the registration of the notice, the company shall be dissolved.

(3) The Secretary of State may, on the application of the official receiver or any other person who appears to the Secretary of State to be interested, give a direction deferring the date at which the dissolution of the company is to take effect for such period as the Secretary of State thinks fit.

(4) An appeal to the court lies from any decision of the Secretary of State on an application for a direction under subsection (3).

(5) Subsection (3) does not apply in a case where the winding-up order was made by the court in Scotland, but in such a case the court may, on an application by any person appearing to the court to have an interest, order that the date at which the dissolution of the company is to take effect shall be deferred for such period as the court thinks fit.

(6) It is the duty of the person—

  (a) on whose application a direction is given under subsection (3);

  (b) in whose favour an appeal with respect to an application for such a direction is determined; or

  (c) on whose application an order is made under subsection (5), within 7 days after the giving of the direction, the determination of the appeal or the making of the order, to deliver to the registrar for registration such a copy of the direction, determination or order as is prescribed.

(7) If a person without reasonable excuse fails to deliver a copy as required by subsection (6), he is liable to a fine and, for continued contravention, to a daily default fine.

CHAPTER X   MALPRACTICE BEFORE AND DURING LIQUIDATION;
PENALISATION OF COMPANIES AND COMPANY OFFICERS;
INVESTIGATIONS AND PROSECUTIONS

Offences of fraud, deception, etc.

206   Fraud, etc. in anticipation of winding up

(1) When a company is ordered to be wound up by the court, or passes a resolution for voluntary winding up, any person, being a past or present officer of the company, is deemed to have committed an offence if, within the 12 months immediately preceding the commencement of the winding up, he has—

  (a) concealed any part of the company's property to the value of £500 or more, or concealed any debt due to or from the company, or

  (b) fraudulently removed any part of the company's property to the value of £500 or more, or

  (c) concealed, destroyed, mutilated or falsified any book or paper affecting or relating to the company's property or affairs, or

  (d) made any false entry in any book or paper affecting or relating to the company's property or affairs, or

  (e) fraudulently parted with, altered or made any omission in any document affecting or relating to the company's property or affairs, or

  (f) pawned, pledged or disposed of any property of the company which has been obtained on credit and has not been paid for (unless the pawning, pledging or disposal was in the ordinary way of the company's business).

(2) Such a person is deemed to have committed an offence if within the period above-mentioned he has been privy to the doing by others of any of the things mentioned in paragraphs (c), (d) and (e) of subsection (1); and he commits an offence if, at any time after the commencement of the winding up, he does any of the things mentioned in paragraphs (a) to (f) of that subsection, or is privy to the doing by others of any of the things mentioned in paragraphs (c) to (e) of it.

(3) For purposes of this section, 'officer' includes a shadow director.

(4) It is a defence—

  (a) for a person charged under paragraph (a) or (f) of subsection (1) (or under subsection (2) in respect of the things mentioned in either of those two paragraphs) to prove that he had no intent to defraud, and

  (b) for a person charged under paragraph (c) or (d) of subsection (1) (or under subsection (2) in respect of the things mentioned in either of those two paragraphs) to prove that he had no intent to conceal the state of affairs of the company or to defeat the law.

(5) Where a person pawns, pledges or disposes of any property in circumstances which amount to an offence under subsection (1)(f), every person who takes in pawn or pledge, or otherwise receives, the property knowing it to be pawned, pledged or disposed of in such circumstances, is guilty of an offence.

(6) A person guilty of an offence under this section is liable to imprisonment or a fine, or both.

(7) The money sums specified in paragraphs (a) and (b) of subsection (1) are subject to increase or reduction by order under section 416 in Part XV.

207   Transactions in fraud of creditors

(1) When a company is ordered to be wound up by the court or passes a resolution for voluntary winding up, a person is deemed to have committed an offence if he, being at the time an officer of the company—

    (a) has made or caused to be made any gift or transfer of, or charge on, or has caused or connived at the levying of any execution against, the company's property, or

    (b) has concealed or removed any part of the company's property since, or within 2 months before, the date of any unsatisfied judgment or order for the payment of money obtained against the company.

(2) A person is not guilty of an offence under this section—

    (a) by reason of conduct constituting an offence under subsection (1)(a) which occurred more than 5 years before the commencement of the winding up, or

    (b) if he proves that, at the time of the conduct constituting the offence, he had no intent to defraud the company's creditors.

(3) A person guilty of an offence under this section is liable to imprisonment or a fine, or both.

208   Misconduct in course of winding up

(1) When a company is being wound up, whether by the court or voluntarily, any person, being a past or present officer of the company, commits an offence if he—

    (a) does not to the best of his knowledge and belief fully and truly discover to the liquidator all the company's property, and how and to whom and for what consideration and when the company disposed of any part of that property (except such part as has been disposed of in the ordinary way of the company's business), or

    (b) does not deliver up to the liquidator (or as he directs) all such part of the company's property as is in his custody or under his control, and which he is required by law to deliver up, or

    (c) does not deliver up to the liquidator (or as he directs) all books and papers in his custody or under his control belonging to the company and which he is required by law to deliver up, or

    (d) knowing or believing that a false debt has been proved by any person in the winding up, fails to inform the liquidator as soon as practicable, or

    (e) after the commencement of the winding up, prevents the production of any book or paper affecting or relating to the company's property or affairs.

(2) Such a person commits an offence if after the commencement of the winding up he attempts to account for any part of the company's property by fictitious losses or expenses; and he is deemed to have committed that offence if he has so attempted at any meeting of the company's creditors within the 12 months immediately preceding the commencement of the winding up.

(3) For purposes of this section, 'officer' includes a shadow director.

(4) It is a defence—

(a) for a person charged under paragraph (a), (b) or (c) of subsection (1) to prove that he had no intent to defraud, and
(b) for a person charged under paragraph (e) of that subsection to prove that he had no intent to conceal the state of affairs of the company or to defeat the law.

(5) A person guilty of an offence under this section is liable to imprisonment or a fine, or both.

209   Falsification of company's books

(1) When a company is being wound up, an officer or contributory of the company commits an offence if he destroys, mutilates, alter or falsifies any books, papers or securities, or makes or is privy to the making of any false or fraudulent entry in any register, book of account or document belonging to the company with intent to defraud or deceive any person.

(2) A person guilty of an offence under this section is liable to imprisonment or a fine, or both.

210   Material omissions from statement relating to company's affairs

(1) When a company is being wound up, whether by the court or voluntarily, any person, being a past or present officer of the company, commits an offence if he makes any material omission in any statement relating to the company's affairs.

(2) When a company has been ordered to be wound up by the court, or has passed a resolution for voluntary winding up, any such person is deemed to have committed that offence if, prior to the winding up, he has made any material omission in any such statement.

(3) For purposes of this section, 'officer' includes a shadow director.

(4) It is a defence for a person charged under this section to prove that he had no intent to defraud.

(5) A person guilty of an offence under this section is liable to imprisonment or a fine, or both.

211   False representations to creditors

(1) When a company is being wound up, whether by the court or voluntarily, any person, being a past or present officer of the company—

(a) commits an offence if he makes any false representation or commits any other fraud for the purpose of obtaining the consent of the company's creditors or any of them to an agreement with reference to the company's affairs or to the winding up, and
(b) is deemed to have committed that offence if, prior to the winding up, he has made any false representation, or committed any other fraud, for that purpose.

(2) For purposes of this section, 'officer' includes a shadow director.

(3) A person guilty of an offence under this section is liable to imprisonment or a fine, or both.

Penalisation of directors and officers

212   Summary remedy against delinquent directors, liquidators, etc.

(1) This section applies if in the course of the winding up of a company it appears that a person who—

(a) is or has been an officer of the company,
(b) has acted as liquidator, *administrator* or administrative receiver of the company, or
(c) not being a person falling within paragraph (a) or (b), is or has been concerned, or has taken part, in the promotion, formation or management of the company,

has misapplied or retained, or become accountable for, any money or other property of the company, or been guilty of any misfeasance or breach of any fiduciary or other duty in relation to the company.

(2) The reference in subsection (1) to any misfeasance or breach of any fiduciary or other duty in relation to the company includes, in the case of a person who has acted as liquidator *or administrator* of the company, any misfeasance or breach of any fiduciary or other duty in connection with the carrying out of his functions as liquidator *or administrator* of the company.

(3) The court may, on the application of the official receiver or the liquidator, or of any creditor or contributory, examine into the conduct of the person falling within subsection (1) and compel him—

(a) to repay, restore or account for the money or property or any part of it, with interest at such rate as the court thinks just, or

(b) to contribute such sum to the company's assets by way of compensation in respect of the misfeasance or breach of fiduciary or other duty as the court thinks just.

(4) The power to make an application under subsection (3) in relation to a person who has acted as liquidator *or administrator* of the company is not exercisable, except with the leave of the court, after *that person* has had his release.

(5) The power of a contributory to make an application under subsection (3) is not exercisable except with the leave of the court, but is exercisable notwithstanding that he will not benefit from any order the court may make on the application.

[*When the Enterprise Act 2002, sch. 17, is brought into force, the words in italics in the Insolvency Act 1986, s. 212(1)(b) and (2), and the words 'or administrator' in s. 212(4), will be repealed, and the words 'that person' in s. 212(4) will be replaced by 'he'.*]

213   Fraudulent trading

(1) If in the course of the winding up of a company it appears that any business of the company has been carried on with intent to defraud creditors of the company or creditors of any other person, or for any fraudulent purpose, the following has effect.

(2) The court, on the application of the liquidator may declare that any persons who were knowingly parties to the carrying on of the business in the manner above-mentioned are to be liable to make such contributions (if any) to the company's assets as the court thinks proper.

214   Wrongful trading

(1) Subject to subsection (3) below, if in the course of the winding up of a company it appears that subsection (2) of this section applies in relation to a person who is or has been a director of the company, the court, on the application of the liquidator, may declare that that person is to be liable to make such contribution (if any) to the company's assets as the court thinks proper.

(2) This subsection applies in relation to a person if—

(a) the company has gone into insolvent liquidation,

(b) at some time before the commencement of the winding up of the company, that person knew or ought to have concluded that there was no reasonable prospect that the company would avoid going into insolvent liquidation, and

(c) that person was a director of the company at that time;

but the court shall not make a declaration under this section in any case where the time mentioned in paragraph (b) above was before 28 April 1986.

(3) The court shall not make a declaration under this section with respect to any person if it is satisfied that after the condition specified in subsection (2)(b) was first satisfied in relation to him that person took every step with a view to minimising the potential loss to the company's creditors as (assuming him to have known that there was no reasonable prospect that the company would avoid going into insolvent liquidation) he ought to have taken.

(4) For the purposes of subsections (2) and (3), the facts which a director of a company ought to know or ascertain, the conclusions which he ought to reach and the steps which he ought to take are those which would be known or ascertained, or reached or taken, by a reasonably diligent person having both—

(a) the general knowledge, skill and experience that may reasonably be expected of a person carrying out the same functions as are carried out by that director in relation to the company, and

(b) the general knowledge, skill and experience that that director has.

(5) The reference in subsection (4) to the functions carried out in relation to a company by a director of the company includes any functions which he does not carry out but which have been entrusted to him.

(6) For the purposes of this section a company goes into insolvent liquidation if it goes into liquidation at a time when its assets are insufficient for the payment of its debts and other liabilities and the expenses of the winding up.

(7) In this section 'director' includes a shadow director.

(8) This section is without prejudice to section 213.

215   Proceedings under ss. 213, 214

(1) On the hearing of an application under section 213 or 214, the liquidator may himself give evidence or call witnesses.

(2) Where under either section the court makes a declaration, it may give such further directions as it thinks proper for giving effect to the declaration; and in particular, the court may—

(a) provide for the liability of any person under the declaration to be a charge on any debt or obligation due from the company to him, or on any mortgage or charge or any interest in a mortgage or charge on assets of the company held by or vested in him, or any person on his behalf, or any person claiming as assignee from or through the person liable or any person acting on his behalf, and

(b) from time to time make such further order as may be necessary for enforcing any charge imposed under this subsection.

(3) For the purposes of subsection (2), 'assignee'—

(a) includes a person to whom or in whose favour, by the directions of the person made liable, the debt, obligation, mortgage or charge was created, issued or transferred or the interest created, but

(b) does not include an assignee for valuable consideration (not including consideration by way of marriage) given in good faith and without notice of any of the matters on the grounds of which the declaration is made.

(4) Where the court makes a declaration under either section in relation to a person who is a creditor of the company, it may direct that the whole or any part of any debt owed by the company to that person and any interest thereon shall rank in priority after all other debts owed by the company and after any interest on those debts.

(5) Sections 213 and 214 have effect notwithstanding that the person concerned may be criminally liable in respect of matters on the ground of which the declaration under the section is to be made.

216   Restriction on reuse of company names

(1) This section applies to a person where a company ('the liquidating company') has gone into insolvent liquidation on or after the appointed day and he was a director or shadow director of the company at any time in the period of 12 months ending with the day before it went into liquidation.

(2) For the purposes of this section, a name is a prohibited name in relation to such a person if—

(a) it is a name by which the liquidating company was known at any time in that period of 12 months, or

(b) it is a name which is so similar to a name falling within paragraph (a) as to suggest an association with that company.

(3) Except with leave of the court or in such circumstances as may be prescribed, a person to whom this section applies shall not at any time in the period of 5 years beginning with the day on which the liquidating company went into liquidation—

  (a) be a director of any other company that is known by a prohibited name, or
  (b) in any way, whether directly or indirectly, be concerned or take part in the promotion, formation or management of any such company, or
  (c) in any way, whether directly or indirectly, be concerned or take part in the carrying on of a business carried on (otherwise than by a company) under a prohibited name.

(4) If a person acts in contravention of this section, he is liable to imprisonment or a fine, or both.

(5) In subsection (3) 'the court' means any court having jurisdiction to wind up companies; and on an application for leave under that subsection, the Secretary of State or the official receiver may appear and call the attention of the court to any matters which seem to him to be relevant.

(6) References in this section, in relation to any time, to a name by which a company is known are to the name of the company at that time or to any name under which the company carries on business at that time.

(7) For the purposes of this section a company goes into insolvent liquidation if it goes into liquidation at a time when its assets are insufficient for the payment of its debts and other liabilities and the expenses of the winding up.

(8) In this section 'company' includes a company which may be wound up under Part V of this Act.

217 Personal liability for debts, following contravention of s. 216

(1) A person is personally responsible for all the relevant debts of a company if at any time—

  (a) in contravention of section 216, he is involved in the management of the company, or
  (b) as a person who is involved in the management of the company, he acts or is willing to act on instructions given (without the leave of the court) by a person whom he knows at that time to be in contravention in relation to the company of section 216.

(2) Where a person is personally responsible under this section for the relevant debts of a company, he is jointly and severally liable in respect of those debts with the company and any other person who, whether under this section or otherwise, is so liable.

(3) For the purposes of this section the relevant debts of a company are—

  (a) in relation to a person who is personally responsible under paragraph (a) of subsection (1), such debts and other liabilities of the company as are incurred at a time when that person was involved in the management of the company, and
  (b) in relation to a person who is personally responsible under paragraph (b) of the subsection, such debts and other liabilities of the company as are incurred at a time when that person was acting or was willing to act on instructions given as mentioned in that paragraph.

(4) For the purposes of this section, a person is involved in the management of a company if he is a director of the company or if he is concerned, whether directly or indirectly, or takes part, in the management of the company.

(5) For the purposes of this section a person who, as a person involved in the management of a company, has at any time acted on instructions given (without the leave of the court) by a person whom he knew at that time to be in contravention in relation to the company of section 216 is presumed, unless the contrary is shown, to have been willing at any time thereafter to act on any instructions given by that person.

(6) In this section 'company' includes a company which may be wound up under Part V.

Investigation and prosecution of malpractice

218   Prosecution of delinquent officers and members of company

(1) If it appears to the court in the course of a winding up by the court that any past or present officer, or any member, of the company has been guilty of any offence in relation to the company for which he is criminally liable, the court may (either on the application of a person interested in the winding up or of its own motion) direct the liquidator to refer the matter—

(a) in the case of a winding up in England and Wales, to the Secretary of State, and

(b) in the case of a winding up in Scotland, to the Lord Advocate.

(3) If in the case of a winding up by the court in England and Wales it appears to the liquidator, not being the official receiver, that any past or present officer of the company, or any member of it, has been guilty of an offence in relation to the company for which he is criminally liable, the liquidator shall report the matter to the official receiver.

(4) If it appears to the liquidator in the course of a voluntary winding up that any past or present officer of the company, or any member of it, has been guilty of an offence in relation to the company for which he is criminally liable, he shall forthwith report the matter—

(a) in the case of a winding up in England and Wales, to the Secretary of State, and

(b) in the case of a winding up in Scotland, to the Lord Advocate,

and shall furnish to the Secretary of State or (as the case may be) the Lord Advocate such information and give him such access to and facilities for inspecting and taking copies of documents (being information or documents in the possession or under the control of the liquidator and relating to the matter in question) as the Secretary of State or (as the case may be) the Lord Advocate requires.

(5) Where a report is made to the Secretary of State under subsection (4) he may, for the purpose of investigating the matter reported to him and such other matters relating to the affairs of the company as appear to him to require investigation, exercise any of the powers which are exercisable by inspectors appointed under section 431 or 432 of the Companies Act to investigate a company's affairs.

(6) If it appears to the court in the course of a voluntary winding up that—

(a) any past or present officer of the company, or any member of it, has been guilty as above-mentioned, and

(b) no report with respect to the matter has been made by the liquidator under subsection (4),

the court may (on the application of any person interested in the winding up or of its own motion) direct the liquidator to make such a report.

On a report being made accordingly, this section has effect as though the report had been made in pursuance of subsection (4).

219   Obligations arising under s. 218

(1) For the purpose of an investigation by the Secretary of State in consequence of a report made to him under section 218(4), any obligation imposed on a person by any provision of the Companies Act to produce documents or give information to, or otherwise to assist, inspectors appointed as mentioned in section 218(5) is to be regarded as an obligation similarly to assist the Secretary of State in his investigation.

(2) An answer given by a person to a question put to him in exercise of the powers conferred by section 218(5) may be used in evidence against him.

(2A) However, in criminal proceedings in which that person is charged with an offence to which this subsection applies—

(a) no evidence relating to the answer may be adduced, and

(b) no question relating to it may be asked,

by or on behalf of the prosecution, unless evidence relating to it is adduced, or a question relating to it is asked, in the proceedings by or on behalf of that person.

(2B) Subsection (2A) applies to any offence other than—

(a) an offence under section 2 or 5 of the Perjury Act 1911 (false statements made on oath otherwise than in judicial proceedings or made otherwise than on oath), or

(b) an offence under section 44(1) or (2) of the Criminal Law (Consolidation) (Scotland) Act 1995 (false statements made on oath or otherwise than on oath).

(3) Where criminal proceedings are instituted by the Director of Public Prosecutions, the Lord Advocate or the Secretary of State following any report or reference under section 218, it is the duty of the liquidator and every officer and agent of the company past and present (other than the defendant or defender) to give to the Director of Public Prosecutions, the Lord Advocate or the Secretary of State (as the case may be) all assistance in connection with the prosecution which he is reasonably able to give.

For this purpose 'agent' includes any banker or solicitor of the company and any person employed by the company as auditor, whether that person is or is not an officer of the company.

(4) If a person fails or neglects to give assistance in the manner required by subsection (3), the court may, on the application of the Director of Public Prosecutions, the Lord Advocate or the Secretary of State (as the case may be) direct the person to comply with that subsection; and if the application is made with respect to a liquidator, the court may (unless it appears that the failure or neglect to comply was due to the liquidator not having in his hands sufficient assets of the company to enable him to do so) direct that the costs shall be borne by the liquidator personally.

PART VI   MISCELLANEOUS PROVISIONS APPLYING TO COMPANIES WHICH ARE INSOLVENT OR IN LIQUIDATION

Office-holders

230   Holders of office to be qualified insolvency practitioners

(1) Where an administration order is made in relation to a company, the administrator must be a person who is qualified to act as an insolvency practitioner in relation to the company.

(2) Where an administrative receiver of a company is appointed, he must be a person who is so qualified.

(3) Where a company goes into liquidation, the liquidator must be a person who is so qualified.

(4) Where a provisional liquidator is appointed, he must be a person who is so qualified.

(5) Subsections (3) and (4) are without prejudice to any enactment under which the official receiver is to be, or may be liquidator or provisional liquidator.

[*When the Enterprise Act 2002, sch. 17, is brought into force, the Insolvency Act 1986, s. 230(1), will be repealed.*]

231   Appointment to office of two or more persons

(1) This section applies if an appointment or nomination of any person to the office of *administrator,* administrative receiver, liquidator or provisional liquidator—

(a) relates to more than one person, or

(b) has the effect that the office is to be held by more than one person.

(2) The appointment or nomination shall declare whether any act required or authorised under any enactment to be done by the *administrator,* administrative receiver, liquidator or provisional liquidator is to be done by all or any one or more of the persons for the time being holding the office in question.

[*When the Enterprise Act 2002, sch. 17, is brought into force, the words in italics in the Insolvency Act 1986, s. 231, will be repealed.*]

232   Validity of office-holder's acts

The acts of an individual as *administrator,* administrative receiver, liquidator or provisional liquidator of a company are valid notwithstanding any defect in his appointment, nomination or qualifications.

[When the Enterprise Act 2002, sch. 17, is brought into force, the word in italics in the Insolvency Act 1986, s. 232, will be repealed.]

Management by administrators, liquidators, etc.

233 Supplies of gas, water, electricity, etc.

(1) This section applies in the case of a company where—

    (a) *an administration order is made in relation to the company, or*

    (b) an administrative receiver is appointed, or

    (ba) a moratorium under section 1A is in force, or

    (c) a voluntary arrangement approved under Part I has taken effect, or

    (d) the company goes into liquidation, or

    (e) a provisional liquidator is appointed;

and 'the office-holder' means the administrator, the administrative receiver, the nominee, the supervisor of the voluntary arrangement, the liquidator or the provisional liquidator, as the case may be.

(2) If the request is made by or with the concurrence of the office-holder for the giving, after the effective date, of any of the supplies mentioned in the next subsection, the supplier—

    (a) may make it a condition of the giving of the supply that the office-holder personally guarantees the payment of any charges in respect of the supply, but

    (b) shall not make it a condition of the giving of the supply, or do anything which has the effect of making it a condition of the giving of the supply, that any outstanding charges in respect of a supply given to the company before the effective date are paid.

(3) The supplies referred to in subsection (2) are—

    (a) a supply of gas by a gas supplier within the meaning of Part I of the Gas Act 1986,

    (b) a supply of electricity by an electricity supplier within the meaning of Part I of the Electricity Act 1989,

    (c) a supply of water by a water undertaker or, in Scotland, a water authority,

    (d) a supply of telecommunication services by a public telecommunications operator.

(4) 'The effective date' for the purposes of this section is whichever is applicable of the following dates—

    (a) *the date on which the administration order was made,*

    (b) the date on which the administrative receiver was appointed (or, if he was appointed in succession to another administrative receiver, the date on which the first of his predecessors was appointed),

    (ba) the date on which the moratorium came into force,

    (c) the date on which the voluntary arrangement took effect,

    (d) the date on which the company went into liquidation,

    (e) the date on which the provisional liquidator was appointed.

(5) The following applies to expressions used in subsection (3)—

    (c) 'water authority' means the same as in the Water (Scotland) Act 1980, and

    (d) 'telecommunication services' and 'public telecommunications operator' mean the same as in the Telecommunications Act 1984, except that the former does not include local delivery services within the meaning of Part II of the Broadcasting Act 1990.

[When the Enterprise Act 2002, sch. 17, is brought into force, the Insolvency Act 1986, s. 233(1)(a), will be replaced by:

    (a) the company enters administration, or

and s. 233(4)(a) will be replaced by:

    (a) the date on which the company entered administration,]

234 Getting in the company's property

(1) This section applies in the case of a company where—
- (a) *an administration order is made in relation to the company, or*
- (b) an administrative receiver is appointed, or
- (c) the company goes into liquidation, or
- (d) a provisional liquidator is appointed;

and 'the office-holder' means the administrator, the administrative receiver, the liquidator or the provisional liquidator, as the case may be.

(2) Where any person has in his possession or control any property, books, papers or records to which the company appears to be entitled, the court may require that person forthwith (or within such period as the court may direct) to pay, deliver, convey, surrender or transfer the property, books, papers or records to the office-holder.

(3) Where the office-holder—
- (a) seizes or disposes of any property which is not property of the company, and
- (b) at the time of seizure or disposal believes, and has reasonable grounds for believing, that he is entitled (whether in pursuance of an order of the court or otherwise) to seize or dispose of that property,

the next subsection has effect.

(4) In that case the office-holder—
- (a) is not liable to any person in respect of any loss or damage resulting from the seizure or disposal except in so far as that loss or damage is caused by the office-holder's own negligence, and
- (b) has a lien on the property, or the proceeds of its sale, for such expenses as were incurred in connection with the seizure of disposal.

[*When the Enterprise Act 2002, sch. 17, is brought into force, the Insolvency Act 1986, s. 234(1)(a), will be replaced by:*
- (a) *the company enters administration, or*]

235 Duty to cooperate with office-holder

(1) This section applies as does section 234; and it also applies, in the case of a company in respect of which a winding-up order has been made by the court in England and Wales, as if references to the office-holder included the official receiver, whether or not he is the liquidator.

(2) Each of the persons mentioned in the next subsection shall—
- (a) give to the office-holder such information concerning the company and its promotion, formation, business, dealings, affairs or property as the office-holder may at any time after the effective date reasonably require, and
- (b) attend on the office-holder at such times as the latter may reasonably require.

(3) The persons referred to above are—
- (a) those who are or have at any time been officers of the company,
- (b) those who have taken part in the formation of the company at any time within one year before the effective date,
- (c) those who are in the employment of the company, or have been in its employment (including employment under a contract for services) within that year, and are in the office-holder's opinion capable of giving information which he requires,
- (d) those who are, or have within the year been, officers of, or in the employment (including employment under a contract for services) of, another company which is, or within that year was, an officer of the company in question, and
- (e) in the case of a company being wound up by the court, any person who has acted as administrator, administrative receiver or liquidator of the company.

(4) For the purposes of subsections (2) and (3), 'the effective date' is whichever is applicable of the following dates—

428   Insolvency Act 1986, Part VI

(a) the date on which the administration order was made,

(b) the date on which the administrative receiver was appointed or, if he was appointed in succession to another administrative receiver, the date on which the first of his predecessors was appointed,

(c) the date on which the provisional liquidator was appointed, and

(d) the date on which the company went into liquidation.

(5) If a person without reasonable excuse fails to comply with any obligation imposed by this section, he is liable to a fine and, for continued contravention, to a daily default fine.

[When the Enterprise Act 2002, sch. 17, is brought into force, the Insolvency Act 1986, s. 235(4)(a), will be replaced by:

(a) the date on which the company entered administration,]

236 Inquiry into company's dealings, etc.

(1) This section applies as does section 234; and it also applies in the case of a company in respect of which a winding-up order has been made by the court in England and Wales as if references to the office-holder included the official receiver, whether or not he is the liquidator.

(2) The court may, on the application of the office-holder, summon to appear before it—

(a) any officer of the company,

(b) any person known or suspected to have in his possession any property of the company or supposed to be indebted to the company, or

(c) any person whom the court thinks capable of giving information concerning the promotion, formation, business, dealings, affairs or property of the company.

(3) The court may require any such person as is mentioned in subsection (2)(a) to (c) to submit an affidavit to the court containing an account of his dealings with the company or to produce any books, papers or other records in his possession or under his control relating to the company or the matters mentioned in paragraph (c) of the subsection.

(4) The following applies in a case where—

(a) a person without reasonable excuse fails to appear before the court when he is summoned to do so under this section, or

(b) there are reasonable grounds for believing that a person has absconded, or is about to abscond, with a view to avoiding his appearance before the court under this section.

(5) The court may, for the purpose of bringing that person and anything in his possession before the court, cause a warrant to be issued to a constable or prescribed officer of the court—

(a) for the arrest of that person, and

(b) for the seizure of any books, papers, records, money or goods in that person's possession.

(6) The court may authorise a person arrested under such a warrant to be kept in custody, and anything seized under such a warrant to be held, in accordance with the rules, until that person is brought before the court under the warrant or until such other time as the court may order.

237 Court's enforcement powers under s. 236

(1) If it appears to the court, on consideration of any evidence obtained under section 236 or this section, that any person has in his possession any property of the company, the court may, on the application of the office-holder, order that person to deliver the whole or any part of the property to the office-holder at such time, in such manner and on such terms as the court thinks fit.

(2) If it appears to the court, on consideration of any evidence so obtained, that any person is indebted to the company, the court may, on the application of the office-holder,

order that person to pay to the office-holder, at such time and in such manner as the court may direct, the whole or any part of the amount due, whether in full discharge of the debt or otherwise, as the court thinks fit.

(3) The court may, if it thinks fit, order that any person who is within the jurisdiction of the court would be liable to be summoned to appear before it under section 236 or this section shall be examined in any part of the United Kingdom where he may for the time being be, or in a place outside the United Kingdom.

(4) Any person who appears or is brought before the court under section 236 or this section may be examined on oath, either orally or (except in Scotland) by interrogatories, concerning the company or the matters mentioned in section 236(2)(c).

Adjustment of prior transactions (administration and liquidation)

238   Transactions at an undervalue (England and Wales)

(1) This section applies in the case of a company where—
(a) *an administration order is made in relation to the company, or*
(b) the company goes into liquidation;
and 'the office-holder' means the administrator or the liquidator, as the case may be.

(2) Where the company has at a relevant time (defined in section 240) entered into a transaction with any person at an undervalue, the office-holder may apply to the court for an order under this section

(3) Subject as follows, the court shall, on such an application, make such order as it thinks fit for restoring the position to what it would have been if the company had not entered into that transaction.

(4) For the purposes of this section and section 241, a company enters into a transaction with a person at an undervalue if—
(a) the company makes a gift to that person or otherwise enters into a transaction with that person on terms that provide for the company to receive no consideration, or
(b) the company enters into a transaction with that person for a consideration the value of which, in money or money's worth, is significantly less than the value, in money or money's worth, of the consideration provided by the company.

(5) The court shall not make an order under this section in respect of a transaction at an undervalue if it is satisfied—
(a) that the company which entered into the transaction did so in good faith and for the purpose of carrying on its business, and
(b) that at the time it did so there were reasonable grounds for believing that the transaction would benefit the company.

[*When the Enterprise Act 2002, sch. 17, is brought into force, the Insolvency Act 1986, s. 238(1)(a), will be replaced by:*
(a) *the company enters administration, or*]

239   Preferences (England and Wales)

(1) This section applies as does section 238.

(2) Where the company has at a relevant time (defined in the next section) given a preference to any person, the office-holder may apply to the court for an order under this section.

(3) Subject as follows, the court shall, on such an application, make such order as it thinks fit for restoring the position to what it would have been if the company had not given that preference.

(4) For the purposes of this section and section 241, a company gives a preference to a person if—

(a) that person is one of the company's creditors or a surety or guarantor for any of the company's debts or other liabilities, and

(b) the company does anything or suffers anything to be done which (in either case) has the effect of putting that person into a position which, in the event of the company going into insolvent liquidation, will be better than the position he would have been in if that thing had not been done.

(5) The court shall not make an order under this section in respect of a preference given to any person unless the company which gave the preference was influenced in deciding to give it by a desire to produce in relation to that person the effect mentioned in subsection (4)(b).

(6) A company which has given a preference to a person connected with the company (otherwise than by reason only of being its employee) at the time the preference was given is presumed, unless the contrary is shown, to have been influenced in deciding to give it by such a desire as is mentioned in subsection (5).

(7) The fact that something has been done in pursuance of the order of a court does not, without more, prevent the doing or suffering of that thing from constituting the giving of a preference.

240   **'Relevant time' under ss. 238, 239**

(1) Subject to the next subsection, the time at which a company enters into a transaction at an undervalue or gives a preference is a relevant time if the transaction is entered into, or the preference given—

(a) in the case of a transaction at an undervalue or of a preference which is given to a person who is connected with the company (otherwise than by reason only of being its employee), at a time in the period of 2 years ending with the onset of insolvency (which expression is defined below),

(b) in the case of a preference which is not such a transaction and is not so given, at a time in the period of 6 months ending with the onset of insolvency, *and*

(c) *in either case, at a time between the presentation of a petition for the making of an administration order in relation to the company and the making of such an order on that petition.*

(2) Where a company enters into a transaction at an undervalue or gives a preference at a time mentioned in subsection (1)(a) or (b), that time is not a relevant time for the purposes of section 238 or 239 unless the company—

(a) is at that time unable to pay its debts within the meaning of section 123 in Chapter VI of Part IV, or

(b) becomes unable to pay its debts within the meaning of that section in consequence of the transaction or preference;

but the requirements of this subsection are presumed to be satisfied, unless the contrary is shown, in relation to any transaction at an undervalue which is entered into by a company with a person who is connected with the company.

(3) *For the purposes of subsection (1), the onset of insolvency is—*

(a) *in a case where section 238 or 239 applies by reason of the making of an administration order or of a company going into liquidation immediately upon the discharge of an administration order, the date of the presentation of the petition on which the administration order was made,*

(aa) *in a case where section 238 or 239 applies by reason of a company going into liquidation following conversion of administration into winding up by virtue of Article 37 of the EC Regulation, the date of the presentation of the petition on which the administration order was made, and*

(b) *in a case where the section applies by reason of a company going into liquidation at any other time, the date of the commencement of the winding up.*

[*When the Enterprise Act 2002, sch. 17, is brought into force, the words in italics in the Insolvency Act 1986, s. 240(1), will be replaced by:*

    (c) *in either case, at a time between the making of an administration application in respect of the company and the making of an administration order on that application, and*

    (d) *in either case, at a time between the filing with the court of a copy of notice of intention to appoint an administrator under paragraph 14 or 22 of Schedule B1 and the making of an appointment under that paragraph.*

and s. 240(3) will be replaced by:

    (3) *For the purposes of subsection (1), the onset of insolvency is—*

    (a) *in a case where section 238 or 239 applies by reason of an administrator of a company being appointed by administration order, the date on which the administration application is made,*

    (b) *in a case where section 238 or 239 applies by reason of an administrator of a company being appointed under paragraph 14 or 22 of Schedule B1 following filing with the court of a copy of a notice of intention to appoint under that paragraph, the date on which the copy of the notice is filed,*

    (c) *in a case where section 238 or 239 applies by reason of an administrator of a company being appointed otherwise than as mentioned in paragraph (a) or (b), the date on which the appointment takes effect,*

    (d) *in a case where section 238 or 239 applies by reason of a company going into liquidation either following conversion of administration into winding up by virtue of Article 37 of the EC Regulation or at the time when the appointment of an administrator ceases to have effect, the date on which the company entered administration (or, if relevant, the date on which the application for the administration order was made or a copy of the notice of intention to appoint was filed), and*

    (e) *in a case where section 238 or 239 applies by reason of a company going into liquidation at any other time, the date of the commencement of the winding up.*]

241 Orders under ss. 238, 239

(1) Without prejudice to the generality of sections 238(3) and 239(3), an order under either of those sections with respect to a transaction or preference entered into or given by a company may (subject to the next subsection)—

    (a) require any property transferred as part of the transaction, or in connection with the giving of the preference, to be vested in the company,

    (b) require any property to be so vested if it represents in any person's hands the application either of the proceeds of sale of property so transferred or of money so transferred,

    (c) release or discharge (in whole or in part) any security given by the company,

    (d) require any person to pay, in respect of benefits received by him from the company, such sums to the office-holder as the court may direct,

    (e) provide for any surety or guarantor whose obligations to any person were released or discharged (in whole or in part) under the transaction, or by the giving of the preference, to be under such new or revived obligations to that person as the court thinks appropriate,

    (f) provide for security to be provided for the discharge of any obligation imposed by or arising under the order, for such an obligation to be charged on any property and for the security or charge to have the same priority as a security or charge released or discharged (in whole or in part) under the transaction or by the giving of the preference, and

    (g) provide for the extent to which any person whose property is vested by the order in the company, or on whom obligations are imposed by the order, is to be able to prove in the winding up of the company for debts or other liabilities which arose from, or were released or discharged (in whole or in part) under or by, the transaction or the giving of the preference.

(2) An order under section 238 or 239 may affect the property of, or impose any obligation on, any person whether or not he is the person with whom the company in question entered into the transaction or (as the case may be) the person to whom the preference was given; but such an order—

(a) shall not prejudice any interest in property which was acquired from a person other than the company and was acquired in good faith and for value, or prejudice any interest deriving from such an interest, and

(b) shall not require a person who received a benefit from the transaction or preference in good faith and for value to pay a sum to the office-holder, except where that person was a party to the transaction or the payment is to be in respect of a preference given to that person at a time when he was a creditor of the company.

(2A) Where a person has acquired an interest in property from a person other than the company in question, or has received a benefit from the transaction or preference, and at the time of that acquisition or receipt—

(a) he had notice of the relevant surrounding circumstances and of the relevant proceedings, or

(b) he was connected with, or was an associate of, either the company in question or the person with whom that company entered into the transaction or to whom that company gave the preference,

then, unless the contrary is shown, it shall be presumed for the purposes of paragraph (a) or (as the case may be) paragraph (b) of subsection (2) that the interest was acquired or the benefit was received otherwise than in good faith.

(3) For the purposes of subsection (2A)(a), the relevant surrounding circumstances are (as the case may require)—

(a) the fact that the company in question entered into the transaction at an undervalue; or

(b) the circumstances which amounted to the giving of the preference by the company in question;

and subsections (3A) to (3C) have effect to determine whether, for those purposes, a person has notice of the relevant proceedings.

(3A) In a case where section 238 or 239 applies by reason of the making of an administration order, a person has notice of the relevant proceedings if he has notice—

(a) of the fact that the petition on which the administration order is made has been presented; or

(b) of the fact that the administration order has been made.

(3B) In a case where section 238 or 239 applies by reason of the company in question going into liquidation immediately upon the discharge of an administration order, a person has notice of the relevant proceedings if he has notice—

(a) of the fact that the petition on which the administration order is made has been presented;

(b) of the fact that the administration order has been made; or

(c) of the fact that the company has gone into liquidation.

(3C) In a case where section 238 or 239 applies by reason of the company in question going into liquidation at any other time, a person has notice of the relevant proceedings if he has notice—

(a) where the company goes into liquidation on the making of a winding-up order, of the fact that the petition on which the winding-up order is made has been presented or of the fact that the company has gone into liquidation;

(b) in any other case, of the fact that the company has gone into liquidation.

(4) The provisions of section 238 to 241 apply without prejudice to the availability of any other remedy, even in relation to a transaction or preference which the company had no power to enter into or give.

[*When the Enterprise Act 2002, sch. 17, is brought into force, the Insolvency Act 1986, s. 241(3A) and (3B), will be replaced by:*

(3A) Where section 238 or 239 applies by reason of a company's entering administration, a person has notice of the relevant proceedings if he has notice that—

(a) *an administration application has been made,*

(b) *an administration order has been made,*

(c) *a copy of a notice of intention to appoint an administrator under paragraph 14 or 22 of Schedule B1 has been filed, or*

(d) *notice of the appointment of an administrator has been filed under paragraph 18 or 29 of that Schedule.*

(3B) Where section 238 or 239 applies by reason of a company's going into liquidation at the time when the appointment of an administrator of the company ceases to have effect, a person has notice of the relevant proceedings if he has notice that—

(a) *an administration application has been made,*

(b) *an administration order has been made,*

(c) *a copy of a notice of intention to appoint an administrator under paragraph 14 or 22 of Schedule B1 has been filed,*

(d) *notice of the appointment of an administrator has been filed under paragraph 18 or 29 of that Schedule, or*

(e) *the company has gone into liquidation.*]

244 Extortionate credit transactions

(1) This section applies as does section 238, and where the company is, or has been, a party to a transaction for, or involving, the provision of credit to the company.

(2) The court may, on the application of the office-holder, make an order with respect to the transaction if the transaction is or was extortionate and was entered into in the period of 3 years ending with the day on which *the administration order was made or (as the case may be) the company* went into liquidation.

(3) For the purposes of this section a transaction is extortionate if, having regard to the risk accepted by the person providing the credit—

(a) the terms of it are or were such as to require grossly exorbitant payments to be made (whether unconditionally or in certain contingencies) in respect of the provision of the credit, or

(b) it otherwise grossly contravened ordinary principles of fair dealing;

and it shall be presumed, unless the contrary is proved, that a transaction with respect to which an application is made under this section is or, as the case may be, was extortionate.

(4) An order under this section with respect to any transaction may contain such one or more of the following as the court thinks fit, that is to say—

(a) provision setting aside the whole or part of any obligation created by the transaction,

(b) provision otherwise varying the terms of the transaction or varying the terms on which any security for the purposes of the transaction is held,

(c) provision requiring any person who is or was a party to the transaction to pay to the office-holder any sums paid to that person, by virtue of the transaction, by the company,

(d) provision requiring any person to surrender to the office-holder any property held by him as security for the purposes of the transaction,

(e) provision directing accounts to be taken between any persons.

(5) The powers conferred by this section are exercisable in relation to any transaction

concurrently with any powers exercisable in relation to that transaction as a transaction at an undervalue or under section 242 (gratuitous alienations in Scotland).

[*When the Enterprise Act 2002, sch. 17, is brought into force, the words in italics in the Insolvency Act 1986, s. 244(2), will be replaced by:*

   the company entered administration or]

245   Avoidance of certain floating charges

(1) This section applies as does section 238, but applies to Scotland as well as to England and Wales.

(2) Subject as follows, a floating charge on the company's undertaking or property created at a relevant time is invalid except to the extent of the aggregate of—

    (a) the value of so much of the consideration for the creation of the charge as consists of money paid, or goods or services supplied, to the company at the same time as, or after, the creation of the charge,

    (b) the value of so much of that consideration as consists of the discharge or reduction, at the same time as, or after, the creation of the charge, of any debt of the company, and

    (c) the amount of such interest (if any) as is payable on the amount falling within paragraph (a) or (b) in pursuance of any agreement under which the money was so paid, the goods or services were so supplied or the debt was so discharged or reduced.

(3) Subject to the next subsection, the time at which a floating charge is created by the company is a relevant time for the purposes of this section if the charge is created—

    (a) in the case of a charge which is created in favour of a person who is connected with the company, at a time in the period of 2 years ending with the onset of insolvency,

    (b) in the case of a charge which is created in favour of any other person, at a time in the period of 12 months ending with the onset of insolvency, *or*

    (c) *in either case, at a time between the presentation of a petition for the making of an administration order in relation to the company and the making of such an order on that petition.*

(4) Where a company creates a floating charge at a time mentioned in subsection (3)(b) and the person in favour of whom the charge is created is not connected with the company, that time is not a relevant time for the purposes of this section unless the company—

    (a) is at that time unable to pay its debts within the meaning of section 123 in Chapter VI of Part IV, or

    (b) becomes unable to pay its debts within the meaning of that section in consequence of the transaction under which the charge is created.

(5) *For the purposes of subsection (3), the onset of insolvency is—*

    (a) *in a case where this section applies by reason of the making of an administration order, the date of the presentation of the petition on which the order was made, and*

    (b) *in a case where this section applies by reason of a company going into liquidation, the date of the commencement of the winding up.*

(6) For the purposes of subsection (2)(a) the value of any goods or services supplied by way of consideration for a floating charge is the amount in money which at the time they were supplied could reasonably have been expected to be obtained for supplying the goods or services in the ordinary course of business and on the same terms (apart from the consideration) as those on which they were supplied to the company.

[*When the Enterprise Act 2002, sch. 17, is brought into force, the words in italics in the Insolvency Act 1986, s. 245(3), will be replaced by:*

    (c) *in either case, at a time between the making of an administration application in respect of the company and the making of an administration order on that application, or*

(d) in either case, at a time between the filing with the court of a copy of notice of intention to appoint an administrator under paragraph 14 or 22 of Schedule B1 and the making of an appointment under that paragraph.
and s. 245(5) will be replaced by:
(5) For the purposes of subsection (3), the onset of insolvency is—
(a) in a case where this section applies by reason of an administrator of a company being appointed by administration order, the date on which the administration application is made,
(b) in a case where this section applies by reason of an administrator of a company being appointed under paragraph 14 or 22 of Schedule B1 following filing with the court of a copy of notice of intention to appoint under that paragraph, the date on which the copy of the notice is filed,
(c) in a case where this section applies by reason of an administrator of a company being appointed otherwise than as mentioned in paragraph (a) or (b), the date on which the appointment takes effect, and
(d) in a case where this section applies by reason of a company going into liquidation, the date of the commencement of the winding up.]

246   Unenforceability of liens on books, etc.

(1) This section applies in the case of a company where—
(a) an administration order is made in relation to the company, or
(b) the company goes into liquidation, or
(c) a provisional liquidator is appointed;
and 'the office-holder' means the administrator, the liquidator or the provisional liquidator, as the case may be.

(2) Subject as follows, a lien or other right to retain possession of any of the books, papers or other records of the company is unenforceable to the extent that its enforcement would deny possession of any books, papers or other records to the office-holder.

(3) This does not apply to a lien on documents which give a title to property and are held as such.
[When the Enterprise Act 2002, sch. 17, is brought into force, the Insolvency Act 1986, s. 246(1)(a), will be replaced by:
(a) the company enters administration, or]

PART VII   INTERPRETATION FOR FIRST GROUP OF PARTS

247   'Insolvency' and 'go into liquidation'

(1) In this Group of Parts, except in so far as the context otherwise requires, 'insolvency', in relation to a company, includes the approval of a voluntary arrangement under Part I, the making of an administration order or the appointment of an administrative receiver.

(2) For the purposes of any provision in this Group of Parts, a company goes into liquidation if it passes a resolution for voluntary winding up or an order for its winding up is made by the court at a time when it has not already gone into liquidation by passing such a resolution.

(3) The reference to a resolution for voluntary winding up in subsection (2) includes a resolution deemed to occur by virtue of an order made following conversion of a voluntary arrangement or administration into winding up under Article 37 of the EC Regulation.
[When the Enterprise Act 2002, sch. 17, is brought into force, the words in italics in the Insolvency Act 1986, s. 247(1), will be replaced by:
or the appointment of an administrator or
and s. 247(3) will be replaced by:
(3) The reference to a resolution for voluntary winding up in subsection (2) includes a reference to a resolution which is deemed to occur by virtue of—

(a) paragraph 83(6)(b) of Schedule B1, or

(b) an order made following conversion of administration or a voluntary arrangement into winding up by virtue of Article 37 of the EC Regulation.]

248 'Secured creditor', etc.

In this Group of Parts, except in so far as the context otherwise requires—

(a) 'secured creditor', in relation to a company, means a creditor of the company who holds in respect of his debt a security over property of the company, and 'unsecured creditor' is to be read accordingly; and

(b) 'security' means—

(i) in relation to England and Wales, any mortgage, charge, lien or other security, and

(ii) in relation to Scotland, any security (whether heritable or movable), any floating charge and any right of lien or preference and any right of retention (other than a right of compensation or set-off).

249 'Connected' with a company

For the purposes of any provision in this Group of Parts, a person is connected with a company if—

(a) he is a director or shadow director of the company or an associate of such a director or shadow director, or

(b) he is an associate of the company;

and 'associate' has the meaning given by section 435 in Part XVIII of this Act.

250 'Member' of a company

For the purposes of any provision in this Group of Parts, a person who is not a member of a company but to whom shares in the company have been transferred, or transmitted by operation of law, is to be regarded as a member of the company, and references to a member or members are to be read accordingly.

251 Expressions used generally

In this Group of Parts, except in so far as the context otherwise requires—

'administrative receiver' means—

(a) an administrative receiver as defined by section 29(2) in Chapter I of Part III, or

(b) a receiver appointed under section 51 in Chapter II of that Part in a case where the whole (or substantially the whole) of the company's property is attached by the floating charge;

'business day' means any day other than a Saturday, a Sunday, Christmas Day, Good Friday or a day which is a bank holiday in any part of Great Britain;

'chattel leasing agreement' means an agreement for the bailment or, in Scotland, the hiring of goods which is capable of subsisting for more than 3 months;

'contributory' has the meaning given by section 79;

'director' includes any person occupying the position of director, by whatever name called;

'floating charge' means a charge which, as created, was a floating charge and includes a floating charge within section 462 of the Companies Act (Scottish floating charges);

'office copy', in relation to Scotland, means a copy certified by the clerk of court;

'the official rate', in relation to interest, means the rate payable under section 189(4);

'prescribed' means prescribed by the rules;

'receiver', in the expression 'receiver or manager', does not include a receiver appointed under section 51 in Chapter II of Part III;

'retention of title agreement' means an agreement for the sale of goods to a company, being an agreement—

(a) which does not constitute a charge on the goods, but

(b) under which, if the seller is not paid and the company is wound up, the seller will have priority over all other creditors of the company as respects the goods or any property representing the goods;

'the rules' means rules under section 411 in Part XV; and

'shadow director', in relation to a company, means a person in accordance with whose directions or instructions the directors of the company are accustomed to act (but so that a person is not deemed a shadow director by reason only that the directors act on advice given by him in a professional capacity);

and any expression for whose interpretation provision is made by Part XXVI of the Companies Act, other than an expression defined above in this section, is to be construed in accordance with that provision.

THE THIRD GROUP OF PARTS   MISCELLANEOUS MATTERS BEARING ON BOTH COMPANY AND INDIVIDUAL INSOLVENCY; GENERAL INTERPRETATION; FINAL PROVISIONS

PART XII   PREFERENTIAL DEBTS IN COMPANY AND INDIVIDUAL INSOLVENCY

386   Categories of preferential debts

(1) A reference in this Act to the preferential debts of a company or an individual is to the debts listed in Schedule 6 to this Act *(money owed to the Inland Revenue for income tax deducted at source; VAT, insurance premium tax, landfill tax, climate change levy, aggregates levy, car tax, betting and gaming duties, beer duty, lottery duty, air passenger duty; social security and pension scheme contributions;* remuneration etc. of employees; levies on coal and steel production); and references to preferential creditors are to be read accordingly.

(2) In that Schedule 'the debtor' means the company or the individual concerned.

(3) Schedule 6 is to be read with Schedule 4 to the Pension Schemes Act 1993 (occupational pension scheme contributions).

[*When the Enterprise Act 2002, s. 251(3), is brought into force, the words in italics in s. 386(1) will be replaced by:*

(contributions to occupational pension schemes;]

387   'The relevant date'

(1) This section explains references in Schedule 6 to the relevant date (being the date which determines the existence and amount of a preferential debt).

(2) For the purposes of section 4 in part I (meetings to consider company voluntary arrangement), the relevant date in relation to a company which is not being wound up is—

(a) *where an administration order is in force in relation to the company, the date of the making of that order, and*

(b) *where no such order has been made, the date on which the voluntary arrangement takes effect.*

(2A) For the purposes of paragraph 31 of Schedule A1 (meetings to consider company voluntary arrangement where a moratorium under section 1A is in force), the relevant date in relation to a company is the date of filing.

(3) *In relation to a company which is being wound up, the following applies—*

(a) *if the winding up is by the court, and the winding-up order was made immediately upon the discharge of an administration order, the relevant date is the date of the making of the administration order;*

(aa) *if the winding up is by the court and the winding-up order was made following conversion* of administration into winding up by virtue of Article 37 of the EC Regulation, the relevant date is the date of the making of the administration order;

(ab) if the company is deemed to have passed a resolution for voluntary winding up by virtue of an order following conversion of administration into winding up under Article 37 of the EC Regulation, the relevant date is the date of the making of the administration order;

(b) if the case does not fall within paragraph (a), (aa) or (ab) and the company—
  (i) is being wound up by the court, and
  (ii) had not commenced to be wound up voluntarily before the date of the making of the winding-up order,
  the relevant date is the date of the appointment (or first appointment) of a provisional liquidator or, if no such appointment has been made, the date of the winding-up order;

(c) if the case does not fall within paragraph (a), (aa), (ab) or (b), the relevant date is the date of the passing of the resolution for the winding up of the company.

(4) In relation to a company in receivership (where section 40 or, as the case may be, section 59 applies), the relevant date is—

(a) in England and Wales, the date of the appointment of the receiver by debenture-holders, and

(b) in Scotland, the date of the appointment of the receiver under section 53(6) or (as the case may be) 54(5).

. . .

[When the Enterprise Act 2002, sch. 17, is brought into force, paras (a) and (b) in the Insolvency Act 1986, s. 387(2), will be replaced by:

(a) if the company is in administration, the date on which it entered administration, and

(b) if the company is not in administration, the date on which the voluntary arrangement takes effect.

and s. 387(3) will be replaced by:

(3) In relation to a company which is being wound up, the following applies—

(a) if the winding up is by the court, and the winding-up order was made immediately upon the discharge of an administration order, the relevant date is the date on which the company entered administration;

(aa) if the winding up is by the court and the winding-up order was made following conversion of administration into winding up by virtue of Article 37 of the EC Regulation, the relevant date is the date on which the company entered administration;

(ab) if the company is deemed to have passed a resolution for voluntary winding up by virtue of an order following conversion of administration into winding up under Article 37 of the EC Regulation, the relevant date is the date on which the company entered administration;

(b) if the case does not fall within paragraph (a), (aa) or (ab) and the company—
  (i) is being wound up by the court, and
  (ii) had not commenced to be wound up voluntarily before the date of the making of the winding-up order, the relevant date is the date of the appointment (or first appointment) of a provisional liquidator or, if no such appointment has been made, the date of the winding-up order;

(ba) if the case does not fall within paragraph (a), (aa), (ab) or (b) and the company is being wound up following administration pursuant to paragraph 83 of Schedule B1, the relevant date is the date on which the company entered administration;

(c) if the case does not fall within paragraph (a), (aa), (ab), (b) or (ba), the relevant date is the date of the passing of the resolution for the winding up of the company.

(3A) In relation to a company which is in administration (and to which no other provision of this section applies) the relevant date is the date on which the company enters administration.]

PART XVI   PROVISIONS AGAINST DEBT AVOIDANCE (ENGLAND AND WALES ONLY)

423   Transactions defrauding creditors

(1) This section relates to transactions entered into at an undervalue; and a person enters into such a transaction with another person if—

    (a) he makes a gift to the other person or he otherwise enters into a transaction with the other on terms that provide for him to receive no consideration;

    (b) he enters into a transaction with the other in consideration of marriage; or

    (c) he enters into a transaction with the other for a consideration the value of which, in money or money's worth, is significantly less than the value, in money or money's worth, of the consideration provided by himself.

(2) Where a person has entered into such a transaction, the court may, if satisfied under the next subsection, make such order as it thinks fit for—

    (a) restoring the position to what it would have been if the transaction had not been entered into, and

    (b) protecting the interests of persons who are victims of the transaction.

(3) In the case of a person entering into such a transaction, an order shall only be made if the court is satisfied that it was entered into by him for the purpose—

    (a) of putting assets beyond the reach of a person who is making, or may at some time make, a claim against him, or

    (b) of otherwise prejudicing the interests of such a person in relation to the claim which he is making or may make.

(4) In this section 'the court' means the High Court or—

    (a) if the person entering into the transaction is an individual, any other court which would have jurisdiction in relation to a bankruptcy petition relating to him;

    (b) if that person is a body capable of being wound up under Part IV or V of this Act, any other court having jurisdiction to wind it up.

(5) In relation to a transaction at an undervalue, references here and below to a victim of the transaction are to a person who is, or is capable of being, prejudiced by it; and in the following two sections the person entering into the transaction is referred to as 'the debtor'.

424   Those who may apply for an order under s. 423

(1) An application for an order under section 423 shall not be made in relation to a transaction except—

    (a) in a case where the debtor has been adjudged bankrupt or is a body corporate which is being wound up or *in relation to which an administration order is in force*, by the official receiver, by the trustee of the bankrupt's estate or the liquidator or administrator of the body corporate or (with the leave of the court) by a victim of the transaction;

    (b) in a case where a victim of the transaction is bound by a voluntary arrangement approved under Part I or Part VIII of this Act, by the supervisor of the voluntary arrangement or by any person who (whether or not so bound) is such a victim; or

    (c) in any other case, by a victim of the transaction.

(2) An application made under any of the paragraphs of subsection (1) is to be treated as made on behalf of every victim of the transaction.

[*When the Enterprise Act 2002, sch. 17, is brought into force, the words in italics in the Insolvency Act 1986, s. 424(1)(a), will be replaced by:*

  is in administration,]

425   Provision which may be made by order under s. 423

(1) Without prejudice to the generality of section 423, an order made under that section with respect to a transaction may (subject as follows)—

(a) require any property transferred as part of the transaction to be vested in any person, either absolutely or for the benefit of all the persons on whose behalf the application for the order is treated as made;

(b) require any property to be so vested if it represents, in any person's hands, the application either of the proceeds of sale of property so transferred or of money so transferred;

(c) release or discharge (in whole or in part) any security given by the debtor;

(d) require any person to pay to any other person in respect of benefits received from the debtor such sums as the court may direct;

(e) provide for any surety or guarantor whose obligations to any person were released or discharged (in whole or in part) under the transaction to be under such new or revived obligations as the court thinks appropriate;

(f) provide for security to be provided for the discharge of any obligation imposed by or arising under the order, for such an obligation to be charged on any property and for such security or charge to have the same priority as a security or charge released or discharged (in whole or in part) under the transaction.

(2) An order under section 423 may affect the property of, or impose any obligation on, any person whether or not he is the person with whom the debtor entered into the transaction; but such an order—

(a) shall not prejudice any interest in property which was acquired from a person other than the debtor and was acquired in good faith, for value and without notice of the relevant circumstances, or prejudice any interest deriving from such an interest, and

(b) shall not require a person who received a benefit from the transaction in good faith, for value and without notice of the relevant circumstances to pay any sum unless he was a party to the transaction.

(3) For the purposes of this section the relevant circumstances in relation to a transaction are the circumstances by virtue of which an order under section 423 may be made in respect of the transaction.

(4) In this section 'security' means any mortgage, charge, lien or other security.

PART XVII   MISCELLANEOUS AND GENERAL

430 Provision introducing Schedule of punishments

(1) Schedule 10 to this Act has effect with respect to the way in which offences under this Act are punishable on conviction.

(2) In relation to an offence under a provision of this Act specified in the first column of the Schedule (the general nature of the offence being described in the second column), the third column shows whether the offence is punishable on conviction on indictment, or on summary conviction, or either in the one way or the other.

(3) The fourth column of the Schedule shows, in relation to an offence, the maximum punishment by way of fine or imprisonment under this Act which may be imposed on a person convicted of the offence in the way specified in relation to it in the third column (that is to say, on indictment or summarily) a reference to a period of years or months being to a term of imprisonment of that duration.

(4) The fifth column shows (in relation to an offence for which there is an entry in that column) that a person convicted of the offence after continued contravention is liable to a daily default fine; that is to say, he is liable on a second or subsequent conviction of the offence to the fine specified in that column for each day on which the contravention is continued (instead of the penalty specified for the offence in the fourth column of the Schedule).

(5) For the purpose of any enactment in this Act whereby an officer of a company who is in default is liable to a fine or penalty, the expression 'officer who is in default' means any

officer of the company who knowingly and wilfully authorises or permits the default, refusal or contravention mentioned in the enactment.

431 Summary proceedings

(1) Summary proceedings for any offence under any of Parts I to VII of this Act may (without prejudice to any jurisdiction exercisable apart from the subsection) be taken against a body corporate at any place at which the body has a place of business, and against any other person at any place at which he is for the time being.

(2) Notwithstanding anything in section 127(1) of the Magistrates' Courts Act 1980, an information relating to such an offence which is triable by a magistrates' court in England and Wales may be so tried if it is laid at any time within 3 years after the commission of the offence and within 12 months after the date on which evidence sufficient in the opinion of the Director of Public Prosecutions or the Secretary of State (as the case may be) to justify the proceedings comes to his knowledge.

(3) Summary proceedings in Scotland for such an offence shall not be commenced after the expiration of 3 years from the commission of the offence.

Subject to this (and notwithstanding anything in section 136 of the Criminal Procedure (Scotland) Act 1995), such proceedings may (in Scotland) be commenced at any time within 12 months after the date on which evidence sufficient in the Lord Advocate's opinion to justify the proceedings came to his knowledge or, where such evidence was reported to him by the Secretary of State, within 12 months after the date on which it came to the knowledge of the latter; and subsection (3) of that section applies for the purpose of this subsection as it applies for the purpose of that section.

(4) For purposes of this section, a certificate of the Director of Public Prosecutions, the Lord Advocate or the Secretary of State (as the case may be) as to the date on which such evidence as is referred to above came to his knowledge is conclusive evidence.

432 Offences by bodies corporate

(1) This section applies to offences under this Act other than those excepted by subsection (4).

(2) Where a body corporate is guilty of an offence to which this section applies and the offence is proved to have been committed with the consent or connivance of, or to be attributable to any neglect on the part of, any director, manager, secretary or other similar officer of the body corporate or any person who was purporting to act in any such capacity he, as well as the body corporate, is guilty of the offence and liable to be proceeded against and punished accordingly.

(3) Where the affairs of a body corporate are managed by its members, subsection (2) applies in relation to the acts and defaults of a member in connection with his functions of management as if he were a director of the body corporate.

(4) The offences excepted from this section are those under sections 30, 39, 51, 53, 54, 62, 64, 66, 85, 89, 164, 188, 201, 206, 207, 208, 209, 210 and 211 and those under paragraphs 16(2), 17(3)(a), 18(3)(a), 19(3)(a), 22(1) and 23(1)(a) of Schedule A1.

433 Admissibility in evidence of statements of affairs, etc.

(1) In any proceedings (whether or not under this Act)—
  (a) a statement of affairs prepared for the purposes of any provision of this Act which is derived from the Insolvency Act 1985, and
  (b) any other statement made in pursuance of a requirement imposed by or under any such provision or by or under rules made under this Act,
may be used in evidence against any person making or concurring in making the statement.

(2) However, in criminal proceedings in which any such person is charged with an offence to which this subsection applies—

(a) no evidence relating to the statement may be adduced, and

(b) no question relating to it may be asked,

by or on behalf of the prosecution, unless evidence relating to it is adduced, or a question relating to it is asked, in the proceedings by or on behalf of that person.

(3) Subsection (2) applies to any offence other than—

(a) an offence under section 22(6), 47(6), 48(8), 66(6), 67(8), 95(8), 98(6), 99(3)(a), 131(7), 192(2), 208(1)(a) or (d) or (2), 210, 235(5), 353(1), 354(1)(b) or (3) or 356(1) or (2)(a) or (b) or paragraph 4(3)(a) of Schedule 7;

(b) an offence which is—

(i) created by rules made under this Act, and

(ii) designated for the purposes of this subsection by such rules or by regulations made by the Secretary of State;

(c) an offence which is—

(i) created by regulations made under any such rules, and

(ii) designated for the purposes of this subsection by such regulations;

(d) an offence under section 1, 2 or 5 of the Perjury Act 1911 (false statements made on oath or made otherwise than on oath); or

(e) an offence under section 44(1) or (2) of the Criminal Law (Consolidation) (Scotland) Act 1995 (false statements made on oath or otherwise than on oath).

(4) Regulations under subsection (3)(b)(ii) shall be made by statutory instrument and, after being made, shall be laid before each House of Parliament.

434   Crown application

For the avoidance of doubt it is hereby declared that provisions of this Act which derive from the Insolvency Act 1985 bind the Crown so far as affecting or relating to the following matters, namely—

(a) remedies against, or against the property of, companies or individuals;

(b) priorities of debts;

(c) transactions at an undervalue or preferences;

(d) voluntary arrangements approved under Part I or Part VIII, and

(e) discharge from bankruptcy.

PART XVIII   INTERPRETATION

435   Meaning of 'associate'

(1) For the purposes of this Act any question whether a person is an associate of another person is to be determined in accordance with the following provisions of this section (any provision that a person is an associate of another person being taken to mean that they are associates of each other).

(2) A person is an associate of an individual if that person is the individual's husband or wife, or is a relative, or the husband or wife of a relative, of the individual or of the individual's husband or wife.

(3) A person is an associate of any person with whom he is in partnership, and of the husband or wife or a relative of any individual with whom he is in partnership; and a Scottish firm is an associate of any person who is a member of the firm.

(4) A person is an associate of any person whom he employs or by whom he is employed.

(5) A person in his capacity as trustee of a trust other than—

(a) a trust arising under any of the second Group of Parts or the Bankruptcy (Scotland) Act 1985, or

(b) a pension scheme or an employees' share scheme (within the meaning of the Companies Act), is an associate of another person if the beneficiaries of the trust include, or the terms of the trust confer a power that may be exercised for the benefit of, that other person or an associate of that other person.

(6) A company is an associate of another company—

(a) if the same person has control of both, or a person has control of one and persons who are his associates, or he and persons who are his associates, have control of the other, or

(b) if a group of two or more persons has control of each company, and the groups either consist of the same persons or could be regarded as consisting of the same persons by treating (in one or more cases) a member of either group as replaced by a person of whom he is an associate.

(7) A company is an associate of another person if that person has control of it or if that person and persons who are his associates together have control of it.

(8) For the purposes of this section a person is a relative of an individual if he is that individual's brother, sister, uncle, aunt, nephew, niece, lineal ancestor or lineal descendant, treating—

(a) any relationship of the half blood as a relationship of the whole blood and the stepchild or adopted child of any person as his child, and

(b) an illegitimate child as the legitimate child of his mother and reputed father; and references in this section to a husand or wife include a former husband or wife and a reputed husband or wife.

(9) For the purposes of this section any director or other officer of a company is to be treated as employed by that company.

(10) For the purposes of this section a person is to be taken as having control of a company if—

(a) the directors of the company or of another company which has control of it (or any of them) are accustomed to act in accordance with his directions or instructions, or

(b) he is entitled to exercise, or control the exercise of, one third or more of the voting power at any general meeting of the company or of another company which has control of it;

and where two or more persons together satisfy either of the above conditions, they are to be taken as having control of the company.

(11) In this section 'company' includes any body corporate (whether incorporated in Great Britain or elsewhere); and references to directors and other officers of a company and to voting power at any general meeting of a company have effect with any necessary modifications.

436   Expressions used generally

In this Act, except in so far as the context otherwise requires (and subject to Parts VII and XI)—

. . .

'the appointed day' means the day on which this Act comes into force under section 443;

'associate' has the meaning given by section 435;

'business' includes a trade or profession;

'the Companies Act' means the Companies Act 1985;

'conditional sale agreement' and 'hire-purchase agreement' have the same meanings as in the Consumer Credit Act 1974;

. . .

'the EC Regulation' means Council Regulation (EC) No. 1346/2000;

'modifications' includes additions, alterations and omissions and cognate expressions shall be construed accordingly;

. . .

'property' includes money, goods, things in action, land and every description of property wherever situated and also obligations and every description of interest, whether present or future or vested or contingent, arising out of, or incidental to, property;

'records' includes computer records and other non-documentary records;

. . .

'subordinate legislation' has the same meaning as in the Interpretation Act 1978; and 'transaction' includes a gift, agreement or arrangement, and references to entering into a transaction shall be construed accordingly.

. . .

436A   Proceedings under EC Regulation: modified definition of property
In the application of this Act to proceedings by virtue of Article 3 of the EC Regulation, a reference to property is a reference to property which may be dealt with in the proceedings.

PART XIX   FINAL PROVISIONS

443   Commencement
This Act comes into force on the day appointed under section 236(2) of the Insolvency Act 1985 for the coming into force of Part III of that Act (individual insolvency and bankruptcy), immediately after that Part of that Act comes into force for England and Wales.
[*The day appointed for the coming into force of part III of the Insolvency Act 1985 was 29 December 1986 (Insolvency Act 1985 (Commencement No. 5) Order 1986 (SI 1986/1924), art. 3).*]

444   Citation
This Act may be cited as the Insolvency Act 1986.

SCHEDULES
SCHEDULE A1   MORATORIUM WHERE DIRECTORS PROPOSE VOLUNTARY ARRANGEMENT

PART I   INTRODUCTORY

Interpretation

1.   In this Schedule—
'the beginning of the moratorium' has the meaning given by paragraph 8(1),
'the date of filing' means the date on which the documents for the time being referred to in paragraph 7(1) are filed or lodged with the court,
'hire-purchase agreement' includes a conditional sale agreement, a chattel leasing agreement and a retention of title agreement,
'market contract' and 'market charge' have the meanings given by Part VII of the Companies Act 1989,
'moratorium' means a moratorium under section 1A,
'the nominee' includes any person for the time being carrying out the functions of a nominee under this Schedule,
'the settlement finality regulations' means the Financial Markets and Insolvency (Settlement Finality) Regulations 1999,
'system-charge' has the meaning given by the Financial Markets and Insolvency Regulations 1996.

Eligible companies

2.—(1)   A company is eligible for a moratorium if it meets the requirements of paragraph 3, unless—

(a) it is excluded from being eligible by virtue of paragraph 4, or

(b) it falls within sub-paragraph (2).

(2) A company falls within this sub-paragraph if—

(a) it effects or carries out contracts of insurance, but is not exempt from the general prohibition, within the meaning of section 19 of the Financial Services and Markets Act 2000, in relation to that activity,

(b) it has permission under Part IV of that Act to accept deposits,

(bb) it has a liability in respect of a deposit which it accepted in accordance with the Banking Act 1979 (c. 37) or 1987 (c. 22),

(c) it is a party to a market contract or any of its property is subject to a market charge or a system-charge, or

(d) it is a participant (within the meaning of the settlement finality regulations) or any of its property is subject to a collateral security charge (within the meaning of those regulations).

(3) Paragraphs (a), (b) and (bb) of sub-paragraph (2) must be read with—

(a) section 22 of the Financial Services and Markets Act 2000;

(b) any relevant order under that section; and

(c) Schedule 2 to that Act.

3.—(1) A company meets the requirements of this paragraph if the qualifying conditions are met—

(a) in the year ending with the date of filing, or

(b) in the financial year of the company which ended last before that date.

(2) For the purposes of sub-paragraph (1)—

(a) the qualifying conditions are met by a company in a period if, in that period, it satisfies two or more of the requirements for being a small company specified for the time being in section 247(3) of the Companies Act 1985, and

(b) a company's financial year is to be determined in accordance with that Act.

(3) Subsections (4), (5) and (6) of section 247 of that Act apply for the purposes of this paragraph as they apply for the purposes of that section.

(4) A company does not meet the requirements of this paragraph if it is a holding company of a group of companies which does not qualify as a small group or a medium-sized group in respect of the financial year of the company which ended last before the date of filing.

(5) For the purposes of sub-paragraph (4) 'group' has the meaning given by section 262 of the Companies Act 1985 (definitions for Part VII) and a group qualifies as small or medium-sized if it qualifies as such under section 249 of the Companies Act 1985 (qualification of group as small or medium-sized).

4.—(1) A company is excluded from being eligible for a moratorium if, on the date of filing—

(a) *an administration order is in force in relation to the company,*

(b) the company is being wound up,

(c) there is an administrative receiver of the company,

(d) a voluntary arrangement has effect in relation to the company,

(e) there is a provisional liquidator of the company,

(f) a moratorium has been in force for the company at any time during the period of 12 months ending with the date of filing and—

(i) no voluntary arrangement had effect at the time at which the moratorium came to an end, or

(ii) a voluntary arrangement which had effect at any time in that period has come to an end prematurely, or

(g) a voluntary arrangement in relation to the company which had effect in pursuance of a proposal under section 1(3) has come to an end prematurely and, during the period of 12 months ending with the date of filing, an order under section 5(3)(a) has been made.

(2) Sub-paragraph (1)(b) does not apply to a company which, by reason of a winding-up order made after the date of filing, is treated as being wound up on that date.

[*When the Enterprise Act 2002, sch. 17, is brought into force, the Insolvency Act 1986, sch. A1, para. 4(1)(a), will be replaced by:*

   (a) *the company is in administration,*

and after para. 4(1)(f) (and before the word 'or') there will be inserted—

      (fa) *an administrator appointed under paragraph 22 of Schedule B1 has held office in the period of 12 months ending with the date of filing,*]

Capital market arrangement

4A.   A company is also excluded from being eligible for a moratorium if, on the date of filing, it is a party to an agreement which is or forms part of a capital market arrangement under which—

   (i) a party has incurred, or when the agreement was entered into was expected to incur, a debt of at least £10 million under the arrangement, and

   (ii) the arrangement involves the issue of a capital market investment.

Public—private partnership

4B.   A company is also excluded from being eligible for a moratorium if, on the date of filing, it is a project company of a project which—

   (i) is a public—private partnership project, and

   (ii) includes step-in rights.

Liability under an arrangement

4C.—(1) A company is also excluded from being eligible for a moratorium if, on the date of filing, it has incurred a liability under an agreement of £10 million or more.

(2) Where the liability in sub-paragraph (1) is a contingent liability under or by virtue of a guarantee or an indemnity or security provided on behalf of another person, the amount of that liability is the full amount of the liability in relation to which the guarantee, indemnity or security is provided.

(3) In this paragraph—

   (a) the reference to 'liability' includes a present or future liability whether, in either case, it is certain or contingent,

   (b) the reference to 'liability' includes a reference to a liability to be paid wholly or partly in foreign currency (in which case the sterling equivalent shall be calculated as at the time when the liability is incurred).

Interpretation of capital market arrangement

4D.—(1) For the purposes of paragraph 4A an arrangement is a capital market arrangement if—

   (a) it involves a grant of security to a person holding it as trustee for a person who holds a capital market investment issued by a party to the arrangement, or

   (b) at least one party guarantees the performance of obligations of another party, or

   (c) at least one party provides security in respect of the performance of obligations of another party, or

   (d) the arrangement involves an investment of a kind described in articles 83 to 85 of the Financial Services and Markets Act 2000 (Regulated Activities) Order 2001 (SI 2001/544) (options, futures and contracts for differences).

(2) For the purposes of sub-paragraph (1)—

    (a) a reference to holding as trustee includes a reference to holding as nominee or agent,

    (b) a reference to holding for a person who holds a capital market investment includes a reference to holding for a number of persons at least one of whom holds a capital market investment, and

    (c) a person holds a capital market investment if he has a legal or beneficial interest in it.

(3) In paragraph 4A, 4C, 4J and this paragraph—

'agreement' includes an agreement or undertaking effected by—

    (a) contract,

    (b) deed, or

    (c) any other instrument intended to have effect in accordance with the law of England and Wales, Scotland or another jurisdiction, and

'party' to an arrangement includes a party to an agreement which—

    (a) forms part of the arrangement,

    (b) provides for the raising of finance as part of the arrangement, or

    (c) is necessary for the purposes of implementing the arrangement.

Capital market investment

4E.—(1) For the purposes of paragraphs 4A and 4D, an investment is a capital market investment if—

    (a) it is within article 77 of the Financial Services and Markets Act 2000 (Regulated Activities) Order 2001 (SI 2001/544) (debt instruments) and

    (b) it is rated, listed or traded or designed to be rated, listed or traded.

(2) In sub-paragraph (1)—

'listed' means admitted to the official list within the meaning given by section 103(1) of the Financial Services and Markets Act 2000 (c. 8) (interpretation),

'rated' means rated for the purposes of investment by an internationally recognised rating agency,

'traded' means admitted to trading on a market established under the rules of a recognised investment exchange or on a foreign market.

(3) In sub-paragraph (2)—

'foreign market' has the same meaning as 'relevant market' in article 67(2) of the Financial Services and Markets Act 2000 (Financial Promotion) Order 2001 (SI 2001/1335) (foreign markets),

'recognised investment exchange' has the meaning given by section 285 of the Financial Services and Markets Act 2000 (recognised investment exchange).

4F.—(1) For the purposes of paragraphs 4A and 4D an investment is also a capital market investment if it consists of a bond or commercial paper issued to one or more of the following—

    (a) an investment professional within the meaning of article 19(5) of the Financial Services and Markets Act 2000 (Financial Promotion) Order 2001,

    (b) a person who is, when the agreement mentioned in paragraph 4A is entered into, a certified high net worth individual in relation to a communication within the meaning of article 48(2) of that order,

    (c) a person to whom article 49(2) of that order applies (high net worth company, &c.),

    (d) a person who is, when the agreement mentioned in paragraph 4A is entered into, a certified sophisticated investor in relation to a communication within the meaning of article 50(1) of that order, and

(e) a person in a State other than the United Kingdom who under the law of that State is not prohibited from investing in bonds or commercial paper.

(2) For the purposes of sub-paragraph (1)—

   (a) in applying article 19(5) of the Financial Services and Markets Act 2000 (Financial Promotion) Order 2001 for the purposes of sub-paragraph (1)(a)—

      (i) in article 19(5)(b), ignore the words after 'exempt person',

      (ii) in article 19(5)(c)(i), for the words from 'the controlled activity' to the end substitute 'a controlled activity', and

      (iii) in article 19(5)(e) ignore the words from 'where the communication' to the end, and

   (b) in applying article 49(2) of that order for the purposes of sub-paragraph (1)(c), ignore article 49(2)(e).

(3) In sub-paragraph (1)—

'bond' shall be construed in accordance with article 77 of the Financial Services and Markets Act 2000 (Regulated Activities) Order 2001 (SI 2001/544), and

'commercial paper' has the meaning given by article 9(3) of that order.

Debt

4G.   The debt of at least £10 million referred to in paragraph 4A—

   (a) may be incurred at any time during the life of the capital market arrangement, and

   (b) may be expressed wholly or partly in a foreign currency (in which case the sterling equivalent shall be calculated as at the time when the arrangement is entered into).

Interpretation of project company

4H.—(1) For the purposes of paragraph 4B a company is a 'project company' of a project if—

   (a) it holds property for the purpose of the project,

   (b) it has sole or principal responsibility under an agreement for carrying out all or part of the project,

   (c) it is one of a number of companies which together carry out the project,

   (d) it has the purpose of supplying finance to enable the project to be carried out, or

   (e) it is the holding company of a company within any of paragraphs (a) to (d).

(2) But a company is not a 'project company' of a project if—

   (a) it performs a function within sub-paragraph (1)(a) to (d) or is within sub-paragraph (1)(e), but

   (b) it also performs a function which is not—

      (i) within sub-paragraph (1)(a) to (d),

      (ii) related to a function within sub-paragraph (1)(a) to (d), or

      (iii) related to the project.

(3) For the purposes of this paragraph a company carries out all or part of a project whether or not it acts wholly or partly through agents.

Public–private partnership project

4I.—(1) In paragraph 4B 'public–private partnership project' means a project—

   (a) the resources for which are provided partly by one or more public bodies and partly by one or more private persons, or

   (b) which is designed wholly or mainly for the purpose of assisting a public body to discharge a function.

(2) In sub-paragraph (1) 'resources' includes—

(a) funds (including payment for the provision of services or facilities),
(b) assets,
(c) professional skill,
(d) the grant of a concession or franchise, and
(e) any other commercial resource.
(3) In sub-paragraph (1) 'public body' means—
(a) a body which exercises public functions,
(b) a body specified for the purposes of this paragraph by the Secretary of State, and
(c) a body within a class specified for the purposes of this paragraph by the Secretary of State.
(4) A specification under sub-paragraph (3) may be—
(a) general, or
(b) for the purpose of the application of paragraph 4B to a specified case.

Step-in rights

4J.—(1) For the purposes of paragraph 4B a project has 'step-in rights' if a person who provides finance in connection with the project has a conditional entitlement under an agreement to—
(i) assume sole or principal responsibility under an agreement for carrying out all or part of the project, or
(ii) make arrangements for carrying out all or part of the project.
(2) In sub-paragraph (1) a reference to the provision of finance includes a reference to the provision of an indemnity.

'Person'

4K.   For the purposes of paragraphs 4A to 4J, a reference to a person includes a reference to a partnership or another unincorporated group of persons.
5.   The Secretary of State may by regulations modify the qualifications for eligibility of a company for a moratorium.

PART II   OBTAINING A MORATORIUM
Nominee's statement

6.—(1) Where the directors of a company wish to obtain a moratorium, they shall submit to the nominee—
(a) a document setting out the terms of the proposed voluntary arrangement,
(b) a statement of the company's affairs containing—
(i) such particulars of its creditors and of its debts and other liabilities and of its assets as may be prescribed, and
(ii) such other information as may be prescribed, and
(c) any other information necessary to enable the nominee to comply with sub-paragraph (2) which he requests from them.
(2) The nominee shall submit to the directors a statement in the prescribed form indicating whether or not, in his opinion—
(a) the proposed voluntary arrangement has a reasonable prospect of being approved and implemented,
(b) the company is likely to have sufficient funds available to it during the proposed moratorium to enable it to carry on its business, and
(c) meetings of the company and its creditors should be summoned to consider the proposed voluntary arrangement.

(3) In forming his opinion on the matters mentioned in sub-paragraph (2), the nominee is entitled to rely on the information submitted to him under sub-paragraph (1) unless he has reason to doubt its accuracy.

(4) The reference in sub-paragraph (2)(b) to the company's business is to that business as the company proposes to carry it on during the moratorium.

Documents to be submitted to court

7.—(1) To obtain a moratorium the directors of a company must file (in Scotland, lodge) with the court—
- (a) a document setting out the terms of the proposed voluntary arrangement,
- (b) a statement of the company's affairs containing—
  - (i) such particulars of its creditors and of its debts and other liabilities and of its assets as may be prescribed, and
  - (ii) such other information as may be prescribed,
- (c) a statement that the company is eligible for a moratorium,
- (d) a statement from the nominee that he has given his consent to act, and
- (e) a statement from the nominee that, in his opinion—
  - (i) the proposed voluntary arrangement has a reasonable prospect of being approved and implemented,
  - (ii) the company is likely to have sufficient funds available to it during the proposed moratorium to enable it to carry on its business, and
  - (iii) meetings of the company and its creditors should be summoned to consider the proposed voluntary arrangement.

(2) Each of the statements mentioned in sub-paragraph (1)(b) to (e), except so far as it contains the particulars referred to in paragraph (b)(i), must be in the prescribed form.

(3) The reference in sub-paragraph (1)(e)(ii) to the company's business is to that business as the company proposes to carry it on during the moratorium.

(4) The Secretary of State may by regulations modify the requirements of this paragraph as to the documents required to be filed (in Scotland, lodged) with the court in order to obtain a moratorium.

Duration of moratorium

8.—(1) A moratorium comes into force when the documents for the time being referred to in paragraph 7(1) are filed or lodged with the court and references in this Schedule to 'the beginning of the moratorium' shall be construed accordingly.

(2) A moratorium ends at the end of the day on which the meetings summoned under paragraph 29(1) are first held (or, if the meetings are held on different days, the later of those days), unless it is extended under paragraph 32.

(3) If either of those meetings has not first met before the end of the period of 28 days beginning with the day on which the moratorium comes into force, the moratorium ends at the end of the day on which those meetings were to be held (or, if those meetings were summoned to be held on different days, the later of those days), unless it is extended under paragraph 32.

(4) If the nominee fails to summon either meeting within the period required by paragraph 29(1), the moratorium ends at the end of the last day of that period.

(5) If the moratorium is extended (or further extended) under paragraph 32, it ends at the end of the day to which it is extended (or further extended).

(6) Sub-paragraphs (2) to (5) do not apply if the moratorium comes to an end before the time concerned by virtue of—
- (a) paragraph 25(4) (effect of withdrawal by nominee of consent to act),

(b) an order under paragraph 26(3), 27(3) or 40 (challenge of actions of nominee or directors), or

(c) a decision of one or both of the meetings summoned under paragraph 29.

(7) If the moratorium has not previously come to an end in accordance with sub-paragraphs (2) to (6), it ends at the end of the day on which a decision under paragraph 31 to approve a voluntary arrangement takes effect under paragraph 36.

(8) The Secretary of State may by order increase or reduce the period for the time being specified in sub-paragraph (3).

Notification of beginning of moratorium

9.—(1) When a moratorium comes into force, the directors shall notify the nominee of that fact forthwith.

(2) If the directors without reasonable excuse fail to comply with sub-paragraph (1), each of them is liable to imprisonment or a fine, or both.

10.—(1) When a moratorium comes into force, the nominee shall, in accordance with the rules—

(a) advertise that fact forthwith, and

(b) notify the registrar of companies, the company and any petitioning creditor of the company of whose claim he is aware of that fact.

(2) In sub-paragraph (1)(b), 'petitioning creditor' means a creditor by whom a winding-up petition has been presented before the beginning of the moratorium, as long as the petition has not been dismissed or withdrawn.

(3) If the nominee without reasonable excuse fails to comply with sub-paragraph (1)(a) or (b), he is liable to a fine.

Notification of end of moratorium

11.—(1) When a moratorium comes to an end, the nominee shall, in accordance with the rules—

(a) advertise that fact forthwith, and

(b) notify the court, the registrar of companies, the company and any creditor of the company of whose claim he is aware of that fact.

(2) If the nominee without reasonable excuse fails to comply with sub-paragraph (1)(a) or (b), he is liable to a fine.

PART III   EFFECTS OF MORATORIUM

Effect on creditors, etc.

12.—(1) During the period for which a moratorium is in force for a company—

(a) no petition may be presented for the winding up of the company,

(b) no meeting of the company may be called or requisitioned except with the consent of the nominee or the leave of the court and subject (where the court gives leave) to such terms as the court may impose,

(c) no resolution may be passed or order made for the winding up of the company,

(d) *no petition for an administration order in relation to the company may be presented,*

(e) no administrative receiver of the company may be appointed,

(f) no landlord or other person to whom rent is payable may exercise any right of forfeiture by peaceable re-entry in relation to premises let to the company in respect of a failure by the company to comply with any term or condition of its tenancy of such premises, except with the leave of the court and subject to such terms as the court may impose,

(g) no other steps may be taken to enforce any security over the company's property, or to repossess goods in the company's possession under any hire-purchase agreement, except with the leave of the court and subject to such terms as the court may impose, and

(h) no other proceedings and no execution or other legal process may be commenced or continued, and no distress may be levied, against the company or its property except with the leave of the court and subject to such terms as the court may impose.

(2) Where a petition, other than an excepted petition, for the winding up of the company has been presented before the beginning of the moratorium, section 127 shall not apply in relation to any disposition of property, transfer of shares or alteration in status made during the moratorium or at a time mentioned in paragraph 37(5)(a).

(3) In the application of sub-paragraph (1)(h) to Scotland, the reference to execution being commenced or continued includes a reference to diligence being carried out or continued, and the reference to distress being levied is omitted.

(4) Paragraph (a) of sub-paragraph (1) does not apply to an excepted petition and, where such a petition has been presented before the beginning of the moratorium or is presented during the moratorium, paragraphs (b) and (c) of that sub-paragraph do not apply in relation to proceedings on the petition.

(5) For the purposes of this paragraph, 'excepted petition' means a petition under—

(a) section 124A of this Act,

(b) section 72 of the Financial Services Act 1986 on the ground mentioned in subsection (1)(b) of that section, or

(c) section 92 of the Banking Act 1987 on the ground mentioned in subsection (1)(b) of that section,

(d) section 367 of the Financial Services and Markets Act 2000 on the ground mentioned in subsection (3)(b) of that section.

[*When the Enterprise Act 2002, sch. 17, is brought into force, the Insolvency Act 1986, sch. A1, para. 12(1)(d), will be replaced by:*

(d) *no administration application may be made in respect of the company,*

(da) *no administrator of the company may be appointed under paragraph 14 or 22 of Schedule B1,*]

13.—(1) This paragraph applies where there is an uncrystallised floating charge on the property of a company for which a moratorium is in force.

(2) If the conditions for the holder of the charge to give a notice having the effect mentioned in sub-paragraph (4) are met at any time, the notice may not be given at that time but may instead be given as soon as practicable after the moratorium has come to an end.

(3) If any other event occurs at any time which (apart from this sub-paragraph) would have the effect mentioned in sub-paragraph (4), then—

(a) the event shall not have the effect in question at that time, but

(b) if notice of the event is given to the company by the holder of the charge as soon as is practicable after the moratorium has come to an end, the event is to be treated as if it had occurred when the notice was given.

(4) The effect referred to in sub-paragraphs (2) and (3) is—

(a) causing the crystallisation of the floating charge, or

(b) causing the imposition, by virtue of provision in the instrument creating the charge, of any restriction on the disposal of any property of the company.

(5) Application may not be made for leave under paragraph 12(1)(g) or (h) with a view to obtaining—

(a) the crystallisation of the floating charge, or

(b) the imposition, by virtue of provision in the instrument creating the charge, of any restriction on the disposal of any property of the company.

14.   Security granted by a company at a time when a moratorium is in force in relation to the company may only be enforced if, at that time, there were reasonable grounds for believing that it would benefit the company.

Effect on company

15.—(1)   Paragraphs 16 to 23 apply in relation to a company for which a moratorium is in force.
(2) The fact that a company enters into a transaction in contravention of any of paragraphs 16 to 22 does not—
(a)   make the transaction void, or
(b)   make it to any extent unenforceable against the company.

Company invoices, etc.

16.—(1)   Every invoice, order for goods or business letter which—
(a)   is issued by or on behalf of the company, and
(b)   on or in which the company's name appears,
shall also contain the nominee's name and a statement that the moratorium is in force for the company.
(2) If default is made in complying with sub-paragraph (1), the company and (subject to sub-paragraph (3)) any officer of the company is liable to a fine.
(3) An officer of the company is only liable under sub-paragraph (2) if, without reasonable excuse, he authorises or permits the default.

Obtaining credit during moratorium

17.—(1)   The company may not obtain credit to the extent of £250 or more from a person who has not been informed that a moratorium is in force in relation to the company.
(2) The reference to the company obtaining credit includes the following cases—
(a)   where goods are bailed (in Scotland, hired) to the company under a hire-purchase agreement, or agreed to be sold to the company under a conditional sale agreement, and
(b)   where the company is paid in advance (whether in money or otherwise) for the supply of goods or services.
(3) Where the company obtains credit in contravention of sub-paragraph (1)—
(a)   the company is liable to a fine, and
(b)   if any officer of the company knowingly and wilfully authorised or permitted the contravention, he is liable to imprisonment or a fine, or both.
(4) The money sum specified in sub-paragraph (1) is subject to increase or reduction by order under section 417A in Part XV.

Disposals and payments

18.—(1)   Subject to sub-paragraph (2), the company may only dispose of any of its property if—
(a)   there are reasonable grounds for believing that the disposal will benefit the company, and
(b)   the disposal is approved by the committee established under paragraph 35(1) or, where there is no such committee, by the nominee.
(2) Sub-paragraph (1) does not apply to a disposal made in the ordinary way of the company's business.
(3) If the company makes a disposal in contravention of sub-paragraph (1) otherwise than in pursuance of an order of the court—

(a) the company is liable to a fine, and

(b) if any officer of the company authorised or permitted the contravention, without reasonable excuse, he is liable to imprisonment or a fine, or both.

19.—(1) Subject to sub-paragraph (2), the company may only make any payment in respect of any debt or other liability of the company in existence before the beginning of the moratorium if—

(a) there are reasonable grounds for believing that the payment will benefit the company, and

(b) the payment is approved by the committee established under paragraph 35(1) or, where there is no such committee, by the nominee.

(2) Sub-paragraph (1) does not apply to a payment required by paragraph 20(6).

(3) If the company makes a payment in contravention of sub-paragraph (1) otherwise than in pursuance of an order of the court—

(a) the company is liable to a fine, and

(b) if any officer of the company authorised or permitted the contravention, without reasonable excuse, he is liable to imprisonment or a fine, or both.

Disposal of charged property, etc.

20.—(1) This paragraph applies where—

(a) any property of the company is subject to a security, or

(b) any goods are in the possession of the company under a hire-purchase agreement.

(2) If the holder of the security consents, or the court gives leave, the company may dispose of the property as if it were not subject to the security.

(3) If the owner of the goods consents, or the court gives leave, the company may dispose of the goods as if all rights of the owner under the hire-purchase agreement were vested in the company.

(4) Where property subject to a security which, as created, was a floating charge is disposed of under sub-paragraph (2), the holder of the security has the same priority in respect of any property of the company directly or indirectly representing the property disposed of as he would have had in respect of the property subject to the security.

(5) Sub-paragraph (6) applies to the disposal under sub-paragraph (2) or (as the case may be) sub-paragraph (3) of—

(a) any property subject to a security other than a security which, as created, was a floating charge, or

(b) any goods in the possession of the company under a hire-purchase agreement.

(6) It shall be a condition of any consent or leave under sub-paragraph (2) or (as the case may be) sub-paragraph (3) that—

(a) the net proceeds of the disposal, and

(b) where those proceeds are less than such amount as may be agreed, or determined by the court, to be the net amount which would be realised on a sale of the property or goods in the open market by a willing vendor, such sums as may be required to make good the deficiency, shall be applied towards discharging the sums secured by the security or payable under the hire-purchase agreement.

(7) Where a condition imposed in pursuance of sub-paragraph (6) relates to two or more securities, that condition requires—

(a) the net proceeds of the disposal, and

(b) where paragraph (b) of sub-paragraph (6) applies, the sums mentioned in that paragraph,

to be applied towards discharging the sums secured by those securities in the order of their priorities.

(8) Where the court gives leave for a disposal under sub-paragraph (2) or (3), the directors shall, within 14 days after leave is given, send an office copy of the order giving leave to the registrar of companies.

(9) If the directors without reasonable excuse fail to comply with sub-paragraph (8), they are liable to a fine.

21.—(1) Where property is disposed of under paragraph 20 in its application to Scotland, the company shall grant to the disponee an appropriate document of transfer or conveyance of the property, and

    (a) that document, or

    (b) where any recording, intimation or registration of the document is a legal requirement for completion of title to the property, that recording, intimation or registration,

has the effect of disencumbering the property of, or (as the case may be) freeing the property from, the security.

(2) Where goods in the possession of the company under a hire-purchase agreement are disposed of under paragraph 20 in its application to Scotland, the disposal has the effect of extinguishing, as against the disponee, all rights of the owner of the goods under the agreement.

22.—(1) If the company—

    (a) without any consent or leave under paragraph 20, disposes of any of its property which is subject to a security otherwise than in accordance with the terms of the security,

    (b) without any consent or leave under paragraph 20, disposes of any goods in the possession of the company under a hire-purchase agreement otherwise than in accordance with the terms of the agreement, or

    (c) fails to comply with any requirement imposed by paragraph 20 or 21,

it is liable to a fine.

(2) If any officer of the company, without reasonable excuse, authorises or permits any such disposal or failure to comply, he is liable to imprisonment or a fine, or both.

Market contracts, etc.

23.—(1) If the company enters into any transaction to which this paragraph applies—

    (a) the company is liable to a fine, and

    (b) if any officer of the company, without reasonable excuse, authorised or permitted the company to enter into the transaction, he is liable to imprisonment or a fine, or both.

(2) A company enters into a transaction to which this paragraph applies if it—

    (a) enters into a market contract,

    (b) gives a transfer order,

    (c) grants a market charge or a system-charge, or

    (d) provides any collateral security.

(3) The fact that a company enters into a transaction in contravention of this paragraph does not—

    (a) make the transaction void, or

    (b) make it to any extent unenforceable by or against the company.

(4) Where during the moratorium a company enters into a transaction to which this paragraph applies, nothing done by or in pursuance of the transaction is to be treated as done in contravention of paragraphs 12(1)(g), 14 or 16 to 22.

(5) Paragraph 20 does not apply in relation to any property which is subject to a market charge, a system-charge or a collateral security charge.

(6) In this paragraph, 'transfer order', 'collateral security' and 'collateral security charge' have the same meanings as in the settlement finality regulations.

PART IV   NOMINEES

Monitoring of company's activities

24.—(1)   During a moratorium, the nominee shall monitor the company's affairs for the purpose of forming an opinion as to whether—
- (a) the proposed voluntary arrangement or, if he has received notice of proposed modifications under paragraph 31(7), the proposed arrangement with those modifications has a reasonable prospect of being approved and implemented, and
- (b) the company is likely to have sufficient funds available to it during the remainder of the moratorium to enable it to continue to carry on its business.

(2) The directors shall submit to the nominee any information necessary to enable him to comply with sub-paragraph (1) which he requests from them.

(3) In forming his opinion on the matters mentioned in sub-paragraph (1), the nominee is entitled to rely on the information submitted to him under sub-paragraph (2) unless he has reason to doubt its accuracy.

(4) The reference in sub-paragraph (1)(b) to the company's business is to that business as the company proposes to carry it on during the remainder of the moratorium.

Withdrawal of consent to act

25.—(1)   The nominee may only withdraw his consent to act in the circumstances mentioned in this paragraph.

(2) The nominee must withdraw his consent to act if, at any time during a moratorium—
- (a) he forms the opinion that—
  - (i) the proposed voluntary arrangement or, if he has received notice of proposed modifications under paragraph 31(7), the proposed arrangement with those modifications no longer has a reasonable prospect of being approved or implemented, or
  - (ii) the company will not have sufficient funds available to it during the remainder of the moratorium to enable it to continue to carry on its business,
- (b) he becomes aware that, on the date of filing, the company was not eligible for a moratorium, or
- (c) the directors fail to comply with their duty under paragraph 24(2).

(3) The reference in sub-paragraph (2)(a)(ii) to the company's business is to that business as the company proposes to carry it on during the remainder of the moratorium.

(4) If the nominee withdraws his consent to act, the moratorium comes to an end.

(5) If the nominee withdraws his consent to act he must, in accordance with the rules, notify the court, the registrar of companies, the company and any creditor of the company of whose claim he is aware of his withdrawal and the reason for it.

(6) If the nominee without reasonable excuse fails to comply with sub-paragraph (5), he is liable to a fine.

Challenge of nominee's actions, etc.

26.—(1)   If any creditor, director or member of the company, or any other person affected by a moratorium, is dissatisfied by any act, omission or decision of the nominee during the moratorium, he may apply to the court.

(2) An application under sub-paragraph (1) may be made during the moratorium or after it has ended.

(3) On an application under sub-paragraph (1) the court may—
    (a) confirm, reverse or modify any act or decision of the nominee,
    (b) give him directions, or
    (c) make such other order as it thinks fit.
(4) An order under sub-paragraph (3) may (among other things) bring the moratorium to an end and make such consequential provision as the court thinks fit.

27.—(1)   Where there are reasonable grounds for believing that—
    (a) as a result of any act, omission or decision of the nominee during the moratorium, the company has suffered loss, but
    (b) the company does not intend to pursue any claim it may have against the nominee, any creditor of the company may apply to the court.
(2) An application under sub-paragraph (1) may be made during the moratorium or after it has ended.
(3) On an application under sub-paragraph (1) the court may—
    (a) order the company to pursue any claim against the nominee,
    (b) authorise any creditor to pursue such a claim in the name of the company, or
    (c) make such other order with respect to such a claim as it thinks fit,
unless the court is satisfied that the act, omission or decision of the nominee was in all the circumstances reasonable.
(4) An order under sub-paragraph (3) may (among other things)—
    (a) impose conditions on any authority given to pursue a claim,
    (b) direct the company to assist in the pursuit of a claim,
    (c) make directions with respect to the distribution of anything received as a result of the pursuit of a claim,
    (d) bring the moratorium to an end and make such consequential provision as the court thinks fit.
(5) On an application under sub-paragraph (1) the court shall have regard to the interests of the members and creditors of the company generally.

Replacement of nominee by court

28.—(1)   The court may—
    (a) on an application made by the directors in a case where the nominee has failed to comply with any duty imposed on him under this Schedule or has died, or
    (b) on an application made by the directors or the nominee in a case where it is impracticable or inappropriate for the nominee to continue to act as such,
direct that the nominee be replaced as such by another person qualified to act as an insolvency practitioner, or authorised to act as nominee, in relation to the voluntary arrangement.
(2) A person may only be appointed as a replacement nominee under this paragraph if he submits to the court a statement indicating his consent to act.

PART V   CONSIDERATION AND IMPLEMENTATION OF
VOLUNTARY ARRANGEMENT

Summoning of meetings

29.—(1)   Where a moratorium is in force, the nominee shall summon meetings of the company and its creditors for such a time, date (within the period for the time being specified in paragraph 8(3)) and place as he thinks fit.
(2) The persons to be summoned to a creditors' meeting under this paragraph are every creditor of the company of whose claim the nominee is aware.

Conduct of meetings

30.—(1) Subject to the provisions of paragraphs 31 to 35, the meetings summoned under paragraph 29 shall be conducted in accordance with the rules.

(2) A meeting so summoned may resolve that it be adjourned (or further adjourned).

(3) After the conclusion of either meeting in accordance with the rules, the chairman of the meeting shall report the result of the meeting to the court, and, immediately after reporting to the court, shall give notice of the result of the meeting to such persons as may be prescribed.

Approval of voluntary arrangement

31.—(1) The meetings summoned under paragraph 29 shall decide whether to approve the proposed voluntary arrangement (with or without modifications).

(2) The modifications may include one conferring the functions proposed to be conferred on the nominee on another person qualified to act as an insolvency practitioner, or authorised to act as nominee, in relation to the voluntary arrangement.

(3) The modifications shall not include one by virtue of which the proposal ceases to be a proposal such as is mentioned in section 1.

(4) A meeting summoned under paragraph 29 shall not approve any proposal or modification which affects the right of a secured creditor of the company to enforce his security, except with the concurrence of the creditor concerned.

(5) Subject to sub-paragraph (6), a meeting so summoned shall not approve any proposal or modification under which—

    (a) any preferential debt of the company is to be paid otherwise than in priority to such of its debts as are not preferential debts, or

    (b) a preferential creditor of the company is to be paid an amount in respect of a preferential debt that bears to that debt a smaller proportion than is borne to another preferential debt by the amount that is to be paid in respect of that other debt.

(6) The meeting may approve such a proposal or modification with the concurrence of the preferential creditor concerned.

(7) The directors of the company may, before the beginning of the period of seven days which ends with the meetings (or either of them) summoned under paragraph 29 being held, give notice to the nominee of any modifications of the proposal for which the directors intend to seek the approval of those meetings.

(8) References in this paragraph to preferential debts and preferential creditors are to be read in accordance with section 386 in Part XII of this Act.

Extension of moratorium

32.—(1) Subject to sub-paragraph (2), a meeting summoned under paragraph 29 which resolves that it be adjourned (or further adjourned) may resolve that the moratorium be extended (or further extended), with or without conditions.

(2) The moratorium may not be extended (or further extended) to a day later than the end of the period of two months which begins—

    (a) where both meetings summoned under paragraph 29 are first held on the same day, with that day,

    (b) in any other case, with the day on which the later of those meetings is first held.

(3) At any meeting where it is proposed to extend (or further extend) the moratorium, before a decision is taken with respect to that proposal, the nominee shall inform the meeting—

(a) of what he has done in order to comply with his duty under paragraph 24 and the cost of his actions for the company, and

(b) of what he intends to do to continue to comply with that duty if the moratorium is extended (or further extended) and the expected cost of his actions for the company.

(4) Where, in accordance with sub-paragraph (3)(b), the nominee informs a meeting of the expected cost of his intended actions, the meeting shall resolve whether or not to approve that expected cost.

(5) If a decision not to approve the expected cost of the nominee's intended actions has effect under paragraph 36, the moratorium comes to an end.

(6) A meeting may resolve that a moratorium which has been extended (or further extended) be brought to an end before the end of the period of the extension (or further extension).

(7) The Secretary of State may by order increase or reduce the period for the time being specified in sub-paragraph (2).

33.—(1) The conditions which may be imposed when a moratorium is extended (or further extended) include a requirement that the nominee be replaced as such by another person qualified to act as an insolvency practitioner, or authorised to act as nominee, in relation to the voluntary arrangement.

(2) A person may only be appointed as a replacement nominee by virtue of sub-paragraph (1) if he submits to the court a statement indicating his consent to act.

(3) At any meeting where it is proposed to appoint a replacement nominee as a condition of extending (or further extending) the moratorium—

(a) the duty imposed by paragraph 32(3)(b) on the nominee shall instead be imposed on the person proposed as the replacement nominee, and

(b) paragraphs 32(4) and (5) and 36(1)(e) apply as if the references to the nominee were to that person.

34.—(1) If a decision to extend, or further extend, the moratorium takes effect under paragraph 36, the nominee shall, in accordance with the rules, notify the registrar of companies and the court.

(2) If the moratorium is extended, or further extended, by virtue of an order under paragraph 36(5), the nominee shall, in accordance with the rules, send an office copy of the order to the registrar of companies.

(3) If the nominee without reasonable excuse fails to comply with this paragraph, he is liable to a fine.

Moratorium committee

35.—(1) A meeting summoned under paragraph 29 which resolves that the moratorium be extended (or further extended) may, with the consent of the nominee, resolve that a committee be established to exercise the functions conferred on it by the meeting.

(2) The meeting may not so resolve unless it has approved an estimate of the expenses to be incurred by the committee in the exercise of the proposed functions.

(3) Any expenses, not exceeding the amount of the estimate, incurred by the committee in the exercise of its functions shall be reimbursed by the nominee.

(4) The committee shall cease to exist when the moratorium comes to an end.

Effectiveness of decisions

36.—(1) Sub-paragraph (2) applies to references to one of the following decisions having effect, that is, a decision, under paragraph 31, 32 or 35, with respect to—

(a) the approval of a proposed voluntary arrangement,

    (b) the extension (or further extension) of a moratorium,

    (c) the bringing of a moratorium to an end,

    (d) the establishment of a committee, or

    (e) the approval of the expected cost of a nominee's intended actions.

(2) The decision has effect if, in accordance with the rules—

    (a) it has been taken by both meetings summoned under paragraph 29, or

    (b) (subject to any order made under sub-paragraph (5)) it has been taken by the creditors' meeting summoned under that paragraph.

(3) If a decision taken by the creditors' meeting under any of paragraphs 31, 32 or 35 with respect to any of the matters mentioned in sub-paragraph (1) differs from one so taken by the company meeting with respect to that matter, a member of the company may apply to the court.

(4) An application under sub-paragraph (3) shall not be made after the end of the period of 28 days beginning with—

    (a) the day on which the decision was taken by the creditors' meeting, or

    (b) where the decision of the company meeting was taken on a later day, that day.

(5) On an application under sub-paragraph (3), the court may—

    (a) order the decision of the company meeting to have effect instead of the decision of the creditors' meeting, or

    (b) make such other order as it thinks fit.

Effect of approval of voluntary arrangement

37.—(1) This paragraph applies where a decision approving a voluntary arrangement has effect under paragraph 36.

(2) The approved voluntary arrangement—

    (a) takes effect as if made by the company at the creditors' meeting, and

    (b) binds every person who in accordance with the rules—

        (i) was entitled to vote at that meeting (whether or not he was present or repre-sented at it), or

        (ii) would have been so entitled if he had had notice of it, as if he were a party to the voluntary arrangement.

(3) If—

    (a) when the arrangement ceases to have effect any amount payable under the arrange-ment to a person bound by virtue of sub-paragraph (2)(b)(ii) has not been paid, and

    (b) the arrangement did not come to an end prematurely, the company shall at that time become liable to pay to that person the amount payable under the arrangement.

(4) Where a petition for the winding up of the company, other than an excepted petition within the meaning of paragraph 12, was presented before the beginning of the moratorium, the court shall dismiss the petition.

(5) The court shall not dismiss a petition under sub-paragraph (4)—

    (a) at any time before the end of the period of 28 days beginning with the first day on which each of the reports of the meetings required by paragraph 30(3) has been made to the court, or

    (b) at any time when an application under paragraph 38 or an appeal in respect of such an application is pending, or at any time in the period within which such an appeal may be brought.

Challenge of decisions

38.—(1) Subject to the following provisions of this paragraph, any of the persons men-tioned in sub-paragraph (2) may apply to the court on one or both of the following grounds—

(a) that a voluntary arrangement approved at one or both of the meetings summoned under paragraph 29 and which has taken effect unfairly prejudices the interests of a creditor, member or contributory of the company,

(b) that there has been some material irregularity at or in relation to either of those meetings.

(2) The persons who may apply under this paragraph are—

(a) a person entitled, in accordance with the rules, to vote at either of the meetings,

(b) a person who would have been entitled, in accordance with the rules, to vote at the creditors' meeting if he had had notice of it, and

(c) the nominee.

(3) An application under this paragraph shall not be made—

(a) after the end of the period of 28 days beginning with the first day on which each of the reports required by paragraph 30(3) has been made to the court, or

(b) in the case of a person who was not given notice of the creditors' meeting, after the end of the period of 28 days beginning with the day on which he became aware that the meeting had taken place,

but (subject to that) an application made by a person within sub-paragraph (2)(b) on the ground that the arrangement prejudices his interests may be made after the arrangement has ceased to have effect, unless it came to an end prematurely.

(4) Where on an application under this paragraph the court is satisfied as to either of the grounds mentioned in sub-paragraph (1), it may do any of the following—

(a) revoke or suspend—

(i) any decision approving the voluntary arrangement which has effect under paragraph 36, or

(ii) in a case falling within sub-paragraph (1)(b), any decision taken by the meeting in question which has effect under that paragraph,

(b) give a direction to any person—

(i) for the summoning of further meetings to consider any revised proposal for a voluntary arrangement which the directors may make, or

(ii) in a case falling within sub-paragraph (1)(b), for the summoning of a further company or (as the case may be) creditors' meeting to reconsider the original proposal.

(5) Where at any time after giving a direction under sub-paragraph (4)(b)(i) the court is satisfied that the directors do not intend to submit a revised proposal, the court shall revoke the direction and revoke or suspend any decision approving the voluntary arrangement which has effect under paragraph 36.

(6) Where the court gives a direction under sub-paragraph (4)(b), it may also give a direction continuing or, as the case may require, renewing, for such period as may be specified in the direction, the effect of the moratorium.

(7) Sub-paragraph (8) applies in a case where the court, on an application under this paragraph—

(a) gives a direction under sub-paragraph (4)(b), or

(b) revokes or suspends a decision under sub-paragraph (4)(a) or (5).

(8) In such a case, the court may give such supplemental directions as it thinks fit and, in particular, directions with respect to—

(a) things done under the voluntary arrangement since it took effect, and

(b) such things done since that time as could not have been done if a moratorium had been in force in relation to the company when they were done.

(9) Except in pursuance of the preceding provisions of this paragraph, a decision taken at a meeting summoned under paragraph 29 is not invalidated by any irregularity at or in relation to the meeting.

Implementation of voluntary arrangement

39.—(1) This paragraph applies where a voluntary arrangement approved by one or both of the meetings summoned under paragraph 29 has taken effect.

(2) The person who is for the time being carrying out in relation to the voluntary arrangement the functions conferred—

(a) by virtue of the approval of the arrangement, on the nominee, or

(b) by virtue of paragraph 31(2), on a person other than the nominee, shall be known as the supervisor of the voluntary arrangement.

(3) If any of the company's creditors or any other person is dissatisfied by any act, omission or decision of the supervisor, he may apply to the court.

(4) On an application under sub-paragraph (3) the court may—

(a) confirm, reverse or modify any act or decision of the supervisor,

(b) give him directions, or

(c) make such other order as it thinks fit.

(5) The supervisor—

(a) may apply to the court for directions in relation to any particular matter arising under the voluntary arrangement, and

(b) is included among the persons who may apply to the court for the winding up of the company or for an administration order to be made in relation to it.

(6) The court may, whenever—

(a) it is expedient to appoint a person to carry out the functions of the supervisor, and

(b) it is inexpedient, difficult or impracticable for an appointment to be made without the assistance of the court,

make an order appointing a person who is qualified to act as an insolvency practitioner, or authorised to act as supervisor, in relation to the voluntary arrangement, either in substitution for the existing supervisor or to fill a vacancy.

(7) The power conferred by sub-paragraph (6) is exercisable so as to increase the number of persons exercising the functions of supervisor or, where there is more than one person exercising those functions, so as to replace one or more of those persons.

PART VI   MISCELLANEOUS

Challenge of directors' actions

40.—(1) This paragraph applies in relation to acts or omissions of the directors of a company during a moratorium.

(2) A creditor or member of the company may apply to the court for an order under this paragraph on the ground—

(a) that the company's affairs, business and property are being or have been managed by the directors in a manner which is unfairly prejudicial to the interests of its creditors or members generally, or of some part of its creditors or members (including at least the petitioner), or

(b) that any actual or proposed act or omission of the directors is or would be so prejudicial.

(3) An application for an order under this paragraph may be made during or after the moratorium.

(4) On an application for an order under this paragraph the court may—

(a) make such order as it thinks fit for giving relief in respect of the matters complained of,

(b) adjourn the hearing conditionally or unconditionally, or

(c) make an interim order or any other order that it thinks fit.

(5) An order under this paragraph may in particular—

(a) regulate the management by the directors of the company's affairs, business and property during the remainder of the moratorium,

(b) require the directors to refrain from doing or continuing an act complained of by the petitioner, or to do an act which the petitioner has complained they have omitted to do,

(c) require the summoning of a meeting of creditors or members for the purpose of considering such matters as the court may direct,

(d) bring the moratorium to an end and make such consequential provision as the court thinks fit.

(6) In making an order under this paragraph the court shall have regard to the need to safeguard the interests of persons who have dealt with the company in good faith and for value.

(7) In relation to any time when an administration order is in force in relation to the company, or the company is being wound up, in pursuance of a petition presented before the moratorium came into force, no application for an order under this paragraph may be made by a creditor or member of the company; but such an application may be made instead by the administrator or (as the case may be) liquidator.

[*When the Enterprise Act 2002, sch. 17, is brought into force, the Insolvency Act 1986, sch. A1, para. 40(7), will be replaced by:*

(7) Sub-paragraph (8) applies where—

(a) the appointment of an administrator has effect in relation to the company and the appointment took effect before the moratorium came into force, or

(b) the company is being wound up in pursuance of a petition presented before the moratorium came into force.

(8) No application for an order under this paragraph may be made by a creditor or member of the company; but such an application may be made instead by the administrator or (as the case may be) the liquidator.]

Offences

41.—(1) This paragraph applies where a moratorium has been obtained for a company.

(2) If, within the period of 12 months ending with the day on which the moratorium came into force, a person who was at the time an officer of the company—

(a) did any of the things mentioned in paragraphs (a) to (f) of sub-paragraph (4), or

(b) was privy to the doing by others of any of the things mentioned in paragraphs (c), and (e) of that sub-paragraph,

he is to be treated as having committed an offence at that time.

(3) If, at any time during the moratorium, a person who is an officer of the company—

(a) does any of the things mentioned in paragraphs (a) to (f) of sub-paragraph (4), or

(b) is privy to the doing by others of any of the things mentioned in paragraphs (c), (d) and (e) of that sub-paragraph,

he commits an offence.

(4) Those things are—

(a) concealing any part of the company's property to the value of £500 or more, or concealing any debt due to or from the company, or

(b) fraudulently removing any part of the company's property to the value of £500 or more, or

(c) concealing, destroying, mutilating or falsifying any book or paper affecting or relating to the company's property or affairs, or

(d) making any false entry in any book or paper affecting or relating to the company's property or affairs, or

(e) fraudulently parting with, altering or making any omission in any document affecting or relating to the company's property or affairs, or

(f) pawning, pledging or disposing of any property of the company which has been obtained on credit and has not been paid for (unless the pawning, pledging or disposal was in the ordinary way of the company's business).

(5) For the purposes of this paragraph, 'officer' includes a shadow director.

(6) It is a defence—
(a) for a person charged under sub-paragraph (2) or (3) in respect of the things mentioned in paragraph (a) or (f) of sub-paragraph (4) to prove that he had no intent to defraud, and
(b) for a person charged under sub-paragraph (2) or (3) in respect of the things mentioned in paragraph (c) or (d) of sub-paragraph (4) to prove that he had no intent to conceal the state of affairs of the company or to defeat the law.

(7) Where a person pawns, pledges or disposes of any property of a company in circumstances which amount to an offence under sub-paragraph (2) or (3), every person who takes in pawn or pledge, or otherwise receives, the property knowing it to be pawned, pledged or disposed of in circumstances which—
(a) would, if a moratorium were obtained for the company within the period of 12 months beginning with the day on which the pawning, pledging or disposal took place, amount to an offence under sub-paragraph (2), or
(b) amount to an offence under sub-paragraph (3), commits an offence.

(8) A person guilty of an offence under this paragraph is liable to imprisonment or a fine, or both.

(9) The money sums specified in paragraphs (a) and (b) of sub-paragraph (4) are subject to increase or reduction by order under section 417A in Part XV.

42.—(1)   If, for the purpose of obtaining a moratorium, or an extension of a moratorium, for a company, a person who is an officer of the company—
(a) makes any false representation, or
(b) fraudulently does, or omits to do, anything, he commits an offence.

(2) Sub-paragraph (1) applies even if no moratorium or extension is obtained.

(3) For the purposes of this paragraph, 'officer' includes a shadow director.

(4) A person guilty of an offence under this paragraph is liable to imprisonment or a fine, or both.

Void provisions in floating charge documents

43.—(1)   A provision in an instrument creating a floating charge is void if it provides for—
(a) obtaining a moratorium, or
(b) anything done with a view to obtaining a moratorium (including any preliminary decision or investigation),
to be an event causing the floating charge to crystallise or causing restrictions which would not otherwise apply to be imposed on the disposal of property by the company or a ground for the appointment of a receiver.

(2) In sub-paragraph (1), 'receiver' includes a manager and a person who is appointed both receiver and manager.

Functions of the Financial Services Authority

44.—(1)   This Schedule has effect in relation to a moratorium for a regulated company with the modifications in sub-paragraphs (2) to (16) below.

(2) Any notice or other document required by virtue of this Schedule to be sent to a creditor of a regulated company must also be sent to the Authority.

(3) The Authority is entitled to be heard on any application to the court for leave under paragraph 20(2) or 20(3) (disposal of charged property, etc.).

(4) Where paragraph 26(1) (challenge of nominee's actions, etc.) applies, the persons who may apply to the court include the Authority.

(5) If a person other than the Authority applies to the court under that paragraph, the Authority is entitled to be heard on the application.

(6) Where paragraph 27(1) (challenge of nominee's actions, etc.) applies, the persons who may apply to the court include the Authority.

(7) If a person other than the Authority applies to the court under that paragraph, the Authority is entitled to be heard on the application.

(8) The persons to be summoned to a creditors' meeting under paragraph 29 include the Authority.

(9) A person appointed for the purpose by the Authority is entitled to attend and participate in (but not to vote at)—

(a) any creditors' meeting summoned under that paragraph,

(b) any meeting of a committee established under paragraph 35 (moratorium committee).

(10) The Authority is entitled to be heard on any application under paragraph 36(3) (effectiveness of decisions).

(11) Where paragraph 38(1) (challenge of decisions) applies, the persons who may apply to the court include the Authority.

(12) If a person other than the Authority applies to the court under that paragraph, the Authority is entitled to be heard on the application.

(13) Where paragraph 39(3) (implementation of voluntary arrangement) applies, the persons who may apply to the court include the Authority.

(14) If a person other than the Authority applies to the court under that paragraph, the Authority is entitled to be heard on the application.

(15) Where paragraph 40(2) (challenge of directors' actions) applies, the persons who may apply to the court include the Authority.

(16) If a person other than the Authority applies to the court under that paragraph, the Authority is entitled to be heard on the application.

(17) This paragraph does not prejudice any right the Authority has (apart from this paragraph) as a creditor of a regulated company.

(18) In this paragraph—

'the Authority' means the Financial Services Authority, and 'regulated company' means a company which—

(a) is, or has been, an authorised person within the meaning given by section 31 of the Financial Services and Markets Act 2000,

(b) is, or has been, an appointed representative within the meaning given by section 39 of that Act, or

(c) is carrying on, or has carried on, a regulated activity, within the meaning given by section 22 of that Act, in contravention of the general prohibition within the meaning given by section 19 of that Act.

Subordinate legislation

45.—(1) Regulations or an order made by the Secretary of State under this Schedule may make different provision for different cases.

(2) Regulations so made may make such consequential, incidental, supplemental and transitional provision as may appear to the Secretary of State necessary or expedient.

(3) Any power of the Secretary of State to make regulations under this Schedule may be exercised by amending or repealing any enactment contained in this Act (including one contained in this Schedule) or contained in the Company Directors Disqualification Act 1986.

(4) Regulations (except regulations under paragraph 5) or an order made by the Secretary of State under this Schedule shall be made by statutory instrument subject to annulment in pursuance of a resolution of either House of Parliament.

(5) Regulations under paragraph 5 of this Schedule are to be made by statutory instrument and shall only be made if a draft containing the regulations has been laid before and approved by resolution of each House of Parliament.

SCHEDULE B1   ADMINISTRATION

[*On 15 June 2003, sch. B1 had not been brought into force.*]

ARRANGEMENT OF SCHEDULE

NATURE OF ADMINISTRATION

Administration

1—(1) For the purposes of this Act 'administrator' of a company means a person appointed under this Schedule to manage the company's affairs, business and property.

(2) For the purposes of this Act—
   (a) a company is 'in administration' while the appointment of an administrator of the company has effect,
   (b) a company 'enters administration' when the appointment of an administrator takes effect,
   (c) a company ceases to be in administration when the appointment of an administrator of the company ceases to have effect in accordance with this Schedule, and
   (d) a company does not cease to be in administration merely because an administrator vacates office (by reason of resignation, death or otherwise) or is removed from office.

2   A person may be appointed as administrator of a company—
   (a) by administration order of the court under paragraph 10,
   (b) by the holder of a floating charge under paragraph 14, or
   (c) by the company or its directors under paragraph 22.

Purpose of administration

3—(1) The administrator of a company must perform his functions with the objective of—
   (a) rescuing the company as a going concern, or

(b)   achieving a better result for the company's creditors as a whole than would be likely if the company were wound up (without first being in administration), or

(c)   realising property in order to make a distribution to one or more secured or preferential creditors.

(2) Subject to sub-paragraph (4), the administrator of a company must perform his functions in the interests of the company's creditors as a whole.

(3) The administrator must perform his functions with the objective specified in sub-paragraph (1)(a) unless he thinks either—

(a)   that it is not reasonably practicable to achieve that objective, or

(b)   that the objective specified in sub-paragraph (1)(b) would achieve a better result for the company's creditors as a whole.

(4) The administrator may perform his functions with the objective specified in sub-paragraph (1)(c) only if—

(a)   he thinks that it is not reasonably practicable to achieve either of the objectives specified in sub-paragraph (1)(a) and (b), and

(b)   he does not unnecessarily harm the interests of the creditors of the company as a whole.

4   The administrator of a company must perform his functions as quickly and efficiently as is reasonably practicable.

Status of administrator

5   An administrator is an officer of the court (whether or not he is appointed by the court).

General restrictions

6   A person may be appointed as administrator of a company only if he is qualified to act as an insolvency practitioner in relation to the company.

7   A person may not be appointed as administrator of a company which is in administration (subject to the provisions of paragraphs 90 to 97 and 100 to 103 about replacement and additional administrators).

8—(1) A person may not be appointed as administrator of a company which is in liquidation by virtue of—

(a)   a resolution for voluntary winding up, or

(b)   a winding-up order.

(2) Sub-paragraph (1)(a) is subject to paragraph 38.

(3) Sub-paragraph (1)(b) is subject to paragraphs 37 and 38.

9—(1) A person may not be appointed as administrator of a company which—

(a)   has a liability in respect of a deposit which it accepted in accordance with the Banking Act 1979 (c. 37) or 1987 (c. 22), but

(b)   is not an authorised deposit taker.

(2) A person may not be appointed as administrator of a company which effects or carries out contracts of insurance.

(3) But sub-paragraph (2) does not apply to a company which—

(a)   is exempt from the general prohibition in relation to effecting or carrying out contracts of insurance, or

(b)   is an authorised deposit taker effecting or carrying out contracts of insurance in the course of a banking business.

(4) In this paragraph—

'authorised deposit taker' means a person with permission under Part IV of the Financial Services and Markets Act 2000 (c. 8) to accept deposits, and

'the general prohibition' has the meaning given by section 19 of that Act.

(5) This paragraph shall be construed in accordance with—

(a) section 22 of the Financial Services and Markets Act 2000 (classes of regulated activity and categories of investment),

(b) any relevant order under that section, and

(c) Schedule 2 to that Act (regulated activities).

APPOINTMENT OF ADMINISTRATOR BY COURT

Administration order

10   An administration order is an order appointing a person as the administrator of a company.

Conditions for making order

11   The court may make an administration order in relation to a company only if satisfied—

(a) that the company is or is likely to become unable to pay its debts, and

(b) that the administration order is reasonably likely to achieve the purpose of administration.

Administration application

12—(1) An application to the court for an administration order in respect of a company (an 'administration application') may be made only by—

(a) the company,

(b) the directors of the company,

(c) one or more creditors of the company,

(d) the justices' chief executive for a magistrates' court in the exercise of the power conferred by section 87A of the Magistrates' Courts Act 1980 (c. 43) (fine imposed on company), or

(e) a combination of persons listed in paragraphs (a) to (d).

(2) As soon as is reasonably practicable after the making of an administration application the applicant shall notify—

(a) any person who has appointed an administrative receiver of the company,

(b) any person who is or may be entitled to appoint an administrative receiver of the company,

(c) any person who is or may be entitled to appoint an administrator of the company under paragraph 14, and

(d) such other persons as may be prescribed.

(3) An administration application may not be withdrawn without the permission of the court.

(4) In sub-paragraph (1) 'creditor' includes a contingent creditor and a prospective creditor.

Powers of court

13—(1) On hearing an administration application the court may—

(a) make the administration order sought;

(b) dismiss the application;

(c) adjourn the hearing conditionally or unconditionally;

(d) make an interim order;

(e) treat the application as a winding-up petition and make any order which the court could make under section 125;

(f) make any other order which the court thinks appropriate.

(2) An appointment of an administrator by administration order takes effect—

(a) at a time appointed by the order, or

(b) where no time is appointed by the order, when the order is made.

(3) An interim order under sub-paragraph (1)(d) may, in particular—

(a) restrict the exercise of a power of the directors or the company;

(b) make provision conferring a discretion on the court or on a person qualified to act as an insolvency practitioner in relation to the company.

(4) This paragraph is subject to paragraph 39.

APPOINTMENT OF ADMINISTRATOR BY HOLDER OF FLOATING CHARGE

Power to appoint

14—(1) The holder of a qualifying floating charge in respect of a company's property may appoint an administrator of the company.

(2) For the purposes of sub-paragraph (1) a floating charge qualifies if created by an instrument which—

(a) states that this paragraph applies to the floating charge,

(b) purports to empower the holder of the floating charge to appoint an administrator of the company,

(c) purports to empower the holder of the floating charge to make an appointment which would be the appointment of an administrative receiver within the meaning given by section 29(2), or

(d) purports to empower the holder of a floating charge in Scotland to appoint a receiver who on appointment would be an administrative receiver.

(3) For the purposes of sub-paragraph (1) a person is the holder of a qualifying floating charge in respect of a company's property if he holds one or more debentures of the company secured—

(a) by a qualifying floating charge which relates to the whole or substantially the whole of the company's property,

(b) by a number of qualifying floating charges which together relate to the whole or substantially the whole of the company's property, or

(c) by charges and other forms of security which together relate to the whole or substantially the whole of the company's property and at least one of which is a qualifying floating charge.

Restrictions on power to appoint

15—(1) A person may not appoint an administrator under paragraph 14 unless—

(a) he has given at least two business days' written notice to the holder of any prior floating charge which satisfies paragraph 14(2), or

(b) the holder of any prior floating charge which satisfies paragraph 14(2) has consented in writing to the making of the appointment.

(2) One floating charge is prior to another for the purposes of this paragraph if—

(a) it was created first, or

(b) it is to be treated as having priority in accordance with an agreement to which the holder of each floating charge was party.

(3) Sub-paragraph (2) shall have effect in relation to Scotland as if the following were substituted for paragraph (a)—

'(a) it has priority of ranking in accordance with section 464(4)(b) of the Companies Act 1985 (c. 6),'.

16   An administrator may not be appointed under paragraph 14 while a floating charge on which the appointment relies is not enforceable.

17   An administrator of a company may not be appointed under paragraph 14 if—

(a) a provisional liquidator of the company has been appointed under section 135, or

(b) an administrative receiver of the company is in office.

Notice of appointment

18—(1) A person who appoints an administrator of a company under paragraph 14 shall file with the court—

(a) a notice of appointment, and

(b) such other documents as may be prescribed.

(2) The notice of appointment must include a statutory declaration by or on behalf of the person who makes the appointment—

(a) that the person is the holder of a qualifying floating charge in respect of the company's property,

(b) that each floating charge relied on in making the appointment is (or was) enforceable on the date of the appointment, and

(c) that the appointment is in accordance with this Schedule.

(3) The notice of appointment must identify the administrator and must be accompanied by a statement by the administrator—

(a) that he consents to the appointment,

(b) that in his opinion the purpose of administration is reasonably likely to be achieved, and

(c) giving such other information and opinions as may be prescribed.

(4) For the purpose of a statement under sub-paragraph (3) an administrator may rely on information supplied by directors of the company (unless he has reason to doubt its accuracy).

(5) The notice of appointment and any document accompanying it must be in the prescribed form.

(6) A statutory declaration under sub-paragraph (2) must be made during the prescribed period.

(7) A person commits an offence if in a statutory declaration under sub-paragraph (2) he makes a statement—

(a) which is false, and

(b) which he does not reasonably believe to be true.

Commencement of appointment

19   The appointment of an administrator under paragraph 14 takes effect when the requirements of paragraph 18 are satisfied.

20   A person who appoints an administrator under paragraph 14—

(a) shall notify the administrator and such other persons as may be prescribed as soon as is reasonably practicable after the requirements of paragraph 18 are satisfied, and

(b) commits an offence if he fails without reasonable excuse to comply with paragraph (a).

Invalid appointment: indemnity

21—(1) This paragraph applies where—

(a) a person purports to appoint an administrator under paragraph 14, and

(b) the appointment is discovered to be invalid.

(2) The court may order the person who purported to make the appointment to indemnify the person appointed against liability which arises solely by reason of the appointment's invalidity.

APPOINTMENT OF ADMINISTRATOR BY COMPANY OR DIRECTORS

Power to appoint

22—(1) A company may appoint an administrator.

(2) The directors of a company may appoint an administrator.

Restrictions on power to appoint

23—(1) This paragraph applies where an administrator of a company is appointed—
    (a) under paragraph 22, or
    (b) on an administration application made by the company or its directors.

(2) An administrator of the company may not be appointed under paragraph 22 during the period of 12 months beginning with the date on which the appointment referred to in sub-paragraph (1) ceases to have effect.

24—(1) If a moratorium for a company under Schedule A1 ends on a date when no voluntary arrangement is in force in respect of the company, this paragraph applies for the period of 12 months beginning with that date.

(2) This paragraph also applies for the period of 12 months beginning with the date on which a voluntary arrangement in respect of a company ends if—
    (a) the arrangement was made during a moratorium for the company under Schedule A1, and
    (b) the arrangement ends prematurely (within the meaning of section 7B).

(3) While this paragraph applies, an administrator of the company may not be appointed under paragraph 22.

25   An administrator of a company may not be appointed under paragraph 22 if—
    (a) a petition for the winding up of the company has been presented and is not yet disposed of,
    (b) an administration application has been made and is not yet disposed of, or
    (c) an administrative receiver of the company is in office.

Notice of intention to appoint

26—(1) A person who proposes to make an appointment under paragraph 22 shall give at least five business days' written notice to—
    (a) any person who is or may be entitled to appoint an administrative receiver of the company, and
    (b) any person who is or may be entitled to appoint an administrator of the company under paragraph 14.

(2) A person who proposes to make an appointment under paragraph 22 shall also give such notice as may be prescribed to such other persons as may be prescribed.

(3) A notice under this paragraph must—
    (a) identify the proposed administrator, and
    (b) be in the prescribed form.

27—(1) A person who gives notice of intention to appoint under paragraph 26 shall file with the court as soon as is reasonably practicable a copy of—
    (a) the notice, and
    (b) any document accompanying it.

(2) The copy filed under sub-paragraph (1) must be accompanied by a statutory declaration made by or on behalf of the person who proposes to make the appointment—
    (a) that the company is or is likely to become unable to pay its debts,
    (b) that the company is not in liquidation, and
    (c) that, so far as the person making the statement is able to ascertain, the appointment is not prevented by paragraphs 23 to 25, and
    (d) to such additional effect, and giving such information, as may be prescribed.

(3) A statutory declaration under sub-paragraph (2) must—
    (a) be in the prescribed form, and
    (b) be made during the prescribed period.

(4) A person commits an offence if in a statutory declaration under sub-paragraph (2) he makes a statement—
    (a) which is false, and
    (b) which he does not reasonably believe to be true.

28—(1) An appointment may not be made under paragraph 22 unless the person who makes the appointment has complied with any requirement of paragraphs 26 and 27 and—

(a) the period of notice specified in paragraph 26(1) has expired, or

(b) each person to whom notice has been given under paragraph 26(1) has consented in writing to the making of the appointment.

(2) An appointment may not be made under paragraph 22 after the period of ten business days beginning with the date on which the notice of intention to appoint is filed under paragraph 27(1).

Notice of appointment

29—(1) A person who appoints an administrator of a company under paragraph 22 shall file with the court—

(a) a notice of appointment, and

(b) such other documents as may be prescribed.

(2) The notice of appointment must include a statutory declaration by or on behalf of the person who makes the appointment—

(a) that the person is entitled to make an appointment under paragraph 22,

(b) that the appointment is in accordance with this Schedule, and

(c) that, so far as the person making the statement is able to ascertain, the statements made and information given in the statutory declaration filed with the notice of intention to appoint remain accurate.

(3) The notice of appointment must identify the administrator and must be accompanied by a statement by the administrator—

(a) that he consents to the appointment,

(b) that in his opinion the purpose of administration is reasonably likely to be achieved, and

(c) giving such other information and opinions as may be prescribed.

(4) For the purpose of a statement under sub-paragraph (3) an administrator may rely on information supplied by directors of the company (unless he has reason to doubt its accuracy).

(5) The notice of appointment and any document accompanying it must be in the prescribed form.

(6) A statutory declaration under sub-paragraph (2) must be made during the prescribed period.

(7) A person commits an offence if in a statutory declaration under sub-paragraph (2) he makes a statement—

(a) which is false, and

(b) which he does not reasonably believe to be true.

30   In a case in which no person is entitled to notice of intention to appoint under paragraph 26(1) (and paragraph 28 therefore does not apply)—

(a) the statutory declaration accompanying the notice of appointment must include the statements and information required under paragraph 27(2), and

(b) paragraph 29(2)(c) shall not apply.

Commencement of appointment

31   The appointment of an administrator under paragraph 22 takes effect when the requirements of paragraph 29 are satisfied.

32   A person who appoints an administrator under paragraph 22—

(a) shall notify the administrator and such other persons as may be prescribed as soon as is reasonably practicable after the requirements of paragraph 29 are satisfied, and

(b) commits an offence if he fails without reasonable excuse to comply with paragraph (a).

33   If before the requirements of paragraph 29 are satisfied the company enters administration by virtue of an administration order or an appointment under paragraph 14—

(a) the appointment under paragraph 22 shall not take effect, and

(b) paragraph 32 shall not apply.

Invalid appointment: indemnity

34—(1) This paragraph applies where—
   (a) a person purports to appoint an administrator under paragraph 22, and
   (b) the appointment is discovered to be invalid.
(2) The court may order the person who purported to make the appointment to indemnify the person appointed against liability which arises solely by reason of the appointment's invalidity.

ADMINISTRATION APPLICATION—SPECIAL CASES

Application by holder of floating charge

35—(1) This paragraph applies where an administration application in respect of a company—
   (a) is made by the holder of a qualifying floating charge in respect of the company's property, and
   (b) includes a statement that the application is made in reliance on this paragraph.
(2) The court may make an administration order—
   (a) whether or not satisfied that the company is or is likely to become unable to pay its debts, but
   (b) only if satisfied that the applicant could appoint an administrator under paragraph 14.

Intervention by holder of floating charge

36—(1) This paragraph applies where—
   (a) an administration application in respect of a company is made by a person who is not the holder of a qualifying floating charge in respect of the company's property, and
   (b) the holder of a qualifying floating charge in respect of the company's property applies to the court to have a specified person appointed as administrator (and not the person specified by the administration applicant).
(2) The court shall grant an application under sub-paragraph (1)(b) unless the court thinks it right to refuse the application because of the particular circumstances of the case.

Application where company in liquidation

37—(1) This paragraph applies where the holder of a qualifying floating charge in respect of a company's property could appoint an administrator under paragraph 14 but for paragraph 8(1)(b).
(2) The holder of the qualifying floating charge may make an administration application.
(3) If the court makes an administration order on hearing an application made by virtue of sub-paragraph (2)—
   (a) the court shall discharge the winding-up order,
   (b) the court shall make provision for such matters as may be prescribed,
   (c) the court may make other consequential provision,
   (d) the court shall specify which of the powers under this Schedule are to be exercisable by the administrator, and
   (e) this Schedule shall have effect with such modifications as the court may specify.
38—(1) The liquidator of a company may make an administration application.
(2) If the court makes an administration order on hearing an application made by virtue of sub-paragraph (1)—
   (a) the court shall discharge any winding-up order in respect of the company,
   (b) the court shall make provision for such matters as may be prescribed,
   (c) the court may make other consequential provision,
   (d) the court shall specify which of the powers under this Schedule are to be exercisable by the administrator, and
   (e) this Schedule shall have effect with such modifications as the court may specify.

Effect of administrative receivership

39—(1) Where there is an administrative receiver of a company the court must dismiss an administration application in respect of the company unless—

    (a) the person by or on behalf of whom the receiver was appointed consents to the making of the administration order,

    (b) the court thinks that the security by virtue of which the receiver was appointed would be liable to be released or discharged under sections 238 to 240 (transaction at undervalue and preference) if an administration order were made,

    (c) the court thinks that the security by virtue of which the receiver was appointed would be avoided under section 245 (avoidance of floating charge) if an administration order were made, or

    (d) the court thinks that the security by virtue of which the receiver was appointed would be challengeable under section 242 (gratuitous alienations) or 243 (unfair preferences) or under any rule of law in Scotland.

(2) Sub-paragraph (1) applies whether the administrative receiver is appointed before or after the making of the administration application.

EFFECT OF ADMINISTRATION

Dismissal of pending winding-up petition

40—(1) A petition for the winding up of a company—

    (a) shall be dismissed on the making of an administration order in respect of the company, and

    (b) shall be suspended while the company is in administration following an appointment under paragraph 14.

(2) Sub-paragraph (1)(b) does not apply to a petition presented under—

    (a) section 124A (public interest), or

    (b) section 367 of the Financial Services and Markets Act 2000 (c. 8) (petition by Financial Services Authority).

(3) Where an administrator becomes aware that a petition was presented under a provision referred to in sub-paragraph (2) before his appointment, he shall apply to the court for directions under paragraph 63.

Dismissal of administrative or other receiver

41—(1) When an administration order takes effect in respect of a company any administrative receiver of the company shall vacate office.

(2) Where a company is in administration, any receiver of part of the company's property shall vacate office if the administrator requires him to.

(3) Where an administrative receiver or receiver vacates office under sub-paragraph (1) or (2)—

    (a) his remuneration shall be charged on and paid out of any property of the company which was in his custody or under his control immediately before he vacated office, and

    (b) he need not take any further steps under section 40 or 59.

(4) In the application of sub-paragraph (3)(a)—

    (a) 'remuneration' includes expenses properly incurred and any indemnity to which the administrative receiver or receiver is entitled out of the assets of the company,

    (b) the charge imposed takes priority over security held by the person by whom or on whose behalf the administrative receiver or receiver was appointed, and

    (c) the provision for payment is subject to paragraph 43.

Moratorium on insolvency proceedings

42—(1) This paragraph applies to a company in administration.
(2) No resolution may be passed for the winding up of the company.
(3) No order may be made for the winding up of the company.
(4) Sub-paragraph (3) does not apply to an order made on a petition presented under—
(a) section 124A (public interest), or
(b) section 367 of the Financial Services and Markets Act 2000 (c. 8) (petition by Financial Services Authority).
(5) If a petition presented under a provision referred to in sub-paragraph (4) comes to the attention of the administrator, he shall apply to the court for directions under paragraph 63.

Moratorium on other legal process

43—(1) This paragraph applies to a company in administration.
(2) No step may be taken to enforce security over the company's property except—
(a) with the consent of the administrator, or
(b) with the permission of the court.
(3) No step may be taken to repossess goods in the company's possession under a hire-purchase agreement except—
(a) with the consent of the administrator, or
(b) with the permission of the court.
(4) A landlord may not exercise a right of forfeiture by peaceable re-entry in relation to premises let to the company except—
(a) with the consent of the administrator, or
(b) with the permission of the court.
(5) In Scotland, a landlord may not exercise a right of irritancy in relation to premises let to the company except—
(a) with the consent of the administrator, or
(b) with the permission of the court.
(6) No legal process (including legal proceedings, execution, distress and diligence) may be instituted or continued against the company or property of the company except—
(a) with the consent of the administrator, or
(b) with the permission of the court.
(7) Where the court gives permission for a transaction under this paragraph it may impose a condition on or a requirement in connection with the transaction.
(8) In this paragraph 'landlord' includes a person to whom rent is payable.

Interim moratorium

44—(1) This paragraph applies where an administration application in respect of a company has been made and—
(a) the application has not yet been granted or dismissed, or
(b) the application has been granted but the administration order has not yet taken effect.
(2) This paragraph also applies from the time when a copy of notice of intention to appoint an administrator under paragraph 14 is filed with the court until—
(a) the appointment of the administrator takes effect, or
(b) the period of five business days beginning with the date of filing expires without an administrator having been appointed.
(3) Sub-paragraph (2) has effect in relation to a notice of intention to appoint only if it is in the prescribed form.
(4) This paragraph also applies from the time when a copy of notice of intention to appoint an administrator is filed with the court under paragraph 27(1) until—

(a) the appointment of the administrator takes effect, or

(b) the period specified in paragraph 28(2) expires without an administrator having been appointed.

(5) The provisions of paragraphs 42 and 43 shall apply (ignoring any reference to the consent of the administrator).

(6) If there is an administrative receiver of the company when the administration application is made, the provisions of paragraphs 42 and 43 shall not begin to apply by virtue of this paragraph until the person by or on behalf of whom the receiver was appointed consents to the making of the administration order.

(7) This paragraph does not prevent or require the permission of the court for—

(a) the presentation of a petition for the winding up of the company under a provision mentioned in paragraph 42(4),

(b) the appointment of an administrator under paragraph 14,

(c) the appointment of an administrative receiver of the company, or

(d) the carrying out by an administrative receiver (whenever appointed) of his functions.

Publicity

45—(1) While a company is in administration every business document issued by or on behalf of the company or the administrator must state—

(a) the name of the administrator, and

(b) that the affairs, business and property of the company are being managed by him.

(2) Any of the following commits an offence if without reasonable excuse he authorises or permits a contravention of sub-paragraph (1)—

(a) the administrator,

(b) an officer of the company, and

(c) the company.

(3) In sub-paragraph (1) 'business document' means—

(a) an invoice,

(b) an order for goods or services, and

(c) a business letter.

PROCESS OF ADMINISTRATION

Announcement of administrator's appointment

46—(1) This paragraph applies where a person becomes the administrator of a company.

(2) As soon as is reasonably practicable the administrator shall—

(a) send a notice of his appointment to the company, and

(b) publish a notice of his appointment in the prescribed manner.

(3) As soon as is reasonably practicable the administrator shall—

(a) obtain a list of the company's creditors, and

(b) send a notice of his appointment to each creditor of whose claim and address he is aware.

(4) The administrator shall send a notice of his appointment to the registrar of companies before the end of the period of 7 days beginning with the date specified in sub-paragraph (6).

(5) The administrator shall send a notice of his appointment to such persons as may be prescribed before the end of the prescribed period beginning with the date specified in sub-paragraph (6).

(6) The date for the purpose of sub-paragraphs (4) and (5) is—

(a) in the case of an administrator appointed by administration order, the date of the order,

(b) in the case of an administrator appointed under paragraph 14, the date on which he receives notice under paragraph 20, and

(c) in the case of an administrator appointed under paragraph 22, the date on which he receives notice under paragraph 32.

(7) The court may direct that sub-paragraph (3)(b) or (5)—
- (a) shall not apply, or
- (b) shall apply with the substitution of a different period.

(8) A notice under this paragraph must—
- (a) contain the prescribed information, and
- (b) be in the prescribed form.

(9) An administrator commits an offence if he fails without reasonable excuse to comply with a requirement of this paragraph.

Statement of company's affairs

47—(1) As soon as is reasonably practicable after appointment the administrator of a company shall by notice in the prescribed form require one or more relevant persons to provide the administrator with a statement of the affairs of the company.

(2) The statement must—
- (a) be verified by a statement of truth in accordance with Civil Procedure Rules,
- (b) be in the prescribed form,
- (c) give particulars of the company's property, debts and liabilities,
- (d) give the names and addresses of the company's creditors,
- (e) specify the security held by each creditor,
- (f) give the date on which each security was granted, and
- (g) contain such other information as may be prescribed.

(3) In sub-paragraph (1) 'relevant person' means—
- (a) a person who is or has been an officer of the company,
- (b) a person who took part in the formation of the company during the period of one year ending with the date on which the company enters administration,
- (c) a person employed by the company during that period, and
- (d) a person who is or has been during that period an officer or employee of a company which is or has been during that year an officer of the company.

(4) For the purpose of sub-paragraph (3) a reference to employment is a reference to employment through a contract of employment or a contract for services.

(5) In Scotland, a statement of affairs under sub-paragraph (1) must be a statutory declaration made in accordance with the Statutory Declarations Act 1835 (c. 62) (and sub-paragraph (2)(a) shall not apply).

48—(1) A person required to submit a statement of affairs must do so before the end of the period of 11 days beginning with the day on which he receives notice of the requirement.

(2) The administrator may—
- (a) revoke a requirement under paragraph 47(1), or
- (b) extend the period specified in sub-paragraph (1) (whether before or after expiry).

(3) If the administrator refuses a request to act under sub-paragraph (2)—
- (a) the person whose request is refused may apply to the court, and
- (b) the court may take action of a kind specified in sub-paragraph (2).

(4) A person commits an offence if he fails without reasonable excuse to comply with a requirement under paragraph 47(1).

Administrator's proposals

49—(1) The administrator of a company shall make a statement setting out proposals for achieving the purpose of administration.

(2) A statement under sub-paragraph (1) must, in particular—
- (a) deal with such matters as may be prescribed, and
- (b) where applicable, explain why the administrator thinks that the objective mentioned in paragraph 3(1)(a) or (b) cannot be achieved.

(3) Proposals under this paragraph may include—
  (a) a proposal for a voluntary arrangement under Part I of this Act (although this paragraph is without prejudice to section 4(3));
  (b) a proposal for a compromise or arrangement to be sanctioned under section 425 of the Companies Act (compromise with creditors or members).

(4) The administrator shall send a copy of the statement of his proposals—
  (a) to the registrar of companies,
  (b) to every creditor of the company of whose claim and address he is aware, and
  (c) to every member of the company of whose address he is aware.

(5) The administrator shall comply with sub-paragraph (4)—
  (a) as soon as is reasonably practicable after the company enters administration, and
  (b) in any event, before the end of the period of eight weeks beginning with the day on which the company enters administration.

(6) The administrator shall be taken to comply with sub-paragraph (4)(c) if he publishes in the prescribed manner a notice undertaking to provide a copy of the statement of proposals free of charge to any member of the company who applies in writing to a specified address.

(7) An administrator commits an offence if he fails without reasonable excuse to comply with sub-paragraph (5).

(8) A period specified in this paragraph may be varied in accordance with paragraph 107.

Creditors' meeting

50—(1) In this Schedule 'creditors' meeting' means a meeting of creditors of a company summoned by the administrator—
  (a) in the prescribed manner, and
  (b) giving the prescribed period of notice to every creditor of the company of whose claim and address he is aware.

(2) A period prescribed under sub-paragraph (1)(b) may be varied in accordance with paragraph 107.

(3) A creditors' meeting shall be conducted in accordance with the rules.

Requirement for initial creditors' meeting

51—(1) Each copy of an administrator's statement of proposals sent to a creditor under paragraph 49(4)(b) must be accompanied by an invitation to a creditors' meeting (an 'initial creditors' meeting').

(2) The date set for an initial creditors' meeting must be—
  (a) as soon as is reasonably practicable after the company enters administration, and
  (b) in any event, within the period of ten weeks beginning with the date on which the company enters administration.

(3) An administrator shall present a copy of his statement of proposals to an initial creditors' meeting.

(4) A period specified in this paragraph may be varied in accordance with paragraph 107.

(5) An administrator commits an offence if he fails without reasonable excuse to comply with a requirement of this paragraph.

52—(1) Paragraph 51(1) shall not apply where the statement of proposals states that the administrator thinks—
  (a) that the company has sufficient property to enable each creditor of the company to be paid in full,
  (b) that the company has insufficient property to enable a distribution to be made to unsecured creditors other than by virtue of section 176A(2)(a), or
  (c) that neither of the objectives specified in paragraph 3(1)(a) and (b) can be achieved.

(2) But the administrator shall summon an initial creditors' meeting if it is requested—

    (a) by creditors of the company whose debts amount to at least 10 per cent of the total debts of the company,

    (b) in the prescribed manner, and

    (c) in the prescribed period.

(3) A meeting requested under sub-paragraph (2) must be summoned for a date in the prescribed period.

(4) The period prescribed under sub-paragraph (3) may be varied in accordance with paragraph 107.

Business and result of initial creditors' meeting

53—(1) An initial creditors' meeting to which an administrator's proposals are presented shall consider them and may—

    (a) approve them without modification, or

    (b) approve them with modification to which the administrator consents.

(2) After the conclusion of an initial creditors' meeting the administrator shall as soon as is reasonably practicable report any decision taken to—

    (a) the court,

    (b) the registrar of companies, and

    (c) such other persons as may be prescribed.

(3) An administrator commits an offence if he fails without reasonable excuse to comply with sub-paragraph (2).

Revision of administrator's proposals

54—(1) This paragraph applies where—

    (a) an administrator's proposals have been approved (with or without modification) at an initial creditors' meeting,

    (b) the administrator proposes a revision to the proposals, and

    (c) the administrator thinks that the proposed revision is substantial.

(2) The administrator shall—

    (a) summon a creditors' meeting,

    (b) send a statement in the prescribed form of the proposed revision with the notice of the meeting sent to each creditor,

    (c) send a copy of the statement, within the prescribed period, to each member of the company of whose address he is aware, and

    (d) present a copy of the statement to the meeting.

(3) The administrator shall be taken to have complied with sub-paragraph (2)(c) if he publishes a notice undertaking to provide a copy of the statement free of charge to any member of the company who applies in writing to a specified address.

(4) A notice under sub-paragraph (3) must be published—

    (a) in the prescribed manner, and

    (b) within the prescribed period.

(5) A creditors' meeting to which a proposed revision is presented shall consider it and may—

    (a) approve it without modification, or

    (b) approve it with modification to which the administrator consents.

(6) After the conclusion of a creditors' meeting the administrator shall as soon as is reasonably practicable report any decision taken to—

    (a) the court,

    (b) the registrar of companies, and

    (c) such other persons as may be prescribed.

(7) An administrator commits an offence if he fails without reasonable excuse to comply with sub-paragraph (6).

Failure to obtain approval of administrator's proposals

55—*(1) This paragraph applies where an administrator reports to the court that—*
- (a) *an initial creditors' meeting has failed to approve the administrator's proposals presented to it, or*
- (b) *a creditors' meeting has failed to approve a revision of the administrator's proposals presented to it.*

(2) The court may—
- (a) *provide that the appointment of an administrator shall cease to have effect from a specified time;*
- (b) *adjourn the hearing conditionally or unconditionally;*
- (c) *make an interim order;*
- (d) *make an order on a petition for winding up suspended by virtue of paragraph 40(1)(b);*
- (e) *make any other order (including an order making consequential provision) that the court thinks appropriate.*

Further creditors' meetings

56—*(1) The administrator of a company shall summon a creditors' meeting if—*
- (a) *it is requested in the prescribed manner by creditors of the company whose debts amount to at least 10 per cent of the total debts of the company, or*
- (b) *he is directed by the court to summon a creditors' meeting.*

(2) An administrator commits an offence if he fails without reasonable excuse to summon a creditors' meeting as required by this paragraph.

Creditors' committee

57—*(1) A creditors' meeting may establish a creditors' committee.*

(2) A creditors' committee shall carry out functions conferred on it by or under this Act.

(3) A creditors' committee may require the administrator—
- (a) *to attend on the committee at any reasonable time of which he is given at least seven days' notice, and*
- (b) *to provide the committee with information about the exercise of his functions.*

Correspondence instead of creditors' meeting

58—*(1) Anything which is required or permitted by or under this Schedule to be done at a creditors' meeting may be done by correspondence between the administrator and creditors—*
- (a) *in accordance with the rules, and*
- (b) *subject to any prescribed condition.*

(2) A reference in this Schedule to anything done at a creditors' meeting includes a reference to anything done in the course of correspondence in reliance on sub-paragraph (1).

(3) A requirement to hold a creditors' meeting is satisfied by conducting correspondence in accordance with this paragraph.

FUNCTIONS OF ADMINISTRATOR

General powers

59—*(1) The administrator of a company may do anything necessary or expedient for the management of the affairs, business and property of the company.*

(2) *A provision of this Schedule which expressly permits the administrator to do a specified thing is without prejudice to the generality of sub-paragraph (1).*

(3) *A person who deals with the administrator of a company in good faith and for value need not inquire whether the administrator is acting within his powers.*

60   *The administrator of a company has the powers specified in Schedule 1 to this Act.*

61   *The administrator of a company—*

(a) *may remove a director of the company, and*

(b) *may appoint a director of the company (whether or not to fill a vacancy).*

62   *The administrator of a company may call a meeting of members or creditors of the company.*

63   *The administrator of a company may apply to the court for directions in connection with his functions.*

64—(1) *A company in administration or an officer of a company in administration may not exercise a management power without the consent of the administrator.*

(2) *For the purpose of sub-paragraph (1)—*

(a) *'management power' means a power which could be exercised so as to interfere with the exercise of the administrator's powers,*

(b) *it is immaterial whether the power is conferred by an enactment or an instrument, and*

(c) *consent may be general or specific.*

Distribution

65—(1) *The administrator of a company may make a distribution to a creditor of the company.*

(2) *Section 175 shall apply in relation to a distribution under this paragraph as it applies in relation to a winding up.*

(3) *A payment may not be made by way of distribution under this paragraph to a creditor of the company who is neither secured nor preferential unless the court gives permission.*

66   *The administrator of a company may make a payment otherwise than in accordance with paragraph 65 or paragraph 13 of Schedule 1 if he thinks it likely to assist achievement of the purpose of administration.*

General duties

67   *The administrator of a company shall on his appointment take custody or control of all the property to which he thinks the company is entitled.*

68—(1) *Subject to sub-paragraph (2), the administrator of a company shall manage its affairs, business and property in accordance with—*

(a) *any proposals approved under paragraph 53,*

(b) *any revision of those proposals which is made by him and which he does not consider substantial, and*

(c) *any revision of those proposals approved under paragraph 54.*

(2) *If the court gives directions to the administrator of a company in connection with any aspect of his management of the company's affairs, business or property, the administrator shall comply with the directions.*

(3) *The court may give directions under sub-paragraph (2) only if—*

(a) *no proposals have been approved under paragraph 53,*

(b) *the directions are consistent with any proposals or revision approved under paragraph 53 or 54,*

(c) *the court thinks the directions are required in order to reflect a change in circumstances since the approval of proposals or a revision under paragraph 53 or 54, or*

(d) *the court thinks the directions are desirable because of a misunderstanding about proposals or a revision approved under paragraph 53 or 54.*

Administrator as agent of company

69   In exercising his functions under this Schedule the administrator of a company acts as its agent.

Charged property: floating charge

70—(1) The administrator of a company may dispose of or take action relating to property which is subject to a floating charge as if it were not subject to the charge.

(2) Where property is disposed of in reliance on sub-paragraph (1) the holder of the floating charge shall have the same priority in respect of acquired property as he had in respect of the property disposed of.

(3) In sub-paragraph (2) 'acquired property' means property of the company which directly or indirectly represents the property disposed of.

Charged property: non-floating charge

71—(1) The court may by order enable the administrator of a company to dispose of property which is subject to a security (other than a floating charge) as if it were not subject to the security.

(2) An order under sub-paragraph (1) may be made only—
  (a) on the application of the administrator, and
  (b) where the court thinks that disposal of the property would be likely to promote the purpose of administration in respect of the company.

(3) An order under this paragraph is subject to the condition that there be applied towards discharging the sums secured by the security—
  (a) the net proceeds of disposal of the property, and
  (b) any additional money required to be added to the net proceeds so as to produce the amount determined by the court as the net amount which would be realised on a sale of the property at market value.

(4) If an order under this paragraph relates to more than one security, application of money under sub-paragraph (3) shall be in the order of the priorities of the securities.

(5) An administrator who makes a successful application for an order under this paragraph shall send a copy of the order to the registrar of companies before the end of the period of 14 days starting with the date of the order.

(6) An administrator commits an offence if he fails to comply with sub-paragraph (5) without reasonable excuse.

Hire-purchase property

72—(1) The court may by order enable the administrator of a company to dispose of goods which are in the possession of the company under a hire-purchase agreement as if all the rights of the owner under the agreement were vested in the company.

(2) An order under sub-paragraph (1) may be made only—
  (a) on the application of the administrator, and
  (b) where the court thinks that disposal of the goods would be likely to promote the purpose of administration in respect of the company.

(3) An order under this paragraph is subject to the condition that there be applied towards discharging the sums payable under the hire-purchase agreement—
  (a) the net proceeds of disposal of the goods, and
  (b) any additional money required to be added to the net proceeds so as to produce the amount determined by the court as the net amount which would be realised on a sale of the goods at market value.

(4) An administrator who makes a successful application for an order under this paragraph shall send a copy of the order to the registrar of companies before the end of the period of 14 days starting with the date of the order.

(5) An administrator commits an offence if he fails without reasonable excuse to comply with sub-paragraph (4).

Protection for secured or preferential creditor

73—(1) An administrator's statement of proposals under paragraph 49 may not include any action which—
  (a) affects the right of a secured creditor of the company to enforce his security,
  (b) would result in a preferential debt of the company being paid otherwise than in priority to its non-preferential debts, or
  (c) would result in one preferential creditor of the company being paid a smaller proportion of his debt than another.

(2) Sub-paragraph (1) does not apply to—
  (a) action to which the relevant creditor consents,
  (b) a proposal for a voluntary arrangement under Part I of this Act (although this sub-paragraph is without prejudice to section 4(3)), or
  (c) a proposal for a compromise or arrangement to be sanctioned under section 425 of the Companies Act (compromise with creditors or members).

(3) The reference to a statement of proposals in sub-paragraph (1) includes a reference to a statement as revised or modified.

Challenge to administrator's conduct of company

74—(1) A creditor or member of a company in administration may apply to the court claiming that—
  (a) the administrator is acting or has acted so as unfairly to harm the interests of the applicant (whether alone or in common with some or all other members or creditors), or
  (b) the administrator proposes to act in a way which would unfairly harm the interests of the applicant (whether alone or in common with some or all other members or creditors).

(2) A creditor or member of a company in administration may apply to the court claiming that the administrator is not performing his functions as quickly or as efficiently as is reasonably practicable.

(3) The court may—
  (a) grant relief;
  (b) dismiss the application;
  (c) adjourn the hearing conditionally or unconditionally;
  (d) make an interim order;
  (e) make any other order it thinks appropriate.

(4) In particular, an order under this paragraph may—
  (a) regulate the administrator's exercise of his functions;
  (b) require the administrator to do or not do a specified thing;
  (c) require a creditors' meeting to be held for a specified purpose;
  (d) provide for the appointment of an administrator to cease to have effect;
  (e) make consequential provision.

(5) An order may be made on a claim under sub-paragraph (1) whether or not the action complained of—
  (a) is within the administrator's powers under this Schedule;
  (b) was taken in reliance on an order under paragraph 71 or 72.

(6) An order may not be made under this paragraph if it would impede or prevent the implementation of—

(a) a voluntary arrangement approved under Part I,

(b) a compromise or arrangement sanctioned under section 425 of the Companies Act (compromise with creditors and members), or

(c) proposals or a revision approved under paragraph 53 or 54 more than 28 days before the day on which the application for the order under this paragraph is made.

Misfeasance

75—(1) The court may examine the conduct of a person who—

(a) is or purports to be the administrator of a company, or

(b) has been or has purported to be the administrator of a company.

(2) An examination under this paragraph may be held only on the application of—

(a) the official receiver,

(b) the administrator of the company,

(c) the liquidator of the company,

(d) a creditor of the company, or

(e) a contributory of the company.

(3) An application under sub-paragraph (2) must allege that the administrator—

(a) has misapplied or retained money or other property of the company,

(b) has become accountable for money or other property of the company,

(c) has breached a fiduciary or other duty in relation to the company, or

(d) has been guilty of misfeasance.

(4) On an examination under this paragraph into a person's conduct the court may order him—

(a) to repay, restore or account for money or property;

(b) to pay interest;

(c) to contribute a sum to the company's property by way of compensation for breach of duty or misfeasance.

(5) In sub-paragraph (3) 'administrator' includes a person who purports or has purported to be a company's administrator.

(6) An application under sub-paragraph (2) may be made in respect of an administrator who has been discharged under paragraph 98 only with the permission of the court.

ENDING ADMINISTRATION

Automatic end of administration

76—(1) The appointment of an administrator shall cease to have effect at the end of the period of one year beginning with the date on which it takes effect.

(2) But—

(a) on the application of an administrator the court may by order extend his term of office for a specified period, and

(b) an administrator's term of office may be extended for a specified period not exceeding six months by consent.

77—(1) An order of the court under paragraph 76—

(a) may be made in respect of an administrator whose term of office has already been extended by order or by consent, but

(b) may not be made after the expiry of the administrator's term of office.

(2) Where an order is made under paragraph 76 the administrator shall as soon as is reasonably practicable notify the registrar of companies.

(3) An administrator who fails without reasonable excuse to comply with sub-paragraph (2) commits an offence.

78—(1) In paragraph 76(2)(b) 'consent' means consent of—

(a) each secured creditor of the company, and

(b) if the company has unsecured debts, creditors whose debts amount to more than 50 per cent of the company's unsecured debts, disregarding debts of any creditor who does not respond to an invitation to give or withhold consent.

(2) But where the administrator has made a statement under paragraph 52(1)(b) 'consent' means—

(a) consent of each secured creditor of the company, or

(b) if the administrator thinks that a distribution may be made to preferential creditors, consent of—

(i) each secured creditor of the company, and

(ii) preferential creditors whose debts amount to more than 50 per cent of the preferential debts of the company, disregarding debts of any creditor who does not respond to an invitation to give or withhold consent.

(3) Consent for the purposes of paragraph 76(2)(b) may be—

(a) written, or

(b) signified at a creditors' meeting.

(4) An administrator's term of office—

(a) may be extended by consent only once,

(b) may not be extended by consent after extension by order of the court, and

(c) may not be extended by consent after expiry.

(5) Where an administrator's term of office is extended by consent he shall as soon as is reasonably practicable—

(a) file notice of the extension with the court, and

(b) notify the registrar of companies.

(6) An administrator who fails without reasonable excuse to comply with sub-paragraph (5) commits an offence.

Court ending administration on application of administrator

79—(1) On the application of the administrator of a company the court may provide for the appointment of an administrator of the company to cease to have effect from a specified time.

(2) The administrator of a company shall make an application under this paragraph if—

(a) he thinks the purpose of administration cannot be achieved in relation to the company,

(b) he thinks the company should not have entered administration, or

(c) a creditors' meeting requires him to make an application under this paragraph.

(3) The administrator of a company shall make an application under this paragraph if—

(a) the administration is pursuant to an administration order, and

(b) the administrator thinks that the purpose of administration has been sufficiently achieved in relation to the company.

(4) On an application under this paragraph the court may—

(a) adjourn the hearing conditionally or unconditionally;

(b) dismiss the application;

(c) make an interim order;

(d) make any order it thinks appropriate (whether in addition to, in consequence of or instead of the order applied for).

Termination of administration where objective achieved

80—(1) This paragraph applies where an administrator of a company is appointed under paragraph 14 or 22.

(2) If the administrator thinks that the purpose of administration has been sufficiently achieved in relation to the company he may file a notice in the prescribed form—

(a) with the court, and

(b) with the registrar of companies.

(3) The administrator's appointment shall cease to have effect when the requirements of sub-paragraph *(2)* are satisfied.

(4) Where the administrator files a notice he shall within the prescribed period send a copy to every creditor of the company of whose claim and address he is aware.

(5) The rules may provide that the administrator is taken to have complied with sub-paragraph *(4)* if before the end of the prescribed period he publishes in the prescribed manner a notice undertaking to provide a copy of the notice under sub-paragraph *(2)* to any creditor of the company who applies in writing to a specified address.

(6) An administrator who fails without reasonable excuse to comply with sub-paragraph *(4)* commits an offence.

Court ending administration on application of creditor

81—*(1)* On the application of a creditor of a company the court may provide for the appointment of an administrator of the company to cease to have effect at a specified time.

(2) An application under this paragraph must allege an improper motive—

    (a) in the case of an administrator appointed by administration order, on the part of the applicant for the order, or

    (b) in any other case, on the part of the person who appointed the administrator.

(3) On an application under this paragraph the court may—

    (a) adjourn the hearing conditionally or unconditionally;

    (b) dismiss the application;

    (c) make an interim order;

    (d) make any order it thinks appropriate (whether in addition to, in consequence of or instead of the order applied for).

Public interest winding-up

82—*(1)* This paragraph applies where a winding-up order is made for the winding up of a company in administration on a petition presented under—

    (a) section 124A (public interest), or

    (b) section 367 of the Financial Services and Markets Act 2000 (c. 8) (petition by Financial Services Authority).

(2) This paragraph also applies where a provisional liquidator of a company in administration is appointed following the presentation of a petition under any of the provisions listed in sub-paragraph *(1)*.

(3) The court shall order—

    (a) that the appointment of the administrator shall cease to have effect, or

    (b) that the appointment of the administrator shall continue to have effect.

(4) If the court makes an order under sub-paragraph *(3)(b)* it may also—

    (a) specify which of the powers under this Schedule are to be exercisable by the administrator, and

    (b) order that this Schedule shall have effect in relation to the administrator with specified modifications.

Moving from administration to creditors' voluntary liquidation

83—*(1)* This paragraph applies in England and Wales where the administrator of a company thinks—

    (a) that the total amount which each secured creditor of the company is likely to receive has been paid to him or set aside for him, and

    (b) that a distribution will be made to unsecured creditors of the company (if there are any).

(2) This paragraph applies in Scotland where the administrator of a company thinks—

(a) that each secured creditor of the company will receive payment in respect of his debt, and

(b) that a distribution will be made to unsecured creditors (if there are any).

(3) The administrator may send to the registrar of companies a notice that this paragraph applies.

(4) On receipt of a notice under sub-paragraph (3) the registrar shall register it.

(5) If an administrator sends a notice under sub-paragraph (3) he shall as soon as is reasonably practicable—

(a) file a copy of the notice with the court, and

(b) send a copy of the notice to each creditor of whose claim and address he is aware.

(6) On the registration of a notice under sub-paragraph (3)—

(a) the appointment of an administrator in respect of the company shall cease to have effect, and

(b) the company shall be wound up as if a resolution for voluntary winding up under section 84 were passed on the day on which the notice is registered.

(7) The liquidator for the purposes of the winding up shall be—

(a) a person nominated by the creditors of the company in the prescribed manner and within the prescribed period, or

(b) if no person is nominated under paragraph (a), the administrator.

(8) In the application of Part IV to a winding up by virtue of this paragraph—

(a) section 85 shall not apply,

(b) section 86 shall apply as if the reference to the time of the passing of the resolution for voluntary winding up were a reference to the beginning of the date of registration of the notice under sub-paragraph (3),

(c) section 89 does not apply,

(d) sections 98, 99 and 100 shall not apply,

(e) section 129 shall apply as if the reference to the time of the passing of the resolution for voluntary winding up were a reference to the beginning of the date of registration of the notice under sub-paragraph (3), and

(f) any creditors' committee which is in existence immediately before the company ceases to be in administration shall continue in existence after that time as if appointed as a liquidation committee under section 101.

Moving from administration to dissolution

84—(1) If the administrator of a company thinks that the company has no property which might permit a distribution to its creditors, he shall send a notice to that effect to the registrar of companies.

(2) The court may on the application of the administrator of a company disapply sub-paragraph (1) in respect of the company.

(3) On receipt of a notice under sub-paragraph (1) the registrar shall register it.

(4) On the registration of a notice in respect of a company under sub-paragraph (1) the appointment of an administrator of the company shall cease to have effect.

(5) If an administrator sends a notice under sub-paragraph (1) he shall as soon as is reasonably practicable—

(a) file a copy of the notice with the court, and

(b) send a copy of the notice to each creditor of whose claim and address he is aware.

(6) At the end of the period of three months beginning with the date of registration of a notice in respect of a company under sub-paragraph (1) the company is deemed to be dissolved.

(7) On an application in respect of a company by the administrator or another interested person the court may—

(a) extend the period specified in sub-paragraph (6),

(b) suspend that period, or

(c) disapply sub-paragraph (6).

(8) Where an order is made under sub-paragraph (7) in respect of a company the administrator shall as soon as is reasonably practicable notify the registrar of companies.

(9) An administrator commits an offence if he fails without reasonable excuse to comply with sub-paragraph (5).

Discharge of administration order where administration ends

85—(1)   This paragraph applies where—
  (a)   the court makes an order under this Schedule providing for the appointment of an administrator of a company to cease to have effect, and
  (b)   the administrator was appointed by administration order.
(2)   The court shall discharge the administration order.

Notice to Companies Registrar where administration ends

86—(1)   This paragraph applies where the court makes an order under this Schedule providing for the appointment of an administrator to cease to have effect.
(2)   The administrator shall send a copy of the order to the registrar of companies within the period of 14 days beginning with the date of the order.
(3)   An administrator who fails without reasonable excuse to comply with sub-paragraph (2) commits an offence.

REPLACING ADMINISTRATOR

Resignation of administrator

87—(1)   An administrator may resign only in prescribed circumstances.
(2)   Where an administrator may resign he may do so only—
  (a)   in the case of an administrator appointed by administration order, by notice in writing to the court,
  (b)   in the case of an administrator appointed under paragraph 14, by notice in writing to the person who appointed him,
  (c)   in the case of an administrator appointed under paragraph 22(1), by notice in writing to the company, or
  (d)   in the case of an administrator appointed under paragraph 22(2), by notice in writing to the directors of the company.

Removal of administrator from office

88   The court may by order remove an administrator from office.

Administrator ceasing to be qualified

89—(1)   The administrator of a company shall vacate office if he ceases to be qualified to act as an insolvency practitioner in relation to the company.
(2)   Where an administrator vacates office by virtue of sub-paragraph (1) he shall give notice in writing—
  (a)   in the case of an administrator appointed by administration order, to the court,
  (b)   in the case of an administrator appointed under paragraph 14, to the person who appointed him,
  (c)   in the case of an administrator appointed under paragraph 22(1), to the company, or
  (d)   in the case of an administrator appointed under paragraph 22(2), to the directors of the company.
(3)   An administrator who fails without reasonable excuse to comply with sub-paragraph (2) commits an offence.

Supplying vacancy in office of administrator

90 Paragraphs 91 to 95 apply where an administrator—
(a) dies,
(b) resigns,
(c) is removed from office under paragraph 88, or
(d) vacates office under paragraph 89.

91—(1) Where the administrator was appointed by administration order, the court may replace the administrator on an application under this sub-paragraph made by—
(a) a creditors' committee of the company,
(b) the company,
(c) the directors of the company,
(d) one or more creditors of the company, or
(e) where more than one person was appointed to act jointly or concurrently as the administrator, any of those persons who remains in office.

(2) But an application may be made in reliance on sub-paragraph (1)(b) to (d) only where—
(a) there is no creditors' committee of the company,
(b) the court is satisfied that the creditors' committee or a remaining administrator is not taking reasonable steps to make a replacement, or
(c) the court is satisfied that for another reason it is right for the application to be made.

92 Where the administrator was appointed under paragraph 14 the holder of the floating charge by virtue of which the appointment was made may replace the administrator.

93—(1) Where the administrator was appointed under paragraph 22(1) by the company it may replace the administrator.

(2) A replacement under this paragraph may be made only—
(a) with the consent of each person who is the holder of a qualifying floating charge in respect of the company's property, or
(b) where consent is withheld, with the permission of the court.

94—(1) Where the administrator was appointed under paragraph 22(2) the directors of the company may replace the administrator.

(2) A replacement under this paragraph may be made only—
(a) with the consent of each person who is the holder of a qualifying floating charge in respect of the company's property, or
(b) where consent is withheld, with the permission of the court.

95 The court may replace an administrator on the application of a person listed in paragraph 91(1) if the court—
(a) is satisfied that a person who is entitled to replace the administrator under any of paragraphs 92 to 94 is not taking reasonable steps to make a replacement, or
(b) that for another reason it is right for the court to make the replacement.

Substitution of administrator: competing floating charge-holder

96—(1) This paragraph applies where an administrator of a company is appointed under paragraph 14 by the holder of a qualifying floating charge in respect of the company's property.

(2) The holder of a prior qualifying floating charge in respect of the company's property may apply to the court for the administrator to be replaced by an administrator nominated by the holder of the prior floating charge.

(3) One floating charge is prior to another for the purposes of this paragraph if—
(a) it was created first, or
(b) it is to be treated as having priority in accordance with an agreement to which the holder of each floating charge was party.

(4) Sub-paragraph (3) shall have effect in relation to Scotland as if the following were substituted for paragraph (a)—

'(a) it has priority of ranking in accordance with section 464(4)(b) of the Companies Act 1985 (c. 6),'.

Substitution of administrator appointed by company or directors: creditors' meeting

97—(1) This paragraph applies where—
- (a) an administrator of a company is appointed by a company or directors under paragraph 22, and
- (b) there is no holder of a qualifying floating charge in respect of the company's property.

(2) A creditors' meeting may replace the administrator.

(3) A creditors' meeting may act under sub-paragraph (2) only if the new administrator's written consent to act is presented to the meeting before the replacement is made.

Vacation of office: discharge from liability

98—(1)   Where a person ceases to be the administrator of a company (whether because he vacates office by reason of resignation, death or otherwise, because he is removed from office or because his appointment ceases to have effect) he is discharged from liability in respect of any action of his as administrator.

(2) The discharge provided by sub-paragraph (1) takes effect—
- (a) in the case of an administrator who dies, on the filing with the court of notice of his death,
- (b) in the case of an administrator appointed under paragraph 14 or 22, at a time appointed by resolution of the creditors' committee or, if there is no committee, by resolution of the creditors, or
- (c) in any case, at a time specified by the court.

(3) For the purpose of the application of sub-paragraph (2)(b) in a case where the administrator has made a statement under paragraph 52(1)(b), a resolution shall be taken as passed if (and only if) passed with the approval of—
- (a) each secured creditor of the company, or
- (b) if the administrator has made a distribution to preferential creditors or thinks that a distribution may be made to preferential creditors—
  - (i)   each secured creditor of the company, and
  - (ii) preferential creditors whose debts amount to more than 50 per cent of the preferential debts of the company, disregarding debts of any creditor who does not respond to an invitation to give or withhold approval.

(4) Discharge—
- (a) applies to liability accrued before the discharge takes effect, and
- (b) does not prevent the exercise of the court's powers under paragraph 75.

Vacation of office: charges and liabilities

99—(1) This paragraph applies where a person ceases to be the administrator of a company (whether because he vacates office by reason of resignation, death or otherwise, because he is removed from office or because his appointment ceases to have effect).

(2) In this paragraph—
'the former administrator' means the person referred to in sub-paragraph (1), and
'cessation' means the time when he ceases to be the company's administrator.

(3) The former administrator's remuneration and expenses shall be—
- (a) charged on and payable out of property of which he had custody or control immediately before cessation, and
- (b) payable in priority to any security to which paragraph 70 applies.

(4) A sum payable in respect of a debt or liability arising out of a contract entered into by the former administrator or a predecessor before cessation shall be—

(a) charged on and payable out of property of which the former administrator had custody or control immediately before cessation, and

(b) payable in priority to any charge arising under sub-paragraph (3).

(5) Sub-paragraph (4) shall apply to a liability arising under a contract of employment which was adopted by the former administrator or a predecessor before cessation; and for that purpose—

(a) action taken within the period of 14 days after an administrator's appointment shall not be taken to amount or contribute to the adoption of a contract,

(b) no account shall be taken of a liability which arises, or in so far as it arises, by reference to anything which is done or which occurs before the adoption of the contract of employment, and

(c) no account shall be taken of a liability to make a payment other than wages or salary.

(6) In sub-paragraph (5)(c) 'wages or salary' includes—

(a) a sum payable in respect of a period of holiday (for which purpose the sum shall be treated as relating to the period by reference to which the entitlement to holiday accrued),

(b) a sum payable in respect of a period of absence through illness or other good cause,

(c) a sum payable in lieu of holiday,

(d) in respect of a period, a sum which would be treated as earnings for that period for the purposes of an enactment about social security, and

(e) a contribution to an occupational pension scheme.

GENERAL

Joint and concurrent administrators

100—(1) In this Schedule—

(a) a reference to the appointment of an administrator of a company includes a reference to the appointment of a number of persons to act jointly or concurrently as the administrator of a company, and

(b) a reference to the appointment of a person as administrator of a company includes a reference to the appointment of a person as one of a number of persons to act jointly or concurrently as the administrator of a company.

(2) The appointment of a number of persons to act as administrator of a company must specify—

(a) which functions (if any) are to be exercised by the persons appointed acting jointly, and

(b) which functions (if any) are to be exercised by any or all of the persons appointed.

101—(1) This paragraph applies where two or more persons are appointed to act jointly as the administrator of a company.

(2) A reference to the administrator of the company is a reference to those persons acting jointly.

(3) But a reference to the administrator of a company in paragraphs 87 to 99 of this Schedule is a reference to any or all of the persons appointed to act jointly.

(4) Where an offence of omission is committed by the administrator, each of the persons appointed to act jointly—

(a) commits the offence, and

(b) may be proceeded against and punished individually.

(5) The reference in paragraph 45(1)(a) to the name of the administrator is a reference to the name of each of the persons appointed to act jointly.

(6) Where persons are appointed to act jointly in respect of only some of the functions of the administrator of a company, this paragraph applies only in relation to those functions.

102—(1) This paragraph applies where two or more persons are appointed to act concurrently as the administrator of a company.

(2) A reference to the administrator of a company in this Schedule is a reference to any of the persons appointed (or any combination of them).

103—(1) Where a company is in administration, a person may be appointed to act as administrator jointly or concurrently with the person or persons acting as the administrator of the company.

(2) *Where a company entered administration by administration order, an appointment under sub-paragraph (1) must be made by the court on the application of—*
- (a) *a person or group listed in paragraph 12(1)(a) to (e), or*
- (b) *the person or persons acting as the administrator of the company.*

(3) *Where a company entered administration by virtue of an appointment under paragraph 14, an appointment under sub-paragraph (1) must be made by—*
- (a) *the holder of the floating charge by virtue of which the appointment was made, or*
- (b) *the court on the application of the person or persons acting as the administrator of the company.*

(4) *Where a company entered administration by virtue of an appointment under paragraph 22(1), an appointment under sub-paragraph (1) above must be made either by the court on the application of the person or persons acting as the administrator of the company or—*
- (a) *by the company, and*
- (b) *with the consent of each person who is the holder of a qualifying floating charge in respect of the company's property or, where consent is withheld, with the permission of the court.*

(5) *Where a company entered administration by virtue of an appointment under paragraph 22(2), an appointment under sub-paragraph (1) must be made either by the court on the application of the person or persons acting as the administrator of the company or—*
- (a) *by the directors of the company, and*
- (b) *with the consent of each person who is the holder of a qualifying floating charge in respect of the company's property or, where consent is withheld, with the permission of the court.*

(6) *An appointment under sub-paragraph (1) may be made only with the consent of the person or persons acting as the administrator of the company.*

Presumption of validity

104   *An act of the administrator of a company is valid in spite of a defect in his appointment or qualification.*

Majority decision of directors

105   *A reference in this Schedule to something done by the directors of a company includes a reference to the same thing done by a majority of the directors of a company.*

Penalties

106—(1)   *A person who is guilty of an offence under this Schedule is liable to a fine (in accordance with section 430 and Schedule 10).*

(2) *A person who is guilty of an offence under any of the following paragraphs of this Schedule is liable to a daily default fine (in accordance with section 430 and Schedule 10)—*
- (a) *paragraph 20,*
- (b) *paragraph 32,*
- (c) *paragraph 46,*
- (d) *paragraph 48,*
- (e) *paragraph 49,*
- (f) *paragraph 51,*
- (g) *paragraph 53,*
- (h) *paragraph 54,*
- (i) *paragraph 56,*
- (j) *paragraph 71,*
- (k) *paragraph 72,*
- (l) *paragraph 77,*
- (m) *paragraph 78,*

    (n) paragraph 80,

    (o) paragraph 84,

    (p) paragraph 86, and

    (q) paragraph 89.

Extension of time limit

107—(1)   *Where a provision of this Schedule provides that a period may be varied in accordance with this paragraph, the period may be varied in respect of a company—*

    (a) *by the court, and*

    (b) *on the application of the administrator.*

(2) *A time period may be extended in respect of a company under this paragraph—*

    (a) *more than once, and*

    (b) *after expiry.*

108—(1)   *A period specified in paragraph 49(5), 50(1)(b) or 51(2) may be varied in respect of a company by the administrator with consent.*

(2) *In sub-paragraph (1) 'consent' means consent of—*

    (a) *each secured creditor of the company, and*

    (b) *if the company has unsecured debts, creditors whose debts amount to more than 50 per cent of the company's unsecured debts, disregarding debts of any creditor who does not respond to an invitation to give or withhold consent.*

(3) *But where the administrator has made a statement under paragraph 52(1)(b) 'consent' means—*

    (a) *consent of each secured creditor of the company, or*

    (b) *if the administrator thinks that a distribution may be made to preferential creditors, consent of—*

        (i)   *each secured creditor of the company, and*

        (ii) *preferential creditors whose debts amount to more than 50 per cent of the total preferential debts of the company, disregarding debts of any creditor who does not respond to an invitation to give or withhold consent.*

(4) *Consent for the purposes of sub-paragraph (1) may be—*

    (a) *written, or*

    (b) *signified at a creditors' meeting.*

(5) *The power to extend under sub-paragraph (1)—*

    (a) *may be exercised in respect of a period only once,*

    (b) *may not be used to extend a period by more than 28 days,*

    (c) *may not be used to extend a period which has been extended by the court, and*

    (d) *may not be used to extend a period after expiry.*

109   *Where a period is extended under paragraph 107 or 108, a reference to the period shall be taken as a reference to the period as extended.*

Amendment of provision about time

110—(1)   *The Secretary of State may by order amend a provision of this Schedule which—*

    (a) *requires anything to be done within a specified period of time,*

    (b) *prevents anything from being done after a specified time, or*

    (c) *requires a specified minimum period of notice to be given.*

(2) *An order under this paragraph—*

    (a) *must be made by statutory instrument, and*

    (b) *shall be subject to annulment in pursuance of a resolution of either House of Parliament.*

Interpretation

111—(1)   *In this Schedule—*

'administrative receiver' has the meaning given by section 251,

'administrator' has the meaning given by paragraph 1 and, where the context requires, includes a reference to a former administrator,

'company' includes a company which may enter administration by virtue of Article 3 of the EC Regulation,

'correspondence' includes correspondence by telephonic or other electronic means,

'creditors' meeting' has the meaning given by paragraph 50,

'enters administration' has the meaning given by paragraph 1,

'floating charge' means a charge which is a floating charge on its creation,

'in administration' has the meaning given by paragraph 1,

'hire-purchase agreement' includes a conditional sale agreement, a chattel leasing agreement and a retention of title agreement,

'holder of a qualifying floating charge' in respect of a company's property has the meaning given by paragraph 14,

'market value' means the amount which would be realised on a sale of property in the open market by a willing vendor,

'the purpose of administration' means an objective specified in paragraph 3, and

'unable to pay its debts' has the meaning given by section 123.

(2) A reference in this Schedule to a thing in writing includes a reference to a thing in electronic form.

(3) In this Schedule a reference to action includes a reference to inaction.

Scotland

112   In the application of this Schedule to Scotland—

(a) a reference to filing with the court is a reference to lodging in court, and

(b) a reference to a charge is a reference to a right in security.

113   Where property in Scotland is disposed of under paragraph 70 or 71, the administrator shall grant to the disponee an appropriate document of transfer or conveyance of the property, and—

(a) that document, or

(b) recording, intimation or registration of that document (where recording, intimation or registration of the document is a legal requirement for completion of title to the property), has the effect of disencumbering the property of or, as the case may be, freeing the property from, the security.

114   In Scotland, where goods in the possession of a company under a hire-purchase agreement are disposed of under paragraph 72, the disposal has the effect of extinguishing as against the disponee all rights of the owner of the goods under the agreement.

115—(1) In Scotland, the administrator of a company may make, in or towards the satisfaction of the debt secured by the floating charge, a payment to the holder of a floating charge which has attached to the property subject to the charge.

(2) In Scotland, where the administrator thinks that the company has insufficient property to enable a distribution to be made to unsecured creditors other than by virtue of section 176A(2)(a), he may file a notice to that effect with the registrar of companies.

(3) On delivery of the notice to the registrar of companies, any floating charge granted by the company shall, unless it has already so attached, attach to the property which is subject to the charge and that attachment shall have effect as if each floating charge is a fixed security over the property to which it has attached.

116   In Scotland, the administrator in making any payment in accordance with paragraph 115 shall make such payment subject to the rights of any of the following categories of persons (which rights shall, except to the extent provided in any instrument, have the following order of priority)—

(a) the holder of any fixed security which is over property subject to the floating charge and which ranks prior to, or pari passu with, the floating charge,

(b) creditors in respect of all liabilities and expenses incurred by or on behalf of the administrator,

(c) the administrator in respect of his liabilities, expenses and remuneration and any indemnity to which he is entitled out of the property of the company,

(d) the preferential creditors entitled to payment in accordance with paragraph 65,

(e) the holder of the floating charge in accordance with the priority of that charge in relation to any other floating charge which has attached, and

(f) the holder of a fixed security, other than one referred to in paragraph (a), which is over property subject to the floating charge.

Sections 14, 42   SCHEDULE 1

POWERS OF ADMINISTRATOR OR ADMINISTRATIVE RECEIVER

1. Power to take possession of, collect and get in the property of the company and, for that purpose, to take such proceedings as may seem to him expedient.

2. Power to sell or otherwise dispose of the property of the company by public auction or private contract or, in Scotland, to sell, feu, hire out or otherwise dispose of the property of the company by public roup or private bargain.

3. Power to raise or borrow money and grant security therefor over the property of the company.

4. Power to appoint a solicitor or accountant or other professionally qualified person to assist him in the performance of his functions.

5. Power to bring or defend any action or other legal proceedings in the name and on behalf of the company.

6. Power to refer to arbitration any question affecting the company.

7. Power to effect and maintain insurances in respect of the business and property of the company.

8. Power to use the company's seal.

9. Power to do all acts and to execute in the name and on behalf of the company any deed, receipt or other document.

10. Power to draw, accept, make and endorse any bill of exchange or promissory note in the name and on behalf of the company.

11. Power to appoint any agent to do any business which he is unable to do himself or which can more conveniently be done by an agent and power to employ and dismiss employees.

12. Power to do all such things (including the carrying out of works) as may be necessary for the realisation of the property of the company.

13. Power to make any payment which is necessary or incidental to the performance of his functions.

14. Power to carry on the business of the company.

15. Power to establish subsidiaries of the company.

16. Power to transfer to subsidiaries of the company the whole or any part of the business and property of the company.

17. Power to grant or accept a surrender of a lease or tenancy of any of the property of the company, and to take a lease or tenancy of any property required or convenient for the business of the company.

18. Power to make any arrangement or compromise on behalf of the company.

19. Power to call up any uncalled capital of the company.

20. Power to rank and claim in the bankruptcy, insolvency, sequestration or liquidation

of any person indebted to the company and to receive dividends, and to accede to trust deeds for the creditors of any such person.

21. Power to present or defend a petition for the winding up of the company.

22. Power to change the situation of the company's registered office.

23. Power to do all other things incidental to the exercise of the foregoing powers.

SCHEDULE 2A

EXCEPTIONS TO PROHIBITION ON APPOINTMENT OF ADMINISTRATIVE RECEIVER: SUPPLEMENTARY PROVISIONS

[On 15 June 2003, sch. 2A had not been brought into force.]

Capital market arrangement

1.—*(1) For the purposes of section 72B an arrangement is a capital market arrangement if—*

(a) *it involves a grant of security to a person holding it as trustee for a person who holds a capital market investment issued by a party to the arrangement, or*

(aa) *it involves a grant of security to—*

(i) *a party to the arrangement who issues a capital market investment, or*

(ii) *a person who holds the security as trustee for a party to the arrangement in connection with the issue of a capital market investment, or*

(ab) *it involves a grant of security to a person who holds the security as trustee for a party to the arrangement who agrees to provide finance to another party, or*

(b) *at least one party guarantees the performance of obligations of another party, or*

(c) *at least one party provides security in respect of the performance of obligations of another party, or*

(d) *the arrangement involves an investment of a kind described in articles 83 to 85 of the Financial Services and Markets Act 2000 (Regulated Activities) Order 2001 (SI 2001/544) (options, futures and contracts for differences).*

(2) For the purposes of sub-paragraph (1)—

(a) *a reference to holding as trustee includes a reference to holding as nominee or agent.*

(b) *a reference to holding for a person who holds a capital market investment includes a reference to holding for a number of persons at least one of whom holds a capital market investment, and*

(c) *a person holds a capital market investment if he has a legal or beneficial interest in it; and*

(d) *the reference to the provision of finance includes the provision of an indemnity.*

(3) In section 72B(1) and this paragraph 'party' to an arrangement includes a party to an agreement which—

(a) *forms part of the arrangement,*

(b) *provides for the raising of finance as part of the arrangement, or*

(c) *is necessary for the purposes of implementing the arrangement.*

Capital market investment

2—*(1) For the purposes of section 72B an investment is a capital market investment if it—*

(a) *is within article 77 of the Financial Services and Markets Act 2000 (Regulated Activities) Order 2001 (SI 2001/544) (debt instruments), and*

(b) *is rated, listed or traded or designed to be rated, listed or traded.*

(2) In sub-paragraph (1)—

'rated' means rated for the purposes of investment by an internationally recognised rating agency,

'listed' means admitted to the official list within the meaning given by section 103(1) of the Financial Services and Markets Act 2000 (c. 8) (interpretation), and

'traded' means admitted to trading on a market established under the rules of a recognised investment exchange or on a foreign market.

(3) In sub-paragraph (2)—

'recognised investment exchange' has the meaning given by section 285 of the Financial Services and Markets Act 2000 (recognised investment exchange), and

'foreign market' has the same meaning as 'relevant market' in article 67(2) of the Financial Services and Markets Act 2000 (Financial Promotion) Order 2001 (SI 2001/1335) (foreign markets).

3—(1) An investment is also a capital market investment for the purposes of section 72B if it consists of a bond or commercial paper issued to one or more of the following—

    (a) an investment professional within the meaning of article 19(5) of the Financial Services and Markets Act 2000 (Financial Promotion) Order 2001,

    (b) a person who is, when the agreement mentioned in section 72B(1) is entered into, a certified high net worth individual in relation to a communication within the meaning of article 48(2) of that order,

    (c) a person to whom article 49(2) of that order applies (high net worth company, etc.),

    (d) a person who is, when the agreement mentioned in section 72B(1) is entered into, a certified sophisticated investor in relation to a communication within the meaning of article 50(1) of that order, and

    (e) a person in a State other than the United Kingdom who under the law of that State is not prohibited from investing in bonds or commercial paper.

(2) In sub-paragraph (1)—

'bond' shall be construed in accordance with article 77 of the Financial Services and Markets Act 2000 (Regulated Activities) Order 2001 (SI 2001/544), and

'commercial paper' has the meaning given by article 9(3) of that order.

(3) For the purposes of sub-paragraph (1)—

    (a) in applying article 19(5) of the Financial Promotion Order for the purposes of sub-paragraph (1)(a)—

        (i) in article 19(5)(b), ignore the words after 'exempt person',

        (ii) in article 19(5)(c)(i), for the words from 'the controlled activity' to the end substitute 'a controlled activity', and

        (iii) in article 19(5)(e) ignore the words from 'where the communication' to the end, and

    (b) in applying article 49(2) of that order for the purposes of sub-paragraph (1)(c), ignore article 49(2)(e).

'Agreement'

4 For the purposes of sections 72B and 72E and this Schedule 'agreement' includes an agreement or undertaking effected by—

    (a) contract,

    (b) deed, or

    (c) any other instrument intended to have effect in accordance with the law of England and Wales, Scotland or another jurisdiction.

Debt

5 The debt of at least £50 million referred to in section 72B(1)(a) or 72E(2)(a)—

    (a) may be incurred at any time during the life of the capital market arrangement or financed project, and

    (b) may be expressed wholly or partly in foreign currency (in which case the sterling equivalent shall be calculated as at the time when the arrangement is entered into or the project begins).

Step-in rights

6—(1) For the purposes of sections 72C to 72E a project has 'step-in rights' if a person who provides finance in connection with the project has a conditional entitlement under an agreement to—
  (a) assume sole or principal responsibility under an agreement for carrying out all or part of the project, or
  (b) make arrangements for carrying out all or part of the project.
(2) In sub-paragraph (1) a reference to the provision of finance includes a reference to the provision of an indemnity.

Project company

7—(1) For the purposes of sections 72C to 72E a company is a 'project company' of a project if—
  (a) it holds property for the purpose of the project,
  (b) it has sole or principal responsibility under an agreement for carrying out all or part of the project,
  (c) it is one of a number of companies which together carry out the project,
  (d) it has the purpose of supplying finance to enable the project to be carried out, or
  (e) it is the holding company of a company within any of paragraphs (a) to (d).
(2) But a company is not a 'project company' of a project if—
  (a) it performs a function within sub-paragraph (1)(a) to (d) or is within sub-paragraph (1)(e), but
  (b) it also performs a function which is not—
    (i) within sub-paragraph (1)(a) to (d),
    (ii) related to a function within sub-paragraph (1)(a) to (d), or
    (iii) related to the project.
(3) For the purposes of this paragraph a company carries out all or part of a project whether or not it acts wholly or partly through agents.

'Resources'

8 In section 72C 'resources' includes—
  (a) funds (including payment for the provision of services or facilities),
  (b) assets,
  (c) professional skill,
  (d) the grant of a concession or franchise, and
  (e) any other commercial resource.

'Public body'

9—(1) In section 72C 'public body' means—
  (a) a body which exercises public functions,
  (b) a body specified for the purposes of this paragraph by the Secretary of State, and
  (c) a body within a class specified for the purposes of this paragraph by the Secretary of State.
(2) A specification under sub-paragraph (1) may be—
  (a) general, or
  (b) for the purpose of the application of section 72C to a specified case.

Regulated business

10—(1) For the purposes of section 72D a business is regulated if it is carried on—
  (a) in reliance on a licence granted to a person under section 7 of the Telecommunications Act 1984 (c. 12) (telecommunications service),

(b) in reliance on a licence under section 7 or 7A of the Gas Act 1986 (c. 44) (transport and supply of gas),

(c) in reliance on a licence granted by virtue of section 41C of that Act (power to prescribe additional licensable activity),

(d) in reliance on a licence under section 6 of the Electricity Act 1989 (c. 29) (supply of electricity),

(e) by a water undertaker,

(f) by a sewerage undertaker,

(g) by a universal service provider within the meaning given by section 4(3) and (4) of the Postal Services Act 2000 (c. 26),

(h) by the Post Office company within the meaning given by section 62 of that Act (transfer of property),

(i) by a relevant subsidiary of the Post Office Company within the meaning given by section 63 of that Act (government holding),

(j) in reliance on a licence under section 8 of the Railways Act 1993 (c. 43) (railway services),

(k) in reliance on a licence exemption under section 7 of that Act (subject to sub-paragraph (2) below),

(l) by the operator of a system of transport which is deemed to be a railway for a purpose of Part I of that Act by virtue of section 81(2) of that Act (tramways, etc.), or

(m) by the operator of a vehicle carried on flanged wheels along a system within paragraph (l).

(2) Sub-paragraph (1)(k) does not apply to the operator of a railway asset on a railway unless on some part of the railway there is a permitted line speed exceeding 40 kilometres per hour.

'Person'

11   A reference to a person in this Schedule includes a reference to a partnership or another unincorporated group of persons.

Sections 165, 167   SCHEDULE 4

POWERS OF LIQUIDATOR IN A WINDING UP

PART I   POWERS EXERCISABLE WITH SANCTION

1.   Power to pay any class of creditors in full.

2.   Power to make any compromise or arrangement with creditors or persons claiming to be creditors, or having or alleging themselves to have any claim (present or future, certain or contingent, ascertained or sounding only in damages) against the company, or whereby the company may be rendered liable.

3.   Power to compromise, on such terms as may be agreed—

(a) all calls and liabilities to calls, all debts and liabilities capable of resulting in debts, and all claims (present or future, certain or contingent, ascertained or sounding only in damages) subsisting or supposed to subsist between the company and a contributory or alleged contributory or other debtor or person apprehending liability to the company, and

(b) all questions in any way relating to or affecting the assets or the winding up of the company,

and take any security for the discharge of any such call, debt, liability or claim and give a complete discharge in respect of it.

3A.   Power to bring legal proceedings under section 213, 214, 238, 239, 242, 243 or 423.

[On 15 June 2003, para. 3A had not been brought into force.]

PART II   POWERS EXERCISABLE WITHOUT SANCTION IN
VOLUNTARY WINDING UP, WITH SANCTION IN WINDING
UP BY THE COURT

4.   Power to bring or defend any action or other legal proceeding in the name and on behalf of the company.

5.   Power to carry on the business of the company so far as may be necessary for its beneficial winding up.

PART III   POWERS EXERCISABLE WITHOUT SANCTION
IN ANY WINDING UP

6.   Power to sell any of the company's property by public auction or private contract with power to transfer the whole of it to any person or to sell the same in parcels.

7.   Power to do all acts and execute, in the name and on behalf of the company, all deeds, receipts and other documents and for that purpose to use, when necessary, the company's seal.

8.   Power to prove, rank and claim in the bankruptcy, insolvency or sequestration of any contributory for any balance against his estate, and to receive dividends in the bankruptcy, insolvency or sequestration in respect of that balance, as a separate debt due from the bankrupt or insolvent, and rateably with the other separate creditors.

9.   Power to draw, accept, make and endorse any bill of exchange or promissory note in the name and on behalf of the company, with the same effect with respect to the company's liability as if the bill or note had been drawn, accepted, made or endorsed by or on behalf of the company in the course of its business.

10.   Power to raise on the security of the assets of the company any money requisite.

11.   Power to take out in his official name letters of administration to any deceased contributory, and to do in his official name any other act necessary for obtaining payment of any money due from a contributory or his estate which cannot conveniently be done in the name of the company.

In all such cases the money due is deemed, for the purpose of enabling the liquidator to take out the letters of administration or recover the money, to be due to the liquidator himself.

12.   Power to appoint an agent to do any business which the liquidator is unable to do himself.

13.   Power to do all such other things as may be necessary for winding up the company's affairs and distributing its assets.

Section 386   SCHEDULE 6

THE CATEGORIES OF PREFERENTIAL DEBTS

[Paragraphs 1 to 7 of sch. 6 will be repealed when the Enterprise Act 2002, s. 251(1), is brought into force.]

Category 1: Debts due to Inland Revenue

1.   Sums due at the relevant date from the debtor on account of deductions of income tax from emoluments paid during the period of 12 months next before that date.

The deductions here referred to are those which the debtor was liable to make under section 203 of the Income and Corporation Taxes Act 1988 (pay as you earn), less the amount of the repayments of income tax which the debtor was liable to make during that period.

2.   Sums due at the relevant date from the debtor in respect of such deductions as are required to be made by the debtor for that period under section 559 of the Income and Corporation Taxes Act 1988 (sub-contractors in the construction industry).

Category 2: Debts due to Customs and Excise

3.   Any value added tax which is referable to the period of 6 months next before the relevant date (which period is referred to below as 'the 6-month period').
For the purposes of this paragraph—

(a) where the whole of the prescribed accounting period to which any value added tax is attributable falls within the 6-month period, the whole amount of that tax is referable to that period; and

(b) in any other case the amount of any value added tax which is referable to the 6-month period is the proportion of the tax which is equal to such proportion (if any) of the accounting reference period in question as falls within the 6-month period;

and in sub-paragraph (a) 'prescribed' means prescribed by regulations under the Value Added Tax Act 1994.

3A.   Any insurance premium tax which is referable to the period of 6 months next before the relevant date (which period is referred to below as 'the 6-month period').
For the purposes of this paragraph—

(a) where the whole of the accounting period to which any insurance premium tax is attributable falls within the 6-month period, the whole amount of that tax is referable to that period; and

(b) in any other case the amount of any insurance premium tax which is referable to the 6-month period is the proportion of the tax which is equal to such proportion (if any) of the accounting period in question as falls within the 6-month period;

and references here to accounting periods shall be construed in accordance with Part III of the Finance Act 1994.

3B.   Any landfill tax which is referable to the period of 6 months next before the relevant date (which period is referred to below as 'the 6-month period').
For the purposes of this paragraph—

(a) where the whole of the accounting period to which any landfill tax is attributable falls within the 6-month period, the whole amount of that tax is referable to that period; and

(b) in any other case the amount of any landfill tax which is referable to the 6-month period is the proportion of the tax which is equal to such proportion (if any) of the accounting period in question as falls within the 6-month period;

and references here to accounting periods shall be construed in accordance with Part III of the Finance Act 1996.

3C.   Any climate change levy which is referable to the period of 6 months next before the relevant date (which period is referred to below as 'the 6-month period').
For the purposes of this paragraph—

(a) where the whole of the accounting period to which any climate change levy is attributable falls within the 6-month period, the whole amount of that levy is referable to that period; and

(b) in any other case the amount of any climate change levy which is referable to the 6-month period is the proportion of the levy which is equal to such proportion (if any) of the accounting period in question as falls within the 6-month period;

and references here to accounting periods shall be construed in accordance with Schedule 6 to the Finance Act 2000.

3D.   Any aggregates levy which is referable to the period of 6 months next before the relevant date (which period is referred to below as 'the 6-month period').
For the purposes of this paragraph—

(a) where the whole of the accounting period to which any aggregates levy is attributable falls within the 6-month period, the whole amount of that levy is referable to that period; and

(b) in any other case the amount of any aggregates levy which is referable to the
6-month period is the proportion of the levy which is equal to such proportion
(if any) of the accounting period in question as falls within the 6-month period;
and references here to accounting periods shall be construed in accordance with Part 2 of the
Finance Act 2001.

4.   The amount of any car tax which is due at the relevant date from the debtor and
which became due within a period of 12 months next before that date.

5.   Any amount which is due—
(a) by way of general betting duty, bingo duty or gaming duty, or
(b) under section 12(1) of the Betting and Gaming Duties Act 1981 (general betting
duty and pool betting duty recoverable from agent collecting stakes),
from the debtor at the relevant date and which became due within the period of 12 months
next before that date.

5A.   The amount of any excise duty on beer which is due at the relevant date from the
debtor and which became due within a period of 6 months next before that date.

5B.   Any amount which is due by way of lottery duty from the debtor at the relevant date
and which became due within the period of 12 months next before that date.

5C.   Any amount which is due by way of air passenger duty from the debtor at
the relevant date and which became due within the period of six months next before that
date.

Category 3: Social security contributions

6.   All sums which on the relevant date are due from the debtor on account of Class 1 or
Class 2 contributions under the Social Security Contributions and Benefits Act 1992 or the
Social Security (Northern Ireland) Act 1975 and which became due from the debtor in the 12
months next before the relevant date.
[*Before an amendment was made by the Social Security (Consequential Provisions) Act 1992, sch. 2,
para. 73, this paragraph referred to the Social Security Act 1975 instead of the Social Security Contributions and Benefits Act 1992. The reference in paragraph 7 to 'either of those Acts of 1975' was not
amended to reflect the amendment made in this paragraph. The reference to the Social Security (Northern Ireland) Act 1975 is to be construed as including a reference to the Social Security Contributions
and Benefits (Northern Ireland) Act 1992 (Social Security (Consequential Provisions) (Northern Ireland) Act 1992, s. 2(4)).*]

7.   All sums which on the relevant date have been assessed on and are due from the
debtor on account of Class 4 contributions under either of those Acts of 1975, being sums
which—
(a) are due to the Commissioners of Inland Revenue (rather than to the Secretary of
State or a Northern Ireland department), and
(b) are assessed on the debtor up to 5 April next before the relevant date,
but not exceeding, in the whole, any one year's assessment.

Category 4: Contributions to occupational pension schemes, etc.

8.   Any sum which is owed by the debtor and is a sum to which Schedule 4 to the Pension
Schemes Act 1993 applies (contributions to occupational pension schemes and state scheme
premiums).

Category 5: Remuneration, etc., of employees

9.   So much of any amount which—
(a) is owed by the debtor to a person who is or has been an employee of the debtor,
and

(b) is payable by way of remuneration in respect of the whole or any part of the period of 4 months next before the relevant date,

as does not exceed so much as may be prescribed by order made by the Secretary of State.

10.   An amount owed by way of accrued holiday remuneration, in respect of any period of employment before the relevant date, to a person whose employment by the debtor has been terminated, whether before, on or after that date.

11.   So much of any sum owed in respect of money advanced for the purpose as has been applied for the payment of a debt which, if it had not been paid, would have been a debt falling within paragraph 9 or 10.

12.   So much of any amount which—

(a) is ordered (whether before or after the relevant date) to be paid by the debtor under the Reserve Forces (Safeguard of Employment) Act 1985, and

(b) is so ordered in respect of a default made by the debtor before that date in the discharge of his obligations under that Act,

as does not exceed such amount as may be prescribed by order made by the Secretary of State.

Interpretation for Category 5

13.—(1)   For the purposes of paragraphs 9 to 12, a sum is payable by the debtor to a person by way of remuneration in respect of any period if—

(a) it is paid as wages or salary (whether payable for time or for piece work or earned wholly or partly by way of commission) in respect of services rendered to the debtor in that period, or

(b) it is an amount falling within the following sub-paragraph and is payable by the debtor in respect of that period.

(2) An amount falls within this sub-paragraph if it is—

(a) a guarantee payment under Part III of the Employment Rights Act 1996 (employee without work to do);

(b) any payment for time off under section 53 (time off to look for work or arrange training) or section 56 (time off for ante-natal care) of that Act or under section 169 of the Trade Union and Labour Relations (Consolidation) Act 1992 (time off for carrying out trade union duties etc.);

(c) remuneration on suspension on medical grounds, or on maternity grounds, under Part VII of the Employment Rights Act 1996; or

(d) remuneration under a protective award under section 189 of the Trade Union and Labour Relations (Consolidation) Act 1992 (redundancy dismissal with compensation).

14.—(1)   This paragraph relates to a case in which a person's employment has been terminated by or in consequence of his employer going into liquidation or being adjudged bankrupt or (his employer being a company not in liquidation) by or in consequence of—

(a) a receiver being appointed as mentioned in section 40 of this Act (debentureholders secured by floating charge), or

(b) the appointment of a receiver under section 53(6) or 54(5) of this Act (Scottish company with property subject to floating charge), or

(c) the taking of possession by debenture-holders (so secured), as mentioned in section 196 of the Companies Act.

(2) For the purposes of paragraphs 9 to 12, holiday remuneration is deemed to have accrued to that person in respect of any period of employment if, by virtue of his contract of employment or of any enactment that remuneration would have accrued in respect of that period if his employment had continued until he became entitled to be allowed the holiday.

(3) The reference in sub-paragraph (2) to any enactment includes an order or direction made under an enactment.

15.   Without prejudice to paragraphs 13 and 14—
   (a) any remuneration payable by the debtor to a person in respect of a period of holiday or of absence from work through sickness or other good cause is deemed to be wages or (as the case may be) salary in respect of services rendered to the debtor in that period, and
   (b) references here and in those paragraphs to remuneration in respect of a period of holiday include any sums which, if they had been paid, would have been treated for the purposes of the enactments relating to social security as earnings in respect of that period.

Category 6: Levies on coal and steel production

15A.   Any sums due at the relevant date from the debtor in respect of—
   (a) the levies on the production of coal and steel referred to in Articles 49 and 50 of the E.C.S.C. Treaty, or
   (b) any surcharge for delay provided for in Article 50(3) of that Treaty and Article 6 of Decision 3/52 of the High Authority of the Coal and Steel Community.

Orders

16.   An order under paragraph 9 or 12—
   (a) may contain such transitional provisions as may appear to the Secretary of State necessary or expedient;
   (b) shall be made by statutory instrument subject to annulment in pursuance of a resolution of either House of Parliament.

SCHEDULE 10

Section 430

PUNISHMENT OF OFFENCES UNDER THIS ACT

Section of Act creating offence	General nature of offence	Mode of prosecution	Punishment	Daily default fine (where applicable)
6A(1)	False representation or fraud for purpose of obtaining members' or creditors' approval of proposed voluntary arrangement.	1. On indictment. 2. Summary.	7 years or a fine, or both. 6 months or the statutory maximum, or both.	
12(2)	Company and others failing to state in correspondence etc. that administrator appointed.	Summary.	One-fifth of the statutory maximum.	
15(8)	Failure of administrator to register office copy of court order permitting disposal of charged property.	Summary.	One-fifth of the statutory maximum.	One-fiftieth of the statutory maximum.
18(5)	Failure of administrator to register office copy of court order varying or discharging administration order.	Summary.	One-fifth of the statutory maximum.	One-fiftieth of the statutory maximum.
21(3)	Administrator failing to register administration order and give notice of appointment.	Summary.	One-fifth of the statutory maximum.	One-fiftieth of the statutory maximum.
22(6)	Failure to comply with provisions relating to statement of affairs, where administrator appointed.	1. On indictment. 2. Summary.	A fine. The statutory maximum.	One-tenth of the statutory maximum.
23(3)	Administrator failing to send out, register and lay before creditors statement of his proposals.	Summary.	One-fifth of the statutory maximum.	One-fiftieth of the statutory maximum.
24(7)	Administrator failing to file court order discharging administration order under s. 24.	Summary.	One-fifth of the statutory maximum.	One-fiftieth of the statutory maximum.

Continued

Schedule 10 continued

Section of Act creating offence	General nature of offence	Mode of prosecution	Punishment	Daily default fine (where applicable)
27(6)	*Administrator failing to file court order discharging administration order under s. 27.*	*Summary.*	*One-fifth of the statutory maximum.*	*One-fiftieth of the statutory maximum.*
30	Body corporate acting as receiver.	1. On indictment. 2. Summary.	A fine. The statutory maximum.	
31	*Undischarged bankrupt acting as receiver or manager.*	1. On indictment. 2. Summary.	2 years or a fine; or both. 6 months or the statutory maximum, or both.	
38(5)	Receiver failing to deliver accounts to registrar.	Summary.	One-fifth of the statutory maximum.	One-fiftieth of the statutory maximum.
39(2)	Company and others failing to state in correspondence that receiver appointed.	Summary.	One-fifth of the statutory maximum.	One-fiftieth of the statutory maximum.
43(6)	Administrative receiver failing to file office copy of order permitting disposal of charged property.	Summary.	One-fifth of the statutory maximum.	One-fiftieth of the statutory maximum.
45(5)	*Administrative receiver failing to file notice of vacation of office.*	*Summary.*	*One-fifth of the statutory maximum.*	*One-fiftieth of the statutory maximum.*
46(4)	Administrative receiver failing to give notice of his appointment.	Summary.	One-fifth of the statutory maximum.	One-fiftieth of the statutory maximum.
47(6)	Failure to comply with provisions relating to statement of affairs, where administrative receiver appointed.	1. On indictment. 2. Summary.	A fine. The statutory maximum.	One-tenth of the statutory maximum.

Section	Description	Mode of prosecution	Punishment	Daily default fine
48(8)	Administrative receiver failing to comply with requirements as to his report.	Summary.	One-fifth of the statutory maximum.	One-fiftieth of the statutory maximum.
. . .				
85(2)	Company failing to give notice in Gazette of resolution for voluntary winding up.	Summary.	One-fifth of the statutory maximum.	One-fiftieth of the statutory maximum.
89(4)	Director making statutory declaration of company's solvency without reasonable grounds for his opinion.	1. On indictment. 2. Summary.	2 years or a fine; or both. 6 months or the statutory maximum, or both.	
89(6)	Declaration under section 89 not delivered to registrar within prescribed time.	Summary.	One-fifth of the statutory maximum.	One-fiftieth of the statutory maximum.
93(3)	Liquidator failing to summon general meeting of company at each year's end.	Summary.	One-fifth of the statutory maximum.	One-fiftieth of the statutory maximum.
94(4)	Liquidator failing to send to registrar a copy of account of winding up and return of final meeting.	Summary.	One-fifth of the statutory maximum.	One-fiftieth of the statutory maximum.
94(6)	Liquidator failing to call final meeting.	Summary.	One-fifth of the statutory maximum.	
95(8)	Liquidator failing to comply with s. 95, where company insolvent.	Summary.	The statutory maximum.	
98(6)	Company failing to comply with s. 98 in respect of summoning and giving notice of creditors' meeting.	1. On indictment. 2. Summary.	A fine. The statutory maximum.	
99(3)	Directors failing to attend and lay statement in prescribed form before creditors' meeting.	1. On indictment. 2. Summary.	A fine. The statutory maximum.	

Continued

Schedule 10 continued

Section of Act creating offence	General nature of offence	Mode of prosecution	Punishment	Daily default fine (where applicable)
105(3)	Liquidator failing to summon company general meeting and creditors' meeting at each year's end.	Summary.	One-fifth of the statutory maximum.	
106(4)	Liquidator failing to send to registrar account of winding up and return of final meetings.	Summary.	One-fifth of the statutory maximum.	One-fiftieth of the statutory maximum.
106(6)	Liquidator failing to call final meeting of company or creditors.	Summary.	One-fifth of the statutory maximum.	
109(2)	Liquidator failing to publish notice of his appointment.	Summary.	One-fifth of the statutory maximum.	One-fiftieth of the statutory maximum.
114(4)	Directors exercising powers in breach of s. 114, where no liquidator.	Summary.	The statutory maximum.	
131(7)	Failing to comply with requirements as to statement of affairs, where liquidator appointed.	1. On indictment. 2. Summary.	A fine. The statutory maximum.	
164	Giving, offering etc. corrupt inducement affecting appointment of liquidator.	1. On indictment. 2. Summary.	A fine. The statutory maximum.	
166(7)	Liquidator failing to comply with requirements of s. 166 in creditors' voluntary winding up.	Summary.	The statutory maximum.	
188(2)	Default in compliance with s. 188 as to notification that company being wound up.	Summary.	One-fifth of the statutory maximum.	One-tenth of the statutory maximum.

Section	General nature of offence	Mode of prosecution	Punishment	Daily default fine
192(2)	Liquidator failing to notify registrar as to progress of winding up.	Summary.	One-fifth of the statutory maximum.	One-fiftieth of the statutory maximum.
201(4)	Failing to deliver to registrar office copy of court order deferring dissolution.	Summary.	One-fifth of the statutory maximum.	One-fiftieth of the statutory maximum.
203(6)	Failing to deliver to registrar copy of directions or result of appeal under s. 203.	Summary.	One-fifth of the statutory maximum.	One-fiftieth of the statutory maximum.
204(7)	Liquidator failing to deliver to registrar copy of court order for early dissolution.	Summary.	One-fifth of the statutory maximum.	One-fiftieth of the statutory maximum.
204(8)	Failing to deliver to registrar copy of court order deferring early dissolution.	Summary.	One-fifth of the statutory maximum.	One-fiftieth of the statutory maximum.
205(7)	Failing to deliver to registrar copy of Secretary of State's directions or court order deferring dissolution.	Summary.	One-fifth of the statutory maximum.	One-fiftieth of the statutory maximum.
206(1)	Fraud etc. in anticipation of winding up.	1. On indictment. 2. Summary.	7 years or a fine, or both. 6 months or the statutory maximum, or both.	
206(2)	Privity to fraud in anticipation of winding up; fraud, or privity to fraud, after commencement of winding up.	1. On indictment. 2. Summary.	7 years or a fine, or both. 6 months or the statutory maximum, or both.	
206(5)	Knowingly taking in pawn or pledge, or otherwise receiving, company property.	1. On indictment. 2. Summary.	7 years or a fine, or both. 6 months or the statutory maximum, or both.	

Continued

Schedule 10 continued

Section of Act creating offence	General nature of offence	Mode of prosecution	Punishment	Daily default fine (where applicable)
207	Officer of company entering into transaction in fraud of company's creditors.	1. On indictment. 2. Summary.	2 years or a fine, or both. 6 months or the statutory maximum, or both.	
208	Officer of company misconducting himself in course of winding up.	1. On indictment. 2. Summary.	7 years or a fine, or both. 6 months or the statutory maximum, or both.	
209	Officer or contributory destroying, falsifying, etc. company's books.	1. On indictment. 2. Summary.	7 years or a fine, or both. 6 months or the statutory maximum, or both.	
210	Officer of company making material omission from statement relating to company's affairs.	1. On indictment. 2. Summary.	7 years or a fine, or both. 6 months or the statutory maximum, or both.	
211	False representation or fraud for purpose of obtaining creditors' consent to an agreement in connection with winding up.	1. On indictment. 2. Summary.	7 years or a fine, or both. 6 months or the statutory maximum, or both.	
216(4)	Contravening restrictions on reuse of name of company in insolvent liquidation.	1. On indictment. 2. Summary.	7 years or a fine, or both. 6 months or the statutory maximum, or both.	
235(5)	Failing to cooperate with officer-holder.	1. On indictment. 2. Summary.	A fine. The statutory maximum.	One-tenth of the statutory maximum.

. . .

Continued

Sch. A1, para. 9(2).	Directors failing to notify nominee of beginning of moratorium.	1. On indictment. 2. Summary.	2 years or a fine, or both. 6 months or the statutory maximum, or both.
Sch. A1, para. 10(3).	Nominee failing to advertise or notify beginning of moratorium.	Summary.	One-fifth of the statutory maximum.
Sch. A1, para. 11(2).	Nominee failing to advertise or notify beginning of moratorium.	Summary.	One-fifth of the statutory maximum.
Sch. A1, para. 16(2).	Company and officers failing to state in correspondence etc. that moratorium in force.	Summary.	One-fifth of the statutory maximum.
Sch. A1, para. 17(3)(a).	Company obtaining credit without disclosing existence of moratorium.	1. On indictment. 2. Summary.	A fine. The statutory maximum.
Sch. A1, para. 17(3)(b).	Obtaining credit for company without disclosing existence of moratorium.	1. On indictment. 2. Summary.	2 years or a fine, or both. 6 months or the statutory maximum, or both.
Sch. A1, para. 18(3)(a).	Company disposing of property otherwise than in ordinary way of business.	1. On indictment. 2. Summary.	A fine The statutory maximum.
Sch. A1, para. 18(3)(b).	Authorising or permitting disposal of company property.	1. On indictment. 2. Summary.	2 years or a fine, or both. 6 months or the statutory maximum, or both.
Sch. A1, para. 19(3)(a).	Company making payments in respect of liabilities existing before beginning of moratorium.	1. On indictment. 2. Summary.	A fine. The statutory maximum.
Sch. A1, para. 19(3)(b).	Authorising or permitting such a payment.	1. On indictment. 2. Summary.	2 years or a fine, or both. 6 months or the statutory maximum, or both.
Sch. A1, para. 20(9).	Directors failing to send to registrar office copy of court order permitting disposal of charged property.	Summary.	One fifth of the statutory maximum.
Sch. A1, para. 22(1).	Company disposing of charged property.	1. On indictment. 2. Summary.	A fine. The statutory maximum.

Schedule 10 continued

Section of Act creating offence	General nature of offence	Mode of prosecution	Punishment	Daily default fine (where applicable)
Sch. A1, para. 22(2).	Authorising or permitting such a disposal.	1. On indictment. 2. Summary.	2 years or a fine, or both. 6 months or the statutory maximum, or both.	
Sch. A1, para. 23(1)(a).	Company entering into market contract, etc.	1. On indictment. 2. Summary.	A fine. The statutory maximum.	
Sch. A1, para. 23(1)(b).	Authorising or permitting company to do so.	1. On indictment. 2. Summary.	2 years or a fine, or both. 6 months or the statutory maximum, or both.	
Sch. A1, para. 25(6).	Nominee failing to give notice of withdrawal of consent to act.	Summary.	One-fifth of the statutory maximum.	
Sch. A1, para. 34(3).	Nominee failing to give notice of extension of moratorium.	Summary.	One-fifth of the statutory maximum.	
Sch. A1, para. 41(2).	Fraud or privity to fraud in anticipation of moratorium.	1. On indictment. 2. Summary.	7 years or a fine, or both. 6 months or the statutory maximum, or both.	
Sch. A1, para. 41(3).	Fraud or privity to fraud during moratorium.	1. On indictment. 2. Summary.	7 years or a fine, or both. 6 months or the statutory maximum, or both.	

Sch. A1, para. 41(7).	Knowingly taking in pawn or pledge, or otherwise receiving, company property.	1. On indictment. 2. Summary.	7 years or a fine, or both. 6 months or the statutory maximum, or both.	
Sch. A1, para. 42(1).	False representation or fraud for purpose of obtaining or extending moratorium.	1. On indictment. 2. Summary.	7 years or a fine, or both. 6 months or the statutory maximum, or both.	
Sch. B1, para. 18(7).	Making false statement in statutory declaration where administrator appointed by holder of floating charge.	1. On indictment. 2. Summary.	2 years, or a fine or both. 6 months or the statutory maximum, or both.	
Sch. B1, para. 20.	Holder of floating charge failing to notify administrator or others of commencement of appointment.	1. On indictment. 2. Summary.	2 years, or a fine or both. 6 months, or the statutory maximum or both.	One-tenth of the statutory maximum.
Sch. B1, para. 27(4).	Making false statement in statutory declaration where appointment of administrator proposed by company or directors.	1. On indictment. 2. Summary.	2 years, or a fine or both. 6 months, or the statutory maximum or both.	
Sch. B1, para. 29(7).	Making false statement in statutory declaration where administrator appointed by company or directors.	1. On indictment. 2. Summary.	2 years, or a fine or both. 6 months, or the statutory maximum or both.	
Sch. B1, para. 32.	Company or directors failing to notify administrator or others of commencement of appointment.	1. On indictment. 2. Summary.	2 years, or a fine or both. 6 months, or the statutory maximum or both.	One-tenth of the statutory maximum.

Continued

Section of Act creating offence	General nature of offence	Mode of prosecution	Punishment	Daily default fine (where applicable)
Sch. B1, para. 45(2).	Administrator, company or officer failing to state in business document that administrator appointed.	Summary.	One-fifth of the statutory maximum.	
Sch. B1, para. 46(9).	Administrator failing to give notice of his appointment.	Summary.	One-fifth of the statutory maximum.	One-fiftieth of the statutory maximum.
Sch. B1, para. 48(4).	Failing to comply with provisions about statement of affairs where administrator appointed.	1. On indictment. 2. Summary.	A fine. The statutory maximum.	One-tenth of the statutory maximum.
Sch. B1, para. 49(7).	Administrator failing to send out statement of his proposals.	Summary.	One-fifth of the statutory maximum.	One-fiftieth of the statutory maximum.
Sch. B1, para. 51(5).	Administrator failing to arrange initial creditors' meeting.	Summary.	One-fifth of the statutory maximum.	One-fiftieth of the statutory maximum.
Sch. B1, para. 53(3).	Administrator failing to report decision taken at initial creditors' meeting.	Summary.	One-fifth of the statutory maximum.	One-fiftieth of the statutory maximum.
Sch. B1, para. 54(7).	Administrator failing to report decision taken at creditors' meeting summoned to consider revised proposal.	Summary.	One-fifth of the statutory maximum.	One-fiftieth of the statutory maximum.
Sch. B1, para. 56(2).	Administrator failing to summon creditors' meeting.	Summary.	One-fifth of the statutory maximum.	One-fiftieth of the statutory maximum.
Sch. B1, para. 71(6).	Administrator failing to file court order enabling disposal of charged property.	Summary.	One-fifth of the statutory maximum.	One-fiftieth of the statutory maximum.
Sch. B1, para. 72(5).	Administrator failing to file court order enabling disposal of hire-purchase property.	Summary.	One-fifth of the statutory maximum.	One-fiftieth of the statutory maximum.
Sch. B1, para. 77(3).	Administrator failing to notify Registrar of Companies of automatic end of administration.	Summary.	One-fifth of the statutory maximum.	One-fiftieth of the statutory maximum.
Sch. B1, para. 78(6).	Administrator failing to give notice of extension by consent of term of office.	Summary.	One-fifth of the statutory maximum.	One-fiftieth of the statutory maximum.
Sch. B1, para. 80(6).	Administrator failing to give notice of termination of administration where objective achieved.	Summary.	One-fifth of the statutory maximum.	One-fiftieth of the statutory maximum.

Sch. B1, para. 84(9).	Administrator failing to comply with provisions where company moves to dissolution.	Summary.	One-fifth of the statutory maximum.	One-fiftieth of the statutory maximum.
Sch. B1, para. 86(3).	Administrator failing to notify Registrar of Companies where court terminates administration.	Summary.	One-fifth of the statutory maximum.	One-fiftieth of the statutory maximum.
Sch. B1, para. 89(3).	Administrator failing to give notice on ceasing to be qualified.	Summary.	One-fifth of the statutory maximum.	One-fiftieth of the statutory maximum.
. . .				

[The entries relating to ss. 12(2), 15(8), 18(5), 21(3), 22(6), 23(3), 24(7) and 27(6) will be repealed when the Enterprise Act 2002, sch. 17, is brought into force. The word 'Undischarged' in the entry for s. 31 will be repealed when the Enterprise Act 2002, sch. 17, is brought into force. The entry in column 5 (daily default fine) relating to s. 45(5) would be repealed if the relevant provision of sch. 24 to the Companies Act 1989 were brought into force. The entries relating to sch. B1 will be inserted when the Enterprise Act 2002, sch. 17 is brought into force.]

Company Directors Disqualification Act 1986
(1986, c. 46)

An Act to consolidate certain enactments relating to the disqualification of persons from being directors of companies, and from being otherwise concerned with a company's affairs.

[25 July 1986]

Preliminary

1   Disqualification orders: general

(1) In the circumstances specified below in this Act a court may, and under sections 6 and 9A shall, make against a person a disqualification order, that is to say an order that for a period specified in the order—

    (a) he shall not be a director of a company, act as receiver of a company's property or in any way, whether directly or indirectly, be concerned or take part in the promotion, formation or management of a company unless (in each case) he has the leave of the court, and

    (b) he shall not act as an insolvency practitioner.

(2) In each section of this Act which gives to a court power or, as the case may be, imposes on it the duty to make a disqualification order there is specified the maximum (and, in section 6, the minimum) period of disqualification which may or (as the case may be) must be imposed by means of the order and, unless the court otherwise orders, the period of disqualification so imposed shall begin at the end of the period of 21 days beginning with the date of the order.

(3) Where a disqualification order is made against a person who is already subject to such an order or to a disqualification undertaking, the periods specified in those orders or, as the case may be, in the order and the undertaking shall run concurrently.

(4) A disqualification order may be made on grounds which are or include matters other than criminal convictions, notwithstanding that the person in respect of whom it is to be made may be criminally liable in respect of those matters.

1A   Disqualification undertakings: general

(1) In the circumstances specified in sections 7 and 8 the Secretary of State may accept a disqualification undertaking, that is to say an undertaking by any person that, for a period specified in the undertaking, the person—

    (a) will not be a director of a company, act as receiver of a company's property or in any way, whether directly or indirectly, be concerned or take part in the promotion, formation or management of a company unless (in each case) he has the leave of a court, and

    (b) will not act as an insolvency practitioner.

(2) The maximum period which may be specified in a disqualification undertaking is 15 years; and the minimum period which may be specified in a disqualification undertaking under section 7 is two years.

(3) Where a disqualification undertaking by a person who is already subject to such an undertaking or to a disqualification order is accepted, the periods specified in those undertakings or (as the case may be) the undertaking and the order shall run concurrently.

(4) In determining whether to accept a disqualification undertaking by any person, the Secretary of State may take account of matters other than criminal convictions, notwithstanding that the person may be criminally liable in respect of those matters.

Disqualification for general misconduct in connection with companies

2   Disqualification on conviction of indictable offence

(1) The court may make a disqualification order against a person where he is convicted of an indictable offence (whether on indictment or summarily) in connection with the promotion, formation, management, liquidation or striking off of a company, with the receivership of a company's property or with his being an administrative receiver of a company.

(2) 'The court' for this purpose means—

(a) any court having jurisdiction to wind up the company in relation to which the offence was committed, or

(b) the court by or before which the person is convicted of the offence, or

(c) in the case of a summary conviction in England and Wales, any other magistrates' court acting for the same petty sessions area;

and for the purposes of this section the definition of 'indictable offence' in Schedule 1 to the Interpretation Act 1978 applies for Scotland as it does for England and Wales.

(3) The maximum period of disqualification under this section is—

(a) where the disqualification order is made by a court of summary jurisdiction, 5 years, and

(b) in any other case, 15 years.

3   Disqualification for persistent breaches of companies legislation

(1) The court may make a disqualification order against a person where it appears to it that he has been persistently in default in relation to provisions of the companies legislation requiring any return, account or other document to be filed with, delivered or sent, or notice of any matter to be given, to the registrar of companies.

(2) On an application to the court for an order to be made under this section, the fact that a person has been persistently in default in relation to such provisions as are mentioned above may (without prejudice to its proof in any other manner) be conclusively proved by showing that in the 5 years ending with the date of the application he has been adjudged guilty (whether or not on the same occasion) of three or more defaults in relation to those provisions.

(3) A person is to be treated under subsection (2) as being adjudged guilty of a default in relation to any provision of that legislation if—

(a) he is convicted (whether on indictment or summarily) of an offence consisting in a contravention of or failure to comply with that provision (whether on his own part or on the part of any company), or

(b) a default order is made against him, that is to say an order under any of the following provisions—

(i) section 242(4) of the Companies Act (order requiring delivery of company accounts),

(ia) section 245B of that Act (order requiring preparation of revised accounts),

(ii) section 713 of that Act (enforcement of company's duty to make returns),

(iii) section 41 of the Insolvency Act (enforcement of receiver's or manager's duty to make returns), or

(iv) section 170 of that Act (corresponding provision for liquidator in winding up),

in respect of any such contravention of or failure to comply with that provision (whether on his own part or on the part of any company).

(4) In this section 'the court' means any court having jurisdiction to wind up any of the companies in relation to which the offence or other default has been or is alleged to have been committed.

(5) The maximum period of disqualification under this section is 5 years.

4   Disqualification for fraud, etc., in winding up

(1) The court may make a disqualification order against a person if, in the course of the winding up of a company, it appears that he—

    (a) has been guilty of an offence for which he is liable (whether he has been convicted or not) under section 458 of the Companies Act (fraudulent trading), or

    (b) has otherwise been guilty, while an officer or liquidator of the company, receiver of the company's property or administrative receiver of the company, of any fraud in relation to the company or of any breach of his duty as such officer, liquidator, receiver or administrative receiver.

(2) In this section 'the court' means any court having jurisdiction to wind up any of the companies in relation to which the offence or other default has been or is alleged to have been committed; and 'officer' includes a shadow director.

(3) The maximum period of disqualification under this section is 15 years.

5   Disqualification on summary conviction

(1) An offence counting for the purposes of this section is one of which a person is convicted (either on indictment or summarily) in consequence of a contravention of, or failure to comply with, any provision of the companies legislation requiring a return, account or other document to be filed with, delivered or sent, or notice of any matter to be given, to the registrar of companies (whether the contravention or failure is on the person's own part or on the part of any company).

(2) Where a person is convicted of a summary offence counting for those purposes, the court by which he is convicted (or, in England and Wales, any other magistrates' court acting for the same petty sessions area) may make a disqualification order against him if the circumstances specified in the next subsection are present.

(3) Those circumstances are that, during the 5 years ending with the date of the conviction, the person has had made against him, or has been convicted of, in total not less than 3 default orders and offences counting for the purposes of this section; and those offences may include that of which he is convicted as mentioned in subsection (2) and any other offence of which he is convicted on the same occasion.

(4) For the purposes of this section—

    (a) the definition of 'summary offence' in Schedule 1 to the Interpretation Act 1978 applies for Scotland as for England and Wales, and

    (b) 'default order' means the same as in section 3(3)(b).

(5) The maximum period of disqualification under this section is 5 years.

Disqualification for unfitness

6   Duty of court to disqualify unfit directors of insolvent companies

(1) The court shall make a disqualification order against a person in any case where, on an application under this section, it is satisfied—

    (a) that he is or has been a director of a company which has at any time become insolvent (whether while he was a director or subsequently), and

    (b) that his conduct as a director of that company (either taken alone or taken together with his conduct as a director of any other company or companies) makes him unfit to be concerned in the management of a company.

(2) For the purposes of this section and the next, a company becomes insolvent if—

    (a) the company goes into liquidation at a time when its assets are insufficient for the payment of its debts and other liabilities and the expenses of the winding up,

    (b) *an administration order is made in relation to the company, or*

    (c) an administrative receiver of the company is appointed;

and references to a person's conduct as a director of any company or companies include, where that company or any of those companies has become insolvent, that person's conduct in relation to any matter connected with or arising out of the insolvency of that company.

(3) In this section and section 7(2), 'the court' means—

(a) where the company in question is being or has been wound up by the court, that court,

(b) where the company in question is being or has been wound up voluntarily, any court which has or (as the case may be) had jurisdiction to wind it up,

(c) *where neither of the preceding paragraphs applies but an administration order has at any time been made, or an administrative receiver has at any time been appointed, in relation to the company in question, any court which has jurisdiction to wind it up.*

(3A) Sections 117 and 120 of the Insolvency Act 1986 (jurisdiction) shall apply for the purposes of subsection (3) as if the references in the definitions of 'registered office' to the presentation of the petition for winding up were references—

(a) in a case within paragraph (b) of that subsection, to the passing of the resolution for voluntary winding up,

(b) *in a case within paragraph (c) of that subsection, to the making of the administration order or or (as the case may be) the appointment of the administrative receiver.*

(3B) Nothing in subsection (3) invalidates any proceedings by reason of their being taken in the wrong court; and proceedings—

(a) for or in connection with a disqualification order under this section, or

(b) in connection with a disqualification undertaking accepted under section 7, may be retained in the court in which the proceedings were commenced, although it may not be the court in which they ought to have been commenced.

(3C) In this section and section 7, 'director' includes a shadow director.

(4) Under this section the minimum period of disqualification is 2 years, and the maximum period is 15 years.

[*When the Enterprise Act 2002, sch. 17, is brought into force, the Company Directors Disqualification Act 1986, s. 6(2)(b), will be replaced by:*

(b) *the company enters administration, or*

and s. 6(3)(c) will be replaced by:

(c) *where neither paragraph (a) nor (b) applies but an administrator or administrative receiver has at any time been appointed in respect of the company in question, any court which has jurisdiction to wind it up.*

and s. 6(3A)(b) will be replaced by:

(b) *in a case within paragraph (c) of that subsection, to the appointment of the administrator or (as the case may be) administrative receiver.*]

7 Disqualification order or undertaking; and reporting provisions

(1) If it appears to the Secretary of State that it is expedient in the public interest that a disqualification order under section 6 should be made against any person, an application for the making of such an order against that person may be made—

(a) by the Secretary of State, or

(b) if the Secretary of State so directs in the case of a person who is or has been a director of a company which is being or has been wound up by the court in England and Wales, by the official receiver.

(2) Except with the leave of the court, an application for the making under that section of a disqualification order against any person shall not be made after the end of the period of 2 years beginning with the day on which the company of which that person is or has been a director became insolvent.

(2A) If it appears to the Secretary of State that the conditions mentioned in section 6(1) are satisfied as respects any person who has offered to give him a disqualification undertaking, he may accept the undertaking if it appears to him that it is expedient in the public interest that he should do so (instead of applying, or proceeding with an application, for a disqualification order).

(3) If it appears to the office-holder responsible under this section, that is to say—

(a) in the case of a company which is being wound up by the court in England and Wales, the official receiver,

(b) in the case of a company which is being wound up otherwise, the liquidator,

(c) in the case of a company *in relation to which an administration order is in force*, the administrator, or

(d) in the case of a company of which there is an administrative receiver, that receiver,

that the conditions mentioned in section 6(1) are satisfied as respects a person who is or has been a director of that company, the office-holder shall forthwith report the matter to the Secretary of State.

(4) The Secretary of State or the official receiver may require the liquidator, administrator or administrative receiver of a company, or the former liquidator, administrator or administrative receiver of a company—

(a) to furnish him with such information with respect to any person's conduct as a director of the company, and

(b) to produce and permit inspection of such books, papers and other records relevant to that person's conduct as such a director,

as the Secretary of State or the official receiver may reasonably require for the purpose of determining whether to exercise, or of exercising, any function of his under this section.

[*When the Enterprise Act 2002, sch. 17, is brought into force, the words in italics in the Company Directors Disqualification Act 1986, s. 7(3)(c), will be replaced by:*

which is in administration,]

8   Disqualification after investigation of company

(1) If it appears to the Secretary of State from investigative material that it is expedient in the public interest that a disqualification order should be made against a person who is, or has been, a director or shadow director of a company, he may apply to the court for such an order.

(1A) 'Investigative material' means—

(a) a report made by inspectors under—

(i) section 437 of the Companies Act 1985;

(ii) section 167, 168, 169 or 284 of the Financial Services and Markets Act 2000; or

(iii) where the company is an open-ended investment company (within the meaning of that Act) regulations made as a result of section 262(2)(k) of that Act; and

(b) information or documents obtained under—

(i) section 447 or 448 of the Companies Act 1985;

(ii) section 2 of the Criminal Justice Act 1987;

(iii) section 28 of the Criminal Law (Consolidation) (Scotland) Act 1995;

(iv) section 83 of the Companies Act 1989; or

(v) section 165, 171, 172, 173 or 175 of the Financial Services and Markets Act 2000.

(2) The court may make a disqualification order against a person where, on an application under this section, it is satisfied that his conduct in relation to the company makes him unfit to be concerned in the management of a company.

(2A) Where it appears to the Secretary of State from such report, information or documents that, in the case of a person who has offered to give him a disqualification undertaking—

(a) the conduct of the person in relation to a company of which the person is or has been a director or shadow director makes him unfit to be concerned in the management of a company, and

(b) it is expedient in the public interest that he should accept the undertaking (instead of applying, or proceeding with an application, for a disqualification order), he may accept the undertaking.

(3) In this section 'the court' means the High Court or, in Scotland, the Court of Session.

(4) The maximum period of disqualification under this section is 15 years.

8A Variation etc. of disqualification undertaking

(1) The court may, on the application of a person who is subject to a disqualification undertaking—

(a) reduce the period for which the undertaking is to be in force, or

(b) provide for it to cease to be in force.

(2) On the hearing of an application under subsection (1), the Secretary of State shall appear and call the attention of the court to any matters which seem to him to be relevant, and may himself give evidence or call witnesses.

(2A) Subsection (2) does not apply to an application in the case of an undertaking given under section 9B, and in such a case on the hearing of the application whichever of the OFT or a specified regulator (within the meaning of section 9E) accepted the undertaking—

(a) must appear and call the attention of the court to any matters which appear to it or him (as the case may be) to be relevant;

(b) may give evidence or call witnesses.

(3) In this section 'the court'—

(a) in the case of an undertaking given under section 9B means the High Court or (in Scotland) the Court of Session;

(b) in any other case has the same meaning as in section 7(2) or 8 (as the case may be).

9 Matters for determining unfitness of directors

(1) Where it falls to a court to determine whether a person's conduct as a director of any particular company or companies makes him unfit to be concerned in the management of a company, the court shall, as respects his conduct as a director of that company or, as the case may be, each of those companies, have regard in particular—

(a) to the matters mentioned in Part I of Schedule 1 to this Act, and

(b) where the company has become insolvent, to the matters mentioned in Part II of that Schedule;

and references in that Schedule to the director and the company are to be read accordingly.

(1A) In determining whether he may accept a disqualification undertaking from any person the Secretary of State shall, as respects the person's conduct as a director of any company concerned, have regard in particular—

(a) to the matters mentioned in Part I of Schedule 1 to this Act, and

(b) where the company has become insolvent, to the matters mentioned in Part II of that Schedule;

and references in that Schedule to the director and the company are to be read accordingly.

(2) Section 6(2) applies for the purposes of this section and Schedule 1 as it applies for the purposes of sections 6 and 7 and in this section and that Schedule 'director' includes a shadow director.

(3) Subject to the next subsection, any reference in Schedule 1 to an enactment contained in the Companies Act or the Insolvency Act includes, in relation to any time before the coming into force of that enactment, the corresponding enactment in force at that time.

(4) The Secretary of State may by order modify any of the provisions of Schedule 1; and such an order may contain such transitional provisions as may appear to the Secretary of State necessary or expedient.

(5) The power to make orders under this section is exercisable by statutory instrument subject to annulment in pursuance of a resolution of either House of Parliament.

Disqualification for competition infringements

9A   Competition disqualification order

(1) The court must make a disqualification order against a person if the following two conditions are satisfied in relation to him.

(2) The first condition is that an undertaking which is a company of which he is a director commits a breach of competition law.

(3) The second condition is that the court considers that his conduct as a director makes him unfit to be concerned in the management of a company.

(4) An undertaking commits a breach of competition law if it engages in conduct which infringes any of the following—

    (a) the Chapter 1 prohibition (within the meaning of the Competition Act 1998) (prohibition on agreements, etc. preventing, restricting or distorting competition);

    (b) the Chapter 2 prohibition (within the meaning of that Act) (prohibition on abuse of a dominant position);

    (c) Article 81 of the Treaty establishing the European Community (prohibition on agreements, etc. preventing, restricting or distorting competition);

    (d) Article 82 of that Treaty (prohibition on abuse of a dominant position).

(5) For the purpose of deciding under subsection (3) whether a person is unfit to be concerned in the management of a company the court—

    (a) must have regard to whether subsection (6) applies to him;

    (b) may have regard to his conduct as a director of a company in connection with any other breach of competition law;

    (c) must not have regard to the matters mentioned in Schedule 1.

(6) This subsection applies to a person if as a director of the company—

    (a) his conduct contributed to the breach of competition law mentioned in subsection (2);

    (b) his conduct did not contribute to the breach but he had reasonable grounds to suspect that the conduct of the undertaking constituted the breach and he took no steps to prevent it;

    (c) he did not know but ought to have known that the conduct of the undertaking constituted the breach.

(7) For the purposes of subsection (6)(a) it is immaterial whether the person knew that the conduct of the undertaking constituted the breach.

(8) For the purposes of subsection (4)(a) or (c) references to the conduct of an undertaking are references to its conduct taken with the conduct of one or more other undertakings.

(9) The maximum period of disqualification under this section is 15 years.

(10) An application under this section for a disqualification order may be made by the OFT or by a specified regulator.

(11) Section 60 of the Competition Act 1998 (c. 41) (consistent treatment of questions arising under United Kingdom and Community law) applies in relation to any question arising by virtue of subsection (4)(a) or (b) above as it applies in relation to any question arising under Part 1 of that Act.

9B   Competition undertakings

(1) This section applies if—

    (a) the OFT or a specified regulator thinks that in relation to any person an undertaking which is a company of which he is a director has committed or is committing a breach of competition law,

    (b) the OFT or the specified regulator thinks that the conduct of the person as a director makes him unfit to be concerned in the management of a company, and

    (c) the person offers to give the OFT or the specified regulator (as the case may be) a disqualification undertaking.

(2) The OFT or the specified regulator (as the case may be) may accept a disqualification undertaking from the person instead of applying for or proceeding with an application for a disqualification order.

(3) A disqualification undertaking is an undertaking by a person that for the period specified in the undertaking he will not—

(a) be a director of a company;

(b) act as receiver of a company's property;

(c) in any way, whether directly or indirectly, be concerned or take part in the promotion, formation or management of a company;

(d) act as an insolvency practitioner.

(4) But a disqualification undertaking may provide that a prohibition falling within subsection (3)(a) to (c) does not apply if the person obtains the leave of the court.

(5) The maximum period which may be specified in a disqualification undertaking is 15 years.

(6) If a disqualification undertaking is accepted from a person who is already subject to a disqualification undertaking under this Act or to a disqualification order the periods specified in those undertakings or the undertaking and the order (as the case may be) run concurrently.

(7) Subsections (4) to (8) of section 9A apply for the purposes of this section as they apply for the purposes of that section but in the application of subsection (5) of that section the reference to the court must be construed as a reference to the OFT or a specified regulator (as the case may be).

9C   Competition investigations

(1) If the OFT or a specified regulator has reasonable grounds for suspecting that a breach of competition law has occurred it or he (as the case may be) may carry out an investigation for the purpose of deciding whether to make an application under section 9A for a disqualification order.

(2) For the purposes of such an investigation sections 26 to 30 of the Competition Act 1998 (c. 41) apply to the OFT and the specified regulators as they apply to the OFT for the purposes of an investigation under section 25 of that Act.

(3) Subsection (4) applies if as a result of an investigation under this section the OFT or a specified regulator proposes to apply under section 9A for a disqualification order.

(4) Before making the application the OFT or regulator (as the case may be) must—

(a) give notice to the person likely to be affected by the application, and

(b) give that person an opportunity to make representations.

9D   Coordination

(1) The Secretary of State may make regulations for the purpose of coordinating the performance of functions under sections 9A to 9C (relevant functions) which are exercisable concurrently by two or more persons.

(2) Section 54(5) to (7) of the Competition Act 1998 (c. 41) applies to regulations made under this section as it applies to regulations made under that section and for that purpose in that section—

(a) references to Part 1 functions must be read as references to relevant functions;

(b) references to a regulator must be read as references to a specified regulator;

(c) a competent person also includes any of the specified regulators.

(3) The power to make regulations under this section must be exercised by statutory instrument subject to annulment in pursuance of a resolution of either House of Parliament.

(4) Such a statutory instrument may—

(a) contain such incidental, supplemental, consequential and transitional provision as the Secretary of State thinks appropriate;

(b) make different provision for different cases.

9E   Interpretation

(1) This section applies for the purposes of sections 9A to 9D.

(2) Each of the following is a specified regulator for the purposes of a breach of competition law in relation to a matter in respect of which he or it has a function—

   (a) the Director General of Telecommunications;
   (b) the Gas and Electricity Markets Authority;
   (c) the Director General of Water Services;
   (d) the Rail Regulator;
   (e) the Civil Aviation Authority.

(3) The court is the High Court or (in Scotland) the Court of Session.

(4) Conduct includes omission.

(5) Director includes shadow director.

Other cases of disqualification

10   Participation in wrongful trading

(1) Where the court makes a declaration under section 213 or 214 of the Insolvency Act that a person is liable to make a contribution to a company's assets, then, whether or not an application for such an order is made by any person, the court may, if it thinks fit, also make a disqualification order against the person to whom the declaration relates.

(2) The maximum period of disqualification under this section is 15 years.

11   Undischarged bankrupts

(1) It is an offence for a person who is an undischarged bankrupt to act as director of, or directly or indirectly to take part in or be concerned in the promotion, formation or management of, a company, except with the leave of the court.

(2) 'The court' for this purpose is the court by which the person was adjudged bankrupt or, in Scotland, sequestration of his estates was awarded.

(3) In England and Wales, the leave of the court shall not be given unless notice of intention to apply for it has been served on the official receiver; and it is the latter's duty, if he is of opinion that it is contrary to the public interest that the application should be granted, to attend on the hearing of the application and oppose it.

12   Failure to pay under county court administration order

(1) The following has effect where a court under section 429 of the Insolvency Act revokes an administration order under Part VI of the County Courts Act 1984.

(2) A person to whom that section applies by virtue of the order under section 429(2)(b) shall not, except with the leave of the court which made the order, act as director or liquidator of, or directly or indirectly take part or be concerned in the promotion, formation or management of, a company.

12A   Northern Irish disqualification orders

A person subject to a disqualification order under Part II of the Companies (Northern Ireland) Order 1989—

   (a) shall not be a director of a company, act as receiver of a company's property or in any way, whether directly or indirectly, be concerned or take part in the promotion, formation or management of a company unless (in each case) he has the leave of the High Court of Northern Ireland, and
   (b) shall not act as an insolvency practitioner.

Consequences of contravention

13   Criminal penalties

If a person acts in contravention of a disqualification order or disqualification undertaking or in contravention of section 12(2) or 12A, or is guilty of an offence under section 11, he is liable—

(a) on conviction on indictment, to imprisonment for not more than 2 years or a fine, or both; and

(b) on summary conviction, to imprisonment for not more than 6 months or a fine not exceeding the statutory maximum, or both.

14   Offences by body corporate

(1) Where a body corporate is guilty of an offence of acting in contravention of a disqualification order or disqualification undertaking or in contravention of section 12A, and it is proved that the offence occurred with the consent or connivance of, or was attributable to any neglect on the part of any director, manager, secretary or other similar officer of the body corporate, or any person who was purporting to act in any such capacity he, as well as the body corporate, is guilty of the offence and liable to be proceeded against and punished accordingly.

(2) Where the affairs of a body corporate are managed by its members, subsection (1) applies in relation to the acts and defaults of a member in connection with his functions of management as if he were a director of the body corporate.

15   Personal liability for company's debts where person acts while disqualified

(1) A person is personally responsible for all the relevant debts of a company if at any time—

(a) in contravention of a disqualification order or disqualification undertaking or in contravention of section 11 or 12A of this Act he is involved in the management of the company, or

(b) as a person who is involved in the management of the company, he acts or is willing to act on instructions given without the leave of the court by a person whom he knows at that time to be the subject of a disqualification order or disqualification undertaking or a disqualification order under Part II of the Companies (Northern Ireland) Order 1989 or to be an undischarged bankrupt.

(2) Where a person is personally responsible under this section for the relevant debts of a company, he is jointly and severally liable in respect of those debts with the company and any other person who, whether under this section or otherwise, is so liable.

(3) For the purposes of this section the relevant debts of a company are—

(a) in relation to a person who is personally responsible under paragraph (a) of subsection (1), such debts and other liabilities of the company as are incurred at a time when that person was involved in the management of the company, and

(b) in relation to a person who is personally responsible under paragraph (b) of that subsection, such debts and other liabilities of the company as are incurred at a time when that person was acting or was willing to act on instructions given as mentioned in that paragraph.

(4) For the purposes of this section, a person is involved in the management of a company if he is a director of the company or if he is concerned, whether directly or indirectly, or takes part, in the management of the company.

(5) For the purposes of this section a person who, as a person involved in the management of a company, has at any time acted on instructions given without the leave of the court by a person whom he knew at that time to be the subject of a disqualification order or disqualification undertaking or a disqualification order under Part II of the Companies (Northern Ireland) Order 1989 or to be an undischarged bankrupt is presumed, unless the contrary is shown, to have been willing at any time thereafter to act on any instructions given by that person.

Supplementary provisions

16   Application for disqualification order

(1) A person intending to apply for the making of a disqualification order by the court

having jurisdiction to wind up a company shall give not less than 10 days' notice of his intention to the person against whom the order is sought; and on the hearing of the application the last-mentioned person may appear and himself give evidence or call witnesses.

(2) An application to a court with jurisdiction to wind up companies for the making against any person of a disqualification order under any of sections 2 to 4 may be made by the Secretary of State or the official receiver, or by the liquidator or any past or present member or creditor of any company in relation to which that person has committed or is alleged to have committed an offence or other default.

(3) On the hearing of any application under this Act made by a person falling within subsection (4), the applicant shall appear and call the attention of the court to any matters which seem to him to be relevant, and may himself give evidence or call witnesses.

(4) The following fall within this subsection—
- (a) the Secretary of State;
- (b) the official receiver;
- (c) the OFT;
- (d) the liquidator;
- (e) a specified regulator (within the meaning of section 9E).

17 Application for leave under an order or undertaking

(1) Where a person is subject to a disqualification order made by a court having jurisdiction to wind up companies, any application for leave for the purposes of section 1(1)(a) shall be made to that court.

(2) Where—
- (a) a person is subject to a disqualification order made under section 2 by a court other than a court having jurisdiction to wind up companies, or
- (b) a person is subject to a disqualification order made under section 5,

any application for leave for the purposes of section 1(1)(a) shall be made to any court which, when the order was made, had jurisdiction to wind up the company (or, if there is more than one such company, any of the companies) to which the offence (or any of the offences) in question related.

(3) Where a person is subject to a disqualification undertaking accepted at any time under section 7 or 8, any application for leave for the purposes of section 1A(1)(a) shall be made to any court to which, if the Secretary of State had applied for a disqualification order under the section in question at that time, his application could have been made.

(3A) Where a person is subject to a disqualification undertaking accepted at any time under section 9B any application for leave for the purposes of section 9B(4) must be made to the High Court or (in Scotland) the Court of Session.

(4) But where a person is subject to two or more disqualification orders or undertakings (or to one or more disqualification orders and to one or more disqualification undertakings), any application for leave for the purposes of section 1(1)(a), 1A(1)(a) or 9B(4) shall be made to any court to which any such application relating to the latest order to be made, or undertaking to be accepted, could be made.

(5) On the hearing of an application for leave for the purposes of section 1(1)(a) or 1A(1)(a), the Secretary of State shall appear and call the attention of the court to any matters which seem to him to be relevant, and may himself give evidence or call witnesses.

(6) Subsection (5) does not apply to an application for leave for the purposes of section 1(1)(a) if the application for the disqualification order was made under section 9A.

(7) In such a case and in the case of an application for leave for the purposes of section 9B(4) on the hearing of the application whichever of the OFT or a specified regulator (within the meaning of section 9E) applied for the order or accepted the undertaking (as the case may be)—

(a) must appear and draw the attention of the court to any matters which appear to it or him (as the case may be) to be relevant;

(b) may give evidence or call witnesses.

[*The second comma in s. 17(4) has been added editorially.*]

18   Register of disqualification orders and undertakings

(1) The Secretary of State may make regulations requiring officers of courts to furnish him with such particulars as the regulations may specify of cases in which—

(a) a disqualification order is made, or

(b) any action is taken by a court in consequence of which such an order or a disqualification undertaking is varied or ceases to be in force, or

(c) leave is granted by a court for a person subject to such an order to do anything which otherwise the order prohibits him from doing, or

(d) leave is granted by a court for a person subject to such an undertaking to do anything which otherwise the undertaking prohibits him from doing;

and the regulations may specify the time within which, and the form and manner in which, such particulars are to be furnished.

(2) The Secretary of State shall, from the particulars so furnished, continue to maintain the register of orders, and of cases in which leave has been granted as mentioned in subsection (1)(c), which was set up by him under section 29 of the Companies Act 1976 and continued under section 301 of the Companies Act 1985.

(2A) The Secretary of State must include in the register such particulars as he considers appropriate of—

(a) disqualification undertakings accepted by him under section 7 or 8;

(b) disqualification undertakings accepted by the OFT or a specified regulator under section 9B;

(c) cases in which leave has been granted as mentioned in subsection (1)(d).

(3) When an order or undertaking of which entry is made in the register ceases to be in force, the Secretary of State shall delete the entry from the register and all particulars relating to it which have been furnished to him under this section or any previous corresponding provision and, in the case of a disqualification undertaking, any other particulars he has included in the register.

(4) The register shall be open to inspection on payment of such fee as may be specified by the Secretary of State in regulations.

(4A) Regulations under this section may extend the preceding provisions of this section, to such extent and with such modifications as may be specified in the regulations, to disqualification orders made under Part II of the Companies (Northern Ireland) Order 1989.

(5) Regulations under this section shall be made by statutory instrument subject to annulment in pursuance of a resolution of either House of Parliament.

Miscellaneous and general

20   Admissibility in evidence of statements

(1) In any proceedings (whether or not under this Act), any statement made in pursuance of a requirement imposed by or under sections 6 to 10, 15 or 19(c) of, or Schedule 1 to, this Act, or by or under rules made for the purposes of this Act under the Insolvency Act, may be used in evidence against any person making or concurring in making the statement.

(2) However, in criminal proceedings in which any such person is charged with an offence to which this subsection applies—

(a) no evidence relating to the statement may be adduced, and

(b) no question relating to it may be asked, by or on behalf of the prosecution, unless evidence relating to it is adduced, or a question relating to it is asked, in the proceedings by or on behalf of that person.

(3) Subsection (2) applies to any offence other than—
  (a) an offence which is—
      (i) created by rules made for the purposes of this Act under the Insolvency Act, and
      (ii) designated for the purposes of this subsection by such rules or by regulations made by the Secretary of State;
  (b) an offence which is—
      (i) created by regulations made under any such rules, and
      (ii) designated for the purposes of this subsection by such regulations;
  (c) an offence under section 5 of the Perjury Act 1911 (false statements made otherwise than on oath); or
  (d) an offence under section 44(2) of the Criminal Law (Consolidation) (Scotland) Act 1995 (false statements made otherwise than on oath).

(4) Regulations under subsection (3)(a)(ii) shall be made by statutory instrument and, after being made, shall be laid before each House of Parliament.

21 Interaction with Insolvency Act

(1) References in this Act to the official receiver, in relation to the winding up of a company or the bankruptcy of an individual, are to any person who, by virtue of section 399 of the Insolvency Act, is authorised to act as the official receiver in relation to that winding up or bankruptcy; and, in accordance with section 401(2) of that Act, references in this Act to an official receiver includes a person appointed as his deputy.

(2) Sections 1A, 6 to 10, 13, 14, 15, 19(c) and 20 of, and Schedule 1 to, this Act and sections 1 and 17 of this Act as they apply for the purposes of those provisions are deemed included in Parts I to VII of the Insolvency Act for the purposes of the following sections of that Act—
  section 411 (power to make insolvency rules);
  section 414 (fees orders);
  section 420 (orders extending provisions about insolvent companies to insolvent partnerships);
  section 422 (modification of such provisions in their application to recognised banks).

(3) Section 434 of that Act (Crown application) applies to sections 1A, 6 to 10, 13, 14, 15, 19(c) and 20 of, and Schedule 1 to, this Act and sections 1 and 17 of this Act as they apply for the purposes of those provisions as it does to the provisions of that Act which are there mentioned. . . .

22 Interpretation

(1) This section has effect with respect to the meaning of expressions used in this Act, and applies unless the context otherwise requires.

(2) The expression 'company'—
  (a) in section 11, includes an unregistered company and a company incorporated outside Great Britain which has an established place of buisness in Great Britain, and
  (b) elsewhere, includes any company which may be wound up under Part V of the Insolvency Act.

(3) Section 247 in Part VII of the Insolvency Act (interpretation for the first Group of parts of that Act) applies as regards references to a company's insolvency and to its going into liquidation; and 'administrative receiver' has the meaning given by section 251 of that Act and references to acting as an insolvency practitioner are to be read in accordance with section 388 of that Act.

(4) 'Director' includes any person occupying the position of director, by whatever name called.

(5) 'Shadow director', in relation to a company, means a person in accordance with

whose directions or instructions the directors of the company are accustomed to act (but so that a person is not deemed a shadow director by reason only that the directors act on advice given by him in a professional capacity).

(6) Section 740 of the Companies Act applies as regards the meaning of 'body corporate'; and 'officer' has the meaning given by section 744 of that Act.

(7) In references to legislation other than this Act—
'the Companies Act' means the Companies Act 1985;
'the Companies Acts' has the meaning given by section 744 of that Act; and
'the Insolvency Act' means the Insolvency Act 1986;
and in sections 3(1) and 5(1) of this Act 'the companies legislation' means the Companies Acts (except the Insider Dealing Act), Parts I to VII of the Insolvency Act and, in Part XV of that Act, sections 411, 413, 414, 416 and 417.

[*Before an amendment was made by the Criminal Justice Act 1993, sch. 5, para. 4, the Companies Act 1985, s. 744, provided: ' "the Insider Dealing Act" means the Company Securities (Insider Dealing) Act 1985'.*]

(8) Any reference to provisions, or a particular provision, of the Companies Acts or the Insolvency Act includes the corresponding provisions or provision of the former Companies Acts (as defined by section 735(1)(c) of the Companies Act, but including also that Act itself) or, as the case may be, the Insolvency Act 1985.

(9) Any expression for whose interpretation provision is made by Part XXVI of the Companies Act (and not by subsections (3) to (8) above) is to be construed in accordance with that provision.

(10) Any reference to acting as receiver—
(a) includes acting as manager or as both receiver and manager, but
(b) does not include acting as administrative receiver;
and 'receivership' is to be read accordingly.

24   Extent
(1) This Act extends to England and Wales and to Scotland.
(2) Nothing in this Act extends to Northern Ireland.

25   Commencement
This Act comes into force simultaneously with the Insolvency Act 1986.

26   Citation
This Act may be cited as the Company Directors Disqualification Act 1986.

SCHEDULES

Section 9   SCHEDULE 1

MATTERS FOR DETERMINING UNFITNESS OF DIRECTORS

PART I   MATTERS APPLICABLE IN ALL CASES

1.   Any misfeasance or breach of any fiduciary or other duty by the director in relation to the company.

2.   Any misapplication or retention by the director of, or any conduct by the director giving rise to an obligation to account for, any money or other property of the company.

3.   The extent of the director's responsibility for the company entering into any transaction liable to be set aside under Part XVI of the Insolvency Act (provisions against debt avoidance).

4.   The extent of the director's responsibility for any failure by the company to comply with any of the following provisions of the Companies Act, namely—

(a) section 221 (companies to keep accounting records);

(b) section 222 (where and for how long records to be kept);

(c) section 288 (register of directors and secretaries);

(d) section 352 (obligation to keep and enter up register of members);

(e) section 353 (location of register of members);

(f) section 363 (duty of company to make annual returns);

(h) sections 399 and 415 (company's duty to register charges it creates).

[*A new subpara. (h) would be substituted if para. 4 of sch. 16 to the Companies Act 1989 were brought into force.*]

5. The extent of the director's responsibility for any failure by the directors of the company to comply with—

(a) section 226 or 227 of the Companies Act (duty to prepare annual accounts), or

(b) section 233 of that Act (approval and signature of accounts).

PART II   MATTERS APPLICABLE WHERE COMPANY HAS BECOME INSOLVENT

6. The extent of the director's responsibility for the causes of the company becoming insolvent.

7. The extent of the director's responsibility for any failure by the company to supply any goods or services which have been paid for (in whole or in part).

8. The extent of the director's responsibility for the company entering into any transaction or giving any preference, being a transaction or preference—

(a) liable to be set aside under section 127 or sections 238 to 240 of the Insolvency Act, or

(b) challengeable under section 242 or 243 of that Act or under any rule of law in Scotland.

9. The extent of the director's responsibility for any failure by the directors of the company to comply with section 98 of the Insolvency Act (duty to call creditors' meeting in creditors' voluntary winding up).

10. Any failure by the director to comply with any obligation imposed on him by or under any of the following provisions of the Insolvency Act—

(a) section 22 (company's statement of affairs in administration);

(b) section 47 (statement of affairs to administrative receiver);

(c) section 66 (statement of affairs in Scottish receivership);

(d) section 99 (directors' duty to attend meeting; statement of affairs in creditors' voluntary winding up);

(e) section 131 (statement of affairs in winding up by the court);

(f) section 234 (duty of any one with company property to deliver it up);

(g) section 235 (duty to cooperate with liquidator, etc.).

Companies Act 1989

(1989, c. 40)

An Act . . . to make new provision with respect to the registration of company charges and otherwise to amend the law relating to companies; . . . and for connected purposes.   [16 November 1989]

[*The Department of Trade and Industry has indicated that the provisions of the Companies Act 1989 which are printed below in italics will not be brought into force.*]

PART IV   REGISTRATION OF COMPANY CHARGES

Introduction

92   Introduction

The provisions of this Part amend the provisions of the Companies Act 1985 relating to the registra-tion of company charges—

    (a) *by inserting in Part XII of that Act (in place of sections 395 to 408 and 410 to 423) new provisions with respect to companies registered in Great Britain, and*

    (b) *by inserting as Chapter III of Part XXIII of that Act (in place of sections 409 and 424) new provisions with respect to oversea companies.*

Registration in the companies charges register

93   Charges requiring registration

The following sections are inserted in Part XII of the Companies Act 1985—

    'Registration in the company charges register

395   Introductory provisions

    (1) The purpose of this Part is to secure the registration of charges on a company's property.

    (2) In this Part—

    'charge' means any form of security interest (fixed or floating) over property, other than an interest arising by operation of law; and

    'property', in the context of what is the subject of a charge, includes future property.

    (3) It is immaterial for the purposes of this Part where the property subject to a charge is situated.

    (4) References in this Part to 'the registrar' are—

        (a) *in relation to a company registered in England and Wales, to the registrar of com-panies for England and Wales, and*

        (b) *in relation to a company registered in Scotland, to the registrar of companies for Scotland;*

and references to registration, in relation to a charge, are to registration in the register kept by him under this Part.

396   Charges requiring registration

    (1) The charges requiring registration under this Part are—

        (a) *a charge on land or any interest in land, other than—*

            (i) *in England and Wales, a charge for rent or any other periodical sum issuing out of the land,*

            (ii) *in Scotland, a charge for any rent, ground annual or other periodical sum pay-able in respect of the land;*

        (b) *a charge on goods or any interest in goods, other than a charge under which the chargee is entitled to possession either of the goods or of a document of title to them;*

        (c) *a charge on intangible movable property (in Scotland, incorporeal movable property) of any of the following descriptions—*

            (i) *goodwill,*

            (ii) *intellectual property,*

            (iii) *book debts (whether book debts of the company or assigned to the company),*

            (iv) *uncalled share capital of the company or calls made but not paid;*

        (d) *a charge for securing an issue of debentures; or*

        (e) *a floating charge on the whole or part of the company's property.*

    (2) The descriptions of charge mentioned in subsection (1) shall be construed as follows—

        (a) *a charge on a debenture forming part of an issue or series shall not be treated as falling within paragraph (a) or (b) by reason of the fact that the debenture is secured by a charge on land or goods (or on an interest in land or goods);*

(b) *in paragraph (b) 'goods' means any tangible movable property (in Scotland, corporeal movable property) other than money;*

(c) *a charge is not excluded from paragraph (b) because the chargee is entitled to take possession in case of default or on the occurrence of some other event;*

(d) *in paragraph (c)(ii) 'intellectual property' means—*

(i)   *any patent, trade mark, registered design, copyright or design right, or*

(ii) *any licence under or in respect of any such right;*

(e) *a debenture which is part of an issue or series shall not be treated as a book debt for the purposes of paragraph (c)(iii);*

(f) *the deposit by way of security of a negotiable instrument given to secure the payment of book debts shall not be treated for the purposes of paragraph (c)(iii) as a charge on book debts;*

(g) *a shipowner's lien on subfreights shall not be treated as a charge on book debts for the purposes of paragraph (c)(iii) or as a floating charge for the purposes of paragraph (e).*

(3) *Whether a charge is one requiring registration under this Part shall be determined—*

(a) *in the case of a charge created by a company, as at the date the charge is created, and*

(b) *in the case of a charge over property acquired by a company, as at the date of the acquisition.*

(4) *The Secretary of State may by regulations amend subsections (1) and (2) so as to add any description of charge to, or remove any description of charge from, the charges requiring registration under this Part.*

(5) *Regulations under this section shall be made by statutory instrument which shall be subject to annulment in pursuance of a resolution of either House of Parliament.*

(6) *In the following provisions of this Part references to a charge are, unless the context otherwise requires, to a charge requiring registration under this Part.*

Where a charge not otherwise requiring registration relates to property by virtue of which it requires to be registered and to other property, the references are to the charge so far as it relates to property of the former description.'.

[In Scotland, the words ', ground annual' in s. 396(1)(a)(ii) will be repealed on the day when the Abolition of Feudal Tenure etc. (Scotland) Act 2000 (asp 5), sch. 12, para. 46, is brought into force, unless the Companies Act 1989, s. 92, has not come into force by that date.]

94   *The companies charges register*
The following section is inserted in Part XII of the Companies Act 1985—

'397   The companies charges register
(1) *The registrar shall keep for each company a register, in such form as he thinks fit, of charges on property of the company.*

(2) *The register shall consist of a file containing with respect to each charge the particulars and other information delivered to the registrar under the provisions of this Part.*

(3) *Any person may require the registrar to provide a certificate stating the date on which any specified particulars of, or other information relating to, a charge were delivered to him.*

(4) *The certificate shall be signed by the registrar or authenticated by his official seal.*

(5) *The certificate shall be conclusive evidence that the specified particulars or other information were delivered to the registrar no later than the date stated in the certificate; and it shall be presumed unless the contrary is proved that they were not delivered earlier than that date.'.*

95   *Delivery of particulars for registration*
The following sections are inserted in Part XII of the Companies Act 1985—

'398   Company's duty to deliver particulars of charge for registration
(1) *It is the duty of a company which creates a charge, or acquires property subject to a charge—*

(a) to deliver the prescribed particulars of the charge, in the prescribed form, to the registrar for registration, and

(b) to do so within 21 days after the date of the charge's creation or, as the case may be, the date of the acquisition;

but particulars of a charge may be delivered for registration by any person interested in the charge.

(2) Where the particulars are delivered for registration by a person other than the company concerned, that person is entitled to recover from the company the amount of any fees paid by him to the registrar in connection with the registration.

(3) If a company fails to comply with subsection (1), then, unless particulars of the charge have been delivered for registration by another person, the company and every officer of it who is in default is liable to a fine.

(4) Where prescribed particulars in the prescribed form are delivered to the registrar for registration, he shall file the particulars in the register and shall note, in such form as he thinks fit, the date on which they were delivered to him.

(5) The registrar shall send to the company and any person appearing from the particulars to be the chargee, and if the particulars were delivered by another person interested in the charge to that person, a copy of the particulars filed by him and of the note made by him as to the date on which they were delivered.

399   Effect of failure to deliver particulars for registration

(1) Where a charge is created by a company and no prescribed particulars in the prescribed form are delivered for registration within the period of 21 days after the date of the charge's creation, the charge is void against—

(a) an administrator or liquidator of the company, and

(b) any person who for value acquires an interest in or right over property subject to the charge,

where the relevant event occurs after the creation of the charge, whether before or after the end of the 21 day period.

This is subject to section 400 (late delivery of particulars).

(2) In this Part 'the relevant event' means—

(a) in relation to the voidness of a charge as against an administrator or liquidator, the beginning of the insolvency proceedings, and

(b) in relation to the voidness of a charge as against a person acquiring an interest in or right over property subject to a charge, the acquisition of that interest or right;

and references to 'a relevant event' shall be construed accordingly.

(3) Where a relevant event occurs on the same day as the charge is created, it shall be presumed to have occurred after the charge is created unless the contrary is proved.

400   Late delivery of particulars

(1) Where prescribed particulars of a charge created by a company, in the prescribed form, are delivered for registration more than 21 days after the date of the charge's creation, section 399(1) does not apply in relation to relevant events occurring after the particulars are delivered.

(2) However, where in such a case—

(a) the company is at the date of delivery of the particulars unable to pay its debts, or subsequently becomes unable to pay its debts in consequence of the transaction under which the charge is created, and

(b) insolvency proceedings begin before the end of the relevant period beginning with the date of delivery of the particulars,

the charge is void as against the administrator or liquidator.

(3) For this purpose—

(a) the company is 'unable to pay its debts' in the circumstances specified in section 123 of the Insolvency Act 1986; and

(b) the 'relevant period' is—

    (i)   two years in the case of a floating charge created in favour of a person connected with the company (within the meaning of section 249 of that Act),

    (ii) one year in the case of a floating charge created in favour of a person not so connected, and

    (iii) six months in any other case.

(4) Where a relevant event occurs on the same day as the particulars are delivered, it shall be presumed to have occurred before the particulars are delivered unless the contrary is proved.'.

96   Delivery of further particulars

The following section is inserted in Part XII of the Companies Act 1985—

'401   Delivery of further particulars

(1) Further particulars of a charge, supplementing or varying the registered particulars, may be delivered to the registrar for registration at any time.

(2) Further particulars must be in the prescribed form signed by or on behalf of both the company and the chargee.

(3) Where further particulars are delivered to the registrar for registration and appear to him to be duly signed, he shall file the particulars in the register and shall note, in such form as he thinks fit, the date on which they were delivered to him.

(4) The registrar shall send to the company and any person appearing from the particulars to be the chargee, and if the particulars were delivered by another person interested in the charge to that other person, a copy of the further particulars filed by him and of the note made by him as to the date on which they were delivered.'.

97   Effect of omissions and errors in registered particulars

The following section is inserted in Part XII of the Companies Act 1985—

'402   Effect of omissions and errors in registered particulars

(1) Where the registered particulars of a charge created by a company are not complete and accurate, the charge is void, as mentioned below, to the extent that rights are not disclosed by the registered particulars which would be disclosed if they were complete and accurate.

(2) The charge is void to that extent, unless the court on the application of the chargee orders otherwise, as against—

(a) an administrator or liquidator of the company, and

(b) any person who for value acquires an interest in or right over property subject to the charge,

where the relevant event occurs at a time when the particulars are incomplete or inaccurate in a relevant respect.

(3) Where a relevant event occurs on the same day as particulars or further particulars are delivered, it shall be presumed to have occurred before those particulars are delivered unless the contrary is proved.

(4) The court may order that the charge is effective as against an administrator or liquidator of the company if it is satisfied—

(a) that the omission or error is not likely to have misled materially to his prejudice any unsecured creditor of the company, or

(b) that no person became an unsecured creditor of the company at a time when the registered particulars of the charge were incomplete or inaccurate in a relevant respect.

(5) The court may order that the charge is effective as against a person acquiring an interest in or right over property subject to the charge if it is satisfied that he did not rely, in connection with the acquisition, on registered particulars which were incomplete or inaccurate in a relevant respect.

(6) For the purposes of this section an omission or inaccuracy with respect to the name of the chargee shall not be regarded as a failure to disclose the rights of the chargee.'.

98 *Memorandum of charge ceasing to affect company's property*
The following section is inserted in Part XII of the Companies Act 1985—

'403 *Memorandum of charge ceasing to affect company's property*
(1) *Where a charge of which particulars have been delivered ceases to affect the company's property, a memorandum to that effect may be delivered to the registrar for registration.*

(2) *The memorandum must be in the prescribed form signed by or on behalf of both the company and the chargee.*

(3) *Where a memorandum is delivered to the registrar for registration and appears to him to be duly signed, he shall file it in the register, and shall note, in such form as he thinks fit, the date on which it was delivered to him.*

(4) *The registrar shall send to the company and any person appearing from the memorandum to be the chargee, and if the memorandum was delivered by another person interested in the charge to that person, a copy of the memorandum filed by him and of the note made by him as to the date on which it was delivered.*

(5) *If a duly signed memorandum is delivered in a case where the charge in fact continues to affect the company's property, the charge is void as against—*
    (a) *an administrator or liquidator of the company, and*
    (b) *any person who for value acquires an interest in or right over property subject to the charge,*
where the relevant event occurs after the delivery of the memorandum.

(6) *Where a relevant event occurs on the same day as the memorandum is delivered, it shall be presumed to have occurred before the memorandum is delivered unless the contrary is proved.'.*

99 *Further provisions with respect to voidness of charges*
The following sections are inserted in Part XII of the Companies Act 1985—

'Further provisions with respect to voidness of charges

404 *Exclusion of voidness as against unregistered charges*
(1) *A charge is not void by virtue of this Part as against a subsequent charge unless some or all of the relevant particulars of that charge are duly delivered for registration—*
    (a) *within 21 days after the date of its creation, or*
    (b) *before complete and accurate relevant particulars of the earlier charge are duly delivered for registration.*

(2) *Where relevant particulars of the subsequent charge so delivered are incomplete or inaccurate, the earlier charge is void as against that charge only to the extent that rights are disclosed by registered particulars of the subsequent charge duly delivered for registration before the corresponding relevant particulars of the earlier charge.*

(3) *The relevant particulars of a charge for the purposes of this section are those prescribed particulars relating to rights inconsistent with those conferred by or in relation to the other charge.*

405 *Restrictions on voidness by virtue of this Part*
(1) *A charge is not void by virtue of this Part as against a person acquiring an interest in or right over property where the acquisition is expressly subject to the charge.*

(2) *Nor is a charge void by virtue of this Part in relation to any property by reason of a relevant event occurring after the company which created the charge has disposed of the whole of its interest in that property.*

406 *Effect of exercise of power of sale*
(1) *A chargee exercising a power of sale may dispose of property to a purchaser freed from any interest or right arising from the charge having become void to any extent by virtue of this Part—*
    (a) *against an administrator or liquidator of the company, or*
    (b) *against a person acquiring a security interest over property subject to the charge; and a purchaser is not concerned to see or inquire whether the charge has become so void.*

(2) *The proceeds of the sale shall be held by the chargee in trust to be applied—*

First, in discharge of any sum effectively secured by prior encumbrances to which the sale is not made subject;

Second, in payment of all costs, charges and expenses properly incurred by him in connection with the sale, or any previous attempted sale, of the property;

Third, in discharge of any sum effectively secured by the charge and encumbrances ranking pari passu *with the charge;*

Fourth, in discharge of any sum effectively secured by encumbrances ranking after the charge; and any residue is payable to the company or to a person authorised to give a receipt for the proceeds of the sale of the property.

(3) *For the purposes of subsection (2)—*

    (a) *prior encumbrances include any encumbrance to the extent that the charge is void as against it by virtue of this Part; and*

    (b) *no sum is effectively secured by a charge to the extent that it is void as against an administrator or liquidator of the company.*

(4) *In this section—*

    (a) *references to things done by a chargee include things done by a receiver appointed by him, whether or not the receiver acts as his agent;*

    (b) *'power of sale' includes any power to dispose of, or grant on interest out of, property for the purpose of enforcing a charge (but in relation to Scotland does not include the power to grant a lease), and references to 'sale' shall be construed accordingly; and*

    (c) *'purchaser' means a person who in good faith and for valuable consideration acquires an interest in property.*

(5) *The provisions of this section as to the order of application of the proceeds of sale have effect subject to any other statutory provision (in Scotland, any other statutory provision or rule of law) applicable in any case.*

(6) *Where a chargee exercising a power of sale purports to dispose of property freed from any such interest or right as is mentioned in subsection (1) to a person other than a purchaser, the above provisions apply, with any necessary modifications, in relation to a disposition to a purchaser by that person or any successor in title of his.*

(7) *In Scotland, subsections (2) and (7) of section 27 of the Conveyancing and Feudal Reform (Scotland) Act 1970 apply to a chargee unable to obtain a discharge for any payment which he is required to make under subsection (2) above as they apply to a creditor in the circumstances mentioned in those subsections.*

407 *Effect of voidness on obligation secured*

(1) *Where a charge becomes void to any extent by virtue of this Part, the whole of the sum secured by the charge is payable forthwith on demand; and this applies notwithstanding that the sum secured by the charge is also the subject of other security.*

(2) *Where the charge is to secure the repayment of money, the references in subsection (1) to the sum secured include any interest payable.'.*

100 *Additional information to be registered*
The following sections are inserted in Part XII of the Companies Act 1985—

'*Additional information to be registered*

408 *Particulars of taking up of issue of debentures*

(1) *Where particulars of a charge for securing an issue of debentures have been delivered for registration, it is the duty of the company—*

    (a) *to deliver to the registrar for registration particulars in the prescribed form of the date on which any debentures of the issue are taken up, and of the amount taken up, and*

    (b) *to do so before the end of the period of 21 days after the date on which they are taken up.*

(2) *Where particulars in the prescribed form are delivered to the registrar for registration under this section, he shall file them in the register.*

(3) *If a company fails to comply with subsection (1), the company and every officer of it who is in default is liable to a fine.*

409   Notice of appointment of receiver or manager, &c.

(1) *If a person obtains an order for the appointment of a receiver or manager of a company's property, or appoints such a receiver or manager under powers contained in an instrument, he shall within seven days of the order or of the appointment under those powers, give notice of that fact in the prescribed form to the registrar for registration.*

(2) *Where a person appointed receiver or manager of a company's property under powers contained in an instrument ceases to act as such receiver or manager, he shall, on so ceasing, give notice of that fact in the prescribed form to the registrar for registration.*

(3) *Where a notice under this section in the prescribed form is delivered to the registrar for registration, he shall file it in the register.*

(4) *If a person makes default in complying with the requirements of subsection (1) or (2), he is liable to a fine.*

(5) *This section does not apply in relation to companies registered in Scotland (for which corresponding provision is made by sections 53, 54 and 62 of the Insolvency Act 1986).*

410   Notice of crystallisation of floating charge, &c.

(1) *The Secretary of State may by regulations require notice in the prescribed form to be given to the registrar of—*
   - (a) *the occurrence of such events as may be prescribed affecting the nature of the security under a floating charge of which particulars have been delivered for registration, and*
   - (b) *the taking of such action in exercise of powers conferred by a fixed or floating charge of which particulars have been delivered for registration, or conferred in relation to such a charge by an order of the court, as may be prescribed.*

(2) *The regulations may make provision as to—*
   - (a) *the persons by whom notice is required to be, or may be, given, and the period within which notice is required to be given;*
   - (b) *the filing in the register of the particulars contained in the notice and the noting of the date on which the notice was given; and*
   - (c) *the consequences of failure to give notice.*

(3) *As regards the consequences of failure to give notice of an event causing a floating charge to crystallise, the regulations may include provision to the effect that the crystallisation—*
   - (a) *shall be treated as ineffective until the prescribed particulars are delivered, and*
   - (b) *if the prescribed particulars are delivered after the expiry of the prescribed period, shall continue to be ineffective against such persons as may be prescribed,*

subject to the exercise of such powers as may be conferred by the regulations on the court.

(4) *The regulations may provide that if there is a failure to comply with such of the requirements of the regulations as may be prescribed, such persons as may be prescribed are liable to a fine.*

(5) *Regulations under this section shall be made by statutory instrument which shall be subject to annulment in pursuance of a resolution of either House of Parliament.*

(6) *Regulations under this section shall not apply in relation to a floating charge created under the law of Scotland by a company registered in Scotland.'.*

Copies of instruments and register to be kept by company

101   Copies of instruments and register to be kept by company
The following sections are inserted in Part XII of the Companies Act 1985—

'Copies of instruments and register to be kept by company

411   Duty to keep copies of instruments and register

(1) Every company shall keep at its registered office a copy of every instrument creating or evidencing a charge over the company's property.

In the case of a series of uniform debentures, a copy of one debenture of the series is sufficient.

(2) Every company shall also keep at its registered office a register of all such charges, containing entries for each charge giving a short description of the property charged, the amount of the charge and (except in the case of securities to bearer) the names of the persons entitled to it.

(3) This section applies to any charge, whether or not particulars are required to be delivered to the registrar for registration.

(4) If a company fails to comply with any requirement of this section, the company and every officer of it who is in default is liable to a fine.

412   Inspection of copies and register

(1) The copies and the register referred to in section 411 shall be open to the inspection of any creditor or member of the company without fee; and to the inspection of any other person on payment of such fee as may be prescribed.

(2) Any person may request the company to provide him with a copy of—

   (a) any instrument creating or evidencing a charge over the company's property, or

   (b) any entry in the register of charges kept by the company, on payment of such fee as may be prescribed.

This subsection applies to any charge, whether or not particulars are required to be delivered to the registrar for registration.

(3) The company shall send the copy to him not later than ten days after the day on which the request is received or, if later, on which payment is received.

(4) If inspection of the copies or register is refused, or a copy requested is not sent within the time specified above—

   (a) the company and every officer of it who is in default is liable to a fine, and

   (b) the court may by order compel an immediate inspection of the copies or register or, as the case may be, direct that the copy be sent immediately.'.

Supplementary provisions

102   Power to make further provision by regulations
The following section is inserted in Part XII of the Companies Act 1985—

'Supplementary provisions

413   Power to make further provision by regulations

(1) The Secretary of State may by regulations make further provision as to the application of the provisions of this Part in relation to charges of any description specified in the regulations.

Nothing in the following provisions shall be construed as restricting the generality of that power.

(2) The regulations may require that where the charge is contained in or evidenced or varied by a written instrument there shall be delivered to the registrar for registration, instead of particulars or further particulars of the charge, the instrument itself or a certified copy of it together with such particulars as may be prescribed.

(3) The regulations may provide that a memorandum of a charge ceasing to affect property of the company shall not be accepted by the registrar unless supported by such evidence as may be prescribed, and that a memorandum not so supported shall be treated as not having been delivered.

(4) The regulations may also provide that where the instrument creating the charge is delivered to the registrar in support of such a memorandum, the registrar may mark the instrument as cancelled before returning it and shall send copies of the instrument cancelled to such persons as may be prescribed.

(5) The regulations may exclude or modify, in such circumstances and to such extent as may be prescribed, the operation of the provisions of this Part relating to the voidness of a charge.

(6) The regulations may require, in connection with the delivery of particulars, further particulars or a memorandum of the charge's ceasing to affect property of the company, the delivery of such supplementary information as may be prescribed, and may—

(a) apply in relation to such supplementary information any provisions of this Part relating to particulars, further particulars or such a memorandum, and

(b) provide that the particulars, further particulars or memorandum shall be treated as not having been delivered until the required supplementary information is delivered.

(7) Regulations under this section shall be made by statutory instrument which shall be subject to annulment in pursuance of a resolution of either House of Parliament.'.

103 Other supplementary provisions
The following sections are inserted in Part XII of the Companies Act 1985—

'414 Date of creation of charge
(1) References in this Part to the date of creation of a charge by a company shall be construed as follows.

(2) A charge created under the law of England and Wales shall be taken to be created—

(a) in the case of a charge created by an instrument in writing, when the instrument is executed by the company or, if its execution by the company is conditional, upon the conditions being fulfilled, and

(b) in any other case, when an enforceable agreement is entered into by the company conferring a security interest intended to take effect forthwith or upon the company acquiring an interest in property subject to the charge.

(3) A charge created under the law of Scotland shall be taken to be created—

(a) in the case of a floating charge, when the instrument creating the floating charge is executed by the company, and

(b) in any other case, when the right of the person entitled to the benefit of the charge is constituted as a real right.

(4) Where a charge is created in the United Kingdom but comprises property outside the United Kingdom, any further proceedings necessary to make the charge valid or effectual under the law of the country where the property is situated shall be disregarded in ascertaining the date on which the charge is to be taken to be created.

415 Prescribed particulars and related expressions
(1) References in this Part to the prescribed particulars of a charge are to such particulars of, or relating to, the charge as may be prescribed.

(2) The prescribed particulars may, without prejudice to the generality of subsection (1), include—

(a) whether the company has undertaken not to create other charges ranking in priority to or pari passu with the charge, and

(b) whether the charge is a market charge within the meaning of Part VII of the Companies Act 1989 or a charge to which the provisions of that Part apply as they apply to a market charge.

(3) References in this Part to the registered particulars of a charge at any time are to such particulars and further particulars of the charge as have at that time been duly delivered for registration.

(4) References in this Part to the registered particulars of a charge being complete and accurate at any time are to their including all the prescribed particulars which would be required to be delivered if the charge were then newly created.

416 Notice of matters disclosed on register
(1) A person taking a charge over a company's property shall be taken to have notice of any matter requiring registration and disclosed on the register at the time the charge is created.

(2) *Otherwise, a person shall not be taken to have notice of any matter by reason of its being disclosed on the register or by reason of his having failed to search the register in the course of making such inquiries as ought reasonably to be made.*

(3) *The above provisions have effect subject to any other statutory provision as to whether a person is to be taken to have notice of any matter disclosed on the register.*

417   Power of court to dispense with signature

(1) *Where it is proposed to deliver further particulars of a charge, or to deliver a memorandum of a charge ceasing to affect the company's property, and—*

(a) *the chargee refuses to sign or authorise a person to sign on his behalf, or cannot be found, or*

(b) *the company refuses to authorise a person to sign on its behalf, the court may on the application of the company or the chargee, or of any other person having a sufficient interest in the matter, authorise the delivery of the particulars or memorandum without that signature.*

(2) *The order may be made on such terms as appear to the court to be appropriate.*

(3) *Where particulars or a memorandum are delivered to the registrar for registration in reliance on an order under this section, they must be accompanied by an office copy of the order.*

In such a case the references in sections 401 and 403 to the particulars or memorandum being duly signed are to their being otherwise duly signed.

(4) *The registrar shall file the office copy of the court order along with the particulars or memorandum.'.*

104   Interpretation, &c.

The following sections are inserted in Part XII of the Companies Act 1985—

'418   Regulations

Regulations under any provision of this Part, or prescribing anything for the purposes of any such provision—

(a) *may make different provision for different cases, and*

(b) *may contain such supplementary, incidental and transitional provisions as appear to the Secretary of State to be appropriate.*

419   Minor definitions

(1) *In this Part—*

'chargee' means the person for the time being entitled to exercise the security rights conferred by the charge;

'issue of debentures' means a group of debentures, or an amount of debenture stock, secured by the same charge; and

'series of debentures' means a group of debentures each containing or giving by reference to another instrument a charge to the benefit of which the holders of debentures of the series are entitled pari passu.

(2) *References in this Part to the creation of a charge include the variation of a charge which is not registrable so as to include property by virtue of which it becomes registrable.*

The provisions of section 414 (construction of references to date of creation of charge) apply in such a case with any necessary modifications.

(3) *References in this Part to the date of acquisition of property by a company are—*

(a) *in England and Wales, to the date on which the acquisition is completed, and*

(b) *in Scotland, to the date on which the transaction is settled.*

(4) *In the application of this Part to a floating charge created under the law of Scotland, references to crystallisation shall be construed as references to the attachment of the charge.*

(5) *References in this Part to the beginning of insolvency proceedings are to—*

(a) *the presentation of a petition on which an administration order or winding-up order is made, or*

(b) *the passing of a resolution for voluntary winding up.*

420   *Index of defined expressions*
The following Table shows the provisions of this Part defining or otherwise explaining expressions used in this Part (other than expressions used only in the same section)—

charge	sections 395(2) and 396(6)
charge requiring registration	section 396
chargee	section 419(1)
complete and accurate (in relation to registered particulars)	section 415(4)
creation of charge	section 419(2)
crystallisation (in relation to Scottish floating charge)	section 419(4)
date of acquisition (of property by a company)	section 419(3)
date of creation of charge	section 414
further particulars	section 401
insolvency proceedings, beginning of	section 419(5)
issue of debentures	section 419(1)
memorandum of charge ceasing to affect company's property	section 403
prescribed particulars	section 415(1) and (2)
property	section 395(2)
registered particulars	section 415(3)
registrar and registration in relation to a charge	section 395(4)
relevant event	section 399(2)
series of debentures	section 419(1).'.

107   *Consequential amendments*
The enactments specified in Schedule 16 have effect with the amendments specified there, which are consequential on the amendments made by the preceding provisions of this Part.

PART V   OTHER AMENDMENTS OF COMPANY LAW

Deregulation of private companies

117   **Power to make further provision by regulations**
   (1) The Secretary of State may by regulations make provision enabling private companies to elect, by elective resolution in accordance with section 379A of the Companies Act 1985, to dispense with compliance with such requirements of that Act as may be specified in the regulations, being requirements which appear to the Secretary of State to relate primarily to the internal administration and procedure of companies.
   (2) The regulations may add to, amend or repeal provisions of that Act; and may provide for any such provision to have effect, where an election is made, subject to such adaptations and modifications as appear to the Secretary of State to be appropriate.
   (3) The regulations may make different provision for different cases and may contain such supplementary, incidental and transitional provisions as appear to the Secretary of State to be appropriate.
   (4) Regulations under this section shall be made by statutory instrument.
   (5) No regulations under this section shall be made unless a draft of the instrument containing the regulations has been laid before Parliament and approved by a resolution of each House.

Miscellaneous

133   *Issue of redeemable shares*
   (1) In Part V of the Companies Act 1985 (share capital, its increase, maintenance and reduction), Chapter III (redeemable shares, purchase by a company of its own shares) is amended as follows.
   (2) After section 159 (power to issue redeemable shares) insert—

'159A   Terms and manner of redemption

(1) Redeemable shares may not be issued unless the following conditions are satisfied as regards the terms and manner of redemption.

(2) The date on or by which, or dates between which, the shares are to be or may be redeemed must be specified in the company's articles or, if the articles so provide, fixed by the directors, and in the latter case the date or dates must be fixed before the shares are issued.

(3) Any other circumstances in which the shares are to be or may be redeemed must be specified in the company's articles.

(4) The amount payable on redemption must be specified in, or determined in accordance with, the company's articles, and in the latter case the articles must not provide for the amount to be determined by reference to any person's discretion or opinion.

(5) Any other terms and conditions of redemption shall be specified in the company's articles.

(6) Nothing in this section shall be construed as requiring a company to provide in its articles for any matter for which provision is made by this Act.'.

(3) In section 160 (financing, &c. of redemption)—

    (a) omit subsection (3) (which is superseded by the new section 159A), and

    (b) in subsection (4) (cancellation of shares on redemption) for 'redeemed under this section' substitute 'redeemed under this Chapter'.

141   Application to declare dissolution of company void

[Subsections (1) to (3) make amendments to the Companies Act 1985, s. 651, which are incorporated in the text of that section in this book.]

(4) An application may be made under section 651(5) of the Companies Act 1985 as inserted by subsection (3) above (proceedings for damages for personal injury, etc.) in relation to a company dissolved before the commencement of this section notwithstanding that the time within which the dissolution might formerly have been declared void under that section had expired before commencement.

But no such application shall be made in relation to a company dissolved more than twenty years before the commencement of this section.

(5) Except as provided by subsection (4), the amendments made by this section do not apply in relation to a company which was dissolved more than two years before the commencement of this section.

142   Abolition of doctrine of deemed notice

(1) In Part XXIV of the Companies Act 1985 (the registrar of companies, his functions and offices), after section 711 insert—

'711A   Exclusion of deemed notice

(1) A person shall not be taken to have notice of any matter merely because of its being disclosed in any document kept by the registrar of companies (and thus available for inspection) or made available by the company for inspection.

(2) This does not affect the question whether a person is affected by notice of any matter by reason of a failure to make such inquiries as ought reasonably to be made.

(3) In this section 'document' includes any material which contains information.

(4) Nothing in this section affects the operation of—

    (a) section 416 of this Act (under which a person taking a charge over a company's property is deemed to have notice of matters disclosed on the companies charges register), or

    (b) section 198 of the Law of Property Act 1925 as it applies by virtue of section 3(7) of the Land Charges Act 1972 (under which the registration of certain land charges under Part XII, or Chapter III of Part XXIII, of this Act is deemed to constitute actual notice for all purposes connected with the land affected).'.

. . .

144 *'Subsidiary', 'holding company' and 'wholly-owned subsidiary'*
[*Subsection (1) substitutes a new s. 736 in the Companies Act 1985, and that substitution has been made in the text of the 1985 Act in this book.*]

(2) Any reference in any enactment (including any enactment contained in subordinate legislation within the meaning of the Interpretation Act 1978) to a 'subsidiary' or 'holding company' within the meaning of section 736 of the Companies Act 1985 shall, subject to any express amendment or saving made by or under this Act, be read as referring to a subsidiary or holding company as defined in section 736 as substituted by subsection (1) above.

This applies whether the reference is specific or general, express or implied.

. . .

(6) So much of section 23(3) of the Interpretation Act 1978 as applies section 17(2)(a) of that Act (presumption as to meaning of references to enactments repealed and re-enacted) to deeds or other instruments or documents does not apply in relation to the repeal and re-enactment by this section of section 736 of the Companies Act 1985.

PART X   MISCELLANEOUS AND GENERAL PROVISIONS

General

215   Commencement and transitional provisions
(1) The following provisions of this Act come into force on Royal Assent—
  (a) in Part V (amendments of company law), section 141 (application to declare dissolution of company void);
  (b) in Part VI (mergers)—
     (i) sections 147 to 150, and
     (ii) paragraphs 2 to 12, 14 to 16, 18 to 20, 22 to 25 of Schedule 20, and section 153 so far as relating to those paragraphs;
  (c) in Part VIII (amendments of the Financial Services Act 1986), section 202 (offers of short-dated debentures);
  (d) in Part X (miscellaneous and general provisions), the repeals made by Schedule 24 in sections 71, 74, 88 and 89 of, and Schedule 9 to, the Fair Trading Act 1973, and section 212 so far as relating to those repeals.

(2) The other provisions of this Act come into force on such day as the Secretary of State may appoint by order made by statutory instrument; and different days may be appointed for different provisions and different purposes.

(3) An order bringing into force any provision may contain such transitional provisions and savings as appear to the Secretary of State to be necessary or expedient.

(4) The Secretary of State may also by order under this section amend any enactment which refers to the commencement of a provision brought into force by the order so as to substitute a reference to the actual date on which it comes into force.

216   Short title
This Act may be cited as the Companies Act 1989.

Section 107	*SCHEDULE 16*
	AMENDMENTS CONSEQUENTIAL ON PART IV

Companies Act 1985 (c. 6)

2.—(1) *Schedule 24 to the Companies Act 1985 (punishment of offences) is amended as follows.*
(2) *For the entries relating to sections 399(3) to 423(3) (offences under Part XII: registration of charges) substitute—*

'398(3)	Company failing to deliver particulars of charge to registrar.	1. On indictment.	A fine.
		2. Summary.	The statutory maximum.
408(3)	Company failing to deliver particulars of taking up of issue of debentures.	Summary.	One-fifth of the statutory maximum.
409(4)	Failure to give notice to registrar of appointment of receiver or manager, or of his ceasing to act.	Summary.	One-fifth of the statutory maximum.
410(4)	Failure to comply with requirements of regulations under s. 410.	Summary.	One-fifth of the statutory maximum.
411(4)	Failure to keep copies of charging instruments or register at registered office.	1. On indictment.	A fine.
		2. Summary.	The statutory maximum.
412(4)	Refusing inspection of charging instrument or register or failing to supply copies.	Summary.	One-fifth of the statutory maximum. '.

Insolvency Act 1986 (c. 45)

3.—(1) The Insolvency Act 1986 is amended as follows.

(2) In section 9(3) (restrictions on making administration order where administrative receiver has been appointed), in paragraph (b) (exceptions) insert—

'(i) be void against the administrator to any extent by virtue of the provisions of Part XII of the Companies Act 1985 (registration of company charges),';

and renumber the existing sub-paragraphs as (ii) to (iv).

(3) In sections 45(5), 53(2), 54(3) and 62(5) (offences of failing to deliver documents relating to appointment or cessation of appointment of receiver) omit the words 'and, for continued contravention, to a daily default fine'.

Company Directors Disqualification Act 1986 (c. 46)

4. In Schedule 1 to the Company Directors Disqualification Act 1986 (matters relevant to determining unfitness of directors), in paragraph 4 (failure of company to comply with certain provisions), for sub-paragraph (h) substitute—

'(h) sections 398 and 703D (duty of company to deliver particulars of charge on its property).'.

<table>
<tr><td>**Section 212**</td><td style="text-align:center">SCHEDULE 24
REPEALS</td></tr>
</table>

Chapter	Short title	Extent of repeal
1986 c. 45.	Insolvency Act 1986.	In sections 45(5), 53(2), 54(3) and 62(5), the words 'and, for continued contravention, to a daily default fine'.
		In Schedule 10, the entries in column 5 relating to sections 45(5), 53(2), 54(3) and 62(5).

Criminal Justice Act 1993

(1993, c. 36)

An Act . . . to implement provisions of the Community Council Directive No. 89/592/EEC and to amend and restate the law about insider dealing in securities; . . . and for connected purposes.

[27 July 1993]

PART V   INSIDER DEALING

The offence of insider dealing

52   The offence

(1) An individual who has information as an insider is guilty of insider dealing if, in the circumstances mentioned in subsection (3), he deals in securities that are price-affected securities in relation to the information.

(2) An individual who has information as an insider is also guilty of insider dealing if—

(a) he encourages another person to deal in securities that are (whether or not that other knows it) price-affected securities in relation to the information, knowing or having reasonable cause to believe that the dealing would take place in the circumstances mentioned in subsection (3); or

(b) he discloses the information, otherwise than in the proper performance of the functions of his employment, office or profession, to another person.

(3) The circumstances referred to above are that the acquisition or disposal in question occurs on a regulated market, or that the person dealing relies on a professional intermediary or is himself acting as a professional intermediary.

(4) This section has effect subject to section 53.

53   Defences

(1) An individual is not guilty of insider dealing by virtue of dealing in securities if he shows—

(a) that he did not at the time expect the dealing to result in a profit attributable to the fact that the information in question was price-sensitive information in relation to the securities, or

(b) that at the time he believed on reasonable grounds that the information had been disclosed widely enough to ensure that none of those taking part in the dealing would be prejudiced by not having the information, or

(c) that he would have done what he did even if he had not had the information.

(2) An individual is not guilty of insider dealing by virtue of encouraging another person to deal in securities if he shows—

(a) that he did not at the time expect the dealing to result in a profit attributable to the fact that the information in question was price-sensitive information in relation to the securities, or

(b) that at the time he believed on reasonable grounds that the information had been or would be disclosed widely enough to ensure that none of those taking part in the dealing would be prejudiced by not having the information, or

(c) that he would have done what he did even if he had not had the information.

(3) An individual is not guilty of insider dealing by virtue of a disclosure of information if he shows—

(a) that he did not at the time expect any person, because of the disclosure, to deal in securities in the circumstances mentioned in subsection (3) of section 52; or

(b) that, although he had such an expectation at the time, he did not expect the dealing to result in a profit attributable to the fact that the information was price-sensitive information in relation to the securities.

(4) Schedule 1 (special defences) shall have effect.

(5) The Treasury may by order amend Schedule 1.

(6) In this section references to a profit include references to the avoidance of a loss.

Interpretation

54   Securities to which Part V applies

(1) This Part applies to any security which—

    (a) falls within any paragraph of Schedule 2; and

    (b) satisfies any conditions applying to it under an order made by the Treasury for the purposes of this subsection;

and in the provisions of this Part (other than that Schedule) any reference to a security is a reference to a security to which this Part applies.

(2) The Treasury may by order amend Schedule 2.

55   'Dealing' in securities

(1) For the purposes of this Part, a person deals in securities if—

    (a) he acquires or disposes of the securities (whether as principal or agent); or

    (b) he procures, directly or indirectly, an acquisition or disposal of the securities by any other person.

(2) For the purposes of this Part, 'acquire', in relation to a security, includes—

    (a) agreeing to acquire the security; and

    (b) entering into a contract which creates the security.

(3) For the purposes of this Part, 'dispose', in relation to a security, includes—

    (a) agreeing to dispose of the security; and

    (b) bringing to an end a contract which created the security.

(4) For the purposes of subsection (1), a person procures an acquisition or disposal of a security if the security is acquired or disposed of by a person who is—

    (a) his agent,

    (b) his nominee, or

    (c) a person who is acting at his direction,

in relation to the acquisition or disposal.

(5) Subsection (4) is not exhaustive as to the circumstances in which one person may be regarded as procuring an acquisition or disposal of securities by another.

56   'Inside information', etc.

(1) For the purposes of this section and section 57, 'inside information' means information which—

    (a) relates to particular securities or to a particular issuer of securities or to particular issuers of securities and not to securities generally or to issuers of securities generally;

    (b) is specific or precise;

    (c) has not been made public; and

    (d) if it were made public would be likely to have a significant effect on the price of any securities.

(2) For the purposes of this Part, securities are 'price-affected securities' in relation to inside information, and inside information is 'price-sensitive information' in relation to securities, if and only if the information would, if made public, be likely to have a significant effect on the price of the securities.

(3) For the purposes of this section 'price' includes value.

57   'Insiders'

(1) For the purposes of this Part, a person has information as an insider if and only if—

    (a) it is, and he knows that it is, inside information, and

    (b) he has it, and knows that he has it, from an inside source.

(2) For the purposes of subsection (1), a person has information from an inside source if and only if—
- (a) he has it through—
    - (i) being a director, employee or shareholder of an issuer of securities; or
    - (ii) having access to the information by virtue of his employment, office or profession; or
- (b) the direct or indirect source of his information is a person within paragraph (a).

58   Information 'made public'

(1) For the purposes of section 56, 'made public', in relation to information, shall be construed in accordance with the following provisions of this section; but those provisions are not exhaustive as to the meaning of that expression.

(2) Information is made public if—
- (a) it is published in accordance with the rules of a regulated market for the purpose of informing investors and their professional advisers;
- (b) it is contained in records which by virtue of any enactment are open to inspection by the public;
- (c) it can be readily acquired by those likely to deal in any securities—
    - (i) to which the information relates, or
    - (ii) of an issuer to which the information relates; or
- (d) it is derived from information which has been made public.

(3) Information may be treated as made public even though—
- (a) it can be acquired only by persons exercising diligence or expertise;
- (b) it is communicated to a section of the public and not to the public at large;
- (c) it can be acquired only by observation;
- (d) it is communicated only on payment of a fee; or
- (e) it is published only outside the United Kingdom.

59   'Professional intermediary'

(1) For the purposes of this Part, a 'professional intermediary' is a person—
- (a) who carries on a business consisting of an activity mentioned in subsection (2) and who holds himself out to the public or any section of the public (including a section of the public constituted by persons such as himself) as willing to engage in any such business; or
- (b) who is employed by a person falling within paragraph (a) to carry out any such activity.

(2) The activities referred to in subsection (1) are—
- (a) acquiring or disposing of securities (whether as principal or agent); or
- (b) acting as an intermediary between persons taking part in any dealing in securities.

(3) A person is not to be treated as carrying on a business consisting of an activity mentioned in subsection (2)—
- (a) if the activity in question is merely incidental to some other activity not falling within subsection (2); or
- (b) merely because he occasionally conducts one of those activities.

(4) For the purposes of section 52, a person dealing in securities relies on a professional intermediary if and only if a person who is acting as a professional intermediary carries out an activity mentioned in subsection (2) in relation to that dealing.

60   Other interpretation provisions

(1) For the purposes of this Part, 'regulated market' means any market, however operated, which, by an order made by the Treasury, is identified (whether by name or by reference to criteria prescribed by the order) as a regulated market for the purposes of this Part.

(2) For the purposes of this Part an 'issuer', in relation to any securities, means any

company, public sector body or individual by which or by whom the securities have been or are to be issued.

(3) For the purposes of this Part—

(a) 'company' means any body (whether or not incorporated and wherever incorporated or constituted) which is not a public sector body; and

(b) 'public sector body' means—

(i) the government of the United Kingdom, of Northern Ireland or of any country or territory outside the United Kingdom;

(ii) a local authority in the United Kingdom or elsewhere;

(iii) any international organisation the members of which include the United Kingdom or another member state;

(iv) the Bank of England; or

(v) the central bank of any sovereign State.

(4) For the purposes of this Part, information shall be treated as relating to an issuer of securities which is a company not only where it is about the company but also where it may affect the company's business prospects.

Miscellaneous

61 Penalties and prosecution

(1) An inividual guilty of insider dealing shall be liable—

(a) on summary conviction, to a fine not exceeding the statutory maximum or imprisonment for a term not exceeding six months or to both; or

(b) on conviction on indictment, to a fine or imprisonment for a term not exceeding seven years or to both.

(2) Proceedings for offences under this Part shall not be instituted in England and Wales except by or with the consent of—

(a) the Secretary of State; or

(b) the Director of Public Prosecutions.

(3) In relation to proceedings in Northern Ireland for offences under this Part, subsection (2) shall have effect as if the reference to the Director of Public Prosecutions were a reference to the Director of Public Prosecutions for Northern Ireland.

62 Territorial scope of offence of insider dealing

(1) An individual is not guilty of an offence falling within subsection (1) of section 52 unless—

(a) he was within the United Kingdom at the time when he is alleged to have done any act constituting or forming part of the alleged dealing;

(b) the regulated market on which the dealing is alleged to have occurred is one which, by an order made by the Treasury, is identified (whether by name or by reference to criteria prescribed by the order) as being, for the purposes of this Part, regulated in the United Kingdom; or

(c) the professional intermediary was within the United Kingdom at the time when he is alleged to have done anything by means of which the offence is alleged to have been committed.

(2) An individual is not guilty of an offence falling within subsection (2) of section 52 unless—

(a) he was within the United Kingdom at the time when he is alleged to have disclosed the information or encouraged the dealing; or

(b) the alleged recipient of the information or encouragement was within the United Kingdom at the time when he is alleged to have received the information or encouragement.

63 Limits on section 52

(1) Section 52 does not apply to anything done by an individual acting on behalf of a public sector body in pursuit of monetary policies or policies with respect to exchange rates or the management of public debt or foreign exchange reserves.

(2) No contract shall be void or unenforceable by reason only of section 52.

64 Orders

(1) Any power under this Part to make an order shall be exercisable by statutory instrument.

(2) No order shall be made under this Part unless a draft of it has been laid before and approved by a resolution of each House of Parliament.

(3) An order under this Part—

(a) may make different provision for different cases; and

(b) may contain such incidental, supplemental and transitional provisions as the Treasury consider expedient.

SCHEDULES

Section 53(4)

SCHEDULE 1
SPECIAL DEFENCES

Market makers

1.—(1) An individual is not guilty of insider dealing by virtue of dealing in securities or encouraging another person to deal if he shows that he acted in good faith in the course of—

(a) his business as a market maker, or

(b) his employment in the business of a market maker.

(2) A market maker is a person who—

(a) holds himself out at all normal times in compliance with the rules of a regulated market or an approved organisation as willing to acquire or dispose of securities; and

(b) is recognised as doing so under those rules.

(3) In this paragraph 'approved organisation' means an international securities self-regulating organisation approved by the Treasury under any relevant order under section 22 of the Financial Services and Markets Act 2000.

Market information

2.—(1) An individual is not guilty of insider dealing by virtue of dealing in securities or encouraging another person to deal if he shows that—

(a) the information which he had as an insider was market information; and

(b) it was reasonable for an individual in his position to have acted as he did despite having that information as an insider at the time.

(2) In determining whether it is reasonable for an individual to do any act despite having market information at the time, there shall, in particular, be taken into account—

(a) the content of the information;

(b) the circumstances in which he first had the information and in what capacity; and

(c) the capacity in which he now acts.

3. An individual is not guilty of insider dealing by virtue of dealing in securities or encouraging another person to deal if he shows—

(a) that he acted—

(i) in connection with an acquisition or disposal which was under consideration or the subject of negotiation, or in the course of a series of such acquisitions or disposals; and

(ii) with a view to facilitating the accomplishment of the acquisition or disposal or the series of acquisitions or disposals; and

(b) that the information which he had as an insider was market information arising directly out of his involvement in the acquisition or disposal or series of acquisitions or disposals.

4.   For the purposes of paragraphs 2 and 3 market information is information consisting of one or more of the following facts—

(a) that securities of a particular kind have been or are to be acquired or disposed of, or that their acquisition or disposal is under consideration or the subject of negotiation;

(b) that securities of a particular kind have not been or are not to be acquired or disposed of;

(c) the number of securities acquired or disposed of or to be acquired or disposed of or whose acquisition or disposal is under consideration or the subject of negotiation;

(d) the price (or range of prices) at which securities have been or are to be acquired or disposed of or the price (or range of prices) at which securities whose acquisition or disposal is under consideration or the subject of negotiation may be acquired or disposed of;

(e) the identity of the persons involved or likely to be involved in any capacity in an acquisition or disposal.

Price stabilisation

5.—(1) An individual is not guilty of insider dealing by virtue of dealing in securities or encouraging another person to deal if he shows that he acted in conformity with the price stabilisation rules.

(2) 'Price stabilisation rules' means rules made under section 144(1) of the Financial Services and Markets Act 2000.

Section 54   SCHEDULE 2

SECURITIES

Shares

1.   Shares and stock in the share capital of a company ('shares').

Debt securities

2.   Any instrument creating or acknowledging indebtedness which is issued by a company or public sector body, including, in particular, debentures, debenture stock, loan stock, bonds and certificates of deposit ('debt securities').

Warrants

3.   Any right (whether conferred by warrant or otherwise) to subscribe for shares or debt securities ('warrants').

Depositary receipts

4.—(1) The rights under any depositary receipt.

(2) For the purposes of sub-paragraph (1) a 'depositary receipt' means a certificate or other record (whether or not in the form of a document)—

(a) which is issued by or on behalf of a person who holds any relevant securities of a particular issuer; and

(b) which acknowledges that another person is entitled to rights in relation to the relevant securities or relevant securities of the same kind.

(3) In sub-paragraph (2) 'relevant securities' means shares, debt securities and warrants.

Options

5. Any option to acquire or dispose of any security falling within any other paragraph of this Schedule.

Futures

6.—(1) Rights under a contract for the acquisition or disposal of relevant securities under which delivery is to be made at a future date and at a price agreed when the contract is made.

(2) In sub-paragraph (1)—

(a) the references to a future date and to a price agreed when the contract is made include references to a date and a price determined in accordance with terms of the contract; and

(b) 'relevant securities' means any security falling within any other paragraph of this Schedule.

Contracts for differences

7.—(1) Rights under a contract which does not provide for the delivery of securities but whose purpose or pretended purpose is to secure a profit or avoid a loss by reference to fluctuations in—

(a) a share index or other similar factor connected with relevant securities;

(b) the price of particular relevant securities; or

(c) the interest rate offered on money placed on deposit.

(2) In sub-paragraph (1) 'relevant securities' means any security falling within any other paragraph of this Schedule.

Electronic Communications Act 2000
(2000, c. 7)

An Act to make provision to facilitate the use of electronic communications and electronic data storage . . . and for connected purposes.   [25 May 2000]

15 General interpretation
(1) . . .
'communication' includes a communication comprising sounds or images or both and a communication effecting a payment;
'electronic communication' means a communication transmitted (whether from one person to another, from one device to another or from a person to a device or vice versa)—

(a) by means of a telecommunication system (within the meaning of the Telecommunications Act 1984); or

(b) by other means but while in an electronic form.

. . .

[*Section 4(1) of the Telecommunications Act 1984 provides:*

In this Act 'telecommunication system' means a system for the conveyance, through the agency of electric, magnetic, electromagnetic, electrochemical or electromechanical energy, of—

(a) *speech, music and other sounds;*
(b) *visual images;*
(c) *signals serving for the impartation (whether as between persons and persons, things and things or persons and things) of any matter otherwise than in the form of sounds or visual images; or*
(d) *signals serving for the actuation or control of machinery or apparatus.*]

Financial Services and Markets Act 2000
(2000, c. 8)

An Act to make provision about the regulation of financial services and markets; to provide for the transfer of certain statutory functions relating to building societies, industrial and provident societies and certain other mutual societies; and for connected purposes.   [14 June 2000]

PART II   REGULATED AND PROHIBITED ACTIVITIES

The general prohibition

19   The general prohibition
(1) No person may carry on a regulated activity in the United Kingdom, or purport to do so, unless he is—
   (a) an authorised person; or
   (b) an exempt person.
(2) The prohibition is referred to in this Act as the general prohibition.

Requirement for permission

20   Authorised persons acting without permission
(1) If an authorised person carries on a regulated activity in the United Kingdom, or purports to do so, otherwise than in accordance with permission—
   (a) given to him by the Authority under Part IV, or
   (b) resulting from any other provision of this Act,
he is to be taken to have contravened a requirement imposed on him by the Authority under this Act.
(2) The contravention does not—
   (a) make a person guilty of an offence;
   (b) make any transaction void or unenforceable; or
   (c) (subject to subsection (3)) give rise to any right of action for breach of statutory duty.
(3) In prescribed cases the contravention is actionable at the suit of a person who suffers loss as a result of the contravention, subject to the defences and other incidents applying to actions for breach of statutory duty.

Financial promotion

21   Restrictions on financial promotion
(1) A person ('A') must not, in the course of business, communicate an invitation or inducement to engage in investment activity.
(2) But subsection (1) does not apply if—
   (a) A is an authorised person; or
   (b) the content of the communication is approved for the purposes of this section by an authorised person.

(3) In the case of a communication originating outside the United Kingdom, subsection (1) applies only if the communication is capable of having an effect in the United Kingdom.

(4) The Treasury may by order specify circumstances in which a person is to be regarded for the purposes of subsection (1) as—

    (a) acting in the course of business;

    (b) not acting in the course of business.

(5) The Treasury may by order specify circumstances (which may include compliance with financial promotion rules) in which subsection (1) does not apply.

(6) An order under subsection (5) may, in particular, provide that subsection (1) does not apply in relation to communications—

    (a) of a specified description;

    (b) originating in a specified country or territory outside the United Kingdom;

    (c) originating in a country or territory which falls within a specified description of country or territory outside the United Kingdom; or

    (d) originating outside the United Kingdom.

(7) The Treasury may by order repeal subsection (3).

(8) 'Engaging in investment activity' means—

    (a) entering or offering to enter into an agreement the making or performance of which by either party constitutes a controlled activity; or

    (b) exercising any rights conferred by a controlled investment to acquire, dispose of, underwrite or convert a controlled investment.

(9) An activity is a controlled activity if—

    (a) it is an activity of a specified kind or one which falls within a specified class of activity; and

    (b) it relates to an investment of a specified kind, or to one which falls within a specified class of investment.

(10) An investment is a controlled investment if it is an investment of a specified kind or one which falls within a specified class of investment.

(11) Schedule 2 (except paragraph 26) applies for the purposes of subsections (9) and (10) with references to section 22 being read as references to each of those subsections.

(12) Nothing in Schedule 2, as applied by subsection (11), limits the powers conferred by subsection (9) or (10).

(13) 'Communicate' includes causing a communication to be made.

(14) 'Investment' includes any asset, right or interest.

(15) 'Specified' means specified in an order made by the Treasury.

Regulated activities

22   The classes of activity and categories of investment

(1) An activity is a regulated activity for the purposes of this Act if it is an activity of a specified kind which is carried on by way of business and—

    (a) relates to an investment of a specified kind; or

    (b) in the case of an activity of a kind which is also specified for the purposes of this paragraph, is carried on in relation to property of any kind.

(2) Schedule 2 makes provision supplementing this section.

(3) Nothing in Schedule 2 limits the powers conferred by subsection (1).

(4) 'Investment' includes any asset, right or interest.

(5) 'Specified' means specified in an order made by the Treasury.

Offences

23 Contravention of the general prohibition

(1) A person who contravenes the general prohibition is guilty of an offence and liable—

(a) on summary conviction, to imprisonment for a term not exceeding six months or a fine not exceeding the statutory maximum, or both;

(b) on conviction on indictment, to imprisonment for a term not exceeding two years or a fine, or both.

(2) In this Act 'an authorisation offence' means an offence under this section.

(3) In proceedings for an authorisation offence it is a defence for the accused to show that he took all reasonable precautions and exercised all due diligence to avoid committing the offence.

24 False claims to be authorised or exempt

(1) A person who is neither an authorised person nor, in relation to the regulated activity in question, an exempt person is guilty of an offence if he—

(a) describes himself (in whatever terms) as an authorised person;

(b) describes himself (in whatever terms) as an exempt person in relation to the regulated activity; or

(c) behaves, or otherwise holds himself out, in a manner which indicates (or which is reasonably likely to be understood as indicating) that he is—

(i) an authorised person; or

(ii) an exempt person in relation to the regulated activity.

(2) In proceedings for an offence under this section it is a defence for the accused to show that he took all reasonable precautions and exercised all due diligence to avoid committing the offence.

(3) A person guilty of an offence under this section is liable on summary conviction to imprisonment for a term not exceeding six months or a fine not exceeding level 5 on the standard scale, or both.

(4) But where the conduct constituting the offence involved or included the public display of any material, the maximum fine for the offence is level 5 on the standard scale multiplied by the number of days for which the display continued.

25 Contravention of section 21

(1) A person who contravenes section 21(1) is guilty of an offence and liable—

(a) on summary conviction, to imprisonment for a term not exceeding six months or a fine not exceeding the statutory maximum, or both;

(b) on conviction on indictment, to imprisonment for a term not exceeding two years or a fine, or both.

(2) In proceedings for an offence under this section it is a defence for the accused to show—

(a) that he believed on reasonable grounds that the content of the communication was prepared, or approved for the purposes of section 21, by an authorised person; or

(b) that he took all reasonable precautions and exercised all due diligence to avoid committing the offence.

Enforceability of agreements

26 Agreements made by unauthorised persons

(1) An agreement made by a person in the course of carrying on a regulated activity in contravention of the general prohibition is unenforceable against the other party.

(2) The other party is entitled to recover—
  (a) any money or other property paid or transferred by him under the agreement; and
  (b) compensation for any loss sustained by him as a result of having parted with it.
(3) 'Agreement' means an agreement—
  (a) made after this section comes into force; and
  (b) the making or performance of which constitutes, or is part of, the regulated activity in question.
(4) This section does not apply if the regulated activity is accepting deposits.

27 Agreements made through unauthorised persons

(1) An agreement made by an authorised person ('the provider')—
  (a) in the course of carrying on a regulated activity (not in contravention of the general prohibition), but
  (b) in consequence of something said or done by another person ('the third party') in the course of a regulated activity carried on by the third party in contravention of the general prohibition,
is unenforceable against the other party.
(2) The other party is entitled to recover—
  (a) any money or other property paid or transferred by him under the agreement; and
  (b) compensation for any loss sustained by him as a result of having parted with it.
(3) 'Agreement' means an agreement—
  (a) made after this section comes into force; and
  (b) the making or performance of which constitutes, or is part of, the regulated activity in question carried on by the provider.
(4) This section does not apply if the regulated activity is accepting deposits.

28 Agreements made unenforceable by section 26 or 27

(1) This section applies to an agreement which is unenforceable because of section 26 or 27.
(2) The amount of compensation recoverable as a result of that section is—
  (a) the amount agreed by the parties; or
  (b) on the application of either party, the amount determined by the court.
(3) If the court is satisfied that it is just and equitable in the circumstances of the case, it may allow—
  (a) the agreement to be enforced; or
  (b) money and property paid or transferred under the agreement to be retained.
(4) In considering whether to allow the agreement to be enforced or (as the case may be) the money or property paid or transferred under the agreement to be retained the court must—
  (a) if the case arises as a result of section 26, have regard to the issue mentioned in subsection (5); or
  (b) if the case arises as a result of section 27, have regard to the issue mentioned in subsection (6).
(5) The issue is whether the person carrying on the regulated activity concerned reasonably believed that he was not contravening the general prohibition by making the agreement.
(6) The issue is whether the provider knew that the third party was (in carrying on the regulated activity) contravening the general prohibition.
(7) If the person against whom the agreement is unenforceable—
  (a) elects not to perform the agreement, or
  (b) as a result of this section, recovers money paid or other property transferred by him under the agreement,
he must repay any money and return any other property received by him under the agreement.

(8) If property transferred under the agreement has passed to a third party, a reference in section 26 or 27 or this section to that property is to be read as a reference to its value at the time of its transfer under the agreement.

(9) The commission of an authorisation offence does not make the agreement concerned illegal or invalid to any greater extent than is provided by section 26 or 27.

29 Accepting deposits in breach of general prohibition

(1) This section applies to an agreement between a person ('the depositor') and another person ('the deposit-taker') made in the course of the carrying on by the deposit-taker of accepting deposits in contravention of the general prohibition.

(2) If the depositor is not entitled under the agreement to recover without delay any money deposited by him, he may apply to the court for an order directing the deposit-taker to return the money to him.

(3) The court need not make such an order if it is satisfied that it would not be just and equitable for the money deposited to be returned, having regard to the issue mentioned in subsection (4).

(4) The issue is whether the deposit-taker reasonably believed that he was not contravening the general prohibition by making the agreement.

(5) 'Agreement' means an agreement—

    (a) made after this section comes into force; and

    (b) the making or performance of which constitutes, or is part of, accepting deposits.

30 Enforceability of agreements resulting from unlawful communications

(1) In this section—

'unlawful communication' means a communication in relation to which there has been a contravention of section 21(1);

'controlled agreement' means an agreement the making or performance of which by either party constitutes a controlled activity for the purposes of that section; and

'controlled investment' has the same meaning as in section 21.

(2) If in consequence of an unlawful communication a person enters as a customer into a controlled agreement, it is unenforceable against him and he is entitled to recover—

    (a) any money or other property paid or transferred by him under the agreement; and

    (b) compensation for any loss sustained by him as a result of having parted with it.

(3) If in consequence of an unlawful communication a person exercises any rights conferred by a controlled investment, no obligation to which he is subject as a result of exercising them is enforceable against him and he is entitled to recover—

    (a) any money or other property paid or transferred by him under the obligation; and

    (b) compensation for any loss sustained by him as a result of having parted with it.

(4) But the court may allow—

    (a) the agreement or obligation to be enforced, or

    (b) money or property paid or transferred under the agreement or obligation to be retained,

if it is satisfied that it is just and equitable in the circumstances of the case.

(5) In considering whether to allow the agreement or obligation to be enforced or (as the case may be) the money or property paid or transferred under the agreement to be retained the court must have regard to the issues mentioned in subsections (6) and (7).

(6) If the applicant made the unlawful communication, the issue is whether he reasonably believed that he was not making such a communication.

(7) If the applicant did not make the unlawful communication, the issue is whether he knew that the agreement was entered into in consequence of such a communication.

(8) 'Applicant' means the person seeking to enforce the agreement or obligation or retain the money or property paid or transferred.

(9) Any reference to making a communication includes causing a communication to be made.

(10) The amount of compensation recoverable as a result of subsection (2) or (3) is—

    (a) the amount agreed between the parties; or

    (b) on the application of either party, the amount determined by the court.

(11) If a person elects not to perform an agreement or an obligation which (by virtue of subsection (2) or (3)) is unenforceable against him, he must repay any money and return any other property received by him under the agreement.

(12) If (by virtue of subsection (2) or (3)) a person recovers money paid or property transferred by him under an agreement or obligation, he must repay any money and return any other property received by him as a result of exercising the rights in question.

(13) If any property required to be returned under this section has passed to a third party, references to that property are to be read as references to its value at the time of its receipt by the person required to return it.

PART III   AUTHORISATION AND EXEMPTION

Authorisation

31   Authorised persons

. . . (2) In this Act 'authorised person' means a person who is authorised for the purposes of this Act.

PART IV   PERMISSION TO CARRY ON REGULATED ACTIVITIES

Application for permission

40   Application for permission

. . . (4) A permission given by the Authority under this Part or having effect as if so given is referred to in this Act as 'a Part IV permission'.

PART VI   OFFICIAL LISTING

The competent authority

72   The competent authority

(1) On the coming into force of this section, the functions conferred on the competent authority by this Part are to be exercised by the Authority.

(2) Schedule 7 modifies this Act in its application to the Authority when it acts as the competent authority.

(3) But provision is made by Schedule 8 allowing some or all of those functions to be transferred by the Treasury so as to be exercisable by another person.

73   General duty of the competent authority

(1) In discharging its general functions the competent authority must have regard to—

    (a) the need to use its resources in the most efficient and economic way;

    (b) the principle that a burden or restriction which is imposed on a person should be proportionate to the benefits, considered in general terms, which are expected to arise from the imposition of that burden or restriction;

    (c) the desirability of facilitating innovation in respect of listed securities;

    (d) the international character of capital markets and the desirability of maintaining the competitive position of the United Kingdom;

    (e) the need to minimise the adverse effects on competition of anything done in the discharge of those functions;

    (f) the desirability of facilitating competition in relation to listed securities.

(2) The competent authority's general functions are—

    (a) its function of making rules under this Part (considered as a whole);

    (b) its functions in relation to the giving of general guidance in relation to this Part (considered as a whole);

    (c) its function of determining the general policy and principles by reference to which it performs particular functions under this Part.

The official list

74   The official list

(1) The competent authority must maintain the official list.

(2) The competent authority may admit to the official list such securities and other things as it considers appropriate.

(3) But—

    (a) nothing may be admitted to the official list except in accordance with this Part; and

    (b) the Treasury may by order provide that anything which falls within a description or category specified in the order may not be admitted to the official list.

(4) The competent authority may make rules ('listing rules') for the purposes of this Part.

(5) In the following provisions of this Part—

'security' means anything which has been, or may be, admitted to the official list; and 'listing' means being included in the official list in accordance with this Part.

Listing

75   Applications for listing

(1) Admission to the official list may be granted only on an application made to the competent authority in such manner as may be required by listing rules.

(2) No application for listing may be entertained by the competent authority unless it is made by, or with the consent of, the issuer of the securities concerned.

(3) No application for listing may be entertained by the competent authority in respect of securities which are to be issued by a body of a prescribed kind.

(4) The competent authority may not grant an application for listing unless it is satisfied that—

    (a) the requirements of listing rules (so far as they apply to the application), and

    (b) any other requirements imposed by the authority in relation to the application,

are complied with.

(5) An application for listing may be refused if, for a reason relating to the issuer, the competent authority considers that granting it would be detrimental to the interests of investors.

(6) An application for listing securities which are already officially listed in another EEA State may be refused if the issuer has failed to comply with any obligations to which he is subject as a result of that listing.

76   Decision on application

(1) The competent authority must notify the applicant of its decision on an application for listing—

    (a) before the end of the period of six months beginning with the date on which the application is received; or

    (b) if within that period the authority has required the applicant to provide further information in connection with the application, before the end of the period of six months beginning with the date on which that information is provided.

(2) If the competent authority fails to comply with subsection (1), it is to be taken to have decided to refuse the application.

(3) If the competent authority decides to grant an application for listing, it must give the applicant written notice.

(4) If the competent authority proposes to refuse an application for listing, it must give the applicant a warning notice.

(5) If the competent authority decides to refuse an application for listing, it must give the applicant a decision notice.

(6) If the competent authority decides to refuse an application for listing, the applicant may refer the matter to the Tribunal.

(7) If securities are admitted to the official list, their admission may not be called in question on the ground that any requirement or condition for their admission has not been complied with.

77   Discontinuance and suspension of listing

(1) The competent authority may, in accordance with listing rules, discontinue the listing of any securities if satisfied that there are special circumstances which preclude normal regular dealings in them.

(2) The competent authority may, in accordance with listing rules, suspend the listing of any securities.

(3) If securities are suspended under subsection (2) they are to be treated, for the purposes of sections 96 and 99, as still being listed.

(4) This section applies to securities whenever they were admitted to the official list.

(5) If the competent authority discontinues or suspends the listing of any securities, the issuer may refer the matter to the Tribunal.

78   Discontinuance or suspension: procedure

(1) A discontinuance or suspension takes effect—
  (a) immediately, if the notice under subsection (2) states that that is the case;
  (b) in any other case, on such date as may be specified in that notice.

(2) If the competent authority—
  (a) proposes to discontinue or suspend the listing of securities, or
  (b) discontinues or suspends the listing of securities with immediate effect,
it must give the issuer of the securities written notice.

(3) The notice must—
  (a) give details of the discontinuance or suspension;
  (b) state the competent authority's reasons for the discontinuance or suspension and for choosing the date on which it took effect or takes effect;
  (c) inform the issuer of the securities that he may make representations to the competent authority within such period as may be specified in the notice (whether or not he has referred the matter to the Tribunal);
  (d) inform him of the date on which the discontinuance or suspension took effect or will take effect; and
  (e) inform him of his right to refer the matter to the Tribunal.

(4) The competent authority may extend the period within which representations may be made to it.

(5) If, having considered any representations made by the issuer of the securities, the competent authority decides—
  (a) to discontinue or suspend the listing of the securities, or
  (b) if the discontinuance or suspension has taken effect, not to cancel it,
the competent authority must give the issuer of the securities written notice.

(6) A notice given under subsection (5) must inform the issuer of the securities of his right to refer the matter to the Tribunal.

(7) If a notice informs a person of his right to refer a matter to the Tribunal, it must give an indication of the procedure on such a reference.

(8) If the competent authority decides—
  (a) not to discontinue or suspend the listing of the securities, or
  (b) if the discontinuance or suspension has taken effect, to cancel it,
the competent authority must give the issuer of the securities written notice.

(9) The effect of cancelling a discontinuance is that the securities concerned are to be readmitted, without more, to the official list.

(10) If the competent authority has suspended the listing of securities and proposes to refuse an application by the issuer of the securities for the cancellation of the suspension, it must give him a warning notice.

(11) The competent authority must, having considered any representations made in response to the warning notice—
  (a) if it decides to refuse the application, give the issuer of the securities a decision notice;
  (b) if it grants the application, give him written notice of its decision.

(12) If the competent authority decides to refuse an application for the cancellation of the suspension of listed securities, the applicant may refer the matter to the Tribunal.

(13) 'Discontinuance' means a discontinuance of listing under section 77(1).

(14) 'Suspension' means a suspension of listing under section 77(2).

Listing particulars

79 Listing particulars and other documents

(1) Listing rules may provide that securities (other than new securities) of a kind specified in the rules may not be admitted to the official list unless—
  (a) listing particulars have been submitted to, and approved by, the competent authority and published; or
  (b) in such cases as may be specified by listing rules, such document (other than listing particulars or a prospectus of a kind required by listing rules) as may be so specified has been published.

(2) 'Listing particulars' means a document in such form and containing such information as may be specified in listing rules.

(3) For the purposes of this Part, the persons responsible for listing particulars are to be determined in accordance with regulations made by the Treasury.

(4) Nothing in this section affects the competent authority's general power to make listing rules.

80 General duty of disclosure in listing particulars

(1) Listing particulars submitted to the competent authority under section 79 must contain all such information as investors and their professional advisers would reasonably require, and reasonably expect to find there, for the purpose of making an informed assessment of—
  (a) the assets and liabilities, financial position, profits and losses, and prospects of the issuer of the securities; and
  (b) the rights attaching to the securities.

(2) That information is required in addition to any information required by—
  (a) listing rules, or
  (b) the competent authority,
as a condition of the admission of the securities to the official list.

(3) Subsection (1) applies only to information—
  (a) within the knowledge of any person responsible for the listing particulars; or
  (b) which it would be reasonable for him to obtain by making enquiries.

(4) In determining what information subsection (1) requires to be included in listing particulars, regard must be had (in particular) to—
- (a) the nature of the securities and their issuer;
- (b) the nature of the persons likely to consider acquiring them;
- (c) the fact that certain matters may reasonably be expected to be within the knowledge of professional advisers of a kind which persons likely to acquire the securities may reasonably be expected to consult; and
- (d) any information available to investors or their professional advisers as a result of requirements imposed on the issuer of the securities by a recognised investment exchange, by listing rules or by or under any other enactment.

81   Supplementary listing particulars

(1) If at any time after the preparation of listing particulars which have been submitted to the competent authority under section 79 and before the commencement of dealings in the securities concerned following their admission to the official list—
- (a) there is a significant change affecting any matter contained in those particulars the inclusion of which was required by—
  - (i)   section 80,
  - (ii) listing rules, or
  - (iii) the competent authority, or
- (b) a significant new matter arises, the inclusion of information in respect of which would have been so required if it had arisen when the particulars were prepared,

the issuer must, in accordance with listing rules, submit supplementary listing particulars of the change or new matter to the competent authority, for its approval and, if they are approved, publish them.

(2) 'Significant' means significant for the purpose of making an informed assessment of the kind mentioned in section 80(1).

(3) If the issuer of the securities is not aware of the change or new matter in question, he is not under a duty to comply with subsection (1) unless he is notified of the change or new matter by a person responsible for the listing particulars.

(4) But it is the duty of any person responsible for those particulars who is aware of such a change or new matter to give notice of it to the issuer.

(5) Subsection (1) applies also as respects matters contained in any supplementary listing particulars previously published under this section in respect of the securities in question.

82   Exemptions from disclosure

(1) The competent authority may authorise the omission from listing particulars of any information, the inclusion of which would otherwise be required by section 80 or 81, on the ground—
- (a) that its disclosure would be contrary to the public interest;
- (b) that its disclosure would be seriously detrimental to the issuer; or
- (c) in the case of securities of a kind specified in listing rules, that its disclosure is unnecessary for persons of the kind who may be expected normally to buy or deal in securities of that kind.

(2) But—
- (a) no authority may be granted under subsection (1)(b) in respect of essential information; and
- (b) no authority granted under subsection (1)(b) extends to any such information.

(3) The Secretary of State or the Treasury may issue a certificate to the effect that the disclosure of any information (including information that would otherwise have to be included in listing particulars for which they are themselves responsible) would be contrary to the public interest.

(4) The competent authority is entitled to act on any such certificate in exercising its powers under subsection (1)(a).

(5) This section does not affect any powers of the competent authority under listing rules made as a result of section 101(2).

(6) 'Essential information' means information which a person considering acquiring securities of the kind in question would be likely to need in order not to be misled about any facts which it is essential for him to know in order to make an informed assessment.

(7) 'Listing particulars' includes supplementary listing particulars.

83 Registration of listing particulars

(1) On or before the date on which listing particulars are published as required by listing rules, a copy of the particulars must be delivered for registration to the registrar of companies.

(2) A statement that a copy has been delivered to the registrar must be included in the listing particulars when they are published.

(3) If there has been a failure to comply with subsection (1) in relation to listing particulars which have been published—

    (a) the issuer of the securities in question, and

    (b) any person who is a party to the publication and aware of the failure, is guilty of an offence.

(4) A person guilty of an offence under subsection (3) is liable—

    (a) on summary conviction, to a fine not exceeding the statutory maximum;

    (b) on conviction on indictment, to a fine.

(5) 'Listing particulars' includes supplementary listing particulars.

(6) 'The registrar of companies' means—

    (a) if the securities are, or are to be, issued by a company incorporated in Great Britain whose registered office is in England and Wales, the registrar of companies in England and Wales;

    (b) if the securities are, or are to be, issued by a company incorporated in Great Britain whose registered office is in Scotland, the registrar of companies in Scotland;

    (c) if the securities are, or are to be, issued by a company incorporated in Northern Ireland, the registrar of companies for Northern Ireland; and

    (d) in any other case, any of those registrars.

Prospectuses

84 Prospectuses

(1) Listing rules must provide that no new securities for which an application for listing has been made may be admitted to the official list unless a prospectus has been submitted to, and approved by, the competent authority and published.

(2) 'New securities' means securities which are to be offered to the public in the United Kingdom for the first time before admission to the official list.

(3) 'Prospectus' means a prospectus in such form and containing such information as may be specified in listing rules.

(4) Nothing in this section affects the competent authority's general power to make listing rules.

85 Publication of prospectus

(1) If listing rules made under section 84 require a prospectus to be published before particular new securities are admitted to the official list, it is unlawful for any of those securities to be offered to the public in the United Kingdom before the required prospectus is published.

(2) A person who contravenes subsection (1) is guilty of an offence and liable—

- (a) on summary conviction, to imprisonment for a term not exceeding three months or a fine not exceeding level 5 on the standard scale;
- (b) on conviction on indictment, to imprisonment for a term not exceeding two years or a fine, or both.

(3) A person is not to be regarded as contravening subsection (1) merely because a prospectus does not fully comply with the requirements of listing rules as to its form or content.

(4) But subsection (3) does not affect the question whether any person is liable to pay compensation under section 90.

(5) Any contravention of subsection (1) is actionable, at the suit of a person who suffers loss as a result of the contravention, subject to the defences and other incidents applying to actions for breach of statutory duty.

86   Application of this Part to prospectuses

(1) The provisions of this Part apply in relation to a prospectus required by listing rules as they apply in relation to listing particulars.

(2) In this Part—

- (a) any reference to listing particulars is to be read as including a reference to a prospectus; and
- (b) any reference to supplementary listing particulars is to be read as including a reference to a supplementary prospectus.

87   Approval of prospectus where no application for listing

(1) Listing rules may provide for a prospectus to be submitted to and approved by the competent authority if—

- (a) securities are to be offered to the public in the United Kingdom for the first time;
- (b) no application for listing of the securities has been made under this Part; and
- (c) the prospectus is submitted by, or with the consent of, the issuer of the securities.

(2) 'Non-listing prospectus' means a prospectus submitted to the competent authority as a result of any listing rules made under subsection (1).

(3) Listing rules made under subsection (1) may make provision—

- (a) as to the information to be contained in, and the form of, a non-listing prospectus; and
- (b) as to the timing and manner of publication of a non-listing prospectus.

(4) The power conferred by subsection (3)(b) is subject to such provision made by or under any other enactment as the Treasury may by order specify.

(5) Schedule 9 modifies provisions of this Part as they apply in relation to non-listing prospectuses.

Sponsors

88   Sponsors

(1) Listing rules may require a person to make arrangements with a sponsor for the performance by the sponsor of such services in relation to him as may be specified in the rules.

(2) 'Sponsor' means a person approved by the competent authority for the purposes of the rules.

(3) Listing rules made by virtue of subsection (1) may—

- (a) provide for the competent authority to maintain a list of sponsors;
- (b) specify services which must be performed by a sponsor;
- (c) impose requirements on a sponsor in relation to the provision of services or specified services;
- (d) specify the circumstances in which a person is qualified for being approved as a sponsor.

(4) If the competent authority proposes—

    (a) to refuse a person's application for approval as a sponsor, or

    (b) to cancel a person's approval as a sponsor,

it must give him a warning notice.

(5) If, after considering any representations made in response to the warning notice, the competent authority decides—

    (a) to grant the application for approval, or

    (b) not to cancel the approval,

it must give the person concerned, and any person to whom a copy of the warning notice was given, written notice of its decision.

(6) If, after considering any representations made in response to the warning notice, the competent authority decides—

    (a) to refuse to grant the application for approval, or

    (b) to cancel the approval,

it must give the person concerned a decision notice.

(7) A person to whom a decision notice is given under this section may refer the matter to the Tribunal.

89 Public censure of sponsor

(1) Listing rules may make provision for the competent authority, if it considers that a sponsor has contravened a requirement imposed on him by rules made as a result of section 88(3)(c), to publish a statement to that effect.

(2) If the competent authority proposes to publish a statement it must give the sponsor a warning notice setting out the terms of the proposed statement.

(3) If, after considering any representations made in response to the warning notice, the competent authority decides to make the proposed statement, it must give the sponsor a decision notice setting out the terms of the statement.

(4) A sponsor to whom a decision notice is given under this section may refer the matter to the Tribunal.

Compensation

90 Compensation for false or misleading particulars

(1) Any person responsible for listing particulars is liable to pay compensation to a person who has—

    (a) acquired securities to which the particulars apply; and

    (b) suffered loss in respect of them as a result of—

        (i) any untrue or misleading statement in the particulars; or

        (ii) the omission from the particulars of any matter required to be included by section 80 or 81.

(2) Subsection (1) is subject to exemptions provided by Schedule 10.

(3) If listing particulars are required to include information about the absence of a particular matter, the omission from the particulars of that information is to be treated as a statement in the listing particulars that there is no such matter.

(4) Any person who fails to comply with section 81 is liable to pay compensation to any person who has—

    (a) acquired securities of the kind in question; and

    (b) suffered loss in respect of them as a result of the failure.

(5) Subsection (4) is subject to exemptions provided by Schedule 10.

(6) This section does not affect any liability which may be incurred apart from this section.

(7) References in this section to the acquisition by a person of securities include references to his contracting to acquire them or any interest in them.

(8) No person shall, by reason of being a promoter of a company or otherwise, incur any liability for failing to disclose information which he would not be required to disclose in listing particulars in respect of a company's securities—

    (a) if he were responsible for those particulars; or

    (b) if he is responsible for them, which he is entitled to omit by virtue of section 82.

(9) The reference in subsection (8) to a person incurring liability includes a reference to any other person being entitled as against that person to be granted any civil remedy or to rescind or repudiate an agreement.

(10) 'Listing particulars', in subsection (1) and Schedule 10, includes supplementary listing particulars.

Penalties

91   Penalties for breach of listing rules

(1) If the competent authority considers that—

    (a) an issuer of listed securities, or

    (b) an applicant for listing,

has contravened any provision of listing rules, it may impose on him a penalty of such amount as it considers appropriate.

(2) If, in such a case, the competent authority considers that a person who was at the material time a director of the issuer or applicant was knowingly concerned in the contravention, it may impose on him a penalty of such amount as it considers appropriate.

(3) If the competent authority is entitled to impose a penalty on a person under this section in respect of a particular matter it may, instead of imposing a penalty on him in respect of that matter, publish a statement censuring him.

(4) Nothing in this section prevents the competent authority from taking any other steps which it has power to take under this Part.

(5) A penalty under this section is payable to the competent authority.

(6) The competent authority may not take action against a person under this section after the end of the period of two years beginning with the first day on which it knew of the contravention unless proceedings against that person, in respect of the contravention, were begun before the end of that period.

(7) For the purposes of subsection (6)—

    (a) the competent authority is to be treated as knowing of a contravention if it has information from which the contravention can reasonably be inferred; and

    (b) proceedings against a person in respect of a contravention are to be treated as begun when a warning notice is given to him under section 92.

92 Warning notices

(1) If the competent authority proposes to take action against a person under section 91, it must give him a warning notice.

(2) A warning notice about a proposal to impose a penalty must state the amount of the proposed penalty.

(3) A warning notice about a proposal to publish a statement must set out the terms of the proposed statement.

(4) If the competent authority decides to take action against a person under section 91, it must give him a decision notice.

(5) A decision notice about the imposition of a penalty must state the amount of the penalty.

(6) A decision notice about the publication of a statement must set out the terms of the statement.

(7) If the competent authority decides to take action against a person under section 91, he may refer the matter to the Tribunal.

93   Statement of policy

(1) The competent authority must prepare and issue a statement ('its policy statement') of its policy with respect to—

    (a) the imposition of penalties under section 91; and

    (b) the amount of penalties under that section.

(2) The competent authority's policy in determining what the amount of a penalty should be must include having regard to—

    (a) the seriousness of the contravention in question in relation to the nature of the requirement contravened;

    (b) the extent to which that contravention was deliberate or reckless; and

    (c) whether the person on whom the penalty is to be imposed is an individual.

(3) The competent authority may at any time alter or replace its policy statement.

(4) If its policy statement is altered or replaced, the competent authority must issue the altered or replacement statement.

(5) In exercising, or deciding whether to exercise, its power under section 91 in the case of any particular contravention, the competent authority must have regard to any policy statement published under this section and in force at the time when the contravention in question occurred.

(6) The competent authority must publish a statement issued under this section in the way appearing to the competent authority to be best calculated to bring it to the attention of the public.

(7) The competent authority may charge a reasonable fee for providing a person with a copy of the statement.

(8) The competent authority must, without delay, give the Treasury a copy of any policy statement which it publishes under this section.

94   Statements of policy: procedure

(1) Before issuing a statement under section 93, the competent authority must publish a draft of the proposed statement in the way appearing to the competent authority to be best calculated to bring it to the attention of the public.

(2) The draft must be accompanied by notice that representations about the proposal may be made to the competent authority within a specified time.

(3) Before issuing the proposed statement, the competent authority must have regard to any representations made to it in accordance with subsection (2).

(4) If the competent authority issues the proposed statement it must publish an account, in general terms, of—

    (a) the representations made to it in accordance with subsection (2); and

    (b) its response to them.

(5) If the statement differs from the draft published under subsection (1) in a way which is, in the opinion of the competent authority, significant, the competent authority must (in addition to complying with subsection (4)) publish details of the difference.

(6) The competent authority may charge a reasonable fee for providing a person with a copy of a draft published under subsection (1).

(7) This section also applies to a proposal to alter or replace a statement.

Competition

95   Competition scrutiny

(1) The Treasury may by order provide for—

    (a) regulating provisions, and

    (b) the practices of the competent authority in exercising its functions under this Part ('practices'),

to be kept under review.

(2) Provision made as a result of subsection (1) must require the person responsible for keeping regulating provisions and practices under review to consider—

    (a) whether any regulating provision or practice has a significantly adverse effect on competition; or

    (b) whether two or more regulating provisions or practices taken together have, or a particular combination of regulating provisions and practices has, such an effect.

(3) An order under this section may include provision corresponding to that made by any provision of Chapter III of Part X.

(4) Subsection (3) is not to be read as in any way restricting the power conferred by subsection (1).

(5) Subsections (6) to (8) apply for the purposes of provision made by or under this section.

(6) Regulating provisions or practices have a significantly adverse effect on competition if—

    (a) they have, or are intended or likely to have, that effect; or

    (b) the effect that they have, or are intended or likely to have, is to require or encourage behaviour which has, or is intended or likely to have, a significantly adverse effect on competition.

(7) If regulating provisions or practices have, or are intended or likely to have, the effect of requiring or encouraging exploitation of the strength of a market position they are to be taken to have, or be intended or be likely to have, an adverse effect on competition.

(8) In determining whether any of the regulating provisions or practices have, or are intended or likely to have, a particular effect, it may be assumed that the persons to whom the provisions concerned are addressed will act in accordance with them.

(9) 'Regulating provisions' means—

    (a) listing rules,

    (b) general guidance given by the competent authority in connection with its functions under this Part.

Miscellaneous

96 Obligations of issuers of listed securities

(1) Listing rules may—

    (a) specify requirements to be complied with by issuers of listed securities; and

    (b) make provision with respect to the action that may be taken by the competent authority in the event of non-compliance.

(2) If the rules require an issuer to publish information, they may include provision authorising the competent authority to publish it in the event of his failure to do so.

(3) This section applies whenever the listed securities were admitted to the official list.

97 Appointment by competent authority of persons to carry out investigations

(1) Subsection (2) applies if it appears to the competent authority that there are circumstances suggesting that—

    (a) there may have been a breach of listing rules;

    (b) a person who was at the material time a director of an issuer of listed securities has been knowingly concerned in a breach of listing rules by that issuer;

    (c) a person who was at the material time a director of a person applying for the admission of securities to the official list has been knowingly concerned in a breach of listing rules by that applicant;

    (d) there may have been a contravention of section 83, 85 or 98.

(2) The competent authority may appoint one or more competent persons to conduct an investigation on its behalf.

(3) Part XI applies to an investigation under subsection (2) as if—
- (a) the investigator were appointed under section 167(1);
- (b) references to the investigating authority in relation to him were to the competent authority;
- (c) references to the offences mentioned in section 168 were to those mentioned in subsection (1)(d);
- (d) references to an authorised person were references to the person under investigation.

98   Advertisements etc. in connection with listing applications

(1) If listing particulars are, or are to be, published in connection with an application for listing, no advertisement or other information of a kind specified by listing rules may be issued in the United Kingdom unless the contents of the advertisement or other information have been submitted to the competent authority and that authority has—
- (a) approved those contents; or
- (b) authorised the issue of the advertisement or information without such approval.

(2) A person who contravenes subsection (1) is guilty of an offence and liable—
- (a) on summary conviction, to a fine not exceeding the statutory maximum;
- (b) on conviction on indictment, to imprisonment for a term not exceeding two years or a fine, or both.

(3) A person who issues an advertisement or other information to the order of another person is not guilty of an offence under subsection (2) if he shows that he believed on reasonable grounds that the advertisement or information had been approved, or its issue authorised, by the competent authority.

(4) If information has been approved, or its issue has been authorised, under this section, neither the person issuing it nor any person responsible for, or for any part of, the listing particulars incurs any civil liability by reason of any statement in or omission from the information if that information and the listing particulars, taken together, would not be likely to mislead persons of the kind likely to consider acquiring the securities in question.

(5) The reference in subsection (4) to a person incurring civil liability includes a reference to any other person being entitled as against that person to be granted any civil remedy or to rescind or repudiate an agreement.

99   Fees

(1) Listing rules may require the payment of fees to the competent authority in respect of—
- (a) applications for listing;
- (b) the continued inclusion of securities in the official list;
- (c) applications under section 88 for approval as a sponsor; and
- (d) continued inclusion of sponsors in the list of sponsors.

(2) In exercising its powers under subsection (1), the competent authority may set such fees as it considers will (taking account of the income it expects as the competent authority) enable it—
- (a) to meet expenses incurred in carrying out its functions under this Part or for any incidental purpose;
- (b) to maintain adequate reserves; and
- (c) in the case of the Authority, to repay the principal of, and pay any interest on, any money which it has borrowed and which has been used for the purpose of meeting expenses incurred in relation to—
  - (i) its assumption of functions from the London Stock Exchange Limited in relation to the official list; and
  - (ii) its assumption of functions under this Part.

(3) In fixing the amount of any fee which is to be payable to the competent authority, no

account is to be taken of any sums which it receives, or expects to receive, by way of penalties imposed by it under this Part.

(4) Subsection (2)(c) applies whether expenses were incurred before or after the coming into force of this Part.

(5) Any fee which is owed to the competent authority under any provision made by or under this Part may be recovered as a debt due to it.

100   Penalties

(1) In determining its policy with respect to the amount of penalties to be imposed by it under this Part, the competent authority must take no account of the expenses which it incurs, or expects to incur, in discharging its functions under this Part.

(2) The competent authority must prepare and operate a scheme for ensuring that the amounts paid to it by way of penalties imposed under this Part are applied for the benefit of issuers of securities admitted to the official list.

(3) The scheme may, in particular, make different provision with respect to different classes of issuer.

(4) Up to date details of the scheme must be set out in a document ('the scheme details').

(5) The scheme details must be published by the competent authority in the way appearing to it to be best calculated to bring them to the attention of the public.

(6) Before making the scheme, the competent authority must publish a draft of the proposed scheme in the way appearing to it to be best calculated to bring it to the attention of the public.

(7) The draft must be accompanied by notice that representations about the proposals may be made to the competent authority within a specified time.

(8) Before making the scheme, the competent authority must have regard to any representations made to it under subsection (7).

(9) If the competent authority makes the proposed scheme, it must publish an account, in general terms, of—

   (a) the representations made to it in accordance with subsection (7); and
   (b) its response to them.

(10) If the scheme differs from the draft published under subsection (6) in a way which is, in the opinion of the competent authority, significant the competent authority must (in addition to complying with subsection (9)) publish details of the difference.

(11) The competent authority must, without delay, give the Treasury a copy of any scheme details published by it.

(12) The competent authority may charge a reasonable fee for providing a person with a copy of—

   (a) a draft published under subsection (6);
   (b) scheme details.

(13) Subsections (6) to (10) and (12) apply also to a proposal to alter or replace the scheme.

101   Listing rules: general provisions

(1) Listing rules may make different provision for different cases.

(2) Listing rules may authorise the competent authority to dispense with or modify the application of the rules in particular cases and by reference to any circumstances.

(3) Listing rules must be made by an instrument in writing.

(4) Immediately after an instrument containing listing rules is made, it must be printed and made available to the public with or without payment.

(5) A person is not to be taken to have contravened any listing rule if he shows that at the time of the alleged contravention the instrument containing the rule had not been made available as required by subsection (4).

(6) The production of a printed copy of an instrument purporting to be made by the

competent authority on which is endorsed a certificate signed by an officer of the authority authorised by it for that purpose and stating—

(a) that the instrument was made by the authority,

(b) that the copy is a true copy of the instrument, and

(c) that on a specified date the instrument was made available to the public as required by subsection (4),

is evidence (or in Scotland sufficient evidence) of the facts stated in the certificate.

(7) A certificate purporting to be signed as mentioned in subsection (6) is to be treated as having been properly signed unless the contrary is shown.

(8) A person who wishes in any legal proceedings to rely on a rule-making instrument may require the Authority to endorse a copy of the instrument with a certificate of the kind mentioned in subsection (6).

102   Exemption from liability in damages

(1) Neither the competent authority nor any person who is, or is acting as, a member, officer or member of staff of the competent authority is to be liable in damages for anything done or omitted in the discharge, or purported discharge, of the authority's functions.

(2) Subsection (1) does not apply—

(a) if the act or omission is shown to have been in bad faith; or

(b) so as to prevent an award of damages made in respect of an act or omission on the ground that the act or omission was unlawful as a result of section 6(1) of the Human Rights Act 1998.

103   Interpretation of this Part

(1) In this Part—

'application' means an application made under section 75;

'issuer', in relation to anything which is or may be admitted to the official list, has such meaning as may be prescribed by the Treasury;

'listing' has the meaning given in section 74(5);

'listing particulars' has the meaning given in section 79(2);

'listing rules' has the meaning given in section 74(4);

'new securities' has the meaning given in section 84(2);

'the official list' means the list maintained as the official list by the Authority immediately before the coming into force of section 74, as that list has effect for the time being;

'security' (except in section 74(2)) has the meaning given in section 74(5).

(2) In relation to any function conferred on the competent authority by this Part, any reference in this Part to the competent authority is to be read as a reference to the person by whom that function is for the time being exercisable.

(3) If, as a result of an order under Schedule 8, different functions conferred on the competent authority by this Part are exercisable by different persons, the powers conferred by section 91 are exercisable by such person as may be determined in accordance with the provisions of the order.

(4) For the purposes of this Part, a person offers securities if, and only if, as principal—

(a) he makes an offer which, if accepted, would give rise to a contract for their issue or sale by him or by another person with whom he has made arrangements for their issue or sale; or

(b) he invites a person to make such an offer.

(5) 'Offer' and 'offeror' are to be read accordingly.

(6) For the purposes of this Part, the question whether a person offers securities to the public in the United Kingdom is to be determined in accordance with Schedule 11.

(7) For the purposes of subsection (4) 'sale' includes any disposal for valuable consideration.

PART VIII   PENALTIES FOR MARKET ABUSE

Market abuse

118   Market abuse

(1) For the purposes of this Act, market abuse is behaviour (whether by one person alone or by two or more persons jointly or in concert)—

(a) which occurs in relation to qualifying investments traded on a market to which this section applies;

(b) which satisfies any one or more of the conditions set out in subsection (2); and

(c) which is likely to be regarded by a regular user of that market who is aware of the behaviour as a failure on the part of the person or persons concerned to observe the standard of behaviour reasonably expected of a person in his or their position in relation to the market.

(2) The conditions are that—

(a) the behaviour is based on information which is not generally available to those using the market but which, if available to a regular user of the market, would or would be likely to be regarded by him as relevant when deciding the terms on which transactions in investments of the kind in question should be effected;

(b) the behaviour is likely to give a regular user of the market a false or misleading impression as to the supply of, or demand for, or as to the price or value of, investments of the kind in question;

(c) a regular user of the market would, or would be likely to, regard the behaviour as behaviour which would, or would be likely to, distort the market in investments of the kind in question.

(3) The Treasury may by order prescribe (whether by name or by description)—

(a) the markets to which this section applies; and

(b) the investments which are qualifying investments in relation to those markets.

(4) The order may prescribe different investments or descriptions of investment in relation to different markets or descriptions of market.

(5) Behaviour is to be disregarded for the purposes of subsection (1) unless it occurs—

(a) in the United Kingdom; or

(b) in relation to qualifying investments traded on a market to which this section applies which is situated in the United Kingdom or which is accessible electronically in the United Kingdom.

(6) For the purposes of this section, the behaviour which is to be regarded as occurring in relation to qualifying investments includes behaviour which—

(a) occurs in relation to anything which is the subject matter, or whose price or value is expressed by reference to the price or value, of those qualifying investments; or

(b) occurs in relation to investments (whether qualifying or not) whose subject matter is those qualifying investments.

(7) Information which can be obtained by research or analysis conducted by, or on behalf of, users of a market is to be regarded for the purposes of this section as being generally available to them.

(8) Behaviour does not amount to market abuse if it conforms with a rule which includes a provision to the effect that behaviour conforming with the rule does not amount to market abuse.

(9) Any reference in this Act to a person engaged in market abuse is a reference to a person engaged in market abuse whether alone or with one or more other persons.

(10) In this section—

'behaviour' includes action or inaction;

'investment' is to be read with section 22 and Schedule 2;

'regular user', in relation to a particular market, means a reasonable person who regularly deals on that market in investments of the kind in question.

119   The code

(1) The Authority must prepare and issue a code containing such provisions as the Authority considers will give appropriate guidance to those determining whether or not behaviour amounts to market abuse.

(2) The code may among other things specify—

(a) descriptions of behaviour that, in the opinion of the Authority, amount to market abuse;

(b) descriptions of behaviour that, in the opinion of the Authority, do not amount to market abuse;

(c) factors that, in the opinion of the Authority, are to be taken into account in determining whether or not behaviour amounts to market abuse.

(3) The code may make different provision in relation to persons, cases or circumstances of different descriptions.

(4) The Authority may at any time alter or replace the code.

(5) If the code is altered or replaced, the altered or replacement code must be issued by the Authority.

(6) A code issued under this section must be published by the Authority in the way appearing to the Authority to be best calculated to bring it to the attention of the public.

(7) The Authority must, without delay, give the Treasury a copy of any code published under this section.

(8) The Authority may charge a reasonable fee for providing a person with a copy of the code.

122   Effect of the code

(1) If a person behaves in a way which is described (in the code in force under section 119 at the time of the behaviour) as behaviour that, in the Authority's opinion, does not amount to market abuse that behaviour of his is to be taken, for the purposes of this Act, as not amounting to market abuse.

(2) Otherwise, the code in force under section 119 at the time when particular behaviour occurs may be relied on so far as it indicates whether or not that behaviour should be taken to amount to market abuse.

Power to impose penalties

123   Power to impose penalties in cases of market abuse

(1) If the Authority is satisfied that a person ('A')—

(a) is or has engaged in market abuse, or

(b) by taking or refraining from taking any action has required or encouraged another person or persons to engage in behaviour which, if engaged in by A, would amount to market abuse,

it may impose on him a penalty of such amount as it considers appropriate.

(2) But the Authority may not impose a penalty on a person if, having considered any representations made to it in response to a warning notice, there are reasonable grounds for it to be satisfied that—

(a) he believed, on reasonable grounds, that his behaviour did not fall within paragraph (a) or (b) of subsection (1), or

(b) he took all reasonable precautions and exercised all due diligence to avoid behaving in a way which fell within paragraph (a) or (b) of that subsection.

(3) If the Authority is entitled to impose a penalty on a person under this section it may, instead of imposing a penalty on him, publish a statement to the effect that he has engaged in market abuse.

Miscellaneous

129   Power of court to impose penalty in cases of market abuse

(1) The Authority may on an application to the court under section 381 or 383 request the court to consider whether the circumstances are such that a penalty should be imposed on the person to whom the application relates.

(2) The court may, if it considers it appropriate, make an order requiring the person concerned to pay to the Authority a penalty of such amount as it considers appropriate.

131   Effect on transactions

The imposition of a penalty under this Part does not make any transaction void or unenforceable.

PART IX   HEARINGS AND APPEALS

132   The Financial Services and Markets Tribunal

(1) For the purposes of this Act, there is to be a tribunal known as the Financial Services and Markets Tribunal (but referred to in this Act as 'the Tribunal').

(2) The Tribunal is to have the functions conferred on it by or under this Act.

PART XVIII   RECOGNISED INVESTMENT EXCHANGES AND CLEARING HOUSES

CHAPTER I   EXEMPTION

General

285   Exemption for recognised investment exchanges and clearing houses

(1) In this Act—

    (a) 'recognised investment exchange' means an investment exchange in relation to which a recognition order is in force; and

    (b) 'recognised clearing house' means a clearing house in relation to which a recognition order is in force.

PART XXV   INJUNCTIONS AND RESTITUTION

Injunctions

381   Injunctions in cases of market abuse

(1) If, on the application of the Authority, the court is satisfied—

    (a) that there is a reasonable likelihood that any person will engage in market abuse, or

    (b) that any person is or has engaged in market abuse and that there is a reasonable likelihood that the market abuse will continue or be repeated,

the court may make an order restraining (or in Scotland an interdict prohibiting) the market abuse.

(2) If on the application of the Authority the court is satisfied—

    (a) that any person is or has engaged in market abuse, and

    (b) that there are steps which could be taken for remedying the market abuse,

the court may make an order requiring him to take such steps as the court may direct to remedy it.

(3) Subsection (4) applies if, on the application of the Authority, the court is satisfied that any person—

    (a) may be engaged in market abuse; or

    (b) may have been engaged in market abuse.

(4) The court make [*sic*] an order restraining (or in Scotland an interdict prohibiting) the person concerned from disposing of, or otherwise dealing with, any assets of his which it is satisfied that he is reasonably likely to dispose of, or otherwise deal with.

(5) The jurisdiction conferred by this section is exercisable by the High Court and the Court of Session.

(6) In subsection (2), references to remedying any market abuse include references to mitigating its effect.

Restitution orders

383   Restitution orders in cases of market abuse

(1) The court may, on the application of the Authority, make an order under subsection (4) if it is satisfied that a person ('the person concerned')—

   (a) has engaged in market abuse, or

   (b) by taking or refraining from taking any action has required or encouraged another person or persons to engage in behaviour which, if engaged in by the person concerned, would amount to market abuse,

and the condition mentioned in subsection (2) is fulfilled.

(2) The condition is—

   (a) that profits have accrued to the person concerned as a result; or

   (b) that one or more persons have suffered loss or been otherwise adversely affected as a result.

(3) But the court may not make an order under subsection (4) if it is satisfied that—

   (a) the person concerned believed, on reasonable grounds, that his behaviour did not fall within paragraph (a) or (b) of subsection (1); or

   (b) he took all reasonable precautions and exercised all due diligence to avoid behaving in a way which fell within paragraph (a) or (b) of subsection (1).

(4) The court may order the person concerned to pay to the Authority such sum as appears to the court to be just having regard—

   (a) in a case within paragraph (a) of subsection (2), to the profits appearing to the court to have accrued;

   (b) in a case within paragraph (b) of that subsection, to the extent of the loss or other adverse effect;

   (c) in a case within both of those paragraphs, to the profits appearing to the court to have accrued and to the extent of the loss or other adverse effect.

(5) Any amount paid to the Authority in pursuance of an order under subsection (4) must be paid by it to such qualifying person or distributed by it among such qualifying persons as the court may direct.

(6) On an application under subsection (1) the court may require the person concerned to supply it with such accounts or other information as it may require for any one or more of the following purposes—

   (a) establishing whether any and, if so, what profits have accrued to him as mentioned in subsection (2)(a);

   (b) establishing whether any person or persons have suffered any loss or adverse effect as mentioned in subsection (2)(b) and, if so, the extent of that loss or adverse effect; and

   (c) determining how any amounts are to be paid or distributed under subsection (5).

(7) The court may require any accounts or other information supplied under subsection (6) to be verified in such manner as it may direct.

(8) The jurisdiction conferred by this section is exercisable by the High Court and the Court of Session.

(9) Nothing in this section affects the right of any person other than the Authority to bring proceedings in respect of the matters to which this section applies.

(10) 'Qualifying person' means a person appearing to the court to be someone—

(a) to whom the profits mentioned in paragraph (a) of subsection (2) are attributable; or

(b) who has suffered the loss or adverse effect mentioned in paragraph (b) of that subsection.

Restitution required by Authority

384   Power of Authority to require restitution

(1) The Authority may exercise the power in subsection (5) if it is satisfied that an authorised person ('the person concerned') has contravened a relevant requirement, or been knowingly concerned in the contravention of such a requirement, and—

(a) that profits have accrued to him as a result of the contravention; or

(b) that one or more persons have suffered loss or been otherwise adversely affected as a result of the contravention.

(2) The Authority may exercise the power in subsection (5) if it is satisfied that a person ('the person concerned')—

(a) has engaged in market abuse, or

(b) by taking or refraining from taking any action has required or encouraged another person or persons to engage in behaviour which, if engaged in by the person concerned, would amount to market abuse,

and the condition mentioned in subsection (3) is fulfilled.

(3) The condition is—

(a) that profits have accrued to the person concerned as a result of the market abuse; or

(b) that one or more persons have suffered loss or been otherwise adversely affected as a result of the market abuse.

(4) But the Authority may not exercise that power as a result of subsection (2) if, having considered any representations made to it in response to a warning notice, there are reasonable grounds for it to be satisfied that—

(a) the person concerned believed, on reasonable grounds, that his behaviour did not fall within paragraph (a) or (b) of that subsection; or

(b) he took all reasonable precautions and exercised all due diligence to avoid behaving in a way which fell within paragraph (a) or (b) of that subsection.

(5) The power referred to in subsections (1) and (2) is a power to require the person concerned, in accordance with such arrangements as the Authority considers appropriate, to pay to the appropriate person or distribute among the appropriate persons such amount as appears to the Authority to be just having regard—

(a) in a case within paragraph (a) of subsection (1) or (3), to the profits appearing to the Authority to have accrued;

(b) in a case within paragraph (b) of subsection (1) or (3), to the extent of the loss or other adverse effect;

(c) in a case within paragraphs (a) and (b) of subsection (1) or (3), to the profits appearing to the Authority to have accrued and to the extent of the loss or other adverse effect

(6) 'Appropriate person' means a person appearing to the Authority to be someone—

(a) to whom the profits mentioned in paragraph (a) of subsection (1) or (3) are attributable; or

(b) who has suffered the loss or adverse effect mentioned in paragraph (b) of subsection (1) or (3).

(7) 'Relevant requirement' means—

    (a) a requirement imposed by or under this Act; and

    (b) a requirement which is imposed by or under any other Act and whose contravention constitutes an offence in relation to which this Act confers power to prosecute on the Authority.

(8) In the application of subsection (7) to Scotland, in paragraph (b) for 'in relation to which this Act confers power to prosecute on the Authority' substitute 'mentioned in paragraph (a) or (b) of section 402(1)'.

[*At the end of s. 384(2) the Queen's Printer's copy mistakenly has a comma instead of a full point.*]

PART XXIX   INTERPRETATION

417   Definitions

(1) In this Act—

. . .

'authorisation offence' has the meaning given in section 23(2);

. . .

'authorised person' has the meaning given in seciton 31(2);

'the Authority' means the Financial Services Authority;

'body corporate' includes a body corporate constituted under the law of a country or territory outside the United Kingdom;

. . .

'director', in relation to a body corporate, includes—

    (a) a person occupying in relation to it the position of a director (by whatever name called); and

    (b) a person in accordance with whose directions or instructions (not being advice given in a professional capacity) the directors of that body are accustomed to act;

. . .

'exempt person', in relation to a regulated activity, means a person who is exempt from the general prohibition in relation to that activity as a result of an exemption order made under section 38(1) or as a result of section 39(1) or 285(2) or (3);

. . .

'general prohibition' has the meaning given in section 19(2);

. . .

'industrial and provident society' means a society registered or deemed to be registered under the Industrial and Provident Societies Act 1965 or the Industrial and Provident Societies Act (Northern Ireland) 1969;

. . .

'market abuse' has the meaning given in section 118;

. . .

'Part IV permission' has the meaning given in section 40(4);

'partnership' includes a partnership constituted under the law of a country or territory outside the United Kingdom;

'prescribed' (where not otherwise defined) means prescribed in regulations made by the Treasury;

. . .

'recognised clearing house' and 'recognised investment exchange' have the meaning given in section 285;

. . .

'regulated activity' has the meaning given in section 22;

. . .

'rule' means a rule made by the Authority under this Act;

. . .

425 Expressions relating to authorisation elsewhere in the single market

(1) In this Act—

    (a) . . . 'EEA State', . . . and 'banking consolidation directive' have the meaning given in Schedule 3; . . .

PART XXX SUPPLEMENTAL

428 Regulations and orders

(1) Any power to make an order which is conferred on a Minister of the Crown by this Act and any power to make regulations which is conferred by this Act is exercisable by statutory instrument.

(2) The Lord Chancellor's power to make rules under section 132 is exercisable by statutory instrument.

(3) Any statutory instrument made under this Act may—

    (a) contain such incidental, supplemental, consequential and transitional provision as the person making it considers appropriate; and

    (b) make different provision for different cases.

429 Parliamentary control of statutory instruments

(1) No order is to be made under—

    (a) section 144(4), 192(b) or (e), 236(5), 404 or 419, or

    (b) paragraph 1 of Schedule 8,

unless a draft of the order has been laid before Parliament and approved by a resolution of each House.

433 Short title

This Act may be cited as the Financial Services and Markets Act 2000.

Section 31(1)(b) and 37   SCHEDULE 3

EEA PASSPORT RIGHTS

PART I DEFINED TERMS

2. 'The banking consolidation directive' means Directive 2000/12/EC of the European Parliament and of the Council of 20 March 2000 relating to the taking up and pursuit of the business of credit institutions.

EEA State

8. 'EEA State' means a State which is a contracting party to the agreement on the European Economic Area signed at Oporto on 2 May 1992 as it has effect for the time being.

Section 72(3)   SCHEDULE 8

TRANSFER OF FUNCTIONS UNDER PART VI

The power to transfer

1.—(1) The Treasury may by order provide for any function conferred on the competent authority which is exercisable for the time being by a particular person to be transferred so as to be exercisable by another person.

(2) An order may be made under this paragraph only if—

    (a) the person from whom the relevant functions are to be transferred has agreed in writing that the order should be made;

    (b) the Treasury are satisfied that the manner in which, or efficiency with which, the functions are discharged would be significantly improved if they were transferred to the transferee; or

    (c) the Treasury are satisfied that it is otherwise in the public interest that the order should be made.

Supplemental

2.—(1) An order under this Schedule does not affect anything previously done by any person ('the previous authority') in the exercise of functions which are transferred by the order to another person ('the new authority').

(2) Such an order may, in particular, include provision—

    (a) modifying or excluding any provision of Part VI, IX or XXVI in its application to any such functions;

    (b) for reviews similar to that made, in relation to the Authority, by section 12;

    (c) imposing on the new authority requirements similar to those imposed, in relation to the Authority, by sections 152, 155 and 354;

    (d) as to the giving of guidance by the new authority;

    (e) for the delegation by the new authority of the exercise of functions under Part VI and as to the consequences of delegation;

    (f) for the transfer of any property, rights or liabilities relating to any such functions from the previous authority to the new authority;

    (g) for the carrying on and completion by the new authority of anything in the process of being done by the previous authority when the order takes effect;

    (h) for the substitution of the new authority for the previous authority in any instrument, contract or legal proceedings;

    (i) for the transfer of persons employed by the previous authority to the new authority and as to the terms on which they are to transfer;

    (j) making such amendments to any primary or subordinate legislation (including any provision of, or made under, this Act) as the Treasury consider appropriate in consequence of the transfer of functions effected by the order.

(3) Nothing in this paragraph is to be taken as restricting the powers conferred by section 428.

3. If the Treasury have made an order under paragraph 1 ('the transfer order') they may, by a separate order made under this paragraph, make any provision of a kind that could have been included in the transfer order.

Section 87(5)   SCHEDULE 9

NON-LISTING PROSPECTUSES

General application of Part VI

1. The provisions of Part VI apply in relation to a non-listing prospectus as they apply in relation to listing particulars but with the modifications made by this Schedule.

References to listing particulars

2.—(1) Any reference to listing particulars is to be read as a reference to a prospectus.

(2) Any reference to supplementary listing particulars is to be read as a reference to a supplementary prospectus.

General duty of disclosure

3.—(1) In section 81(1), for 'section 79' substitute 'section 87'.

(2) In section 80(2), omit 'as a condition of the admission of the securities to the official list'.

Supplementary prospectuses

4. In section 81(1), for 'section 79 and before the commencement of dealings in the securities concerned following their admission to the official list' substitute 'section 87 and before the end of the period during which the offer to which the prospectus relates remains open'.

Exemption from liability for compensation

5.—(1) In paragraphs 1(3) and 2(3) of Schedule 10, for paragraph (d) substitute—

'(d) the securities were acquired after such a lapse of time that he ought in the circumstances to be reasonably excused and, if the securities are dealt in on an approved exchange, he continued in that belief until after the commencement of dealings in the securities on that exchange.'

(2) After paragraph 8 of that Schedule, insert—

'Meaning of "approved exchange"

9. "Approved exchange" has such meaning as may be prescribed.'

Advertisements

6. In section 98(1), for 'If listing particulars are, or are to be, published in connection with an application for listing,' substitute 'If a prospectus is, or is to be, published in connection with an application for approval, then, until the end of the period during which the offer to which the prospectus relates remains open,'.

Fees

7. Listing rules made under section 99 may require the payment of fees to the competent authority in respect of a prospectus submitted for approval under section 87.

Section 90(2) and (5)   SCHEDULE 10

COMPENSATION: EXEMPTIONS

Statements believed to be true

1.—(1) In this paragraph 'statement' means—

(a) any untrue or misleading statement in listing particulars; or

(b) the omission from listing particulars of any matter required to be included by section 80 or 81.

(2) A person does not incur any liability under section 90(1) for loss caused by a statement if he satisfies the court that, at the time when the listing particulars were submitted to the competent authority, he reasonably believed (having made such enquiries, if any, as were reasonable) that—

(a) the statement was true and not misleading, or

(b) the matter whose omission caused the loss was properly omitted,

and that one or more of the conditions set out in sub-paragraph (3) are satisfied.

(3) The conditions are that—

    (a) he continued in his belief until the time when the securities in question were acquired;

    (b) they were acquired before it was reasonably practicable to bring a correction to the attention of persons likely to acquire them;

    (c) before the securities were acquired, he had taken all such steps as it was reasonable for him to have taken to secure that a correction was brought to the attention of those persons;

    (d) he continued in his belief until after the commencement of dealings in the securities following their admission to the official list and they were acquired after such a lapse of time that he ought in the circumstances to be reasonably excused.

Statements by experts

2.—(1) In this paragraph 'statement' means a statement included in listing particulars which—

    (a) purports to be made by, or on the authority of, another person as an expert; and

    (b) is stated to be included in the listing particulars with that other person's consent.

(2) A person does not incur any liability under section 90(1) for loss in respect of any securities caused by a statement if he satisfies the court that, at the time when the listing particulars were submitted to the competent authority, he reasonably believed that the other person—

    (a) was competent to make or authorise the statement, and

    (b) had consented to its inclusion in the form and context in which it was included,

and that one or more of the conditions set out in sub-paragraph (3) are satisfied.

(3) The conditions are that—

    (a) he continued in his belief until the time when the securities were acquired;

    (b) they were acquired before it was reasonably practicable to bring the fact that the expert was not competent, or had not consented, to the attention of persons likely to acquire the securities in question;

    (c) before the securities were acquired he had taken all such steps as it was reasonable for him to have taken to secure that that fact was brought to the attention of those persons;

    (d) he continued in his belief until after the commencement of dealings in the securities following their admission to the official list and they were acquired after such a lapse of time that he ought in the circumstances to be reasonably excused.

Corrections of statements

3.—(1) In this paragraph 'statement' has the same meaning as in paragraph 1.

(2) A person does not incur liability under section 90(1) for loss caused by a statement if he satisfies the court—

    (a) that before the securities in question were acquired, a correction had been published in a manner calculated to bring it to the attention of persons likely to acquire the securities; or

    (b) that he took all such steps as it was reasonable for him to take to secure such publication and reasonably believed that it had taken place before the securities were acquired.

(3) Nothing in this paragraph is to be taken as affecting paragraph 1.

Corrections of statements by experts

4.—(1) In this paragraph 'statement' has the same meaning as in paragraph 2.

(2) A person does not incur liability under section 90(1) for loss caused by a statement if he satisfies the court—

(a) that before the securities in question were acquired, the fact that the expert was not competent or had not consented had been published in a manner calculated to bring it to the attention of persons likely to acquire the securities; or

(b) that he took all such steps as it was reasonable for him to take to secure such publication and reasonably believed that it had taken place before the securities were acquired.

(3) Nothing in this paragraph is to be taken as affecting paragraph 2.

Official statements

5.   A person does not incur any liability under section 90(1) for loss resulting from—

(a) a statement made by an official person which is included in the listing particulars, or

(b) a statement contained in a public official document which is included in the listing particulars,

if he satisfies the court that the statement is accurately and fairly reproduced.

False or misleading information known about

6.   A person does not incur any liability under section 90(1) or (4) if he satisfies the court that the person suffering the loss acquired the securities in question with knowledge—

(a) that the statement was false or misleading,

(b) of the omitted matter, or

(c) of the change or new matter,

as the case may be.

Belief that supplementary listing particulars not called for

7.   A person does not incur any liability under section 90(4) if he satisfies the court that he reasonably believed that the change or new matter in question was not such as to call for supplementary listing particulars.

Meaning of 'expert'

8.   'Expert' includes any engineer, valuer, accountant or other person whose profession, qualifications or experience give authority to a statement made by him.

Section 103(6)   SCHEDULE 11

OFFERS OF SECURITIES

The general rule

1.—(1) A person offers securities to the public in the United Kingdom if—

(a) to the extent that the offer is made to persons in the United Kingdom, it is made to the public; and

(b) the offer is not an exempt offer.

(2) For this purpose, an offer which is made to any section of the public, whether selected—

(a) as members or debenture holders of a body corporate,

(b) as clients of the person making the offer, or

(c) in any other manner,

is to be regarded as made to the public.

Exempt offers

2.—(1) For the purposes of this Schedule, an offer of securities is an 'exempt offer' if, to the extent that the offer is made to persons in the United Kingdom—
   (a) the condition specified in any of paragraphs 3 to 24A is satisfied in relation to the offer; or
   (b) the condition specified in one relevant paragraph is satisfied in relation to part, but not the whole, of the offer and, in relation to each other part of the offer, the condition specified in a different relevant paragraph is satisfied.
(2) The relevant paragraphs are 3 to 8, 12 to 18 and 21.

Offers for business purposes

3.   The securities are offered to persons—
   (a) whose ordinary activities involve them in acquiring, holding, managing or disposing of investments (as principal or agent) for the purposes of their businesses, or
   (b) who it is reasonable to expect will acquire, hold, manage or dispose of investments (as principal or agent) for the purposes of their businesses,
or are otherwise offered to persons in the context of their trades, professions or occupations.

Offers to limited numbers

4.—(1) The securities are offered to no more than fifty persons.
(2) In determining whether this condition is satisfied, the offer is to be taken together with any other offer of the same securities which was—
   (a) made by the same person;
   (b) open at any time within the period of 12 months ending with the date on which the offer is first made; and
   (c) not an offer to the public in the United Kingdom by virtue of this condition being satisfied.
(3) For the purposes of this paragraph—
   (a) the making of an offer of securities to trustees or members of a partnership in their capacity as such, or
   (b) the making of such an offer to any other two or more persons jointly,
is to be treated as the making of an offer to a single person.

Clubs and associations

5.   The securities are offered to the members of a club or association (whether or not incorporated) and the members can reasonably be regarded as having a common interest with each other and with the club or association in the affairs of the club or association and in what is to be done with the proceeds of the offer.

Restricted circles

6.—(1) The securities are offered to a restricted circle of persons whom the offeror reasonably believes to be sufficiently knowledgeable to understand the risks involved in accepting the offer.
(2) In determining whether a person is sufficiently knowledgeable to understand the risks involved in accepting an offer of securities, any information supplied by the person making the offer is to be disregarded, apart from information about—
   (a) the issuer of the securities; or
   (b) if the securities confer the right to acquire other securities, the issuer of those other securities.

Underwriting agreements

7.   The securities are offered in connection with a genuine invitation to enter into an underwriting agreement with respect to them.

Offers to public authorities

8.—(1) The securities are offered to a public authority.
(2) 'Public authority' means—
- (a) the government of the United Kingdom;
- (b) the government of any country or territory outside the United Kingdom;
- (c) a local authority in the United Kingdom or elsewhere;
- (d) any international organisation the members of which include the United Kingdom or another EEA State; and
- (e) such other bodies, if any, as may be specified.

Maximum consideration

9.—(1) The total consideration payable for the securities cannot exceed 40,000 euros (or an equivalent amount).
(2) In determining whether this condition is satisfied. the offer is to be taken together with any other offer of the same securities which was—
- (a) made by the same person;
- (b) open at any time within the period of 12 months ending with the date on which the offer is first made; and
- (c) not an offer to the public in the United Kingdom by virtue of this condition being satisfied.

(3) An amount (in relation to an amount denominated in euros) is an 'equivalent amount' if it is an amount of equal value, calculated at the latest practicable date before (but in any event not more than 3 days before) the date on which the offer is first made, denominated wholly or partly in another currency or unit of account.

Minimum consideration

10.—(1) The minimum consideration which may be paid by any person for securities acquired by him pursuant to the offer is at least 40,000 euros (or an equivalent amount).
(2) Paragraph 9(3) also applies for the purposes of this paragraph.

Securities denominated in euros

11.—(1) The securities are denominated in amounts of at least 40,000 euros (or an equivalent amount).
(2) Paragraph 9(3) also applies for the purposes of this paragraph.

Takeovers

12.—(1) The securities are offered in connection with a takeover offer.
(2) 'Takeover offer' means—
- (a) an offer to acquire shares in a body incorporated in the United Kingdom which is a takeover offer within the meaning of the takeover provisions (or would be such an offer if those provisions applied in relation to any body corporate);
- (b) an offer to acquire all or substantially all of the shares, or of the shares of a particular class, in a body incorporated outside the United Kingdom; or
- (c) an offer made to all the holders of shares, or of shares of a particular class, in a body corporate to acquire a specified proportion of those shares.

(3) 'The takeover provisions' means—
  (a) Part XIIIA of the Companies Act 1985; or
  (b) in relation to Northern Ireland, Part XIVA of the Companies (Northern Ireland) Order 1986.

(4) For the purposes of sub-paragraph (2)(b), any shares which the offeror or any associate of his holds or has contracted to acquire are to be disregarded.

(5) For the purposes of sub-paragraph (2)(c), the following are not to be regarded as holders of the shares in question—
  (a) the offeror;
  (b) any associate of the offeror; and
  (c) any person whose shares the offeror or any associate of the offeror has contracted to acquire.

(6) 'Associate' has the same meaning as in—
  (a) section 430E of the Companies Act 1985; or
  (b) in relation to Northern Ireland, Article 423E of the Companies (Northern Ireland) Order 1986.

Mergers

13. The securities are offered in connection with a merger (within the meaning of Council Directive No. 78/855/EEC).

Free shares

14.—(1) The securities are shares and are offered free of charge to any or all of the holders of shares in the issuer.

(2) 'Holders of shares' means the persons who at the close of business on a date—
  (a) specified in the offer, and
  (b) falling within the period of 60 days ending with the date on which the offer is first made,
were holders of such shares.

Exchange of shares

15. The securities—
  (a) are shares, or investments of a specified kind relating to shares, in a body corporate, and
  (b) are offered in exchange for shares in the same body corporate, and the offer cannot result in any increase in the issued share capital of the body corporate.

Qualifying persons

16.—(1) The securities are issued by a body corporate and are offered—
  (a) by the issuer, by a body corporate connected with the issuer or by a relevant trustee;
  (b) only to qualifying persons; and
  (c) on terms that a contract to acquire any such securities may be entered into only by the qualifying person to whom they were offered or, if the terms of the offer so permit, any qualifying person.

(2) A person is a 'qualifying person', in relation to an issuer, if he is a genuine employee or former employee of the issuer or of another body corporate in the same group or the wife, husband, widow, widower or child or stepchild under the age of eighteen of such an employee or former employee.

(3) In relation to an issuer of securities, 'connected with' has such meaning as may be prescribed.

(4) 'Group' and 'relevant trustee' have such meaning as may be prescribed.

Convertible securities

17.—(1) The securities result from the conversion of convertible securities and listing particulars (or a prospectus) relating to the convertible securities were (or was) published in the United Kingdom under or by virtue of Part VI or such other provisions applying in the United Kingdom as may be specified.

(2) 'Convertible securities' means securities of a specified kind which can be converted into, or exchanged for, or which confer rights to acquire, other securities.

(3) 'Conversion' means conversion into or exchange for, or the exercise of rights conferred by the securities to acquire, other securities.

Charities

18.   The securities are issued by—
   (a) a charity within the meaning of—
      (i)   section 96(1) of the Charities Act 1993, or
      (ii) section 35 of the Charities Act (Northern Ireland) 1964,
   (b) a recognised body within the meaning of section 1(7) of the Law Reform (Miscellaneous Provisions) (Scotland) Act 1990,
   (c) a housing association within the meaning of—
      (i)   section 5(1) of the Housing Act 1985,
      (ii) section 1 of the Housing Associations Act 1985, or
      (iii) Article 3 of the Housing (Northern Ireland) Order 1992,
   (d) an industrial or provident society registered in accordance with—
      (i)   section 1(2)(b) of the Industrial and Provident Societies Act 1965, or
      (ii) section 1(2)(b) of the Industrial and Provident Societies Act 1969, or
   (e) a non-profit making association or body, recognised by the country or territory in which it is established, with objectives similar to those of a body falling within any of paragraphs (a) to (c),
and the proceeds of the offer will be used for the purposes of the issuer's objectives.

Building societies etc.

19.   The securities offered are shares which are issued by, or ownership of which entitles the holder to membership of or to obtain the benefit of services provided by—
   (a) a building society incorporated under the law of, or of any part of, the United Kingdom;
   (b) any body incorporated under the law of, or of any part of, the United Kingdom relating to industrial and provident societies or credit unions; or
   (c) a body of a similar nature established in another EEA State.

Euro-securities

20.—(1) The securities offered are Euro-securities and no advertisement relating to the offer is issued in the United Kingdom, or is caused to be so issued—
   (a) by the issuer of the Euro-securities;
   (b) by any credit institution or other financial institution through which the Eurosecurities may be acquired pursuant to the offer; or
   (c) by any body corporate which is a member of the same group as the issuer or any of those institutions.

(2) But sub-paragraph (1) does not apply to an advertisement of a prescribed kind.

(3) 'Euro-securities' means investments which—

    (a) are to be underwritten and distributed by a syndicate at least two of the members of which have their registered offices in different countries or territories;

    (b) are to be offered on a significant scale in one or more countries or territories, other than the country or territory in which the issuer has its registered office; and

    (c) may be acquired pursuant to the offer only through a credit institution or other financial institution.

(4) 'Credit institution' means a credit institution as defined in Article 1(1)(a) of the banking consolidation directive.

(5) 'Financial institution' means a financial institution as defined in Article 1(1)(a) of the banking consolidation directive.

(6) 'Underwritten' means underwritten by whatever means, including by acquisition or subscription, with a view to resale.

Same class securities

21.   The securities are of the same class, and were issued at the same time, as securities in respect of which a prospectus has been published under or by virtue of—

    (a) Part VI;

    (b) Part III of the Companies Act 1985; or

    (c) such other provisions applying in the United Kingdom as may be specified.

Short date securities

22.   The securities are investments of a specified kind with a maturity of less than one year from their date of issue.

Government and public securities

23.—(1) The securities are investments of a specified kind creating or acknowledging indebtedness issued by or on behalf of a public authority.

(2) 'Public authority' means—

    (a) the government of the United Kingdom;

    (b) the government of any country or territory outside the United Kingdom;

    (c) a local authority in the United Kingdom or elsewhere;

    (d) any international organisation the members of which include the United Kingdom or another EEA State; and

    (e) such other bodies, if any, as may be specified.

Non-transferable securities

24.   The securities are not transferable.

Units in a collective investment scheme

24A.   The securities are units (as defined by section 237(2)) in a collective investment scheme.

General definitions

25.   For the purposes of this Schedule—

'shares' has such meaning as may be specified; and

'specified' means specified in an order made by the Treasury.

Limited Liability Partnerships Act 2000
(2000, c. 12)

An Act to make provision for limited liability partnerships.   [20 July 2000]

Introductory

1   Limited liability partnerships

(1) There shall be a new form of legal entity to be known as a limited liability partnership.

(2) A limited liability partnership is a body corporate (with legal personality separate from that of its members) which is formed by being incorporated under this Act; and—

   (a) in the following provisions of this Act (except in the phrase 'oversea limited liability partnership'), and

   (b) in any other enactment (except where provision is made to the contrary or the context otherwise requires),

references to a limited liability partnership are to such a body corporate.

(3) A limited liability partnership has unlimited capacity.

(4) The members of a limited liability partnership have such liability to contribute to its assets in the event of its being wound up as is provided for by virtue of this Act.

(5) Accordingly, except as far as otherwise provided by this Act or any other enactment, the law relating to partnerships does not apply to a limited liability partnership.

(6) The Schedule (which makes provision about the names and registered offices of limited liability partnerships) has effect.

Incorporation

2   Incorporation document etc.

(1) For a limited liability partnership to be incorporated—

   (a) two or more persons associated for carrying on a lawful business with a view to profit must have subscribed their names to an incorporation document,

   (b) there must have been delivered to the registrar either the incorporation document or a copy authenticated in a manner approved by him, and

   (c) there must have been so delivered a statement in a form approved by the registrar, made by either a solicitor engaged in the formation of the limited liability partnership or anyone who subscribed his name to the incorporation document, that the requirement imposed by paragraph (a) has been complied with.

(2) The incorporation document must—

   (a) be in a form approved by the registrar (or as near to such a form as circumstances allow),

   (b) state the name of the limited liability partnership,

   (c) state whether the registered office of the limited liability partnership is to be situated in England and Wales, in Wales or in Scotland,

   (d) state the address of that registered office,

   (e) state the name and address of each of the persons who are to be members of the limited liability partnership on incorporation, and

   (f) either specify which of those persons are to be designated members or state that every person who from time to time is a member of the limited liability partnership is a designated member.

(2A) Where a confidentiality order, made under section 723B of the Companies Act 1985 as applied to . . . limited liability partnerships, is in force in respect of any individual named as a member of a limited liability partnership under subsection (2) that subsection shall have effect as if the reference to the address of the individual were a reference to the address for the time being notified by him under the Limited Liability Partnerships (Particulars of Usual Residential Address) (Confidentiality Orders) Regulations 2002 to any limited liability partnership of which he is a member or if he is not such a member either the address specified in his application for a confidentiality order or the address last notified by him under such a confidentiality order as the case may be.

(2B) Where the incorporation document or a copy of such delivered under this section includes an address specified in reliance on subsection (2A) there shall be delivered with it or the copy of it a statement in a form approved by the registrar containing particulars of the usual residential address of the member whose address is so specified.

(3) If a person makes a false statement under subsection (1)(c) which he—

(a) knows to be false, or

(b) does not believe to be true,

he commits an offence.

(4) A person guilty of an offence under subsection (3) is liable—

(a) on summary conviction, to imprisonment for a period not exceeding six months or a fine not exceeding the statutory maximum, or to both, or

(b) on conviction on indictment, to imprisonment for a period not exceeding two years or a fine, or to both.

[*The three points in s. 2(2A) indicate the editorial removal of the superfluous word 'a'.*]

3   Incorporation by registration

(1) When the requirements imposed by paragraphs (b) and (c) of subsection (1) of section 2 have been complied with, the registrar shall retain the incorporation document or copy delivered to him and, unless the requirement imposed by paragraph (a) of that subsection has not been complied with, he shall—

(a) register the incorporation document or copy, and

(b) give a certificate that the limited liability partnership is incorporated by the name specified in the incorporation document.

(2) The registrar may accept the statement delivered under paragraph (c) of subsection (1) of section 2 as sufficient evidence that the requirement imposed by paragraph (a) of that subsection has been complied with.

(3) The certificate shall either be signed by the registrar or be authenticated by his official seal.

(4) The certificate is conclusive evidence that the requirements of section 2 are complied with and that the limited liability partnership is incorporated by the name specified in the incorporation document.

Membership

4   Members

(1) On the incorporation of a limited liability partnership its members are the persons who subscribed their names to the incorporation document (other than any who have died or been dissolved).

(2) Any other person may become a member of a limited liability partnership by and in accordance with an agreement with the existing members.

(3) A person may cease to be a member of a limited liability partnership (as well as by death or dissolution) in accordance with an agreement with the other members or, in the absence of agreement with the other members as to cessation of membership, by giving reasonable notice to the other members.

(4) A member of a limited liability partnership shall not be regarded for any purpose as employed by the limited liability partnership unless, if he and the other members were partners in a partnership, he would be regarded for that purpose as employed by the partnership.

5   Relationship of members etc.

(1) Except as far as otherwise provided by this Act or any other enactment, the mutual rights and duties of the members of a limited liability partnership, and the mutual rights and duties of a limited liability partnership and its members, shall be governed—

  (a) by agreement between the members, or between the limited liability partnership and its members, or

  (b) in the absence of agreement as to any matter, by any provision made in relation to that matter by regulations under section 15(c).

(2) An agreement made before the incorporation of a limited liability partnership between the persons who subscribe their names to the incorporation document may impose obligations on the limited liability partnership (to take effect at any time after its incorporation).

6   Members as agents

(1) Every member of a limited liability partnership is the agent of the limited liability partnership.

(2) But a limited liability partnership is not bound by anything done by a member in dealing with a person if—

  (a) the member in fact has no authority to act for the limited liability partnership by doing that thing, and

  (b) the person knows that he has no authority or does not know or believe him to be a member of the limited liability partnership.

(3) Where a person has ceased to be a member of a limited liability partnership, the former member is to be regarded (in relation to any person dealing with the limited liability partnership) as still being a member of the limited liability partnership unless—

  (a) the person has notice that the former member has ceased to be a member of the limited liability partnership, or

  (b) notice that the former member has ceased to be a member of the limited liability partnership has been delivered to the registrar.

(4) Where a member of a limited liability partnership is liable to any person (other than another member of the limited liability partnership) as a result of a wrongful act or omission of his in the course of the business of the limited liability partnership or with its authority, the limited liability partnership is liable to the same extent as the member.

7   Ex-members

(1) This section applies where a member of a limited liability partnership has either ceased to be a member or—

  (a) has died,

  (b) has become bankrupt or had his estate sequestrated or has been wound up,

  (c) has granted a trust deed for the benefit of his creditors, or

  (d) has assigned the whole or any part of his share in the limited liability partnership (absolutely or by way of charge or security).

(2) In such an event the former member or—

  (a) his personal representative,

  (b) his trustee in bankruptcy or permanent or interim trustee (within the meaning of the Bankruptcy (Scotland) Act 1985) or liquidator,

  (c) his trustee under the trust deed for the benefit of his creditors, or

  (d) his assignee,

may not interfere in the management or administration of any business or affairs of the limited liability partnership.

(3) But subsection (2) does not affect any right to receive an amount from the limited liability partnership in that event.

8   Designated members

(1) If the incorporation document specifies who are to be designated members—

(a) they are designated members on incorporation, and

(b) any member may become a designated member by and in accordance with an agreement with the other members,

and a member may cease to be a designated member in accordance with an agreement with the other members.

(2) But if there would otherwise be no designated members, or only one, every member is a designated member.

(3) If the incorporation document states that every person who from time to time is a member of the limited liability partnership is a designated member, every member is a designated member.

(4) A limited liability partnership may at any time deliver to the registrar—

(a) notice that specified members are to be designated members, or

(b) notice that every person who from time to time is a member of the limited liability partnership is a designated member,

and, once it is delivered, subsection (1) (apart from paragraph (a)) and subsection (2), or subsection (3), shall have effect as if that were stated in the incorporation document.

(5) A notice delivered under subsection (4)—

(a) shall be in a form approved by the registrar, and

(b) shall be signed by a designated member of the limited liability partnership or authenticated in a manner approved by the registrar.

(6) A person ceases to be a designated member if he ceases to be a member.

9   Registration of membership changes

(1) A limited liability partnership must ensure that—

(a) where a person becomes or ceases to be a member or designated member, notice is delivered to the registrar within fourteen days, and

(b) where there is any change in the name or address of a member, notice is delivered to the registrar within 28 days.

(2) Where all the members from time to time of a limited liability partnership are designated members, subsection (1)(a) does not require notice that a person has become or ceased to be a designated member as well as a member.

(3) A notice delivered under subsection (1)—

(a) shall be in a form approved by the registrar, and

(b) shall be signed by a designated member of the limited liability partnership or authenticated in a manner approved by the registrar,

and, if it relates to a person becoming a member or designated member, shall contain a statement that he consents to becoming a member or designated member signed by him or authenticated in a manner approved by the registrar.

(3A) Where a confidentiality order under section 723B of the Companies Act 1985 as applied to limited liability partnerships is made in respect of an existing member, the limited liability partnership must ensure that there is delivered within 28 days to the registrar notice in a form approved by the registrar containing the address for the time being notified to it by the member under the Limited Liability Partnerships (Particulars of Usual Residential Address) (Confidentiality Orders) Regulations 2002.

(3B) Where such a confidentiality order is in force in respect of a member the requirement in subsection (1)(b) to notify a change in the address of a member shall be read in relation to that member as a requirement to deliver to the registrar, within 28 days, notice of—

(a) any change in the usual residential address of that member; and

(b) any change in the address for the time being notified to the limited liability partnership by the member under the Limited Liability Partnerships

(Particulars of Usual Residential Address) (Confidentiality Orders) Regulations 2002,

and the registrar may approve different forms for the notification of each kind of address.

(4) If a limited liability partnership fails to comply with subsection (1), the partnership and every designated member commits an offence.

(5) But it is a defence for a designated member charged with an offence under subsection (4) to prove that he took all reasonable steps for securing that subsection (1) was complied with.

(6) A person guilty of an offence under subsection (4) is liable on summary conviction to a fine not exceeding level 5 on the standard scale.

Regulations

14   Insolvency and winding up

(1) Regulations shall make provision about the insolvency and winding up of limited liability partnerships by applying or incorporating, with such modifications as appear appropriate, Parts I to IV, VI and VII of the Insolvency Act 1986.

(2) Regulations may make other provision about the insolvency and winding up of limited liability partnerships, and provision about the insolvency and winding up of oversea limited liability partnerships, by—

- (a) applying or incorporating, with such modifications as appear appropriate, any law relating to the insolvency or winding up of companies or other corporations which would not otherwise have effect in relation to them, or
- (b) providing for any law relating to the insolvency or winding up of companies or other corporations which would otherwise have effect in relation to them not to apply to them or to apply to them with such modifications as appear appropriate.

(3) In this Act 'oversea limited liability partnership' means a body incorporated or otherwise established outside Great Britain and having such connection with Great Britain, and such other features, as regulations may prescribe.

15   Application of company law etc.

Regulations may make provision about limited liability partnerships and oversea limited liability partnerships (not being provision about insolvency or winding up) by—

- (a) applying or incorporating, with such modifications as appear appropriate, any law relating to companies or other corporations which would not otherwise have effect in relation to them.
- (b) providing for any law relating to companies or other corporations which would otherwise have effect in relation to them not to apply to them or to apply to them with such modifications as appear appropriate, or
- (c) applying or incorporating, with such modifications as appear appropriate, any law relating to partnerships.

16   Consequential amendments

(1) Regulations may make in any enactment such amendments or repeals as appear appropriate in consequence of this Act or regulations made under it.

(2) The regulations may, in particular, make amendments and repeals affecting companies or other corporations or partnerships.

17   General

(1) In this Act 'regulations' means regulations made by the Secretary of State by statutory instrument.

(2) Regulations under this Act may in particular—

- (a) make provision for dealing with non-compliance with any of the regulations (including the creation of criminal offences),

(b) impose fees (which shall be paid into the Consolidated Fund), and

(c) provide for the exercise of functions by persons prescribed by the regulations.

(3) Regulations under this Act may—

   (a) contain any appropriate consequential, incidental, supplementary or transitional provisions or savings, and

   (b) make different provision for different purposes.

(4) No regulations to which this subsection applies shall be made unless a draft of the statutory instrument containing the regulations (whether or not together with other provisions) has been laid before, and approved by a resolution of, each House of Parliament.

(5) Subsection (4) applies to—

   (a) regulations under section 14(2) not consisting entirely of the application or incorporation (with or without modifications) of provisions contained in or made under the Insolvency Act 1986,

   (b) regulations under section 15 not consisting entirely of the application or incorporation (with or without modifications) of provisions contained in or made under Part I, Chapter VIII of Part V, Part VII, Parts XI to XIII, Parts XVI to XVIII, Part XX or Parts XXIV to XXVI of the Companies Act 1985,

   (c) regulations under section 14 or 15 making provision about oversea limited liability partnerships, and

   (d) regulations under section 16.

(6) A statutory instrument containing regulations under this Act shall (unless a draft of it has been approved by a resolution of each House of Parliament) be subject to annulment in pursuance of a resolution of either House of Parliament.

Supplementary

18 Interpretation

In this Act—

'address', in relation to a member of a limited liability partnership, means—

   (a) if an individual, his usual residential address, and

   (b) if a corporation or Scottish firm, its registered or principal office,

'business' includes every trade, profession and occupation,

'designated member' shall be construed in accordance with section 8,

'enactment' includes subordinate legislation (within the meaning of the Interpretation Act 1978),

'incorporation document' shall be construed in accordance with section 2,

'limited liability partnership' has the meaning given by section 1(2),

'member' shall be construed in accordance with section 4.

'modifications' includes additions and omissions,

'name' in relation to a member of a limited liability partnership, means—

   (a) if an individual, his forename and surname (or, in the case of a peer or other person usually known by a title, his title instead of or in addition to either or both his forename and surname), and

   (b) if a corporation or Scottish firm, its corporate or firm name,

'oversea limited liability partnership' has the meaning given by section 14(3),

'the registrar' means—

   (a) if the registered office of the limited liability partnership is, or is to be, situated in England and Wales or in Wales, the registrar or other officer performing under the Companies Act 1985 the duty of registration of companies in England and Wales, and

   (b) if its registered office is, or is to be, situated in Scotland, the registrar or other officer performing under that Act the duty of registration of companies in Scotland, and

'regulations' has the meaning given by section 17(1).

19   Commencement, extent and short title

(1) The preceding provisions of this Act shall come into force on such day as the Secretary of State may by order made by statutory instrument appoint; and different days may be appointed for different purposes.

(2) The Secretary of State may by order made by statutory instrument make any transitional provisions and savings which appear appropriate in connection with the coming into force of any provision of this Act.

(3) For the purposes of the Scotland Act 1998 this Act shall be taken to be a pre-commencement enactment within the meaning of that Act.

(4) Apart from sections 10 to 13 (and this section), this Act does not extend to Northern Ireland.

(5) This Act may be cited as the Limited Liability Partnerships Act 2000.

SCHEDULE   NAMES AND REGISTERED OFFICES

PART I   NAMES

Name to indicate status

2.—(1) The name of a limited liability partnership must end with—
  (a) the expression 'limited liability partnership', or
  (b) the abbreviation 'llp' or 'LLP'.

(2) But if the incorporation document for a limited liability partnership states that the registered office is to be situated in Wales, its name must end with—
  (a) one of the expressions 'limited liability partnership' and 'partneriaeth atebolrwydd cyfyngedig', or
  (b) one of the abbreviations 'llp', 'LLP', 'pac' and 'PAC'.

Registration of names

3.—(1) A limited liability partnership shall not be registered by a name—
  (a) which includes, otherwise than at the end of the name, either of the expressions 'limited liability partnership' and 'partneriaeth atebolrwydd cyfyngedig' or any of the abbreviations 'llp', 'LLP', 'pac' and 'PAC'.
  (b) which is the same as a name appearing in the index kept under section 714(1) of the Companies Act 1985,
  (c) the use of which by the limited liability partnership would in the opinion of the Secretary of State constitute a criminal offence, or
  (d) which in the opinion of the Secretary of State is offensive.

(2) Except with the approval of the Secretary of State, a limited liability partnership shall not be registered by a name which—
  (a) in the opinion of the Secretary of State would be likely to give the impression that it is connected in any way with Her Majesty's Government or with any local authority, or
  (b) includes any word or expression for the time being specified in regulations under section 29 of the Companies Act 1985 (names needing approval),
and in paragraph (a) 'local authority' means any local authority within the meaning of the Local Government Act 1972 or the Local Government etc. (Scotland) Act 1994, the Common Council of the City of London or the Council of the Isles of Scilly.

Change of name

4.—(1) A limited liability partnership may change its name at any time.

(2) Where a limited liability partnership has been registered by a name which—

    (a) is the same as or, in the opinion of the Secretary of State, too like a name appearing at the time of registration in the index kept under section 714(1) of the Companies Act 1985, or

    (b) is the same as or, in the opinion of the Secretary of State, too like a name which should have appeared in the index at that time,

the Secretary of State may within twelve months of that time in writing direct the limited liability partnership to change its name within such period as he may specify.

(3) If it appears to the Secretary of State—

    (a) that misleading information has been given for the purpose of the registration of a limited liability partnership by a particular name, or

    (b) that undertakings or assurances have been given for that purpose and have not been fulfilled,

he may, within five years of the date of its registration by that name, in writing direct the limited liability partnership to change its name within such period as he may specify.

(4) If in the Secretary of State's opinion the name by which a limited liability partnership is registered gives so misleading an indication of the nature of its activities as to be likely to cause harm to the public, he may in writing direct the limited liability partnership to change its name within such period as he may specify.

(5) But the limited liability partnership may, within three weeks from the date of the direction apply to the court to set it aside and the court may set the direction aside or confirm it and, if it confirms it, shall specify the period within which it must be complied with.

(6) In sub-paragraph (5) 'the court' means—

    (a) if the registered office of the limited liability partnership is situated in England and Wales or in Wales, the High Court, and

    (b) if it is situated in Scotland, the Court of Session.

(7) Where a direction has been given under sub-paragraph (2), (3) or (4) specifying a period within which a limited liability partnership is to change its name, the Secretary of State may at any time before that period ends extend it by a further direction in writing.

(8) If a limited liability partnership fails to comply with a direction under this paragraph—

    (a) the limited liability partnership, and

    (b) any designated member in default,

commits an offence.

(9) A person guilty of an offence under sub-paragraph (8) is liable on summary conviction to a fine not exceeding level 3 on the standard scale.

Notification of change of name

5.—(1) Where a limited liability partnership changes its name it shall deliver notice of the change to the registrar.

(2) A notice delivered under sub-paragraph (1)—

    (a) shall be in a form approved by the registrar, and

    (b) shall be signed by a designated member of the limited liability partnership or authenticated in a manner approved by the registrar.

(3) Where the registrar receives a notice under sub-paragraph (2) he shall (unless the new name is one by which a limited liability partnership may not be registered)—

    (a) enter the new name in the index kept under section 714(1) of the Companies Act 1985, and

    (b) issue a certificate of the change of name.

(4) The change of name has effect from the date on which the certificate is issued.

Effect of change of name

    6.   A change of name by a limited liability partnership does not—

        (a) affect any of its rights or duties,

        (b) render defective any legal proceedings by or against it,

and any legal proceedings that might have been commenced or continued against it by its former name may be commenced or continued against it by its new name.

Improper use of 'limited liability partnership' etc.

    7.—(1) If any person carries on a business under a name or title which includes as the last words—

        (a) the expression 'limited liability partnership' or 'partneriaeth atebolrwydd cyfyn-gedig', or

        (b) any contraction or imitation of either of those expressions,

that person, unless a limited liability partnership or oversea limited liability partnership, commits an offence.

    (2) A person guilty of an offence under sub-paragraph (1) is liable on summary conviction to a fine not exceeding level 3 on the standard scale.

Similarity of names

    8.   In determining for the purposes of this Part whether one name is the same as another there are to be disregarded—

    (1) the definite article as the first word of the name,

    (2) any of the following (or their Welsh equivalents or abbreviations of them or their Welsh equivalents) at the end of the name—

    'limited liability partnership',

    'company',

    'and company',

    'company limited',

    'and company limited',

    'limited',

    'unlimited',

    'public limited company',

    'investment company with variable capital', and

    'open-ended investment company', and

    (3) type and case of letters, accents, spaces between letters and punctuation marks, and 'and' and '&' are to be taken as the same.

PART II   REGISTERED OFFICES

Situation of registered office

    9.—(1) A limited liability partnership shall—

        (a) at all times have a registered office situated in England and Wales or in Wales, or

        (b) at all times have a registered office situated in Scotland,

to which communications and notices may be addressed.

    (2) On the incorporation of a limited liability partnership the situation of its registered office shall be that stated in the incorporation document.

    (3) Where the registered office of a limited liability partnership is situated in Wales, but the incorporation document does not state that it is to be situated in Wales (as opposed to England and Wales), the limited liability partnership may deliver notice to the registrar stating that its registered office is to be situated in Wales.

(4) A notice delivered under sub-paragraph (3)—
- (a) shall be in a form approved by the registrar, and
- (b) shall be signed by a designated member of the limited liability partnership or authenticated in a manner approved by the registrar.

Change of registered office

10.—(1) A limited liability partnership may change its registered office by delivering notice of the change to the registrar.

(2) A notice delivered under sub-paragraph (1)—
- (a) shall be in a form approved by the registrar, and
- (b) shall be signed by a designated member of the limited liability partnership or authenticated in a manner approved by the registrar.

PART II

Statutory Instruments

Company and Business Names Regulations 1981
(1981 No. 1685)

The Secretary of State, in exercise of his powers under sections 31 and 32 of the Companies Act 1981 hereby makes the following regulations—

1.   These Regulations may be cited as the Company and Business Names Regulations 1981 and shall come into operation on 26 February 1982.

2.   In these Regulations, unless the context otherwise requires, 'the Act' means the Companies Act 1981.

3.   The words and expressions stated in column (1) of the Schedule hereto (together with the plural and the possessive forms of those words and expressions) are hereby specified as words and expressions for the registration of which as or as part of a company's corporate name the approval of the Secretary of State is required by section 22(2)(b) of the Act or for the use of which as or as part of a business name his approval is required by section 28(2)(b) of the Act.

4.   Subject to Regulation 5, each Government department or other body stated in column (2) of the Schedule hereto is hereby specified as the relevant body for the purposes of section 31(2) and (3) of the Act in relation to the word or expression (and the plural and the possesive forms of that word or expression) opposite to it in column (1).

5.   Where two Government departments or other bodies are specified in the alternative in Column (2) of the Schedule hereto the second alternative is to be treated as specified,

   (a)   in the case of the corporate name of a company,
      (i)   if the company has not yet been registered and its principal or only place of business in Great Britain is to be in Scotland or, if it will have no place of business in Great Britain, its proposed registered office is in Scotland, and
      (ii)   if the company is already registered and its principal or only place of business in Great Britain is in Scotland or, if it has no place of business in Great Britain, its registered office is in Scotland, and
   (b)   in the case of a business name, if the principal or only place of the business carried on or to be carried on in Great Britain is or is to be in Scotland,

and the first alternative is to be treated as specified in any other case.

Regulations 3, 4 and 5   SCHEDULE

SPECIFICATION OF WORDS, EXPRESSIONS AND
RELEVANT BODIES

Column (1)	Column (2)
Word or expression	Relevant body
Abortion	Department of Health and Social Security
Apothecary	Worshipful Society of Apothecaries of London or Pharmaceutical Society of Great Britain
Association	
Assurance	
Assurer	
Authority	
Benevolent	
Board	
British	
Chamber (or Chambers) of Business (or their Welsh equivalents, Siambr Fusnes; Siambrau Busnes)	
Chamber (or Chambers) of Commerce (or their Welsh equivalents, Siambr Fasnach; Siambrau Masnach)	
Chamber (or Chambers) of Commerce and Industry (or their Welsh equivalents, Siambr Masnach a Diwydiant; Siambrau Masnach a Diwydiant)	
Chamber (or Chambers) of Commerce, Training and Enterprise (or their Welsh equivalents, Siambr Masnach, Hyfforddiant a Menter; Siambrau Masnach, Hyfforddiant a Menter)	
Chamber (or Chambers) of Enterprise (or their Welsh equivalents, Siambr Fenter; Siambrau Menter)	
Chamber (or Chambers) of Industry (or their Welsh equivalents, Siambr Ddiwydiant; Siambrau Diwydiant)	
Chamber (or Chambers) of Trade (or their Welsh equivalents, Siambr Fasnach; Siambrau Masnach)	
Chamber (or Chambers) of Trade and Industry (or their Welsh equivalents, Siambr Masnach a Diwydiant; Siambrau Masnach a Diwydiant)	
Chamber (or Chambers) of Training (or their Welsh equivalents, Siambr Hyfforddiant; Siambrau Hyfforddiant)	
Chamber (or Chambers) of Training and Enterprise (or their Welsh equivalents, Siambr Hyfforddiant a Menter; Siambrau Hyfforddiant a Menter)	
Charitable	
Charity	} Charity Commission or the Scottish Ministers
Charter	
Chartered	
Chemist	
Chemistry	

Column (1)	Column (2)
Word or expression	Relevant body
Contact Lens	General Optical Council
Co-operative	
Council	
Dental	} General Dental Council
Dentistry	
District Nurse	Panel of Assessors in District Nurse Training
Duke	Home Office or the Scottish Ministers
England	
English	
European	
Federation	
Friendly Society	
Foundation	
Fund	
Giro	
Great Britain	
Group	
Health Centre	} Department of Health and Social Security
Health Service	
Health Visitor	Council for the Education and Training of Health Visitors
Her Majesty	} Home Office or the Scottish Ministers
His Majesty	
Holding	
Industrial and Provident Society	
Institute	
Institution	
Insurance	
Insurer	
International	
Ireland	
Irish	
King	Home Office or the Scottish Ministers
Midwife	} Central Midwives Board or Central
Midwifery	Midwives Board for Scotland
National	
Nurse	} General Nursing Council for England and
Nursing	Wales or General Nursing Council for Scotland
Patent	
Patentee	
Police	Home Office or the Scottish Ministers
Polytechnic	Department for Education and Skills
Post Office	
Pregnancy Termination	Department of Health and Social Security
Prince	
Princess	} Home Office or the Scottish Ministers
Queen	
Reassurance	
Reassurer	
Register	
Registered	
Reinsurance	
Reinsurer	
Royal	

Column (1)	Column (2)
Word or expression	Relevant body
Royale Royalty Scotland Scottish Sheffield	} Home Office or the Scottish Ministers
Society Special School Stock Exchange Trade Union Trust United Kingdom	Department for Education and Skills
University Wales Welsh	The Privy Council
Windsor	Home Office or the Scottish Ministers

Note: The reference in Column (2) to the Home Office shall be treated as a reference to the Lord Chancellor's Department in relation to the following entries in Column (1)—

(a) Duke,
(b) Her Majesty,
(c) His Majesty,
(d) King,
(e) Prince,
(f) Princess,
(g) Queen,
(h) Royal,
(i) Royale,
(j) Royalty, and
(k) Windsor.

Companies (Registers and Other Records) Regulations 1985

(1985 No. 724)

The Secretary of State, in exercise of his powers under section 723(4) of the Companies Act 1985, and of all other powers enabling him in that behalf, hereby makes the following Regulations—

Citation, commencement, revocation and interpretation

1.—(1) These Regulations may be cited as the Companies (Registers and other Records) Regulations 1985 and shall come into operation on 1 July 1985.

(2) In these Regulations, unless the context otherwise requires—

'the Act' means the Companies Act 1985;

'the place for inspection' means, in relation to a register, or a register of holders of debentures of a company, which is kept by recording the matters in question otherwise than in a legible form, the place where the duty to allow inspection of the register is for the time being performed in accordance with these Regulations;

'register' means a register or other record as is mentioned in section 722(1) of the Act or regulation 20 of the 2001 Regulations;

'the register of directors' interests' means the register required to be kept under section 325(1) of the Act;

'the 2001 Regulations' means the Uncertificated Securities Regulations 2001; and expressions defined in the 2001 Regulations shall have the same meaning in these Regulations.

(3) Any reference in these Regulations to the duty to allow inspection of a register, or of the register of holders of debentures, is a reference to the duty provided for in section 723(3) of the Act to allow inspection of, or to furnish, a reproduction of the recording of the register, or of the relevant part of the recording in a legible form.

(4) Any reference in these Regulations to the register of interests in voting shares shall be construed as including a reference to the separate part of that register referred to in section 213(1) of the Act.

(5) The Companies (Registers and other Records) Regulations 1979 are hereby revoked.

Requirements with respect to registers kept otherwise than in a legible form

2.—(1) This Regulation applies with respect to any register specified in Schedule 1 to these Regulations which is kept by a company by recording the matters in question otherwise than in a legible form.

(2) The company shall perform the duty to allow inspection of any register to which this Regulation applies at a place specified in the said Schedule 1 in relation to that register.

(3) In the case of any register to which this Regulation applies, the company shall not be required—

    (a) to keep the register in any place where it is required to be kept under the Act,

    (b) to give any notice to the registrar of companies required to be given under the Act of the place where the register is kept, or of any change in that place, or

    (c) to include in its annual return any statement required to be given under the Act of the address of the place where the register is kept.

(4) Where provision is made in the Act with respect to default in complying with any requirement of that Act regarding the place where a register specified in Schedule 1 to these Regulations is to be kept, the provision shall have effect in relation to any such register to which this Regulation applies as if there were substituted for the reference therein to such default, a reference to default in complying with the requirements of paragraph (2) above.

(5) This Regulation applies with respect to an issuer [register] of members and a record of uncertificated shares which is kept by a company by recording the matters in question otherwise than in legible form—

    (a) as it applies to a register of members under the Act which is kept in like fashion; and

    (b) as if references to the Act were references to the 2001 Regulations.

(6) This Regulation applies with respect to an index kept by virtue of paragraph 7 of Schedule 4 to the 2001 Regulations which is kept by a company by recording the matters in question otherwise than in legible form—

    (a) as it applies to an index of a register of members under the Act which is kept in like fashion; and

    (b) as if references to the Act were references to the 2001 Regulations.

[*The word 'register' seems to have been accidentally omitted from reg. 2(5).*]

Notification of place for inspection of registers

3.—(1) Subject to the provisions of paragraph (3) below, where a company keeps any register specified in paragraph (2) below by recording the matters in question otherwise than in a legible form, the company shall send to the registrar of companies notice, in the form indicated in Part I of Schedule 2 to these Regulations, of the place for inspection of that register and of any change in that place.

(2) The registers referred to in paragraph (1) above are

    (a) the register of members,

    (b) an overseas branch register, and

    (c) the register of directors' interests.

(3) The company shall not be obliged to give notice under paragraph (1) above—

  (a) where the company changes from keeping a register in a legible form to keeping it otherwise than in a legible form and the place for inspection of the register immediately following the change is the same as the place where the register was kept in a legible form immediately prior to the change, or

  (b) in the case of a register specified in paragraph 2(a) or (c) above, where since the register first came into existence—

    (i) it has been kept by recording the matters in question otherwise than in a legible form, and

    (ii) the place for inspection has been the registered office of the company.

(4) Where the register of members of a company is kept by recording the matters in question otherwise than in a legible form and the place for inspection of that register is elsewhere than at the registered office, the company shall include in its annual return a statement of the address of the place for inspection of that register.

(5) Subsection (4) of section 353 of the Act shall apply with respect to any default in complying with paragraph (1) above as it applies in relation to a default in complying with subsection (2) of that section; and subsection (7) of section 363 of the Act shall apply with respect to any failure to comply with paragraph (4) above as it applies in relation to a failure to comply with that section.

(6) In the case of a company which is a participating issuer, references in this regulation to the register of members shall be taken to be a reference to the company's issuer register of members and record of uncertificated shares.

Requirements with respect to a register of debenture holders kept otherwise than in a legible form

4.—(1) This Regulation applies to any register of holders of debentures of a company which is kept by a company by recording the matters in question otherwise than in a legible form.

(2) A company registered in England and Wales shall not perform the duty to allow inspection of a register to which this Regulation applies in Scotland and a company registered in Scotland shall not perform such duty in England and Wales.

(3) A company shall not perform the duty to allow inspection of a register to which this Regulation applies in England and Wales, in the case of a company registered in England and Wales, or in Scotland, in the case of a company registered in Scotland, elsewhere than at—

  (a) the registered office of the company,

  (b) any other office of the company at which the work of ensuring that the register is duly made up is done, or

  (c) if the company arranges with some other person for the carrying out of the work referred to in (b) above to be undertaken on behalf of the company by that other person, the office of that other person at which the work is done.

(4) The requirements of section 190 of the Act (provisions as to registers of debenture holders) and sections 363 and 364 of and Schedule 15 to that Act (annual returns) shall not apply to a register to which this Regulation applies in so far as they relate to any of the following matters—

  (a) the place where the register is permitted to be kept,

  (b) the giving of notice to the registrar of companies of the place where the register is kept, or of any change in that place, and

  (c) the inclusion in the annual return of a statement of the address of the place where the register is kept.

Notification of the place for inspection of registers of debenture holders

5.—(1) Subject to paragraph (2) below, where the place for inspection of a register to which Regulation 4 above applies is in England and Wales or Scotland, the company shall send to the registrar of companies, notice in the form indicated in Part II of Schedule 2 to these Regulations of the place for inspection of that register and of any change in that place.

(2) The company shall not be obliged to give notice under paragraph (1) above—

(a) where a company changes from keeping the register in a legible form to keeping it otherwise than in a legible form and the place for inspection of the register immediately following the change is the same as the place where the register was kept in a legible form immediately prior to the change, or

(b) where since the register first came into existence—

(i) it has been kept by recording the matters in question otherwise than in a legible form, and

(ii) the place for inspection has been the registered office of the company.

(3) Where the place for inspection of a register to which Regulation 4 above applies is situated in England and Wales, in the case of a company registered in England and Wales, or in Scotland, in the case of a company registered in Scotland, elsewhere than at the registered office of the company, the company shall include in its annual return a statement of the address of that place.

(4) Subsection (7) of section 363 of the Act shall apply with respect to any failure to comply with paragraph (3) above as it applies in relation to a failure to comply with that section.

Other provisions relating to registers kept otherwise than in a legible form

6.—(1) Where a register or a register of holders of debentures is kept by recording the matters in question otherwise than in a legible form, any reference to such register in any provision of the Act or the 2001 Regulations relating to the place where a duplicate of such register, another register or duplicate of another register is required to be kept, shall be construed as a reference to the place for inspection of the first mentioned register.

(2) Where the place for inspection of the register of members is the office of some person other than the company and by reason of any default of that person the company fails to comply with—

(a) the provisions of Regulation 2 above relating to the duty to allow inspection of the index of the register of members, or

(b) the provisions of Regulation 3 above relating to the register of members, section 357 of the Act (consequences of failure to comply with requirements as to register owing to agent's default) shall apply with respect to such failure as it applies in relation to a failure to comply with the provisions specified in that section by reason of any default of the person other than the company, at whose office the register of members is kept.

(2A) In the case of a company which is a participating issuer, paragraph (2) shall apply as if—

(a) references to the register of members were references to the company's issuer register of members and record of uncertificated shares; and

(b) the reference to the index of the register of members were a reference to an index kept by virtue of paragraph 7 of Schedule 4 to the 2001 Regulations.

(3) Where an overseas branch register is kept by a company by recording the matters in question otherwise than in a legible form, paragraphs 2(2) and 3(1) of Schedule 14 to the Act shall have effect as if, for the references to the country or territory where that register is kept, there were substituted references to the country or territory where the place for inspection of the register is situated.

(4) Where the register of directors' interests is kept by a company by recording the matters in question otherwise than in a legible form, paragraph 29 of Schedule 13 to the Act shall have effect as if, for the reference to that register, there were substituted a reference to a reproduction of the recording of that register in a legible form.

(5) Where the accounting records of a company are kept otherwise than in a legible form and the place for inspection of such records is outside Great Britain, section 222(2) of the Act shall have effect as if, for the references to the accounting records being kept at a place outside Great Britain, there were substituted references to the place for inspection of such records being at a place outside Great Britain.

Regulation 2
SCHEDULE 1
PLACES FOR PERFORMANCE OF DUTY TO ALLOW INSPECTION OF REGISTERS KEPT OTHERWISE THAN IN A LEGIBLE FORM

Statutory Provision	Register	Place
COMPANIES ACT 1985 Section 211(8)	Register and any associated index of interests in voting shares	(a) Where the register of directors' interests is kept otherwise than in a legible form, the place for inspection of that register. (b) Where the register of directors' interests is kept in a legible form, the place where it is so kept.
Section 222(1)	Accounting records	The registered office of the company or such other place as the directors of the company think fit.
Section 288(1)	Register of directors and secretaries	The registered office of the company.
Section 353(1)	Register of members	The registered office of the company provided that— (a) if the work of ensuring that the requirements of the Act with regard to entries in the register are complied with is done at another office of the company, the place for inspection may be that other office and (b) if the company arranges with some other person for the carrying out of the work referred to in (a) above to be undertaken on behalf of the company by that other person, the place for inspection may be the office of that other person at which the work is done; so however that the place for inspection shall not, in the case of a company registered in England and Wales, be at a place outside England and Wales and, in the case of a company registered in Scotland, be at a place outside Scotland.
Section 354(3)	Index of the register of members	(a) Where the register of members is kept otherwise than in a legible form, the place for inspection of that register. (b) Where the register of members is kept in a legible form, the place where it is so kept.
Section 362(1)	Overseas branch register	Any place where, but for these Regulations, the register would be permitted to be kept under section 362(1) of the Act.
Sections 407(1) and 422(1)	Register of charges	The registered office of the company.
Schedule 13, paragraph 25	Register of directors' interests	(a) Where the register of members is kept otherwise than in a legible form:

Statutory Provision	Register	Place
		(i) that register is the registered office of the company, that office, and
		(ii) if not, the place for inspection of that register or the registered office of the company.
		(b) Where the register of members is kept in a legible form:
		(i) registered office of the company, that office, and
		(ii) if that register is not so kept, the place where that register is kept or the registered office of the company.
Schedule 13, paragraph 28	Index of the register of directors' interests	(a) Where the register of directors' interests is kept otherwise than in a legible form, the place for inspection of that register.
		(b) Where the register of directors' interests is kept in a legible form, the place where it is so kept.
Schedule 14, paragraph 4(1)	Duplicate of overseas branch register	(a) Where the register of members is kept otherwise than in a legible form, the place for inspection of that register.
		(b) Where the register of members is kept in a legible form, the place where it is so kept.

Companies (Disclosure of Directors' Interests) (Exceptions) Regulations 1985

(1985 No. 802)

The Secretary of State, in exercise of the powers conferred by section 324(3) of the Companies Act 1985 and of all other powers enabling him in that behalf, hereby makes the following Regulations:—

1.   These Regulations may be cited as the Companies (Disclosure of Directors' Interests) (Exceptions) Regulations 1985 and shall come into operation on 1 July 1985.

2.   Section 324(1) and (2) of the Companies Act 1985 shall not require notification of—

  (a)   interests in shares or debentures of any person in his capacity as trustee or personal representative of any trust or estate of which the Public Trustee is also a trustee (otherwise than as custodian trustee) or, as the case may be, a personal representative;

  (b)   interests in shares in, or debentures of, a society registered under the Industrial and Provident Societies Act 1965 or deemed to be so registered by virtue of section 4 of that Act;

  (c)   interests in shares or debentures of a person in his capacity as trustee of, or as beneficiary under, a trust relating exclusively to—

    (i)   any retirement benefits scheme which is an approved scheme or a statutory scheme as defined in section 26(1) of the Finance Act 1970, and any retirement benefit scheme which is treated as being two or more separate retirement benefit schemes under section 25(3) of that Act where any of those separate schemes is an approved scheme or a statutory scheme, or

(ii) a superannuation fund to which section 36 of the Finance Act 1980 applies;

(d) any event occurring in relation to any person in any such capacity as is mentioned in paragraph (a) or (c) of this Regulation or in relation to any such shares or debentures as are mentioned in paragraph (b);

(e) interests in shares or debentures which a person is taken to have under paragraph 4 of Part I of Schedule 13 to the Companies Act 1985 where the body corporate referred to in that paragraph is interested in those shares or debentures in its capacity as trustee of any such trust as is mentioned in paragraph (c) of this Regulation;

(f) any event occurring in relation to any person as a result of which he is taken to have any such interest as is mentioned in paragraph (e) of this Regulation;

(g) interests in shares in a body corporate which arise solely on account of any limitation imposed by the memorandum or articles of association of the body corporate on a person's right to dispose of a share.

3.—(1) The said section 324(1) and (2) shall not require notification—

(a) to a company which is the wholly owned subsidiary of a body corporate incorporated outside Great Britain of interests in shares in, or debentures of, that body corporate or any other body corporate so incorporated, or of any event occurring in relation to any such shares or debentures;

(b) to a company by a director of the company who is also the director of a body corporate of which the company is the wholly owned subsidiary and which is itself required to keep a register under section 325(1) of the Companies Act 1985, of interests in any shares or debentures or of any event occurring in relation to any shares or debentures.

(2) For the purposes of paragraph (1) of this Regulation, a company shall be deemed to be the wholly owned subsidiary of another body corporate if it has no members but that other and that other's wholly owned subsidiaries and its or their nominees.

4. The Companies (Disclosure of Directors' Interests) (Exceptions) No. 1 Regulations 1967, the Companies (Disclosure of Directors' Interests) (Exceptions) No. 2 Regulations 1968 and the Companies (Disclosure of Directors' Interests) (Exceptions) No. 3 Regulations 1968 are hereby revoked.

Companies (Tables A to F) Regulations 1985
(1985 No. 805)

The Secretary of State, in exercise of the powers conferred by section 454(2) of the Companies Act 1948 and now vested in him, of the powers conferred by sections 3 and 8 of the Companies Act 1985 and of all other powers enabling him in that behalf, hereby makes the following Regulations—

1. These Regulations may be cited as the Companies (Tables A to F) Regulations 1985 and shall come into operation on 1 July 1985.

2. The regulations in Table A and the forms in Tables B, C, D, E and F in the Schedule to these Regulations shall be the regulations and forms of memorandum and articles of association for the purposes of sections 3 and 8 of the Companies Act 1985.

3. The Companies (Alteration of Table A etc.) Regulations 1984 are hereby revoked.

SCHEDULE
TABLE A   REGULATIONS FOR MANAGEMENT OF A
COMPANY LIMITED BY SHARES
INTERPRETATION

1.   In these regulations—
'the Act' means the Companies Act 1985 including any statutory modification or re-enactment thereof for the time being in force.
'the articles' means the articles of the company.
'clear days' in relation to the period of a notice means that period excluding the day when the notice is given or deemed to be given and the day for which it is given or on which it is to take effect.
'communication' means the same as in the Electronic Communications Act 2000.
'electronic communication' means the same as in the Electronic Communications Act 2000.
'executed' includes any mode of execution.
'office' means the registered office of the company.
'the holder' in relation to shares means the member whose name is entered in the register of members as the holder of the shares.
'the seal' means the common seal of the company.
'secretary' means the secretary of the company or any other person appointed to perform the duties of the secretary of the company, including a joint, assistant or deputy secretary.
'the United Kingdom' means Great Britain and Northern Ireland.
Unless the context otherwise requires, words or expressions contained in these regulations bear the same meaning as in the Act but excluding any statutory modification thereof not in force when these regulations become binding on the company.

SHARE CAPITAL

2.   Subject to the provisions of the Act and without prejudice to any rights attached to any existing shares, any share may be issued with such rights or restrictions as the company may by ordinary resolution determine.
3.   Subject to the provisions of the Act, shares may be issued which are to be redeemed or are to be liable to be redeemed at the option of the company or the holder on such terms and in such manner as may be provided by the articles.
4.   The company may exercise the powers of paying commissions conferred by the Act. Subject to the provisions of the Act, any such commission may be satisfied by the payment of cash or by the allotment of fully or partly paid shares or partly in one way and partly in the other.
5.   Except as required by law, no person shall be recognised by the company as holding any share upon any trust and (except as otherwise provided by the articles or by law) the company shall not be bound by or recognise any interest in any share except an absolute right to the entirety thereof in the holder.

SHARE CERTIFICATES

6.   Every member, upon becoming the holder of any shares, shall be entitled without payment to one certificate for all the shares of each class held by him (and, upon transferring a part of his holding of shares of any class, to a certificate for the balance of such holding) or several certificates each for one or more of his shares upon payment for every certificate after

the first of such reasonable sum as the directors may determine. Every certificate shall be sealed with the seal and shall specify the number, class and distinguishing numbers (if any) of the shares to which it relates and the amount or respective amounts paid up thereon. The company shall not be bound to issue more than one certificate for shares held jointly by several persons and delivery of a certificate to one joint holder shall be a sufficient delivery to all of them.

7.   If a share certificate is defaced, worn-out, lost or destroyed, it may be renewed on such terms (if any) as to evidence and indemnity and payment of the expenses reasonably incurred by the company in investigating evidence as the directors may determine but otherwise free of charge, and (in the case of defacement or wearing-out) on delivery up of the old certificate.

LIEN

8.   The company shall have a first and paramount lien on every share (not being a fully paid share) for all moneys (whether presently payable or not) payable at a fixed time or called in respect of that share. The directors may at any time declare any share to be wholly or in part exempt from the provisions of this regulation. The company's lien on a share shall extend to any amount payable in respect of it.

9.   The company may sell in such manner as the directors determine any shares on which the company has a lien if a sum in respect of which the lien exists is presently payable and is not paid within fourteen clear days after notice has been given to the holder of the share or to the person entitled to it in consequence of the death or bankruptcy of the holder, demanding payment and stating that if the notice is not complied with the shares may be sold.

10.   To give effect to a sale the directors may authorise some person to execute an instrument of transfer of the shares sold to, or in accordance with the directions of, the purchaser. The title of the transferee to the shares shall not be affected by any irregularity in or invalidity of the proceedings in reference to the sale.

11.   The net proceeds of the sale, after payment of the costs, shall be applied in payment of so much of the sum for which the lien exists as is presently payable, and any residue shall (upon surrender to the company for cancellation of the certificate for the shares sold and subject to a like lien for any moneys not presently payable as existed upon the shares before the sale) be paid to the person entitled to the shares at the date of the sale.

CALLS ON SHARES AND FORFEITURE

12.   Subject to the terms of allotment, the directors may make calls upon the members in respect of any moneys unpaid on their shares (whether in respect of nominal value or premium) and each member shall (subject to receiving at least fourteen clear days' notice specifying when and where payment is to be made) pay to the company as required by the notice the amount called on his shares. A call may be required to be paid by instalments. A call may, before receipt by the company of any sum due thereunder, be revoked in whole or part and payment of a call may be postponed in whole or part. A person upon whom a call is made shall remain liable for calls made upon him notwithstanding the subsequent transfer of the shares in respect whereof the call was made.

13.   A call shall be deemed to have been made at the time when the resolution of the directors authorising the call was passed.

14.   The joint holders of a share shall be jointly and severally liable to pay all calls in respect thereof.

15.   If a call remains unpaid after it has become due and payable the person from whom it is due and payable shall pay interest on the amount unpaid from the day it became due and payable until it is paid at the rate fixed by the terms of allotment of the share or in the notice

of the call or, if no rate is fixed, at the appropriate rate (as defined by the Act) but the directors may waive payment of the interest wholly or in part.

16.   An amount payable in respect of a share on allotment or at any fixed date, whether in respect of nominal value or premium or as an instalment of a call, shall be deemed to be a call and if it is not paid the provisions of the articles shall apply as if that amount had become due and payable by virtue of a call.

17.   Subject to the terms of allotment, the directors may make arrangements on the issue of shares for a difference between the holders in the amounts and times of payment of calls on their shares.

18.   If a call remains unpaid after it has become due and payable the directors may give to the person from whom it is due not less than fourteen clear days' notice requiring payment of the amount unpaid together with any interest which may have accrued. The notice shall name the place where payment is to be made and shall state that if the notice is not complied with the shares in respect of which the call was made will be liable to be forfeited.

19.   If the notice is not complied with any share in respect of which it was given may, before the payment required by the notice has been made, be forfeited by a resolution of the directors and the forfeiture shall include all dividends or other moneys payable in respect of the forfeited shares and not paid before the forfeiture.

20.   Subject to the provisions of the Act, a forfeited share may be sold, re-allotted or otherwise disposed of on such terms and in such manner as the directors determine either to the person who was before the forfeiture the holder or to any other person and at any time before sale, re-allotment or other disposition, the forfeiture may be cancelled on such terms as the directors think fit. Where for the purposes of its disposal a forfeited share is to be transferred to any person the directors may authorise some person to execute an instrument of transfer of the share to that person.

21.   A person any of whose shares have been forfeited shall cease to be a member in respect of them and shall surrender to the company for cancellation the certificate for the shares forfeited but shall remain liable to the company for all moneys which at the date of forfeiture were presently payable by him to the company in respect of those shares with interest at the rate at which interest was payable on those moneys before the forfeiture or, if no interest was so payable, at the appropriate rate (as defined in the Act) from the date of forfeiture until payment but the directors may waive payment wholly or in part or enforce payment without any allowance for the value of the shares at the time of forfeiture or for any consideration received on their disposal.

22.   A statutory declaration by a director or the secretary that a share has been forfeited on a specified date shall be conclusive evidence of the facts stated in it as against all persons claiming to be entitled to the share and the declaration shall (subject to the execution of an instrument of transfer if necessary) constitute a good title to the share and the person to whom the share is disposed of shall not be bound to see to the application of the consideration, if any, nor shall his title to the share be affected by any irregularity in or invalidity of the proceedings in reference to the forfeiture or disposal of the share.

TRANSFER OF SHARES

23.   The instrument of transfer of a share may be in any usual form or in any other form which the directors may approve and shall be executed by or on behalf of the transferor and, unless the share is fully paid, by or on behalf of the transferee.

24.   The directors may refuse to register the transfer of a share which is not fully paid to a person of whom they do not approve and they may refuse to register the transfer of a share on which the company has a lien. They may also refuse to register a transfer unless—

(a)   it is lodged at the office or at such other place as the directors may appoint and is accompanied by the certificate for the shares to which it relates and such other evidence as the directors may reasonably require to show the right of the transferor to make the transfer;

(b) it is in respect of only one class of shares; and

(c) it is in favour of not more than four transferees.

25.   If the directors refuse to register a transfer of a share, they shall within two months after the date on which the transfer was lodged with the company send to the transferee notice of the refusal.

26.   The registration of transfers of shares or of transfers of any class of shares may be suspended at such times and for such periods (not exceeding thirty days in any year) as the directors may determine.

27.   No fee shall be charged for the registration of any instrument of transfer or other document relating to or affecting the title to any share.

28.   The company shall be entitled to retain any instrument of transfer which is registered, but any instrument of transfer which the directors refuse to register shall be returned to the person lodging it when notice of the refusal is given.

TRANSMISSION OF SHARES

29.   If a member dies the survivor of survivors where he was a joint holder, and his personal representatives where he was a sole holder or the only survivor of joint holders, shall be the only persons recognised by the company as having any title to his interest; but nothing herein contained shall release the estate of a deceased member from any liability in respect of any share which had been jointly held by him.

30.   A person becoming entitled to a share in consequence of the death or bankruptcy of a member may, upon such evidence being produced as the directors may properly require, elect either to become the holder of the share or to have some person nominated by him registered as the transferee. If he elects to become the holder he shall give notice to the company to that effect. If he elects to have another person registered he shall execute an instrument of transfer of the share to that person. All the articles relating to the transfer of shares shall apply to the notice or instrument of transfer as if it were an instrument of transfer executed by the member and the death or bankruptcy of the member had not occurred.

31.   A person becoming entitled to a share in consequence of the death or bankruptcy of a member shall have the rights to which he would be entitled if he were the holder of the share, except that he shall not, before being registered as the holder of the share, be entitled in respect of it to attend or vote at any meeting of the company or at any separate meeting of the holders of any class of shares in the company.

ALTERATION OF SHARE CAPITAL

32.   The company may by ordinary resolution—

(a) increase its share capital by new shares of such amount as the resolution prescribes;

(b) consolidate and divide all or any of its share capital into shares of larger amount than its existing shares;

(c) subject to the provisions of the Act, subdivide its shares, or any of them, into shares of smaller amount and the resolution may determine that, as between the shares resulting from the subdivision, any of them may have any preference or advantage as compared with the others; and

(d) cancel shares which, at the date of the passing of the resolution, have not been taken or agreed to be taken by any person and diminish the amount of its share capital by the amount of the shares so cancelled.

33.   Whenever as a result of a consolidation of shares any members would become entitled to fractions of a share, the directors may, on behalf of those members, sell the shares representing the fractions for the best price reasonably obtainable to any person (including, subject to the provisions of the Act, the company) and distribute the net proceeds of sale in due proportion among those members, and the directors may authorise some person to execute an instrument of transfer of the shares to, or in accordance with the directions of, the purchaser. The transferee shall not be bound to see to the application of the purchase money nor shall his title to the shares be affected by any irregularity in or invalidity of the proceedings in reference to the sale.

34.   Subject to the provisions of the Act, the company may by special resolution reduce its share capital, any capital redemption reserve and any share premium account in any way.

PURCHASE OF OWN SHARES

35.   Subject to the provisions of the Act, the company may purchase its own shares (including any redeemable shares) and, if it is a private company, make a payment in respect of the redemption or purchase of its own shares otherwise than out of distributable profits of the company or the proceeds of a fresh issue of shares.

GENERAL MEETINGS

36.   All general meetings other than annual general meetings shall be called extraordinary general meetings.

37.   The directors may call general meetings and, on the requisition of members pursuant to the provisions of the Act, shall forthwith proceed to convene an extraordinary general meeting for a date not later than eight weeks after receipt of the requisition. If there are not within the United Kingdom sufficient directors to call a general meeting, any director or any member of the company may call a general meeting.

NOTICE OF GENERAL MEETINGS

38.   An annual general meeting and an extraordinary general meeting called for the passing of a special resolution or a resolution appointing a person as a director shall be called by at least twenty-one clear days' notice. All other extraordinary general meetings shall be called by at least fourteen clear days' notice but a general meeting may be called by shorter notice if it is so agreed—

(a)   in the case of an annual general meeting, by all the members entitled to attend and vote thereat; and

(b)   in the case of any other meeting by a majority in number of the members having a right to attend and vote being a majority together holding not less than ninety-five per cent in nominal value of the shares giving that right.

The notice shall specify the time and place of the meeting and the general nature of the business to be transacted and, in the case of an annual general meeting, shall specify the meeting as such.

Subject to the provisions of the articles and to any restrictions imposed on any shares, the notice shall be given to all the members, to all persons entitled to a share in consequence of the death or bankruptcy of a member and to the directors and auditors.

39.   The accidental omission to give notice of a meeting to, or the non-receipt of notice of a meeting by, any person entitled to receive notice shall not invalidate the proceedings at that meeting.

PROCEEDINGS AT GENERAL MEETINGS

40.   No business shall be transacted at any meeting unless a quorum is present. Two persons entitled to vote upon the business to be transacted, each being a member or a proxy for a member or a duly authorised representative of a corporation, shall be a quorum.

41.   If such a quorum is not present within half an hour from the time appointed for the meeting, or if during a meeting such a quorum ceases to be present, the meeting shall stand adjourned to the same day in the next week at the same time and place or to such time and place as the directors may determine.

42.   The chairman, if any, of the board of directors or in his absence some other director nominated by the directors shall preside as chairman of the meeting, but if neither the chairman nor such other director (if any) be present within fifteen minutes after the time appointed for holding the meeting and willing to act, the directors present shall elect one of their number to be chairman and, if there is only one director present and willing to act, he shall be chairman.

43.   If no director is willing to act as chairman, or if no director is present within fifteen minutes after the time appointed for holding the meeting, the members present and entitled to vote shall choose one of their number to be chairman.

44.   A director shall, notwithstanding that he is not a member, be entitled to attend and speak at any general meeting and at any separate meeting of the holders of any class of shares in the company.

45.   The chairman may, with the consent of a meeting at which a quorum is present (and shall if so directed by the meeting), adjourn the meeting from time to time and from place to place, but no business shall be transacted at an adjourned meeting other than business which might properly have been transacted at the meeting had the adjournment not taken place. When a meeting is adjourned for fourteen days or more, at least seven clear days' notice shall be given specifying the time and place of the adjourned meeting and the general nature of the business to be transacted. Otherwise it shall not be necessary to give any such notice.

46.   A resolution put to the vote of a meeting shall be decided on a show of hands unless before, or on the declaration of the result of, the show of hands a poll is duly demanded. Subject to the provisions of the Act, a poll may be demanded—

(a) by the chairman; or

(b) by at least two members having the right to vote at the meeting; or

(c) by a member or members representing not less than one-tenth of the total voting rights of all the members having the right to vote at the meeting; or

(d) by a member or members holding shares conferring a right to vote at the meeting being shares on which an aggregate sum has been paid up equal to not less than one-tenth of the total sum paid up on all the shares conferring that right;

and a demand by a person as proxy for a member shall be the same as a demand by the member.

47.   Unless a poll is duly demanded a declaration by the chairman that a resolution has been carried or carried unanimously, or by a particular majority, or lost, or not carried by a particular majority and an entry to that effect in the minutes of the meeting shall be conclusive evidence of the fact without proof of the number or proportion of the votes recorded in favour of or against the resolution.

48.   The demand for a poll may, before the poll is taken, be withdrawn but only with the consent of the chairman and a demand so withdrawn shall not be taken to have invalidated the result of a show of hands declared before the demand was made.

49.   A poll shall be taken as the chairman directs and he may appoint scrutineers (who need not be members) and fix a time and place for declaring the result of the poll. The result of the poll shall be deemed to be the resolution of the meeting at which the poll was demanded.

50.   In the case of an equality of votes, whether on a show of hands or on a poll, the chairman shall be entitled to a casting vote in addition to any other vote he may have.

51.   A poll demanded on the election of a chairman or on a question of adjournment shall be taken forthwith. A poll demanded on any other question shall be taken either forthwith or at such time and place as the chairman directs not being more than thirty days after the poll is demanded. The demand for a poll shall not prevent the continuance of a meeting for the transaction of any business other than the question on which the poll was demanded. If a poll is demanded before the declaration of the result of a show of hands and the demand is duly withdrawn, the meeting shall continue as if the demand had not been made.

52.   No notice need be given of a poll not taken forthwith if the time and place at which it is to be taken are announced at the meeting at which it is demanded. In any other case at least seven clear days' notice shall be given specifying the time and place at which the poll is to be taken.

53.   A resolution in writing executed by or on behalf of each member who would have been entitled to vote upon it if it had been proposed at a general meeting at which he was present shall be as effectual as if it had been passed at a general meeting duly convened and held and may consist of several instruments in the like form each executed by or on behalf of one or more members.

VOTES OF MEMBERS

54.   Subject to any rights or restrictions attached to any shares, on a show of hands every member who (being an individual) is present in person or (being a corporation) is present by a duly authorised representative, not being himself a member entitled to vote, shall have one vote and on a poll every member shall have one vote for every share of which he is the holder.

55.   In the case of joint holders the vote of the senior who tenders a vote, whether in person or by proxy, shall be accepted to the exclusion of the votes of the other joint holders; and seniority shall be determined by the order in which the names of the holders stand in the register of members

56.   A member in respect of whom an order has been made by any court having jurisdiction (whether in the United Kingdom or elsewhere) in matters concerning mental disorder may vote, whether on a show of hands or on a poll, by his receiver, curator bonis or other person authorised in that behalf appointed by the court, and any such receiver, curator bonis or other person may, on a poll, vote by proxy. Evidence to the satisfaction of the directors of the authority of the person claiming to exercise the right to vote shall be deposited at the office, or at such other place as is specified in accordance with the articles for the deposit of instruments of proxy, not less than 48 hours before the time appointed for holding the meeting or adjourned meeting at which the right to vote is to be exercised and in default the right to vote shall not be exercisable.

57.   No member shall vote at any general meeting or at any separate meeting of the holders of any class of shares in the company, either in person or by proxy, in respect of any share held by him unless all moneys presently payable by him in respect of that share have been paid.

58.   No objection shall be raised to the qualification of any voter except at the meeting or adjourned meeting at which the vote objected to is tendered, and every vote not disallowed at the meeting shall be valid. Any objection made in due time shall be referred to the chairman whose decision shall be final and conclusive.

59.   On a poll votes may be given either personally or by proxy. A member may appoint more than one proxy to attend on the same occasion.

60.   The appointment of a proxy shall be executed by or on behalf of the appointor and shall be in the following form (or in a form as near thereto as circumstances allow or in any other form which is usual or which the directors may approve)—

PLC/Limited

I/We,   , of

, being a
member/members of the above-named company, hereby appoint
of
, or failing him
of   , as my/our proxy to vote in my/our name[s] and on my/our
behalf at the annual/extraordinary general meeting of the company to be
held on   19   , and at any adjournment
thereof.
Signed on   19.

61. Where it is desired to afford members an opportunity of instructing the proxy how he
shall act the appointment of a proxy shall be in the following form (or in a form as near
thereto as circumstances allow or in any other form which is usual or which the directors may
approve)—

PLC/Limited

I/We,   , of

, being a
member/members of the above-named company, hereby appoint
of
, or failing him
of   , as my/our proxy at the annual/extraordinary general
meeting of the company to be held on   19   , and at any
adjournment thereof.
This form is to be used in respect of the resolutions mentioned below as follows:

    Resolution No. 1 *for *against
    Resolution No. 2 *for *against
*Strike out whichever is not desired.
Unless otherwise instructed, the proxy may vote as he thinks fit or abstain from voting.
Signed this   day of   19   .

62. The appointment of a proxy and any authority under which it is executed or a
copy of such authority certified notarially or in some other way approved by the directors
may—

    (a) in the case of an instrument in writing be deposited at the office or at such other
place within the United Kingdom as is specified in the notice convening the meeting or in any instrument of proxy sent out by the company in relation to the
meeting not less than 48 hours before the time for holding the meeting or
adjourned meeting at which the person named in the instrument proposes to
vote; or

    (aa) in the case of an appointment contained in an electronic communication, where
an address has been specified for the purpose of receiving electronic communications—

        (i) in the notice convening the meeting, or
        (ii) in any instrument of proxy sent out by the company in relation to the meet-
ing, or
        (iii) in any invitation contained in an electronic communication to appoint a
proxy issued by the company in relation to the meeting,

be received at such address not less than 48 hours before the time for holding the meeting or
adjourned meeting at which the person named in the appointment proposes to vote;

    (b) in the case of a poll taken more than 48 hours after it is demanded, be deposited or
received as aforesaid after the poll has been demanded and not less than 24 hours
before the time appointed for the taking of the poll; or

(c) where the poll is not taken forthwith but is taken not more than 48 hours after it was demanded, be delivered at the meeting at which the poll was demanded to the chairman or to the secretary or to any director;

and an appointment of proxy which is not deposited, delivered or received in a manner so permitted shall be invalid.

In this regulation and the next, 'address', in relation to electronic communications, includes any number or address used for the purposes of such communications.

63.   A vote given or poll demanded by proxy or by the duly authorised representative of a corporation shall be valid notwithstanding the previous determination of the authority of the person voting or demanding a poll unless notice of the determination was received by the company at the office or at such other place at which the instrument of proxy was duly deposited or, where the appointment of the proxy was contained in an electronic communication, at the address at which such appointment was duly received before the commencement of the meeting or adjourned meeting at which the vote is given or the poll demanded or (in the case of a poll taken otherwise than on the same day as the meeting or adjourned meeting) the time appointed for taking the poll.

NUMBER OF DIRECTORS

64.   Unless otherwise determined by ordinary resolution, the number of directors (other than alternate directors) shall not be subject to any maximum but shall be not less than two.

ALTERNATE DIRECTORS

65.   Any director (other than an alternate director) may appoint any other director, or any other person approved by resolution of the directors and willing to act, to be an alternate director and may remove from office an alternate director so appointed by him.

66.   An alternate director shall be entitled to receive notice of all meetings of directors and of all meetings of committees of directors of which his appointor is a member, to attend and vote at any such meeting at which the director appointing him is not personally present, and generally to perform all the functions of his appointor as a director in his absence but shall not be entitled to receive any remuneration from the company for his services as an alternate director. But it shall not be necessary to give notice of such a meeting to an alternate director who is absent from the United Kingdom.

67.   An alternate director shall cease to be an alternate director if his appointor ceases to be a director; but, if a director retires by rotation or otherwise but is reappointed or deemed to have been reappointed at the meeting at which he retires, any appointment of an alternate director made by him which was in force immediately prior to his retirement shall continue after his reappointment.

68.   Any appointment or removal of an alternate director shall be by notice to the company signed by the director making or revoking the appointment or in any other manner approved by the directors.

69.   Save as otherwise provided in the articles, an alternate director shall be deemed for all purposes to be a director and shall alone be responsible for his own acts and defaults and he shall not be deemed to be the agent of the director appointing him.

POWERS OF DIRECTORS

70.   Subject to the provisions of the Act, the memorandum and the articles and to any directions given by special resolution, the business of the company shall be managed by the

directors who may exercise all the powers of the company. No alteration of the memorandum or articles and no such direction shall invalidate any prior act of the directors which would have been valid if that alteration had not been made or that direction had not been given. The powers given by this regulation shall not be limited by any special power given to the directors by the articles and a meeting of directors at which a quorum is present may exercise all powers exercisable by the directors.

71. The directors may, by power of attorney or otherwise, appoint any person to be the agent of the company for such purposes and on such conditions as they determine, including authority for the agent to delegate all or any of his powers.

DELEGATION OF DIRECTORS' POWERS

72. The directors may delegate any of their powers to any committee consisting of one or more directors. They may also delegate to any managing director or any director holding any other executive office such of their powers as they consider desirable to be exercised by him. Any such delegation may be made subject to any conditions the directors may impose, and either collaterally with or to the exclusion of their own powers and may be revoked or altered. Subject to any such conditions, the proceedings of a committee with two or more members shall be governed by the articles regulating the proceedings of directors so far as they are capable of applying.

APPOINTMENT AND RETIREMENT OF DIRECTORS

73. At the first annual general meeting all the directors shall retire from office, and at every subsequent annual general meeting one-third of the directors who are subject to retirement by rotation or, if their number is not three or a multiple of three, the number nearest to one-third shall retire from office; but, if there is only one director who is subject to retirement by rotation, he shall retire.

74. Subject to the provisions of the Act, the directors to retire by rotation shall be those who have been longest in office since their last appointment or reappointment, but as between persons who became or were last reappointed directors on the same day those to retire shall (unless they otherwise agree among themselves) be determined by lot.

75. If the company, at the meeting at which a director retires by rotation, does not fill the vacancy the retiring director shall, if willing to act, be deemed to have been reappointed unless at the meeting it is resolved not to fill the vacancy or unless a resolution for the reappointment of the director is put to the meeting and lost.

76. No person other than a director retiring by rotation shall be appointed or reappointed a director at any general meeting unless—
  (a) he is recommended by the directors; or
  (b) not less than fourteen nor more than thirty-five clear days before the date appointed for the meeting, notice executed by a member qualified to vote at the meeting has been given to the company of the intention to propose that person for appointment or reappointment stating the particulars which would, if he were so appointed or reappointed, be required to be included in the company's register of directors together with notice executed by that person of his willingness to be appointed or reappointed.

77. Not less than seven nor more than twenty-eight clear days before the date appointed for holding a general meeting notice shall be given to all who are entitled to receive notice of the meeting of any person (other than a director retiring by rotation at the meeting) who is recommended by the directors for appointment or reappointment as a director at the meeting or in respect of whom notice has been duly given to the company of the intention to propose

him at the meeting for appointment or reappointment as a director. The notice shall give the particulars of that person which would, if he were so appointed or reappointed, be required to be included in the company's register of directors.

78. Subject as aforesaid, the company may by ordinary resolution appoint a person who is willing to act to be a director either to fill a vacancy or as an additional director and may also determine the rotation in which any additional directors are to retire.

79. The directors may appoint a person who is willing to act to be a director, either to fill a vacancy or as an additional director, provided that the appointment does not cause the number of directors to exceed any number fixed by or in accordance with the articles as the maximum number of directors. A director so appointed shall hold office only until the next following annual general meeting and shall not be taken into account in determining the directors who are to retire by rotation at the meeting. If not reappointed at such annual general meeting, he shall vacate office at the conclusion thereof.

80. Subject as aforesaid, a director who retires at an annual general meeting may, if willing to act, be reappointed. If he is not reappointed, he shall retain office until the meeting appoints someone in his place, or if it does not do so, until the end of the meeting.

DISQUALIFICATION AND REMOVAL OF DIRECTORS

81. The office of a director shall be vacated if—
  (a) he ceases to be a director by virtue of any provision of the Act or he becomes prohibited by law from being a director; or
  (b) he becomes bankrupt or makes any arrangement or composition with his creditors generally; or
  (c) he is, or may be, suffering from mental disorder and either—
    (i) he is admitted to hospital in pursuance of an application for admission for treatment under the Mental Health Act 1983 or, in Scotland, an application for admission under the Mental Health (Scotland) Act 1960, or
    (ii) an order is made by a court having jurisdiction (whether in the United Kingdom or elsewhere) in matters concerning mental disorder for his detention or for the appointment of a receiver, curator bonis or other person to exercise powers with respect to his property or affairs; or
  (d) he resigns his office by notice to the company; or
  (e) he shall for more than six consecutive months have been absent without permission of the directors from meetings of directors held during that period and the directors resolve that his office be vacated.

REMUNERATION OF DIRECTORS

82. The directors shall be entitled to such remuneration as the company may by ordinary resolution determine and, unless the resolution provides otherwise, the remuneration shall be deemed to accrue from day to day.

DIRECTORS' EXPENSES

83. The directors may be paid all travelling, hotel, and other expenses properly incurred by them in connection with their attendance at meetings of directors or committees of directors or general meetings or separate meetings of the holders of any class of shares or of debentures of the company or otherwise in connection with the discharge of their duties.

DIRECTORS' APPOINTMENTS AND INTERESTS

84.   Subject to the provisions of the Act, the directors may appoint one or more of their number to the office of managing director or to any other executive office under the company and may enter into an agreement or arrangement with any director for his employment by the company or for the provision by him of any services outside the scope of the ordinary duties of a director. Any such appointment, agreement or arrangement may be made upon such terms as the directors determine and they may remunerate any such director for his services as they think fit. Any appointment of a director to an executive office shall terminate if he ceases to be a director but without prejudice to any claim to damages for breach of the contract of service between the director and the company. A managing director and a director holding any other executive office shall not be subject to retirement by rotation.

85.   Subject to the provisions of the Act, and provided that he has disclosed to the directors the nature and extent of any material interest of his, a director notwithstanding his office—

(a)   may be a party to, or otherwise interested in, any transaction or arrangement with the company or in which the company is otherwise interested;

(b)   may be a director or other officer of, or employed by, or a party to any transaction or arrangement with, or otherwise interested in, any body corporate promoted by the company or in which the company is otherwise interested; and

(c)   shall not, by reason of his office, be accountable to the company for any benefit which he derives from any such office or employment or from any such transaction or arrangement or from any interest in any such body corporate and no such transaction or arrangement shall be liable to be avoided on the ground of any such interest or benefit.

86.   For the purposes of regulation 85—

(a)   a general notice given to the directors that a director is to be regarded as having an interest of the nature and extent specified in the notice in any transaction or arrangement in which a specified person or class of persons is interested shall be deemed to be a disclosure that the director has an interest in any such transaction of the nature and extent so specified; and

(b)   an interest of which a director has no knowledge and of which it is unreasonable to expect him to have knowledge shall not be treated as an interest of his.

DIRECTORS' GRATUITIES AND PENSIONS

87.   The directors may provide benefits, whether by the payment of gratuities or pensions or by insurance or otherwise, for any director who has held but no longer holds any executive office or employment with the company or with any body corporate which is or has been a subsidiary of the company or a predecessor in business of the company or of any such subsidiary, and for any member of his family (including a spouse and a former spouse) or any person who is or was dependent on him, and may (as well before as after he ceases to hold such office or employment) contribute to any fund and pay premiums for the purchase or provision of any such benefit.

PROCEEDINGS OF DIRECTORS

88.   Subject to the provisions of the articles, the directors may regulate their proceedings as they think fit. A director may, and the secretary at the request of a director shall, call a meeting of the directors. It shall not be necessary to give notice of a meeting to a director who is absent from the United Kingdom. Questions arising at a meeting shall be decided by a majority of votes. In the case of an equality of votes, the chairman shall have a second or

casting vote. A director who is also an alternate director shall be entitled in the absence of his appointor to a separate vote on behalf of his appointor in addition to his own vote.

89.   The quorum for the transaction of the business of the directors may be fixed by the directors and unless so fixed at any other number shall be two. A person who holds office only as an alternate director shall, if his appointor is not present, be counted in the quorum.

90.   The continuing directors or a sole continuing director may act notwithstanding any vacancies in their number, but, if the number of directors is less than the number fixed as the quorum, the continuing directors or director may act only for the purpose of filling vacancies or of calling a general meeting.

91.   The directors may appoint one of their number to be the chairman of the board of directors and may at any time remove him from that office. Unless he is unwilling to do so, the director so appointed shall preside at every meeting of directors at which he is present. But if there is no director holding that office, or if the director holding it is unwilling to preside or is not present within five minutes after the time appointed for the meeting, the directors present may appoint one of their number to be chairman of the meeting.

92.   All acts done by a meeting of directors, or of a committee of directors, or by a person acting as a director shall, notwithstanding that it be afterwards discovered that there was a defect in the appointment of any director or that any of them were disqualified from holding office, or had vacated office, or were not entitled to vote, be as valid as if every such person had been duly appointed and was qualified and had continued to be a director and had been entitled to vote.

93.   A resolution in writing signed by all the directors entitled to receive notice of a meeting of directors or of a committee of directors shall be as valid and effectual as if it had been passed at a meeting of directors or (as the case may be) a committee of directors duly convened and held and may consist of several documents in the like form each signed by one or more directors; but a resolution signed by an alternate director need not also be signed by his appointor and, if it is signed by a director who has appointed an alternate director, it need not be signed by the alternate director in that capacity.

94.   Save as otherwise provided by the articles, a director shall not vote at a meeting of directors or of a committee of directors on any resolution concerning a matter in which he has, directly or indirectly, an interest or duty which is material and which conflicts or may conflict with the interests of the company unless his interest or duty arises only because the case falls within one or more of the following paragraphs—

(a) the resolution relates to the giving to him of a guarantee, security, or indemnity in respect of money lent to, or an obligation incurred by him for the benefit of, the company or any of its subsidiaries;

(b) the resolution relates to the giving to a third party of a guarantee, security, or indemnity in respect of an obligation of the company or any of its subsidiaries for which the director has assumed responsibility in whole or part and whether alone or jointly with others under a guarantee or indemnity or by the giving of security;

(c) his interest arises by virtue of his subscribing or agreeing to subscribe for any shares, debentures or other securities of the company or any of its subsidiaries, or by virtue of his being, or intending to become, a participant in the underwriting or sub-underwriting of an offer of any such shares, debentures, or other securities by the company or any of its subsidiaries for subscription, purchase or exchange;

(d) the resolution relates in any way to a retirement benefits scheme which has been approved, or is conditional upon approval, by the Board of Inland Revenue for taxation purposes.

For the purposes of this regulation, an interest of a person who is, for any purpose of the Act (excluding any statutory modification thereof not in force when this regulation becomes binding on the company), connected with a director shall be treated as an interest of the director and, in relation to an alternate director, an interest of his appointor shall be treated as an interest of the alternate director without prejudice to any interest which the alternate director has otherwise.

95.   A director shall not be counted in the quorum present at a meeting in relation to a resolution on which he is not entitled to vote.

96.   The company may by ordinary resolution suspend or relax to any extent, either generally or in respect of any particular matter, any provision of the articles prohibiting a director from voting at a meeting of directors or of a committee of directors.

97.   Where proposals are under consideration concerning the appointment of two or more directors to offices or employments with the company or any body corporate in which the company is interested the proposals may be divided and considered in relation to each director separately and (provided he is not for another reason precluded from voting) each of the directors concerned shall be entitled to vote and be counted in the quorum in respect of each resolution except that concerning his own appointment.

98.   If a question arises at a meeting of directors or of a committee of directors as to the right of a director to vote, the question may, before the conclusion of the meeting, be referred to the chairman of the meeting and his ruling in relation to any director other than himself shall be final and conclusive.

SECRETARY

99.   Subject to the provisions of the Act, the secretary shall be appointed by the directors for such term, at such remuneration and upon such conditions as they may think fit; and any secretary so appointed may be removed by them.

MINUTES

100.   The directors shall cause minutes to be made in books kept for the purpose—
  (a) of all appointments of officers made by the directors; and
  (b) of all proceedings at meetings of the company, of the holders of any class of shares in the company, and of the directors, and of committees of directors, including the names of the directors present at each such meeting.

THE SEAL

101.   The seal shall only be used by the authority of the directors or of a committee of directors authorised by the directors. The directors may determine who shall sign any instrument to which the seal is affixed and unless otherwise so determined it shall be signed by a director and by the secretary or by a second director.

DIVIDENDS

102.   Subject to the provisions of the Act, the company may by ordinary resolution declare dividends in accordance with the respective rights of the members, but no dividend shall exceed the amount recommended by the directors.

103.   Subject to the provisions of the Act, the directors may pay interim dividends if it appears to them that they are justified by the profits of the company available for distribution. If the share capital is divided into different classes, the directors may pay interim dividends on shares which confer deferred or non-preferred rights with regard to dividend as well as on shares which confer preferential rights with regard to dividend, but no interim dividend shall be paid on shares carrying deferred or non-preferred rights if, at the time of payment, any

preferential dividend is in arrear. The directors may also pay at intervals settled by them any dividend payable at a fixed rate if it appears to them that the profits available for distribution justify the payment. Provided the directors act in good faith they shall not incur any liability to the holders of shares conferring preferred rights for any loss they may suffer by the lawful payment of an interim dividend on any shares having deferred or non-preferred rights.

104.   Except as otherwise provided by the rights attached to shares, all dividends shall be declared and paid according to the amounts paid up on the shares on which the dividend is paid. All dividends shall be apportioned and paid proportionately to the amounts paid up on the shares during any portion or portions of the period in respect of which the dividend is paid; but, if any share is issued on terms providing that it shall rank for dividend as from a particular date, that share shall rank for dividend accordingly.

105.   A general meeting declaring a dividend may, upon the recommendation of the directors, direct that it shall be satisfied wholly or partly by the distribution of assets and, where any difficulty arises in regard to the distribution, the directors may settle the same and in particular may issue fractional certificates and fix the value for distribution of any assets and may determine that cash shall be paid to any member upon the footing of the value so fixed in order to adjust the rights of members and may vest any assets in trustees.

106.   Any dividend or other moneys payable in respect of a share may be paid by cheque sent by post to the registered address of the person entitled or, if two or more persons are the holders of the share or are jointly entitled to it by reason of the death or bankruptcy of the holder, to the registered address of that one of those persons who is first named in the register of members or to such person and to such address as the person or persons entitled may in writing direct. Every cheque shall be made payable to the order of the person or persons entitled or to such other person as the person or persons entitled may in writing direct and payment of the cheque shall be a good discharge to the company. Any joint holder or other person jointly entitled to a share as aforesaid may give receipts for any dividend or other moneys payable in respect of the share.

107.   No dividend or other moneys payable in respect of a share shall bear interest against the company unless otherwise provided by the rights attached to the share.

108.   Any dividend which has remained unclaimed for twelve years from the date when it became due for payment shall, if the directors so resolve, be forfeited and cease to remain owing by the company.

ACCOUNTS

109.   No member shall (as such) have any right of inspecting any accounting records or other book or document of the company except as conferred by statute or authorised by the directors or by ordinary resolution of the company.

CAPITALISATION OF PROFITS

110.   The directors may with the authority of an ordinary resolution of the company—

    (a) subject as hereinafter provided, resolve to capitalise any undivided profits of the company not required for paying any preferential dividend (whether or not they are available for distribution) or any sum standing to the credit of the company's share premium account or capital redemption reserve;

    (b) appropriate the sum resolved to be capitalised to the members who would have been entitled to it if it were distributed by way of dividend and in the same proportions and apply such sum on their behalf either in or towards paying up the amounts, if any, for the time being unpaid on any shares held by them respectively, or in paying up in full unissued shares or debentures of the company of a nominal amount equal to that sum, and allot the shares or debentures credited as fully paid to those members, or as they may direct, in those proportions, or partly in one way and partly in the other: but the share premium account, the capital redemption reserve, and any profits which are not available for distribution may, for the purposes of this regulation, only be applied in paying up unissued shares to be allotted to members credited as fully paid;

(c) make such provision by the issue of fractional certificates or by payment in cash or otherwise as they determine in the case of shares or debentures becoming distributable under this regulation in fractions; and

(d) authorise any person to enter on behalf of all the members concerned into an agreement with the company providing for the allotment to them respectively, credited as fully paid, of any shares or debentures to which they are entitled upon such capitalisation, any agreement made under such authority being binding on all such members.

NOTICES

111.   Any notice to be given to or by any person pursuant to the articles (other than a notice calling a meeting of the directors) shall be in writing or shall be given using electronic communications to an address for the time being notified for that purpose to the person giving the notice.

In this regulation, 'address', in relation to electronic communications, includes any number or address used for the purposes of such communications.

112.   The company may give any notice to a member either personally or by sending it by post in a prepaid envelope addressed to the member at his registered address or by leaving it at that address or by giving it using electronic communications to an address for the time being notified to the company by the member. In the case of joint holders of a share, all notices shall be given to the joint holder whose name stands first in the register of members in respect of the joint holding and notice so given shall be sufficient notice to all the joint holders. A member whose registered address is not within the United Kingdom and who gives to the company an address within the United Kingdom at which notices may be given to him, or an address to which notices may be sent using electronic communications, shall be entitled to have notices given to him at that address, but otherwise no such member shall be entitled to receive any notice from the company.

In this regulation and the next, 'address', in relation to electronic communications, includes any number or address used for the purposes of such communications.

113.   A member present, either in person or by proxy, at any meeting of the company or of the holders of any class of shares in the company shall be deemed to have received notice of the meeting and, where requisite, of the purposes for which it was called.

114.   Every person who becomes entitled to a share shall be bound by any notice in respect of that share which, before his name is entered in the register of members, has been duly given to a person from whom he derives his title.

115.   Proof that an envelope containing a notice was properly addressed, prepaid and posted shall be conclusive evidence that the notice was given. Proof that a notice contained in an electronic communication was sent in accordance with guidance issued by the Institute of Chartered Secretaries and Administrators shall be conclusive evidence that the notice was given. A notice shall be deemed to be given at the expiration of 48 hours after the envelope containing it was posted or, in the case of a notice contained in an electronic communication, at the expiration of 48 hours after the time it was sent.

116.   A notice may be given by the company to the persons entitled to a share in consequence of the death or bankruptcy of a member by sending or delivering it, in any manner

authorised by the articles for the giving of notice to a member, addressed to them by name, or by the title of representatives of the deceased, or trustee of the bankrupt or by any like description at the address, if any, within the United Kingdom supplied for that purpose by the persons claiming to be so entitled. Until such an address has been supplied, a notice may be given in any manner in which it might have been given if the death or bankruptcy had not occurred.

WINDING UP

117.   If the company is wound up, the liquidator may, with the sanction of an extraordinary resolution of the company and any other sanction required by the Act, divide among the members in specie the whole or any part of the assets of the company and may, for that purpose, value any assets and determine how the division shall be carried out as between the members or different classes of members. The liquidator may, with the like sanction, vest the whole or any part of the assets in trustees upon such trusts for the benefit of the members as he with the like sanction determines, but no member shall be compelled to accept any assets upon which there is a liability.

INDEMNITY

118.   Subject to the provisions of the Act but without prejudice to any indemnity to which a director may otherwise be entitled, every director or other officer or auditor of the company shall be indemnified out of the assets of the company against any liability incurred by him in defending any proceedings, whether civil or criminal, in which judgment is given in his favour or in which he is acquitted or in connection with any application in which relief is granted to him by the court from liability for negligence, default, breach of duty or breach of trust in relation to the affairs of the company.

TABLE B   A PRIVATE COMPANY LIMITED BY SHARES
MEMORANDUM OF ASSOCIATION

1.   The company's name is 'The South Wales Motor Transport Company cyfyngedig'.
2.   The company's registered office is to be situated in Wales.
3.   The company's objects are the carriage of passengers and goods in motor vehicles between such places as the company may from time to time determine and the doing of all such other things as are incidental or conducive to the attainment of that object.
4.   The liability of the members is limited.
5.   The company's share capital is £50,000 divided into 50,000 shares of £1 each. We, the subscribers to this memorandum of association, wish to be formed into a company pursuant to this memorandum; and we agree to take the number of shares shown opposite our respective names.

Names and Addresses of Subscribers	Number of shares taken by each Subscriber
1. Thomas Jones, 138 Mountfield Street, Tredegar.	1
2. Mary Evans, 19 Merthyr Road, Aberystwyth.	1
Total shares taken	2

Dated   19   .
Witness to the above signatures,
Anne Brown, 'Woodlands', Fieldside Road, Bryn Mawr.
. . .

TABLE F   A PUBLIC COMPANY LIMITED BY SHARES
MEMORANDUM OF ASSOCIATION

1.   The company's name is 'Western Electronics Public Limited Company'.
2.   The company is to be a public company.
3.   The company's registered office is to be situated in England and Wales.
4.   The company's objects are the manufacture and development of such descriptions of electronic equipment, instruments and appliances as the company may from time to time determine, and the doing of all such other things as are incidental or conducive to the attainment of that object.
5.   The liability of the members is limited.
6.   The company's share capital is £5,000,000 divided into 5,000,000 shares of £1 each.

We, the subscribers to this memorandum of association, wish to be formed into a company pursuant to this memorandum; and we agree to take the number of shares shown opposite our respective names.

Names and Addresses of Subscribers	Number of shares taken by each Subscriber
1. James White, 12 Broadmead, Birmingham.	1
2. Patrick Smith, 145A Huntley House, London Wall, London EC2.	1
Total shares taken	2

Dated   19

Witness to the above signatures,
Anne Brown, 13 Hute Street, London WC2.

Insolvency Proceedings (Monetary Limits) Order 1986
(1986 No. 1996)

The Secretary of State, in exercise of the powers conferred by sections 416 and 418 of, and paragraphs 9 and 12 of Schedule 6 to, the Insolvency Act 1986, hereby makes the following Order:

1.—(1) This Order may be cited as the Insolvency Proceedings (Monetary Limits) Order 1986 and shall come into force on 29 December 1986.

(2) In this Order 'the Act' means the Insolvency Act 1986.

4.   The amount prescribed for the purposes of paragraphs 9 and 12 of Schedule 6 to the Act (maximum amount for preferential status of employees' claims for remuneration and under the Reserve Forces (Safeguard of Employment) Act 1985) is £800.

Accounting Standards (Prescribed Body) Regulations 1990
(1990 No. 1667)

The Secretary of State, in exercise of the powers conferred on him by section 256 of the Companies Act 1985, hereby makes the following Regulations:

1.   These Regulations may be cited as the Accounting Standards (Prescribed Body) Regulations 1990 and shall come into force on 20 August 1990.

2.   The Accounting Standards Board Limited is hereby prescribed for the purposes of section 256(1) of the Companies Act 1985.

Companies (Defective Accounts) (Authorised Person) Order 1991
(1991 No. 13)

Whereas it appears to the Secretary of State that the Financial Reporting Review Panel Limited is a person:
(a) having an interest in, and to have satisfactory procedures directed to securing, compliance by companies with the accounting requirements of the Companies Act 1985;
(b) having satisfactory procedures for receiving and investigating complaints about the annual accounts of companies; and
(c) otherwise to be a fit and proper person to be authorised.
The Secretary of State, in exercise of the powers conferred on him by section 245C of the Companies Act 1985 and of all other powers enabling him in that behalf, hereby makes the following Order:
1.   This Order may be cited as the Companies (Defective Accounts) (Authorised Person) Order 1991 and shall come into force on 1 February 1991.
2.   The Financial Reporting Review Panel Limited is hereby authorised for the purposes of section 245B of the Companies Act 1985.

Companies (Inspection and Copying of Registers, Indices and Documents) Regulations 1991
(1991 No. 1998)

The Secretary of State, in exercise of the powers conferred on him by section 723A of the Companies Act 1985, the provisions of the Companies Act 1985 listed in Schedule 1 to these Regulations and of all other powers enabling him in that behalf, hereby makes the following Regulations:

Citation and commencement
1.   These Regulations may be cited as the Companies (Inspection and Copying of Registers, Indices and Documents) Regulations 1991 and shall come into force on 1 November 1991.

Interpretation
2.   In these Regulations:
'the Act' means the Companies Act 1985;
'business day' means, in relation to a company subject to any provision of these Regulations, any day except a Saturday or Sunday, Christmas Day, Good Friday and any other day which is a bank holiday in the part of Great Britain where that company is registered (or in the case of a company that is a body corporate to which section 723A of the Act is applied by section 718 thereof, the part of Great Britain where its principal office was situated on 5 January 1976 or if it was incorporated after that date, the part of Great Britain where its principal office was situated immediately after incorporation); and
'company' includes a body corporate to which section 723A of the Act is applied by any enactment.

Inspection

3.—(1) This Regulation applies to an obligation to make a register, index or document available for inspection imposed on a company by sections 169(5) (contract for purchase by company of its own shares), 175(6) (statutory declaration and auditors' report relating to payment out of capital), 191(1) (register of debenture holders), 219(1) (register of interests in shares &c.), 288(3) (register of directors and secretaries), 318(7) (directors' service contracts), 356(1) (register and index of members) and 383(1) (minute books) of the Act, as well as to section 325 of, and paragraph 25 of Part IV of Schedule 13 to, the Act (register of directors' interests).

(2) The company shall:

(a) make the register, index or document available for such inspection for not less than two hours during the period between 9 a.m. and 5 p.m. on each business day; and

(b) permit a person inspecting the register, index or document to copy any information made available for inspection by means of the taking of notes or the transcription of the information.

(3) Paragraph (2)(b) shall not be construed as obliging a company to provide any facilities additional to those provided for the purposes of facilitating inspection.

Registers of members and debenture holders: presentation and extraction of entries

4.—(1) This Regulation applies to a company's register of members maintained under section 352 of the Act, to an index of the names of the company's members maintained under section 354 thereof and to a register of debenture holders maintained under section 190 thereof.

(2) A company is not obliged:

(a) by virtue of section 356(1) of the Act to present for inspection its register of members or an index of Members' names; or

(b) by virtue of section 191(1) of the Act to present for inspection a register of debenture holders maintained by it,

in a manner which groups together entries by reference to whether a member or (as the case may be) a debenture holder has given an address in a particular geographical location, is of a particular nationality, has a holding of a certain size, is a natural person or not or is of a particular gender.

(3) Nor is a company obliged:

(a) by virtue of section 356(3) of the Act, in providing a copy of a part of its register of members; or

(b) by virtue of section 191(2) of the Act, in providing a copy of a part of a register of debenture holders,

to extract entries from the register by reference to whether a member or (as the case may be) a debenture holder has given an address in a particular geographical location, is of a particular nationality, has a holding of a certain size, is a natural person or not or is of a particular gender.

Fees

5. Schedule 2 to these Regulations prescribes the fees payable for the purposes of the provisions of the Act listed therein.

SCHEDULE 1

Sections 191(1), 191(2), 191(3), 219(2), 288(3), 325(5) (together with paragraphs 25 and 26(1) of Part VI of Schedule 13), 356(1), 356(3) and 383(3).

Regulation 5   SCHEDULE 2

Fees in respect of inspections of registers by non-members
  1. The fee prescribed for the purposes of the following provisions of the Act:
      (a) section 191(1) (Fee for inspection of register of debenture holders);
      (b) section 288(3) (Fee for inspection of register of directors and secretaries);
      (c) section 325(5) and paragraph 25 of Part IV of Schedule 13 (Fee for inspection of register of directors' interests in shares or debentures); and
      (d) section 356(1) (Fee for inspection of register of members and index); is £2.50 for each hour or part thereof during which the right of inspection is exercised.

Fees for provision of copies and entries in registers and copies of reports
  2. The fee prescribed for the purposes of the following provisions of the Act:
      (a) section 191(2) (Fee for copies of entries in the register of debentures);
      (b) section 219(2) (Fees for copies of entries in the register of interests in shares or copies of reports or part of reports made pursuant to section 215(7));
      (c) section 325(5) and paragraph 26(1) of Part IV of Schedule 13 (Fee for copies of entries in the register of directors' interests in shares or debentures); and
      (d) section 356(3) (Fee for copies of entries in the register of members);
is:
      (i)   for the first 100 entries,
            or part thereof copied, ...£2.50;
      (ii) for the next 1000 entries,
            or part thereof copied, ...£20.00;
            and
      (iii) for every subsequent 1000 entries,
            or part thereof copied, ...£15.00.

Fees for copies of other documents
  3. The fee prescribed for the purposes of the following provisions of the Act—
      (a) section 191(3) (Fee for copies of trust deeds); and
      (b) section 383(3) (Fee for copies of minutes)
is 10 pence per hundred words, or part thereof, copied.

Companies (Single Member Private Limited Companies) Regulations 1992
(1992 No. 1699)

Whereas a draft of these Regulations has been approved by resolution of each House of Parliament in pursuance of paragraph 2(2) of Schedule 2 to the European Communities Act 1972.

  Now, therefore, the Secretary of State, being a Minister designated for the purposes of section 2(2) of that Act in relation to measures relating to single member private companies limited by shares or by guarantee, in exercise of the powers conferred by that section hereby makes the following Regulations:

Citation and commencement
  1. These Regulations may be cited as the Companies (Single Member Private Limited Companies) Regulations 1992 and shall come into force on the day after the day on which they were made.
[The Regulations were made on 14 July 1992.]

Single member private companies limited by shares or by guarantee

2.—(1) Notwithstanding any enactment or rule of law to the contrary, a private company limited by shares or by guarantee within the meaning of section 1 of the Companies Act 1985 may be formed by one person (in so far as permitted by that section as amended by these Regulations) and may have one member; and accordingly—

(a) any enactment or rule of law which applies in relation to a private company limited by shares or by guarantee shall, in the absence of any express provision to the contrary, apply with such modification as may be necessary in relation to such a company which is formed by one person or which has only one person as a member as it does in relation to such a company which is formed by two or more persons or which has two or more persons as members. . . .

(2) In this regulation 'enactment' shall include an enactment comprised in subordinate legislation and 'subordinate legislation' shall have the same meaning as in section 21(1) of the Interpretation Act 1978.

Transitional provision

3.   A person who, before the coming into force of these Regulations, is liable by virtue of section 24 of the Companies Act 1985 for the payment of the debts of a private company limited by shares or by guarantee, shall not be so liable for the payment of the company's debts contracted on or after the day on which these Regulations come into force.

Insider Dealing (Securities and Regulated Markets) Order 1994

(1994 No. 187)

Whereas a draft of this Order has been approved by a resolution of each House of Parliament pursuant to section 64(2) of the Criminal Justice Act 1993;

Now, therefore, the Treasury, in exercise of the powers conferred on them by sections 54(1), 60(1), 62(1) and 64(3) of that Act and of all other powers enabling them in that behalf, hereby make the following Order:

Title, commencement and interpretation

1.   This Order may be cited as the Insider Dealing (Securities and Regulated Markets) Order 1994 and shall come into force on the twenty eighth day after the day on which it is made.

[*The Order was made on 1 February 1994.*]

2.   In this Order a 'State within the European Economic Area' means a State which is a member of the European Communities and the Republics of Austria, Finland and Iceland, the Kingdoms of Norway and Sweden and the Principality of Liechtenstein.

Securities

3.   Articles 4 to 8 set out conditions for the purposes of section 54(1) of the Criminal Justice Act 1993 (securities to which Part V of the Act of 1993 applies).

4.   The following condition applies in relation to any security which falls within any paragraph of Schedule 2 to the Act of 1993, that is, that it is officially listed in a State within the European Economic Area or that it is admitted to dealing on, or has its price quoted on or under the rules of, a regulated market.

5.   The following alternative condition applies in relation to a warrant, that is, that the right under it is a right to subscribe for any share or debt security of the same class as a share or debt security which satisfies the condition in article 4.

6.   The following alternative condition applies in relation to a depositary receipt, that is, that the rights under it are in respect of any share or debt security which satisfies the condition in article 4.

7.   The following alternative conditions apply in relation to an option or a future, that is, that the option or rights under the future are in respect of—
   (a) any share or debt security which satisfies the condition in article 4, or
   (b) any depositary receipt which satisfies the condition in article 4 or article 6.

8.   The following alternative condition applies in relation to a contract for differences, that is, that the purpose or pretended purpose of the contract is to secure a profit or avoid a loss by reference to fluctuations in—
   (a) the price of any shares or debt securities which satisfy the condition in article 4, or
   (b) an index of the price of such shares or debt securities.

Regulated markets

9.   The following markets are regulated markets for the purposes of Part V of the Act of 1993—
   (a) any market which is established under the rules of an investment exchange speci-fied in the Schedule to this Order;
   (b) the market known as OFEX.

United Kingdom regulated markets

10.   The regulated markets which are regulated in the United Kingdom for the purposes of Part V of the Act of 1993 are any market which is established under the rules of—
   (a) the London Stock Exchange Limited;
   (b) LIFFE Administration & Management;
   (c) OMLX, the London Securities and Derivatives Exchange Limited;
   (d) virt-x Exchange Limited;
   (e) the exchange known as COREDEALMTS;
together with the market known as OFEX.

Article 9   SCHEDULE

                              REGULATED MARKETS

Any market which is established under the rules of one of the following investment exchanges:
Amsterdam Stock Exchange.
Antwerp Stock Exchange.
Athens Stock Exchange.
Barcelona Stock Exchange.
Bavarian Stock Exchange.
Berlin Stock Exchange.
Bilbao Stock Exchange.
Bologna Stock Exchange.
Bremen Stock Exchange.
Brussels Stock Exchange.
Copenhagen Stock Exchange.
The exchange known as COREDEALMTS.
Dusseldorf Stock Exchange.
The exchange known as EASDAQ.
Florence Stock Exchange.
Frankfurt Stock Exchange.
Genoa Stock Exchange.

Hamburg Stock Exchange.
Hanover Stock Exchange.
Helsinki Stock Exchange.
Iceland Stock Exchange.
The Irish Stock Exchange Limited.
Lisbon Stock Exchange.
LIFFE Administration & Management.
The London Stock Exchange Limited.
Luxembourg Stock Exchange.
Lyon Stock Exchange.
Madrid Stock Exchange.
Milan Stock Exchange.
Naples Stock Exchange.
The exchange known as NASDAQ.
The exchange known as the Nouveau Marché.
OMLX, the London Securities and Derivatives Exchange Limited.
Oporto Stock Exchange.
Oslo Stock Exchange.
Palermo Stock Exchange.
Paris Stock Exchange.
Rome Stock Exchange.
Stockholm Stock Exchange.
Stuttgart Stock Exchange.
The exchange known as SWX Swiss Exchange.
Trieste Stock Exchange.
Turin Stock Exchange.
Valencia Stock Exchange.
Venice Stock Exchange.
Vienna Stock Exchange.
virt-x Exchange Limited.

Companies (EU Political Expenditure) Exemption Order 2001

(2001 No. 445)

The Secretary of State, in exercise of the powers conferred on him by section 347B of the Companies Act 1985 and of all other powers enabling him in that behalf, hereby makes the following Order, of which a draft has been laid before Parliament in accordance with section 347B(11) of that Act and approved by a resolution of each House of Parliament:

Citation, commencement and interpretation

1.—(1) This Order may be cited as the Companies (EU Political Expenditure) Exemption Order 2001.

(2) This Order shall come into force on 16 February 2001.

(3) In this Order references to 'the Act' are references to the Companies Act 1985.

Exemption from authorisation under sections 347C, D and E

2. A company or subsidiary undertaking of the description specified in article 3 is exempted from the need to be authorised as mentioned in sections 347C(1), 347D(2), 347D(3) and 347E(2) of the Act (prohibition on donations and political expenditure by companies, special rules for subsidiaries and special rule for parent company of non-GB subsidiary under-

taking) in respect of, and only in respect of, the description of EU political expenditure specified in article 4.

Description of company or subsidiary undertaking

3.—(1) Any company or subsidiary undertaking whose ordinary course of business includes, or is proposed to include, the preparation, publication or dissemination to the public, or any part of the public, of material relating to news, and to public and political affairs and events, and to views, opinion and comment on the news and on public and political affairs and events.

(2) For the purposes of paragraph (1) above it is to be irrelevant—
(a) by which means or modes the material described in that paragraph is to be prepared, published or disseminated; or
(b) where the public, or any part of the public, to which such material is published or disseminated, is located or the identity or description of the public or any part of it.

Description of EU political expenditure

4. Any EU political expenditure incurred by a company or subsidiary undertaking specified in article 3 in respect of the preparation, publication or dissemination of such material as is specified in article 3(1) where that material contains matter which would render that preparation, publication or dissemination on the part of the company or subsidiary undertaking an activity of that company or subsidiary undertaking within the meaning of section 347A(5)(b) of the Act.

Financial Services and Markets Act 2000 (Prescribed Markets and Qualifying Investments) Order 2001
(2001 No. 996)

The Treasury, in exercise of the powers conferred upon them by section 118(3) of the Financial Services and Markets Act 2000, hereby make the following Order:

Citation

1. This Order may be cited as the Financial Services and Markets Act 2000 (Prescribed Markets and Qualifying Investments) Order 2001.

Commencement

2. This Order comes into force on the day on which section 123 of the Act (power to impose penalties in cases of market abuse) comes into force.
[*The Financial Services and Markets Act 2000, s. 123, came into force on 1 December 2001.*]

Interpretation

3. In this Order—
'the Act' means the Financial Services and Markets Act 2000; and
'UK recognised investment exchange' means a body corporate or unincorporated association in respect of which there is in effect a recognition order made under section 290(1)(a) of the Act (recognition orders in respect of investment exchanges other than overseas investment exchanges).

Prescribed markets

4. There are prescribed, as markets to which section 118 of the Act applies, all markets which are established under the rules of a UK recognised investment exchange.

4A. There is prescribed, as a market to which section 118 of the Act applies, the market known as OFEX.

Qualifying investments

5.   There are prescribed, as qualifying investments in relation to the markets prescribed by article 4, all investments of a kind specified for the purposes of section 22 of the Act.

Financial Services and Markets Act 2000 (Official Listing of Securities) Regulations 2001

(2001 No. 2956)

The Treasury, in exercise of the powers conferred upon them by sections 75(3), 79(3), 103(1), 417(1) and 428(3) of, and paragraph 9 of Schedule 10 and paragraphs 16(3), 16(4) and 20(2) of Schedule 11 to, the Financial Services and Markets Act 2000, hereby make the following Regulations:

PART 1   GENERAL

Citation and commencement

1.   These Regulations may be cited as the Financial Services and Markets Act 2000 (Official Listing of Securities) Regulations 2001 and come into force on the day on which section 74(1) comes into force.

[*The Financial Services and Markets Act 2000, s. 74(1), came into force on 1 December 2001.*]

Interpretation

2.—(1) In these Regulations—

'the Act' means the Financial Services and Markets Act 2000;

'competent authority' is to be construed in accordance with section 72;

'the Financial Promotion Order' means the Financial Services and Markets Act 2000 (Financial Promotion) Order 2001;

'issuer' has the same meaning as is given, for the purposes of section 103(1), in regulation 4 below;

'non-listing prospectus' has the meaning given in section 87(2); and

'the Regulated Activities Order' means the Financial Services and Markets Act 2000 (Regulated Activities) Order 2001.

(2) Any reference in these Regulations to a section or Schedule is, unless otherwise stated or unless the context otherwise requires, a reference to that section of or Schedule to the Act.

PART 2   MISCELLANEOUS MATTERS PRESCRIBED FOR THE PURPOSES OF PART VI OF THE ACT

Bodies whose securities may not be listed

3.   For the purposes of section 75(3) (which provides that no application for listing may be entertained in respect of securities issued by a body of a prescribed kind) there are prescribed the following kinds of body—

    (a) where the securities are securities within the meaning of the Regulated Activities Order, a private company within the meaning of section 1(3) of the Companies Act 1985 or article 12(3) of the Companies (Northern Ireland) Order 1986;

    (b) an old public company within the meaning of section 1 of the Companies Consolidation (Consequential Provisions) Act 1985 or article 3 of the Companies Consolidation (Consequential Provisions) (Northern Ireland) Order 1986.

Meaning of 'issuer'

4.—(1) For the purposes of section 103(1), 'issuer' has the meaning given in this regulation.

(2) In relation to certificates or other instruments falling within article 80 of the Regulated Activities Order (certificates representing certain securities), 'issuer' means—

    (a) for the purposes of paragraph 16 of Schedule 11 (exemption from prospectus requirement for securities issued by a body corporate and offered to qualifying persons), the person by whom the certificates or instruments have been or are to be issued;

    (b) for all other purposes, the person who issued or is to issue the securities to which the certificates or instruments relate.

(3) In relation to any other securities, 'issuer' means the person by whom the securities have been or are to be issued.

Meaning of 'approved exchange'

5.   For the purposes of paragraph 9 of Schedule 10, 'approved exchange' means a recognised investment exchange approved by the Treasury for the purposes of the Public Offers of Securities Regulations 1995 (either generally or in relation to dealings in securities).

[*By virtue of an approval dated 16 June 1995, the London Stock Exchange was approved by the Treasury for the purposes of the Public Offers of Securities Regulations 1995 with effect from 19 June 1995, in relation to securities within the meaning of Part II of those Regulations which are admitted to dealings on, or are the subject of an application for admission to dealings on, the Alternative Investment Market. (The approval also related to dealings in securities on the Unlisted Securities Market, but that market no longer operates.)*]

PART 3   PERSONS RESPONSIBLE FOR LISTING PARTICULARS, PROSPECTUSES AND NON-LISTING PROSPECTUSES

Responsibility for listing particulars

6.—(1) Subject to the following provisions of this Part, for the purposes of Part VI of the Act the persons responsible for listing particulars (including supplementary listing particulars) are—

    (a) the issuer of the securities to which the particulars relate;

    (b) where the issuer is a body corporate, each person who is a director of that body at the time when the particulars are submitted to the competent authority;

    (c) where the issuer is a body corporate, each person who has authorised himself to be named, and is named, in the particulars as a director or as having agreed to become a director of that body either immediately or at a future time;

    (d) each person who accepts, and is stated in the particulars as accepting, responsibility for the particulars;

    (e) each person not falling within any of the foregoing sub-paragraphs who has authorised the contents of the particulars.

(2) A person is not to be treated as responsible for any particulars by virtue of paragraph (1)(b) above if they are published without his knowledge or consent and on becoming aware of their publication he forthwith gives reasonable public notice that they were published without his knowledge or consent.

(3) When accepting responsibility for particulars under paragraph (1)(d) above or authorising their contents under paragraph (1)(e) above, a person may state that he does so only in relation to certain specified parts of the particulars, or only in certain specified respects, and in such a case he is responsible under paragraph (1)(d) or (e) above—

    (a) only to the extent specified; and

    (b) only if the material in question is included in (or substantially in) the form and context to which he has agreed.

(4) Nothing in this regulation is to be construed as making a person responsible for any particulars by reason of giving advice as to their contents in a professional capacity.

(5) Where by virtue of this regulation the issuer of any shares pays or is liable to pay compensation under section 90 for loss suffered in respect of shares for which a person has subscribed no account is to be taken of that liability or payment in determining any question as to the amount paid on subscription for those shares or as to the amount paid up or deemed to be paid up on them.

Securities issued in connection with takeovers and mergers

7.—(1) This regulation applies where—
- (a) listing particulars relate to securities which are to be issued in connection with—
  - (i) an offer by the issuer (or by a wholly-owned subsidiary of the issuer) for securities issued by another person ('A');
  - (ii) an agreement for the acquisition by the issuer (or by a wholly-owned subsidiary of the issuer) of securities issued by another person ('A'); or
  - (iii) any arrangement whereby the whole of the undertaking of another person ('A') is to become the undertaking of the issuer (or of a wholly-owned subsidiary of the issuer, or of a body corporate which will become such a subsidiary by virtue of the arrangement); and
- (b) each of the specified persons is responsible by virtue of regulation 6(1)(d) above for any part ('the relevant part') of the particulars relating to A or to the securities or undertaking to which the offer, agreement or arrangement relates.

(2) In paragraph (1)(b) above the 'specified persons' are—
- (a) A; and
- (b) where A is a body corporate—
  - (i) each person who is a director of A at the time when the particulars are submitted to the competent authority; and
  - (ii) each other person who has authorised himself to be named, and is named, in the particulars as a director of A.

(3) Where this regulation applies, no person is to be treated as responsible for the relevant part of the particulars under regulation 6(1)(a), (b) or (c) above but without prejudice to his being responsible under regulation 6(1)(d).

(4) In this regulation—
- (a) 'listing particulars' includes supplementary listing particulars; and
- (b) 'wholly-owned subsidiary' is to be construed in accordance with section 736 of the Companies Act 1985 (and, in relation to an issuer which is not a body corporate, means a body corporate which would be a wholly-owned subsidiary of the issuer within the meaning of that section if the issuer were a body corporate).

Specialist securities

9.—(1) This regulation applies where listing particulars relate to securities of a kind specified by listing rules for the purposes of section 82(1)(c), other than securities which are to be issued in the circumstances mentioned in regulation 7(1)(a) above.

(2) No person is to be treated as responsible for the particulars under regulation 6(1)(a), (b) or (c) above but without prejudice to his being responsible under regulation 6(1)(d).

(3) 'Listing particulars' includes supplementary listing particulars.

Responsibility for prospectuses and non-listing prospectuses

10.—(1) This part of these Regulations applies in relation to a prospectus required by listing rules in accordance with section 84(1), or to a non-listing prospectus, as it applies in relation to listing particulars, but as if—
- (a) any reference to listing particulars were a reference to a prospectus and any reference to supplementary listing particulars were a reference to a supplementary prospectus; and

(b) notwithstanding the definition of 'issuer' given in regulation 2(1) above, any reference in this Part (other than in regulation 6(1)(b) or (c) or in paragraph (2) below) to the issuer of securities included a reference to the person offering or proposing to offer them.

(2) In the application of regulation 6 above to a prospectus or non-listing prospectus in accordance with this regulation, a person is not responsible under regulation 6(1)(a) where—

(a) he is not the issuer, but is making the offer in association with the issuer; and

(b) the prospectus or supplementary prospectus was drawn up primarily by the issuer, or by one or more persons acting on behalf of the issuer.

PART 4   MATTERS PRESCRIBED FOR THE PURPOSES OF SCHEDULE 11 (OFFERS NOT TO BE TREATED AS PUBLIC OFFERS OF SECURITIES)

Offers of securities to 'qualifying persons': definitions

11.—(1) For the purposes of paragraph 16(3) of Schedule 11 (offers of securities to 'qualifying persons') and for the purposes of paragraph (2) below, a body corporate is 'connected with' another body corporate if—

(a) they are in the same group; or

(b) one is entitled, either alone or with any other body corporate in the same group, to exercise or control the exercise of a majority of the voting rights attributable to the share capital which are exercisable in all circumstances at any general meeting of the other body corporate or its holding company.

(2) For the purposes of paragraph 16(4) of Schedule 11, 'relevant trustee' means a person holding shares in or debentures of a body corporate as trustee, in pursuance of arrangements made by that body corporate (or by another body corporate connected with it) for the purpose of enabling or facilitating the holding of such shares or debentures by or for the benefit of qualifying persons (within the meaning of paragraph 16(2) of Schedule 11), or enabling or facilitating transactions in such shares or debentures between or for the benefit of such persons.

(3) In paragraph (2) above, 'shares' and 'debentures' include—

(a) any investment of the kind specified by article 76 of the Regulated Activities Order (shares) or article 77 of that Order (instruments creating or acknowledging indebtedness);

(b) any investment of the kind specified by article 79 or 80 of that Order (instruments giving entitlements to investments, and certificates representing certain securities) so far as relevant to articles 76 and 77; and

(c) any investment of the kind specified by article 89 of that Order (rights to or interests in investments) so far as relevant to investments of the kind mentioned in sub-paragraph (a) or (b) above.

(4) For the purposes of paragraph 16(4) of Schedule 11 and for the purposes of paragraph (1) above, 'group', in relation to a body corporate, means that body corporate, any other body corporate which is its holding company or subsidiary, and any other body corporate which is a subsidiary of that holding company, together with any body corporate in which a member of the group holds a qualifying capital interest.

(5) In this regulation—

(a) 'equity share capital' is to be construed in accordance with section 744 of the Companies Act 1985 (or, in relation to a company registered in Northern Ireland, in accordance with article 2(3) of the Companies (Northern Ireland) Order 1986);

(b) 'holding company' and 'subsidiary' are to be construed in accordance with section 736 of the Companies Act 1985 (or, in relation to a company registered in

Northern Ireland, in accordance with article 4 of the Companies (Northern Ireland) Order 1986);

(c) 'qualifying capital interest', in relation to a body corporate, means an interest, in relevant shares of the body corporate, which is held on a long-term basis for the purpose of securing a contribution to the holder's own activities by the exercise of control or influence arising from that interest, and a holding of 20 per cent or more of the nominal value of the relevant shares of a body corporate is to be presumed to be a qualifying capital interest unless the contrary is shown; and

(d) 'relevant shares', in relation to a body corporate, means shares, comprised in the equity share capital of the body corporate, of a class carrying rights to vote in all circumstances at general meetings of the body.

Financial Services and Markets Act 2000 (Offers of Securities) Order 2001

(2001 No. 2958)

The Treasury, in exercise of the powers conferred upon them by section 87(4) of and paragraphs 8(2), 15, 17, 21, 22, 23 and 25 of Schedule 11 to the Financial Services and Markets Act 2000, hereby make the following Order:

Citation and commencement

1. This Order may be cited as the Financial Services and Markets Act 2000 (Offers of Securities) Order 2001 and comes into force on the day on which section 74(1) comes into force.

[*The Financial Services and Markets Act 2000, s. 74(1), came into force on 1 December 2001.*]

Interpretation

2.—(1) In this Order—

'the Act' means the Financial Services and Markets Act 2000;

'the Public Offers of Securities Regulations' means the Public Offers of Securities Regulations 1995; and

'the Regulated Activities Order' means the Financial Services and Markets Act 2001 (Regulated Activities) Order 2001.

(2) Any reference in this Order to a section or Schedule is, unless otherwise stated or unless the context otherwise requires, a reference to that section of or Schedule to the Act.

Listing rules about non-listing prospectuses

3. For the purposes of section 87(4) there are specified, as provisions to which the power of the competent authority to make listing rules about the timing and manner of publication of a non-listing prospectus is subject, the provisions of the Public Offers of Securities Regulations.

Public authorities

4. For the purposes of paragraphs 8(2)(e) and 23(2)(e) of Schedule 11 (bodies which are included within the category of 'public authority') there are specified the following bodies—

(a) the National Assembly for Wales;
(b) a Northern Ireland department; and
(c) the Scottish Administration.

Exchange of shares

5. For the purposes of paragraph 15 of Schedule 11 (exchange of shares) there are specified the following kinds of investments relating to shares—

(a) any investment of the kind specified by article 79 of the Regulated Activities Order (instruments giving entitlements to investments) in so far as relating to investments of the kind specified by article 76 of that Order (shares); and

(b) any investment of the kind specified by article 80 of the Regulated Activities Order (certificates representing securities) in so far as relating to investments of the kind specified by article 76 of that Order (shares).

Convertible securities

6.—(1) For the purposes of paragraph 17(1) of Schedule 11 (convertible securities) there are specified the provisions of—

(a) Part III of the Companies Act 1985; and

(b) the Public Offers of Securities Regulations.

(2) For the purposes of paragraph 17(2) of Schedule 11 (convertible securities) there is specified any security which is—

(a) an investment of the kind specified by article 77 of the Regulated Activities Order (instruments creating or acknowledging indebtedness);

(b) an investment of the kind specified by article 79 of the Regulated Activities Order (instruments giving entitlements to investments) in so far as relating to investments of the kind specified by article 76 of that Order (shares); or

(c) an investment of the kind specified by article 80 of the Regulated Activities Order (certificates representing securities) in so far as relating to investments of the kind specified by article 76 of that Order (shares).

(3) For the purposes of paragraph 2(b) and (c) above, paragraph (3) of article 76 of the Regulated Activities Order (exclusion relating to building societies, industrial and provident societies, credit unions, and equivalent bodies in other EEA States) is to be disregarded.

Same class securities

7. For the purposes of paragraph 21 of Schedule 11 (same class securities) there are specified the provisions of the Public Offers of Securities Regulations.

Short date securities

8. For the purposes of paragraph 22 of Schedule 11 (short date securities) there are specified investments of the kind specified by article 77 of the Regulated Activities Order (instruments creating or acknowledging indebtedness).

Government securities

9. For the purposes of paragraph 23(1) of Schedule 11 (Government and public securities) there are specified the following kinds of investments, namely loan stock, bonds and other instruments.

Shares

10. For the purposes of paragraph 25 of Schedule 11 (definition of shares) 'shares' means any investment of the kind specified by article 76 of the Regulated Activities Order (shares).

Uncertificated Securities Regulations 2001
(2001 No. 3755)

Whereas a draft of these Regulations has been approved by resolution of each House of Parliament

Now, therefore, the Treasury, in exercise of the powers conferred by section 207 of the Companies Act 1989 and now vested in them, and of all other powers enabling them in that behalf, hereby to make the following Regulations:

PART 1   CITATION, COMMENCEMENT, AND INTERPRETATION

Citation and commencement

1.   These Regulations may be cited as the Uncertificated Securities Regulations 2001 and shall come into force on 26th November 2001.

Purposes and basic definition

2.—(1) These Regulations enable title to units of a security to be evidenced otherwise than by a certificate and transferred otherwise than by a written instrument, and make provision for certain supplementary and incidental matters; and in these Regulations 'relevant system' means a computer-based system, and procedures, which enable title to units of a security to be evidenced and transferred without a written instrument, and which facilitate supplementary and incidental matters.

(2) Where a title to a unit of a security is evidenced otherwise than by a certificate by virtue of these Regulations, the transfer of title to such a unit of a security shall be subject to these Regulations.

Interpretation

3.—(1) In these Regulations—

'the 1985 Act' means the Companies Act 1985;

'the 1986 Act' means the Financial Services Act 1986;

'the 2000 Act' means the Financial Services and Markets Act 2000; . . .

'the 1974 Regulations' means the Local Authority (Stocks and Bonds) Regulations 1974; and 'local authority' has the same meaning as it has in those Regulations;

'the 1995 Regulations' means the Uncertificated Securities Regulations 1995;

'the Authority' means the Financial Services Authority referred to in section 1 of the 2000 Act;

'certificate' means any certificate, instrument or other document of, or evidencing, title to units of a security;

'company' means a company within the meaning of section 735(1) of the 1985 Act;

'dematerialised instruction' means an instruction sent or received by means of a relevant system;

'designated agency' has the meaning given by regulation 11(1);

'enactment' includes an enactment comprised in any subordinate legislation within the meaning of the Interpretation Act 1978, and an enactment comprised in, or in an instrument made under, an Act of the Scottish Parliament;

'generate', in relation to an Operator-instruction, means to initiate the procedures by which the Operator-instruction comes to be sent;

'guidance', in relation to an Operator, means guidance issued by him which is intended to have continuing effect and is issued in writing or other legible form, which if it were a rule, would come within the definition of a rule;

'instruction' includes any instruction, election, acceptance or any other message of any kind;

'interest in a security' means any legal or equitable interest or right in relation to a security, including—

    (a) an absolute or contingent right to acquire a security created, allotted or issued or to be created, allotted or issued; and

    (b) the interests or rights of a person for whom a security is held on trust or by a custodian or depositary;

'issue', in relation to a new unit of a security, means to confer title to a new unit on a person;

'issuer-instruction' means a properly authenticated dematerialised instruction attributable to a participating issuer;

'issuer register of members' has the meaning given by regulation 20(1)(a);
'issuer register of securities'—
   (a) in relation to shares, means an issuer register of members; and
   (b) in relation to units of a security other than shares, means a register of persons
        holding the units, maintained by or on behalf of the issuer or, in the case of
        public sector securities, by or on behalf of the person specified in regulation
        21(3);
'local authority security' means a security which, when held in certificated form, is transferable in accordance with regulation 7 of the 1974 Regulations and title to which must be
registered in accordance with regulation 5 of those Regulations;
'officer', in relation to an Operator or a participating issuer, includes—
   (a) where the Operator or the participating issuer is a company, such persons as are
        mentioned in section 744 of the 1985 Act;
   (b) where the Operator or the participating issuer is a partnership, a partner; or in the
        event that no partner is situated in the United Kingdom, a person in the United
        Kingdom who is acting on behalf of a partner; and
   (c) where the Operator or the participating issuer is neither a company nor a partner-
        ship, any member of its governing body; or in the event that no member of its
        governing body is situated in the United Kingdom, a person in the United King-
        dom who is acting on behalf of any member of its governing body;
'Operator' means a person approved by the Treasury under these Regulations as Operator
of a relevant system (and in Schedule 1 includes a person who has applied to the Treasury
under regulation 4 for their approval of him as an Operator);
'Operator-instruction' means a properly authenticated dematerialised instruction attrib-
utable to an Operator;
'Operator register of corporate securities' has the meaning given by regulation 22(2)(a)(i);
'Operator register of members' has the meaning given by regulation 20(1)(b);
'Operator register of public sector securities' has the meaning given by regulation 21(1)(a);
'Operator register of securities'—
   (a) in relation to shares, means an Operator register of members;
   (b) in relation to units of a security other than shares, means an Operator register
        of corporate securities, an Operator register of public sector securities or, as the
        case may be, a register maintained by an Operator by virtue of regulation
        22(3)(a);
'Operator's conversion rules' means the rules made and practices instituted by the Operator in order to comply with paragraph 18 of Schedule 1;
'Operator-system' means those facilities and procedures which are part of the relevant
system, which are maintained and operated by or for an Operator, by which he generates
Operator-instructions and receives dematerialised instructions from system-participants and
by which persons change the form in which units of a participating security are held;
'participating issuer' means (subject to paragraph (3)) a person who has issued a security
which is a participating security;
'participating security' means a security title to units of which is permitted by an Operator
to be transferred by means of a relevant system;
'public sector securities' means UK Government securities and local authority securities;
'record of uncertificated public sector securities' has the meaning given by regulation
21(2)(a);
'record of securities' means any of a record of uncertificated corporate securities, a record
of uncertificated shares and a record of uncertificated public sector securities;
'record of uncertificated corporate securities' has the meaning given by regulation
22(2)(b)(ii);
'record of uncertificated shares' has the meaning given by regulation 20(6)(a);

'register of members' means either or both of an issuer register of members and an Operator register of members;

'record of securities' means either or both of an issuer register of securities and an Operator register of securities;

'relevant system' has the meaning given by regulation 2(1); and 'relevant system' includes an Operator-system;

'rules', in relation to an Operator, means rules made or conditions imposed by him with respect to the provision of the relevant system;

'securities' means shares, stock, debentures, debenture stock, loan stock, bonds, units of a collective investment scheme within the meaning of section 235 of the 2000 Act, rights under a depositary receipt within the meaning of paragraph 4 of Schedule 2 to the Criminal Justice Act 1993, and other securities of any description, and interests in a security;

'settlement', in relation to a transfer of uncertificated units of a security between two system-members by means of a relevant system, means the delivery of those units to the transferee and, where appropriate, the creation of any associated obligation to make payments, in accordance with the rules and practices of the Operator; and 'settle' shall be construed accordingly;

'settlement bank', in relation to a relevant system, means a person who has contracted to make payments in connection with transfers of title to uncertificated units of a security by means of that system;

'share' means share (or stock) in the share capital of a company;

'system-member', in relation to a relevant system, means a person who is permitted by an Operator to transfer by means of that system title to uncertificated units of a security held by him, and shall include, where relevant, two or more persons who are jointly so permitted;

'system-member instruction' means a properly authenticated dematerialised instruction attributable to a system-member;

'system-participant', in relation to a relevant system, means a person who is permitted by an Operator to send and receive properly authenticated dematerialised instructions; and 'sponsoring system-participant' means a system-participant who is permitted by an Operator to send properly authenticated dematerialised instructions attributable to another person and to receive properly authenticated dematerialised instructions on another person's behalf;

'system-user', in relation to a relevant system, means a person who as regards that system is a participating issuer, a system-member, system-participant or settlement bank;

'UK Government security' means a security issued by Her Majesty's Government in the United Kingdom or by a Northern Ireland department;

'uncertificated', in relation to a unit of a security, means (subject to Regulation 42(11)(a)) that title to the unit is recorded on the relevant Operator register of securities, and may, by virtue of these Regulations, be transferred by means of a relevant system; and 'certificated', in relation to a unit of a security, means that the unit is not an uncertificated unit;

'unit', in relation to a security, means the smallest possible transferable unit of the security (for example a single share);

'wholly dematerialised security' means—

    (a) a strip, in relation to any stock or bond, within the meaning of section 47(1B) of the Finance Act 1942; or

    (b) a participating security whose terms of issue (or, in the case of shares, where its terms of issue or the articles of association of the company in question) provide that its units may only be held in uncertificated form and title to them may only be transferred by means of a relevant system;

and other expressions have the meanings given to them by the 1985 Act.

  (2) For the purposes of these Regulations—

    (a) a dematerialised instruction is properly authenticated if it complies with the specifications referred to in paragraph 5(3) of Schedule 1; or if it was given, and not withdrawn, before these Regulations came into force and was properly authenticated within the meaning of regulation 3(2)(a) of the 1995 Regulations;

(b) a dematerialised instruction is attributable to a person if it is expressed to have been sent by that person, or if it is expressed to have been sent on behalf of that person, in accordance with the rules and specifications referred to in paragraph 5(4) of Schedule 1; and a dematerialised instruction may be attributable to more than one person. . . .

PART 2   THE OPERATOR

Approval and compliance

Applications for approval

4.—(1) Any person may apply to the Treasury for their approval of him as Operator of a relevant system. . . .

Grant and refusal of approval

5.— . . . (5) Provided that it had not been withdrawn before these Regulations came into force, an approval granted to a person under regulation 5 of the 1995 Regulations shall be treated as having been granted under this regulation.

Supervision

Withdrawal of approval

7.—(1) The Treasury may withdraw an Operator's approval at the request, or with the consent, of the Operator.

(2) If it appears to the Treasury that—

(a) any requirement of Schedule 1 is not satisfied in relation to an Operator; or

(b) an Operator is failing or has failed to comply with any obligation imposed on him by or under these Regulations,

they may withdraw approval from that Operator by written instrument even though the Operator does not wish his approval to be withdrawn. . . .

Delegation of Treasury functions

11.—(1) . . . the Treasury may by instrument in writing delegate all or any of the functions conferred by this Part of these Regulations to the Authority; and references in these Regulations to the 'designated agency' are references to the Authority so far as such functions are so delegated.

PART 3   PARTICIPATING SECURITIES

PARTICIPATION BY ISSUERS

Participation in respect of shares

14. Where—

(a) an Operator permits title to shares of a class in relation to which regulation 15 applies, or in relation to which a directors' resolution passed in accordance with regulation 16 is effective, to be transferred by means of a relevant system; and

(b) the company in question permits the holding of shares of that class in uncertificated form and the transfer of title to any such shares by means of a relevant system,

title to shares of that class which are recorded on an Operator register of members may be transferred by means of that relevant system.

15. This regulation applies to a class of shares if the company's articles of association are in all respects consistent with—

    (a) the holding of shares of that class in uncertificated form;

    (b) the transfer of title to shares of that class by means of a relevant system; and

    (c) these Regulations.

16.—(1) This regulation applies to a class of shares if a company's articles of association in any respect are inconsistent with—

    (a) the holding of shares of that class in uncertificated form;

    (b) the transfer of title to shares of that class by means of a relevant system; or

    (c) any provision of these Regulations.

(2) A company may resolve, subject to paragraph (6)(a), by resolution of its directors (in this Part referred to as a 'director's resolution') that title to shares of a class issued or to be issued by it may be transferred by means of a relevant system.

(3) Upon a directors' resolution becoming effective in accordance with its terms, and for as long as it is in force, the articles of association in relation to the class of shares which were the subject of the directors' resolution shall not apply to any uncertificated shares of that class to the extent that they are inconsistent with—

    (a) the holding of shares of that class in uncertificated form;

    (b) the transfer of title to shares of that class by means of a relevant system; or

    (c) any provision of these Regulations.

(4) Unless a company has given notice to every member of the company in accordance with its articles of association of its intention to pass a directors' resolution before the passing of such a resolution, it shall give such notice within 60 days of the passing of the resolution.

(5) Notice given by the company before the coming into force of these Regulations of its intention to pass a directors' resolution which, if it had been given after the coming into force of these Regulations would have satisfied the requirements of paragraph (4), shall be taken to satisfy the requirements of that paragraph.

(6) In respect of a class of shares, the members of a company may by ordinary resolution—

    (a) if a directors' resolution has not been passed, resolve that the directors of the company shall not pass a directors' resolution;

    (b) if a directors' resolution has been passed but not yet come into effect in accordance with its terms, resolve that it shall not come into effect;

    (c) if a directors' resolution has been passed and is effective in accordance with its terms but the class of shares has not yet been permitted by the Operator to be a participating security, resolve that the directors' resolution shall cease to have effect; or

    (d) if a directors' resolution has been passed and is effective in accordance with its terms and the class of shares has been permitted by the Operator to be a participating security, resolve that the directors shall take the necessary steps to ensure that title to shares of the class that was the subject of the directors' resolution shall cease to be transferable by means of a relevant system and that the directors' resolution shall cease to have effect,

and the directors shall be bound by the terms of any such ordinary resolution.

(7) Such sanctions as apply to a company and its officers in the event of a default in complying with section 376 of the 1985 Act shall apply to a participating issuer and his officers in the event of a default in complying with paragraph (4).

(8) A company shall not permit the holding of shares in such a class as is referred to in paragraph (1) in uncertificated form, or the transfer of title to shares in such a class by means of a relevant system, unless in relation to that class of shares a directors' resolution is effective.

(9) This regulation shall not be taken to exclude the right of the members of a company to amend the articles of association of the company, in accordance with the articles, to allow

the holding of any class of its shares in uncertificated form and the transfer of title to shares in such a class by means of a relevant system.

17.—(1) A class of shares in relation to which, immediately before the coming into force of these Regulations—

(a) regulation 15 of the 1995 Regulations applied; or

(b) a directors' resolution passed in accordance with regulation 16 of the 1995 Regulations was effective,

shall be taken to be a class of shares in relation to which regulation 15 of these Regulations applies or, as the case may be, a directors' resolution passed in accordance with regulation 16 is effective.

(2) On the coming into force of these Regulations a company's articles of association in relation to any such class of shares, and the terms of issue of any such class of shares, shall cease to apply to the extent that they are inconsistent with any provision of these Regulations.

Interpretation of regulations 15, 16 and 17

18. For the purposes of regulations 15, 16 and 17 any shares with respect to which share warrants to bearer are issued under section 188 of the 1985 Act shall be regarded as forming a separate class of shares.

Participation in respect of securities other than shares

19.—(1) Subject to paragraph (2), where—

(a) an Operator permits title to a security other than a share to be transferred by means of a relevant system; and

(b) the issuer permits the holding of units of that security in uncertificated form and the transfer of title to units of that security by means of a relevant system,

title to units of that security which are recorded on an Operator register of securities may be transferred by means of that relevant system.

(2) In relation to any security other than a share, if the law under which it is constituted is not the law of England and Wales, Northern Ireland or Scotland, or if the current terms of its issue are in any respect inconsistent with—

(a) the holding of title to units of that security in uncertificated form;

(b) the transfer of title to units of that security by means of a relevant system; or

(c) subject to paragraph (3), these Regulations,

the issuer shall not permit the holding of units of that security in uncertificated form, or the transfer of title to units of that security by means of a relevant system.

(3) On the coming into force of these Regulations the current terms of issue of a relevant participating security shall cease to apply to the extent that they are inconsistent with any provision of these Regulations.

(4) For the purposes of this regulation—

(a) a relevant participating security is a participating security (other than a share) the terms of issue of which, immediately before the coming into force of these Regulations, were in all respects consistent with the 1995 Regulations; and

(b) the terms of issue of a security shall be taken to include the terms prescribed by the issuer on which units of the security are held and title to them is transferred.

KEEPING OF REGISTERS AND RECORDS

Entries on registers and records in respect of shares

20.—(1) In respect of every company which is a participating issuer, there shall be—

(a) a register maintained by the participating issuer, and such a register is referred to in these Regulations as an 'issuer register of members'; and

(b) a register maintained by the Operator, and such a register is referred to in these Regulations as an 'Operator register of members'.

(2) A participating issuer which is a company shall keep and enter up the issuer register of members in accordance with paragraph 2 of Schedule 4.

(3) In respect of every company which is a participating issuer, the Operator shall keep and enter up the Operator register of members in accordance with paragraph 4 of Schedule 4.

(4) References in any enactment or instrument to a company's register of members shall, unless the context otherwise requires, be construed in relation to a company which is a participating issuer as referring to the company's issuer register of members and Operator register of members.

(5) Paragraph (4) does not apply in relation to a company's issuer register of members to the extent that any of the particulars entered in that register in accordance with paragraph 2(1) of Schedule 4 are inconsistent with the company's Operator register of members.

(6) A participating issuer which is a company shall—

(a) maintain a record of the entries made in its Operator register of members; and such a record is referred to in these Regulations as a 'record of uncertificated shares'; and

(b) keep and enter up that record in accordance with paragraph 5 of Schedule 4.

(7) Such sanctions as apply to a company and its officers in the event of a default in complying with section 352 of the 1985 Act shall apply to—

(a) a company which is a participating issuer and its officers in the event of a default in complying with paragraph (1)(a) or (6)(a), or

(b) an Operator and his officers in the event of a default in complying with paragraph (1)(b).

Entries on registers and records in respect of public sector securities

21.—(1) In respect of every participating security which is a public sector security the Operator shall—

(a) maintain a register, and such a register is referred to in these Regulations as an 'Operator register of public sector securities'. . . .

(2) The person specified in paragraph (3) shall—

(a) maintain a record of the entries made in an Operator register of public sector securities; and such a record is referred to in these Regulations as a 'record of uncertificated public sector securities'. . . .

(3) The person referred to in paragraph (2) is the Bank of England, except where the security to which an Operator register of public sector securities relates is a local authority security, in which case it is—

(a) the relevant local authority; or

(b) if the local authority has appointed another person to act as registrar for the purpose of the 1974 Regulations in respect of that security, the person so appointed. . . .

Entries on registers and records in respect of other securities

22.—(1) Paragraph (2) applies where a participating issuer is required by or under an enactment or instrument to maintain in the United Kingdom a register of persons holding securities (other than shares or public sector securities) issued by him.

(2) Where this paragraph applies, then in so far as the register in question relates to any class of security which is a participating security—

(a) the Operator shall—

(i) maintain a register, and such a register is referred to in these Regulations as an 'Operator register of corporate securities'; and

(ii) keep and enter up the Operator register of corporate securities in accordance with paragraph 14 of Schedule 4.

(b) the participating issuer—

(i) shall not maintain the register to the extent that it relates to securities held in uncertificated form;

(ii) shall maintain a record of the entries made in any Operator register of corporate securities, and such a record is referred to in these Regulations as a 'record of uncertificated corporate securities'; and

(iii) shall keep and enter up that record in accordance with paragraph 15 of Schedule 4.

(3) Where a participating issuer is not required by or under an enactment or instrument to maintain in the United Kingdom in respect of a participating security issued by him a register of persons holding units of that participating security, the Operator shall—

(a) maintain a register in respect of that participating security; and

(b) record in that register—

(i) the names and addresses of the persons holding units of that security in uncertificated form, and

(ii) how many units of that security each such person holds in that form.

(4) Such sanctions as apply to a company and its officers in the event of a default in complying with section 352 of the 1985 Act shall apply to an Operator and his officers in the event of a default in complying with paragraph (2)(a)(i) or (3).

(5) Such sanctions as apply in the event of a default in complying with the requirement to maintain a register imposed by the relevant enactment or instrument referred to in paragraph (1) shall apply to a participating issuer and his officers in the event of a default in complying with paragraph (2)(b)(ii).

General provisions concerning keeping registers and records

23.—(1) The obligations of an Operator to maintain and to keep and enter up any register of securities, imposed by these Regulations—

(a) shall not give rise to any form of duty or liability on the Operator, except such as is expressly provided for in these Regulations or as arises from fraud or other wilful default, or negligence, on the part of the Operator;

(b) shall not give rise to any form of duty or liability on a participating issuer, other than where the Operator acts on the instructions of that participating issuer, in the absence of fraud or other wilful default, or negligence, on the part of that participating issuer; and

(c) shall not give rise to any form of duty or liability enforceable by civil proceedings for breach of statutory duty.

(2) Without prejudice to paragraph (1) or to any lesser period of limitation and to any rule as to the prescription of rights, liability incurred by a participating issuer or by an Operator arising—

(a) from the making or deletion of an entry in a register of securities or record of securities pursuant to these Regulations; or

(b) from a failure to make or delete any such entry,

shall not be enforceable more than 20 years after the date on which the entry was made or deleted or, in the case of a failure, the failure first occurred.

(3) No notice of any trust, expressed, implied or constructive, shall be entered on an Operator register of securities, or a part of such a register, or be receivable by an Operator.

(4) Schedule 4 (which provides for the keeping of registers and records of participating securities, and which excludes, or applies with appropriate modifications, certain provisions of the 1985 Act) shall have effect.

Effect of entries on registers

24.—(1) Subject to regulation 29 and to paragraphs (2) and (3) below, a register of members is prima facie evidence, and in Scotland sufficient evidence unless the contrary is shown, of any matters which are by these Regulations directed or authorised to be inserted in it.

(2) Paragraph (1) does not apply to a company's issuer register of members to the extent that any of the particulars entered in that register in accordance with paragraph 2(1) of Schedule 4 are inconsistent with the company's Operator register of members.

(3) The entry of a person's name and address in a company's issuer register of members shall not be treated as showing that person to be a member of the company unless—

    (a) the issuer register of members also shows him as holding shares in the company in certificated form;

    (b) the Operator register of members shows him as holding shares in the company in uncertificated form; or

    (c) he is deemed to be a member of the company by regulation 32(6)(b).

(4) Section 361 of the 1985 Act shall not apply with respect to a company which is a participating issuer. . . .

(6) Subject to regulation 29, an entry on an Operator register of corporate securities which records a person as holding units of a security in uncertificated form shall be evidence of such title to the units as would be evidenced if the entry on that register—

    (a) were an entry on the part maintained by the participating issuer of such register as is mentioned in regulation 22(1); and

    (b) where appropriate, related to units of that security held in certificated form.

(7) Subject to regulation 29, an entry on a register maintained by virtue of regulation 22(3)(a) shall (where the units are capable of being held in certificated form) be prima facie evidence, and in Scotland sufficient evidence unless the contrary is shown, that the person to whom the entry relates has such title to the units of the security which he is recorded as holding in uncertificated form as he would have if he held the units in certificated form.

Rectification of registers of securities

25.—(1) Unless the circumstances described in paragraph (2) apply, a participating issuer shall not rectify an issuer register of securities if such rectification would also require the rectification of an Operator register of securities.

(2) The circumstances referred to in paragraph (1) are that the rectification of an issuer register of securities is effected—

    (a) with the consent of the Operator; or

    (b) by order of a court in the United Kingdom.

(3) A participating issuer who rectifies an issuer register of securities in order to give effect to an order of a court in the United Kingdom shall immediately give the Operator written notification of the change to the entry, if any rectification of the Operator register of securities may also be required (unless the change to the issuer register is made in response to an Operator-instruction).

(4) An Operator who rectifies an Operator register of securities shall immediately—

    (a) generate an Operator-instruction to inform the relevant participating issuer of the change to the entry (unless the change is made in response to an issuer-instruction); and

    (b) generate an Operator-instruction to inform the system-members concerned of the change to the entry.

Closing registers

26. Notwithstanding section 358 of the 1985 Act or any other enactment, a participating issuer shall not close a register of securities relating to a participating security without the consent of the Operator.

Registration by an Operator of transfers of securities

27.—(1) Except where relevant units of a security are transferred by means of a relevant system to a person who is to hold them thereafter in certificated form (and subject to paragraphs (2) and (4))—

(a) upon settlement of a transfer of uncertificated units of a security in accordance with his rules;

(b) following receipt of an issuer-instruction notifying him that the circumstances specified in regulation 33(2)(b) have arisen in respect of a transfer of units of a participating security; or

(c) following receipt of an issuer-instruction given under Regulation 42(8)(b),

an Operator shall register on the relevant Operator register of securities the transfer of title to those units of that security.

(2) An Operator shall refuse to register a transfer of title to units of a participating security in accordance with a system-member instruction or an issuer-instruction (as the case may be) if he has actual notice that the transfer is—

(a) prohibited by order of a court in the United Kingdom;

(b) prohibited or avoided by or under an enactment;

(c) a transfer to a deceased person; or

(d) where the participating issuer is constituted under the law of Scotland, prohibited by or under an arrestment.

(3) Notwithstanding that an Operator has received, in respect of a transfer of title to units of a participating security, actual notice of the kind referred to in paragraph (2), the Operator may register that transfer of title on the relevant Operator register of securities if at the time that he received the actual notice it was not practicable for him to halt the process of registration.

(4) Without prejudice to his rules, an Operator may refuse to register a transfer of title to units of a participating security in accordance with a system-member instruction or an issuer-instruction (as the case may be) if the instruction requires a transfer of units—

(a) to an entity which is not a natural or legal person;

(b) to a minor (which, in relation to a participating issuer constituted under the law of Scotland, shall mean a person under 16 years of age);

(c) to be held jointly in the names of more persons than is permitted under the terms of the issue of the security; or

(d) where, in relation to the system-member instruction or the issuer-instruction (as the case may be), the Operator has actual notice of any of the matters specified in regulation 35(5)(a)(i) to (iii).

(5) An Operator shall not register a transfer of title to uncertificated units of a security on an Operator register of securities otherwise than in accordance with paragraph (1) unless he is required to do so by order of a court in the United Kingdom or by or under an enactment.

(6) Paragraph (5) shall not be taken to prevent an Operator from entering on an Operator register of securities a person who is a system-member to whom title to uncertificated units of a security has been transmitted by operation of law.

(7) Immediately upon—

(a) the registration by an Operator of the transfer of title to units of a participating security in accordance with—

(i) paragraph (1);

(ii) an order of a court in the United Kingdom; or

(iii) a requirement arising by or under an enactment; or

(b) the making or deletion by an Operator of an entry on an Operator register of securities—

(i) following the transmission of title to uncertificated units of a security by operation of law; or

(ii) upon the transfer of uncertificated units of a security to a person who is to hold them thereafter in certificated form,

the Operator shall generate an Operator-instruction to inform the relevant participating issuer of the registration, or of the making or deletion of the entry (as the case may be); and where appropriate the participating issuer shall register the transfer or transmission of title to those units on an issuer register of securities in accordance with regulation 28.

(8) Subsection (5) of section 183 of the 1985 Act shall apply in relation to a refusal by an Operator to register a transfer of securities in any of the circumstances specified in paragraphs (2) and (4), as it applies in relation to a refusal by a company to register a transfer of shares or debentures; and in that subsection as it so applies—

    (a) the reference to the date on which the transfer was lodged with the company shall be taken to be a reference to the date on which the relevant system-member instruction or issuer-instruction (as the case may be) was received by the Operator; and

    (b) the reference to a notice of the refusal shall be taken to be a reference to an Operator-instruction, or written notification from the Operator, informing the relevant system-member or participating issuer (as the case may be) of the refusal.

(9) Such sanctions as apply to a company and its officers in the event of a default in complying with subsection (5) of section 183 of the 1985 Act shall apply to an Operator and his officers in the event of a default in complying with that subsection as applied by paragraph (8).

Registration by a participating issuer of transfers of securities upon conversion into certificated form

28.—(1) Paragraphs (2) to (5) apply where relevant units of a security are transferred by means of a relevant system to a person who is to hold them thereafter in certificated form.

(2) Subject to paragraphs (3) and (4), a participating issuer shall (where appropriate) register a transfer of title to relevant units of a security on an issuer register of securities in accordance with an Operator-instruction.

(3) A participating issuer shall refuse to register a transfer of title to relevant units of a security in accordance with an Operator-instruction if he has actual notice that the transfer is—

    (a) prohibited by order of a court in the United Kingdom;

    (b) prohibited or avoided by or under an enactment;

    (c) a transfer to a deceased person; or

    (d) where the participating issuer is constituted under the law of Scotland, prohibited by or under an arrestment.

(4) A participating issuer may refuse to register a transfer of title to relevant units of a security in accordance with an Operator-instruction if the instruction requires a transfer of units—

    (a) to an entity which is not a natural or legal person;

    (b) to a minor (which, in relation to a participating issuer constituted under the law of Scotland, shall mean a person under 16 years of age);

    (c) to be held jointly in the names of more persons than is permitted under the terms of the issue of the security; or

    (d) where, in relation to the Operator-instruction, the participating issuer has actual notice from the Operator of any of the matters specified in regulation 35(5)(a)(i) to (iii).

(5) A participating issuer shall notify the Operator by issuer-instruction whether he has registered a transfer in response to an Operator-instruction to do so.

(6) A participating issuer shall not register a transfer of title to relevant units of a security on an issuer register of securities unless he is required to do so—

    (a) by an Operator-instruction;

    (b) by an order of a court in the United Kingdom; or

    (c) by or under an enactment.

(7) A unit of a security is a relevant unit for the purposes of this regulation if, immediately before the transfer in question, it was held by the transferor in uncertificated form.

(8) Subsection (5) of section 183 of the 1985 Act shall apply in relation to a refusal by a participating issuer to register under paragraph (2) a transfer of securities in any of the

circumstances specified in paragraphs (3) and (4), as it applies in relation to a refusal by a company to register a transfer of shares or debentures; and in that subsection as it so applies the reference to the date on which the transfer was lodged with the company shall be taken to be a reference to the date on which the Operator-instruction was received by the participating issuer.

(9) Such sanctions as apply to a company and its officers in the event of a default in complying with subsection (5) of section 183 of the 1985 Act shall apply to a participating issuer and his officers in the event of a default in complying with that subsection as applied by paragraph (8).

[*In reg. 28(4)(d) the Queen's Printer's copy mistakenly has a full point instead of a comma after 'in relation to the Operator-instruction'.*]

Registration to be in accordance with regulations 27 and 28

29.   Any purported registration of a transfer of title to an uncertificated unit of a security other than in accordance with regulation 27 or 28 shall be of no effect.

Registration of linked transfers

30.—(1) Paragraph (2) applies where an Operator receives two or more system-member instructions requesting him to register two or more transfers of title to uncertificated units of a security, and it appears to the Operator—

    (a) either—

        (i)   that there are fewer units of the security registered on an Operator register of securities in the name of a person identified in any of the system-member instructions as a transferor than the number of units to be transferred from him under those system-member instructions; or

        (ii) that it has not been established in accordance with paragraph 21(1)(c) of Schedule 1, in relation to any of the transfers taken without regard to the other transfers, that a settlement bank has agreed to make a payment; and

    (b) that registration of all of the transfers would result in each of the persons identified in the system-member instructions as a transferor having title to a number of uncertificated units of a security equal to or greater than nil; and

    (c) that the combined effect of all the transfers taken together would result in paragraph 21(1)(c) of Schedule 1 being satisfied.

(2) Where this paragraph applies, the Operator may either—

    (a) register the combined effect of all the transfers taken together; or

    (b) register all the transfers simultaneously,

unless one or more of those transfers may not be registered by virtue of the fact that the Operator has actual notice of any of the circumstances specified in regulation 27(2), or is to be refused registration by virtue of regulation 27(4).

(3) Notwithstanding that an Operator has received, in respect of two or more such system-member instructions as are referred to in paragraph (1), actual notice of the kind referred to in paragraph (2), the Operator may register all the transfers in question or their combined effect if at the time that he received the actual notice it was not practicable for him to halt the process of registration.

Position of a transferee prior to entry on an issuer register of securities

31.—(1) Paragraph (2) applies when an Operator deletes an entry on an Operator register of securities in consequence of which—

    (a) the Operator must generate an Operator-instruction in accordance with regulation 27(7); and

    (b) by virtue of that instruction a participating issuer must register, on an issuer register of securities, a transfer of title to units of a participating security constituted under the law of England and Wales or Northern Ireland.

(2) Where this paragraph applies—
   (a) subject to—
      (i) sub-paragraph (b); and
      (ii) any enactment or rule of law,
      the transferor shall, notwithstanding the deletion of the entry in the Operator register of securities, retain title to the requisite number of units of the relevant participating security until the transferee is entered on the relevant issuer register of securities as the holder thereof; and
   (b) the transferee shall acquire an equitable interest in the requisite number of units of that security. . . .

(5) The requisite number for the purposes of this regulation is the number of units which are to be specified in the Operator-instruction which the Operator must generate in accordance with regulation 27(7).

(6) This regulation has effect notwithstanding that the units to which the deletion of the entry in the Operator register of securities relates, or in which an interest arises by virtue of paragraph (2)(b) or (4)(b), or any of them, may be unascertained. . . .

(8) Subject to paragraphs (6) and (7), this regulation shall not be construed as conferring a proprietary interest (whether of the kind referred to in paragraph (2)(b) or (4)(b), or of any other kind) in units of a security if the conferring of such an interest at the time specified in these Regulations would otherwise be void by or under any enactment or rule of law.

(9) In this regulation—
   (a) 'the transferee' means the person to be identified in the Operator-instruction as the transferee; and
   (b) 'the transferor' means the person to be identified in the Operator-instruction as the transferor.

CONVERSIONS AND NEW ISSUES

Conversion of securities into certificated form

32.—(1) Except as provided in regulation 42, a unit of a participating security shall not be converted from uncertificated form into certificated form unless an Operator generates an Operator-instruction to notify the relevant participating issuer that a conversion event has occurred; and in this regulation such an Operator-instruction is referred to as a 'rematerialisation notice'.

(2) A conversion event occurs—
   (a) where such a conversion is permitted by the Operator's conversion rules; or
   (b) following receipt by an Operator of a system-member instruction requiring the conversion into certificated form of uncertificated units of a participating security registered in the name of the system-member; or
   (c) following receipt by an Operator of written notification from a participating issuer which is a company requiring the conversion into certificated form of uncertificated units of a participating security, issued by that participating issuer and registered in the name of a system-member, and which contains a statement that the conversion is required to enable the participating issuer to deal with the units in question in accordance with provisions in that participating issuer's memorandum or articles or in the terms of issue of the units in question.

(3) An Operator—
   (a) may generate a rematerialisation notice following a conversion event occurring in the circumstances specified in paragraph (2)(a);
   (b) shall generate a rematerialisation notice following a conversion event occurring in the circumstances specified in paragraph (2)(b) unless the participation in the relevant system, by the system-member in whose name the uncertificated units in question are registered, has been suspended pursuant to the Operator's rules; and

   (c) shall generate a rematerialisation notice following a conversion event occurring in the circumstances specified in paragraph (2)(c).

(4) On the generation of a rematerialisation notice, the Operator shall delete any entry in an Operator register of securities which shows the relevant system-member as the holder of the unit or units specified in the rematerialisation notice.

(5) On receipt of a rematerialisation notice, the participating issuer to whom the rematerialisation notice is addressed shall, where relevant, enter the name of the system-member on an issuer register of securities as the holder of the unit or units specified in the rematerialisation notice.

(6) During any period between the deletion of any entry in an Operator register of securities required to be made by paragraph (4) and the making of the entry in an issuer register of securities required to be made by paragraph (5)—

   (a) the relevant system-member shall retain title to the units of the security specified in the rematerialisation notice notwithstanding the deletion of any entry in the Operator register of securities; and

   (b) where those units are shares, the relevant system-member shall be deemed to continue to be a member of the company.

(7) Following—

   (a) the making of an entry in an issuer register of securities in accordance with paragraph (5); or

   (b) registration of a transfer of title to units of a security in accordance with regulation 28,

the relevant participating issuer shall, where the terms of issue of the security in question provide for a certificate to be issued, issue a certificate in respect of the units of the security to the relevant person.

(8) Subsection (1)(b) of section 185 of the 1985 Act shall apply in relation to the issue of a certificate by a participating issuer pursuant to paragraph (7) as it applies in relation to the completion and having ready for delivery by a company of share certificates, debentures or certificates of debenture stock; and in that subsection as it so applies the reference to the date on which a transfer is lodged with the company shall be a reference to the date on which the participating issuer receives the relevant rematerialisation notice in accordance with this regulation, or the relevant Operator-instruction in accordance with regulation 27(7).

(9) Such sanctions as apply to a company and its officers in the event of a default in complying with subsection (5) of section 183 of the 1985 Act shall apply—

   (a) to an Operator and his officers in the event of a default in complying with paragraph (4); and

   (b) to a participating issuer and his officers in the event of a default in complying with paragraph (5).

(10) Such sanctions as apply to a company and its officers in the event of a default in complying with subsection (1) of section 185 of the 1985 Act shall apply to a participating issuer and his officers in the event of a default in complying with paragraph (7) in accordance with the requirements laid down in paragraph (8).

Conversion of securities into uncertificated form

33.—(1) A unit of a participating security shall not be converted from certificated form into uncertificated form unless the participating issuer notifies the Operator by means of an issuer-instruction that any of the circumstances specified in paragraph (2) have arisen; and in this regulation such an issuer-instruction is referred to as a 'dematerialisation notice'.

(2) The circumstances referred to in paragraph (1) are—

   (a) where the unit of the participating security is held by a system-member, that the participating issuer has received—

    (i)   a request in writing from the system-member in the form required by the Operator's conversion rules that the unit be converted from certificated form to uncertificated form; and

    (ii) subject to paragraph (4), the certificate relating to that unit; or

  (b) where the unit of the participating security is to be registered on an Operator register of securities in the name of a system-member following a transfer of the unit to him, that the participating issuer—

    (i)   subject to paragraph (3), has received (by means of the Operator-system unless the Operator's conversion rules permit otherwise) a proper instrument of transfer in favour of the system-member relating to the unit to be transferred;

    (ii) subject to paragraph (4), has received (by means of the Operator-system unless the Operator's conversion rules permit otherwise) the certificate relating to that unit; and

    (iii) may accept by virtue of the Operator's conversion rules that the system-member to whom the unit is to be transferred wishes to hold it in uncertificated form.

(3) The requirement in paragraph (2)(b)(i) that the participating issuer shall have received an instrument of transfer relating to the unit of the participating security shall not apply in a case where for a transfer of a unit of that security no instrument of transfer is required.

(4) The requirements in paragraphs (2)(a)(ii) and (2)(b)(ii) that the participating issuer shall have received a certificate relating to the unit of the participating security shall not apply in a case where the system-member or transferor (as the case may be) does not have a certificate in respect of the unit to be converted into uncertificated form because no certificate has yet been issued to him or is due to be issued to him in accordance with the terms of issue of the relevant participating security.

(5) Subject to paragraphs (3) and (4), a participating issuer shall not give a dematerialisation notice except in the circumstances specified in paragraph (2).

(6) Upon giving a dematerialisation notice, a participating issuer shall delete any entry in any issuer register of securities which evidences title to the unit or units of the participating security in question.

(7) Following receipt of a dematerialisation notice, an Operator shall enter the name of the relevant system-member on an Operator register of securities as the holder of the relevant unit or units of the participating security in question, provided that this obligation shall be subject to regulation 27 if the notice was given in the circumstances specified in paragraph (2)(b).

(8) When a dematerialisation notice is given, the relevant system-member, or the transferor of the unit or units of the security in question, as the case may be, shall (without prejudice to any equitable interest which the transferee may have acquired in the unit or units in question)—

  (a) retain title to the units of the security specified in the dematerialisation notice notwithstanding the deletion of any entry in any issuer register of securities required to be made by paragraph (6); and

  (b) where those units are shares, be deemed to continue to be a member of the company.

(9) Where a dematerialisation notice is given in the circumstances specified in paragraph (2)(b), such title shall be retained, and (where appropriate) such membership shall be deemed to continue, until the time at which the Operator enters the name of the relevant system-member on an Operator register of securities in accordance with paragraph (7).

(10) Within 2 months of receiving a dematerialisation notice, an Operator shall generate an Operator-instruction informing the participating issuer whether an entry has been made in an Operator register of securities in response to the dematerialisation notice.

(11) Such sanctions as apply to a company and its officers in the event of a default in complying with subsection (5) of section 183 of the 1985 Act shall apply—

(a) to a participating issuer and his officers in the event of a default in complying with paragraph (6); and

(b) to an Operator and his officers in the event of a default in complying with paragraph (7) or (10).

New issues in uncertificated form

34.—(1) For the purposes of an issue of units of a participating security, a participating issuer may require the Operator to enter the name of a person in an Operator register of securities as the holder of new units of that security in uncertificated form if, and only if, that person is a system-member; and provided that compliance with any such requirement shall be subject to the rules of the Operator.

(2) For the purposes of calculating the number of new units to which a system-member is entitled a participating issuer may treat a system-member's holdings of certificated and uncertificated units of a security as if they were separate holdings.

(3) A requirement made by a participating issuer under paragraph (1) may be made by means of an issuer-instruction and shall specify the names of the persons to be entered in the Operator register of securities as the holders of new uncertificated units of the security, and the number of such units to be issued to each of those persons.

(4) An Operator who receives a requirement made by a participating issuer under paragraph (1) shall notify the participating issuer, by Operator-instruction or in writing, if he has not entered the name of any one or more of the persons in question in the Operator register of securities as the holder of new units of the security.

PART 4   DEMATERIALISED INSTRUCTIONS ETC.

Properly authenticated dematerialised instructions, etc.

35.—(1) This regulation has effect for the purpose of determining the rights and obligations of persons to whom properly authenticated dematerialised instructions are attributable and of persons to whom properly authenticated dematerialised instructions are addressed, when such instructions relate to an uncertificated unit of a security, or relate to a right, benefit or privilege attaching to or arising from such a unit, or relate to the details of a holder of such a unit.

(2) Where a properly authenticated dematerialised instruction is expressed to have been sent on behalf of a person by a sponsoring system-participant or the Operator—

(a) the person on whose behalf the instruction is expressed to have been sent shall not be able to deny to the addressee—

(i) that the properly authenticated dematerialised instruction was sent with his authority; or

(ii) that the information contained in the properly authenticated dematerialised instruction is correct; and

(b) the sponsoring system-participant or the Operator (as the case may be) shall not be able to deny to the addressee—

(i) that he has authority to send the properly authenticated dematerialised instruction; or

(ii) that he has sent the properly authenticated dematerialised instruction.

(3) Where a properly authenticated dematerialised instruction is expressed to have been sent by a person, and the properly authenticated dematerialised instruction is not expressed to have been sent on behalf of another person, the person shall not be able to deny to the addressee—

(a) that the information contained in the properly authenticated dematerialised instruction is correct; or

(b) that he has sent the properly authenticated dematerialised instruction.

(4) An addressee who receives (whether directly, or by means of the facilities of a sponsoring system-participant acting on his behalf) a properly authenticated dematerialised instruction may, subject to paragraph (5), accept that at the time at which the properly authenticated dematerialised instruction was sent or at any time thereafter—

    (a) the information contained in the instruction was correct;

    (b) the system-participant or the Operator (as the case may be) identified in the instruction as having sent the instruction sent the instruction; and

    (c) the instruction, where relevant, was sent with the authority of the person on whose behalf it is expressed to have been sent.

(5) Subject to paragraph (6), an addressee may not accept any of the matters specified in paragraph (4) if at the time he received the properly authenticated dematerialised instruction or at any time thereafter—

    (a) he was a person other than a participating issuer or a sponsoring system-participant receiving properly authenticated dematerialised instructions on behalf of a participating issuer, and he had actual notice—

        (i) that any information contained in it was incorrect;

        (ii) that the system-participant or the Operator (as the case may be) expressed to have sent the instruction did not send the instruction; or

        (iii) where relevant, that the person on whose behalf it was expressed to have been sent had not given to the Operator or the sponsoring system-participant (as the case may be), identified in the properly authenticated dematerialised instruction as having sent it, his authority to send the properly authenticated dematerialised instruction on his behalf; or

    (b) he was a participating issuer, or a sponsoring system-participant receiving properly authenticated dematerialised instructions on behalf of a participating issuer, and—

        (i) he had actual notice from the Operator of any of the matters specified in sub-paragraph (a)(i) to (iii); or

        (ii) if the instruction was an Operator-instruction requiring the registration of a transfer of title, he had actual notice of any of the circumstances specified in regulation 28(3); or

    (c) he was an Operator and the instruction related to a transfer of units of a security which was in excess of any limit imposed by virtue of paragraph 15 of Schedule 1; or

    (d) he was an Operator and he had actual notice of any of the circumstances specified in regulation 27(2) in a case where the instruction was—

        (i) a system-member instruction requesting him to settle a transfer in accordance with his rules; or

        (ii) an issuer-instruction given in the circumstances specified in regulation 33(2)(b) requesting him to register a transfer of title.

(6) Notwithstanding that an addressee has received, in respect of a properly authenticated dematerialised instruction, actual notice of the kind referred to in paragraph (5), the addressee may accept the matters specified in paragraph (4) if at the time that he received the actual notice it was not practicable for him to halt the processing of the instruction.

(7) Subject to paragraph (8), this regulation has effect without prejudice to the liability of any person for causing or permitting a dematerialised instruction—

    (a) to be sent without authority; or

    (b) to contain information which is incorrect; or

    (c) to be expressed to have been sent by a person who did not send it.

(8) Subject to paragraph (9), a person who is permitted by this regulation to accept any matter shall not be liable in damages or otherwise to any person by reason of his having relied on the matter that he was permitted to accept.

(9) The provisions of paragraph (8) do not affect—

    (a) any liability of the Operator to pay compensation under regulation 36; or

    (b) any liability of a participating issuer under regulation 46 arising by reason of a default in complying with, or contravention of, regulation 28(6).

(10) For the purposes of this regulation—

    (a) a properly authenticated dematerialised instruction is expressed to have been sent by a person or on behalf of a person if it is attributable to that person; and

    (b) an addressee is the person to whom a properly authenticated dematerialised instruction indicates it is addressed in accordance with the rules and specifications referred to in paragraph 5(5) of Schedule 1.

(11) Nothing in this regulation shall be taken, in respect of any authority, to modify or derogate from the protections to a donee or third person given by or under any enactment or to prohibit a donee or third person so protected from accepting any of the matters specified in paragraph (4).

(12) Paragraphs (2) to (4), (5)(a), (6) to (9) and (11) of this regulation shall apply in relation to a written notification given under regulation 25(3) or 32(2)(c) as if—

    (a) each reference to a properly authenticated dematerialised instruction were to such a notification which has been authenticated by the Operator in accordance with rules made and practices instituted by the Operator in order to comply with paragraph 25(g) of Schedule 1;

    (b) each reference to information contained in the properly authenticated dematerialised instruction being correct (or incorrect) included, in the case of written notification given under sub-paragraph (c) of regulation 32(2), a reference to any statement of the sort referred to in that sub-paragraph being true (or untrue, as the case may be);

    (c) each reference to an addressee were a reference to the Operator; and

    (d) the reference in paragraph (6) to the processing of the instruction were to acting on the written notification.

Liability for forged dematerialised instructions, induced amendments to Operator registers of securities, and induced Operator-instructions

36.—(1) For the purpose of this regulation—

    (a) a dematerialised instruction is a forged dematerialised instruction if—

      (i) it was not sent from the computers of a system-participant or the computers comprising an Operator-system; or

      (ii) it was not sent from the computers of the system-participant or the computers comprising an Operator-system (as the case may be) from which it is expressed to have been sent;

    (b) an act is a causative act if, not being a dematerialised instruction and not being an act which causes a dematerialised instruction to be sent from the computer of a system-participant, it unlawfully causes the Operator—

      (i) to make, delete or amend an entry on an Operator register of securities; or

      (ii) to send an Operator-instruction to a participating issuer;

    (c) an entry on, deletion from, or amendment to an Operator register of securities is an induced amendment if it is an entry on, deletion from, or amendment to an Operator register of securities which results from a causative act or a forged dematerialised instruction; and

    (d) an Operator-instruction is an induced Operator-instruction if it is an Operator-instruction to a participating issuer which results from a causative act or a forged dematerialised instruction.

(2) If, as a result of a forged dematerialised instruction (not being one which results in an induced amendment to an Operator register of securities or an induced Operator-instruction),

an induced amendment to an Operator register of securities, or an induced Operator-instruction, any one or more of the following events occurs—

(a) the name of any person remains on, is entered on, or is removed or omitted from, a register of securities;

(b) the number of units of a security in relation to which the name of any person is entered on a register of securities is increased, reduced, or remains unaltered;

(c) the description of any units of a security in relation to which the name of any person is entered on a register of securities is changed or remains unaltered,

and that person suffers loss as a result, he may apply to the court for an order that the Operator compensate him for his loss.

(3) It is immaterial for the purposes of sub-paragraphs (a) to (c) of paragraph (2) whether the event is permanent or temporary.

(4) The court shall not make an order under paragraph (2)—

(a) if the Operator identifies a person as being responsible (whether alone or with others) for the forged dematerialised instruction (not being one which results in an induced amendment to an Operator register of securities or an induced Operator-instruction) or the causative act or forged dematerialised instruction resulting in the induced amendment to the Operator register of securities or the induced Operator-instruction (as the case may be) notwithstanding that it is impossible (for whatever reason) for the applicant to obtain satisfactory compensation from that person; or

(b) if the Operator shows that a participating issuer would be liable under regulation 46 to compensate the applicant for the loss in respect of which the application is made, by reason of the participating issuer's default in complying with, or contravention of, regulation 28(6).

(5) Subject to paragraphs (6) and (7), the court may award to an applicant compensation for—

(a) each forged dematerialised instruction (not being one which results in an induced amendment to an Operator register of securities or an induced Operator-instruction);

(b) each induced amendment to an Operator register of securities; and

(c) each induced Operator-instruction,

resulting in an event mentioned in sub-paragraph (a), (b) or (c) of paragraph (2).

(6) The court shall not under paragraph (5) award to an applicant—

(a) more than £50,000 for each such forged dematerialised instruction, induced amendment to an Operator register of securities, or induced Operator-instruction;

(b) compensation for both an induced amendment to an Operator register of securities and an induced Operator-instruction if that induced amendment and that induced Operator-instruction resulted from the same causative act or the same forged dematerialised instruction.

(7) In respect of liability arising under this regulation the court shall—

(a) in awarding compensation only order the Operator to pay such amount of compensation as it appears to it to be just and equitable in all the circumstances having regard to the loss sustained by the applicant as a result of the forged dematerialised instruction, induced amendment to the Operator register of securities, or induced Operator-instruction;

(b) in ascertaining the loss, apply the same rules concerning the duty of a person to mitigate his loss as apply to damages recoverable under the common law of England and Wales, Northern Ireland, or Scotland, (as the case may be); and

(c) where it finds that the loss was to any extent caused or contributed to by any act or omission of the applicant, reduce the amount of the award by such proportion as it thinks just and equitable having regard to that finding.

(8) An application to the court for an order under paragraph (2) shall not prejudice any right of the Operator to recover from a third party any sum that he may be ordered to pay.

(9) An event mentioned in sub-paragraph (a), (b) or (c) of paragraph (2) shall not give rise to any liability on the Operator other than such as is expressly provided for in this regulation, except such as may arise from fraud or other wilful default, or negligence, on the part of the Operator.

(10) Subject to paragraph (9), this regulation does not affect—

(a) any right which any person may have other than under this regulation (not being a right against the Operator); or

(b) any liability which any person other than the Operator may incur other than under this regulation.

(11) Where an application is made under paragraph (2), and the Operator receives from the applicant a request for information or documents relating to—

(a) a forged dematerialised instruction;

(b) an induced amendment to an Operator register of securities; or

(c) an induced Operator-instruction,

in respect of which the application is made, the Operator shall, in so far as he is able, and in so far as the request is reasonable, within one month give the applicant the information and documents.

(12) The applicant shall, in so far as he is able, within one month give the Operator such information or documents as the Operator reasonably requests in connection with an application under paragraph (2) with respect to—

(a) steps taken by the applicant to prevent the giving of any forged dematerialised instruction (whether of the kind referred to in paragraph (2) or of any other kind); and

(b) steps taken by the applicant to mitigate the loss suffered by him,

provided that the applicant need not give information or documents pursuant to this paragraph until the Operator has complied with any request made by virtue of paragraph (11).

(13) Neither the Operator nor the applicant shall be required to disclose any information by virtue of, respectively, paragraph (11) or (12) which would be privileged in the course of civil proceedings, or, in Scotland, which they would be entitled to refuse to disclose—

(a) on grounds of confidentiality as between client and professional legal adviser in proceedings in the Court of Session; or

(b) on grounds of confidentiality of communications made in connection with, or in contemplation of, such proceedings and for the purposes of those proceedings.

(14) The jurisdiction conferred by this regulation shall be exercisable, in the case of a participating security constituted under the law of England and Wales, or Northern Ireland, by the High Court; and in the case of a participating security constituted under the law of Scotland by the Court of Session.

PART 5   MISCELLANEOUS AND SUPPLEMENTAL

MISCELLANEOUS

Construction of references to transfers etc.

37.   References in any enactment or rule of law to a proper instrument of transfer or to a transfer with respect to securities, or any expression having like meaning, shall be taken to include a reference to an Operator-instruction to a participating issuer to register a transfer of title on the relevant issuer register of securities in accordance with the Operator-instruction.

Certain formalities and requirements not to apply

38.—(1) Any requirements in an enactment or rule of law which apply in respect of the transfer of securities otherwise than by means of a relevant system shall not prevent—

    (a) an Operator from registering a transfer of title to uncertificated units of a security upon settlement of a transfer of such units in accordance with his rules; or

    (b) an Operator-instruction from requiring a participating issuer to register a transfer of title to uncertificated units of a security.

(2) Subject to regulation 32(7), notwithstanding any enactment, instrument or rule of law, a participating issuer shall not issue a certificate in relation to any uncertificated units of a participating security.

(3) A document issued by or on behalf of a participating issuer purportedly evidencing title to an uncertificated unit of a participating security shall not be evidence of title to the unit of the security; and in particular—

    (a) section 186 of the 1985 Act shall not apply to any document issued with respect to uncertificated shares; . . .

(4) Any requirement in or under any enactment to endorse any statement or information on a certificate evidencing title to a unit of a security—

    (a) shall not prohibit the conversion into, or issue of, units of the security in uncertificated form; and

    (b) in relation to uncertificated units of the security, shall be taken to be a requirement for the relevant participating issuer to provide the holder of the units with the statement or information on request by him.

(5) Sections 53(1)(c) and 136 of the Law of Property Act 1925 (which impose requirements for certain dispositions and assignments to be in writing) shall not apply (if they would otherwise do so) to—

    (a) any transfer of title to uncertificated units of a security by means of a relevant system; and

    (b) any disposition or assignment of an interest in uncertificated units of a security title to which is held by a relevant nominee.

(6) In paragraph (5) 'relevant nominee' means a subsidiary undertaking of an Operator designated by him as a relevant nominee in accordance with such rules and practices as are mentioned in paragraph 25(f) of Schedule 1.

(7) Subsection (4) of section 183 of the 1985 Act shall not apply in relation to the transfer of uncertificated units of a security by means of a relevant system.

Fees charged by Operators

39.—(1) Subject to paragraph (2), nothing in these Regulations prevents an Operator from charging a fee for carrying out any function under Part 3 of these Regulations.

(2) An Operator may not charge a fee to a participating issuer for maintaining or keeping and entering up an Operator register of securities.

Trusts, trustees and personal representatives etc.

40.—(1) Unless expressly prohibited from transferring units of a security by means of any computer-based system, a trustee or personal representative shall not be chargeable with a breach of trust or, as the case may be, with default in administering the estate by reason only of the fact that—

    (a) for the purpose of acquiring units of a security which he has the power to acquire in connection with the trust or estate, he has paid for the units under arrangements which provide for them to be transferred to him from a system-member but not to be so transferred until after the payment of the price;

    (b) for the purpose of disposing of units of a security which he has power to dispose of in connection with the trust or estate, he has transferred the units to a system-member under arrangements which provide that the price is not to be paid to him until after the transfer is made; or

(c) for the purpose of holding units of a security belonging to the trust or estate in uncertificated form and for transferring title to them by means of a relevant system, he has become a system-member.

(2) Notwithstanding section 192 of the 1985 Act, a trustee of a trust deed for securing an issue of debentures shall not be chargeable with a breach of trust by reason only of the fact that he has assented to an amendment of the trust deed only for the purposes of—

(a) allowing the holding of debentures in uncertificated form;

(b) allowing the exercise of rights attaching to the debentures by means of a relevant system; or

(c) allowing the transfer of title to the debentures by means of a relevant system, provided that he has given or caused to be given notice of the amendment in accordance with the trust deed not less than 30 days prior to its becoming effective to all persons registered as holding the debentures on a date not more than 21 days before the dispatch of the notice.

(3) Without prejudice to regulation 23(3) or section 360 of the 1985 Act, the Operator shall not be bound by or compelled to recognise any express, implied or constructive trust or other interest in respect of uncertificated units of a security, even if he has actual or constructive notice of the said trust or interest. . . .

Notices of meetings etc.

41.—(1) For the purposes of determining which persons are entitled to attend or vote at a meeting, and how many votes such persons may cast, the participating issuer may specify in the notice of the meeting a time, not more than 48 hours before the time fixed for the meeting, by which a person must be entered on the relevant register of securities in order to have the right to attend or vote at the meeting.

(2) Changes to entries on the relevant register of securities after the time specified by virtue of paragraph (1) shall be disregarded in determining the rights of any person to attend or vote at the meeting, notwithstanding any provisions in any enactment, articles of association or other instrument to the contrary.

(3) For the purposes of—

(a) serving notices of meetings, whether under section 370(2) of the 1985 Act, any other enactment, a provision in the articles of association or any other instrument; or

(b) sending copies of the documents required to be sent to any person by section 238 of the 1985 Act,

a participating issuer may determine that persons entitled to receive such notices, or copies of such documents (as the case may be), are those persons entered on the relevant register of securities at the close of business on a day determined by him.

(4) The day determined by a participating issuer under paragraph (3) may not be more than 21 days before the day that the notices of the meeting, or the copies of the documents as the case may be, are sent.

(5) This regulation is without prejudice to the protection afforded—

(a) by paragraph 5(3) of Schedule 4, to a participating issuer which is a company; and

(b) by paragraph 13(4) or 15(3) of Schedule 4, to a participating issuer.

Notices to minority shareholders

42.—(1) Paragraphs (2) to (4) shall apply in relation to any uncertificated units of a security (other than a wholly dematerialised security) to which a notice given under section 429 of the 1985 Act relates, in place of the provisions of section 430(6) of that Act.

(2) Immediately on receipt of a copy sent under section 430(5)(a) of the 1985 Act of a notice given under section 429 relating to uncertificated units of a participating security

(whether or not it also relates to certificated units of the security), a company which is a participating issuer shall—
  (a) by issuer-instruction—
      (i) inform the Operator that the copy notice has been received, and
      (ii) identify the holding of uncertificated units of the participating security to which the notice relates; and
  (b) enter the name of the relevant system-member on an issuer register of securities as the holder of those uncertificated units.

(3) On receipt of an issuer-instruction under paragraph (2)(a), the Operator shall delete any entry in an Operator register of securities which shows the relevant system-member as the holder of the uncertificated units of the participating security to which the notice relates.

(4) On registration on an issuer register of securities (in accordance with paragraph (2)(b)) of the relevant system-member as the holder of the uncertificated units of the participating security to which the notice relates, the participating issuer—
  (a) shall be under the same obligation to enter the offeror on that register as the holder of those units, in place of the relevant system-member, as it would be if it had received an Operator-instruction under regulation 28(2) requiring it to register a transfer of title to those units in that manner; and regulation 28(9) shall have effect accordingly; and
  (b) where the terms of issue of the security in question provide for a certificate to be issued, shall issue to the offeror a certificate in respect of those units.

(5) Subsection (1)(b) of section 185 of the 1985 Act shall apply in relation to the issue of a certificate by a participating issuer pursuant to paragraph (4)(b) as it applies in relation to the completion and having ready for delivery by a company of share certificates, debentures or certificates of debenture stock; and in that subsection as it so applies the reference to the date on which a transfer is lodged with the company shall be a reference to the date on which the participating issuer receives the copy notice sent under section 430(5)(a) of the 1985 Act.

(6) Such sanctions as apply to a company and its officers in the event of a default in complying with subsection (1) of section 185 of the 1985 Act shall apply to a participating issuer and his officers in the event of a default in complying with paragraph (4)(b) in accordance with the requirements laid down in paragraph (5).

(7) Paragraphs (8) to (11) shall apply in relation to any units of a wholly dematerialised security to which a notice given under section 429 of the 1985 Act relates, in place of the provisions of section 430(6) of that Act.

(8) Immediately on receipt of a copy sent under section 430(5)(a) of the 1985 Act of a notice given under section 429 relating to units of a wholly dematerialised security, a company which is a participating issuer shall—
  (a) by issuer-instruction—
      (i) inform the Operator that the copy notice has been received; and
      (ii) identify the holding of units of the wholly dematerialised security to which the notice relates; and
  (b) by a further issuer-instruction, inform the Operator of the name of the transferee.

(9) On receipt of an issuer-instruction under paragraph (8)(a), the Operator shall delete any entry in an Operator register of securities which shows the relevant system-member as the holder of the units to which the notice relates.

(10) On receipt of an issuer-instruction under paragraph (8)(b), the Operator shall enter the transferee on the relevant Operator register of securities as the holder of the units to which the notice relates, in place of the relevant system-member.

(11) Where an Operator deletes an entry in an Operator register of securities pursuant to paragraph (9)—
  (a) the units of the wholly dematerialised security to which the notice relates shall notwithstanding that deletion, continue to be regarded as uncertificated units for

the purposes of these Regulations until the Operator enters the transferee on the relevant Operator register of securities as the holder of those units;

(b) subject to—

(i) sub-paragraph (c) or (d), as the case may be; and

(ii) any enactment or rule of law,

the relevant system-member shall, notwithstanding that deletion, retain title to the units of the wholly dematerialised security to which the notice relates until the transferee is entered on the relevant Operator register of securities pursuant to paragraph (10);

(c) in the case of a security constituted under the law of England and Wales or Northern Ireland, the transferee shall acquire an equitable interest in the units of the wholly dematerialised security to which the notice relates;

(d) in the case of a security constituted under the law of Scotland, the relevant system-member shall hold the units of the wholly dematerialised security to which the notice relates on trust for the benefit of the transferee.

(12) Such sanctions as apply to a company and its officers in the event of a default in complying with subsection (5) of section 183 of the 1985 Act shall apply—

(a) to a participating issuer and his officers in the event of a default in complying with paragraph (2)(b) or (8); and

(b) to an Operator and his officers in the event of a default in complying with paragraph (3), (9) or (10).

(13) For the purposes of this regulation—

(a) 'offeror' has the meaning given by section 428(8) of the 1985 Act as construed in accordance with section 430D(5) of that Act;

(b) 'relevant system-member' means the system-member identified in the copy notice sent under section 430(5)(a) of the 1985 Act as the holder of the uncertificated units, or as the case may be the units of the wholly dematerialised security, to which the notice relates; and

(c) 'transferee' means the offeror or, if the offeror is not a system-member, the system-member in whose name the units of the wholly dematerialised security to which the notice given under section 429 of the 1985 Act relates are to be registered on the Operator register of securities.

(14) The reference in section 430D(5) of the 1985 Act to section 430(6) shall be taken to include a reference to the provisions of paragraphs (4), (8) and (9).

Irrevocable powers of attorney

43.—(1) This regulation applies where the terms of an offer for all or any uncertificated units of a participating security provide that a person accepting the offer creates an irrevocable power of attorney in favour of the offeror, or a person nominated by the offeror, in the terms set out in the offer.

(2) An acceptance communicated by properly authenticated dematerialised instruction in respect of uncertificated units of a security shall constitute a grant of an irrevocable power of attorney by the system-member accepting the offer in favour of the offeror, or person nominated by the offeror, in the terms set out in the offer.

(3) Where the contract constituted by such offer and acceptance as are referred to in paragraphs (1) and (2) respectively is governed by the law of England and Wales, section 4 of the Powers of Attorney Act 1971 shall apply to a power of attorney constituted in accordance with this regulation.

(4) A declaration in writing by the offeror stating the terms of a power of attorney and that it has been granted by virtue of this regulation and stating the name and address of the grantor shall be prima facie evidence, and in Scotland sufficient evidence unless the contrary is shown, of the grant; and any requirement in any enactment, rule of law, or instrument to produce a

copy of the power of attorney, or such a copy certified in a particular manner, shall be satisfied by the production of the declaration or a copy of the declaration certified in that manner. . . .

Actual notice

44. For the purpose of determining under these Regulations whether a person has actual notice of a fact, matter or thing that person shall not under any circumstances be taken to be concerned to establish whether or not it exists or has occurred.

Participating securities issued in uncertificated form

45. Nothing in these Regulations shall require—

(a) a participating issuer or its officers to maintain a register which records how many units of a wholly dematerialised security are held in certificated form; or

(b) an Operator or participating issuer, or their officers, to take any action to change a unit of a wholly dematerialised security from uncertificated form to certificated form or vice versa.

DEFAULTS AND CONTRAVENTIONS

Breaches of statutory duty

46.—(1) A default in complying with, or a contravention of, regulation 16(8), 19(2), 25(1), 26, 28(5) or (6), 32(5), 33(5), or 42(2) or (8) shall be actionable at the suit of a person who suffers loss as a result of the default or contravention, or who is otherwise adversely affected by it, subject to the defences and other incidents applying to actions for breach of statutory duty.

(2) Paragraph (1) shall not affect the liability which any person may incur, nor affect any right which any person may have, apart from paragraph (1).

Liability of officers for contraventions

47.—(1) In regulation 16(7), 20(7), 21(5), 22(5), 28(9), 32(9) or (10), 33(11) or 42(6) or (12) an officer of a participating issuer shall be in default in complying with, or in contravention of, the provision mentioned in that regulation if, and only if, he knowingly and wilfully authorised or permitted the default or contravention.

(2) In regulation 20(7), 21(4), 22(4), 27(9), 32(9), 33(11) or 42(12) an officer of an Operator shall be in default in complying with, or in contravention of, the provision mentioned in that regulation if, and only if, he knowingly and wilfully authorised or permitted the default or contravention.

Exemption from liability

48. Regulations 21(5), 28(9), 32(9) and (10), and 33(11) shall not apply to any of the following or its officers—

(a) the Crown;

(b) any person acting on behalf of the Crown;

(c) the Bank of England; or

(d) in respect of a security which immediately before it became a participating security was transferable by exempt transfer within the meaning of the Stock Transfer Act 1982, a participating issuer.

SCHEDULE 1 REQUIREMENTS FOR APPROVAL OF A PERSON AS OPERATOR

[schedule introduced by reg. 5(1)]

Arrangements and resources

1. An Operator must have adequate arrangements and resources for the effective monitoring and enforcement of compliance with his rules or, as respects monitoring, arrangements

providing for that function to be performed on his behalf (and without affecting his responsibility) by another body or person who is able and willing to perform it.

Financial resources

2.   An Operator must have financial resources sufficient for the proper performance of his functions as an Operator.

Promotion and maintenance of standards

3.   An Operator must be able and willing to promote and maintain high standards of integrity and fair dealing in the operation of the relevant system and to cooperate, by the sharing of information or otherwise, with the Treasury and any other authority, body or person having responsibility for the supervision or regulation of investment business or other financial services.

Operation of the relevant system

4.—(1) Except in the circumstances referred to in sub-paragraph (2), where an Operator causes or permits a part of the relevant system which is not the Operator-system to be operated by another person (other than as his agent) the Operator—

  (a) shall monitor compliance by the person and that part with the requirements of this Schedule; and

  (b) shall have arrangements to ensure that the person provides him with such information and such assistance as he may require in order to meet his obligations under these Regulations.

(2) Where a part of the relevant system which is not the Operator-system comprises procedures which enable dematerialised instructions to be authenticated in accordance with paragraph 5(3)(b), the Operator shall have arrangements to ensure that he is provided with such information and such assistance as he may require in order to keep under review his agreement to the specifications by which those dematerialised instructions may be authenticated.

System security

5.—(1) A relevant system must be so constructed and operate in such a way that it satisfies the requirements of sub-paragraphs (2) to (6).

(2) The relevant system must minimise the possibility of unauthorised access to, or modification of, any program or data held in any computer forming part of the Operator-system.

(3) Each dematerialised instruction must be authenticated—

  (a) in accordance with the specifications of the Operator, and those specifications shall provide that each dematerialised instruction—

      (i) is identifiable as being from the computers of the Operator or of a particular system-participant; and

      (ii) is designed to minimise fraud and forgery; or

  (b) if it is sent to the Operator by, or by the Operator to, a depositary, a clearing house or an exchange, in accordance with specifications of that depositary, clearing house or exchange to which the Operator has agreed and which provide that each dematerialised instruction—

      (i) is identifiable as being from the computers of the Operator or of the depositary, clearing house or exchange which sent it; and

      (ii) is designed to minimise fraud and forgery.

(4) Each dematerialised instruction must, in accordance with any relevant rules of

the Operator and with the specifications of the Operator or the specifications referred to in sub-paragraph (3)(b) (as the case may be), express by whom it has been sent and, where relevant, on whose behalf it has been sent.

(5) Each dematerialised instruction must, in accordance with any relevant rules of the Operator and with the specifications of the Operator or the specifications referred to in sub-paragraph (3)(b) (as the case may be), indicate—

(a) where it is sent to a system-participant or the Operator, that it is addressed to that system-participant or the Operator;

(b) where it is sent to a person who is using the facilities of a sponsoring system-participant to receive dematerialised instructions, that it is addressed to that person and the sponsoring system-participant; and

(c) where it is sent to the Operator in order for him to send an Operator-instruction to a system-participant, that it is addressed to the Operator, to the system-participant and, if the system-participant is acting as a sponsoring system-participant, to the relevant person on whose behalf the sponsoring system-participant receives dematerialised instructions [.]

(6) The relevant system must minimise the possibility for a system-participant to send a dematerialised instruction on behalf of a person from whom he has no authority.

(7) For the purposes of this paragraph—

'clearing house' means a body or association—

(a) which is a recognised clearing house within section 285(1)(b) of the 2000 Act;

(b) which is authorised under that Act to provide clearing services in the United Kingdom; or

(c) which provides services outside the United Kingdom which are similar in nature to those provided by any such body or association, and which is regulated or supervised in the provision of those services by a regulatory body or agency of government;

'depositary' means a body or association carrying on business outside the United Kingdom with whom an Operator has made arrangements—

(a) to enable system-members to hold (whether directly or indirectly) and transfer title to securities (other than participating securities) by means of facilities provided by that body or association; or

(b) to enable that body or association to permit persons to whom it provides services in the course of its business to hold (whether directly or indirectly) and transfer title to participating securities by means of the Operator's relevant system; and

'exchange' means a body or association—

(a) which is a recognised investment exchange within section 285(1)(a) of the 2000 Act;

(b) which is authorised under that Act to provide a facility for the matching and execution of transactions in securities in the United Kingdom; or

(c) which provides services outside the United Kingdom which are similar in nature to those provided by any such body or association, and which is regulated or supervised in the provision of those services by a regulatory body or agency of government

[*In sch. 1, para. 5(5), the Queen's Printer's copy has '; and' instead of a full point at the end of sub-para. (c).*]

System capabilities

6.   A relevant system must ensure that the Operator-system can send and respond to properly authenticated dematerialised instructions in sufficient volume and speed.

7.   Before an Operator registers a transfer of title to uncertificated units of a security, a relevant system must be able to establish—
   (a) that the transferor has title to such number of units of the security as is in aggregate at least equal to the number to be transferred; or
   (b) that the transfer is one of two or more transfers which may be registered in accordance with regulation 30(2).

8.   Before an Operator-instruction to a participating issuer to register a transfer of title to uncertificated units of a security is generated, a relevant system must be able to establish that the transferor has title to such number of units of the security as is in aggregate at least equal to the number to be transferred.

9.   A relevant system must enable an Operator to comply with his obligations to keep all necessary Operator registers of securities in accordance with these Regulations.

10.   A relevant system must maintain adequate records of all dematerialised instructions.

11.   A relevant system must—
   (a) enable each system-member to obtain a copy of any records relating to him as are maintained by the relevant system in order to comply with paragraph 7(a), 8 or 10; and
   (b) be able to make correcting entries in such records as are maintained in order to comply with paragraph 7(a) or 8 which are inaccurate.

12.   A relevant system must be able to permit each participating issuer to inspect the entries from time to time appearing in an Operator register of securities relating to any participating security issued by him.

13.   A relevant system must be able to establish, where there is a transfer of uncertificated units of a security to a system-member for value, that a settlement bank has agreed to make payment in respect of the transfer, whether alone or taken together with another transfer for value.

14.   A relevant system must ensure that the Operator-system is able to generate Operator-instructions—
   (a) requiring participating issuers to amend the appropriate issuer registers of securities kept by them;
   (b) informing participating issuers in a way which enables them to amend the appropriate records of securities kept by them; and
   (c) informing settlement banks of their payment obligations.

15.   A relevant system must—
   (a) enable a system-member—
       (i) to grant authority to a sponsoring system-participant to send properly authenticated dematerialised instructions on his behalf; and
       (ii) to limit such authority by reference to the net value of the units of the securities to be transferred in any one day; and
   (b) prevent the transfer of units in excess of that limit.

16.   For the purposes of paragraph 15(a)(ii), once authority is granted pursuant to a system charge (within the meaning of regulation 3 of the Financial Markets and Insolvency Regulations 1996) a limit of such authority shall not be imposed or changed without the consent of the donee of that authority.

17.   Nothing in paragraph 15 or 16 shall be taken, in respect of an authority, to modify or derogate from the protections given by or under any enactment to a donee of the authority or a third person.

18.   A relevant system must enable system-members—
   (a) to change the form in which they hold units of a participating security; and
   (b) where appropriate, to require participating issuers to issue certificates relating to units of a participating security held or to be held by them.

19.   Paragraph 18 shall not apply to any wholly dematerialised security.

Operating procedures

20. A relevant system must comprise procedures which provide that it responds only to properly authenticated dematerialised instructions which are attributable to a system-user or an Operator.

21.—(1) Subject to sub-paragraphs (2) to (5), a relevant system must comprise procedures which provide that an Operator only registers a transfer of title to uncertificated units of a security or generates an Operator-instruction requiring a participating issuer to register such a transfer, and only generates an Operator-instruction informing a settlement bank of its payment obligations in respect of such a transfer, if—

  (a) it has—
    (i) received a system-member instruction which is attributable to the transferor; or
    (ii) been required to do so by a court in the United Kingdom or by or under an enactment;
  (b) it has—
    (i) established that the transferor has title to such number of units as is in aggregate at least equal to the number to be transferred; or
    (ii) established that the transfer is one of two or more transfers which may be registered in accordance with regulation 30(2);
  (c) in the case of a transfer to a system-member for value, it has established that a settlement bank has agreed to make payment in respect of the transfer, whether alone or taken together with another transfer for value; and
  (d) the transfer is not in excess of any limit which by virtue of paragraph 15(a)(ii) the transferor has set on an authority given by him to a sponsoring system-participant.

(2) Sub-paragraph (1)(a) shall not prevent the registration by an Operator of a transfer of title to uncertificated units of a security, or the generation of an Operator-instruction, in accordance with procedures agreed between the Operator and the transferor to enable the transfer by means of a relevant system of uncertificated units of a security provided that such transfer is for the purpose of, or relates to, facilitating the provision of financial credit or financial liquidity to the transferor by a settlement bank, the Bank of England, the European Central Bank, any other central bank, or any other body having functions as a monetary authority.

(3) A relevant system must comprise procedures which provide that—

  (a) the Operator may amend an Operator register of securities; and
  (b) an Operator-instruction requiring a participating issuer to register a transfer of uncertificated units of a security, or informing a settlement bank of its payment obligations in respect of such a transfer, may be generated,

if necessary to correct an error and if in accordance with the rules made and practices instituted by the Operator in order to comply with this Schedule.

(4) A relevant system must comprise procedures which provide that—

  (a) the Operator may amend an Operator register of securities; and
  (b) an Operator-instruction requiring a participating issuer to register a transfer of units of a wholly dematerialised security, or informing a settlement bank of its payment obligations in respect of such a transfer, may be generated,

if necessary to effect a transfer of such units, on the termination of participation in the relevant system by the system-member by whom those units are held and if in accordance with the rules made and practices instituted by the Operator in order to comply with this Schedule, to a person nominated under the Operator's rules.

(5) Sub-paragraph (1)(a) shall not prevent the registration by an Operator of a transfer of title to uncertificated units of a security, or the generation of an Operator-instruction, in order to give effect to the procedures referred to in sub-paragraph (3) or (4).

22.—(1) Subject to sub-paragraph (2), a relevant system must comprise procedures which provide that an Operator-instruction to a participating issuer relating to a right, privilege or benefit attaching to or arising from an uncertificated unit of a security, is generated only if it has—

    (a) received a properly authenticated dematerialised instruction attributable to the system-member having the right, privilege or benefit requiring the Operator to generate an Operator-instruction to the participating issuer; or

    (b) been required to do so by a court in the United Kingdom or by or under an enactment.

    (2) A relevant system must comprise procedures which provide that an Operator-instruction to a participating issuer relating to a right, privilege or benefit attaching to or arising from an uncertificated unit of a security, may be generated if necessary to correct an error and if in accordance with the rules made and practices instituted by an Operator in order to comply with this Schedule.

    23.   A relevant system must comprise procedures which ensure that, where participating issuers keep records of securities, those records are regularly reconciled with the relevant Operator registers of securities.

    24.   A relevant system must comprise procedures which—

    (a) enable system-users to notify the Operator of an error in or relating to a dematerialised instruction; and

    (b) ensure that, where the Operator becomes aware of an error in or relating to a dematerialised instruction, he takes appropriate corrective action.

Rules and practices

    25.   An Operator's rules and practices—

    (a) must bind system-members and participating issuers—

      (i) so as to ensure the efficient processing of transfers of title to uncertificated units of a security in response to Operator-instructions; and

      (ii) as to the action to be taken where transfer of title in response to a system-member instruction or an Operator-instruction cannot be effected;

    (b) must make provision as to the manner in which a system-member or the relevant participating issuer may change the form in which that system-member holds units of a participating security (other than a wholly dematerialised security);

    (c) must make provision for a participating issuer to cease to participate in respect of a participating security so as—

      (i) to minimise so far as practicable any disruption to system-members in respect of their ability to transfer the relevant security; and

      (ii) to provide the participating issuer with any relevant information held by the Operator relating to the uncertificated units of the relevant security held by system-members;

    (d) must make provision for the orderly termination of participation by system-members and system-participants whose participation is disruptive to other system-members or system-participants or to participating issuers;

    (e) must make provision—

      (i) as to which of the Operator's records are to constitute an Operator register of securities in relation to a participating security, or a participating security of a particular kind; and

      (ii) as to the times at which, and the manner in which, a participating issuer may inspect an Operator register of securities in accordance with paragraph 12;

    (f) if they make provision for the designation of a subsidiary undertaking as a relevant nominee, must require that the relevant nominee maintain adequate records of—

      (i) the names of the persons who have an interest in the securities it holds; and

      (ii) the nature and extent of their interests; and

(g) must make provision for the authentication by the Operator of any written notification given under regulation 25(3) or 32(2)(c).

26. An Operator's rules and practices must require—

(a) that each system-participant is able to send and receive properly authenticated dematerialised instructions;

(b) that each system-member has arrangements—

(i) for properly authenticated dematerialised instructions attributable to him to be sent;

(ii) for properly authenticated dematerialised instructions to be received by or for him; and

(iii) with a settlement bank for payments to be made, where appropriate, for units of a security transferred by means of the relevant system; and

(c) that each participating issuer is able to respond with sufficient speed to Operator-instructions.

27. An Operator must have rules which require system-users and former system-users to provide him with such information in their possession as he may require in order to meet his obligations under these Regulations.

SCHEDULE 4   KEEPING OF REGISTERS AND RECORDS OF PARTICIPATING SECURITIES

[schedule introduced by reg. 23(4)]

Interpretation

1. In this Schedule—

'uncertificated shares' means shares title to which may be transferred by means of a relevant system; and

'certificated shares' means shares which are not uncertificated shares; and 'uncertificated stock' means stock title to which may be transferred by means of a relevant system; and 'certificated stock' means stock which is not uncertificated stock.

2.—(1) Every participating issuer which is a company shall enter in its issuer register of members—

(a) the names and addresses of the members;

(b) the date on which each person was registered as a member; and

(c) the date at which any person ceased to be a member.

(2) With the names and addresses of the members there shall be entered a statement—

(a) of the certificated shares held by each member, distinguishing each share by its number (so long as the share has a number) and, where the company has more than one class of issued shares, by its class; and

(b) of the amount paid or agreed to be considered as paid on the certificated shares of each member.

(3) Where the company has converted any of its shares into stock and given notice of the conversion to the registrar of companies, the issuer register of members shall show the amount and class of the certificated stock held by each member, instead of the amount of shares and the particulars relating to shares specified in sub-paragraph (2).

(4) Subject to sub-paragraph (5), section 352 of the 1985 Act shall not apply to a company which is a participating issuer, other than as respects any overseas branch register.

(5) Section 352(5) of the 1985 Act shall apply to a participating issuer which is a company which makes default in complying with this paragraph and every officer of it who is in default as if such a default were a default in complying with section 352 of the Act.

(6) An entry relating to a former member of the company may be removed from the

issuer register of members after the expiration of 20 years beginning with the day on which he ceased to be a member.

(7) For the purposes of this paragraph references to an issuer register of members shall not be taken to include an overseas branch register.

3.   Section 352A of the 1985 Act shall apply to a participating issuer which is a private company limited by shares as if references therein to the company's register of members were references to its issuer register of members.

4.—(1) In relation to every participating issuer which is a company, an Operator of a relevant system shall, in respect of any class of shares which is a participating security for the purposes of that system, enter on an Operator register of members—

(a) the names and addresses of the members who hold uncertificated shares in the company;

(b) with those names and addresses a statement of the uncertificated shares held by each member and, where the company has more than one class of issued uncertificated shares, distinguishing each share by its class; and

(c) where the company has converted any of its shares into stock and given notice of the conversion to the registrar of companies, the Operator register of members shall show the amount and class of uncertificated stock held by each member, instead of the amount of shares and the particulars relating to shares specified in sub-paragraph (b).

(2) An entry relating to a member of a company who has ceased to hold any uncertificated shares in the company may be removed from the Operator register of members after the expiration of 20 years beginning with the day on which he ceased to hold any such shares.

(3) For the purposes of this paragraph references to an Operator register of members shall not be taken to include an overseas branch register.

(4) Members of a company who hold shares in uncertificated form may not be entered as holders of those shares on an overseas branch register.

Records of uncertificated shares

5.—(1) Every participating issuer which is a company shall enter in its record of uncertificated shares—

(a) the same particulars, so far as practicable, as are required by paragraph 4(1) to be entered in the Operator register of members; and

(b) a statement of the amount paid or agreed to be considered as paid on the uncertificated shares of each member.

(2) A company to which this paragraph applies shall, unless it is impracticable to do so by virtue of circumstances beyond its control, ensure that the record of uncertificated shares is regularly reconciled with the Operator register of members.

(3) Provided that it has complied with sub-paragraph (2), a company shall not be liable in respect of any act or thing done or omitted to be done by or on behalf of the company in reliance upon the assumption that the particulars entered in any record of uncertificated shares which the company is required to keep by these Regulations accord with the particulars entered in its Operator register of members.

(4) Section 352(5) of the 1985 Act shall apply to a participating issuer which is a company which makes default in complying with this paragraph and every officer of it who is in default as if such a default were a default in complying with section 352 of that Act.

Location of issuer register of members and records of uncertificated shares, and ancillary matters

6.—(1) Subject to sub-paragraph (2), a company's issuer register of members and its record of uncertificated shares shall be kept at its registered office, except that—

(a) if the work of making up the issuer register of members or the record of uncertificated shares is done at another office of the company, they may be kept there; and

(b) if the company arranges with some other person for the making up of the issuer register of members or the record of uncertificated shares to be undertaken on its behalf by that other, they may be kept at the office of the other at which the work is done;

but the issuer register of members must not be kept, in the case of a company registered in England and Wales, at any place elsewhere than in England and Wales or, in the case of a company registered in Scotland, at any place elsewhere than in Scotland.

(2) A company's issuer register of members and its record of uncertificated shares shall at all times be kept at the same place.

(3) Subject as follows, every participating issuer which is a company shall send notice in the prescribed form to the registrar of companies of the place where its issuer register of members and its record of uncertificated shares are kept, and of any change in that place, provided that any notice sent by such a company in accordance with section 353(2) of the 1985 Act, and which has effect on the coming into force of these Regulations, shall be treated as being a notice sent in compliance with this sub-paragraph.

(4) The notice need not be sent if the issuer register of members and the record of uncertificated shares have at all times since they came into existence been kept at the company's registered office.

(5) Subject to sub-paragraph (6), sections 353 and 357 of the 1985 Act shall not apply to a company which is a participating issuer.

(6) Section 353(4) of the 1985 Act shall apply to a participating issuer which is a company which makes default in complying with sub-paragraph (2) at any time, or makes default for 14 days in complying with sub-paragraph (3), and every officer of it who is in default as if such a default were a default in complying with section 353(2) of that Act.

7.—(1) Every participating issuer which is a company having more than 50 members shall, unless the particulars required by paragraph 2(1) to be entered in the issuer register of members are kept in such a form as to constitute in themselves an index, keep an index of the names of the members of the company and shall, within 14 days after the date on which any alteration is made in the issuer register of members or the Operator register of members, make any necessary alteration in the index.

(2) The index shall in respect of each member contain a sufficient indication to enable the account of that member in the issuer register of members and, in the case of a member who holds uncertificated shares in the company, in the record of uncertificated shares, to be readily found.

(3) The index shall be at all times kept at the same place as the issuer register of members and the record of uncertificated shares.

(4) Subject to sub-paragraph (5), section 354 of the 1985 Act shall not apply to a company which is a participating issuer.

(5) Section 354(4) of the 1985 Act shall apply to a participating issuer which is a company which makes default in complying with this paragraph and every officer of it who is in default as if such a default were a default in complying with section 354 of that Act.

8. Section 355 of the 1985 Act shall apply to a company which is a participating issuer as if references in that section to the company's register of members were references instead to its issuer register of members.

9. Section 356 of, and paragraph 25 of Schedule 13 to, the 1985 Act shall apply to a company which is a participating issuer as if—

(a) references in those provisions to the company's register of members were references to its issuer register of members and its record of uncertificated shares; and

    (b) references in section 356 to the company's index of members were references to the index required to be kept by paragraph 7,

and references to the 1985 Act in the Companies (Inspection and Copying of Registers, Indices and Documents) Regulations 1991 shall be construed accordingly.

    10. Where under paragraph 6(1)(b), a company's issuer register of members and record of uncertificated shares is kept at the office of some person other than the company, and by reason of any default of his the company fails to comply with—

    paragraph 6(2) (record of uncertificated shares to be kept with issuer register of members);

    paragraph 6(3) (notice to registrar);

    paragraph 7(3) (index to be kept with issuer register of members and record of uncertificated shares); or

    section 356 of the 1985 Act (inspection),

or with any requirement of the 1985 Act as to the production of the register of members or any part thereof, that other person is liable to the same penalties as if he were an officer of the company who was in default, and the power of the court under section 356(6) of the 1985 Act extends to the making of orders against that other and his officers and servants.

    11. Where, under section 359 of the 1985 Act, the court orders rectification of the register of members of a company which is a participating issuer, it shall not order the payment of any damages under subsection (2) of that section to the extent that such rectification relates to the company's Operator register of members and does not arise from an act or omission of the Operator on the instructions of that company or from fraud or other wilful default, or negligence, on the part of that company.

Registers of corporate securities

    14.—(1) Where an Operator of a relevant system is required to maintain an Operator register of corporate securities, that register shall comprise the following particulars which the Operator shall enter on it, namely—

    (a) the names and addresses of the persons holding units of the relevant participating security in uncertificated form; and

    (b) how many units of that security each such person holds in that form.

    (2) Sections 190 and 191 of the 1985 Act shall not apply to any part of an Operator register of corporate securities.

Records of uncertificated corporate securities

    15.—(1) A participating issuer shall enter in a record of uncertificated corporate securities the same particulars, so far as practicable, as are required by paragraph 14(1) to be entered in the relevant Operator register of corporate securities.

    (2) A participating issuer to which this paragraph applies shall, unless it is impracticable to do so by virtue of circumstances beyond its control, ensure that the record of uncertificated corporate securities is regularly reconciled with the Operator register of corporate securities.

    (3) Provided that it has complied with sub-paragraph (2), a participating issuer shall not be liable in respect of any act or thing done or omitted to be done by it or on its behalf in reliance upon the assumption that the particulars entered in any record of uncertificated corporate securities which the participating issuer is required to keep by these Regulations accord with particulars entered in any Operator register of corporate securities relating to it.

    (4) In the case of a participating issuer which is a company, the record of uncertificated corporate securities shall be kept at the same place as the part of any register of debenture holders maintained by the company would be required to be kept.

    (5) Section 191(1), (2), (4) and (5) of the 1985 Act shall apply in relation to a record of uncertificated corporate securities maintained by a participating issuer which is a company, so far as that record relates to debentures, as it applies or would apply to any register of debenture

holders maintained by the company; and references to the 1985 Act in the Companies (Inspection and Copying of Registers, Indices and Documents) Regulations 1991 shall be construed accordingly.

(6) Any provision of an enactment or instrument which requires a register of persons holding securities (other than shares or public sector securities) to be open to inspection shall also apply to the record of uncertificated corporate securities relating to any units of those securities which are participating securities.

Miscellaneous

16.—(1) Every register which an Operator is required to maintain by virtue of these Regulations shall be kept in the United Kingdom.

(2) Provided that it is kept in the United Kingdom, any such register which relates to securities issued by a company shall be deemed to be kept—
  (a) in the case of a company registered in England and Wales, in England and Wales; or
  (b) in the case of a company registered in Scotland, in Scotland.

17.—(1) An entry in a register of securities or in a record of securities relating to a person who no longer holds the securities which are the subject of the entry may be removed from the register or the record (as the case may be) after the expiration of 20 years beginning with the day on which the person ceased to hold any of those securities.

(2) Sub-paragraph (1) does not apply in respect of an entry in a register of members.

18. Sections 722 and 723(1) and (2) of the 1985 Act shall apply—
  (a) to any register, record or index required to be kept by any person in accordance with these Regulations as they apply to any register, record or index required by the Companies Acts to be kept by a company; and
  (b) to an Operator and its officers as they apply to a company and its officers.

19.—(1) Such sanctions as apply to a company and its officers in the event of a default in complying with section 352 of the 1985 Act shall apply to an Operator and his officers in the event of a default in complying with paragraph 4, 12 or 14. . . .

(3) Such sanctions as apply in the event of a default in complying with the requirement to maintain a register imposed by the relevant enactment or instrument referred to in Regulation 22(1) shall apply to—
  (a) a participating issuer other than a company; and
  (b) a participating issuer which is a company, in relation to so much of the record of uncertificated corporate securities as does not relate to debentures,
and his officers in the event of a default in complying with paragraph 15.

(4) Sub-paragraphs (2) and (3) shall not apply to any of the following or its officers—
  (a) the Crown;
  (b) any person acting on behalf of the Crown;
  (c) the Bank of England; or
  (d) in respect of a security which immediately before it became a participating security was transferable by exempt transfer within the meaning of the Stock Transfer Act 1982, a participating issuer.

20. An officer of a participating issuer shall be in default in complying with, or in contravention of paragraph 2, 5, 6, 7, 13 or 15, or section 722(2) of the 1985 Act as applied by paragraph 18, if, and only if, he knowingly and wilfully authorised or permitted the default or contravention.

21. An officer of an Operator shall be in default in complying with, or in contravention of, the provisions referred to in paragraph 19(1) of this Schedule, or of section 722(2) of the 1985 Act as applied by paragraph 18, if, and only if, he knowingly and wilfully authorised or permitted the default or contravention.

Companies (Particulars of Usual Residential Address) (Confidentiality Orders) Regulations 2002

(2002 No. 912)

The Secretary of State, in exercise of the powers conferred on her by sections 723B to E of the Companies Act 1985 and of all other powers enabling her in that behalf, hereby makes the following Regulations, of which a draft has been laid before Parliament in accordance with section 723F(5) of that Act and approved by a resolution of each House of Parliament:

Citation, commencement and interpretation

1.—(1) These Regulations may be cited as the Companies (Particulars of Usual Residential Address) (Confidentiality Orders) Regulations 2002.

(2) These Regulations shall come into force on 2 April 2002.

(3) In these Regulations—

'the 1985 Act' means the Companies Act 1985;

'the LLP Regulations' mean the Limited Liability Partnerships (Particulars of Usual Residential Address) (Confidentiality Orders) Regulations 2002;

'beneficiary of an order' means an individual in relation to whom a confidentiality order is in force;

'company' means a relevant company within the meaning of section 723D of the 1985 Act and a company incorporated outside Great Britain proposing to establish a place of business, or open a branch in Great Britain, which would require that company to deliver for registration the information specified in section 691 of the 1985 Act, or Schedule 21A, as the case may be;

'competent authority' means any authority specified in Schedule 1 to these Regulations;

'police force' means a police force within the meaning of section 101(1) of the Police Act 1996 or section 50 of the Police (Scotland) Act 1967;

'service address' means the address specified pursuant to regulation 2(2)(b) in an application made under section 723B(1) of the 1985 Act or, if another address has been substituted under regulation 7, the address most recently substituted under that regulation; and

'working day' means any day other than a Saturday, a Sunday, Christmas Day, Good Friday or a day which is a bank holiday in any part of England or Wales under or by virtue of the Banking and Financial Dealings Act 1971.

PART I APPLICATIONS FOR CONFIDENTIALITY ORDERS UNDER SECTION 723B OF THE 1985 ACT

2.—(1) An application for a confidentiality order shall be made to the Secretary of State.

(2) An application for a confidentiality order shall:

(a) be in such form and contain such information and be accompanied by such evidence as the Secretary of State may from time to time direct;

(b) specify each company of which the applicant is or proposes to become a director, secretary or permanent representative and shall specify an address complying with regulation 9;

(3) The Secretary of State may from time to time direct different information or evidence be provided for different cases or categories of application.

(4) The Secretary of State may require any information or evidence delivered by an applicant to be verified in such manner as she may direct.

(5) The Secretary of State may require any application to be supported by a statement by any company to which the application relates that that company wishes a confidentiality order to be made in respect of the applicant together with the statement of the reasons for that wish.

(6) At any time after receiving an application and before determining it, the Secretary of State may require that any applicant deliver additional information or evidence including the delivery by a company of a statement complying with paragraph (5).

(7) Subject to paragraph (8) each application shall be accompanied by a fee of £100, and the Secretary of State may reject any application without considering it unless it is accompanied by such fee.

(8) No fee shall be payable where an application is made by an applicant—

(a) who at the same time has made an application for a confidentiality order under the LLP Regulations, and where a fee has been paid in respect of that application; or

(b) in respect of whom, at the time of the application, a confidentiality order made under the LLP Regulations is in force.

(9) An applicant may withdraw his application, by notice delivered to the Secretary of State, at any time before the Secretary of State makes a decision on the application, and the Secretary of State may retain the fee paid in respect of that application.

Referral of questions for the purposes of the determination of an application

3.—(1) The Secretary of State may, in respect of any application or category of applications, refer to a relevant body any question relating to an assessment, in the case of such application or category of applications, of the nature and extent of any risk of violence or intimidation considered by the applicant as likely to be created in relation to the applicant, or any person living with him, by virtue of the availability for inspection by members of the public of particulars of his usual residential address.

(2) The Secretary of State may also refer to a relevant body any question as to the nature or extent of any risk of violence or intimidation likely to be created in relation to any applicant or category of applicants or persons living with them as a result of their involvement in the activities of a particular company or category of companies or of a particular sector of commerce or industry.

(3) The Secretary of State may accept any answer to a question referred in accordance with paragraph (1) or (2) as providing sufficient evidence of the nature and extent of any risk relevant to an applicant or any person living with him for the purposes of any determination under section 723B(3) or (4) of the 1985 Act.

(4) In this regulation, 'relevant body' means any police force and any other person whom the Secretary of State considers may be able to assist in answering a question referred to that person under paragraph (1) or (2).

Notification of the outcome of an application

4. The Secretary of State shall send the applicant at his usual residential address, as stated in his application, notice of her decision under section 723B(3) or (4) of the 1985 Act and such notice shall be sent within five working days of the decision being made.

Appeals

5.—(1) An applicant who has received notice under regulation 4 that his application for a confidentiality order has been unsuccessful may appeal to the High Court or the Court of Session on the grounds that the decision—

(a) is unlawful;

(b) is irrational or unreasonable; or

(c) has been made on the basis of a procedural impropriety or otherwise contravenes the rules of natural justice.

(2) No appeal under this regulation may be brought unless the leave of the court has been obtained.

(3) An applicant must bring an appeal within 21 days of the sending of the notice under regulation 4 or, with the court's permission, after the end of such period, but only if the court is satisfied:

    (a) where permission is sought before the end of that period, that there is good reason for the applicant being unable to bring the appeal in time; or

    (b) where permission is sought after that time, that there was a good reason for the applicant's failure to bring the appeal in time and for any delay in applying for permission.

(4) The court determining an appeal may—

    (a) dismiss the appeal; or

    (b) quash the decision,

and where the court quashes a decision it may refer the matter to the Secretary of State with a direction to reconsider it and to make a determination in accordance with the findings of the court.

PART II   SERVICE ADDRESSES

6.   Where an application for a confidentiality order is made by a director, secretary or permanent representative, that individual shall notify to each of the companies specified in the application the service address specified in the application pursuant to regulation 2(2)(b).

7.   If a beneficiary of an order wishes to substitute another address, complying with regulation 9, for an address specified by him under regulation 2(2)(b) or previously notified by him under this regulation, he shall do so by notifying every company of which he is a director, secretary or permanent representative of the address to be substituted.

8.   Where the beneficiary of an order—

    (a) becomes a director, secretary or permanent representative of a company; or

    (b) is to be named in a statement delivered under section 10(2) of the 1985 Act as a director or secretary of a company to be formed under the 1985 Act; or

    (c) is a director, secretary or permanent representative of a company at the time when it establishes a place of business in Great Britain requiring registration of information under section 691 of the 1985 Act or opens a branch in Great Britain requiring registration of information under Schedule 21A to the 1985 Act, or proposes to establish such a place of business or open such a branch

that beneficiary shall, in a case falling within (a) or (c) above notify to the company the service address, and in a case falling within (b) above notify the service address to be included in the statement as provided in Schedule 1 to the 1985 Act.

9.—(1) Where an applicant for a confidentiality order or a beneficiary of an order holds, or proposes to hold, office as a director, secretary or permanent representative of more than one company the service address specified by that applicant or beneficiary in relation to each such company must be the same, and that address shall have effect for all offices held, or proposed to be held, by that applicant or beneficiary.

(2) A service address must be at a place at which service of documents may be effected by physical delivery other than a PO or a DX Box Number and where that delivery is capable of being recorded by the obtaining of an acknowledgement of delivery by any person.

(3) A service address must be situated within a state within the European Economic Area, and 'a state within the European Economic Area' means a state which is a member of the European Communities and the Republic of Iceland, the Kingdom of Norway and the Principality of Liechtenstein.

PART III   DURATION AND RENEWAL OF A CONFIDENTIALITY ORDER

10.—(1) Subject to paragraphs (2), (3), and (4) a confidentiality order shall remain in force for the period of five years from the date on which it is made unless revoked earlier under regulation 11.

(2) Where the beneficiary of a confidentiality order ('the existing order') delivers an application under section 723B(1) of the 1985 Act for a further confidentiality order ('the new order') before the expiry of the existing order ('the expiry date') and the Secretary of State decides before the expiry date to make a new order under section 723B(3) of the 1985 Act, the new order shall come into force on the expiry of the existing order.

(3) Where the beneficiary of an existing order delivers an application under section 723B(1) of the 1985 Act for a new order before the expiry date and the Secretary of State has not made a decision under section 723B(3) or (4) of the 1985 Act before that date, the existing order shall continue in force until—

(a) the Secretary of State makes a decision under section 723B(3) of the 1985 Act and the new order is made; or

(b) the application is dismissed under section 723B(4) of the 1985 Act.

(4) Where a confidentiality order is made in relation to an application in respect of which no fee has been paid pursuant to paragraph (8) of regulation 2 that order shall remain in force for a period equal to the period for which the confidentiality order referred to in paragraph (8) of regulation 2, made under the LLP Regulations, is to remain in force.

Revocation of a confidentiality order

11.—(1) The Secretary of State may revoke a confidentiality order at any time if she is satisfied that—

(a) the beneficiary of the order, or any other person, in purported compliance with any provision of these Regulations, has furnished the Secretary of State with false, misleading or inaccurate information; or

(b) the registrar has not received, within the period of 28 days beginning with the date on which the beneficiary of the order was sent notice under regulation 4 of the Secretary of State's decision, in relation to each company of which that beneficiary is a director, secretary or permanent representative, the information in respect of the service address required to be delivered to the registrar under sections 288, 692 or Schedule 21A of the 1985 Act, as the case may be, by virtue of the making of the order; or

(c) the registrar has not received within the period of 28 days from—

(i) any change or alteration among, or to, the directors, the secretary or permanent representatives by virtue of the appointment of a beneficiary of any order; or

(ii) any change in the particulars of the usual residential address or the service address of the beneficiary of an order, in relation to each company of which that beneficiary is a director, secretary or permanent representative,

the information required to be delivered to the registrar under sections 288, 692 or Schedule 21A of the 1985 Act, as the case may be, of any such change or alteration, whether that change or alteration occurred before or after the making of the confidentiality order; or

(d) any statement delivered to the registrar under section 10(2) of the 1985 Act naming an individual in respect of whom a confidentiality order under section 723B of that Act has been made did not contain the service address of the beneficiary or was not accompanied by a statement under section 10(2A) containing the usual residential address of the beneficiary; or

(e) any return required to be delivered to the registrar under section 691(1)(b)(i) of, or paragraph 1(1) of Schedule 21A to, the 1985 Act does not contain the service address of the beneficiary or any return required to be delivered to the registrar under sub-section (5) of section 691 of, or paragraph 9 of Schedule 21A to, the 1985 Act is not so delivered; or

(f) any address purporting to be the service address of a beneficiary of an order which has been notified to the registrar under any provision of the 1985 Act which does not comply with all the requirements of regulation 9.

(2) Where a beneficiary of an order is also the beneficiary of a confidentiality order made under the LLP Regulations which is revoked under those Regulations, the order made under section 723B of the 1985 Act is also revoked.

(3) If the Secretary of State proposes to revoke an order under this regulation, other than one revoked under paragraph (2), she shall send the beneficiary of the order notice.

(4) The notice must—

(a) state the grounds on which it is proposed to revoke the order;

(b) inform the beneficiary that he may, within the period of 21 days beginning with the date of the notice, deliver representations to the Secretary of State; and

(c) state that if representations are not received by the Secretary of State within that period, the order will be revoked at the expiry of that period.

(5) If the beneficiary delivers representations as to why the order should not be revoked within the period specified in paragraph (4), the Secretary of State shall have regard to the representations in determining whether to revoke the order, and shall send the beneficiary notice of her decision, and such notice shall be sent within five working days of the decision being made.

(6) Any communication by the Secretary of State in respect of the revocation or proposed revocation of a confidentiality order shall be sent to the beneficiary at his usual residential address.

Notification of cessation of a confidentiality order

12.   On a confidentiality order ceasing to have effect, for whatever reason, the beneficiary of that order shall notify every relevant company within the meaning of section 723D(1)(a) of the 1985 Act of which he is a director or secretary, of that order ceasing to have effect within five days of its so ceasing to have effect.

PART IV   ACCESS TO CONFIDENTIAL RECORDS

13.—(1) Subject to paragraph (2) a competent authority is entitled to inspect, and take copies of, confidential records.

(2) The circumstances in which a competent authority may inspect, and take copies of, confidential records are that the registrar has made a determination, in respect of that competent authority, as to the manner in which that competent authority and its officers, servants and representatives may inspect, and take copies of, confidential records.

(3) The registrar may from time to time vary or revoke any determination with the consent of the competent authority in respect of whom it has been made.

Disclosure of relevant information

14.—(1) Subject to regulation 13 the disclosure of relevant information by any person is prohibited in the following circumstances—

(a) where the information disclosed was delivered to the registrar, after the making of a confidentiality order in relation to the beneficiary of an order to whom the information relates, in the course of the performance of the duties of the registrar under the 1985 Act in respect of that information and the information was obtained by the person disclosing it from the registrar;

(b) where the information disclosed was provided to a company, of which the beneficiary of the order to which the information relates was a director, secretary or permanent representative, after the making of that order, for the purpose of enabling the company to comply with sections 288, 289, 290, 691, 692 and Schedule 21A of the 1985 Act, as the case may be, and the information was obtained by the person disclosing it from the company.

(2) Paragraph (1) does not prohibit the disclosure of relevant information by a competent authority which is made for the purpose of facilitating the carrying out of a public function and 'public function' includes—

(a) any function conferred by or in accordance with any provision contained in any enactment or subordinate legislation;

(b) any function conferred by or in accordance with any provision contained in the Community Treaties or any Community instrument;

(c) any similar function conferred on persons by or under provisions having effect as part of the law of a country or territory outside the United Kingdom;

(d) any function exercisable in relation to the investigation of any criminal offence or for the purposes of any criminal proceedings,

and disclosure for the purpose of facilitating the carrying out of a public function includes disclosure in relation to, and for the purpose of, any proceedings whether civil, criminal or disciplinary in which the competent authority engages while carrying out its public functions.

(3) Paragraph (1) does not prohibit the disclosure of relevant information where the disclosure—

(a) facilitates the creation and maintenance of confidential records, the protected part of the register of a company, any return by an oversea company of information which is to form part of confidential records and the provision of facilities for the inspection and copying of confidential records; or

(b) is by the registrar, or any person performing functions on his behalf, of any relevant information obtained in the circumstances described in sub-paragraph (1)(a), included in any document delivered to the registrar under any provision of the 1985 Act where that document is prescribed in respect of the delivery to the registrar of any information which is not relevant information and that document is made available for inspection and copying as if that were required by section 709(1) of the 1985 Act; or

(c) is by any person of any relevant information obtained by that person from any document as is referred to in sub-paragraph (b).

(4) Paragraph (1) does not prohibit the disclosure by any person of relevant information obtained in the course of the performance of their duties or functions, where that disclosure occurred notwithstanding the exercise by that person of the due care and diligence in maintaining the confidentiality, required by the 1985 Act and these Regulations, of that information, that could reasonably be expected of a person performing those duties and functions.

(5) In this regulation—

'enactment' includes—

(a) an Act of the Scottish Parliament;

(b) Northern Ireland legislation;

'subordinate legislation' has the meaning given in the Interpretation Act 1978 and also includes an instrument made under an Act of the Scottish Parliament or under Northern Ireland legislation.

PART V   FORM AND DELIVERY OF NOTICES ETC.

15.—(1) Any notice—

(a) by the Secretary of State under regulation 4, 11(3) or 11(5); or

(b) to the Secretary of State under regulation 2(9);

and any representations made to the Secretary of State under regulation 11 shall be in legible form.

(2) Where any notice is required to be sent by the Secretary of State to the usual residential address of any person, that notice is validly sent if sent to the address of that person,

shown in the records of the registrar available for inspection or copying under section 709 of the 1985 Act or the confidential records as the case may be when the notice is sent.

Offences and penalties

17.—(1) Any person who, in an application under section 723B of the 1985 Act, makes a statement which he knows to be false in a material particular, or recklessly makes a statement, which is false in a material particular, shall be guilty of an offence.

(2) Any person who discloses information in contravention of regulation 14 shall be guilty of an offence.

(3) A person guilty of an offence under paragraph (1) or (2) shall be liable—

(a) on conviction on indictment, to imprisonment for a term not exceeding two years or to a fine or to both; and

(b) on summary conviction, to imprisonment not exceeding six months, or to a fine not exceeding the statutory maximum or to both.

SCHEDULE 1   COMPETENT AUTHORITIES

[schedule introduced by reg. 1]

the Secretary of State;

the registrar and the registrar of companies for Northern Ireland;

an inspector appointed under Part XIV of the Companies Act 1985 or regulation 30 of the Open-Ended Investment Companies Regulations 2001;

any person authorised to exercise powers under section 447 of the Companies Act 1985, or section 84 of the Companies Act 1989;

any person exercising functions conferred by Part VI of the Financial Services and Markets Act 2000 or the competent authority under that Part;

a person appointed to make a report under section 166 of the Financial Services and Markets Act 2000;

a person appointed to conduct an investigation under section 167 or 168(3) or (5) of the Financial Services and Markets Act 2000;

an inspector appointed under section 284 of the Financial Services and Markets Act 2000;

the Department of Enterprise, Trade and Investment in Northern Ireland;

the Scottish Executive;

the Scotland Office;

the National Assembly for Wales;

the Wales Office (Office of the Secretary of State for Wales);

the Treasury;

the Commissioners of HM Customs and Excise;

the Commissioners of Inland Revenue;

the Bank of England;

the Director of Public Prosecutions and the Director of Public Prosecutions in Northern Ireland;

the Serious Fraud Office;

the Secret Intelligence Service;

the Security Service;

the Financial Services Authority;

the Competition Commission;

the Occupational Pensions Regulatory Authority;

the Panel on Takeovers and Mergers;

the Chief Registrar of Friendly Societies and the Registrar for Credit Unions and Industrial and Provident Societies for Northern Ireland;

the Director General of Fair Trading;

the Office of the Information Commissioner;

the Friendly Societies Commission;

a local weights and measures authority;

the Charity Commission;

an official receiver appointed under section 399 of the Insolvency Act 1986;

a person acting as an insolvency practitioner within the meaning of section 388 of the Insolvency Act 1986;

an inspector appointed under Part XV of the Companies (Northern Ireland) Order 1986 or Regulation 22 of the Open-Ended Investment Companies (Companies with Variable Capital) Regulations (Northern Ireland) 1997;

any person authorised to exercise powers under Article 440 of the Companies (Northern Ireland) Order 1986;

the Official Receiver for Northern Ireland;

a police force;

any procurator fiscal;

an overseas regulatory authority within the meaning of section 82 of the Companies Act 1989.

SOURCES OF AMENDMENTS

The text of the legislation set out in this book is the text in force on 10 June 2003. Where this differs from the text as originally enacted, the following list identifies the legislation which made the amendment or repeal which has been taken into account. The list does not include amendments made before a repeal, unless necessary to identify what has been repealed. The following abbreviations are used: CA89 = Companies Act 1989; CDDA86 = Company Directors Disqualification Act 1986; FSA86 = Financial Services Act 1986; IA85 = Insolvency Act 1985; IA86 = Insolvency Act 1986; IA00 = Insolvency Act 2000. A reference in the form 1992/1699 is to a statutory instrument number (or, before 1948, statutory rules and orders number).

Partnership Act 1890
S. 1: Statute Law (Repeals) Act 1998, sch. 1, part X, group 1. **S. 3:** Decimal Currency Act 1969, s. 10(1). **S. 9:** 1923/405, art. 2. **S. 22:** repealed in England and Wales by Trusts of Land and Appointment of Trustees Act 1996, sch. 4. **S. 23(1):** Statute Law Revision Act 1908; differently worded in Northern Ireland because of Judgments (Enforcement) Act (Northern Ireland) 1969, sch. 4, part II, and 1981/226 (NI 6), sch. 2, para. 8. **S. 23(2):** Courts Act 1971, sch. 11, part II; differently worded in Northern Ireland because of Judgments (Enforcement) Act (Northern Ireland) 1969, sch. 4, part II, and sch. 6. **S. 23(4):** repealed by Statute Law (Repeals) Act 1998, sch. 1, part X, group 1. **S. 35(a):** repealed in England and Wales by Mental Health Act 1959, sch. 8. **S. 36(2):** 1921/1804, art. 7; 1923/405, art. 2. **S. 47:** omitted (applies to Scotland only). **Ss. 48, 49 and sch.:** repealed by Statute Law Revision Act 1908.

Stock Transfer Act 1963
S. 1(4)(b)–(f): omitted. **S. 2(2) and (3):** Companies Consolidation (Consequential Provisions) Act 1985, sch. 2; see note at end of section. **S. 2(4):** omitted (applies to Scotland only and has been repealed there by Requirements of Writing (Scotland) Act 1995, sch. 5). **S. 3(5):** Stock Exchange (Completion of Bargains) Act 1976, s. 6. **S. 4(1):** 2001/3649, art. 271; definitions of terms not used in provisions printed in this book omitted. **S. 5:** omitted (applies to Northern Ireland only). **S. 6(2):** omitted.

Companies Act 1985
S. 1(3A): 1992/1699, sch., para. 1. **S. 2(6):** 2000/3373, art. 2; omitted words apply to Scotland only and have been repealed there by Requirements of Writing (Scotland) Act 1995, sch. 5. **S. 2(6A):** 2000/3373, art. 2(3). **S. 3A:** CA89, s. 110(1). **S. 4:** CA89, s. 110(2). **S. 5:** 2003/1116, sch., para. 1. **S. 7(3):** 2000/3373, art. 3; omitted words apply to Scotland only and have been repealed there by Requirements of Writing (Scotland) Act 1995, sch. 5. **S. 7(3A):** 2000/3373, art. 3(3). **S. 8A:** CA89, s. 128. **S. 10:** 2002/912, sch. 2, para. 1. **S. 12:** 2000/3373, art. 4. **S. 13(4):** IA86, sch. 13, part I. **S. 21:** repealed by Welsh Language Act 1993, s. 30(2) and sch. 2. **S. 23:** CA89, s. 129(1); 1990/1392, art. 8; 1990/1707, art. 8(2); 1997/2306, regs 2 and 3; 2001/3649, art. 4. **S. 24:** 1992/1699, sch., para. 2; 2003/1116, sch., para. 2. **S. 26:** 1996/2827, sch. 8, para. 4; 2001/1090, sch. 5, para. 8; 2001/1228, sch. 7, para. 3. **S. 29:** 2000/3373, art. 31(1). **S. 30:** 2000/3373, art. 5. **Ss. 35, 35A, 35B:** CA89, s. 108(1); Charities Act 1993, sch. 6, para. 20. **S. 36:** CA89, s. 130(1). **S. 36A:** CA89, s. 130(2). **S. 36B:** omitted (applies to Scotland only; inserted by CA89, s. 130(3), and substituted by Law Reform (Miscellaneous Provisions) (Scotland) Act 1990, s. 72(1); differently worded in Scotland because of Requirements of Writing (Scotland) Act 1995, sch. 4, para. 51). **S. 36C:** CA89, s. 130(4). **S. 38(1):** words inserted by CA89, sch. 17, para. 1, were repealed by Law Reform (Miscellaneous Provisions) Scotland Act 1990, sch. 8, para. 33(2) and sch. 9. **S. 38(2):** CA89, sch. 17, para. 1. **S. 38(3):** omitted (extends to Scotland only). **S. 39(1) and (2):** CA89, sch. 17, para. 2. **S. 39(2A):** omitted (extends to Scotland only). **S. 39(3):** words inserted by CA89, sch. 17, para. 2(4), were repealed by Law

Reform (Miscellaneous Provisions) Scotland Act 1990, sch. 8, para. 33(3) and sch. 9; differently worded in Scotland because of Requirements of Writing (Scotland) Act 1995, sch. 4, para. 53(b). **S. 40:** CA89, sch. 17, para. 3; differently worded in Scotland because of Requirements of Writing (Scotland) Act 1995, sch. 4, para. 54. **S. 41:** CA89, sch. 17, para. 4. **S. 43:** 2000/3373, art. 6. **S. 44(7):** IA86, sch. 13, part I. **S. 46:** CA89, sch. 10, para. 1. **S. 47:** 2000/3373, art. 7. **S. 49:** 2000/3373, art. 8. **S. 54:** 2003/1116, sch., para. 3. **Ss. 56–79:** repealed by FSA86, sch. 17; repeals of ss. 58–60 and 62 brought into force for certain purposes only; ss. 59 and 60 repealed for all remaining purposes by 2001/3649, art. 5; see notes after ss. 58 and 62. **S. 60(8):** 1991/ 2000, reg. 5(1). **S. 80:** CA89, s. 115(1). **S. 80A:** CA89, s. 115(1). **S. 81:** see note at the end of the section. **Ss. 82 and 83:** see note at the end of s. 82. **Ss. 84 and 85:** see note at the end of s. 81. **Ss. 86 and 87:** Repealed by FSA86, sch. 17, part I. **S. 89:** 2003/1116, sch., para. 4. **S. 94:** 2003/ 1116, sch., para. 5. **S. 95:** 2003/1116, sch., para. 6. **S. 97:** see note after s. 81; amendments made by FSA86, sch. 16, para. 16, were never brought into force and were repealed by 1995/ 1537, sch. 2, para. 5(e). **S. 103(4):** 2003/1116, sch., para. 7. **S. 103(7):** IA86, sch. 13, part I. **S. 111A:** CA89, s. 131(1). **S. 116:** CA89, s. 131(2). **S. 117:** 2000/3373, art. 9. **S. 125:** 2003/1116, sch., para. 8. **S. 127:** 2003/1116, sch., para. 9. **S. 131(1):** CA89, sch. 19, para. 1. **S. 131(4):** 2003/1116, sch., para. 10. **S. 131(7):** IA86, sch. 13, part I. **S. 140(2):** IA86, sch. 13, part I. **S. 143:** 2003/1116, sch., para. 11. **S. 153(3)(f):** IA86, sch. 13, part I. **S. 153(3)(g):** IA85, sch. 6, para. 8; IA86, sch. 13, part I. **S. 153(4)(b):** CA89, s. 132. **S. 153(4)(bb):** FSA86, s. 196(2). **S. 153(5):** FSA86, s. 196(3); CA89, sch. 18, para. 33(3). **S. 155:** 2000/3373, art. 10. **S. 156:** IA86, sch. 13, part I; 2000/3373, art. 11. **S. 158:** 2000/3373, art. 31(2). **S. 159A:** CA89, s. 133(2). **S. 160:** CA89, s. 133(3). **S. 161:** repealed by Finance Act 1988, sch. 14, part XI. **S. 162:** CA89, s. 133(4); 2003/1116, reg. 2. **Ss. 162A–162G:** 2003/1116, reg. 3. **S. 163:** FSA86, sch. 16, para. 17; 2001/3649, art. 6. **S. 169:** CA89, s. 143(2) and sch. 24; 2003/1116, sch., para. 12. **S. 169A:** 2003/1116, sch., para. 13. **S. 170:** 2003/1116, sch., para. 14. **S. 171(5):** 1997/220, reg. 7(1). **S. 173(4):** IA86, sch. 13, part I. **S. 175(6):** CA89, s. 143(3) and sch. 24. **S. 178(7):** repealed by IA85, sch. 10, part II. **S. 182(1):** 1995/3272, reg. 40(1); amendment duplicated by 2001/3755, sch. 7, para. 7. **S. 183:** 1995/3272, reg. 40(2); amendment duplicated by 2001/3755, sch. 7, para. 8. **S. 185:** FSA86, s. 194(5); 2001/3649, art. 7. **S. 186:** CA89, sch. 17, para. 5; Law Reform (Miscellaneous Provisions) (Scotland) Act 1990, sch. 8, para. 33(4) and sch. 9; differently worded in Scotland because of Requirements of Writing (Scotland) Act 1995, sch. 4, para. 55. **S. 188:** CA89, sch. 17, para. 6; Law Reform (Miscellaneous Provisions) (Scotland) Act 1990, sch. 8, para. 33(5) and sch. 9; differently worded in Scotland because of Requirements of Writing (Scotland) Act 1995, sch. 4, para. 56. **S. 189:** omitted (applies to Scotland only). **S. 191:** CA89, s. 143(4) and sch. 24. **S. 196:** IA86, sch. 13, part I. **S. 197:** omitted (applies to Scotland only). **S. 198:** 1993/1819, reg. 3; 2003/1116, sch., para. 15. **S. 199:** 1993/1819, reg. 4; 1996/2827, sch. 8, para. 5; 2001/1228, sch. 7, para. 4; 2001/3649, art. 8. **S. 200:** 1993/1819, reg. 5. **S. 201:** repealed by CA89, sch. 24. **S. 202(1):** CA89, s. 134(3) and sch. 24. **S. 202(2):** 1993/1819, reg. 6(1). **S. 202(2A) and (2B):** 1993/1819, reg. 6(2). **S. 202(4):** CA89, s. 134(3). **S. 203(1):** In Scotland the words 'pupil or minor' are replaced by 'person under the age of 18 years' by Age of Legal Capacity (Scotland) Act 1991, sch. 1, para. 39. **S. 206(3), (3A) and (3B):** 1993/1819, reg. 7. **S. 206(8):** CA89, s. 134(3). **S. 209:** 1993/1819, reg. 8. **S. 209(1):** 1996/2827, sch. 8, para. 6; 2001/1228, sch. 7, para. 5. **S. 209(2):** 2001/3649, art. 9; 2002/765, reg. 2(1). **S. 209(2A)–(2C):** 1993/2689; 2001/3649, art. 9. **S.209(9A):** 1996/1560, reg. 2. **S. 209(9B):** 1996/1560, reg. 2; 2001/3755, sch. 7, para. 9; **S. 209(10)(b):** Church of Scotland (Properties and Investments) Order Confirmation Act 1994, sch., para. 42(1). **S. 209(10)(d):** repealed by Law of Property (Miscellaneous Provisions) Act 1994, sch. 2. **S. 210(5A):** 1991/ 1646, reg. 3. **S. 210A:** CA89, s. 134(5). **S. 211(9):** CA89, sch. 10, para. 3. **S. 214:** 2003/1116, sch., para. 16. **S. 215(4):** CA89, sch. 10, para. 3. **S. 216:** 1991/1646, reg. 4. **S. 219:** CA89, s. 143(5) and sch. 24. **S. 220(1):** 1993/1819, reg. 9; 1996/2827, sch. 8, para. 7; 2000/2952, reg. 2; 2001/1228, sch. 7, para. 6; 2001/3649, art. 10(1)–(8). **S. 220(1A):;** 2001/3649, art. 10(9). **Ss. 221–62A:** CA89, s. 1. **Ss. 221–2:** CA89, s. 2. **S. 223:** CA89, s. 3. **S. 224:** CA89, s. 3; 1990/

355, art. 15; 1996/189, reg. 2. **S. 225:** CA89, s. 3; 1996/189, reg. 3; Enterprise Act 2002, sch. 17, para. 4. **S. 226:** CA89, s. 4(1). **S. 227:** CA89, s. 5(1). **Ss. 228–9:** CA89, s. 5(3). **S. 228(2)(b):** 1992/3178, reg. 4; 1993/3246, sch. 2, para. 1. **S. 228(2)(d):** repealed by 1996/189, reg. 4. **S. 228(2)(f):** Welsh Language Act 1993, s. 30(3). **S. 230:** CA89, s. 5(4). **S. 231:** CA89, s. 6(1); 1993/1820, reg. 11(1); 1996/189, reg. 15(1). **S. 232:** CA89, s. 6(3); 2002/1986, reg. 2. **S. 233:** CA89, s. 7. **S. 234:** CA89, s. 8(1); 1996/189, reg. 5; 1997/571, reg. 2(1). **S. 234A:** CA89, s. 8(1). **Ss. 234B and 234C:** 2002/1986, reg. 3. **S. 235:** CA89, s. 9; 2002/1986, reg. 4. **S. 236:** CA89, s. 9. **S. 237:** CA89, s. 9; 1996/189, reg. 6; 2002/1986, regs 5, 6 and 10(2). **S. 238:** CA89, s. 10; 2000/3373, art. 12; 2002/1986, reg. 10(3)–(5). **S. 239:** CA89, s. 10; 2000/3373, art. 13; 2002/1986, reg. 10(6). **S. 240:** CA89, s. 10; 1994/1935, sch. 1, para. 1. **S. 241:** CA89, s. 11; 2002/1986, reg. 10(7). **S. 241A:** 2002/1986, reg. 7. **S. 242:** CA89, s. 11; Welsh Language Act 1993, s. 30(4); 2002/1986, reg. 10(8); words inserted by 1992/1083, reg. 2(2), were repealed by Welsh Language Act 1993, sch. 2. **S. 242A:** CA89, reg. 11. **S. 242B:** 1992/2452, reg. 3. **S. 243:** CA89, s. 11; Welsh Language Act 1993, s. 30(4); words inserted by 1992/1083, reg. 2(3), were repealed by Welsh Language Act 1993, sch. 2. **S. 244:** CA89, s. 11. **S. 245:** CA89, s. 12; 2002/1986, reg. 10(9). **S. 245A:** CA89, s. 12. **S. 245B:** CA89, s. 12; 2002/1986, reg. 10(10). **S. 245C:** CA89, s. 12. **S. 246:** CA89, s. 13(1); 1997/220, reg. 2(1); 1997/570, reg. 6(1); 2000/1430, reg. 8(1). **S. 246A:** 1997/220, reg. 3. **S. 247:** CA89, s. 13(1); 1992/2452, reg. 5; 1996/189, reg. 8; 1997/220, reg. 7(2). **S. 247A:** 1997/220, reg. 4; 2001/3649, art. 11. **S. 247B:** 1997/220, reg. 5; 2000/1430, reg. 8(2). **S. 248:** CA89, s. 13(3); 2001/3649, art. 12. **S. 248(3) and (4):** repealed by 1996/189, reg. 9. **S. 248A:** 1997/220, reg. 6. **S. 249:** CA89, s. 13(3); 1992/2452, reg. 6. **S. 249A:** 1994/1935, reg. 2; 1997/936, reg. 2; 2000/1430, reg. 2. **S. 249AA:** 2000/1430, reg. 3; 2001/3649, art. 13. **S. 249B:** 1994/1935, reg. 2; 1996/189, reg. 10; 1997/936, reg. 3; 2000/1430, reg. 4; 2001/1283, art. 3(3)(a); 2001/3649, art. 14. **Ss. 249C and 249D:** omitted (apply to charities only; inserted by 1994/1935, reg. 2). **S. 249E:** 1994/1935, reg. 2; 2000/1430, reg. 8(5). **S. 249E(2):** omitted (applies to charities only). **S. 250:** repealed by 2000/1430, reg. 8(6). **S. 251:** CA89, s. 15; 1992/3003, reg. 3; 2000/3373, art. 14; 2001/3649, art. 15; 2002/1986, reg. 8. **S. 252:** CA89, s. 16. **S. 253:** CA89, s. 16; 2000/3373, art. 15. **S. 254:** CA89, s. 17; 1991/2705, sch. 2, para. 1; 1993/1820, reg. 10; 1993/3246, sch. 2, para. 2. **Ss. 255, 255A and 255B:** omitted (apply only to banking and insurance companies; inserted by CA89, s. 18(1); substituted by 1991/2705, reg. 3; amended by 1993/3246, regs 2 and 3, 1994/233, reg. 3, and 1996/189, reg. 15(2)). **S. 255C:** repealed by 1993/3246, sch. 2, para. 3. **S. 255D:** omitted (concerns banking companies only; inserted by CA89, s. 18(2)). **S. 255E:** repealed by Welsh Language Act 1993, s. 35(2). **S. 256:** CA89, s. 19. **S. 257:** CA89, s. 20. **S. 258:** CA89, s. 21. **S. 259:** CA89, s. 22. **S. 260:** CA89, s. 22; 1991/2705, reg. 2; 1993/3246, sch. 2, para. 4; 1997/220, reg. 4(5). **S. 261:** CA89, s. 22. **S. 262:** CA89, s. 22; 1992/3178, reg. 7; 2000/2952, reg. 2; 2000/3373, art. 16(1); 2002/765, reg. 2(2); 2002/1986, reg. 10(11); words inserted by 1996/189, reg. 12(1), were repealed by 1997/2306, reg. 4(2). **S. 262A:** CA89, s. 22; 1991/2705, sch. 2, para. 3; 1994/233, reg. 4(2); 1993/3246, sch. 2, para. 5; 1994/1935, sch. 1, para. 3; 1997/220, reg. 7(6); 2000/3373, art. 16(2); 2002/1986, reg. 10(12); words inserted by 1996/189, reg. 12(2), were repealed by 1997/2306, reg. 4(4). **S. 265:** FSA86, sch. 16, para. 19; 1999/2770, reg. 2; 2001/3649, art. 17. **S. 266:** Finance Act 1988, s. 117(3); 1999/2770, reg. 3. **S. 268:** omitted (concerns insurance companies only). **S. 269(2):** 1997/220, reg. 7(7). **S. 271:** CA89, sch. 10, para. 4. **S. 272(3):** CA89, sch. 10, para. 5. **S. 272(5):** CA89, sch. 10, para. 6; Welsh Language Act 1993, s. 30(4). **S. 273(7):** CA89, sch. 10, para. 6; Welsh Language Act 1993, s. 30(4). **S. 276:** CA89, sch. 10, para. 7; 1997/220, reg. 7(8). **S. 279:** omitted (applies only to banking and insurance companies). **S. 287:** CA89, s. 136. **S. 288:** CA89, s. 143(6) and sch. 24; Criminal Justice and Police Act 2001, s. 45(1) and (3); 2002/912, sch. 2, para. 2. **S. 288A:** 2002/915, sch. 2, para. 2. **S. 289:** CA89, sch. 10, para. 9, and sch. 19, para. 2; 2000/1430, reg. 8(7); 2002/912, sch. 2, para. 3. **S. 290:** CA89, sch. 19, para. 3; 2002/912, sch. 2, para. 4. **Ss. 295–9:** repealed by CDDA86, sch. 4. **S. 300:** repealed by IA85, sch. 10, part II. **Ss. 301–2:** repealed by CDDA86, sch. 4. **S. 305:** CA89, sch. 19, para. 4. **S. 310(3):** CA89, s. 137(1). **S. 318(7):** CA89, s. 143(7) and sch. 24. **S. 320(2):**

1990/1393. **S. 321(4):** CA89, sch. 19, para. 8; 2001/3649, art. 19. **S. 322A:** CA89, s. 109(1). **S. 322B:** 1992/1699, sch., para. 3(1). **S. 327(2)(b):** In Scotland the words 'pupil or minor' are replaced by 'person under the age of 18 years' by Age of Legal Capacity (Scotland) Act 1991, sch. 1, para. 39. **S. 328(8):** In Scotland the words 'pupil or minor' are replaced by 'person under the age of 18 years' by Age of Legal Capacity (Scotland) Act 1991, sch. 1, para. 39. **S. 329:** FSA86, sch. 16, para. 20; 2001/3649, art. 20. **S. 331(5):** repealed by Banking Act 1987, sch. 7, part 1. **S. 332(1)(b):** CA89, s. 138(a). **S. 334:** CA89, s. 138(b). **S. 335(1):** 1990/1393. **S. 337(3):** 1990/1393. **S. 338(4):** Banking Act 1987, sch. 6, para. 18(6); CA89, sch. 10, para. 10; CA89, s. 138(c). **S. 338(6):** CA89, s. 138(c). **S. 339(4):** Banking Act 1987, sch. 6, para. 18(6); CA89, sch. 10, para. 10. **S. 340(7):** 1990/1393. **Ss. 343 and 344:** omitted (apply to banking companies only). **S. 346:** 2003/1116, sch., para. 17. **Ss. 347A to 347K:** Political Parties, Elections and Referendums Act 2000, sch. 19. **S. 350(1):** CA89, sch. 17, para. 7. **S. 351(3), (4) and (5)(c):** repealed by Welsh Language Act 1993, s. 31 and sch. 2. **S. 352:** 2003/1116, sch., para. 18. **S. 352A:** 1992/1699, sch., para. 4(1). **S. 356:** CA89, sch. 24 and s. 143(8). **S. 362(4) and (5):** omitted (concern extension of s. 362 to British overseas territories). **Ss. 363–5:** CA89, s. 139(1). **S. 363(5):** 1990/1707, art 7. **S. 364(1):** 1999/2322. **S. 366A:** CA89, s. 115(2); 2000/3373, art. 17. **S. 368:** CA89, sch. 19, para. 9; 2003/1116, sch., para. 19. **S. 369:** CA89, s. 115(3); 2000/3373, art. 18; 2003/1116, sch., para. 20. **S. 370:** 2003/1116, sch., para. 21. **S. 370A:** 1992/1699, sch., para. 5. **S. 372:** 2000/3373, art. 19. **S. 373:** 2000/3373, art. 20; 2003/1116, sch., para. 22. **S. 376:** 2003/1116, sch., para. 23. **S. 378:** CA89, s. 115(3); 2003/1116, sch., para. 24. **S. 379A:** CA89, s. 116(2); 1996/1471, art. 2; 2000/3373, art. 21. **S. 380(4)(bb):** CA89, s. 116(3). **S. 380(4)(j):** IA86, sch. 13, part I. **S. 380(4)(l) and (m):** 1995/3272, reg. 40(3); duplicated, with amendment, by 2001/3755, sch. 7, para. 10. **S. 380(4A):** 2003/1116, sch., para. 25. **Ss. 381A–C:** CA89, s. 113(2). **S. 381A(5):** 1996/1471, art. 3(2)(a). **S. 381B:** 1996/1471, art. 3. **S. 381C(1):** 1996/1471, art. 4. **S. 382A:** CA89, s. 113(3). **S. 382B:** 1992/1699, sch., para. 6(1). **S. 383:** CA89, s. 143(9) and sch. 24. **Ss. 384–8A:** CA89, s. 119(1). **S. 384(1):** 1994/1935, sch. 1, para. 4. **S. 386:** 2000/1430, reg. 8(8). **S. 388A:** 1994/1935, reg. 3; 2000/1430, reg. 8(9). **S. 389:** repealed by CA89, sch. 24. **S. 389A:** CA89, s. 120(1). **S. 390:** CA89, s. 120(1); 1996/1471, art. 3(2); 2000/3373, art. 31(3). **Ss. 390A and 390B:** CA89, s. 121. **Ss. 391–3:** CA89, s. 122(1). **Ss. 394 and 394A:** CA89, s. 123(1). **S. 395(1):** IA85, sch. 6, para. 10. **S. 396:** Copyright, Designs and Patents Act 1988, sch. 7, para. 31(2); Trade Marks Act 1994, sch. 5. **S. 403:** 2000/3373, art. 22. **Ss. 409–24:** omitted (s. 409 concerns oversea companies only; ss. 410–24 apply to Scotland only). **S. 425(1):** IA85, sch. 6, para. 11; Enterprise Act 2002, sch. 17, para. 5. **S. 425(5):** omitted (applies to Scotland only; differently worded in Scotland because of Court of Session Act 1988, sch. 2). **S. 426(6):** IA85, sch. 6, para. 12. **S. 427A:** 1987/1991; CA89, s. 114(2); Enterprise Act 2002, sch. 17, para. 4. **S. 428:** FSA86, s. 172 and sch. 12. **S. 429:** FSA86, s. 172 and sch. 12; 2003/1116, sch., para. 26. **S. 430:** FSA86, s. 172 and sch. 12. **S. 430A:** FSA86, s. 172 and sch. 12; 2003/1116, sch., para. 27. **Ss. 430B–430F:** FSA86, s. 172 and sch. 12. **S. 431:** 2003/1116, sch., para. 28. **S. 432(2A):** CA89, s. 55. **S. 433(2):** repealed by FSA86, sch. 13, para. 7. **S. 434:** CA89, s. 56(2)–(5); Youth Justice and Criminal Evidence Act 1999, sch. 3, paras 4 and 5; Criminal Justice and Police Act 2001, sch. 2, para. 17. **S. 435:** repealed by CA89, sch. 24. **S. 436(1):** CA89, s. 56(6). **S. 437(1A):** FSA86, sch. 13, para. 7. **S. 437(1B) and (1C):** CA89, s. 57. **S. 438(1):** CA89, s. 58. **S. 439:** CA89, s. 59. **S. 440:** repealed by CA89, s. 60(1) and sch. 24. **S. 441(1):** CA89, s. 61; IA85, sch. 6, para. 3; IA86, sch. 13, part I. **S. 442(3)–(3C):** CA89, s. 62. **S. 443(4):** repealed by CA89, sch. 24. **S. 445:** 1991/1646, reg. 5. **S. 446(3):** FSA86, sch. 13, para. 8(a); CA 89, sch. 24. **S. 446(4) and (4A):** FSA86, sch. 16, para. 21; 2001/3649, art. 21. **S. 446(5) and (6):** repealed by FSA86, sch. 17, part I. **S. 446(7):** repealed by CA89, sch. 24. **S. 447(1):** repealed by CA89, s. 63 and sch. 24. **S. 447(8A) and (8B):** Youth Justice and Criminal Evidence Act 1999, sch. 3, paras 4 and 6. **S. 447(9):** Criminal Justice and Police Act 2001, sch. 2, para. 17. **S. 448:** CA89, s. 64(1). **S. 449(1):** CA89, s. 65(2) and sch. 24; FSA86, sch. 13, para. 9(1); IA85, sch. 6, para. 4; IA86, sch. 13, part I; 1994/1696, sch. 8, para. 9(2); 1992/1315, sch. 4, para. 1; Criminal Justice Act 1993, sch. 5, para. 4(2);

FSA86, sch. 17, part I; Friendly Societies Act 1992, sch. 21, para. 7(1); Pensions Act 1995, sch. 3, para. 12; Banking Act 1987, sch. 6, para. 18(7); Bank of England Act 1998, sch. 5, para. 62; 2001/1283, art. 3(3)(b); 2001/3649, art. 22(1)–(5). **S. 449(1A):** FSA86, sch. 13, para. 9(2); CA89, s. 65(3); 2001/3649, art. 22(1) and (7). **S. 449(1B):** FSA86, sch. 13, para. 9(2); CA89, s. 65(4). **S. 449(1C):** FSA86, sch. 13, para. 9(2). **S. 449(1D):** inserted by FSA86, sch. 13, para. 9(2); repealed by 2001/3649, art. 22(1) and (8). **S. 449(2):** CA89, s. 65(5). **S. 449(3):** CA89, s. 65(6); Friendly Societies Act 1992, sch. 21, para. 7(2) and sch. 22; Bank of England Act 1998, sch. 5, para. 62; 1999/1820, sch. 2, para. 78; 2001/3649, art. 22(1) and (9)–(12). **S. 449(3A):** CA89, s. 65(6). **S. 449(4):** FSA86, sch. 13, para. 9(3); CA89, s. 65(7). **S. 450:** CA89, s. 66; 2001/3649, art. 23. **S. 451:** CA89, s. 67. **S. 451A:** CA89, s. 68; 1994/1696, sch. 8, para. 9(3); 2001/3649, art. 24. **S. 452:** CA89, s. 69; 1994/1696, sch. 8, para. 9(4); 2001/3649, art. 25. **S. 453:** CA89, s. 70. **S. 454:** 1991/1646, reg. 6; CA89, sch. 19, para. 10(2). **S. 455:** 1991/1646, reg. 7. **S. 456:** 1991/1646, reg. 8; CA89, sch. 19, para. 10(1). **S. 459(1):** CA89, sch. 19, para. 11. **S. 459(3):** Water Act 1989, sch. 25, para. 71(3); Water Consolidation (Consequential Provisions) Act 1991, sch. 1, para. 40(2); s. 459(3) extends to England and Wales only. **S. 460:** 1994/1696, sch. 8, para. 9(5); CA89, sch. 19, para. 11 and sch. 24; 2001/3649, art. 26. **S. 461(6):** IA85, sch. 6, para. 24; IA86, sch. 13, part I. **Ss. 462–6:** omitted (extend to Scotland only). **Ss. 467–85:** repealed by IA86, sch. 12. **Ss. 486–7:** omitted (extend to Scotland only). **Ss. 488–94:** repealed by IA86, sch. 12. **Ss. 495–7:** repealed by IA85, sch. 10, part II. **Ss. 498–525:** repealed by IA86, sch. 12. **Ss. 526–31:** repealed by IA85, sch. 10, part II. **S. 532:** repealed by IA86, sch. 12. **Ss. 533–4:** repealed by IA85, sch. 10, part II. **S. 535:** repealed by IA86, sch. 12. **S. 536:** repealed by IA85, sch. 10, part II. **S. 537–40:** repealed by IA86, sch. 12. **Ss. 541–3:** repealed by IA85, sch. 10, part II. **S. 544:** repealed by IA85, sch. 10, part I. **Ss. 545–8:** repealed by IA85, sch. 10, part II. **Ss. 549–50:** repealed by IA86, sch. 12. **S. 551:** repealed by IA85, sch. 10, part II. **Ss. 552–5:** repealed by IA86, sch. 12. **S. 556:** repealed by IA85, sch. 10, part II. **Ss. 557–60:** repealed by IA86, sch. 12. **S. 561:** repealed by IA85, sch. 10, part II. **S. 562:** repealed by IA86, sch. 12. **Ss. 563–4:** repealed by IA85, sch. 10, part II. **Ss. 565–7:** repealed by IA86, sch. 12. **S. 568:** repealed by IA85, sch. 10, part II. **S. 569:** repealed by IA86, sch. 12. **S. 570:** repealed by IA85, sch. 10, part IV. **Ss. 571–82:** repealed by IA86, sch. 12. **S. 583:** repealed by IA85, sch. 10, part II. **Ss. 584–5:** repealed by IA86, sch. 12. **S. 586:** repealed by IA85, sch. 10, part II. **S. 587:** repealed by IA86, sch. 12. **S. 588:** repealed by IA85, sch. 10, part II. **Ss. 589–600:** repealed by IA86, sch. 12. **S. 601:** repealed by IA85, sch. 10, part II. **Ss. 602–5:** repealed by IA86, sch. 12. **Ss. 606–15:** repealed by IA85, sch. 10, part II. **S. 615A and 615B:** repealed by IA86, sch. 12. **Ss. 616–18:** repealed by IA85, sch. 10, part II. **S. 619:** repealed by IA86, sch. 12. **S. 620:** repealed by IA85, sch. 10, part II. **Ss. 621–30:** repealed by IA86, sch. 12. **S. 631:** repealed by IA85, sch. 10, part II. **Ss. 632–3:** repealed by IA86, sch. 12. **S. 634:** repealed by IA85, sch. 10, part II. **Ss. 635–9:** repealed by IA86, sch. 12. **S. 640:** repealed by IA85, sch. 10, part II. **S. 641:** repealed by IA86, sch. 12. **S. 642:** repealed by IA85, sch. 10, part II. **Ss. 643–50:** repealed by IA86, sch. 12. **S. 651(1):** CA89, sch. 24. **S. 651(4)–(7):** CA89, s. 141(3). **S. 652A:** Deregulation and Contracting Out Act 1994, sch. 5, para. 2. **S. 652B:** Deregulation and Contracting Out Act 1994, sch. 5, para. 2; Enterprise Act 2002, sch. 17, para. 7. **S. 652C:** Deregulation and Contracting Out Act 1994, sch. 5, para. 2; Enterprise Act 2002, sch. 17, para. 8. **Ss. 652D–F:** Deregulation and Contracting Out Act 1994, sch. 5, para. 2. **S. 653:** Deregulation and Contracting Out Act 1994, sch. 5, para. 3. **S. 657(2):** IA85, sch. 6, para. 46; IA86, sch. 13, part I. **S. 658(1):** IA85, sch. 6, para. 47; IA86, sch. 13, part I. **Ss. 659–74:** repealed by IA86, sch. 12. **Ss. 676–8:** omitted as of limited interest. **S. 680:** 1992/1699, sch., para. 7. **S. 684:** CA89, sch. 19, para. 12. **S. 685:** 1991/1997, reg. 53; 2000/3373, art. 24. **S. 686:** CA89, sch. 19, para. 5; 2000/3373, art. 25. **Ss. 690A–697:** omitted (concern oversea companies). **S. 698:** 1992/3179, sch. 2, para. 13; definitions of terms not used in provisions printed in this book omitted. **Ss. 699–703R:** omitted (concern oversea companies). **S. 704(7) and (8):** Deregulation and Contracting Out Act 1994, sch. 16, para. 8. **S. 705:** CA89, sch. 19, para. 14; 1992/3179, sch. 3, para. 5. **S. 705A:** omitted (concerns oversea companies; inserted by 1992/3179, reg. 3(2)). **S. 706:** CA89, s.

125(1); 1992/3179, sch. 3, para. 6; 2000/3373, art. 31(4)(a). **S. 707:** repealed by 2000/3373, art. 31(4). **S. 707A:** CA89, s. 126(1). **S. 707B:** 2000/3373, art. 27. **S. 708:** CA89, s. 127(2) and sch. 24. **S. 709:** CA89, s. 126(2); Civil Evidence Act 1995, sch. 1, para. 10; Youth Justice and Criminal Evidence Act 1999, sch. 6; Criminal Justice and Police Act 2001, s. 45(1) and (4). **S. 710:** CA89, s. 126(2). **S. 710A:** CA89, s. 126(2). **S. 710B:** Welsh Language Act 1993, s. 30(6). **S. 711(1):** CA89, sch. 10, para. 14; 1987/1991, reg. 2(b); 1992/3179, sch. 3, para. 7; 2000/3373, art. 31(5). **S. 711(2):** IA86, sch. 13, part I. **S. 712:** repealed by CA89, s. 127(3) and sch. 24. **S. 713:** CA89, s. 127(4). **S. 714:** 1992/3179, sch. 3, para. 8; Limited Liability Partnerships Act 2000, sch., para. 1. **S. 715:** repealed by CA89, s. 127(3) and sch. 24. **S. 715A:** CA89, s. 127(1). **Ss. 716 and 717:** repealed by 2002/3203, art. 2. **S. 718:** omitted (concerns unregistered companies). **S. 720:** omitted (concerns insurance companies). **S. 723A:** CA89, s. 143(1). **Ss. 723B–F:** Criminal Justice and Police Act 2001, s. 45(1) and (2). **S. 724:** repealed by IA86, sch. 12. **S. 730(5):** CA89, sch. 19, para. 17. **S. 731(3):** Criminal Procedure (Consequential Provisions) (Scotland) Act 1995, sch. 4, para. 56(3). **S. 733:** IA85, sch. 6, para. 7; IA86, sch. 13, part I; CA89, s. 123(3) and sch. 24. **S. 734(1):** CA89, s. 120(2) and s. 123(4). **S. 734(4):** Criminal Procedure (Consequential Provisions) (Scotland) Act 1995, sch. 4, para. 56(4). **S. 734(5) and (6):** CA89, sch. 19, para. 18. **S. 735A:** IA86, sch. 13, part II; CA89, s. 127(5) and sch. 24; Deregulation and Contracting Out Act 1994, sch. 16, para. 9; 2000/3373, art. 31(4)(b). **S. 735B:** CA89, s. 127(6); Deregulation and Contracting Out Act 1994, sch. 16, para. 10; 2001/ 3649, art. 28. **Ss. 736 and 736A:** CA89, s. 144(1). **S. 736B:** CA89, s. 144(3). **S. 741(3):** 1992/ 1699, sch., para. 3(2). **S. 742:** CA89, sch. 10, para. 15; 2000/3373, art. 28. **Ss. 742A–C:** 2001/ 3649, art. 29. **S. 743A:** omitted (applies to Scotland only). **S. 744:** CA89, sch. 10, para. 16 and sch. 24; Criminal Justice Act 1993, sch. 5, para. 4(1) and (2); IA85, sch. 10, part II; Banking Act 1987, sch. 7, part I; FSA86, sch. 17, part I; 1997/2306, reg. 4(1); 2000/3373, art. 29; 2001/3649, art. 30. **S. 744A:** CA89, sch. 19, para. 20; Criminal Justice Act 1993, sch. 5, para. 4(2); 1997/ 2306, reg. 4(3); 2000/3373, art. 30; 2001/3649, art. 31; 2003/1116, sch., para. 29. **S. 746:** CA89, sch. 24. **Sch. 1:** CA89, sch. 10, para. 17 and sch. 19, para. 7; 2000/1430, reg. 8(10); 2002/912, sch. 2, para. 7. **Sch. 2:** omitted. **Sch. 3:** see note in text. **Sch. 4, para. 3(7):** 1996/189, sch. 1, para. 2. **Sch. 4, part I, section B:** CA89, sch. 1, paras 2–4; 1996/189, sch. 1, para. 3. **Sch. 4, para. 11:** CA89, sch. 1, para. 5. **Sch. 4, para. 12:** CA89, sch. 10, para. 20. **Sch. 4, para. 34:** CA89, sch. 1, para. 6; 1996/189, sch. 1, para. 4. **Sch. 4, paras 35–59A:** omitted. **Sch. 4, paras 60–9:** repealed by CA89,sch. 24. **Sch. 4, paras 71–3:** omitted. **Sch. 4, paras 74, 75 and 77–81:** repealed by CA89, sch. 24. **Sch. 4, para. 84:** FSA86, sch. 16, para. 23(b); 2001/ 3649, art. 32. **Sch. 4, paras 87 and 90–2:** repealed by CA89, sch. 24. **Sch. 4, para. 94:** 1996/ 189, sch. 1, para. 16. **Sch. 4, para. 95:** repealed by CA89, sch. 24. **Schedules 4A and 5:** omitted. **Sch. 6 title:** CA89, sch. 4, para. 2. **Sch. 6, paras 1–14:** CA89, sch. 4, para. 3; 1997/ 570; 2001/3649, art. 33; 2002/1986, reg. 10(13). **Sch. 6, paras 15–30:** omitted. **Sch. 7, para. 1:** 1996/189, regs 14(4)(a) and 15(3). **Sch. 7, paras 2, 2Aand 2B:** CA89, sch. 5, para. 3. **Sch. 7, paras 3 to 5:** Political Parties, Elections and Referendums Act 2000, s. 140. **Sch. 7, para. 5A:** inserted by CA89, s. 137(2), repealed by 1996/189, reg. 14(4)(b). **Sch. 7, para. 6:** CA89, sch. 5, para. 2(2); 1992/3178, reg. 3. **Sch. 7, para. 9:** Disability Discrimination Act 1995, sch. 6, para. 4. **Sch. 7, para. 10:** repealed by 1996/189, reg. 14(4)(c). **Sch. 7, para. 12:** 1996/189, reg. 14(5); 1997/571, reg. 2(2). **Sch. 7A:** 2002/1986, reg. 9 and sch. **Schedules 8, 8A, 9 and 9A:** omitted. **Sch. 10:** repealed by 1993/3246, sch. 2, para. 7. **Sch. 10A:** CA89, s. 21(2) and sch. 9. **Sch. 11:** omitted. **Sch. 12:** repealed by CDDA86, sch. 4. **Sch 13, para. 11:** FSA86, sch. 16, para. 25; Charities Act 1992, sch. 6, para. 11; Charities Act 1993, sch. 6, para. 20; 2001/ 3649, art. 37. **Sch. 13, para. 12:** Church of Scotland (Properties and Investments) Order Confirmation Act 1994, sch., para. 42. **Sch. 13, para. 25:** CA89,s. 143(10)(a) and sch. 24. **Sch. 13, para. 26:** CA89,s. 143(10)(b). **Sch. 14, part I:** 1997/1313. **Sch. 14, part III:** omitted (concerns oversea companies). **Sch. 15:** repealed by CA89, sch. 24. **Sch. 15A:** CA89, s. 114(1). **Sch. 15B:** omitted. **Sch. 16:** repealed by IA86, sch. 12. **Schedules 17, 18, 19 and 20, part I:** repealed by IA85, sch. 10, part II. **Sch. 20, part II:** omitted (applies to Scotland only). **Schedules 21, 21A, 21B, 21C, 21D, 22 and 23:** omitted. **Sch. 24:** Statute Law (Repeals) Act 1993, sch. 1, part XIV, group 2; FSA86, sch. 16, para. 27 and sch. 17; CA89, ss. 63(8), 64(2), 119(2), 120(3), 122(2), 123(2) and 139(3), sch. 10, para. 24 and sch. 24; CDDA86, sch. 4; 1992/1699, sch., paras 3(3), 4(2) and 6(2); 1996/1471, art. 3(2)(c); IA85, sch. 10, parts I and II; IA86, sch. 12; Deregulation and Contracting Out Act 1994, sch. 5, para. 4; 2000/3373, art. 31(6); 2002/1986, reg. 10(14); 2003/1116, sch., para. 33; omitted entries relate to sections of Act not printed in this book; see also note at end of schedule. **Sch. 25:** omitted.

Business Names Act 1985
S. 1(1): 2001/1090, sch. 5, para. 10. **S. 2(1):** 1999/1820, sch. 2, para. 79. **S. 4:** 2001/1090, sch. 5, para. 11. **S. 8(1):** Statute Law (Repeals) Act 1993, sch. 1, part XIV, group 2.

Insolvency Act 1986
S. 1: IA00, sch. 2, paras 1 and 2; 2002/1240, reg. 4; Enterprise Act 2002, sch. 17, para. 10. **S. 1A:** IA00, sch. 1, paras 1 and 2. **S. 2:** IA00, sch. 1, paras 1 and 3 and sch. 2, paras 1 and 3. **S. 4:** IA00, sch. 2, paras 1 and 4. **S. 4A:** IA00, sch. 2, paras 1 and 5. **S. 5:** IA00, sch. 2, paras 1 and 6 and sch. 5; Enterprise Act 2002, sch. 17, para. 11. **S. 6:** IA00, sch. 2, paras 1 and 7; Enterprise Act 2002, sch. 17, para. 12. **S. 6A:** IA00, sch. 2, paras 1 and 8. **S. 7:** IA00, sch. 2, paras 1 and 9. **Ss. 7A and 7B:** IA00, sch. 2, paras 1 and 10. **S. 8:** Banking Act 1987, sch. 6, para. 25(1); 2001/3649, arts 303 and 304; 2002/1240, reg. 5; 2002/1555, art. 14. **S. 9(1):** Criminal Justice Act 1988, s. 62(2); Access to Justice Act 1999, sch. 13, para. 133. **Ss. 10 and 11:** IA00, s. 9. **S. 16:** omitted (applies only to Scotland). **S. 19:** Insolvency Act 1994, s. 1. **S. 27:** IA00, sch. 1, para. 5, and sch. 5. **S. 44:** Insolvency Act 1994, s. 2. **Ss. 50–71:** omitted (extend to Scotland only). **Ss. 72A–72H:** Enterprise Act 2002, s. 250(1). **S. 100:** Enterprise Act 2002, sch. 17, para. 14. **S. 110:** 2001/1090, sch. 5, para. 15; s. 110(4) is differently worded in Scotland by SSI 2001/128, sch. 4, para. 1. **S. 113:** omitted (applies to Scotland only). **S. 117:** 2002/1240, reg. 6. **Ss. 120–1:** omitted (apply to Scotland only). **S. 122(1):** 1992/1699, sch., para. 8; IA00, sch. 1, para. 6. **S. 124(1):** Criminal Justice Act 1988, s. 62(2); Access to Justice Act 1999, sch. 13, para. 133; 2002/1240, reg. 8. **S. 124(3A):** IA00, sch. 1, para. 7. **S. 124(4):** CA89, s. 60(2). **S. 124A:** CA89, s. 60(3); 2001/3649, art. 305. **S. 127:** Enterprise Act 2002, sch. 17, para. 15. **S. 129:** Enterprise Act 2002, sch. 17, para. 16. **S. 138:** omitted (applies to Scotland only). **S. 140:** Enterprise Act 2002, sch. 17, para. 17. **S. 142:** omitted (applies to Scotland only). **S. 155(3):** 1999/1820, sch. 2, para. 85. **Ss. 157 and 161–2:** omitted (apply to Scotland only). **S. 168(5A)–(5C):** omitted (concern members of insolvent partnerships). **S. 169:** omitted (applies to Scotland only). **S. 176A:** Enterprise Act 2002, s. 252. **S. 184(3):** 1986/1996, art. 2 and sch. part I. **Ss. 190–1:** omitted. **S. 193:** omitted (applies to Scotland only). **Ss. 196–200:** omitted. **S. 204:** omitted (applies to Scotland only). **S. 206(1):** 1986/1996, art. 2 and sch. part I. **S. 212:** Enterprise Act 2002, sch. 17, para. 18, and sch. 26. **S. 218:** IA00, s. 10(1)–(6) and sch. 5. **S. 219:** IA00, ss. 10(7) and 11. **Ss. 220–9:** omitted (winding up of unregistered companies). **S. 230:** Enterprise Act 2002, sch. 17, para. 19, and sch. 26. **S. 231:** Enterprise Act 2002, sch. 17, para. 20. **S. 232:** Enterprise Act 2002, sch. 17, para. 21, and sch. 26. **S. 233:** Water Act 1989, sch. 25, para. 78(1); Electricity Act 1989, sch. 16, para. 35(1) and (2); Broadcasting Act 1990, sch. 20, para. 43; Gas Act 1995, sch. 4, para. 14(1) and (2) and sch. 6; Utilities Act 2000, sch. 6, para. 47; IA00, sch. 1, para. 8; Enterprise Act 2002, sch. 17, para. 22. **S. 234:** Enterprise Act 2002, sch. 17, para. 23. **S. 235:** Enterprise Act 2002, sch. 17, para. 24. **S. 238:** Enterprise Act 2002, sch. 17, para. 25. **S. 240:** 2002/1240, reg. 11; Enterprise Act 2002, sch. 17, para. 26, and sch. 26. **S. 241:** Insolvency (No. 2) Act 1994, s. 1; Enterprise Act 2002, sch. 17, para. 27. **Ss. 242–3:** omitted (apply to Scotland only). **S. 244:** Enterprise Act 2002, sch. 17, para. 30. **S. 245:** Enterprise Act 2002, sch. 17, para. 31, and sch. 26. **S. 246:** Enterprise Act 2002, sch. 17, para. 32. **S. 247:** 2002/1240, reg. 12; Enterprise Act 2002, sch. 17, para. 33. **Ss. 252–385:** omitted (insolvency of individuals; bankruptcy). **S. 386(1):** Finance Act 1994, sch. 7, para. 7(2); Finance Act 1996, sch. 5, para. 12; Finance Act 1991, sch. 2, para 21A (inserted by Finance (No. 2) Act 1992, s. 9(2)); Finance Act 1993, s. 36(1); Finance Act 1995, s. 17; 1987/2093, reg. 2(2); Finance Act 2000, sch. 7, para. 3;

Finance Act 2001, sch. 5, para. 17; Enterprise Act 2002, s. 251(3). **S. 386(3):** Pension Schemes Act 1993, sch. 8, para. 18. **S. 387(2):** IA00, sch. 2, para. 11; Enterprise Act 2002, sch. 17, para. 34(1) and (2). **S. 387(2A):** IA00, sch. 1, para. 9. **S. 387(3):** 2002/1240, reg. 16; Enterprise Act 2002, sch. 17, para. 34(1) and (3). **S. 387(3A):** Enterprise Act 2002, sch. 17, para. 34(1) and (4). **S. 387(5) and (6) and ss. 388–422:** omitted. **Ss. 426–9:** omitted. **S. 431(3):** Criminal Procedure (Consequential Provisions) (Scotland) Act 1995, sch. 4, para. 61. **S. 432:** IA00, sch. 1, para. 11. **S. 433:** Youth Justice and Criminal Evidence Act 1999, sch. 3, para. 7. **S. 436:** 2002/1037, reg. 4; definitions (added by 1994/2421, art. 2(1) and (2)) not relevant to provisions printed in this book are omitted. **S. 436A:** 2002/1240, reg. 18. **Ss. 437–42:** omitted. **Sch. A1:** IA00, sch. 1, para. 4. **Sch. A1, para. 1:** 2002/1555, art. 28(1) and (2). **Sch. A1, para. 2:** 2002/1555, arts 28(1) and (3) and 29. **Sch. A1, para. 3:** 2002/1990, reg. 3(1) and (2). **Sch. A1, para. 4:** Enterprise Act 2002, sch. 17, para. 37(1) and (2). **Sch. A1, paras 4A to 4K:** 2002/1990, reg. 3(1) and (3). **Sch. A1, para. 12:** 2002/1555, art. 30; Enterprise Act 2002, sch. 17, para. 37(1) and (3). **Sch. A1, para. 23:** 2002/1555, art. 28(1) and (4). **Sch. A1, para. 40:** Enterprise Act 2002, sch. 17, para. 37(1) and (4). **Sch. 2:** omitted (applies to Scotland only). **Sch. 2A:** Enterprise Act 2002, s. 250(2) and sch. 18. **Sch. 2A, para. 1:** 2003/1468. **Sch. 3:** omitted (applies to Scotland only). **Sch. 4, para. 3A:** Enterprise Act 2002, s. 253. **Sch. 5:** omitted (concerns bankrupcy). **Sch. 6, paras 1–7:** to be repealed by Enterprise Act 2002, s. 251(1), and sch. 26. **Sch. 6, paras 1 and 2:** Income and Corporation Taxes Act 1988, sch. 29, para. 32. **Sch. 6, para. 3:** Value Added Tax Act 1994, sch. 14, para. 8. **Sch. 6, para. 3A:** Finance Act 1994, sch. 7, para. 7(2). **Sch. 6, para. 3B:** Finance Act 1996, sch. 5, para. 12. **Sch. 6, para. 3C:** Finance Act 2000, sch. 7, para. 3. **Sch. 6, para. 3D:** Finance Act 2001, sch. 5, para. 17. **Sch. 6, para. 5:** Finance Act 1997, sch. 2, para. 6 and sch. 18, part II. **Sch. 6, para. 5A:** Finance Act 1991, sch. 2, para. 22. **Sch. 6, para. 5B:** Finance Act 1993, s. 36(2). **Sch. 6, para. 5C:** Finance Act 1994, sch. 6, para. 13(1). **Sch. 6, para. 6:** Social Security (Consequential Provisions) Act 1992, sch. 2, para. 73. **Sch. 6, para. 8:** Pension Schemes Act 1993, sch. 8, para. 18. **Sch. 6, para. 13(2):** Employment Rights Act 1996, sch. 1, para. 29. **Sch. 6, para. 15A:** 1987/2093, reg. 2(1). **Schedules 7, 8 and 9:** omitted. **Sch. 10:** Statute Law (Repeals) Act 1993, sch. 1, part XIV, group 2; IA00, sch. 1, para. 12, and sch. 2, para. 12; Enterprise Act 2002, sch. 17, para. 39, sch. 23, para. 17, and sch. 26; entries relating to sections not printed in this book omitted; see also note at end of schedule. **Schedules 11–14:** omitted.

Company Directors Disqualification Act 1986

S. 1: IA00, s. 5(1) and (2) and sch. 4, paras 1 and 2; Enterprise Act 2002, s. 204(1) and (3). **S. 1A:** IA00, s. 6(1) and (2). **S. 2(1):** Deregulation and Contracting Out Act 1994, sch. 11, para. 6; IA00, sch. 4, paras 1 and 3. **S. 3(3):** CA89, sch. 10, para. 35. **S. 4:** IA00, sch. 4, paras 1 and 4. **S. 6:** IA00, sch. 4, paras 1 and 5; Enterprise Act 2002, sch. 17, paras 40 and 41. **S. 7:** IA00, s. 6(1) and (3) and sch. 4, paras 1 and 6; Enterprise Act 2002, sch. 17, paras 40 and 42. **S. 8(1):** FSA86, s. 198(2); Criminal Justice Act 1988, s. 145(b); Criminal Justice (Scotland) Act 1987, s. 55(b); Criminal Procedure (Consequential Provisions) (Scotland) Act 1995, sch. 4, para. 62; CA89, s. 79; 2001/3649, art. 39. **S. 8(1A):** 2001/3649, art. 39. **S. 8(2A):** IA00, s. 6(1) and (4). **S. 8A:** IA00, s. 6(1) and (5); Enterprise Act 2002, s. 204(1), (4) and (5). **S. 9:** IA00, s. 6(1) and (6), sch. 4, paras 1 and 7 and sch. 5. **Ss. 9A–9E:** Enterprise Act 2002, s. 204(1) and (2). **S. 12A:** IA00, s. 7(1). **S. 13:** IA00, sch. 4, paras 1 and 8. **S. 14:** IA00, sch. 4, paras 1 and 9. **S. 15:** IA00, sch. 4, paras 1 and 10. **S. 16:** IA00, sch. 4, paras 1 and 11; Enterprise Act 2002, s. 204(1), (6) and (7). **S. 17:** IA00, sch. 4, paras 1 and 12; Enterprise Act 2002, s. 204(1), (8), (9) and (10). **S. 18:** IA00, sch. 4, paras 1 and 13; Enterprise Act 2002, s. 204(1) and (11). **S. 19:** omitted (savings from repealed Acts). **S. 20:** Youth Justice and Criminal Evidence Act 1999, sch. 3, para. 8. **S. 21(2):** CA89, s. 24; IA00, sch. 4, paras 1 and 14(1) and (2). **S. 21(3):** IA00, sch. 4, paras 1 and 14(1) and (3). **S. 21(4):** omitted (applies to Scotland only). **S. 22:** IA00, s. 5(3), sch. 4, paras 1 and 15 and sch. 5. **Ss. 22A, 22B and 23:** omitted (application of Act to building societies and incorporated friendly societies, transitional provisions, savings and repeals). **Sch. 1, para. 4:**

CA89, s. 139(4); see note at end of paragraph. **Sch. 1, para. 5:** CA89, sch. 10, para. 35(3). **Sch. 1, para. 5A:** omitted (application of Act to open-ended investment companies). **Schedules 2, 3 and 4:** omitted (savings, transitional provisions and repeals).

Companies Act 1989
Only extracts from this Act are included in this book. The omissions and repeals noted here are only those from the sections or schedules printed. Much of the Companies Act 1989 makes amendments to other Acts printed in this book. Where those amendments have been brought into force they have been incorporated in the text of those Acts printed in this book. Amendments which had not been brought into force when this edition went to press and which are not expected to be abandoned are noted at appropriate places in the text of the Companies Act 1985 in this book. **S. 93:** Trade Marks Act 1994, sch. 5. **S. 133(4):** repealed by 2003/1116, sch., para. 34. **S. 142(2):** omitted. **Sch. 16:** only amendments of provisions printed in this book are included. **Sch. 24:** only entries which have not been brought into force and which relate to provisions printed in this book are included.

Criminal Justice Act 1993
Only Part V and its associated schedules are included in this book. **Sch. 1, paras 1 and 5:** 2001/3649, art. 341.

Financial Services and Markets Act 2000
Only extracts from this Act are included in this book. **S. 425(1):** 2000/2952, reg. 8(1) and (4). **Sch. 3, para. 2:** 2000/2952, reg. 8(1) and (5)(b). **Sch. 11, para. 2:** 2001/2955, reg. 2(a). **Sch. 11, para. 20:** 2000/2952, reg. 8(6); 2002/765, reg. 4. **Sch. 11, para. 24A:** 2001/2955, reg. 2(b).

Limited Liability Partnerships Act 2000
S. 2: 2002/915, sch. 2, para. 1. **S. 9:** 2002/915, sch. 2, para. 3. **Ss. 10–13:** omitted (amendment of tax statutes). **Sch., para. 1:** omitted (amendment of Companies Act 1985 incorporated in the text of that Act in this book). **Sch., para. 8:** 2001/1228, sch. 7, para. 11.

SI 1981/1685
Under the Companies Consolidation (Consequential Provisions) Act 1985, s. 31(2), these Regulations are to be treated as made and having effect under the Companies Act 1985, s. 29, and the Business Names Act 1985, s. 3. **Reg. 3:** 1992/1196, reg. 2(2). **Reg. 4:** 1992/1196, reg. 2(3). **Sch.:** 1982/1653, reg. 3; 1992/1196, reg. 2(4) and (5); 1995/3022, reg. 3; 1999/1820, sch. 2. para. 139; 2001/259, reg. 3; 2001/3500, sch. 2, para. 14; 2002/1397, sch., para. 17.

SI 1985/724
Regs 1, 2, 3 and 6: 2001/3755, sch. 7, para. 17.

SI 1985/805
Sch., Table A, reg. 1: 2000/3373, sch. 1, para. 1. **Sch., Table A, regs 4 and 41:** 1985/1052. **Sch., Table A, regs 60, 61, 62, 63, 111 and 112:** 2000/3373, sch. 1, paras 2–7. **Sch., Table A, reg. 115**: 1985/1052; 2000/3373, sch. 1, para. 8. **Sch., Tables C, D and E:** omitted.

SI 1986/1996
Art. 2 and sch., part I: omitted (amendments to IA86 incorporated in the text of the Act in this book). **Art. 3 and sch., part II:** omitted (concern bankruptcy).

SI 1992/1699
Reg. 2(1)(b) and sch.: omitted (amendments to Companies Act 1985 and Insolvency Act 1986 which have been incorporated in the text of the Acts in this book).

SI 1994/187
Art. 9: 2000/1923, art. 2; 2002/1874, art. 2. **Art. 10:** 1996/1561, art. 3; 2000/1923, art. 2; 2002/1874, art. 2. **Sch.:** 1996/1561, art. 4; 2000/1923, art. 2; 2002/1874, art. 2.

SI 2001/996
Art. 4A: 2001/3681, art. 2.

SI 2001/2956
Reg. 3: 2001/3439. **Reg. 8:** omitted (concerns electricity privatisation). **Reg. 12:** omitted (concerns Euro-securities).

SI 2001/3755
Reg. 3(1): definitions of terms not used in provisions printed in this book omitted. **Reg. 3(3):** omitted (concerns public sector securities). **Regs 4(2)–(5), 5(1)–(4), 6, 7(3)–(6), 8–10, 11(2)–(11), 12 and 13:** omitted (concern approval and supervision of the Operator). **Regs 21(1)(b), (2)(b), (4) and (5) and 24(5):** omitted (concern public sector securities). **Reg. 31(3), (4) and (7):** omitted (relate to Scotland only). **Reg. 38(3):** omitted (concerns public sector securities). **Regs 40(4) and 43(5):** omitted (relate to Scotland only). **Reg. 49:** omitted (concerns application to Northern Ireland). **Regs 50, 51 and 52:** omitted (transitory provisions, amendments and revocations). **Sch. 2 and sch. 3:** omitted. **Sch. 4, para. 19(2):** omitted (concerns local authority securities). **Sch. 5, sch. 6 and sch. 7:** omitted.

SI 2002/912
Reg. 16 and sch. 2: omitted (amendments of the Companies Act 1985 incorporated in the text of that Act in this book)

INDEX